THE NEW INTERNATIONAL COMMENTARY ON
THE NEW TESTAMENT

F. F. BRUCE, *General Editor*

The First Epistle
to the
CORINTHIANS

by

GORDON D. FEE

WILLIAM B. EERDMANS PUBLISHING COMPANY
GRAND RAPIDS, MICHIGAN

FOR
WAYNE KRAISS
with appreciation

Library of Congress Cataloging-in-Publication Data

Fee, Gordon D.
The First Epistle to the Corinthians.

(The New international commentary on the New Testament)
Includes indexes.
1. Bible. N.T. Corinthians, 1st—Commentaries.
I. Title. II. Series.
BS2675.3.F43   1987   227'.2077   87-9270
ISBN 0-8028-2288-6

CONTENTS

Editor's Preface   *vii*

Author's Preface   *ix*

Abbreviations   *xiii*

Selected Bibliography   *xxi*

INTRODUCTION   1

   I.   THE CITY AND ITS PEOPLE   1

   II.   THE CHURCH AND ITS APOSTLE   4

   III.   SOME CRITICAL QUESTIONS   15

   IV.   THEOLOGICAL CONTRIBUTIONS   16

ANALYSIS OF 1 CORINTHIANS (with page references)   21

TEXT, EXPOSITION, AND NOTES   27

   I.   INTRODUCTION (1:1-9)   27

   II.   IN RESPONSE TO REPORTS (1:10–6:21)   46

   III.   IN RESPONSE TO THE CORINTHIAN LETTER (7:1–16:12)   266

   IV.   CONCLUDING MATTERS (16:13-24)   825

INDEXES

Subjects   *841*

Authors   *845*

Scripture References   *854*

Early Extrabiblical Literature   *876*

EDITOR'S PREFACE

In accordance with the policy of keeping the New International Commentary on the New Testament up to date, by revision or replacement, a new volume on 1 Corinthians is now presented.

The original NICNT volume on 1 Corinthians was one of the earliest in the series: it was published in 1953, and was the work of the veteran Dutch scholar Dr. F. W. Grosheide, who for over forty years had been Professor of New Testament at the Free University of Amsterdam. Since its appearance a full generation has elapsed. The study of 1 Corinthians—one of the most exciting of Paul's letters—has been energetically pursued. New problems have emerged and new questions have been asked, and on all of these today's reader expects to find some help.

Dr. Gordon Fee is fully abreast of these issues and is well qualified to give the required help. He is best known in the world of New Testament scholarship for his expertise in textual criticism, but his exegetical gifts have been continuously exercised during his years of teaching at Wheaton College, Gordon-Conwell Theological Seminary, and now Regent College, Vancouver, as well as in his commentary on the Pastoral Epistles.

He treats the successive sections of 1 Corinthians with an eye to the place of each in the overall development of the letter and its argument; he treats the letter itself in the context of the epistolary exchanges between Paul and the Corinthian church as well as in its historical, cultural, and social setting. Some elusive questions arise with regard to the Corinthian Christians' unexpressed presuppositions—presuppositions of which Paul had to take account when he was dictating the letter and of which we must be made aware when reading it. This is a real letter (not a literary composition disguised as a letter): in it Paul interacts with living, articulate, and argumentative men and women. Readers who try to use it as a manual of church order, a directory of public worship, or a digest of canon law for today will miss its point; but under Dr. Fee's guidance they will grasp, and perhaps even apply, its abiding message.

F. F. BRUCE

AUTHOR'S PREFACE

The story of the events that led me to write this commentary is long and need not be recounted in full here. It began with my teaching a course in 1 Corinthians at Wheaton College in 1970, something I have done almost every year since, first at Wheaton and then at Gordon-Conwell Theological Seminary. Close work with the text and the literature over the years made me think that there might be a place for yet another commentary—of a slightly different kind and from a slightly different point of view from others. As I wrote the *Study Guide* for the college level course through the International Correspondence Institute (Brussels) during the summer of 1977 the dream became more real, and I hinted at my desire to write such a commentary in the preface of that work. But it was at the annual meeting of the *Studiorum Novi Testamenti Societas* in Toronto in August 1980 that the dream began to move toward reality. Since the publisher of the present series was in the process of replacing some of its earlier volumes, I approached Professor Bruce at that meeting with the suggestion of replacing the second volume in the series, Professor F. W. Grosheide's commentary on 1 Corinthians. That conversation resulted in an offer from Wm. B. Eerdmans, Jr., to write the present volume.

A word about the commentary itself. My basic assumption is that it is primarily for pastors, teachers, and students. Therefore, I have tried above all else to provide a readable exposition of the text, in which the flow of Paul's ideas, their theological relevance, and the meaning of the various parts make good sense as one reads. Commentaries that are more difficult to understand than the English translation on which they are based are anathema. At the same time, however, I am well aware of the scholarly community, to whom I am greatly indebted and who hopefully will also find it worthwhile to consult this work. Since I have been engaged in this enterprise for so many years, I have interacted considerably with much of the literature; that dimension of the enterprise is found in the footnotes. As I was nearing the end of the writing, Professor John Ziesler's discussion of commentaries on 1 Corinthians in English appeared in *The Expository Times* (97 [1986],

263-67). I concur with his judgment that of the commentaries published prior to 1986 Barrett's is the best, while Conzelmann's is indispensable for the advanced reader. I have consciously tried to incorporate the best elements of both of these works.

The present commentary displays several unique features. First, the nature of 1 Corinthians makes it imperative for the reader to see how everything fits into the historical/literary context both of the individual paragraphs and the larger sections. Since my own exegetical urgencies lie here, and since the lack of such contextual exegesis has been my complaint with commentaries in general, one will find here a tendency to err on the other side. Every major section is introduced, as is every paragraph, with an attempt to reconstruct the historical background and to trace the flow of Paul's argument. Most of the individual verses also receive this kind of treatment. Second, and related to the first, is a concern to exegete the whole book from a consistent perspective as to the historical situation. This perspective is the key to much of my understanding of the letter and will be found in the Introduction under the section "The Church and Its Apostle." Third, since my own field of expertise is textual criticism, I have discussed every exegetically significant variant, some at considerable length. Finally, in addition to dropping hints from time to time within the exposition itself, I have concluded almost every paragraph with some observations about application. My own deep concern that the Word of God be a living word for today is reflected in these notes.

I have based the entire exposition on my own exegesis and my class notes (which were often full of notations of what others had said). But only a fool would not regularly consult the work of others. What I thought at times were new insights were usually found somewhere in the literature before me; and frequently, of course, I had to rewrite sections in light of that work. Since 1953 (the year of Grosheide's commentary) the literature on 1 Corinthians has burgeoned beyond the ability of any one person to master it all— especially one whose primary calling is teaching and preaching. A complete bibliography would include over 2,000 items. I have tried to call attention to the most significant of these works by way of the footnotes. Since the commentary is intended for an English-speaking readership, the bibliography, which includes items up to June 1986, is heavily weighted in that direction. One will need to consult the "Index of Authors" for this material, since a volume of this size could not sustain a more complete bibliography as well. The items found in the "Select Bibliography" include commentaries and specialized works that deal in whole or in part with 1 Corinthians. Besides the two commentaries already mentioned, I found the older works by Godet, Findlay, Parry, and Weiss full of insight. My debt to many others will be apparent to all. I apologize in advance to those whom I have overlooked—a problem that will undoubtedly lead to some embarrassment on my part. Perhaps I should also apologize to those with whom I have disagreed. I do not apologize for disagreeing, but some trial runs with the material have given me a great concern lest at times I have not represented opposing views as adequately as I should have.

At this point I should make two further remarks about assumptions. First, I have believed for many years that a former generation of scholars had a more plausible understanding of the order of Pauline letters than many—especially evangelical—scholars do today. This is particularly true with regard to Galatians. I began writing under the assumption that 1 and 2 Thessalonians were Paul's earliest letters and that Galatians *follows* both 1 and 2 Corinthians. After writing the commentary, this has become a settled conviction. For this reason, I have placed all references to Paul's letters in that assumed chronological sequence, since the dating of many references is important. As I argued in my commentary on the Pastoral Epistles, despite the acknowledged difficulties involved, I think those letters also come ultimately from Paul himself. That position, too, is reflected in the notes.

Second, since exegesis cannot be done in a vacuum, I note without apology that I am a believer whose theological tradition is both pentecostal and evangelical. Like many others before me I have written out of my own tradition. Each of these traditions has insights to offer that are sometimes neglected by others. Nonetheless, I have done my best to keep those viewpoints from intruding on the exegesis itself. In particular these traditions have in common the deep conviction that this Epistle is the Word of God written. I have brought that conviction to this work with great passion. Why else write such a commentary, unless it is to help the church better to hear the word of the living God and thereby to be better equipped for obedience in the present age?

It is impossible to thank the many others, besides the scholarly community, who have helped to make this work become a reality. Above all I must mention my dear friend Wayne Kraiss, president of Southern California College, who overheard my moaning a couple of years ago that I had the contract to write but no time in which to do it. Through the generous auspices of a special fund from the college, I was enabled to take a leave of absence from Gordon-Conwell for the academic year 1985-86. Thanks also go to the seminary for granting the leave, and for the generous use of its facilities throughout the year, even though, as it turned out, this was to be my final year there. And what can I say about my wife Maudine, for whom the year was basically a time of endurance as I worked at the writing task on the average of twelve hours a day, six days a week, for a period of fourteen months? Yet she was a constant source of encouragement and frequently engaged in helpful discussions on the meaning of some of the truly difficult texts.

Two other groups of people deserve special mention. First, several members of my local church community, Church of the Redeemer in Hamilton, Massachusetts, took it upon themselves to pray for me and this work on a daily basis. To them, and especially to Bob McManus, who headed this project, I am eternally grateful. Second, several friends and colleagues read sections of the commentary to make sure it was heading in the directions outlined above. These include a former student assistant, Patrick Alexander, who has read it through in its entirety, present Gordon-Conwell Seminary student Rikki Watts, plus my Gordon-Conwell colleagues Gregory Beale, T. David Gordon, Roger Nicole, and David Wells. The indexes were prepared by my teaching assistants at Regent College, Gary Thomas, who carried the bulk of the task, and Steve Tompkins.

I express my appreciation here to the Zondervan Corporation for allowing me to use the NIV and to make my own "corrections" at several places where I personally found the NIV not fully adequate. Finally, a word of thanks to the series editor, F. F. Bruce, for inviting this commentary into the series, and to my editor at Eerdmans, Milton Essenburg, whose encouragement both early on and toward the end were of inestimable help—and to both of them for allowing changes in the format of the series so that I could fit in my own deep concerns.

GORDON D. FEE

ABBREVIATIONS

For text-critical symbols see the Introduction to Erwin Nestle and Kurt
Aland, *Novum Testamentum Graece* (26th ed.).

AB	Anchor Bible
Abot R.Nat.	*Abot de Rabbi Nathan*
ACQ	*American Church Quarterly*
adj.	adjective
adv.	adverb
AGJU	Arbeiten zur Geschichte des Antiken Judentums und des Urchristentums
AJA	*American Journal of Archaeology*
AJT	*American Journal of Theology*
AnBib	Analecta Biblica
ANF	The Ante-Nicene Fathers
ANRW	H. Temporini, ed., *Aufstieg und Niedergang der römischen Welt*
Apoc.Abr.	*Apocalypse of Abraham*
Apoc.Mos.	*Apocalypse of Moses*
Appian	
Maced.	*Macedonian Affairs* (History of Rome)
Aristot.	Aristotle
Pol.	*Politica*
Artemidorus	
oneir.	*Oneirocriticus*
As.Mos.	*The Assumption of Moses*
ASNU	Acta seminarii neotestamentici upsaliensis
ASV	American Standard Version
ATANT	Abhandlungen zur Theologie des Alten und Neuen Testaments
ATR	*Anglican Theological Review*
AusBR	*Australian Biblical Review*
AUSSDS	Andrews University Seminary Studies Dissertation Series
b.Abod.Zar.	Babylonian Talmud, tractate *Aboda Zara*
Abot.	*Aboth*
B.Mes.	*Baba Mesiah*

Ber.	*Berakot*
Git.	*Gittim*
Hul.	*Hullin*
Ketub.	*Ketuboth*
Moed Qat.	*Moed Qatan*
Qidd.	*Qiddusin*
Peah	*Peah*
Pes.	*Pesahim*
Rosh.Hash.	*Rosh Hashanah*
Sabb.	*Sabbath*
Sanh.	*Sanhedrin*
Sot.	*Sotah*
Suk.	*Sukkah*
Taan.	*Taanith*
BA	*Biblical Archaeologist*
BAGD	W. Bauer, W. F. Arndt, F. W. Gingrich, F. Danker, *Greek-English Lexicon of the New Testament* (2d ed., Chicago, 1979)
Bar.	*Baraita* (for tractates see under *b.*)
BARev	*Biblical Archaeology Review*
BDF	F. Blass, A. Debrunner, and R. W. Funk, *A Greek Grammar of the NT* (Chicago, 1961)
BETS	See *JETS*
BG	M. Zerwick, *Biblical Greek* (Rome, 1963)
Bib	*Biblica*
BibRes	*Biblical Research*
BibSac	*Bibliotheca Sacra*
BibTrans	*The Bible Translator*
BJRL	*Bulletin of the John Rylands Library*
BTB	*Biblical Theology Bulletin*
BZ	*Biblische Zeitschrift*
c.	century
ca.	*circa,* about
CBC	The Cambridge Bible Commentary
CBQ	*Catholic Biblical Quarterly*
CBSC	The Cambridge Bible for Schools and Colleges
cf.	*confer,* compare
CGTSC	Cambridge Greek Testament for Schools and Colleges
chap(s).	chapter(s)
Cicero	
Acad.	*Academica*
Att.	*Epistulae ad Atticum*
Cluent.	*Pro Cluentio*
Fin.	*de Finibus*
CJT	*Canadian Journal of Theology*
CQR	*Church Quarterly Review*

CT	*Christianity Today*
CTJ	*Calvin Theological Journal*
CTM	*Concordia Theological Monthly*
CurTM	*Currents in Theology and Mission*
Cyril	Cyril of Alexandria
Arcad.	*de recta fide ad Arcadiam et Marinam*
Danby	H. Danby, *The Mishnah, Translated from the Hebrew with Introduction and Brief Explanatory Notes*
Demos.	Demosthenes
or.	*orations*
Did.	The *Didache*
Dio Chrys.	Dio Chrysostom
or.	*orations*
Diod.Sic.	Diodorus Siculus
Diog.L.	Diogenes Laertius
Vit.	*Vita* (Life)
Dion.Hal.	Dionysius Halicarnassus
Ditt. *Syl.*	Dittenberger, ed., *Sylloge Inscriptionum Graecorum*
DSB	The Daily Study Bible
EBC	The Expositor's Bible Commentary
EBib	Etudes Bibliques
ed.	editor, edited by
e.g.	*exempli gratia,* for example
EGT	The Expositor's Greek Testament
Ep.	*epistula,* letter
ep.Ar.	Epistle of Aristeas
Epict.	Epictetus
esp.	especially
ET	English translation
ETL	*Ephemerides theologicae lovanienses*
EvQ	*Evangelical Quarterly*
EvT	*Evangelische Theologie*
Exp	*The Expositor*
ExpT	*The Expository Times*
FBBS	Facet Books, Biblical Series
FRLANT	Forschungen zur Religion und Literatur des Alten und Neuen Testaments
Gk.	Greek
GNB	Good News Bible
GNC	Good News Commentary
Heb.	Hebrew
HeyJ	*Heythrop Journal*
HistR	*History of Religions*
HKNT	Handkommentar zum Neuen Testament
HNT	Handbuch zum Neuen Testament
HNTC	Harper's NT Commentaries

HSW	E. Hennecke, W. Schneemelcher, R. W. Wilson, *New Testament Apocrypha*
HTR	*Harvard Theological Review*
IB	Interpreter's Bible
IBS	*Irish Biblical Studies*
ICC	International Critical Commentary
IDBSup	G. A. Buttrick, ed., *Interpreter's Dictionary of the Bible, Supplement*
impf.	imperfect tense
impv.	imperative
incl.	including
Int	*Interpretation*
Irenaeus	
Haer.	*adversus haereses*
ITQ	*Irish Theological Quarterly*
JAAR	*Journal of the American Academy of Religion*
JB	The Jerusalem Bible
JBL	*Journal of Biblical Literature*
JBR	*Journal of the Bible and Religion*
Jerome	
vir.ill.	*de viris illustribus*
JJS	*Journal of Jewish Studies*
Jos.	Josephus
Ant.	*Jewish Antiquities*
c.Ap.	*Contra Apion (Against Apion)*
War	*The Jewish War*
Jos. et As.	*Joseph and Asenath*
JSNT	*Journal for the Study of the New Testament*
JSOT	*Journal for the Study of the Old Testament*
JSS	*Journal of Semitic Studies*
JTC	*Journal for Theology and the Church*
JTS	*Journal of Theological Studies*
Jub.	Book of Jubilees
Justin	Justin Martyr
Apol.	*Apology*
Dial.	*Dialogue with Trypho*
KJV	King James Version
LAE	A. Deissmann, *Light from the Ancient East*
LB	The Living Bible
LCC	Library of Christian Classics
LingBib	*Linguistica Biblica*
lit.	literally
Livy	
hist.	*History of Rome*
Loeb	Loeb Classical Library
LSJ	Liddell-Scott-Jones, *Greek-English Lexicon* (Oxford)

Luc.	Lucian
Alex.	Alexander the False Prophet
dial.het.	*Dialogoi Hetairikoi* (Dialogues of the Courtesans)
fug.	*Fugitivi* (The Runaways)
Tim.	*Timon* (or The Misanthrope)
LumV	*Lumière et Vie*
LWC	The Living Word Commentary
LXX	The Septuagint
m.Abot, etc.	*Mishnah* (for tractates see under *b.*)
MajT	The Majority Text
Marc.Aur.Ant.	Marcus Aurelius Antoninus
Mek.Ex.	*Mekilta Exodus*
mg.	margin (the reading found in the margin)
Midr.Num.	*Midrash on Numbers*
Midr.Ps.	*Midrash on Psalms*
Midr.Qoh.	*Midrash on Qoheleth* (Ecclesiastes)
MKNT	H. A. W. Meyer, *Kritisch-exegetischer Kommentar über das Neue Testament*
MM	J. H. Moulton, G. Milligan, *The Vocabulary of the Greek Testament* (1930)
MNTC	Moffatt New Testament Commentary
MS(S)	Manuscript(s)
MTZ	*Münchener theologische Zeitschrift*
n. (nn.)	note (notes)
NA²⁶	E. Nestle, K. Aland, *Novum Testamentum Graece* (26th ed.)
NAB	New American Bible
NAG	*Nachrichten von der Akademie der Wissenschaften in Göttingen*
NASB	New American Standard Bible
NCB	New Century Bible
NEB	New English Bible
NESTThRev	*Near Eastern School of Theology Theological Review*
NIC	New International Commentary on the New Testament
NIDNTT	C. Brown, ed., *The New International Dictionary of New Testament Theology*
NIV	New International Version
NouvRT	*Nouvelle Revue Théologique*
NovT	*Novum Testamentum*
NovTSup	Novum Testamentum, Supplements
n.s.	new series
NT	New Testament
NTD	Das Neue Testament Deutsch
NTM	The New Testament Message
NTS	*New Testament Studies*
Or.Sib.	The Sibylline Oracles
OT	Old Testament

OTP	J. H. Charlesworth, ed., *The Old Testament Pseudepigrapha*
O-W	Orr-Walther (commentary; see bibliography)
p. (pp.)	page(s)

Philo

Abr.	*De Abrahamo*, On Abraham
agric.	*De Agricultura*, On Husbandry
cher.	*De Cherubim*, On the Cherubim
congr.qu.er.	*De Congressu quaerendae Eruditionis gratia*, On Preliminary Studies
det.pot.ins.	*Quod Deterius Potiori insidiari solet*, The Worse Attacks the Better
gig.	*De Gigantibus*, On the Giants
leg.ad Gai.	*De Legatione ad Gaium*, On the Embassy to Gaius
leg.all.	*Legum Allegoriarum*, Allegorical Interpretation
Mos.	*De Vita Mosis*, Life of Moses
mut.nom.	*De Mutatione Nominum*, On the Change of Names
omn.prob.lib.	*Quod Omnis Probus Liber sit*, Every Good Man is Free
op.mund.	*De Opificio Mundi*, On the Creation
post.Cain.	*De Posteritate Caini*, On the Posterity and Exile of Cain
praem.	*De Praemiis et Poenis*, On Rewards and Punishments
quis rer.div.	*Quis Rerum Divinarum Heres*, Who Is the Heir
sacr.AC	*De Sacrificiis Abelis et Caini*, On the Sacrifices of Abel and Cain
somn.	*De Somniis*, On Dreams
spec.leg.	*De specialibus legibus*, On Special Laws
virt.	*De Virtutibus*, On the Virtues

Philostr.   Philostratus

V.Soph.	*Vitae Sophistarum*

Plato

gorg.	*Gorgias*
leg.	*Leges*
Lys.	*Lysis*
Phaed.	*Phaedrus*

Pliny

panegyr.	*panegyricus*

Plutarch

Alex.M.	Life of Alexander the Great
Fort.Rom.	*On the Fortunes of the Romans*
mor.	*Moralia*

Polycarp

Phil.	*Epistle to the Philippians*

POxy	The Oxyrynchus Papyri
PRS	*Perspectives in Religious Studies*
ptc.	participle
PTR	*Princeton Theological Review*

Q	Qumran
1QPH	*Pesher on Habakkuk*
1QS	Rule of the Community
4QFlor	*Florilegium*
q.v.	*quod vide*, which see
RB	*Revue Biblique*
RefThRev	*Reformed Theological Review*
repr.	reprint(ed)
RestQ	*Restoration Quarterly*
RevExp	*Review and Expositor*
RHE	*Revue d'histoire ecclésiastique*
RHPR	*Revue d'histoire et de philosophie religieuses*
R-P	Robertson-Plummer (commentary; see bibliography)
RSR	*Recherches des science religieuse*
RSV	Revised Standard Version
RTP	*Revue de Théologie et de Philosophie*
RV	Revised Version
Sallust	
Jug.	*Bellum Iugurthinum*
SBLDS	Society of Biblical Literature Dissertation Series
SBLTT	Society of Biblical Literature Texts and Translations
SBT	Studies in Biblical Theology
ScEs	*Science et esprit*
Scr	*Scripture*
SD	Studies and Documents
SEÅ	*Svensk exegetisk årsbok*
Seneca	
benef.	*De Beneficiis*
ep.	*Epistulae*
prov.	*De Providentia*
SJT	*Scottish Journal of Theology*
SNTSMS	Society for New Testament Studies Monograph Series
ST	*Studia Theologica*
Stobaeus	
Ecl.	*Eclogae*
Str-B	H. Strack and P. Billerbeck, *Kommentar zum Neuen Testament*
StudEv	*Studia Evangelica*
t.Suk., etc.	*The Tosephta*, for tractates see under Babylonian Talmud (*b.*)
T.Benj.	*The Testament of Benjamin*
T.Job	*The Testament of Job*
T.Jud.	*The Testament of Judah*
T.Lev.	*The Testament of Levi*
T.Naph.	*The Testament of Naphtali*
T.Reub.	*The Testament of Reuben*

Tacitus	
Germ.	*Germania*
TCNT	The Twentieth Century New Testament
TDNT	G. Kittel and G. Friedrich, eds., *Theological Dictionary of the New Testament*
Tert.	Tertullian
pudic.	*de pudicitia* (On Chastity)
res.	*de Resurrectione mortuorum* (On the Resurrection of the Dead)
Teub.	Bibliotheca Scriptorum Graecorum et Romanorum Teubneriana (Leipzig)
Tg.Ps.-J.	*Targum Pseudo-Jonathan*
ThDig	*Theology Digest*
Theod.	Theodotion
ThLZ	*Theologische Literaturzeitung*
THNT	Theologischer Handkommentar zum Neuen Testament
ThRev	*Theological Review*
TNTC	The Tyndale New Testament Commentaries
TR	The Textus Receptus
transl.	translation, or translated by
TrinJ	*Trinity Journal*
TS	*Theological Studies*
TSK	*Theologische Studien und Kritiken*
TU	Texte und Untersuchungen
TynB	*Tyndale Bulletin*
TZ	*Theologische Zeitschrift*
UBS[3]	United Bible Societies Greek New Testament (3d ed.)
v. (vv.)	verse (verses)
VigC	*Vigiliae Christianae*
VoxR	*Vox Reformata*
WC	Westminster Commentaries
WH	Westcott-Hort Greek New Testament
WMANT	Wissenschaftliche Untersuchungen zum Neuen Testament
WPC	Westminster Pelican Commentaries
WTJ	*Westminster Theological Journal*
Xenophon	
apol.	*apologia Socratis*
de Rep.Lac.	*de Republica Lacedaemoniorum*
mem.	*memorabilia*
ZKG	*Zeitschrift für Kirchengeschichte*
ZKT	*Zeitschrift für Katholische Theologie*
ZNW	*Zeitschrift für die neutestamentliche Wissenschaft*
ZTK	*Zeitschrift für Theologie und Kirche*

SELECT BIBLIOGRAPHY

The bibliography on 1 Corinthians runs into several thousand items. Most of these will be discovered through use of the Index of Authors. The items included here are referred to in the commentary simply by the author's last name. Section III is a list of "short titles" for two authors (R. A. Horsley; J. Murphy-O'Connor) whose works might be otherwise difficult to find because of their extensive number.

I. COMMENTARIES

Allo, P. E.-B. *Saint Paul Première Épitre aux Corinthiens*, EBib (Paris, 1934).

Bachmann, Philipp. *Der erste Brief des Paulus an die Korinther* (3d Aufl., Leipzig, 1921).

Barclay, William. *The Letters to the Corinthians*, DSB (2d ed., Philadelphia, 1956).

Barrett, C. K. *A Commentary on the First Epistle to the Corinthians*, HNTC (New York, 1968).

Bruce, F. F. *1 and 2 Corinthians*, NCB (London, 1971).

Calvin, John. *The First Epistle of Paul to the Corinthians* (ET, Grand Rapids, 1960).

Conzelmann, Hans. *1 Corinthians*, Hermeneia (ET, Philadelphia, 1975).

Craig, C. T. *The First Epistle to the Corinthians*, IB (New York, 1953).

Edwards, T. C. *A Commentary on the First Epistle to the Corinthians* (3d ed., London, 1897).

Fascher, Erich. *Der erste Brief des Paulus an die Korinther*, Erster Teil, THNT (3d Aufl., Berlin, 1984).

Findlay, G. G. *St. Paul's First Epistle to the Corinthians*, EGT (London, 1900; repr. Grand Rapids, 1961).

Godet, F. *Commentary on the First Epistle to the Corinthians*, 2 vols. (ET, Edinburgh, 1886; repr. Grand Rapids, 1957).

Goudge, H. L. *The First Epistle to the Corinthians*, WC (London, 1903).

Gromacki, R. G. *Called to Be Saints, An Exposition of I Corinthians* (Grand Rapids, 1977).

Grosheide, F. W. *Commentary on the First Epistle to the Corinthians*, NIC (Grand Rapids, 1953).

Héring, Jean. *The First Epistle of Saint Paul to the Corinthians* (ET, London, 1962).

Hodge, Charles. *An Exposition of the First Epistle to the Corinthians* (New York, 1857; repr. Grand Rapids, 1974).

Holladay, Carl. *The First Letter of Paul to the Corinthians*, LWC (Austin, 1979).

Lenski, R. C. H. *The Interpretation of St. Paul's First and Second Epistle to the Corinthians* (Columbus, OH, 1937).

Kugelman, R. "The First Letter to the Corinthians," in *The Jerome Biblical Commentary* (Englewood Cliffs, NJ, 1968).

Lias, J. J. *The First Epistle to the Corinthians*, CBSC (Cambridge, 1896).

Lietzmann, Hans. *An die Korinther I/II*, HNT (ed. W. G. Kümmel; Tübingen, 1949).

Lightfoot, J. B. *Notes on the Epistles of St Paul from unpublished commentaries* (London, 1895; repr. Grand Rapids, 1957).

MacArthur, John F. *I Corinthians* (Chicago, 1984).

Mare, W. H. *1 Corinthians*, EBC (Grand Rapids, 1976).

Moffatt, James. *The First Epistle of Paul to the Corinthians*, MNTC (New York, 1938).

Morris, Leon. *The First Epistle of Paul to the Corinthians*, TNTC (London, 1958).

Murphy-O'Connor, Jerome. *1 Corinthians*, NTM (Wilmington, DE, 1979).

Orr, W. F. and J. A. Walther (O-W). *I Corinthians*, AB (Garden City, 1976).

Parry, R. St John. *The First Epistle of Paul the Apostle to the Corinthians*, CGTSC (2d ed., Cambridge, 1926).

Prior, David. *The Message of I Corinthians* (Downers Grove, 1985).

Ramsay, William. "Historical Commentary on the Epistles to the Corinthians," *Exp* 6th series (1898-99), I, 19-31; 91-111; 203-17; 273-89; 380-87; II, 287-302; 368-81; 429-44; III, 93-110; 220-40; 343-60.

Robertson, A. and A. Plummer (R-P). *A Critical and Exegetical Commentary on the First Epistle of St Paul to the Corinthians*, ICC (2d ed., Edinburgh, 1914).

Ruef, John. *Paul's First Letter to Corinth*, WPC (Philadelphia, 1971).

Schlatter, Adolf. *Die Korintherbriefe* (Stuttgart, 1962).

Senft, Christophe. *La Première Épitre de Saint-Paul aux Corinthiens* (Neuchâtel, 1979).

Thrall, M. E. *The First and Second Letters of Paul to the Corinthians*, CBC (Cambridge, 1965).

Weiss, Johannes. *Der erste Korintherbrief*, MKNT (9 Aufl., Göttingen, 1910).

Wendland, H. D. *Die Briefe an die Korinther*, NTD (Göttingen, 1968).

Wilson, G. B. *1 Corinthians, A Digest of Reformed Comment* (Edinburgh, 1978).

Wolff, Christian. *Der erste Brief des Paulus an die Korinther*, Zweiter Teil, THNT (2d Aufl., Berlin, 1982).

II. OTHER SIGNIFICANT WORKS

Bartchy, S. S. *ΜΑΛΛΟΝ ΧΡΗΣΑΙ: First-Century Slavery and the Interpretation of 1 Corinthians 7:21*, SBLDS 11 (Missoula, MT, 1973).

Bittlinger, Arnold. *Gifts and Graces, A Commentary on I Corinthians 12–14* (ET, Grand Rapids, 1967).

Dahl, M. E. *The Resurrection of the Body, A Study of I Corinthians 15*, SBT (London, 1962).

Davis, J. A. *Wisdom and Spirit, An Investigation of 1 Corinthians 1.18–3:20 Against the Background of Jewish Sapiential Traditions in the Greco-Roman Period* (Lanham, MD, 1984).

Dungan, D. L. *The Sayings of Jesus in the Churches of Paul* (Philadelphia, 1971).

Ellis, E. E. *Prophecy and Hermeneutic in Early Christianity: New Testament Essays* (Grand Rapids, 1978).

Grudem, W. A. *The Gift of Prophecy in 1 Corinthians* (Washington, 1982).

Gundry, R. H. *SŌMA in Biblical Theology with emphasis on Pauline Anthropology*, SNTSMS 29 (Cambridge, 1976).

Hurd, J. C. *The Origin of I Corinthians* (2d ed., Macon, GA, 1983).

Hurley, J. B. "Man and Woman in 1 Corinthians" (unpubl. diss. Cambridge University, 1973).

Lincoln, A. T. *Paradise Now and Not Yet: Studies in the Role of the Heavenly Dimension in Paul's Thought with Special Reference to his Eschatology*, SNTSMS 43 (Cambridge, 1981).

Martin, R. P. *The Spirit and the Congregation: Studies in 1 Corinthians 12–15* (Grand Rapids, 1984).

Metzger, B. M. *A Textual Commentary on the Greek New Testament* (London, 1971).

Moule, C. F. D. *An Idiom Book of New Testament Greek* (2d ed., Cambridge, 1963).

O'Brien, P. T. *Introductory Thanksgivings in the Letters of Paul* (Leiden, 1977).

Pearson, B. A. *The Pneumatikos-Psychikos Terminology in 1 Corinthians, A Study in the Theology of the Corinthian Opponents of Paul and Its Relation to Gnosticism*, SBLDS 12 (Missoula, MT, 1973).

Schmithals, W. *Gnosticism in Corinth, An Investigation of the Letters to the Corinthians* (ET, Nashville, 1971).

Theissen, Gerd. *The Social Setting of Pauline Christianity: Essays on Corinth* (ET, Philadelphia, 1982).

Wilckens, U. *Weisheit und Torheit* (Tübingen, 1959).

Willis, W. L. *Idol Meat in Corinth, The Pauline Argument in 1 Corinthians 8 and 10*, SBLDS 68 (Chico, CA, 1985).
Zuntz, G. *The Text of the Epistles* (London, 1953).

III. ARTICLES

A. *R. A. Horsley*

"Background" = "The Background of the Confessional Formula in 1 Kor 8:6," *ZNW* 69 (1978), 130-35.

"Consciousness" = "Consciousness and Freedom among the Corinthians: 1 Corinthians 8–10," *CBQ* 40 (1978), 574-89.

"Elitism" = "'How can some of you say there is no resurrection of the dead?' Spiritual Elitism in Corinth," *NovT* 20 (1978), 203-31.

"Gnosis" = "Gnosis in Corinth: 1 Corinthians 8.1-6," *NTS* 27 (1980), 32-51.

"Marriage" = "Spiritual Marriage with Sophia," *VigC* 33 (1979), 30-54.

"Pneumatikos" = "Pneumatikos vs. Psychikos: Distinctions of Spiritual Status among the Corinthians," *HTR* 69 (1976), 269-88.

"Wisdom" = "Wisdom of Word and Words of Wisdom in Corinth," *CBQ* 39 (1977), 224-39.

B. *J. Murphy-O'Connor*

"Baptized" = "'Baptized for the Dead' (I Cor., XV,29). A Corinthian Slogan?" *RB* 88 (1981), 532-43.

Corinth = *St. Paul's Corinth, Texts and Archaeology* (Wilmington, DE, 1983).

"Cosmology" = "I Cor., VIII,6: Cosmology or Soteriology?" *RB* 85 (1978), 253-67.

"Divorced" = "The Divorced Woman in 1 Cor 7:10-11," *JBL* 100 (1981), 601-06.

"Eucharist" = "Eucharist and Community in First Corinthians," *Worship* 51 (1977), 56-69.

"Food" = "Food and Spiritual Gifts in 1 Cor 8:8," *CBQ* 41 (1979), 292-98.

"Freedom" = "Freedom or the Ghetto (*1 Cor.*, VIII,1-13; X,23–XI,1)," *RB* (1978), 543-74.

"Interpolations" = "Interpolations in 1 Corinthians," *CBQ* 48 (1986), 81-84.

"Sex" = "Sex and Logic in 1 Corinthians 11:2-16," *CBQ* 42 (1980), 482-500.

"Slogans" = "Corinthian Slogans in 1 Cor 6:12-20," *CBQ* 40 (1978), 391-96.

"Tradition" = "Tradition and Redaction in 1 Cor 15:3-7," *CBQ* 43 (1981), 582-89.

"V,3-5" = "1 Corinthians, V,3-5," *RB* 84 (1977), 239-45.

"Works" = "Works Without Faith in I Cor., VII,14," *RB* 84 (1977), 349-61.

INTRODUCTION

I. THE CITY AND ITS PEOPLE

As much as for any other document in the NT—and more so than for most—the various sociological, economic, and religious factors that make up the environment of the city of Corinth have a profound influence on one's understanding of Paul's letters to the church there. Its strategic location as sentry of the four-and-one-half-mile (5,950-meter) Isthmus that bridged the Peloponnese and the mainland and separated the Saronic and Corinthian gulfs insured for it a long and illustrious history.[1] It controlled both the overland commercial traffic and that between Italy and Asia, which for the most part found it safer and more convenient to take this "inland" route than to go around the Peloponnese.[2]

The city's history is essentially in two parts. As a Greek city-state it flourished both before and after the golden years of Athens (5th c. B.C.). But as leader of the Achaean League in the mid-second century B.C., it came into conflict with Rome and was destroyed by the Roman consul Lucius Mummius in 146 B.C. The site lay dormant for one hundred years, until it was refounded in 44 B.C. by Julius Caesar as a Roman colony.[3] The reason for its

---

[1]It is located on a terrace at the southern gate of the Isthmus, about two miles from the Gulf of Corinth and at the foot of the 1,886-foot (575-meter)-high Acrocorinth. For descriptions of the city, see esp. Strabo, *Geography* 8.6.20-23 (written *ca.* 7 B.C.) and Pausanias, *Description of Greece, Book II: Corinth* (*ca.* A.D. 170). These texts, and many others, are conveniently brought together and discussed in Murphy-O'Connor, *Corinth*. For the history of Corinth during the Roman period one should consult J. Wiseman, "Corinth and Rome I: 228 B.C.-A.D. 267," in *ANRW* VII/1, pp. 438-548.

[2]Cf. Strabo, *Geography* 8.6.20: "Corinth is called 'wealthy' because of its commerce since it is situated on the Isthmus and is master of two harbours, of which the one [Cenchreae] leads straight to Asia, and the other [Lechaeum] to Italy; and it makes easy the exchange of merchandise from both countries that are so far distant from each other. . . . And also the duties on what by land was exported from the Peloponnesus and what was imported to it fell to those who held the keys" (Loeb, IV, 189-91).

[3]In fact Latin was its official language well beyond the time of Paul. See Murphy-O'Connor, *Corinth*, 5.

1

refounding was probably twofold. First, its strategic location for commerce (described by Strabo) made its refounding almost inevitable. All the necessary ingredients for economic boom were available: a natural defense in the Acrocorinth; adequate water supply from springs; the relationship to Rome; being master of the two harbors for East-West commerce; and control of the Isthmian games, which ranked just below the Olympian in importance (see on 9:24-27). Second, according to Strabo (8.6.23c), Corinth was repopulated by freedmen from Rome. Since their status was just above that of the slave,[4] and since Rome often tended to be overpopulated with such, this was a convenient way for Rome to rid itself of potential trouble, on the one hand, and for the freedman to seize an opportunity for socioeconomic advancement, on the other.

As the description by Strabo some fifty years later makes abundantly clear, prosperity returned to the city almost immediately. Since money attracts people like dead meat attracts flies, Corinth quickly experienced a great influx of people from both West and East,[5] along with all the attendant gains and ills of such growth. The Romans were dominant; they brought with them not only their laws but also their culture and religions. But the Roman world had been thoroughly Hellenized; and since Corinth was historically Greek, it maintained many of those ties—religion, philosophy, the arts. And from the East came the mystery cults of Egypt and Asia and the Jews with their synagogue and "peculiar" belief in a single God.

Since Corinth lacked a landed aristocracy, an aristocracy of money soon developed, along with a fiercely independent spirit. But not all would strike it rich, hence thousands of artisans and slaves made up the bulk of the population. Most likely, however, the splendid wealth of the city spilled over to the advantage of these people as well.

As often happens in such centers, vice and religion flourished side by side. Old Corinth had gained such a reputation for sexual vice that Aristophanes (ca. 450-385 B.C.) coined the verb korinthiazō (= to act like a Corinthian, i.e., to commit fornication). The Asclepius room in the present museum in Corinth provides mute evidence of this facet of city life; here on one wall are a large number of clay votives of human genitals that had been offered to the god for the healing of that part of the body, apparently ravaged by venereal disease. This aspect of Corinthian life, however, has tended to be overplayed by most NT scholars, relying on Strabo's (surely erroneous) description of the thousand temple prostitutes who were alleged to have plied their trade at the temple of Aphrodite on the Acrocorinth. In the first

[4]See the discussion and bibliography on 7:22.

[5]No scientific attempt has been made to estimate its population. See Murphy-O'Connor, *Corinth*, 31-32. Nonetheless, after Rome and Alexandria, it would certainly have vied for distinction as the third city of the Empire.

place Strabo was speaking of Old Corinth, and even then it is doubtful whether his information was accurate.[6] Sexual sin there undoubtedly was in abundance; but it would have been of the same kind that one would expect in any seaport where money flowed freely and women and men were available.

The religious expression of Corinth was as diverse as its population. Pausanias describes at least 26 sacred places (not all were temples) devoted to the "gods many" (the Roman-Greek pantheon) and "lords many" (the mystery cults) mentioned by Paul in 1 Cor. 8:5—and Pausanias does not mention the Jewish synagogue, whose partial lintel with the inscription "synagogue of the Hebrews" has been discovered.[7] Although there is no direct evidence for it, the very wealth that attracted artisans and tradesmen undoubtedly also lured to Corinth artists and philosophers of all kinds, in search of patronage. The latter would also have included a fair share of itinerants and charlatans.[8]

All of this evidence together suggests that Paul's Corinth was at once the New York, Los Angeles, and Las Vegas of the ancient world.

The scattered pieces of evidence from Acts, 1 Corinthians, and Romans[9] suggest that the church was in many ways a mirror of the city. In 1 Cor. 12:13 Paul interrupts his argument to emphasize the diversity of those who have all become one body—Jew, Greek, slave, free. This mix is substantiated in other ways as well. Of the people who are named, at least three are Jews (Aquila, Priscilla, Crispus), even though they bear Latin names. Three (or four) others who also have Latin names are probably Romans (Fortunatus, Quartus, Gaius, Titius Justus),[10] at least one (or two) of whom (Gaius, Titius Justus) were among the wealthier members. The others bear Greek names (Stephanas, Achaicus, Erastus), and of these at least Stephanas and Erastus were probably well-to-do. According to 1:26, however, *not many* of them came from the upper socioeconomic strata; indeed, the evidence of 7:20-24 suggests that some were slaves. The mention of Stephanas's household (1:16) probably reflects a situation where besides his family there were slaves or attached freedmen (see on 16:15-17). If our interpretation of 11:17-34 is correct (q.v.), some of the tensions in the community were between the well-to-do and the poor.[11]

[6]This has been demonstrated by H. Conzelmann, "Korinth und die Mädchen der Aphrodite. Zur Religionsgeschichte der Stadt Korinth," *NAG* 8 (1967-68), 247-61. Cf. Murphy-O'Connor, *Corinth*, 55-57.

[7]Cf. Murphy-O'Connor, *Corinth*, 78-80.

[8]For the significance of this see on 1:10-17 and 9:3-14.

[9]Acts 18:1-8; 1 Cor. 1:10-17; 16:15-17; Rom. 16:23.

[10]Some believe Gaius Titius Justus to be the full name of one person; see n. 71 on 1:16.

[11]Cf. Theissen, 69-174, whose overall thesis is that this tension is the basic cause of the divisions in the church—although he sees it more specifically as a rivalry among the rich.

Although there were some Jews in the community, very little in the letter suggests a Jewish background.[12] At least three texts that speak of their former way of life explicitly indicate that they were former idolaters and therefore chiefly Gentiles (6:10-11; 8:7; 12:2). Other items imply the same: e.g., the whole matter of going to the temple feasts in 8:1–10:22 is a strictly Gentile phenomenon; the attitude toward marriage, thinking it to be a sin, in chap. 7 scarcely fits Judaism, even Hellenistic Judaism; going to the proconsul, or city magistrates, for adjudication (6:1-11) fits the normal processes of the Greeks and Romans within the city, whereas the Jews were forbidden to ask Gentiles for judgments. Their arguing for the right to go to the prostitutes (6:12-20) and their denial of a future bodily resurrection (15:1-58) also sound more Hellenistic than Jewish.

Thus, the picture that emerges is one of a predominantly Gentile community, the majority of whom were at the lower end of the socioeconomic ladder, although there were two or three wealthy families. As former pagans they brought to the Christian faith a Hellenistic worldview and attitude toward ethical behavior. Although they were the Christian church in Corinth, an inordinate amount of Corinth was yet in them, emerging in a number of attitudes and behaviors that required radical surgery without killing the patient. This is what 1 Corinthians attempts to do.

II. THE CHURCH AND ITS APOSTLE

The Problem. Our 1 Corinthians is an occasional, *ad hoc* response to the situation that had developed in the Corinthian church between the time Paul left the city, sometime in A.D. 51-52,[13] and the writing of our letter approx-

---

[12]From time to time some have argued for such. See, e.g., J. M. Ford, "The First Epistle to the Corinthians or the First Epistle to the Hebrews," *CBQ* 28 (1966), 402-16 (for other items see Index) and the dissertation by J. B. Hurley (see bibliography). Cf. also the arguments for Philonic background by B. Pearson, R. A. Horsley, and J. A. Davis discussed below (pp. 13-14). But such a view runs aground on the explicit evidence of the letter.

Hurley's dissertation is an especially interesting, but unconvincing, piece of scholarly logic. There is in fact no *explicit* indication of any kind that 1 Corinthians is addressed to Jews; whereas there are several such indications that the believers were Gentiles. Thus Hurley attempts two things: (1) to show that both the explicit and implicit references do not *necessarily* require a Gentile congregation (here he is especially unconvincing); and (2) to show that by *assuming* a Jewish audience one can make sense of the various items. On the latter he has more success with some (e.g., 11:2-16) than with others (6:12-20; 7:1-40; 8–10). It is striking that the self-confessed "apostle to the Gentiles," when writing to the most thoroughly Hellenistic city in the NT, should be thought to be writing to a Diaspora Jewish congregation. All the evidence suggests otherwise.

[13]This is one of the few certain dates in the NT, and the one from which most Pauline dates are ultimately derived. That this is so is the result of the Gallio inscription

imately three years later. The difficulty in determining the nature of that situation is intrinsic to the text. Paul addresses, in response to reports (1:11; 5:1; 11:18) or to their letter (cf. 7:1), at least eleven different, somewhat disparate concerns, ten of which are behavioral; only chap. 15 is theological as such, and even there he concludes both major sections with ethical warnings and imperatives (vv. 33-34, 58). But in every case his greater concern is the theological stance behind the behavior. Our difficulty at this distance is threefold: (1) to discover the relationship, if indeed there is one, of these various items to one another; (2) to determine the relationship of the community to Paul; and (3) to determine what influences/positions in the Corinthian "theology" allowed them not only to adopt such behavior but also to argue for the right to do it.

For the most part, historically, these matters were resolved (if noted at all) in terms either of Paul's *informing* or *correcting* the Corinthians in areas where they were deficient or had gone astray. As such our letter has usually been understood as a *response to their division into parties,* wherein Paul takes the side of one over against the other (or sometimes, it is argued, he speaks to both groups).[13a] There are, however, a number of difficulties with this point of view:

(a) That there is some form of internal division in the church is evident from three texts: 1:10-12; 3:4-5; and 11:18-19. That this division is at least along socioeconomic lines is indicated by Paul's response in 11:17-34 (cf. 1:26; 7:20-24; 12:13); but whether it is also along spiritual/theological lines is moot. In any case, nothing in chaps. 7–16, where Paul is responding to their letter, suggests as much. Indeed, it is probably quite wrong to envision the church as split into "parties" at all,[14] since nothing in the letter itself gives much in the way of hints as to how these might be viewed.[15]

(b) Apart from 7:1-40 and 11:2-16—and even here he stands over against their point of view—the language and style of 1 Corinthians are

(see the discussion in Murphy-O'Connor, *Corinth,* 141-52) and the references in Acts 18:12, which place Paul and Gallio in Corinth at some point between A.D. 50 and 52.

[13a]For a classical presentation of this point of view, see K. Prümm, "Die pastorale Einheit des Ersten Korintherbriefes," *ZKT* 64 (1940), 202-14.

[14]On this see especially the introduction to 1:10–4:21 and the commentary on 1:12. Cf. also the introductions to 2:6-16 and 12–14, which have also been understood, quite incorrectly it would seem, as revealing "groups" within the church itself. But in fact Paul says nothing of the kind, and the exegesis of these passages reveals a considerably different kind of issue in each case.

[15]It is common to understand the "weak" and "gnostics" of chaps. 8–10 as belonging to the "parties" of 1:11. But that is highly questionable, and in any case there is no hint of any kind in those chapters that the church is internally divided on that matter. See the commentary (intro. to 8:1–11:1).

especially rhetorical and combative. Paul is taking them on at every turn. There is little to suggest that he is either informing or merely correcting; instead, he is attacking and challenging with all the weapons in his literary arsenal. If 1 Corinthians is a response to their letter, in which they are asking Paul to arbitrate their differences, then one must judge him to have misread their letter rather considerably.

(c) The letter in its entirety is addressed to the whole church, with no suggestion that he is speaking now to one group, and then to another. Nearly everything is in the second person plural, except for a few instances where he shifts to the second singular, perhaps with some specific person(s) in view.[16] If Paul were settling differences among them, one would expect at least some word to that effect. But there is none.

These factors together suggest that the traditional viewpoint comes up lacking at crucial points. What is needed is a way of looking at the letter that will hold all these items together within a more consistent framework.

A Proposed Reconstruction. The basic stance of the present commentary is that the *historical situation* in Corinth was *one of conflict between the church and its founder.* This is not to deny that the church was experiencing internal strife, but it is to argue that the greater problem of "division" was between Paul and some in the community who were leading the church as a whole into an anti-Pauline view of things. For Paul this conflict presents a twofold crisis—over his authority and his gospel. Furthermore, the key issue between Paul and them, which created both of these crises, has to do with the Corinthian understanding of what it means to be "spiritual" *(pneumatikos).* Several factors go into this view of things:

(a) *The occasion of 1 Corinthians.* Our letter records Paul's third dealings with this church. The most plausible understanding of these relationships is that 1 Corinthians is the third in an exchange of letters between Paul and Corinth. Thus:

(i) Paul's first association with them was the founding visit mentioned in Acts 18 (*ca.* A.D. 49-51), a visit that had a unique feature to it—the length of stay. Although both Acts 18 and 1 Corinthians give us some information about the makeup of the community, we learn nothing as to its size, its place(s) and times of meeting, nor the nature of its leadership.

(ii) A couple of years later, while Paul was in Ephesus, he wrote the Previous Letter to the community mentioned in 1 Cor. 5:9. Although one cannot be sure as to what prompted this letter, he at least dealt with some problems of sexual immorality: he told them not to associate with fornicators, by which he intended that they should not associate with *brothers* who were acting in such a way. Besides fornicators, he also mentions in 5:10 the

[16]See on 4:7; cf. 7:21, 27; 8:9-10; 14:16-17; 15:36-37.

covetous, robbers, and idolaters. Were these also dealt with in the Previous Letter? The best guess would seem to be yes, at least on the matter of idolatry, because this problem also emerges in our letter in a way that makes most sense if Paul had already spoken to it in the former letter.

If in fact the Previous Letter dealt at least with two of the issues that resurface in this one, namely fornication and idolatry, then most likely that letter was also written as a response of some kind to the situation in Corinth. It is clear from 1 Corinthians 5 that the Corinthians themselves have misunderstood the letter; it seems more than likely that they have in fact disregarded it (see on 5:9-11).

(iii) That leads, then, to our 1 Corinthians, which was occasioned primarily by a letter brought to Paul by Stephanas, Fortunatus, and Achaicus (16:15-17), a letter that makes most sense when viewed under very ordinary circumstances—*as a response on their part to his letter*.[17] Given the combative nature of so much of his response, it seems highly likely that in their letter they have taken considerable exception to several of his positions and/or prohibitions. Paul's attitude toward their letter, and thus toward the Corinthians, is further exacerbated by an oral communication from some believers from Chloe's household (1:11), who filled his ears with information about what was going on in Corinth that Paul probably suspected from their letter but which he now knows for certain. The coming of Chloe's people *at least* helps Paul better to understand their letter.[18]

Paul's difficulties in writing this letter are essentially twofold: On the one hand, he must reassert his authority in a situation where it has severely eroded. This is made the more difficult by his use of servant imagery as the model of leadership in the church (3:5-9; 4:1-5)—how shall he reassert his own authority over them and not destroy the perspective of that imagery?[19] On the other hand, he must convince them to change both their theology and their behavior to conform to his, since they are moving toward positions that threaten the gospel itself—every bit as much as the Judaizers in Galatia were doing in another direction.

(b) *The opposition*. The available data make it clear that between Paul's leaving the church, recorded in Acts 18:18, and his writing of our 2 Corinthians, some "bad blood" had developed between Paul and this

---

[17]Although much of his reconstruction of the relationship between Paul and Corinth is less than convincing, it is to Hurd's credit that he took seriously this eminently reasonable historical probability (see esp. pp. 50-58). The majority of commentators tend to overlook any relationship between Paul's first letter to them and their letter to him.

[18]This order of events cannot be proved, of course, but it seems to make good sense of the data. It also helps to make sense of the apparent discrepancies between what is really going on in the church and the "official" stance presented in their letter (as, e.g., in 11:2).

[19]See especially on 4:14-21.

church. These tensions apparently come to a head in an unexpected visit that he makes to them, noted in 2 Cor. 2:1-4. The evidence of 1 Corinthians indicates that the problem had already been brewing before that "painful" visit. The question is, Where does 1 Corinthians fit into this scheme?

(i) Quite in contrast to 2 Corinthians and Galatians, this letter yields little or no evidence that the church has yet been invaded by the outsiders mentioned in 2 Cor. 10–13. In fact, the mention in 1 Cor. 9:12 of some "others" who share the Corinthians' provisions is the one possible reference to outsiders, and such an understanding is not demanded by the context. Thus it is not quite proper to speak of Paul's "opponents" in the ordinary sense of that word, as referring to outside agitators.[20] Rather, the opposition is led by "some among you" (15:12; cf. 4:18).

(ii) Our 1 Corinthians reflects the problem at a middle stage. The situation is not good; the relationship between Paul and the church is visibly deteriorating, but apparently it has not yet resulted in open hostility. They are still communicating by letter. Nonetheless, a decidedly anti-Pauline sentiment has developed in the church. *Initiated by a few*,[21] this sentiment is infecting *nearly the whole*.[22] Therefore, although there are certainly divisions within the community itself (probably along sociological lines), the most serious form of "division" is that between the *majority* of the community and Paul himself. They stand over against him on almost every issue. The key issue here is their calling his authority into question. What right does he have to speak to them as he did in the Previous Letter, since there is considerable doubt, based on their own criteria, whether he is truly *pneumatikos* (spiritual) or a prophet (cf. 14:37)?

One cannot be certain how such a situation developed. The evidence from chaps. 1–4, 9, and 14 suggests that it was a combination of several factors. (1) In chaps. 1–4, perhaps as a result of the ministry of Apollos, it seems certain that the Corinthians have begun to think of their new faith in terms of *sophia* (wisdom), as though, in comparison with others, it were the ultimate expression of divine *sophia*. Under these new criteria, neither Paul nor his gospel fared well. As to the *content* of wisdom, they considered his

---

[20]To this extent Ellis, 103, is correct in arguing that "in 1 Corinthians . . . there are . . . no opponents." But he seems to overlook too much in this letter to reject the notion of opposition altogether.

[21]See on 1:12; 4:3, 6, 18-20; 9:3; 10:29-30; 14:37; 15:12.

[22]It should be noted in this regard that although Paul at times refers to those in the community who oppose him (e.g., 4:18-20; 9:3), the letter itself is addressed to the whole church; and with but two exceptions (7:1-40; 11:2-16), they come under some pretty heavy fire (cf. 1:10–4:21, with its mixture of irony, rhetoric, and sarcasm; or 5:1-13 and 6:1-11, where he takes on the whole church far more than the guilty parties [especially with the stinging sarcasm of 6:5]; or 8:1–11:1, where he parries with them using every form of argumentation).

gospel and preaching to be something like "milk" for babes, whereas they had moved on to headier stuff designed for the "mature" (see 2:6; 3:1). Likewise as to the *form* of wisdom, they were particularly repelled by his lack of the rhetorical skills that ordinarily accompanied *sophia* (cf. 1:17; 2:1-5).

It should be noted at this point that the argument of 1:10–4:21 does *not* conclude at 3:18-23, as most commentators tend to see it, but with the rather considerable defense of his apostolic ministry found in 4:1-21.[23] This suggests that the "divisions" that have preceded are not simply a matter of playing favorites with regard to their various teachers. They are at the same time decidedly over against Paul. According to v. 3, they have been sitting in judgment on him. In v. 6 he notes that they have been puffed up *for* the one (Apollos) and *against* the other (Paul). At the end of the argument he says that he has sent Timothy to them so that they might once again be reminded of *his* ways, and that they might return to them. He concludes on a final hot note about some who have been arrogant about him and his coming to them, and asks the whole church how he wants his next coming to be— with a rod, or in a spirit of gentleness? As is argued in the commentary, the whole of chaps. 5–6 is also best understood as reflecting this same crisis of authority over his rights to direct their affairs.

(2) The same kind of fierce defense emerges again in chap. 9, in the middle of an argument where he and they seem clearly to be at loggerheads. Again, he accuses them of "sitting in judgment" on him (v. 3). The issue at hand is their rejection of his prior prohibition of their attending idol feasts in the pagan shrines (see the introduction to 8:1–11:1). Their rejection seems to have been expressed at least in part as the result of what they perceived to be his vacillation in behavior with regard to marketplace food: he ate such food in some settings, but abstained in others (see on 9:19-23; cf. 10:29-33). Indeed, he seems to take a considerable swipe at his opponents on this matter at the conclusion of the argument in 10:30: "If I take part in the meal with thankfulness, why am I denounced because of something I thank God for?"

In defending these actions of his, however, he also takes up another area of tension between them—his working with his own hands at the demeaning (for a "wise man") task of tent-making with his concomitant refusal to accept patronage from them (see on 9:3-14). That this issue emerges again in 2 Corinthians (cf. 11:8-9; 12:13) indicates that it was a festering sore between them. Apparently they were either offended by his not accepting their patronage or they questioned the apostleship of one who acted thus—or perhaps both!

---

[23]Very likely 2:15 is something of a sideswipe at their accusation: "The *pneumatikos* [meaning himself in this case] . . . is not subject to anyone's judgment."

(3) Finally, in 14:37, in another passage where he and they are at odds, he asserts in an *ad hominem* way: "If anyone thinks that he is a prophet or *pneumatikos,* let him acknowledge that what I am writing to you is the Lord's command." And he concludes by pronouncing judgment on those who fail to recognize his word as authority among them.

A man who talks thus, and this is the tenor of the whole argument (except for chaps. 7 and 11:2-16), is *not* attempting to *inform* his readers because of their deficient understanding; nor is he trying to reconcile warring factions. Furthermore, the letter is not written to one group, nor directed against the ringleaders of the opposition.[24] Rather, Paul is on the attack, contending with them, arguing with them, trying to convince them that he is right and they are wrong. Over and again he resorts to rhetoric ("Do you not know that. . . ?" [ten times]; or "If anyone thinks that he/she is . . ." [three times]), to sarcasm, to irony. Thus the letter is basically the apostle Paul vis-à-vis the whole Corinthian congregation.

(c) *The point(s) of contention.* Most likely the insurgents are not only calling his authority into question, but also are modifying the gospel toward Hellenism. For Paul these two crises always overlap. It is not his own person that is at stake in their denial of his authority, but the gospel he preaches. To deny the one is to deny the other. Most likely the key issue between them is a basic theological problem, what it means to be *pneumatikos.* The problem here is not so much a matter of elitism among themselves—there is not a hint of such in chaps. 12–14 (i.e., that some feel superior to others because of their gifts, or that others feel inferior for the lack thereof). This habitually given answer is not based on anything explicit in the text, but is read in from the outside.

More likely the problem is that they think of themselves as *pneumatikoi,* but are not so sure about the apostle Paul (cf. 14:37). Here indeed some odious comparisons may have been made between him and Apollos (although 16:12 makes it clear that neither of them was party to such a rift). In any case Paul seems to feel a need to explain, indeed glory in, his weaknesses as a demonstration of his gospel (cf. 2:1-5; 4:9-13; 15:8-11).

Although one cannot be sure, their understanding of being *pneumatikos* is most likely related to their experience of Spirit inspiration, especially their overemphasis on the gift of tongues (see especially the introduction to chaps. 12–14). In 14:23, somewhat rhetorically but nonetheless realistically, Paul says that if they all come together at the same place and all speak in tongues, the outsider will declare them mad. This, plus the very need to order that gift to "one at a time" and not more than two or three in

[24]Only 4:18; 9:3; and 15:12 single them out—although they are probably also in view in the threefold "if anyone thinks he is (wise, full of knowledge, spiritual)" (3:18; 8:2; 14:37).

sequence, suggests that they were both overly and singularly enthusiastic about this gift. If, as suggested in 13:1, "speaking the tongues of angels" reflects their own understanding of this gift, then one can begin to appreciate how they made it the basic criterion for their understanding of spirituality. Glossolalia was for them the evidence that they had already assumed the spiritual existence of the angels.

This in turn is probably related to their interest in *sophia* and *gnōsis* (wisdom and knowledge), two words that occur primarily in the context of specific behavioral aberrations (chaps. 1–4 and 8–10 respectively). Both of these "gifts" have become their special possession by means of the Spirit. They are spiritually endowed, hence they have special wisdom and superior knowledge. It is probably no accident that the statement "if anyone thinks that he/she is . . ." (3:18; 8:1; 14:37) is found in each of the three major sections of the letter (chaps. 1–4; 8–10; 12–14) and reflects these three crucial Corinthian terms ("wisdom," "knowledge," and "spiritual").

Further related to this is their apparently "spiritual" understanding of the sacraments, whereby the one who has been baptized and partakes of the "spiritual food" of the Lord's Table also finds security (10:1-5), so that behavior in this present life has little or no effect on one's true spirituality.

All of this, of course, stands over against both Paul and his gospel in radical ways and results in *kauchēsis* ("boasting" or false confidence). Hence they are "puffed up" (4:6, 18; 5:2) and full of arrogance (5:6), and even have gross immorality in their midst—so little is their true spiritual condition affected by such things.

Closely related to this are two further crucial theological aberrations: (i) Their worldview has been "tainted" (ingrained by a lifetime) by Hellenistic dualism. Because they were "spiritual," they took a dim view of continuing existence in the material world, including the body.[25] This is the element seized on by Walther Schmithals[26] and others (e.g., U. Wilckens[27] and R. Jewett[28]), who argue that the Corinthians were "Gnostics." But such language is not only anachronistic,[29] it fails adequately to describe this element in the Corinthian spirituality. None of the essential phenomena of Gnosticism is present in this letter except the dualism itself, which can be explained on other grounds.

---

[25]If this is so, and all the evidence seems to point in this direction, then the play on the terms "of the flesh" (= made of fleshly stuff) and "of the flesh" (= living from the old-age point of view) in 3:1-3 is particularly telling. See the commentary.

[26]*Gnosticism* (see bibliography).

[27]*Weisheit* (see bibliography).

[28]*Paul's Anthropological Terms, A Study of Their Use in Conflict Settings* (AGJU 10; Leiden, 1971).

[29]See the critique, *inter alia*, in R. McL. Wilson, "How Gnostic Were the Corinthians?" *NTS* 19 (1972/73), 65-74; and Pearson, 51-81.

Despite their continuing existence in the body, the Corinthians consider themselves to be the "spiritual ones," already as the angels. Hence, since from their perspective the body is eschatologically insignificant (cf. 6:13; 15:12), neither does it have present significance. This attitude toward corporeal existence is at least in part responsible for such things as the denial of a future bodily resurrection (15:12) and both the affirmation of sexual immorality and the denial of sexual relations within marriage (6:12-20 and 7:1-6).

(ii) Finally, and probably very closely related to the former, is the likelihood that they had a considerably "overrealized" eschatological view of their present existence,[30] for which I have coined the inelegant expression "spiritualized eschatology." This would follow directly from their view of being *pneumatikoi* (people of the Spirit, whose present existence is to be understood in strictly spiritual terms). The Spirit belongs to the Eschaton, and they are already experiencing the Spirit in full measure. If tongues is understood as the "language of angels," then their experience of glossolalia is evidence for them that they have already arrived (already they speak the language of heaven).

It is doubtful, however, whether they also have a Jewish apocalyptic view of the End; rather, they have probably translated such a view into their framework of "spirituality," in which they regarded their present spiritual existence as an assumption of that which is to be, minus the physical body. From their point of view it would not so much be the "time" of the future that has become a present reality for them, as the "existence" of the future. They are now experiencing a kind of ultimate spirituality in which they live *above* the merely material existence of the present age.

If the Lukan version of the saying of Jesus on resurrection and marriage (Luke 20:35) is the one known in the Pauline churches ("Those who are considered worthy of taking part in that age and in the resurrection from the dead will neither marry nor be given in marriage, and they can no longer die; for they are like the angels"), then Robin Scroggs may well be right that part of the problem in chaps. 7 and 11 is with some "eschatological women," who are already living as if they had totally entered the new age.[31]

This would also explain in part their attitude toward Paul (whose weaknesses make it obvious that he had *not* arrived), and why Paul so often views their present existence in light of the future, since neither have they yet arrived (1:5-8; 3:13-15, 17; 4:5; 5:5; 6:13-14; 7:26-31; 11:26, 32; 15:24, 51-56; 16:22). Thus, with fine sarcasm Paul in 4:8 takes the measure of their

---

[30]On this matter see esp. A. C. Thiselton, "Realized Eschatology at Corinth," *NTS* 24 (1977/78), 510-26.

[31]See the introduction to chaps. 7 and 11:2-16.

present attitude ("already" they are rich, full, and reigning) and in light of present apostolic existence finds it wanting (4:9-13).

(d) *The source of their false spirituality*. Although not all would put the various components together in this way, there is a growing consensus among scholars that these are the basic components of the Corinthian false theology. But that is scarcely so on the question of the source of the problem, both in its anti-Pauline and theological dimensions. Several suggestions have been made:

(i) J. C. Hurd[32] suggested that most of the problems stem from Paul himself. In a scheme that totally disregards the historical value of Acts in terms of dating Paul's activities, Hurd proposes that the Previous Letter (5:9) was written as a result of the Apostolic Decree (Acts 15:29). In this letter Paul made some decided changes from his earlier preaching in Corinth as a form of accommodation to Jerusalem. The net result is that the Corinthians in their letter to him are more faithful to the early Paul than he was in his own letter. Our 1 Corinthians turns out to be a middle ground, in which he avoids the excessive caution of the Previous Letter and the extremes of his earlier preaching, which are now found in the Corinthian positions. Despite a considerable number of helpful insights into the relationship between Paul and Corinth, this thesis, when tested against the hard evidence of 1 Corinthians and the letters on either side (1 and 2 Thessalonians; 2 Corinthians, Romans,[33] and Galatians), is found wanting, especially in terms of Paul's radical shift of positions from extreme freedom (earlier preaching [thesis]) to restrictions (Previous Letter [antithesis]) to moderation (1 Corinthians [synthesis]).[34]

(ii) More recently Birger Pearson, Richard Horsley, and James Davis[35] have argued that the Corinthian error derives from wisdom speculation in Hellenistic Judaism, either of the personified wisdom associated with Philo (Horsley) or with Torah-wisdom of the type found in Sirach and Qumran (Davis). These scholars have mustered considerable evidence to show possible parallels between the language assumed to be from the Corinthians and that of this literature. What is less certain is that the parallels reflect what is essential to Judaism in this tradition rather than its hellenization. At best the parallels only allow that the Corinthian errors *may* derive

---

[32]*Origin*, 213-96.

[33]J. R. Richards's argument that Romans precedes 1 Corinthians is quite unconvincing ("Romans and 1 Corinthians: Their Chronological Relationship and Comparative Dates," *NTS* 13 [1966/67], 14-30).

[34]Among others, see the critique by Barrett, 7-8. Despite some intriguing suggestions, the alleged parallels between our 1 Corinthians and the Decree are viable only on the hypothesis of certain exegetical conclusions, which are doubtful at best. Although brilliantly conceived, Hurd's thesis has been unable to attract many followers.

[35]See the bibliography.

from this source.[36] What remains unprovable—and improbable—is that they in fact do.

The basic problem with this approach lies with the explicitly Gentile features of this letter, noted above (p. 4), that emerge at several crucial points. In 8:1–10:22 the Corinthians are arguing for the right to attend pagan feasts in the idol temples, and some among them are unable to do so precisely because they were "formerly accustomed" to eating in the idol's presence as though it were a god (8:7). One can scarcely imagine the context in which a Diaspora Jew would so argue—even Philo would be horrified here. In 1:22 Paul explicitly says of "wisdom" that this is the Greek quest, while Jews demand "miraculous signs." It does no good, as Davis argues, to assign this statement merely to Paul's rhetoric.[37] Even as rhetoric, the statement is quite explicit, while the idea that the section reflects a Jewish midrashic homily against wisdom is speculative at best. Furthermore, in 12:2, again addressing the whole church, in the context of their misguided emphasis on tongues, Paul says that they formerly were led astray to mute idols—hardly the stuff of an essentially Hellenistic Jewish error.

(iii) Most likely, therefore, most of the error comes from their former paganism. Little or no Jew-Gentile tension is in fact perceptible in the letter. As noted above, at least three texts explicitly point out how things were in their former pagan days (6:9-11; 8:7; 12:1-3). Perhaps in part related to the coming and going of Paul and Apollos, and especially to Apollos's eloquence, they probably began to think of their teachers in terms similar to itinerant philosophers. Thus they began to view their new faith as the new *sophia*—the divine *sophia*. In this light, and in light of their experience of the Spirit, they considered themselves to have arrived at *sophia* itself. Under such new criteria, neither the gospel nor the apostle Paul comes off very well. Hence their rejection of Paul, and with that their tacit rejection of his gospel. Under such conditions one can understand Paul's great urgency to reassert the gospel as the message of a crucified Messiah and himself as the apostle of such a Messiah and message.

In any case, nothing in the letter *cannot* be explained in light of its Greco-Roman origins; whereas several items are extremely difficult to explain on the hypothesis of Hellenistic Jewish origins.

---

[36]Cf. Davis, 81: "Our investigation . . . has disclosed that it is quite possible to interpret the manifestation of wisdom at Corinth . . . against the background of later sapiential Judaism." One may grant that, but what he feels is confirmed by the analysis of 2:6–3:20 is likewise only possible. If Paul is attacking a form of Hellenized Judaism, it is most perceptible as Hellenism, not Judaism. The inability to carry this scheme through the entire letter—or to gainsay the explicitly pagan nature of so much of their argument—is what finally defeats it, attractive as some of its features are.

[37]P. 189 n. 26.

(iv) Finally, a "source" solution of a considerably different type should be noted. Gerd Theissen has argued that the basic tensions both within the community and between some of the community and Paul are best explained along sociological lines. Since the wealthy would be responsible for patronage both for the house churches and for the itinerant teachers, Theissen has suggested that the rival factions represent rival house churches and "patrons." Again, there are some especially helpful insights here; in fact, this suggestion can be modified toward rivalry between the "patrons" and Paul, some of whom are the leaders of the anti-Pauline sentiments in the church, and many things fall into place, including their dabbling in *sophia,* their "examination" of Paul because he refused to accept patronage (9:1-19), and their abuse of the poor at the Lord's Table.

The present commentary proceeds from this perspective. Its advantages are (1) that it takes seriously all the data of the letter, in terms of both content and style, and (2) that it can be consistently maintained throughout the letter, tying together the various parts in a coherent way.[38]

III. SOME CRITICAL QUESTIONS

In general 1 Corinthians is remarkably free of the kinds of questions that fit under this rubric. Discussions may be found in the standard Introductions. The letter may be safely dated in the Spring (see on 16:8), *ca.* A.D. 53-55, depending on the time of Paul's departure from Corinth (Acts 18:18) and the length of his stay in Ephesus. The single issue of significance is whether or not the letter is a unity. For various reasons several scholars have divided it (along with 2 Corinthians) into various letters sent to Corinth by Paul.[39] The starting point is Paul's mention of the Previous Letter in 5:9, which is assumed to be visible in some sections of 2 Corinthians. Then, on the basis of alleged contradictions between some sections of our 1 Corinthians, the letter has been broken up into three letters.

But these theories run aground at four points: (1) The very fact that there is so little agreement in the theories suggests that the various reconstructions are not as viable as their proponents would lead one to believe. (2) The alleged contradictions are invariably resolvable exegetically. For example, as argued in the present commentary, the tensions that some find between 8:1-13 and 10:23-33 are the result of Paul's speaking to two quite different, though related, issues. (3) Related to this, these theories miss a

---

[38]The attempt to do this may be found especially in the various introductions, both to the major sections of the letter and to the smaller parts.

[39]See especially the discussion in Hurd, 43-47.

basic form of argumentation in this letter, the "A-B-A" pattern.[40] In each case the first "A" section puts the matter into a larger, more general theological perspective; the "B" section is an explanatory digression of some kind, yet crucial to the argument as a whole; and the second "A" section is the very specific response to the matter at hand.[41] (4) When one can make perfectly good sense of the document as it comes to us, such theories are as unnecessary as they are unprovable. As Hurd concludes (p. 47), the evidence does not seem "strong enough to support the burden of proof which this kind of theory must always bear."

IV. THEOLOGICAL CONTRIBUTIONS

Although 1 Corinthians is not often consulted, except by scholars, for Pauline theology, its theological contributions are writ large in the history of the church. For here Paul is doing what he does best, bringing the gospel to bear in the marketplace. For him the truth of his gospel is finally tested in its ability to work its way out in the exigencies of everyday life in some very ticklish situations. Much could be said here; the present observations are limited to three areas, each of which is also crucial to a good understanding of the letter as a whole.

1. Eschatology. As much as in any of his writings, the essentially eschatological framework of Paul's theological thinking stands out in bold relief in this letter. For Paul this thinking has its focus in the event of Christ, his death and resurrection, and the subsequent gift of the Spirit. Christ's resurrection marks the turning of the ages; the subsequent gift of the eschatological Spirit is certain evidence that the End has begun. But the fact that we still live in bodies subject to decay (15:49-53), and that there is yet a future Parousia of the Lord (11:26; 15:23) with a subsequent resurrection (15:20-28), is also clear evidence that what has begun has not yet been fully brought to consummation. Thus for Paul, believers are thoroughly eschatological people, determined and conditioned by the reality of the future that has already begun, but still awaiting the final glory. We are therefore both "already" and "not yet."

This framework is thoroughgoing in Paul, yet nowhere more evident than here. This is true not only of his language (e.g., the kingdom of God is both now [4:20] and not yet [6:10-11; 15:50]) and of his expectations (e.g.,

---

[40]See on chaps. 1-3; 7:25-40; 8-10; 12-14. Cf. J. Collins, "Chiasmus, the 'ABA' Pattern and the Text of Paul," in *Studia Paulinorum Congressus Internationalis Catholicus* (Rome, 1963), vol. 2, pp. 575-84.

[41]Thus (a) 8:1-13/(b) 9:1-27/(a) 10:1-22; (a) 1:10-2:5/(b) 2:6-16/(a) 3:1-23; (a) 7:15-28/(b) 29-35/(a) 36-40; (a) 12/(b) 13/(a) 14.

the gifted Corinthians still await the revelation of the Lord Jesus [1:4-8]; at the Lord's Table we proclaim his death until he comes [11:26]), but especially of his understanding of present Christian life. On the one hand, because the future has already been set in motion, one's entire present existence is determined by this reality (7:29-31). God's people live "as if not"; they are not, as others, conditioned by the present order that is passing away. Such a point of view controls Paul's ethical imperatives at every step. Believers may not take one another to pagan courts because in light of their eschatological existence such things as redressing one's grievances are mere trivialities (6:1-6); Christians may not attend pagan feasts because the judgments against idolatry of a former time have been written down to warn those on whom the end of the ages has come (10:11). All merely human values and behavior have already been judged by God in Christ; already the present age is passing away (1:26-28; 7:31). Thus believers must exercise internal judgments in the present (5:12-13); the church must cleanse out the old leaven so that it may be a new loaf (5:7-8).

On the other hand, the future that has begun and absolutely conditions present existence still awaits its final consummation. But such a future is as certain as life itself. Again, this certainty has been guaranteed by the resurrection. Just as God raised up the Lord, so he will raise us up (6:14; 15:1-28). Christ is the firstfruits, God's own surety of the full harvest. When Christ comes again, not only will he raise the dead and transform the living, but by these events he will also have finally destroyed the last enemy, death itself (15:24-28, 54-57).

But neither the certain future nor the reality of eschatological existence in the present means that one has already fully arrived. Death is ours (3:22), but some still die (11:30); the present and future are ours (3:22), but the paradigm of present ethical life is our crucified Messiah (4:10-13). Thus, Christian life is paradox, apparent contradictions held together in tension. The guarantee rests not in present circumstances, but in the absolute certainty of the future that has already determined our present existence as well. The whole of our letter must be understood as flowing out of this essential framework (see on 4:1-5; 6:1-6; 7:29-31; 15:12-28, 35-38).

2. The Gospel and Ethical Life. Related to the eschatological framework just noted is Paul's insistence on radical obedience to Christ as the norm of Christian existence. If Romans and Galatians make it plain that one is not saved by obedience to the law, 1 Corinthians makes it equally plain that the saved are expected to live out their lives in obedience to the "commandments of God" (7:19) and the "law of Christ" (9:21). If such obedience is not required for entry into faith, it is nonetheless required as the outflow of faith.

Paul understands Christian ethics in terms of "becoming what you are," a perspective that emerges in 1 Corinthians in a number of ways. He is never short on the imperative, but he always sets it in the context of God's prior action on our behalf in Christ. Thus Paul commands the Corinthians to clean out the old leaven that they may become a new loaf, because in Christ our Passover they have already become a new loaf (5:7-8); they cannot go to the prostitutes because their bodies have already been set apart for Christ through his resurrection and they are already one S/spirit with him (6:14-17); they must cease acting as in their former pagan way of life or else they will not inherit the kingdom, but at the same time they are reminded that such were some of them and they are so no longer through Christ and the Spirit (6:9-11).

In such ethics there are some absolutes, precisely because some sins are quite incompatible with life in Christ (sexual immorality, 6:12-20; attending temple feasts, 10:14-22). This is not law, in the sense of gaining right standing with God. But it is absolute since some behavior is absolutely contradictory to the character of God. On the other hand, merely religious scruples—circumcision (7:19); marketplace idol food (9:19-13; 10:23-30)—are irrelevant to the believer since they have been done away with in Christ. The only exception is when such behavior offends another (10:31-33).

The pattern for all behavior is Christ himself (11:1) as his life is mediated through the life of the apostle (4:16-17; 11:1). Thus the gospel is not turned into law, but neither is it divested of its true response. All is of grace, but grace brings the Spirit who enables the imitation of Christ.

3. The Church. Perhaps the single greatest theological contribution of our letter to the Christian faith is Paul's understanding of the nature of the church, especially in its local expression. If the gospel itself is at stake in the Corinthians' theology and behavior, so also is its visible expression in the local community of redeemed people. The net result is more teaching on the church here than in any of Paul's letters.

Two great images predominate. First, the local church is God's temple in Corinth (3:16-17). With this imagery Paul makes several points: (a) As the temple of God they are expected to live as his alternative both to the pagan temples and to the way of life that surrounds them. Indeed, this is precisely the concern throughout so much of the letter, that there are so many gray areas that the Corinthian Christians are hardly distinguishable from the Corinth in which they live (cf. 5:1; 6:7; 10:32; 14:23). (b) What makes them God's temple is the presence of the Holy Spirit in their midst. Thus, in contrast to the mute idols that surround them, they are themselves the sanctuary of the living God by his Spirit. And when God's Spirit is manifested among them by prophetic utterance, pagans will have their hearts searched and judged and they will come to recognize that God is among his people (14:24-25). (c) So sacred to God is his temple that those who would destroy it—as they are doing by their quarrels and worldly wisdom—will themselves be destroyed by God (3:17). This understanding of their existence as a people among whom God is powerfully present by his Spirit makes possible our understanding of 5:1-13, where the church is purified by removing the incestuous man, yet he himself will experience salvation through such an action. Apparently being removed from such a community will lead to his repentance.

Second, the church is the body of Christ (10:17; 11:29; 12:12-26). With this image Paul makes essentially two points: (a) Underlying the imagery is the necessity of unity. As with the preceding image, the key to this unity is their common experience of the Spirit (12:13). Whether Jew or Greek, slave or free, they are one in Christ through the Spirit. Precisely because they are *one* body in Christ, the rich must cease abusing the poor at the Lord's Table (11:22, 29); and those who are more visible may not say to the less visible, "we have no need of you" (12:21-26). God has so arranged the body that all the members are essential to one another. (b) But his greater concern with this imagery is the concomitant necessity of diversity. Rather than the uniformity that the Corinthians value, Paul urges that they recognize the need for all the various manifestations of the one Spirit. Otherwise there is no body, only a monstrosity (12:15-20).

Given this concern, therefore, it is of some interest that there is no teaching on church order as such. There is no mention of "elders" or of the "overseers" and "deacons" of Phil. 1:1. Moreover, there is not a hint as to the nature, times, and leadership of their gatherings for worship. Two expressions of worship emerge. According to 11:17-34 they gather at the same place for a meal that is held in conjunction with the Lord's Supper. But we know nothing as to how often they ate this meal together, nor of its relationship to the expression of vocal worship referred to in 14:26, whether the latter happened in conjunction with the former (very likely) or reflected a separate gathering of its own. In either case, Paul emphasizes the truly corporate nature of such worship. Provision is to be made for "each one" to participate so that the whole body may be edified. The purpose of such worship is twofold. On the one hand, singing, praying, and thanksgiving are directed toward God (11:13; 14:14-17); on the other hand, utterances of various kinds are directed toward the community so that it may be built up.

A final word needs to be said about the considerable importance of this letter to today's church. The cosmopolitan character of the city and church, the strident individualism that emerges in so many of their behavioral aberrations, the arrogance that attends their understanding of spirituality, the accommodation of the gospel to the surrounding culture in so many ways—these and many other features of the Corinthian church are but mirrors held up before the church of today. Likewise the need for discipleship modeled after the "weakness" of Christ (4:9-13), for love to rule over all (13:1-13), for edification to be the aim of worship (14:1-33), for sexual immorality to be seen for what it is (5:1-13; 6:12-20), for the expectation of marriages to be permanent (7:1-40)—these and many others are every bit as relevant to us as to those to whom they were first spoken. It is my prayer that this commentary may help us hear the voice of Paul, inspired by the Spirit, in a still clearer way in our own day.

ANALYSIS OF 1 CORINTHIANS

I. INTRODUCTION (1:1-9)   27
  A. SALUTATION (1:1-3)   27
  B. THANKSGIVING (1:4-9)   35

II. IN RESPONSE TO REPORTS (1:10–6:20)   46
  A. A CHURCH DIVIDED—INTERNALLY AND AGAINST
    PAUL (1:10–4:20)   47
    1. The Problem—Division over Leaders in the Name
    of Wisdom (1:10-17)   51
    2. The Gospel—A Contradiction to Wisdom (1:18–2:5)   66
      a. God's folly—a crucified Messiah (1:18-25)   67
      b. God's folly—the Corinthian believers (1:26-31)   78
      c. God's folly—Paul's preaching (2:1-5)   88
    3. God's Wisdom—Revealed by the Spirit (2:6-16)   97
    4. On Being Spiritual and Divided (3:1-4)   121
    5. Correcting a False View of Church and Ministry (3:5-17)   128
      a. Leaders are merely servants (3:5-9)   129
      b. The church must be built with care (3:10-15)   135
      c. Warning to those who would destroy the church,
        God's temple in Corinth (3:16-17)   145
    6. Conclusion of the Matter—All Are Christ's (3:18-23)   150
    7. The Corinthians and Their Apostle (4:1-21)   156
      a. On being a servant and being judged (4:1-5)   157
      b. The marks of true apostleship (4:6-13)   164
      c. Appeal and exhortation (4:14-21)   182
  B. IMMORALITY AND LITIGATION: TEST CASES OF
    THE CRISIS OF AUTHORITY AND GOSPEL (5:1–6:20)   194
    1. The Case of the Incestuous Man (5:1-13)   196
      a. Paul's judgment—he must be expelled (5:1-5)   198
      b. Argument by analogy—the passover (5:6-8)   214
      c. Correcting a "misunderstanding" (5:9-13)   220
    2. A Case of Litigation (6:1-11)   228
      a. Shame on the church (6:1-6)   229

·

b. Shame on the plaintiff and warning against
    the wrongdoer (6:7-11) 239
3. *On Going to the Prostitutes (6:12-20)* 249

III. IN RESPONSE TO THE CORINTHIAN LETTER
     (7:1–16:12) 266
A. MARRIAGE AND RELATED MATTERS (7:1-40) 267
    1. *To the Married (or Formerly Married)—Stay as You Are*
        (7:1-16) 270
        a. No abstinence within marriage (7:1-7) 271
        b. Either singleness or marriage for the "unmarried"
            and widows (7:8-9) 286
        c. No divorce for Christian partners (7:10-11) 290
        d. No divorce for mixed marriages (7:12-16) 296
    2. *The Guiding Principle—Stay as One Was When Called*
        (7:17-24) 306
    3. *About the "Virgins" (7:25-40)* 322
        a. Singleness is preferable but not required (7:25-28) .. 324
        b. Paul's reasons for singleness (7:29-35) 334
        c. But marriage is no sin (7:36-40) 349
B. FOOD SACRIFICED TO IDOLS (8:1–11:1) 357
    1. *The Basis of Christian Conduct—Love, Not Knowledge*
        (8:1-13) 363
        a. The way of love and the way of knowledge (8:1-3) .. 364
        b. The content of the way of knowledge (8:4-6) 369
        c. The criterion—care for a brother (8:7-13) 376
    2. *Paul's Apostolic Defense (9:1-27)* 392
        a. In defense of his apostleship (9:1-2) 394
        b. Paul's apostolic rights (9:3-14) 397
        c. Paul's apostolic restraint (9:15-18) 414
        d. Paul's apostolic freedom (9:19-23) 422
        e. Exhortation and example (9:24-27) 433
    3. *Conclusion—No Going to the Temples (10:1-22)* 441
        a. The example of Israel (10:1-5) 441
        b. Application of the example—warning against idolatry
            (10:6-13) 450
        c. The prohibition and its basis (10:14-22) 462
    4. *On the Eating of Marketplace Food (10:23–11:1)* 475
C. WOMEN AND MEN IN WORSHIP (11:2-16) 491
    1. *An Argument from Culture and Shame (11:2-6)* 498
    2. *An Argument from Creation (11:7-12)* 512
    3. *An Argument from Propriety (11:13-16)* 524
D. ABUSE OF THE LORD'S SUPPER (11:17-34) 531
    1. *The Problem—Abuse of the Poor (11:17-22)* 534
    2. *The Problem—Abuse of the Lord (11:23-26)* 545

  3. The Answer—Discern the Body (11:27-32)   558
  4. The Answer—Wait for One Another (11:33-34)   567
 E. SPIRITUAL GIFTS AND SPIRITUAL PEOPLE
  (12:1–14:40)   569
  1. The Criterion—Jesus Is Lord (12:1-3)   574
  2. The Need for Diversity (12:4-31)   582
   a. Diversity in the godhead and the gifts (12:4-11)   583
   b. The body—diversity in unity (12:12-14)   600
   c. A twofold application of the metaphor (12:15-26)   607
   d. Once more—the fact of diversity (12:27-31)   616
  3. The More Excellent Way (13:1-13)   625
   a. The necessity of love (13:1-3)   628
   b. The character of love (13:4-7)   635
   c. The permanence of love (13:8-13)   641
  4. The Need for Intelligibility in the Assembly (14:1-25)   652
   a. The "greater gift"—prophecy (14:1-5)   653
   b. Analogies that argue for intelligibility (14:6-12)   660
   c. Application to the believing community (14:13-19)   667
   d. Application for the sake of unbelievers (14:20-25)   676
  5. The Ordering of Gifts (14:26-40)   688
   a. The ordering of tongues and prophecy (14:26-33)   689
   b. [[The ordering of women (14:34-35)]]   699
   c. Conclusion—confrontation and summary (14:36-40)   708
 F. THE RESURRECTION OF BELIEVERS (15:1-58)   713
  1. The Basis—The Resurrection of Christ (15:1-11)   717
  2. The Certainty of Resurrection (15:12-34)   737
   a. If Christ is NOT raised (15:12-19)   738
   b. But Christ IS raised (15:20-28)   745
   c. *Ad hominem* arguments for resurrection (15:29-34)   760
  3. The Resurrection Body (15:35-49)   775
   a. Analogies of seeds and "bodies" (15:35-44)   778
   b. Application of the analogies (15:45-49)   786
  4. The Assurance of Triumph (15:50-58)   795
 G. ABOUT THE COLLECTION (16:1-11)   809
  1. Arrangements for the Collection (16:1-4)   810
  2. Travel Plans—Paul's and Timothy's (16:5-11)   817
 H. ABOUT THE COMING OF APOLLOS (16:12)   823

IV. CONCLUDING MATTERS (16:13-24)   825
 A. CONCLUDING EXHORTATIONS (16:13-18)   826
 B. FINAL GREETINGS (16:19-24)   833

The First Epistle
to the
CORINTHIANS

Text, Exposition, and Notes

I. INTRODUCTION (1:1-9)

Almost all letters from the Greco-Roman period begin with a threefold salutation: Name of the Writer, to the Addressee, Greetings.[1] Very often the next item in the letter would be a thanksgiving and/or prayer to the gods for the health or well-being of the addressee.[2] Paul's letters follow this standard form; however, in his hands even these formal items are touched by the gospel so as to become distinctively Christian.

A. SALUTATION (1:1-3)

1 *Paul, called to be an apostle of Christ Jesus[3] by the will of God, and our brother Sosthenes,*

2 *To the church of God in Corinth, to those sanctified in Christ Jesus and called to be holy,[4] together with all those everywhere who call on the name of our Lord Jesus Christ—their Lord and ours:*

[1]All the true "letters" in the NT follow this pattern (including the letter from James in Acts 15:23-29), except for 3 John, which lacks the standard greeting.

For a considerable collection of examples of these salutations from papyri, see F. X. J. Exler, *The Form of the Ancient Greek Letter of the Epistolary Papyri (3rd c. B.C.-3rd c. A.D.)* (Chicago, 1923), pp. 23-68.

[2]Paul usually has a thanksgiving, in several of which he includes a prayer-report (see, e.g., 1 Thess. 1:2-5; Phil. 1:3-11). For the closest Christian example of the actual prayer in the NT, see 3 John 2: "Dear friend, I pray that you may enjoy good health and that all may go well with you, even as your soul is getting along well" (NIV).

[3]Some early MSS (ℵ A b) and all the later ones have the reverse word order, Jesus Christ (see KJV). That word order, however, rarely occurs in Paul when he is referring to our Lord by name (except in the standard formula "our Lord Jesus Christ," in which it is always in this order). See 2:2 and 3:11, which are exceptions; but in both cases the emphasis is on the earthly Jesus and his crucifixion, not, as here, on the name of the exalted Lord who has commissioned his apostle.

[4]The earliest and best MSS both East and West (P46 B D F G b m; Ambrosiaster) have the difficult word order ἡγιασμένοις ἐν Χριστῷ Ἰησοῦ τῇ οὔσῃ ἐν Κορίνθῳ. Both Zuntz, 91-92, and Metzger, 543, consider this reading "intrinsically too difficult"

3 *Grace and peace to you from God our Father and the Lord Jesus Christ.*

Paul's two earlier letters (1 and 2 Thessalonians) elaborate very little on the three parts of the salutation. With the elaborations of this letter Paul begins a habit that will carry through to the end. In each case the elaborations reflect, either directly or subtly, many of the concerns about to be raised in the letter itself. Even as he formally addresses the church in the salutation, Paul's mind is already at work on the critical behavioral and theological issues at hand.

1 The two letters to the Thessalonians begin simply "Paul and Silvanus and Timothy." Here Paul is joined by a coworker, "our brother Sosthenes." But before he adds the name of Sosthenes to his own, he affirms that he himself is "called to be an apostle of Christ Jesus by the will of God." This word order almost certainly excludes the possibility of Sosthenes's being an apostle; but Paul's reason for the insertion lies elsewhere. The Corinthians are a church at odds with their founder: they are judging him (4:1-5) and examining him as to his apostleship (9:1-23). Later (4:15; 9:1-2) he will present further evidence for his apostleship (he founded the church; he saw the Risen Lord), but because this church is questioning that apostleship, he begins by asserting its divine origins.[5] Since such an assertion would ordinarily be quite unnecessary (see, e.g., 1 and 2 Thessalonians, Philippians, and Philemon), and given the considerable tensions between them and Paul, it seems unlikely that this emphasis would have escaped notice in Corinth.[6]

Paul stresses three items in this assertion. First, his apostleship is by divine "call" (elsewhere only in Romans). Although the words "to be" are

and too "un-Pauline" to be original and suggest an "accidental omission of one or more phrases and their subsequent reintroduction at the wrong position" (Zuntz). However, in this case preference for the "more difficult reading" as the original should prevail. One can more easily imagine later scribes to have "corrected" Paul's own rough order than earlier ones to have omitted and then "corrected" in this bizarre fashion. Furthermore, how does one explain how this "corruption," brought about by a *double* error, became the dominant reading both East and West, while the more Pauline "original" lay dormant for so many years and that no form of the earlier corruptions from which this sprang survived in any form?

[5]Godet, 38, thinks otherwise, that there is here no "polemical intention against parties that might deny his apostleship." But a comparison of 1 and 2 Thessalonians with 1 Corinthians suggests that this assertion is in fact motivated by the recent events in this church.

[6]Cf. the similar elaboration in Galatians, the other letter where the questioning of Paul's apostleship is part of the problem being addressed in the letter. He also refers to himself as an apostle in Colossians, Ephesians, and the Pastoral Epistles, each for its own set of reasons. See, e.g., G. D. Fee, *1 and 2 Timothy, Titus* (GNC; San Francisco, 1984), p. 1.

not in the Greek text, nothing else could be meant by the juxtaposed words "called apostle." He does not intend this as a title to which he has the right and by which he is properly to be called, as in "Paul, called an apostle" (cf. 15:9, where this usage occurs in a negative sense: he is not worthy to be called an apostle). Rather he is insisting that this is his "calling," his divine vocation, just as he will go on in v. 2 to affirm that being "God's holy people" is their calling.[7]

Second, Paul emphasizes the divine origin of his apostleship with the addition "by the will of God."[8] Such an addition may seem redundant to his being called;[9] however, with this phrase Paul grounds his apostleship, beyond its historical realization in his "call," in its ultimate origins in the divine purposes. For Paul salvation itself has its point of origin, and therefore its certainty, in the divine will (cf. Gal. 1:4; Eph. 1:3-11), as does the apostleship that through the Spirit's effectual working announces that salvation to others. In all of this Paul is affirming that God's action is always the prior one. His own position in Christ, as well as his ministry, is predicated on God's call, which is but the expression of God's prior will.[10] Above all else, this sense of call based on God's will is what fills the apostle with such confidence in his ministry. It also leads to the apparent ambiguity that so many moderns find in him. On the one hand, he can be completely self-effacing in terms of his own person or personal role; on the other hand, he can be absolutely unyielding when it comes to his ministry as such. The latter issues from his confidence that his apostleship had come not by his own choosing but strictly "by the will of God."

Third, he describes the nature of his vocation as an "apostle of Christ

---

[7]In this letter in particular the concepts of *calling* as "vocation" and *calling* as "election" tend to blur somewhat. In 1:1 and 2 the concept of "vocation" predominates. In 1:9 and 24 the "calling" is the divine invitation to God's "family." In the extended usage in 7:15-24 the idea is less clear. The calling is first that of becoming believers, but it seems also inherently to have the idea of "one's station in life," thus meaning more than simply "vocation," that is, what one *does*. In any case the ideas are always closely related in Paul. One is *called* of God "into the fellowship of his Son" (1:9), and such a call means that one lives out the implications of that calling as "God's holy people" (1:2), which also involves being and doing what one is and does as one who has been "called" of God so to be and do (1:1; 7:15-24). For further reflections on "Paul's theology of calling as a response to the Corinthian *Pneumatikoi*," see chap. 3 in Bartchy, 127-59.

[8]Gk. διά with the genitive to denote "efficient cause" (BAGD III.1d). Cf. 2 Corinthians, Colossians, Ephesians, and 2 Timothy, where this phrase stands alone in the superscription.

[9]Indeed Héring, 1, suggests that " 'called' is duplicated by . . . 'the will of God,' and perhaps the latter should be deleted." But this is to miss Paul's usage rather widely.

[10]There has been some discussion (e.g., Barrett, 30-31) as to whether "by the will of God" modifies "called" or Paul's apostleship. More likely it includes both ideas. That is, Paul has been called to become an apostle because that is God's prior will. Cf. Conzelmann, 20.

Jesus." Paul had already used this term in 1 Thess. 2:7 as a designation for himself and his coworkers; its several occurrences in 1 Corinthians demonstrate that it had already become a fixed term in the church to designate a certain group of authoritative people.[11] It obviously includes the Twelve, but also goes considerably beyond them (15:5-7). Part of the problem with the term is that it has a sense of function as well as that of office or position. That is, it primarily had to do with some who were "sent" by Christ to preach the gospel (cf. 1:17).[12] But those who were so sent, and especially those who founded churches as a result of their evangelizing, came to be known as *apostles,* a designation that had inherent in it a sense of position as well (especially for those who were directly associated with Christ in his earthly ministry). In Paul the functional and positional usages nearly coalesce. The emphasis in this instance clearly falls on his position of authority in relationship to the church in Corinth; but that position is predicated on his relationship to "Christ Jesus," as one who was sent by Christ to found this (and other) church(es). Thus the phrase "of Christ Jesus," although perhaps a possessive, is more likely a subjective genitive, emphasizing the origin of Paul's apostleship more than his belonging to Christ.

To his own name Paul adds that of "our brother Sosthenes" (lit. "Sosthenes the brother"). Although Paul frequently is joined by others in the writing of his letters (eight times in all), this is a rare phenomenon in antiquity, and one cannot be certain what to make of it.[13] In the letters to Thessalonica Silas and Timothy are probably to be regarded as joining in the actual writing of the letter, since the verbs and pronouns throughout are in the first person plural ("*we* give thanks," "be imitators of *us*" [cf. 1 Cor. 4:16!], etc.). So also with 2 Corinthians. But this letter has little or none of that.[14] Sosthenes is not further heard from as a companion or coworker of Paul, either in this letter or elsewhere. That he is probably to be considered a

---

[11]The literature on this term and the nature of the "office" is large. Among other items, see K. H. Rengstorf, *TDNT* I, 407-45; chap. 2 in H. von Campenhausen, *Ecclesiastical Authority and Spiritual Power in the Church of the First Three Centuries* (ET Stanford, 1969; 1st Ger. ed. 1953), pp. 12-29; R. Schnackenburg, "Apostles Before and During Paul's Time," in *Apostolic History and the Gospel* (ed. W. W. Gasque, R. P. Martin; Grand Rapids, 1970), pp. 287-303; and J. A. Kirk, "Apostleship since Rengstorf: Towards a Synthesis," *NTS* 21 (1974/75), 249-64. For an overview of the literature on its origins, see F. H. Agnew, "The Origin of the NT Apostle-Concept: A Review of Research," *JBL* 105 (1986), 75-96.

[12]For the eschatological role played by the apostle, see the important discussion by A. Fridrichsen, *The Apostle and His Message* (Uppsala, 1947). Cf. P. R. Jones, "1 Corinthians 15:8: Paul the Last Apostle," *TynB* 36 (1985), 3-34.

[13]For a brief discussion of this phenomenon see G. J. Bahr, "Paul and Letter Writing in the First Century," *CBQ* 28 (1966), 476-77. The only other known instance of joint authorship of a letter is in Cicero, *Att.* 11.5.1.

[14]See the comments on 1:23 and 2:6-16.

coworker is suggested by the absolute use of "*the* brother" (cf. 16:12; 2 Cor. 1:1; etc.),[15] although in this case, since Sosthenes seems to have had nothing to do with the letter as such, it may be merely the means of identifying one of Paul's present companions who is well known to the Corinthians.[16] Perhaps in this case he is also serving as Paul's secretary (cf. 16:21), but that too is conjecture.

The identification of this Sosthenes is also uncertain. It may be that he is the Sosthenes mentioned in Acts 18:17, the ruler of the synagogue in Corinth, who was beaten in the presence of Gallio. If so, then he would have become a believer and was now with Paul in Ephesus. This identification is made the more probable by the simple designation of him as "our brother," implying that at least he was known to the Corinthians.

2   If the superscription (v. 1) is subtly directed toward the situation in Corinth, even more so is the address proper. The letter is addressed to "the church of God in Corinth." In his earlier two letters Paul had written to the church *of* the Thessalonians *in* God. Here they are the church *of* God *in* Corinth. The church belongs to God (cf. 3:9), not to them or to Paul (or Apollos), and by this slight change in the address Paul disallows at the outset one of their tendencies—to think too highly of themselves.[17]

The letter is addressed to the whole church, with no indication of parties or factions. Furthermore, one finds no mention of leaders, nor any appeal to them in the body of the letter, as one does in Phil. 1:1 and 4:3.[18] Rather, the entire community is addressed, and what is said here and throughout is said to all.

The use of the term "church" *(ekklēsia)* to designate these early Christian communities was ready-made for them. It already had been used in

---

[15]On this matter see Ellis, 13-18, and C. H. Dodd, "New Testament Translation Problems I," *BibTrans* 27 (1976), 301-11.

[16]Although the term "brother/sister" is found in pagan social and religious life (see BAGD 2), it also had a history in Judaism that almost certainly forms the background for its adoption in early Christianity (see H. F. von Soden, *TDNT* I, 145-46). Among Christians, of course, it had increased significance through Jesus' use of *Abba* ("dear Father") as his standard address of God—indicating his own unique sonship—and his inviting his disciples to use that address after him (Luke 11:2; cf. Gal. 4:6; Rom. 8:15). In the new relationship with God and the new community brought about by Christ Jesus all of the old social, sexual, and racial distinctions are broken down (Gal. 3:28); all are "born" into God's family and equally become sisters and brothers. The designation is found some 130 times in Paul for fellow believers, 39 of them in 1 Corinthians.

[17]This shift would have escaped the Corinthians, of course; but it probably says something about Paul and his relationship to this church.

[18]The suggestion by M. Guerra that πᾶσιν τοῖς ἐπικαλουμένοις refers to the governing body charged with directing the community and that ἐν παντὶ τόπῳ means their "position" is not supported by the philological or contextual evidence ("1 Cor 1, 1-3: los ministros en la comunidad de Corinto. Análisis filológico y traducción de protocolo de la Primera Carta a los Corintios," *Scripta Theologica* 9 [1977], 761-96).

the LXX to refer to Israel as a gathered people (see Deut. 4:10 and scores of other references), and in the Greek world it was used especially of the body politic, assembled to conduct the affairs of state (hence the concern for the illegal *ekklēsia* in Acts 19:39). In its use as a term for the local community of believers the emphasis still often lay on their being a gathered community (cf. 5:1-5; 11:18; 14:23), but it also came to serve as the primary designation for themselves as the newly constituted, eschatological people of God, who had submitted to the Risen Christ as Lord, and thus awaited his return.

This is the only case in the extant letters of Paul of an extensive elaboration of the address. He says first that they are "sanctified in Christ Jesus."[19] As with Paul's apostleship, the emphasis lies on their becoming God's people as the result of divine activity. What God has done "in Christ Jesus" makes them his new people.[20] The verb "sanctified"[21] probably should be understood as a metaphor for Christian conversion (cf. 6:11 and 1:30). However, the choice of this particular metaphor is hardly accidental. Believers are set apart for God, just as were the utensils in the Temple. But precisely because they are "set apart" for God, they must also bear the character of the God who has thus set them apart. Thus holiness forms part of God's intention in saving his people (cf. 1 Thess. 4:3; 5:23). Paul's concept of holiness regularly entails observable behavior. That will be particularly the case in this letter, which is addressed to a community whose "spirituality" and "higher wisdom" have been largely divorced from ethical consequences. Thus at the outset his readers are singularly identified as the "church of God, *sanctified* in Christ Jesus."

They are also "called to be holy." As with v. 1, this may sound redundant. The difficulty lies in finding a proper English translation for *hagiois* ("holy").[22] The traditional translation, "saints," contains too many misleading connotations to be of value. The term has its origins in Exod. 19:5-6, where the people of God are called his "holy people," an expression that in later Judaism referred to the elect who were to share in the blessings of

[19]With this phrase, which probably immediately follows "church of God" (see n. 4), there is a shift to the plural, but not as a means of particularizing or individualizing. Rather, the people collectively are in view.

[20]Thus the phrase ἐν Χριστῷ Ἰησοῦ is probably not locative here, but a kind of instrumental: "By what God has accomplished through Christ they have been sanctified."

[21]Gk. ἡγιασμένοις. This verb has a rich OT background, whereby what was formerly profane or ordinary had been consecrated, and thus set apart, strictly for divine purposes. In Paul it has clearly ethical implications in its first appearance (1 Thess. 5:23). In 1 Cor. 7:14 it seems to keep its original cultic/ritual sense; but here and in 1:30 and 6:11 it serves as an additional metaphor, among many others found in the apostle, to describe the many-splendored event of the salvation that is in Christ Jesus.

[22]This difficulty is nicely illustrated in the NIV, which here translates "holy," but in 16:15 (cf. Eph. 1:1) translates "saints," and in 16:1 (cf. Rom. 12:13) translates "God's people."

the messianic kingdom (Dan. 7:18-27; Ps. Sol. 17; Qumran).[23] Thus it is another OT term for Israel, especially Israel as God's elect, which has been appropriated by the NT writers for the new people of God. Again, the use of this particular term, with its root concept of being "holy," cannot be incidental. The best translation, therefore, is probably "God's holy people," which captures both ideas. Thus, just as Paul is an apostle by divine calling, so the Corinthian believers are God's new people by divine calling, who as such are to reflect God's character. One might note in passing that this is *not* their strong suit; in too many ways they look far more *like* Corinth than they do God's holy people *in* Corinth.

But what exactly did Paul intend by the next phrase, "together with all those everywhere who call on the name of our Lord Jesus Christ—their Lord and ours"?[24] Grammatically it could go either with Paul and Sosthenes, suggesting that the whole church universal is somehow to be seen as joining in the writing of this letter (which seems unlikely),[25] or with "called to be God's holy people," or with "the church of God in Corinth." Similar usage in 2 Cor. 1:1 and Phil. 1:1 suggests that the latter is intended. But what can it mean in this case? Surely not, as in the other two instances, that the letter is addressed to all Christians everywhere. Despite the difficulty with the syntax, Paul's own point seems clear enough. The *pneumatikoi* in Corinth seem to have struck an independent course, both from Paul and therefore also from the rest of the churches (see 4:17; 11:16; 14:33; and esp. 14:36). So Paul starts by giving them a gentle nudge to remind them that their own calling to be God's people belongs to a much larger picture. In the new people that God is creating for himself in the coming age that has already dawned, the Corinthians have a share with all the saints, fellow believers "in every place" who also "call on the name of our Lord Jesus Christ," that is, who have put their trust in him and pray to and worship him.[26] What Paul will say to the Corinthians, he reminds them regularly, is what he has said to all the churches.

---

[23]See the helpful discussion by O. E. Evans, "New Wine in Old Skins: XIII. The Saints," *ExpT* 86 (1975), 196-200.

[24]Weiss, 4, conjectures that the entire phrase is a secondary addition by a final redactor of the Pauline corpus, who was trying to make the letter more universal in its application. But such radical surgery is unnecessary. The "addition" is Pauline in every way, and the unusual "theirs and ours" at the end seems hardly the kind of awkwardness a redactor would create.

[25]U. Wickert, following Theodore of Mopsuestia, argues that the phrase includes both Paul and the Corinthians ("Einheit und Eintracht der Kirche im Präskript des ersten Korintherbriefes," *ZNW* 50 [1959], 73-82); but it is difficult to see how Paul would think of all other Christians as joining him in writing the letter. The concern is with the independence/exclusivism being exhibited by the Corinthian pneumatics.

[26]"To call upon the name of the Lord" is another OT phrase (by way of the LXX) that was appropriated by early Christians to express their existence. The verb ἐπικαλέω

The universal nature of the church is further emphasized by the phrase "everywhere" (lit. "in every place"). "Everywhere" is probably not quite the nuance of Paul's Greek, which rather implies "in every meeting-place."[27] Thus the Corinthians are being reminded that they are not alone; rather there are those all over the world who call on the name of the Lord when they meet together. That this is Paul's point seems certain by the final addition of "theirs and ours,"[28] which probably in this instance is intended to go beyond his own churches to all the churches of the saints. The one whom the Corinthians call "Lord" is also Lord of the whole church, and as such is finally to have his way among them as he does in the other churches.

Thus in a variety of little ways, even in the salutation, Paul scores points he must make later in specific ways in response to their attitudes and actions.

3 The salutation proper had already achieved its basic form in Paul's two earlier letters. In 1 Thessalonians the simple "grace to you and peace" appears. In 2 Thessalonians Paul adds the source, "from God the Father and the Lord Jesus Christ," the form (with the addition of "our") it would take thereafter (except for Colossians).

Here is a marvelous example of Paul's Christianizing whatever he put his hand to. The traditional greeting in the Hellenistic world was *chairein*—the infinitive of the verb "to rejoice," but in salutations meaning simply "Greetings!" (see Acts 15:23; Jas. 1:1). In Paul's hands this now becomes *charis* ("grace"), to which is added the traditional Jewish greeting *shalom* ("peace"). Thus instead of "greetings," it is "grace to you—and peace." In a sense this sums up the whole of Paul's theological outlook. The sum total of all God's activity toward his human creatures is found in the

---

properly means "to name" in the sense of "giving a name to." In the middle voice it came to mean "call on someone for aid," as in 2 Cor. 1:23. However, most often it referred to calling on God for salvation (e.g., Joel 3:5) or deliverance (Ps. 50:15), or simply to calling on him as the one in whom people have put their trust (e.g., Gen. 4:26), and therefore especially in prayer (e.g., Gen. 12:8). The latter two uses are those especially appropriated by the early Christians, to the point that, as here, the phrase became a near synonym for "believers" (cf. Acts 9:14). Cf. W. C. van Unnik, "'With All Who Call on the Name of the Lord,'" in *The New Testament Age, Essays in Honor of Bo Reicke* (ed. W. C. Weinrich; Macon, GA, 1984), II, 533-51, who emphasizes the element of prayer in distress as a common bond among believers, and P.-E. Langevin, "'Ceux qui invoquent le nom du Seigneur' (1 Co 1,2)," *ScEs* 19 (1967), 373-407; 20 (1968), 113-26; 21 (1969), 71-122.

[27]See Barrett, 33, who so translates.

[28]The two pronouns, "theirs and ours," immediately follow the Greek word τόπῳ ("place") and could modify it (as Grosheide, 24). But this gives a nearly intolerable sense. Ruef, 2-3, would also make them modify τόπῳ, but translates the latter to mean "station" or "status." Thus "in every status, theirs and ours." But besides giving a sense to τόπος that is not well attested, this completely misses Pauline usage.

word "grace"; God has given himself to them mercifully and bountifully in Christ.[29] Nothing is deserved; nothing can be achieved. "'Tis mercy all, immense and free." And the sum total of those benefits as they are experienced by the recipients of God's grace is found in the word "peace," meaning "well-being, wholeness, welfare." The one flows out of the other, and both together flow from "God our Father" (see n. 16) and were made effective in human history through our "Lord Jesus Christ."

The collocation of Father and Son in such texts as these must not be overlooked. If in 8:6, 11:3, and 15:26-28 there is a functional subordination of the Son to the Father in terms of his work, texts such as this one, and 1 Thess. 3:11 and 1 Cor. 12:4-6, make it clear that in Paul's mind the Son is truly God and works in cooperation with the Father in the redemption of his people.

A final note, therefore, about the salutation as a whole, namely its christological emphasis.[30] Paul is an apostle *of Christ Jesus;* the Corinthians have become believers ("were sanctified") *in Christ Jesus;* Christians universal are designated as those who call on the name of *our Lord Jesus Christ;* and grace and peace from God the Father are effected through *our Lord Jesus Christ.* A similar emphasis will be seen in the following thanksgiving.

B. THANKSGIVING (1:4-9)

4 *I always thank God[1] for you because of his grace given you in Christ Jesus.* 5 *For in him you have been enriched in every way—in all your speaking and in all your knowledge—*6 *because our testimony about Christ[2] was confirmed in you.* 7 *Therefore you do not lack any spiritual gift as you eagerly wait for our Lord Jesus Christ to be revealed.* 8 *He will keep you strong to the end, so that you will be blameless on the day[3] of our Lord Jesus Christ.[4]* 9 *God, who has*

---

[29]Cf. J. D. G. Dunn, *Jesus and the Spirit* (Philadelphia, 1975), p. 202: "It is important to grasp . . . that for Paul 'grace' does not mean an attitude or disposition of God; it denotes rather the wholly generous *act* of God."

[30]This emphasis is also noted by W. Grundmann, *TDNT* IX, 554-55; but he seems quite wrong in seeing it as an attempt by Paul to correct a Gnostic Christology on the part of the Corinthians.

[1]The NIV follows ℵ B eth Ephraim here in omitting μου. But this is a case where accidental omission is far more likely than a nearly universal addition on the part of many early scribes, especially since the wording does not naturally lend itself to the addition of "my."

[2]Several MSS, incl. B* F G 81 1175, read θεοῦ, probably an assimilation to the wording of 2:1 (q.v.).

[3]The Western MSS D F G read παρουσίᾳ instead of ἡμέρᾳ.

[4]The word Χριστοῦ is not found in P[46] B. This is probably a very early accidental omission (based on the juxtaposition and abbreviation of ΙΥ ΧΥ). For a fuller discussion see Zuntz, 184, who tends to favor the shorter text.

called you into fellowship with his Son Jesus Christ our Lord, is faithful.

Paul's thanksgivings generally follow the same pattern: I (1) give thanks, (2) to God, (3) always, (4) for the recipients, and (5) for certain reasons, which are then elaborated.[5] This thanksgiving is more clearly defined than the thanksgivings of 1 and 2 Thessalonians (and some of the later ones as well), and lacks any mention of intercessory prayer for the recipients. As with the salutation, it contains a number of items that anticipate the body of the letter.

What is remarkable here is the apostle's ability to thank God for the very things in the church that, because of the abuses, are also causing him grief. Some in fact have suggested that this is irony.[6] But such a view tends to miss some vital features in Paul's theology. Unlike many contemporary Christians, whose tendency is to domesticate the faith by eliminating anything that could be troublesome, the apostle recognizes that the problem lies not in their gifts, but in their attitude toward these gifts.[7] Precisely because the gifts come from God, Paul is bound to give thanks for them. After all, they are good things that have gone sour.[8] In this thanksgiving, therefore, Paul accomplishes two things: he gives genuine thanks to God both for the Corinthians themselves and for God's having "gifted" them, but at the same time he redirects their focus.

This redirection has two emphases: (1) The Corinthians are genuinely "gifted," but as the letter reveals they are also self-satisfied and creature-oriented, boasting in mere human beings. The whole of the thanksgiving is God-oriented and Christ-centered. Everything comes *from God* and is given *in Christ Jesus*. (2) The second emphasis is eschatological. They lack no spiritual gift, but they have not yet arrived. They *await* the revelation (v. 7). Christ will establish them so that they *will be blameless* on the Day of the Lord (v. 8). This eschatological tension between their present giftedness (spirituality) and the final glory will emerge again in this letter (e.g., 4:8-13; 13:8-13).

Although vv. 4-8 form a single, somewhat convoluted, sentence, the flow of thought can be easily traced. The verb "I thank" controls the whole.

---

[5]See P. Schubert, *Form and Function of the Pauline Thanksgivings* (Berlin, 1939); and now esp. O'Brien, 107-37.

[6]See, e.g., Craig, 18; Allo, 4.

[7]Cf. the observation of O'Brien, 114: "The Corinthians had forgotten that what they had received were 'gifts' (note the biting words of 4:7, 'What have you that you did not receive? If then you received it, why do you boast as if it were not a gift?'), sovereignly distributed by the Holy Spirit (12:4-11, esp. v. 11) and that their purpose was 'for the common good' (12:7), or that the church might be edified (14:5)."

[8]Cf. Lightfoot, 148: "St Paul here gives thanks for their use: he afterward condemns their abuse."

The grounds for the thanksgiving are stated in v. 4 ("for grace given you in Christ"). V. 5 elaborates the grounds in terms of some specific gifts, which also serve as confirmation of the gospel among them (v. 6). As a result of God's confirming the gospel among them in this way, they lack no gift available in the present age as they await the final consummation at the coming of Christ (v. 7). V. 8 then brings the sentence to a fitting conclusion by shifting the focus from past "graces" to what God will yet do for them at the final eschatological event, namely "confirm them completely to the end." The whole is then set off with the exclamation of v. 9, which emphasizes the faithfulness of God to accomplish the future glory (of vv. 7-8) in light of their prior "calling."

4 It is Paul's regular habit ("always") to give thanks for his converts, as well as for other Christians.[9] Indeed, his ability to give thanks for these Christians probably says much about his own character. If he must speak strongly to them, indeed at times be sarcastic and shame them, he nonetheless never ceases to be thankful for them; for in the final analysis, even though he feels responsible for them as a father for his children (4:14-21), they are God's people, not his own. In every redeemed person there is evidence of the grace of God, and that brings forth Paul's gratitude, both *to God* and *for them*. To delight in God for his working in the lives of others, even in the lives of those with whom one feels compelled to disagree, is sure evidence of one's own awareness of being the recipient of God's mercies. So it was with Paul. The self-sufficient are scarcely so disposed.

The specific basis of Paul's thanksgiving in their case is God's "grace given you in Christ Jesus." Commonly this is viewed as a thanksgiving for grace as such, i.e., the gracious outpouring of God's mercy in Christ toward the undeserving. However, for Paul *charis* ("grace") very often is closely associated with *charisma/charismata* ("gift/gifts") and in such instances refers to concrete expressions of God's gracious activity in his people.[10] Indeed, the word "grace" itself sometimes denotes these concrete manifestations, the "graces" (gifts), of God's grace. So, e.g., in 1 Cor. 16:3 and 2 Cor. 8-9, *charis* refers not only to the "grace of giving" on the part of the Corinthians, but concretely to their gifts as well.

Such a "concrete" understanding of grace seems to be what is in view here, since vv. 5-7 specify its manifestations in terms of certain *charismata* ("gifts"), which in fact the Corinthians tended to prize very highly. Paul's emphasis, of course, differs considerably from theirs. They

---

[9]See 1 Thess. 1:2; 2:13; 2 Thess. 1:3; 2:13; Rom. 1:8; Col. 1:3; Phil. 1:3; Phlm. 4. Thanksgiving becomes doxology in 2 Corinthians and Ephesians. All of this is conspicuously absent from Galatians.

[10]Cf., e.g., Rom. 12:6, where believers are given differing *charismata*, according to the *charis given* to them.

stressed the gifts per se; he the gracious activity of *God*, who would so gift his people. Precisely because they are "given" by God[11] and are "grace" (unmerited by the recipients), there can be no grounds for boasting on their part. Paul's dilemma in this letter is to convince the Corinthians to share his view of these benefits, since they arrogantly boast over the very things that as gifts may *not* be the source of personal boasting (cf. 4:7).

5   Paul next enumerates specifically the "graces" for which he is giving thanks.[12] They "have been enriched," he says, "in every way."[13] Yet it is clear from the phrases that follow that his focus is much narrower, namely, "in all your speaking *(logos)* and in all your knowledge *(gnōsis)*." Ordinarily, these would not be the only—or ordinary—things for which one might give thanks among a group of new Christians. In fact, it is often noted that Paul does not in their case mention such things as love, faith, or hope (as, e.g., in 1 Thessalonians, Philippians, or Colossians).[14] This is true, of course, but it does not necessarily imply that they lack these; after all, in a nearly parallel passage in 2 Cor. 8:7 the two items mentioned here are again included, along with faith, earnestness, and love.

Paul selects these almost certainly because they were noticeably evident in the community. But they also happen to be items that function in some very negative ways in the church. What Paul appears to be doing, then, is redirecting their focus from their "graces" (good things in themselves because they edify the church) to God, who has given them, and to Christ, "in whom" they have been made available.[15] This is true even of the imagery expressed in the verb "you have been enriched." In similar contexts, both in earlier and later letters, Paul most often uses the verb "to abound" to speak of the overflow in the Christian life. What is significant here is that, although the concept of God's having "riches" recurs in his letters,[16] the imagery of being "enriched in (or by) Christ" is unique to the Corinthian letters. In each case it occurs in contrast to "poverty"—of Christ

---

[11]Who is the implied subject of all the passive verbs in this paragraph.

[12]The ὅτι that joins this clause to v. 4 is probably explicative, indicating that what follows modifies v. 4 by spelling out in detail the meaning of the phrase "because of the grace of God given you in Christ Jesus." It could therefore also be translated "in that." Thus, "I always thank God . . . because of his grace given you in Christ Jesus, in that in everything you have been enriched in him." Many (e.g., BAGD, Conzelmann, 25 n. 3) take the ὅτι to go with the verb εὐχαριστῶ (either "I thank God . . . because," or "I thank God . . . that"), but the structure of the sentence as a whole and the context seem to rule in favor of an explicative ὅτι here.

[13]Gk. ἐν παντί; for this usage see BAGD 2aβ.

[14]See, among others, Héring, 3; Craig, 19; O-W, 144.

[15]"In him" refers back to "in Christ Jesus" in v. 4, and is similar in usage to v. 2: "by what God has done in Christ Jesus."

[16]This is true especially of Romans, Colossians, Ephesians, and Philippians. Thus he has "riches of grace," "riches of kindness," "riches in glory," etc.

whose "poverty" effected their "enrichment" (2 Cor. 8:9), or of Paul whose preaching made it possible (4:8-13; 2 Cor. 6:10). Given the sarcastic sense in which the imagery appears in 4:8, one wonders whether this is not one of *their* terms that Paul is now using in its positive sense, precisely because in Christ Jesus their experience of spiritual gifts is a genuine enrichment.

But what are the specific "graces" intended by the words *logos* (the NIV's "all your speaking" seems to miss the point) and *gnōsis* ("knowledge")?[17] Considerable discussion has arisen concerning the meaning of these two words,[18] but the context of 1 Corinthians itself supplies all the help one needs. Both terms occur far more often in 1 and 2 Corinthians than in all the other Pauline letters,[19] and in contexts that make it clear that they are Corinthian terms. Significantly, both words appear positively as gifts of the Spirit in chaps. 12–14, but also negatively in another context in the letter. The term *logos* here (cf. 12:8) probably means something akin to "in every kind of 'spiritual utterance,' " and refers especially to the many gifts of utterance noted in chaps. 12–14 (knowledge, wisdom, tongues, prophecy, etc.)—even though as those chapters make clear their interest in "speech" is more singular. But in chaps. 1–4, the term refers in a pejorative sense to what is merely human in contrast to the *logos* of the cross (1:17-18; cf. 2:1-4). So also with *gnōsis*. As a *charisma* in chaps. 12–14 it refers to the gift of special knowledge, probably related to prophetic revelation (12:8; 13:2; 14:6).[20] Yet in 8:1-13 it serves as their basis for Christian conduct, and as such comes under severe criticism from Paul.

[17]With abstract nouns πᾶς usually has the sense of "every kind of." See BAGD 1aβ. Cf. Barrett, 36-37, and O'Brien, 117.

[18]Lightfoot, 147, followed by O'Brien, 118, lists four possibilities: (1) that λόγος refers to the lower, γνῶσις to the higher knowledge (which they rightly dismiss as impossible); (2) that λόγος refers to the gift of tongues, γνῶσις to prophecy (which is also to be dismissed as too narrow a view); (3) that λόγος refers to the gospel which came to them, and γνῶσις to their hearty acceptance of it (which is discredited by the whole context of 1 Corinthians); and (4) the position they prefer, that λόγος refers to the outward expression, γνῶσις to the inward conviction and apprehension of the gospel. But this latter also seems to miss the point in the context of 1 Corinthians. Other options have been offered: Zuntz, 101, suggests that one refers to "rational" and the other to "ecstatic" gifts, which again seems to miss the actual data of 1 Corinthians. K. Grayston suggests, even less convincingly, that λόγος refers to those who were insisting on following the remembered words of Jesus in a legalistic way (they had traded one form of law for another), while γνῶσις refers to those who had "an awareness of the cosmic relationships between God the Father, the Lord Jesus Christ, and the Christian," so that they were, through Christ, absolved from "the conventional rules" ("Not With a Rod," *ExpT* 88 [1976], 13-16).

[19]The word λόγος occurs 26 times in 1 and 2 Corinthians, 38 in the other eight letters (plus 20 in the Pastorals). The word γνῶσις occurs 16 times in 1 and 2 Corinthians, seven in the other letters (including the Pastorals).

[20]See 8:1 for a further discussion of this word.

What then is Paul doing here? He seems to be picking up on two of their own terms, items in their spirituality about which they are perhaps a bit too *self*-confident. In the places where they boast in such things as "utterance" or "knowledge," Paul argues that they are acting in merely human ways, and thus are not "in Spirit" at all. Nonetheless, these same items appear as legitimate gifts of the Spirit that belong to the present age (12:8-11; 13:8-12), and set in proper perspective they will edify the church (14:1-6). Precisely because they are spiritual gifts (v. 7), given by God in Christ Jesus, Paul can be genuinely grateful for them.

6 It is difficult to determine the precise sense of the conjunction[21] that begins this clause, and thus also to determine the relationship of these words to what has just been said. Most often, as in the NIV, it is seen as a causal clause, which "explains the reason for the richness of spiritual endowment the Corinthians possessed. That cause was a testimony centred on Christ."[22] More likely, however, the Greek *kathōs* carries its ordinary comparative sense ("just as," "even as"). In this case it would be used very much as in 1 Thess. 1:5, where after Paul asserts that his gospel came among them with power, he adds the reminder, "just as you yourselves know." Here, therefore, he is probably suggesting that their gifts, for which he is genuinely thankful, are the *evidence* that "our testimony about Christ was confirmed in you."[23] If we take seriously that the implied subject of the passive verb is "God," then the clause says that God himself confirmed Paul's witness to Christ among them by giving them these spiritual gifts, which is exactly what v. 7 will go on to reaffirm.

Although not common in Paul (cf. 2:1; 2 Thess. 1:10; 2 Tim. 1:8), the term "testimony" refers to the gospel itself and is probably used because of the verb "confirmed." The whole clause thus functions as a metaphor, taken from commercial law.[24] In preaching the gospel in Corinth, Paul bore witness to the good news about Christ, especially his death (1:18-25; 2:1-2) and resurrection (15:1-11);[25] God himself "guaranteed" the truth of the

---

[21]Gk. καθώς. Cf. 1 Thess. 1:5; Phil. 1:7.

[22]O'Brien, 120.

[23]This position was also taken by Godet, 53-54, and Lightfoot, 148. Cf. the translation by Moffatt: "all of which verifies the testimony we bore to Christ when we were with you."

[24]The verb βεβαιόω ("confirmed"), which ordinarily had the meaning of "make firm" or "strengthen," became a technical term in the Hellenistic period for guaranteeing legal contracts (see the discussion in A. Deissmann, *Biblical Studies* [ET, Edinburgh, 1901], pp. 101-05; cf. MM, p. 108). Some have stressed the legal aspect here in a more literal sense (esp. H. Schlier, *TDNT* I, 600-03), but that is to lose the richness of the metaphor itself, which is used again by Paul in 2 Cor. 1:21 to speak of the certainty of their existence together in Christ.

[25]The NIV properly understands the genitive "the testimony of Christ" to be objective here; that is, Christ is the "object," not the "subject," of the verbal idea in the word "testimony" (cf. GNB, NAB, NASB, RSV).

message by enriching them with every kind of spiritual gift.[26] This means also that "in you" carries the sense here of "among you," or "in your midst" (cf. RSV, NAB).

As throughout the thanksgiving, therefore, the emphasis in this clause is on Christ. Nonetheless, one might also see here a hidden reference to his own ministry among them, since for Paul in this community these two stand or fall together.

7 This clause functions to bring closure to the point that has been made thus far, namely, Paul's gratitude for their spiritual gifts, which serve as God's confirmation both of the gospel itself and Paul's preaching of it in Corinth. But by adding the eschatological note at the end, Paul also now attempts to set their present giftedness in the proper eschatological perspective of "already/not yet."[27]

The clause itself is a result clause[28] that modifies v. 6,[29] so that vv. 6 and 7 together recapitulate by way of historical reminder what was said in vv. 4-5. Thus, "I thank God he bestowed 'grace' on you (v. 4), in that he 'enriched' you with specific spiritual gifts (v. 5), *just as* historically it worked out in your midst by God's confirming our testimony about Christ (v. 6) *so that* you came short in no spiritual gift (v. 7)."

It is not certain what precisely is intended by "you do not lack any spiritual gift." The verb "lack" ordinarily takes a genitive for its object and in that case would mean, as the NIV has it, that they potentially have at their disposal all the gifts of God. But here the verb is modified by a prepositional phrase,[30] as in v. 5 ("in every way"), and therefore could mean that they do not come short, either in comparison with others or with normal expectations of Christians who have the Spirit, in any of the gifts that they do possess. Although many prefer the latter option (because of the grammar),[31] it is

---

[26]G. W. MacRae has made the tentative suggestion that this verse should be translated, "since the testimony to Christ has grown strong among you to the point that you lack no spiritual gift" (see "A Note on 1 Corinthians 1:4-9," in *Eretz-Israel*, vol. 16 [Orlinsky *Festschrift*] [Jerusalem, 1982], pp. 171-75). Although it is an intriguing suggestion, MacRae comes to it through a desire to make the verb βεβαιόω mean nearly the same thing in both vv. 6 and 8. But as is noted in v. 8, that is not necessary, nor does it make the best sense of Paul's own play on words here.

[27]For this essential framework to Paul's theology, see the Introduction, pp. 16-17.

[28]Even though in classical Greek ὥστε with the infinitive ordinarily signaled a potential, rather than actual, result (which took the indicative), this distinction had broken down considerably in the late Hellenistic period. It was common among the older commentaries (e.g., Lightfoot, Findlay, R-P) to keep this distinction, but both common usage and the context here demand that the result had already been actualized in Corinth.

[29]The RSV reflects a view that sees v. 6 as parenthetical and v. 7 therefore as modifying v. 5. Conzelmann, 27, argues that v. 7 modifies both vv. 5 and 6. Neither of these makes as much sense of the syntax nor of the argument as the position adopted here.

[30]Gk. ἐν μηδενὶ χαρίσματι (= you are lacking *in no spiritual gift*).

[31]See, e.g., Lightfoot, 148; Barrett, 38; and O'Brien, 123-24.

more likely that the syntax here is influenced by v. 5 ("enriched in every way").[32] Thus the clause merely repeats in a negative way what was already affirmed positively in v. 5. This also means that the word *charisma* ("spiritual gift"),[33] which could be seen to refer more broadly to the gracious gift of redemption,[34] is as in v. 5 to be understood more specifically to refer to those special endowments of the Holy Spirit mentioned in chaps. 12–14 (cf. Rom. 12:6).

But thanksgiving for present gifts is not the final—nor the only— word. Such gifts are ever to be realized in the context of "eagerly awaiting the revelation of our Lord Jesus Christ." Indeed, there is perhaps a correlation between the contemporary church's general loss of such "graces" and its general lack of eager expectation of the final consummation. It should be noted here that even though Paul's theological perspective is thoroughly eschatological, a comparison of this thanksgiving with that in 1 Thess. 1:2-5 indicates that an eschatological note is not a necessary element in the Pauline thanksgivings (in fact it occurs only in Philippians and Colossians in the later letters).[35]

Why, then, this additional note about the coming of Christ? It may of course mean nothing more than that such a concern is ever present with the apostle himself, since salvation for Paul was primarily an eschatological reality, begun with Christ's coming and to be consummated by his imminent return. But it is also probable in this instance that that ever present concern is heightened by the Corinthians' own apparently overrealized eschatological understanding of their existence, which for them was related in particular to their experience of the "spiritual gift" of tongues (see on 13:1). Paul's gratitude for their giftedness, therefore, includes a reminder that they still *await* the final glory, since it seems to be the case that some among them do not have such eager expectation (see on 4:8 and 15:12).

What they eagerly await[36] is "for our Lord Jesus Christ to be revealed." Although Paul ordinarily speaks of Christ's return in terms of his "coming" *(parousia),* he has previously in 2 Thess. 1:7 also referred to it as Christ's "revelation." In this case the choice of nouns is probably less dictated by any nuance of ideas between "coming" and "revelation" than

[32]So Conzelmann, 27.

[33]On this word see on 12:4; cf. the discussion in Dunn, *Jesus,* pp. 205-07.

[34]As, e.g., in Rom. 5:15-16 and 6:23. This is the view of a large number of commentators (e.g., Calvin, 22; O'Brien, 124).

[35]Thus O'Brien, 124, does not seem quite precise when he speaks of "the customary eschatological climax of the introductory thanksgivings." This perspective is the result of analyzing the thanksgiving periods *formally* without giving chronology its due. Eschatology is missing in 1 Thessalonians, Romans, and Philemon.

[36]Paul uses the verb ἀπεκδέχομαι only in eschatological contexts of looking forward to the End (Gal. 5:5; Rom. 8:19, 23, 25; Phil. 3:20).

by the general sense of the entire paragraph, which has God as its subject. Thus God will consummate the ages by the final "revelation" of his Son; it is this final christological revelation that the Corinthians are being reminded they yet await.

8 With this clause Paul finally brings to a conclusion the long sentence that began in v. 4. He does so by elaborating on the eschatological note struck at the end of v. 7, now in terms of what it means for the Corinthians themselves. It is noteworthy that the *language* of this clause resembles that of the prayer found in 1 Thess. 3:13. It is possible, therefore, that the clause is intended to function very much like the prayer-reports in the other thanksgivings—however, with the significant difference that this is a strong affirmation, not simply a wish-prayer.[37] Paul is here confident that God will indeed "confirm" them to the end.

Significantly, he makes this affirmation by repeating the verb "to confirm," which appeared in the metaphor of v. 6. Thus, instead of his usual "he will strengthen, or establish, you,"[38] Paul says that in the same way that God first "guaranteed" our testimony to Christ while we were with you, he will *also*[39] "guarantee" or "confirm" you "to the end."[40] That this is a purposeful repeating of the legal metaphor from v. 6 is further evidenced by the word "blameless," which carries the sense of their being guiltless (with reference to the law) when appearing before God at the final judgment because Christ's righteousness has been given to them.[41] Finally, the use of the phrase "on the day of our Lord Jesus Christ" also points to the final judgment. The OT eschatological expression "the day of the Lord" (see Amos 5:18-20; Joel 2:31) is appropriated by Paul and made christological. It is still "the day of the Lord," but "the Lord" is none other than Jesus Christ (see also 3:13-15; 5:5; cf. 1 Thess. 5:2).

What is remarkable is that Paul should express such confidence about a community whose current behavior is anything but blameless and

---

[37]G. P. Wiles has suggested that "this is a possible wish-prayer, using the future indicative to express a wish: '*May he sustain* you to the end . . .'" (*Paul's Intercessory Prayers* [SNTSMS 24; Cambridge, 1974], p. 35; see also pp. 97-101). But to do so he must not only neglect the clear grammar of the sentence but also disallow that the thanksgiving is genuine—hence the need to conclude with prayer, that these things shall really be so.

[38]Gk. στηρίζω; see 1 Thess. 3:2, 13; 2 Thess. 2:17; 3:3; Rom. 1:11; 16:25.

[39]A καί is unfortunately left out of the NIV. It means "also" here and thus refers back to the former ἐβεβαιώθη in v. 6.

[40]The phrase ἕως τέλους could possibly mean "completely" here. Some (e.g., Grosheide, 31; Barrett, 39; O'Brien, 129) think it has a twofold sense here: "completely to the end." Perhaps so, but the primary reference is temporal, not one of degrees.

[41]Gk. ἀνέγκλητος, found also in a "last judgment" passage in Col. 1:22 (cf. 1 Tim. 3:10; Tit. 1:6,7). In other contexts Paul uses either ἄμεμπτος or ἄμωμος, words that carry more of the moral or religious sense.

whom on several occasions he must exhort with the strongest kinds of warning. The secret, of course, lies in the subject of the verb, "he" (= God).[42] If Paul's confidence lay in the Corinthians themselves, then he is in trouble. But just as in 5:6-8 and 6:9-11, in Paul's theology the indicative (God's prior action of grace) always precedes the imperative (their obedience as response to grace) and is the ground of his confidence.

Not all, however, are agreed that the subject of "he" is "God." In fact the most natural antecedent is "our Lord Jesus Christ," which immediately precedes it.[43] Nonetheless, good reasons exist for thinking that Paul intended "God" as the subject. First, because God, to whom Paul is giving thanks, is the implied subject of all the passive verbs in the paragraph. Second, and in particular, God is the implied subject of the prior occurrence of the verb "confirm" in v. 6, thus indicating that he is *also* the one who will confirm the Corinthians themselves at the end. Third, in the final exclamation, God again is acknowledged as faithful in bringing all of this to pass.

Thus even though Paul is concerned to remind the church that they have not yet arrived, at the same time he holds out before them his great confidence that by God's own action they will indeed make it in the end. Consequently, by means of thanksgiving Paul redirects their confidence from themselves and their own giftedness toward God, from whom and to whom are all things.

9 All that has preceded in the thanksgiving, both God's prior act of grace in their behalf and his future "guaranteeing" of them on the day of judgment, is now summed up in this glorious exclamation. In a way very similar to 1 Thess. 5:24, Paul joins the reality of God's faithfulness to his calling of believers. How can he be sure that they, of all people, will be found guiltless on that day? Because "God is faithful,"[44] he assures them, predicating his confidence on one of the more deeply rooted motifs about God found in the OT. The God of Israel was a faithful God, always reliable, always true to himself, who could therefore be counted on to fulfill all his promises (Deut. 7:9; Ps. 144:13).[45]

In this case, however, the affirmation of God's character does not

---

[42]Gk. relative pronoun ὅς.

[43]Almost all of the earlier commentaries go this way. Godet, e.g., says: "The pron. . . . refers of course to the person of *Jesus Christ*" (p. 58). Among more recent commentaries that also adopt this position, see Barrett, 39, and Ruef, 6. Most recent commentaries take the position argued for here.

[44]For this expression in Paul see 10:13; 2 Cor. 1:18; cf. 1 Thess. 5:24; 2 Thess. 3:3.

[45]W. C. van Unnik suggests that these words are reminiscent of the *Haftarah* in the synagogue, which speaks of "the faithful God who speaks and acts" ("Reisepläne und Amen-Sagen, Zusammenhang und Gedankfolge in 1 Korinther 1:15-24," in *Studia Paulina in honorem J. de Zwaan* [Haarlem, 1953], p. 221). It has also been suggested, both because of the language and because of the place of this exclamation at the end of the

depend on OT realities, but on his more recent work in Corinth itself, whereby he "called [them] into fellowship with his Son Jesus Christ our Lord."[46] God's faithfulness in having called and redeemed them now serves as the grounds for Paul's hope of their final salvation at the end. These words pick up the theme of "calling" from vv. 1 and 2 (q.v.), especially God's calling of the Corinthians themselves to become believers (cf. also 1:24).[47] Thus again Paul redirects their focus from themselves to God, who by calling them is responsible for their very existence as a community of faith.

The call here is expressed in terms of "fellowship with his Son."[48] Although this language recurs in a sacramental passage in 10:16, it is doubtful that it alludes to the sacrament here. The reference is to what took place at their conversion. The calling *to* Christ is a calling to be *in fellowship with* Christ through the Spirit (cf. 2 Cor. 13:13; Phil. 2:1). Thus in all likelihood this language is to be understood not only positionally, but also relationally. Believers are not only *in* Christ, and as such freed from the guilt of their sins, but are also *in fellowship with* Christ, and as such are privileged to commune with him through the Spirit.[49] Such language, however, for Christian conversion or Christian life is unusual in Paul, and, in light of what is about to be said in the very next sentence, may have been chosen so as also to reflect the idea of the fellowship of believers that has been formed in his Son,[50] but that seems doubtful in light of the soteriological use of "call."

---

thanksgiving period, that the whole sentence is liturgical in its form and content (see, e.g., J. T. Sanders, "The Transition from Opening Epistolary Thanksgiving to Body in the Letters of the Pauline Corpus," *JBL* 81 [1962], 361-62). The liturgical character of the language is perhaps possible, but in its present form the whole has been so adapted to the present context that any discovery of prior expressions is not particularly useful for finding its meaning here (cf. O'Brien, 131). For this kind of "pan-liturgism" see also on 16:20-24.

[46]The Greek text here has the unusual expression, totally lost in the NIV, that it is God *through* whom (δι' οὗ) they were called, rather than *by* whom (ὑφ' οὗ). Ordinarily, one expects God the Father to be the primary cause and the Son to be the agent of mediation. Nonetheless, Paul can speak of God as the one "from whom, through whom, and unto whom are all things" (Rom. 11:33). Here the reason for God himself serving as agent is that the purpose of the call is expressed in terms of the Son.

[47]On the OT background of "call" see L. Coenen, *NIDNTT* I, 272-73. In Paul the one who "calls" is always God the Father.

[48]On the use of the term "Son of God" in Paul, as well as a discussion of its origins in early Christianity, see M. Hengel, *The Son of God* (ET, Philadelphia, 1976). In 1 Corinthians it appears only here and in 15:28. These two texts demonstrate that Hengel is basically correct, "that for Paul the *soteriological* rather than the speculative significance of the term stands in the foreground" (p. 8).

[49]Cf. F. Hauck, *TDNT* III, 804; and G. Panikulam, *Koinōnia in the New Testament, A Dynamic Expression of Christian Life* (AnBib 85; Rome, 1979), pp. 13-15.

[50]So Barrett, 40; cf. Willis, 209-10, who follows J. Y. Campbell, "Κοινωνία and Its Cognates in the New Testament," *JBL* 51 (1932), 380 (repr. *Three New Testament Studies* [Leiden, 1965], pp. 1-28). But see the discussion in O'Brien, 131-32, who understands it in terms of participation in the spiritual blessings made available in his Son.

Finally, it must be noted again that God is the subject of all the actions of the thanksgiving. And in every case that work is mediated by or focused on "his Son Jesus Christ our Lord." Thus the christological emphasis that began in the salutation is carried through in an even more emphatic way in this introductory thanksgiving. Everything God has done, and will do, for the Corinthians is done expressly in "Jesus Christ our Lord."

With these great cadences the introductory matters to this letter come to an end. But one can learn much from these words. Not only do they anticipate the letter itself, but they do so in such a way as to disclose a good deal about Pauline theology and his own pastoral care. As the letter will reveal, there are some strained relationships in this church, both between the church and Paul and internally within the membership. Moreover, the cause of many of these tensions is that some gifts of God are being badly abused by them. Nonetheless, Paul can still open with honest thanksgiving, both for the Corinthians themselves and for their gifts, which for Paul serve as evidence of God's confirming his preaching among them. Eventually, Paul must speak to the abuses; for now he is grateful. His concern here is to redirect their focus—from themselves to God and Christ and from an over-realized eschatology to a healthy awareness of the glory that is still future.

For much of its life the church has suffered through the opposite of the Corinthian problem, namely an "underrealized" eschatological perspective, in which very little is expected from God in the present age. The twentieth century, through both the traditional Pentecostal and more recent charismatic movements, has witnessed a resurgence of many of the more visible gifts of the Spirit. Among some Christians there has been a Corinthian-like focus on the more spectacular gifts, leading at times to spiritual pride, while others in their own form of pride have rejected altogether such gifting as a possibility for the contemporary church. From this thanksgiving we should learn both to be thankful for such gifts, as evidence of God's confirmation of the gospel, and to make sure that our focus is Paul's—on God and Christ, from whom and through whom are all things.

II. IN RESPONSE TO REPORTS (1:10–6:20)

Even though the people from Chloe's household probably reached Paul after the Corinthian letter,[1] the news he received from them is of such a critical nature that he feels compelled to address these behavioral items first. He takes up four such matters before responding to their letter. The items in

[1]See the Introduction, p. 7.

1:10–4:21 and 5:1-13 have explicitly been brought to his attention by way of report (see 1:11 and 5:1). For the relationship of the two matters in chap. 6 to those in chaps. 5 and 7, see below, pp. 194-96.

A. A CHURCH DIVIDED—INTERNALLY AND AGAINST PAUL (1:10–4:21)

The problem that Paul addresses at the outset of this letter is probably the best known of them all.[2] Moreover, because our own experience is of a church divided, and especially because we have also experienced painfully destructive quarrels within the church in various ways, we instinctively feel ourselves immediately in touch with their problem.

Nonetheless, this is an extremely complex issue,[3] made so especially by two further pieces of data in the letter: (1) On the one hand, because this is the first item to which Paul speaks, most people tend to read the rest of the letter in light of chaps. 1–4; that is, behind every issue (e.g., 7:1-16 or 8:1–11:1) they see the Corinthians divided into parties. On the other hand, scarcely anything explicit is said in chaps. 5–16 to indicate the existence of actual parties within the church,[4] nor is there any mention of Apollos or Cephas of the kind that would suggest that they are rallying points for such parties.[5]

(2) Although the Corinthians were quarreling with one another over their leaders (1:10-12), nothing in chaps. 1–4 indicates that they were deeply divided on issues as such. This is not to say that they were not; it is to say that nothing in 1:10–4:21 explicitly so indicates. Furthermore, anyone

---

[2]It is in fact the earliest specific item from Paul's letters mentioned outside the NT (1 Clem. 47:1-4 [*ca.* A.D. 95]).

[3]The range of scholarly opinion is far broader and more diverse here than for any other issue in the letter (see the discussion in Hurd, 95-107). Much of how one views the whole letter is determined by one's approach to this issue; hence its considerable importance.

[4]There can be little question that in certain areas some within the believing community were abusing or taking advantage of others (e.g., 6:1-11; 7:5; 8:10; 11:2-16; 11:20-22), but in none of these do the differences appear to be along party lines. In fact very few of the issues raised are spoken to in such a way that one might even conjecture that there were deep differences within the community itself on these matters.

[5]On this whole question see J. Munck, *Paul and the Salvation of Mankind* (ET, London, 1959), chap. 5, "The Church without Factions, Studies in I Corinthians 1-4." Although Munck has perhaps slightly overstated the case, he seems to be correct in deemphasizing the role of actual parties in the church. Cf. Hurd's assessment: "Now the perplexing fact is that the remainder of I Corinthians [chaps. 5–16] does not seem to give any information about the issues which separated these four parties about which Paul was so concerned when he began to write. I Corinthians apparently was addressed by Paul to a single, more or less unified, opposing point of view" (96). See further the discussion in the Introduction, pp. 6-10.

reading this section with the presupposition that the problem basically involved parties within the church must always feel a lack of coherence to Paul's answer, since so little of it speaks directly to that matter. The question persists, then, as to whether, or how much, the issue in 1:10–4:21 affects our understanding of the other problems in the church.

What then is the problem? A careful reading of 1:10–4:21 indicates that at least four issues are involved:[6] (1) There is "quarreling" and "divisiveness" among them, with their various teachers as rallying points. That this is so is indicated by explicit statements in 1:10-12, 3:3-4, and 3:21, plus indirect statements in 3:5-9 and 4:1-2 as to how they should regard these teachers. However, there is not the slightest hint that the teachers were themselves party to this quarreling; indeed, Paul's affirmations of Apollos in 3:5-9 and 16:12 indicate the very opposite.

(2) This quarreling is in some way being carried on in the name of "wisdom." The Greek word group *sophia/sophos* ("wisdom"/"wise") dominates the discussion throughout chaps. 1–3. The high incidence in these three chapters of this otherwise infrequent word group,[7] plus the fact that in most cases the word is used in a pejorative sense, is a sure indication that this is a Corinthian way of speaking, not Paul's.[8]

(3) Related to these first two items are the repeated references to the Corinthians' "boasting" (1:29-31; 3:21; 4:7) and being "puffed up" (4:6, 18-19). Their quarrels took the form of boasting in mere men, apparently in the name of wisdom (3:18-21; cf. 4:6). The problem, however, probably goes much deeper than that. As Munck observes: "Their view of Christian leaders as teachers of wisdom really ministers to their own exaltation. It is true that they boast about these great names, but only to boast about themselves."[9]

(4) Apart from 3:5-23 the whole response has a decidedly apologetic

[6]Cf. the analysis by N. A. Dahl, "Paul and the Church at Corinth According to 1 Corinthians 1:10–4:21," in *Christian History and Interpretation, Studies Presented to John Knox* (ed. W. R. Farmer, C. F. D. Moule, and R. R. Niebuhr; Cambridge, 1967), 313-35. Dahl sees the same four issues, but states them slightly differently.

[7]The word group appears 44 times in the first ten epistles (plus one in the Pastorals); 28 of these are in 1 Corinthians, 26 in chaps. 1–3! Of the remaining 16 occurrences, ten are in Colossians and Ephesians, where the peculiar nature of that "heresy" also has dictated the language used. All of this indicates that Paul does not ordinarily think of the gospel or Christ in terms of "wisdom."

[8]Otherwise Ellis, 44-62, who first of all rejects the notion that 1 Corinthians reflects "an adversary theology, *i.e.*, a theology incorporating ideas of his opponents that are modified and redirected against them" (p. 46). He then argues on the basis of 2:6-16 and 12:8 that "wisdom" is basically a positive term for Paul, a gift belonging to those who are *pneumatikoi* (not all the Corinthian believers, but a gifted few). The background to such an understanding is OT prophecy and Jewish apocalyptic.

[9]*Paul*, p. 157.

ring to it, in which Paul is defending not only his own past ministry among them (1:16-17; 2:1–3:4), but also his present relationship to them, since he is being "judged" by them (4:1-21). Given the express statement in 4:18 that some are "puffed up" against Paul, and the indication in 4:6 that some are "puffed up" *for* one (apparently Apollos in this case), *against* the other (probably Paul), it seems altogether likely that the quarreling over their leaders is not just *for* Apollos or Cephas, but is decidedly *over against* Paul at the same time.[10]

The question remains as to how these four elements comprise a single issue. Although the answer to this is largely speculative, nonetheless some good guesses can be made. Interpreters commonly see the emphasis on wisdom as stemming from their response to the ministry of Apollos, either from his content or his style, or perhaps both.[11] This has much to commend it and very well may be so. But since very little in the church in Corinth, as seen in this letter, reflects a Jewish background,[12] it seems better to see the problem as stemming from Hellenistic influences.[13] In this case, therefore, it is possible that the key lies with the phenomenon in the Hellenistic world of the itinerant philosopher, many of whom were sophists—more concerned with polished oration than with significant content. The coming and going in turn of Paul, Apollos, and Peter (if indeed he had visited the church), and especially some marked contrasts in style and content among them, had perhaps led the Corinthians themselves to begin to think of their new-found faith as an expression of *sophia*—the divine *sophia*, to be sure, but *sophia* nonetheless. Within this kind of context they were quarreling over their leaders as teachers of wisdom, boasting in one or the other, and judging them from this merely human perspective. From this perspective neither Paul nor his gospel comes off very well. The message of a crucified Messiah, preached by an apostle who lived in considerable weakness, is hardly designed to impress the "wise," as they now considered themselves. In any case—and this is the crucial item for these chapters—the greater issue for

[10]The apologetic nature of 1:10–4:21 is the basic thesis of Dahl's argument (see n. 6). This position has been taken up and argued for as a literary form, but less convincingly, by J. B. Chance, "Paul's Apology to the Corinthians," *PRS* 9 (1982), 145-55. See also the favorable remarks by Hurd in his preface to the new edition of *Origin*, p. xx.

[11]This has been not only the traditional way of viewing things, but also the repeated suggestion of R. A. Horsley (see bibliography).

[12]See the Introduction, pp. 4, 13-14.

[13]Even if it came from Apollos by way of Alexandrian Judaism, exhibited, e.g., in Philo, this marriage of Moses and Plato was decidedly in favor of Plato and Hellenism, not Jewishness. On this whole question Munck correctly asserts: "I Cor. 1-4 shows us something taken from a Hellenistic *milieu* which has received the Gospel, but which introduces into the Gospel certain elements of that *milieu* which falsify the Gospel" (*Paul*, p. 152).

Paul is not the division itself; that is merely a symptom. The greater issue is the threat posed to the gospel, and along with that to the nature of the church and its apostolic ministry. Thus, in a more profound way than is usually recognized, this opening issue is the most crucial in the letter, not because their "quarrels" were the most significant error in the church, but because the nature of this particular strife had as its root cause their false theology, which had exchanged the theology of the cross for a false triumphalism that went beyond, or excluded, the cross.

In Paul's argument with them, therefore, three things needed to be squared away: (1) their radical misunderstanding (or confusion) about the nature of the gospel; (2) their misguided perception as to the nature of the church and their teachers—and the latter's relationship to the gospel; and (3) to accomplish both of these while both reasserting his own authority over them and yet not destroying the very thing he has argued with them as to the role of leadership. The reassertion of his authority, of course, is crucial to the whole letter, since his very ability to pronounce authoritative judgments on their behavior is dependent on this.[14]

The argument itself follows these lines. The opening paragraph (1:10-17) states the problem and serves as a transition to the argument proper. Then in three separate paragraphs Paul argues that the nature of the gospel itself (1:18-25), their own experience of it as the new people of God (1:26-31), and Paul's preaching that brought about their existence (2:1-5) all stand in contradiction to their new stance based on (merely human) wisdom. In 2:6–3:4 he notes that for those who have the Spirit this former preaching of the cross *was* divine wisdom, since it was revealed as such by the Spirit; but alas the Corinthians, contrary to their most cherished notions, have been acting just like those who do *not* have the Spirit. This last paragraph (3:1-4) also serves as a transition for him to speak to their radical misunderstanding of the nature of the church and the role of leadership (3:5-17). This part of the argument concludes in 3:18-23 with his forbidding their "boasting in mere humans" and redirecting their focus christologically. In chap. 4 he finally

---

[14]This would seem to make more sense of the "apologetic" aspect of chaps. 1–4 than to adopt the position of Dahl or Chance (see nn. 6 and 10). Both see these chapters as being essentially preparatory for the authoritative pronouncements of the rest of the letter, but especially of chaps. 5–6 (cf. J. H. Schütz, *Paul and the Anatomy of Apostolic Authority* [SNTSMS 26; Cambridge, 1975], pp. 187-203). They also tend to deemphasize the fact that the gospel itself is at stake—as always for Paul—even when defending his apostleship. Chance, e.g., says of 1:18-25 that "in vv. 18-25 Paul defends his refusal to promote himself. . . . Paul has [thus] laid the foundation for his statements in 2:1-5 that it is because he is weak and foolish that he can serve as a spokesman for Christ" (pp. 150-51). That seems to miss the content of the paragraph and to turn the relationship of those two paragraphs on its head.

turns to the problem of their rejection of him and tells them that they may not judge someone else's "servant" (vv. 1-5). He then assails their pride by setting his own apostolic ministry, with its theology of the cross, against their false theology that has allowed them to judge him in the first place (vv. 6-13), and finally he reasserts his authority, but does so by changing images to that of father and children (vv. 14-21).[15]

1. The Problem—Division over Leaders in the Name of Wisdom (1:10-17)

10 *I appeal to you, brothers, in the name of our Lord Jesus Christ, that all of you agree with one another so that there may be no divisions[16] among you and that you may be perfectly united in mind and thought.* 11 *My brothers, some from Chloe's household have informed me that there are quarrels among you.* 12 *What I mean is this: One of you says, "I follow Paul"; another, "I follow Apollos"; another, "I follow Cephas[a]"; still another, "I follow Christ."*

13 *Is Christ divided?[17] Was Paul crucified for you? Were you baptized into[b] the name of Paul?* 14 *I am thankful[18] that I did not baptize any of you except Crispus and Gaius,* 15 *so no one can say that you were baptized into my name.* 16 *(Yes, I also baptized the household of Stephanas; beyond that, I don't remember if I baptized anyone else.)* 17 *For Christ did not send me to baptize, but to preach the gospel—not with words of human wisdom, lest the cross of Christ be emptied of its power.*

[a]That is, Peter
[b]Or *in;* also in verse 15

---

[15]On the A-B-A pattern of argumentation in this letter (here 1:18–2:5/2:6–3:4/3:5-23 [4:1-23]), see the Introduction, pp. 15-16. Cf. on 7:25-40; 8:1–10:22; 12–14. For a different understanding of the chiasmus in the present chapters, see P. F. Ellis, "Salvation Through the Wisdom of the Cross," in *Sin, Salvation and the Spirit* (ed. D. Durken; Collegeville, MN, 1979), pp. 324-33.

[16]P46 33 and a few others have the singular here, which is due to the dropping of a syllable with the same ending (σχίσμα/ματα).

[17]For the sake of clarity and in conformity to the questions that follow, P46 and a few others have added the negative particle μή at the beginning of the sentence, thus making certain it is read as a question—expecting a negative answer.

[18]It is not easy to decide whether Paul's original read as the NIV, "I am thankful" (א* B 6 1739 cop^pt), or as the MajT, "I thank God." Although supported only by the heart of the Egyptian tradition, the text without τῷ θεῷ is more likely original, in that the addition is easy to account for on the basis of Paul's ordinary usage (there is no other instance of the absolute use of εὐχαριστῶ [10:30 is of a different order]). Omission here, however, could have been accidental (ΕΥΧΑΡΙΣΤΩΤΩΘΩ), so a final decision is not possible.

In the structure of the letter and in Paul's present argument this section fulfills a threefold purpose. First, it introduces the body of the letter.[19] Second, it states in a very specific way the nature of the problem that is first to be taken up and the source of Paul's information about it. Third, vv. 13-17 in particular offer an initial apologetic, which at the same time serves as a means of shifting the focus from the problem of "divisions over leaders" to the greater theological issue underlying its visible expression.

10 With this sentence Paul makes an immediate transition from the thanksgiving to the body of the letter proper. This particular "request formula"[20] occurs commonly in antiquity, both in personal letters and in more official documents.[21] Paul already used the formula in 1 Thessalonians (4:1, 10; 5:14); it will appear again in 1 Cor. 4:16 and 16:15. The use of the vocative ("brothers") and the accompanying authorizing prepositional phrase ("in the name of our Lord Jesus Christ") indicate that for Paul, as Bjerkelund suggests, it belongs more to the "official" category than to the simple request formula. Here Paul is appealing to them with his full apostolic authority.

Nonetheless, it is still "appeal," or exhortation, not demand—although the circumstances could certainly warrant the latter. The reason for this is not simply that his own authority is being called into question, so he dare not demand in such a context. Rather, from a perspective consistent throughout the letter, Paul urges them as "brothers (and sisters)"[22] to conform their behavior to the gospel, not as law but as a response to the grace

---

[19]On this matter see esp. J. T. Sanders, "The Transition from Opening Epistolary Thanksgiving to Body in the Letters of the Pauline Corpus," *JBL* 81 (1962), 348-62; J. L. White, "Introductory Formulae in the Body of the Pauline Letter," *JBL* 90 (1971), 91-97; and C. J. Bjerkelund, *Parakalô: Form, Funktion und Sinn der parakalo-Sätze in den Paulinischen Briefen* (Oslo, 1967).

[20]This is the language of White, "Formulae." However, his including it in the same category as that of Phlm. 8 and the papyrus examples he cites or refers to does not seem quite precise. In this case it fits far better with the more official documents cited by Bjerkelund (see next note).

[21]For a full analysis of the data, as well as the Pauline usage, see Bjerkelund, *Parakalô.* See also K. Grayston, "A Problem of Translation. The Meaning of *parakaleō, paraklēsis* in the New Testament," *Scripture Bulletin* 11 (1980), 27-31.

[22]The vocative ἀδελφοί occurs more times (21) in 1 Corinthians than in any of the other letters, although proportionately it appears more often in 1 Thessalonians (14) and 2 Thessalonians (7). It occurs at a shift in the argument 17 times; four times in conclusions (7:24; 11:33; 14:39; 15:58). Although it means "brothers," it is clear from the evidence of this letter (11:2-16) and Phil. 4:1-3 that women were participants in the worship of the community and would have been included in the "brothers" being addressed. The latter passage is particularly telling since in v. 1 Paul uses the vocative ἀδελφοί, and then directly addresses two women in the very next sentence. It is therefore not pedantic, but culturally sound and biblically sensitive, for us to translate this vocative "brothers and sisters." See also n. 16 on 1:1.

that is in Christ. Here, therefore, the appeal is made "in the name of our Lord Jesus Christ" (cf. 2 Thess. 3:6). This phrase picks up the christological emphasis from the thanksgiving,[23] and thus serves as the ground of the appeal.[24] Possibly the use of the phrase "in the name of" anticipates the baptismal argument in v. 13. That is, they belong to Christ alone, having been baptized in his name, not in the name of Paul or one of the others. More likely, however, this usage reflects that of 2 Thess. 3:6, where the authority of the name is the basis of the appeal.

The content of the appeal is expressed both positively and negatively. In the structure of Paul's sentence the verb "I appeal" is followed by a single "that" clause, which functions as the object of the verb, but at the same time moves very close to a purpose clause.[25] The "that" controls all three verbs that follow, which alternate between positive and negative ways of getting at the same concern. Thus:

I urge *that*
   A. you all say the same thing,
       B. that is,[26] that there be no divisions[27] among you,
   A. rather,[28] that you be knit together in the same mind and the same opinion.

Positively, Paul urges unity by thrice repeating "the same"—that they might all say the *same thing* and that they might be "knit together" in *the same* mind[29] and *the same* opinion.[30] Although the words "mind" and "opinion" (NIV "thought") imply that at least they must agree on the fundamental nature of the gospel, as will be spelled out in 1:18–3:23, they do not thereby imply that in the Christian faith unity demands uniformity; the argument for the need for diversity in chap. 12, not to mention Paul's argument in Gal. 2:1-10, rules that out. What, then, can it mean for him to appeal that they all be of the *same* mind and opinion? The answer lies in what

[23]In much the same way as "God's mercy," spelled out in chaps. 1–11 in Romans, becomes the ground of the ethical appeal in 12:1. See Cranfield, *ICC,* vol. 2, p. 596.

[24]Gk. διά with the genitive, which ordinarily reflects "means" or "agent," here moves closer to the sense of "on the basis of."

[25]Gk. ἵνα. For a discussion of this idiom see Zerwick, *BG,* 406-08.

[26]Gk. καί; for this usage see BAGD 3.

[27]Gk. σχίσματα; only here and in 11:18 and 12:25 in Paul. The context suggests it means something closer to dissensions here than schism.

[28]The Gk. δέ is thus slightly adversative here.

[29]Gk. νοῦς, which here means something close to "disposition" (J. Behm, *TDNT* IV, 958) or "way of thinking" (BAGD). Cf. 2:16, where in contrast to the people of the world who do not have the Spirit, Paul says, "But *we* have the νοῦν Χριστοῦ," which in this case means something closer to the actual thinking or plans of Christ.

[30]Gk. γνώμη; cf. 7:25 and 40.

he says negatively, which reflects the actual situation in Corinth: "that there may be no divisions among you." Although the Greek word for "divisions" *(schismata)* is that from which we derive the English word "schism," it does not in fact mean that, at least not in the sense of a "party" or "faction." The word properly means "tear/rent" (cf. Mark 2:21) or the "plowing" of a field. The best illustration of the present usage is found in the Gospel of John (7:40-43; 9:16; 10:19-21), where various groups are said to have divided opinions about Jesus, meaning they were arguing with one another as to his significance. Thus Paul does not refer to distinctly formed groups or "parties" here, but to divided opinions over their various leaders, which according to v. 11 and 3:3 have developed into jealousy and quarrels. Appropriately, therefore, Paul goes on to urge that they rather be "knit together" (NIV, "perfectly united"), the same word found in Mark 1:19 for the "mending/restoring" of the nets.[31]

11 Paul now proceeds to explain to them how he came to know about their divisions: he was "informed" by "some from Chloe's household."[32] Although one cannot be sure, it is unlikely that these informants were themselves members of the *Corinthian* community.[33] The church had sent as representatives to Paul Stephanas, Fortunatus, and Achaicus (16:15-17), who had almost certainly also carried their letter to him. Had Chloe's people been members at Corinth, they would most likely have been among those who "followed Paul." Yet Paul is not at all pleased by this slogan. Furthermore, Paul's informants are here being quoted as trustworthy witnesses. Had they been "Paul's people," it would hardly have served his own interests for him to quote them as his authorities on the situation there. Most likely, therefore, Chloe was a wealthy Asian—whether a Christian or not cannot be known—whose business interests caused her agents to travel between Ephesus and Corinth. Some of them had become Christians and were members of the church in Ephesus. Having been to Corinth on business, they visited the church there, and on their return to Ephesus had given Paul an "earful" as to the *real* situation.[34]

---

[31]Gk. καταρτίζω. The rendering "knit together" is from *The Centenary Translation* (Helen Barrett Montgomery).

[32]Gk. ὑπὸ τῶν Χλόης, lit. "by those of Chloe." One cannot tell whether her "household" was intended, or her "business," although the two could be one in this case. These people could be either family, slaves, or freedmen; there is no way to tell, although slaves or freedmen is more likely, since, as Theissen, 57, points out, "members of a family would have used their father's name, even if he were deceased"; cf. the further discussion on pp. 92-94.

[33]Theissen, 92-93, thinks otherwise; but his reasons are based on the (probably faulty) assumption that Rom. 16 was written to Ephesus and they are not mentioned.

[34]This point of view was argued by Ramsay, 103-05. From time to time it has been adopted by others (e.g., Héring). Barrett, 42, is more cautious: "They had travelled between Corinth and Ephesus, but may have been based on either the one city or the other."

What they have informed Paul is that "there are quarrels[35] among you." It is noteworthy that Paul must be informed by outsiders about these quarrels. This seems to corroborate what was argued in the Introduction (pp. 5-7), that their letter to Paul does not itself reflect intramural tensions within a divided community who were asking his judgment on various issues where they had differences. Indeed, it is quite the opposite. The very nature of their slogans in v. 12, including the existence of those who "follow Paul"—but without his blessing—implies that such a community would scarcely be asking him to arbitrate their internal differences. Rather, the community in general (or many within the community) stands over against its apostle on those various issues. The point is that Paul has now been informed about the true condition of the community, which probably differs considerably from what he would have picked up from their letter, although the three official delegates who brought it may also have given him an "earful." He would have known from that letter that they were decidedly *not* about to follow his instructions; what he probably did not know until informed by Chloe's people was the true nature of the opposition and some of the thinking that lay behind it. That will now be replayed for their hearing in v. 12.[36]

12 This verse is a crux in terms of how one is going to understand 1 Corinthians as a whole and especially the historical situation of the church to which Paul is writing.[37] Hence it is important to establish what can actually be known (which is not too much) from what is explicitly said.

What is known is that the quarrels are being generated in the names of their various leaders, although it is altogether unlikely that the leaders themselves are party to it. This is obviously true of Paul and Christ; the evidence of 16:12 demands that Paul did not think that Apollos was guilty in any way. Of Peter and his presence there, nothing certain can be known.

But the exact nature of this quarreling and how it took shape in the community are matters on which far more certainty is expressed in the

---

[35]Gk. ἔρις, a Pauline word in the NT (3:3; 2 Cor. 12:20; Gal. 5:20; Rom. 1:29; 13:13; Phil. 1:15; 1 Tim. 6:4; Tit. 3:9), found most often in vice lists of various kinds.

[36]The phrase that begins v. 12, λέγω δὲ τοῦτο ὅτι, is properly translated by the NIV (cf. Barrett, Conzelmann) as "what I mean is this," not as the RV, "Now I say this."

[37]We may dismiss at the outset a very old interpretation that goes back to Chrysostom and was defended by F. Field, *Notes on the Translation of the New Testament* (Cambridge, 1899), pp. 169-70 (cf. Lias, 51). Based on a singular interpretation of the verb μετεσχημάτισα in 4:6 (q.v.), this interpretation suggests that in 1:12 Paul has replaced the names of the actual protagonists (members of the church in Corinth) with those of himself, Apollos, and Cephas as a legitimate "fiction" in order to keep from having his rebukes take a personal form. Thus in 4:6 he intended: "I have spoken the truth in the disguised form of Apollos and myself, etc." But this is to put too much weight on a singular, and not necessary, interpretation of a single word that flies full in the face of the whole argument. After all, the plain statements in 3:5-9 about his and Apollos's ministries are hardly "in disguise."

literature than is actually warranted by what is explicit in the text. Paul says that "each one of you is saying," by which he probably does not mean that every individual is involved in the sloganeering, but that the whole church has been affected by it. The slogans literally read "I am of (Paul)," which means something like "I am Paul's person," or as the NIV has it, "I follow Paul." But in what way and for what reason? Here we are left with a good deal of guesswork.

Paul begins with those who claim him as their teacher of wisdom. Are these loyalists, who have stood by him in the face of opposition? Or are they sloganeering in his name, but without his knowledge, nor perhaps fully understanding his own position? We simply do not know. We do know, both from v. 13 and 3:4-9, that he is scarcely pleased to have his name used in this way. In any case, as Barrett has noted, the very existence of those who lay claim to Paul "itself implies opposition to Paul in Corinth."[38] This is an especially important point, for although he *begins* his response by taking on the distortion of the gospel and the church revealed by these quarrels, he *concludes* the argument by defending his apostleship and his authority over them (4:1-21).

As to the nature of the other slogans, our best guesses lie with the reference to *Apollos*.[39] He is the one teacher who certainly followed Paul in Corinth (see Acts 18:24-28). Moreover, he is the one to whom Paul repeatedly refers in his own response (3:4-9, 22; 4:6). Indeed, the most natural understanding of 4:6 is that Paul for all practical purposes has narrowed the issue in chaps. 1–4 to himself and Apollos and that the Corinthians are "puffed up" in favor of the one (Apollos) against the other (Paul). According to Acts 18:24 he was "a learned [or eloquent][40] man, with a thorough knowledge of the Scriptures," whose own defective understanding of the Christian faith had been repaired by two of Paul's colleagues, Priscilla and Aquila. Paul acknowledges in 3:5-9 that Apollos's work was not in competition with his own, but rather that it "watered" what he had "sown." How, then, did some within the community see it differently? Most likely the contrasts in 2:1-5 fit here, as well as the emphasis in the community on *sophia* (wisdom). It is not so much that Apollos himself advocated under-

---

[38]Barrett, 43.

[39]Cf. the discussion in Hurd, 97-99. Because of the information from Acts and the repeated mention of him in these chapters, it has been natural—and traditional—to take this stance. See, e.g., the considerable, sometimes speculative, reconstruction by J. H. A. Hart, "Apollos," *JTS* 7 (1906), 16-28, esp. 22-28. Not all have done so, however. T. W. Manson, e.g., would dismiss Apollos altogether as having any relevance (see "St. Paul in Ephesus: (3) The Corinthian Correspondence," *BJRL* 26 (1941), 101-20 (repr. in *Studies in the Gospels and Epistles* [Manchester, 1962], pp. 190-209).

[40]The Gk. λόγιος can mean either "educated" or "eloquent." The earlier versions all preferred "eloquent," probably on the basis of their understanding of 1 Corinthians. This may very well be right, but certainty is not available.

standing the gospel in terms of wisdom—although this cannot be ruled out, given his origins in Alexandria, the home of his contemporary, the Jewish Platonist Philo—but that the Corinthians themselves had become enamored with *sophia* and saw Apollos as best fitting their new understanding. This would be especially so if their love of wisdom included a fascination for the values of the Greek philosophical, rhetorical tradition (see on 2:1-5).

The presence of *Peter*[41] in Corinth is less certain.[42] The most probable evidence in favor of it is the reference in 9:5, where it is presupposed that the Corinthians knew that he traveled about with his wife. That would make most sense had he visited Corinth, although enough was probably known about the early apostles in the various churches to make one properly hesitant.[43] What is more important, however, is the question as to whether his influence was of such a nature in Corinth as to have created a "Cephas party." In this case, all the evidence of 1 Corinthians seems to speak against it. Whatever some meant when they said, "I follow Cephas," it had not brought about the theological divisions in the church envisioned by F. C. Baur, and frequently repeated thereafter.[44] Despite the opinions of many, not a single item in 1 Corinthians[45] explicitly suggests a Judaizing faction in the church;[46] and the one issue that might point to such, namely the food sacrificed to idols in chaps. 8–10, explicitly says that those who are "defiled" by the Corinthian "gnostics" are people who had formerly been

[41]Paul usually refers to him by his Aramaic name Κηφᾶς (cf. 3:22; 9:5; 15:5; Gal. 1:18; 2:9, 11, 14), although Gal. 2:7-8 plainly shows that for him the Greek and Aramaic are interchangeable, as they probably were in all the churches.

[42]For the debate on this question see O. Cullmann, *Peter* (Philadelphia, 1953), pp. 53-54 (esp. his n. 55).

[43]On the question of how much about the apostles might have been known in the early churches, see J. Jervell, "The Problem of Traditions in Acts," in *Luke and the People of God* (ET, Minneapolis, 1972), pp. 19-39.

[44]See F. C. Baur, *Paul* (ET, London, 1873), pp. 268-320. Baur condensed the four into two: a Paul-Apollos party opposed by a Judaizing Peter-Christ party. The influence of a Judaizing group under Peter has been a commonly held position since. For more recent advocacy see Manson, "Corinthian Correspondence"; C. K. Barrett, "Cephas and Corinth," in *Abraham unser Vater, Festschrift für Otto Michel* (Leiden, 1963), pp. 1-12; and P. Vielhauer, "Paulus und die Kephaspartei in Korinth," *NTS* 21 (1974/75), 341-52. Common to these latter three is the view that the "Peter-party" represents the greater threat to the community, and that there are veiled allusions to him in the silence in 3:1-9 and 4:6, and in the person who was laying another foundation in 3:11. See the discussion on these verses for a refutation of this view (cf. the excursus in Fascher, 34-37).

[45]It is not by accident, therefore, that many of the scholars who have advocated this position start their investigation with 2 Corinthians 10–13. See, e.g., W. L. Knox, *Paul and the Church of Jerusalem* (Cambridge, 1939), pp. 311, 320-22; and H. J. Schoeps, *Paul* (ET, Philadelphia, 1961), pp. 78-82. See further the disussion by Hurd, 99-101.

[46]Cf. the judgment of Dahl ("Paul," p. 315), who after reviewing various scholarly options concludes: "There is a wide . . . agreement that in I Corinthians Paul is not opposing Judaizers."

accustomed to idols (8:7) and are therefore clearly Gentiles. This is not to say that Peter had not left his mark on some in the church, but it does not seem to have been an indelible, or visible, theological mark. More likely there is a personal allegiance factor here, involving some who had been converted and baptized under his ministry,[47] or perhaps the issue is related to Paul's apostleship vis-à-vis that of Peter.

Most difficult of all is the slogan "I follow Christ." The difficulties stem from several factors: (1) the very placing of Christ's name alongside those of merely human leaders, (2) the probability that all the groups would equally believe that they were following Christ, (3) the fact that this is what Paul would certainly want them all to do, (4) the lack of a single further explicit allusion to such a group, and (5) the fact that the rhetorical questions in v. 13 that are intended to show the absurdity of their quarreling in this fashion could in each instance be answered favorably by such a group. It is our lack of certain information that has allowed the guesses about this group to run the gamut:[48] to deny altogether that there was such a group;[49] to see it as Paul's own position over against theirs;[50] to apply to them what is applied by others to Apollos; to see them as Jewish extremists;[51] to see them as Gnostics who curse Jesus (12:3) but affirm Christ as the true "Spiritual Man";[52] to see them as enthusiasts, the Corinthian *pneumatikoi,* who have an exaltation Christology that has avoided the cross.[53]

What, then, shall one say to all this? The grammar of the passage seems to demand that there were in fact Corinthians saying such a thing.[54]

---

[47]Bachmann, 67, believes that Peter had not been in Corinth, but that some converts of his from the East had moved to Corinth. This possibility, of course, cannot be ruled out.

[48]See the summary in Allo, 9-10, and his Excursus IV, 80-87; cf. the discussion in Hurd, 101-06. For a more recent survey, especially of German scholarship, see Fascher, 90-92.

[49]Hurd tends to favor this position, especially for reason 5.

[50]That is, "Each of you says, 'I am of Paul, etc.,' but I am of Christ." See, e.g., K. Lake, *The Earlier Epistles of Paul: Their Motive and Origin* (2nd ed., London, 1914), p. 127.

[51]See the large number of options listed by Allo, 80-87. Usually it has been argued that this is a group from James, and that the Peter-party would therefore be the moderates. Recent advocates include S. G. F. Brandon, *The Fall of Jerusalem and the Christian Church* (London, 1957), p. 140; and W. O. Fitch, "Paul, Apollos, Cephas, Christ," *Theology* 74 (1971), 18-24.

[52]A view first presented by W. Lütgert (*Freiheitspredigt und Schwarmgeister in Korinth* [Gütersloh, 1908]). It has been vigorously advocated in recent years by Schmithals in his *Gnosticism in Corinth*.

[53]See esp. Conzelmann's Excursus, 33-34. Cf. Moffatt, 10, and Murphy-O'Connor, 11-12, among others.

[54]Despite the attractiveness of Lake's translation (n. 50), it has against it the clear listing intended by the μέν, δέ, δέ, δέ, with no signal that there is a break with the

But beyond that all is speculation, including the suggestion that this was a party with a definable theology.[55] If such were the case, Conzelmann's position is particularly attractive, but his own confidence in it seems to outrun the evidence itself. In the long run the popular view may still be the best one: here are some people who form no distinct group at all, but who in their own attempt to rise above the rest, those boasting in mere men, have fallen into their own brand of spiritual elitism that makes them no better than the others.

But do these slogans represent actual "parties" within the community? Probably not, since nothing else in chaps. 1–4 nor in the rest of the letter so indicates.[56] As Munck has insightfully noted: "At bottom it is only the word 'I', in the sentences 'I belong to Paul' etc. against which he argues."[57] As Munck further suggests, the whole church has fallen prey to a love for disputation, in which various members exalt themselves ("boast") by supposing that their wisdom has been taken over from one of their renowned leaders, one of those close or well known to them, or in some cases even from Christ himself. This solution makes the most sense of the argument that follows,[58] including Paul's rejection in vv. 13-17 of those who so use his name.[59]

13   Paul is aghast at what he has learned from Chloe's people; and

---

fourth member, not to mention that the first question in v. 13 seems to suppose that the fourth slogan is one of theirs (see below).

[55]The statement in 2 Cor. 10:7, "If anyone is confident that he belongs to Christ . . . ," is often seen as further evidence for this party and its continuing existence as the real trouble in the church; but that seems to miss the real point of the 2 Corinthians passage. There some outsiders ("super-apostles") are claiming to be Christ's servants (11:23), and Paul is simply answering their claim by arguing that he, too, belongs to Christ. Cf. Dahl, "Paul," p. 323, and V. P. Furnish, *II Corinthians* (AB 32A, Garden City, NY, 1984), p. 476.

[56]Otherwise Conzelmann, 34, who argues that one cannot "dismiss the group question as being merely a matter of harmless squabbles. The energy Paul expends upon it is too great for that." However, I do not argue that these are "harmless squabbles." As noted above (pp. 49-50), they reflect a serious misunderstanding of the gospel itself, as well as of the church and its leaders; hence the energy expended, since for Paul everything else is subordinate to the gospel.

[57]*Paul,* p. 150.

[58]Cf. the alternatives to this solution proposed by Dahl ("Paul," pp. 322-25) and Theissen, 99-110. Dahl suggests that the division arose over whether or not to write to Paul, since, as some asserted (4:18), he had promised to return but did not. They were arguing, therefore, that they should contact one of their other teachers. Theissen suggests that the division is really between some well-to-do converts, who had "entertained" the various leaders while they were in Corinth and who, because of social status, exercised considerable influence on others who were of lower classes.

[59]Cf. 4:15 where their "countless guides" would include the Corinthians themselves, who are trying to continue Paul's work, each in his own way (cf. Munck, *Paul,* p. 152).

often in such moments he turns to rhetoric, designed to help his readers/listeners to see the total absurdity of their own position.[60] Despite some debate over the meaning of the first one, the point of these questions is clear. In each case they represent logical extensions of their slogans, yet in each case the question also demands a strongly negative response on the part of the Corinthians.[61]

The first question is the more difficult. Although it could be read as an exclamation: "Christ is divided!"[62] it seems more likely that it is a rhetorical question, leading off the series.[63] But what can it possibly mean? Most often the verb is translated as a passive (NIV, "Is Christ divided?"), with Christ as a metonym for the church (as in 12:12). Thus by their divisions they are dividing Christ himself. The difficulty with this view is how it could have been the natural question to follow out of the fourth slogan, especially since it would be favorable to this group ("Of course Christ is not divided," they would answer; "We are following him"). The alternative is to give the verb its more natural meaning—"to apportion out," or "to separate into component parts." In this case the implication is not so much that Christ is being divided into parts and apportioned out as that he has been apportioned out as only one among many. Thus Paul is asking, in direct response to the final slogan, "Absurd! Can Christ be made a party in the same breath as the others?" or "Do you mean to say that Christ has been apportioned out so that only one group has him?"

The next questions take on the absurdity of their slogans, which are in the name of mere men. By parceling out Christ as one among others, and by saying "I am of Paul, etc.," they must allow then that Paul, too, could have been crucified for them or that they had been baptized into Paul's name. This of course is *reductio ad absurdum,* and is intended to demolish their slogans. Tactfully, he chooses to use his own name; by implication what he says is obviously true for Apollos and Peter. By means of the final question on baptism, however, he is also able to make the transition to his apologetic for the gospel, and his own role in its proclamation.

---

[60]This is a frequent device in 1 Corinthians. See, e.g., 4:7; 6:1-5; 10:22; 14:36; etc.

[61]R. W. Funk, *Language, Hermeneutic, and Word of God* (New York, 1966), pp. 161-62, has suggested that the three questions and the rest of 1:15–4:21 are a form of chiasm, being responded to in reverse order: 1:14-16 responds to the third question; 1:18–2:16 to the second; 3:1–4:21 to the third. This seems doubtful, especially since 1:18–2:16 scarcely *responds* to the question, "Was Paul crucified for you?"

[62]A few translations so render it; "Christ has been divided into groups" (GNB); "And so, in effect, you have broken Christ into many pieces" (LB); "You have rent the Christ in pieces!" (TCNT).

[63]The earliest MS of 1 Corinthians (P[46]) has so understood it, by adding the negative μή. See n. 17 above.

What is less apparent is how much one is to make of the question about baptism. The crucifixion of Jesus and the baptism of the believer are ideas that seem to flow together naturally in Paul (e.g., Rom. 6:2-3; Col. 2:12-15). One must not make too much of the collocation here, however, as some have done, and suggest that by baptism one has appropriated the work of the cross.[64] Not only is that foreign to Paul's purposes, but the rest of the paragraph stands in firm opposition to it. Paul's reason for this question probably flows out of their slogans. To be baptized "into the name of" someone means that the baptisand has turned over allegiance, has given himself/herself, to the one named in the rite.[65] The Corinthian slogans at least imply such an understanding. But since they were *not* baptized into Paul's name, by that very fact they cannot say "I am of Paul." It also seems probable, on the basis of Paul's arguments in both 10:1-6 and 15:29, that the Corinthians themselves held a somewhat "magical" view of baptism. With such a view they perhaps also held in high regard those who had baptized them. Hence again their ability to say "I am of Apollos," etc. Thus Paul in the rest of the paragraph disabuses them altogether of the importance of the person doing the baptizing and at the same time puts into proper perspective this initiatory rite whereby one in faith responded to the gospel and thus gave oneself totally to Christ.[66]

14-15 In what follows Paul is not trying to work out a theology of baptism, nor is he in effect negating baptism. Rather, having just mentioned the absurd—that anyone should be baptized in his name—he goes on to say how grateful[67] he is for a simple, uncalculated historical reality, namely that he baptized so few. This at least, he says, works in my favor, lest those baptized by him turn about and say the very absurdity of v. 13, that they had

---

[64]See, among others, O. Cullmann, *Baptism in the New Testament* (ET, London, 1950), who rather boldly asserts: ". . . in I Cor. 1.13 . . . Baptism is *clearly* conceived as participation in the Cross of Christ. . . . Here the two expressions 'you were baptised' and 'another was crucified for you' are *treated as synonymous"* (p. 15; italics mine). This seems to miss Paul's point, and to exceed the evidence considerably. Not only does Paul treat the two questions separately (baptism, vv. 14-16; the preaching of the cross, vv. 17-25), but in v. 17 he deliberately separates them as two distinct events. J. D. G. Dunn rightly assesses: "While the association of the two questions in v. 13 is suggestive, any link between the event of the cross and that of baptism must be based on firmer ground than 1.13 affords" (*Baptism in the Holy Spirit* [London, 1970], p. 118).

[65]See the discussion in Dunn, *Baptism,* p. 117.

[66]It seems altogether likely, especially on the basis of Acts 2:38; 8:16; 10:48 (perhaps; see n. 35 on 6:11); and 19:5 (cf. Rom. 6:3), that the early church baptized only in the name of Jesus, rather than in the Trinitarian formula of Matt. 28:19. This text could add to that evidence; however, one needs to be cautious here, since the concern is so obviously of another kind that one cannot be sure that it adequately reflects the precise formula for Christian baptism. It at least *included* the name of the Lord Jesus.

[67]For this use of "I thank God," see also 14:18.

been baptized into him—and thereby form something of a sect in his name. Was Paul skittish here, as though by now he would put nothing beyond the Corinthian believers? Perhaps; but it is also possible, as v. 17 implies, that he really does feel a need to put the rite into proper perspective, at least in relationship to the proclamation of the gospel.

No doubt the two exceptions are related to the fact that both men were very early converts in the city.[68] "Crispus" is almost surely the Jewish synagogue ruler of that name mentioned in Acts 18:8. "Gaius" is most likely to be identified with the "Gaius, host to me and to the whole church," of Rom. 16:23, since Paul was apparently in Corinth when he wrote the letter to Rome.[69] This means that Gaius scarcely fits the description of the majority of believers given in 1:26-29. The fact that he hosted the church means that he was a man of substance;[70] it probably also means that he belonged to that class of Roman freedmen who had come to Corinth and had "made it big" in the commercial enterprises of the city.[71]

16 And then Paul remembers—or his memory has been jogged by Stephanas himself (cf. 16:15-17): "Ah yes," he interrupts, "I also baptized the household[72] of Stephanas," an interjection that shows how truly *ad hoc*

[68]This is further strengthened by the mention of Stephanas in v. 16, since Paul explicitly refers to him and his household as the "first converts in Achaia" (16:15).

[69]This is the standard view, based on the fact that the collection that was anticipated by Paul's third visit to Corinth (2 Cor. 8–9) had now been received from Achaia (Rom. 15:26). On the Roman destination of chap. 16, see H. Gamble, *The Textual History of the Letter to the Romans* (Grand Rapids, 1977).

[70]On this whole question and its significance for various issues in this letter, see Theissen, 69-119, who argues convincingly that Crispus and Stephanas were also from the upper classes.

[71]Bruce, 34, notes the suggestion that he might be identified with the God-fearer Titius Justus of Acts 18:7, whose house was next to the synagogue and the place where the church gathered after it had been excluded from the synagogue. Thus his full Roman name would have been Gaius Titius Justus. This is intriguing and plausible, in light of the fact that he was almost certainly one of the early converts in the city.

[72]Although it is quite beside Paul's point, a great amount of ink has been spilt over Paul's use of οἶκος here (cf. 16:15, where οἰκία is used), whether this baptism also included infants and small children. Much of the more recent debate has centered on whether the terms οἶκος/οἰκία (both translated "household" in the NIV) in other sources have normally included infants. A. Strobel ("Der Begriff des 'Hauses' im griechischen und römischen Privatrecht," *ZNW* 56 [1965], 91-100) has argued that οἰκία would be a broader term that would often include slaves, while οἶκος was used in a narrower sense for those within a family who possessed legal rights, thus excluding slaves and usually minor children. But even he admits that this evidence is inconclusive; and Theissen, 83-87, has pointed out that the terms are more interchangeable than Strobel allows. In sum, it is the nearly universal judgment of NT scholarship that a biblical case for infant baptism cannot be decided on the basis of these "house-formulae." This judgment comes from scholars on both sides of the issue. See, e.g., G. Delling, "Zur Taufe von 'Häusern' im Urchristentum," *NovT* 7 (1965), 285-311, who thus bases the practice on the sole efficacy of the grace of God as it is given in Christ. The notable exception is J. Jeremias,

this letter is. Having thus had his memory jogged once, and as if to cover his tracks lest it fail him further about something he obviously did not consider important, he adds: "beyond that, I don't remember[73] if I baptized anyone else." Nothing more is known of Stephanas, except what we learn in 16:15-17, that he and his family were the first converts in the province and that he was obviously a leader in the church. The language of 16:16 suggests that Paul still approves of his leadership, which makes his role in the dissensions very difficult to assess.

17 With the aside about Stephanas the argument has started to slip away somewhat; so with this sentence Paul gets himself back on track. The "for" that begins the sentence refers to the final words of v. 16: "I don't remember whether I baptized anyone else." *For,* he goes on to explain, that is not my calling—nor my point. His point has been to jolt the Corinthians into seeing the folly of their kind of allegiance to mere humans—something to which he will return in 3:3-9. But for now, having made it clear what he did *not* come to do ("to baptize"), he moves on to what he *did* come to do ("preach the gospel"), and he makes this point in terms of his own apostleship ("Christ sent me").[74] This in turn will serve as the turning point in the argument, whereby he sets out to contrast their present concern, "wisdom," with what should be their concern, namely the gospel, with its focus on "the cross of Christ."

In saying "Christ did not send me to baptize" Paul does not intend to minimize Christian baptism; his use of this imagery in Rom. 6:3-7 would forever rule that out. The reason for expressing his own calling in this negative way has been dictated by the nature of the argument. Not only were they not baptized into his name (v. 13), but he actually baptized very few of them, which was to his great advantage lest some begin to think in these terms (vv. 14-16); in any case this discussion of who baptized whom is quite beside the point (v. 17a), so let us get on to the real issue, which has to do with the nature of the gospel itself (v. 17b).

Nonetheless, it is possible—probable, it would seem to me—that "who baptized whom" was part of their divisions. Thus Paul does separate the act of baptizing from the proclamation of the gospel, a fact that must also be taken into account as part of his understanding of baptism. It seems clear from this passage that Paul does not understand baptism to *effect* salvation.

Infant Baptism in the First Four Centuries (ET, London, 1960), and *The Origins of Infant Baptism, A Further Study in Reply to Kurt Aland* (ET, Naperville, IL, 1962). Aland's study was entitled *Did the Early Church Baptize Infants?* (ET, Philadelphia, 1963). On this whole question, both historically and biblically, see chap. 6 in G. R. Beasley-Murray, *Baptism in the New Testament* (London, 1963).

[73]Gk. οἶδα, "know," in the sense of "recall"; cf. 16:15.
[74]Gk. ἀπέστειλεν, the verb form of the noun ἀπόστολος.

The preaching of the cross does that—when of course it is accompanied by the effectual work of the Spirit.[75] But it would be quite wrong to go on, as some do, and say that baptism is a purely secondary matter.[76] Surely Paul would not have so understood it. For him baptism comes *after* the hearing of the gospel, but it does so as the God-ordained mode of faith's response to the gospel.

Paul describes his own task as that of "preaching the gospel," which he here elaborates with a striking contrast: "not with words of human wisdom, lest the cross of Christ be emptied of its power." The very way this is said, plus the long elaboration of it in 1:18–2:16, makes it probable that "words of human wisdom" is a Corinthian value. Thus Paul's general intent with these words seems clear: to set forth his own ministry, both its content and form, in sharp contrast to their present stance. It also thereby serves apologetic purposes. But the precise meaning of the negative phrase, which literally reads "not in *sophia* [wisdom] of *logos* [word]," is not quite so clear. Is the emphasis on the content (wisdom) or form (word), or perhaps both?[77] In light of the contrastive purpose clause that follows, the genitive, "of word," is most likely descriptive, and means something like "not with a kind of *sophia* that is characterized by rhetoric (or perhaps reason or logic)." Thus the emphasis is first of all on content; Paul is about to set out the divine wisdom of the cross in contrast to merely "human wisdom." But it probably also includes a concern over form, since according to 2:1-5 the human wisdom with which they are most enamored is that characterized by the Greek philosophical, rhetorical tradition.[78] This seems to be corroborated by the way the following argument flows out of this phrase.

This is the first occurrence of *sophia* in the letter; the argument that follows indicates that this is the real issue. What exactly the Corinthians themselves would have meant by it is a matter of considerable debate.[79]

---

[75]Cf. the similar conclusion in Dunn, *Baptism,* pp. 118-20; see also Beasley-Murray, *Baptism,* pp. 177-81.

[76]See, e.g., Lietzmann, 9.

[77]Recent scholarship has been so enamored with *sophia* as content (hypostatic Wisdom as the way of salvation) that it has generally neglected *sophia* as speech and rhetoric. For a corrective, see Horsley, "Wisdom," although his own enthusiasm for Philonic parallels causes him to reach some debatable conclusions about the Corinthians' own role in this matter. Cf. R. Scroggs, "Paul: ΣΟΦΟΣ and ΠΝΕΥΜΑΤΙΚΟΣ," *NTS* 14 (1967/68), 36.

[78]A concern to establish his message as *not* something merely human, i.e., merely a matter of rhetoric or speech, had already exercised Paul considerably in Thessalonica (see 1 Thess. 1:5; 2:3-6, 13). But there are clear differences between the concern in 1 Thessalonians and the one expressed here. There *logos* is seen positively, as a part of the whole of the witness. Here it is totally pejorative.

[79]Traditionally it was assumed that it reflects the Greek philosophical or sophist tradition. The most comprehensive recent advocacy of this position can be found in

Since Paul does not speak of a "higher" wisdom (the NIV at 2:1 is somewhat misleading), or use language that would seem to reflect a personification of wisdom (see comment on 1:24 and 30 below), but rather speaks of it as "of this world" (1:20), or "merely human" (1:25), most likely it reflects the current philosophical milieu, with its emphasis both on human understanding and rhetorical skill. Given the way that Paul in 2:1-5 sets his own preaching in contrast to this "wisdom of word," it probably also reflects the position from which they are currently judging him and his ministry (cf. 4:1-5).

But here the contrast, which begins as though it might be similar to 2:1-5 (cf. 1 Thess. 1:5), makes a surprising turn toward the *content* of the preaching, not its manner or effect. In so doing Paul also sets up the powerful cadences that follow, a fact that is blurred in most English translations. "Christ sent me to preach," he says, "not wisdom characterized by *logos*." But there is another *logos*, he goes to argue in v. 18, the *logos* of the cross, which is foolishness to the perishing, who are doing so because they think existence is predicated on wisdom. Thus he concludes his sentence, "lest the cross[80] of Christ be emptied of its power."[81] The other contrast, the question of form and manner, between preaching in such a way as "to distinguish

---

Munck (*Paul*, pp. 148-54); it is the position basically adopted in this commentary. Some who see the background as Greek argue for a hypostatic (personal) understanding of *sophia*. Thus they see the Corinthians as having equated Sophia with the so-called heavenly redeemer of Gnosticism (see esp. Wilckens, 68-76). Others have viewed the emphasis on wisdom as belonging to the Jewish wisdom tradition, either the personified wisdom of Proverbs (e.g., 8:1–9:6) and Sirach (e.g., 1:4, 9) or its Hellenized form in Philo of Alexandria (see Pearson, 27-39; Horsley, "Wisdom" and "Marriage"; and Davis [see bibliography]). But the problems with these views are twofold: (1) There does not seem to be any viable evidence that the Corinthians had a personalized view of wisdom; indeed, the evidence goes in the other direction (see commentary on 1:24 and 30); (2) the background seems unlikely to be Jewish, since Paul explicitly says that the *Jews* demand *signs* and it is the Greeks who seek for wisdom. Davis, 189 n. 26, calls this objection "misguided." But to do so he must dismiss Paul's explicit statement in favor of a highly speculative midrashic analysis of the text. Whether rhetorical or not, Paul's clear *statement* is that *Greeks*, not Jews, pursue wisdom. Some of course (e.g., Ellis, 45-62) reject wisdom as a Corinthian concern and see it as Paul's own point of view, which is then argued for as having a Jewish background. But the context of the whole argument seems to speak too strongly against this option. Even Paul's affirmations of wisdom in 2:6-16 seem to have been dictated by the position of the church. Elsewhere he simply does not reflect this emphasis or understanding. Cf. the statistics in n. 7.

80This is the first occurrence of the terms "cross" and "crucified" in the Pauline corpus. They do not occur in Paul as often as one might be led to think ("cross" ten times; "crucify" eight). Most of these are in conflict settings. Otherwise Paul tends to speak of Christ's having "died" for us.

81The NIV adds the words "of its power," on the basis of the context in v. 18. This is almost certainly the correct understanding of the usage, which also might be translated "rendered ineffective" or "invalidated."

myself in *logos* and *sophia"* (2:1) and "with a demonstration of the Spirit's power" (2:5), is a real one and must be spoken to. But the more urgent concern is between *sophia* itself and the message of the cross. To have come with the former, Paul says, in effect would have been totally to negate the latter. Therefore it is to this issue that he will first turn (vv. 18-25).

It is easy to see the urgency of a paragraph like this for the contemporary church, which not only often experiences quarrels such as these at the local level, but also is deeply fragmented at every other level. We have churches and denominations, renewal movements that all too often are broken off and become their own "church of Christ," and every imaginable individualistic movement and sect. Even in a day of various kinds of ecumenism, the likelihood of total visible unity in the church is more remote than ever. This fragmentation is both a shame on our house and a cause for deep repentance. If there is a way forward, it probably lies less in structures and more in our readiness to recapture Paul's focus here—on the preaching of the cross as the great divine contradiction to our merely human ways of doing things.

2. The Gospel—A Contradiction to Wisdom (1:18–2:5)

Having set up the contrast in v. 17 between the "wisdom of *logos*" and the cross, Paul now moves to a series of arguments that will have this contrast as its point of reference. Their "boasting" in men in the name of wisdom ultimately impacts the nature of the gospel itself. In a series of three paragraphs, therefore, Paul tries to get the Corinthians to see that their own existence as Christians, especially in regard to their Christian beginnings, stands in total contradiction to their present "boasting." Each of the paragraphs is predicated on the same reality, namely that the cross is not something to which one may add human wisdom and thereby make it superior; rather, the cross stands in absolute, uncompromising contradiction to human wisdom. The cross in fact is folly to wisdom humanly conceived; but it is God's folly, folly that is at the same time his wisdom and power.[1]

---

[1]Some have detected a midrashic pattern to this section, similar to some patterns found in Qumran and Philo. See W. Wuellner, "Haggadic Homily Genre in I Corinthians 1-3," *JBL* 89 (1970), 199-204; Ellis, 213-20; J. I. H. MacDonald, *Kerygma and Didache. The Articulation and Structure of the Earliest Christian Message* (Cambridge, 1980), pp. 37-68; V. P. Branick, "Source and Redaction Analysis of 1 Corinthians 1-3," *JBL* 101 (1982), 251-69; and Davis, 67-70. While this may be helpful in seeing the milieu of Paul's own basically Jewish thought patterns, it says little about the Corinthians themselves, as Davis, e.g., proposes. Furthermore, the advocates of this theory go considerably beyond the evidence when they also suggest that the homily may have already existed and that Paul is here adapting it (Ellis) or that "the exegesis of this homily can no longer be made with certainty in reference to the conditions in the church in Corinth"

Thus he says in effect, "So you think the gospel is a form of *sophia?* How foolish can you get? Look at its *message;* it is based on the story of a crucified Messiah. Who in the name of wisdom would have dreamed that up? Only God is so wise as to be so foolish" (1:18-25); "Furthermore, look at its *recipients*. Yourselves! Who in the name of wisdom would have chosen you to be the new people of God?" (1:26-31); "Finally, remember my own *preaching*. Who in the name of wisdom would have come in such weakness? Yet look at its results" (2:1-5).

a. God's folly—a crucified Messiah (1:18-25)

18 *For the message of the cross is foolishness to those who are perishing, but to us[2] who are being saved it is the power of God.* 19 *For it is written:*

"I will destroy the wisdom of the wise;
the intelligence of the intelligent I will frustrate."[a]

20 *Where is the wise man? Where is the* expert in the law?[3] *Where is the philosopher of this age? Has not God made foolish the wisdom of the world[4]?* 21 *For since in the wisdom of God the world through its wisdom did not know him, God was pleased through the foolishness of what was preached to save those who believe.* 22 *Jews demand miraculous signs and Greeks look for wisdom,* 23 *but we preach Christ crucified: a stumbling block to Jews and foolishness to Gentiles,[5]* 24 *but to those whom God has called, both Jews and Greeks, Christ the power of God and the wisdom of God.* 25 *For the*

(Branick, p. 267). Since it is so thoroughly Pauline in its present "adaptation," it is nearly irrelevant to suggest that it may have had prior existence; and to argue that it may not *fit* the present context seems both to miss the true nature of the problem in Corinth and to plead for irrationality in exegesis. If Paul did not intend all this to speak directly to the Corinthians, then we must argue that authors are nonintentional, and the whole question of the meaning of an author's words becomes moot.

On a different tack, K. Bailey has found intricate poetic patterns in 1:17–2:2, consisting of a 13-part chiasm, with v. 23 as the middle member ("Recovering the poetic structure of I Cor. i 17–ii 2. A Study in Text and Commentary," *NovT* 17 [1975], 265-96). There can be little question, it would seem, that much of Paul's argumentation takes on the patterns of semitic parallelism; but this is a reflection of how his mind works. The "chiasm" that Bailey has discovered is less than convincing, since he must omit what doesn't fit (in this case, vv. 27-28) and seems to miss the obvious structures of Paul's own argumentation (a section of poetry that has 1:17 and 2:2 as its beginning and ending makes little sense of the flow of Paul's thought, nor of his conjunctions and particles).

[2]The Latin tradition omits ἡμῖν, probably a translational variant.

[3]NIV "scholar"; the translation here is that of BAGD.

[4]P[11] (7th c.) and the later MajT add τούτου to conform the text to the more common Pauline usage.

[5]The MajT reads "Greeks" here, an assimilation to vv. 22 and 24. Here is clear evidence that these two terms can become nearly synonymous in Paul.

foolishness of God is wiser than man's wisdom, and the weakness of
God is stronger than man's strength.

ᵃIsaiah 29:14

This paragraph is crucial not only to the present argument (1:10–4:21) but to the entire letter as well. Indeed, it is one of the truly great moments in the apostle Paul. Here he argues, with OT support, that what God had always intended and had foretold in the prophets, he has now accomplished through the crucifixion: He has brought an end to human self-sufficiency as it is evidenced through human wisdom and devices. No, Paul argues with his Corinthian friends, the gospel is not some new *sophia* (wisdom, or philosophy), not even a new divine *sophia*. For *sophia* allows for human judgments or evaluations of God's activity. But the gospel stands as the divine antithesis to such judgments. No mere human, in his or her right mind or otherwise, would ever have dreamed up God's scheme for redemption—through a crucified Messiah. It is too preposterous, too humiliating, for a God.

It is altogether likely, of course, that Paul's Corinthian opponents would also have sensed the humiliation of that message, and that that is why they had "moved on" to "higher" things, far beyond the mere "milk" that Paul had offered them. But Paul recognizes that to move beyond the cross is not to "move on" at all, but is to abandon Christ altogether. Hence he here argues that the message of the cross is absolute—and fundamental—and as such stands over against the merely human wisdom of their present position.

18 The "for" that begins this sentence ties it to v. 17 as an explanation of the final clause in that verse. Unfortunately our paragraph break and the limits of English tend to cause us to miss the subtle contrast that Paul intends. At the end of v. 17 he had said (literally): "not in the wisdom of *logos* (word, rhetoric, reason), lest the cross of Christ be invalidated." Now he says, "For the *logos* (word, message) of the cross is foolishness to those who are perishing." There is a *logos* (speech) that belongs to wisdom and there is a *logos* (message) whose content is the cross; but they are mutually exclusive.

From the standpoint of his new position in Christ, Paul with this sentence sets forth the two basic groups of humankind. Formerly, as a Jew, it was Jew and Gentile (just as for the Greco-Roman it was Greek/Roman and barbarian). Now it is "us who are being saved"[6] and "those who are perishing."[7] The former groups, Jew and Gentile, continue to exist (indeed, in

---

[6]Gk. σωζομένοις; cf. v. 21. Although not frequent in this letter (3:15; 5:5; 7:16; 9:22; 10:33; 15:2), this is probably the most comprehensive word in Paul's vocabulary for God's redemptive event. His use of the verb has its roots in the OT; see G. Fohrer, *TDNT* VII. 970-80. The NIV properly captures the nuance of the present tense for both verbs.

[7]Gk. ἀπολλυμένοις; cf. 8:11; 10:9-10; 15:18. The verb means to experience eternal loss.

v. 22 they will serve as representatives for the two most common human "idolatries"), but apart from Christ they now both belong to the "perishing." In Pauline theology the new division is not so much predicated on their *response* to the message of the cross as it is on the *event* of the cross and resurrection itself. That is, the crucifixion and resurrection of Jesus for Paul marked the "turning of the ages," whereby God decisively judged and condemned the present age and is in process of bringing it to an end.[8] Those who still belong to it, therefore, are in process of "perishing" with it. From this "old-age" point of view the message of the cross is foolishness.

On the other hand, those who are "being saved," because they have been called (v. 24) and believe (v. 21), have come to see their present existence as the result of God's power, which was also effected by God through the cross and resurrection of Jesus. For Paul, of course, it is not just "those" who are being saved, but *us,* a word that includes himself but especially serves to remind the Corinthians of who they are.

The contrast between "foolishness" and "power" is not precise, of course. The greater precision (between folly and wisdom, power and weakness) will come later in the paragraph (vv. 22-25). For now the contrast has been set up by the language of v. 17, between "*wisdom* of word" and "the cross being emptied" (the NIV rightly adds "of its *power*").[9]

19   Paul now moves on to argue that this folly of God, with its message of the cross, is in fact God's way of doing what he said he would do: set aside and destroy human wisdom. For him to say "For it is written" is sufficient argument.[10] God has already spoken on this issue; he is now merely bringing it to pass.

The citation itself is of Isa. 29:14,[11] chosen because, containing the

---

[8]This essentially eschatological framework, in which salvation *and* judgment are both "already" and "not yet," is absolutely crucial to any proper understanding of Paul. See, e.g., H. Ridderbos, *Paul: An Outline of His Theology* (ET, Grand Rapids, 1975), p. 39: ". . . one can speak of a growing consensus insofar that scholars are more and more finding the point of departure for an adequate approach to the whole in the *redemptive-historical, eschatological character of Paul's proclamation*" (italics his). It is thoroughgoing in this letter, touching almost every part. See the Introduction, pp. 16-17.

[9]This is one of the sure evidences that the problem from Paul's perspective is soteriological, not christological (*pace* Wilckens). Thus the contrast is stated this way, *not* so as to avoid a misunderstanding of what wisdom means for him (as Wilckens and Schütz, *Paul,* p. 196 would have it), but precisely because the Corinthians are turning the gospel into a form of wisdom in which the death of Christ is being emptied of its power.

[10]The absolute use of γέγραπται in Paul is always a reference to the OT Scriptures. See E. E. Ellis, *Paul's Use of the Old Testament* (Edinburgh, 1957), pp. 22-25. Those who see this section as midrash consider this to be the text for the sermon. See Wuellner, "Haggadic Homily," p. 201; and Ellis, 213. Since all of this flows out of the contrasts set up in v. 17, however, it seems far more likely that in this case the text has been determined by the context, not the other way around.

[11]Although the citation is basically from the LXX, Paul has altered the final word from κρύψω ("I will hide") to ἀθετήσω, perhaps, as has often been suggested, on the

word "wisdom" as it does, it makes precisely the point Paul wants to press here. In its original context this passage belongs to that grand series of texts that regularly warn Israel, or someone in Israel, not to try to match wits with God (cf. Isa. 40:12-14, 25; Job 38–42). Yet it is the folly of our human machinations that we think we can outwit God, or that lets us think that God ought to be at least as smart as we are. Paul sees this Isaiah passage as now having eschatological fulfillment. In the cross, the promised "great reversal" has been played out before human eyes in its ultimate way.

20 After the manner of Isa. 33:18 (cf. Isa. 19:11-12),[12] Paul turns to rhetoric to advance his own position against the Corinthians. What is not clear is what Paul himself intended by these questions. Was he inviting the various "wise ones" of the world to step forth and take cognizance of what God had done in the cross? If so, then Paul is now beginning a debate with his hypothetical disputants, and in such a summons, of course, the Corinthians themselves are expected to participate. In this view the final question would thus begin the debate. As attractive as this alternative is, especially in light of vv. 22-25, it seems more likely that these questions, rather than beginning the argument or explanation proper, continue the point of the quotation in v. 19. In this case Paul would be reflecting the sarcasm of a passage like Isa. 19:12, in which the prophet asks in light of what God was about to do, "Where *now* are your wise men?" Thus Paul is asking rhetorically, "In view of what God *has done* in the cross, what is left of the wise of this present age? Where now are all the teachers of wisdom, both Jew and Greek; has not God by this deed not only rendered the wise as foolish but also nullified their very wisdom itself?"

Despite the dismissal of the idea by some,[13] the questions them-

---

basis of Ps. 33:10 ("The Lord . . . thwarts the purposes of the people"). In any case, the word "hide" is probably a Hebrew idiom that in the Isaiah passage is correctly rendered by the NIV "will vanish." Thus, as Davis, 71-72, has rightly pointed out, it should here carry its basic meaning of "set aside," rather than "thwart" or "frustrate."

[12]Some have argued that this verse, too, is a quotation from Isaiah and therefore see Paul here, along with the allusions to Jer. 9:23-24 in vv. 26-31, using a florilegium (a prior collection of "testimonies" to Christ that the early church had gathered from various places in the OT). See H. St. John Thackeray, *The Septuagint and Jewish Worship* (London, 1921), pp. 95-100; L. Cerfaux, "Vestiges d'un florilege dans I Cor. 1.18–3.24?", *RHE* 27 (1931), 521-34; and E. Peterson, "1 Korinther 1,18f. und die Thematic des jüdischen Busstages," *Bib* 32 (1951), 97-103. Peterson advanced the argument in particular as a result of the Qumran discoveries (see esp. 4QFlor). This is a matter still very much up for grabs in NT scholarship. Two things may be said about it here: (1) One can neither prove nor disprove that Paul had such a collection available to him. (2) But in any case v. 20 is *not* a quotation from Isaiah. At best the questions are allusions; more likely they are a "free formulation on Paul's part in reminiscence of passages from Isaiah" (Conzelmann, 42).

[13]See, e.g., Conzelmann, 43 n. 32, who thinks that the suggestion is "too subtle."

selves probably reflect the various "wise ones" of the ancient world. "Where is the wise man?" would refer to the Greek thinker or philosopher (or it could be the general term of which the next two are the specific expressions). The second question is the one that makes this suggestion seem certain: "Where is the expert in the law [not "scholar" as in the NIV and Barrett]?" The Greek word *grammateus* is that used among Jews for their rabbis, the teachers of the law (cf. the Gospels, where it was traditionally translated "scribe"; hence the KJV for this passage: "Where is the scribe?"); it is simply not found among Greeks for their scholars or teachers.[14] Paul by these two designations is anticipating the distinctions of v. 22, where the Jews demand signs and the Greeks ask for wisdom.[15]

The third question then probably generalizes for the sake of the Corinthians themselves.[16] This noun is a rare one,[17] but its corresponding verb and abstract noun are common. Literally it means "debater"; given the nature of much that went under the name of philosophy in the contemporary world, the translation "philosopher" is probably not far off. The qualification "of this age"[18] stands only with the third term, but is probably intended to reflect all three.[19] The various wise ones all belong to this present age that has been judged by God and is on its way out.

With the final rhetorical question Paul sets his own argument in motion. The question appeals to what God has done in Christ: "Has not God made foolish[20] the wisdom of the world[21]?" As Conzelmann rightly notes:

[14]In ordinary Greek vocabulary it refers to a civil officer, e.g., the "town-clerk" of Acts 19:35. See BAGD; cf. Lightfoot, 159.

[15]Otherwise Davis, 73 (following R. G. Hamerton-Kelly, *Pre-Existence, Wisdom, and the Son of Man* [Cambridge, 1973], p. 119), who argues that all three questions assume a Jewish milieu. Given the argument that follows, one would need particularly strong evidence for such, which is not forthcoming.

[16]The alternative to this interpretation, favored, e.g., by Godet and Wilckens, is to see the first as the general term, including both Jew and Greek, while the latter two narrow the focus. This is altogether possible. What seems beyond question is that Paul himself was thinking in these terms, and thereby anticipating the rest of the argument.

[17]Gk. συζητητής; found only here and in Ignatius, *Eph.* 18:1, in all of Greek literature.

[18]Gk. τοῦ αἰῶνος τούτου. This is clearly eschatological language, reflecting the terms "this age" and "the coming age" in rabbinic and apocalyptic Judaism. For Paul, therefore, it becomes an ethical/moral term. Since in Christ God has ushered in the future, which will be consummated at the Parousia, the present age has been judged, and therefore condemned, by God. All who live under its aegis and share in its point of view likewise live under the judgment of God and are passing away. Hence, they belong to *this* age, as over against the new age that God is bringing in.

[19]Cf. Conzelmann, 43.

[20]Gk. ἐμώρανεν; cf. the discussion by G. Bertram, *TDNT* IV, 845-47.

[21]In this instance Paul uses τοῦ κόσμου. This is a clear indication that the two terms αἰων ("age") and κόσμος ("world") had come to merge in his own thinking. Both have become eschatological terms, conditioned by God's ultimate event in Christ, his

"The judgment on the [world] is passed . . . not by reasoning, but by asserting an act of God" (p. 43). The cross is foolishness to the perishing (v. 18), but by means of it God himself has rendered as foolish the world's wisdom, wisdom that belongs merely to the sphere of human self-sufficiency. God has not simply made such wisdom *appear* foolish; he has by means of the cross actually turned the tables on such wisdom altogether, so that it has been made into its very opposite—foolishness.[22] It is not presently self-evident that God has done so, of course, so the rest of the paragraph is Paul's explication of how this is so.

21 Paul now sets out to explain to the Corinthians how what he has just asserted by way of a rhetorical question is true.[23] He begins with a proposition on which he assumes he and they will agree, namely that "the world through its wisdom[24] did not [come to] know[25] [God]." The *kosmos* ("world") is now personified and represents the whole human order of things in its fallenness. On their own, especially through the "wisdom" that belongs to them in their creaturely, fallen existence, human beings failed to know God altogether. Again, this is an assertion based on what for Paul is a self-evident reality. As he will elaborate in Rom. 1:18-31, left to themselves mere creatures cannot find out the living God. The best they can do is to create gods in the likeness of created things, or, as so often happens, in their own distorted likenesses. The true knowledge of God, meaning not so much a proper apprehension of God's being and character as a correct understanding of what God is doing in the world,[26] can come only by revelation—through the Spirit. It is precisely this point that Paul will pick up in 2:6-16.

Paul asserts that it was within the province of God's own wisdom that

---

cross and resurrection. Both the κόσμος, the world order that has been under the domination of Satan, and the present age have been judged by God in Christ and are thus in the process of passing away (see esp. 7:29-31). On this term see J. Guhrt, *NIDNTT* I, 521-26, and H. Sasse, *TDNT* III, 868-95.

[22]Note Godet's nice touch: "He has, as it were, *befooled* wisdom" (p. 94).

[23]The γάρ that connects this sentence to v. 20 is what makes our choice as to the meaning of v. 20 seem certain. This conjunction implies that v. 21 explains the final question of v. 20. Had that final question been the beginning of a debate with the hypothetical "wise ones," one would have expected a different syntax here (a δέ or no particle at all).

[24]The Greek literally reads "through wisdom." Some have understood this to refer to something like a "system of *sophia*," and therefore to a kind of quasi-Gnostic understanding of the world. Thus σοφία here is understood more in terms of content than mode or way of viewing things. But the latter understanding is to be preferred (hence the NIV: "through *its* wisdom"), since the phrase διὰ τῆς σοφίας stands in contrast in this sentence to the διὰ τῆς μωρίας τοῦ κηρύγματος in the following, companion clause.

[25]Gk. ἔγνω, probably an inceptive aorist.

[26]At this point Paul's Jewish understanding of "knowing God" comes to the fore (cf. E. D. Schmitz, *NIDNTT* II, 395-97). The phrase in the next clause, "to save those who believe," is therefore the proper commentary on this one.

he so arranged things.[27] He does not explain how so here, but the reason seems clear. A God discovered by human wisdom will be both a projection of human fallenness and a source of human pride, and this constitutes the worship of the creature, not the Creator. The gods of the "wise" are seldom gracious to the undeserving, and they tend to make considerable demands on the ability of people to understand them; hence they become gods only for the elite and "deserving." It should be noted that Paul is here acknowledging that there is another *sophia,* God's wisdom, which he is about to explicate (see v. 24); but that wisdom turns out to be the exact opposite of human wisdom. Again, *how* all of this is God's wisdom, and how we come to know it, is what 2:6-16 will take up in detail.

On the contrary, Paul says, "God was pleased"[28] to bring people into a proper relationship with himself "through the foolishness of what was preached." The word *kērygma* (KJV, "preaching") here means not the act of preaching itself,[29] but the content of that proclamation, namely the message of a crucified Messiah. This is confirmed by vv. 22-25, which go on to explicate "the foolishness of what was preached." God's purpose in all of this is "to save those who believe." This is the first clear expression[30] in the Pauline letters of what was certainly central to his theology, namely that God himself has initiated salvation for those whom he calls (cf. vv. 24, 27), and their response to that call of grace is to "believe." But believing does not mean simply giving assent to; it means putting one's whole trust in as well. Thus, in contrast to the present Corinthian emphasis on wisdom, Paul insists—as they should well remember from their own experience—that salvation does not come "through wisdom" but "through the foolishness of the event of the cross." And precisely because it stands in contradiction to

[27]Some take the phrase ἐν τῇ σοφίᾳ τοῦ θεοῦ to be a quasi-instrumental, making it mean "The world did not know God by means of the wisdom of God displayed in the created order" (e.g., Kümmel, Héring). But that not only puts considerable strain on the context, it seems to miss the significance of the word order. This phrase stands first here and is something of an absolute usage (i.e., it does not modify "the world did not know," but an understood "God so arranged things in his own wisdom that the world did not know"). Cf. A. J. M. Wedderburn, "ἐν τῇ σοφίᾳ τοῦ θεοῦ—1 Kor 1 ₂₁," *ZNW* 64 (1973), 132-34, who, following Moule, 79, calls this usage circumstantial.

[28]Gk. εὐδόκησεν, a word that in Paul implies strong volition, as well as taking pleasure in. See BAGD; G. Schrenk, *TDNT* II, 740-42.

[29]Ruef, 13, suggests that it refers to both. But cf. G. Friedrich (*TDNT* III, 714-17), who notes: "It is worth considering whether the reference in 1 C. 1:21 might not be to the act, namely, that it pleased God through something foolish, i.e., human preaching, to save men. But the context . . . favours the sense of content in v. 21." Cf. 15:14.

[30]As elsewhere this is predicated on the view that Galatians was written after 1 Corinthians, but before Romans. See the "Author's Preface," p. xi. The expression in 2 Thess. 2:14, "to be saved . . . through belief in the truth," puts the emphasis more on believing the gospel to be true—in contrast to those in vv. 8-12 who "believe the lie"—than on personal trust in Christ.

ordinary human wisdom, it is only for "those who believe," for those who will take the risk and put their whole trust in God to save in this way.

22 The rest of the paragraph now picks up the theme of "the foolishness of the cross" from v. 18, by way of v. 21, and reinforces the two points Paul wants to make in refutation of the present Corinthian stance: (1) Wisdom (their thing) and the cross (God's thing) stand in absolute contradiction one to the other; (2) the "foolish thing" (the cross) is where God was pleased to demonstrate his saving power and redeeming grace on behalf of humankind. But Paul makes these points in grand style.

First, the contrasts of v. 18 (foolishness/power) are now picked up and given precision. This Paul does by dividing the "perishing" into two basic classes, chosen partly because they reflect his Jewish view of the world, but mostly because they reflect the two basic ways that humanity in its "right mind" (i.e., through wisdom) is religious. Thus the "Jews" and "Greeks" here illustrate the basic idolatries of humanity. God must function as the all-powerful or the all-wise, but always in terms of our best interests— power in our behalf, wisdom like ours! For both the ultimate idolatry is that of insisting that God conform to our own prior views as to how "the God who makes sense" ought to do things.[31]

Thus "Jews demand miraculous signs." This reflects Jewish messianic expectations. God had acted powerfully in their behalf in history; the promised Messiah would restore the former glory by acting powerfully on their behalf once again. "Show us a sign," they repeatedly demand of Jesus (Matt. 11:38-39; Mark 8:11; Luke 11:16; John 6:30), "authenticate yourself; validate your messianic credentials with powerful displays." And who can blame them? They had been down a long time and were looking for a mighty deliverer. They knew how God had acted in the past—with a mighty hand and an outstretched arm. Their idolatry was that they now had God completely figured out; he would simply repeat the Exodus, in still greater splendor.

"Greeks look for wisdom." This, too, was a national characteristic.[32] As early as Herodotus it is said of them: "All Greeks were zealous for

---

[31]Cf. Barrett: "It implies a refusal to take God on trust; he must present his credentials in the form of visible and identifiable acts in which his claim upon man . . . [is] validated" (p. 54); and Conzelmann: "In this way they set themselves up as an authority that can pass judgment upon God. . . . They expect God to submit himself to their criteria" (p. 47).

[32]It is this clear statement of Paul's that makes it so difficult to root the use of wisdom in this passage in the Jewish wisdom tradition as many do (see n. 79 on v. 17). The fact that Paul identifies it as a Greek characteristic and then uses all his rhetorical energy *against* "the wisdom of this world," which the *Greeks* seek, seems to demand a Hellenistic derivation of the Corinthian position; unless, of course, it is to be found, as Horsley argues, in Hellenistic Judaism, which Paul perceived to be more Greek than Jewish. But that, too, seems doubtful.

every kind of learning."[33] Again, who can fault them? Theirs were the advances of civilization as none before. Indeed, it was their very advances in learning that caused many to abandon the traditional gods and turn to *sophia,* or *philosophia.* Their idolatry was to conceive of God as ultimate Reason, meaning of course what *we* deem to be reasonable.

These, then, are the two basic idolatries; and they are ever with us. The demand for power and the insistence on wisdom, always for us or from our point of view, are still the basic idolatries of our fallen world.

23 To the seekers of signs and wisdom Paul now presents the ultimate divine contradiction: "But we[34] preach Christ crucified."[35] Rather than giving them the signs and wisdom they demand—and God has plenty of both—they get weakness and folly. Indeed, "Christ crucified" is a contradiction in terms, of the same category as "fried ice." One may have a Messiah, or one may have a crucifixion; but one may not have both—at least not from the perspective of merely human understanding. *Messiah* meant power, splendor, triumph; *crucifixion* meant weakness, humiliation, defeat. Little wonder that both Jew and Greek were scandalized by the Christian message. During Roman times crucifixion was the ultimate penalty, reserved mainly for rebellious subjects of various kinds (insurrectionists and the like) and slaves.[36] Jesus died as a state criminal,[37] a scandal[38] to Jew, Greek, and Christian alike.

To the Jew the message of a crucified Messiah was the ultimate scandal. Although in Roman times the Jews did not crucify, they did afterward hang those who had been stoned, especially blasphemers and idola-

---

[33]*History* 4.77 (Loeb).

[34]This is the first appearance of a first person plural verb in the letter. Cf. the comments on 1:1 and 2:6. One should note how natural it is for Paul to slip into this usage; note also that it tends to happen in such places as this, where Paul would be concerned to imply that such preaching is not unique to himself. See 15:10-11.

[35]Gk. perfect, ἐσταυρωμένον. Perhaps the perfect reflects, as W. C. Robinson, Jr. ("Word and Power," *Soli Deo Gloria, Essays for W. C. Robinson* [ed. J. M. Richards; Richmond, 1968], p. 71), and Ellis, 74, believe, the possibility that for Paul the exalted Lord "in his exaltation, remains the crucified one" (Ellis, 73). On the other hand, it is an adjective here (cf. 2:2) and one wonders what other form the adjective might have taken.

[36]On this whole subject, including both the actual historical data on crucifixion in the Roman world and the meaning of Jesus' crucifixion for both Christian and pagan, see M. Hengel, *Crucifixion* (ET, Philadelphia, 1977).

[37]Cf. Tacitus (*Annals* 15.44): "Christus, the founder of the name [Christian], had undergone the death penalty in the reign of Tiberius, by sentence of the procurator Pontius Pilate" (Loeb).

[38]The Greek word translated "stumbling block" is σκάνδαλον, from which we derive our word "scandal." "Scandal" is in fact closer to the sense than "stumbling block," since the word does not so much mean something that one is tripped up by as something that offends to the point of arousing opposition (see BAGD).

ters.[39] They saw hanging therefore as the fulfillment of Deut. 21:23, "because anyone who is hung on a tree is under God's curse." This also helps to explain the deep rage of the apostle himself against Christ; he was infuriated that fellow Jews should honor as God one whom God himself had obviously cursed by having him hanged (cf. Gal. 1:13-14; 3:13). There is simply no way that "Christ crucified" could be fitted into their understanding either of God or of Scripture. Hence, "a stumbling block to Jews."

To the "Gentiles"[40] the message of "Christ crucified" was a "pernicious superstition"[41] and utter "foolishness." As Hengel notes, Paul's word for folly here "does not denote either a purely intellectual defect nor a lack of transcendental wisdom. Something more is involved," something more closely akin to "madness."[42] It is hard for those in the christianized West, where the cross for almost nineteen centuries has been the primary symbol of the faith, to appreciate how utterly mad the message of a God who got himself crucified by his enemies must have seemed to the first-century Greek or Roman. But it is precisely the depth of this scandal and folly that we *must* appreciate if we are to understand both why the Corinthians were moving away from it toward wisdom and why it was well over a century before the cross appears among Christians as a symbol of their faith.

24 Since the Jews seek signs and the Greeks look for wisdom, and since God is all-wise and all-powerful, why not, one might wonder, give them signs and wisdom rather than this "pernicious superstition" that will offend them both? Paul's reason lies in the double reality that (1) the nasty business of a crucified messiah was in fact the ultimate expression of God's "power" and "wisdom," and (2) as such it is available for those whom "God has called, both Jews and Greeks." Again, Paul brings the Corinthians back to viewing things from above, rather than from below, from their own perspective of wisdom.

From any merely human perspective the central message of the Christian gospel must always appear as folly. But to people from both groups this folly turns out to be the very place where God is powerfully at work, calling out a people for his name. Those who are "being saved" (v. 18), the "believing ones" (v. 21), are so because of God's prior action;

---

[39]See *m.Sanh.* 6.4: "All that have been stoned must be hanged. But the Sages say: None is hanged save the blasphemer and idolater" (Danby).

[40]One should perhaps not make too much of it, but the subtle shift of terms from "Greeks" to "Gentiles" in this clause seems noteworthy. While under most of this discussion the two terms could be interchangeable, it was especially the "Greek" who sought after wisdom. On other hand, not only the Greek, but the Roman in particular, would find a crucified messiah utter nonsense.

[41]This is the language of Tacitus (see n. 37). Cf. the younger Pliny: "a perverse, extravagant superstition" (*Ep.* 10.96.8).

[42]*Crucifixion*, p. 1.

they are "those whom God has called" (see 1:1-2, 9). For them the preaching of "Christ crucified" is effectual; it is "Christ the power of God and the wisdom of God." Paul's concern here is not so much on their being able to *perceive* the cross as wisdom (that will be explained in 2:6-16), but on the actual *effective work* of the cross in the world. Thus in saying that Christ is the "wisdom of God," he is not using philosophical categories, nor is he personifying wisdom in Christ;[43] rather, this is an evangelical statement, i.e., a statement about the effectual working of the Christian evangel. Christ is the "wisdom of God" precisely because he is "the power of God for the salvation of everyone who believes" (Rom. 1:16; cf. v. 30 below).

25 Christ crucified as God's power, and therefore God's wisdom, at work in the world is the ultimate contradiction. Paul now brings closure to his argument by grounding the historical outworking of that reality in a theological axiom: God is both wiser and more powerful than mere human beings. But he says that by keeping intact the paradoxical language of the paragraph. To the perishing the cross is folly; and so it is—*God's* folly, which because it is God's thing turns out to be "wiser than [human] wisdom." In the cross God "outsmarted" his human creatures and thereby nullified their wisdom. In the same cross God also "overpowered" his enemies, with lavish grace and forgiveness, and thereby divested them of their strength.

Thus played out before human eyes is the scandalous and contradictory wisdom of God. Had God consulted us for wisdom we could have given him a more workable plan, something that would attract the sign-seeker and the lover of wisdom. As it is, in his own wisdom he left us out of the consultation. We are thus left with the awful risk: trust God and be saved by his wise folly, or keep up our pretensions and perish. Better the former, because this "weakness of God is stronger than [human] strength"; it accomplishes that which all human pretensions cannot do. It brings one into "fellowship with his Son Jesus Christ our Lord" (v. 9).

One can scarcely conceive of a more important—and more difficult—passage for the church today than this one. It is difficult, for the very reason it was in Corinth. We simply cannot abide the scandal of God's doing things his way, without our help. And to do it by means of such weakness and folly! But we have often succeeded in blunting the scandal by symbol, or

---

[43]This oft-repeated suggestion needs to be laid to rest. In fact, such an idea would be at odds with Paul's concern here. This is *not* a christological statement, such as one finds in Col. 2:2-3, for example. Rather, it is a soteriological statement, just as is v. 30 (q.v.). After all, it begins, "Christ the *power* of God," in direct response to the quest of the Jews in vv. 22-23. One may as well argue that a personified Dynamis Christology lies behind the Corinthian folly.

creed, or propositions. God will not be so easily tamed, and, freed from its shackles, the preaching of the cross alone has the power to set people free. Paul does not tell us how so here, but the whole story makes it plain. In the death of his Son, God has judged us who were responsible for it. Christ has thereby not only taken on himself our sins and guilt and "removed them." He has disarmed us in the divine presence by forgiving us when we richly deserved death. Thus forgiven we are set free not only from our sins but to become his new people in the world. It thus achieves what the god of human expectations cannot achieve—it creates disciples who will trust in him for life. Such "weakness" in God is scandalous to those who think of themselves as righteous and thus in no need of forgiveness; but to those who recognize themselves as in need of mercy this is the good news that sets us free to follow him. Thus this weakness is also the ultimate power, and therefore the final wisdom of God.

b. God's folly—the Corinthian believers (1:26-31)

26 *Brothers, think of what you were when you were called. Not many of you were wise by human standards; not many were influential; not many were of noble birth.* 27 *But God chose the foolish things of the world to shame the wise; God chose the weak things of the world to shame the strong.* 28 *He chose the lowly things of this world and the despised things—and[1] the things that are not—to nullify the things that are,* 29 *so that no one may boast before him.* 30 *It is because of him that you are in Christ Jesus, who has become for us wisdom from God—that is, our righteousness, holiness and redemption.* 31 *Therefore, as it is written: "Let him who boasts boast in the Lord."[a]*

[a]Jer. 9:24

To further his argument that the gospel he preached stands in direct contradiction to human expectations about God, Paul turns from the content of the gospel to the existence of the Corinthians themselves as believers. Not from the world's "beautiful people," but from the lower classes, the "nobodies," God chose those who for the most part would make up his new people. Thus they themselves evidence the foolishness of God that confounds the wise. This paragraph scarcely flatters their self-exaltation; it thereby serves all the more to demolish their boasting in mere men. "Boasting" is the new theme that is picked up here, not only because that is what they were doing by their quarrels over their leaders, but also because it is the main theme of the passage from Jer. 9:23-24 that serves as the framework for the argument.

[1]B syr vg Origen, followed by the later MajT, read a καί here; it is missing in the majority of early sources East and West. Its addition is easily accounted for, for the same reasons that the NIV translates with an "and."

The paragraph opens by reminding them of their own humbler origins (v. 26); in vv. 27-28 this is turned into a theological statement, in which God's choosing people like them is asserted to have the same design as the cross itself—to save them, but at the same time to "shame" and "nullify" the very values in which they are currently boasting. The election of such people reveals the ultimate divine intent (v. 29): to obliterate completely all human grounds for "boasting"—for self-sufficiency—and thereby to cast one completely in trust upon the living God (v. 31). This was made possible through the work of Christ, whom God made to become the true "wisdom" for us, in that he effected redemption for us, thereby making us right with God (v. 30).

26 A turn in the argument is signaled by the vocative, "brothers [and sisters]" (cf. 1:10), and by an untranslated "for."[2] The latter is an inferential or explanatory conjunction, indicating that this paragraph (and the next) will offer specific illustrations further to demonstrate the point of vv. 18-25. Thus he bids them "think[3] what you were when you were called" (lit. "consider your calling"), picking up from v. 24 the motif of their being "called" (cf. vv. 1-2, 9). Ordinarily this word[4] refers to the act of calling.[5] However, the context here demands a meaning very much like that of the NIV. That is, even though it refers to their call to salvation, Paul is concerned with who they were at the time of that call, just as in 7:17-24. Perhaps the Pauline nuance could be captured by paraphrasing: "Look at what was involved in the fact of *your* being called by God; who you were when he called you." His point in getting them so to consider themselves is that in calling out a people for his name God showed no regard for their present values—worldly wisdom or merit. Indeed, in calling *them* he chiefly chose those who are a living contradiction to those values.

What follows spells out in (rhetorical) detail their status at the time of their call: "Not many were wise *(sophoi)* by human standards; not many were influential *(dynatoi);* not many were of noble birth *(eugeneis)*." The prepositional phrase "by human standards,"[6] which qualifies "wise," is intended for all three terms (cf. "of this age" in v. 20) and reflects the

---

[2]D F G have replaced the γάρ with an οὖν, but as Barrett, 56, correctly points out, this inverts the argument.

[3]Although he acknowledges that the difference is slight, Barrett, 56, follows Schlatter here in seeing this βλέπετε as an indicative. The imperative is to be preferred, as elsewhere in this letter (8:9; 10:18; 16:10).

[4]Gk. κλῆσις, in form a verbal noun, thus emphasizing the act more than the acquired status resulting from it.

[5]Despite BAGD there is no evidence that it ever referred to vocation or station in life. See Bartchy, 136 n. 482.

[6]Gk. κατὰ σάρκα; for the use of σάρξ in Paul see E. Schweizer, *TDNT* VII, 125-38; for a more popular treatment see W. Barclay, *Flesh and Spirit* (Nashville, 1962), pp. 16-22.

perspective of their current thinking. This is the first appearance of "flesh" *(sarx)* in Paul's extant letters; eventually it will serve as the basic term to describe our present, "this-worldly" existence, which most often refers to humanity in its fallenness over against God (e.g., Gal. 5; Rom. 8). The irony of their present situation is that they are judging Paul and his gospel from this point of view, which, were they to apply it to themselves, would only serve to show how insignificant *they* really are. So Paul will apply it for them, to show how different God's perspective is from their own.

But what specifically did he intend by the choice of the terms "wise, influential, well born"? The first two seem to have been dictated by the argument itself. These are the adjectives of the two nouns that describe Christ crucified in v. 24; he is the wisdom *(sophia)* and power *(dynamis)* of God, and therefore stands in contradiction to those who are *sophoi* and *dynatoi* by the standards of this age. At the same time this play on terms reflects the first two items in Jer. 9:23; however, in Jeremiah the LXX (rightly) translates the second term by *ischyros,* with the implication of strength or might (cf. vv. 25 and 27).[7] *Dynatos,* on the other hand, which can also suggest might, when applied to people more often carries the sense, as it does here, of the "prominent and influential," those who "carry the clout" in any sociological setting.[8] Thus before their conversion the majority of the believers did not belong to the "wise" and "influential" in Corinth.

Nor did they have distinguished ancestry: "not many were well born." This is the more surprising term. Jeremiah has "wealthy" to complete his triad; and it might be argued, given the origins of Roman Corinth,[9] that very few people in that city were "well born." But the *nouveaux riches* form their own aristocracy, and the majority of the Corinthian believers did not belong to it. It may be that this word was chosen in place of "wealthy" because it is more sociologically determinative: Some of them may have been wealthy, but few would have been well born. On the other hand, Munck has mustered a considerable amount of evidence to show that part of the "boast" of the Sophists was precisely that they belonged to the "wise, powerful, and well born."[10]

---

[7]But cf. the addition to the prayer of Hannah (1 Sam. 2:10) in the LXX, which has φρόνιμοι and δύνατοι for the σοφοί and ἰσχυροί of Jeremiah.

[8]Cf. Acts 25:5; Jos. *War* 1.242; Philo, *Mos.* 1.49. Cf. D. Sänger, "Die *dynatoi* in 1 Kor 1:26," *ZNW* 76 (1985), 285-91.

[9]It was populated chiefly by freedmen from Italy. See the Introduction, p. 2.

[10]*Paul,* pp. 162-63 n. 2: "While we can take it without further evidence, that the sophists are σοφοί, there are various examples of their having parents or ancestors who are δύνατοι and εὐγενεῖς." The examples that follow are both numerous and convincing, and seem to disallow that the terms are merely sociological, as Theissen, 70-71,

This passage has long held interest for understanding the social status of the early Hellenistic Christian communities. Traditionally, it was understood to say that the Christian faith appealed primarily to the "dregs" of society. Hence, more than a century later the antagonist Celsus sneered:

> Their injunctions are like this. "Let no one educated, no one wise, no one sensible draw near. For these abilities are thought by us to be evils. But as for anyone ignorant, anyone stupid, anyone uneducated, anyone who is a child, let him come boldly." By the fact that they themselves admit that these people are worthy of their God, they show that they want and are able to convince only the foolish, dishonourable and stupid, and only slaves, women, and children.[11]

In recent years some have argued for quite the opposite, that despite this statement of Paul's, which is dismissed as rhetoric, the early Hellenistic believers "came by and large from fairly well-to-do bourgeois circles with a fair percentage also from upper class people as well as the very poor."[12] Recent sociological studies, especially those by E. A. Judge[13] and G. Theissen,[14] are more judicious and have demonstrated that the truly unique feature of early Christianity was its nonhomogeneous character, that it cut across all sociological lines and accepted as "brothers" slave and free, Jew and Gentile, male and female.[15]

---

argues. Both Pearson, 40, and Horsley, "Pneumatikos," 282-83, have argued that Philo also uses such terminology for those advanced in wisdom (cf. the enthusiastic endorsement by Davis, 191 n. 42, who asserts that their examples "show the true provenance of this terminology"). But in fact none of their examples brings this set, nor anything quite like it, together. Nor does Philo use this language in such a way as to build confidence that he is the source of a Corinthian usage.

[11]Quoted by Origen in *Contra Celsum* 3.44 (transl. H. Chadwick; Cambridge, 1965, p. 158). Origen rightly goes on to respond, on the basis of 1 Cor. 1:26, that this is not the whole picture, but in so doing he quite neglects Paul's own point.

[12]W. Wuellner, "The Sociological Implications of I Corinthians 1:26-28 Reconsidered," *StudEv* 6 (TU 112; Berlin, 1973), p. 672. Unfortunately Wuellner's position is predicated primarily on grammatical grounds, which in this case are shaky at best, and lacks the more solid approach of sociology. Cf. also K. Schreiner, "Zur biblischen Legitimation des Adels: Auslegungsgeschichte zu 1. Kor. 1,26-29," *ZKG* 85 (1975), 317-57.

[13]See esp. *The Social Patterns of Christian Groups in the First Century* (London, 1960), pp. 49-61.

[14]See esp. the articles that form chaps. 2–4 of *Social Setting*.

[15]The more moot point in their analyses is the contention that although the majority were from the lower strata, they were by and large influenced by the dominant minority who were from the upper classes. Theissen, in fact, makes this his general thesis about the church in Corinth, and sees 1 Corinthians, therefore, as addressed primarily to this upper-class minority, who by their own frictions are responsible for dividing the church. Thus he sees Paul's statement in 4:10 as a reflection of sober reality, that they were indeed "wise, strong, and honored." He must therefore treat v. 26 as not addressing the recipients directly; rather it is intended to remind them of how the majority are. But this

In saying "not many,"[16] of course, Paul is well aware that some of their number were in fact well off by human standards (e.g., Crispus, Gaius, Erastus, Stephanas). Some of them indeed had their own houses and, according to 11:17-22, were abusing the "have-nots" at the Lord's Table. But primarily the community was composed of people who were not "upper class," although from this statement one cannot determine how many would have belonged to the truly "poor"—slaves and poor freedmen—and how many would have been artisans and craftsmen, such as Paul was himself.

But sociology is not Paul's concern; his is theological, and he is capitalizing on the less-than-pretentious social standing of the majority—which at the same time may have had philosophical overtones—to make his point. What Celsus saw as the shame of Christianity, Paul saw as its greater glory. By bringing "good news to the poor" through his Son, God has forever aligned himself with the disenfranchised; at the same time he has played out before our eyes his own overthrow of the world's false standards. Every middle-class or upper-class domestication of the gospel is therefore a betrayal of that gospel.

27-28 With these sets of contrasts Paul now goes on to display the "greater glory" of the gospel. The Corinthians did not stumble onto a great thing in hearing the good news as it was preached by Paul, rather "God chose"[17] the likes of them; and he did so in order to shame the world, and finally to bring it to nothing. In the final analysis, therefore, this sentence (vv. 26-29) is not so much a demeaning of the Corinthians as it is an exaltation of the marvelous grace of God.

The contrasts themselves echo the language of vv. 22-25, but now by way of v. 26, to which they directly correspond. God chose not the "wise," but the "foolish things[18] of the world"; not the "influential," but the "weak

___

seems to turn the two passages upside down. The argument in 4:8-11 is filled with so much irony that it is difficult to take it for sober reality; on the other hand, this passage addresses the church directly, and says "Look at *your* calling, brothers." This is the sober reality. Otherwise, the whole force of the argument is lost. Rhetoric, after all, derives its force from the agreement it assumes and to which it refers.

[16]Cf. the reflection on this verse attributed to Lady Huntington: "Saved by an 'm'. Paul did not say, 'not any,' but 'not many'."

[17]Gk. ἐξελέξατο, the word for election. The emphasis here is not on election as such, but on the sovereignty of God who elects as he wills, and whom he wills.

[18]In each case in vv. 27-28 the "foolish, weak, and lowly" are neuter plural, while the first contrasting noun, "the wise," is masculine and the others are neuter. This presents an unusual sentence in the Greek, but it is understandable nonetheless. The older commentators (e.g., Lightfoot, Godet) tended to make too much of these gender differences. The best solution is that Paul is here generalizing. Not only did he choose "foolish" people, but in all his ways he has chosen what the world deems as foolish (including the cross). Cf. Barrett, 58, who translates: "what the world counts foolish." This seems to catch Paul's point.

things of the world"; not the "well born," but the "lowly things[19] of the world." What God did in the cross and in calling the "lowly" Corinthians not only exhibits his own character, that he is gracious, but also illustrates that he is not beholden to the world: "Whatever the Lord pleases he does" (Ps. 135:6, RSV [in the context of "choosing" Israel as his own possession!]). Thus he is not only not accountable to the "wise" of this world, but by his gracious activity in Christ he has actually "shamed" the wise. By this latter term Paul does not mean something subjective, the "feelings of shame" that the wise are now to feel. Rather, he has here picked up an OT theme that expresses the vindication of God over his enemies (or over the enemies of the righteous), a vindication that is related to God's righteous judgments (e.g., Ps. 6:10; 31:17; 35:4, 26-27).[20] With Paul this vindication has become eschatological; in choosing the Corinthians God has already begun the final vindication over his enemies. He has already "disgraced" them by overturning their warped perspective.

Paul's eschatological perspective is made clear by the final contrasts. He begins with "lowly," to which he adds "the despised things" (cf. 6:4);[21] then in typical rhetorical fashion he labels these, including the Corinthians, as "the things that are not"—the "nothings"—which God chose in order "to nullify the things that are." The verb "to nullify"[22] is what makes certain that this is rhetorical, eschatological language, not philosophical.[23] This verb occurs throughout 1 Corinthians in decidedly eschatological contexts to express Paul's conviction that in Christ God has already set the future in motion, whereby the present age is "on its way out," is being done away with by God himself.[24] Through Christ crucified, and by God's subsequent calling of the Corinthians to be participants in the "glory" (2:7), God has already chosen "the things that are not" to render ineffective "the things that are" (the wise, with their "this age," merely human point of view).

[19]Gk. ἀγενῆ, the opposite of εὐγενεῖς, but most often meaning not "low born," but simply "insignificant" or "base."

[20]Cf. H. C. Kee, "The Linguistic Background of 'Shame' in the New Testament," in *On Language, Culture, and Religion: In Honor of Eugene A. Nida* (ed. M. Black and W. A. Smalley; The Hague, 1974), pp. 133-47.

[21]This term in particular must weigh heavily in one's understanding of the sociological dimensions of the church discussed above in v. 26. This is a deliberate word choice by Paul to elaborate further the meaning of "not well-born." Not only are such people "poorly related," but they are also scorned by those who are. It makes little sense in this context if this does not reflect the lower-class status of the majority.

[22]Gk. καταργέω.

[23]This expression is used in Judaism to refer to the doctrine of creation *ex nihilo* (out of nothing; cf. 2 Macc. 7:28; Philo, *spec.leg.* 4.187) and of conversion as the new creation (*Jos. et As.* 8.15). But as Conzelmann notes (51 n. 23), nothing like this is in Paul's mind, since "the things that are" belong "to the negative side."

[24]See 2:6; 6:13; 13:8 (2x); 13:10; 15:24, 26.

29 With this clause Paul expresses the ultimate purpose[25] of the divine folly: "so that no one[26] may boast before him."[27] God, it turns out, deliberately chose the foolish things of the world, the cross and the Corinthian believers, so that he could remove forever, from every human creature, any possible grounds on their part of standing in the divine presence with something in their hands. The ground is level at the foot of the cross; not a single thing that any of us possesses will advantage him/her before the living God—not brilliance, "clout," achievement, money, or prestige. By choosing the lowly Corinthians God declared that he has forever ruled out every imaginable human system of gaining his favor. It is all—"trust him completely" (v. 31)—or nothing.

The verb "boast," which is a predominantly Pauline word in the NT,[28] occurs here for the first time, most likely because of its prior usage in Jer. 9:23-24, which Paul is about to quote (v. 31). This word presents considerable difficulty for translation. It can mean "to take pride in" or "to glory in," hence "boast." But at times, especially here, it comes very close to the concept of "trust," that is, "to put one's full confidence in." We "boast" in that in which we have risked everything in order to secure ourselves. There is an interesting fluctuation between positive and pejorative usages in Paul; but there is no problem in finding the key. For him the watershed is the grace of God manifested in the death of Christ for sinners, whereby God has eliminated every human pretension and all self-sufficiency. Thus one must put full confidence, one must "boast, glory" in the Lord and his mercy. Every other form of "boasting" is thereby abolished (cf. 3:21; 4:7; Rom. 2:23; 3:27), except that which reflects the "weakness" and "foolishness" of God (e.g., Rom. 5:3; 2 Cor. 12:9).

30-31 The opening sentences of this paragraph reminded the Corinthians that their own calling, like the cross itself, expresses the "foolishness" of God that is "wiser than human wisdom." But all of that was said negatively: God was thereby intent on "shaming" and "bringing to an end" human wisdom, so that no mere creature may have grounds for boasting in

---

[25]Paul's sentence (vv. 27-29) has three ἵνα clauses (which ordinarily express purpose), each following an instance of the repeated "God chose," and concludes with this ὅπως clause (also expressing purpose). The three ἵνα clauses express the "realized" purpose of God (Conzelmann, 50), i.e., the process that is currently being worked out in the world. The final ὅπως clause of this verse, then, expresses God's ultimate aim in all of this.

[26]Gk. μὴ πᾶσα σάρξ. This awkward expression is a Hebraism, the πᾶσα σάρξ reflecting the OT idiom kal-basar. Thus, despite the word order, the μή negates the verb, giving the less than felicitous "so that all flesh may not boast."

[27]Gk. ἐνώπιον τοῦ θεοῦ, lit. "in the presence of God."

[28]The word group καυχάομαι-καύχησις-καύχημα occurs 55 of 59 times in Paul in the NT; 39 of the 55 occur in 1 and 2 Corinthians (ten in 1 Corinthians; 29 in 2 Corinthians), the vast majority of which are pejorative.

his presence. Now, by way of contrast, he addresses the Corinthians directly to express positively what God has done in calling them. The sentence is strictly soteriological and corresponds to vv. 26-29 in the same way that v. 24 does to vv. 22-23.

The contrasts themselves, which stand out in the Greek text, are difficult to transfer into English. Literally, Paul says, "*but*[29] of him[30] you are, in Christ Jesus.*" Paul's point is clear: In contrast to the world, you owe *your* existence[31] to the prior activity of God, which has been effected in history through Christ Jesus. As in the preceding sentence all the emphasis falls on God's activity,[32] activity expressed most vividly in human history "in Christ Jesus."[33]

The way Paul expresses this divine activity in Christ has had a long history of misinterpretation in the church, related in part to the translation of the KJV ("who of God is made unto us wisdom, and righteousness, and sanctification, and redemption")—as though this were a christological statement—and in part to reading it in light of Col. 2:2-3 and Jas. 1:5. Thus Christ is seen as the source of wisdom for Christians, whereby they either come to know God or are enlightened about his ways;[34] in other words, Christ became wisdom for us so that we might thereby become wise. But that is to miss Paul's point by a wide margin. In keeping with v. 24, he asserts that God made[35] Christ to become true "wisdom" for us[36]—which is then

[29]A clearly contrastive δέ has been left out of the NIV. "But as for you," Paul says, "in contrast to what has been said about the world in the preceding sentences. . . ."

[30]Gk. ἐξ αὐτοῦ, picking up the last word in v. 29: . . . τοῦ θεοῦ. ἐξ αὐτοῦ δὲ. . . .

[31]The ὑμεῖς ἐστε is also emphatic.

[32]What is not clear is the precise nuance of the phrase "of him," which expresses either "grounds" (NIV; cf. Conzelmann, 51, "by his act") or "source" (RSV, "He is the source of your life in Christ Jesus"). The former has the difficulty of being an unusual sense for the NT (cf. further Lightfoot, 167). The latter was the unanimous interpretation of the Greek commentators. See, e.g., Chrysostom: "For ye are the children of Him in whose presence it is not meet to glory, having become so through Christ Jesus" (cf. Barrett, "you are related to God").

[33]Thus as in v. 2 the phrase ἐν Χριστῷ ᾿Ιησοῦ is probably not locative, but semi-instrumental. By what God has accomplished "in Christ Jesus" they have become his children.

[34]An interpretation still perpetuated by Mare, 197.

[35]Gk. ἀπὸ θεοῦ, rightly translated "from God." But it is not "wisdom from God" that Christ was made for us; rather it is "wisdom *for us* from God"; i.e., God made him wisdom on our behalf.

[36]The shift from "you" to "us" is significant here. The sentence begins as a direct word to the Corinthians, as to their existence in Christ Jesus over against the wise of the world. But at this point the perspective broadens to include all who are Christ's. As Godet remarks: "And this because the matter in question now is, what Christ is objectively to [people], and not the subjective appropriation of Him by believers" (p. 116). Cf. the similar shift in 2:6-16.

immediately interpreted in historical-soteriological terms, "that is, our righteousness, holiness and redemption." Thus Paul is not suggesting, as the KJV implies, that Christ has been made these four things for believers. Rather, God has made him to become *wisdom*—but not of the kind with which the Corinthians are now enamored. True wisdom is to be understood in terms of the three illustrative metaphors, which refer to the saving event of Christ.

The metaphors themselves lack what we might ordinarily consider logical sequence (i.e., "redemption" brings about our "righteousness" [= right standing with God], followed by "holiness").[37] But that misses Paul's present concern. These are not three different steps in the saving process; they are rather three different metaphors for the same event (our salvation that was effected in Christ), each taken from a different sphere and each emphasizing a different aspect of the one reality (cf. 6:11). The fact that he uses nouns to describe this event, rather than verbs, is dictated by the fact that they stand in apposition to the noun "wisdom."

This is the first appearance of "righteousness" (= "justification") in Paul. As a result of the later[38] "Judaizing" controversy in Galatia it becomes the dominant metaphor. But the usage here and in 6:11 suggests two things: (1) It was already a common metaphor for Paul to express the saving work of Christ; and (2) it functioned in this period as one among other metaphors to connote the rich breadth of that work.[39] "Righteousness," therefore, is not so much an ethical term here as it is forensic, and highlights the believer's undeserved stance of right standing before God, despite his/her guilt from having broken his law. We have already met the term "holiness" in 1:2. This is a "religious" metaphor, and in this kind of list it moves us into the ethical sphere. It is a recurring motif in 1 and 2 Thessalonians and is picked up again in 6:11. The term "redemption" is a metaphor from slavery, and had a rich history among the Jews to express their own deliverance from the bondage of Egypt. The emphasis is more on the deliverance of captives unto freedom than it is on the concept of "ransom" by payment;[40] in Pauline

---

[37]Cf. Conzelmann: "The three soteriological concepts are not systematically arranged" (p. 52).

[38]For this perspective note the "Author's Preface," p. xi.

[39]This is not the common interpretation. For a slightly different approach, which argues for the centrality of justification even here, see R. Y.-K. Fung, "Justification by Faith in 1 & 2 Corinthians," in *Pauline Studies: Essays Presented to Professor F. F. Bruce on his 70th Birthday* (ed. D. A. Hagner and M. J. Harris; Grand Rapids, 1980), pp. 246-61.

[40]Besides the discussions in *TDNT* IV, 351-56 (F. Büchsel) and *NIDNTT* III, 195-200 (C. Brown), see L. L. Morris, *The Apostolic Preaching of the Cross* (Grand Rapids, 1955), pp. 9-59; D. Hill, *Greek Words and Hebrew Meanings* (SNTSMS 5; Cambridge, 1967), pp. 49-81; and I. H. Marshall, "The Development of the Concept of Redemption in the New Testament," in *Reconciliation and Hope* (ed. R. Banks; Grand Rapids, 1974), pp. 153-69.

usage (e.g., Rom. 3:24; Col. 1:14) it usually refers to deliverance from the bondage of sin.

Thus there is "wisdom" with God, to be sure. But it is of another kind from what the Corinthians currently delight in and squabble over. Wisdom does not have to do with "getting smart," nor with status or rhetoric. God's wisdom—the real thing—has to do with salvation through Christ Jesus. In a community where "wisdom" was part of a higher spirituality divorced from ethical consequences, Paul says that God has made Christ to become "wisdom" for us all right, but that means he has made him to become for us the one who redeems from sin and leads to holiness— ethical behavior that is consonant with the gospel. All of this is made clear by the final purpose clause of v. 31.[41] Just as the ultimate goal in God's choosing the "foolish things" of the world was to eradicate human boasting in his presence, so on the positive side the final goal of the work of Christ was to make possible the one true ground for boasting: "Let him who boasts, boast in the Lord." With other grounds for confidence now swept aside by the "divine contradiction," we are left with the ultimate "risk"—to trust God with our lives, and thus to "boast" in him.

The OT citation is from Jer. 9:24, but as usual in Paul it has been adapted to the present context. In place of the "in this" of Jeremiah, which points ahead to the clause that follows ("that he understands and knows me"), Paul has substituted "in the Lord," which of course is close to Jeremiah's overall sense, if not his precise intent. "The Lord" in this adaptation refers to Christ,[42] especially to the work of Christ in our behalf spelled out in v. 30. Thus human boasting is eliminated by God himself in favor of boasting in Christ's redemptive work, wherein alone one has favor with God.

The conclusion of this paragraph, "no human boasting" but rather "boasting in Christ" through whom God has effected salvation for us, continues (rightly) to play a significant role in the church. All of this is quite in keeping with the grand cadences of Romans and Galatians, with which the Protestant tradition is so familiar. Unfortunately, the *means* (the cross as the divine scandal) and the *evidence* (God's choice of the lowly) for this conclusion do not always get the same hearing. It is not that God cannot, or will not, save the affluent. But for Paul the glory of the gospel does not lie there; rather, it lies in his mercy toward the very people whom most of the affluent tend to write off—the foolish, the weak, the despised. Such people do not fit well into the "suburban captivity of the church." This paragraph must serve

---

[41]Gk. ἵνα, translated "therefore" in the NIV. The sentence itself is elliptical; probably a form of "to be" is to be understood: "in order that it might be (confirmed) even as it is written."

[42]As always in Paul unless the context clearly rules otherwise.

as a continual warning against our remaking into our own more comfortable images God's distinctly revealed priorities of mercy for the helpless—as part of the evidence that his ways are not ours.

c. God's folly—Paul's preaching (2:1-5)

1 *When I came to you, brothers, I did not come with eloquence or superior wisdom as I proclaimed to you the testimony about God.*[a1] 2 *For I resolved to know nothing while I was with you except Jesus Christ and him crucified.* 3 *I came to you in weakness and fear, and with much trembling.* 4 *My message and my preaching were not with wise and persuasive words,*[2] *but with a demonstration of the Spirit's*

[1]P46 ℵ* A C 88 436 a r syp bo Epiphanius Ambrosiaster read ὑμῖν τὸ μυστήριον (NIV mg. "as I proclaimed to you God's mystery"). Despite the arguments by Metzger, 545, the reading μαρτύριον is to be preferred on all counts. Metzger argues that μυστήριον is to be preferred "from an exegetical point of view" (thus basically on internal grounds), in that it "here prepares for its usage in ver. 7." But that, of course, is precisely why it was substituted for the less common—and less colorful—μαρτύριον of the majority. In fact, it is difficult under any circumstances to imagine that scribes of the second to fourth centuries, for whom the Pauline usage of "mystery" had become a commonplace, substituted "witness" in its place. This alleged substitution is supposed to have been influenced by the usage in 1:6; but that usage is (1) not the same (there it is "the witness *of Christ*"); (2) too distant to have carried the kind of influence suspected, so that it happened both early and extensively in the early church; and (3) too uncommon to have caused such extensive substitution. Furthermore, as both Barrett, 62-63, and Zuntz, 101, point out, had Paul used "mystery" here in anticipation of its usage in v. 7, he would have both nullified his present point and caused the word "in the latter place [to] lose much of its force" (Zuntz).

[2]Later MSS, on the analogy of v. 13, add ἀνθρωπίνης ("human"), which is obviously secondary. But after that, there is considerable difficulty in deciding the original text. The NIV reflects the text of (ℵ*) B D 33 181 1175 1506 1739 1881 pc πειθοῖς σοφίας λόγοις (cf. NA26, Lietzmann, Barrett, Conzelmann). The difficulty with this reading is the word πειθοῖς, apparently the dative of πειθός, a word that is otherwise unknown in all of Greek literature (see the discussion of πειθός and πειθώ in BAGD). Paul, of course, is capable of creating such a word, and the early Greek Fathers do not have difficulty with it. The problem, however, is complicated by the reading of P46 F G, πειθοῖς σοφίας. Zuntz has (cogently) argued that this reading alone makes sense of how the various corruptions arose (pp. 23-25). The σ at the end of πειθοῖς is a result of the simple corruption of doubling the initial σ of σοφίας. The λόγοις was then added, also on the analogy of v. 13, to make sense of what had now become an adjective. With some reluctance this is the position taken in this commentary, for two reasons: (1) this reading is unquestionably the *lectio difficilior* and more easily explains how the others came about than vice versa. It is extremely difficult to account for the "omission" of λόγοις on any grounds; and in this case it would need to have happened twice, once each in the ancestors of P46 and F G; (2) the complete absence of the word πειθός in the entire Greek rhetorical tradition is difficult to explain had there ever been such a word; whereas the regular adj. πιθανός is common. On the other hand, the noun πειθώ is plentiful in this tradition. Given the fact that Paul is here reflecting so much of the language of this tradition, a Pauline creation seems less likely than a scribal corruption. Thus the text would read: "My message and my preaching were not with the persuasion of wisdom, but with the Spirit's power."

power, 5 so that your faith might not rest on men's wisdom, but on God's power.

^aSome manuscripts *as I proclaimed to you God's mystery*

With this paragraph Paul concludes his argument that the message of the cross and the Corinthians' very existence as believers stand in contradiction to their present stance. Along with 1:26-31 it demonstrates the point of 1:18-25,[3] this time in terms of Paul's effective ministry among them despite his weaknesses and failure to rely on the kind of "powerful" speech with which they are enamored. Thus, not only the *means* (the cross) and the *people* (the church in Corinth), but also the *preacher* (Paul) declare that God is in the process of overturning the world's systems.[4] At the same time, of course, the entire paragraph has a strong apologetic overtone. By its results, his own ministry has been justified before them.

The paragraph is replete with themes from 1:17-25,[5] signaling its closest possible ties to what has preceded. The argument has two parts (vv. 1-2, 3-5), both of which begin with "and I." The first two verses, which pick up the language of 1:17 and 23, remind them of the *content* of his

---

[3]It is possible, though not argued for as obvious or certain, that Paul intended this paragraph to be an illustration of the second part of 1:25 ("the weakness of God is stronger than [human] strength"), just as vv. 26-31 would have illustrated the first part ("the foolishness of God is wiser than [human] wisdom"). The *content* of each paragraph certainly moves in this direction; and the *structure* of the three paragraphs could also be seen to support it. An explanatory γάρ ties vv. 26-31 to v. 25. The κἀγώ that begins this paragraph would then join these two paragraphs to one another. Note that the paratactic καί (joining sentences or sections with the conjunction "and") is extremely rare in Paul and that both paragraphs also begin with the vocative.

[4]Cf. Conzelmann, 53: "Just as the attitude of the community must accord with the word of the cross, so also must the form of the preaching and the bearing of the preacher." This seems to make more sense of the argument as a whole than the assertions of those who see this paragraph as somewhat independent from 1:18-31 (e.g., Barrett, Mare, Murphy-O'Connor). Those who see the larger section as a midrashic homily (see n. 1 on 1:18-25) have conflicting opinions about this paragraph. Ellis, 213-14, views it as the "application" of the midrash (in his view, vv. 18-31); this has more to commend it than Wuellner's view that it is a "halakic" digression. The difficulties with Ellis's position are two: (1) vv. 26-31 just as certainly apply 17-25 to their situation as do 2:1-5; (2) the themes of 2:1-5 are all found in 17-25, but not one of them is found in 26-31; therefore, it does *not* in fact "apply" 26-31.

Cf. the discussion in L. Hartman, "Some Remarks on 1 Cor. 2:1-5," *SEÅ* 34 (1974), 109-20. Here in particular the suggestion that Jewish wisdom speculation lies behind the Corinthian theology must yield to the more certain evidence that Paul is reflecting on the Greek rhetorical tradition.

[5]V. 1, "not in word or wisdom" (cf. 1:17); v. 2, "Jesus Christ and him crucified" (1:23); v. 3, I came "in weakness" (1:25); v. 4, my preaching was not in "persuasion of wisdom" (1:17) but in "demonstration of power" (1:23-25); v. 5, that your faith might not rest "on [human] wisdom, but on God's power" (1:25).

preaching, but now emphasizing that it was a deliberate act on his part. Vv. 3-4 then remind them of the *form* of the preacher and his preaching, which bears the same character as the message itself—"weakness." Nonetheless, as in 1:22-25, in this "weakness" the power of God is at work, now expressed in terms of the Spirit. A final purpose clause in v. 5 gives the reason for all this, that their faith might be of God and in God alone and not in human wisdom (cf. 1:31).

In every possible way Paul has tried to show them the folly of their present fascination with wisdom, which has inherent within it the folly of self-sufficiency and self-congratulation. Even the preacher whom God used to bring them to faith had to reject self-reliance. One senses that for Paul this is not merely a historical replay of his time with them, but also functions as something of a paradigm for his understanding of Christian ministry, a paradigm that will be spelled out in greater detail in 4:11-13 and especially in 2 Cor. 2:14–6:13.

1 Paul needs to rehearse one more piece of history with them[6]—his own preaching when he was among them,[7] both its form and content. Like 1:26, the new paragraph is signaled by the vocative ("brothers [and sisters]"; see 1:10) and an untranslated conjunction (lit. "and I").[8] In this case the conjunction suggests the closest possible tie to v. 31: "In the cross and in choosing you, God in effect eliminated human boasting, so that the only boast left is in the Lord. *And I, for my part,* when I came to you, evidenced the same reality.[9] I was totally stripped of self-reliance, so that God's power could be manifested and so that your faith might rest on him alone."

In a way similar to 1:17 Paul describes his preaching as (lit.) "not according to excellence of word or wisdom." Paul's point is clear enough; the precise nuances are less so. The NIV is misleading in suggesting that "excellence" is an adjective modifying "wisdom," and especially in translating the phrase "superior wisdom." "According to excellence" most likely refers to his manner of preaching,[10] hence "not in such a way as to distinguish myself" (Conzelmann). The two kinds of "excellence" that he rejected are terms we have already met (see 1:5 and 17). As before it is not certain whether "word" emphasizes form or content, or both. Probably here

---

[6]Highlighted in the Greek by the awkward "When I came, I came. . . ." Cf. Rom. 15:29. This is not comparable to the Hebrew idiom "seeing, I saw"; rather, it reflects the *ad hoc* nature of the letter. Cf. Lightfoot, 170.

[7]Note the repeated "to you" (v. 1), "to you" (v. 1), "with you" (v. 2), "to you" (v. 3), all of which have "your faith" (v. 5) as their goal.

[8]Gk. κἀγώ; rare in Paul (as a paratactic conjunction only here, in v. 3, and in 3:1 in the extant letters).

[9]See also Hartman, "Remarks," p. 114, who translates, "so it was also with me."

[10]Gk. κατὰ ὑπεροχήν. See BAGD on ὑπεροχή and κατά (II.5b).

it leans toward form (hence "eloquence"), while "wisdom" reflects content; as v. 4 indicates, however, it too could refer to form in this context. In either case, Paul is once more picking up their terms and negating them in light of Christ crucified.[11] Those who seek wisdom may sound as if they are involved in a noble affair; in reality they are engaged in various forms of self-congratulatory, and therefore divisive, competition over "excellence" of speech, rhetoric, or profundity, "full of sound and fury, signifying nothing."

Paul would have none of that, precisely because he came to them to "proclaim . . . the testimony about God." Despite its acceptance by an increasing number of scholars,[12] the reading "mystery" is unlikely to be original. That choice of words at this point would seem to deflect his present concern. To be sure, Paul uses such language at v. 7 (and 4:1), but that reflects the considerable shift of argument in 2:6-16. Here he is recalling, as he did in 1:6, his initial preaching among them, preaching that took the form of "proclaiming"[13] the "testimony of God." Although this latter expression is not common in Paul,[14] it had already been used in 2 Thess. 2:10 (and 1 Cor. 1:6, q.v.) to refer to his preaching of the gospel. Thus it is a happy choice of terms to recall what he was about when he first preached among them. Rather than engaging in rhetoric or philosophy, Paul was bearing witness to God, i.e., what God had done in Christ to effect salvation,[15] as v. 2 now goes on to explain.

---

[11]Cf. Hartman, "Remarks," who shows convincingly that the rejected terms throughout this paragraph are from Greek rhetoric.

[12]Besides the NA[26] and UBS[3] noted above (n. 1), see the commentaries by Lietzmann, Moffatt, Héring, O-W, Mare, and Senft; cf. G. Bornkamm, *TDNT* IV, 819; R. E. Brown, *The Semitic Background of the Term "Mystery" in the New Testament* (FBBS; Philadelphia, 1968), pp. 48-49; Wilckens, 45; R. W. Funk, "Word and Word in I Corinthians 2:6-16," in *Language*, p. 295; Schütz, *Paul*, p. 91; Hartman, "Remarks," p. 112; A. A. Trites, *The New Testament Concept of Witness* (SNTSMS 31; Cambridge, 1977), p. 203.

[13]Gk. καταγγέλλω, but less "preaching" as "bearing tidings." Bornkamm, *TDNT* IV, 819, makes the somewhat irrelevant observation that "the linking of μαρτύριον with καταγγέλλειν . . . is unusual in the NT." Neither is this verb used with μυστήριον. Given its meaning elsewhere as announcing or proclaiming the gospel (cf. 9:14 and throughout Acts), the case can be made that μαρτύριον fits best as its object here.

[14]And therefore all the more likely to have been changed, than vice versa. See n. 1 above.

[15]With Barrett, 63 (NIV; R-P, 30), against Lightfoot, 171 (Godet, 124; Holladay, 39), I take this to be an objective genitive. Lightfoot sees the expression in 1:6 as objective (Christ is the object of the preaching); thus this one is subjective (or source), since the testimony to Christ has been borne first of all by God. While that is attractive, the interpretation offered seems less complex, that Paul is bearing witness to God himself and to what he has done.

2 The "for" that begins this sentence is explanatory; Paul is offering reasons for the behavior outlined in v. 1. He did not attempt to distinguish himself in either eloquence or philosophical reasoning because he had already "resolved to know nothing . . . except Jesus Christ and him crucified." This is the "testimony about God" to which he bore witness while he was among them. "To know nothing" does not mean that he left all other knowledge aside, but rather that he had the gospel, with its crucified Messiah, as his singular focus and passion while he was among them. It has often been speculated that this sentence is to be understood as his (somewhat negative) response to the recent ministry in Athens, as recorded in Acts 17:16-34. The problem with that suggestion is that (1) it misreads the evidence of Acts as being a failure of sorts,[16] and (2) it assumes that this resolve on the part of Paul was a change of strategy, or a return to a former strategy, neither of which is implied by what is actually said. To say "I resolved"[17] means nothing more than that he purposed to continue his regular practice (cf. Gal. 3:1). After all, according to Acts 18:1-8 his preaching began in the synagogue among Jews and God-fearers, where it was always his practice to begin by preaching "Jesus Christ" (cf., e.g., Acts 13:26-42, which Luke sets forth as the primary exhibit of Paul's proclaiming Christ in such a setting). Neither does the addition "and him crucified" suggest a new strategy. For Paul that was simply part of proclaiming Christ; it is added from 1:23 for emphasis—and to tie what is said here to 1:18-25. If any contrast is implied in the words "I resolved," it would be with the wandering sophists and orators, with whom he is now being compared, rather than with his own preaching before and after Athens. If anything, that resolve would have been increased by the experience in Thessalonica, where he had already had to put distance between himself and such itinerant "flatterers" and "man-pleasers" (1 Thess. 2:1-10).

3 With another "and I" Paul resumes the description of his preaching; but now it focuses less on the form of preaching and more directly on the "form" of the preacher. The verb[18] can mean either "I came to you," emphasizing that this is how he was when he arrived, or "I was with you," suggesting that he manifested "weakness" in his ongoing relationship with them. The latter is to be preferred for two reasons: (1) There is a precise analogy in 16:10, which speaks of Timothy's *coming* and not fearing while he *is with you* (the same combination of verbs and prepositional phrase as

---

[16]It is clear from 17:34 that Luke did not so regard it; it is idle psychologizing, and from the distance of nearly two thousand years at that, to think that one can enter into the mind of Paul regarding this experience from what Luke reports.

[17]Gk. οὐ ἔκρινα. This can mean "I refused"; but more likely, despite the unusual word order, Paul intends the οὐ to negate the whole clause, which in effect negates either "to know" or "anything." Otherwise Field, *Notes*, p. 167.

[18]Gk. ἐγενόμην πρὸς ὑμᾶς. The word order of the sentence is emphatic: (lit.) "And I in weakness and in fear and in much trembling became toward you."

here and in v. 1); (2) vv. 1-2 emphasize his resolve when he came to them; here the emphasis is on the ongoing visit.[19]

From this distance it is impossible to know the exact nature of Paul's being with them "in weakness."[20] He is most likely referring to some observable physical condition.[21] In any case his intent seems clear: for him there was a genuine correspondence between his own personal weaknesses and his gospel (cf. Col. 1:24). At the heart of his preaching stood the "weakness of God" (1:25), the story of a crucified Messiah (v. 2). His own weaknesses served as a further visible demonstration of the same message, but even more to demonstrate that the message was of divine, not human, origin (see esp. 2 Cor. 4:7 and 13:4). Thus the apostle regularly glories in his weaknesses,[22] not because he "enjoyed ill health" but because they were a sure evidence that the power was of God and not of himself. Apparently this became a point of genuine contention between Paul and this church, as the long apologetic sections of 2 Cor. 4:7–5:10 and 11:17–12:10 reveal. Possibly Paul has already gotten inklings of the problem from his informants; hence this passage, and especially 4:8-13.

Along with "weakness" he adds "and in fear and much trembling,"[23] but it is not at all clear what this means. The two words often occur together in the LXX (e.g., Exod. 15:16; Isa. 19:16), usually to express the

[19]Cf. Godet, 128, Lightfoot, 172; Findlay, 776; R-P, 32; Bachmann, 112 n. 1; Grosheide, 60; otherwise Barrett, 64; Conzelmann, 53. Conzelmann suggests that "πρός, 'to,' is too strong"; but that is not quite accurate, since the preposition regularly means "be (in company) with someone" (BAGD III.7). Barrett seems to miss the force of the analogy with 16:10.

[20]Hartman, "Remarks," p. 115, suggests that the language is a reflection of the context of the Jeremiah citation in 1:31.

[21]A metaphorical meaning here would not comport with the rest of the evidence in the Corinthian correspondence. What precisely the "weakness" might have been, however, lies beyond our abilities to recapture. The word ἀσθενεία is the ordinary one for "illness." Since Paul had some time previously preached in Galatia as the result of an illness (Gal. 4:13-14), and since later to the Corinthians themselves he will speak of "carrying about in his body the death of Jesus" (2 Cor. 4:10) and of a long-lasting "thorn in his flesh" (2 Cor. 12:7; for an excellent recent discussion of this perplexing text, see Furnish, II Corinthians, pp. 547-50), it is possible that there was a recurrence of such an illness while he was among them. Yet in 1 Cor. 4:9-13, when recounting what it meant for him to be "weak," he mentions only external hardships (hunger, persecution, brutal treatment, working with his own hands [for the possibility that it refers to his tentmaking, which in the eyes of others would have been considered "weakness," see R. F. Hock, The Social Context of Paul's Ministry (Philadelphia, 1980), p. 60]). In any case the word here most likely refers not to inner feelings, but to how he appeared in the eyes of others. Probably the best we can do is take "weakness" to refer to his "sufferings" or "hardships" and be content not to know precisely what that meant for him here.

[22]Cf. 4:9-13; Gal. 4:13-14; 2 Cor. 4:7-12; 6:4-10; 11:30; 12:7-10; Rom. 8:17-27; Phil. 1:29-30; Col. 1:24-27.

[23]For reasons not easy to decipher, the NIV joins "weakness and fear" and then adds "and with much trembling." The latter two words, despite the adj. "much" attached only to the "trembling," regularly occur together, and are certainly intended so here.

dread that people (esp. enemies) are to sense in the presence of God and his activity in the world. The combination is unique to Paul in the NT (2 Cor. 7:15; Phil. 2:12; Eph. 6:5), but elsewhere does not seem to refer to people over against God. Most likely here it reflects the general picture given in Acts 18:9-11, where for reasons unknown to us Paul seems overwhelmed by the task of evangelizing in this great city.[24] In any case it is a condition which he is gladly willing that the Corinthians should now recall, so that they will be reminded of how unlike the sophists his preaching and appearance truly were.

4-5 But Paul does not glory in his weaknesses for their own sake, nor simply to contrast himself to the sophists. Rather, he does so to remind the Corinthians, as they should well remember, that the real power does not lie in the person or presentation of the preacher but in the work of the Spirit, as is evidenced by their own existence. Thus, to what he has just said about himself, he adds[25] words about his preaching that recall v. 1; however, in this case the negative "not with the persuasion of wisdom"[26] receives its corresponding counterpart "but with a demonstration of the Spirit's power."

His preaching is first described by their term, *logos* ("word"; cf. 1:17 and 2:1). Although it was not to *their* liking, he does have a *logos,* the *logos* of the cross (1:18; 2:2). But unlike the Corinthians, who attached wisdom to *logos,* Paul attaches *kērygma* ("preaching" or "proclamation"; cf. 1:21). *Logos* and *kērygma* therefore probably refer to the content and form of Paul's actual delivery (hence "message and preaching"). He deliberately avoided the very thing that now fascinates them, "the persuasion of wisdom." But his preaching did not thereby lack "persuasion." What it lacked was the kind of persuasion found among the sophists and rhetoricians, where the power lay in the person and his delivery. Paul's preaching, on the other hand, despite his personal appearance and whatever its actual form,[27] produced the desired results, namely it brought about the faith of the Corinthians.

---

[24]On the other hand, Hartman, "Remarks," pp. 117-18, has argued that these terms are deliberately chosen vis-à-vis the Greek rhetorical tradition (as evidenced, e.g., in Quintilian 12.5.1), thus presenting himself to them as a kind of "anti-rhetor," so that the "demonstration" will be of the Spirit, not of "wisdom."

[25]The sentence begins with one of the rare cases in Paul where καί is used as a paratactic conjunction.

[26]For this phrase see n. 2 above.

[27]As many have pointed out, "methinks the man protesteth too much." His letters, which at times have all the character of speech, are in fact powerful examples of rhetoric and persuasion. Nonetheless Paul can confidently assert before those who have come to care about such things that his preaching was not of this kind. This seems to make certain that it is not rhetoric in general, but rhetoric of a very specific and well-known kind, that he is disavowing.

What accompanied Paul's preaching was "a demonstration[28] of the Spirit's power." Is Paul now in danger of rebuilding what he has been tearing down, as some suggest? Hardly. His intent is clear from the context: Even though he was weak and his preaching lacked "rhetoric" and "wisdom," their very coming to faith demonstrated that it did not lack power.[29]

Thus, very much in keeping with the message itself (cf. 1:23-25), his preaching exhibited "the weakness of God" that is stronger than human strength (1:25). What is less certain is to what specific "proof" he might be referring. The Greek literally reads "of the Spirit and power,"[30] which some see as referring to two realities, "spiritual gifts and miracles."[31] But in Paul the terms "Spirit" and "power" are at times nearly interchangeable (cf. 5:4). To speak of the Spirit is automatically to speak of power (cf. Rom. 15:13, 19). The combination here is probably very close to a hendiadys (the use of two words to express the same reality: "the Spirit, that is, Power"), hence the NIV's "the Spirit's power." But to what powerful demonstration of the Spirit does this refer? It is possible, but not probable given the context of "weakness," that it reflects the "signs and wonders" of 2 Cor. 12:12. More likely it refers to their actual conversion, with its concomitant gift of the Spirit, which was probably evidenced by spiritual gifts, especially tongues.[32] This seems to be more in keeping with Paul's concern. The evidence lies not in external "proofs" that Paul will muster against mere wisdom and rhetoric. Rather, the evidence lies with the Corinthians themselves and their own experience of the Spirit as they responded to the message of the gospel.[33]

[28] Gk. ἀποδόξει (a NT hapax legomenon), a word suggesting more than simply "manifestation," something akin to "evidence" or "proof." In Greek rhetoric it was a technical term for a compelling conclusion drawn from the premises. Cf. Quintilian 5.10.7 ("an ἀπόδειξις is clear proof" [Loeb, II, 205]) and Cicero, *Acad.* 2:8 ("Therefore this is the definition of logical proof, in Greek ἀπόδειξις: 'a process of reasoning that leads from things perceived to something not previously perceived'" [Loeb, XIX, 501]). Paul thus turns this word on its head, arguing that the "proof" lies not in compelling rhetoric, but in the accompanying *visible* ἀπόδειξις of the Spirit's power. Cf. Hartman, "Remarks," pp. 116-17; Dunn, *Spirit*, pp. 226-27.

[29] So also Dunn, *Jesus*, pp. 226-27.

[30] The genitives are at least objective (= evidence that the Spirit is present in power); Barrett, 65, suggests that they are subjective as well (= the manifested Spirit and power bring proof and conviction).

[31] Recently, Ellis, 64-65.

[32] Cf. E. Schweizer, *TDNT* VI, 423: The Spirit is understood as "something whose reception may be verified."

[33] Cf. Robinson, "Word," pp. 68-82. However, he is too intent on emphasizing their conversion to the exclusion of their own experience of the gifts of the Spirit. That concern probably reflects a later time in the church when the coming of the Spirit is less visibly manifested than seems to have been the case in the NT. It is hard to imagine the Corinthians' being able to make the distinction. For them to hear the words "the Spirit and power" would automatically have recalled the visible evidences of the Spirit's presence.

This is the first specific mention of the Spirit in 1 Corinthians, although the gifts of the Spirit were alluded to in the thanksgiving (1:4-7). In the Introduction (pp. 10-13) I argued that this is the crucial point of difference between Paul and the "arrogant" who have opposed him (4:18). For them "Spirit" meant the gift of tongues; it meant to have arrived in the "excellence of wisdom" (v. 1; cf. 4:8, 10), to have entered into a new existence that raised them above merely earthly existence, quite unrelated to genuine ethical behavior. For Paul, on the other hand, "Spirit" *included* inspired utterances—as long as they edified—but for him the emphasis lay on the Spirit's *power*, power to transform lives (as here), to reveal God's secret wisdom (2:6-16), to minister in weakness (4:9-13), and to effect holiness in the believing community (5:3-5). In other words, the purpose of the Spirit's coming was not to transport one above the present age, but to empower one to live within it.

With the concluding purpose clause of v. 5 the argument that began in 1:18 now comes full circle. The message of the cross, which is folly to the "wise," is the saving power of God to those who believe. The goal of all the divine activity, both in the cross and in choosing them, and now in Paul's preaching that brought the cross and them together, has been to disarm the wise and powerful so that those who believe must trust God alone and completely. Thus, as v. 31 concludes vv. 26-31, so v. 5 concludes this paragraph: "so that your faith might not rest on [human] wisdom, but on God's power." In another context this might seem to suggest that faith rests on evidences; but that would scarcely make sense here. Throughout this passage the power of God has the cross as its paradigm. The true alternative to wisdom humanly conceived is not "signs" but the gospel, which the Spirit brings to bear on our lives in powerful ways.

This paragraph has had an interesting history of application in the church, depending on where the emphasis has been placed. Some emphasize what Paul did *not* do, that is, preach with excellence of word and wisdom, and glory in a more rough-hewn presentation (which, interestingly enough, is often accompanied by a kind of bombast that seems intent on persuasion of a rhetorical kind, despite protests to the contrary). Others wish to emphasize the "positive," the "proofs" of the Spirit's power, which they see as in contrast to mere preaching. On the other hand, the polished oratory sometimes heard in American pulpits, where the sermon itself seems to be the goal of what is said, makes one wonder whether the text has been heard at all. Paul's own point needs a fresh hearing. What he is rejecting is not preaching, not even persuasive preaching; rather, it is the real danger in all preaching—self-reliance. The danger always lies in letting the form and content get in the way of what should be the single concern: the gospel proclaimed through human weakness but accompanied by the powerful work of the Spirit so that lives are changed through a divine-human encounter. That is hard to teach in a course in homiletics, but it still stands as the true need in genuinely Christian preaching.

3. God's Wisdom—Revealed by the Spirit (2:6-16)

6 *We do, however, speak a message of wisdom among the mature, but not the wisdom of this age or of the rulers of this age, who are coming to nothing.* 7 *No, we speak of God's secret wisdom, a wisdom that has been hidden and that God destined for our glory before time began.* 8 *None of the rulers of this age understood it, for if they had, they would not have crucified the Lord of glory.* 9 *However, as it is written:*

"No eye has seen,
no ear has heard,
no mind has conceived
what God has prepared for those who love him" ª—

10 *but¹ God has revealed it to us by his² Spirit.*

The Spirit searches all things, even the deep things of God. 11 *For who among men knows the thoughts of a man except the man's spirit³ within him? In the same way no one knows the thoughts of God except the Spirit of God.* 12 *We have not received the spirit of the world but the Spirit who is from God, that we may understand what God has freely given us.* 13 *This is what we speak, not in words taught us by human wisdom but in words taught by the Spirit,⁴ expressing spiritual truths in spiritual words.* ᵇ 14 *The man without the Spirit does not accept the things that come from the Spirit of God,⁵ for they*

---

¹The NIV here reflects the text of NA²⁶-UBS³ (δέ), following ℵ A C D F G Maj latt sy. The γάρ of P⁴⁶ B 6 88 181 326 365 1739 1877 2127 2492 m sa bomss Clement is to be preferred on all counts. It is the *lectio difficilior* (a copyist would scarcely have deliberately created a text with three γάρ's in a row, whereas the substitution of a δέ for a γάρ would have been natural and could have been deliberate or accidental; see the note on v. 11); it fits Pauline style (cf. Rom. 15:3-4); and it makes better sense of the argument (see the commentary).

²The NIV is probably translating the τοῦ of τοῦ πνεύματος as "his." An αὐτοῦ does in fact appear in the majority of witnesses, incl. D F G latt (probably as a "translational" variant; i.e., a variant that came about through translation into Latin). The text without αὐτοῦ is supported by P⁴⁶ ℵ* A B C 630 1739 1881 pc cop.

³A few Western MSS (F G a b Pel) omit the words τοῦ ἀνθρώπου, resulting in a text that translates "except the spirit (Spirit?) within him."

⁴The MajT, with no early Greek or versional support, adds ἁγίου to πνεύματος.

⁵On the basis of the citations from several Fathers, Zuntz, 221-23, argues that τοῦ θεοῦ is an interpolation (cf. the "C" rating in the UBS³). This illustrates a highly questionable use of patristic evidence to support a "shorter text" (cf. G. D. Fee, "The Text of John in The Jerusalem Bible: A Critique of the Use of Patristic Citations in New

are foolishness to him, and he cannot understand them, because they are spiritually discerned. 15 *The spiritual man makes judgments about all things,6 but he himself is not subject to any man's judgment:*

16 *"For who has known the mind of the Lord
that he may instruct him?"c*

But we have the mind of Christ.7

a Isaiah 64:4
b Or *Spirit, interpreting spiritual truths to spiritual men*
c Isaiah 40:13

To this point Paul has been rather hard on "wisdom"—because he is arguing against a Corinthian attitude toward it that has placed him and his gospel in a less than favorable light. But not all is pejorative. He also asserted that God acted by means of his own wisdom (1:21) and that he made Christ to become "wisdom" for us; but in so doing Paul transformed "wisdom" from a philosophical, rhetorical term into a historical, soteriological one (1:24, 30). Taking up the language of vv. 4-5 ("not in the persuasion of wisdom, but with a demonstration of the Spirit's power"), he now makes a turn in the argument in order to reassert that the gospel he preaches is in fact the wisdom of God. But it cannot be perceived as such by those who are pursuing *sophia;* it is recognized only by those who have the Spirit.

As with much of 1:18–2:5, the argument of this paragraph is full of bite. The Corinthians, enamored by wisdom and thinking of themselves as "spiritual," are less than enchanted with Paul's message, which they regard as mere "milk." With fine irony Paul demolishes these various misperceptions and false boastings. The gospel of the crucified Messiah is wisdom all right, he affirms, but not of the kind they are now pursuing. True wisdom is indeed for those who are "spiritual," for those who have the Spirit, who has revealed what God has really accomplished in Christ. Because they do have the Spirit, and thus the mind of Christ, they should have seen the cross for what it is—God's wisdom—and thereby have been able to make true judgments. By pursuing *sophia* they are acting just like those without the Spirit,

---

Testament Textual Criticism," *JBL* 90 [1971], 170-72). Not one of the patristic citations is more than probable; none is certain. Internal considerations support the full description, which is carefully balanced with what is said about the believer in v. 12. See the commentary.

6The majority of MSS replace the τά of τὰ πάντα with a μέν, thus conforming the πάντα to v. 10 and placing the emphasis on the second clause. See the discussion in Metzger, 547, and Zuntz, 109-10 and 198.

7A few MSS (B D* F G 81 it) replace Χριστοῦ with κυρίου, assimilating Paul to the citation of Isa. 40:13.

who are likewise pursuing wisdom but see the cross as foolishness. The net result—and the irony—is that they are "spiritual," yet "unspiritual"; they are pursuing "wisdom," yet missing the very wisdom of God.

The argument, which is in three parts, can be easily traced: (1) Vv. 6-10a set forth the nature of God's wisdom in terms of the basic contrast between those for whom it was destined and those who cannot perceive it. God's wisdom, predestined by him to bring *us* to glory, was therefore held "in mystery" ("secret"), hidden from the present age and its leaders. (2) Vv. 10b-13 explain how we are let in on the secret, and why the others are left out. We have received the Spirit, who knows the mind of God and has revealed to us what God is up to. (3) Vv. 14-16 conclude by reaffirming all this in terms of "natural" and "spiritual" people. The people of this age, who are pursuing mere "wisdom" and so consider the cross "foolishness," do not have the Spirit; therefore, they cannot understand true wisdom (v. 14) nor make valid judgments (v. 15), an activity that is properly available only to those who have the Spirit. The paragraph concludes with a citation from Isa. 40:13, which offers biblical support for people's inability to comprehend, a situation that is now reversed for those who have the Spirit and therefore the "mind of Christ."

Despite what appears to be a simple—and explicable—turn in the argument, this paragraph has suffered much in the church, both at the hand of scholars and in popular preaching and Bible reading. The reasons for this have to do partly with the language (e.g., wisdom, mystery, hidden, rulers of this age, deep things of God, spiritual/natural man, the mind of Christ) and partly with the several *contrasts* set up both in this paragraph and in 3:1-4. As a result the paragraph has been variously viewed as an example of Paul's playing the Corinthians' game after all—that he really argues that those who are truly spiritual do possess a "deeper wisdom," and that he thereby establishes two classes within the church—one "spiritual" and "mature"; the other "natural" (or "worldly") and "immature" (or "babes").[8] But such a view runs counter not only to the argument as a whole

---

[8]This has taken several forms. Traditionally (e.g., Goudge, 16), Paul is seen to be arguing that despite what he has said in 2:1-5, he nevertheless does have "deep truth to reveal," which "requires a developed spiritual character for its appreciation." Those who continue to take some form of this approach see Paul as addressing a special group ("the mature" or "the spiritual"), the differences having to do with how the special group is perceived. See, e.g., Conzelmann: "The section is dominated by a pneumatic enthusiasm, a distinction between two classes. The pneumatics here do not comprise all Christians, but only a superior class" (p. 57); cf. R. Bultmann, "Karl Barth, *The Resurrection of the Dead,*" in *Faith and Understanding* (ET, New York, 1969), pp. 70-72; and Wilckens, 52-96. R. Scroggs argues convincingly against Wilckens's basic position (that Paul is here adopting the position of his Gnostic opponents and thus betrays his own theology), but continues to promote the idea that Paul "must have had an esoteric wisdom

(not to mention this paragraph), but also to the whole of Pauline theology. Indeed, such an argument would effectively destroy the very point of everything said in 1:18–2:5.[9] Paul is not here rebuilding what he has just torn down. He is retooling their understanding of the Spirit and spirituality, in order that they might perceive the truth of what he has been arguing to this point.

While it is true that much of the *language* of this paragraph is not common to Paul, the explanation of this phenomenon is, as before, to be found in his using *their* language but filling it with his own content and thus refuting them.[10] The theology, however, is his own, and it differs radically from theirs. For Paul—as for them—the Spirit is the key to everything. For him the Spirit is an eschatological reality, marking the turning of the ages. This becomes crucial for understanding the several *contrasts* in the passage. On the one hand, those who are still of *this* age, who have not received the Spirit, do not understand the wisdom of God in Christ crucified. But their wisdom is under divine judgment and already on its way out. Those who have the Spirit, on the other hand, have "the mind of Christ" and thus understand God's activity, revealed to them by the Spirit. This is why Paul comes down so hard on his Corinthian friends. They do have the Spirit; they are part of the new age that God is ushering in. But their present conduct and stance toward wisdom betray them. Paul includes them among the "spir-

---

teaching entirely separate from his kerygma" ("Paul," p. 35). Ellis, 25-26, on the other hand, sees Paul as addressing only the πνευμάτιχοι here, who are defined as those who with Paul possess spiritual gifts. The position argued for in this commentary is in essential agreement with Funk, "Word," pp. 275-305; cf. B. E. Gärtner, "The Pauline and Johannine Idea of 'To Know God' Against the Hellenistic Background," *NTS* 14 (1967/68), 215-21; and J. Francis, "'As Babes in Christ'—Some Proposals regarding 1 Corinthians 3.1-3," *JSNT* 7 (1980), 41-60.

[9]Both Wilckens and Conzelmann admit this (see previous note). They see Paul as using the ideas and language of his opponents, or of a prior "schema," which he fails adequately to integrate, thus creating tension or paradox. The logic of this position is finally taken by M. Widmann ("1 Kor 2:6-16: Ein Einspruch gegen Paulus," *ZNW* 70 [1979], 44-53), who argues that the passage is a gloss introduced by Paul's Corinthian opponents as a reply to Paul. See the response by Murphy-O'Connor, "Interpolations," 81-84.

[10]Cf. Funk, "Word," p. 300 n. 107: "Paul has simply turned their language, and thus their expectations, inside out in the interest of bringing them face to face with the word of the cross." However, one must exercise due caution here—not every new term must come from them loaded with foreign nuances—but this seems to make the most sense of the data.

Both the source of their language and Paul's use of it are hotly debated. Wilckens, Bultmann, and Conzelmann see it as Gnostic terminology that Paul has less than successfully incorporated so that he comes out looking far more Gnostic than Christian (see n. 8 above). Scroggs in particular has shown the weaknesses in this approach, especially as it appears in Wilckens. Others see the background as Jewish Hellenism of the type found in Philo; cf. Pearson, 27-37, and Horsley, "Pneumatikos."

itual" (vv. 7-13), yet later addresses them as "fleshly" and "merely human" because their quarrels indicate that they are acting just like those who do not have the Spirit (3:1-4). The real contrast is therefore between Christian and non-Christian, between those who have and those who do not have the Spirit. Paul's concern throughout is to get the Corinthians to understand who they are—in terms of the cross—and to stop acting as non-Spirit people. At the same time, as with 2:1-5, an unmistakable note of personal apologetic lies just below the surface, if not right in the open.[11]

6 The "however"[12] that begins this sentence marks a decisive turn in the argument; but it also closely ties what follows to what has immediately preceded in vv. 4-5. Despite the insistence that his preaching was *not* with the "persuasion of wisdom" so that their faith might not rest on "human wisdom," Paul says "we[13] nevertheless do speak wisdom."[14] In so asserting, his first concern is to ensure that he is not misunderstood. By "wisdom" he does *not* refer to what is fascinating the Corinthians: wisdom that belongs strictly to this age and its rulers, who are already "coming to nothing."

What, then, does he mean by "wisdom"? Whatever else, the emphasis now is on the *content* of *sophia*,[15] not its *form*, as in vv. 1-5; nonetheless, he says very little that actually describes this content. The reason for this, of course, is first of all that Paul assumes his readers will pick that up from

---

[11]It should be noted, finally, that those who see this section as a previously independent midrash, adapted by Paul to its present context (e.g., Wuellner and Ellis; see n. 1 on 1:18–2:5), seem to push the meaning of the term midrash beyond recognizable limits—not to mention rather generally miss the point of the paragraph in its present context. *Midrash* minimally means an exposition *based on* OT texts; the texts cited here are *not* the basis of the argument but are used as supporting evidence only and are in no way the crucial matter.

[12]Gk. δέ, clearly adversative here and thus rightly translated "however" (cf. "yet" in RSV, GNB, NAB).

[13]One of the commonly noted phenomena of this paragraph is the shift to the first person plural throughout. Some have argued that this signals a switch to a special group. See, e.g., Ellis, 24-26, esp. n. 17, who sees it as "the signature of pneumatics," those special persons with "spiritual gifts." But that is to make too much of a common Pauline feature (see, e.g., E. Stauffer, *TDNT* II, 356-58). The shift in this first instance (and in vv. 7 and 13) represents his common editorial "we," and refers at least to Paul, and perhaps to other preachers/teachers. To that degree it therefore also reflects his underlying apologetic: "But despite what you may think, I do preach wisdom." Beginning with "our" in v. 7, including "those who love him" in v. 9 and "to us" in v. 10, and continuing through "we" in v. 16, we meet a usage that Funk calls "inclusive-exclusive"; i.e., "on the one hand, it attempts to pull his readers into his own orbit, to embrace them, as it were, within the fold of the faithful. On the other hand, given the polemical context, it verges on exclusion," which motif "erupts in 3:1f. as the singular" ("Word," p. 300 n. 107; cf. p. 286 n. 46).

[14]For the structure of this kind of argumentation cf. 1:17 and 18, where the wisdom characterized by *logos* sets up the contrast with the *logos* of the cross.

[15]Hence the NIV's addition, "the message" of wisdom.

1:23-24 and 30 (cf. 2:2). He has already declared: "We preach Christ *crucified* . . . the wisdom of God."[16] That this is the basic thrust of its content is confirmed by the otherwise unnecessary reference to the crucifixion (not simply "killed") in v. 8. With *a crucified Messiah as its assumed content,* Paul's present concern is to explain the *nature* of this wisdom, which made it impossible for those in pursuit of merely human wisdom to recognize it as such.

What has caused some to think that Paul is dealing with "deeper truths" is the phrase "among the *teleioi* (mature),"[17] which anticipates the "mere infants" of 3:1. Since Paul says that he speaks this "wisdom" among "the mature" and that he could not so address them, it is thus assumed that there are hidden depths of Christian truth that he did indeed possess, but kept to himself in Corinth because of their lack of maturity. But the rest of the paragraph indicates that such is not the case. The equation in 3:1, where "infants" is the opposite of "spiritual," indicates that the *teleioi* of this verse are those who have received the Spirit (v. 12) and are therefore the "spiritual" of v. 15. The argument of the whole paragraph, especially the language "for *our* glory" (v. 7), "for those who love him" (i.e., "*us*"; v. 9), "revealed it to *us*" (v. 10), and "we have received the Spirit who is from God" (v. 12), implies that Paul is, as earlier, addressing the whole church and drawing them all into the orbit of what he is saying. Most likely the terminology is theirs.[18] In their rejection of Paul they think he is treating

[16]Scroggs, "Paul," pp. 35-37, tries to drive a wedge between Paul's "kerygma and his sophia," which he calls "clear-cut." While such a distinction might possibly be made, in the sense that the implications of what one "preaches" in order to evangelize might be more fully explicated when one teaches, to draw a sharp line between these in Paul is to miss rather widely his singular passion for the gospel. On this question see esp. Gärtner, "Idea," p. 219: "What is in view is not an intellectual or theoretical, rational knowledge as the Stoics would have understood it. It has nothing to do with an insight into God's secrets, disclosed in ecstasy or in a mystical way, as Philo explained Abraham's or Moses' knowledge of God. . . . *Sophia* is rather the profound content of God's revelation . . . [and] in one way can be identified with Christ the Son of God whose death on the cross was an essential expression of the 'depths of God'." See also the argument in Funk, "Word," pp. 291-94. Cf. Bornkamm, *TDNT* IV, 820: ". . . .2:6-16 remains within the sphere of the λόγος τοῦ σταυροῦ. It is misleading to seek in this section thoughts which are not included in the *kerygma* itself."

[17]Gk. ἐν τοῖς τελείοις. Turner (*Syntax,* p. 264) suggests that the ἐν here could stand "pleonastically for the normal dat[ive], *to* or *for.*" But as Barrett, 69, has pointed out, that does not at all accord with Pauline usage. Barrett's own distinction, that this "implies that all may speak" (as in 12:8), is not so apparent. On the use of "we," see n. 13 above. Paul probably intends nothing significant by this preposition except to describe those *among whom* God's wisdom is spoken.

[18]In this case it probably reflects either Hellenistic philosophy (e.g., Plato) or Hellenistic Judaism of the type found in Philo. See P. J. Du Plessis, *ΤΕΛΕΙΟΣ: The Idea of Perfection in the New Testament* (Kampen, 1959), pp. 36-121; cf. Pearson, 27-30, and Horsley, "Pneumatikos," 281-83, who opt for Philonic influence.

them like mere babes, feeding them only with milk, while they perceive themselves to have advanced to maturity (cf. 4:8). A similar usage in 14:20 suggests that "infants" and "grown-ups" is the basic intent of the imagery. Therefore, the usage is at least partly ironical. Those "in Christ" (1:30) are "the mature,"[19] and thus the Corinthians are included. But their behavior indicates that they are very much mere babes. Paul's concern, as in 14:20, is to persuade them to adopt the thinking that goes along with being "mature" in Christ.

The wisdom of which Paul is now speaking, he is quick to reassert, is of a radically different kind from that which the Corinthians are currently pursuing, which is "of this age" (cf. 1:20). However, in this case he adds "or of the rulers of this age, who are coming to nothing." This latter verb is the eschatological one from v. 28; the "rulers of this age," and therefore by implication the age itself, are "coming to nothing," that is, they are in the process of "being abolished." But who are the "rulers of this age"? and why are they brought in here? The answer to the second question is twofold: partly it anticipates what will be said in v. 8, where they represent the people of this age who fail to recognize the wisdom of God and who thereby stand in contrast to those who are destined for glory; but it also seems to reflect an early expression of the Christian *kērygma* as it was preached in the Pauline circle.[20] As to the first question, there has been a growing consensus over many years that the "rulers" are demonic powers,[21] or at least that by these words Paul wants the Corinthians to see demonic powers as lying behind the activity of the earthly rulers.[22] This oft-repeated assertion needs finally to be

---

It has also been common to see Paul as here influenced either by the terminology of the mystery cults (Reitzenstein, Bultmann) or by Gnosticism (Wilckens, Conzelmann) to refer to "the initiates." But this has been effectively refuted by Pearson and others. The mystery rites never use this adjective in this way, and the data from Gnosticism are at least a century or more later.

[19]For this sense of the term, see esp. Du Plessis, *ΤΕΛΕΙΟΣ*, pp. 178-85; cf. Weiss, 53.

[20]See, e.g., Luke 24:20; Acts 3:17; 13:27 (note the "ignorance" motif in the latter two instances, both sermons). For this observation I am indebted to W. Carr, "The Rulers of This Age—I Corinthians II.6-8," *NTS* 23 (1976/77), 20-35, esp. pp. 25-27.

[21]The literature here is immense. Among commentators, see Weiss, Moffatt, Lietzmann, Héring, Barrett, Conzelmann. Among others, see R. Bultmann, *Theology of the New Testament* (ET, London, 1952), I, 259; Wilckens, 60-63; Scroggs, "Paul," p. 41; BAGD.

[22]This view is espoused by such various scholars as O. Cullmann, *Christ and Time* (ET, London, 1962), pp. 191-206; G. B. Caird, *Principalities and Powers* (Oxford, 1956), pp. 80-82; G. H. C. MacGregor, "Principalities and Powers. The Cosmic Background of St Paul's Thought," *NTS* 1 (1954/55), 17-28; W. J. P. Boyd, "I Cor. 2:8," *ExpT* 68 (1957), 158; and Bruce, 38. As Carr has pointed out, this view has almost nothing in its favor. Cullmann's basis for so arguing rests on a faulty view of the angels of the nations; and the linguistic evidence itself is completely lacking.

laid to rest[23] since the linguistic evidence, the context, and Pauline theology all argue against it.[24] Given the evidence of v. 8, the "rulers" here at least include those responsible for the crucifixion. But in this first instance the term probably also intends the "leaders" of this age in the broader sense, including the various "wise ones" of 1:20 and 26. Those to whom the Corinthians would especially give deference do not really know true wisdom; indeed, they are themselves "coming to nothing."

7-8 In these verses Paul elaborates the two sides of v. 6. V. 7 explains the *nature* of God's wisdom that made it impossible for the wise of this age to grasp it; v. 8 repeats the failure of the "rulers" in terms of their responsibility for the crucifixion.

He begins with a sharp contrast to the negative side of v. 6. "No,"[25] he says, "we speak *God's* wisdom,"[26] which he immediately qualifies in four ways. The first three describe its nature, so as to distinguish it from the wisdom of this age. First, it is wisdom "in mystery" (NIV, "secret wisdom").[27] One cannot be certain whether this phrase modifies "wisdom" as

---

[23]Despite the evidence against it, it will probably not die easily, since those interpretations that see Gnostic backgrounds to much of what is being said here are particularly dependent on this interpretation to make them work.

[24]The linguistic evidence is decisive: (1) the term ἄρχοντες is never equated with the ἀρχαί of Col. 1:16 and Eph. 6:12; (2) when ἄρχων appears in the singular it sometimes refers to Satan; but (3) there is no evidence of any kind, either in Jewish or Christian writings until the second century, that the term was used of demons; and (4) in the NT it invariably refers to earthly rulers and unambiguously does so in Paul in Rom. 13:3. See G. D. Fee, *New Testament Exegesis* (Philadelphia, 1983), pp. 87-89. Some see the qualifier "of this age" to be determinative, since Satan is referred to in John's Gospel as "the ruler of the world" (12:3; 14:30; 16:11); but that seems a remote connection at best, since the phrase in John belongs to his special vocabulary. Nothing like it appears in Paul (esp. not in Eph. 2:2). While the "powers" do play a significant role in Pauline theology, there is no evidence that they are responsible for the death of Christ; rather, Christ triumphed over them by his death (Col. 2:15). On this whole question see G. Miller, "APXONTΩN TOY AIΩNOY TOYTOY—A New Look at 1 Corinthians 2:6-8," *JBL* 91 (1972), 522-28; and esp. Carr, "Rulers," which also appears in somewhat abbreviated form in *Angels and Principalities, The Background, Meaning and Development of the Pauline Use of* hai archai kai hai exousiai (SNTSMS 42; Cambridge, 1981), pp. 118-20.

[25]Gk. ἀλλά, the strong adversative.

[26]The θεοῦ is emphatic, θεοῦ σοφίαν; the genitive is probably possessive in this case, although it may also lean toward source, i.e., wisdom that not only belongs to God, but also comes from God. The NIV's addition, "of" (God's wisdom), is unnecessary and probably slightly misleading.

[27]This is another phrase that has caused some to see Paul as reflecting the mystery cults or Gnosticism. But again that not only misses Paul's own Jewish background, but the whole point of the argument as well. On the unlikelihood of the mystery cults influencing the NT at all, see G. Wagner, *Pauline Baptism and the Pagan Mysteries* (ET, Edinburgh, 1967). On the term "mystery" in Paul see R. E. Brown, *Semitic Background;* cf. G. Bornkamm, *TDNT* IV, 817-24: "In sum, μυστήριον . . . in the NT . . . betrays no relation to the mystery cults."

an adjective (hence the NIV's "secret wisdom") or the verb "we speak" as an adverb.[28] The former seems preferable. God's wisdom is not some inaccessible teaching, spoken in secret. As Paul will develop more fully in Colossians and Ephesians,[29] in the singular the term "mystery" ordinarily refers to something formerly hidden in God from *all* human eyes but now revealed in history through Christ and made understandable to his people through the Spirit.[30] The seeds of this idea are sown here for the first time in Paul; in particular it embraces the paradox of the crucifixion of "the Lord of glory" (v. 8).[31]

Second, and to clarify the phrase "in mystery," God's wisdom—salvation through a crucified Messiah—"has been hidden." The perfect tense, plus the phrase that follows ("before time began"), indicates that such wisdom has been hidden in God from eternity until such a time ("now") as he was ready to reveal it. What follows in v. 8 suggests further that God's "secret" remains hidden from the "rulers," the representatives of the "wise" of this age.

Third, God's secret wisdom, long hidden—and still hidden to some—was "destined" by God himself "for our glory before time began." This is the clause that begins to clarify both the content of "wisdom" and the identity of the "mature" in v. 6. The verb "destined"[32] is an intensified form of the ordinary verb for "determining." The emphasis lies on "deciding upon beforehand" (BAGD); therefore, to "predestine." As in 1:1, God's call is the expression of his prior will, which in this case is further intensified by the phrase "before time began" (lit. "before the ages"). What God determined *"before* the ages" has been worked out in the *present* age, which is being brought to its conclusion as the *final glorious* age has dawned and is awaiting its consummation —"for our glory." What has been predestined technically is God's wisdom; the larger context indicates that Paul has in view God's gracious activity in Christ, whereby through the crucifixion he determined eternal salvation for his people—including especially the

---

[28]It would then refer to the *form* of the instruction that would be accessible to the τέλειοι, but inaccessible to the νήπιοι. As we have noted throughout, that is contextually an unlikely interpretation. For an advocacy of the adverbial understanding, see B. Frid, "The Enigmatic ΑΛΛΑ in 1 Corinthians 2.9," *NTS* 31 (1985), 605.

[29]See Col. 1:26-27; 2:2; 4:3; Eph. 1:9; 3:3, 4, 9; 6:19. In these letters "mystery" especially, though not exclusively, refers to the inclusion of the Gentiles in the salvation of God.

[30]Three times in 1 Corinthians it appears in the plural (4:2; 13:2; 14:2). The latter two in particular reflect the idea of things still hidden, but revealed or expressed in the form of spiritual gifts. On the usage in 14:2 and 15:51 see the commentary *ad loc*.

[31]For further discussion of "mystery" in this passage and in Paul, see S. Kim, *The Origin of Paul's Gospel* (Tübingen, 1981), pp. 75-78.

[32]Gk. προορίζω; cf. Rom. 8:29-30; Eph. 1:5, 11; Acts 4:28.

Corinthian believers. Just as God *chose* the foolish and weak for salvation and thereby "shamed" the wise and powerful, who are being brought to nothing (1:26-28), so now Paul repeats that God "destined" his people for glory (not shame), and has done so in contrast to the rulers of this age who are "coming to nothing." "For our glory" is eschatological language, referring to the final goal of salvation, namely that God's people should share in his own glory.[33] Hence the crucified one is in this context also called "the Lord of glory" (v. 8).

Fourth (v. 8a),[34] God's wisdom is something that "none of the rulers of this age[35] understood." With this clause Paul elaborates the negative side of v. 6, but now in light of the preceding description of God's wisdom. The reason for their failure is that it was "hidden in God" and could only be grasped by a revelation of the Spirit (v. 10). The reason for repeating this idea seems to be twofold: first, to reestablish the contrast between "us" and "them" that is crucial to his argument; and second, to confirm their part in the historical event itself, which both demonstrated their "ignorance" of God's ways and implicated them in the carrying out of his plan.[36] What they did not understand was the nature of true wisdom—God's wisdom, as spelled out in 1:18–2:5—which stands in contradiction to human understanding; and because they were thus "ignorant" they did what human "wisdom" demanded—they crucified the one who for them was one more messianic pretender. Thus the divine irony: The very ones who were trying to do away with Jesus by crucifying him were in fact carrying out God's prior will—"destined for our glory before time began." Instead of crucifying a messianic pretender, they killed "the Lord of glory" himself,[37] the very one

---

[33]Cf. 1 Thess. 2:12; 2 Thess. 1:10, and esp. Rom. 8:17 and 8:29-30.

[34]The NIV (correctly, given their translational theory of dynamic equivalency) treats v. 8a as a new sentence. In fact, it is a relative clause that marks the fourth qualification of God's wisdom.

[35]For the meaning of "rulers of this age" see above on v. 6.

[36]Given this concern on Paul's part to root God's wisdom in the historical event of Christ's death, and the rulers' implication in that death, it is surprising to see this clause interpreted by some as the key to a Gnostic, mythological understanding of the whole passage. The "ignorance" motif is alleged to be a reflection of the Gnostic Redeemer myth, where the Aeons were ignorant of who Christ really was, namely "the Lord of Glory," which is also seen as mythological language. For this view see especially Wilckens, 70-80; it is repeated in Conzelmann, 63, and even finds a surprising, though greatly qualified, supporter in Barrett, 71-72. Besides the lack of certainty that there ever was such a myth, nothing in the language or context of this verse even remotely hints at such a mythological understanding. The "rulers" are not demonic powers; and even if they were, the evidence of the Gospels, which reflects the view of the early church, is that the demons were the only ones who did in fact recognize Jesus. Moreover, in this context it is not Jesus about whom the "rulers" are ignorant, but about God's wisdom, which was displayed in the very crucifixion for which they were responsible.

[37]Cf. the similar irony in the Peter speech in Acts 3:15, "you killed the author of life"! See also Acts 2:22-25.

who, as Lord of all the ages, is therefore Lord of the final glory that is both his and his people's ultimate destiny. The Pauline irony, of course, is that the Corinthians in pursuing *sophia* are pursuing what belongs to *this* age, which is passing away and whose rulers were implicated in the divine irony.

9 In typical style Paul concludes the argument to this point with scriptural support. In this case, however, there are considerable difficulties with the "citation."[38] First, *what* is he citing? and second, *how does it function* in the argument? These questions are made more difficult by the fact that the "citation" occurs in two parts, which as they now stand form an *anacolouthon* in the Greek sentence (grammar that "doesn't follow"). Literally the text reads:

line 1: *"What* eye did not see,
line 2:   and ear did not hear,
line 3:   and did not enter into the heart of *man* (= "no human mind conceived"),[39]
line 4: *"What* God prepared for those who love him."

Of the two difficulties, the *function* of the quotation is the more easily resolved. Paul cites two realities, which sustain the two parts of the preceding argument. First, Scripture supports the fact that people in the present age do not understand what God accomplished in Christ: God's ways (his "wisdom") are not even conceivable by the merely human mind. Second, what they are ignorant of is the salvation that God "has prepared for those who love him." Lines 1-3, therefore, support what is said in vv. 6b and 8; line 4 supports v. 7, that God has destined eternal salvation for us. At the same time, line 4 anticipates the next section of the argument, which is picked up immediately in v. 10.

That much seems clear enough. Paul's syntax also indicates that the clause functions to *conclude* the argument to this point.[40] The introductory

---

[38]These difficulties have led to a nearly impossible interpretation at both the popular and scholarly level, to the effect that the content of the passage speaks to what is yet future. Thus, "eye has not *yet* seen, etc., what God yet has in store for those who love him." But that not only misses what is actually said, but also misses the context rather widely.

[39]The NIV has correctly captured the sense of the Hebrew idiom, but has unfortunately left out the word ἀνθρώπου, which in this context therefore misses the point altogether. God's wisdom is something that no *human* mind has conceived.

[40]What the syntax does not seem to allow is an interpretation such as one finds in the RSV and NEB, which sees the quotation as the beginning of the next section of the argument (RSV: "But, as it is written, 'What no eye has seen, nor ear heard, nor the heart of man conceived, what God has prepared for those who love him,' God has revealed to us through the Spirit"). In this view the entire quotation functions as the object of the verb "revealed" in v. 10. But this destroys Paul's syntax altogether by missing the adversative force of the ἀλλά of v. 9 and running roughshod over the explanatory γάρ that begins v. 10.

formula, "however, as it is written," is identical to Rom. 15:3. As in that passage, the "however" is a strong adversative to the preceding negatives (v. 8), especially the first one.[41] Thus he says, "the rulers of this age did *not* understand, *but* even as it stands written. . . ." This structural observation also helps, despite the *anacolouthon,* to make sense of how the two clauses go together. The NIV disregards the relative pronoun, "what things," of line 1 and makes the relative clause of line 4 the object of the verbs in lines 1 to 3. More likely the reverse of this is intended, with lines 1 to 3 being the object clause of the anticipated verb "prepared" in line 4 (cf. Moffatt: *"What* no eye has ever seen, etc., God has prepared *all that* for those who love him"). In this case the emphasis lies with line 4, which is precisely the point of the argument that began in v. 6. Paul thus argues: "We speak God's wisdom, salvation through Christ crucified, which none of the rulers of this age understood; but even as it is written: What no one could see, hear, or understand about God's ways, these things[42] God has prepared for those who love him."[43] The next part of the paragraph goes on to explain *how* those who love God understand his "wisdom."

But *what* is he quoting? First of all, no OT passage resembles this one in its entirety. The closest thing to it is Isa. 64:4 (LXX 64:3), which contains some close verbal similarities to lines 1 and 2.[44] In that case line 4 might be a free adaptation of "what things you will do for those who wait for mercy."[45] The closest parallel to line 3 is to be found in the LXX of Isa. 65:16: "and it shall not enter their hearts." Because no exact parallel is to be found in the OT, and because the citation appears to be complete in its present form,

---

[41]This ἀλλά has been a major source of difficulty for many. For a helpful discussion of the alternatives, see Frid, "Enigmatic ΑΛΛΑ," pp. 603-06. The one view that does not seem likely is that it repeats the ἀλλά of v. 7 and that v. 9 should then have an understood λαλοῦμεν as its verb: "But even if it is in mystery, we speak etc." As Frid rightly notes, this makes meaningless the ἀλλά of v. 9.

[42]Thus the second ἅ functions very much like a ταῦτα.

[43]Frid, "Enigmatic ΑΛΛΑ," p. 610 n. 45, who also recognizes the parallel with Rom. 15:3 and that v. 9 therefore stands in contrast to v. 8a, offers a slightly different solution, which has a similar net result. He sees the sentence as an ellipse and would add the verb from v. 8, "we know." Thus: "None of them knew, but, as it is written, what things etc., these things we do know."

[44]LXX:

ἀπὸ τοῦ αἰῶνος οὐκ ἠκούσαμεν
οὐδὲ οἱ ὀφθαλμοὶ ἡμῶν εἶδον . . .
ἃ ποιήσεις τοῖς ὑπομένουσιν ἔλεον.

"From eternity we have not heard,
nor have our eyes seen. . . ,
what things you shall do for those who wait for mercy."

[45]The phrase "for those who love God" appears again in Rom. 8:28 (and possibly 1 Cor. 8:3, q.v.), thus suggesting that Paul is comfortable with it. It has a rich OT background (e.g., Exod. 20:6; Deut. 5:10; 7:9, and scores of others), but nowhere does anything like the present clause appear in this form.

several alternative suggestions have been presented: e.g., an unknown apocalyptic writing,[46] a prior Jewish collation of OT passages, or a prior apocalyptic amalgam of OT ideas.[47] The fact that the passage appears in this same form in the Ascension of Isaiah suggests most strongly that Paul himself is not freely paraphrasing the OT. Most likely the "citation" is an amalgamation of OT texts that had already been joined and reflected on in apocalyptic Judaism, which Paul knew either directly or indirectly. In any case, the introductory formula, "as it is written," makes it certain that he considered the citation to be God's Word,[48] and therefore the twin points of vv. 6-8 have previously been announced by God and are now seen as having come to pass.

10a   If the main point of the citation in v. 9 was to support the argument of vv. 6-8, the final line of the citation, "what God has prepared for those who love him," prepares the way for the main concern of the entire passage, namely that God's wisdom can be known only by God's people because they alone have the Spirit. But there is some difference of opinion, based on a textual difference,[49] as to how this sentence is syntactically related to what has preceded. If "but" is the correct reading, then the sentence stands (as in the NIV) as an adversative to the whole of v. 9, with special emphasis on the contrast between their inability and "our" ability to grasp God's wisdom. That is, v. 10 basically stands in contrast to lines 1-3 of v. 9. But on the analogy of Rom. 15:3-4 and on the basis of its excellent support, an explanatory "for" is the preferred reading. In this case, the explanation picks up the emphasis on line 4 in the citation. The others could not understand the things that "God has prepared *for those who love him*, for *to us* God has revealed[50] [them] by the Spirit." The contrast, therefore, despite the emphatic position of "to us,"[51] lies not so much between "us" and "them" as on the reason they could not, but we can, understand the

---

[46]See the evidence mustered by M. Stone and J. Strugnell that the citation is from an otherwise unknown *Apocalypse of Elijah* (*The Books of Elijah, Parts 1-2* [SBLTT 18; Missoula, 1979]).

[47]See Ellis, *Use*, p. 35, for a discussion and bibliography. For more recent work, see A. Feuillet, "L'enigme de I Cor., II,9," *RB* 70 (1963), 52-74 (Digest in Eng. in *ThDig* 14 [1966], 143-48); and K. Berger, "Zur Diskussion über die Herkunft von I Cor. ii.9," *NTS* 24 (1977/78), 170-83.

[48]Cf. Ellis, *Use*, pp. 22-25.

[49]See n. 1 above.

[50]Gk. ἀπεκάλυψεν, the verb that became the technical one for the "divine revelation of certain supernatural secrets" (BAGD); see, e.g., Ps. 98:2 (LXX 97:2). This becomes a particularly well-developed idea in Jewish and Christian "apocalyptic," e.g., Dan. 2:22 (cf. vv. 19 and 28 Theod.). For Paul this is the ordinary verb for supernatural revelation of any kind.

[51]The emphatic position of ὑμῖν is not so much to contrast "us" with those who cannot perceive God's ways, but to place "us" in immediate juxtaposition with "those who love him." Thus: "For to us, namely those who love him, God has revealed what is otherwise hidden." On the significance of the first person plural here, see n. 13 above.

things that God has prepared for his people. That is, as vv. 10b-13 make clear, the emphasis lies on the *means* of revelation, the Spirit, not on the recipients themselves, although the latter of course are always in view, an emphasis that will be picked up again in vv. 14-16.

10b-11 With the second sentence of v. 10, Paul begins the main part of his argument. The key to understanding God's wisdom lies with the Spirit.[52] The basis of the argument that follows is the Greek philosophic principle of "like is known only by like,"[53] that is, humans do not on their own possess the quality that would make it possible to know God or God's wisdom. Only "like is known by like"; only God can know God. Therefore, the Spirit of God becomes the link between God and humanity, the "quality" from God himself who makes the knowing possible. This of course is for Paul a fortuitous bit of reasoning, for two reasons: (1) This is what he really believes about our ability to know the ways of God that are otherwise "past finding out"; left to themselves, the natural man/woman cannot know God by reason or intuition, as Paul affirms in v. 14. (2) This is precisely the linkage he needs in his argument with the Corinthians. By their own experience of the Spirit of God, they consider themselves to be "spiritual." Apparently they have thought of spirituality mostly in terms of ecstasy and experience, which has led some of them to deny the physical body, on the one hand, and to a sense of "having arrived" (cf. 4:8), on the other. What Paul is about to do is to present the Spirit as the key to the proper understanding of the gospel itself, especially of his preaching (v. 13) and their own gifts (v. 12); and in this context, as always, the gospel, God's wisdom, is the message of salvation through the crucified one.

The sentence begins with an untranslated "for," which links the

---

[52]Although Paul does not so designate him here, the argument of the entire passage confirms that he is referring to the Holy Spirit, the Third Person of the Trinity. The ease with which Paul flows in and out of the language "Spirit" and "Holy Spirit" makes this decisive. Cf., e.g., 1 Thess. 1:5 and 1 Cor. 2:4, where in similar contexts Paul in the earlier letter designated him as "Holy Spirit," but not in the latter. In this letter, see 6:11 and 19 and esp. 12:3. On the other hand, one must be careful not to read too much later Christian theology back into Paul's language here. From what is said in this paragraph one may conclude that the Spirit is divine, but it goes beyond Paul's concern to address the question whether the Holy Spirit is a distinct Person. Nonetheless passages like this one, and 12:4-6, serve as the "stuff" out of which the later full Trinitarian formulations are (legitimately) mined. On this question see D. W. Martin, "'Spirit' in the Second Chapter of First Corinthians," *CBQ* 5 (1943), 181-95.

[53]On this question see esp. Gärtner, "Idea" (see n. 8). Whether the actual "source" of Paul's usage is his own experience or an adaptation from the Corinthians themselves is a moot point. In either case, two things are certain: (1) this is the only occurrence of this principle in the extant Pauline corpus, and (2) as usual he has so thoroughly adapted it to his own theology that the question of source becomes nearly irrelevant.

explanation that follows as a kind of commentary to the first assertion, that God has revealed (his wisdom)[54] to us through the Spirit. The Spirit is first of all linked with God: "The Spirit searches all things, even the deep things of God." Although somewhat unusual language for Paul, it is not inexplicable. Elsewhere he speaks of the "depth of the riches of the wisdom and knowledge of God" (Rom. 11:33), reflecting his sense of the profound greatness of God, which is part of Paul's Jewishness, both OT and apocalyptic.[55] The idea of the Spirit's "searching" all things, even the depths of God, is best understood in light of Paul's own explanation in v. 11.[56] Perhaps this sentence, too, has a tinge of irony. They considered Paul's preaching to be "milk"; on the contrary, he implies, redemption through the cross comes from the profound depths of God's own wisdom, which his Spirit, given to those who love him, has searched out and revealed to us.

In v. 11, with yet another explanatory "for,"[57] Paul offers a supporting analogy for the fact that the Spirit knows the things of God, and makes the further point that he *alone* knows them. Here in particular the principle of "like is known by like" is spelled out in detail, in this case influenced by the OT motif that no one has ever seen God. The analogy itself is a simple one, and insists that just as the only person who knows what goes on inside one's own mind is oneself, so only God knows the things of God.[58] Paul makes that point by use of the word "spirit" because first of all he is talking about the Holy Spirit and secondly because it is for him a common word for the interior expression of the human person.[59] Thus, while Paul

---

[54]There is no object to the verb ἀπεκάλυψεν in Paul's sentence. Probably, as Godet, 147, observes, that is because the emphasis lies on the *fact* of revelation here, not on what is revealed. The context makes it certain that something very much like "his wisdom" is in view.

[55]See, e.g., a passage like Dan. 2:20-23. Although there is no mention of the Spirit as the agent of revelation, the linguistic parallels with v. 22 ("God reveals deep and hidden things") are of such a nature that one scarcely needs to search Greek or Gnostic sources for this terminology.

[56]What lies behind such an idea can be illustrated from Rom. 8:27, where God is called the One who searches people's hearts (an epithet with deep OT roots: e.g., 1 Sam. 16:7; Ps. 139:1, 2, 23). In this passage the fact that he searches the hearts of others functions as the presupposition that he must *a fortiori* also know the unspoken desires of his own Spirit. On this see Cranfield, *Romans,* I, 424.

[57]Gk. γάρ. This piling up of γάρ's is a typical feature of Pauline style. Cf. 1:17, 18, 19, 21; 3:3, 4; 9:15, 16, 17; and many others.

[58]The one difference between the two parts of the sentence has to do with the verb "to know" (οἶδεν/ἔγνωκεν). The older commentators suggested that the differences have to do with the capacity for "knowing" itself (e.g., Lightfoot, 179; R-P, 44); more likely ἔγνωκεν is chosen in the second instance because it constitutes a truer perfect and suggests the sense of "no one has ever known" (cf. Barrett, 74).

[59]The phrase "the man's spirit within him" is almost identical to the LXX of Zech. 12:1: πνεῦμα ἀνθρώπου ἐν αὐτῷ.

would undoubtedly understand the human "spirit" as a distinguishable constituent of the human personality, this sentence is *not* trying to make a
definitive anthropological statement,[60] nor is it suggesting that the analogy
of the Trinity fits the human personality. Moreover, Paul is not trying to
make a definitive pneumatological statement. It is analogy, pure and simple.
And the analogy does not have to do with the constituents of personality;
rather, it has to do with our common experience of personal reality. At the
human level, I alone know what I am thinking, and no one else, unless I
choose to reveal my thoughts in the form of words. So also only God knows
what God is about. God's Spirit, therefore, who as God knows the mind of
God, becomes the link to our knowing him also, because as v. 12 goes on to
affirm: "we have received the Spirit *of God.*"

12 With this sentence and the next we come to the central issue in
the entire paragraph.[61] The argument began with the assertion that Paul does
indeed speak wisdom among the "grown-ups" of God's people. That wisdom, which is not esoteric knowledge of deeper truths about God but simply
his own plan for saving his people, is contrasted to that of the leaders of the
present age, who cannot know God's wisdom because it is his "secret,
hidden" wisdom, destined for, and finally revealed to, those who love him.
That revelation has been given by the Spirit, who alone knows the inner
secrets of God, and whom, as this verse now affirms, "we have received."
Since "like is known by like," the Spirit, who alone knows the thoughts of
God, becomes the link on the human side for our knowing the thoughts of
God.

As in vv. 6-9 Paul makes that point once again by way of antithesis to
those of the present age.[62] He is forever reminding the Corinthians that they
belong to a different world order, a different age, and therefore must not do
as they are now doing—pursue or think in terms of merely human *sophia.*[63]

---

[60]It seems clear in this case that the word πνεῦμα is another expression for νοῦς.
Cf. v. 16, where to have the Spirit of God is the same as to have the νοῦν of Christ.

[61]The δέ that joins the sentence to what precedes is "consecutive" or "resumptive." It should be translated "now," resuming the point of v. 10a, after the mild digression of vv. 10b-11.

[62]Note again the interchangeability of αἰών ([this] "age") and κόσμος ([this]
"world"). See above on 1:20.

[63]As throughout the passage the interpretation of the "we" is crucial to one's
understanding of the sense of the whole passage. Those who see this as polemical (in the
sense of the Corinthians vis-à-vis Paul) suggest that he is here arguing with them that he,
too, has the Spirit and not they alone (e.g., Conzelmann, 66-67). There can be little
question, of course, that Paul is included in the "we" of this verse, and in a secondary
sense it may reflect this polemic (as vv. 15-16 also probably do); but the language "what
God has freely given us" echoes "our glory" in v. 7 and "to us who love him" in vv. 9
and 10 and seems to make most sense as referring especially to the Corinthians.

The usage in vv. 7-10, plus the connection of this verse with v. 10 by means of

In receiving the Spirit,[64] it was not "the spirit of the world" that "we have received." Made to walk on all fours, this can be seen as unusual language. But Paul's point is simple. He is not suggesting that there is a "spirit" of the world comparable to the Holy Spirit, nor is he referring to demonic "spirits."[65] He is rather saying something about the Holy Spirit. The Spirit whom we have received is not "of this world"; rather, he is "the Spirit who is from God."[66] The implication, of course, is that since they have the Holy Spirit, who is not of this world, they should desist thinking like this world.

The final clause of the sentence picks up the point of vv. 6 and 10 and thereby gives the reason, in *this* context, for our having received the Spirit, namely, "that we may understand[67] what God has freely given us." This latter phrase in particular picks up the motif of v. 9, "what God has prepared for those who love him," and gives us a clear glimpse into the *content* of the wisdom that God has revealed to his people by his Spirit. The verb *(charizomai)* seems to be a deliberate allusion to the "grace" *(charis)* of God, or the "gift" *(charisma)* of salvation (as in Rom. 6:23);[68] it appears here in the neuter plural ("what things have been freely bestowed") because it is reflecting the neuter plurals of v. 9. Therefore, this language seems determinative that Paul, in talking about God's wisdom in this passage, is referring to salvation through the crucified one (as in 1:23-24; 2:2). And God's people "understand" that precisely because they have received the Spirit.

---

the resumptive δέ (see n. 61) and the fact that in Paul the language "receive the Spirit" elsewhere refers only to believers in general (see the following note), seems also to deny the force of the assertion by W. C. Kaiser that "Paul is not talking about the Spirit that animates believers, but about the Holy Spirit's operation in delivering the Scripture to the apostle" (see "A Neglected Text in Bibliology Discussions: I Corinthians 2:6-16," *WTJ* 43 [1981], 301-19; the quotation is from p. 315). Kaiser's concern is indeed picked up in v. 13, although the language "delivering the Scripture to the apostle" seems to be a considerable distance from Paul's own concern and intent.

[64]This is ordinary NT language for the gift of the Spirit; cf. Acts 2:38; 10:47; 19:2; 2 Cor. 11:4; Gal. 3:2, 14; Rom. 8:15. In Paul it refers primarily to Christian conversion.

[65]This was suggested, e.g., by Ellis, 29-30, on the assumption that it is related to "the rulers of this age" in vv. 6 and 8, whom he incorrectly understands to be demonic powers. Cf. Barrett, 75.

[66]The NIV has thus correctly caught the sense of the contrast in this sentence, but by so translating it is also forced to miss the exact repetition of the designation from v. 11. Thus: ". . . except *the Spirit of God;* and we have . . . received *the Spirit of God.*"

[67]Gk. εἰδῶμεν, picking up the verbs from v. 11.

[68]Conzelmann, 67, candidly acknowledges as much, but is so enamored with Hellenistic parallels in the paragraph that he immediately qualifies it by saying that "χάρις, too, can assume the tenor of the mysteries and denote the power within the pneumatic, thus becoming synonymous with πνεῦμα. It will therefore be necessary to look for further indications." But why should one do so when both the argument itself and the terminology are so thoroughly Pauline?

13 Having been arguing that their common gift of the Spirit is what enables them to understand God's wisdom, Paul now returns to his own preaching of that wisdom, first mentioned in vv. 6 and 7, and links it to the same reception of the Spirit. This sentence, therefore, not only continues the argument at hand,[69] but also recalls the preceding paragraph (2:1-5) with its underlying apologetic motif. "What we preached to you was God's wisdom all right," he asserted (vv. 6-7), despite what they may think. Now he returns to that assertion by way of the explanation of vv. 10-12. Just as we have all received the Spirit so as to understand the gift of salvation, so also the message "I"[70] preach is given "in words taught by the Spirit."[71] The Spirit is thus the key to everything—Paul's preaching (vv. 4-5, 13), their conversion (vv. 4-5, 12), and especially their understanding of the content of his preaching as the true wisdom of God (vv. 6-13). As throughout the paragraph—and the entire argument beginning with 1:17—what he says positively about his own ministry is placed in antithesis to what is merely human: "not in words *(logois)* taught by human *sophia*."[72] The ties to 2:1-5 are obvious. "Words" of course does not mean simply language itself, but the meaning, or message, contained in the words as they give expression to the gospel.

What is less obvious is the further explanation of this teaching. Did Paul intend "expressing spiritual truths in spiritual words" (NIV), or "interpreting spiritual truths to spiritual men" (NIV mg.), or "comparing spiritual things with spiritual" (KJV, RSV mg.)?[73] The problems are two: (1) finding

---

[69]Gk. ἃ καὶ λαλοῦμεν, lit. "what things *also* we speak." "What things," of course, refers to "what God has freely given us." λαλοῦμεν is a repetition of the verb from vv. 6 and 7, and therefore seems clearly resumptive.

[70]Since λαλοῦμεν repeats the verb of vv. 6 and 7, it is also likely that the "we" here picks up the editorial "we" of those sentences. Hence "I." See n. 13 above.

[71]The noun πνεύματος lacks the definite article, thus indicating that the presence or absence of the article with πνεῦμα does not determine whether Paul intends *the* Spirit in any given instance. Otherwise N. Turner, *Grammatical Insights into the New Testament* (Edinburgh, 1965), pp. 17-22. The clue to this usage, both in Paul and in Luke-Acts, is probably related to various constructions with certain cases and has nothing to do with the Spirit's personality. Cf. the usage of the article with personal names in the Gospel of John (G. D. Fee, *NTS* 17 [1970/71], 168-83).

[72]O-W, 158, suggest the alternative possibility of "learned words of human wisdom," but they make too much of the subtle shades of meaning. Héring, 20, on the unfounded assertion that the common translation would only be possible if διδακτός were a noun, adopts a conjectural omission of λόγοις and thus translates: "amongst people instructed in human philosophy." But such conjectures are unnecessary, especially since the "subjective" or "agency" use of the genitive with this adjective is found also in John 6:45, which Héring overlooks.

[73]Gk. πνευματικοῖς πνευματικὰ συγκρίνοντες. The KJV translates "comparing spiritual things with spiritual," giving rise to the use of this text at the popular level to support the analogy of Scripture, i.e., comparing one text with another so as to derive its meaning from within Scripture itself. That is a useful hermeneutical principle, based on

a proper meaning for the verb *synkrinontes,* and (2) determining whether the word *pneumatikois* refers to the just-mentioned "words taught by the Spirit" or means "spiritual people" and anticipates the antitheses of vv. 14-15.[74] On this second matter the possibility that it anticipates what follows has in its favor the immediate contrast of the "nonspiritual person" in v. 14. In this context that could make a lot of sense. Nonetheless, the grammar would seem to favor the view that Paul is giving further explication of what he has just said.[75] "We speak words taught by the Spirit," he asserts, "which means that we [explain] spiritual things [probably referring to the "things freely given us by God," v. 12] by means of, or with, the spiritual words taught us by the Spirit."

As to the meaning of the verb, Paul is the only one to use it elsewhere in the NT, in 2 Cor. 10:12 (twice), where it plainly means "compare," a meaning that does not seem appropriate here. Some have argued that it should carry its classical sense of "combining";[76] however, Paul's septuagintal background seems determinative in favor of "explaining" or "interpreting." Most likely therefore he intended something like "explaining the things of the Spirit [as described in v. 12] by means of the words taught by the Spirit," that is, as Holladay (p. 47) suggests, "in language appropriate to the message, not with human wisdom."

14 In a sense the argument to this point has been consummated with v. 13. Both the "what" (God's hidden wisdom, salvation through the cross) and the "how" (revelation by means of the Spirit) of God's wisdom "have been sketched in antithetical language."[77] With vv. 14-16 Paul now picks up the negative side of the antithesis, in light of what has been argued positively about the work of the Spirit in vv. 10-13. At the same time he seems to be setting up the Corinthians for the polemic of 3:1-4.

---

belief in the common inspiration by the Spirit of all Scripture, but it is quite beside Paul's present point.

[74]It is possible, though less probable, that it is neuter and simply means something like "spiritual means" or "spiritual things" in general.

[75]The participial construction, modifying λαλοῦμεν, argues for the closest possible tie to what has already been said, not a loose addition anticipating what follows. Furthermore, one would expect the definite article with πνευματικοῖς if "those who are spiritual" were intended.

[76]Most recently Kaiser, "Bibliology," p. 318, and MacArthur, 63; cf. Lightfoot, 180-81, and Goodspeed (translation). Kaiser does so on the basis of the not totally relevant assertion, borrowed from Godet, that "the meaning of 'interpreting' for this verb is foreign in the N.T. and Classical Greek." Nor is there any NT usage meaning "combine"; and the comparison with classical Greek is particularly irrelevant since the word was regularly used with the meaning of "interpreting" or "explaining" in the LXX (e.g., Gen. 40:8, 16, 22; 41:12, 13, 15; Num. 15:34; Dan. 5:7), but never in the "classical" sense.

[77]This is the language of Funk, "Word," p. 296.

The thrust of v. 14 is an elaboration of the negative side of vv. 6 and 8-9 (also 12 and 13) in terms of the people of this age who miss out on God's wisdom; only the language is new. Those who belong to this age are now called *psychikoi* (NASB, NAB, "the natural man/woman") in contrast to those with the Spirit, who are called *pneumatikoi* (v. 15; cf. 15:44-46). There has been considerable debate over this term, mostly in terms of its origins and why Paul uses it. Whatever else, the ensuing description demonstrates that it refers to those who do not have the Spirit, and thus to the merely human. But why this usage, since Paul elsewhere prefers some form of *sarx* ("flesh") when making a contrast with *pneuma* ("Spirit"), as he does in the polemical paragraph that immediately follows? Perhaps it is a Corinthian term that he is picking up and turning against them.[78] But in this case it is difficult to see how they might have been using it, unless they were describing Paul in this manner. More likely it comes out of his own Jewish background, where the Greek noun *psychē* has been used to translate Heb. *nepeš*, which often simply denotes humanity in its natural, physical existence.[79] This seems to be his present point. With this term he is designating people who are not now, nor have they ever been, believers. They are strictly people who know only the "wisdom of this age" (v. 6). When he turns to address the Corinthians, who are in fact acting just like these people without the Spirit, he calls them *sarkinoi* (3:1), which will have have a different nuance altogether.

The *psychikoi* are described in three ways, each in terms of their relationship—or lack thereof—to the Spirit. First, they do "not accept the things that come from *the Spirit of God.*" This description stands in conspicuous contrast to the "we [who] have received . . . the Spirit of God" of v. 12. The verb in this case is the ordinary one for "receiving" or "accepting" another person. The implication is not that *psychikos* persons are simply incapable of understanding the things of the Spirit, but that, because of their being "merely human" (i.e., without the help of the Spirit), they "reject" the things of the Spirit.

Second, the reason for this "not accepting/rejecting" is that the things of the Spirit "are foolishness to [them]." Because they have not received the Spirit, in the sense of v. 12, their view of everything is from the bottom up, twisted and distorted. This is another sure indication that Paul is still pursuing the argument of 1:18–2:5, where the preaching of Christ

---

[78]This is the view of Wilckens, 89-91, who sees it as a Gnostic term being taken over by Paul; cf. Pearson, 38-39; Horsley, "Pneumatikos"; and Davis, 117-25, who see it as evidence of Philonic influences.

[79]See the discussion of these terms in *TDNT* IX, 608-63 (E. Schweizer), and *NIDNTT* III, 676-86 (G. Harder).

crucified, God's wisdom, is rejected as foolishness by those who are perishing (1:18, 23). People are revealed for who they are by their response to the cross; to see it as foolishness means to stand over against God and his ways—and to stand under his judgment as without his Spirit and therefore apart from "what he has freely given us."

Third, again in antithesis to v. 12, the "natural man/woman *cannot* understand" the very things that the one who has received the Spirit *can*. Here the emphasis lies on their inability. Again it is "like is known by like" (see v. 11); without the Spirit they lack the one essential "quality" necessary for them to know God and his ways—"because they are spiritually discerned." This last phrase demonstrates the fluidity of Paul's use of language. The word "spiritual" is now an adverb;[80] but the context makes it clear that Paul intends "by means of the Spirit," not by some intuitive process. For Paul, "to be spiritual" and "to discern spiritually" simply means to have the Spirit, who so endows and enables.

The verb translated "discern"[81] is a crucial one. The fact that it occurs only in this letter in the Pauline corpus (ten times), and that in every case but one (14:24) it appears in a polemical or ironical context, makes one think that it is probably a Corinthian word that Paul is taking up against them. Finding a proper meaning for it is difficult. Technically it can mean to "examine" in a judicial sense, and it clearly has that meaning in the two instances where he charges them with "judging" him (4:3-4; 9:3).[82] Here there seems to be a play on the word; many think it is also ironical, anticipating the usage in 4:3-4. Probably it means something very close to "discern" in the sense of being able to make appropriate "judgments" about what God is doing in the world; and the person "without the Spirit" obviously cannot do that. As such it is immediately picked up in v. 15 as the one proper activity of the truly "spiritual" person.

15-16   With these sentences the argument of the present paragraph, as well as that of the whole section that began in 1:17, is brought to its conclusion. At the same time they serve to lead into the strong polemical application of all this to the Corinthians and their quarreling (3:1-4). The four parts seem to form an ABBA pattern:

A The spiritual person examines all things;
  B But he/she in turn is examined by no one.
  B′ For who has known the mind of the Lord that he may instruct him?
A′ But we have the mind of Christ.

---

[80]Gk. πνευματικῶς.

[81]Gk. ἀνακρίνω; cf. v. 15 (2x); 4:3 (2x), 4; 9:3; 10:25, 27; 14:24.

[82]The emphasis lies on the process of examining, rather than the verdict itself, implied in the root verb κρίνω.

117

The first line stands in sharp contrast[83] to the final word about the *psychikos* person in v. 14. That person is totally unable to understand the things of the Spirit because such things are "examined" by spiritual means, that is, they are examined, discerned, so as to be understood by means of the Spirit, whom the *psychikos* does not have. But the *pneumatikos,* the "spiritual person" (= the person with the Spirit),[84] is not at such a disadvantage. This person can "make judgments about all things." Such a statement of course must not be wrested from its context. It is the Spirit who "searches all things, even the depths of God" (v. 10); therefore the person who has the Spirit can discern God's ways. Not necessarily all things, of course, but all things that pertain to the work of salvation, matters formerly hidden in God but now revealed through the Spirit.

The second line, which stands in contrast to the first, reverses the order of things in light of what has just been said in v. 14. But here there seems to be a play on the word "discern." The person lacking the Spirit cannot discern what God is doing; the one with the Spirit is able to do so because of the Spirit; therefore, the one without the Spirit cannot "examine," or "make judgments" on, the person with the Spirit. In its first instance this simply means that the person who belongs to this age is not in a position to judge as "foolish" the person who belongs to the age to come. As someone has said, "The profane person cannot understand holiness; but the holy person can well understand the depths of evil." Those whose lives are invaded by the Spirit of God can discern all things, including those without the Spirit; but the inverse is not possible. Here is another sentence that, taken out of its context, has suffered much in the church. There are always some who consider themselves full of the Spirit in such a way as to be beyond discipline or the counsel of others. Such a reading of the text is an unfortunate travesty, since these people are usually among those most needing such discipline.

But one wonders whether with these words the argument does not also move subtly toward the next paragraph, and even more so toward the conclusion to be reached in 4:1-5. The Corinthians regard themselves as "spiritual" and as such they are also "examining" the apostle. Paul allows that the truly "spiritual" person, the one who understands what God has done in Christ crucified, discerns, "examines" all things. Thus he himself will be able to make the necessary judgments about them that follow. Indeed, the whole of this letter will be the spelling out of the principle detailed in line A. But also because he has so understood "the mind of Christ," he

---

[83]Set off in the Greek text by an adversative δέ.

[84]The context seems to demand such a meaning for πνευματικός. To suggest, as does Grudem, 158, that it here means "spiritually mature" seems to miss Paul's argument.

disallows their making judgments on him. To the contrary, by their actions they have proved themselves to be less than truly "spiritual," indeed "fleshly," acting like mere humans who do not have the Spirit. Thus as a "spiritual person" he himself is "not subject to any man's judgment." As he will insist in 4:3-4, he is not subject to any merely human court because he belongs to the Lord, who alone will judge him, as well as all others.

The third line (B') gives scriptural support for the assertion of the second (B). But it does so without an introductory formula (e.g., "it is written"). Thus Paul reworks Isa. 40:13[85] in such a way that in its present form it serves as a rhetorical question, demanding the answer "No one."[86] "For," he asks rhetorically in light of line B, "who has known the mind of the Lord that he may instruct him?" Again, in the context of the argument this probably has a double intent. On the one hand, it simply asks rhetorically of the *psychikoi* how they can expect to know true wisdom, and thereby pass judgment on the one who has the Spirit, when they do not have the mind of the Lord. "Who is the person who wants to match wits with God?" he asks. But surely this, too, is directed now at his Corinthian friends themselves. "Who among his detractors, now enamored with human wisdom and passing judgment on Paul, is so capable of knowing the mind of the Lord that he/she can bypass the very wisdom of God itself as it is revealed in the cross?" Indeed, whoever would pursue wisdom so as to avoid the story of the cross fares no better than the person who would commit the ultimate folly of thinking he or she could instruct the Lord himself.

The final line (A') corresponds to the first assertion in v. 15, but now in direct response to the rhetorical question of v. 16a. "But," in contrast to those who lack the Spirit and thereby do *not* know the mind of the Lord, *"we* have the mind of Christ."[87] By "mind" he probably means the thoughts of Christ as they are revealed by the Spirit. In fact in the Greek Bible that Paul

---

[85]He has left out the middle line of three ("who has become his advisor?"), since it would fail to serve his present purpose. According to Robertson (*Grammar*, p. 724), the ὅς that introduces the second line of the quotation "denotes a consecutive idea, 'so as to.'"

[86]Cf. Wilckens, 95. This line is often interpreted otherwise, namely as support of line A, implying that the question from Isaiah is open-ended at this point, to be answered by the next line. That is, "The spiritual person judges all things, . . . for who has known the mind of Christ? The answer? We have." But that puts too much stress on the grammar (the δέ of the final line is better understood as an adversative, especially in light of the emphatic *"we"* and the change to "mind *of Christ"*), and does not fit the argument as well.

[87]The substitution of "Christ" for the "Lord" of the Isaiah passage probably has no significance for the present argument, but it does indicate something of Paul's own Christology! For him Christ is Lord; therefore when the OT speaks of the Lord, he sees in such language references to Christ himself. See also in this regard the interchange of the "Spirit of God" and the "Spirit of Christ" in Rom. 8:9.

cites, the word "mind" translates the Heb. *rûaḥ*, which ordinarily means "spirit."

Thus the argument is brought full circle. Paul began by insisting that his message was in fact an expression of wisdom—God's own wisdom, revealed as such by the Spirit. He at least—in contrast to the merely *psychikos* person, the mere human being without the Spirit—understands the mind of Christ. As those who possess the Spirit the Corinthians also potentially possess that same mind. However, as he will now point out, their behavior betrays them. They do, but they don't. The concern from here on will be to force them to acknowledge the folly of their "wisdom," which is expressing itself in quarrels and thereby destroying the very church for which Christ died.

＊

This paragraph has endured a most unfortunate history of application in the church. Paul's own point has been almost totally lost in favor of an interpretation nearly 180 degrees the opposite of his intent. Almost every form of spiritual elitism, "deeper life" movement, and "second blessing" doctrine has appealed to this text. To receive the Spirit according to their special expression paves the way for people to know "deeper truths" about God. One special brand of this elitism surfaces among some who have pushed the possibilities of "faith" to the extreme, and regularly make a "special revelation" from the Spirit their final court of appeal. Other "lesser" brothers and sisters are simply living below their full privileges in Christ. Indeed, some advocates of this form of spirituality bid fair to repeat the Corinthian error in its totality. What is painful about so much of this is not simply the improper use of this passage, but that so often it is accompanied by a toning down of the message of the cross. In fact one is hard-pressed to hear the content of "God's wisdom" ever expounded as the paradigm for truly Christian living.

Paul's concern needs to be resurrected throughout the church. The gift of the Spirit does not lead to special status among believers; rather, it leads to special status vis-à-vis the world. But it should do so always in terms of the centrality of the message of our crucified/risen Savior. The Spirit should identify God's people in such a way that their values and worldview are radically different from the wisdom of this age. They do know what God is about in Christ; they do live out the life of the future in the present age that is passing away; they are marked by the cross forever. As such they are the people of the Spirit, who stand in bold contrast to those who are merely human and do not understand the scandal of the cross. Being spiritual does not lead to elitism; it leads to a deeper understanding of God's profound mystery—redemption through a crucified Messiah.

4. On Being Spiritual and Divided (3:1-4)

1 *Brothers, I could not address you as spiritual but as worldly[1]—mere infants in Christ.* 2 *I gave you milk, not solid food, for you were not yet ready for it. Indeed, you are still[2] not ready.* 3 *You are still worldly.[3] For since there is jealousy and quarreling[4] among you, are you not worldly? Are you not acting like mere men?* 4 *For when one says, "I follow Paul," another, "I follow Apollos," are you not mere men[5]?*

The argument that began as a directive against quarrels and division (1:10-13) appears at first glance to have gone astray in what followed in 1:17–2:16. As was noted, however, the long discussion of wisdom and the cross is not a digression, but almost certainly the real issue. The church is indeed at stake, but even more so is the gospel itself. The wisdom that they are now pursuing strips the gospel of its real power; at the same time, their very pursuit of it has led to the divisions. With this paragraph, therefore, Paul makes the transition from the one argument (over the nature of the

---

[1]Gk. σαρκίνοις ("fleshly" = composed of flesh). In v. 3 Paul shifts to σαρκικός ("fleshly" = having the characteristics of flesh; associated with flesh). Paul keeps this distinction in his use of σάρκινος in 2 Cor. 3:3 (". . . but on tablets of human hearts," i.e., on hearts composed of flesh) and σαρκικός in 2 Cor. 1:12 ("worldly wisdom"; i.e., wisdom based on the point of view of the sinful nature). The later witnesses, not surprisingly, read σαρκικοῖς here against the σαρκίνοις of P46 ℵ A B C* D* 6 33 945 1175 1739 pc). For the possible significance see the commentary on v. 1.

[2]ἔτι is omitted in P46 B 0185. Cf. Zuntz, 40: "In I Cor. iii.2 the omission, by P46 B, of ἔτι after οὐδέ so greatly improves the style as to make the assumption of a mere scribal error difficult. . . . I find it hard to accept the current assertion that οὐδὲ ἔτι νῦν means 'and not even now': this would be οὐδὲ νῦν. The majority text to me suggests the meaning 'but not any longer'. The scribes may have anticipated ἔτι from the following clause. If Paul actually wrote it, he conflated two expressions: (1) 'not even now (οὐδὲ νῦν) you are able', and (2) 'even now (ἔτι καὶ νῦν) you are still unable'." Most likely Paul is responsible for it, and P46 B represent an Alexandrian "improvement."

[3]In the two instances of σαρκικοί in this verse, the Western MSS D F G, joined by P46 in the second instance, read σάρκινοι. Zuntz, 99, prefers this reading, since Paul generally uses σάρκινος to refer to human beings. But here the word takes on the moral overtones of σάρξ.

[4]P46 D F G 33 Maj a b sy have the additional words καὶ διχοστασίαι ("and dissensions"), against P11 ℵ A B C P Ψ 81 630 1175 1506 1739 1881 r vg sy Clement Origen Didymus. This is not an easy decision. An early and widespread "omission" of these words is particularly difficult to account for. But so is an "addition," which is best explained as an intrusion from Gal. 5:20 (although the two words are not juxtaposed there). On the whole, despite the early combination of P46 with the Western MSS, interpolation seems more easily accounted for than omission, since the latter could scarcely have been accidental, and one cannot imagine a reason for deliberate excision.

[5]The MajT, against all early evidence both East and West, substitutes σαρκικοί for ἄνθρωποι, a patent corruption that misses Paul's point by a wide margin.

121

gospel and the meaning of true "wisdom") to the other (about division in the name of their leaders).[6] The transition itself is marked by the twin clauses in v. 2: "You were not yet ready. . . . Indeed, you are still not ready."

But this paragraph is far more than simply a transition. It certainly *functions* that way; but in its own right it is fully part of the argument itself. Two concerns drive the apostle, both noted in the title given to this section: "On Being Spiritual and Divided." These, of course, for Paul are mutually exclusive options. The problem is that the Corinthians *think* of themselves as the one—"spiritual"—while *in fact* they are the other—"divided." Thus Paul does two things, which flow directly out of 2:6-16 and lead directly into 3:5-17.[7]

First, picking up the theme of being "spiritual" from what has just preceded, Paul makes a frontal attack and pronounces the Corinthians as not spiritual at all. Indeed, they are just the opposite; they are "fleshly"—still thinking like mere human beings, those who do not have the Spirit. With this charge Paul exposed himself to centuries of misunderstanding. But his concern is singular: not to suggest classes of Christians or grades of spirituality, but to get them to stop *thinking* like the people of this present age.[8]

Secondly, he wants them to stop *behaving* like the people of the present age, which is the point at hand. In the argument, therefore, their quarrels become Exhibit A of the charge in vv. 1 and 2.[9] Their behavior is

---

[6]Note especially the change of themes from wisdom, folly, and cross to spiritual, babes, and mere humans, with the concept of being "spiritual" as the link between the two.

[7]These two items are brought together again in the preliminary "conclusion" of 3:18-23: "If anyone thinks he is wise, . . . So then, no more boasting about men!"

[8]This seems by far the best answer to the question whether Paul himself makes distinctions between believers within the congregation, an idea that almost all commentators, including those who believe so, recognize as inherently problematic—given the current problem of divisiveness within the congregation and Paul's own theology as seen elsewhere. See the commentary on 2:6-16. Cf. Funk, "Word," p. 299: "Does Paul nevertheless make a distinction within the congregation? Indeed he does! The question is what kind of distinction and on what basis?" After giving a theological basis for what Funk refers to as a "dialectical" tension, he says of this passage: "Thus it may be said that Christians both have (insofar as they walk according to the spirit) and do not have (insofar as they fall short of the norm) the spirit." On the other hand, to suggest *two* meanings for πνευματικός (as, e.g., du Plessis, *ΤΕΛΕΙΟΣ*, pp. 183-85, and Mare, 204) misses Paul's point. What Mare suggests as necessitating a different meaning here from 2:14-15 can better be subsumed under the ironical usage argued for here, without the difficulties of the other view.

[9]He then proceeds to address this question directly for three paragraphs, but interestingly not in terms of quarreling per se, but in terms of their misunderstanding of the nature and role of leadership in the church (3:5-15), which in turn reflects their misunderstanding of the nature of the church itself (3:16-17). See below on 3:5-17.

that of "mere humans." Is it not true, then, that they are not "spiritual" but "fleshly"?

Paul, of course, does not mean to say they do not have the Spirit. They do; and that's the problem, because they are thinking and behaving otherwise. The argument has considerable bite, therefore, because his ultimate point is: "Stop it! People of the Spirit simply must stop behaving the way you are."

1-2a   With another untranslated "and I" (cf. 2:1) and accompanying vocative, Paul proceeds to a direct application of the argument of 2:6-16 to the Corinthian situation. "We who have received the Spirit do indeed have the mind of Christ and understand the wisdom of the folly of God. And I, for my part, brothers and sisters, was not able to address[10] you as *pneumatikoi* ('spiritual')." The use of the vocative ("brothers [and sisters]"; see 1:10) and the second person plural pronouns throughout make it clear that he is not addressing a faction within the congregation, but the church as a whole. Not all may be guilty, but all are defiled by the actions of the many. Also, the use of the aorist in vv. 1-2a ("I could not . . . because you could not") with the corresponding change to the present in 2b indicates that he is still, as in 1:18-2:5, reflecting on his former time with them. This, then, is his personal response to their reported disenchantment with him.

By saying that he "could not address [them] as spiritual," he seems to be allowing that there are "unspiritual" Christians—which is both true and not true. It is *not* true in the sense that the Spirit is the crucial factor in whether one is or is not a believer; one cannot be a Christian and be devoid of Spirit (cf. Rom. 8:9; Gal. 3:2-3; Tit. 3:5-7). On the other hand, the Corinthians are involved in a lot of unchristian behavior; in that sense they are "unspiritual," not because they lack the Spirit but because they are thinking and living just like those who do. But these theological niceties that so often concern us are quite beside Paul's point. He is "after them," as it were; and he uses their language, now based on his own content that has just been given, to shame them into reality (despite the demurrer of 4:14).

They consider themselves *pneumatikoi,* whatever else. They are less sure about Paul and have probably communicated as much to him. From Paul's perspective, however, their current thinking and behavior betray them. And how it is expressed! Not only could he not address them as "spiritual," but they were in fact quite the opposite—"fleshly." For those whose spirituality had denigrated present physical existence to the point of denying a future bodily resurrection (15:12), this word can only be biting

---

[10]Gk. λαλῆσαι, the infinitive of the same verb used about his preaching in 2:6, 7, and 13.

irony. For this reason the translation "worldly" is a bit unfortunate, and misses Paul's own change of words in v. 3.[11] The word used here, *sarkinoi,* emphasizes especially their humanness and the physical side of their existence as over against the spiritual. The change to *sarkikoi* in v. 3 only adds to the blow. They were not only "of the flesh" when Paul first was among them, but even now their behavior is "fleshly," a word with clear ethical overtones of living from the perspective of the present age, therefore out of one's sinfulness. Furthermore, *sarkinoi* is *not* a synonym for *psychikos* in 2:14. The change is deliberate. The latter word had just been used to describe the person totally devoid of Spirit, who could not even follow Paul's present argument because the whole would be folly to him/her. Because the Corinthians had received the Spirit, he could not call them *psychikoi*—even if they were acting that way. So the shift to *sarkinoi* is fitting in every way. He avoids accusing them of not having the Spirit altogether, but at the same time he bitingly forces them to have to face up to their true condition.

Immediately, however, he shifts images, to pick up on their (apparent) accusation that he fed them only with milk, not with "wisdom." This is the imagery that has created tensions for interpretation, especially his elaboration of it in v. 2a. Even though the language probably came from them, the question remains as to what Paul himself intends by it as he directs it toward their prior relationship with him. The problem is twofold: (1) What does he mean by "mere infants"? and (2) what is the significance of "milk" and "solid food"?

First, he calls them "mere infants in Christ," which harks back to the "grown-ups" of 2:6. This is common imagery in antiquity, most often reflecting the theme of "progressing in understanding," i.e., moving from an elementary grasp of truth to a more mature knowledge of the deeper things of a system.[12] It is common to see this as Paul's intent as well.[13] The problem with this view is that it does not fit the argument or Paul's use of the imagery elsewhere.[14] Paul regularly uses the imagery of "children" in a

[11]See n. 1. This stands against the commonly held view that these words mean basically the same thing. If so, then one wonders why Paul himself uses two words. If the difference is somewhat subtle, it is nonetheless by Paul's own choice and needs to be taken seriously. See, e.g., R-P, 52; Moulton, *Grammar,* II, 378.

[12]For Hellenism, see Epict. 2.16.39: "Are you not willing, at this late date, like children, to be weaned and to partake of more solid food?" (Loeb, I, 333); for Hellenistic Judaism, see Philo, *agric.* 9: "But seeing that for babes (νηπίοις) milk (γάλα) is food, but for grown men (τελείοις) wheaten bread, there must also be soul-nourishment, such as is milk-like suited to the time of childhood, . . . and such as is adapted to grown men in the shape of instructions leading the way through wisdom and temperance and all virtue" (Loeb, III, 113); cf. *congr.qu.er.* 19 and *omn.prob.lib.* 160.

[13]See, e.g., W. Grundmann, "Die *nēpioi* in der urchristlichen Paränese," *NTS* 5 (1958/59), 188-205, and most of the commentaries.

[14]In this regard see esp. Francis, "Babes," pp. 43-48.

positive sense to reflect his own apostolic relationship with his converts. In such cases the word is always *teknon* ("child");[15] the word used here (*nēpios*, "baby" or "mere infant") almost always has a pejorative sense, in contrast with being adult, and refers to thinking or behavior that is not fitting.[16] That is certainly his concern here. It is not so much that they have not made progress—that is part of the problem, they think they have—but that they are "adults" of the wrong kind, hence "mere infants." Thus he is simply continuing the argument of the entire passage, but with new imagery. Just as they think of themselves as "spiritual"—and are in one sense—but by their thinking and behavior demonstrate that they are "fleshly,"[17] so too they think of themselves as "full-grown," and should be since they are "in Christ" (cf. 2:6). However, by considering Paul's teaching "milk for babes" they show that they are "mere infants"; they have abandoned the gospel for something that may look like "solid food" but is without nutritional value. Paul allows that they are indeed "in Christ" because they are believers after all; his concern, however, is not that they "progress" into deeper teaching from the rudimentary, but that they abandon their present "childish" behavior altogether so that they may appreciate the "milk" for what it is, "solid food."

That means, secondly, that the images of "milk" and "solid food" must also be understood in light of this antithesis. The argument of 2:6-16 implies that for Paul the gospel of the crucified one is both "milk" and "solid food." As milk it is the good news of salvation; as solid food it is understanding that the entire Christian life is predicated on the same reality—and those who have the Spirit should so understand the "mystery." Thus the Corinthians do not need a change in diet but a change in perspective. As Morna Hooker nicely puts it: "Yet while he uses their language, the fundamental contrast in Paul's mind is not between two quite different diets which he has to offer, but between the true food of the Gospel with which he has fed them (whether milk or meat) and the synthetic substitutes which the Corinthians have preferred."[18]

This imagery, therefore, is of a kind with those that have preceded; and Paul's point remains the same—to move the Corinthians from their

[15]Cf. 1 Thess. 2:7, 11; 1 Cor. 4:14-16; 2 Cor. 6:13; Gal. 4:19; Phil. 2:22; Phlm. 10.

[16]So also 13:12, although the imagery there is not quite so pejorative. There is behavior appropriate to infancy; what is not appropriate is for an adult so to behave. Cf. 14:20.

[17]The same antithesis occurs throughout chaps. 1–4. E.g., Paul affirms that they are "enriched in every way" in 1:4-5; but he says it sarcastically in 4:8. So also with the use of "wise" and "fool" in the earlier part of the argument. The wise are foolish, and the foolish wise, depending on how they hear the message of Christ crucified.

[18]"Hard sayings, I Corinthians 3:2," *Theology* 69 (1966), 21.

present fascination with wisdom back to the pure gospel of the crucified Christ. The problem, he insists, is not on his side, but on theirs. "I could not" (explain the cross as God's wisdom in mystery) "because you could not" (so understand it, given your "advancement" in the wrong direction).[19] The problem, it turns out, is not with the message at all, but with those who had put themselves in a position so as not to be able to hear and understand what was being said to them.[20]

2b-3 With the words "you were not yet able," Paul brings to a conclusion the long rehearsal of his former association with them. Both his preaching and their response to it are living evidence of the power and wisdom of the gospel. If they failed to see its wisdom, the fault was theirs, not his. Now he moves to their present situation as the evidence that the problem lay with them, not with him. He begins by repeating what he has just said, but now in the present tense. "Indeed,[21] you are still not ready," i.e. "you are not even now able."[22]

As proof that they cannot even now understand the true nature of the gospel as truly "spiritual" people should, he confronts them with their present "jealousy and quarreling." With these words he returns to the language of 1:11. To "quarreling"[23] he now adds "jealousy,"[24] which here means something close to "rivalry,"[25] as evidenced in their bickerings over their leaders. These are not the activities of those who live in the Spirit, but are the behavior of people who are still living "in the flesh."

He begins his explanation of their present inability by using the imagery with which the paragraph began. "For[26] you are still fleshly." Only now, as was pointed out above, the word has been changed to *sarkikoi*, "of the flesh," a word with clear ethical overtones. They are not only *not* giving

---

[19]Unfortunately, the NIV fails to keep the play on words that begins and ends these two sentences: "For my part I was not able (ἠδυνήθην), because you were not yet able (ἐδύνασθε)."

[20]Again, Hooker, p. 20: "The Corinthians' failure to understand the wisdom spoken in a mystery is not due to the fact that Paul is withholding it from them, but is the result of their own inability to digest what he is offering them."

[21]Gk. ἀλλά; Turner, *Syntax*, III, 330: "Introducing a strong addition, ἀλλά . . . may be *yes, indeed*."

[22]See n. 2 above.

[23]Gk. ἔρις; see on 1:10.

[24]Gk. ζῆλος. The combination also occurs in 2 Cor. 12:20; Gal. 5:20; Rom. 13:13. In Paul the word can be either positive (= "zeal") or negative, depending on the context. Here it is clearly pejorative, "the kind of zeal that does not try to help others, but to harm them, the predominant concern being for personal advancement" (A. Stumpff, *TDNT* II, 882). Cf. 13:4: "Love οὐ ζηλοῖ."

[25]So BAGD.

[26]Another explanatory γάρ. As in 2:10-12, there is here a piling up of γάρ's, one sentence giving way to the next, as one explanation follows hard on the heels of the former.

evidence of life in the Spirit, but far worse, their quarrels and rivalry confirm that their behavior belongs to the present age, with its fallen, twisted values. Whatever they may be saying about themselves, their behavior belies it. They may indeed be "spiritual"; unfortunately they are "living like the devil."

The sentence concludes with a rhetorical question that brings all of this into perspective. "For inasmuch as there are in fact rivalry and quarreling among you, is this not clear evidence that you are yet living from the old age point of view?" To make sure that they catch the proper sense of *sarkikoi,* he adds "that is,[27] are you not acting like mere men?" With this question the former paragraph and this one are now brought together. Those who do not have the Spirit are mere humans; thus they consider the cross folly. At the same time their behavior stems from a merely human, thoroughly self-centered point of view. The Corinthians have the Spirit, but are behaving precisely like people who do not, like "mere humans." Being human is not a bad thing in itself, any more than being *sarkinoi* is (v. 1). What is intolerable is to have received the Spirit, which makes one more than merely human, and to continue to live as though one were nothing more. Receiving the Spirit puts one in the new age, in which life is to be lived according to the Spirit, not according to the flesh ("sinful nature"). The verb translated "acting"[28] (lit. "walking") is used regularly in Paul for "the walk of life," that is, one's way of living (cf. 7:17). For him the basic imperative of the Christian life is "Walk [live] by the Spirit, and you will not gratify the desires of the sinful nature" (Gal. 5:16).[29] He simply has no patience for belief that does not issue in proper behavior.

4 Finally, with one more explanatory "for" Paul brings the argument back to where it began in 1:10-12. Just as in 1:11-12, their slogans specifically illustrate their quarrels, which are the evidence that they are walking according to the flesh (v. 3). In this instance, however, only the first two (Paul and Apollos) are mentioned. As argued above (1:12), not too much should be made of this. Most likely it reflects the probability that the source of much of what Paul has been arguing against up to this point stems from those who think of themselves as "following Apollos." In any case, Paul will take up these two slogans and use Apollos and himself as examples with which to correct their false view of leadership within the church.

---

[27]The καί is pleonastic in this instance: "Are you not still of the flesh, that is, are you not behaving like mere men?"

[28]Gk. περιπατεῖτε; see H. Seesemann, *TDNT* V, 944-45. See also n. 36 on 4:17.

[29]Cf. the variations on the theme in 1 Thess. 2:12; 4:1,12; 1 Cor. 7:17; Rom. 6:4; 8:1,4; 13:13; Col. 2:6; Eph. 2:10; 4:1; 5:2.

Like 2:6-16 this paragraph has had its own history of unfortunate application. Very often the text has been used in the debate over eternal salvation, or whether the saved can ever be lost. The implication is often that because these people are believers, yet "carnal," it is therefore permissible to be "carnal Christians." That, of course, is precisely the wrong application. There is no question that Paul considers his Corinthian friends believers and that they are in fact acting otherwise. But Paul's whole concern is to get them to change, not to allow that such behavior is permissible since not all Christians are yet mature. Paul's language is ironical, not permissive. The eternal destiny of such people, were they to persist in their "merely human" ways, depends on how one views the various warning texts in this letter (e.g., 6:9-11; 10:1-13). But this text is not speaking to that question. We would do well to let it carry Paul's own point, not to use it for a theological concern of our own making. Spiritual people are to walk in the Spirit. If they do otherwise, they are "worldly" and are called upon to desist. *Remaining worldly* is not one of the options.

5. Correcting a False View of Church and Ministry (3:5-17)

Although at times it may seem otherwise, the argument to this point has nonetheless been dealing with the problem of strife in the church, strife being carried on in the name of wisdom with their leaders as reference points. The argument in chap. 1 is determinative: The cross, God's wisdom, precludes all human boasting, including boasting in men. Since this wisdom is available to those who have the Spirit, the Corinthians themselves should have known it. Instead they have been carrying on from the point of view of the "flesh," as those who have missed the meaning of the cross. Their quarreling represents the old ways—living as mere humans.

At issue, however, is not simply quarreling. That was just addressed in 3:1-4 with polemic and irony. At issue is their radically misguided perception of the nature of the church and its leadership, in this case especially the role of the teachers. In a series of three paragraphs, using images from agriculture and architecture, Paul proceeds to address three closely related issues. With the farming metaphor of vv. 5-9 he takes up the question of how they are to regard their teachers, since their slogans are out. Apostles are servants, each with his own task and reward; but everything is God's—farm, workers, and the growth of crops. By implication, boasting in "mere servants of the farm" is folly in its own right. Shifting to a building metaphor (vv. 10-15), he addresses the teachers themselves, but seems to speak especially to those currently responsible for the church in Corinth. In the strongest possible terms he warns them to build the church with imperishable materials corresponding to the foundation—Christ crucified. From that warning he moves naturally (vv. 16-17) to the matter of the nature of the building itself. The church is God's temple in Corinth; they are resolutely warned against destroying it (as their present fascination with wisdom and divisions is doing).

With vv. 18-23 the argument that began at 1:10 is brought to a preliminary conclusion. Picking up the two basic strands of the argument—wisdom/folly, boasting in men—he weaves them together into a final christological-soteriological tapestry that is designed to raise them above their petty boastings. What fools these "mere humans" be, boasting in men when all things are theirs in Christ Jesus.

a. Leaders are merely servants (3:5-9)

5 *What,[1] after all, is Apollos? And what is Paul?[2] Only servants,[3] through whom you came to believe—as the Lord has assigned to each his task. 6 I planted the seed, Apollos watered it, but God made it grow. 7 So neither he who plants nor he who waters is anything, but only God, who makes things grow. 8 The man who plants and the man who waters have one purpose, and each will be rewarded according to his own labor. 9 For we are God's fellow workers; you are God's field, God's building.*

This paragraph picks up directly from the rhetorical questions that concluded vv. 1-4. Besides evidencing a misapprehension of the gospel itself, the Corinthians' slogans bespeak a totally inadequate perception of the church and its ministry. They are boasting in their individual teachers as though they could "belong" to them in some way. This paragraph attempts, by way of analogy, to disabuse them of this perception.

Apollos and Paul are "only servants," he asserts (v. 5), and by implication, therefore, not "masters" to whom they may belong. But he does not pursue that implication as such; rather, he takes up the imagery of "servant" and places it in the familiar setting of the farm, where God is at

---

[1]The MajT, supported by P46 C D F G, reads τίς in both instances ("Who . . . Who"), thus emphasizing the personalities. The context emphasizes their functions, and is therefore decisive for τί . . . τί (as is the answer in v. 7: οὐ . . . ἐστίν τι). The masculine, although very early, was probably the result of conforming to the immediately following masculine διάκονοι. See Metzger, 548, and Zuntz, 131-32.

[2]The MajT, against P46 א A B C D* F G P 048 33 81 629 1739 pc latt co, has the reverse order, "Who, then, is Paul? Who is Apollos?" This is an assimilation to v. 4, and reflects a tendency to give Paul greater prominence.

[3]The awkwardness of this sentence was mitigated in the later textual tradition by the addition of ἀλλ᾽ ἤ, so that the answer becomes part of the question in the TR. Thus the KJV: "Who then is Paul, and who is Apollos, but servants by whom ye believed, even as the Lord gave to every man?"

once both responsible for growth (vv. 6-7) and the owner of the field (v. 9). The point of the analogy is finally pressed in v. 9: Both workers and farm belong to God, who is therefore the one to whom all are accountable. But in making that point, he also stresses both the unity and diversity of the laborers. Their aim is one, the harvest; but they have differing tasks (v. 8). With this part of the analogy Paul also affirms the ministry of Apollos and absolves him of any personal role in the quarrels.

5 Not only is their boasting in Paul and Apollos evidence that they are "mere humans," and therefore not yet truly "spiritual"—in the necessary sense, where belief and behavior concur—but their boasting quite misses the point of truly Christian ministry.[4] "What, after all,[5] is Apollos? What is Paul?" This is rhetoric,[6] and it expresses disdain. "You are of Paul, or Apollos? Are they lords of some kind to whom you may attach yourselves, to whom you may belong? Do you not know, after all, what Apollos and Paul really are?"

The answer is in two parts, the second dependent on the first. First, "servants, through whom you came to believe." *Servant* is common imagery in Paul for himself and his coworkers.[7] Under a different metaphor, he will pick it up again in 4:1-5. This particular imagery controls Paul's understanding of his relationship both to his Lord and his gospel. He is God's servant, and as such is a servant of the gospel. This terminology was ready-made for him and the early church, flowing out of the teaching of Jesus himself (cf. Mark 10:41-45; Luke 22:25-27). Jesus was among them as one who served (Luke 22:27), and in the ultimate expression of servanthood "gave his life a ransom for the many" (Mark 10:45). On the other hand, the Greek attitude toward leadership is expressed by Jesus in Mark 10:42 ("their rulers lord it over them").[8] Hence the irony in Paul's response continues.

---

[4]As Munck put it: "The Corinthians have chosen to regard the Christian teachers as teachers of wisdom. Their valuation of them is at once too high and too low. Too high, because they have given them the stamp of authority without regard to their position as servants of God and Christ, and at the same time too low because they have subjected them to their own (the Corinthians') judgment" (*Paul*, p. 157).

[5]Gk. οὖν. The NIV has a nice touch here and precisely captures the force of the particle in its context. Cf. BAGD, 3 and 1cβ.

[6]Reflecting elements of the diatribe (chiasm with v. 5; rhetorical objection); cf. Conzelmann, 73.

[7]See 2 Cor. 3:6; 6:4; 11:23; Rom. 16:1; Col. 1:7, 23, 25; 4:7; Eph. 3:7; 6:21; 1 Tim. 4:6. If one were to add the noun and verb, which describe his work as "ministry," the count is even greater. Eventually it became a technical term for an "office" in the church ("deacon," Phil. 1:1; 1 Tim. 3:8). On this question see esp. Ellis, 6-15, although he tends to see the term as more specialized than the data warrant, and H. W. Beyer, *TDNT* II, 81-93.

[8]Cf. the contemptuous attitude toward serving found in Plato, in the words of Socrates' antagonist Callicles: "How can a man be happy if he is servant to anybody at all?" (*gorg.* 492b). It should be noted that some of the Cynic philosophers considered

The cross is not only the paradigm of the gospel, and of God's ways that stand in contradiction to human ways, but it also serves as the basic model for ministry. It stands as the divine contradiction to a merely human understanding of the role of leaders, such as the Corinthians were exhibiting.

Paul and Apollos were servants "through whom" the Corinthians came to believe. The aorist of the verb "believed" refers to their point of conversion. This would naturally refer to Paul's own ministry among them, as the following imagery indicates, but it has no intention of excluding Apollos. Rather, the emphasis is on the fact that the Corinthians did not believe *in* Paul or Apollos, but *through* them came to believe in Christ.

The clause that forms the second part of the answer is abbreviated, and therefore somewhat ambiguous. Literally it says, "and to each one as the Lord gave." The difficulty lies with "to each." Does this refer to the gift of faith given to each of the Corinthians who came to believe through the ministry of the servants,[9] or to the differing tasks given to the servants themselves (as the NIV)? The context demands the latter. Paul is thus anticipating the division of labor that he will speak to in vv. 6-8, and means something like: "and each servant worked according to the task given him by Christ himself."[10] His concern is twofold: (1) that they recognize that the differences between Apollos and himself, which had become occasions for strife, are in fact Christ-appointed for their *common good;* and (2) that they focus not on the servants, but on the Lord himself, whose servants they are all to be. Both of these points will now be elaborated in detail by means of the agricultural analogy that follows.

6 The analogy itself is general and does not necessarily presuppose a certain kind of farming (grains or vineyard).[11] As v. 9 and the rest of the

---

themselves servants to other Cynics and in the "service of God." See, e.g., Epict. 3.22.63-109, although his "service" was not in ministering directly to the needs of others but in keeping himself aloof so as to render greater service by "having leisure for the public interest." This is a far cry from Paul's use of the imagery.

[9]Implied in the KJV: "even as the Lord gave to every man," and probably in the NASB: "even as the Lord gave *opportunity* to each one"; cf. TCNT: "and that only as the Lord helped each of you." No English, German, or French commentator seems to have opted for this interpretation (MacArthur is based on the NASB, but does not comment on this clause).

[10]Taking ὁ κύριος to refer to Christ, as it almost always does when used absolutely.

[11]Although H. Riesenfeld thinks otherwise, noting that the use of γεώργιος in the LXX ordinarily reflects a vineyard, and the frequent use of this image for Israel made it a natural in this case. See "Parabolic Language in the Pauline Epistles," in *The Gospel Tradition* (ET, Philadelphia, 1970), pp. 197-99. Analogies of various kinds from farming are well known in antiquity, not least from Jesus himself. The fourth-century sophist Libanius uses language almost identical to Paul's first two lines: "I planted the good seed; you water it; the world plucks its fruit" (cf. Loeb, I, 33).

argument indicate, Paul is not thinking of the conversion of individual Corinthians, but of the planting of the church as such (v. 9, "you [plural] are God's field"). There are four particulars: (1) the one who "planted the seed" = Paul who founded the church; (2) the one who "watered (or irrigated, cultivated) it" = Apollos who continued a teaching ministry among them; (3) the one who "made it grow"[12] = God, to whom they all belong (v. 9); and (4) the "field" or farm = the church in Corinth. The analogy itself therefore functions both to affirm the ministry of Apollos and to put Paul and Apollos on equal footing from the perspective of their mutual servanthood. At the same time, as the application in v. 7 indicates, it is intended to redirect their focus from the servants to the one God, whom both equally serve, and to whom they all belong.[13]

7 The first application of the analogy is signaled by the strong inferential conjunction "so then,"[14] and moves Paul back to the argument of vv. 4 and 5. In effect, it further elaborates the first part of the answer to the rhetorical questions of v. 5: "only servants, through whom you came to believe." The problem in Corinth is with perspective. They are viewing things from below, and as a result think altogether too highly of their teachers. In response to that perspective, the questions "What, after all, is Apollos? And what is Paul?" are answered with a resounding "Nothing!" As the final clause of v. 5 and its corresponding elaboration in v. 8 reveal, this is not the only thing to be said. Paul and Apollos do have essential tasks to perform, for which they will receive their own rewards. But they have no independent importance;[15] from the perspective of ultimate responsibility for the Corinthians' existence as the people of God, Paul and Apollos count for nothing. Without God's prior activity bringing them to faith and causing them to grow, there is no church at all. Hence the point is clear: Stop quarreling over those whose tasks are nothing in comparison with the activity of God.[16] Focus on him alone, for he alone saves and sanctifies.

8 With this sentence Paul moves to a second application of the analogy of v. 6, which corresponds to the second part of the answer in v. 5: "as the Lord has assigned to each his task." For the Corinthians' ultimate

[12]The change to the imperfect should not be missed, as the NIV tends to. The NASB, however, is too stilted: "but God was causing the growth." The imperfect implies that God was in the activity of both, and continues to be so even now.

[13]As Conzelmann, 73, comments (although I would put less emphasis on "party" as such): "The result of this conception of [ministry] is to break up both the Paul party and the Apollos party alike. Both lose their heads."

[14]Gk. ὥστε. The argumentative nature of this epistle calls forth this conjunction, used in this way, several times: 3:21; 4:5; 5:8; 7:38; 10:12; 11:27, 33; 14:22, 39; 15:58; cf. Phil. 2:12. For this usage see Moule, 144.

[15]The language is Barrett's (p. 85).

[16]In Paul's sentence the word θεός functions in apposition to the substantive ὁ αὐξάνων: "but the one who makes things grow—God."

existence as a church, God alone counts. Those over whom the Corinthians are bickering only serve under God. Therefore, *their* mutual concern is singular: the growth of the crop to a rich harvest. This point is not spelled out that clearly in Paul's own language, but in keeping with the analogy makes the only logical sense of "he who plants and he who waters are one."[17] In putting it in this language, of course, Paul emphasizes the mutuality of himself and Apollos, probably over against the divisiveness that the Corinthians would bring to their ministries.

If the first half of this verse emphasizes the *unity* of their (Paul's and Apollos's) individual labors, the second half emphasizes their *diversity*, as in vv. 5b and 6. But it does so not by differentiating the tasks, but in terms of pay: each being "rewarded according to his own labor." In the context of the analogy, Paul's present point is not immediately obvious. Probably it emphasizes again the servant nature of the workers. They labor under another who also determines their pay. If so, it anticipates the argument of 4:1-5 that disallows the Corinthians to judge another's servant. But the *language* here also anticipates the argument to follow, that each worker is to take care how he/she builds (v. 10b), since fire will test the work of each and thereby determine the reward (vv. 13-15). In this case Paul is less concerned about himself and Apollos as such, although that is not to be discounted, as he is about those who are currently "at work" in the church in Corinth. For the significance of "reward" in Paul, see the comment on v. 14.

9   With an explanatory "for,"[18] Paul picks up the main points of the analogy (that Paul and Apollos are workers together in a common cause and belong to God, and that the Corinthians, therefore, do not belong to Paul and Apollos because they, too, belong to God) and drives them home with terse, but pointed, epigrams: "We are God's fellow workers; you are God's field." At the same time he shifts images, "You are God's building,"[19] and

---

[17] Thus the "have one purpose" of the NIV captures the sense of the language in the context of the analogy; cf. NAB: "work to the same end," and NEB, "they work as a team." The latter puts a bit more emphasis on their being equal, as does the RSV ("are equal").

[18] This γάρ may also be causal, giving the grounds for the preceding statements. There has been some debate over its precise reference point, v. 8a or 8b. But as Conzelmann, 74, notes, that is an unnecessary disjuncture. More likely, given the second clause ("You the church are God's field"), it reaches back through v. 8 to embrace the entire argument of the paragraph.

[19] For the significance of this metaphor in Paul, see n. 16 on v. 10. Some (e.g., Conzelmann, 74-75; Riesenfeld, "Parabolic Language," p. 199) have noted the juxtaposition of these two images in Judaism (see Jer. 1:10; 24:6; Sir. 49:7; cf. Jesus' own parables of planting and building). But it is doubtful whether any of this influenced Paul here. The images are common ones; given its greater frequency in his letters, he seems more comfortable with the image of building than that of farming, which probably reflects his urban rather than rural upbringing.

thus sets in motion a new argument, which will be spelled out in vv. 10-15 and 16-17.

In speaking of himself and Apollos as "fellow workers," Paul uses another of his favorite terms to describe those who labor with him in ministry.[20] Usually it refers to someone who has worked as Paul's companion; here he extends the term to refer to another who in a more distant way joins him in the ministry of the gospel. In the Greek text the emphasis is altogether on God: "God's we are, being fellow workers; God's field, God's building, you are." Some have suggested that Paul here intends, as the KJV has it, "we are laborers together *with* God."[21] But everything in the context speaks against it: The emphatic position of the genitive ("God's") suggests possession,[22] as do the following, equally emphatic, genitives, which are unambiguously possessive; the argument of the whole paragraph emphasizes their unity in fellow labor *under* God, an argument that would be undercut considerably if he were now emphasizing that they worked *with* God in Corinth; and finally, these new "slogans" serve as the climax of the whole paragraph, in which the emphasis is decidedly on God's ownership, not on Paul's and Apollos's working with him in Corinth.

Thus the whole paragraph is tersely summarized with these emphatic words. Everything is God's—the church, its ministry, Paul, Apollos—everything. Therefore, it is absolutely not permissible to say "I belong to Paul," since the only legitimate "slogan" is "we all belong to God."

Because the imagery of ministry presented here is so common in Paul, and because it so clearly reflects the teaching of Jesus as well, one may be certain that Paul would intend these words to go beyond their particular historical circumstances to apply to the church at all times in all settings. Whatever *form* ministry finally takes, and on that we have been divided for centuries, there can be no mistake as to its *nature*—servanthood, of the kind exhibited by the Lord himself and his apostle. There simply is no other paradigm.

Paul's points need regularly to be underscored, both for clergy and laity alike. The church belongs to its Lord, and to him alone; and its ministers must function in his church in the posture of servants. Paul's intent here of course is to correct a misguided perception of ministry on the part of a church that was making too much of its ministers. Our need to hear it

---

[20]Gk. συνεργός. Cf. 1 Thess. 3:2; 2 Cor. 1:24; 8:23; Phil. 2:25; 4:3; Col. 4:11; Phlm. 1, 24. On the use of this term in Paul, see G. Bertram, *TDNT* VII, 874-75, and Ellis, 5-7.

[21]E.g., Godet, 177; Morris, 66; and more recently, Ellis, 6.

[22]The "with" comes from the σύν in συνεργός. Paul's usage elsewhere makes this a plausible meaning; but here the context is absolutely determinative. See V. P. Furnish, "'Fellow Workers in God's Service,'" *JBL* 80 (1961), 364-70.

probably reflects the same realities, although most would think of themselves as above the Corinthian attitude.

All too often those "in charge," be they clergy, boards, vestry, sessions, or what have you, tend to think of the church as "theirs." They pay lip-service to its being "Christ's church, after all," then proceed to operate on the basis of very pagan, secular structures, and regularly speak of "my" or "our" church. Nor does the church belong to the people, especially those who have "attended all their lives," or who have "supported it with great sums of money," as though that gave them special privileges. The church belongs to Christ, and all other things—structures, attitudes, decisions, nature of ministry, everything—should flow out of that singular realization.

Moreover, those "in charge" must be ever mindful of who is really in charge. To be a servant does *not* mean the abdication of leadership, nor, on the other hand, does it mean to become everyone's "errand boy or girl." It has to do with attitude, perspective, not with one's place on the organizational chart. And as Paul will make clear in 4:8-17, it must be "like priest, like people." Servant leadership is required precisely because servanthood is the basic stance of all truly Christian behavior.

b. The church must be built with care (3:10-15)

10 *By the grace God[1] has given me, I laid[2] a foundation as an expert builder, and[3] someone else is building on it. But each one should be careful how he builds.* 11 *For no one can lay any foundation other than the one already laid, which is Jesus Christ.* 12 *If anyone[4] builds on this[5] foundation using gold, silver,[6] costly stones,*

[1]The τοῦ θεοῦ is missing in P46 0142 81 1962 2495 pc b f vgmss Clement. Metzger, 549, argues that "the words were eliminated as repetitious." Zuntz, 47, on the other hand, argues for an interpolation by the majority on the basis of Pauline style (when referring to "grace" as a particular charism bestowed on an individual [Rom. 12:3; Gal. 2:9], he does not include the genitive). "God" is the implied subject of the passive verb (hence the NIV), so the net result is the same in either case, although Zuntz probably has the better of it in terms of the original text.

[2]D and the MajT have replaced the ἔθηκα with the perfect τέθεικα, thus emphasizing its enduring condition. The original conforms to the aorist in v. 6, and refers to Paul's founding visit.

[3]P46 D 1827 omit the δέ. Zuntz, 189, argues that this is the original, the δέ being a "natural addition." This, he argues, "adds enormously to the emphasis of Paul's words." The clauses would thus punctuate: ". . . as an expert builder. Someone else is building on it: let each one take care. . . ." Although this is persuasively argued, the overwhelming MS evidence on the other side gives good reason to pause.

[4]NIV "any man," which is unnecessarily sexist, and not found in the Greek text.

[5]A "this" is found in most of the early versional evidence, as well as in D and the MajT. One cannot tell whether the NIV is translating this text, or whether the "this" is "versional" here as well. In any case, the τοῦτον is secondary and deflects Paul's emphasis, which is no longer on the foundation but the superstructure.

[6]On the variants χρυσόν/χρυσίον, ἄργυρον/ἀργύριον see Zuntz, 133, 209. χρυσόν and ἄργυρον are to be preferred.

wood, hay or straw, 13 each person's[7] *work will be shown for what it is, because the Day will bring it[8] to light. It will be revealed with fire, and the fire will test the quality of each* person's[9] *work.* 14 *If what he has built survives, he will receive his reward.* 15 *If it is burned up, he will suffer loss; he himself will be saved, but only as one escaping through the flames.*

At the end of the preceding analogy Paul made an abrupt change of metaphors (to "God's building"), which he now sets out to elaborate. At the same time, though dealing still with the same general topic of the church and its leadership, he clearly shifts emphasis. Picking up the theme of each one's being "rewarded according to his own labor" (v. 8b), he is concerned to warn, in the strongest possible language, those who are currently "building the church." The paragraph opens with the imagery itself (v. 10a), followed immediately by the warning (v. 10b). After returning to his role and emphasizing again the heart of his gospel—Jesus Christ (v. 11), he then uses the imagery in striking fashion to urge them to build with imperishable materials (vv. 12-13) because there will come a day when each person's work will be tested and his/her reward thereby determined (vv. 14-15).

The paragraph is dominated by the indefinite pronouns "someone else," "no one," "each one," and "anyone."[10] Since Apollos is not mentioned, and since the urgency both here and in the further application of the metaphor that follows (vv. 16-17) is specifically with what was happening in the church at the time of Paul's writing, the particulars therefore shift from Paul and Apollos to Paul and those responsible for the current "wood, hay or straw" of *sophia* (wisdom). Thus the argument continues to be a frontal attack against the division and those primarily responsible for it.[11]

Here is another paragraph that has suffered much in the church (cf. 2:6-16; 3:1-4): from those who would decontextualize it in terms of individualistic popular piety (i.e., how I build my own Christian life on Christ),[12] to

---

[7]NIV, "his." See n. 4.

[8]A large number of MSS omit this αὐτό (incl. P[46] ℵ D latt Maj), most likely because it looks like an unnecessary intrusion. See Zuntz, 132; cf. Metzger, 549. An "addition" in this case almost certainly would have followed the verb. It is also possible that Paul intended the intensive "the fire itself," but as Conzelmann, 71 n. 19, points out, one cannot see why, since there is no emphasis on fire in the passage.

[9]NIV, "man's." See n. 4.

[10]Gk. ἄλλος once (v. 10); οὐδείς once (v. 11); ἕκαστος three times (vv. 10, 13 [2x]); τις three times (vv. 12, 14, 15).

[11]C. W. Fishburne ("I Corinthians III. 10-15 and the Testament of Abraham," *NTS* 17 [1969/70], 109-15) suggests that the central point of this analogy is the same as that of vv. 5-9, but that Paul *also* issues a warning along the way (see pp. 109 and 114). This seems to miss rather widely both the reason for the change of metaphors and the urgency of the present paragraph.

[12]A perspective still expressed, e.g., in the popular expositions by Barclay, Prior, and MacArthur.

certain Protestants who have used it as grist for the Calvinist-Arminian debate over the security of the believer, to those in the Roman Catholic tradition who have found in it the single piece of NT evidence for the doctrine of purgatory. Paul addresses none of these issues, not even indirectly. His concern is singular, that those currently leading the church take heed because their present work will not stand the fiery test to come, having shifted from the imperishable "stuff" of Jesus Christ and him crucified.[13]

10 The opening sentences of the paragraph form a chiasm:

A Paul laid the foundation for the church;
  B Someone else is now building on it;
  B' But let that "someone" take care how he/she builds;
A' The foundation Paul laid is Jesus Christ.

Together these sentences set out the particulars of the new analogy (lines A and B)[14] and state its point by warning the builders (line B') and by specifying the foundation on which they are to build (line A').

Three of the particulars remain the same as in the preceding analogy.[15] (1) The church in Corinth, not the individual Christian, is the building,[16] and (2) God is the owner (v. 9). (3) Paul again is presented as the founder of the church, in this analogy as the one who "laid a foundation as an expert builder." He defines/elaborates this task in two ways, and even here anticipates the greater concern of the paragraph.

First, he did so "according to the *charis* (grace) given him." Although this might be a general allusion to God's prior act of grace in Christ Jesus as it relates to his apostolic ministry (cf. 15:9-10), more likely, as in 1:4, "grace" refers to a specific charism "given me" by God. Here it would

---

[13]For a succinct but helpful expression of the position taken here, cf. K. Donfried, "Justification and Last Judgment in Paul," *Int* 30 (1976), 148-49.

[14]As with the preceding analogy, this is a common one in antiquity, ready at hand for Paul's own adaptation. See, e.g., Epict. 2.15.8 ("Do you not wish to make your beginning and your foundation [θεμέλιον] firm, . . . and only after you have done that proceed to rear thereon [ἐποικοδομεῖν] the structure of your determination?" Loeb, I, 317); and Philo, *somn.* 2.8 ("So much by way of a foundation [θεμελίων]. As we go on to build the superstructure [ἐποικοδομῶμεν] let us follow the directions of Allegory, that wise Master-builder [σοφῆς ἀρχιτέκτονος]"; Loeb, V, 445, 447). Cf. further Philo, *gig.* 30; *mut.nom.* 211; Plutarch, *Fort.Rom.* 320b.

[15]As argued below, the fourth particular changes from Apollos to those in Corinth responsible for promoting "wisdom."

[16]Gk. οἰκοδομή; used also as an analogy for the church in Eph. 2:21. The Greek word has the same noun/verb ambiguity that one finds in the English word "building," which can refer either to the finished product or to the process. In v. 9 it refers to the church as the "structure," which is then specified in v. 16 as the temple of God. In vv. 10-15 the emphasis lies on the process of "building" the building (the verb ἐποικοδομέω is repeated four times). Elsewhere in 1 Corinthians the simple verb (οἰκοδομέω) and the noun οἰκοδομή are used for the concept of "building up, edifying" the church (1 Cor. 8:1, 10; 10:23; 14:3-5, 12, 17, 26).

refer especially to his apostolic task of founding churches. This is what makes him an apostle as far as the Corinthian church in particular is concerned, a point to which he feels compelled to return regularly (see 4:15-17; 9:1-2; 2 Cor. 3:1-3; 10:12-16; cf. Rom. 15:20). In either case, the specific notation of "grace given" continues the emphasis from vv. 5-9 on God as the primary ground of their existence.

Second, he laid the foundation "as an expert (*sophos* = 'wise') builder."[17] This choice of words is directly related to the context and especially to what he has just argued in 2:6-16. By laying the foundation he did—Jesus Christ and him crucified—he was the truly "wise" master-builder in contrast to the "wise" in Corinth,[18] who are building the church of totally incongenial materials and are therefore in danger of attempting to lay another foundation as well. This latter point will be elaborated in v. 11; but before that he gives the fourth particular in the analogy: "someone else is building on it."

With this clause, and especially with its accompanying warning "but each one should be careful how he/she builds," Paul is once again directing his aim at the Corinthians themselves, and in particular those who are leading the way in their strife and divisions.[19] That he does not now intend Apollos,[20] or Peter,[21] seems certain from various strands of evidence: First, that would contradict what he has just said in vv. 5-9, where he sees Apollos and himself as "one in a common cause" (v. 8), each of whom has been given his own task from the Lord himself. Second, the warning of the paragraph would fall on deaf ears, since Apollos is not now in Corinth (6:12); it seems too indirect for Paul somehow to want the Corinthians to catch such a warning so that they would not exalt Apollos too highly. Third, Apollos is not mentioned in the paragraph, as he is in the preceding one.

---

[17]Gk. ἀρχιτέκτων, a word that, as the papyrus and inscriptional evidence put forward in MM indicates, refers not simply to a "carpenter," τέκτων, but to the one who serves as both architect and chief engineer. Hence the rendering "master-builder" in many modern translations (RSV, NAB, NASB, NEB). The word is also found in Isa. 3:3 (LXX); cf. Philo, *somn.* 2.8.

[18]A point missed by the otherwise adequate rendering of the NIV.

[19]Cf. Munck (*Paul,* pp. 150-51): "Paul therefore does not contrast himself with the other Christian leaders who have performed a task in Corinth after him. . . . [Rather], the Corinthians and the apostle are contrasted with each other. The apostle has laid the proper foundation, . . . but it is of decisive importance how the Corinthians continue to build on it." Among the commentaries, see Goudge, R-P, Parry, Holladay, O-W, although the latter mysteriously miss the specific context of chaps. 1–4.

[20]This is a common view; cf., e.g., Lightfoot, Weiss, Lietzmann, Mare. Grosheide, Senft, and others see it as a more general description of any and all who followed Paul in Corinth.

[21]See n. 44 on 1:12. Among commentators it is given a favorable hearing by Moffatt, Craig, Barrett, and Bruce.

Finally, everything in the analogy, including what has been said about Paul as the "wise" master-builder, Jesus Christ as the foundation, and the warnings of vv. 13-15, points to a direct confrontation between Paul and the church over their stance on "wisdom." This is confirmed by the further direct application of the imagery to them in vv. 16-17. Thus the indefinite pronouns refer to the Corinthians themselves and the whole point of the analogy is to warn them of the consequences of persisting on their present course.

11 This sentence is something of an intrusion into the analogy proper,[22] which has to do with the superstructure now being built (vv. 12-15) on Paul's properly laid foundation, not with whether they are actually laying another foundation as such. But if it intrudes into the analogy (as a fifth particular, not available nor a concern in the preceding one), it is not an intrusion into the argument. The sentence functions in two ways: to remind the Corinthians once again of the argument to this point, and to anticipate the following elaboration by insisting that the reason for care in building the superstructure is related to the character of the foundation.

This sentence seems to be sure evidence that he is once again addressing his argument directly toward the Corinthians themselves, who by their pursuit of *sophia* are leading the church toward total destruction (cf. v. 17).[23] Not only must they take care how they build the superstructure, but they are also reminded that there cannot be "any foundation other than[24] the one already laid, which is Jesus Christ." The foundation is not proper doctrine,[25] the concern of a later period, but the gospel itself, with its basic content of salvation through Jesus Christ. Since this seems so clearly to hark back to the argument of 1:18–2:16, we may rightly assume that he intends them to hear "Jesus Christ and him crucified" (1:23; 2:2).

---

[22]Even the γάρ ("for") that joins the clause to v. 10 is less easy to account for. It undoubtedly has in the first instance a causal relationship to the last clause of v. 10 (line B'); but in terms of the analogy proper that does not follow, since the point of the warning is "building upon" the foundation, not the laying of the foundation itself. Its function, therefore, must be to point forward to the rest of the analogy as it is elaborated in v. 12, and thus the emphasis is on "Jesus Christ."

[23]Some have seen this sentence as an allusion to Peter (see n. 21), in light of the logion in Matt. 16:18, that "on this rock will I build my church," which it is argued was the perspective being promoted by the so-called Cephas-party. But not only does this make the unwarranted assumption that a logion peculiar to Matthew's Gospel would have been known in a Pauline church, but it also implies that the foundation has to do with personalities (Paul, Peter, etc.) rather than with the gospel vis-à-vis *sophia*, which seems to be more in keeping with the context of the argument as a whole.

[24]Gk. παρὰ τὸν κείμενον. The παρά here is comparative, following ἄλλος (BAGD, III.3). The present τὸν κείμενον probably implies something like "the one already in place." Cf. Barrett, 87.

[25]Suggested at times in commentaries. See, e.g., Mare, 207.

12 With the words "if anyone is building[26] on the foundation," Paul proceeds to elaborate the second part of v. 10, the identification of the fourth particular in the analogy and its accompanying warning. This is the primary concern of the paragraph. However, it flows out of the momentary digression in v. 11, with its emphasis on the gospel of Christ crucified. The point is that the quality of the superstructure must be appropriate to the foundation.

But what did Paul intend by listing the six building materials, "gold, silver, costly stones, wood, hay or straw"? Regarding this question several observations should be made: (1) The analogy itself, and especially this list of materials, easily lends itself to allegory; and such have been forthcoming on a regular basis in the church. But Paul's own point lies elsewhere. He did not "mean" anything by "gold" or "straw" as such. (2) The concern of the metaphor is not in this instance with the building per se, but with those who are doing the building. Therefore, any application of the "meaning" of the materials must be consonant with that concern, and with Paul's own explicit statements. (3) Although this is indeed a "studied scale of descending value,"[27] Paul's own use of the analogy makes no point of it. Nor does he place emphasis on the "value" (i.e., costliness) of the first three in contrast to the last three. His own elaboration in vv. 13-15 picks up a singular theme, namely that some materials endure fire while others are consumed. His concern, then, is not with the individual items, but with the *imperishable* quality of some over against the others. (4) With Paul's own concern in view, and in light of the context of the argument as a whole, one may rightly argue, therefore, that for Paul the "gold, silver, and costly stones" represent what is compatible with the foundation, the gospel of Jesus Christ and him crucified; what will perish is *sophia* in all of its human forms. It belongs only to this age, and this age is passing away, along with all that belongs to it.[28] (5) Finally, it is probably not irrelevant that "gold, silver, and costly stones" recur regularly in the OT to describe the building materials of the Temple.[29] Therefore, Paul does not have some "fabulous building"[30] in view, but the

[26]The conditional sentence here is almost certainly a particular, not a general, supposition, and should be so translated. Paul's concern is not with what at any time might occur "if ever anyone builds," but with what is actually, or presumably, going on in Corinth at the present time. On this matter see Burton, *Moods,* p. 101.

[27]BDF 461 (p. 241).

[28]It is simply to press the analogy too hard to say, e.g., as does Gromacki (p. 48): "Since the foundation is a person, then the materials must also be persons." That may seem logical, but it scarcely recognizes the nature and function of metaphor. Furthermore, when that interpretation is pressed, it creates some strange conclusions for vv. 14-15.

[29]They occur in various combinations: "gold and silver" frequently (cf. Hag. 2:8), as in 1 Chr. 22:14, 16, which also mentions "stones," but not "precious stones"; 1 Chr. 29:2 has "gold, silver, and fine stone"; 2 Chr. 3:6 has "gold and precious stones."

[30]This is the language of Conzelmann, 76. Again he is too enamored by Greek sources; the context and Paul's own Jewish background are determinative here.

OT description of Solomon's temple, thus anticipating the imagery of vv. 16-17.[31]

13 The rest of the paragraph now explains the warning of v. 10b in light of the imagery of v. 12. A day of judgment is coming, and it will test everyone's "building," that is, *how* one has built, whether of perishable or imperishable materials. The test, with its resultant disclosure of the quality of the materials, will determine the reward. The fact of the sure and, from Paul's perspective, soon-to-come Day of Judgment serves as the *ground* of the warning, just as it will serve in 4:3-5 as the ground for their not judging him. Perhaps one also finds here an accent on the *future* reality of the judgment, in light of their own enchantment with present "spirituality."

The first part of v. 13, as the NIV indicates, is the conclusion (apodosis) of Paul's conditional sentence. In this kind of condition the apodosis states the obvious conclusion to the supposition found in the protasis (the "if" part of the clause).[32] Paul simply affirms what for him is a self-evident reality, that the kind of building one constructs, that is, the kind of "stuff" that goes into the workmanship,[33] will eventually be clearly seen[34] for what it is. The rest of the verse gives the eschatological grounds for this conviction.[35]

Paul begins by emphasizing the element of "exposure" that the previous sentence had asserted. As "day" brings everything "to light," so a great Day is lying before all, when everyone's work will be exposed and seen from the divine perspective. The "Day," of course, refers to *the* Day (cf. 1:8), the OT Day of the Lord, a term taken over by Jewish apocalyptic

---

[31]This also determines the debate over λίθους τιμίους, whether it means building stones as such (e.g., marble) or the precious gems that adorn the Temple. The LXX uses this combination in the singular to refer to costly construction stones (e.g., 1 Chr. 29:2, "all kinds of fine stone and marble"), but the plural in 2 Chr. 3:6 for adorning the Temple "with precious stones."

[32]This type of conditional sentence is of the same category as "If you stand out in the rain, you will get wet." No surprises, just common sense. If the one condition prevails, then the other is inevitable.

[33]The word for the building process, ἔργον ("work"), carries the same ambiguity as the word "building" (see n. 16 above). The word often appears in Paul to denote what he and others do in serving Christ and the gospel (e.g., 1 Thess. 5:13; 1 Cor. 9:1; 15:58; 16:10; Rom. 15:18; Phil. 2:30); cf. κόπος and κοπάω. In this case ἔργον means something close to "workmanship," with a view especially to the final product of the working process.

[34]Gk. φανερὸν γενήσεται; the two other occurrences of this combination in 1 Corinthians (11:19; 14:25) imply the revealing in the present (by the Spirit) of what has been hidden; the usage here is eschatological, as the rest of the paragraph makes plain.

[35]Fishburne, "I Corinthians III. 10-15," has argued that Paul is dependent on the Testament of Abraham 13. The crucial point of the argument, of course, is the dating and provenance of the Testament. On this matter he is less than convincing and has overlooked some crucial sources that point in the other direction. See E. P. Sanders, "Testament of Abraham," in OTP, I, 871-80.

and then by Christians to express their conviction that a time for ultimate divine justice lay still in the future. For Christians that day was made more certain because divine judgment, as well as the life of the future, had already begun in the death and resurrection of Jesus Christ.[36]

But the "revelation" of one's workmanship is not Paul's real concern with this imagery, so he quickly moves on to an accompanying metaphor, "fire." Fire not only "reveals," it also "tests," and in the testing the true revelation takes place (vv. 14-15). There are two grammatical difficulties with the first clause: the present tense of the verb ("it is being revealed") and the lack of an expressed subject: either he intends "the work of each" or "the Day." The two items are interrelated and are of ready solution. Almost certainly he intended "the Day" to be the subject of the verb;[37] otherwise the next clause is redundant. That means that the whole clause functions in Paul's sentence as a general maxim, which the second clause picks up and applies to the argument. Thus he says: "For the Day of Judgment will expose every person's workmanship, whether gospel or *sophia,* because that Day, when it comes, manifests itself[38] with fire; and the fire will test the quality of each person's work."

"Fire" was a natural motif that came to be associated with judgment; it occurs throughout the literature of Judaism, especially in the prophetic and apocalyptic traditions.[39] The imagery can refer either to "purifying" or to "testing." The language here, and its further application in vv. 14-15, makes it clear that Paul's concern is the "testing" quality of fire. It will not "purify" the worker (see on v. 15); rather, it will judge his/her workmanship to see whether it has been made of "quality" material.

14-15 With a set of antithetical parallels, plus an additional explanation at the end of the second one, Paul spells out the results of the "testing by fire." The two kinds of material listed in v. 12 serve as the points of reference. On the one hand, those who stay with the gospel as Paul preached it, who build the church in Corinth with "gold, silver, and costly stones,"

---

[36]Cf. 1:8. Paul has various expressions for this "Day." For him it involves the Parousia, the resurrection, and judgment. Hence it is above all "the day of the Lord" (1 Thess. 5:2 [cf. v. 4!]; 2 Thess. 2:2; 1 Cor. 5:5), which OT term he transformed into "the day of our Lord Jesus (Christ)" (1:8; 2 Cor. 1:14; Phil. 1:6, 10; 2:16). Although there is no distinction in these terms as to what aspect of the future Paul is emphasizing, that of judgment tends to dominate. See G. Delling, *TDNT* II, 943-53; cf. H. Ridderbos, *Paul,* pp. 551-62; G. Vos, *The Pauline Eschatology* (Grand Rapids, 1961), pp. 261-87.

[37]A few commentaries (e.g., Parry) take τὸ ἔργον to be the subject, but they do not really wrestle with the grammar, nor the distinct flow of Paul's thought.

[38]Taking the verb to be a middle (as Grosheide), rather than a passive. The alternative, expressed by R-P, is to translate "The day is (to be) revealed in fire," expressing "a common use of the present tense, to indicate that a coming event is so certain that it may be spoken of as already here" (p. 63).

[39]Paul himself uses it in apocalyptic fashion in 2 Thess. 1:8. For the biblical use of the metaphor for judgment, see *TDNT* VI, 928-52 (F. Lang).

will see their work "survive" the test, and they "will receive their reward."
On the other hand, those who persist in pursuing *sophia,* who are building
with "wood, hay, or straw," will see their work consumed and they themselves "will suffer loss"—although their loss, he is quick to qualify, does
not refer to their salvation.

The theme of "reward" harks back to v. 8, and suggests that appropriate "pay" will be given for appropriate labor. For some this has been a
difficult idea to reconcile with Paul's gospel of grace, God's *unmerited* favor
being lavished on the *undeserving.* How can grace receive "pay"? The
answer to this is complex, since Paul is a complex man. But the solution is to
be found in two directions: First, on this matter Paul reflects his Jewish
heritage and stands in thoroughgoing opposition to the Hellenistic world.[40]
The difference between Paul and his heritage is that for him the "reward" is
"according to grace," not "according to obligation" (Rom. 4:4-5). The
very concept of eschatology, with its final salvation and judgment, had
inherent in it the concept of final "reward." But the "reward" is not deserved, even though it is according to "works" (i.e., based in part on what
one has done); rather, it too is part of the gift. Second, and very importantly,
Paul stood just as firmly over against every form of libertinism and nonethical "spirituality" as he did against every form of legalism. Salvation for him
was both "now" and "not yet." What began in the present as gift is to be
persevered in, righteously, and thus consummated at the final glory, which
is also a gift. For Paul righteousness is both *Gabe* and *Aufgabe* (gift and
responsibility). Without the latter, one might surely question the reality of
the former. But, again, both are gifts.[41] Thus, as surely as there is final
judgment, there are also "reward" and "loss." What is *not* known, either
from this passage or elsewhere, is the nature of the reward.[42] This text only
affirms its certainty.

The nature of the loss,[43] however, is determined by the context. First
of all, one's work itself "is burned up." In this context that must refer in

[40]On this matter, and others in this paragraph, see H. Preisker and E. Würthwein, *TDNT* IV, 695-728.

[41]See further Donfried, "Justification," pp. 140-52.

[42]However, cf. 4:5, where the final verdict is to "receive praise from God."
What more reward, one wonders in the context of bounteous grace, could one desire than
the pronouncement of "Well done, good and faithful servant" by the Master (Matt. 25:21,
23)? Even here, however, there is the implication of something more. Cf. 5:5 n. 33.

[43]The verb ζημιωθήσεται can mean either "to be punished" (the choice of
BAGD) or "suffer loss or damage." All other occurrences in the NT carry the second
meaning, including Paul in 2 Cor. 7:9 and Phil. 3:8. Since the context, and especially the
stylistic feature of antithetic parallels, also favor this meaning, one is hard-pressed to find
any good reason for the former meaning here. Parry, 67, translates "he will be fined,"
keeping the metaphor of "work" and "pay" (cf. Lightfoot, followed *inter alia* by R-P and
Barrett, "mulcted of his pay"). But that emphasizes the wrong aspect of the metaphor,
which is not "work," but the "fire" of judgment.

some way to the church itself, which, as v. 17 goes on to warn, is in the process of being destroyed by the Corinthians' *sophia* and divisions. Again, the precise nature of that "loss" is not spelled out. The "destruction" in v. 17 seems to imply the church's failure to function any longer as a viable alternative to Corinth, by manifesting the nature and fruit of the gospel within totally pagan surroundings. In such a case, there will also be terrible loss on the Day of Judgment, in which many who thought of themselves as God's people are revealed to be otherwise. As for the "workers" involved, they also, by implication, suffer loss of "reward," whatever that will be.

To clarify further that it is the "work" that is consumed (because it was built of perishable material) and not the laborer herself/himself, Paul adds a final quasi-proverbial note: "He himself will be saved, but only as one escaping through the flames."[44] This sentence is often seen as expressing a purifying element to the judgment, and has served as the NT support for the concept of purgatory.[45] But that is to miss Paul by a wide margin. This is metaphor, pure and simple,[46] probably reflecting something like Amos's "firebrand plucked from the burning" (4:11).[47] The implication is that the person persisting in his present course of "worldly wisdom" is in grave danger, and that he "will be pulled out of his rubble heap just in the nick of time."[48]

Thus Paul is not so much making a soteriological statement as he is warning his Corinthian friends. He obviously, as elsewhere (e.g., 6:11), sees them as within the context of the faith; salvation after all is by grace, not by one's own works. But also as elsewhere he expects the warnings to be

---

[44]Chrysostom, *hom. 9 in 1 Cor.*, argues that this means that he will be preserved in the fire of hell, so that he will not experience annihilation. But this was to preserve his own prior understanding of the analogy. The verb σώζω in this context will not sustain a nonsoteriological meaning.

[45]This understanding of the text goes back at least as far as Origen. For the full discussion of the patristic data, see J. Gnilka, *Ist I Cor. 3,10-15 ein Schriftzeugnis für das Fegfeuer? Eine exegetisch-historische Untersuchung* (Düsseldorf, 1955). He answers his question ("Is 1 Cor. 3:10-15 a scriptural witness to the doctrine of purgatory?") with a No; it simply cannot be exegetically sustained. A more modern expression of the traditional point of view may be found in B. Bartmann, *Purgatory* (ET, London, 1936).

[46]The Greek construction οὕτως δέ ὡς makes this certain: "thus, as it were, only through fire."

[47]Cf. Zech 3:2, and the English proverb "saved by the skin of one's teeth." For Greek and Roman parallels, see Weiss, 83 n. 1.

[48]Donfried, "Justification," p. 149, and most commentators. J. T. Townsend doubts the "figure of speech" interpretation in favor of Paul's having been a former Shammaite, who in this passage reflects their belief, described in *Bar.Rosh.Hash.* 16b-17a, that such people "will pass through hell fire before their final salvation" (see "1 Corinthians 3:15 and the School of Shammai," *HTR* 61 [1968], 500-04). But the differences, which Townsend slights, between v. 15 and the Shammaites are so great as to preclude indebtedness.

taken seriously. Here the word of warning and the word of hope are one. He wants them to desist from their current worldly wisdom; he wants them, with him, to be saved and to experience reward. But their current behavior is so seriously aberrant that he must warn them yet once more (in vv. 16-17), this time in the strongest terms yet: those who persist in these activities and attitudes are in fact in eternal danger.

This text has singular relevance to the contemporary church. It is neither a challenge to the individual believer to build his or her life well on the foundation of Christ, nor is it grist for theological debate. Rather, it is one of the most significant passages in the NT that warn—and encourage— those responsible for "building" the church of Christ. In the final analysis, of course, this includes all believers, but it has particular relevance, following so closely as it does vv. 5-9, to those with teaching/leadership responsibilities. Paul's point is unquestionably warning. It is unfortunately possible for people to attempt to build the church out of every imaginable human system predicated on merely worldly wisdom, be it philosophy, "pop" psychology, managerial techniques, relational "good feelings," or what have you. But at the final judgment, all such building (and perhaps countless other forms, where systems have become more important than the gospel itself) will be shown for what it is: something merely human, with no character of Christ or his gospel in it. Often, of course, the test may come this side of the final one, and in such an hour of stress that which has been built of modern forms of *sophia* usually comes tumbling down.

But the good news of the passage is that one does not need to build badly. That which has the character of the foundation, Jesus Christ crucified and risen, will not only survive any present hour of testing, but will enter the final judgment as a glorious church; and those responsible for such building will receive their due reward, which in itself is an expression of grace.

c. Warning to those who would destroy the church, God's temple in Corinth (3:16-17)

16 *Don't you know that you yourselves are God's temple and that God's Spirit lives in you?* 17 *If anyone destroys God's temple, God will destroy[1] him; for God's temple is sacred, and you are that temple.*

Since v. 5 Paul has been trying to correct the Corinthians' false view of church leadership, by redirecting their focus from the teachers themselves to God, who owns all and whose alone they are. At the same time he must correct their understanding of the nature of the church itself. Thus the

---

[1]"Influenced by the preceding word, several witnesses, chiefly Western, read the present tense φθείρει (D^{gr} G^{gr} L P 81 [pc]) instead of φθερεῖ" (Metzger, 549).

argument now takes another slight turn, in which he carries the imagery of vv. 9b-15 a step further by specifying the *kind* of building that he and the others have been erecting, namely God's *temple* in Corinth. With this imagery he does two things: (1) he tries to help the Corinthians to see the nature and significance of their being God's people in Corinth, and (2) by picking up the imagery of judgment from vv. 13-15, he sternly warns those who are in process of destroying the church by their divisions. Thus he presents us with remarkable imagery describing the nature of the local church, as well as with the strongest warning in the NT against those who would take the church lightly and destroy it by worldly wisdom and division.

16 The turn in the argument, and the strong feeling with which he will argue his next point, is achieved with a rhetorical device that occurs here for the first time in Paul: "Do you not know that . . . ?" The fact that he will use this device ten times in this letter,[2] chiefly in contexts where he is exercised, and that it occurs only one other time in his letters (Rom. 6:16), probably says much about his feelings toward the Corinthians and their behavior.[3] In the Thessalonian letters his way of reminding them of what they should or did already know was to say, "For even as you yourselves know. . . ." But in this letter he turns to rhetoric, less to remind the Corinthians of something they had already been told[4] than to point to a reality that they should know by the very nature of things. "Do you not know who you are?" he asks them. And it is clear from their current behavior that they do not know, or at least have not seriously considered the implications of who they are as God's people in Corinth.

The imagery of the church as God's temple,[5] which occurs twice more in Paul (2 Cor. 6:16; Eph. 2:21), is a pregnant one both for the Jewish Paul and the Gentile Corinthians. The word used *(naos)* refers to the actual sanctuary, the place of the deity's dwelling, in contrast to the word *hieron*, which referred to the temple precincts as well as to the sanctuary.[6] For Paul

---

[2]3:16; 5:6; 6:2, 3, 9, 15, 16, 19; 9:13, 24.

[3]Given their own emphasis on wisdom and knowledge, this may be more than simply a rhetorical device here, moving closer to irony or sarcasm: "Can it be that you who boast in γνῶσις do not know that?"

[4]Some have suggested that Paul's question implies that Paul had previously given them this image. See, e.g., Weiss, 84; B. Gärtner, *The Temple and the Community in Qumran and the New Testament* (SNTSMS 1; Cambridge, 1965), p. 57. But that is to put too much weight on the language of what seems rather to be a rhetorical device in this letter.

[5]J. M. Ford, "You Are God's 'Sukkah' (I Cor. iii.10-17)," *NTS* 21 (1973/74), 139-42, argues that the imagery here is that of building the "tabernacle" during the Feast of Tabernacles. But the alleged parallels are so remote and the temple imagery in Paul so fixed that this seems destined to be an item of curiosity at best.

[6]See O. Michel in *TDNT* IV, 880-90. The distinctions between the two words do not necessarily hold in all the Greek of the NT period, but the usage in the LXX, where the distinction is common, seems to have influenced Paul here.

the imagery reflects the OT people of God. Although they are never called God's temple as such, they are his people among whom he chose to "dwell" by tabernacling in their midst.[7] It is possible, though by no means certain, that the imagery also had eschatological overtones for Paul.[8] Such an understanding would flow from two sources: Jewish eschatological hopes as reflected in a variety of sources,[9] and a tradition, which seems to go back to Jesus himself, that he would rebuild the temple "in three days."[10] The present experience of the church as the place where the (eschatological) Spirit dwells would thus be the restored temple of Ezekiel's vision (chaps. 40–48), where God promised "to live among them forever" (43:9) and out of which flowed the river of fresh water that restored the land (47:1-12).

The imagery of the church as temple would have been easily understood by the Corinthians as well, although perhaps not with its rich OT overtones. As practicing pagans (see 6:9; 8:7) most of them would have frequented the many pagan temples and shrines (naoi) in their city. Indeed, some of them were arguing for the right to do so still (see chaps. 8–10). But now Paul is calling their attention to the fact that since there is only one God, he can have only one temple in Corinth, and they are it.[11] They became that new temple by the fact that "God's Spirit lives in you." Most likely Paul meant by this not that the Spirit dwelt in each of them, true as that would be for him (cf. 6:19), but that the Spirit of God "lives in your midst." That is, Paul is here reflecting on the church as the corporate place of God's dwelling, who, when gathered in Jesus' name, experienced the presence and power of the Lord Jesus in their midst (5:4-5). Again, as in 2:10-13 (cf. 2:4-5), the Spirit is the key, the crucial reality, for life in the new age. The presence of the Spirit, and that *alone,* marks them off as God's new people, his temple, in Corinth.

---

[7]Cf., e.g., Ps. 114:2: "Judah became his sanctuary," plus the rich imagery of God's dwelling in their midst in the desert.

[8]This suggestion has been frequently made, and it is probably correct, given the Qumran eschatological parallels (see Gärtner, *Temple*) and Paul's overall eschatological frame of reference; but nothing in Paul's usage itself demands such an understanding. See, among others, Weiss, Barrett, Bruce, Conzelmann, Senft.

[9]E.g., Isa. 28:16 (cf. 1 Cor. 3:10); Ezek. 40–48; *Jub.* 1:17; 1 Enoch 91:13; 4QFlor.

[10]As represented in the charges of the false witnesses in Mark 14:58. The "falseness" does not have to do with the statement, but with what would have been meant by it. The same tradition is reflected in John 2:19-21, and probably among the Hellenists in Acts (whence arose Paul), who rejected the temple in Jerusalem as "made with hands" (Acts 6:13; 7:48-50).

[11]Although one perhaps should not make too much of it, Paul's word order, ναὸς θεοῦ ἐστε, is probably both emphatic and an illustration of "Colwell's rule" (that predicate nouns that precede the verb are usually definite, even if they do not have the definite article). If so, then Paul is saying, "Do you not know that you are *the* temple of God in Corinth?"

17 As God's temple in Corinth, the church was to be his alternative to Corinth, both its religions and vices. But the Corinthians, by their worldly wisdom, boasting, and divisions, were in effect banishing the Spirit and thus about to destroy the only alternative God had in their city. Hence, following the rhetoric that calls attention to who they are, Paul solemnly warns those who were thus wreaking havoc in the church: "If anyone destroys[12] God's temple, God will destroy that person." As E. Käsemann has pointed out, this has all the earmarks of a "sentence of holy law,"[13] in which the *lex talionis* and chiasm combine to express the fearful judgment of God on the last Day.[14] One can scarcely circumvent the awful nature of the warning. Those who are responsible for dismantling the church[15] may expect judgment in kind; it is difficult to escape the sense of eternal judgment in this case, given its close proximity to vv. 13-15.[16] Although in the formal character of casuistic law, this is a strongly prophetic word in the apostle,[17] and needs to be heard accordingly.

Some interpreters are dismayed that Paul can now speak of a person within the community as "being destroyed," especially after the provision of escape was given in v. 15. In fact it is common to suggest that Paul is dealing with two different groups of people in the two passages.[18] But neither rhetoric nor prophetic threat—not to mention Paul—is so logical. This threat takes the warning of vv. 10-15 to its next step. The whole is addressed to the church. If a distinction is to be made between the "anyone" of this passage and that of vv. 10-15, it would be that the focus here is more specifically on those few who seem to be the prime movers of the present quarrelings.[19] The *reason* for such a dire threat is given in the final clause:

---

[12]As in vv. 12-13, this is almost certainly a present particular supposition: "If anyone is destroying. . . ."

[13]"Sätze Heiligen Rechts im Neuen Testament," *NTS* 1 (1954/55), 248-60; ET, *New Testament Questions of Today* (Philadelphia, 1969), pp. 66-81, esp. 66-68. But see the critique by D. E. Aune, *Prophecy in Early Christianity and the Ancient Mediterranean World* (Grand Rapids, 1983), pp. 167, 237.

[14]Note especially the near wordplay brought about by the juxtaposition of the two verbs: φθείρει/φθερεῖ ("If anyone the temple of God destroys, destroy this person will God").

[15]According to BAGD, the imagery is that of "the destruction of a house."

[16]On this question R-P are worth quoting in full: "But . . . φθερεῖ here . . . must [not] be pressed to mean annihilation (see on v. 5). Nor, on the other hand, must it be watered down to mean mere physical punishment (cf. xi.30). The exact meaning is nowhere revealed in Scripture; but terrible ruin and eternal loss of some kind seems to be meant" (p. 67). Cf. BAGD and G. Harder, *TDNT* IX, 93-106.

[17]Cf. Käsemann, "Sentences," p. 68; cf. C. J. Roetzel, "The Judgment Form in Paul's Letters," *JBL* 88 (1969), 305.

[18]So, e.g., Godet, MacArthur, and Barrett (to a lesser extent).

[19]The theological question as to whether a true "believer" could be destroyed by God lies beyond Paul's present concern. In any case, one must be careful not to let the

"for God's temple is sacred,[20] and you are that temple."[21] The word "sacred" maintains the imagery of the temple, which was set apart for God and was not to be desecrated in any way. But again, the language means not simply ritual holiness (cf. 1:2), but "holy" in the moral-ethical sense. Thus the statement, although an indicative referring to the imagery of the temple, becomes a functional imperative through the addition of "and that temple you are." God is holy; his temple is therefore also holy, set apart for his purposes; and as his temple, you are by implication also to be holy. As this letter reveals, this is not one of their strong suits. So the threat, which is real, is at the same time turned into an invitation for them to become what in fact they are by the grace of God, "God's *holy* temple in Corinth."[22]

This passage has endured a long history of unfortunate interpretation in the church. Because the imagery of the temple is reapplied in 6:19-20 to the individual Corinthian who was going to the prostitutes, many have read that usage back into this passage as though it were a word of warning to individual Christians as to how they are to treat their bodies or live out their individual Christian lives. Both the context and the grammar disallow such interpretations, even by "extended application." This is all the more unfortunate because this is one of the few texts in the NT where we are exposed both to an understanding of the nature of the local church (God's temple indwelt by his Spirit) and where the warning of v. 17 makes it clear how important the local church is to God himself.

One of the desperate needs of the church is to recapture this vision of what it is by grace, and therefore also what God intends it to be. In most Protestant circles one tends to take the local parish altogether too lightly.

"logic" of one's system (as in the case of MacArthur, 86) prejudge the plain meaning of Paul's words. That these people were members of the Corinthian community seems beyond reasonable doubt; that Paul is also serving up a genuine threat of eternal punishment seems also the plain sense of the text. The theological resolution of such tension will lie either with the concept of the visible church being composed of more than the real church, destined by God for glory, or with the supposition that some, who by all appearances do belong to the community of faith, have, for reasons beyond our understanding, opted out and are once again pursuing a path leading to destruction. The net result is the same in either case. Paul does not consider any of the Corinthian "bent ones" to be there—yet; and the warning is intended to keep it from happening.

[20]Gk. ἅγιος, "holy."

[21]This translation reflects what is most likely the correct understanding of a difficult Greek construction, οἵτινές ἐστε ὑμεῖς. The plural compound relative pronoun οἵτινες does not have a proper antecedent, and can refer either to "temple" or "holy." The reason for the plural is attraction to the following ὑμεῖς (cf. Phil. 1:28; 1 Tim. 3:15). The antecedent is most likely "temple," which rounds off the sentence by referring again to v. 16. To emphasize that "holy" is what they in fact are seems to ask too much of the context.

[22]Cf. Käsemann, "Sentences," p. 68.

Seldom does one sense that it is, or can be, experienced as a community that is so powerfully indwelt by the Spirit that it functions as a genuine alternative to the pagan world in which it is found. It is perhaps not too strong to suggest that the recapturing of this vision of its being, both in terms of its being powerfully indwelt by the Spirit and of its thereby serving as a genuine alternative ("holy" in the most holistic sense) to the world, is its single greatest need.

6. Conclusion of the Matter—All Are Christ's (3:18-23)

> 18 *Do not deceive yourselves.[1] If any one of you thinks he is wise by the standards of this age, he should become a "fool" so that he may become wise.* 19 *For the wisdom of this world is foolishness in God's sight. As it is written: "He catches the wise in their craftiness"[a]; * 20 *and again, "The Lord knows that the thoughts of the wise are futile."[b]* 21 *So then, no more boasting about men! All things are yours,* 22 *whether Paul or Apollos or Cephas[c] or the world or life or death or the present or the future—all are yours,* 23 *and you are of Christ, and Christ is of God.*

> a Job 5:13
> b Psalm 94:11
> c That is, Peter

Paul now gathers up the various threads of the argument to this point and brings it to a preliminary conclusion, a conclusion which makes certain that the long argument of 1:18–3:4 was not some mere sermonic or rhetorical aside, but rather spoke to the root of the problem of their strife. The paragraph is in two parts (vv. 18-20, 21-23), each marked in the Greek text by an identical opening exhortation ("Let no one . . ."), and each thereby bringing closure to the first two parts of the problem (*quarreling* in the name of their leaders; but doing so under the guise of *wisdom*).[2]

First he insists that none of them be deceived by what appears to be wisdom but is not. Their *sophia* belongs only to the present age and has no standing whatsoever with God himself; indeed, it is foolishness to him. All of this recalls and applies the argument of 1:18–2:16. This motif in turn is tied to the theme of "boasting" in men, thus picking up the problem of the strife itself, especially as it has been carried on in the name of their various leaders. This recalls 3:5-9, which pointed out the folly of following mere men, "servants of the farm" as it were.

---

[1]The Greek is singular here and should be so translated: "Let no one deceive himself" (RSV).
[2]See above, p. 48. The final part of the problem, which is also the most sensitive one, namely their attitude toward Paul himself, is finally addressed in chap. 4.

As the reason why they must not "boast" in their teachers, Paul turns their slogans end for end. It is not that the Corinthians belong to Apollos or Paul, but that Paul and Apollos—and everything else—belong to the Corinthians; indeed, all things are theirs because they are Christ's and Christ is God's. Thus the main point of 3:5-17 is restated with breathtaking crescendo.

18 Following hard on the heels of the severe warning in v. 17, Paul exhorts: "Let no one delude[3] himself" (NAB). Those who persist in pursuing *sophia*, who are thereby destroying, not building, the church, are self-deceived[4]—and a fearful judgment threatens them. Their present course, because it is the way of deception, will lead ultimately to destruction. Hence he urges that they abandon it in favor of one that brings them back to God's folly, which is true wisdom. The rest of vv. 18-20 spells out this concern by recapitulating the basic paradoxes of 1:18-2:16.

The opening salvo is irony once again: "If any one of you thinks he is wise by the standards of this age." Of course they do; that is quite the point. This same formula will appear three more times in this letter,[5] two of which (8:2; 14:37), along with this one, speak to the heart of the attitudinal problems that plague the church. They think of themselves as wise, as having arrived at knowledge (8:2), and as being spiritual (14:37). That is precisely their problem. And in each case Paul must disabuse them of such opinions; otherwise the church is up for grabs.

This passage helps to bolster the conviction that much of the language of the argument is theirs, but that it is picked up by Paul and used against them. They think of themselves as the "wise." But for Paul such wisdom is strictly "according to the standards of this age." Paul is an eschatological man, and this age is under God's judgment and on its way out (cf. 1:20, 27-29; 2:6, 8). In the cross and resurrection of Christ, God has "befooled" wisdom. Everything is end for end: wisdom is folly, folly is wisdom; weakness is power; leaders are servants; God's people are nobodies, yet possess all things (vv. 22-23; 2 Cor. 6:9-10). Not everything that has been so reversed is now plainly visible; but the cross and resurrection are evidence of its certainty. Therefore, God's people must abandon confidence in the securities of the present age; they must trust in God's folly—"he

---

[3]Gk. ἐξαπατάτω, a Pauline word in the NT (2 Thess. 2:3; 2 Cor. 11:3; Rom. 7:11; 16:18; 1 Tim. 2:14). Cf. the μὴ πλανᾶσθε in 6:9 and 15:33.

[4]This kind of warning further indicates that the problem in Corinth had not yet been the work of outsiders. There is no hint in this letter that they are being deceived by someone from the outside. In Gal. 3:1 and 2 Cor. 11:2-3, on the other hand, the work of outsiders has deceived God's people.

[5]8:2; 11:16; 14:37; cf. Gal. 6:3; Phil. 3:4. In each case the formula introduces a position actually held by his "opponents" and thus functions as a form of irony to dissuade them, or to get them to hear his argument on the other side.

should become a 'fool' "—and thereby become truly wise. Nothing new is said here; this is simply the argument of 1:18–3:4 reinforced.

19-20 Paul now gives the theological basis for the preceding exhortation, plus its scriptural support. The way of stating it is the reverse of 1:18-25. There he set out to demonstrate that "the wisdom of God [Christ crucified] is foolishness to the world." Here he says, "The wisdom of this world[6] is foolishness in God's sight." Exactly the same point is made, but now in terms of the divine perspective, which ultimately is the only one that counts. If before they were being shown the foolishness of *their* "wisdom," because God and his ways stand in contradiction to it, now they are being urged to adopt God's perspective altogether, since their "wisdom" is, after all, folly.

And how do we know? Because once again, as in 1:19, there is sufficient evidence from what "is written" that God has always so regarded human efforts to understand his ways. In this case two texts are cited, Job 5:13[7] and Ps. 94:11 (LXX 93:11),[8] brought together under the keyword "the wise," along with God's attitude toward such. The citations together illustrate the utter futility of "the wise," hence the fact that their "wisdom is foolishness in God's sight." The first text is expressed in the imagery of hunting, in which the hunter uses the very craftiness, or cunning, of the prey as the means of capture.[9] The ultimate irony is that people are cunningly avoiding the God with whom they have to do; but God has used that very cunning to ensnare them. Thinking themselves to be wise, they are in fact fools. The second text emphasizes their ultimate futility. God knows their reasonings,[10] that they are futile. The obvious point for Paul, therefore, is that the Corinthians are themselves fools if they do not take seriously this divine view of things.

21a With a final emphatic "So then" (see on 3:7), Paul brings the present argument to its conclusion, which is at once exhortation, theology,

[6]Note again the interchange of αἰών and κόσμος, just as in 1:20 (q.v.).

[7]The only direct citation of Job in the NT (cf. Rom. 11:35). Even though these are the words of Eliphaz, they are the common assumption of all the "players" in the book of Job, which is what makes the dialogue possible, and in Eliphaz's case also reflects the divine irony. This much of his speech at least is true!

[8]The two texts together serve as a good place to observe Paul's use of the OT. The citation of Job is closer to the Hebrew than to the LXX. Paul seems to be translating on his own, although the word πανουργία reflects v. 12 of the LXX. The citation of the Psalm is exactly as in the LXX, except for the exchange of the crucial word σόφος for ἄνθρωπος. This is probably an example of Paul's *appeal* to Scripture being at the same time an interpretation of it (cf. Eph. 4:8). See Ellis, *Use*, p. 144; and A. M. Harmon, "Aspects of Paul's Use of the Psalms," *WTJ* 32 (1969), 22. The sense is exactly that of the Psalm.

[9]Cf. NEB: "He traps the wise in their own cunning" (cf. GNB).

[10]Gk. διαλογισμούς, which refers to human machinations more than simply "thoughts."

and doxology. The passage has a kind of grandeur that makes one hesitant to comment on it; nonetheless, to see what makes up that grandeur may cause the hearing of it to be all the greater. He begins with exhortation (v. 21a), proceeds to give the theological basis for it (vv. 21b-23), and concludes with a near-doxology (v. 23) in which everything is grounded in the ultimate theological truth—the unity of God. Before such majesty their divisions and worldly wisdom are altogether silenced and brought to nothing.

First, then, the exhortation: "Let no one boast of men" (RSV). With these words the appeal of 1:10-12 is finally addressed directly, by the weaving together of two threads: their sloganeering in the name of their teachers (1:12; 3:4) and their boasting, as though they were self-sufficient (1:29, 31). At the same time it flows directly out of the immediately preceding predicate, that God knows the reasonings of the wise to be futile. In light of all that has been said—about the power of God's wisdom in the cross, about servant leadership that reflects the character of the cross, about God's contempt for the futility of worldly wisdom—in light of all that, let no one among you still be bold enough to say "I belong to Paul," or "I belong to Apollos." That is to ground one's confidence in the creature, mere mortals all. Rather, Paul will now direct their focus one final time to the Creator, who is God over all.

21b-22   This sentence begins with an untranslated "for,"[11] which gives the theological basis for "no more boasting about men." Why not? Because "all things are yours." These words are predicated on the final theological conclusion of v. 23, in which this statement is repeated and the ultimate basis added: "All things are yours, and you are of Christ, and Christ is of God." With these words Paul completely transforms their slogans. They say (lit.), "*I* am *of Paul,* etc." With the analogy of the field (vv. 5-9) Paul changed that to "*you* are *of God.*" Now he makes the further transformation, "*All things* are *of you,* including Paul, Apollos, and Cephas." This turns their slogans completely on their head, with the significant difference that the pronoun is plural, not singular. Thus, they may not say "I belong to Paul, or Apollos, or Cephas," not only because that is to boast in mere men, but because that is the precise opposite of reality in Christ. In him, as Eph. 1 will say in lofty cadences, God has begun what he will eventually bring to full consummation, namely "to bring all things in heaven and earth under one head, even Christ" (Eph. 1:10); therefore, *all things are yours* (plural).

The list of "all things" begins with the three "men"[12] in 1:12 around

---

[11]Gk. γάρ, causal or explanatory in this case. Cf. RSV, NASB, Moffatt.

[12]This is the only other mention of "Cephas" in the entire section. This means either that he is less important (the position adopted in this commentary) or that the silence elsewhere is an indirect way of indicating that his "faction" is more serious, which seems less likely. See on 1:12 (n. 44) and 3:11.

whose names the Corinthians are clustering in some form of jealousy and strife (3:3). This of course is the point of everything. One is therefore not quite prepared for the sudden expansion of the list, which really does include *all things.* One wonders whether Paul himself had all this in mind when the sentence began. Nonetheless it is altogether true to his theology. These five items, "the world, life, death, the present, and the future," are the ultimate tyrannies of human existence, to which people are in lifelong bondage as slaves. For Paul the death and resurrection of Jesus marked the turning of the ages in such a way that nothing lies outside Christ's jurisdiction.[13] In the form of the cross God has planted his flag on planet Earth and marked it off as his own possession; hence the "world" is his. So also with the whole of existence ("life" and "death"), which are immediately placed into eschatological perspective ("the present and the future").[14] Because in Christ Jesus both "life" itself and therefore "the future" are ours, "death" is ours as well, as is "the present." We die, but "life" cannot be taken from us; we live the life of the future in the present age, and therefore the present has become our own possession. For those in Christ Jesus, what things were formerly tyrannies are now their new birthright. This is the glorious freedom of the children of God. They are free lords of all things,[15] not bound to the whims of chance or the exigencies of life and death. The future is no cause for panic; it is already theirs. In light of such expansive realities, how can the Corinthians say, "I am of Paul, or Apollos"? That is too narrow, too constricted a view. Apollos—and Paul, and Peter, and the whole universe—is yours. You do not belong to them; they belong to you, as your servants, because "you— and they—are Christ's, and Christ is God's."

23 These final words come close to doxology: "All things are yours, and[16] you are Christ's, and Christ is God's." As already noted, they serve as the ultimate theological basis for what has preceded. They are also its proper qualification. It is not that "all things are yours" willy-nilly, or selfishly, or in the same sense as they were to the Stoic, who regarded "possession of all things" as making him "self-sufficient"[17]—and there-

---

[13]Except the continuing expression of death itself. This is the point of 15:23-28. When this final enemy is subdued, *then* comes the End, when all is turned over to the Father.

[14]These last two also form pairs in the similar listing in Rom. 8:38, where nothing can separate God's people from his love as it is given to them in Christ Jesus.

[15]The language is Barrett's. Cf. JB, which tries to capture this sense of the passage, as well as to tie it to vv. 5-9, by translating: "Paul, Apollos, Cephas, the world, life and death, the present and the future, are all your servants."

[16]The two δέ's in this and the next clause are consecutive, not adversative, and thus correctly translated "and."

[17]The language "all things are yours" is identical to statements among the Stoics, but its point for them was that they were thereby αὐτάρκης, "self-sufficient."

fore ultimately independent and self-centered. They are yours because you belong to Christ; and all things are his (cf. 15:23-28). Thus it is only in him that the believer possesses all things; but *in him* the believer does indeed possess all things.

The final crescendo resounds: "and Christ is God's." For some this text has raised moments of concern; for Paul it is simply the final note of triumph. The point of the whole argument has been "possession." Paul's Jewish heritage had taught him well: God is one (Deut. 6:4). God is therefore the ultimate reality, the one who possesses all things and outside of whose ultimate control lies nothing. Everything Paul understands about the work of Christ is predicated on that singular reality. This is therefore a soteriological statement, not a christological one (in terms of his being). In keeping with the rest of the NT, most such soteriological statements, when they include words about the Father and Son, express subordination (cf. 8:6; 15:27-28). But it is functional subordination, not ontological, that is, just as in 15:23-28 it has to do with his function as savior, not with his being as God. God is one; and Christian existence, brought about by the death and resurrection of Christ, is ultimately to be found in the one God. It cannot get any better than that.

On this high note Paul's response to the Corinthian pride in man and wisdom has come to a fitting conclusion. But the problem is larger still; so he turns next to deal with their attitudes toward him in particular. But that's the next chapter.

The Corinthian error is an easy one to repeat. Not only do we all have normal tendencies to turn natural preferences into exclusive ones, but in our fallenness we also tend to consider ourselves "wise" enough to inform God through whom he may minister to his people. Our slogans take the form of "I am of the Presbyterians," or "of the Pentecostals," or "of the Roman Catholics." Or they might take ideological forms: "I am of the liberals," or "of the evangelicals," or "of the fundamentalists." And these are also used as weapons: "Oh, he's a fundamentalist, you know." Which means that we no longer need to listen to him, since his ideology has determined his overall value as a spokesman for God. It is hardly possible in a day like ours that one will not have denominational, theological, or ideological preferences. The

---

See, e.g., Seneca, *benef.* 7.2.5; 7.3.2; 7.4.1; Diog. L., *Vit.* 7.125; Cicero, *Fin.* 3.22.75-76. On this matter see Weiss, 90-91, and esp. H. Braun, "Exegetische Randglossen zum I Korintherbrief," in *Gesammelte Studien zum Neuen Testament und seiner Umwelt* (Tübingen, 1967), 182-86. Paul's own radically different meaning for the phrase is another clear indication that finding the "source" of his language is not always significant, since his "in Christ" existence so thoroughly transforms everything, even the language he uses, and gives it new meaning.

difficulty lies in allowing that it might really be true that "all things are ours," including those whom we think God would do better to be without. But God is full of surprises; and he may choose to minister to us from the "strangest" of sources, if we were but more truly "in Christ" and therefore free in him to learn and to love.

This does not mean that one should not be discriminating; after all, Paul has no patience for that teaching in Corinth which had abandoned the pure gospel of Christ. But to be "of Christ" is also to be free from the tyrannies of one's own narrowness, free to learn even from those with whom one may disagree.

7. The Corinthians and Their Apostle (4:1-21)

Given the concluding nature of the exhortations of 3:18-23, and especially their crowning doxological note, one might well wonder why Paul feels compelled to continue. But the present section makes it clear that not all has been said.[1] The Corinthians' theological misunderstanding of the gospel and church, and the role of their teachers, have now been addressed. But at the heart of much of this is the attitude of many toward Paul himself. These people are not simply *for* Apollos or Peter; they are decidedly *anti*-Paul. They are rejecting both his teaching *and* his authority.

This presents Paul with a genuine dilemma. On the one hand, he must reassert his authority—going the way of his gospel is *not* optional; on the other hand, he must do that without blunting the force of his argument to this point, especially his contention as to the *servant* role of an apostle.

The first paragraph (vv. 1-5) leads the way by making an application of the servant model and showing how that relates to their treatment of him. He changes images from farm to household and insists that he is *God's* servant, not theirs; and they are not allowed to judge another's servant. While on the theme of judgment, he gently broadens the perspective to remind them again of the future judgment that all must experience.

In vv. 6-13 he directly applies the argument to them and their attitudes. With rhetoric full of sarcasm and irony he goes for the jugular. His own apostleship, which he portrays in bold relief, contrasting his own "shame" with their perceived "high station," is alone consonant with a theology of the cross.

Finally, in vv. 14-21 he reasserts his apostolic authority, his right to correct their bad behavior and bad theology. But he does so with consum-

---

[1]Some would divide the letter into three somewhat coordinate sections, 1:18–2:5, 2:6–3:4, and 3:5–4:5, but that misses the apologetic thrust of the argument almost completely, which seems to mitigate this arrangement. See, e.g., B. Fiore, "'Covert Allusion' in 1 Corinthians 1-4," *CBQ* 47 (1985), 85-102.

mate skill—by changing the metaphor to father and children and thus appealing to them. But appeal is still apology, so he concludes on a final note of warning. If the father's "gentleness" will not change their attitudes, then the "rod" must. So how will they have it? Will this letter and Timothy's visit do it? or must he himself visit them with a "rod" in his hand?

In some ways this is one of Paul's finest hours. Here for the first time in his letters we catch a glimpse of the man himself, and what makes him run. Above everything else, Paul is "of Christ" (3:23), or "in Christ Jesus" (4:17). This means that he is thoroughly eschatological, but not simply awaiting the end. For him it means that the future (Christ's return and reign) has been determined by the past (Christ's death and resurrection), and that that certain future (guaranteed by the gift of the Spirit) determines the present. The resurrection of Jesus from the dead was not a matter of creed for him; it was the singular reality that conditioned his entire existence. But not his alone. By the resurrection God himself had set the future inexorably in motion; the "coming" of Christ and subsequent "judgment" are inevitable corollaries, as sure as life itself. For Paul, therefore, those sure events radicalize present Christian existence. All merely human judgments are nothing in light of the final judgment; all merely human values, which weigh things heavily at the apparently favorable end of the scale, have already been judged and are now reversed by Christ himself.

Paul's problem is that in their own way the Corinthians were also eschatological people, for they too had received the Spirit. But for them this meant not so much that the future determined one's present life as that one had entered into a new realm of being altogether. They had already arrived, but in all the wrong ways (4:8). What Paul is trying to do above all else is to get the Corinthians to enter his orbit, to see things from his eschatological perspective. Therefore, it is not simply a matter of his being right and their being wrong on certain specific issues. It has to do with one's whole existence, one's whole way of looking at life, since "you are Christ's, and Christ is God's." Without this perspective ourselves much of what is said here can be enigma; but it need not be, once one has been drawn into Paul's orbit by his/her own encounter with the living Christ.

a. On being a servant and being judged (4:1-5)

1 *So then, men ought to regard us as servants of Christ and as those entrusted with the secret things of God.* 2 *Now it is required² that*

---

²Several significant MSS (P⁴⁶ ℵ A C D F G P 6 33 1739 1881 pc) read ζητεῖτε for ζητεῖται. This is doubly complex: on the one hand it may simply be an itacism (the ε/αι interchange is frequent in the earlier centuries); on the other hand, if the second plural were actually intended, was it indicative or imperative (probably the former = "Now then you seek in stewards, etc.")? In either case, the second plural is probably secondary.

those who have been given a trust prove faithful. 3 *I care very little if I am judged by you or by any human court; indeed, I do not even judge myself.* 4 *My conscience is clear, but that does not make me innocent. It is the Lord who judges me.* 5 *Therefore judge nothing before the appointed time; wait till the Lord comes. He will bring to light what is hidden in darkness and will expose the motives of men's hearts. At that time each will receive his praise from God.*

This paragraph brings together two items from the preceding argument: the apostles as servants (3:5-9) and the coming judgment (3:13-15). At the same time it picks up the language of "examining/judging" from 2:14-16 and makes explicit what one may have only suspected heretofore, namely that the Corinthians were in fact passing judgment on the apostle. This brings into focus several other items from before as well: his preaching not being with the wisdom of *logos* (1:17); the tension over his presence with them in weakness (2:3); the nature of his former preaching as being "milk" for "infants" (3:2); the insistence that he was among them as a "wise" master-builder (3:10). They have almost certainly been passing judgment on him over these very things, thereby reflecting their new understanding of spirituality and disdaining his own theology of the cross.

The argument of the paragraph is easily traced. Changing the metaphor to household stewards entrusted with "the divine mysteries," Paul says that the Corinthians are to regard him and Apollos in the terms just described, as servants. But his new point is that although he "belongs" to them (since he is Christ's servant for them), he is not accountable to them. What is required of household stewards is faithfulness (v. 2), and only the master of the house can make that determination (vv. 4b, 5c). So, he argues, in one sense what you are currently saying about me is of little consequence (v. 3); but neither is his own clear conscience (v. 4). They must desist, he enjoins, because what does matter is the return of Christ, who at that time will judge not only Paul but them as well (v. 5).

1 The new turn in the argument is marked by asyndeton (lack of a joining conjunction).[3] But it is not a new topic; rather, Paul is going back to the point of 3:5-9, now by way of vv. 21-23. Paul, Apollos, and Cephas do indeed "belong" to them; but that is to be understood in light of v. 9, where Paul had asserted that they first belong to God. *This* is how "people[4] ought to

---

[3]The "so then" of the NIV seems to miss Paul's Greek. He has οὕτως ("thus"), which is correlative with the ὡς ("as") that follows (cf. 3:15; 9:26). There are plenty of examples of οὕτως referring to what precedes, but in such cases it is used absolutely (cf., e.g., 8:12). Conzelmann, 82 n. 1, shares the view of the NIV, but disregards οὕτως . . . ὡς as correlative. He sees the οὕτως as pointing backward, the ὡς as object of the verb λογιζέσθω.

[4]Gk. ἄνθρωπος, used here as a form of the indefinite pronoun (see BAGD 3aγ).

regard us, *as* servants of Christ." The plurals in vv. 1-2 (us, servants, etc.) must be taken seriously as flowing directly from v. 22 above (cf. v. 6 below). Paul is describing not only his own ministry but that of his fellow servants as well. However, as vv. 3-5 and the rest of the chapter reveal,[5] his real concern here is to set forth his own ministry in the context of his struggle with the Corinthians.

What is significant for this paragraph is the change of metaphors. In 3:5-9 the word *diakonoi* was used, emphasizing the servant nature of their task under God, with secondary emphasis on the division of labor. Now the metaphor changes to that of a household. The first word, *hypēretas* ("servants [of Christ]"),[6] is a more general term, but often refers to one who has the duties of administering the affairs of another. That this was Paul's intent is verified by the second word, *oikonomos,* which denotes a "steward" (often a slave) who has been "entrusted with" managing a household.[7] This is a happy change of metaphors for Paul (cf. 9:17); not only is it pregnant with the notion of accountability that is in the forefront of this paragraph, but it inherently conveys the motif of delegated authority as well, the other concern of this chapter. Thus apostles are to be regarded as "servants of Christ," reemphasizing their humble position and their belonging to Christ alone; at the same time they are "stewards of the mysteries of God" (RSV), emphasizing both their trusted position and their accountability to God.

The "authority" aspect of the metaphor is here brought out in the object of the trust, "the secret things of God." We have already met this word in the singular in 2:7. Here it is plural, as also in 13:2 and 14:2; but it seems to carry a more general connotation here than in those two instances.[8] The reason for this choice of words at this point indeed remains a mystery—

---

[5]Even though he reverts to the first plurals in vv. 8-13, the very direct application of that picture to himself personally, with the attendant appeal that they also be like him, indicates that even there the emphasis is not on apostleship in general but on his own apostleship in particular.

[6]This word originated to describe the slaves who rowed in the lower tier of a trireme. Eventually it came to be used of any who were in a subservient position, with emphasis on the relationship of one who served a superior. K. H. Rengstorf, *TDNT* VIII, 542, seems to miss the context of the argument considerably in suggesting that the word comes very close to ἀπόστολος here. That is to capture the "authority" motif without catching the real point of the imagery, servanthood.

[7]The word came to have a much broader range, referring to any person in a position of trust, but accountable to others. On the pre-Christian use of the term, see J. Reumann, "'Servants of God'—Pre-Christian Religious Application of OIKONOMOΣ in Greek," *JBL* 77 (1958), 339-49; for Pauline usage see *idem,* "Οἰκονομία-Terms in Paul in Comparison with Lucan *Heilsgeschichte,*" *NTS* 13 (1966/67), 147-67.

[8]In the two instances in 12-14, in the context of spiritual gifts, it almost certainly refers to special revelation(s) given by the Spirit. Here the context requires that *the* revelation is in view (cf. Conzelmann, 83).

in our ordinary English sense of the word. Some have seen here an allusion to the pagan mystery cults, wherein Paul has taken a word with which the Corinthians would have been familiar and has given it new meaning, referring to the Christian "mysteries" as over against those of Isis, etc. The problem is complicated by how the Corinthians themselves would have understood it, given their own thoroughly pagan background and environment.[9] Most likely, as in 2:7, it reflects again Paul's own semitic usage, in which he, as one who has the Spirit, has been given to understand God's plan of salvation, long hidden to human minds but now revealed in Christ.[10] Thus the "mysteries of God" means the revelation of the gospel, now known through the Spirit and especially entrusted to the apostles to proclaim.[11]

2 This sentence is joined to v. 1 by a complex set of adverbial particles,[12] whose purpose is clearer than their precise meaning. Bauer suggests something like "in this connection, then,"[13] which nicely fits the intent of the clause: to elaborate the metaphor in the direction of Paul's primary concern. What is sought[14] in[15] "stewards" is faithfulness, that[16] they be trustworthy (in the true sense of that word: "worthy of the trust that has been placed in their care"). Not eloquence, nor wisdom (nor "initiative," nor "success"—our more standard requirements), but faithfulness to the trust, is what God requires of his servants. For Paul this means absolute fidelity to the gospel as he received it and preached it (cf. 15:1-11). His intent, of course, is not to provide a general maxim for Christian ministry—although it is still the only valid criterion—but to set up the singular criterion by which God alone could be his judge and which would therefore rule out the Corinthian "examination" of him and his ministry.

3 Paul now applies the general maxim of v. 2 specifically to himself and the Corinthians' attitude toward him. They have been "examining/judging" him (see on 2:15).[17] As noted before, this word does not so

---

[9]This point is made especially by A. E. Harvey, "The Use of Mystery Language in the Bible," *JTS* n.s. 31 (1980), 331-32.

[10]See the references to Brown and Bornkamm in n. 27 on 2:7.

[11]The suggestion of some that it means "dispenser of the sacraments" is so far removed from both the literary and historical context as not to need refutation.

[12]Gk. ὧδε λοιπόν (lit. "here, in addition").

[13]BAGD, λοιπόν, 3b; cf. Moule, 161: "on that showing (ὧδε, referring back to the preceding verse where the apostles have been called stewards) it follows that (λοιπόν) what is looked for in stewards is that . . ." (cf. Parry, 74). For a complete discussion, see M. E. Thrall, *Greek Particles in the New Testament* (Grand Rapids, 1962), pp. 26-28.

[14]Gk. ζητεῖται, which in cases like this can move over to the sense of "required" (BAGD 2c; NIV, Barrett, Conzelmann). The sense seems proverbial.

[15]According to Turner, *Syntax*, p. 265, this ἐν functions as a dative of reference.

[16]This ἵνα-clause is epexegetic, not final, functioning as the object of the verb "to seek."

[17]Ellis, 46, suggests on the basis of his interpretation of 2:6-16 that this "examination" of Paul does "not represent an opposition"; rather, the Corinthians "only wish to subject Paul to the testing usually given to a fellow pneumatic." But see n. 13 on 2:6-16.

much refer to a verdict that has been handed down, as to the process of "examining" that leads to the verdict. Their attitude toward him, either generally speaking or in some specific way, amounts to a judicial inquiry (cf. 9:3); they are "investigating" him, bringing him before themselves as the grand jury, as it were. But for Paul the application of the criterion of v. 2 forbids such activity.

The sentence begins "But it is a matter of the least consequence to me,[18] that I am judged by you." The relationship of this clause to what has preceded, which is less than transparent, is based on an assumption within the metaphor itself, finally spelled out in v. 4 ("It is the Lord who judges me"). The assumption is that since the criterion is faithfulness to a committed trust, only the one from whom he had received the trust can judge him— not his fellow servants nor in this case those who might be "under him," the Corinthians themselves. But by this statement Paul is not being flip or arrogant. The addition of the next phrase, "or by any human court" (lit. "by any human *day*"), puts it into perspective. The word "day," which is similar to our expression "having one's day in court,"[19] is to be understood in light of *the* Day already mentioned in 3:13, but now also anticipating the "day" of final judgment in v. 5. This is not a criticism of the Roman judicial system; Paul is once again being thoroughly eschatological. The only judgment that counts is the final one (v. 5); in light of our present eschatological existence, in which we are already determined by the future and the present age is recognized as under the judgment of God and thus passing away, all human systems amount to nothing (cf. 6:2-4).

Therefore, for Paul all merely human judgments against him, be they of the Corinthians or of any others who may so judge him, are of little or no consequence whatsoever. The only judgment that counts is the final eschatological judgment administered by Christ himself. So much is this so that Paul includes personal "judgments" of himself as equally inconsequential. He does not "even judge himself," not because he is irresponsible, or intends to be so, but because he is in the service of another. His personal evaluations of his own performance are irrelevant; what his master thinks is what counts. Besides, any such judgments also belong to this age. Paul stands too close to the consummation to be exercised by self-examination.

4 The reason Paul can make such bold statements as those in v. 3 are finally given at the end of this verse ("It is the Lord who judges me"), which in turn leads to the final exhortation of v. 5. But before he gets there, he feels compelled to add a qualifier to the remarkable statement at the end of the last sentence, "I do not even judge myself"—which he must have realized could play into their hands. In Thessalonica he had already been

---

[18]Gk. ἐμοὶ δὲ εἰς ἐλάχιστόν ἐστιν; on the idiom see BAGD, εἰμι III.2.
[19]On this usage see BAGD, ἡμέρα, 3bβ.

scored for alleged hidden motives (1 Thess. 2:1-12), and apparently some of that had surfaced in this church as well (9:1-19; cf. 2 Cor. 2:17–3:4 and passim). Having renounced even personal evaluation of his stewardship, he now adds,[20] I do not intend to suggest that I really do have hidden agenda that have yet to be revealed. As far as my discharging the responsibilities of my stewardship is concerned,[21] "my conscience is clear."[22] He says as much again in 7:25: "I give my judgment as one who by the Lord's mercy is trustworthy" (the same adjective as in v. 2).

But the qualifier itself is quickly qualified, lest the point of the imagery be lost. "With regard to my stewardship my own conscience is clear. But so what? That does not mean that I am thereby[23] actually vindicated, or acquitted."[24] The NIV is slightly misleading. It is not the presence or absence of innocence that concerns Paul. Rather, he is simply keeping the metaphor going. Personal evaluation of his own stewardship is irrelevant in light of his ultimate accountability only to the Lord. Not that he is aware of any breach of duty, he is quick to add. Now he simply gets back to the point: The fact that he knows of no failure with regard to his trust likewise means nothing, for that simply puts it back onto the level of a merely human court. His own clear conscience, therefore, does not acquit him before God.

The reason? "It is the Lord[25] who judges me." In saying this Paul has arrived at the point of the imagery that began in v. 1. As v. 5 indicates, "the Lord" is Christ,[26] the metaphor itself having dictated this choice of

---

[20]A difficult γάρ joins this clause to the preceding one. The NEB takes it as causal ("Why [ἀλλ'], I do not even pass judgement on myself, for I have nothing on my conscience"), but that seems to miss the force of the three clauses together. More likely this is an illustration of γάρ having the force of δέ. See BAGD 4; cf. Zerwick, *BG*, 473.

[21]The sentence must be kept in this context. To make it a general statement about his interior life simply goes beyond the present concern.

[22]Lit. "I know nothing with myself." The verb σύνοιδα, found only here and in Acts 5:2 in the NT, is the root from which comes the noun συνείδησις, "conscience" (see on 8:7).

[23]Gk. ἐν τούτῳ; a causal usage: "on this account," or "because of this." See Moule, 51.

[24]Gk. δεδικαίωμαι; the first occurrence of this verb in the extant Pauline letters. Its only other occurrence in 1 Corinthians is in 6:11, where it has its well-known theological meaning of right standing with God. Although it is used here in keeping with the metaphor, it does not necessarily lose its theological flavor altogether. Nonetheless, the emphasis here is on the final judgment, not on a judgment previously carried out through Christ's death.

[25]The noun κύριος does not have the article, but this is a clear case of Colwell's rule (see on 3:17), where a definite predicate noun that precedes the verb does not need the definite article.

[26]Holladay, 60, thinks otherwise, that it refers to God, who is mentioned at the end of v. 5. But ordinary Pauline usage ("Lord" used absolutely almost always refers to Christ) and the language "the Lord comes" in v. 5, which refers exclusively to Christ, seem determinative.

titles: Only the Lord *(kyrios)*, the master *(kyrios)* of the house, to whom alone I am accountable, may examine me *(anakrinō,* v. 4) and hand down a verdict *(krinō,* v. 5) as to the faithfulness with which I discharge my duties. The obvious conclusion, therefore, will be pronounced in the next sentence: "You must stop judging me."

5   With yet another emphatic "So then,"[27] Paul brings the imagery of this paragraph to its conclusion in the form of a strong imperative: "judge nothing before the appointed time." In light of their actual situation, revealed in v. 3 and 9:3, this injunction should probably be given its full force as a present prohibition:[28] "So then, *stop* reaching a verdict[29] on anything before the appointed time." By "anything" Paul does not mean that they are to make no judgments. In 5:12, in the context of flagrant immorality in their midst, they are commanded to "judge those on the inside," and in 6:5 they are expected to be able to judge disputes between brothers within the community. Rather, the kinds of "judgments" that must cease are those they are currently making about Paul and his ministry, judgments that reflect their lack of genuine eschatological perspective. Such judgments are "before the appointed time,"[30] when[31] the Lord, the "master of the household," will himself come and hand down the verdict: "At that time each will receive his praise from God."[32] Thus their own judgments are inconsequential both because only the Lord can judge his own servants (v. 4b), and also because only the final eschatological judgment counts for anything.

Paul's point is now made; nonetheless he proceeds to qualify the coming of the Lord by appending a description of the Judge: "He will bring to light what is hidden in darkness and will expose the motives of men's hearts" (cf. 14:24). Using the language of his Jewish heritage,[33] in the form

---

[27]Gk. ὥστε. See on 3:7 and 21a, properly translated "therefore" in the NIV.

[28]On this usage, see Turner, *Syntax,* p. 76. Cf. the translation by Williams: "So you must stop forming. . . ."

[29]The verb has now changed to κρίνω. It will change again to διακρίνω in v. 7. This same play on κρίνω words occurs again in 11:27-34, and is nearly impossible to reproduce in English.

[30]Gk. πρὸ καιροῦ (cf. Matt. 8:29); this could possibly mean "ahead of time" = "too early" (cf. NEB, Phillips, "premature"), but the next clause, which defines the "time" intended, makes it clear that Paul means the appointed time (= the Day) of judgment.

[31]Gk. ἕως ἄν, which means "that the commencement of an event is dependent on circumstances" (BAGD I.1b). The circumstance here is the coming of the Lord, which thereby defines the "appointed time."

[32]On the possibility that this is what Paul means by "reward," see also on 3:14.

[33]It is axiomatic in Judaism that God knows and searches human hearts. See, e.g., 1 Sam. 16:7; 1 Chr. 28:9; Ps. 139:1, 11-12; Jer. 17:10; Matt. 6:4, 6, 18; Heb. 4:12-13; Sir. 1:30; *Midr.Ps.* 14:1; *Bar.Sota* 3a; Jos. *War* 5.413. Cf. Paul himself in 14:25; 1 Thess. 2:4; 2 Cor. 4:2-4; Rom. 2:16.

of semitic parallelism (cf. 3:15),[34] he reflects on the reality that nothing can be hidden from the God with whom we have to do. He will expose ("bring to light") all things because he already dwells in inaccessible light, where there is nothing "hidden in darkness,"[35] including the inner recesses of one's own thoughts—the motives that lie behind the visible actions. Paul's primary reason for this description of the coming Judge seems to be to reinforce what he suggested in v. 4, that he really has nothing to hide. Indeed, what is remarkable about Paul's use of this language is its positive application, that it will result in his—and others'—receiving "praise from God." At the same time, since he expands the application to "each person" (cf. 3:10-15), it also serves as an invitation to the Corinthians to "come clean." They, too, are candidates to "receive praise from God" when the Lord comes. On the other hand, if they do not correct their ways, it obviously could also function as a veiled threat. Christ "will bring to light what is hidden in darkness and will expose the motives of men's hearts." A sure future lies before them as well. Take heed.

The application of this paragraph to the contemporary church seems self-evident. On the one hand, it is a word to those in the church who are forever "examining" their ministers, and who in any case tend to do so on the wrong grounds. Corinth is not the only church that ever became disillusioned with its minister because he or she lacked enough "charismatic" qualities. But God's Word to us is that faithfulness, not success, is what God requires of his servants. On the other hand, although not intended so by Paul, by implication it is also a word to those who preach and teach, that they recognize themselves as "under trust." Their "trustworthiness" is finally going to be judged by the Lord himself, on the grounds of their being faithful to the trust itself, the gospel. In that hour none of our self-evaluations as to our worth in the kingdom is going to count for a thing, only our faithfulness to the gospel itself.

b. The marks of true apostleship (4:6-13)

6 *Now, brothers, I have applied these things to myself and Apollos for your benefit, so that you may learn from us the meaning of the*

---

[34]This is a piece of typical semitic poetry, in the form of synonymous parallelism. Therefore, one must be careful of "overexegeting" the two lines. In such poetry a single reality is being expressed, even though the two lines say it in slightly different ways.

[35]Turner, *Insights*, pp. 131-32, argues that it is "not the things that darkness hides," but "the concealing darkness itself" that is brought to light. His concern is well taken, that the very darkness that allows the Corinthians their misjudgments needs to be destroyed at Christ's coming. Nonetheless, this concept is so common in Jewish antiquity that it seems overly subtle to suggest that Paul intended something other than bringing to light "the things that darkness hides." Cf. Barrett, 103.

saying, "Do not go beyond what is written." [1] Then you will not take pride in the one over against the other.[2] 7 For who makes you different from anyone else? What do you have that you did not receive? And if you did receive it, why do you boast as though you did not?

8 Already you have all you want! Already you have become rich! You have become kings—and that without us! How I wish that you really had become kings so that we might be kings with you! 9 For it seems to me that[3] God has put us apostles on display at the end of the procession, like men condemned to die in the arena. We have been made a spectacle to the whole universe, to angels as well as to men. 10 We are fools for Christ, but you are so wise in Christ! We are weak, but you are strong! You are honored, we are dishonored! 11 To this very hour we go hungry and thirsty, we are in rags, we are brutally treated, we are homeless. 12 We work hard with our own hands. When we are cursed, we bless; when we are persecuted, we endure it; 13 when we are slandered,[4] we answer kindly. Up to this moment we have become the scum of the earth, the refuse of the world.

Paul herewith applies the foregoing figures (from 3:5–4:5) directly to the situation in Corinth. But how he applies them! The section is dominated by two themes: their pride (vv. 6-8, 10) and his weaknesses (vv. 9, 11-13). He begins by going right to the root of the matter—their pride—which has caused them to be "puffed up" against Paul (v. 6). After trying to deflate them through a series of rhetorical questions (v. 7), he launches into an *ad hominem* argument against both their exalted status and their improper view of apostleship. The contrasts are stark: They have "arrived" (v. 8); he is like a man condemned to die in the arena (v. 9). They are wise, strong, and honored; he is foolish, weak, and dishonored (v. 10). The paragraph then concludes with a catalogue of apostolic tribulations (vv. 11-13), in which he "boasts" in the very things about himself that they disdain. The irony is devastating: How they perceive themselves, masterfully overstated in vv. 8 and 10, is undoubtedly the way they think *he* ought to be. But the way he actually is, set forth in the rhetoric of vv. 11-13, is the way *they* all ought to be.

[1]The Syriac versions and the MajT add φρονεῖν after γέγραπται. Not only does this lack any early support, but there is no way to explain its universal early omission if it were original. Here is a clear case of "the more difficult" reading being the original.

[2]NIV, "one man over against another." See the commentary.

[3]The MajT has added a ὅτι here for the sake of improving Paul's Greek: δοκέω followed by an indicative ordinarily prefers the expressed "that"; so does English, hence the "that" in most English versions.

[4]P68 B D F G Ψ Maj read the more common βλασφημούμενοι for the much rarer δυσφημούμενοι of P46 ℵ* A C P 33 81 1175 1506 pc. Again, the more difficult reading is to be preferred.

Paul is here applying the theology of the cross, set forth in 1:18–2:16, to the Christian life. It is true that this paragraph speaks of his apostleship in particular, but it is equally true that the whole point of the next paragraph (vv. 14-17) is to urge them to "imitate" him, that is, to follow his "way of life in Christ Jesus." For Paul, as we have seen, to be a servant means to be a servant of Christ Jesus. It means to go the way of the cross. As the poet put it: "It is the way the master trod; should not the servant tread it still?"

6 With this sentence Paul proceeds to tell the Corinthians expressly *why* he has been using the various preceding analogies about himself and Apollos. It was "for your benefit," he tells them, which is then spelled out in two purpose clauses. The first one is a notoriously difficult crux: "that you may learn from us the meaning of the saying, 'Do not go beyond what is written.'" Whatever that means, the aim of everything that has preceded, as the rest of the argument demonstrates, is the final purpose clause:[5] that "you will not take pride in the one over against the other."[6] They have been "boasting in men," and this has involved them in strife and quarrels. Here we learn that they are in fact "puffed up" in favor of "the one" (probably Apollos, as we shall note momentarily) and over against "the other" (Paul). It is this pride of theirs, plus their being over against Paul, that he will address in the rest of the paragraph.

That the argument has reached the moment of truth is signaled first of all by the way it begins: with the words "these things" placed in the emphatic position, followed by the transitional particle *de* (NIV, "now") and the vocative "brothers [and sisters]" (see on 1:10). As the verb and the specific mention of Paul and Apollos indicate, "these things" refer to the various images that have made up the argument, beginning at 3:5 and continuing to 4:5. The sentence also seems to imply that whatever role Peter may have had in the community, he was not being followed vis-à-vis Paul in the same way that Apollos was (see on 1:12 and 3:22).[7] The verb translated "I have

---

[5] Morna Hooker suggests otherwise: "that the first will refer to the basic trouble which has given rise to the situation described in the second" ("'Beyond the Things which are Written': An Examination of I Cor. iv.6," *NTS* 10 [1963/64], 128). But the rest of the argument puts the focus on the second clause. Vv. 7-13 take up the matter of "pride" and vv. 18-21 speak to their arrogance against Paul in particular.

[6] What is less clear, and in fact cannot be decided, is whether the second ἵνα-clause is coordinate with the first and thus dependent on the verb μετεσχημάτισα or subordinate to μάθητε as an object clause, giving the content of what they should have learned. The latter is probably to be preferred, but the former cannot be ruled out. In either case the net result is the same: it all points to the final clause as the ultimate concern.

[7] Otherwise Barrett, 106, following T. W. Manson (see n. 44 on 1:12). He suggests: ". . . Paul means that he has made the argument of the last few paragraphs . . . look as if it applied (or applied only) to himself and Apollos." The rest of the sentence, especially the "*for* the one, *against* the other," makes this view difficult to sustain. See n. 26 below.

applied" ordinarily means "to change the outward appearance of anything, the thing itself remaining the same."[8] But despite a very old tradition going back to Chrysostom that would make the verb mean that here, it makes very little sense to do so.[9] The context and the emphatic position of "these things" demand a meaning wherein the figures, not the persons, are what have "changed form."[10] That is, he has gone from metaphor to metaphor, changing images as he went along, but always intending them (at least most of them), as he now says, to apply "to myself and Apollos."[11] In other words, in case they have somehow missed it, he now expressly tells them that he has been carrying on the argument with its various images about himself and Apollos so that they might *learn* something and as a result desist from their current "pride in persons."

But what is it that he wanted them to "learn" from the preceding metaphors? This clause is particularly difficult to pin down. Literally it reads: "in order that you may learn in us the not beyond what is written," a text that some see as so obscure that they despair of finding its meaning.[12] One solution would emend the text by eliminating altogether the five troublesome words, *to mē hyper ha gegraptai* ("the: not above[13] what is written"), suggesting that they are a gloss.[14] But Ockham's razor must prevail in

---

[8]Gk. μετασχηματίζω (cf. 2 Cor. 11:13-15; Phil. 3:21). This definition is from Field, *Notes*, p. 169. For the most thorough discussions of the verb, see F. H. Colson, "Μετεσχημάτισα in I Cor. iv 6," *JTS* 17 (1916), 379-84, and Hooker (n. 5 above).

[9]Cf. n. 37 on 1:12.

[10]Fiore ("'Covert Allusion,'" pp. 94-95) renews the suggestion that ταῦτα refers to Paul and Apollos, who "become figures themselves, to which the community is to look for their own improvement." This study, which is otherwise a very helpful analysis of the use of "indirect speech" as a rhetorical device in antiquity, is seriously marred by its failure to recognize the apologetic element in chap. 4.

[11]This meaning is solidly attested in the noncompounded form of the verb σχηματίζω, putting emphasis on the word σχῆμα. See the discussion by Hooker and Colson (n. 8 above); cf. BAGD. For a discussion of the noncompounded form as referring to "indirect speech" in rhetoric, see Fiore, "'Covert Allusion,'" pp. 88-93.

[12]Cf. Moffatt, 46, who leaves out the troublesome words by translating, "to teach you . . . that you are not to be puffed up." He comments: "But between *teach you* and *that* in Greek five . . . words are inserted whose meaning lies beyond recovery." Cf. Conzelmann, 86: "The phrase τὸ μὴ ὑπὲρ ἃ γέγραπται is unintelligible"; Senft, 67.

[13]This would be the singular biblical example (although of course from this view it is not biblical) of ὑπέρ having a local sense, meaning "above" or "over."

[14]The conjecture has the following steps: (1) Paul originally wrote ἵνα ἐν ἡμῖν μάθητε ἵνα μὴ εἷς etc. (2) In the next copy μή was dropped out accidentally. (3) In that copy or the next someone inserted μή between the lines above the α in ἵνα. (4) In that copy or the next, someone wrote in the margin τὸ μὴ ὑπὲρ ἃ γέγραπται, i.e., "the μή is written above the α." (5) This copy fell into the hands of the copyist responsible for all succeeding copies of 1 Corinthians, who inserted the whole marginal gloss into the text in this form.

The conjecture originated with J. M. S. Baljon, *De Tekst der Brieven van Paulus aan de Romeinen, de Corinthiërs en de Galatiërs als voorwerp van de conjecturaalkritiek beschouwd* (Utrecht, 1884), pp. 49-51. Although not always properly at-this case; the solution is defeated by its very ingenuity and complexity.[15] Given that the text as we have it is what Paul wrote, the structure itself is easy enough to discern, even if the final sense is not. The neuter article *to* in this instance reflects a standard usage: to introduce quoted material (cf. 14:16).[16] This in itself eliminates those interpretations suggesting that "what stands written" refers to the whole argument to this point.[17] The NIV, therefore, has properly caught the sense of Paul's Greek: "that you may learn . . . the meaning of the saying, 'Do not go beyond what is written.' "

But that solves only half the problem—the easier half at that. What does the saying itself mean? And where does it come from—from the Corinthians or from Paul? Here the NIV is ambiguous, keeping very close to what Paul has actually said without attempting to interpret. There are two basic options: (1) Taking their clue from the verb *gegraptai*, which refers throughout Paul's letters to the citing of scripture, most interpreters think that the saying means something like "live according to scripture" (RSV).[18] This is an attractive option, but it leaves one with the difficulty of deciding

---

tributed to him, and in some cases taking slightly different forms, it was adopted in the commentaries by Schmiedel, Bousset, Héring, Williams, and Murphy-O'Connor (Weiss, R-P, and Conzelmann are tempted); and in the following studies: W. F. Howard, "1 Corinthians iv.6 (Exegesis or Emendation?)," *ExpT* 33 (1921/22), 479-80; J. T. Hudson, "1 Cor. iv.6," *ExpT* 35 (1923/24), 332 (tempted); A. Legault, "'Beyond the Things which are written' (I Cor. iv.6)," *NTS* 18 (1971/72), 227-31; and esp. J. Strugnell, "A Plea for Conjectural Emendation in the New Testament, with a Coda on 1 Cor 4:6," *CBQ* 36 (1974), 543-58, who tries to remove some of the difficulties posited by Ross and others (see next note) by suggesting that the scribe who wrote the gloss in the margin intended to tell his readers that he added a μή "beyond what stands written," i.e., it wasn't in his text at all, but the sense needed it so he marked the text accordingly. Strugnell's position has been viewed favorably by D. R. MacDonald, "A Conjectural Emendation of 1 Cor 15:31-32: or the Case of the Misplaced Lion Fight," *HTR* 93 (1980), 261; and Murphy-O'Connor, "Interpolations," 85.

[15]See especially the objections by J. M. Ross, "Not Above What is Written. A Note on 1 Cor 4:6," *ExpT* 82 (1971), 215-17. The problem is compounded by two factors: (1) It takes at least five steps (fewer in Strugnell's case) to get from an original without the words to the text as we now have it, and (2) it had to have happened so close to the source that all of these changes took place before a single copy of the original was able to be copied without the inserted gloss. Ross also notes regarding Baljon's conjecture that the glossator would almost surely have written τὸ μὴ ὑπὲρ τὸ ἃ γέγραπται. For a considerable response to Strugnell, but more on the whole question of conjectural emendation than on this text per se, see G. D. Kilpatrick, "Conjectural Emendation in the New Testament," in *New Testament Textual Criticism, Its Significance for Exegesis. Essays in Honour of Bruce M. Metzger* (ed. E. J. Epp and G. D. Fee; Oxford, 1981), 349-60.

[16]See BAGD ὅ 8 a. Illustrations are legion, especially in the early Greek Fathers' citations of the Bible. In the NT see Matt. 19:18; Luke 22:37; Rom. 13:9; Gal. 5:14.

[17]As, e.g., in Phillips: "that you might learn from what I have said about us."

[18]Cf. Barrett ("Nothing beyond what stands written"); JB ("Keep to what is written"), Williams ("Never go beyond what is written").

what "scripture" refers to: the texts specifically cited in chaps. 1 and 3?[19] or the OT in some overall, but vague, sense?[20] Of these two options the former is to be preferred, but it is still not clear how the Corinthians would have understood the cited texts as something they were "not to go beyond." (2) The second option sees the saying as a popular proverb, which both he and the Corinthians knew, that meant something like "Keep within the rules" (NEB).[21] This, too, is attractive; but again it is not certain what the proverb would have meant in this context. Probably something like "The way you are treating me vis-à-vis Apollos is not playing within the rules of the game, as it were." Of these solutions, the one that sees Paul as referring to previously cited scripture is more likely.[22] If so, then this first purpose clause would be speaking again to the matter of wisdom and boasting, that they should "live according to scripture" and not boast illegitimately (1:29, 31), nor be caught up by the "wise" whom God has ensnared (1:19; 3:19-20). But on this matter we must finally plead ignorance. Here is a case where the apostle and his readers were on a wavelength that will probably be forever beyond our ability to pick up.

But if what they were to learn "from us" cannot finally be determined,[23] the final goal of the learning seems certain.[24] They[25] were to stop "boasting" in "the one" in such a way as to be "over against the other." Here we come to the root of the problem. Although this may simply be a general statement against the whole scene of quarreling as expressed in 1:12, it seems more likely that "the one" here is Apollos and "the other" Paul. Two items support this interpretation. First, the word for pride in this case, which means to be "puffed up" (similar to our idiom from balloons, "filled with hot air"), occurs again in v. 18 ("arrogant," NIV), specifically in a context where some stand over against the apostle because he had not returned to visit them. Second, the combination of "*the* one" and "*the*

---

[19]This is argued for especially by Hooker, " 'Beyond,' " and Ellis, 61, 69, 74-75, 214.

[20]As, e.g., Mare, 212: "[It] seems to be a general statement advising the Corinthians not to go beyond any written doctrine in the OT."

[21]Cf. GNB, "Observe the proper rules." Another alternative of this kind was suggested by Parry, 78-79, namely that γέγραπται carries the technical sense of a contract or agreement. Hence he is telling them " 'not to go beyond the terms,' i.e. of the commission as teacher."

[22]Chiefly on the grounds of Paul's use of γέγραπται elsewhere.

[23]Gk. ἐν ἡμῖν, either "in our case" or "by means of us," referring to the preceding analogies.

[24]On this matter Conzelmann, 86, is too skeptical in suggesting that "the second ἵνα-clause . . . is likewise difficult to fathom. Here the general sense is certainly plain, but the expression is not."

[25]The Greek text reads εἷς φυσιοῦσθε, the εἷς in this case functioning much like a ἕκαστος (= each of you is puffed up); cf. 1:12, "each of you is saying."

other," where they follow the mention of two specific people, would ordinarily refer back to the two people, not to "one" and "another" in general.[26] It may be, of course, that the two could alternate, depending on whose side one was on (i.e., a person saying "I belong to Paul" could also be over against "the other," who in that case would be Apollos). And that may have been so; but the inescapable implication of the rest of the argument in this chapter is that some of them at least were decidedly against Paul, and he now turns to take them on for the pride exhibited in their being opposed to him.

7 The "for" that connects these questions with v. 6 indicates that Paul is about to give reasons—by way of rhetoric—why those who are "puffed up" against him are out of place.[27] Their pride in persons reflects a lack of proper perspective,[28] a lack of gratitude. The Fall has given us all too high a view of ourselves, with a correspondingly low view of others. Instead of offering humble thanksgiving for gifts received (see on 1:4), the Corinthians have allowed the gifts to become a sign of status and a source of dissension. With these questions, then, Paul is trying to give them perspective.

The exact intent of the first question, however, is not immediately transparent. The difficulty lies with the meaning of the verb *diakrinei* ("discern, distinguish"), which is probably something of a wordplay on the *anakrinō* ("examine") and *krinō* ("judge") of vv. 3-5. It is common to see it as referring to the Corinthians' being "puffed up" against one another within the community. Thus: "Who makes you different from anyone else?" (NIV). The implication is that there are no grounds for anyone's exalting himself/herself over another, since any differences are ultimately attributable to God.[29] But this places the emphasis on the internal quarrels in the community, which do not otherwise seem to surface at this point in the argument, where Paul is trying to correct their attitude toward himself.

[26]Cf. Matt. 6:24: "two masters, . . . the one, . . . the other"; Luke 17:34: "two people in bed, the one taken, the other left"; Luke 18:10: "two men, . . . the one a Pharisee, the other a tax collector." When Paul wants to say "one for another," as in 1 Thess. 5:11, it is simply εἰς τὸν ἕνα. This grammatical phenomenon also rules out the interpretation that sees the text as a general teaching on learning humility from the example of Paul and Apollos.

[27]The questions unexpectedly appear in the second person singular, which in this case probably picks up "each one" from v. 6 and at the same time reflects Paul's semitic background, in which the OT legal materials, spoken to all of Israel, are often given force by appearing in the singular: "Thou shalt, or shalt not." This same kind of movement from a second plural to a second singular occurs again in 7:27-28; 8:9-10; 14:16-17; and 15:36.

[28]Pride generally results from an improper perspective, both about oneself (whether of achievement or status) and about one's true stance before God (deserving rather than helpless).

[29]Or perhaps irony would be intended: "You may think of yourself as better than another, but in reality there are no significant differences between you in God's sight."

The alternative is to see the question as directly related to v. 6 and their pride vis-à-vis Paul. In this case the question would mean, "Who distinguishes *you*?"[30] On what possible grounds do you boast in this manner? The implication is that their boasting in wisdom, which allows them to "examine" Paul, is strictly self-proclaimed. The English equivalent to such rhetoric would be, "Who in the world do you think you are, anyway? What kind of self-delusion is it that allows you to put yourself in a position to judge another person's servant?"

If the first question marks the Corinthian conceit as *presumptuous,* the second marks it as *ungrateful*[31]—and is singularly devastating: "What do you have that you did not receive?" This is an invitation to experience one of those rare, unguarded moments of total honesty, where in the presence of the eternal God one recognizes that everything—absolutely everything— that one "has" is a gift.[32] All is of grace; nothing is deserved, nothing earned. Those who so experience grace also live from a posture of unbounded gratitude. Those, such as the Corinthians, who think of themselves as especially gifted with the Spirit and wisdom, thereby enabling them to judge another, reflect a total misunderstanding of grace, and quite miss the "humility of God" expressed in the crucified One.

In case they miss the point, Paul drives the second question home with a third, which assumes the answer "nothing" to the second: "And since[33] you *did* receive it, why do you boast as though you did not?" Here is the telling word. Their "boasting"[34] is sure evidence that they have missed the gospel of grace. Instead of recognizing everything as a gift and being filled with gratitude, they *possessed* their gifts—saw them as their own— and looked down on the apostle who seemed to lack so much. Grace leads to gratitude; "wisdom" and self-sufficiency lead to boasting and judging. Grace has a leveling effect; self-esteem has a self-exalting effect. Grace means humility; boasting means that one has arrived. Precisely because their boasting reflects such an attitude, Paul turns to irony to help them see the folly of their "boasting."

8 As a contrast to the stance of gratitude and humility urged by the rhetorical questions of v. 7, Paul now begins a series of antitheses between

---

[30]Cf. BAGD: "Who concedes you any superiority?" and Moffatt, 48: "Who in the world sees anything special in *you*?"

[31]So Findlay, 800.

[32]The question belongs alongside those equally devastating questions in the OT in which one is brought face to face with the truth about oneself before God: e.g., Isa. 40:14: "Whom did the Lord consult to enlighten him?" ("You who know so much as now to question his ways?" being the implied response). Cf. Job 38.

[33]Gk. εἰ δὲ καί ("but if indeed"), which does not imply that they may not have received it, but reinforces the fact that they did indeed.

[34]Gk. καυχᾶσαι again; cf. 1:29-31.

them and himself to which shame is the only suitable response.[35] With three staccato sentences, the rhetoric punctuated by asyndeton,[36] Paul goes straight to the heart of the matter. The words are full of biting irony, attacking their own view of themselves (cf. Rev. 3:17), which is at once true and false. It is true in the sense of 12:13 and 1:5, that in Christ they have all drunk deeply of the Spirit and have been enriched with every kind of spiritual gift. But such gifts must be forever humbling, for they finally lead to a discipleship that goes the way of the cross, not the way of a false triumphalism.

The three verbs attack not just their pride in general, but specifically their view of spirituality, which reflects an "overrealized" eschatology.[37] Paul's perspective, which he shares with the rest of the NT writers, is one of "already but not yet" held in tension; theirs is one of "already" with little room for "not yet." Having received the Spirit, they have already arrived; for them spirituality means to have been transported into a whole new sphere of existence where they are "above" the earthly, and especially "fleshly," existence of others. Thus, "already you have all you want," a verb that means to eat to the full.[38] Not only do they boast in what is a gracious gift, but they are "satiated" with their gifts, including "wisdom."[39] "Already you have become rich!" (cf. 1:5),[40] a second metaphor for spiritual giftedness. In both cases they are gifted indeed, but not in the way they think.

The emphatic position of the adverb "already" marks the first two

[35]Despite the demurrer of v. 14 (q.v.).

[36]As with many modern translations (e.g., RSV, NAB, NEB), the NIV marks the irony and rhetoric with exclamation points. It is possible, as many do (e.g., TCNT, GNB, JB, Moffatt), to take the sentences as a continuation of the rhetorical questions of v. 7. Hence, "Do you already have everything you need? Are you already rich? Have you become kings, even though we are not?" (GNB). This has some attraction to it; however, the change in style from v. 7 is especially pronounced and probably therefore suggests staccato indicatives. In either case, it is all irony.

[37]Ellis, 77-79, doubts that this verse reflects an overrealized eschatology on the part of the Corinthians. See the response by A. C. Thiselton, "Realized Eschatology at Corinth," *NTS* 24 (1976/77), 510-26.

[38]Gk. κορέννυμι, a verb that is often used metaphorically in the religious and philosophical writers. Cf., e.g., Philo, *leg.all.* 3.111 ("we have glutted ourselves with immoderate pleasure"; cf. 183); *post.Cain.* 145 ("wherefore God ever causes his earliest gifts to cease before their recipients are glutted").

[39]Although one cannot be sure that Paul intended it, it is difficult not to connect this imagery with that of 3:1-2, where he has had to treat them as "babies" because they were not "grown up" enough to recognize the cross as the heart of all things that God is about in the new age. They think of themselves as adults, and Paul now allows that to the point of their being "stuffed" with rich food. But they gorge themselves on what eventually brings only leanness of soul.

[40]Gk. πλουτέω ("become rich") rather than the πλουτίζω ("be made rich") of 1:5. The change from the perfect in the first sentence to the aorist with this and the next verb is not significant. The two aorists are ingressive: "you have become; you have begun. . . ."

exclamations as eschatological; the language of the third does the same: "You have become kings—and that without us!" Despite the support of many commentators and translators, the NIV reflects a slightly skewed nuance for the verb, which in Paul's sentence refers to their activity of reigning,[41] not to their status as kings. Hence the NAB: "You have launched upon your reign" (cf. NEB, Barrett). The differences may seem slight; the point is that Paul's language here is thoroughly eschatological and reflects his Jewish heritage,[42] which viewed the saints as sharing the reign at the End, but not themselves as becoming kings.[43] For Paul the long-awaited messianic kingdom had been inaugurated by the coming of Jesus. The kingdom of God is both a present reality (v. 20) and a future hope (6:9). Paul thus sees their present boasting in spiritual status as tantamount to their supposing the final reign of God already to have begun. As with the spiritual gifts with which they have been enriched, so also with the kingdom of God. They have indeed entered the kingdom, of which the Spirit is the evidence. But they have not yet fully realized the End, of which the resurrection will be the evidence (cf. chap. 15).

In the Greek text the "without us" stands in the same emphatic position as the "already" in the previous two sentences. As the NIV suggests, it means not "apart from our help,"[44] but, as the next sentence implies, "without our having a share in it." The use of the plural "us" here and throughout the rest of this passage needs to be noted. By this designation Paul is first of all referring to himself. But the use of "us," especially "us apostles" in v. 9, indicates that the Corinthians are being set over against *all*

[41]As always in Paul; see 15:25; Rom. 5:14, 17, 21; 6:12. Even the RSV instinctively recognizes this, for even though the first instance is translated "without us you have become kings," the following clause is more correctly rendered: "And would that you did reign, so that we might share the rule with you."

[42]Cf. especially how the argument of this section concludes with language about the kingdom of God (v. 20), which picks up the language of this verse.

[43]Dan. 7:27; cf. Jesus in Luke 22:29-30 and the parable in Luke 19:17. See also Rev. 5:10; 20:4, 6; 22:5. Some (e.g., Findlay, Weiss, Conzelmann) have suggested that this is a reflection of Stoic parallels, perhaps adopted by the Corinthians, in which "the wise person is king." The parallels are indeed striking (see esp. Philo, *Abr.* 261: "The kingdom of the wise person comes by the gift of God," and Plutarch, *Tranq. an.* 472a: "In their [the Stoics'] sect the wise man . . . is a rich man and a king"). But one of the differences between these parallels and the Jewish heritage of Paul is in the static, positional character of the Stoic over against the Jewish apocalyptic emphasis on the dynamic character of the kingdom.

[44]Findlay, 801, interprets the adverb ἤδη to mean "so soon" and the following χωρὶς ἡμῶν ("without us") to mean "without our help" (cf. NAB). The whole, therefore, is seen not as eschatological but as Paul's reflecting on their stance toward him over against their other teachers. "So soon you have become full, without our aid; etc." It might have been possible to understand the first two in this way, but the addition of the third, with its distinctively eschatological language, rules decisively in the other direction.

their teachers. Again, the plural "you" may not necessarily include all believers, but the fact that the church as a whole is being contrasted to Paul— and his view of how other apostles also ought to be—implies that the infections of "some" have spread widely among them.

The final sentence brings things into perspective. "How I wish that you really had begun to reign"; that would mean that the End which we all await had in fact truly come. It would mean, he says somewhat wistfully,[45] that we also[46] have entered the final kingdom with you. Instead, he remains as they know him to be, full of weaknesses. But in contrast to them, he will capitalize on the very things they disdain, because these weaknesses reflect the true nature of discipleship, discipleship that is consonant with his preaching of the cross.

9 The final sentence of v. 8 sets up the contrasts of the rest of the paragraph, contrasts not only between them and himself, but also between their opposing views of apostleship—and discipleship. Paul has *not* in fact entered the time of reigning, and neither by implication have they. This latter point, however, is not his immediate concern. Rather, he first sets forth in its starkest form the *evidence* that he and the other apostles have not yet begun to reign. To do so he uses the figure of those condemned to die in the arena. We apostles are like them, he says, not like those who have the places of honor in the box seats.

The metaphor reads (lit.): "For it seems to me that God has appointed us the apostles[47] to be last, as those condemned to die." Most interpreters understand the words "to be last" to suggest the last events of the spectacles, whose participants were those condemned to die,[48] either as gladiators or those simply thrown to the beasts. The NIV, on the other hand, understands them in terms of the Roman triumph, in which a conquering general staged a splendid parade that included not only his armies but the booty as well.[49] At the very "end of the procession" were those captives who had been "condemned to die in the arena." In that way they became a spectacle[50] for all to

---

[45]Gk. καὶ ὄφελόν γε, indicating an unfulfillable wish.

[46]The NIV leaves out an emphatic καί here, "even we."

[47]For Paul's use of the term "apostle" see on 1:1. In this context it must include Apollos as well as Peter. This is further evidence that for Paul, at least at this stage, the term was more functional than official. At least it included far more than the Twelve, as 15:7 also implies.

[48]Gk. ἐπιθανατίους; cf. similar usage in the LXX of Bel 31, referring to those who were condemned to be thrown to the lions, two at a time, daily, and in Dion.Hal. 7.35 to the condemned who were thrown from a high rock overlooking the Forum.

[49]This is a widely attested phenomenon. See, e.g., Dio Cassius, *Roman History*, VI; Jos. *War* 7.132-57. For a full discussion, see H. S. Versnel, *Triumphus: An Inquiry into the Origin, Development, and Meaning of the Roman Triumph* (Leiden, 1970).

[50]Gk. θέατρον; lit. "what one sees at a theater," thus a play or a spectacle. It is common to note the Stoic use of this term, as found, e.g., in Seneca (*prov.* 2.9, 11; *ep.*

see. Since Paul will utilize this imagery again in 2 Cor. 2:14, also in connection with his apostleship,[51] it seems likely that this is also in view here. In either case, the metaphor is a striking one, intended to begin the series with the same sense of utter humiliation with which it will conclude (v. 13). The scandal of the cross is written large over Paul's vision of his own apostleship. For him it truly was "like master, like servant" (cf. Luke 20:26-27).[52]

The Corinthians' pride in spiritual status apparently included a degree of embarrassment over Paul's lack thereof, not to mention his lack of wisdom and eloquence. It was perhaps doubtful from their perspective whether he was an apostle with much standing.[53] With a final thrust at this pride he affirms not only that he is like one condemned to die in the arena, but that the spectacle is for the whole world[54] to behold. Indeed, in words that must have aimed at their discomfort, Paul says that there is a cosmic dimension to the spectacle: He is on display before the whole universe, as it were—not just human beings, but the angels as well.[55] That seems to be the point of the reference to angels, which is otherwise not entirely discernible. Angels are referred to elsewhere in 1 Corinthians in 6:2; 10:11; and 13:1.[56] In each case some exegetical difficulties are attached to the references. Paul here assumes more than he explains for the sake of his later readers! We may assume that he means those messengers of God whom we would call "good angels," since Paul does not call those who are evil "angels," but "principalities and powers."

10 The contrasts begun in vv. 8-9, in the context of eschatology,

---

64.4-6); but Seneca thought of the Stoic as a "spectacle" of courage and strength before the gods, and thus for him it was a matter of pride. That is a far cry from Paul's usage here. It is therefore probably not quite precise, and in any case irrelevant, to say that Paul has "taken over" the "Stoic picture of the philosopher's struggle as a spectacle for the world" (Conzelmann, 88; cf. G. Kittel, *TDNT* III, 43; V. C. Pfitzner, *Paul and the Agon Motif* [NovTSup 16; Leiden, 1967], p. 189). See J. Sevenster, *Paul and Seneca* (NovTSup 4; Leiden, 1961), pp. 115-16. Other Latin writers use the imagery, in a way similar to Paul, to express the "tragedy" of their lives; e.g., Sallust, *Jug.* 14.23; Pliny, *panegyr.* 33.3.

[51]This is not a universal view about 2 Cor. 2:14. See the helpful discussion in Furnish, *II Corinthians*, pp. 174-75. The argument by P. Marshall in this case seems conclusive ("A Metaphor of Social Shame: THRIAMBEUEIN in 2 Cor. 2:14," *NovT* 25 [1983], 302-17), especially since Egan's entire argument is predicated on the use of a compound, not the simple verb itself ("Lexical Evidence on Two Pauline Passages," *NovT* 19 [1977], 34-62).

[52]On this see below on vv. 16-17.

[53]Note especially how 2 Corinthians carries on this theme in several sections, e.g., 2:14–6:13 and 10:1–13:10.

[54]Gk. κόσμος, translated "universe" by the NIV because of the inclusion of "angels" as well as people.

[55]G. Kittel, *TDNT* III, 43, suggests reminiscences to Job, whose sufferings were a spectacle to Satan; this would therefore imply fallen angels, which seems doubtful.

[56]If we are correct that part of their misguided view of spirituality included the motif of being as the angels, then there might be some "punch" to this reference.

are now resumed in an extraordinary way. With three antitheses similar to those in 1:26, Paul sets the Corinthians and himself (and other apostles) in bold relief, again with total irony.[57] The majority of the Corinthians are not among the "wise, powerful, or honored"; but they are acting as if they were. In one sense Paul would allow that they are, since they are "in Christ." But they are all of these things in the wrong way; so as before, the purpose of this irony, as well as the tribulation list that follows (vv. 11-13), is both didactic and apologetic. Their "theology of glory" must finally yield to that which alone is Christian, the theology of the cross. At the same time they must stop disregarding his apostleship.

The first set flows directly out of v. 9, but repeats the themes from 1:18-25 and 3:18-19. The apostles' being a spectacle of cosmic proportions makes them "fools for[58] Christ." Yet there is obvious double entendre: They also thereby reflect the truth of the gospel, which is folly in the eyes of the worldly wise. The Corinthians, on the other hand, find themselves in the "seat of the scornful": "You are so[59] wise[60] in Christ." The addition "in Christ," which probably occurs to balance the "for Christ" in the first clause, only adds to the irony. It is true that they are "in Christ"; but they are altogether missing Christ (see 2:6-16). Those who are in Christ should be "sensible" indeed, but for Paul that means to take his view of the gospel, not the view of the worldly wise, who are not in Christ.

The second set also picks up the themes of 1:18-25, which are repeated in 2:3-5. "We are weak." That of course is the problem from the Corinthian perspective (cf. 2:1-3). But again there is double entendre: Paul's weaknesses reflect the "weakness of God," which is displayed in the cross as his saving power; and in 2:4-5 they are seen as the proper channels through which God's power might be manifested. On the other hand, "you are strong!" In light of 1:26-28 this is the ultimate irony. They are not in fact among the powerful and influential in Corinth, but by their judging Paul they are assuming the seat of such. Yet again, in Christ they should be among the truly "strong."

The final set is put in reverse order, probably to create a smooth transition to vv. 11-13, which will deal only with the apostles. The shift from

---

[57]Theissen, 72-73, seems to miss both the irony and the point of the argument by suggesting that the terms in this passage are also intended primarily to be sociological. It is true that these three terms reflect the sociological terms of 1:26, but that's quite the point of the irony. If they were intended to be sociological, that would make them "true" in another sense, and the irony would be lost.

[58]Gk. διά, "for Christ's sake," as in almost all English translations.

[59]This is not in the Greek text; it is the NIV's attempt, along with the exclamation point, to emphasize the ironic character of the antitheses.

[60]Gk. φρόνιμοι, a synonym of σοφία, with perhaps greater emphasis on the "sensible" character of the "wise" person. It is usually pejorative in Paul, as it is here (cf. 2 Cor. 11:19; Rom. 11:25; 12:16).

the "well-born" of 1:26 is noteworthy. He could not say that about them, precisely because so few would have been.[61] But they can be called "the honored," partly because in Christ it is true—they are destined for glory (2:7). In their case, however, it is self-honor. The worldly wise, whose theology they are emulating, would scarcely afford honor to those who make up the majority of the Christian community in Corinth. Besides being a play on 1:26, this pair also echoes v. 9. The position in which God has placed the apostles, at the end of the procession as those condemned to die in the arena, is the ultimate humiliation of the "dishonored." The Corinthians, on the other hand, would be among those in the procession or the throng, "the honored," who would watch the "dishonored" go to their deaths. But Paul is "dishonored" only before the world, who also dishonor Christ—which again puts the Corinthians in a position of jeopardy. The rest of the passage proceeds to detail the nature of the "dishonor" that befalls those who bear the message of the cross.

11-13   Paul now abandons irony for straight talk. This tribulation list, which spells out in detail the "dishonor" that attends Paul's apostolic ministry, reflects a common phenomenon in antiquity.[62] Such lists can be found elsewhere in Paul himself,[63] as well as in Stoic philosophers,[64] Jewish apocalyptists,[65] Josephus,[66] the Greek biographers and historians,[67] and the later Gnostics[68] (cf. also Heb. 11:33-38). What Paul has in common with such lists is the phenomenon itself, plus an incidental use of language here

---

[61]This is the point that Theissen (n. 57 above) misses; but it is crucial. If Paul were truly addressing the well-born in the community, then that would still be the appropriate word. But he does not do so because the letter is not to those people, but to the community as a whole, of whom the majority are not well-born. But they can be ironically called "the honored."

[62]On this matter see esp. R. Hodgson, "Paul the Apostle and First Century Tribulation Lists," *ZNW* 74 (1983), 59-80.

[63]Especially in 2 Corinthians (4:8-9; 6:4-5, 8-10; 11:23-29; 12:10); cf. Rom. 8:35.

[64]E.g., Epict. 2.19.24: "Show me a man who though sick is happy, though in danger is happy, though dying is happy, though condemned to exile is happy, though in disrepute is happy. Show him! By the gods I would fain see a Stoic!" (Loeb, I, 367); cf. 2.10.17. See esp. R. Bultmann, *Der Stil der paulinischen Predigt und die kynisch-stoische Diatribe* (Göttingen, 1910), pp. 71-72.

[65]E.g., the longer recension of 2 Enoch 66:6: "Walk, my children, in *long-suffering*, in meekness, in *affliction*, in *distress*, in faithfulness, in truth, in hope, in *weakness*, in *derision*, in *assaults*, in *temptation*, in *deprivation*, in *nakedness*, having love for one another, until you go out from this age of suffering" (OTP, I, 194). See W. Schrage, "Leid, Kreuz und Eschaton. Die Peristasenkataloge als Mermale paul-inischer theologia crucis und Eschatologie," *EvT* 34 (1974), 141-75.

[66]He puts into the mouth of Ananus the high priest these words (*War* 4.165): "When plundered you submit, when beaten you are silent, nay over the murdered none dares audibly to groan!" (Loeb, III, 51); cf. *War* 2.151-53.

[67]See the collection in Hodgson (n. 62 above), pp. 76-80.

[68]*Ibid.*, pp. 72-74.

and there. The content of this list is adapted both to his circumstances as a missionary of the gospel of Christ and to his struggles with the Corinthians. The great difference between this list and its companions in 2 Corinthians is the didactic purpose of this one. As vv. 14-17 go on to say, this is a model in kind, if not in specifics, of what the Corinthians also are to be.

The three verses hold together as a single piece, beginning and ending on the same note: "To this very hour/up to this moment."[69] This looks like a deliberate contrast to the Corinthians' overrealized eschatology addressed in v. 8, again emphasizing the harsh realities of Christian life between the ages, over against their having begun to reign. The catalogue is in three parts: (1) a list of five commonplace items, expressing the missionary's deprivations and ill-treatment (v. 11), to which is added a sixth that seems especially to be an area where Paul's behavior has rubbed the Corinthians the wrong way (v. 12a); (2) a set of three antitheses, expressing the apostle's responses to his ill-treatment (vv. 12b-13a); (3) a final metaphor of humiliation, similar in intent to v. 9 but even more extreme in expression (v. 13b).

There is nothing remarkable about the list of commonplace items. Deprivation occurs as a regular motif in such catalogues. However, in this case they stand in direct and stark contrast to the "filled, rich, and reigning" Corinthians (v. 8). Hunger and thirst[70] "up to this very hour" are set over against their "already" being satiated. Dressed "in rags" (cf. RSV, "ill-clad"), which appears as "nakedness" in 2 Cor. 11:27 and Rom. 8:35 and in both instances means to be inadequately clothed, is the obvious opposite of "already being rich." The final two items might seem to be out of order since "homeless" belongs to the first three while ill-treatment picks up another theme altogether. But these are the two that are expanded on in vv. 12-13a, in chiastic order. Hence he next lists "brutally treated," which will be addressed again in the antitheses of vv. 12b-13a. The word literally means "to strike with the fist."[71] Here it seems to denote mistreatment in

---

[69]Gk. ἄχρι τῆς ἄρτι ὥρας . . . ἕως ἄρτι. This structural item seems intentional; however, it is probably going beyond the evidence to see the whole as an expression of chiasm, as does M. L. Barré, "Paul as 'Eschatologic Person': A New Look at 2 Cor 11:29," *CBQ* 37 (1975), 520-22. The "pairs" of verbs in vv. 11b-12a seem forced and their corresponding relationship to the pairs in 12b-13a is not at all self-evident.

[70]These words recur in the more complete list in 2 Cor. 11:23-29 (v. 27); they are also reflected elsewhere in the "famine" of Rom. 8:35 and the "hunger" and "want" of Phil. 4:12.

[71]Gk. κολαφιζόμεθα (cf. 2 Cor. 12:7, denoting the messenger of Satan who "buffeted" Paul), a rare word, occurring chiefly in Christian authors. It may have a ring of being "cuffed . . . in an insulting manner," as Barrett, 111, suggests, but there is nothing inherent in the word nor the context to demand this further nuance. See K. L. Schmidt, *TDNT* III, 818-21.

general, although it may also include bodily harm since the list in 2 Cor. 11:23-29 explicitly includes both bodily blows and words of a more general nature expressing mistreatment. Finally, he lists "homelessness," which in particular reminds them of the itinerant nature of the missionaries, who thus declare that they have no permanent dwelling here (cf. Heb. 11:13-16). Brutal treatment and homelessness hardly describe those who have already come to reign.

The sixth item, "we work with our own hands," seems out of place since it does not fit the same category of "hardship" as the others.[72] It obviously indicates that he had not yet begun to reign! But it is probably included here for further reasons. At least as early as the mission to Thessalonica, what was originally a necessity had developed into a studied expression of his mission (cf. 1 Thess. 2:9; 4:11; 2 Thess. 3:6-13).[73] We know from the present letter (9:4-18) and from 2 Cor. 11:9 and 12:13-17 that "working with his hands" was not only his practice in Corinth, but had become a point of contention between him and them (see on 9:4-18). Thus he lists it here as part of his "apostolic hardships" to let them know that his "depriving" them of the privilege of helping him was first of all in keeping with his overall stance as a disciple of the crucified one.

The three antitheses of vv. 12b-13a go beyond the mere cataloguing of hardships to express his response to ill-treatment. One wonders whether this is not his way of indirectly indicating to them not only his response to what they have been doing to him, but also the kind of responses that they too need to learn. In any case, they are clear reflections of the teaching of Jesus, and as such anticipate the "imitation of Christ" motif in the next paragraph.[74] The first one, "when we are cursed, we bless," is a direct echo both of the teaching (Luke 6:28)[75] and example of Jesus (Luke 23:34). This ethical theme recurs in Paul (1 Thess. 5:15; Rom. 12:17). It is perhaps of some significance that the verb translated "curse" appears in its noun form in 5:11 ("slanderer") as one of the kinds of behavior that is to result in dissociation from a "brother" who persists in it. Very likely this was hap-

---

[72]Except in the case of a missionary for whom it might be an added burden of time and energy. It may well be, of course, that the hunger, etc., are partly the result of his refusal to accept patronage and thus are directly related to his "working with his own hands."

[73]On this question see esp. chap. 4 ("Tentmaking and Apostleship: The Debate at Corinth") in R. F. Hock, *Social Context,* pp. 50-65.

[74]The same rhetorical style appears in the antitheses of 2 Cor. 4:8-9, but the nature and purpose of those are considerably different from these.

[75]Paul: λοιδορούμενοι εὐλογοῦμεν; Luke: εὐλογεῖτε τοὺς καταρωμένους ὑμᾶς. But note esp. the language of Rom. 12:14: εὐλογεῖτε καὶ μὴ καταρᾶσθε. Here is another example of Paul and Luke reflecting the same language of the Jesus tradition, which is what one might well expect (cf. 11:23-25; 1 Tim. 5:18; et al.).

pening to Paul himself in this church. The second antithesis, "when we are persecuted, we endure it," is not found in Jesus' teaching, but again mirrors his example, especially in the trial and crucifixion. The third one, "when we are slandered, we answer kindly," is similar to the first, but with a change of language. The verb translated "we answer kindly" is Paul's common one for urging, or appealing to, the churches for obedience (cf. 1:10; 4:16). It is a word with a broad range of meanings, and following "when we are slandered" may certainly mean something close to "conciliate" (RSV). The NEB, however, renders it "we humbly make our appeal," which in the present context may be closer to Paul's intent. Some of them are "slandering" him, but he is herewith "humbly making his appeal" to them to desist and follow Christ.

Finally, he concludes with the most unflattering of metaphors, indicating the world's reaction to this way of living. We who follow Christ in these ways, Paul says, do not receive the accolades of the worldly wise. To the contrary, we are to them "the scum of the earth, the refuse of the world."[76] This translation is probably very close to Paul's intent. The two words, which are nearly synonymous, refer to the "off-scouring" that is removed in the process of cleansing, either sweepings from the floor *(perikatharmata)* or dirt removed from the body *(peripsēma)*. Both words, therefore, came to be used metaphorically for anything that is contemptible.[77] However, on the basis of the use of *perikatharmata* in Prov. 21:18 ("a ransom for the righteous") and some late references to *peripsēma* as a technical term for one of the "unfortunates" of society who was offered to the gods to ward off some calamity, many interpreters have seen in these words a veiled reference to Paul's sufferings as being a kind of "sacrifice"; that is, as one of the "dregs" he is in his weaknesses a kind of "scapegoat" for the world (Col. 1:24 is often brought in as an example).[78] Although this view has some attraction, especially as a further elaboration of v. 9, the lexical evidence is not as strong as its proponents make it out to be, and the ordinary usage to refer to what is contemptible fits the context without the need for expiatory overtones.

---

[76]Cf. Lam. 3:45: "You have made us scum and refuse among the nations." Although the Greek words used by Paul, περικαθάρματα and περίψημα, are not used in the LXX, his metaphor here is remarkably similar to the notion in the Lamentations text. See A. Hanson, "1 Corinthians 4:13b and Lamentations 3:45," *ExpT* 93 (1982), 214-15.

[77]For περικαθάρματα see, e.g., Epict. 3.22.78: "And did Priam, who begot fifty sons, all rascals (περικαθάρματα)?" (Loeb, II, 159); cf. Philo, *virt.* 174, who lists it as one among several such terms as to how the arrogant regard others.

[78]Cf. BAGD and F. Hauck, *TDNT* III, 430-31 on περικαθάρματα, and BAGD and G. Stählin, *TDNT* VI, 84-93 on περίψημα. Among commentators, see Lightfoot, Weiss, Héring, Barrett, and Bruce (the latter two cautiously). This interpretation is rejected altogether by R-P, Allo, and Conzelmann.

Paul's point is singular. In contrast to the Corinthians, who are "filled, rich, ruling, wise, powerful, honored," he and his fellow apostles look far more like their Lord, who fits well the picture of Isa. 53:2b-3: "He had no beauty or majesty to attract us to him, nothing in his appearance that we should desire him. He was despised and rejected by men, a man of sorrows and familiar with suffering. Like one from whom men hide their faces, he was despised and we esteemed him not." Thus a series of contrasts that began with the apostles as those condemned to die in the arena as a spectacle before the whole universe concludes on the same note (lit.): "as the scum of the world we have become, the offscourings of all people[79] up to this moment." Not a pretty picture, but with powerful imagery this catalogue carries the theme of the folly of God as wiser than merely human wisdom to a fitting conclusion.

Finally, this catalogue is not merely rhetoric for Paul. Although stated rhetorically, it fits well his theology, in two ways. First, as noted before, Paul was thoroughly eschatological. That did not mean that he could handle suffering because he expected the imminent return of Christ, and therefore imminent relief. Rather, for him it meant absolute certainty about the future, which God had set in motion through the resurrection of Jesus and which completely determined his present existence. The tribulations catalogued here belong to the present age, which has already been judged by God and therefore has no hold on him. These things are simply not worth comparing with the glory that awaits. For Paul everything is seen in light of that glory (2 Cor. 4:16-17).

Second, Paul took seriously that his sufferings and weaknesses were a genuine participation in Christ himself. For him discipleship entailed fellowship in the sufferings of Christ (Rom. 8:17; Phil. 3:10); but that did not mean that one must suffer in order to be a genuine disciple. His own lot, and that of so many with him, entailed great suffering as the direct result of belonging to Christ. So much was this so that he considered it the norm (cf. 1 Thess. 3:3; Phil. 1:29). But this norm was first of all theologically predicated—on the "great reversal" that God had already effected through the cross. Thus for Paul discipleship meant "sharing in the sufferings of Christ," not in its expiatory sense but in its *imitatio* sense (v. 16)—being in the world as Christ was in the world. Christ was really like this; those who would follow him must expect that they, too, will be like this.

This is an admittedly difficult text to hear well in the contemporary church, especially in Western cultures. In fact one feels a certain sense of

---

[79]Gk. πάντων could be either masculine, "all people," or neuter, "all things." The "of the world" of the NIV is not quite precise.

personal dissonance commenting on it while sitting at a word-processor surrounded by books and other modern conveniences. The rhetorical questions of v. 7 come through loud and clear. They still have their powerfully disarming effect, no matter who one is or in what circumstances. Life, all of life, is a gift; and it is all the more so for one who knows the Giver: "For out of His infinite riches in Jesus, He giveth and giveth and giveth again."[80] But what do we do with the rhetoric and irony of vv. 8-13? Some would easily dismiss it as rhetoric; others simply read it and leave it in the first century (Paul may have been like that, but so what?); still others read it, but are greatly puzzled as to how it might speak to them. How does one avoid either guilt, on the one hand, because we are not like that, or a martyr complex, on the other, in which one loves to suffer because he/she does it so well?

Two observations might be made: (1) We need to become more aware of the Corinthian side of this text than we tend to. That is, we try desperately to identify with Paul, when in fact we are probably much more like the Corinthians than any of us dare admit. We are rich, well-filled, etc.; and all too often that blinds us to our desperate needs. As Barrett notes (p. 113), between Paul's and the Corinthians' views of ministry "there can be little doubt which conception . . . corresponds more closely to the Lord's command (e.g. Mark viii.34f.)." (2) Perhaps if we were truly more like our Lord, standing more often in opposition to the status quo with its worldly wisdom and more often in favor of justice, we too would know more about what it means to be scum in the eyes of the world's "beautiful" or "powerful" people. In any case, we greatly need to recapture Paul's eschatological perspective so that neither wealth nor want tyrannizes us.

c. Appeal and exhortation (4:14-21)

14 *I am not writing this to shame you, but to warn[1] you, as my dear children.* 15 *Even[2] though you have ten thousand guardians in Christ, you do not have many fathers, for in Christ Jesus[3] I became your father through the gospel.* 16 *Therefore I urge you to imitate*

---

[80]From Annie Johnson Flint, "He Giveth More Grace."

[1]The evidence is divided between νουθετῶ (P[46] B D F G Ψ Maj latt) and νουθετῶν (P[11vid] ℵ A C P 6 33 104 365 630 945 1175 1739 pc). In this case P[46] and B seem to have abandoned the rest of the Egyptian tradition. The add/omit of the ν could have been accidental in either direction. The question must finally be decided on the grounds of Pauline style, which favors the participle. The οὐ/ἀλλά formula ordinarily contrasts coordinates in Paul, in this case "not shaming"/"but admonishing." Otherwise Barrett, 113, who offers no explanation for his choice.

[2]The NIV leaves out an explanatory γάρ, which is omitted by a few witnesses (P[46] pc g).

[3]B and 1506 omit 'Ιησοῦ, probably in conformity to the ἐν Χριστῷ that has just preceded it.

me.⁴ 17 *For this reason⁵ I am sending to you Timothy, my son whom I love, who is faithful in the Lord. He will remind you of my way of life in Christ Jesus,⁶ which agrees with what I teach everywhere in every church.*

18 *Some of you have become arrogant, as if I were not coming to you.* 19 *But I will come to you very soon, if the Lord is willing, and then I will find out not only how these arrogant people are talking, but what power they have.* 20 *For the kingdom of God is not a matter of talk but of power.* 21 *What do you prefer? Shall I come to you with a whip, or in love and with a gentle spirit?*

The argument that began in 1:10 is now finished; but Paul is not. The most delicate issue still remains: In light of all that has been said, how is he to reestablish his authority over them? True, the letter itself, and its argumentation, is an expression of authority; nonetheless, since his status seems to have been called into question (see on 1:1; 4:3; 9:1-3)—and, as we have argued, is a part of the strife itself—he needs to address the matter directly. But how shall he do that without losing the force of the argument to this point? Typically, with another change of metaphors.

The imagery of father and children has all the needed ingredients. It continues the important motif of his having founded the church (cf. 3:6 and 10); and the inherent authority of the father/child relationship allows him alternately to "admonish" (v. 14), to "urge" behavioral change (vv. 16-17), and, if all else fails, to threaten discipline (vv. 18-21).

What becomes transparent in this final appeal is that for Paul right thinking simply is not enough. The gospel must result in appropriate behavior as well. Thus he exhorts them to "imitate" him (v. 16), which means to return to his "way of life in Christ Jesus" (v. 17). This is the reason for sending Timothy (v. 17); this explains his own coming to them in the near future (vv. 18-21); and, of course, this underlies the reason for the letter—not only what has been said, but also what will yet be said. This paragraph,

---

⁴A few late MSS add the words καθὼς κἀγὼ Χριστοῦ from 11:1. Although not original, they do capture Paul's intent.

⁵A few of the Egyptian MSS (P¹¹ ℵ* A P 33 81 1175 2495) add an αὐτό, which would strengthen the conjunction to mean "for this very reason." Both the word order and Pauline style rule against it. Paul always has εἰς αὐτὸ τοῦτο for this idiom (cf. Zuntz, 63). Probably it represents a dittography.

⁶The exact wording of the name here is more complex than in v. 15 (see n. 3). The alternatives are: (1) Χριστῷ 'Ιησοῦ (P⁴⁶ ℵ C 6 33 81 104 629 630 1175 1739 1881 pc a bo); (2) κυρίῳ 'Ιησοῦ (D F G); or (3) simply Χριστῷ (A B Ψ Maj b sa). Variant (2) is secondary; it has been influenced by the immediately preceding κυρίῳ. A case can be made for either (1) or (3) as conformation to one of the forms in v. 15. See Zuntz, 181, for the argument for the longer reading.

therefore, brings chaps. 1–4 to a fitting conclusion and at the same time prepares them for what is coming next.

14 In light of the irony and sarcasm of the preceding paragraph, how can Paul now deny that he was intending to "shame"[7] them? The very fact of this demurrer is evidence that he realized they should have been ashamed; they would seem beyond hope if they were not. But that was not the *reason* for what has preceded. A moment will come when their behavior will be so distressing to him that he will openly admit to trying to shame them into Christian sanity (6:5; cf. 15:34). But for now the purpose behind his writing "this"[8] has been "to warn you, as my dear children."[9]

The verb translated "to warn" is a Pauline word in the NT.[10] "Admonish" catches the nuance a little better. It has the primary connotation of trying to have a corrective influence on someone, an "admonition that is designed to correct while not provoking or embittering."[11] Such correction may include "warning," but it also implies counsel and appeal. It is a fitting word for the imagery "as my dear[12] children."

This imagery, which is especially conciliatory after what has just been said, had a long history in Judaism, where it often depicted the relationship of a teacher to his disciple(s).[13] The term "disciples," however, never appears in Paul's letters. The people in his churches are his "children" because they are his converts (v. 15; Phlm. 10), and because they are his children in this sense, he can exhort and encourage (1 Thess. 2:11), or chide (2 Cor. 6:13; 12:14; Gal. 4:19), or appeal, as here.

---

[7]Gk. ἐντρέπων, a word that originally meant to "turn in," hence "to hang one's head," either in respect (cf. Matt. 21:37) or in shame (as here). The word is to be distinguished from καταισχύνω in 1:27, which connotes "disgrace."

[8]Gk. ταῦτα, "these things." It is possible that this includes the whole of what has preceded; at least its antecedent is vv. 6-13. B. Sanders, "Imitating Paul: 1 Cor 4:16," *HTR* 74 (1981), 353-63, sees it as recalling the ταῦτα of v. 6, hence "the description of Paul's and Apollos's role as servants according to 3:5–4:13" (p. 354). Fiore, "'Covert Allusion,'" pp. 97-98, would make it refer to the "admonitions of the whole hortatory section [i.e., 1:10–4:13]." But it is not emphatic here, as is the case in v. 6. Sanders's concern is the correct one; he is perhaps asking the pronoun to carry too much weight.

[9]In Eph. 6:4 the proper duty of the parent is to bring up the child in the νουθεσία of the Lord. Cf. Wis. 11:10, ὡς πατὴρ νουθετῶν ("admonishing as a father").

[10]Gk. νουθετῶ; cf. 1 Thess. 5:12, 14; 2 Thess. 3:15; Rom. 15:14; Col. 1:28; 3:16 (and in the Pauline speech in Acts 20:31); see also νουθεσία (1 Cor. 10:11; Eph. 6:4; Tit. 3:10).

[11]J. Behm, *TDNT* IV, 1021.

[12]Gk. ἀγαπητά, "beloved," a favorite adjective in Paul. It is used absolutely in 10:14 ("my beloved") and with ἀδελφοί in 15:58 ("my beloved brothers").

[13]E.g., in the Wisdom literature the term "my Son" is used for the one who is instructed in the way of Wisdom (see, e.g., Prov. 1:8, 10; 2:1; 3:1, etc.; Eccl. 12:12; Sir. 2:1; 3:1; etc.). For rabbinic examples see Str-B, III, 339-41.

15 Having called them his "dear children," he proceeds to make use of this imagery in two ways: first, in this verse, to reestablish his unique, and therefore authoritative, relationship to them as their founder; second, in vv. 16-17, to urge them to conform their behavior to the "father's" example. In this first instance, he not only reminds them that he is their father—because he gave them birth[14] "in Christ Jesus through the gospel"—but also emphasizes that his relationship to them is unique in this regard—he is their *only* father. This latter point is made first, in unusually hyperbolic language: "Even though you *may end up*[15] having *countless thousands*[16] of guardians in Christ, *at least*[17] you do not have many fathers." The "guardian"[18] was ordinarily a trusted slave, distinguished from a "teacher,"[19] to whom a father turned over his children (usually sons), whom the guardian was to conduct to and from school and whose conduct in general he was to oversee. This is not intended to be a putdown of their other teachers, of whom Paul has thus far spoken favorably. Rather, the metaphor intends simply to distinguish his own relationship to them from that of all others, including of course Apollos and Peter,[20] but also those within their community who are currently exercising influence, not to mention all others who ever would. His unique relationship to them was that of "father," and that gave him a special authority over and responsibility toward them. With this language, therefore, he is both reasserting his authority and appealing to their loyalty, which had obviously eroded in this church.

To explain this point, Paul adds: "for in Christ Jesus I became your father through the gospel."[21] This first of all elaborates on the words "not many fathers." But the emphasis lies on the more significant relationship

---

[14]Gk. ἐγέννησα, the regular verb for begetting children and referring either to the father's or the mother's role.

[15]This is an attempt to give to ἐάν with the subjunctive the sense of a contemplated future result suggested by Robertson, *Grammar,* p. 1018.

[16]Gk. μυρίος; the NIV's "ten thousand" is probably too literal here. It may mean that, but in this kind of context it means "innumerable, countless" (cf. 14:19).

[17]See Turner, *Syntax,* 330 for this meaning of ἀλλά in a conditional sentence.

[18]Gk. παιδαγωγός (cf. Gal. 3:24). Cf. J. B. Lightfoot, *The Epistle of St. Paul to the Galatians* (repr. Grand Rapids, 1957), pp. 148-49.

[19]See, e.g., Xenophon, *de rep.Lac.* 3.2; Plato, *Lys.* 208c; Diog. L. 3.92; Philo, *leg.ad Gai.* 53.

[20]That they in particular were intended is the standard view. If so, then it would seem that Paul is hereby retracting much that has been said. Therefore, several have argued that the "countless number of guardians in Christ" refers especially to those within the community who are presently leading them astray. They are the "some who are arrogant" of v. 18. See Parry, 83; Furnish, "Fellow Workers," p. 370; and Munck, *Paul,* p. 152. This makes more sense of the full data of the argument. But in either case it should not be read quite so pejoratively.

[21]Cf. *b.Sanh.* 19b: "R. Samuel . . . said . . . : He who teaches the son of his neighbour the Torah, Scripture ascribes it to him as if he had begotten him."

brought about by their "birth," namely that they are "in Christ Jesus." Paul's concern from beginning to end is the gospel. That is why he can move so easily from vv. 11-13 to this passage, without losing stride. Everything has been said and done for Christ Jesus. He has "fathered" them so that they might be *in Christ Jesus*. He has sent Timothy, who is also his son *in the Lord,* so that they might learn to walk *in Christ Jesus* (v. 17). This is the point of everything for Paul, and the other details of the argument must never obscure for us that singular passion of his. The means of their birth into Christ, as always, is "through the gospel." This is how the argument began in 1:17; with these words it is being brought full circle. The content of the gospel, of course, is what was argued in 1:18-31 against their worldly wisdom.

16 This clause now takes the father-child imagery a step further, and in so doing enunciates the point of the entire paragraph. Since they have but one father, Paul, who gave them birth in Christ Jesus through the gospel, "therefore[22] I urge[23] you to imitate me."[24] The picture is one of a father who has instructed his children in proper behavior by his own example. They are to be "like father, like children." The immediate context for this exhortation is the tribulation list of vv. 11-13, in which Paul describes his own life and ministry in terms consonant with the gospel of a crucified Messiah. It therefore functions as one more item in the long argument of 1:10–4:13 that appeals to the servant nature of discipleship over against their "boasting" and worldly wisdom.[25] However, by implication, especially from what is

---

[22]Gk. inferential οὖν, somewhat rare in 1 Corinthians.

[23]Gk. παρακαλῶ. See on 1:10; it is probably to make too much of this verb to see it as key to the structure of the entire passage as Dahl does ("Paul," p. 319), followed by Fiore, " 'Covert Allusion.' " To make a technical term of what in this context is simply an appropriate verb, fitting nicely the argument of the paragraph but not necessarily reaching all the way back to 1:10, is to put a straightjacket on an author's use of language.

[24]As an expression of the relationship both between teachers and pupils and between a worshiper and his deity, this word had a long history in both the Greco-Roman and Jewish worlds. See W. Michaelis, *TDNT* IV, 659-74. For Paul's own Jewish background see Wis. 4:2 (imitating wisdom); *ep.Ar.* 188, 210, 281 (imitating God); 4 Macc. 9:23 (imitating a holy martyr); Jos. *Ant.* 1.68 (descendants of Seth who imitated his ways); 8.315 (Asa, who imitated David); Philo, *virt.* 66 (Joshua imitating Moses); *congr.qu.er.* 70. Philo's own understanding of the concept is found in this latter reference: "for the practiser must be the imitator of a life, not the hearer of words, since the latter is the characteristic mark of the recipient of teaching, and the former of the strenuous self-exerciser" (Loeb, IV, 493). The term does not refer to one who mimics, nor even to one who follows as a disciple, but to one who actually internalizes and lives out the model that has been set before her/him.

[25]See Sanders (n. 8 above), who rightly urges that the nature of much in this section, as well as in the letter as a whole, points to a breakdown in communal life, which the coming of Timothy in part is intended to correct by a different example from what is currently going on among them.

said further in v. 17, the concern is now also being raised to the much broader level of their behavior in general, as it is reflected throughout the rest of the letter.

The language "imitate me" has considerable significance also for the larger question of Pauline ethical instruction.[26] The lack of specific references to the teaching of Jesus in the Pauline letters has been an ongoing puzzle,[27] the best solution to which lies with this concept. That Paul was long on behavioral concerns (ethics is the proper theological category) is writ large in his letters. He is never satisfied simply to change people's thinking. That is obviously important because the one (right behavior) flows out of the other (correct theology); but in his letters he never leaves them with an argument that does not have its corresponding parenesis (ethical instruction). It is therefore impossible to imagine that he did not do the same when he was present with the young converts in these newly formed Christian communities. 1 Thess. 4:1 in fact makes it clear that he did. But what shape did that instruction take? Here is where the teaching of Jesus and the example of the missionary coalesce. In 11:1 Paul says as much: They are to follow him as he follows Christ, which in that case most likely refers both to the example and the teaching of Christ.[28] Thus Paul's actual ethical instruction as it appears in his Epistles rarely uses the *language* of Jesus as it is recorded in the Gospels;[29] but on every page it reflects his example and his teaching, as we shall have occasion to note throughout (cf. 4:12). It may seem somewhat prosaic to add that such an exhortation probably tells us far

[26]There is a considerable bibliography on this motif in Paul. Among other items, see esp. W. Michaelis, *TDNT* IV, 659-74; D. M. Stanley, " 'Become Imitators of Me': The Pauline Conception of Apostolic Tradition," *Bib* 40 (1959), 859-77; W. P. de Boer, *The Imitation of Paul* (Kampen, 1960), pp. 92-196; and H. D. Betz, *Nachfolge und Nachahmung Jesu Christi im Neuen Testament* (Tübingen, 1967).

[27]An extreme view, influenced especially by R. Bultmann (e.g., "The Significance of the Historical Jesus for the Theology of Paul," in *Faith and Understanding* [ET, New York, l966], pp. 220-46), and one that was for years almost a byword in German and American scholarship, has argued that, to all intents and purposes, the teaching of Jesus was irrelevant to Paul. But the historical evidence seems to be largely against this. See, e.g., W. D. Davies, "The Moral Teaching of the Early Church," in *Jewish and Pauline Studies* (Philadelphia, 1984), pp. 278-88. For a brief, but helpful, survey of this debate, see Dungan, xvii-xxxiii.

[28]Paul had earlier affirmed that the Thessalonians had "imitated" the example of both Christ and the missionaries. This passage is especially instructive. The commendation lies in the fact that "in spite of severe suffering they welcomed the message with the joy given by the Holy Spirit." This seems to be a certain allusion to the content of Luke 6:22-23 (// Matt. 5:11- 12).

[29]Grayston's position ("Rod," pp. 13-16), that Paul had been "stung" so badly by his former association with the law that he also rejected any form of the teachings of Jesus that might take the form of law, seems to go a bit too far, especially in light of the parenetic sections of Paul's letters.

more about the apostle's own ethical life than we could have ever picked up from a biographer.

17 This concern over their behavior, and especially that they follow his example, is now posited as the reason for Paul's having sent Timothy to them. The reason for this visit is easier to determine than the event itself,[30] which receives first mention. "For this reason[31] I am sending to you Timothy"; or is it, "I sent to you Timothy" (RSV, cf. NAB, NEB)? Although the verb could be an epistolary aorist, and therefore a present as in the NIV,[32] this is probably an event that had already taken place.[33] Two things support this supposition: (1) the fact that Timothy is not mentioned in 1:1, which makes it improbable in the highest degree that he was still with Paul while he was writing the letter; and (2) the suppositional nature of the reference in 16:10 (q.v.), which makes it unlikely that he is the bearer of our letter. Nothing more is known of this mission by Timothy apart from these two somewhat oblique references.

The description of Timothy is especially remarkable since he would have been so well known to the Corinthians. He was with Paul during at least some of the mission to that city; and they would also have known that he had been something of a "trouble-shooter" for Paul.[34] Why then this description? The implication of 16:10-11 is that Paul is not certain about the kind of reception Timothy might have. If the Corinthians have been "examining" and rejecting Paul, what might they do to his younger companion? This verse implies that Timothy is going in Paul's stead, and therefore that he is to be regarded by them as though Paul himself were present among them. Thus

---

[30]Including its relationship to his mission to Macedonia at about this same time, mentioned in Acts 19:22.

[31]K. E. Bailey, "Structure," would begin the second "essay" of the letter at this point (4:17–7:40), which he entitles "Men and Women in the Human Family (sex)." To do so, he argues that the τοῦτο ("this reason") in this διὰ τοῦτο points forward to Timothy's reminding them of his ways, rather than to v. 16. In a sense that is true, but the whole reason for v. 17 is v. 16. A major structural break here is quite arbitrary and has too many contextual and structural strikes against it, not to mention problems with content and flow of thought.

[32]In Greek letters the aorist is often used for events taking place at the time of writing, which when read by the recipients will already have taken place. Thus the aorist is often used for such references. A clear example is the νῦν δὲ ἔγραψα in 5:11, where the "now" means the letter he is currently writing (1 Corinthians).

[33]At least the *sending;* whether Timothy ever arrived is a moot point. J. B. Lightfoot thinks not, since it is not mentioned in 2 Cor. 12:17-18 and since Acts 19:22 and 2 Cor. 1:1 imply that Timothy got only as far as Macedonia (2 Corinthians was apparently written from Macedonia). See "The Mission of Titus to the Corinthians," in *Biblical Essays* (London, 1893), pp. 271-84.

[34]Cf. Acts 18:5 and 1 Thess. 1:1 for evidence of his presence in Corinth; at least the return portion of the mission to Thessalonica mentioned in 1 Thess. 3:1-6 took place in Corinth.

Paul reminds them that Timothy, as they are (v. 14), is his "beloved son[35] in the Lord." As such he bears family resemblance "in the Lord," that is, he can be counted on to walk in the ways of his spiritual father. This is especially brought out in the word "faithful," the one requirement of the Lord's servants (v. 2). Paul's point, then, is not to inform the Corinthians about someone they already know, but to reinforce Timothy's own relationship to Paul so that they will pay attention to what he says.[36]

Timothy's singular task is "to remind you of my way of life in Christ Jesus," so that they might "imitate" him. The word translated "way of life" is literally "ways" (pl.) and implies both behavior and teaching, which in Paul are intimately bound together.[37] The sending of Timothy for such a task indicates the significance Paul placed on his own presence to guide or correct the community, as the need may be. In light of his inability to be present at the moment, he did the next best thing; he sent Timothy to be there in his place. But now that the Corinthians have written to him and Chloe's people have filled out the picture for him as to the real situation in Corinth, he in turn writes to them—and expects the letter also to take the place of his presence.[38] Given the nature of the aberrations in Corinth, it is important, as he does regularly in this letter,[39] to remind them that what he and Timothy have taught them is in keeping with what is taught in the church universally, at least in all the Pauline churches. This is another gentle nudge to remind them that they, not he, are embarking on a maverick course.

18 In the context of his own anticipated coming,[40] Paul concludes the long section begun in 1:10 by sounding a warning directly at the troublemakers in the community. The words "some of you have become arrogant"[41] indicate at least two things: First, the trouble that Paul has been

---

[35]Gk. ἀγαπητός, as in v. 14.

[36]Cf. the description in Phil. 2:19-23, in a passage that functions differently from this one. There Timothy is to be understood as the bearer of the letter, and the passage functions as the "epistolary commendation" of the letter-bearer.

[37]Gk. ὁδούς. This word almost certainly reflects Paul's Jewish background, in which the teaching of Torah is *halakah* (lit. "a way of walking"); cf. Paul's use of the verb περιπατεῖν ("to walk") as a basic metaphor for ethical behavior (e.g., 3:3; 7:17; Gal. 5:16). Some would limit Paul's "ways" to his doctrinal instruction only, on the basis of the last clause, "even as I teach everywhere in every church" (e.g., Weiss, 119-20; W. Michaelis, *TDNT* V, 87-88). But that is to miss Paul's own understanding too widely. For him "doctrine" includes ethics, or it is no doctrine at all.

[38]On this whole question see esp. R. W. Funk, "The Apostolic *Parousia:* Form and Significance," in *Christian History and Interpretation, Studies Presented to John Knox* (ed. W. R. Farmer, C. F. D. Moule, and R. R. Niebuhr; Cambridge, 1967), pp. 249-68.

[39]See on 1:2; cf. 7:17; 11:16; 14:33, 36.

[40]For the details of the proposed visit see on 16:5-9.

[41]Gk. ἐφυσιώθησαν. The aorist is used because the situation has been reported to him as a definite fact; it does not exclude the present reality, hence the English perfect is permissible.

having comes from within the community itself, not from outside agitators. The verb is identical to that in v. 6, where some are "puffed up" for Apollos over against Paul. This sentence verifies what we have argued right along, that the problem is not simply internal division because they are "playing favorites" with their leaders. Some in the community are decidedly anti-Paul.

Second, although the entire community has been infected, probably in varying degrees, the instigators of the trouble are a smaller group among them.[42] It is noteworthy that at the end of this long argument, carried on against the entire community indiscriminately, Paul should finally zero in on these people in particular. As we have noted, they were probably in view in several references throughout the argument (2:15; 3:12-15, 17, 18; 4:3, 6-7). The problem, of course, is that they have had considerable influence on the entire community, so that the majority, it seems likely from the tenor of the argument throughout, are on the side of these malcontents, or at least are being influenced by them. But at the end of the argument he singles out the ringleaders and threatens them with his own coming. These are the people who have disdained both Paul's authority and his theology. To the degree that the community as a whole has tolerated (or adopted) so much unchristian behavior as the result of this sub-Christian theology, they too are at fault. Hence the letter is addressed to the church; but continually, as here, it evidences tension between the "some" and the whole (see on 1:26). This tension is especially important for the understanding of what follows in chaps. 5 and 6, not to mention the rest of the letter.

The precise nuance of the qualifying clause "as if I were not coming to you" lacks certainty. It could mean that he had previously communicated that he would come, but was delayed for some reason (cf. 1 Thess. 2:17–3:5), and this is now being held against him.[43] More likely, his failure to return after some years[44] had caused some of them to treat him with disdain, "as if I were not coming [back] to you [at all]."[45] His failure to return had perhaps increased in their minds the comparison with the itinerant philosopher; his own lack of wisdom and eloquence (from their perspective) and failure to return combine to give both him and his gospel a poor showing.

---

[42]On the identification of these people, see the Introduction, pp. 7-15.

[43]He is at least anticipating this kind of difficulty in 2 Cor. 1:12-24.

[44]One cannot be certain how long this was. According to Acts 19:8-10, Paul was in Ephesus for at least three months over two years. According to 1 Cor. 16:5-9, Paul feels that his time in Ephesus is coming to an end.

[45]Dahl ("Paul," pp. 325-29) has offered the intriguing hypothesis that the squabble within the community was related to this issue as an internal fight as to whether even to write their letter to him, since he had shown no interest in returning. "Why write to *him*?" some were arguing.

19-20 The sending of Timothy and this letter might have the force of playing right into the hands of the "arrogant," so Paul quickly affirms his own plans to return to Corinth. The details of this plan are given in 16:5-9. That passage also indicates that "very soon" is a relative term.[46] He does intend to come, and it will be "without delay," which here must mean as soon as it is possible for him to do so. The emphasis is on the *certainty* of the visit, not its immediacy. In any case, all such plans are contingent on "if the Lord is willing" (cf. 16:7; Jas. 4:15). Paul's previous experiences of promising a return but having "Satan hinder" him (1 Thess. 2:18), plus his own untoward circumstances in Ephesus (15:31-32; 16:9), have made him properly cautious. He plans to come; but his plans are always subject to the divine will.

The reason for the emphasis on the certainty (from his present perspective) of his coming is expressed in the last clause: "And I will find out not only how these arrogant people are talking, but what power they have." Hidden in this translation are two expressions that tie this final section to everything that has preceded. First, "how these arrogant people are talking" is probably too free a rendering of "the *logos* of those who are puffed up." *Logos* might have referred simply to "how they are talking," if it were not contrasted to *dynamis* ("power") and qualified by "those who are puffed up." They are "puffed up" against Paul (v. 6) partly because he lacks significant *logos* ("word, speech"; see esp. 1:17 and 2:1-5). But in contrast to the *logos* characterized by wisdom that they demand of him, he has already reminded them of his real *logos* ("preaching"), which was not "with persuasion of wisdom" but was accompanied by the *dynamis* of God, i.e., by the powerful work of the Spirit (cf. 2:4-5). Now he threatens the arrogant. When he returns, will they have merely *logos,* or will they also be able to demonstrate the *dynamis* of God in their worldly wisdom? They claim to have the Spirit; will they evidence what for Paul is the crucial matter, namely the powerful, dynamic presence of the Spirit among them to save and to sanctify (cf. 5:1-5)? Obviously he has little fear of the outcome of such a confrontation!

Some have expressed concern that Paul appears to be undoing what he has been arguing earlier, especially in 1:18–2:5 and 3:5–4:13, about the servant nature of his gospel and his own ministry. But that is a false fear, and misses the point of this text. The gospel of Christ crucified in all of its apparent weakness is nonetheless the power of God unto salvation for those who believe. Paul is not challenging the arrogant, therefore, on their grounds, but on his own. What their present stance lacks is the true power of

---

[46]Gk. ταχέως.

the Spirit, which gives people birth to new life in Christ (v. 15), which can change people's lives—can "take the poor lost sinner, lift him from the miry clay and set him free," as the gospel song has it.

That this is the nature of the challenge he sets before the "puffed up" is confirmed by the explanatory word of v. 20: "For the kingdom of God is not a matter of *logos* but of *dynamis.*" The real action is not where they are currently trying to place it, in merely human wisdom that "boasts" in men. What Paul is concerned about is "the kingdom of God." This is one of the rare occurrences in Paul of this term that dominates the ministry and teaching of Jesus.[47] But the very casual way in which it here appears indicates that it was a regular part of his own understanding of the gospel. In most instances in Paul the term refers to the consummation of the kingdom at the coming of Christ (cf., e.g., 6:9-10; 15:50); but this passage, along with Rom. 14:17, makes it certain that for him the kingdom was "now" as well as "not yet." The kingdom that has already been inaugurated by the resurrection of Jesus and the coming of the Spirit is characterized by the *power* of the Spirit. Here is the line of ultimate demarcation between their view of spirituality and Paul's. They were living in the Spirit as though the future had dawned in its fullness, hence they were above the weaknesses that characterized Paul's life and ministry. Paul, on the other hand, lived in the kinds of weaknesses that characterized his Lord, but through those weaknesses the power and grace of God were still at work in the world bringing people to a salvation that put them currently in God's kingdom (cf. Col. 1:13) and assured them of that same kingdom as their inheritance (6:9-10).

21 With one further use of the father-child metaphor,[48] Paul ties the challenge of vv. 18-20 to the appeal of vv. 14-17. But the tone is less conciliatory. Being reminded by what he has just said about the opposition of "some" to him, he concludes with the threat of discipline—which the church is in no danger of exercising among themselves, as what immediately follows attests! It is arguable that this threat is directed especially against the "arrogant" of vv. 18-20. But that would miss the function of this final sentence as a lead-in to the argument that follows, especially to 5:1-13 and 6:1-11. What is remarkable about both of those passages, as we shall see, is that the heavy guns are aimed in each case at the community itself, not at the wrongdoers. That seems to be sure evidence of the pervasive influence of the

---

[47]Cf. 6:9-10; 15:24, 50; 2 Thess. 1:5; Gal. 5:21; Rom. 14:17; Col. 1:13; 4:11; Eph. 5:5; 2 Tim. 4:18.

[48]Craig, 59, says that this is "the schoolmaster's whip," apparently following the argument of C. Schneider, *TDNT* VI, 966-70 (cf. Lightfoot, 201). But this is an unfortunate breaking of the imagery, as well as lexically unsound, as D. Daube has shown. See "Paul a Hellenistic Schoolmaster?" in *Studies in Rationalism, Judaism and Universalism in Memory of Leon Roth* (ed. R. Loewe; London, 1966), pp. 67-71.

"some who are arrogant" in their midst (v. 18). It probably also indicates—as we have argued concerning this section in general and this final paragraph in particular—that Paul's own apostleship, his capacity to speak prophetically among them, comprises a key point of tension between him and the Corinthians, both the ringleaders and the community as a whole that has been influenced by them.

"What do you prefer?" he asks. "Shall I come to you with a *rod*?"[49] Must I come as a father who has to mete out discipline? Or will you allow this letter and Timothy's coming to serve as the proper inducement to correcting your behavior? In that case, then, he may come the way a father would prefer, "in love and with a gentle spirit." Love, of course, is what must control all Christian conduct. One should not make too much of the fact that it seems to be set in contrast to coming with a rod of discipline. Paul is simply continuing the father-child metaphor; his contrasts relate to the *manner* of his coming, not the motive, which would express love in either case. The "gentle spirit" (lit. "spirit of gentleness"[50]) reflects the picture given in the list in vv. 11-13. The word "gentleness" also echoes the teaching of Jesus, who described himself as "gentle in heart" (Matt. 11:29; cf. 2 Cor. 10:1) and pronounced God's congratulatory blessing on those who are likewise (Matt. 5:5).[51] As such it stands again in stark contrast to the arrogance of the Corinthians. The phrase could mean "the Spirit who brings gentleness," but here that would seem to ask the word "spirit" to carry too much weight. In Paul, however, "the thought of [the Spirit] is latent in every reference to the 'spirit' of a Christian man"[52] (cf. 5:3-4 and 14:14-15). Thus, although the phrase in one sense is simply a further expression of the metaphor, it is so as a reflection of our Lord himself, whose earthly life of "gentleness" was lived out in the power of the Spirit.

With these words the long argument of 1:10–4:21 is concluded. Even though at times Paul seems to be weaving in and out of several topics, the concern throughout is singular: to stop a current fascination with "wisdom" on the part of the Corinthians that has allowed them not only to "boast," but to stand over against Paul and his gospel. With a variety of turns to the argument he sets forth his gospel over against their "wisdom"

[49]The NIV has "whip," apparently also under the influence of Schneider (see previous note). The imagery is the "rod of correction," found throughout the OT (Exod. 21:20; 2 Sam. 7:14; Prov. 10:13; 22:15; Isa. 10:24; Lam. 3:1). Cf. also Plato, *leg.* 3.700c; Plut. *mor.* 268D, 693F.

[50]Gk. πνεύματι πραΰτητος; cf. Gal. 6:1.

[51]For a thorough discussion of this term both for Jesus and for the Christian ethic in general, see R. Guelich, *The Sermon on the Mount* (Waco, 1982), pp. 79-83.

[52]Findlay, 806; cf. H. D. Betz, *Galatians* (Hermeneia; Philadelphia, 1979), p. 297 n. 48, who says of the identical phrase in Gal. 6:1 that "it refers both to the divine and to the human spirit."

and tries to reshape their understanding of ministry and church. At last he has also reasserted his authority over them. The clear implication is that they have no choice but to give heed to what he is saying. Their behavior as well as their theology needs shaping up. From here he will address some other items that have been made known to him before he gets to their letter to him.

The changes of tone in this passage reveal some of the real tensions that continue to exist in Christian ministry. How to be prophetic without being harsh or implying that one is above the sins of others. How to get people to change their behavior to conform to the gospel when they think too highly of themselves. There is no easy answer, as this passage reveals. But one called to minister in the church must ever strive to do it; calling people to repentance is part of the task.

Perhaps the greater difficulty for most people in ministry is with the words "Imitate me." These words surely heighten the responsibility that Christians have toward new converts universally. Perhaps our ability to put "the Book" in their hands has been partly responsible for our unfortunately too frequent apology that they should do as we say, not as we do. When the basic way of learning ethical instruction is by example, the obedience factor on the part of the "instructor" is bound to increase! May God give his people grace and courage so to do.

B. IMMORALITY AND LITIGATION: TEST CASES OF THE CRISIS OF AUTHORITY AND GOSPEL (5:1–6:20)

With 5:1 Paul clearly turns to a new problem, a case of incest that is being either tolerated or condoned within the church. The new topic is conceptually so unlike what has preceded[1] that most scholars see the two sections as related only in terms of how Paul knew about the situation—that this, too, was reported to him (5:1; cf. 1:11). But that is to overlook some of the other ties between this section and 4:14-21, especially (1) the "arrogance" of "some" in 4:18-19 and the "arrogance" of the church in 5:2 and 6, and (2) the lack of "power" among the arrogant in 4:19-20 vis-à-vis the "power of our Lord Jesus" in 5:4.[2] These may give more logic to the sequence than one

[1]The sudden shift from topic to topic without preparation, transparent internal ties, or logic is one of the reasons why some scholars see our letter as a compilation of letters to Corinth. See the Introduction, pp. 15-16.

[2]See Hurd, 89 n. 1, to whom I am indebted for this observation, although he notes only the thematic ties, not the distinction between the "some" of the former section and the whole church of this one. For other insights into the relationship between chaps. 1–4 and 5–6, see Dahl, "Paul," pp. 329-33; and esp. P. S. Minear, "Christ and the Congregation: 1 Corinthians 5-6," *RevExp* 80 (1983), 341-50, whose suggestions are the stimulation behind some of this presentation.

might perceive at first glance. In the final paragraph of the preceding argument Paul finally reasserted his apostolic authority, in the context of those who were "puffed up" against him and his "coming very soon" in order to find out their "power." What seems to be at stake in the next three sections (5:1-13; 6:1-11; 6:12-20) is the *crisis of authority* that was a large part of what lay behind 1:10–4:21, and especially the authority of Paul vis-à-vis the "arrogant" who were responsible for leading the church in its new direction, both theologically and over against Paul.

As in 1:10–4:21, however, it is once more Paul versus the church, not against the instigators of the problem as such. He has just threatened to come and "find out the power" of the latter (4:19-20); but he has also threatened the whole church that he will come with a rod (4:21) if they do not change their direction back toward him and his gospel. These next sections amount to something of a test on this very issue. In fact what is most remarkable about 5:1-13 and 6:1-11 is how little time he devotes to the "sins" (and "sinners"). He does threaten the latter with the grave consequences of their wrongdoing, but he is far more exercised in both cases with the church and its attitudes. The question is, Will they pay attention to him on these matters when he is "with them in Spirit and the power of the Lord Jesus," or will they continue to follow their new prophets who are remaking the gospel into worldly wisdom divorced from truly Christian ethics?

This crisis of authority, then, is what seems to hold chaps. 1–6 together. It should be noted, however, that there is also a conceptual tie between 6:1-11 and 5:1-13. Paul concludes the argument at the end of chap. 5 by stating that believers are not to judge those outside the church; rather, they are to judge those inside, meaning of course the incestuous man. That seems to trigger the next item, in which believers had actually gone to outsiders for judgments that Paul is convinced should have been handled within the believing community. This issue seems to be another that had been reported to him, although he does not specifically say so.

What is less clear is how 6:12-20 follows any of this. It deals with sexual immorality again, to be sure, but it is a considerably different concern from 5:1-13;[3] furthermore, it appears to have more affinities with 7:1-7 and

---

[3]A common view sees chaps. 5 and 6 as dealing basically with sexual immorality, with 6:1-11 as a digression. Thus 5:1-13 has to do specifically with incest, and its final remarks on "judging" send Paul off on an aside (6:1-11); but he returns to his theme in 6:12-20 with some general teaching on the subject of sexual sin. The problem with this, of course, is that 6:12-20 is every bit as specific as 5:1-13 and deals with a different item altogether. But see J. H. Bernard, "The Connexion between the Fifth and Sixth Chapters of 1 Corinthians," *Exp* 7:3 (1907), 433-43, who would tie together all of chaps. 5, 6, and 7 in terms of the problem of the incestuous man.

8:1–10:22 than it does with either 5:1-13 or 6:1-11.[4] Without stating the problem, or how he found out about it, Paul suddenly quotes what appear to be Corinthian slogans, but he sharply qualifies them. This is probably the key to its place in the letter; the crisis of authority is now expressed at a specific theological/behavioral point where he and they (both the instigators and the church that has followed them) are at loggerheads. At the same time it serves as the link to the first section of the letter, all of which deals with the double crisis of authority and gospel, and to his response to their letter to him, in which a somewhat different "official" stance has been assumed between them, but one that still reflects the same double crisis.

1. The Case of the Incestuous Man (5:1-13)

This particular matter has created an enormous number of problems for moderns. On the one hand, the problem itself and Paul's solution are rather easy to identify, even though several of the details are puzzling. But for us the perplexing questions are, How could such a thing possibly have happened in the first place? and how does the remedy offered apply to the church today?

The problem for Paul is twofold: that a believer is living in an incestuous relationship that even pagans disallowed is bad enough; but far worse is the church's relaxed attitude toward it—they are arrogant. What is not clear is the relationship of their arrogance to the problem. Are they arrogant *in spite of* what is going on among them, or *because of* it? That is, is their attitude one of mere tolerance, or has this matter become for them a kind of cause célèbre in which they have asserted their freedom or new existence in Christ?

Most Christians find it difficult even to imagine that such a thing could have been happening in a Christian church. But that is because of our tacit assumption, as the result of the Judeo-Christian heritage, that people generally took a dim view of sexual irregularity, even if they did not attach religious significance to it. But such is not the case. In a culture where one could matter-of-factly say, "Mistresses we keep for the sake of pleasure, concubines for the daily care of the body, but wives to bear us legitimate children,"[5] the Judeo-Christian moral restrictions on human sexuality were

---

[4]But see P. Richardson, wno argues that the two items in chap. 6 reflect the same problem, i.e., that the sexual immorality of 6:12-20 is the matter that has been taken to public litigation in 6:1-11 ("Judgment in Sexual Matters in 1 Corinthians 6:1-11," *NovT* 25 [1983], 37-58). Cf. the discussion on 6:1. Less persuasive is K. Bailey's analysis, which, using rhetorical criticism, sees 6:9-11 as being introductory to 6:12-20 ("Paul's Theological Foundation for Human Sexuality: I Cor. 6:9-20 in the Light of Rhetorical Criticism," *ThRev* 3 [1980], 27-41).

[5]Demos., *or.* 59.122 (Loeb, VI, 445, 447 slightly modified).

not easily absorbed by pagan converts. Paul therefore had to address this question regularly in the Gentile churches (cf. 1 Thess. 4:1-8; Col. 3:5-7; Eph. 5:3-13). From 6:9-10 we learn that sexual immorality had been part of the Corinthians' previous life-style; on the basis of 5:9, 6:12-20, 7:2, and 10:8 (cf. 2 Cor. 12:21), we may deduce that they had carried that life-style into their new existence in Christ.[6] The problem, however, is not simply a relaxed attitude toward this sin, but whether they also tried to give a theological basis for it and thereby to condone it.

As is so often the case in this letter, the argument itself and the point of the argument are easier to determine than some of the details. Vv. 1-2 state what Paul knows about the problem and give his basic solution to it: they are to put this man outside the believing community—a command that is repeated no less than four times (vv. 2, 4-5, 7, 13). In a passage that is full of exegetical difficulties (vv. 3-5) he outlines how and why they are to carry out the expulsion, and in vv. 6-8 he offers by way of analogy his own theological basis for it. He returns to the church's attitude in vv. 9-13 and ties it directly to their misunderstanding or disregard of his former letter, in which he had already spoken to these matters. He offers a clarification that concludes the argument as it began: They are "to judge those inside" and expel the incestuous man from the community.

As noted earlier, apart from v. 1 neither the man himself nor his sin is directly addressed. Paul's own revulsion toward the matter underlies the whole and surfaces often; but the argument is addressed almost entirely to the church and its arrogance. What is at stake is not simply a low view of sin; rather, it is the church itself: Will it follow Paul's gospel with its ethical implications? or will it continue in its present "spirituality," one that tolerates such sin and thereby destroys God's temple in Corinth (3:16-17)? Thus Paul uses this concrete example both to assert his authority and to speak to the larger issue of sexual immorality.[7] What we may learn about "church discipline" will be noted at the end of the section.

[6]Hurd, 277, considers this reconstruction to be something of an "illusion" on the part of commentators. He is willing to argue that no sexual aberration actually existed in the community (this one being interpreted as a "spiritual marriage"). But to do so he must not only overlook the implications of these texts, esp. 2 Cor. 12:21, but he must also interpret 6:12-20 as merely hypothetical (see the comm. on this passage). Hurd's case is predicated on the main thesis of his book, that Paul himself introduced prohibitions against sexual immorality in his previous letter when he was communicating to them the content of the "apostolic decree."

[7]It is not clear what Conzelmann, 96 n. 24, means when he says: "Paul's lack of concern for the general moral aspects of the case is shown by the fact that he pronounces no judgment on the woman. She seems not to have belonged to the community." The latter sentence is precisely the point. Paul is obviously concerned with the moral aspects of the case for the *Christian* community; God judges those on the outside (v. 13), which of course implies a considerable moral judgment on pagans.

a. Paul's judgment—he must be expelled (5:1-5)

1 *It is actually reported that there is sexual immorality among you, and of a kind that does not occur[8] even among pagans: A man has his father's wife.* 2 *And you are proud! Shouldn't you rather have been filled with grief and have put out of your fellowship[9] the man who did this?[10]* 3 *Even though[11] I am not physically present, I am with you in spirit. And I have already passed judgment on the one who did this, just as if I were present.* 4 *When you are assembled in the name of the Lord Jesus[12] and I am with you in spirit, and the power of our Lord Jesus[13] is present,* 5 *hand this man over to Satan, so that the sinful nature[a] may be destroyed and his spirit saved on the day of the Lord.[14]*

a Or *that his body;* or *that his flesh*

[8]There is no verb in the Greek text. Later MSS (the 7th-c. P[68] being the earliest) add ὀνομάζεται, which is clearly secondary since no good reason could be given for its universal omission in the early church had it been original.

[9]The MajT has ἐξαρθῇ for ἀρθῇ, thus conforming the verb to the citation from the LXX in v. 13.

[10]Did Paul write ποιήσας (P[46] P[68] B D F G Ψ Maj; favored by Zuntz, 130-31) or πράξας (P[11vid] ℵ A C 33 81 104 326 1175 2464; favored by NA[26]; cf. Metzger, 550)? There is no difference in meaning, although πράξας is more literary. Paul himself interchanges the verbs for apparently stylistic reasons in Rom. 1:32 and 2:2-3. The question is not easily resolved, depending mostly on how one views the external evidence.

[11]The concessive force of the participle ἀπών is heightened in the later MSS by the addition of a ὡς.

[12]The MSS are divided between (1) "the Lord Jesus" (A Ψ 2495 pc); (2) "the Lord Jesus Christ" (ℵ a); (3) "our Lord Jesus" (B D* 1175 1739 pc b d); and (4) "our Lord Jesus Christ" (P[46] F G Maj). This is further complicated by the similar corruptions at the end of the verse (see next note). The addition of Χριστός is probably also related to the syntactical problem of finding which verb form the prepositional phrase modifies (see comm.). *Contra* Zuntz, 235, Χριστός most likely is an addition, probably by a scribe who interpreted the passage the way Zuntz and the RSV (and the present comm.) do: to heighten the solemn words of judgment ("I have pronounced judgment in the name of our Lord Jesus Christ"); an "omission," on the other hand, could only have happened by accident. The judgment on the word ἡμῶν is more difficult, although the MS evidence seems to support its presence. It fits well with "the Lord Jesus" here, and could easily have been omitted with the addition of "Christ." On the other hand, it could have been added on the analogy of the next phrase.

[13]Cf. the previous note. A similar set of variants occurs: (1) "our Lord Jesus" (ℵ A B D* sa); (2) "the Lord Jesus" (P[46] P Ψ 629 2495 pc); (3) "the Lord" (630 1739); and (4) "our Lord Jesus Christ" (F G Maj). In this case variants (1) and (2) are to be preferred to the others (Zuntz, 235, leans toward the reading of 1739, but its reading can easily be explained as an accidental omission due to homoeoteleuton). Of these two, the inclusion of ἡμῶν is preferred on exegetical grounds. See the commentary.

[14]The MSS variously add Ἰησοῦ (ℵ Ψ Maj), Ἰησοῦ Χριστοῦ (D pc), and ἡμῶν Ἰησοῦ Χριστοῦ (A F G P 33 104 365 1881 pc). The translated text is that of P[46] B 630 1739 pc Tert Epiph. Although this may look like more of the same (see the two previous notes), it is not so. Here the use of "the day of the Lord" in Paul is the decisive factor (cf. 1 Thess. 5:2; 2 Thess. 2:2); the very variety of the additions indicates that the shorter reading is the original.

This opening paragraph follows hard on the heels of 4:14-21, where Paul had urged the Corinthians to "imitate" him and follow "his ways," and where he had threatened those who were "puffed up" against him because he had not returned. Although he cannot now come in person, he has learned of some behavior in the church that calls for his presence; so he lets this letter function in his place. He is present all right—in Spirit—and they need to pay attention to his judgments. The paragraph is a bold expression of his apostolic authority in the church, calling them to conform to his ways. He has also written about this previously (vv. 9-11).

Paul begins by expressing dismay at the church and its relaxed attitude toward a "brother" who is living in incest. Rather than being "puffed up," they should have experienced the deep mourning of the penitent. Since they had done nothing at all, Paul makes the considerable point that even though he is *not* present, he has nonetheless exercised his proper authority: he has pronounced judgment on the man. What the church is now to do, in the context of the gathered community where both he and the Lord Jesus are present by the Spirit, is to carry out the verdict that he has pronounced.

1 The two sides to the problem are expressed in vv. 1-2. V. 1 indicates the nature of the deed itself; v. 2 moves to the greater issue, the church's response—or lack thereof—to this sin in their midst. Paul begins on a note of horror: "It is actually reported that there is sexual immorality among you." On the basis of the opening adverb[15] and the verb,[16] some have argued that Paul intends "it is universally reported," and that the horror rests in how widely this thing is known.[17] But Paul's use of this adverb in 6:7 and 15:29 indicates that it moves closer to the idea of "altogether," hence "actually." The horror lies in the fact that there is sexual immorality among them, but they are taking no action. All of this has been "reported" to him. "In case any are wondering whether I might need to come with rod in hand," Paul is suggesting, "listen to what else has been reported to me about you." The report was "that there is sexual immorality among you."[18] The

---

[15]Gk. ὅλως, ordinarily meaning "totally" or "completely"; hence "universally," "in general," or "in a word."

[16]Gk. ἀκούεται, lit. "it is being heard," hence "it was learned" (Mark 2:1), or "it came to one's attention" (Matt. 28:14).

[17]KJV, "it is reported commonly"; cf. Weiss, 124; Héring, 34; Conzelmann, 94: "in general there are reports." Mare, 217, suggests that the present tense of the verb "helps convey the idea that the report is continually spreading." But that is not likely; rather, it indicates that the sexual aberration to which he is referring is going on presently.

[18]The prepositional phrase ἐν ὑμῖν immediately follows the verb; some (e.g., Lightfoot, 202; R-P, 95) take it therefore to modify "reported," i.e., the report is circulating among them, and from them is being noised abroad. But here is a case where word order means little or nothing. The phrase stands in clear contrast to the next one, οὐδὲ ἐν τοῖς ἔθνεσιν ("not even among the pagans").

word *porneia* ("sexual immorality") in the Greek world simply meant "prostitution," in the sense of going to the prostitutes and paying for sexual pleasure. The Greeks were ambivalent on that matter, depending on whether one went openly to the brothels or was more discreet and went with a paramour.[19] But the word had been picked up in Hellenistic Judaism, always pejoratively, to cover all extramarital sexual sins and aberrations, including homosexuality. It could also refer to any of these sins specifically, as it does here. In the NT the word is thus used to refer to that particular blight on Greco-Roman culture, which was almost universally countenanced, except among the Stoics.[20] That is why *porneia* appears so often as the first item in the NT vice lists, not because Christians were sexually "hung up," nor because they considered this the primary sin, the "scarlet letter," as it were. It is the result of its prevalence in the culture, and the difficulty the early church experienced with its Gentile converts breaking with their former ways, which they did not consider immoral.

But in this instance the problem is not just *porneia* in general. Paul seems to have had trouble with that previously in Corinth and addressed it in an earlier letter (v. 9). What exercises him in this instance is that the form of *porneia* they are tolerating is of a kind that was not condoned "even among pagans," whose standards were otherwise not high: "A man has his father's wife." The problem is incest, a man taking a wife of his father other than his own mother and living with her sexually in an ongoing relationship. This is made clear from two points of usage: (1) The language "father's wife" is taken directly from the LXX of Lev. 18:7-8, where this specific sin is forbidden.[21] (2) The verb "to have," when used in sexual or marital contexts, is a euphemism for an enduring sexual relationship, not just a passing fancy or a "one-night stand."[22] By his "having" her, Paul means that the brother is "living with" (RSV) her sexually. What cannot be known is what had happened to the father, whether there had been divorce or death.[23] In either case what is forbidden by all ancients, both Jewish and pagan, is the cohabiting of father and son with the same woman.[24] The fact that the

[19]On this whole question see F. Hauck and S. Schulz, *TDNT* VI, 579-95; cf. W. Barclay, *Flesh and Spirit, An Examination of Galatians 5.19-23* (Nashville, 1962), 24-28.

[20]See the previous note.

[21]Since 18:7 forbids sexual relations with one's *mother*, the "father's wife" with whom intercourse is forbidden in v. 8 refers to a woman other than one's mother, a second wife of some kind.

[22]See especially on 7:2 below and the evidence given there.

[23]What is less likely is that both are simultaneously living with her.

[24]For Jewish law, see Lev. 18:7-8 and 20:11; cf. Amos 2:7b, "father and son sleeping with the same girl." Cf. also Jos., *Ant.* 3.274; Philo, *spec.leg.* 3.12-21; *m.Sanh.* 7.4; *b.Sanh.* 54a; *T. Reub.* passim.

For Greco-Roman law, see the *Institutes* of Gaius 1.63: "Neither can I marry her

woman herself is not mentioned, especially since women are more often condemned for sexual sins than men (cf. John 8:1-11), is a sure indication that only the man was a member of the Christian community. Given the full mutuality of men and women in the marital issues addressed in chap. 7, it is nearly impossible that she could have been a member of the community and not in v. 5 have been brought under the same judgment as her lover.

For us the more perplexing question is the one that cannot finally be answered: How could a Christian man have done such a thing in the first place? While it is true, as Hurd (p. 278) points out, that from this distance one cannot tell whether he and the church considered the relationship innocent or not, it is equally true that Paul perceived it as heinous. This, plus the clear sexual overtones in the idiom "to have a woman," rules out Hurd's own suggestion that this may have been a "spiritual marriage." Most likely the man's action is related to the arrogance of the whole community noted in the next verse.

2 If for us the problem is how a man could have done such a thing, the greater problem for Paul is the fact that with this sin in their midst they are "proud"[25] and "boasting" (v. 6).[26] These two words appear together in chaps. 1–4 (esp. 4:6-7) to describe their current attitude toward Paul, apparently based on their giftedness (4:7), hence reflecting their new spirituality. As noted in 1:29-31, their present stance on wisdom and Spirit had led to self-sufficiency rather than total dependence on Christ. What is not clear from this distance is the precise nuance of the exclamation[27] "And you are proud!" Is this simply referring back to what had been said earlier, expressing a kind of contempt over their being puffed up with such grievous sin in their midst, as in "And in spite of this incest in your midst, you continue to hold your heads high toward me as you have been doing? What right do you have to pride with this kind of thing going on and no one doing anything about it?"

Or is it a direct attack on their pride as it is more closely related to the sin itself? Given their theological stance articulated in 6:12-13 and their

---

who has aforetime been my mother-in-law or step-mother, or daughter-in-law or step-daughter"; the use of "aforetime" is explained as assuming the ban against polygamy (transl. by J. Muirhead [Edinburgh, 1880], pp. 24-25). On Roman attitudes see Cicero, *Cluent.* 6, of the marriage of a woman with her son-in-law: "Oh! to think of the woman's sin, unbelievable, unheard of in all experience save for this single instance!" (Loeb, I, 237).

25Gk. πεφυσιωμένοι ἐστέ ("you are puffed up"), the same word as "take pride in" (4:6) and "arrogant" (4:18).

26Gk. καύχημα; cf. 1:29, 31; 3:21; 4:7

27The NIV follows a long tradition in this regard. Others (e.g., Barrett, 122; Conzelmann, 94) consider the whole sentence to be a question, not just the second half. Thus, "Are you in these circumstances puffed up? Did you not rather go into mourning, that he who had committed this deed might be taken away from you?" (Barrett).

sense of superiority to Paul, and therefore to Paul's ethical instructions given in his previous letter, it is just possible, nay probable it would seem, that this sin in their midst is something over which they have taken a certain amount of pride: "In Christ, through whom we have received the Spirit who has lifted us above the merely earthly, 'all things are lawful.' How can what Paul calls *porneia* be of any consequence to the truly spiritual person?"[28] One cannot be sure of such a reconstruction, of course, but it does fit their attitude as a whole, and it would particularly do so if the man were carrying on the relationship "in the name of the Lord Jesus," although this seems less likely (see vv. 3-4).

Whatever the actual relationship of their pride to the incest, it has blinded them both to the fallen brother's true condition and to their own. Rather than demonstrating pride, "shouldn't you have been filled with grief and put out[29] of your fellowship the man who did this?"[30] The verb "filled with grief" probably refers to the kind of "mourning," that deep anguish of soul frequently related to true repentance, that the righteous experience because of their own sins and the sins of others.[31] "Mourning" is the proper

[28]D. Daube ("Pauline Contributions to a Pluralistic Culture: Re-Creation and Beyond," in *Jesus and Man's Hope* [2 vols.; eds. D. G. Miller and D. K. Hadidian; Pittsburgh, 1971], pp. 223-27) suggests a different reason for the Corinthian attitude, related to the rabbinic doctrine that in conversion a proselyte is like a newborn child; hence all former relations are dissolved, and a man may take his father's wife because "in Christ" this old relationship no longer exists since "all things have become new." As Daube points out, there is certainly a sense in which Paul himself believed this. What he would then be objecting to here is their taking it too far, so that they went beyond even pagan law. This suggestion is difficult to evaluate. On the one hand, such a view may very well have been part of the Corinthians' new spirituality, that "in Christ" all former relationships no longer exist. This can be neither proved nor disproved; but such a stance could help to explain how such a relationship might have been started in the first place. On the other hand, Daube misses Paul by a long way in suggesting that the real issue is pagan law. For Paul the issue is sin, pure and simple, over which the community should mourn and which for the sake of the community must be removed from their midst.

[29]This translation, which understands the ἵνα to be imperatival (see Turner, *Syntax*, 95; Moule, 144-45; Zerwick, *BG*, 415), may be correct, but it covers up a very complex grammatical decision. Barrett, 122; Conzelmann, 96, and many others take it as a consecutive, similar to ὥστε. Thus their mourning should have resulted in the man's expulsion from the community.

[30]This aorist does not contradict what was said about the force of ἔχειν in v. 1. The aorist here (also in v. 3) is constative, summing up the matter as a whole.

[31]As in Matt. 5:4; cf. 1 Esdr. 8:69; Ezra 10:6; *T.Reub.* 1:10. It is just possible that it reflects the kind of mourning one experiences at the death of a loved one. The man's sin and therefore the necessity of his expulsion from the community if he did not repent would have resulted in their having gone into "mourning" at the loss of a brother. See, e.g., V. C. Pfitzner, "Expulsion from the community according to Matthew 18:15-18 and 1 Corinthians 5:1-5," *AusBR* 30 (1982), 42. The γάρ that introduces the next clause suggests that mourning over sin is what is in view, since it must result in such action on their part.

response to such sin in their midst, not pride; and true mourning of this kind would have as its concomitant result that the man would have been "put out of your fellowship."

There are always some who see this action as harsh and unloving; but such criticism comes from those who do not appreciate the biblical view of God's holiness, and the deep revulsion to sin that that holiness entails. When Isaiah sees the exalted Lord, and hears the trisagion "Holy, holy, holy" (Isa. 6), he bows in deep personal and national repentance; and in such moments the removal of sin is the natural consequence.[32] Thus Paul is not here dealing with "church discipline" as such;[33] rather, out of his Jewish heritage he is expressing what should be the *normal* consequences of being the people of God, who are called to be his holy people (1:2). It is this lack of a sense of sin, and therefore of any ethical consequences to their life in the Spirit, that marks the Corinthian brand of spirituality as radically different from that which flows out of the gospel of Christ crucified.[34] And it is precisely this failure to recognize the depth of their corporate sinfulness due to their arrogance that causes Paul to take such strong action as is described in the next sentence (vv. 3-5).

3-4 With an emphatic "and I for my part,"[35] which stands in contrast to "and *you* are puffed up," Paul begins a sentence whose overall point is clear enough, but whose syntax is particularly complex, and whose concluding action (5a) and ultimate purpose (5b) are shrouded in mystery. In contrast to the Corinthians, who because they are "puffed up" have done nothing, not even mourned the man's sin, Paul takes decisive action. But the action cannot be his alone. It must be effected in the context of the gathered assembly, where both he and the power of Christ are present by the Spirit. In

---

[32]The removal of sinful objects is always a concomitant of national repentance in Israel. See, e.g., 2 Kgs. 23:4-5 in the context of 22:11, 19; Zech. 13:2 in the context of 12:10-14; Ezra 10:3 in the context of 10:1.

[33]That is why any comparison with the rite of removal in Qumran is ultimately irrelevant. See, e.g., S. E. Johnson, "The Dead Sea Manual of Discipline and the Jerusalem Church of Acts," in *The Scrolls and the New Testament* (ed. K. Stendahl; New York, 1957), p. 139. See esp. the "penal code" and the judgments in 1QS 6:24–7:25. Theirs was a rite of discipline that had missed the "awful" character of God's holiness and the deeply fallen character of human sinfulness, and therefore was purely ascetic. That is hardly what Paul is dealing with here. Cf. G. Forkman, *The Limits of Religious Community: Expulsion from the Religious Community within the Qumran Sect, within Rabbinic Judaism, and within Primitive Christianity* (Lund, 1972), 75-78.

[34]See pp. 96, 627. Note that Paul does not miss this point: 1:30, "God made Christ to become 'wisdom' for us, that is, to become righteousness, holiness, and redemption"; 6:11, "but such *were* some of you; now you are washed, sanctified, justified in Christ by the Spirit"; 15:3, "Christ died for our sins." See the comm. on these passages.

[35]Gk. ἐγὼ μέν, not picked up in the NIV. The μέν has no coordinate δέ, but contrasts the ἐγώ of this sentence with the ὑμεῖς of the preceding one.

such a gathering the church is to put the man back out into the sphere of Satan for some form of "destruction" that has his salvation as its ultimate goal. All of that seems easy enough; but the details form one of the difficult cruxes in the letter.

Paul begins by noting that even though he is not "physically present," he is present "in spirit." On the basis of the obvious contrast of "body" and "spirit," plus Paul's use of similar language in Col. 2:5,[36] this could possibly be similar to our own use of this idiom, whereby we mean something like "you are in my thoughts."[37] Here, however, Paul intends something more: in a way that is not altogether clear to us he understood himself actually to be present "in spirit/Spirit" in the gathered community.[38] This is confirmed first by the phrase in the next clause, usually translated "just as if I were present," which in light of v. 4 must mean "as actually present."[39] That is, he is not allowing that because he is not physically present he is not truly present and therefore he must act *as though* he were. Rather, he is emphasizing the fact that he is indeed present in Spirit, and that is *why* he can act as he does.

The phrase "and my spirit" in v. 4, with its emphatic use of "my"[40] and the fact that it serves with "you" as the compound subject of the verb "when assembled," is what finally makes this clear. What exactly he understood this to mean is more difficult to pin down, but it is undoubtedly related to his understanding of life in the Spirit. The believer in the new age has "received the Spirit of God" (2:12-13), has "become one spirit with the Lord" (6:17), so that he/she is a "temple of the Holy Spirit, which [referring to the Spirit] one has from God" (6:19). Related to this kind of "receiving/having/being joined to the Spirit" language, Paul further speaks of "my spirit" in ways that seem ambiguous. Sometimes he simply means his own

[36]The language is not exact, but close. Here Paul contrasts τῷ σώματι ("in the body") with τῷ πνεύματι ("in the spirit"); in Colossians the first member is τῇ σαρκί ("in the flesh"), which in this instance means the same thing.

[37]Cf. Barrett, 123, "Paul is using the word in a 'quite popular sense' (Weiss), that is, psychologically rather than theologically. . . . Paul refers to his thoughts, and his concern for the Corinthian church." Of v. 4 he says further: "He will make his contribution, as the Corinthians reflect on what they remember of his convictions, character, and ways, and on what they know of his mind in the present matter" (p. 124). This seems to miss the dynamic character of their gathering in the power of the Spirit.

[38]Cf. Wiles, *Intercessory,* pp. 145-46.

[39]Gk. ὡς παρών; cf. Findlay, 808, who is one of the few commentators to catch the significance of this insertion: "ὡς παρών means 'as being present,' not 'as though present'—which rendering virtually surrenders the previous ἀπών . . . παρὼν δέ"; and Murphy-O'Connor, "V,3-5," 244 n. 20: "There is no justification for translating *hōs parōn* by 'as if present.' . . . Hence, 'as one who is present.'"

[40]Gk. ἐμοῦ, the possessive adjective serving as possessive pronoun in the emphatic position. This is seldom noted by commentators, but it must not be overlooked. Elsewhere with this idiom Paul uses the simple, unemphatic μου (14:14; 2 Cor. 2:13; Rom. 1:9).

person with no reference to the Spirit of God (e.g., 2 Cor. 2:13); but in 1 Cor. 14:14-15 ("my spirit prays") he means that his own spirit prays as the Holy Spirit gives the utterance. In this case we might then translate, "my S/spirit prays." Something very much like that seems to be intended here. Thus, in saying "when you and my S/spirit are assembled together, along with the power of the Lord Jesus," Paul does not mean that in some vague way they are to think about him as though he were actually among them, but is not really so.[41] Rather, when the Corinthians are assembled, the Spirit is understood to be present among them (see on 3:16); and for Paul that means that he, too, is present among them by that same Spirit.[42] If all of that is not easy for us to grasp, we must nonetheless not try to make Paul think or talk like us. This letter, of course, communicates his prophetic word to them on this matter; he probably therefore thinks of the reading of the letter in the gathered assembly as the tangible way in which the Spirit communicates his prophetic-apostolic ministry in their midst (cf. 2 Cor. 10:10-11).

His actual presence by the Spirit probably harks back to the "arrogance" of those who say that he is not returning (4:18). "To the contrary," Paul says, "I am present among you in Spirit, whereby I speak the prophetic word of judgment in your midst."[43] Thus he has "already passed judgment[44] on the one who did this," that this man is to be handed over to Satan

[41]The NIV seems especially to fall into this trap. By eliminating all reference to the Spirit, it makes the whole text mean either "physically" = "actually" present, or "spiritually" = but not really. Thus they translate the first clause "I am with you in spirit," meaning "I am not really present because I am not there physically." The next clause then makes this "not really" clearer by translating "just as if I were present," implying "but I am not because I am only with you in spirit" (v. 4). But this misses Paul by a wide margin, and is an especially unfortunate rendering of καὶ τοῦ ἐμοῦ πνεύματος, which functions in Paul's sentence as the compound subject, along with ὑμῶν, of the verb συναχθέντων ("when you and my S/spirit are assembled").

[42]Cf. E. Schweizer, *TDNT* VI, 434-35; for a somewhat different view see Jewett, *Terms,* pp. 184-97, 451-53.

[43]For the probability that we are dealing with a prophetic judgment, as in 3:17, see Käsemann, "Sentences," pp. 70-71.

[44]Gk. ἤδη κέκρικα; Conzelmann, 94, translates "I have now already resolved . . . to consign this man," commenting that it does not mean "'have passed judgment'; otherwise the infinitive remains hanging in the air." That is not quite so, and reflects Conzelmann's own desire to have the entire action be Paul's, with no community involvement: "The community merely constitutes the forum; it does not share in the action" (p. 97). The sentence is convoluted, but its general syntax is manageable. The τὸν οὕτως τοῦτο κατεργασάμενον is the object of the verb κέκρικα, not of the infinitive that follows some four lines later. But the man is also the object of the *action* that is pursuant to Paul's judgment; hence Paul repeats the object in the form of τὸν τοιοῦτον. The infinitive is a simple instance of indirect discourse; thus, "I have already passed judgment on the one who has perpetrated this deed, that you are to hand over such a one to Satan." The "you" that functions as the subject of the infinitive is implied in the preceding genitive absolute συναχθέντων ὑμῶν ("when you are assembled"). Cf. O-W, 186. On this whole question see the discussion in Murphy-O'Connor, "V, 3-5," 242-45, who comes to a similar conclusion but handles the grammar slightly differently.

(v. 5). But the action is not to be Paul's alone; nor is it to be understood as some sort of ecclesiastical tribunal.[45] Rather, it is to be a community action, carried out in the context of the Spirit, where "you and my S/spirit are assembled together, along with[46] the power of the Lord Jesus." As noted earlier (2:4-5; 4:19-20), the term "power" in a context like this is a reference to the Spirit, who is dynamically present among them when they are assembled together. In such a context Paul's word of prophetic judgment is to be heard and acted upon. The whole community must carry out the action because the "leaven" has affected them as a community; and as a community of the Spirit (3:16) they must act in accordance with the Spirit's direction that has now been given them through Paul.

But there remains a further difficulty, one that rather substantially affects the meaning of the sentence: the phrase in v. 4, "in the name of our Lord Jesus," may qualify either of three verb forms:[47] (1) "When you are assembled in the name of the Lord Jesus" (NIV, JB, NEB);[48] (2) "I have already pronounced judgment in the name of our Lord Jesus" (RSV, GNB, NAB, Moffatt, Montgomery); or (3) ". . . on the one who perpetrated this deed in the name of our Lord Jesus."[49] Option 1 has much to commend it. It

---

[45]This is an especially popular position in the nonexegetical literature, although it can at times be found elsewhere. See, e.g., C. J. Roetzel, *Judgment in the Community* (Leiden, 1972), pp. 113-24, who simply assumes that juridical procedures are in view and discusses the passage accordingly.

[46]One of the syntactical difficulties in the sentence is to determine what this prepositional phrase modifies, either the participle συναχθέντων or the infinitive παραδοῦναι. In this case, however, usage is determinative. The preposition σύν is duplicating the σύν in the compound verb συν-άγω and means what it ordinarily does, "together with" (cf. 1:2). Furthermore, the preposition seldom carries an instrumental sense, and never so in Paul; therefore it can hardly go with παραδοῦναι, where such a sense would be necessary. *Contra* I. Havener, "A Curse for Salvation—1 Corinthians 5:1-5," in *Sin, Salvation and the Spirit* (ed. D. Durken; Collegeville, MN, 1979), pp. 336-37. The parallels adduced by A. Yarbro Collins ("The Function of 'Excommunication' in Paul," *HTR* 73 [1980], 256) from the magical papyri are not in fact parallel, despite A. Deissmann's assertion to the contrary (LAE, p. 303 n. 1).

[47]Another option sometimes suggested is that it modifies παραδοῦναι. But this is ruled out both by word order and by the lack of a need to go this way; the same point is made in option 2, namely the emphasis on the authority of Christ in carrying out the exclusion.

[48]Argued for, vis-à-vis Murphy-O'Connor (next note), by Havener, "Curse," 335-36, although he translates: ". . . assembled under the invocation of our Lord Jesus."

[49]I first heard this view presented in a paper by Frederick Danker at the annual meeting of the SBL in St. Louis, 1976. It was so translated by Elaine Pagels, *The Gnostic Paul* (Philadelphia, 1975), p. 64; and it has been argued for in some detail by Murphy-O'Connor, "V, 3-5," now followed by S. D. MacArthur, "'Spirit' in Pauline Usage: 1 Corinthians 5.5," in *Studia Biblica 1978, III. Papers on Paul and Other New Testament Authors* (ed. E. A. Livingstone; Sheffield, 1980), pp. 249-56; and Yarbro Collins, "Function," p. 253. Cf. O-W, 186, who allow it as "another interesting possibility."

corresponds to the teaching of Jesus recorded in Matt. 18:20, which became the early church's normal understanding of their gatherings, that he himself is present in the midst of two or more "gathered in his name." In this case it would further emphasize the nature of the assembled gathering, as being in the presence of God. On the other hand, this makes the phrase seem redundant to the next one, "with the power of the Lord Jesus," as well as overloads the verb "assembled."[50] What is mostly against it, however, is the word order. Not only does this phrase elsewhere in Paul follow its verb,[51] but also where this kind of prepositional phrase precedes its verb, it is demonstrably emphatic (cf. 1:21), which does not seem to be the case here.

It is less easy to decide between the other two options. Option 3 has in its favor that it immediately follows this verb form and is therefore the more natural reading. In fact, it is fair to say that this would have been the normal understanding were it not for the difficulty instinctively felt with someone's doing such a thing "in the name of the Lord Jesus." Since Murphy-O'Connor has shown how easily those who considered themselves "spiritual" might have been able to say this about such behavior,[52] that objection is less formidable than it once might have seemed. There are, however, still problems with this option. First, there is the difficulty of his using the actual wording "in the name of the Lord Jesus,"[53] which would be even greater if the reading "our"[54] is authentic; he would more likely have used an "in Christ" formula of some kind.[55] More difficult still is its role in the sentence; it seems an overstatement on Paul's part to have added this considerable phrase in the midst of a sentence whose primary concern is not the basis on which the incestuous man is acting, but the authority on which Paul himself is acting while present with them in Spirit.

This means, therefore, that although option 3 is possible, option 2 is more likely what Paul was intending. Part of the problem, after all, is a crisis of authority in the church. Paul is hereby speaking a prophetic judgment on the perpetrator of this deed; but his authority is not his own. Rather, as in 2 Thess. 3:6, he speaks "by the authority of our Lord Jesus" (Moffatt). The

---

[50]See n. 46 above for the argument that the phrase σὺν τῇ δυνάμει τοῦ κυρίου ἡμῶν Ἰησοῦ almost certainly modifies συναχθέντων.

[51]1 Cor. 6:11; 2 Thess. 3:6; Col. 3:17.

[52]See n. 48 above.

[53]Murphy-O'Connor, "V, 3-5," 241, recognizes this problem and argues that "it is not necessary that the offender should have used precisely these words." While that is true, one wonders then why Paul used such a formula at all, if it were not the offender's that he was using.

[54]See n. 12.

[55]This assumes, with others, that a part of their spirituality expressed itself in a kind of exaltation Christology. As Christ was raised and now lives "spiritually," so too they are "in Christ" and therefore live above merely earthly affairs.

fact that the phrase is somewhat removed from its verb is not as significant as some would make out;[56] its distance is simply the result of the direct object being somewhat wordy. Those who see this as a kind of "curse" formula are probably more enamored with ancient parallels than such a phrase actually warrants.[57] To do something in someone's name is to act with that person's authority, which is precisely the point of Paul's concern here.[58]

Thus the sentence through v. 4 says: "As for my part, even though not physically present, I am present with you in S/spirit, and as such I have already, by the authority of our Lord Jesus, pronounced sentence on the man who has perpetrated this deed; so that when you and my S/spirit are assembled together along with the power of the Lord Jesus. . . ." But what exactly were they to do in this setting? That is given in v. 5.

5 These words bring us to the statement of the actual judgment, both its nature and its intended result. In the context of "the power of our Lord Jesus" the community[59] is to "hand this man over to Satan for the destruction of the flesh in order that the spirit might be saved on the day of the Lord."[60] Apart from the similar usage in 1 Tim. 1:20, the language "to hand over to Satan" is not found elsewhere as an act of expulsion from a religious community. There are some remote parallels in the magical papyri,[61] but these are personal execrations spoken directly to the god of the underworld. It may be that Paul was influenced by the LXX of Job 2:6 ("Behold, I hand him over to you"). But whatever the source of the language, the similar usage in 1 Tim. 1:20[62] suggests that for Paul this was quasitechnical language for some kind of expulsion from the Christian com-

---

[56]E.g., Murphy-O'Connor, "V, 3-5," 240, who says, "but elsewhere in Paul this phrase is never so far away from the verb it qualifies." He adds, "This would not be a difficulty if there were an appreciable gain in meaning, but such is not in fact the case here." But the question finally has to do with the main point of the sentence, which this interpretation clearly supports.

[57]See, e.g., Conzelmann, 97, who refers to L. Brun, *Segen und Fluch im Urchristentum* (Oslo, 1932), pp. 106ff.

[58]Some readers may note that this is a change of position from the author's *Study Guide,* pp. 95-96.

[59]That they are the intended subject of the verb "to hand over" is argued in n. 44 above.

[60]This more literal "translation" is intended to help identify some of the problems.

[61]E.g., "Demon of the dead, . . . I hand over to you ($\pi\alpha\rho\alpha\delta\iota\delta\omega\mu\iota$) so-and-so [the name is missing], in order that. . . ." See Deissmann, LAE, p. 302 (my transl.).

[62]This is true whether Paul actually wrote 1 Timothy or not. Remarkably, some scholars would eliminate this text as having relevance because they think Paul did not write the Pastoral Epistles, yet will allow that the remotest of parallels from pagan literature influenced him (e.g., Yarbro Collins, "Function"). But the Pastorals are Pauline even if he didn't write them; here then is relevant usage of the most important kind. See Fee, *1 and 2 Timothy,* pp. 23-24.

munity,[63] probably from the gatherings of the assembly for worship, including the meals and supper in honor of the Lord (see on v. 11). Thus we are not dealing with an "execration" formula, nor is it probable that Paul intends the language to be taken literally, in the sense of personally handing the man to Satan to "go to work on him," as it were.[64] More likely, the language means to turn him back out into Satan's sphere. This does not mean that Satan would not directly attack him in some way, but that is incidental to the language, not its primary intent. In contrast to the gathered community of believers who experience the Spirit and power of the Lord Jesus in edifying gifts and loving concern for one another, this man is to be put back out into the world, where Satan and his "principalities and powers" still hold sway over people's lives to destroy them.[65] By this action the church was to clean out the old leaven that it might become a new loaf without leaven (vv. 6-8).

But what Paul expected to happen to the man himself is more difficult to determine. The problem is twofold: (1) What does "flesh" mean in the phrase "for the destruction of the flesh"? and (2) what is the nature of the contrast between "flesh" and "spirit"? Unfortunately, no solution is without difficulties.

First, a grammatical note. It is common to see the prepositional phrase "for the destruction of the flesh" as expressing purpose, followed by a final purpose clause, "in order that the spirit might be saved." As a matter of grammar, however, the expressed *purpose* of the action, which alone qualifies the verb "to hand over," is the final matter only, his salvation. The preposition *eis* ("for") sometimes expresses purpose, but it may also express anticipated result,[66] which seems far more likely here.[67] What the grammar suggests, then, is that the "destruction of his flesh" is the anticipated result of the man's being being put back out into Satan's domain, while the express purpose of the action is his redemption.[68]

[63]This seems true despite Godet's arguments to the contrary (242-55); cf. MacArthur, "'Spirit,'" 249-50. The Jewish parallels for this activity are of some interest, but the language is not the same, nor is the intent of the action. On this matter see Forkman, *Limits,* pp. 87-108.

[64]This is the common view, and can be found in most of the literature. It goes hand in hand with the interpretation of "the destruction of the flesh" as referring to physical suffering or death. See below.

[65]Cf. Calvin, 108: "While Christ reigns within, so Satan reigns outside, the Church"; Barrett, 126; Murphy-O'Connor, 41-42.

[66]BAGD 4e.

[67]Paul is not averse to doubling purpose clauses, but he does so by twin clauses, not by this preposition and a final clause. See, e.g., ἵνα . . . ὅπως (1:28-29; 2 Thess. 1:11-12; 2 Cor. 8:14); εἰς τό . . . ἵνα (Rom. 7:4; 15:16); ἵνα . . . ἵνα (1 Cor. 4:6; 7:5). The only expression similar to this is in Rom. 6:4, but the εἰς τόν does not express purpose.

[68]This is unfortunately missed in the NIV; the point is also neglected in most of the literature.

But what did Paul actually expect as the result of his being returned to the sphere of Satan's power "for the destruction of the flesh"? Most scholars understand this phrase to refer at least to physical suffering,[69] and most likely to death itself.[70] This is the most natural understanding of the word "destruction."[71] Physical suffering from the hand of Satan, but for God's ultimate purposes, is found in the Book of Job (esp. 2:4-10) and in Paul's own "thorn in the flesh," carried out by a messenger of Satan (2 Cor. 12:7). That the "destruction" might entail death is supported by the incident of Ananias and Sapphira (Acts 5:1-10). Indeed, the combination of suffering and death is found within 1 Corinthians itself, in 11:30-32, where the sickness and death of some are viewed as consequences of "unworthy" participation at the Lord's Table.

Despite this evidence, however, and the large number of scholars who take this view, the idea that Paul expected the man's death seems too difficult to maintain—and not simply because the punishment does not fit the "crime."[72] There are several problems. First, related to the grammatical note, the emphasis in Paul's own sentence, and therefore presumably his intent, lies not on "the destruction of the flesh," but on the final purpose clause, "that the spirit might be saved on the day of the Lord."[73] The former phrase, therefore, must be seen as part of the *remedial* process; otherwise the interpretation seems doomed to fail. It is especially difficult to see how an expected result of death can be understood as remedial.[74]

[69]See *inter alia* Lightfoot, 204 ("physical suffering of some kind is implied, the purpose being remedial"); Morris, 88-89; and G. W. H. Lampe, "Church Discipline and the Interpretation of the Epistle to the Corinthians," in *Christian History and Interpretation, Studies Presented to John Knox* (eds. W. R. Farmer, C. F. D. Moule, and R. R. Niebuhr; Cambridge, 1967), pp. 337-61.

[70]Some express greater confidence in this conclusion than the text allows. BAGD, e.g., give death as the only option; cf. J. Schneider, *TDNT* V, 169; and Käsemann, "Sentences," p. 71, who says this "obviously entails the death of the guilty." This is the almost universal opinion of the commentators. Exceptions are Grosheide, 123; Barclay, 49; and Murphy-O'Connor, 41-42; cf. R-P, 99, who combine physical punishment with destroying his sinful lusts.

[71]Gk. ὄλεθρον; see the previous note.

[72]Unless of course one wants to maintain that only such "shock" treatment would move the Corinthians past their arrogance. It is often implied that the notion that such a man should die is "repugnant" to moderns, and that we must not let our worldview shape our exegesis, so that we reject what Paul is saying because it is repugnant to us. This is indeed true; but the question is not one of "repugnance," but whether in light of Paul's own theology such a view can be maintained.

[73]This is unfortunately missed in the NIV. Literally Paul's Greek says, "to hand him over to Satan for the destruction of the flesh, in order that the spirit might be saved on the Day of the Lord." The whole sentence leads to this final purpose clause.

[74]See in this regard the various suggestions by Barrett, 126-27. The problem with these suggestions, however, is that they do not seem to reflect Pauline theology as we meet it elsewhere.

Second, apart from a literal sense of "handing over to Satan," the word "destruction" is the only thing that supports such a view; but there are several reasons for wondering whether the language can be pressed here,[75] since this interpretation seems to run counter to Paul's own theology in so many ways. For example, nowhere else does Paul express death in terms of "destruction of the flesh." If the phrase were by itself, without the following purpose clause, a case for death could clearly be made; but the phrase is *not* by itself. Here it stands in contrast to the saving of "the spirit"; and it is simply foreign to Paul's usage for the "flesh/spirit" contrast to refer to the body as doomed to destruction but the "spirit" (inner, real person?) as destined for salvation. Such a view stands in contradiction to Paul's express doctrine of the resurrection of the body and in fact would fit nicely into the Corinthians' own view (see on 6:12-14).[76] This has been regularly recognized as the great difficulty with this view, so much so that some have tried to find a different meaning for "spirit" so as to make it compatible with "destruction of the flesh" in the sense of death.[77] In the final analysis Pauline usage is far more significant for interpretation than the word "destruction," which is capable of a metaphorical sense.

Third, the relationship with 11:30-32 is not as comparable as one might be led to believe. There Paul is making a judgment *after* the fact, as it were—indeed, after two facts. They are destroying the Table; and some of them are sickly, or have even died. Paul, by inspiration of the Spirit, prophetically tells them that these two "facts" are related in a consequential

---

[75]In this regard see esp. the arguments in A. C. Thiselton, "The Meaning of ΣΑΡΞ in 1 Corinthians 5.5: A Fresh Approach in the Light of Logical and Semantic Factors," *SJT* 26 (1973), 204-28.

[76]Jewett, *Terms,* p. 124, recognizes this, but resolves it by assuming the compilation-of-letters hypothesis of Weiss and Schmithals and then arguing that Paul himself at an earlier stage used this "gnostic" terminology, which he would later abandon. But that will not do, since this is not just a matter of terminology, but of Paul's fundamental worldview, which derives from his Jewish heritage.

[77]See, e.g., von Campenhausen, *Authority,* p. 135 n. 50; Donfried, "Justification," pp. 150-52; and Yarbro Collins, "Function," pp. 257-62, who interpret it as the Spirit within the community: if the Corinthians allow this man's sin to remain unchecked in their midst, "the Spirit will be lost to the community" (Yarbro Collins, 260). But such a view does violence to the soteriological aspect of the verb "saved," which has to mean something like "be kept safe for." The eschatological reference to "the Day of the Lord" rules out such a possibility.

Another tack is taken by MacArthur, "'Spirit,'" who argues on the basis of the flexibility of the word πνεῦμα in Paul that it could refer to the man from the perspective of his being dead, hence "that the dead [man] might be saved." It seems far better to find more flexibility in εἰς ὄλεθρον τῆς σαρκός, which is linguistically verifiable, than to resort to such options, which appear to be not readily available to the Corinthians themselves.

way. But that is far from "excommunicating" for the very purpose that the man might suffer physically unto death.[78]

Fourth, the further instruction in v. 11, that they are not to associate with this man, not even to eat with him, implies that no immediate death is in purview.

Finally, it is out of character with Paul's theology as we meet it elsewhere that one who sins within the Christian community should be so punished in the present age that he lies beyond the redemptive, restorative love of that community. Paul in fact is found on the other side of things.[79] To these same Corinthians who have been too harsh on a brother who needed correction (2 Cor. 2:5-11), he argues that "punishment by the majority is sufficient" and that they should now restore him. Despite a long history of interpretation that has believed otherwise, this is probably not the same man as in our present passage.[80] Nevertheless it reveals how Paul thinks the community should treat offenders, who previously had to experience some form of "punishment" (cf. Gal. 6:1; 2 Thess. 3:14-15).[81]

With some degree of confidence, therefore, we may put aside the idea that Paul intended that the man should die. The possibility that some form of remedial suffering was in view is not thereby ruled out, although such a view presses the noun "destruction" beyond its ordinary limits. What this means, then, is that we have a typically Pauline contrast between "flesh" and "spirit," although not necessarily typically expressed. What Paul was desiring by having this man put outside the believing community was the destruction of what was "carnal" in him, so that he might be "saved" eschatologically.[82] In this case, as most often in Paul, "flesh" and "spirit" designate "the whole person as viewed from different angles. 'Spirit' means the whole person as oriented towards God. 'Flesh' means the whole person as oriented away from God."[83] The "destruction" of one's sinful nature would thus belong to the same kind of imagery as in "crucifying" it (Gal. 5:24; cf. Rom. 7:5-6).

[78]Cf. Yarbro Collins, "Function," pp. 258-59.

[79]To be sure, he does warn those who persist in their former sins that they may not inherit the eternal kingdom (6:9-11); but even that warning holds out the invitation to stop sinning so that such will not happen.

[80]For a full discussion, see Furnish, *II Corinthians*, pp. 160-68.

[81]On this point, as well as several others in this presentation, see also J. Cambier, "La Chair et l'Esprit en 1 Cor v. 5," *NTS* 15 (1968/69), 221-32.

[82]Apart from Tertullian (*pudic.* 13-15), who knew his view was contrary to common opinion, this was the standard view in the early church, being found explicitly in Origen, Chrysostom, and Theodore of Mopsuestia.

[83]Murphy-O'Connor, 42. The view of Havener, "Curse," p. 340, that "spirit" = the "spiritual body" of 15:44 is too difficult to sustain. One wonders how the Corinthians, without some clue in the present passage, could possibly have so understood it.

The intent of this action, therefore, is the man's salvation. He is not being "turned over to Satan for destruction," an idea that is quite foreign both to Paul and the rest of the NT, but is being excluded from the Christian community with its life in the Spirit. The inevitable consequence is that he is back out in Satan's domain, where, Paul hopes, his "flesh" may be destroyed so that he may be saved on the Day of the Lord. By this latter term Paul does not intend that he must wait until the final Day to be saved. Rather, this is one of Paul's ordinary ways of expressing salvation. Salvation is primarily an eschatological reality, experienced in the present to be sure, but to be realized fully at the Day of the Lord (on this term see on 3:15 and 4:5).

What Paul does not tell us is *how* he perceived this "destruction" of his flesh to take place. In fact, this is the most frequent objection to this view: Satan would then be envisioned as working against his own interests.[84] But that objection is equally true for the other views, since whatever the activity is, it is ultimately against Satan's own interests, given that the aim is the man's eschatological salvation. Perhaps we have been too quick to assume that Paul looked on Satan and his hosts as directly involved in the "destruction." More likely, whatever kind of buffeting from satanic forces he may experience "out there," the actual separation from the fellowship of the people of God, God's "Spirit people," who are living out the life of the future while they await the consummation, would in itself lead to his putting aside his sins so that he might once more join the community. The text itself does not say this, but the rest of Pauline theology certainly supports such a view.

How, then, does all this function as God's Word for us? First, the very complexities of the passage, which has just enough ambiguity to keep one from being certain on key issues, should make us properly hesitant about remaking the text into some kind of canon law. This is an *ad hoc* case of church discipline, similar in kind to that suggested for the idlers/busybodies in 2 Thess. 3:6-15.

But that does not mean that it does not speak to our situation. Indeed, quite the opposite. In a day when the church tolerates every kind of sin ("because we who are sinners must not be judgmental"), the need for discipline within the context of the Spirit's power is perhaps greater than ever. But lest one too quickly start a process of excommunication that finally eliminates us all, a few observations about the text in general are in order.

First, in this text church discipline is not the affair of one or a few.

---

[84]See, e.g., Morris, 88, "But it is difficult to see how handing a man over to Satan would have such a purifying effect. Rather we would expect the reverse, the stimulation of those lusts."

Even though Paul as an apostle pronounced the sentence prophetically, the sin itself was known by all and had contaminated the whole; so the action was to be the affair of all.

Second, the ultimate reason for such discipline is remedial, not judgmental. For such to take place, one needs an especially loving, redemptive community, where the power of the Lord Jesus is a regular part of corporate life.

Third, according to the rest of the passage, the problem was truly affecting the life of the whole community. Probably discipline of this kind should be reserved for such "contaminating" sins.

Finally, the great problem with such discipline in most Christian communities in the Western world is that one can simply go down the street to another church. Not only does that say something about the fragmented condition of the church at large, but it also says something about those who would quickly welcome one who is under discipline in another community.

Perhaps it should be added that if one were to be so disciplined in our day, too often the person could "take it or leave it" as far as the church is concerned—and that probably says more about the condition of the church itself than about the person who is dissociated. Maybe the most significant thing we can learn from such a text is how far many of us are removed from a view of the church in which the dynamic of the Spirit was so real that exclusion could be a genuinely redemptive action.

b. Argument by analogy—the Passover (5:6-8)

6 *Your boasting is not good. Don't you know that a little yeast works through[1] the whole batch of dough? 7 Get[2] rid of the old yeast that you may be a new batch without yeast—as you really are. For Christ, our Passover lamb, has been sacrificed.[3] 8 Therefore let us keep the Festival, not with the old yeast, the yeast of malice and wickedness, but with bread without yeast, the bread of sincerity and truth.*

With this striking set of images, Paul now gives the theological basis for the action of vv. 1-5. He begins with the basic problem—their boasting, which is totally out of place in light of their present sick condition. What they fail to realize is how this man's sin had infected the whole community, which as a

---

[1]Both here and in Gal. 5:9 D reads δολοῖ, a corruption probably influenced by the Latin.

[2]The MajT and a few earlier witnesses (C Ψ 048 a sy^h) relieve Paul's asyndeton by adding an οὖν ("therefore").

[3]Following the lead of the Sahidic and Syriac versions, the MajT adds ὑπὲρ ἡμῶν ("for us"), which cannot have been original since it is impossible to account for "omission" in all the early evidence.

community must be God's temple in Corinth. Paul's metaphor, however, is not illness, but a proverbial saying about "leaven" (v. 6), which in turn calls forth related imagery from the Feast of Unleavened Bread and the Passover (v. 7). They are to get rid of the "old leaven," the incestuous man, so that they might become what they really are, a "new batch of dough." With a shift of metaphors he reminds them of what made them unleavened bread: the sacrifice of God's Paschal Lamb. In v. 8 he applies the festal metaphor once more to their present situation, but broadens it to include their attitudes and behavior in general, which have been the greater issue right along. Although the metaphors get slightly mixed (the church alternately is the purified house, the new batch of dough, and the celebrants of the Feast), Paul's point is clear. They must remove the man for their own sake, so that they may truly be the new people of God in Corinth.

This passage serves as a splendid illustration of Pauline parenesis (ethical instruction). In his use of the leaven imagery, Paul states the imperative in a way that seems to belie his theology. So he immediately corrects the false impression by making the event of the crucified One the grounds for ethical behavior. V. 7, therefore, functions as a compendium of Paul's gospel in metaphor. The death of Christ makes them new; yet they must get rid of the old in order to be new, precisely because in Christ they already are new!

6 In the preceding long sentence Paul reasserted his apostolic authority by placing himself in their midst in S/spirit and pronouncing his verdict on the incestuous man, which the community, gathered in the presence of the Lord, was to carry out. Although the stated aim of that action was this man's redemption, Paul's greater concern lay with the community itself. He now returns to that concern by picking up the theme of their boasting from v. 2. This "boasting"[4] of theirs "is not good,"[5] which of course is true in itself, especially when it is predicated on self-confidence, as theirs was, and not on the Lord (cf. 1:29-31). But the present concern centers not on their boasting in general; rather, it focuses on their boasting as it relates to this sin in their midst (cf. v. 2). As Barrett nicely puts it: "a church exposed to corruption would do well to sing in a lower key" (p. 127).

By means of the rhetorical device "Do you not know that?" (cf. 3:16), Paul attempts to show them the absurdity of their headiness when they are in such imminent danger of being "spoiled" by fermentation. What they should know in this case comes in the form of a proverb: "A little leaven

---

[4]Gk. καύχημα, the noun of the verb that occurs in 1:29, 31; 3:21; 4:7. In this context it is a synonym of φυσιόω in v. 2. The shift from φυσιόω to καυχάομαι also occurred in 4:6 and 7.

[5]Gk. οὐ καλόν; καλός here means something closer to "praiseworthy" than to morally righteous. Cf. on 7:1, 8, 26.

leavens the whole batch of dough" (cf. Gal. 5:9). Although there is no other evidence for it in antiquity, the saying is probably a piece of Jewish folk wisdom, similar to our "A bad apple spoils the whole barrel." What is in view is not "yeast" (as in the NIV), which was not plentiful in antiquity, and which in any case is fresh and wholesome. "Leaven" was not so.[6] It consisted of keeping back a "little" portion of last week's dough, allowing it to ferment, then adding it to this week's dough, which in turn was thoroughly fermented to give it lightness (= sourdough bread). Although the OT does not expressly so specify, the Feast of Unleavened Bread, as well as being a religious celebration, was probably a health provision. Because of the fermentation process, which week after week increased the dangers of infection, the Israelites were commanded once a year to purge their homes of all leaven (Exod. 12:14-20). During the Feast they would bake only unleavened bread, from which dough they would then start up the process again after the Feast. Thus in the NT leaven became a symbol of the process by which an evil spreads insidiously in a community until the whole has been infected by it (cf. Mark 8:15). So it was in Corinth. Their problem was that they were not taking this matter seriously, either the evil itself or their danger of being thoroughly contaminated by it.

7 The mention of "leaven" in v. 6 naturally suggests imagery from Paul's own history as a law-abiding Jew, namely the two religious rituals of Passover. He begins with a direct allusion to the ceremonial removal of all leaven from their homes (Exod. 12:15), which in turn prompts an allusion to the most important event of all, the sacrifice of the Paschal Lamb (Exod. 12:6).

Thus he shifts from the "small" leaven and "whole" batch (of dough) in the proverb to "old" leaven and "new" batch (of dough) from the Feast of Unleavened Bread. The imagery is expressed as an imperative, similar to that which had long been a part of his Jewish experience:[7] "Get rid[8] of the old leaven." In this context, of course, this refers to the removal of the incestuous man in v. 5; but as v. 8 indicates, the very use of such imagery has the possibility of broader application.[9] The purpose of this removal of the "leaven" reflects the process of starting over with a new

[6]On this matter, and for much of the discussion that follows, see C. L. Mitton, "New Wine in Old Wine Skins: IV. Leaven," *ExpT* 84 (1972/73), 339-43; cf. also J. K. Howard, " 'Christ our Passover': A Study of the Passover-Exodus Theme in I Corinthians," *EvQ* 41 (1969), 97-108.

[7]See *m.Pes.* 1.1: "On the night of the 14th [of Nisan] the *hametz* [anything made from grains in which fermentation took place] must be searched for by the light of a lamp"; cf. the long discussion by the rabbis in the rest of the tractate. As a boy Paul had undoubtedly taken part in this annual ceremony. Chrysostom *(hom. 15 in 1 Cor.)* alludes to their searching out even mouseholes, but one cannot tell whether that has a basis in fact.

[8]Gk. ἐκκαθάρατε, lit. "clean out, cleanse."

[9]This seems closer to Paul's intent than the suggestion of some that he is dealing with "the old low level of heathen moral judgments" (Parry, 90; cf. Lightfoot, 204-05).

batch of unleavened dough, and is applied directly to the corporate life of the community: "that you may be a new batch," that is, that they might be a people without the leaven of such sin in their midst.

In so applying the imagery, however, Paul expresses himself in a way that is foreign to his own theology; so he immediately qualifies it with "even as you really are." As always in Paul, the imperative, even though it must be obeyed, cannot be turned into a piece of legal material, obedience to which gives favor with God. Right at the point where the imperative sounds as if it comes first ("*Get rid of* the old *so that* you may be new"), he reminds them that what they must become is what they already are by the grace of God. "Become what you are" is the basic nature of Paul's parenesis. He is simply too steeped in the religious heritage of the OT to allow a *divorce* of ethics from the gift of God's favor. But he has been too badly burned by his former pharisaism to allow that ethics *leads to* that gift of favor. The indicative always comes first: "You are a new loaf (God's people) by sheer grace and mercy." But without the imperative the former has failed to be the power of God unto salvation. Hence, "Now become what you are, God's 'new loaf' in Corinth."[10] The application to our own lives and church, of course, is universal.

Still keeping the imagery of Passover, but shifting over to the second ritual, Paul proceeds to explain *how* they became God's "new loaf" in Corinth: "for indeed[11] our[12] Passover Lamb[13] has been sacrificed,[14] even Christ." Although this is the only occurrence of this imagery in Paul,[15] that

[10]Cf. Barrett, 128: "The people of God have been freed from sin; because this is so, they must now avoid sin and live in obedience to God's command. The imperative is unthinkable without the indicative, which makes the otherwise impossible obedience possible; the indicative is emasculated if the imperative, which gives it moral bite, is wanting."

[11]Gk. καὶ γάρ; cf. Lightfoot, 205, Barrett, 128, "for besides."

[12]Note the shift to the first plural, common in this letter, when he begins to speak of the larger Christian realities of which both he and the church are a part (cf. 2:7; 6:3, etc.).

[13]Gk. τὸ πάσχα, lit. "the Passover." The word can have other points of reference (e.g., to the whole Feast or the meal; see Mark 14:1 and 16), but the language of "being sacrificed" indicates that this is an allusion to the Paschal lamb. See the discussion in Jeremias, *TDNT* V, 895-903; cf. D. O. Wenthe, "An Exegetical Study of I Corinthians 5:7b," *Springfielder* 38 (1974), 134-40.

[14]Wenthe (see the previous note) suggests that the passive indicates that God is to be considered the active subject. But that seems an unlikely inference; starting with τὸ πάσχα as the grammatical subject forces this passive.

What is more significant is the use of the aorist, which points to the once-for-all event of the cross, not to any re-expression of it in the liturgy. On this matter, Lietzmann, 24, was more wishful than the data of the text allow.

[15]Some have argued on the basis of 16:8 that the imagery was suggested to Paul by the season in which the letter was being written (cf. Lightfoot, 206; Weiss, 137; Findlay, 811; R-P, 102; Allo, 125-27; Barrett, 129-30; see the discussion in Hurd, 138-41). The point is moot; the mention of waiting till Pentecost in 16:8 makes it likely

only shows how limited our availability to him is on the basis of his few letters. He clearly assumes that his Gentile readers will understand this thoroughly Jewish imagery.[16] As in John's Gospel, this is a direct application of the death of Christ to the slaughter of the Paschal lambs on the first day of Unleavened Bread.[17] The slaying of the lamb is what led to the Jews' being "unleavened." So too with us, Paul says. Our Lamb has been sacrificed; through his death we have received forgiveness from the past and freedom for new life in Christ. This emphasis on the sacrifice of Christ as the basis of their transfer from the old to the new is the point Paul will elaborate in v. 8, in the final application of the metaphor.

8 With yet another strongly inferential "so then" (see on 3:7), Paul brings this part of the argument to its logical conclusion. They are to remove the incestuous man, which is like cleansing the house of leaven, in order that they might become what they are, God's "new loaf" in Corinth. What makes them God's new people is the sacrifice of "our Passover Lamb, Christ himself." Still keeping the imagery of the Feast ("let us keep the Festival"[18]), Paul broadens the application of the death of Christ to Christian life as a whole.

But what is the Christian equivalent to the Jewish celebration? In its first instance it reflects the prolonged seven-day festival, during which the Jews were forbidden to eat anything leavened. In the same way, on the basis of the crucifixion of Christ, God's people are to keep an ongoing feast of the celebration of God's forgiveness by holy living. This is further confirmed by the specific, purely ethical application of the imagery in the rest of the sentence. Most likely Paul's own intent, therefore, was simply, by way of imperative, to extend the metaphor to its broadest possible implications. It is just possible, however, that this further reference to celebrating the Feast also includes an allusion to their sitting at the Table of the Lord.[19] There is no way to tell for sure, although an allusion to the Table in the context of expelling a brother would certainly be fitting, especially in light of the command in v. 11 that they not even eat with him.

---

that the letter was written around Passover. The pronoun "our" may then be in contrast to "their," referring to the Jews. On the other hand, the imagery here did not begin as a reference to Passover but with the proverb of v. 6, and therefore may simply have flowed naturally from one image to the next. Cf. Parry, 91: "The analogical character of the whole passage forbids any conclusion as to the date of the Epistle."

[16]Cf. Conzelmann, 98 n. 48.

[17]There has been a long debate as to whether from this one can establish where Paul stood on the matter of the date of Christ's death. But this text is of no help on this matter. See, e.g., H. Montefiore, "When Did Jesus Die?" *ExpT* 72 (1960/61), 53-54.

[18]Gk. ἑορτάζωμεν, a NT hapax legomenon; the present tense is significant, implying the continual celebration of the Feast.

[19]This has been suggested by several scholars. Cf. Héring, 37; Lias, 61; O-W, 187; and Wiles, *Intercessory,* 143 n. 3 and 146-47.

In any case, Paul's immediate concern is not with the Table, but with their overall behavior. They are to celebrate their new life in Christ minus the "old leaven," a command that ties the present broader imperative to the earlier specific one. This at least includes an elimination of the kinds of sexual immorality represented by the excluded man. But now the "old leaven" is further qualified in terms of "malice and wickedness."[20] These two words are synonyms, which gather under their umbrella every form of iniquity. The death of Christ has freed us from sin; thus we are to live as those who have been set free.

The "unleavened" expression of their new existence is described in terms of "sincerity[21] and truth." These two words do not generalize Christian behavior in quite the same fashion as do the two negatives.[22] In fact they move toward the motivation of behavior rather than its actual outworking. Both words imply behavior that is fully authentic, without sham or deceit, that can stand the full test of the light of day. Perhaps by these words Paul was reflecting on their attitudes toward his own conduct, that he was one thing with Jews and another with Gentiles.[23] Thus he would be calling them to behavior that is the opposite of what they have accused him of; by implication he is suggesting that their boasting is covering up behavior that is completely sham, without either purity of motive or a basis in the truth of the gospel.

This final application of the metaphor, therefore, is a further reflection on the call to holiness with which the letter began (1:2). The present sin is not their only one; and the death of Christ should have made a difference in their lives. They are to become what they are, God's holy temple in Corinth (3:16-17), his alternative to the "malice and wickedness" that surround them. They must celebrate their Christian expression of the Feast by becoming the people of God, which they are in fact by grace.

In an age in which ethics is too often modified to fit one's present cultural existence—greed, e.g., is easily subsumed under Christian patriotism—these words need once more to be heard distinctly in the church. Christ has died for us not simply to give us passage to heaven but to re-create us in his own image, so that both individually and corporately we may express the character of God by the way we live in a world whose behavior is "polished nice" but which lacks the purity and truth of the gospel. It is

[20]Gk. κακίας καὶ πονηρίας.

[21]Gk. εἰλικρινείας, a Pauline word used especially in dealing with the Corinthians (see 2 Cor. 1:12; 2:17; cf. Phil. 1:10).

[22]Contra Conzelmann, "their corresponding opposites" (p. 99). The proper opposites of κακία and πονηρία are "goodness" and "righteousness."

[23]See the comm. on 9:19-27.

extremely unfortunate when God's own people, as in this case, look more like their surroundings than they do their Lord himself.

c. Correcting a "misunderstanding" (5:9-13)

9 *I wrote[1] you in my letter not to associate with sexually immoral people—* 10 *not[2] at all meaning the people of this world who are immoral, or the greedy and[3] swindlers, or idolaters. In that case you would have to leave this world.* 11 *But now[4] I am writing you that you must not associate with anyone who calls himself a brother but is sexually immoral or greedy, an idolater or a slanderer, a drunkard or a swindler. With such a man do not even eat.*

12 *What business is it of mine[5] to judge those outside the church? Are you not[6] to judge those inside?* 13 *God will judge[7] those outside. "Expel[8] the wicked man from among you."*[a]

[a]Deut. 17:7; 19:19; 22:21, 24; 24:7

At first glance this paragraph seems to move in a new direction, clearing up their misunderstanding of a former letter. But not so. Paul is resolving an issue from a former letter, to be sure, but one that is integrally related to the present concern. That he is still dealing with their "boasting" in the context of the incestuous man is indicated by several items: (1) The matter of associating with one who is sexually immoral is both the point of their

---

[1]NIV, "I have written." See the comm. on v. 9 n. 12.

[2]The MajT has attempted to alleviate a rough construction (see the dash in the NIV) with a καί before the οὐ. The KJV translated the καί as a slight adversative ("yet").

[3]An early variant conformed the whole list by changing this καί to an ἤ (P46 Maj lat sy co). The translated text is almost certainly the original, where the words "greedy" and "swindlers" form a pair (P61vid ℵ* A B C D F G P 048 33 81 1175 1739 al).

[4]For the νῦν ("now") of the majority of witnesses, a few (ℵ C D 6 104 365 629 pm) have added an iota (νυνί), thus changing it from a temporal to a logical "now," implying that the first ἔγραψα in v. 9 is also an epistolary aorist. Conzelmann considers the νῦν to be logical, translating "in actual fact I wrote you" (p. 102); but that presses the logical νῦν past recognizable limits.

[5]D Ψ Maj add a καί ("also"), implying, as vv. 3-5 suggest, that he does have the right to judge those on the inside, but that right does not extend *also* to those on the outside. But this would put the emphasis on *Paul* as the one who judges, which is not his intent here.

[6]P46 syp and copbo omit the οὐχί, thus turning the sentence into an imperative: "You judge those on the inside."

[7]Since the original text and earliest MSS did not have accents, one cannot tell whether Paul's κρινει here should be read κρίνει ("God judges"; cf. L Ψ 629 1241s 2464 al d) or κρινεῖ ("God will judge"; as the majority, including most versions). In light of the eschatological judgments about to be mentioned in 6:2-4, the future is more likely.

[8]In typical fashion the MajT harmonizes to the LXX of Deut. 17:7 by adding a paratactic καί and changing the verb to a future ("and you shall . . .").

"misunderstanding" of the previous letter and of their present "boasting" with a well-known *pornos* ("sexually immoral person") in their midst. (2) The clarification in v. 11 intends to forbid any kind of association with a man who calls himself a *brother* but who is a *pornos,* which is precisely what vv. 1-8 are all about. (3) The paragraph, and therefore the whole section, concludes with a citation of Deut. 17:7, which explicitly repeats the injunctions of vv. 2, 5, and 7.

This suggests, then, that the rather abrupt introduction of the former letter is part of the present argument. Their arrogance and boasting are probably related in part to their disregard or deliberate misinterpretation of Paul's former instructions. Indeed, such an interpretation helps to clarify most of the material in this chapter: e.g., why the church's boasting is the primary concern throughout, rather than the sinner himself; why he reasserts his apostolic authority in dealing with this particular issue; and why the clarification of the former letter is brought in right at this point.[9]

The present argument is basically in three parts. First, the former letter had forbidden "association with sexually immoral people." In vv. 9-10 Paul explains what he did *not* mean by that, namely dissociation from people in the world who were sexually immoral, because that would mean leaving the world altogether. Second, in v. 11 he specifies what he *did* mean, which is precisely what they are now disregarding, namely that they are to dissociate from a *brother* who lives as though he were still in the world. Third, in a quatrain of short sentences dominated by the verb "judge" (vv. 12-13), he gives the reasons for the first two points. Christians take the world as they find it (v. 12a); God will finally judge those on the outside (v. 13a). But inside is a different matter. Here there is to be the kind of "judgment" argued for throughout this passage (v. 12b), which then concludes with the imperative to put the incestuous man outside (v. 13b). These last four sentences also serve as the lead-in to the section on "judging" that follows.

9-10 The abrupt way this paragraph is introduced[10] argues for the reconstruction just noted. Its content indicates that Paul is still dealing with the church's failure to have done something about the incestuous man. This sentence tells us that that failure is related to their misunderstanding of a

---

[9]On the larger issue of this letter and its role in the whole of the writing of 1 Corinthians, see the Introduction, pp. 6-7. The apparent disdain with which they have treated Paul in this matter helps to explain several of the other items in chaps. 7–16. Their letter back to him, mentioned in 7:1, is almost certainly their response to the previous letter, in which for the most part they are taking exception to what he has told them in that letter.

[10]Marked both by the subject matter and asyndeton.

former letter:[11] "I wrote[12] you in my letter not to associate with sexually immoral people." At first blush this sounds a bit harsh, and one might well understand why the Corinthians had trouble with it. The key, however, lies in the verb "to associate with" and Paul's previous use of it in 2 Thess. 3:14 with regard to the idlers/busybodies. The verb literally means to "mix up together"; in the context of social intercourse it means to "mingle with," or "associate with" in a close way.[13] In 2 Thessalonians this prohibition occurs only as a last resort; that is, if the idlers/busybodies do not give heed to what is now a second warning (cf. 1 Thess. 4:11-12; 5:14), they are to be shunned in terms of close fellowship in the believing community. But even so, he adds, they are not to be treated as enemies, but as brothers. Most likely that is what Paul had intended in his former letter to Corinth, a letter written not too long after 2 Thessalonians.

Since that is almost certainly what Paul intended, how did their misunderstanding arise, and especially a misunderstanding that implied that he was talking about not associating "with the people of this world"? The best answer lies with the "some who are arrogant" of 4:18. Most likely by the time Paul's letter had reached the church, these people were already at work in the community, urging that Paul's was not the only legitimate, or the best, understanding of the gospel. Perhaps they seized on the ambiguity of wording in his letter in order to discredit him.[14] In any case, one can surmise that there was a bit of ridicule in their stance: "How can he possibly mean that we are not to associate with the sexually immoral? Does that mean we can no longer go even to the marketplace? How can one live in Corinth and not rub shoulders with some who are like this?" Paul allows here that if he had meant that, then they are right, one would

---

[11]What cannot be known from this distance is whether this previous letter was in response to something already going on in Corinth, or whether Paul initiated the correspondence. The latter is the main thesis of Hurd's *Origin,* in particular that by the former letter Paul communicated to them for the first time the content of the Apostolic Decree of Acts 15. This is a moot point, but is not the necessary conclusion of much else that Hurd has argued rather convincingly—especially that their letter to Paul (see 7:1) is basically a response to this former letter, and therefore that our 1 Corinthians is in turn a response to their letter. See the Introduction, pp. 6-7.

[12]Gk. ἔγραψα. This must be a true aorist, not an epistolary aorist as in v. 11. The νῦν in v. 11, plus the prepositional phrase ἐν τῇ ἐπιστολῇ in this sentence, makes that clear. The English perfect in the NIV, "I have written," defies explanation. Unfortunately it allows that they may not yet have received that communication. Everything in the chapter argues otherwise.

[13]Gk. συναναμίγνυσθαι; cf. Hos. 7:8 and Philo, *Mos.* 1.278.

[14]This was the suggestion of W. L. Knox (*St. Paul and the Church of Jerusalem* [Cambridge, 1925], p. 320), quoted with approval by Hurd, p. 151.

indeed "have to leave this world." But as he elaborates in v. 11, and as they surely must have known, he did not mean that. He meant exactly the opposite; they are not to continue the kinds of associations in which they are now boasting.[15]

In any case, he is ready to clarify, first by telling them what he did *not* intend: "not at all meaning the people of this world who are immoral." By "not at all,"[16] he could mean what the NIV suggests, that there has been an absolute misunderstanding on their part,[17] or more likely that in a qualified way he did not "in general"[18] intend what they have taken it to mean. There are associations with the world that Paul will disallow (e.g., 10:14-22); but his first concern has been with the Christian fellowship as such. Indeed, from Paul's point of view, the only way they can be a viable alternative *to* the world is for them to be *in* the world, but not *of* it (cf. John 17:15-16). To be that alternative, however, they must discipline those wishing to belong to the fellowship but who at the same time insist on continuing their former pagan practices.

The content of that former letter can only be surmised.[19] The way Paul mentions the next three items, plus the evidence from the rest of 1 Corinthians, suggests that it included at least these items. For example, the argument of chaps. 8–10 indicates that the previous letter had already dealt with the special problem of "idolatry" addressed there, namely the insistence on the right of believers to continue to attend meals at the pagan temples.[20] The more surprising items are "the greedy and swindlers,"[21] surprising because to our way of thinking such sins seem less egregious than sexual immorality or idolatry, and certainly less culpable of exclusion

---

[15]This reconstruction seems to make more sense of the data, both in this section and in the letter as a whole, than that the Corinthian response to Paul's letter had been either a polite request for clarification or an unintentional misunderstanding, the two most commonly held positions. The former is articulated by G. G. Findlay, "The Letter of the Corinthian Church to St. Paul," *Exp* 6/1 (1900), 401-07. For the latter, see, among the commentaries, Moffatt, 60; Grosheide, 128; Morris, 91. Neither of these can account for the vigorous rhetorical style of Paul's response, nor for the special nature of this response in attacking their pride as the primary issue.

[16]Gk. οὐ πάντως.

[17]This position is argued for by Lightfoot, 208.

[18]This is Conzelmann's translation; cf. Parry, 92, "not meaning absolutely." For a discussion see Findlay, 810.

[19]On this question see esp. Hurd, 213-39. His is a maximal view, taking all of 1 Corinthians into account, and is very likely generally correct.

[20]On this matter see G. D. Fee, "Εἰδωλόθυτα Once Again: An Interpretation of 1 Corinthians 8-10," *Bib* 61 (1980), 172-97.

[21]Gk. πλεονέκταις καὶ ἅρπαξιν.

from the Christian community.[22] But the ancient world, both pagan and Judeo-Christian, had a special loathing for avarice that hundreds of years of legitimized greed in our culture have mitigated. "Greed," usually translated "covetousness" and called "idolatry" in Col. 3:5, means not just to desire what is not one's own, but often carries the sense of carrying through on the desire to the point of defrauding or taking advantage of someone else. One way in which avarice expresses itself is through robbery or swindling. Since "the greedy and swindlers" here are joined by an "and,"[23] suggesting that in this instance they reflect a single difficulty, it seems likely that Paul is at least anticipating the problem in 6:1-11 and is herewith serving warning on the one who caused the legal action to become necessary in the first place. What is less clear is how this may already have been addressed in the first letter. It should be noted that all three of these sins—sexual immorality, idolatry, and greed—were particularly prevalent in the Corinth of the mid-fifties A.D.

11 So that there will be no further possibility of misunderstanding, Paul proceeds to outline his former position in explicit terms. "But now I am writing you that you must not associate with anyone who calls himself a brother" and who acts in the ways spoken of in the former letter. Paul is not advocating that only the sinless can be members of the Christian community; rather, he is concerned about those who persist in the very activities from which they have been freed through the sacrifice of the Paschal Lamb (v. 7). Christians belong to the new age; their lives have been invaded by the Holy Spirit. They are therefore to "celebrate the Feast," that is, to live out on a continuing basis the ethics of the new people of God. They are to look like their Lord in their behavior, for which purpose the example of the apostle has been given to them (4:16-17). Because in Christ all things are new by the Spirit (2 Cor. 5:14-17), those who belong to Christ must put off their former way of life (Col. 3:5-11). Those who persist in that former way of life, not those who simply struggle with former sins, do not belong to this new community. By their own actions they have opted out; the community must distance itself from such people for its own sake. This is not the rigorism of a Tertullian; it is a reflection of the essential nature of the community of the Spirit, which is to be different from the world in which it lives.

To the four sins mentioned in v. 10, two more are now added, and

---

[22]Chrysostom also recognized this and made the greedy the main focus of his Homily 15. It was clearly a courageous thing for him to do, just as it would be in most Western congregations in our day.

[23]See n. 3 above.

"the greedy" and "swindlers" are separated.[24] This is the first of the vice lists in the Pauline letters. Such lists were a common feature of Hellenistic Judaism,[25] and they regularly recur in Paul in a variety of contexts.[26] Although the list of four items in v. 10 seems especially related to Paul's relationship to the Corinthians, there is no evidence that the additional items here or in 6:9-10 are so to be understood. What is noteworthy again is how characteristic of Corinth the list is.[27]

The word "slanderer"[28] covers all forms of verbal abuse—to malign, revile, slander[29]—and reflects the kind of coarse talk often associated with the rabble. The more difficult word for us is "drunkards," especially in cultures where there is extensive alcoholism. Here the church should be a place of healing, not of rejection. Ancients seldom reflect on those whom we would call alcoholic. By and large, we are dealing with "wine cultures," in which the abstainer is the rare person, and is seldom admired for such. In fact the pagan world in general had very little to say in a negative way about drunkenness,[30] except as it led to other vices—violence, public scolding of servants, unseemly sexuality.[31] Even in Judaism what is said against drunkenness assumes the regular use of wine with meals and is more concerned with other behavior to which drunkenness leads.[32] What is

[24]Cf. 6:9-10, which includes these six (in a different sequence), plus four more.

[25]They are also found among the philosophers; but that simply reflects what a common phenomenon this had become by the time of Paul. The classic study of the phenomenon is A. Vögtle, *Die Tugend- und Lasterkataloge im Neuen Testament* (Münster/W., 1936); cf. the excursus in Conzelmann, 100-101. Among the more relevant texts see 1 Enoch 91:6-7; 3 Bar. 8:5; 13:4; *Or.Sib.* 2.254-83; Philo, *sacr.AC* 32 (the ultimate list!); *det.pot.ins.* 34.

[26]1 Cor. 6:10-11; 2 Cor. 12:20-21; Gal. 5:19-21; Rom. 1:29-31; Col. 3:5, 8; Eph. 5:3-5; 1 Tim. 1:9-11; 2 Tim. 3:2-5; Tit. 3:3; cf. Mark 7:21-22; 1 Pet. 2:1; 4:3; Rev. 21:8; 22:15.

[27]The search for a "source" is futile, including the note by Deissmann, LAE, p. 316, that most of these words are found in their corresponding Latin form on the "counters" of what was apparently a very popular game. The Pauline lists are so diverse as to defy explanation. The only two from the longer list in 6:9-10 that are found in Gal. 5 are sexual immorality and idolatry; otherwise there are a couple of synonyms. So also with the list in Rom. 1.

[28]Gk. λοίδορος; the adjective of the verb used in 4:12 to describe Paul's treatment by those who hold a radically different worldview from his.

[29]Cf. the section in Sir. 23:7-15 for a Jewish view of sins of speech. λοίδορος is the first item mentioned. Cf. also the NT as a whole, which shows great concern over matters of speech (cf. Mark 7:22; 2 Cor. 12:20; Rom. 1:29-30; Col. 3:8; 4:6; Eph. 4:29; 5:4; 1 Tim. 6:4; Jas. 3:1-12; 1 Pet. 2:23; 3:15-16). For the close connection of this vice with drunkenness, see Philo, *somn.* 2.164-69.

[30]At least as it is seen among men. It was considered a vice for women.

[31]For an example, see Lucian, *Tim.* 54-55.

[32]See *T.Jud.* 14-16; 3 Bar. 4:17; Philo, *cher.* 92; *somn.* 2.164-69.

in view here is almost certainly that kind of person who is regularly given to drunkenness and the various forms of carousing with which it is associated.[33]

The intent of the final prohibition, "With such a man do not even eat," is not certain. At the very least it means that the incestuous man is to be excluded from Christian fellowship meals, including the Lord's Table (see on 11:17-34). As in Jude 12, such a person would be "a blemish on their love-feasts." The question is whether eating meals in more private circumstances is also in view. It is arguable that limiting it to the Lord's Table would make the "not even" unnecessary;[34] that is, one may assume that he would not partake of *the* Table; they are "not even" to carry on ordinary social intercourse with him. However, Paul's concern throughout does not seem to be that the church as individual members dissociate from the incestuous man, but that he be excluded from the *community* as it gathers for worship and instruction. The point cannot be finally resolved, although the similar text about dissociation in 2 Thess. 3:15 implies that private fellowship may not have been included in the ban.[35]

12-13 The argument is basically over. With these short sentences, Paul concludes both the present paragraph and the entire section. The theme of "judging" dominates, in the same sense that the verb was used of Paul's action in v. 3. On the one hand, this is what the church must be about in the case of the incestuous man; on the other hand, they may not be about the kind of litigious "judging" that is about to be addressed in 6:1-11. The quatrain of sentences is given in nicely balanced pairs, with an AB/AB structure. First (v. 12) there are two rhetorical questions about those whom the church does not and does "judge," and these questions are given their appropriate responses in the two statements of v. 13.

The first question picks up the motif from vv. 9-10 of their "misunderstanding" the former letter. "What business is it of mine to judge those outside the church[36]?" The "mine" in this sentence is the unemphatic "me"[37] and implies that Paul is not dealing with himself personally, but with himself as he represents the Christian community. Neither he nor they are to pass sentence on the people of the world in their present existence.

[33]Cf. esp. Rom. 13:13 and the list of "night" sins; cf. the similar list of "night" sins in Philo, *cher*. 92-93. See also Eph. 5:18; 1 Tim. 3:3; 3:8; Tit. 1:5.

[34]See, e.g., Findlay, 812.

[35]It should be noted that the parallel is not exact, and that the discipline may be more drastic here than in Thessalonica.

[36]The words "the church" are not in the text, but are added for clarification. The language "outside" and "inside" belongs to Paul's Jewish heritage. Jews applied it to Gentiles; Jesus himself used it to refer to those who were not his disciples (Mark 4:11). Paul applies it to non-Christians, whether Jews or Gentiles (cf. 1 Thess. 4:12; Col. 4:5).

[37]Cf. n. 40 on vv. 3-4.

The reason for that is simple: "God will judge those outside." His judgment is future, a judgment in which the church will also participate (6:2). But for now, the church takes the world as it finds it. As God's temple in the "world," it is to offer a striking alternative to the world, and in that sense it must always be "judging" the world.[38] But it is not ours to bring sentence against those who belong to another worldview, to another age altogether. The time for that judgment is coming.

Exactly the opposite, however, must obtain within the Christian community itself. "Are you not to judge those inside?" This, of course, is what the entire passage has been arguing, in the actual sentence given in vv. 3-5 as well as in the analogy of vv. 6-7 and in the clarification of the former letter in v. 11. Therefore, the final word is given in the form of a quotation from Deut. 17:7: "Expel the wicked man from among you." Thus the section concludes the way it began. The believing community must act responsibly, and boasting is not responsible. For their own sake, as well as for his, they are to put the incestuous man outside.

This passage presents more than its share of difficulties for us: How does one reconcile vv. 12-13 with Jesus' words in Matt. 7:1-5? or with Paul's in 4:3? And how does one reconcile it with 6:2 that follows? Let us begin with what seems unmistakable: Paul is not a separatist, at least not in the ordinary ascetic sense of that word that is one of the hallmarks of sectarian groups. The Pauline principle is simple: Free association outside the church, precisely because God, not the church, judges those on the outside; but strict discipline within the church, because in its free association with the world it may not take on the character of the world in which it freely lives.

It does not take too much observation to note that all too often the opposites have tended to prevail in the church. On the one hand are those who advocate the strictest separation from the world, but who allow many of the sins Paul condemns in vv. 10-11 to thrive in their midst. On the other hand are many who adopt the Corinthian attitude almost totally, usually on the basis that "all are sinners, after all." Thus they live in the world as those who would also be of the world, so that the distinctions between those "inside" and those "outside" are razor-thin, if they exist at all. In such cases the church ends up judging neither those inside nor those out-

---

[38]Indeed, the passage by no means intends that the church should not speak prophetically to the world, "judging" it for its injustices and unrighteousness. That is why God will eventually judge it, after all. The prophetic warning of God's always imminent judgment must ever be a part of the church's proclamation. This sentence has to do with not judging the world in the way they are to judge the incestuous man. In that sense the church has nothing to do with the world.

side. The key to reformation still lies with the work of the Spirit, and to our heeding the indicative-imperative relationship expressed in v. 7.

Finally, Paul is not dealing with the kind of "judging" disallowed by Jesus in Matt. 7:1-5, where the person with a beam in his/her eye condemns the one with merely a mote. Jesus is dealing with personal criticism of one's brother or sister, which is always disallowed, even by Paul (cf. 4:3). This is dealing with persistent wrongdoing of a kind wherein someone wants to have it both ways, to belong to the Christian community without leaving his/her former behavior behind. Such persistence demands discipline for the sake of both the person involved and the community.

The apparent contradiction with 6:2 is resolved eschatologically. We do not pass sentence on the world because that is God's prerogative alone. But when he does pass sentence, his people are going to be involved in the process.

2. A Case of Litigation (6:1-11)

Paul concludes the previous argument by insisting that the church is not to judge those "outside" but must judge those "inside." That had to do first of all with the expulsion of the incestuous man; but it also has to do with another kind of "judgment" that must take place within the Christian community, namely in matters of everyday life where one member has a grievance against another. He now turns to such a matter, one apparently reported to him.[1] Everything in this church is in reverse order. If the church does not "judge" those outside, neither does it go outside with inside affairs.

In this case the problem is easy to reconstruct. Apparently one brother (Man A) had defrauded another (Man B) in some way.[2] To redress his grievances Man B took Man A before the civil magistrates at the *bēma* ("judgment seat"), which was publicly located in the heart of the mar-

---

[1]Nothing in the text says this. The reason for so believing lies in the subject matter (it is nearly impossible, given the nature of the rhetoric with which Paul responds, even to imagine how they may have framed a question or statement about this matter), as well as in its place in the total letter (the mention of their letter does not occur until 7:1). Cf. Hurd, 84-85.

[2]The nature of the matter is not mentioned, nor hinted at. Bernard, "Connexion," argues that this continues the matter of chap. 5—Man A is the incestuous man, whose "wronged" father has taken him to court. But this leaves one with the difficult conclusion that Paul raises the father's act to the same level of wrongdoing as that of his son, and indeed is more severe on him. Richardson, "Judgment," would also make it a sexual matter, tying it to the sin of 6:12-20. The difficulty here is that (1) nothing in the language of 6:1-11 makes this probable (the sexual sins of the vice list do not help since that list also includes greed and robbery); (2) there is insufficient evidence of such matters being brought before civil magistrates; and (3) the specific problem in 6:12-20 has to do with believers going to the prostitutes, not with one man wronging another over sexual irregularities.

ketplace (cf. Acts 18:12-17).[2a] The event is a defeat for the church in every way (v. 7), for the community as a whole as well as for the two brothers.

The whole scene fills Paul with indignation, so much so that there is scarcely any argument at all. He alternates between statements of horror (vv. 1 and 6), rhetorical questions (vv. 2-4, 5b-6, 7b), sarcasm (v. 5), and threat (vv. 8-11). As in the preceding matter, the heavier artillery is aimed at the community itself for allowing such a thing to happen. They are addressed in a series of rhetorical questions (vv. 2-6) that include the most biting sarcasm in the letter (v. 5). In v. 7b he briefly addresses Man B with rhetorical questions, challenging him with the ethics of Christ. Finally, in vv. 8-10 he warns Man A, and the church as a whole, that those who act as he has are in grave danger of forfeiting their inheritance of the kingdom. But as usual in Paul, the threat is followed by a word of assurance (v. 11) that also functions as an invitation to repentance.

Although the passage bristles with Paul's apostolic authority, it seems to be less a reassertion of that authority than was 5:1-13. Here the aggravation comes from two factors: (1) that they have so little self-understanding as to who they are in Christ (vv. 2-4), and (2) that this action so totally destroys the community before the world (v. 6). As always in Paul, but with clear and forceful articulation here, the eschatological framework of his thinking and of the church's existence is the presupposition of the whole.

The question of the sociological dimension of the problem needs to be noted even if final answers cannot be given. If the problem is related to material possessions, as is argued in v. 1, then very likely the two men are among the few in the congregation who have property. That also suggests that they very likely were leaders in the community, which would exacerbate the problem all the more. How this might be further related to the quarrels in chaps. 1–4 and to the anti-Paul sentiment on the part of so many is moot, but the possibility that it is appears to be a live option.

a. Shame on the church (6:1-6)

1 *If any of you has a dispute with another, dare he take it before the ungodly for judgment instead of before the saints?* 2 *Do[3] you not know that the saints will judge the world? And if you are to judge the world, are you not competent to judge trivial cases?* 3 *Do you not*

[2a]For discussions of the broader issues of justice under Roman law, which were based on privilege and status, not individual equality, see J. Crook, *Law and Life of Rome* (Ithaca, NY, 1967), and P. Garnsey, *Social Status and Legal Privilege in the Roman Empire* (Oxford, 1970).

[3]Both here and in v. 9 the NIV has left out the connecting particle ἤ ("or"). This is a translational omission, which is in fact attested in a few MSS (D² L 6 614 629 1241 pm).

*know that we will judge angels? How much more the things of this
life!* 4 *Therefore, if you have disputes about such matters, appoint as
judges even men of little account in the church!*[a] 5 *I say this to shame
you. Is[4] it possible that there is nobody among you wise enough to
judge a dispute between believers?[5]* 6 *But instead, one brother goes
to law against another—and this in front of unbelievers!*

[a]Or *matters, do you appoint as judges men of little account in the church?*

This opening paragraph is as sharp as it is abrupt. Like 5:1-8 it begins as
though it were a word to the offender, but instead it becomes a word to the
church as a whole. It turns out that the failure of the two men is primarily a
failure of the church to be the church. The "argument" comes basically in
the form of a series of rhetorical questions,[6] whose structure seems best
understood as follows:

Q[uestion] 1 (v. 1): presents the basic ingredients of the problem

Q2[1] and Q2[2] (v. 2): A set of questions that minimizes lawsuits in the
present age in light of eschatological realities

Q3[1] and Q3[2] (vv. 3-4): A set of questions that minimizes pagan
courts in the light of further eschatological realities

Indicative 1 (v. 5a): "I say this to shame you"

Q4[1] and Q4[2] (vv. 5b-6): A set of questions designed to shame them
by sarcasm (the second question also recalls v. 1, with special
emphasis on their doing this before pagans)

Crucial to the whole argument is Paul's view of the church as an
eschatological community, whose existence as God's future people absolutely determines its life in the present age (see on 4:1-5). In light of these
eschatological realities, matters of everyday life are trivial, and the pagan
courts who concern themselves with such trivialities are themselves trivialized. Such people have no standing at all with the people of God. The
absurdity of the Corinthian position is that the saints will someday judge the
very world before whom they are now appearing and asking for a judgment.
Not only does such an action give the lie to who they are as the people of
God, but it is done in the presence of unbelievers, the very people to whom
the church is to be God's alternative.

[4]For the rarer ἔνι several MSS substitute ἐστιν (P[11] D F G 6 104 365 630 1739
1881 al).

[5]The Greek text reads ἀνὰ μέσον τοῦ ἀδελφοῦ αὐτοῦ (lit. "between his
brother"). Both J. H. Moulton, *Prolegomena*, 99, and Zuntz, 15, argue that this represents a primitive corruption of ἀνὰ μέσον τοῦ ἀδελφοῦ καὶ τοῦ ἀδελφοῦ αὐτοῦ (cf.
the latter's "The Critic Correcting the Author," *Philologus* 99 [1955], 295-303). Otherwise it is an ellipsis; cf. G. M. Lee, "1 Corinthians vi.5," *ExpT* 79 (1967/68), 310.

[6]This is also the view of NA[26], as well as the TR, WH, Bover, and Nestle.
Otherwise, the NIV, RSV, NEB, and others.

1 The opening salvo of Question 1 reveals both the nature of the problem and the depth of Paul's feelings toward it. He is simply horrified by what he has heard. This is indicated by the very way the question is asked (especially the presence of the verb first, which is difficult to put into good English): "*Dare*[7] anyone,[8] having a case against another, take it for judgment before the ungodly and not before the saints?" The gall of such a man! What he has done seems less of an affront to most modern Christians. The phrase translated "has a dispute" is a technical term for a lawsuit, or legal action;[9] and the verb *krinō* ("judge") in the middle voice can carry the sense of "going to law," or "bringing something for judgment," as it does here. Thus we are dealing with a recurring phenomenon in human society, namely that someone who has been wronged seeks adjudication in the courts.[10] The problem here is that the case was brought "before the ungodly instead of before the saints." The reason for the depth of Paul's horror is brought out in the ensuing sets of questions.

The action for which Paul argues, that such matters be brought before "the saints," reflects Paul's Jewish heritage,[11] but his reasons will be new. For the use of "the saints," which is especially appropriate here as a contrast with "the ungodly," see on 1:2.

---

[7]Gk. τολμάω (BAGD, "dare, have courage, be brave enough"); cf. 2 Cor. 10:12; 11:21 (ironic usage) and Rom. 5:9. The comment by Mare, 221 ("By 'dare'. . . , he strongly admonishes rather than commands Christians to take their legal grievances for settlement before qualified Christians"), is about as far removed from Paul's concern as it is possible to get. Mare's entire comment on this verse is designed to justify going to secular courts to secure church property rather than to listen to Paul's own concerns, which seem to be exactly the opposite—that the securing of property is of zero value for an eschatological people.

[8]Gk. τις ὑμῶν (lit. "any one of you"), with the ὑμῶν functioning as a partitive. This τις probably means "a certain one," as in 5:1 (cf. the singulars in vv. 5-6). It is common among commentators to speak as if there were several such cases going on in the community (e.g., Craig, 69; Grosheide, 133; Mare, 221). Despite the generalized plurals in vv. 7-8, it seems far more likely, as in 5:1-13, that he received reports of a single case that reflected on the whole congregation, especially if the two brothers were also leaders in the community. See Hurd, 86.

[9]Gk. πρᾶγμα ἔχων, with the preposition πρός. See the two illustrations in MM: ἁπλῶς μηδὲν ἔχουσα πρᾶγμα πρὸς ἐμέ (". . . having no legal case at all against me"); μὴ ἔχοντας πᾶν πρᾶγμα πρὸς ἐμέ (". . . not having any case against me").

[10]Cf. the OT where such adjudication was to be brought before the elders at the "gates" (e.g., Judg. 8:16; Ruth 4:2; Job 29:7-8).

[11]On the basis of Exod. 21:1 the rabbis had concluded that it was unlawful for Jews to bring their cases before Gentile law courts. Cf. *b.Git.* 88b: "R. Tarfon used to say: In any place where you find heathen law courts, even though their law is the same as the Israelite law, you must not resort to them since it says, 'These are the judgments which thou shalt bring before them,' that is to say, 'before them' and not before heathens" (Soncino). For regulations see the Mishnaic tractate *Sanhedrin*. By the time of Paul, the Romans had granted the Jews liberty of settling internal matters, at least in Jerusalem; see E. Schürer, *The History of the Jewish People in the Age of Jesus Christ* (rev. ed. G. Vermes, F. Millar, and M. Black; Edinburgh, 1979), II, 208-09.

By calling them "the ungodly" (lit. "unjust")[12] Paul does not intend to demean the Roman courts, to which he himself had recourse more than once,[13] as if they were corrupt. The substitution of "unbelievers" in the identical phrase in v. 6 suggests that this is its basic intent here as well. Moreover, Paul regularly uses *adikoi* to refer to those who break God's laws, and therefore it comes to mean something close to "ungodly," or "unrighteous."[14] In this instance the choice of words is predicated on the special eschatological realities to which he is about to appeal. They are the "unrighteous," who in contrast to "the saints" will not inherit the kingdom of God (v. 9). Indeed, they will themselves be judged by "the saints" at the great eschatological judgment (v. 3). For Paul the absurdity of this matter lies right at this point: "Here are those who will not inherit the kingdom, whom God through his people is going to *judge,* and you are allowing lawsuits to be brought before *them!*"

2 Although the question in v. 1 was directed toward the plaintiff (Man B), the rest of the paragraph is addressed to the whole community for its own failure in allowing this to have happened in the first place. Vv. 2-4 raise two sets of questions, both introduced by the rhetorical formula "Do you not know that?" (see on 3:16),[15] and both giving the new, theological grounds for not going before the ungodly: not because Christians are exclusive (cf. 5:9-10), but because they are eschatological people, who will themselves be involved in God's final judgments on the world.[16] Thus we have another wordplay on "judging" (cf. 4:3-5, 7). Formerly they were "judging" ("investigating") Paul, which was disallowed in light of God's final "judgment." Here they are "judging" in the courts (vv. 1, 6), which is disallowed because of the participation of the saints in the final "judging." Whether the Corinthians would have previously known the specifics of these

---

[12]Gk. ἄδικοι, the opposite of δίκαιος ("just, righteous"). The verb especially has the sense of acting unfairly toward someone (cf. v. 8).

[13]See Acts 16:37-39; 25:10-12.

[14]Cf. H. H. B. Ayles, "1 Corinthians vi.1," *ExpT* 27 (1915/16), 334.

[15]Along with starting the questions with Τολμᾷ, the repeated use of this formula (vv. 2, 3, 9) here suggests the influence of the "diatribe," a literary form popular with the pagan moralists in which the writer/speaker engaged the audience in an imaginary debate. See Bultmann, *Stil;* cf. S. K. Stowers, "A Critical Reassessment of Paul and the Diatribe: The Dialogical Elements in Paul's Letter to the Romans" (Ph.D. diss., Yale, 1979).

[16]This seems to make far more sense of the argumentation of these verses than to suppose that the greater urgency is "to prevent the private scandals of the community from being known by judges who did not share their faith" (M. Delcor, "The Courts of the Church of Corinth and the Courts of Qumran," in *Paul and Qumran* [ed. J. Murphy-O'Connor; Chicago, 1968], p. 69). Delcor's otherwise useful essay is considerably marred by his presupposition that the point of this passage was to set up an internal judicatory within the Christian community.

presuppositions is a moot point.[17] In either case, the presuppositions speak of a reality larger than their details, for which the Corinthians may be held accountable. Here is a clear illustration of the "already but not yet" framework of Pauline theology. The future realities, which for Paul are as certain as the present itself, condition everything the church is and does in the present.

The first eschatological presupposition (Q2[1]) picks up a common motif from Jewish apocalyptic eschatology: "the saints will judge the world." The motif begins with the LXX of Dan. 7:22, ". . . judgment was given to the saints of the Most High." It was thereafter picked up in a whole variety of texts, including Qumran.[18] Paul does not explain what this now means in the Christian context, nor does anyone else in the NT; rather, it is something assumed to have carried over and is here simply asserted as the presupposition of the second question in the set (Q2[2]). In some ways it sounds contradictory to 5:12a. The difference lies in perspective. In 5:12 Paul was speaking of *present* judgments on the people who make up the world, which were none of his business. Here he is speaking of the *final* judgment on "the world" as a whole, the entire anti-God system of things that will come under God's judgment, in which God's people are in some way to be involved.

Given this eschatological reality, Paul makes his first point: the triviality of lawsuits in the present age. The "saints" are now identified as "you,"[19] God's people in Corinth. The apodosis of this sentence reads literally, "Are you unworthy of the most insignificant tribunals?" This means either (1) "Are you unfit to form even the most insignificant courts?"[20] or (2) "Are you not competent to judge trivial cases?"[21] The problem lies

[17]Conzelmann, 104-05, thinks so, considering it to be part of established elementary teaching, on the basis of 1 Thess. 5:1-11. But that passage only indicates that the return of Christ, expressed sometimes in apocalyptic motifs, was part of that teaching. In any case, the way the question is asked assumes that it is something they *should* know, whether they had been informed or not. It is certainly not intended to be flattering, as Hurd, 86, notes. "Can it be that you do not even know. . . ?"

[18]Cf. Wis. 3:7-8: "They shall judge nations and rule over peoples"; 1 Enoch 1:9: "He will arrive with ten million of his holy ones (ἄγιοι) to execute judgment"; 95:3: "You righteous one, fear not the sinners! For the Lord will again deliver them into your hands, so that you may carry out against them anything that you desire"; 1QpHab 5.4: "But God will judge all the nations by the hand of his elect." Cf. Rev. 20:4 and Matt. 19:28//Luke 22:30, which imply "judging" during the messianic age in the OT sense of the elders in the community, rather than executing sentences against the enemies of God.

[19]The text reads: εἰ ἐν ὑμῖν κρίνεται ὁ κόσμος. The ἐν ὑμῖν in forensic settings can be either strictly instrumental ("by you"; cf. Ditt. *Syl.* 1.195.57-59, quoted by Conzelmann, 103, and favored by him) or somewhat local ("before you," i.e., "in your court"; Parry, 95; Lightfoot, 210-11; BDF 219[1]).

[20]Cf. NASB; Barrett, 136.

[21]Most translations and commentaries.

with the word *kritērion,* which properly means a court of justice; but there is sufficient evidence that it also denotes the legal action itself,[22] which is preferable here. In the first instance the emphasis is on the community's failure to function as the proper place for such "judgments." In the second the emphasis lies on the "trifling nature" (NEB) of the present lawsuit. This seems better to fit Paul's point in the eschatological presupposition, which is not that of trying to shame the community into handling such matters in the present in light of the future, but of trying to shame them for having lawsuits at all. Such matters are "trivial";[23] they add up to zero in light of the eschatological judgment. Such people are simply after the wrong things.

3-4 The question in v. 3 (Q3[1]) asserts the second eschatological presupposition: "Do you not know that we[24] will judge angels?"[25] This probably reflects an apocalyptic motif as to the judgment of fallen angels,[26] and thereby intensifies the point of v. 2. So inclusive will be our participation in God's eschatological judgment that not only the world but even the angels will be judged by the newly formed eschatological people of God.

All are agreed on the punctuation to this point, but with the next phrase, "not to mention everyday affairs,"[27] interpreters begin to differ. The NIV and most English translations separate it from the preceding question and make it an exclamation: "How much more the things of this life!" Grammatically, however, it belongs to the question itself: "Do you not know that we will judge angels, not to mention everyday affairs?" The reason for breaking it from the question is obvious: Paul has begun to move from eschatological judgments to temporal ones and thus to the case at hand, all in the same sentence. His point is: "In the eschaton we will sit in on ultimate judgments—even on angels—which of course means that I need not even mention the fact that we should also be able to handle 'mere matters of business.'"[28] The latter term (NIV "the things of this life") is

---

[22]See the two inscriptions cited by BAGD; cf. Diod.Sic. 36.3.3.

[23]Gk. ἐλαχίστων ("least"), here elative, meaning "totally insignificant."

[24]On this shift to the first plural see on 5:7; cf. 11:31.

[25]Cf. 4:9. If for now Paul is a spectacle to the world, both angels and men, in these two questions the roles have been reversed!

[26]Cf. 2 Pet. 2:4; Jude 6; 1 Enoch 67–69. The text in 1 Enoch 91:15 that is often cited here is corrupt; it is not clear whether the angels are being judged or doing the judging (cf. OTP, I, 73 n. 12).

[27]Gk. μήτι γε; cf. BDF 427(3): "Elliptical μήτιγε 1 C 6:3 = πόσῳ γε μᾶλλον 'not to speak of.'"

[28]Gk. βιωτικά, a recurring word in the Greek world for matters of everyday life. Philostr. (*V.Soph.* 1.25.3) uses it to distinguish disputes over matters of everyday life (something close to "civil" cases), which should be settled at home, from graver offenses that need to be settled in court.

not ordinarily pejorative. What gives it such a sense here is not that one should not engage in everyday affairs, but that they should hold a place of significance in the lives of those who belong to a different age.

In the question of v. 4 (Q3²) two words from the previous clauses ("cases," v. 2; "matters of this life," v. 3) are joined as adjective and noun: "Therefore, if you have *disputes about such matters*. . . ."²⁹ But the rest of the sentence presents considerable difficulties: first, whether it is a question or an imperative; second, the meaning of the verb; and third, who is intended by the designation "those of little account" (lit. "those who are despised"), believers or the pagan judges.³⁰ There are two basic solutions:³¹

(1) In making the clause an ironic imperative, the NIV follows a long interpretive tradition. In this case the verb must take the meaning of "appoint judges" and the object must refer to insiders, "those of little account" within the church itself. However, this interpretation faces the nearly insuperable difficulties of having an imperative appear as the final word in a sentence, especially in an instance where irony is the intent, and of Paul's using such pejorative language—even in irony—to speak of fellow believers (see below).

(2) The alternative, also adopted by a long line of scholars and translations, is to see the sentence as a question and the object as outsiders, "those who have no standing at all in the church." Thus: "If therefore you have such business disputes, how can you entrust jurisdiction to outsiders, men who count for nothing in our community?" (NEB). The structure of the whole paragraph, and especially of the two eschatological arguments, seems to favor this point of view. The two sets of questions are basically balanced pairs:

Q2¹—Do you not know that (A)?
　　Q2²—If (A) is true, then why (B)?
Q3¹—Do you not know that (C), not to mention (D)?
　　Q3²—If (D) does happen, then why (E)?

---

²⁹The conditional sentence in this case has ἐάν with the subjunctive in the protasis, indicating a present general condition; i.e., whenever such a situation prevails. . . .

³⁰Gk. τοὺς ἐξουθενημένους. The verb is especially pejorative, meaning "to despise" or "reject with contempt." It is used by Paul in 1:28 to refer to those whom God has chosen "to nullify the things that are" and in 1 Thess. 5:20 about rejecting prophesyings with contempt; cf. Rom. 14:3, 10; 2 Cor. 10:10; Gal. 4:14.

³¹But see Findlay, 815, who would punctuate differently, making the opening βιωτικὰ μὲν οὖν κριτήρια an absolute phrase, and τοὺς ἐξουθενημένους the object of ἔχετε. Thus: "Well, then, for secular tribunals—if you have men that are made of no account in the Church, set these on the bench!" But this seems forced; it is hard to imagine the Corinthians picking that up in their own reading of the letter.

In the final question there has been a shift in the protasis from the eschatological supposition to what is actually happening in Corinth; but the predicate that makes the action in (E) absurd is still the eschatological reason given in (C). This makes excellent sense of the structure of the argument, and it explains the reasons for the slight shifts between the two sets of questions.

But this view is not without difficulties. The first concerns the verb, which ordinarily means "to appoint judges." The objection is that believers "had no voice in the appointment of judges."[32] But this problem is minimal since there is sufficient evidence that the verb also means "to sit for a judgment, or make a ruling."[33] The latter seems to be the intent here; Paul is scarcely concerned in the midst of this kind of rhetoric to establish rules for Christian jurisprudence.

The more difficult item is the object, "those held in disdain"; but this is true for either interpretation. In fact, as noted before, it is difficult to imagine Paul, even in irony, so referring to fellow believers—especially in light of 12:21-25, where he attempts to disabuse the Corinthians of viewing the body of Christ in such a way. Furthermore, the softening to "even men of little account" simply has no lexical basis.[34] In the view adopted here, Paul would not mean that Christians despise the pagan judges—that, too, is a totally un-Pauline view—but that they are those people whose values and judgments the church has rejected by its adoption of totally different standards. To go to pagan courts is to ask those to make a ruling among Christians who have absolutely "no standing within the church" (GNB, NAB), which has been determined by eschatological verities through Christ.

If this is the correct understanding, then with this set of questions Paul is trivializing the pagan courts in the same way that he trivialized the affair itself in v. 2: "In light of our existence in Christ and our participation in the eschatological judgments, how can one care about such trifling matters in the first place, and in any case how can one bring them before those who have no standing in the church and therefore will not have a share in those judgments?"

5 With the first indicative in the paragraph, "I say this to shame you" (cf. 15:34), Paul punctuates the point of the first two sets of questions.

---

[32]Field, *Notes*, p. 171. Cf. A. Stein, who finds this problem so formidable that he offers a more improbable solution yet, that the "ungodly" before whom the Corinthians had taken their case were Jewish rabbis ("Wo trugen die korinthischen Christen ihre Rechtshandel aus?" *ZNW* 59 [1968], 86-90).

[33]Cf. Jos., *Ant.* 13.75: "They requested the king to sit in council (καθίσαντα) with his friends and to hear their arguments on these matters" (Loeb, VII, 263).

[34]One solution for this point of view is to see the word as designating believers from the pagan point of view, as in 1:28. But in such a case it would still divide the house, as it were, and the irony would be completely lost.

Earlier (4:14) he had maintained that his object was not to shame them, but to warn them. Here the object is shame, pure and simple. The matter itself shames them; and in light of their eschatological existence their failure to have acted shames them. In case they do not understand that, he now says it outright.

But the word of shame also points forward to the next question (Q4[1]). In a church full of pride and arrogance, where "wisdom," suggesting superior spirituality, was a watchword, "is it so[35] with you that there is nobody among you who is *sophos* ("wise"),[36] so that he/she might render a decision[37] between the brothers[38]?" This is biting sarcasm, which scarcely needs further comment.[39] As with so much that has been said up to this point, Paul is trying to help the Corinthians see their true condition over against their perceived one. A trial between two brothers before pagan courts is no "innocent" matter; it reveals how lacking in truly Christian wisdom they are, and therefore how poorly they understand their true place in Christ.

6 Not only so, but all of this happens right in the open, "in front of unbelievers." It is not certain whether this sentence is designed to be an exclamation (as in the NIV) or a question (as in the RSV). The meaning is the same in either case. What favors a question is the conjunction "but,"[40] which would function as the second part of a "not . . . but" formula, which is so frequent in Paul's style.

As in v. 1 the prepositional phrase "in front of unbelievers" involves bringing such matters before the civil magistrates in Corinth. But here the emphasis lies with the fact that the church is thereby airing its dirty linen in the public forum. This concern is not often expressed in Paul (cf. 10:32; 1 Thess. 4:11-12), although it becomes a major factor in the ethical imperatives in the Pastoral Epistles (cf. 1 Tim. 6:2; Tit. 2:8, 10; 3:1). As with so many items in this letter, the imagery from 3:16-17, the church as God's temple in Corinth, dominates his perspective even if it is not expressed.

---

[35]Gk. οὕτως, omitted in the NIV; it appears first in the sentence and is therefore emphatic, pointing to the condition that will be expressed in what follows.

[36]See on 1:17 and 3:18; this is the last occurrence of the word group in 1 Corinthians (except in the list of the Spirit's manifestations in 12:8). It is replaced in chap. 8 by its companion, γνῶσις.

[37]Note the change from κρίνω, which in this context has meant either "go to law" or "eschatological judgment," to διακρίνω, "to render a decision."

[38]On this difficult wording, see n. 5 above.

[39]It is just possible that Paul is also referring to the Jewish ḥākām, the scholar a step below the rabbi who could hear cases. See E. Dinkler, "Zum Problem der Ethik bei Paulus. Rechtsnahme und Rechtsversicht. 1 Kor 6.1-11," in *Signum Crucis. Aufsätze zum Neuen Testament* (Tübingen, 1967), p. 208. But that is to make the clause too juridical, when the point is clearly to shame them.

[40]Gk. ἀλλά.

This is obviously still a very difficult word for believers, who not only do not generally think and live within the NT's eschatological categories, but whose values tend to place such a high priority on property that a number of hermeneutical ploys have been established to get around the plain sense of the text. There are simply too many of us with vested interests in the present age for us to have any desire to hear it applied to the contemporary church. This is even more so when the rhetorical questions of v. 7 are also kept in view. So much is this true that many (e.g., Mare) spend most of their time trying to justify actions that are openly contrary to what the text says.[41] But a few hermeneutical remarks should be made.

First, the two great urgencies for Paul are the church's self-understanding as God's eschatological people and its witness before the world. The difficulties with our "hearing" this text are related primarily to our general lack of a biblical self-understanding, especially in terms of the essential eschatological framework of our existence as the people of the future who are to be totally conditioned by that future as we live in the present. Therefore, our priorities tend to be warped toward the values of this age rather than of the age to come. Here we have great need of deep reformation. Most legal actions on the part of Christians are predicated on "rights" and "the pursuit of property" in the present age. Until our thinking is genuinely overhauled on these matters, our approach to the text will be supine neglect, circuitous exegesis, or canon law (the latter is not wrong; rather, it allows people to relegate the text to church jurisprudence and thereby dismiss its implications for our self-understanding).

Second, in terms of specifics, it needs to be noted that the text is dealing with a matter between two Christians as they take it before the public courts for settlement. On this matter Paul's responses in the next paragraph are particularly relevant. What the text does not deal with is a Christian's response to pagans who defraud her/him. But even here there are Christian ways of responding, of which public litigation would hopefully be the last resort. In light of our eschatological outlook, one should always be prepared to ask *why* he/she would do so. If it is out of concern for the one who defrauded and for all others who might be so taken in, then one might seem fully justified. But if it is for the sake of one's own possessions alone, then one surely needs to ask about proper motives and priorities.

---

[41]For a history of exegesis and application in the church see L. Vischer, *Die Auslegungsgeschichte von I Kor. 6,1-11* (Tübingen, 1955). See also S. Meuter, *Das Recht im Dienst der Versöhnung und des Friedens, Studie zur Frage des Rechts nach dem Neuen Testament* (Zürich, 1972), who argues on the basis of this passage that Christians at all costs should avoid the secular courts, since they are based on the principle of retaliation for wrongs done.

b. Shame on the plaintiff and warning against the wrongdoer (6:7-11)

7 *The very fact¹ that you have lawsuits² among you means that you have been completely defeated already. Why not rather be wronged? Why not rather be cheated?* 8 *Instead, you yourselves cheat and do wrong,³ and you do this⁴ to your brothers.*

9 *Do you not know that the wicked will not inherit the kingdom of God? Do not be deceived: Neither the sexually immoral nor idolaters nor adulterers nor male prostitutes nor homosexual offenders* 10 *nor thieves nor the greedy nor drunkards nor slanderers nor swindlers will inherit the kingdom of God.* 11 *And that is what some of you were. But you were washed, you were sanctified, you were justified in the name of the Lord Jesus Christ⁵ and by the Spirit of our God.*

Paul now turns his attention directly to the two men involved in the litigation, but speaks to them in such a way that the entire community is also addressed. The actions of both men are a total defeat, shaming both the church and themselves (v. 7a). Far better, Paul argues by way of rhetoric, for the man who initiated the proceedings to conform to the nonretaliation ethic of the Christian faith (v. 7b). Then in v. 8, using the same verbs from v. 7 but now in the active, he shames the defendant, who did the cheating in the first place, and in vv. 9-10 he proceeds to warn him (and the church) that those who do such things are in danger of forfeiting their inheritance. But as in 5:7 the imperative, though it comes first in the argument, must be understood to follow the indicative, which in this case comes in v. 11 in the form of an affirmation of their conversion.

Although the deeds of the two men are primarily in view, the entire passage is written in the second person plural, thus broadening the perspective to include them all, especially so in vv. 9-11. The NIV's paragraph

---

¹The majority of MSS (including P¹¹vid A B C) read μὲν οὖν here, against the simple μέν of P⁴⁶ ℵ* D* 6 33 630 1739 1881 2495 pc. The latter is to be preferred (cf. Zuntz, 193). μὲν οὖν is a conformation to v. 4. The asyndeton marks a break in the argument; the solitary μέν implies a contrast that must be supplied from the context (in this case the following rhetorical questions).

²A few MSS (ℵ 629 1241 1881 pc) have the singular κρίμα, probably due to the dropping of a syllable through homoeoteleuton.

³The NIV has these two verbs in reverse order, probably for reasons of English style.

⁴The MajT reads ταῦτα, thus making the "wronging" and "cheating" two separate acts. Paul's τοῦτο implies that we are dealing with a single deed.

⁵As in the three instances in 5:4-5, there is a range of options, including the addition of "our" (B P 33 1739 al), which is probably an assimilation to the following phrase, and the omission of "Christ" (A ℵ Maj). An omission could have happened due to homoeoteleuton; more likely "Christ" was added for liturgical reasons.

break at v. 9 is unfortunate.[6] The connection with v. 8 is made both with the conjunction "or" ("or do you not know?") and the word "wicked" (the same word as "ungodly" in v. 1), which is the noun of the verb "do wrong" in vv. 7-8. This broadening of the perspective in these final verses has the effect of moving the text away from the individuals who have sinned to the larger problems that afflict the entire community, to which he will speak once again in 6:12-20.

7 From the word of shame on the whole community in vv. 5-6, who have disregarded their own position in Christ by allowing such a thing to happen before the pagans, Paul turns to shame the two litigants themselves. This opening sentence is something of a broadside against both of them. The emphasis in the Greek, which is nearly impossible to put into good English, is on the utter defeat that this action represents: "Already (i.e., whatever the result of the lawsuit) it is altogether[7] a defeat[8] to you, that you have lawsuits[9] with one another." Paul's point is directed especially at Man B (the plaintiff): "Whether you win or lose, the action itself is already a loss. For even if you win, you lose by not being able to endure injury, and the church loses by your action before the public tribunal." From this he will proceed to the rhetorical questions, which imply that by enduring "loss" he would have truly "won." At the same time the sentence anticipates the words to Man A (the defendant) in vv. 8-10: "By your wrongdoing which precipitated the lawsuit, you, too, have suffered defeat; for even if you have gained some temporal advantage, you stand in greater danger of losing your eternal inheritance." Thus, even before a verdict is reached in the court, the action itself is an utter defeat for all parties.

Since this is so, he asks the plaintiff[10] rhetorically, "Why not rather be wronged? Why not rather be cheated?" Why not, indeed! For one living in the old age, where selfishness in all of its sordid as well as domesticated forms still rules, one can give a thousand reasons why not; but they all begin with the word "but" (as in, "But you don't know what he did to me") and

---

[6]Even more so is K. E. Bailey's attempt to make vv. 9-11 begin the argument of 6:12-20. See "Paul's Theological Foundation for Human Sexuality: I Cor. 6:9-20 in the Light of Rhetorical Criticism," *NESTThRev* 3 (1980), 27-41. In this case both the grammar of v. 9 and the content of vv. 9-11 stand quite against it.

[7]Gk. ὅλως; see on 5:1.

[8]Gk. ἥττημα, found only here and in Rom. 11:12 and Isa. 31:8 (LXX) in the entire body of Greek literature. The verb means to "be overcome"; the noun implies defeat in the sense of suffering great loss. See Field, *Notes,* pp. 160-61, 171-72.

[9]Gk. κρίματα, which ordinarily means a judicial verdict, must here mean the lawsuit itself (cf. Exod. 18:22 LXX).

[10]This is true even though the verbs are in the second plural. The plurals follow those of the first sentence, which had at least the two men in view; probably it also reflects the broadening of perspective noted above.

are motivated by some form of self-protection or self-gain. This is another sure instance of the influence of the teaching of Jesus on Paul (cf. 4:16-17).[11] Paul regularly enjoins that one not return evil for evil (1 Thess. 5:15; Rom. 12:17), a direct reflection of the teaching and example of Jesus (see on 4:12-13). By "overcoming" evil with good, even if it meant personal loss, this brother not only could have staved off real defeat, but could have experienced the greater "gain" of Christian ethics: by enduring undeserved injury he enters into the real meaning of the cross (cf. 1 Pet. 2:19-21).

The two verbs help us only a little to discover the nature of the wrongdoing. The first one, "be wronged,"[12] is the verb for the noun translated "ungodly" in v. 1 (and "wicked" in v. 9). It covers the whole range of activity that injures or does injustice to another person. What was first applied to outsiders has now been brought to bear on their own behavior. The second verb, "be cheated," tends to narrow the perspective to "robbing, cheating, defrauding" someone out of what is rightfully his/hers (cf. 7:5).[13] This word in particular suggests that some kind of property or business dealing is the problem.[14] It also gives substance to the words "the greedy and swindlers" in the vice list in 5:10-11, now repeated in v. 10.

8 Without breaking stride, Paul turns (using the strong adversative[15]) and speaks a word of shame to the one who did the defrauding in the first place. The repetition of the two verbs from v. 7, now changed from the middle/passive[16] to the active, implies that the one whose defrauding of a brother precipitated all this in the first place is primarily in view. Nonetheless the emphatic "you" that begins the sentence suggests that Paul is now broadening the perspective to speak once more to the church as a whole: "But you, even though you should know better and not be like them, are just like the pagans who surround you. You have greed and fraud (not to mention

---

[11]Which makes the observations by many (e.g., Héring, 41 n. 5; Conzelmann, 106) as to the somewhat parallel moral standards in the pagan philosophers of interest but generally irrelevant.

[12]Gk. ἀδικέω.

[13]Gk. ἀποστερέω. Cf. the addition to the commandments from the Decalogue in Mark 10:19 ("Do not defraud," probably with reference to property rights of others), and Jas. 5:4, of wages that have been swindled from workers.

[14]The usage in 7:5 where one partner in a marriage is "defrauding" the other of sexual relationships is seen by Richardson as a "sexual" tie to this passage ("Judgment," pp. 44-46). But the usage is quite unrelated and would be purely coincidental even if some kind of sexual wrongdoing were involved in this instance.

[15]Gk. ἀλλά; the "instead" of the NIV gives one the impression that these words might be addressed to the same person; but the change from the passive to active disallows that.

[16]Field, *Notes,* p. 172, following Alford, suggests that the verbs in v. 7 are middle (= "allow yourself to be wronged"); but that is also the sense they must take if they are passive.

241

sexual immorality and idolatry) going on in your own midst, and that with brothers." The implication of the warning that follows is that such behavior is not only shameful but simply cannot be tolerated in the Christian community.

9-10 With these sentences Paul ties together a number of items in 5:1-13 and 6:1-8. The first sentence flows directly out of vv. 7-8 with another rhetorical "Or do you not know that?" (cf. vv. 2 and 4 above).[17] Likewise, with the word *adikoi* ("wicked") Paul ties these words of warning to the "wrongdoing" of vv. 7-8, and at the same time ties both to v. 1. The "wicked" in v. 1 are those in the world who are going to be judged by the saints (v. 2), a judgment now expressed in terms of their not inheriting the kingdom. Here is a piece of eschatological teaching about which one can be sure the Corinthians had previously been informed: "The 'wicked' will not inherit the kingdom of God." This of course refers to the eschatological consummation of the kingdom that is "not yet," just as the same phrase in 4:20 referred to the kingdom as it is "already" being realized in the present age. The failure of the wicked to "inherit the kingdom of God" is the other side of their being judged in v. 2; this is what that judgment leads to.

Paul's point in all this is to warn "the saints," not only the man who has wronged his brother, but the whole community, that if they persist in the same evils as "the wicked" they are in the same danger of not inheriting the kingdom. Some theologies have great difficulty with such warnings, implying that they are essentially hypothetical since God's children cannot be "disinherited." But such a theology fails to take seriously the genuine tension of texts like this one. The warning is real; the wicked will not inherit the kingdom. That first of all applies to the "unsaved." Paul's concern is that the Corinthians must "stop[18] deceiving themselves" or "allowing themselves to be deceived."[19] By persisting in the same behavior as those already destined for judgment they are placing themselves in the very real danger of that same judgment. If it were not so, then the warning is no warning at all. Paul's own response to such, of course, is v. 11, in which he invites them to change their behavior by reminding them that they do indeed belong to God through the gracious work of Christ and the Spirit.

The warning character of this passage is supported by yet another tie to what has gone before: the fact that Paul defines "the wicked" in terms of the six sins from 5:10-11—to which he now adds four more. The list here

---

[17]As in v. 2, an ἤ ties this rhetorical question directly to v. 8. This especially mitigates the probability that a new section is starting here (see n. 6 above).

[18]As in 4:5 and 7:5 (q.v.) this is a present prohibition, which implies that they are to stop something that is already going on.

[19]Gk. μὴ πλανᾶσθε (cf. 15:33; 3:18 has a different verb). As with the verbs in v. 7 this can be either passive or middle; in either case it comes out at the same point.

begins with two from before, "the sexually immoral" and "idolaters," which in turn reflect the problems of 5:1-13 and 6:12-20 (sexual immorality) and 8:1–11:1 (idolatry).[20] These are followed by the four new items, three of which are sexual ("adulterers, male prostitutes, homosexual offenders"), and therefore tie in with the material in chap. 5. The other, "thieves,"[21] belongs to the matters of this section (although it ordinarily refers to actual robbery rather than to the kind of underhanded stealing suggested by our word "defraud").

The word "adulterers" means precisely that (married persons having sexual relations—of any kind—outside marriage) and needs no further comment. The next two words, however, translated "male prostitutes" and "homosexual offenders" in the NIV, require considerable comment. The first word, *malakoi,* has the basic meaning of "soft"; but it also became a pejorative epithet for men who were "soft" or "effeminate," most likely referring to the younger, "passive" partner in a pederastic relationship[22]— the most common form of homosexuality in the Greco-Roman world.[23] In

---

[20]R. Scroggs (*The New Testament and Homosexuality* [Philadelphia, 1983], pp. 101-09) has argued that the lists here and in chap. 5 have no special relationship to the context. But that is not quite true. Not all may be related to the immediate context, but most of them at least can be shown to relate especially to the problems Paul is encountering in this church. See above on 5:9-10. On the other side, the attempt by Bailey ("Foundation," pp. 27-29) to divide the list into two sets of five each, the first dealing with sexual sins and the second with disorders at the Lord's Table, not only misses the present context altogether but presses "idolatry" into a meaning it cannot sustain ("sacred prostitution"), not to mention missing its clear relationship to 10:1-22.

[21]Gk. κλέπται, the standard word for all such crime, is covered by our word "thief."

[22]See the papyrus cited by Deissmann, LAE, 164: Ζηνόβιον τὸν μαλακόν ("Zenobius the effeminate"); and Dion.Hal. 7.2.4, who describes Aristodemus, the tyrant of Cumae, as "a man of no obscure birth, who was called by the citizens Malacus or 'Effeminate' . . . either because when a boy he was effeminate and allowed himself to be treated as a woman, as some relate, or because he was of a mild nature and slow to anger" (Loeb, IV, 151). Dionysius's first option is surely pejorative and thus helps us with its meaning here, despite J. Boswell's arguments to the contrary (see *Christianity, Social Tolerance and Homosexuality* [Chicago, 1980], pp. 339-40). What makes this certain is a passage like Philo's *spec.leg.* 3.37-39, in which he gives a biting description of pederasty, and is especially harsh on the youths who deck themselves out as women for such purposes. One of the nouns he uses to describe such degeneracy is *malakia* ("Furthermore he [speaking of the 'lover,' the active male partner] sees no harm in becoming a tutor and instructor in the grievous vices of unmanliness and effeminacy [μαλακία]" [Loeb, VII, 499-501]).

[23]On this matter, and for many other items in this discussion, see Scroggs, *Homosexuality,* whose presentation is a model of fairness to all sides. He seems to be basically correct at this point; it is less likely that his case can be held that this is the only kind of homosexuality that is condemned in the NT. The very fact that Paul includes women in Rom. 1:26 tells against Scroggs's whole reconstruction of this matter. The appeal to silence in this instance is especially weak.

many instances young men sold themselves as "mistresses" for the sexual pleasure of men older than themselves. The problem is that there was a technical word for such men, and *malakos* is seldom, if ever, so used. Since it is not the ordinary word for such homosexual behavior, one cannot be sure what it means in a list like this, where there is no further context to help. What is certain is that it refers to *behavior* of some kind, not simply to an attitude or characteristic.[24]

What makes "male prostitute" (in the sense of "effeminate call-boy")[25] the best guess is that it is immediately followed by a word that does seem to refer to male homosexuality, especially to the active partner. This word *(arsenokoitai),* however, is also difficult. This is its first appearance in preserved literature, and subsequent authors are reluctant to use it, especially when describing homosexual activity. The word is a compound of "male" and "intercourse." There is no question as to the meaning of the *koitai* part of the word; it is vulgar slang for "intercourse" (which probably accounts for its seldom being found in the literature).[26] What is not certain is whether "male" is subject (= "males who have intercourse"; thus a word for male prostitutes of all kinds) or object (= "intercourse with males"; therefore male homosexual). In light of these ambiguities, Boswell[27] has argued that neither word can be certainly made to denote homosexuality. His argument, however, seems to be a case of "divide and conquer." What may be true of the words individually is one thing. But here they are not individual; they appear side by side in a vice list that is heavily weighted toward sexual sins. Although one cannot be certain, it is very likely that the NIV is moving toward a proper understanding by translating "male prostitute" and "homosexual offender," with the proviso that "male prostitute" most likely denotes a consenting homosexual youth. For Paul's attitude toward homosexuality in general one need refer only to his own Jewish background with its abhorrence of such,[28] plus his description of such activity (Rom. 1:26-27).

---

[24]This seems certain from the rest of the words in the list, and especially from the first sentence in v. 11: "Such *were* some of you," implying that behavioral change had taken place.

[25]This designation is from Scroggs, *Homosexuality;* see especially his discussion of this word on pp. 62-65.

[26]This is precisely the point that Boswell misses in his long discussion of this word (*Christianity,* pp. 341-52). He himself points out the vulgarity of the word by offering a modern English equivalent; but his equivalent is seldom found in literature of the kind that is preserved for posterity for the same reason this one is avoided: It would ordinarily have offended good taste. Paul apparently is not above the use of such if it will make its proper impact (see 4:13; cf. Phil. 3:8).

[27]*Christianity,* pp. 335-53.

[28]See the chapter on Judaism in Scroggs, *Homosexuality,* pp. 66-98.

After these additional four items, Paul concludes with the other four from 5:10 and 11 (q.v.). Again he repeats: Those who do such things, meaning those who persist in such sins, will not inherit the kingdom. The implication of the warning to believers themselves seems patent. But as always in Paul, warning or imperative is not the last—nor the first—word. What is said here must be kept in tension with what follows in v. 11.

11 Paul cannot bring himself to conclude on the note of warning struck in vv. 8-10,[29] especially since it might leave the impression that the Corinthians were actually still among "the wicked." Thus he brings this whole matter to a conclusion by reaffirming: "And these things[30] are what some of you were." This sentence, therefore, functions in a way similar to the indicative of 5:7 ("Christ our Passover Lamb has been sacrificed"). Just as the imperative in that passage was intended to be taken seriously, so too with the warning in this one. But the predicate in each case is God's prior action in Christ Jesus. The previous list is what the wicked are like still, and because of that they will not inherit the kingdom. Those who persist in the same activities are in similar danger. "But that is what some of you *were*. Now in Christ Jesus you are something different, so live like it. Stop defrauding, living in sexual sin, etc., because you are no longer among those who do."

The rest of the verse gives the soteriological basis for this premise: "But you were washed,[31] you were sanctified, you were justified in the name of the Lord Jesus Christ and by the Spirit of our God." As such it is also one of the more important theological statements in the epistle. Paul's concern is singular: "Your own conversion, effected by God through the work of Christ and the Spirit, is what has removed you from being among the wicked, who will not inherit the kingdom." By implication there is an inherent imperative: "Therefore, live out this new life in Christ and stop being like the wicked."

The *structure* of the sentence seems certain. It begins with three

---

[29]Note how often in this letter Paul concludes on a positive note after such an argument or warning: e.g., 3:22-23; 4:14-17 (as a conclusion to all of 1:18–4:21); 5:7; 6:20; 10:13; 11:32.

[30]Gk. ταῦτα, referring to the whole list. The neuter is striking; one would expect τοιοῦτοι. The neuter functions in a more dramatic way to express horror or contempt (= "these abominations").

[31]Gk. ἀπελούσασθε (only here and in Acts 22:16 in the NT). Some make a considerable point of the fact that the verb is middle and offer such forced translations as "you had yourselves washed," giving further theological significance to this being a voluntary act on the part of the one being baptized (e.g., Beasley-Murray, *Baptism*, p. 163; Fung, "Justification," p. 250; R-P, 119). But much of that discussion will not "wash," since the verb occurs almost altogether in the middle. This is a middle that functions like a passive. Cf. Dunn, *Baptism*, p. 123, and most English translations.

verbs, each introduced with the strong adversative "but," which gives additional force to the "once you were, but now you are not" emphasis of the sentence. As in 1:30, the three verbs are primarily metaphors of salvation, each expressing a special facet of their conversion in light of the preceding sentences: they had been "washed" from the filth of their former life-styles expressed in the preceding list; they had been "sanctified," set apart by God for holy, godly living that stands in stark contrast to their former wickedness; though formerly "unjust,"[32] they had been justified, so that now right with God they may inherit the kingdom that before they could not. Each of the verbs is thus chosen for contextual, not dogmatic, reasons; and their sequence is theologically irrelevant.[33] "Washed" probably comes first because that most naturally follows the "filth" of the vice catalogue. Finally, since the three verbs refer to the same reality, and since each of them has "God" as the implied subject, the two prepositional phrases are to be understood as modifying all three verbs.[34] The latent Trinitarianism of the sentence, therefore, is difficult to escape. God has effected salvation "in the name of the Lord Jesus Christ and by the Spirit."

It is possible, but not as certain as most interpreters imply, that the verb "you were washed" is also an allusion to baptism—similar to the possible secondary reference to the Lord's Table in the imperative "let us celebrate the Feast" in 5:8. Paul does not in fact say "you were baptized," which he was perfectly capable of doing if baptism were his concern. This verb is not used elsewhere in the NT to denote baptism (it is joined to baptism in Acts 22:16, but is not the actual verb for baptism itself). The argument most frequently used in favor of a reference to baptism, besides the connotation in the verb "washed" itself, is the association with the first prepositional phrase, "in the name of the Lord Jesus Christ." But this is to read Paul through the eyes of Luke. There are in fact two matters of usage that suggest otherwise: (1) The use of *en* with "baptism" does not correspond to Paul's usage elsewhere. Indeed, in the NT *en* with "baptize" refers to the element

---

[32]It is difficult to resist seeing in this verb (δικαιόω) something of a wordplay on the adj. ἄδικοι in vv. 1 and 9 and the verb ἀδικέω in vv. 7-8.

[33]Some are anxious about the ordering of these verbs, as if Paul were thereby making some kind of theological statement that does not seem to fit our own dogmatic categories. This is true even of C. A. A. Scott's attempt to read the verbs in reverse order (i.e., behind each action lay the former one; see *Christianity according to St. Paul* [Cambridge, 1927], p. 120).

[34]The repetition of ἀλλά before each verb also argues for this (cf. Fung, "Justification," p. 251). *Contra* Scott (previous note). Cf. the less than convincing presentation by Bailey, "Foundation," pp. 28-29, who argues that the sentence has step parallelism, with each verb corresponding in sequence to the persons of the Trinity mentioned in the prepositional phrases (washed = Christ; sanctified = Spirit; justified = God). This destroys Paul's own parallelism found in the two nicely balanced prepositional phrases.

into which one has been baptized (cf. 12:13); with "baptize" Paul uses the preposition *eis:* one is "baptized *into* the name" (cf. 1:13-15)[35] or "into Christ" (Gal. 3:28).[36] (2) The two prepositions and three verbs all go together; and there is no parallel in Paul's usage to the assertion that one is "baptized in the name of Christ and in the Spirit of our God," or that one is sanctified or justified at baptism. This is not to say that for Paul the verb may not have carried with it an indirect allusion to baptism; but it is to say that Paul is not here concerned with the Christian initiatory rite, but with the spiritual transformation made possible through Christ and effected by the Spirit. The three metaphors emphasize the aspects of Christian conversion found in the theological terms "regeneration, sanctification, and justification";[37] and for Paul these are the work of the Spirit in the believer's life, not the result of baptism.[38]

The precise nuance of the two prepositional phrases is not certain. But since they together modify the three verbs, it seems most likely that they are both to be understood in an instrumental sense (cf. GNB, NEB). The reference to "the name" of Christ, as in 1:10 and 5:4 (cf. 2 Thess. 3:6), probably refers to the authority of Christ on behalf of the believer, especially in terms of his saving work; and the reference to the Spirit reflects Paul's understanding of the Spirit as the means whereby God in the new age effects the work of Christ in the believer's life. Together, then, the two prepositions refer to what God has done *for* his people in Christ, which he has effected *in* them by the Spirit.

Once more, therefore, as in 5:6-8, Paul is urging the Corinthians to become what they are; and he predicates that imperative on the prior work of Christ. In this case, however, the imperative is only implied; and the empha-

---

[35]This is standard usage in the NT, except for Acts 2:38, which has ἐπί; one wonders, therefore, whether the ἐν τῷ ὀνόματι Ἰησοῦ Χριστοῦ of Acts 10:48 goes with βαπτισθῆναι or, as elsewhere in the NT, with the verb "command."

[36]It should perhaps also be pointed out that the collocation of "the name of Jesus" with baptism does not occur in Paul. In the name of Jesus one "commands" (2 Thess. 3:6), "appeals" (1 Cor. 1:10), "judges" (5:3), "does all things" (Col. 3:17), "gives thanks" (Eph. 5:20), and "is washed, sanctified, justified" (here); but nowhere is one "baptized" ἐν τῷ ὀνόματι of Jesus.

[37]For these latter two verbs see the discussion on 1:30; for "sanctify" see also on 1:2, and for "justify" see on 4:4. Some have argued that the verb here does not have the full theological significance that it will obtain in Galatians and Romans (e.g., Bultmann, *Theology,* I, 136); but there are no valid lexical or contextual grounds for so arguing. See the discussion in Fung, "Justification," pp. 250-51; cf. Conzelmann, 107.

[38]For a similar view see Dunn, *Baptism,* pp. 120-23; cf. Barrett, 141, who allows that "baptism is in mind," but that "it is the inward meaning rather than the outward circumstances of the rite that is important to Paul." For the view that it refers to baptism see Beasley-Murray, *Baptism,* 162-67, and most of the other literature on baptism, as well as most commentaries.

sis on the work of Christ is less on the objective reality of his sacrifice than on their experience of that reality by means of the Spirit. They are to *be* and *behave* differently from the wicked, because God in his mercy has already removed the stains of their past sins, has already begun the work of ethical transformation, and has already given them forgiveness and right standing with himself. Although this refers primarily to the issues of 5:1-13 and 6:1-11, it obviously functions as the basis for all the imperatives in this letter, including the one that immediately follows.

Although this entire passage is singularly addressed to the problem of two brothers appearing before the civil magistrates in Corinth, the net result for us is a marvelous blend of Pauline theology and ethics getting their workout in the marketplace. Theology for Paul is not an abstraction, but the application of the gospel to life in the real world. As such this text serves as a model for working through the "tension" between the indicative and the imperative in the life of the believer. One really is expected to obey the rhetorical questions of v. 7; and one really must take seriously the warnings of vv. 8-10. But these are both predicated on the prior work of Christ and the application of that work to our lives by the Spirit.

For Paul there is to be the closest possible relationship between the experience of grace and one's behavior that evidences that experience of grace. Paul himself is as concerned as anyone that the latter (right behavior) should not be perceived as coming first or as leading to the former (the experience of grace). But those who concern themselves with grace without equal concern for behavior have missed Paul's own theological urgencies. It is precisely for these reasons that the warning texts in Paul must be taken with real seriousness. Security in Christ there is, to be sure, but it is a false security that would justify sinners who have never taken seriously "but such *were* some of you." That is to whitewash the sinner without regeneration or transformation; Paul simply would not understand such theology.

What is most often missing in such theologies is the central ingredient in Paul, the transforming work of the Spirit. And in his case that is not simply to be understood as theological jargon. It is rather predicated on the Spirit's coming into the world, signifying the turning of the ages, so that the realities of the future are already at work *in power* in the present age. The Corinthian problem was not with their experience of the Spirit, but with their misunderstanding of what it meant to be Spirit people. Our problems are usually of another kind. The Spirit belongs to the creed and to our theology; but he is all too often left there, so that his genuinely transforming and empowering work is often left until the Eschaton, rather than experienced in the present.

3. On Going to the Prostitutes (6:12-20)

12 *"Everything is permissible for me"—but not everything is beneficial. "Everything is permissible for me"—but I will not be mastered by anything.* 13 *"Food for the stomach and the stomach for food"—but God will destroy them both. The body is not meant for sexual immorality, but for the Lord, and the Lord for the body.[1]* 14 *By his power God raised the Lord from the dead, and he will raise[2] us also.* 15 *Do you not know that your bodies are members of Christ himself? Shall I take[3] the members of Christ and unite them with a prostitute? Never!* 16 *Do[4] you not know that he who unites himself with a prostitute is one with her in body? For it is said, "The two will become one flesh."[a]* 17 *But he who unites himself with the Lord is one with him in spirit.*

18 *Flee from sexual immorality. All other sins a man commits are outside his body, but he who sins sexually sins against his own body.* 19 *Do you not know that your body[5] is a temple of the Holy Spirit, who is in you, whom you have received from God? You are not your own;* 20 *you were bought at a price. Therefore[6] honor God with your body.[7]*

[a]Gen. 2:24

---

[1]Marcion attests an interesting addition: "so that the Temple is for God, and God for the Temple." This is a commentary on the text in light of 3:16 and 6:19.

[2]There are three variants for this verb: ἐξήγειρεν (P[46] [2nd corr.] B 6 1739 pc it); ἐξεγειρεῖ (P[11] P[46]* A D P 1241 pc); ἐξεγερεῖ (P[46] [1st corr.] ℵ C Ψ Maj vg sy[h] co Iren Tert Epiph Ambrst). The first reading is a conformation to the preceding aorist; the second probably is a misreading of the third. The parallelism of the sentences requires the future; otherwise the argument is lost. See the commentary.

[3]Several MSS (F G P Ψ 81 104 pc) drop the σ from ἄρας so that it reads ἄρα οὖν, probably due to the frequency of this combination in Romans. Héring, 43, adopts this reading, but his argument is not convincing.

[4]The evidence is evenly divided over whether this clause begins with an ἤ ("or"; cf. 6:2 and 9). This is not easily decided; cf. the discussion in Zuntz, 195, who concludes, "On the balance, then, the shorter reading would appear to be original."

[5]A number of MSS (A L Ψ 33 81 104 365 1175 1181 1495 pc) read the plural here. This represents an attempt to clarify what is certainly Paul's intent. On the grammar, see below (n. 65).

[6]In some early MSS Paul's δή was changed to ἄρα γε; this in turn was misread in the West so that almost the entire Latin tradition has an addition, "and bear," that is the result of reading ἄρα γε as ἄρατε. See Metzger, 552-53; Zuntz, 169.

[7]The MajT, with no early Greek support, has the addition καὶ ἐν τῷ πνεύματι ὑμῶν, ἅτινά ἐστιν τοῦ θεοῦ ("and your spirit, which are God's," KJV). This addition, which misses the whole point of the argument, reflects the influence of Greek dualism on the later church, which had great trouble with the body.

How this section relates to what immediately precedes is not at all certain. Sexual immorality was also at the head of the vice list of vv. 9-10, which included adultery as well. Apparently such matters are still in the forefront. Following his insistence that they remove the incestuous man—a case in which they had failed to "judge" properly, Paul turned his attention to another instance of their failure to "judge" properly—the case of two brothers going to the pagan courts for "judgment." But he is not through with matters of sexual immorality; just as suddenly he returns to that question, although now the issue is entirely different.[8]

Two words dominate the present argument: "sexual immorality" *(porneia)* and "body";[9] and two passages specifically indicate that the problem involves the two together: "the body is not meant for sexual immorality" (v. 13c); "he who engages in sexual immorality sins against his own body" (v. 18c). But his concern is not with *porneia* in general.[10] Vv. 15-17 argue that one may not "take the members of Christ and unite them with a prostitute," implying that this is the specific expression of *porneia* with which Paul is here dealing.[11] Apparently some men within the Christian community are going to prostitutes and are arguing for the right to do so. Being people of the Spirit, they imply, has moved them to a higher plane, the realm of spirit, where they are unaffected by behavior that has merely to do

[8]It should also be noted that both the nature of the argumentation and the content have strong affinities to 7:1-7, which immediately follows. For the first time in the letter Paul quotes and corrects a Corinthian position, a form of argument that occurs several times again in chaps. 7–16, where he is responding to their letter. Furthermore, there seems to be more than just a casual tie between this section and the "sexual immoralities" of 7:2 and "lack of self-control" in 7:5, which are related specifically to some who are "depriving" their marriage partners of sexual relations, apparently because they think they have "authority over their own bodies" even in the marriage relationship (7:3-4). Is this deprivation the reason why some of the men are visiting the prostitutes?

[9]πορνεία occurs two times; πόρνη ("prostitute") two times; πορνεύω ("practice prostitution") one time; σῶμα ("body") eight times. On the Greek attitude toward *porneia* see the introduction to 5:1-13 and the comments on 5:1 (pp. 196-200).

[10]This is the standard view, found in most of the older commentaries. After an aside over the matter of lawsuits, Paul returns to the issue of sexual immorality from 5:1-13, for which he is now giving a general theological argument. See, e.g., R-P, 121; Grosheide, 143; Lenski, 233.

[11]Otherwise, Hurd, 86, who asserts that "in this passage he does not refer to any specific action of the Corinthians." But the combination of their arguments in vv. 12-13 with the explicit mention of intercourse with prostitutes in vv. 15-16 is as specific as anything that has preceded.

A completely different tack is taken by R. Kempthorne ("Incest and the Body of Christ: A Study of I Corinthians VI.12-20," *NTS* 14 [1967/68], 568-74; cf. M. Miguens, "Christ's 'Members' and Sex (1 Cor 6, 12-20)," *Thomist* 39 [1975], 42-48, who cites it approvingly), who on the basis of a few linguistic ties suggests that Paul is here returning to the problem of 5:1-13. This is highly unlikely; the case rests on an accumulation of possible, but mostly improbable, interpretations.

with the body. So Paul proceeds from the affirmation of v. 11 to an attack on this theological justification.[12]

As before, the gospel itself is at stake, not simply the resolution of an ethical question. The Corinthian pneumatics' understanding of spirituality has allowed them both a false view of freedom ("everything is permissible") and of the body ("God will destroy it"), from which basis they have argued that going to prostitutes is permissible because the body doesn't matter. Paul's response to this is in three parts: (1) In vv. 12-14 he argues directly against their false premises, in v. 12 against their distortion of Christian freedom, and in vv. 13-14 against their misunderstanding of the nature of the body. In v. 13 he makes the basic assertion that controls most of the rest of the argument: "The body is for the Lord, and the Lord for the body," which is demonstrated by the resurrection—both Christ's and ours (v. 14). (2) In vv. 15-17 he then builds on this theological base and argues against prostitution. They have completely missed the nature both of sexual intercourse ("the two become one flesh") and of Christian conversion ("one is joined to the Lord so as to become one with him in spirit"), and that these two "unions" are mutually exclusive. (3) Finally, in vv. 18-20, in case they have not yet quite heard it, he expressly forbids sexual immorality (v. 18a), but again on a theological basis—that such sin is against their bodies (v. 18c), which are not their own but belong to God through "divine purchase" (vv. 19-20).[13]

The net result is one of the more important theological passages in the NT about the human body. It should forever lay to rest the implicit dualism of so much that has been passed off as Christian, where the body is rejected, subdued, or indulged because it is of no significance for—or is even a hindrance to—"real salvation," which has to do with the "soul."

12 As in the preceding two sections, Paul comes out arguing. In contrast to those sections, however, he does not begin by attacking their illicit behavior; rather, he confronts the theology on which that behavior is predicated. "Everything is permissible for me" is almost certainly a Corinthian theological slogan.[14] This is confirmed by the way Paul cites it again in 10:23; in both cases he qualifies it so sharply as to negate it—at least as a

---

[12]G. Snyder, "The Literalization of the Apocalyptic Form in the New Testament Church," *BibRes* 14 (1969), 5-18, divides the section between vv. 12 and 13, a division that is not self-evident.

[13]It should be noted that the passage is full of unique, and in some cases difficult, expressions, which in turn have given rise to equally unique interpretations. Much of the problem here lies with the nature of the argumentation, in which Paul's rhetorical forms sometimes dictate the way the language appears. The difficulties arise when such language is pressed beyond its intent in the argument itself.

[14]C. Spicq, *Théologie Morale du Nouveau Testament* (Paris, 1965), II, 654, thinks otherwise.

theological absolute. The source of the slogan is debatable.[15] Possibly the Corinthians had turned a Pauline position into a slogan for their own purposes. If so, their error would lie in making absolute what for Paul would always have been qualified by his "in Christ" perspective.[16] For him it is only as one is in Christ that "everything is permitted me," and in any case that would have to do with *adiaphora* (the nonessentials: food, drink, days, circumcision, etc.), not with Christian ethics.

With this slogan we encounter for the first time in this letter another of its crucial terms, *exestin/exousia/exousiazō* (basically = "right to determine," hence "authority"). Along with its companions ("wisdom," "knowledge," "spiritual"), this is an area of tension between the Corinthians and Paul. In 8:9 he speaks bitingly of "this *exousia* of yours," which some were using to abuse others in the matter of going to the pagan temples; and the entire argument in 9:3-18 is over his own *exousia* to act in ways that had displeased them. What we have here, then, is a crisis of "authority" of another kind—over their "freedom to act as they pleased" without restraint.[17] For Paul that is not freedom at all, but a form of bondage worse than before.

With the first qualifier Paul turns *exousia* on its head. Freedom is not to be for self but for others. The real question is not whether an action is "lawful" or "right" or even "all right," but whether it is good, whether it benefits.[18] In light of the full context of this section that may mean, "to one's own benefit."[19] Elsewhere in 1 Corinthians, however, this word denotes benefiting someone else (it is parallel with "build up" in 10:23; cf. 10:33). Probably that is what lies behind the qualification here as well.[20] Truly Christian conduct is not predicated on whether I have the right to do something, but whether my conduct is helpful to those about me.

The second qualifier constitutes a wordplay on *exousia*—nearly impossible to carry over into English—that gets at the heart of the present matter. They are saying, "I have *exousia* (freedom to act) with regard to *all*

---

[15]This is a key idea among the Cynics, Stoics, and Gnostics. The latter, of course, are too late to influence Paul's Corinth; but the terminology has close affinities with Stoicism-Cynicism. See J. Dupont, *Gnosis* (Louvain, 1960), pp. 298-308; cf. the discussion in Conzelmann, 108-10.

[16]Cf. Conzelmann, 110: "What Paul here presents is nothing else but the πάντα ὑμῶν—ὑμεῖς δὲ Χριστοῦ, 'all things are yours—but you are Christ's,' of 3:21ff."

[17]Hurley, 93, makes a considerable jump in the use of language to see this word group as having to do with tension between Paul and them over the Mosaic *law*. This is simply not Paul's ordinary forensic vocabulary.

[18]Gk. συμφέρει, found only in the Corinthian letters in Paul. This, too, is a Stoic word, but Paul is using it differently. See Diog.L. 7.98; Epict. 1.22.1.

[19]Cf. NEB ("not everything is for my good"); Daube, "Pauline," p. 229; Findlay, 818.

[20]So Lightfoot, 214; R-P, 123; Conzelmann, 109; Holladay, 84.

things"; Paul qualifies, "Yes, but I will not be *mastered*[21] by *any*thing (or anybody)." At this distance one cannot be sure what Paul intends by this. Does he mean that one should not prate "freedom" with regard to sexual sin when in fact one is enslaved to the very thing that he is arguing is under his own authority? In such a case, the sinner is merely deceiving himself. Perhaps the "thing" Paul will not be enslaved to is *exousia* itself. There is a kind of self-deception that inflated spirituality promotes, which suggests to oneself that he/she is acting with freedom and authority, but which in fact is an enslavement of the worst kind—to the very freedom one thinks one has.[22] An especially attractive option, however, which ties this qualification specifically to the problem as it appears in vv. 15-16, is to understand the verb in light of 7:4, its only other appearance in Paul. As the married partner "has authority over" the other's body, so this might refer to coming under the "power" of the prostitute. That is, by being joined to her in *porneia* the believer constitutes someone else, outside of Christ, as the unlawful lord over one's own body.[23] In any case, their first slogan is simply not true—at least not as an absolute.

13-14   These two verses mark an abrupt change of direction. Paul, who has been talking about Christian freedom, suddenly shifts to the stomach and food, then moves to a theological statement about the body, followed by an affirmation of Christ's and our resurrection. None of this seems to follow.[24] Despite appearances, however, this is a very tight argument against the Corinthians' position about the human body, which they appear to have brought in alongside their stance on freedom.

The key lies in an analysis of the structure. Except for the crucial words of contrast in v. 13 ("not for sexual immorality, but"), the sentences form a perfect parallelism (with chiasm in the first member of each):[25]

Proposition I:
1. Food for the stomach,   A B
     and the stomach for food   B A
    de ("and")

---

[21]Gk. ἐξουσιασθήσομαι (= will not be enslaved, mastered, over*powered*); cf. 7:4.

[22]As Barrett, 146, nicely puts it: "Christian liberty is not licence, for licence is not more but less than liberty."

[23]See Bachmann, 240-41; W. Foerster, *TDNT* II, 575; Kempthorne, "Incest," p. 569; Miguens, "Christ's," p. 38.

[24]The difficulties here can be seen by comparing several English translations. The NIV in particular seems to miss the structure of Paul's argument.

[25]This formal structure has also been recognized by C. H. Giblin, *In Hope of God's Glory, Pauline Theological Perspectives* (New York, 1970), p. 141; cf. Hurley, 87; Murphy-O'Connor, "Slogans," 394; and Bailey, "Foundation," p. 31.

> 2. God will destroy both the one (stomach)   B
>   and the other (food)   A
>   *de* ("But" = the same will not hold true for the body)
> Proposition II:
>   1. The body [not for sexual immorality,
>   but] for the Lord,   A B
>   and the Lord for the body   B A
>   *de* ("and")
>   2. God both[26] has raised the Lord   B
>   and   will raise us   A
>   by his power (referring to both)

Such striking parallelism indicates that the structure itself is purposeful, which in turn offers clues to many of the difficulties. First, the three *de*'s, which have given so much trouble to translators, are readily explained. The *de* between the two propositions (unfortunately left out of the NIV) can only be adversative. Moreover, the clearly consecutive *de* in v. 14 determines that its less clear parallel in v. 13b is also consecutive.

Second, the two propositions are in obvious contrast to each other. Both this arrangement and the rest of the argument make it plain that Paul's concern is with the second one. The matter of food therefore is no issue here at all; rather, it is intended to set up the issue of the body and sexual immorality. This suggests that, as in v. 12, Proposition I is best understood as a Corinthian slogan,[27] which apparently they have carried over to the body and sexual relations with prostitutes.[28]

---

[26]This is the only other structural difference between the two parts: The καί—καί (both—and) must precede the verb in this instance, rather than the object proper, because of the change of tense in the verbs. This is one of the sure clues that the future is the correct reading (see n. 2 above).

[27]This slogan seems to be closely related to the issue of idol food in chaps. 8–10. It has especially close affinities with 8:8, which also seems to reflect a Corinthian position. Whether Paul is himself bringing that argument of theirs to bear here, or whether they had used the same argument for both food and sex, cannot be known. Probably the latter.

[28]This is the view of the majority of commentators. See the chart in Hurd, 68. What is less certain is how much of it constitutes that slogan. On the one hand, the rhythmic chiasm of Part 1 suggests perhaps only that much (cf. RSV). This may be so, but that would mean that Part 2 is Paul's own addition to their slogan, indicating not only his agreement with it, but his readiness to press it to its logical conclusion. Thus the NEB: "'Food is for the belly and the belly for food', you say. True, and one day God will put an end to both." On the other hand, since the whole of Proposition I sets up the contrast in II, it is possible that it represents the Corinthian position in its entirety—although in its present form it comes from Paul's own hand. In this case one would put quotation marks around the whole (cf. NAB; Héring, 46; Hurley, 87-88; Murphy-O'Connor, "Slogans," 394).

What does not seem to make any sense is to take Part 1 as a slogan, and Part 2 as its qualification (as the NIV, GNB). Under this view the slogan would be an extension of their libertine argument: "Not only is everything permitted me, but food is for the stomach

In contrast to v. 12, however, where Paul does not agree with their slogan in its absolute form, here he is in essential agreement. Both food and the stomach belong to the present age, and "God will do away with[29] them both in the end" (NAB).[30] What he will not let them do is take *that* slogan, which has to do with the irrelevancy of food restrictions, and apply it to illicit sexual relations. Paul's construction of the otherwise balanced sentence in Part 1 of Proposition II, following hard on the heels of I as it does, implies that their reasoning went like this: "Since everything is permitted, and since food is for the stomach and the stomach for food (after all, God will destroy them both in the end), and since all bodily appetites are pretty much alike, that means that the body is for sex and sex for the body[31]—because God will destroy them both in the end as well." But their conclusions are dead wrong—on both counts: The body is not for *porneia* but for the Lord; and it is not destined for destruction but for resurrection, the proof of which is Christ's resurrection.

Paul thus counters their argument with his own theological construct, formulated after the manner of theirs: "The body is for the Lord, and the Lord for the body." The rest of the argument will work out what this means. "The body is for the Lord" in the sense explained in vv. 14 and

---

and the stomach for food, so let's live it up and eat anything and anywhere we please." Paul then qualifies this libertine position by pointing to eschatological realities. While this might well fit their attitude at various points, such a reconstruction does not fit the argument here. First, it makes their libertine attitude the whole point, which it is not; second, it gives the point about eating independent value in the middle of an argument that has nothing to do with eating; third, this kind of qualification on Paul's part would play right into their hands, rather than truly modify their position. The fact that neither food nor stomach has any eschatological significance would be quite in keeping with their libertine point of view!

[29]Gk. καταργήσει; see the discussion on 1:28.

[30]This is in keeping with Paul's own view in chap. 15 that the resurrected body is not somatic (i.e., composed of its present material form), but pneumatic (i.e., transformed into a "spiritual body"); see on 15:42-49. The one is mortal, the other immortal; the one is lowly, the other glorious (cf. Phil. 3:21). Such a body has no need for the stomach and food.

For a different view, see Gundry, 54-59 (supported by Murphy-O'Connor, "Slogans," 394-95), who argues that by the reformulation in Proposition II Paul is intending to deny the Corinthian position in Proposition I as to the stomach as well. That is, "stomach" here stands as a synecdoche for "body" and Paul is saying, "Not so, the 'stomach/body' is not intended for destruction; it is 'for the Lord' and therefore intended for resurrection." This would be more attractive if the qualification of Proposition II were simply: "But the Lord is for the body, and the body for the Lord." As it is, this Proposition has its own internal qualification, "not for *porneia*, but," which makes the contrast not simply between the body destined for destruction and the body destined for resurrection, but between stomach/food and body/*porneia*.

[31]Hurley, 90, makes the puzzling extrapolation that their slogan would have run, "any man for any woman, and any woman for any man." Not only is that not parallel, but the context explicitly designates the problem as *men* going to *female* prostitutes.

19-20. The work of redemption includes the whole person, which in the Jewish view of things includes the body.[32] If the stomach is irrelevant for future existence, the body itself is not. Through Christ's own resurrection it has been stamped as belonging to eternity; it is destined for resurrection. Thus it is also "for the Lord" in the present.

The second part, "and the Lord for the body," is not so easy. This obviously cannot mean in the same complementary way that food and the stomach are meant for each other. The statement itself was purposely created out of their slogan; therefore, it is not intended to be pressed in detail.[33] This is not say that it is not true, but that it is not precise. Whatever else, it is not so much a statement about the Lord as it is a further statement about the body. Probably it means that the body belongs to the Lord because in his death and resurrection he has given himself for the body as part of that redemptive work.[34]

The affirmation of the resurrection in v. 14 corresponds to v. 13b and serves as the theological basis for "the body is for the Lord, and the Lord for the body." As such it anticipates the more detailed argument in chap. 15, where some are denying a future resurrection of believers (15:12).[35] As in that argument, our resurrection is predicated on the resurrection of Christ: "God both raised the Lord, and he will raise us."[36] Both are effected "by his

[32]Basing their comments on Weiss, 160-61, both Bultmann (*Theology*, I, 194-95) and J. A. T. Robinson (*The Body. A Study in Pauline Theology* [London, 1952], p. 29) argue that "body" is Paul's basic term for the whole person, meaning something close to "personality." This has become such a byword in NT studies that almost everyone writing on this text since then has either assumed or explicitly stated that that is what "body" means throughout this passage. But that conjecture has no basis in this passage whatsoever; Gundry has demonstrated convincingly that it is not true of Paul in general (cf. Murphy-O'Connor, "Slogans," 392-93). In this case it totally misses Paul's own concern, which stands over against the false view of the Corinthians that the physical body has no eternal significance.

[33]This is especially where a large number of convoluted interpretations have taken place (see n. 13 above). Cf. Murphy-O'Connor, "Slogans," 394-95, who says of these attempts that "they must be classified as unintelligibly pretentious, or ingeniously imaginative, or intolerably pious."

[34]The idea that the "body of Christ," the church, might also be in view here, even in a secondary way, is completely gratuitous. See Bailey, "Foundation," p. 32.

[35]As long as v. 14 was treated as a separate theological statement, somewhat unrelated to the rest of the paragraph, it was inevitable that one day someone would argue that it was a gloss. See U. Schnelle, "1 Kor 6:14—eine nachpaulinische Glosse," *NovT* 25 (1983), 217-19. Cf. the rebuttal in Murphy-O'Connor, "Interpolations," 85-87.

[36]Some have seen the replacement of the personal pronoun ἡμᾶς for σώματα as evidence that σῶμα here means "whole person" (see n. 32 above). But that is to miss Paul's usage altogether. Here is another case where the *language* is dictated by the *structure* of the parallels. The reason for the shift has to do with his use of τὸν κύριον in the first clause, with which ἡμᾶς is in balance, not σώματα. The context, plus the argument of chap. 15, makes it clear that Paul here intends: God raised the Lord *bodily*, and he will raise us *bodily*. Cf. Gundry, 60; Murphy-O'Connor, "Interpolations," 87.

power" (cf. Rom. 1:4). This affirmation stands in bold contrast to the Corinthian view of spirituality, which looked for a "spiritual" salvation that would finally be divested of the body. Lying behind this form of spirituality is a Greek view of the world that placed little or no value on the material order.[37] Out of such a view developed the idea of the "immortality of the soul," that is, that the spirit is somehow immortal, but the body, along with the rest of the material order, is destined for destruction. This is a totally pagan view; the Christian creed says rather: "I believe . . . in the resurrection of the body." In stark contrast to the Greek view, the OT declares that at creation God looked on the universe that he had made and pronounced it good. The final consummation looks for a new heaven and a new earth; and in that new order the body is raised so that God's people will experience the final wholeness that God intended.

15 In vv. 15-17 Paul explains his reformulation of their slogan "the body is *not* for *porneia,* but for the Lord" by applying it directly to their going to the prostitutes. The argument is in two parts, both introduced by the formula "Do you not know that?" (see on 3:16). V. 15 asserts, on the basis of v. 14, that the bodies of believers are "members" of the "body" of the Lord and therefore cannot be joined to a prostitute, to become "members" of her body. Vv. 16-17 further explain v. 15, asserting on the basis of Gen. 2:24 that in sexual intercourse two bodies become one, which is how a man becomes a "member" of her body. This in turn is contrasted to the union with Christ's "body," now expressed in terms of the Spirit. The result is another chiasm:

A Their bodies are members of Christ's body;
  B therefore, they may not be members of a prostitute's.
  B' Joined to a prostitute they become one body with her;
A' joined to Christ they become one S/spirit with him.

The argument is tight: Both are "bodily" relationships that imply a form of "union," the one with Christ through his resurrection; the other with the prostitute through intercourse. Paul's point, of course, is that the two are mutually exclusive; therefore they must "flee from sexual immorality" (v. 18).

The assertion of v. 15 flows directly out of the theological formulation of v. 14. Paul argues that their *bodies* (i.e., the bodies of all believers individually) "are members of Christ himself"; therefore they may not take

---

[37]Hurley, 80-86, argues quite unconvincingly that the present passage is addressed to Jewish converts. But he appeals to nothing in *this* text as supporting such a view; rather, he urges that such might be true elsewhere (which is most unlikely) and therefore should be so here as well. See n. 12 in the Introduction (p. 4).

away from[38] Christ what is united to him and "make them members of a prostitute."[39] The word "members"[40] is a term for the parts of the body, thus suggesting in a metaphorical way that the believer is an integral part of the "body" of Christ. This usage, however, moves in a completely different direction from that in 12:12-26,[41] where the "body" refers to the church, and the concern is with the relationship of the "members" to one another. Here the concern is with one's relationship to the Lord himself. The body of the believer is *for* the Lord because through Christ's resurrection God has set in motion the reality of our own resurrection. This means that the believer's physical body is to be understood as "joined" to Christ's own "body" that was raised from the dead.[42]

Paul's thinking here is fluid, but it is not strained. His concern throughout has the double foci of their view of the body and of *porneia*. He is arguing that the physical body counts; it is *for* the Lord. The resurrection has absolutely determined that. He is also aware that the seventh commandment has never been abrogated, that sexual immorality is absolutely wrong. Since sexual immorality involves bodily union, he gets at the prohibition of the one (sexual immorality) through metaphorical implications from the other (the "parts" of the body). Thus, joined to Christ himself through the resurrection, it is unthinkable ("God forbid!" KJV; NIV, "Never!")[43] that one

[38]Gk. ἄρας; "take up" or "take away," not simply "take," which would be λάβων. Cf. Lightfoot, 216, et al.

[39]This literal rendering of the text shows the linguistic connection between the two parts of the sentence missing in the NIV's "unite them with a prostitute."

The question as to whether the problem involves temple or brothel prostitution is moot. In favor of the former is the use of temple imagery in vv. 19-20 and the apparently close tie between idolatry and committing sexual immorality in 10:7 and 8, plus the similar prohibitions in 6:18 and 10:14. On the other hand, temple *prostitution* as such is unknown in the Greek city-states. See Murphy-O'Connor, *Corinth*, 55-57. Most likely, therefore, this refers to brothels or courtesans.

[40]Gk. μέλος, referring specifically to the "limbs" and "organs" of the body. Once "body" came to be used metaphorically, this word naturally followed. See J. Horst, *TDNT* IV, 555-68.

[41]This has been commonly suggested. See, e.g., L. Cerfaux, *The Church in the Theology of St. Paul* (ET, New York, 1959), pp. 279-80; B. M. Ahern, "The Christian's Union with the Body of Christ in Cor, Gal, and Rom," *CBQ* 23 (1961), 202; Kempthorne, "Incest," pp. 570-72; Bailey, "Foundation," pp. 35-36.

[42]Those who try to connect this passage with 12:12-26 not only miss this very significant difference, but also then miss the point of the present argument.

[43]Gk. μὴ γένοιτο; the first appearance in the extant letters, and the only appearance in 1 Corinthians. It is thoroughgoing in Galatians and Romans. The phrase is common in the diatribe. But see A. J. Malherbe, "MH ΓΕΝΟΙΤΟ in the Diatribe and Paul," *HTR* 73 (1980), 231-40, who has argued that its use in Paul is very little like the diatribe in general, but is like Epictetus's use in particular, where it functions not as the termination of an argument, but rather as a transition: "It may therefore be the case that this way of rejecting an objection or false conclusion is more characteristic of the type of schoolroom instruction in which Epictetus engaged than street corner preaching" (p. 239).

should "take away" a part of the body of Christ and make it a part of the body of a prostitute.

16-17 With a repetition of the formula "Do you not know that?" Paul proceeds to explain v. 15, starting with the sexual union of a man with a prostitute. Since it is unthinkable that one should take away the "limbs" of Christ and make them "limbs" of a prostitute's body, what could have prompted the latter idea in the first place? The answer has to do with the biblical view of sexual intercourse: "He who unites himself[44] with a prostitute[45] is one with her in body." How so? "Because[46] it is said,[47] 'The two will become one flesh.' "[48] While the union of man and wife as "one flesh" implies far more than merely physical union,[49] Paul's concern here is strictly with the physical aspects of the union.[50] To have sexual intercourse with a prostitute involves an illicit sexual joining of one's body to that of another (literally). It is not the sexual union itself that is incompatible with union

---

[44]Gk. κολλώμενος; the verb in Gen. 2:24 is προσκολλᾶσθαι. Since the non-compounded form does not ordinarily imply sexual imagery, some scholars have argued that Paul "by simply removing a prefix, takes the directly sexual reference away from these two verses" (J. I. Miller, "A Fresh Look at I Corinthians 6.16 f.," *NTS* 27 [1980], 127; cf. Miguens, "Christ's 'Members,'" pp. 44-45). But that is to miss Paul's point completely. First, the noncompounded form is used for a similar relationship with a harlot in Sir. 19:2; second, the choice of this verb, which can go either way, is predicated on the second sentence, the relationship with Christ, where the verb from Genesis would be less appropriate.

[45]The Greek text has the article, "*the* prostitute." She is no longer thought of as an individual, but as a member of a class.

[46]Gk. γάρ; clearly explanatory here.

[47]Gk. φησίν; a common classical idiom, but found only here as an introductory formula in the Pauline letters. Ellis, *Use*, p. 23, suggests, without argument, that Paul intends God as the speaker, even though the OT does not so indicate. However, Paul's use of φησίν in 2 Cor. 10:10 is almost certainly impersonal and argues for such a meaning here.

[48]Paul is citing the LXX, which, along with the Samaritan Pentateuch and the Targum of Jonathan, adds the words οἱ δύο. Hurley, 109-10, argues that Paul is here responding to Jewish Christians who have rejected the Mosaic law; hence his appeal to Gen. 2:24 is an appeal to "pre-fall material," which Paul classed "differently from the Law and retained as a foundational element in his thought." Both this assertion and the presupposition on which it is based cannot be substantiated exegetically.

[49]See esp. Eph. 5:25-33. Because this is true, and especially because of the widely held view that σῶμα refers to the "whole person" (see n. 32 above), some have argued that the greater union is also in view here. See, e.g., R. Batey, "The ΜΙΑ ΣΑΡΞ Union of Christ and the Church," *NTS* 13 (1966/67), 270-81; cf. W. J. Bartling, "Sexuality, Marriage, and Divorce in 1 Corinthians 6:12-7:16: A Practical Exercise in Hermeneutics," *CTM* 39 (1968), 362. Despite the use of the same text from Genesis, however, the application in Ephesians has such a different point from this one that Batey's argument for this text is nearly irrelevant. Even further off the mark are the questions by T. A. Burkill, in response to Batey, since they assume concerns on Paul's part that are either unfounded or quite beside the point of this text. See "Two into One: The Notion of Carnal Union in Mark 10:8; 1 Cor. 6:16; Eph. 5:31," *ZNW* 62 (1971), 115-20.

[50]*Contra* Hurley, 102-07.

with Christ; it is such a union *with a prostitute*. This constitutes bodily union with a person who is not herself a member of Christ, whose own body therefore is not destined for resurrection.

In a parallel sentence, with "Lord" substituted for "prostitute" and "spirit" for "body," the illicit union is now contrasted to the believer's union with Christ: "But he who unites himself with the Lord is one with him in spirit." In light of vv. 19-20, Paul probably is referring to the work of the Spirit, whereby through the "one Spirit" the believer's "spirit" has been joined indissolubly with Christ.[51] The believer is united to the Lord and thereby has become one S/spirit with him (see on 5:3-4). This does not mean that Paul is now abandoning his concern over the body; vv. 18-20 indicate that he is not. As with v. 13c above, this is another instance where the language has been dictated by its parallel. Since the union to which this is in contrast was constituted through sexual intercourse, he could scarcely describe it in terms of becoming "one body" with the Lord. Even though the concern is still with the physical body of the believer that belongs to the Lord on the basis of his resurrection, the union in this case is of a different kind; the way to express that union is in terms of the Spirit.

Thus Paul's point is singular. It does not have to do with the union of whole persons in sexual relations—which is true in marriage but irrelevant here; nor does it have to do with the "mystical" union of the believer to Christ, and through Christ to his body the church—which is also irrelevant here. Paul's point is that the physical union of a believer with a prostitute is not possible because the believer's body already belongs to the Lord, through whose resurrection one's body has become a "member" of Christ by his Spirit.

18 To this point Paul has been arguing against the pneumatics' invalid theological slogans. Inherent in that argument was the prohibition now explicitly stated:[52] "Flee from[53] *porneia*." An identical prohibition of idolatry appears in 10:14. The express statement of 5:9-11 implies that both of these are matters to which Paul had previously spoken; the present argument and that of chaps. 8–10 suggest that they had taken exception to his former rulings. In both cases he replies first to their theological stance; but

---

[51]Cf. Dunn, *Baptism*, pp. 123-24. For a considerable argument against those who would see this usage as contrasting "spirit" with "body," with the latter being a lesser union, see Gundry, 65-69. Such an idea is so foreign to the context that one wonders how anyone could have convinced himself/herself of its validity.

[52]Conzelmann, 112, suggests that v. 18 "gives the impression of an intrusion: a rational argument inserted into the pneumatological argument of vv. 17 and 19." But this misses the urgency of the situation, not to mention the connection with the rest of the context, which has to do with sinning against one's body, which is "for the Lord."

[53]Gk. φεύγετε; present imperative, implying "keep running from." Cf. 2 Tim. 2:22 and Gen. 39:12.

also in both cases there can be no wavering on the behavior itself. They must absolutely "flee from sexual immorality."

But prohibition is never Paul's final word. So he offers one further theological reason, closely related to what has already been said. "The body is for the Lord," he had postulated. Now he argues that sexual immorality in particular is a sin against one's own body, which is "for the Lord" because it is also a "temple of the Spirit." All of that can be easily discerned; however, the argument is introduced by a notorious crux that is not at all easy.

With a double asyndeton Paul says (literally): "Flee from sexual immorality. Every sin, whatever it is a man commits, is outside the body, but he who commits sexual immorality sins against his own body." Paul's concern is with the final clause, that in sexual immorality a man sins against his own body—which turns out to be his own but not his own. But what did he intend by the preceding clause which set that up? The problems are two: (1) The phrase "*every* sin, whatever it is that a man commits" is especially strong. Taken at face value it would seem to include even sexual immorality, which makes the next clause difficult. Moreover, the statement has long exercised Christians, who see other sins as also "against one's body."[54] (2) That leads one to ask what "outside the body" means, especially since the next clause specifically singles out sexual immorality as being *against*[55] one's own body.

Although Allo suggests that as many as 20 or 30 solutions have been offered, the viable options may be narrowed to two.[56] The first is to see the first clause as a Corinthian slogan, which Paul then qualifies in the second clause, as in vv. 12-13.[57] This would go something like: "All sin, whatever it is that a man commits, is outside the body," you say (or, you say?). "To the contrary, there is one sin in particular that is against one's own physical body, namely sexual immorality." There are several things in favor of this

---

[54]This is the most common difficulty. See the expression of it in Best, *One Body*, p. 75, who mentions drunkenness, gluttony, and suicide as sins "against the body."

[55]Gk. εἰς, the ordinary idiom with the verb ἁμαρτάνω. It is just possible, as Gundry, 73, argues, that the sense of "within" is intended, as opposed to ἐκτός, "without."

[56]As noted above, to make the "body" refer to the "body of Christ, the church," does not seem viable. See esp. Kempthorne, "Incest," p. 572; and K. Romaniuk, "Exégèse du Nouveau Testament et ponctuation," *NovT* 23 (1981), pp. 199-205. The difficulties in making sense of "his own body" in the second clause are what defeats this option, not to mention its lack of support from the context itself.

[57]Apparently this was first suggested by W. J. Conybeare and J. S. Howson, *The Life and Epistles of St. Paul* (New York, 1874), II, 43. More recent advocacy can be traced to Moule, 196-97. The most thorough argument in its favor is Murphy-O'Connor, "Slogans." Cf. Hurley, 112-14, and the commentaries by Murphy-O'Connor, 50-51, and Thrall, 49. Both Kempthorne and Romaniuk (see the preceding note) also favor it, although the latter argues that it should be read as a question.

option: (1) Paul has already argued with positions of theirs in the present context; (2) it has formal similarity with vv. 13-17, where he cites their slogan, then qualifies it and elaborates on the qualification theologically (vv. 13ab/13c-14/15-17 and 18b/18c/19-20); (3) it preserves the unqualified sense of "all sin"; (4) it corresponds to the generic use of *anthrōpos* ("man") in the slogan in 7:1 (cf. 7:26); and (5) it gets Paul off the hook for having made what appears to be a less than precise theological dictum. On this view their sentence would mean: "The body has nothing to do with sin."[58] This is an attractive option, and may well be right. Nonetheless it is an abrupt word to follow the prohibition,[59] there are no immediate internal clues to suggest it,[60] and the emphasis on "his *own* body" does not seem to respond to their slogan as such, which emphasizes the noncorporeal nature of all sin.[61]

The second option is to see it as a Pauline construct, formulated in the larger context of vv. 13-20 and especially as a means of setting up by way of contrast the real concern, that "he who sins sexually sins against his own body." In this view the *de* ("but") is exceptive, qualifying "every sin" to mean "every other sin" except the one spoken of in this clause. Paul's urgency, however, is not with "other sins"; rather, he is arguing that "every other sin is apart from the body" in the sense that no other sin is directed specifically toward one's own body in the way that sexual immorality is. How so? The answer lies with what has already been said in vv. 15-17 in light of what he will say about "one's own body" in 7:4. His concern is not with what affects and does not affect the body per se, but with the special character of sexual immorality and how that sin is directed especially against the body as "for the Lord." In fornicating with a prostitute a man removes his body (which is a temple of the Spirit, purchased by God and destined for resurrection) from union with Christ and makes it a member of her body, thereby putting it under her "mastery" (v. 12b; cf. 7:4). Every other sin is apart from (i.e., not "in") the body in this singular sense.[62]

[58]Murphy-O'Connor, "Slogans," 393. As he notes, this more than adequately answers Gundry's objection (pp. 73-74) to Moule that if it were a Corinthian libertine slogan, it would need to have said: "All sin is outside the spirit."

[59]At this point the formal correspondence with vv. 13-17 is not quite precise, since this paragraph *begins* with the prohibition, to which this statement as a Corinthian slogan does not seem to have an immediate connection.

[60]If it were a quotation from them, of course, they would not find it as abrupt as we tend to.

[61]This is the primary objection in B. Byrne, "Sinning against One's Own Body: Paul's Understanding of the Sexual Relationship in 1 Corinthians 6:18," *CBQ* 45 (1983), 608-16.

[62]Cf. Byrne, "Sinning," who would add a nuance to "body" from an insight of Käsemann's to the effect that the body is the tangible vehicle of communication between people.

That this moves in the direction of Paul's intent seems verified by the argument in vv. 19-20, which flows directly out of this one. Even though the body is "one's own," it is more properly God's since it is a temple of the Spirit and has been purchased through redemption. Thus the unique nature of sexual sin is not so much that one sins against one's own self,[63] but against one's own body as *viewed in terms of its place in redemptive history*.

19-20   With yet another "Or do you not know that?"[64] Paul gives theological justification for the prohibition of v. 18a and theological explanation of v. 18bc. At the same time the content of this question serves to reinforce and elaborate the theology of the body expressed in vv. 13-17. With the use of two images (temple and purchase of slaves = the Spirit and the cross) he reasserts that the body in its present existence belongs to God. Thus the body is included in the full redemptive work of Christ—crucifixion, resurrection, and the present work of the Spirit. All of which leads to the final inferential imperative: They must therefore glorify God in their bodies, which of course in this context means no sexual immorality.

The tie to what has immediately preceded is achieved with the conjunction "or" (again omitted from the NIV). "The one who sins sexually sins against his own body," he has just affirmed, by which he means his own body as it is "for the Lord." "Or do you not know that your body[65] is a[66] temple of the Holy Spirit,[67] who is in you, whom you have received from God, and that you are not your own?" As in this translation, the final clause should be included in the question.[68] The two parts complement each other. The body is the present habitation of God's Spirit, which means by implication that one belongs to the God whose Spirit dwells within. At the same time the second part results in a shift of metaphors, so that God's proper ownership of the body is affirmed in terms of their being "bought at a price." The emphasis, therefore, is especially on the body as "for the Lord" in the sense of being God's rightful possession, which is evidenced both through the indwelling Spirit and the redemptive work of Christ. This, of course, stands in stark contrast to the pneumatics' view that the body is destined for destruction and therefore has no present or eternal significance.

[63]This is the position of those who see the body here as representing the whole person. It may be profoundly true, but it simply is not Paul's point.

[64]See on 3:16; see esp. vv. 2, 3, 9, 15, and 16 in the present and preceding sections.

[65]Gk. τὸ σῶμα ὑμῶν. For the grammar see Turner, *Syntax*, pp. 23-24; this reflects semitic preference for a distributive singular, where "something belonging to each person in a group of people is placed in the singular." Cf. Rom. 8:23.

[66]Probably "*the* temple," another illustration of Colwell's rule (see on 3:16).

[67]On the possibility that this imagery is prompted by temple prostitution, see n. 39 above. Cf. Gundry, 76.

[68]This is not demanded by the Greek text, but makes far better sense of it. See Findlay, 821; Barrett, 151.

In referring to the body as the temple of the Spirit, Paul has taken the imagery that properly belongs to the church as a whole (cf. 3:16; 2 Cor. 6:16; Eph. 2:21-22) and applied it to the individual believer.[69] On the imagery itself, see on 3:16. The use of the possessives reflects something of the difference. The church through the Spirit is *God's* temple in Corinth, in contrast to all the pagan temples and shrines. Through the phenomenon of the indwelling Spirit, Paul now images the body as the *Spirit's* temple, emphasizing that it is the "place" of the Spirit's dwelling in the individual believers' lives. In the same way that the temple in Jerusalem "housed" the presence of the living God, so the Spirit of God is "housed" in the believer's body. This is imagery pure and simple, in which the significance of the body for the present is being affirmed; it is not intended to be a statement of Christian anthropology, as though the body were the mere external casing of the spirit or Spirit.

The Spirit's indwelling is the presupposition of the imagery, reinforced here by the two modifiers, "who is in you"[70] and "whom you have received[71] from God." What Paul seems to be doing is taking over their own theological starting point, namely that they are "spiritual" because they have the Spirit, and redirecting it to include the sanctity of the body. The reality of the indwelling Spirit is now turned against them. They thought the presence of the Spirit meant a negation of the body; Paul argues the exact opposite: The presence of the Spirit in their present bodily existence is God's affirmation of the body.

Paul moves easily from the fact that the Spirit is "from God" to his final point: Do you not know that the presence of God's Spirit in you means that "you are not you own," that is, that your bodies are not your own to do with as you wish in the matter of sexuality? This is the final punctuation of the original affirmation that the "body is for the Lord." As evidence for this final assertion,[72] Paul shifts metaphors once more, this time to the slave market, imagery to which he will return in the concrete situation of the slave in 7:22. That passage makes it clear that the imagery here is that of slavery; the verb "bought"[73] with its accompanying genitive of quantity, "at a

---

[69]Otherwise Kempthorne, "Incest," pp. 572-73; see the refutation in Gundry, 76.

[70]Gk. ἐν ὑμῖν; in contrast to 3:16 this is distributive, referring to the Spirit in the life of each of them.

[71]The Greek has simply οὗ ἔχετε ἀπὸ θεοῦ ("which you have from God"), but since the emphasis here is not on "possession" but source, the addition "received" is legitimate.

[72]The sentence has an explanatory γάρ, omitted in the NIV.

[73]Gk. ἀγοράζω. On the use of this verb in slave "buying" see the discussion by W. Elert, "Redemptio ab hostibus," *ThLZ* 72 (1947), 267; see also the discussion in Bartchy, 124 n. 450.

price," places it squarely in the slave market.[74] In contrast to the use of this metaphor elsewhere in the NT, where redemption for freedom is in view (e.g., Gal. 3:13; 4:5; Rev. 5:9; 14:3), this passage images their new position as "slaves" of God, bought with a price to do his will.[75] Although some have argued otherwise,[76] the related usage in Galatians and especially the liturgical passage in Rev. 5:9 indicate that Paul has the cross in view, whereby at the "cost" of his life ("by your blood," Rev. 5:9) Christ purchased us for God. His point here is that even the body is included in that purchase. Thus at the end of the argument he joins the cross to the resurrection, along with the present gift of the Spirit, as evidence that the "body is for the Lord, and the Lord for the body."

The final imperative flows directly out of the argument from the two preceding images. The body is the shrine of the indwelling Spirit and is therefore not one's own but God's, who purchased it through the work of the cross. "Therefore[77] honor[78] God with[79] your body." At the same time, it serves to bring the entire argument to its conclusion. This is the positive side of the imperative of v. 18a: "Flee from sexual immorality." Because the body is God's, one must *not* use it in illicit intercourse; instead, one must make it a chaste temple whereby to honor God.

The later addition of "and in your spirit, which are God's"[80] may have been the result of early Christian liturgy, as Lightfoot (p. 218) suggests. Unfortunately, it also became Scripture to generations of Christians and had the net result of deflecting Paul's point toward the position of the Corinthian pneumatics. Not that the addition is untrue; rather, it completely misses the concern of the present argument, which stands over against the Corinthian view that the body counts for nothing and therefore it does not matter what one does with it. To the contrary, Paul argues throughout, the

---

[74]Otherwise, Deissmann, *LAE*, pp. 318-30, who argues that the imagery of sacral manumission of slaves, such as one finds at Delphi, is in view, thus emphasizing the "purchase for freedom" aspect of the metaphor. In this he has been followed by BAGD and others (e.g., Bailey, "Foundation," pp. 33-34), but this has been thoroughly refuted by Elert (see the preceding note) and others. For a overview of the discussion, see Bartchy, 121-25; cf. Conzelmann, 113.

[75]Cf. D. H. Field, *NIDNTT* I, 267-68.

[76]E.g., Conzelmann, 113. While it is true that the metaphor "is not developed," it is too restricting to assert further "that the metaphor should not be pressed." It is not a question of "pressing" a metaphor, but of recognizing what is inherent in the use of the metaphor in the first place.

[77]Gk. δή; used with the imperative to strike a note of urgency. Cf. R-P, 129, "be sure to glorify."

[78]Gk. δοξάζω.

[79]Gk. ἐν; more likely Paul intends "in your body," that is, in the personal activities of the body. Cf. Parry, 107 ("the ἐν perhaps not strictly instrumental, but to mark the sphere of action"); Findlay, 822.

[80]See n. 7 above.

body is included in the redemptive work of God and therefore may not be involved in sexual immorality.

Two points from this passage need to be emphasized in the contemporary church. First, in most Western cultures, where sexual mores have blatantly moved toward pagan standards, the doctrine of the sanctity of the body needs to be heard anew within the church. Sexual immorality is still sin, even though it has been justified under every conceivable rationalization. Those who take Scripture seriously are not prudes or legalists at this point; rather, they recognize that God has purchased us for higher things. Our bodies belong to God through the redemption of the cross; and they are destined for resurrection. Part of the reason why Christians flee sexual immorality is that their bodies are for the Lord, who is to be honored in the deeds of the body as well as in all other behavior and attitudes.

Second, this passage needs to be heard again and again over against every encroachment of Hellenistic dualism that would negate the body in favor of the soul. God made us whole people; and in Christ he has redeemed us wholly. In the Christian view there is no dichotomy between body and spirit that either indulges the body because it is irrelevant or punishes it so as to purify the spirit. This pagan view of physical existence finds its way into Christian theology in a number of subtle ways, including the penchant on the part of some to "save souls" while caring little for people's material needs. The Christian creed, based on NT revelation, is not the immortality of the soul, but the resurrection of the body. That creed does not lead to crass materialism; rather, it affirms a holistic view of redemption that is predicated in part on the doctrine of creation—both the physical and spiritual orders are good because God created them—and in part on the doctrine of redemption, including the consummation—the whole fallen order, including the body, has been redeemed in Christ and awaits its final redemption.

III. IN RESPONSE TO THE CORINTHIAN LETTER (7:1–16:12)

With the words "Now for the matters you wrote about," Paul moves on to the second part of the letter, his response to a letter from Corinth. For the perspective on that letter from which this commentary proceeds, see the Introduction, pp. 6-10. Rather than a friendly exchange, in which the new believers in Corinth are asking spiritual advice of their mentor in the Lord,[1]

---

[1]This is the perspective of the vast majority of commentaries; but for any number of reasons it does not seem to be an adequate understanding of the various data of 1 Corinthians itself. See the Introduction.

their letter was probably a response to Paul's Previous Letter mentioned in 5:9, in which they were taking exception to his position on point after point. In light of their own theology of spirit, with heavy emphasis on "wisdom" and "knowledge," they have answered Paul with a kind of "Why can't we?" attitude, in which they are looking for his response.

So he takes up the items in their letter one by one, most of them introduced by *peri de* ("now about"; 7:1, 25; 8:1 [cf. 8:4]; 12:1; 16:1, 12), and at an appropriate place inserts one more item about which he had been informed (11:17-34). Since there is a certain logic to the whole presentation, the present sequencing is probably Paul's own and is not dictated by their letter. The matters on marriage in chap. 7 follow directly from the concerns over sexual immorality in 5:1-13 and 6:12-20; chaps. 8–10 return to the matter of "idolatry," specifically that of eating meals in the pagan temples, which has a large number of affinities to the issue of "sexual immorality" in 6:12-20 (see on 5:10-11). This item of "false worship" is followed by a series of items dealing with Christian worship (11:2-16, which sets up 11:17-34, followed by the issue of tongues in worship in 12–14). This in turn is followed by the matter of their denying the resurrection of believers, which is a key theological issue behind chaps. 12–14 as well as much of the rest of the letter. Chap. 16 then takes up a number of "house cleaning" items, some of which also come from their letter. Not every item is equally combative (e.g., chaps. 8–10 are much more so than 7:1-24 or 7:25-40); nonetheless in every case he takes exception to *their* position, or at least to the position of some among them who have influenced the whole.

A. MARRIAGE AND RELATED MATTERS (7:1-40)

The first two items Paul takes up (7:1-24 and 7:25-40) are directly related to each other as well as to the issue in 6:12-20. Both sections deal with matters related to marriage (sexual relations, divorce, second marriages, marriage itself). What is less clear is *how* the two sections are related to each other, not to mention the relationship of the individual items within each; indeed, the traditional interpretation (found, e.g., in Findlay or Grosheide) tends to see most of the argument as a digression from the basic question as to whether people should get married or not.[2] But for several reasons that is an inadequate view. Unless there are convincing reasons to the contrary, a recon-

---

[2]A few have seen the issue to be whether or not sexual intercourse within marriage is desirable (see Lietzmann, 29; Héring, 48). In more recent years this view has often taken the form of the Corinthians' asking four separate questions about marriage and divorce. See Hurd, 157.

struction that evidences an inner logic to the whole, as is usual in Paul, is to be preferred.[3]

For such a reconstruction several items need to be noted: (1) On the basis of its usage elsewhere, one may rightfully assume that the *peri de* of 7:25 is to be taken seriously as the start of a different issue from those spoken to in 7:1-24. (2) This is further confirmed by the repeated occurrence of "virgins" (six times) and the verbs for "getting married" (eight times) in 7:25-40, while the former does not appear at all and the latter only twice in 7:1-24. (3) In the former section, vv. 8, 10, and 12 take up items in a kind of sequence that suggests that 7:1-7 should be viewed as the first in that sequence. (4) Although both sections are about "items related to marriage," the controlling motif of Paul's answer is: "Do not seek a change in status." This occurs in every subsection (vv. 2, 8, 10, 11, 12-16, 26-27, 37, 40) and is the singular theme of the paragraph that ties the two sections together (vv. 17-24)—although in each case an exception is allowed.[4] (5) Therefore, even though the issues are slightly different in the two sections, the same theological motivation on the part of the Corinthians almost certainly lies behind their argument in both.

To get at the problem(s) being addressed, one needs first to see the structure of the whole. We may begin with what appears to be the anomaly in the argument, vv. 17-24, whose point seems clear: "Remain in the place you were at the time of your call." What is of interest is that neither of the specifics in that section (circumcision and slavery) is related to the *subject* matter of chap. 7; nonetheless, the thrice-repeated "Let each abide in his/her calling" dominates every paragraph. Thus:

vv. 1-7 —to the married: stay married with full conjugal rights
vv. 8-9 —to the "unmarried" and widows: it is good to remain unmarried
vv. 10-11—to the married (both partners believers): remain married
vv. 12-16—to those with an unbelieving spouse: remain married
vv. 25-38—to "virgins": it is good to remain unmarried
vv. 39-40—to married women (and widows): the married are bound to the marriage; when widowed it is good to remain that way

[3]Among others who attempt such a solution, see W. F. Orr, "Paul's Treatment of Marriage in 1 Corinthians 7," *Pittsburgh Perspective* 8 (1967), 5-22; J. K. Elliott, "Paul's Teaching on Marriage in I Corinthians: Some Problems Considered," *NTS* 19 (1972/73), 219-25; Bartchy, 161-72; G. D. Fee, "1 Corinthians 7:1 in the *NIV*," *JETS* 23 (1980), 307-14; Murphy-O'Connor, "Divorced"; J. Moiser, "A Reassessment of Paul's View of Marriage with Reference to 1 Cor. 7," *JSNT* 18 (1983), 103-22; D. E. Garland, "The Christian's Posture Toward Marriage and Celibacy: 1 Corinthians 7," *RevExp* 80 (1983), 351-62. Not all of these agree on all the details, but they do agree that the two sections deal with essentially different topics and that the whole is a logical, basically consistent argument.

[4]Although in the case of those already married, vv. 1-7, 10-11, and 12-16, the exceptions are more apparent than real. For example, the married woman in v. 10 is "allowed" divorce, provided she remain unmarried or be reconciled to her husband!

This suggests that vv. 1-16 deal basically with those who are already married, or who have formerly been married but whose marriages have been dissolved by death; whereas vv. 25-38 speak to a special group who have yet to be married, to which is added a final word to married women, who are to remain as they are until their husbands' death.

The question that needs to be answered is, Why all this, both the individual sections and the recurring motif? A careful look at each of the parts as outlined above indicates that in both sections there has been some considerable pressure within the church to dissolve or abstain from marriage. Paul's response on both sides is the same: "Stay as you are." For the married there are no real exceptions; here he has the command of the Lord. But for the never-before married and widows/widowers, he allows genuine exceptions, even though singleness is clearly his own preference. Precisely because of his own responses in vv. 1-16, he therefore affirms in the second section that "marriage is no sin."[5] What he does instead is to give his own reasons for singleness—the eschatological urgency of our present existence.

What, then, was the Corinthian position? Almost certainly it was not whether to get married or not (the traditional approach); rather, the answer lies in what appears to be Paul's quotation from their letter in v. 1 ("It is good for a man not to have sexual relations with a woman"), plus his insistence in 7:28 that the "virgin" who marries has not sinned (cf. v. 36). Such a view would put pressure on the married to dissolve their marriages—or abstain from sexual relations within marriage—and on the engaged and widows not to marry at all. What would seem to lie behind this position is once again their present pneumatic existence, which has Hellenistic dualism at its roots and their own brand of "spiritualized eschatology" as its repeated expression. As those who are "spiritual" they are above the merely earthly existence of others; marriage belongs to this age that is passing away. One wonders further whether we do not have here the first evidence for the so-called "eschatological women" in Corinth,[6] who think of themselves as having already realized the "resurrection from the dead" by being in spirit and thus already as the angels (cf. 11:2-16; 13:1), neither marrying nor giving in marriage (cf. Luke 20:35; see the comments on vv. 1-7 and 10).[7]

Two other features about the nature of the argument need to be noted: First, along with 11:2-16, this is one of the least combative sections of the

[5]For a selection of opinions that Paul had a very low view of marriage, see Moiser, "Reassessment," pp. 103-04, and W. E. Phipps, "Is Paul's Attitude towards Sexual Relations Contained in I Cor. 7.1?" *NTS* 28 (1982), 129-30. As the commentary points out, this is to miss Paul by a long way.

[6]See, e.g., R. Scroggs, "Paul and the Eschatological Women," *JAAR* 40 (1972), 283-303; W. A. Meeks, "The Image of the Androgyne: Some Uses of a Symbol in Earliest Christianity," *History of Religions* 13 (1974), 165-208; Bartchy, 127-55.

[7]Cf. Bartchy, 128-32.

letter. Indeed, after the argumentation of 1:10–6:20, this section is altogether placid. Furthermore, also along with 11:2-16, this is one of the least "authority-conscious" sections in all of his letters. Phrases like "I say this by way of concession, not of command" (v. 6), "it is good for them" (vv. 8, 26), "I have no command, but I give my opinion" (v. 25; cf. 40) are not your standard Paul.[8] Second, in a way quite unlike anything else in all his letters, the argument alternates between men and women (12 times in all). And in every case there is complete mutuality between the two sexes.

These two phenomena further support the conjecture that the problem came basically from the "eschatological women." Paul saw clearly, and taught, that in Christ there is neither male nor female (Gal. 3:28), that is, that the old distinctions between the sexes that tended to eliminate women from worship and significance had been broken down by the cross, resurrection, and gift of the Spirit. This was seized by some of the women in this fellowship and taken in some wrong directions. So Paul is responding to them; but he does so, on the one hand, without negating their basic stance in Christ (hence the mutuality throughout), and without yielding to their position, on the other. Indeed, he agrees with one dimension of their position, namely that singleness is preferable, but he totally disagrees with their reasons, hence he finally stands over against them with the strongest kinds of affirmations of marriage.[9]

The net result is a section of considerable importance for the ongoing church, for marriage-related questions are addressed here as nowhere else in the NT. Yet apart from the command in v. 10, the whole is filled with what is acknowledged by the apostle as his personal opinion. That does not mean that it lacks authority or may be disregarded. But much of it functions more at the level of biblical guidelines than biblical mandate, and in using these texts one needs to keep that distinction in view.

1. To the Married (or Formerly Married)—Stay as You Are (7:1-16)

If our reconstruction of the problem is correct, then this first section is basically a response to some who have argued for cessation of sexual relations within marriage on the basis of their slogan: "It is good for a man not to have relations with a woman." Three such situations are addressed: (1) in

---

[8]Cf. the discussion in P. Richardson, " 'I Say, not the Lord': Personal Opinion, Apostolic Authority and the Development of Early Christian Halakah," *TynB* 31 (1980), 65-86, who argues, not altogether persuasively, that this reflects the "rabbi" Paul developing Christian "halakah."

[9]Although recognizing many of the features outlined here, Hurley, 125-41, offers the particularly improbable reconstruction that the concern was basically Jewish and had to do with discarding/not discarding Levitical regulations for purity.

vv. 2-7 Paul forbids the practice of depriving a marriage partner (probably husbands) of sexual relations (which may explain why in 6:12-20 some of them are going to the prostitutes);[10] (2) in vv. 10-11 he forbids those who would eliminate the problem of sexual relations altogether by separating from a believing spouse; and (3) in vv. 12-16 he speaks to the "rest," those who have an unbelieving spouse, and makes basically the same ruling: the Christian should not initiate a divorce.

Since these three issues can all be seen to arise out of the same theological stance quoted in v. 1, it seems most likely that they were all spoken to in the Corinthian letter. That is, on the basis of the slogan that it is *good* not to have sexual relations, they were arguing for abstinence within marriage; and since abstinence might be difficult for some, then divorce was being recommended as a viable alternative—most certainly so when the marriage partner "one touches" is an unbeliever. Not only does Paul say No in each case, but even his exceptions are no real exceptions (temporary abstinence for prayer in the first instance; remaining single or remarrying the same spouse in the case of Christians; and acquiescing to the pagan partner who decides to divorce).

In light of this analysis, then, the question of the place of vv. 8-9 remains. Part of the problem is to determine to whom Paul is speaking. In any case, these verses seem to flow directly out of v. 7; the "unmarried" and widows are spoken to here partly because they provide a natural contrast to the married in vv. 2-7 (how they are to "remain as they are"), and partly in anticipation of this kind of question in vv. 25-40.

a. No abstinence within marriage (7:1-7)

1 *Now for the matters you wrote[11] about: "It is good for a man not to have relations with a woman."*[12] 2 *But because of the instances*[13] *of sexual immorality,*[14] *each man should have his own wife, and*

---

[10]But see Murphy-O'Connor, "Divorced." To illustrate the difficulties with such reconstructions, it may be noted that Murphy-O'Connor and I are in basic—and independent—agreement on both the nature of the problem (i.e., the Corinthian position) and the structure of Paul's answer. Yet he sees the woman as the offended party; I see her as part of the cause of the problem. The differences lie with our understanding of v. 10 (q.v.).

[11]Many of the early versions and the MajT add μοι ("to me"). It is absent in P[46] ℵ B C 33 1739 1881 2464 pc r, which is nearly impossible to account for had μοι been original. This is a clear case of scribes' clarifying an author's intent.

[12]NIV, without quotation marks, "It is good for a man not to marry" (cf. GNB). The third edition mg. reads: Or "It is good for a man not to have sexual relations with a woman." On this translation see the commentary; cf. Fee, "1 Corinthians 7:1."

[13]The Latin tradition alleviated the difficulty of the plural τὰς πορνείας by reading the singular (F G latt sy); cf. KJV, "to avoid fornication"!

[14]NIV: "But since there is so much immorality."

each woman her own husband. 3 The husband should fulfill his marital duty[15] to his wife, and likewise the wife to her husband. 4 The wife's body does not belong to her alone but also to her husband. In the same way, the husband's body does not belong to him alone but also to his wife. 5 Do not deprive each other, unless perhaps[16] *by mutual consent and for a time, so that you may devote yourselves to prayer.[17] Then come together[18] again so that Satan will not tempt you because of your lack of self-control. 6 I say this as a concession, not as a command. 7 I[19] wish that all* people[20] *were as I myself am. But each* person[21] *has his own gift from God; one[22] has this gift, another has that.*

This opening paragraph is crucial to one's understanding of the entire chapter, yet it is full of notorious difficulties that should make any interpreter

[15]Instead of ὀφειλήν ("duty"), the later Syriac versions and the MajT (the 9th c. K and L being the earliest extant Greek evidence) read ὀφειλομένην εὔνοιαν ("the kindness that is her due"). This is the first of several variants in this paragraph in which ascetic elements in the early church influenced the text itself. Not all later Christians shared Paul's view on the obligatory nature of mutual sexual fulfillment in marriage!

[16]NIV, "except." See the commentary on v. 5.

[17]The Syriac versions and MajT (K L again being the earliest Greek evidence) collaborate in adding νηστείᾳ καὶ τῇ ("fasting and") before "prayer." This is the second "ascetic" variant, which in this case runs counter to Paul's own clear instructions. With this addition, abstinence becomes a good thing rather than a concession.

[18]The best text reads ἦτε (P[11vid] ℵ A B C D F G 33 81 365 630 1175 1739 1881 2464 pc b r); the MajT has a reading that goes back as early as P[46] (συνέρχησθε; P[46] P pc have the impv. συνέρχεσθε), which reflects Paul's intent but is unlikely what he actually wrote. This is an assimilation to Paul's usage in 11:20 and 14:23. Was it also ascetically inspired? "Being together" as the norm is stronger than "coming back together."

[19]The NIV tends to leave many Greek conjunctions and particles untranslated. In this case there is variation between a δέ ("now, but," P[46] ℵ* A C D F G 81 326 pc) and a γάρ ("for," B Ψ Maj vg[cl] Cyprian), which is probably another in the string of "ascetic" variants. Here the δέ is almost certainly original (cf. Zuntz, 205; Metzger, 554). By the end of the second century most of the church was reading the text ascetically (= the traditional interpretation). Thus a γάρ in v. 7, which explains why he concedes marriage in v. 6, would be such a natural reading that it is difficult to imagine how anyone would have substituted a δέ—especially since the preceding δέ in v. 6 is already adversative, making a δέ in this clause cumbersome (both would have been adversative to the whole of what had preceded, which explains why the second one was changed).

[20]NIV, "men"; Gk. ἀνθρώπους, which is surely intended to be generic here.

[21]NIV, "man"; since the rest of the argument exhibits a perfect balance between men and women, the NIV is unnecessarily sexist.

[22]For the ὁ μέν . . . ὁ δέ of ℵ* A B C D F G P 6 33 81 630 1739 1881 2464 pc, P[46] and the MajT have ὃς μέν . . . ὃς δέ (favored by Zuntz, 52, on the grounds that it is an Atticism, which scribes would not likely have rejected). The original is almost certainly ὁ μέν . . . ὁ δέ. But since this would otherwise be the only exception to the rule in the NT that the relative, not the article, is used in the indefinite "the one–the other," probably it should be accented ὃ μέν . . . ὃ δέ, referring to χάρισμα, rather than to the differences in people as such.

properly cautious: What is the meaning of v. 1b? Whose statement is it? How then does v. 2 relate to it? What is the force of the prohibition in v. 5? What is the antecedent of "this" in v. 6? And, finally, how does v. 7 respond to the whole?

There are two basic ways of understanding the text, neither of which is totally without difficulties. The traditional view sees the entire paragraph as Paul's position on marriage in general, in response to their query as to its advisability. Thus v. 1b sets forth Paul's basic response as to whether or not one should get married: It is good not to. But that is an ideal that few attain, so as a prophylactic against illicit sexual relations such as he had just addressed in 6:12-20, he encourages them to marry (v. 2). Once married they should give themselves to full conjugal responsibility, with the one exception of mutual, but not prolonged, abstinence for times of prayer. But this is a concession, not a command (v. 6), meaning that marriage (v. 2) is a concession in light of realities, whereas celibacy (v. 1b) is still the ideal. This in effect is the point of v. 7, where Paul wishes that all were celibate as he is; but he recognizes that not all are, so he affirms those who are not. Vv. 8-9 then repeat all this, v. 8 corresponding to vv. 7 and 1b, and v. 9 to vv. 2-6.[23]

According to this view the problem lay within Corinth itself, reflecting a discussion between libertine and ascetic elements.[24] In light of Paul's prior prohibition of sexual immorality (cf. 5:9-10), they had wondered whether sexual intercourse was permitted at all. Although possible, this reconstruction has a large number of difficulties, both in terms of its view of their letter to Paul and in many of the details. Furthermore, it has some difficulty with why Paul would address the question again in a somewhat different vein in vv. 25-38.

The alternative is the one adopted here. V. 1b is seen as a quotation from their letter,[25] with which Paul would be in some agreement.[26] But he

---

[23]Although this is a collage, it represents the view of all the older commentaries (see esp. Godet, Lightfoot, Findlay), as well as many of the more recent ones (e.g., Grosheide, Morris, Conzelmann, Mare).

[24]See Conzelmann, 115.

[25]This view is at least as old as Origen (early 3rd c.). In English it appeared as early as F. W. Farrar, *The Life and Work of St. Paul* (New York, 1879), p. 390. It was adopted, or approved, in several of the earlier commentaries: Goudge, 53; R-P, 132; Parry, 109. Recent advocacy can be traced to J. Jeremias, "Zur Gedankenführung in den paulinischen Briefen: (3) Die Briefzitate in I. Kor 8, 1-13," in *Studia Paulina in Honorem Johannis de Zwaan Septuagenarii* (ed. J. N. Sevenster and W. C. van Unnik; Haarlem, 1953), pp. 151-53. It is probably the currently prevailing view, although D. L. Balch's assertion that "it is generally accepted" is perhaps an overstatement (see "Backgrounds of I Cor. vii: Sayings of the Lord in Q; Moses as an Ascetic θεῖος ἀνήρ in II Cor. iii," *NTS* 18 [1971/72], 352).

[26]C. H. Giblin ("1 Corinthians 7—A Negative Theology of Marriage and Celi-

does not agree with how they are using it. The imperative in v. 5, if taken at face value, does not anticipate deprivation on the part of the "ascetics," but speaks to the actual situation: "Stop depriving one another"—implying that this is what some are doing. Vv. 2 and 6 are crucial. According to this view, v. 2 directs those already married not to go along with sexual abstinence within marriage; rather, they should not only "have their own spouses" but should afford them full conjugal rights (vv. 3-4). The reason for this lies with the *porneia* addressed in 6:12-20. In prohibiting their stance in v. 5, he does allow that temporary, mutually agreed upon abstinence for prayer might be all right, but it should never be the rule. Again the reason is the lack of self-control (= the instances of *porneia* in v. 2), which is now clearly within the marriage relationship. But temporary abstinence is only a concession (the only express concession in the paragraph!); even for something as worthy as prayer it is not a normal part of Christian marriage and is thus not a command. At the end Paul states his own position on the whole matter. He would prefer that they were as he is, and thus could all go along with their slogan, but that is not the reality of Christian existence in terms of gifts. These differ, hence their slogan does not apply to the married state. The married are to stay as they are.

This view seems to be supported by almost all the details in the text itself. It is also supported by the overall structure, which sees vv. 2-5, the heart of the paragraph, as its main point, not a digression after a concession.

1 The new section of the letter is signaled by the opening prepositional phrase, "Now for the matters you wrote about." This "now about" formula appears five more times (7:25; 8:1 [8:4]; 12:1; 16:1; 16:12). Almost certainly these pick up subsequent items in their letter to Paul,[27] but as suggested above not necessarily in order.[28]

The sentence that immediately follows—without prior warning or introduction—is one of the more difficult in the letter, and certainly one of the most misused in the history of the church.[29] The problems are two: (1) What does it mean? and (2) whose statement is it, Paul's or the Corinthian pneumatics'?

---

bacy?" *Bible Today* 41 [1969], 2839-55; cf. *Hope*, pp. 145-49) argues that the quotation also includes v. 2, but both the structure of vv. 2-4 and the lack of a qualifying conjunction in v. 3 speak against this option. Cf. the further objections in Murphy-O'Connor, "Divorced," 603 n. 13.

[27]The only thing comparable to this in the Pauline corpus is found in 1 Thess. 4:9 and 5:1 (but see 4:13). But a letter from Thessalonica to Paul is most unlikely (cf. the commentaries by Best, Marshall, and Bruce).

[28]On the letter itself see the discussion in the Introduction, pp. 6-10 (cf. 5:9 and the introduction to this chapter).

[29]For a brief history of its use, especially as justification for the Christian ascetic tradition, see Phipps, "Attitude."

The first issue can be resolved beyond reasonable doubt. "To touch a woman" is a euphemism for sexual intercourse, for which a comparable English usage would be: "It is good for a man[30] not to have relations with a woman." This is demonstrated both by the linguistic evidence and the universal understanding of it in the early church. The idiom "to touch a woman" occurs nine times in Greek antiquity, ranging across six centuries and a variety of writers, and in every other instance, without ambiguity it refers to having sexual intercourse.[31] There is no evidence of any kind that it can be extended or watered down to mean, "It is good for a man not to marry."[32] Although the phrase "It is good" in this kind of expression may mean morally good, which would fit the Corinthian point of view,[33] more likely in its present Pauline form it means something closer to "It is desirable, or to one's advantage" (cf. vv. 8, 26).[34] In either case, there can be little question that the statement is promoting an ascetic ideal,[35] not simply celibacy per se.

The second issue is more problematic. Traditionally it has been interpreted at face value as Paul's own position, in which he is seen to affirm not only celibacy but a basically ascetic position toward sex and marriage. In this he is viewed as standing over against his own Jewish heritage (Gen. 2:18: "It is *not* good for the man to be alone"),[36] possibly because of his expectation of the nearness of the End (cf. vv. 29-31).[37] Nonetheless, because of the problems already noted in 6:12-20, he accedes to marriage

---

[30]Gk. ἄνθρωπος, the generic term, but intended to be masculine here. The slogan is expressed in the broadest general terms; Paul's qualification will deal with the specifics of husbands and wives.

[31]See Plato, *leg.* 8.840a; Aristot., *Pol.* 7.14.12; Gen. 20:6 (LXX); Ruth 2:9 (LXX); Prov. 6:29 (LXX); Plutarch, *Alex.M.* 21.4; Jos., *Ant.* 1.163; Marc.Aur.Ant. 1.17.6. These are given in English translation in Fee, "1 Corinthians 7:1," p. 308.

[32]See, e.g., Godet, 321; Grosheide, 155; Morris, 105. This is in fact a position held by the cynics. Cf. Stobaeus, *Ecl.* 4.22.28, "It is not good to marry" (οὐκ ἀγαθὸν τὸ γαμεῖν).

[33]Hurd, 160-61, followed by Murphy-O'Connor, "Divorced," 603 n. 11, argues strongly for this meaning, but he fails to take seriously enough the genuine exceptions as to what is καλόν in vv. 8 and 26, and especially that in the latter it is placed totally in the context of what is to their advantage (v. 35) in light of the present distress. This would seem to temper the suggestion that καλός is the antonym of κακός.

[34]Cf. BAGD 3; W. Grundmann, *TDNT* III, 549. Even though such a usage has very little support in the Greek world, it is already found in the LXX (cf. Gen. 2:18; Jon. 4:3, 8).

[35]Schmithals, 235, asserts otherwise, but as Conzelmann observes, "This is to attribute to the community a high degree of ignorance of language and morals—even to the point of stupidity" (p. 115).

[36]Except for Qumran and the Essenes, marriage was the rule in Judaism, both expected and at times thought to be commanded.

[37]See, e.g., Craig, 76.

(v. 2) and insists on full conjugal relationships within that marriage (vv. 3-5). Besides the obvious advantage of taking a text at face value, what else supports the sentence as a Pauline position is the language of the slogan, which has similarities to vv. 8 and 26.[38]

The difficulties with this view, however, seem far to outweigh its advantages. Besides the context and several details that make more sense of it as a Corinthian position, there is the considerable problem that Paul was simply not an ascetic.[39] This is especially so with regard to food and drink (cf. 9:19-23; 10:25-26, 29b-30; Rom. 14). Indeed, in later letters he express-ly condemns asceticism (Col. 2:20-21 and 1 Tim. 4:3) and takes a strongly positive attitude toward marriage (Eph. 5:25-33).[40] Not only so, but in light of his Jewish heritage the idea that marriage might be thought of as a sin in vv. 28 and 36 can scarcely express a Pauline sentiment, but makes a great deal of sense as being over against their point of view.

Most likely, therefore, as in 6:12-13 and 8:1 and 4, Paul is here quoting from the letter itself, if not in actual language at least in sentiment. This also best explains its abruptness following the mention of their letter.[41] If so, here is another expression of their "spirituality" with its negative attitude toward the material world and the body (see on 6:13; cf. 15:12).[42] In such a case, their position would have gone something like: "Since you yourself are unmarried, and are not actively seeking marriage, and since you have denied *porneia* in your letter to us, is it not so that one is better off not to have sexual intercourse at all? After all, in the new age which we have already entered by the Spirit, there is neither marrying nor giving in mar-riage. Why should we not 'be as the angels' now? Besides, since the body counts for nothing, if some wish to fulfill physical needs there are always the prostitutes."

Paul's own attitude toward their slogan is very similar to that in 6:12.

[38]This is the matter that seems finally to convince Conzelmann, 115 n. 10.

[39]Otherwise Dungan, *passim*, whose whole interpretation is based on Paul's alleged asceticism.

[40]The letters are widely held to be inauthentic, 1 Timothy and Ephesians more so than Colossians. For arguments for authenticity see the commentaries by O'Brien on Colossians (Waco, 1982), Fee on 1 Timothy (San Francisco, 1984), and M. Barth on Ephesians (Garden City, 1974). In any case, the thought and content of the letters are thoroughly Pauline; it is well-nigh unimaginable that later "Paulinists" would "correct" their master on this issue, since the entire history of the early church moves in the other direction.

[41]This point is seldom noted by those who advocate the traditional point of view. But in contrast to the rest of the letter, where the new topics are introduced to them in some fashion, this one has the same abruptness as in 6:12.

[42]Other suggested backgrounds for their attitude on the basis of Philonic influ-ence are given by Balch, "Backgrounds," pp. 351-64; and Horsley, "Marriage." Both of these are full of intriguing suggestions but on the whole are less than convincing.

In certain situations, for example, for those gifted with celibacy and vis-à-vis *porneia,* he obviously would salute it, but as a slogan to justify "spiritual marriages," divorce, or not getting married at all, Paul will have none of it. As he will affirm in v. 7, celibacy is a *charisma* ("spiritual gift") and therefore cannot be a higher good than another *charisma,* even though he might have his own personal preferences based on his own experience.

2 This verse is crucial to one's understanding of v. 1b. The "but" with which the sentence begins is clearly adversative to v. 1b. Traditionally it has been held to be a condescension to marriage because of the prevalence of sexual immorality in Corinth. This view, however, runs into considerable difficulties with the *language* of the sentence. More likely it is the beginning of an extended qualification of their position, in which Paul strongly urges that such abstinence as they are arguing for within marriage is strictly forbidden. The structure of vv. 2-4 supports this understanding. After the prepositional phrase "because of the instances of sexual immorality," there are three sets of balanced pairs—each with asyndeton, suggesting that they belong together:

2) Each man should have his *own* wife,	A
and	
Each woman should have her *own* husband	B
3) The husband should give to his wife her due,	A
likewise	
The wife to her husband	B
4) The wife does not have authority over her own body,	A
but her husband does,	
likewise	
The husband does not have authority over his own body,	B
but his wife does.	

If vv. 3-4 were an added explanation to v. 2, as the traditional view maintains, then one would expect some kind of particle or conjunction to make that relationship clear. As it is, the three pairs belong together as a singular qualification to v. 1b, each adding a further dimension to the insistence on full sexuality within marriage.

The reason for this injunction is (literally) "because of the sexual immoralities." This unusual plural has been variously understood,[43] usually as reflecting the enormity of this evil in Corinth itself,[44] and also as implying

---

[43]Cf. the following translations: The NASB renders it literally ("because of immoralities"); NAB ("to avoid immorality"; cf. KJV); NIV, GNB, NEB ("because there is so much immorality"); Lamsa ("because of the danger of immorality"); Norlie ("because of the temptation to impurity").

[44]See, e.g., Lightfoot, 221: "The phrase hints at the profligacy of all kinds which prevailed in the dissolute city."

fornication ("illicit sexual relations between unmarried persons"). The word can certainly denote the latter,[45] but in the immediately preceding paragraph it refers specifically to cases of prostitution. Since the similar phrase in 7:5, "because of your lack of self-control," speaks to those who are already married, it is arguable that because some husbands are being deprived of sexual relations (v. 5a), they are going to the prostitutes.[46] That easily accounts for the plural, which under any circumstances should refer to sexual immoralities that are occurring, not that are anticipated.[47]

His response to their slogan—and remedy for the cases of *porneia*—is (literally): "Let each man be having his own wife, and each woman be having her own husband." This sentence in particular presents considerable difficulties for the traditional view. First, it does not say that people should get married, a verb Paul is obviously willing to use in this section when he intends that (v. 9). Second, there is no known evidence that the idiom "to have a wife" means "to take a wife."[48] In fact this idiom is common in biblical Greek[49] and usually means either to "have sexually" (Exod. 2:1; Deut. 28:30; Isa. 13:16) or simply to *be* married or to be in continuing sexual relations with a man or woman (see esp. 5:1 and 7:29; cf. Mark 6:18; John 4:18).[50] Third, the terms "each man/woman" and "his/her own"[51] should

---

[45]This despite B. Malina, "Does *Porneia* mean Fornication?" *NovT* 14 (1972), 10-17, who has only demonstrated that it does not necessarily mean fornication. Thus he misses Paul's own understanding by a wide mark. Cf. J. Jensen, "Does *porneia* mean Fornication? A Critique of Bruce Malina," *NovT* 20 (1978), 161-84.

[46]Murphy-O'Connor thinks just the opposite. See n. 10 above.

[47]The latter would be suggested by the use of the singular; but the plural, plus the definite article, points to actual occurrences. Cf. M. Hill, "Paul's Concept of 'En-krateia,'" *RefThRev* 36 (1977), 74 n. 24.

[48]When such an idea needs to be expressed it is usually with a form of λαμβάνω. See the Western variant in 7:28 which substitutes λάβῃς γυναῖκα for the γαμήσῃς of the rest. Two texts are instructive here: *T.Lev.* 9:9-10: "Be on your guard against the spirit of promiscuity (τῆς πορνείας), . . . therefore take (λάβε) for yourself a wife (γυναῖκα) while you are still young"; Tobit 4:12: "Beware, my son, of all immorality (πάσης πορνείας). First of all take a wife (γυναῖκα λάβε) from among the descendants of your fathers." In both cases πορνεία (singular) is seen as a reason for getting married (λάβε γυναῖκα). Paul's usage is clearly different from these. Furthermore, the suggestion that a woman "take a husband" is quite foreign to first-century cultures.

[49]It occurs eight times in the LXX (Exod. 2:1; Deut. 28:30; 2 Chr. 11:21; 1 Esdr. 9:12, 18; Tob. 3:8 [BA]; Isa. 13:16; 54:1) and nine times in the NT (Mark 6:18; 12:33 [= Matt. 20:23; 22:28]; Luke 20:28; John 4:18 [twice]; 1 Cor. 5:1; 7:29).

[50]For these data see Fee, "1 Corinthians 7:1," pp. 310-11.

[51]Lightfoot, 221, argues that the distinctions between ἑαυτοῦ and ἴδιον imply that the husband "is considered the lord of the wife"; cf. Grosheide, 155 n. 1. While it is true that Paul is consistent with this usage, and that he does indeed reflect the normal way of speaking in antiquity, to make these kinds of distinctions, which are not warranted by the words themselves, is to fly full in the face of the clearly opposite point of view in vv. 3-4.

mean that Paul intends everyone in the community to get married.[52] Since the rest of the chapter contradicts that, this is read in other ways: to "imply monogamy"[53] or to mean "as a general rule."[54]

When the clauses are taken at face value, however, giving all the words their normal usage, then Paul is saying No to their slogan as far as married partners are concerned. Thus he means: "Let each man who is already married continue in relations with his own wife, and each wife likewise." And that means a *full* conjugal life, which is what vv. 3-5 will now argue in detail. Even though not specifically enunciated here, this is the first in a series of admonitions on "Stay as you are."

3-4 In two balanced pairs of sentences, now marked by chiasm, Paul elaborates on v. 2, that "having one's own spouse" means full, mutual sexual relations. The sentences emphasize two things: (1) that sexual relations are a "due" within marriage (v. 3) because (2) the body is not one's free possession but belongs to one's spouse (v. 4). Although one can make sense of these two emphases in the traditional view (because of the temptation to immorality, marriage must be fully sexual),[55] they are especially understandable if Paul is responding to the rejection of the marriage bed on the part of some. As noted above, this also explains the asyndeton of both pairs: All three sentences belong together as a single, expanded qualification of their position. This also makes sense of the emphasis on mutuality: The way to correct an abuse of mutual relations is not to make demands on the offending party only, but to emphasize the mutual responsibility of each.

The language of obligation, literally "the payment of what is due,"[56] implies that married couples are indebted to one another sexually. Such language has often been found offensive,[57] both by the ascetic (who sees abstinence as a higher good) and the "liberated" person (who sees "obligation" as a demeaning way to speak of such a relationship). This usage, however, is to be explained in light of v. 5, where some are in fact depriving their spouses of sexual relations. Although not primarily a duty, there are times when the duty aspect needs to be heard for the sake of the marriage.

---

[52]Despite every kind of attempt to get around it, the verb ἐχέτω is an imperative and should be so understood.

[53]E.g., R-P, 133; Grosheide, 155.

[54]Hodge, 109; cf. Lenski, 274, who combines the two suggestions.

[55]But it is never made clear why either (1) it was necessary to say this at all (after all, people who get married to fulfill sexual desire would not seem to need this admonition), or (2) Paul makes such a point of mutuality (full sexuality could easily have been stressed without this emphasis).

[56]Gk. τὴν ὀφειλὴν ἀποδιδότω; used frequently in the papyri for the payment of debts.

[57]See the textual variation, n. 13 above.

And Paul's emphasis, it must be noted, is not on "You owe me," but on "I owe you."

The second pair elaborates the first. Not only are sexual relations a "due" within marriage, but they are so because through the unique giving of oneself in Christian marriage one comes under the "authority" of the other. For this verb see 6:12; it implies authority over something in such a way as to do with it as one sees fit.[58] Here the implication is that in the mutuality of sexual relations the body of the one is the "free" possession of the other. But this, too, needs to be heard in light of v. 5. The emphasis is not on "possessing" the body of the other; rather, in marriage I do not have authority over my own body, to do with it as I please. Therefore, one cannot *deprive* the other (v. 5). If we are correct in seeing the problem as stemming primarily from the "eschatological women," then the first concern is that the wife give herself sexually to her husband. But in responding as he does, with emphasis on the full mutuality of sexuality within marriage, Paul puts sexual relations within Christian marriage on much higher ground than one finds in most cultures,[59] including the church, where sex is often viewed as the husband's privilege and the wife's obligation. For Paul the marriage bed is both unitive (cf. 6:16) and an affirmation that the two belong to one another in total mutuality.

5 The prohibition with which this verse begins seems to confirm the point of view argued for to this point.[60] Although it could imply nothing more than "while we are on the subject, do not forbid sex to one another either,"[61] both the verb used to express the prohibition and the concession in the rest of the verse seem to ask too much of such a view.[62] The structure of Paul's sentence, and its emphases, can perhaps best be seen visually:

---

[58]The NIV is less than precise here: "The wife's body does not belong to her *alone*, but *also* to her husband." The italicized words are neither in the text, nor are they implied.

[59]However, see Musonius: "The husband and wife, he used to say, should come together for the purpose of making a life in common and of procreating children, and furthermore of regarding all things in common between them and nothing peculiar or private to one or the other, not even their own bodies. . . . But in marriage there must be above all perfect companionship and mutual love of husband and wife" (transl. C. Lutz, 89).

[60]Even Grosheide, 157, allows that "this shows that there was abstinence in marriage at Corinth," although he does not easily fit that into what he sees as the point of the passage.

[61]Again it is difficult to understand why *this* prohibition, if people were being encouraged to *get* married because of sexual need or as a prophylactic against fornication.

[62]The difficulties for this view can be seen, e.g., in Conzelmann, 117-18, who argues that the prohibition "results from v. 4" as "a prohibition against turning abstinence [Paul's own position] into a matter of principle," but then has considerable difficulty making sense of the rest of the verse.

> Stop defrauding one another (in this matter)
>   *unless perhaps*
>   by mutual consent
>   for a set time
>   *in order that*
>   you may devote time to prayer
>   *and*
>   may be together again
>   *in order that*   (or *lest*
>   Satan might not tempt you   Satan tempt you)
>   *because* of your incontinence

Several grammatical-lexical notes should be made here: (1) Although the present imperative in a prohibition does not demand "Stop defrauding," this is its ordinary sense, in contrast to the aorist subjunctive, which has the sense of "Never defraud." Just as in 4:5, the ordinary nuance of the present tense fits the context perfectly.

(2) The use of the verb "deprive" is especially striking. This is the same verb used in 6:7-8 for the man who had defrauded another. It is a pejorative word for taking away what rightfully belongs to another (cf. Jas. 5:4). Had Paul intended the traditional interpretation, one would have expected the ordinary, "Do not *abstain* from sexual relations."[63]

(3) The particle combination "unless perhaps" implies "a hypothetical modification."[64] Therefore, what follows is intended as a concession—and a hypothetical one at that—to the prohibition. In this case, Paul is thus allowing their point of view, but only by concession, and only under two conditions: that *both* agree to it,[65] and that it be for a set time.[66] This stands quite over against the perspective of the NIV, which implies that the emphasis lies with the exception, rather than with the prohibition itself ("Do not deprive each other except by mutual consent and for a time, so that you may devote yourselves to prayer").

(4) This means further that the purpose clause ("in order that you may devote time to prayer") does not modify the imperative, but the concession with its unexpressed but understood subjunctive.[67] This singular ex-

---

[63] As in *T.Naph.* 8:8: "There is a time for having intercourse with one's wife, and a time to abstain for the purpose of prayer."

[64] Gk. εἰ μήτι ἄν (the ἄν is omitted in P⁴⁶ B r [perhaps the earliest attempt to give it the meaning of the NIV!]); see BDF 376.

[65] Gk. ἐκ συμφώνου ("on the basis of agreement"), a NT hapax legomenon, but see the papyrus examples in MM.

[66] Gk. πρὸς καιρόν, as over against an indefinite time.

[67] Cf. Lightfoot, 221, who would supply γένηται. R. Hanna (*A Grammatical Aid to the Greek New Testament* [Grand Rapids, 1983], p. 295) is considerably misleading here. He indicates that Moule, 145, considers the first ἵνα clause to be imperatival,

pression of purpose for temporary and mutual abstinence from sexual relations may reflect the concern expressed in vv. 33-34. More likely it indicates that the early church placed value on concerted times for prayer, uninterrupted by other normal pursuits.[68]

(5) Grammatically, the verb "may be together again" is a second statement of purpose. However, it is extremely awkward to the sense, so much so that most English translations turn it into an imperative.[69] Most likely the two expressions of purpose conceptually modify the two conditions for temporary abstention; that is, "unless perhaps [it be] by mutual consent so that you may devote time to prayer, and only for a set time so that you may then be together again." In any case, Paul's emphasis lies on this last clause, as is evidenced by the final purpose clause, "so that Satan will not tempt you because of your lack of self-control."

(6) This final clause has been seen as an imperative,[70] but that is not necessary to the sense. This clause is the point of the whole sentence; it modifies the opening prohibition by way of the immediately preceding purpose clause. This is why they must *stop* defrauding one another in this matter—precisely so that it will not put one's spouse at the ready disposal of the Tempter; and that is also why any mutual abstinence for prayer must be for a set time—so that they may be together again and the "defrauded" one not be so tempted.

The net result of all this is (a) that Paul seems almost certainly to be forbidding something that is already going on, and (b) that he altogether eliminates abstention as a normal practice, acceding to it only hypothetically and under certain conditions, on the basis of his Jewish background. His concern is that some have been yielding to the temptations of Satan, the believers' "ancient foe" (cf. Gen. 3:1-15), who is intent on separating people from God through disobedience.[71] The disobedience in this case has

---

which he does not (Moule cites an article by Cadoux in *JTS* [1941], 170, who suggests the *final* ἵνα clause, following Moffatt). Hanna then proposes that "the clause introduced by ἵνα is dependent upon the impv. ἀποστερεῖτε. Consequently, ἵνα has an imperatival sense, although that idea is not inherent within the particle itself ('do not deprive each other . . . except . . . that you may')." This seems to be what lies behind the NIV, but it is grammatically impossible if one reads the ἄν, and improbable even without it.

[68]See *T.Naph.* 8:8, cited above (n. 62). The comment of Sevenster, *Paul,* p. 50, could scarcely be further from Paul's intent ("It is of great benefit to marital relations now and then to set aside time for prayer").

[69]The NEB is an exception, but still makes it an independent clause: "Afterwards you may come together again." The NASB in its wooden literalness is ambiguous.

[70]Moffatt, "You must not let Satan tempt you through incontinence"; cf. n. 66 above.

[71]See H. Seesemann, *TDNT* VI, 23-36; cf. Hill, " 'Enkrateia,' " p. 73. Cf. the story of Jesus' testings in the wilderness, and the final petition of the Lord's Prayer ("but deliver us from the evil one"); cf. 1 Thess. 3:5, where Paul calls Satan "the Tempter."

to do with *porneia* ("sexual immorality"). But Satan can so tempt them only because of their own "lack of self-control,"[72] which leads to incontinence. Thus this final clause leads back to the phrase with which this entire response began (v. 2, "because of the instances of sexual immorality").

6 With the pronoun "this" in the emphatic position, "*This* I say," Paul inserts into the argument that what has just been said is a concession[73] to them (meeting them partway), *not* a command. As with so much else, this sentence is especially difficult for the traditional view, which must make either v. 2[74] or all of vv. 2-5[75] a concession to his own preference for celibacy. The problems with this are several: (1) It makes the "this" jump over the one certain concession in the passage (the "unless perhaps" clause of v. 5, which immediately precedes the pronoun), for something earlier that is not clearly an "indulgence." (2) If it did refer to v. 2 or 2-5 together, then the real concession, it must be pointed out, is not to marriage, but to their incontinence and resultant sexual immoralities. (3) Despite protests to the contrary,[76] the verbs in vv. 2, 3, and 5 are in fact imperatives. If they lack the kind of apodictic expression of "Do this" or "Don't do this," they nonetheless function as "commands" within the present context.[77]

Because of these difficulties, some have argued that this sentence begins the next paragraph (through v. 9) and that the "this" points forward, as often in Paul.[78] But that is not the obvious reading of the text, and it requires the variant "for" in v. 7 (see n. 14) in order for it to work.

As throughout the paragraph, the ordinary sense of the words in their immediate context offers the best understanding of the sentence. Their letter has argued for abstinence from sexual relations within marriage, to which Paul in vv. 2-5a has responded with an emphatic No. That leads to inconti-

---

[72]Gk. ἀκρασία; self-indulgence, not having ἐγκράτεια. On this word group in Paul, and especially its use here and in v. 9, see Hill, " 'Enkrateia.' "

[73]Gk. συγγνώμην; a NT hapax legomenon. In the papyri it more often has the extended meaning of pardon; but in the LXX and Josephus it carries the sense of being indulgent to someone.

[74]E.g., Hodge, 110-11; Findlay, 824; Grosheide, 158; Mare, 229.

[75]E.g., R-P, 135; Morris, 107; Conzelmann, 118.

[76]See, e.g., the assertions in Conzelmann, 118, that "the imperatives must not be pressed." But that is to argue against grammar on the basis of prior conclusions.

[77]Interestingly, Grosheide made this his very point for rejecting the "this" as referring to v. 5, "since the words *by way of concession* do not fit the peremptory words: *defraud ye not*" (158). But the command, of course, is *not* part of the concession, which begins with "unless perhaps."

[78]Orr, "Treatment," p. 11; followed by Garland, "Posture," p. 354, who offer 7:26 and 11:17 as examples. But these are not helpful examples, since in the first case the following ὅτι clause functions epexegetically, "This . . . namely that . . . ," as is most often the case with this idiom in Paul. The example of 11:17 might serve, but one would then need the variant γάρ in v. 7. It is simply not true, however, as Garland maintains (p. 360 n. 23), that if γάρ were original then this τοῦτο must point forward.

nence, he says in v. 5c, and the cases of sexual immorality that already are a plague on your house. So stop defrauding one another in this matter, he commands, unless perhaps there is temporary abstinence by mutual consent at set times for prayer. But[79] *this* is a concession to you; you are *not* to take it as a command. Thus even such a good thing as temporary abstinence for prayer will not be raised to the level of command, precisely because of (1) the difficulties that already persist in the church over this matter, and (2) the fact that such matters belong to the category of "gift" not requirement, as he will go on to say in v. 7.

7 With this sentence Paul brings this first item to its conclusion. This reflection on his own status, and his preference for it both for himself and others, is best explained if the Corinthians themselves had appealed to it in making their own case.[80] "To be sure,"[81] he says, "I wish all people[82] to be as I am."[83] But in sharp contrast to them, who on the basis of his nonmarried state would turn what is at best a questionable principle into law, he qualifies it in terms of spiritual gifts.

What is not clear is precisely what about himself he is referring to. Most interpreters read this in light of vv. 8-9, plus his clear preference in vv. 26-38 for singleness, as a wish on his part that people did not have to get married at all. In light of the argument to this point, however, it is much more likely that he is referring to his actual gift of celibacy, which would mean celibacy in its true sense—not referring to singleness as such (after all, many who are "celibate" in this sense wish they were otherwise), but to that singular gift of freedom from the desire or need of sexual fulfillment that made it possible for him to live without marriage in the first place.

Therefore, despite personal preference for his own status, he recognizes that his celibacy is a *charisma* ("gracious gift"),[84] not a requirement;

---

[79]This view also has the advantage of taking this δέ seriously—as a clear adversative to the immediately preceding concession: ". . . unless perhaps. . . . *But*. . . ."

[80]The traditional view, of course, sees this sentence as capping Paul's argument for celibacy by appealing to his own example. Thus in v. 1 he states a general principle in favor of celibacy. After conceding marriage because of their fallenness, he now comes back to that principle by way of his own personal preferences; but here too he concedes marriage, only now in terms of "gifts."

[81]This is Conzelmann's translation of δέ, which makes more sense of the whole paragraph as sequential than as adversative.

[82]Gk. ἀνθρώπους, again, as in v. 1, the generic term. Does it also imply "men" as such, or is it as elsewhere simply reflecting the basic perspective of the culture? Surely it is the latter.

[83]Barrett, 158, makes the attractive suggestion, based on Paul's usage elsewhere, that he does not intend an unattainable wish here ("I wish it were, but it cannot be"); rather, he is wishing that they all were as he actually is in obedience to his gift. Although this does correspond to Paul's usage, the strongly adversative "but" (ἀλλά) that follows implies that he is referring to status, not to obedience as such.

[84]See on 1:7 and 12:4.

and that places the whole question on an entirely different plane. They were urging celibacy for the married, using his situation as part of the reason for it. But Paul says No; celibacy is for the celibate, and as such it is strictly a matter of *charisma*. Such gifts can neither be reduced to principle, nor can any one of them be required across the board for all, as apparently they were trying to do. Thus he concludes, "Even though I could wish that all were as I am, the fact is that each one has his/her own gift, one gift of one kind, another gift of another kind." In this context it is difficult to avoid the conclusion that sexual life in marriage is the "gift of another kind."[85]

The whole argument, therefore, is summed up in these final words. In another context he will argue that singleness, even without the gift of celibacy in this sense, may be the preferred option for the presently single—but not for their reasons (vv. 25-38). But in the present context he is both affirming his own celibate—and single—status and denying that those who are already married may also be celibate (vv. 2-6) or single (vv. 10-16). They are to "remain as they are." But before he addresses this latter item, this reference to his own situation has caused him first of all to reflect on how that affects some others who are "as he is" but without his gift (vv. 8-9).

Here is a passage that has suffered much in the church, partly because the traditional interpretation has often caused people to approach the text with an agenda in hand different from Paul's own. Interest has been deflected away from his, over no celibacy within marriage, to questions about marriage itself, and especially whether marriage might be a less "spiritual" calling than celibacy. Thus the truly "spiritual" are celibate; for the rest there is the "concession" to marriage, which exists basically to curb illicit desire. But Paul would have none of this. For him both marriage and celibacy are gifts, and despite his own preference for his gift, he certainly does not raise it to a higher spirituality. That is to fly full in the face of the text itself.

On the other hand, the real point of the text, the abusing of sexual relationships within marriage, needs especially to be heard anew in the church. Since Paul by the Spirit can be forthright on this matter, so should we. First, the affirmation of sexual relations within marriage as such is a much-needed corrective to some who still follow Augustine and treat sexuality itself as part of the Fall. God made us sexual creatures; and because

---

[85]Moiser, "Reassessment," pp. 106-07, takes a different view. On the basis of Pauline usage elsewhere, he suggests that it "need be no more than a general reference to the different responses of individual Christians, each living the new life in his or her own way in matters where important principles are not at stake." Cf. Dunn, *Jesus*, pp. 206-07. To the contrary, the usage here is so specific that it probably means that we will need to broaden our understanding of what constitute so-called spiritual gifts.

God made us so, sex is good. Within Christian marriage it is the most intimate celebration of life together in Christ. Second, the mutuality of sexual relations, and of marriage itself, also needs to be heard. Too many still treat sex as though it were the privilege of the husband and the duty of the wife. But not so. It is the privilege and duty of both together. Each belongs mutually to the other. In sexual intercourse, as nowhere else, husbands and wives symbolically express both their unity and mutuality. Finally, perhaps it needs also to be noted that v. 5 not only prohibits the "defrauding" of one another in this matter, but also, by the very fact of the mutuality argued for in vv. 3-4, prohibits the holding back of sexual relations as a means of manipulation within the marriage relationship. That both abuses sex and destroys mutual love and respect.

b. Either singleness or marriage for the "unmarried" and widows (7:8-9)

8 *Now to the unmarried and the widows I say: It is good for them to stay unmarried, as I am.* 9 *But if they* are not practicing continence,[1] *they should marry,*[2] *for it is better to marry than to burn.*[3]

The way this paragraph begins is similar in form to the beginning of vv. 10 and 12. Each has a connective *de* ("now"), a verb of speaking or commanding in the first person singular, and the people addressed in the dative. This suggests that Paul is taking up a series of situations to which he will apply the general rule, "Stay as you are."

This first one, however, presents several difficulties, partly because of its location in the argument but mostly because we tend to recoil at what our English translations universally tell us it means: Marriage is a grudging condescension to those who burn with sexual passion and cannot be continent.

---

[1]NIV, "if they cannot control themselves."

[2]Most MSS read γαμῆσαι (including P⁴⁶ B D F G 1739 Maj); ℵ* A C* P 33 81 945 2495 read γαμεῖν. The questions are two: which is original, and whether there is a distinction in meaning. Both Turner, *Syntax*, 79, and Barrett, 159, 161, read γαμεῖν and suggest that it means to be in a married state, rather than simply to get married. Conzelmann, 119, on the basis of 1 Tim. 5:14 and a similar interchange with χωρίζομαι in v. 10, rejects that nuance for the present tense. However, his use of the variation in v. 10 is irrelevant (despite his exclamation point) since the same nuance could have prevailed for the copyists there as well. Even the passage in 1 Timothy may be putting emphasis on living in the married state rather than on simply getting married. What cannot be known is whether such nuances influenced either Paul or subsequent scribes. Since internal evidence is not decisive (scribes may have conformed an aorist to the following present, or a present to the preceding aorist), the external evidence tends to prevail here in favor of γαμῆσαι.

[3]NIV, "burn with passion."

Unfortunately, what Paul himself intended is not clear. The first question is the contextual one, What is this passage doing here? The surrounding materials deal in their entirety with those who are trying to dissolve marriage, either by abstinence or divorce. Paul's word to them is to remain as they were at the time of their call. Vv. 8-9, on the other hand, speak to people who are not now married and urge them also to remain that way (v. 8), although a genuine exception is allowed (recommended?) in v. 9. As such this seems to have more in common with vv. 25-38, although the reasons for marriage are not similar. This problem is further complicated by the fact that one cannot be sure either to whom this is addressed or what is the exact nature of the exception in v. 9.

Most likely the contextual question is to be resolved in light of v. 7, where Paul has just spoken both to his own personal preference for celibacy (as a genuine gift of freedom from sexual need) and to his awareness that his is not the only gift. Thus he speaks to those who are in his situation—not now married, but without his gift—before he comes back to the further question of the dissolution of marriages. As such the passage also anticipates the question about the "virgins" in vv. 25-38.

8 The series begins with a word to "the unmarried and the widows." The question is, To whom does the word *agamois* ("unmarried") refer? Traditionally this has been seen as addressing all categories of the unmarried, especially the never-before married, to whom Paul adds the special category of widows. So much is this so that the RSV translated both this word and the word *parthenōn* ("virgins") in v. 25 as "unmarried." But this presents several difficulties. Since from this point of view Paul has already advised the unmarried to get married (v. 2), why this repetition? and why pick it up again in vv. 25-38? The answer usually has been that vv. 1-7 give the general principle, which is now being specifically addressed in these two verses. But that founders on the following sections, which are structurally tied to this one but which do not deal with getting married at all.

On the other hand, several items favor the suggestion that *agamois* should be translated "widowers":[4] First, since being "widowed" in antiquity created special problems for women, most cultures had a word for widows; however, they did not always have a word for the male counterpart.[5] Greek has such a word, but it appears seldom to have been used, and

---

[4]This was suggested, apparently independently, by J. M. Ford, *A Trilogy on Wisdom and Celibacy* (South Bend, 1967), pp. 82-84; and Orr, "Treatment," pp. 12-14. It has been adopted, *inter alia,* by Giblin, *Hope,* pp. 153-54; E. Arens, "Was St. Paul Married?" *Bible Today* 66 (1973), pp. 1188-91; Moiser, "Reassessment," p. 108; and Garland, "Posture," p. 354.

[5]Note that even in English, where in most male/female words the root is male and the female counterpart has the suffix (e.g., host/hostess), widow/widower is precisely the opposite.

never in the *koine* period, in which *agamos* served in its place.[6] Second, since throughout the entire passage Paul deals with husbands and wives in mutuality (12 times in all), it would seem to fit naturally into the total argument to see that pattern here as well. After all, if *agamois* refers to all the unmarried, then why add widows? Third, this word appears again in v. 11 for a woman separated from her husband, and in v. 34 in contrast to the "virgin" (one who was never before married), indicating that in his regular usage it denotes not the "unmarried" in general, but the "demarried," those formerly but not now married. On balance, "widower" seems to be the best understanding of the word here. That would also help to explain the presence of these verses in this context, where all of the cases in vv. 1-16 deal with those presently or formerly married, while vv. 25-38 take up the issue of the never-before married.

To those whose marriages have been dissolved through death, Paul advises that "It is good for them to stay unmarried, even as I do."[7] If our understanding of v. 7 is correct, then it is at least possible that the language "it is good" reflects the Corinthian appeal to Paul's present unmarried state as reason for abstention from sexual relations.[8] In the case of abstention on the part of the formerly married by not getting married, Paul would stand in full agreement (cf. vv. 39-40 for attitudes toward the remarriage of widows). Here is the first specific articulation in the argument of the principle, "Remain as you are." But in v. 9 he also articulates the first genuine exception, namely that such people should get married if they are not living in continence.

9 For many later Christians this has been the troubling verse. Paul is seen to be arguing in v. 8 for all singles to stay that way, then as making allowance for marriage for those who cannot remain continent, for it is better to be married than to be consumed with sexual passion. But it is doubtful whether Paul's point is quite so stark. In the first place, Paul does not say (as

---

[6]See, e.g., LSJ.

[7]The grammar seems to require this sense (cf. RSV, GNB, NAB) rather than the "I am" of the NIV. The κἀγώ assumes the repetition of the verb μένω. Thus: "If they remain as I also remain (unmarried being implied)."

On the thorny question of whether Paul was ever married (which includes the related question of whether he was a rabbi—he almost certainly was, and therefore had to have been married), see J. Jeremias, "War Paulus Witwer?" *ZNW* 25 (1926), 310-12; *idem,* "Nochmals: War Paulus Witwer?" *ZNW* 28 (1929), 321-22; Ford, *Trilogy,* pp. 82-84; Arens, "Married?"; all of these argue that Paul was both a rabbi and a widower. Hurd, 275, thinks otherwise, but his case rests on his dubious reconstruction of the earlier teaching of Paul in Corinth. That Paul is not now married is certain; that is supported both by this text and the normal reading of 9:5. But this passage suggests that formerly he very well may have been married.

[8]A position also argued by Hurd, 166.

the NIV), "if they *cannot* control themselves." Rather he says, "if they do not, or are not practicing continence (or exercising self-control)."[9] The implication is that some of these people are doing the same as some of the married in vv. 1-7, practicing "sexual immorality," that is, probably also going to the prostitutes. The antidote for such sin is to get married[10] instead.

With an explanatory "for" Paul appends a reason: "It is better to marry (or to be married)[11] than to burn." This final word is the difficult one. The usage is clearly metaphorical, but it could refer either to burning with desire or burning in judgment (cf. 3:15). Since both of these can be supported from Jewish sources,[12] that evidence is not decisive.[13] The question must finally be decided contextually, and by Paul's usage in 2 Cor. 11:29,[14] which is almost certainly a metaphor for inner passion. Even though the larger context, including the warning in 6:9-10, could be argued to support the judgment metaphor, such an idea is missing from the immediate context altogether. It seems more likely, therefore, that Paul intended that those who are committing sexual sins should rather marry than be consumed by the passions of their sins.

In this case, then, Paul is not so much offering marriage as the remedy for the sexual desire of "enflamed youth," which is the most common way of viewing the text, but as the proper alternative for those who are already consumed by that desire and are sinning.

---

[9]Not only is this what the verb means, but the conditional clause (εἰ with the present indicative) is present particular, emphasizing the reality of the assumption. Cf. Barrett, 161; M. L. Barré, "To Marry or to Burn: πυροῦσθαι in 1 Cor 7:9," *CBQ* 36 (1974), 193-202; Hill, "'Enkrateia,'" p. 75; K. C. Russell, "That Embarrassing Verse in First Corinthians!" *Bible Today* 18 (1980), 338-41.

[10]Gk. γαμέω, the two occurrences in this verse being the only ones in vv. 1-25 (the occurrence in v. 10 refers not to getting married but to the already married).

[11]See n. 2 above.

[12]For "burning" with sexual desire, see esp. Sir. 23:16 (LXX 23:17) (referring to incest): "The soul heated like a burning fire (πῦρ) will not be quenched until it is consumed; a man who commits fornication with his near of kin will never cease until the fire (πῦρ) burns him up" (RSV). On the other hand, the verb πυρόω is used regularly in the LXX to denote the purifying fire that burns away the dross (e.g., Isa. 1:25; Jer. 9:7; Dan. 11:35). Barré, "Marry," p. 194, suggests that some of these latter texts refer to judgment, which they do; but it is never final judgment, only the judgment that purifies. A closer example is *m.Abot.* 1.5: "He that talks much with womenkind brings evil upon himself . . . and at last will inherit Gehenna" (Danby, p. 446).

[13]This stands over against the study by Barré, "Marry," in which he makes the methodological mistake of tracing only the verb πυρόω and the noun πύρωσις. But since the usage is metaphorical, the search needs to be broadened to include all words for burning to see whether they carry these metaphors as well. They do.

[14]Barré recognizes this and in a further article argues for a similar meaning in this text as well. See "Paul as an 'Eschatologic Person': A New Look at 2 Cor 11:29," *CBQ* 37 (1975), 500-526. But see the refutation in Furnish, *II Corinthians*, pp. 520, 538.

A text like this one is difficult for moderns. But if our interpretation is correct, then its advice is twofold. On the one hand, consistent with the general view in Jewish and Christian antiquity, Paul urges the formerly married to remain in their present single state. He will encourage that again in vv. 39-40. But he also clearly recognizes that that represents what he thinks is "good"; it may not be elevated to the position of a commandment. On the other hand, it is a strong word against the formerly married who are not living in continence. For them, marriage is the proper alternative to their being consumed by their sins.

c. No divorce for Christian partners (7:10-11)

10 *To the married I give this command (not I, but the Lord): A wife must not separate[1] from her husband.* 11 *But if she does, she must remain unmarried or else be reconciled to her husband. And a husband must not divorce his wife.*

This is the second in the series of directives that began with v. 8. It is also the second directive (along with vv. 1-7) to those who are already married to "remain as they are." Just as they may not reject sexual relations within marriage, so they may not dissolve their marriages through divorce.

As throughout the chapter Paul addresses both men and women. The order of Paul's concern, which is addressed first and primarily to the women, lends credence to the suggestion that the problem stems basically from some "eschatological women" (see above, pp. 269-70) who were using their slogan (v. 1b) to reject sexual relations with their husbands (v. 5), and arguing for divorce if it came to that.[2]

---

[1]In place of the more difficult aorist passive χωρισθῆναι read by the majority (incl. P[11vid] ℵ B C Ψ), a few MSS read the present passive (or middle) χωρίζεσθαι (A D F G 1181 2495); P[46] 614 pc have the present impv. χωρίζεσθε.

[2]Cf. Findlay, 825; Moffatt, 78. But see Murphy-O'Connor, "Divorced," who argues the exact opposite, namely that an ascetic husband has divorced his wife and this is Paul's word to the wife that she should resist the divorce, and especially not remarry, for the sake of reconciliation. As Murphy-O'Connor himself recognizes, v. 15 creates difficulties for this view, to which he replies that Paul is simply not consistent. The more traditional approach sees these verses as an answer to a polite inquiry about whether divorce is permissible; but that does not take seriously enough either the order of this answer or its relationship to their slogan in v. 1b. Dungan, 83-93, 128-29, 132, comes to the improbable conclusion that the real point is the exception itself (v. 11a), that is, that "Paul intends a prohibition of remarriage, with this rejection of divorce" (p. 132), "wording to the contrary notwithstanding" (p. 128). But Dungan's exegesis is based on some questionable assertions taken over as fact (e.g., that Paul is an ascetic who barely tolerates marriage [cf. n. 41 on 7:34]; a nonverifiable sense to the present general condition [see n. 23 below]); he also misses the place of the "exception" clauses (eight in all) in the argument as a whole, as well as the prevailing motif to remain as one is, not to mention the structure of these two verses in particular. Yet another view is offered by H. H. Rex,

Paul's response, along with that of Jesus in the Synoptic Gospels, has served as the basis for canon law in the church on the whole question of divorce and remarriage. But one must remember that the original intent of the passage was not to establish canon law but to address a specific situation in Corinth—their apparent rejection of marriage on ascetic grounds. The text needs to be heard in its own historical context before it is applied to broader contexts.

10 In speaking to "the married,"[3] Paul is presupposing in this first instance that both partners are believers. This is made certain by vv. 12-16, where, in a way that balances with vv. 10-11, he addresses "the rest," whom that context defines as believers married to unbelievers. Along with the imperatives in vv. 2-5a, this is the only "command"[4] in the entire chapter. While Paul displays ambivalence toward whether widowers and widows should get married (vv. 8-9), he consistently rejects the notion that the married may dissolve their marriages.

But in saying "I give this command," he remembers that Jesus himself spoke to this question, so he appeals to his authority.[5] It is "not I" from whom this command comes, "but the Lord." This is one of the rare instances in Paul's extant letters when he appeals directly to the teaching of Jesus (cf. 9:14; 11:23; 1 Tim. 5:18), which fact means neither that Paul lacks authority nor that Jesus does not ordinarily count as authority for him. The clue is to be found in v. 12, where in contrast to this parenthetical insertion he says, "I, not the Lord." Christ is always Paul's ultimate authority. When he has no direct command, he still speaks as one who is trustworthy (v. 25) because he has the Spirit of God (v. 40). Two reasons suggest themselves as to why he does not appeal more often directly to Jesus: (1) From his point of view his ethical instructions *all* come from the Lord. If he does not appeal more often to the sayings of Jesus themselves, that is because such teachings are the *presupposition* of his own. The "ways" of Jesus are lived out and taught in the "ways" of the apostle (see on 4:16; cf.

"An Attempt to Understand I Cor. 7," *RefThRev* 14 (1955), 44-46, who suggests that not real divorce, but the "separation" in vv. 1-7, is in view. He reconciles the two by making these verses refer only to the widows and widowers of vv. 8-9.

[3]Moiser ("Reassessment," pp. 108-09) makes a point of the perfect as indicating that they were already married (to a pagan) when converted. That is moot. How else might Paul have addressed the already married if not with the perfect?

[4]Gk. παραγγέλλω (cf. 11:17; 1 Thess. 4:11; 2 Thess. 3:4, 6, 10, 12; 1 Tim. 1:3; 4:11; 6:13, 17). The word is used in almost all cases in the NT with regard to the Christian walk. Cf. O. Schmitz, *TDNT* V, 761-65.

[5]Cf. R. L. Omanson, "Some Comments about Style and Meaning: 1 Corinthians 9.15 and 7.10," *BibTrans* 34 (1983), 135-39, who argues that "the words 'not I, but the Lord' are an afterthought on Paul's part, and to translate this verse as if Paul planned from the outset to exhort the readers with the authority of a teaching of Jesus is to alter subtly the meaning by masking the train of Paul's thought" (p. 139).

11:1). Hence he feels no need for such an appeal. Those ways have already been taught before he writes his letters, so that he simply appeals to prior instructions (cf. 1 Thess. 4:1, 11-12).[6] (2) But for many other issues that arose in the Gentile churches, Paul speaks on his own authority (which of course derives from the Lord), precisely because Jesus did not address such questions. However, in this present matter, on which Paul probably had *not* previously given instruction,[7] there is a Jesus word, so he appeals to it. In vv. 12-16, on the other hand, where the issue lies outside the province of Jesus' own life-setting, it is Paul who speaks, not the Lord.[8]

As to the "saying" itself, it is irrelevant to pursue its precise origins in the tradition[9] since Paul's concern is with the point of the saying, not its language.[10] The divorce sayings come to us in two forms: one in Mark 10:11 (// Matt. 19:9) and one in the double tradition (= Q; Luke 16:16 // Matt. 5:32). In each case the form is casuistic law (If, or Whoever . . . then . . .), and the matter that Jesus ultimately addresses is the seventh commandment, not the divorce provision per se. Both versions of the saying have: "Whoever divorces his wife and marries another woman commits adultery"[11]; the "Q" version concludes with a further remarriage saying: "Whoever marries the divorced wife commits adultery." In both cases the man is in view: he

---

[6]A similar position, but on different grounds, has been strongly urged by Dungan, 139-50.

[7]Dungan, 139-50, takes the opposite view, that this saying was already known in the Corinthian community. Cf. J. M. Robinson and D. L. Balch (n. 23 on 7:25). The point is moot, although the contrasts in vv. 12 and 25 would seem to suggest that even this one was not previously known. Cf. Conzelmann, 120, who wonders that it "should have remained unknown in Corinth. At all events it is expressed in such a way that it sounds as if Paul was making it known for the first time."

[8]These twin data from vv. 10 and 12 speak in their own way to the basic authenticity of the Synoptic tradition. It has become common in NT scholarship to assume that early Christian prophets created many of the Jesus sayings as need arose in the churches. These two texts suggest otherwise. Paul himself was a prophet, yet he felt no constraint to have Jesus speak to the new situations he faced. Very likely the early church shared his perspective. In any case these two statements serve as hard evidence for this question and must not be ignored, as they often are. Cf. the discussion in D. R. Catchpole, "The Synoptic Divorce Material As a Traditio-historical Problem," *BJRL* 57 (1974), 92-127. Especially in light of vv. 10 and 12, it is something of a surprise for P. Richardson (" 'I Say,' " pp. 71-72) to consider the present saying a word of the risen Lord rather than of the historical Jesus.

[9]Cf. the discussion in Dungan, *Sayings,* pp. 133-34, who concludes, "The question . . . must be left open."

[10]Since we know how Paul used the OT—sometimes precisely, but more often in an adapted form—we may assume that he would do the same with the *oral* materials from Jesus.

[11]Matthew has two unique features: (1) in the double tradition (Q) version he concludes, "he makes her to become adulterous"; and (2) the excepting clause for sexual immorality, of which Paul shows no knowledge. Mark, on the other hand, expands the saying to include women divorcing men, indicating the basically Greco-Roman milieu of his Gospel.

commits adultery by marrying someone other than his wife, or by marrying someone else's wife. Jesus' own point, especially in the Markan-Matthean conflict setting, is to reject the pharisaic attitude toward divorce altogether.[12] Although his concern was with the *why* of divorce within his own culture (to be rid of a wife in order to have another) by placing marriage back within the creational mandate of Gen. 2:24, Jesus in effect interpreted the seventh commandment to mean no divorce. This is the perspective that Paul picks up. Since his concern is strictly with divorce, he remolds the saying into its apodictic form ("You shall not . . .")[13] and, as Mark will in his Gospel (in reverse order), applies it to both wives and husbands.

Paul addresses the wives first, "A wife must not separate[14] from her husband." Much has been made of the use of the verb "to separate oneself from,"[15] in distinction from the verb used in vv. 12-13, "to divorce."[16] But that probably reflects our own urgencies for greater precision. Divorce in Greco-Roman culture could be "legalized" by means of documents; but more often it simply happened. In this culture divorce was divorce, whether established by a document or not. Either the man sent his wife away (= "divorce" in the sense of v. 12), or else either of them "left" the other (= "to separate").[17] But the evidence is ambiguous as far as the verbs are

[12]The Hillelites and Shammaites debated the allowable grounds of divorce on the basis of the meaning of "something indecent about her" in Deut. 24:1. See esp. *m.Git.* 9.10. The Hillelites took the extreme view, which allowed divorce even for a spoiled dish, a mole (*b.Ketub.* 75a), or if the husband found one fairer to his eyes. This is nothing more than a "hypocritically legalized caving in before the pressure of sexual passion" (Dungan, 121), and Jesus opposed it vigorously.

[13]This would be the direct form of the indirect command in Paul's Greek (εἰ with the infinitive following a verb of command).

[14]Gk. χωρισθῆναι. No point can be made of the passive, as Murphy-O'Connor argues ("Divorced," 601-02). The passive of this verb functions as a middle when used of "divorce" ("be separated from" = "separate oneself from") and does not imply that the other person is the initiator of the action; cf. κοιμάω ("fall asleep"), which is invariably passive when referring to death. See BAGD and the papyrus texts listed in MM; cf. the discussion in R. L. Roberts, "The Meaning of *Chorizō* and *Douloō* in 1 Corinthians 7:10-17," *RestQ* 8 (1965), 179-84.

[15]E.g., R-P, 140; Deissmann, *Bible Studies*, p. 247; Elliott, "Teaching," pp. 223-24; R. C. Campbell, "Teachings of Paul Concerning Divorce," *Foundations* 6 (1963), 362-66.

[16]Gk. ἀφίημι. This is the rarer word; the one used in the Gospels, which is the more common synonym of this one, is ἀπολύω.

[17]Through the kind service of Prof. E. A. Judge, D. C. Barker of Macquarrie University made available to me a section of the draft of his dissertation entitled "Divorced wives living in the household of their ex husbands." Mr. Barker has shown that there is some evidence from papyrus census declarations in Egypt that divorced wives sometimes remained in the households of their husbands (P.Berl.Leibg. 1.17; P.Flor. 3.301). If this were a common and more widespread phenomenon, some aspects of the present text would make a great deal of sense. However, as Mr. Barker points out, one must use great caution here since in both cases the divorced wife was also a sister of the husband, so that her remaining in the household might be on those grounds.

concerned. Ordinarily when the wife "divorces" she simply leaves her husband ("is separated" from him); the same verb is used in v. 15 of a pagan partner of either sex who leaves, and occurs regularly in the papyri for mutual divorce (agreeing to "separate from each other").[18] On the other hand, a man ordinarily "divorced" his wife ("sent her away"); nonetheless in v. 13 the wife can do the same.

What needs to be noted is that such an action by a woman was generally not allowed among the Jews.[19] Divorce was the man's prerogative, and for almost any reason whatsoever.[20] That is the issue Jesus was addressing. But women could, and did, divorce their husbands in the Greco-Roman world, although for obvious socio-economic reasons it was not common for them to do so.[21] Under any circumstances—and especially if Paul were merely answering questions put by the Corinthians on the permissibility of divorce—it is remarkable that Paul should begin his response by speaking to the wife, and speak primarily to her, while the word to the husband in v. 11 appears almost as an afterthought. Thus he applies the word of Jesus to her and "commands" that she not "separate from her husband." She is to "remain as she is."

11 Given the circumstances in Corinth, the exception allowed in this passage also seems remarkable. "No divorce" is what is "commanded" for believers; nonetheless, just as in all the other situations addressed in this chapter, Paul allows an exception: "but if indeed[22] she is separated." This is

[18]See the texts cited in MM. E.g., P.Ryl. II.154[25]: "but if any difference arises between them and they separate from one another (χωρίζονται ἀπ' ἀλλήλων)."

[19]See, e.g., *m.Yeb.* 14.1: "The man that divorces is not like to the woman that is divorced; for a woman is put away with her consent or without it, but a husband can put away his wife only with his own consent" (Danby, p. 240); cf. Jos., *Ant.* 15.259: "Some time afterwards Salome had occasion to quarrel with Costobarus and soon sent him a document dissolving their marriage, which was not in accordance with Jewish law. For it is (only) the man who is permitted by us to do this, and not even a divorced woman may marry again on her own initiative unless her former husband consents" (Loeb, VIII, 123). There has been considerable debate on this question as to whether a wife could initiate a divorce, which seems to be the case, but only in the sense of getting her husband to do the actual divorcing. See J. D. M. Derrett, *Law in the New Testament* (London, 1970), pp. 386-88; and B. Brooten, "Konnten Frauen im alten Judentum die Scheidung betreiben? überlegungen zu Mk 10,11-12 und 1 Kor 7,10-11," *EvT* 42 (1982), 65-80, and "Zur Debatte über das Scheidungsrecht der jüdischen Frau," *EvT* 43 (1983), 466-78.

[20]See above, n. 12.

[21]This, despite Seneca's bitter complaint: "Is there any woman that blushes at divorce now that certain illustrious and noble ladies reckon their years, not by the number of consuls, but by the number of their husbands, and leave home in order to marry, and marry in order to be divorced?" (*benef.* 3.16.2; Loeb, III, 155). This reflects the Roman moralist's remorse over the breakdown of Roman custom that historically forbade divorce altogether, and deals essentially with the citizen class.

[22]Allo, 163, following Weiss, 178, suggests that this implies that an action has already occurred or is known; cf. Dungan, 90 n. 1, who cites this approvingly. But it does

a present general condition (cf. 6:4), indicating "if for any reason this condition may possibly occur."[23] In this kind of construction, where the general condition qualifies what has already been said, the previous sentence expresses the ideal situation (in this case, no divorce), while the following conditional clause introduced by a *de* ("but") "describes the alternative possibility which is permissible but not ideal"[24] (in this case separation, but without remarriage). Thus "no divorce" is not turned into law, and the woman who does so is not put out of the community. What is disallowed is precisely what one finds in the teaching of Jesus: no adultery.[25] Hence if she does separate, she must continue to follow the dictum "Stay as you are," meaning now "Remain unmarried."

Even though divorce in the Corinthians' case was at first predicated on precisely the opposite concern—not to be married at all—with the exception clause Paul is now generalizing and probably no longer has their reason for separation in mind. The wife who may happen to divorce her husband may not use her present unmarried condition as an excuse for remarriage to someone else. If she does in fact desire to remarry, she must "be reconciled to her husband."[26] This is in keeping with Paul's view expressed elsewhere that for believers marriage is permanent, from its inception until the decease

---

no such thing. The combination ἐὰν (εἰ) δὲ καί occurs elsewhere in this same pattern, where it repeats but qualifies a previous verb or idea (4:7; 7:28; 2 Cor. 4:3; 7:9). In each case it merely emphasizes the repeated verb (see Burton, *Moods*, 282; and M. E. Thrall, *Greek Particles in the New Testament* [Grand Rapids, 1962], pp. 78-82). The present general condition, as opposed to the present particular, belies this suggestion (see the following note).

[23]Both Dungan and Murphy-O'Connor (see n. 2 above) rest their cases on this clause, which they argue represents a single case that was already going on in the church. Dungan (p. 89) suggests that this clause can also be translated "but if she has separated," which, he asserts, is "equally possible" with a future sense (cf. Conzelmann, 120). But that is simply not true. Paul uses present and past particular conditions on numerous occasions when such is the case; but the present general condition has nothing to do with the tense of the verb (this is the point of O'Connor's argument, which equally comes to grief grammatically), and it regularly represents for him a hypothetical "if ever such a condition exists." For clear examples see 7:28 and 39. Cf. the review of Dungan by B. A. Pearson in *Int* 26 (1972), 350-51.

[24]Thrall, *Particles*, p. 81. Dungan, 89-93, sees this as contradictory, which in a certain logical sense is true. But the *ad hoc* formulation of responses such as this does not always yield to our own views of logic. To press for the ideal, and even to urge it as a command of the Lord, does not make it binding law; and the possibility that exceptions will occur is simply a concession to reality. But if the exception does indeed occur, it may not turn about and become an excuse for adultery.

[25]This is not stated, of course; but since Paul is appealing to the teaching of Jesus, in which this is the central issue in the matter of remarriage, one would be hard-pressed to argue that for Paul it did not mean the same.

[26]This would be even more understandable if divorced wives sometimes remained in the households of their ex-husbands (see n. 17 above); but the point is moot.

of one of the partners (7:39; Rom. 7:1-3). Thus the priorities of the directive are clear: she is to remain as she is and not divorce her husband; but if she were to disobey this first directive, then she must again remain as she is and not commit adultery by remarrying someone else. If she does not like her new unmarried status, then she must be reconciled to her husband.

What is true of the wife, Paul adds, is likewise true of the husband: "And a husband must not divorce his wife." The lack of an exception here suggests that this is not where the problem lay; and in any case, what is said of the wife would apply to the husband as well.

In a culture in which divorce has become the norm, this text has become a bone of contention. Some find Paul and Jesus too harsh and try to find ways around the plain sense of the text. Others turn the text into law and make divorce the worst of all sins in the church. Neither of these seems an appropriate response. On the one hand, there is little question that both Paul and Jesus disallowed divorce between two believers, especially when it served as grounds for remarriage. Paul does not give reasons for that here, but his view of marriage in Eph. 5:22-33 indicates that it is related to his view of the unitive aspect of marriage and the mutuality of Christian love, which makes it very similar to the reasons Jesus gives.

On the other hand, Paul does not raise this norm to law. Divorce may happen, and such a person is not ostracized from the community. But it must also be remembered that in this setting divorce was being sought for ascetic reasons, which is almost the precise opposite of most such situations in our own culture! What is *not* allowed is remarriage, both because for him that presupposes the teaching of Jesus that such is adultery and because in the Christian community reconciliation is the norm. If the Christian husband and wife cannot be reconciled to one another, then how can they expect to become models of reconciliation before a fractured and broken world?

d. No divorce for mixed marriages (7:12-16)

12 *To the rest I say this (I, not the Lord): If any brother has a wife who is not a believer and she is willing to live with him, he must not divorce her.* 13 *And if[1] a woman has a husband who is not a believer and he is willing to live with her, she must not divorce him.[2]* 14 *For the unbelieving husband has been sanctified through his wife,[3] and*

---

[1]On the decision between εἴ τις and ἥτις, see Metzger, 554.

[2]The NIV (correctly) translates τὸν ἄνδρα ("her husband") by the pronoun, for the same reason that the MajT, against all early evidence, made the same change.

[3]The Western tradition (D F G latt Iren Tert) balances the clause by adding "believing" to "wife."

the unbelieving wife has been sanctified through the brother.*4 Otherwise your children would be unclean, but as it is, they are holy.*

15 *But if the unbeliever leaves, let him do so.* The brother or the sister*5 is not bound in such circumstances; God has called us6 to live in peace.* 16 *How do you know, wife, whether you will save your husband? Or, how do you know, husband, whether you will save your wife?*

With yet another "I speak now to . . ." Paul moves to the third in the series of directives that began in v. 8. In this case the issue is clearly defined by the content; it continues the matter of divorce, this time when one partner is Christian and the other pagan.7 The answer is consistent with vv. 10-11; they are to "stay as they are." The believer may not initiate divorce (vv. 12-13), for which in this instance a reason is added (v. 14). But as before, there is an exception; if the pagan chooses to leave, then the believer is not bound to maintain the marriage (v. 15ab).8 But God's call is to "peace" (v. 15c), which means further that one should maintain the marriage in the hope of the unbelieving spouse's conversion (v. 16). As throughout, the entire section forms balanced pairs between men and women.

4NIV, "her believing husband." The word "brother" is unexpected here, where the contrasts have been ἀνήρ and γυνή; so much so that the MajT text assimilated by reading ἀνδρί.

5NIV, "A believing man or woman."

6Even though ἡμᾶς is supported by P46 B D F G Ψ Maj latt sy sa, the editors of UBS3/NA26 (cf. GNB, NAB, JB) prefer the ὑμᾶς of ℵ* A C K 81 326 1175, on the grounds of "the general tendency of scribes . . . to make modifications in the interest of generalizing the reference of aphorisms" (Metzger, 555). On the other hand, given the weakness of the external evidence for this reading, it is just as easy to imagine scribes' particularizing a typical Pauline "us" to fit the context.

7This is generally recognized by all commentators. Moiser ("Reassessment," pp. 109-10) makes the improbable suggestion that vv. 10-11 deal with mixed marriages where the believer has abandoned the pagan partner and this section with believers who have been abandoned by pagan partners. That flies full in the face of vv. 12-13, not to mention that v. 15 specifically makes such an option the exception to the rule given in vv. 12-14. More improbable still is the suggestion by Ford, *Trilogy,* pp. 73-82, that purely Jewish questions lie behind the Corinthian letter to Paul and that ἄπιστος here means "of doubtful stock" or "half-breed Jew." Indeed, Paul's regular use of ἄπιστος (see n. 10) to refer to unbelieving pagans makes both Hurley's, 122-78, and her positions tenuous in the extreme.

8Elliott ("Teaching," p. 224) argues on the basis of a differentiation between ἀφίημι and χωρίζομαι that vv. 15-16 "concern a new problem." Vv. 12-14 are written to those wanting to separate; vv. 15-16 to those fighting separation. Cf. S. Kubo ("I Corinthians vii.16: Optimistic or Pessimistic?" *NTS* 24 [1978], 539-44), who arrives at a similar conclusion on the basis of his interpretation of v. 16 as pessimistic. However, the overall structure, with directives to "stay as you are" modified by exceptions, speaks against viewing it in this way. See on v. 15.

Almost certainly this issue came from their letter. The argument in vv. 14c and 16 takes the form of debate; it makes best sense if Paul is over against them on this issue. As before, their position would follow from the slogan in v. 1b. But in this case they have not only argued for the suspension of sexual relations by divorce, but most likely they have added the grounds that the pagan partner contaminates the marriage (see on v. 14). Quite the contrary, Paul argues: mixed marriages are essentially Christian marriages (v. 14) and, when maintained, they afford an opportunity for the unbelieving partner to be saved (v. 16). Thus, as throughout, the exception (v. 15) is real but not ideal; it is allowed but is not to be pursued.

12-13 After the "unmarried" and "widows" have been addressed in vv. 8-9 and the "married" in vv. 10-11, one might well wonder who can be left to constitute "the rest"![9] But what follows makes it clear; they are believers who are married to unbelievers.[10] Since such concerns lay outside the province of Jesus' own life-setting, Paul himself speaks[11] to this matter, not the Lord (see on v. 10 above).

With two sets of perfectly balanced sentences,[12] Paul sets forth his judgments, this time in the order of husband and wife. What he has already said in vv. 10-11, as the Lord's command, continues to hold for mixed marriages. Believers are not to initiate divorce. If there is a distinction between the verbs, then in this case he envisions a more active putting away of the pagan partner (cf. the husband in v. 11); whereas the wife in v. 10 and the pagan spouse in v. 15 separate themselves from the relationship (see on v. 10). Here the clauses are simple particulars ("If such and such is the case, then abide by this ruling"), implying the actual existence of such cases in the community.

But at the same time, these sentences anticipate the exception of v. 15: "If any brother has a wife who is not a believer *and she is willing to*[13]

---

[9]On the basis of 1 Thess. 4:13; 5:6 (and Eph. 2:3), where Paul refers to pagans as "the rest," Dungan, 93, following Lightfoot, 225, suggests that it refers to pagans here ("the nonbelievers who are the mates of the Christians"). However, it is specifically addressed *to* "the rest," which can only mean Christians.

[10]Gk. ἄπιστοι; Miss Ford notwithstanding (see n. 7 above), this word in Paul most often refers to pagans, who have not come to faith (cf. 6:6; 10:27; 14:22-24; 2 Cor. 4:4; 6:14-15).

[11]Gk. λέγω, as in vv. 6, 8, and 35. As elsewhere in the chapter, with the single exception of v. 10, Paul does not lay down rules, but speaks as one to be trusted (v. 25) because he has the Spirit of God (v. 40).

[12]The only exceptions are: (1) The man is called "a brother," the woman "a wife"; nothing can be made of this since in v. 15 he speaks of the two believers as "the brother or the sister." (2) The final object in v. 13 repeats the noun "husband" rather than the pronoun, as at the end of v. 12.

[13]The verb συνευδοκέω implies more than simply "being willing" in a rather passive sense; it also means "agreeing with" it or "consenting to" it.

298

live with him." Already this places the initiative with the unbeliever if the marriage is to be dissolved. What it also demonstrates is that not all conversions were household conversions, as in the case of Stephanas (16:15). Illustrations of both phenomena abound in the Greco-Roman world (i.e., where the family took on the religion of the head of the household or where only one, especially in the case of wives, became the devotee of a deity other than that of the spouse). In this case Paul has the latter in view, in which the spouse has at least tolerated conversion.

14 Picking up the two relationships from vv. 12-13, but now in reverse order,[14] Paul explains why[15] the directive in those verses has been given. Both the argument and the language of this passage are unusual for Paul.[16] The problem lies with the use of the word "sanctified"[17] of the spouse and "holy"[18] of the children, words that in Paul ordinarily carry moral/ethical implications.[19] The word in fact has already been used in 1:30 and 6:11 as a metaphor for salvation itself. But whatever it means here, it cannot carry that force, not only because the idea that marriage can effect salvation for the pagan partner would be nonsense to Paul but also because v. 16 completely disallows such a sense. The question, then, is what sense it does carry.

Among many options,[20] the most viable seems to be one that (1) ties

---

[14]Together the three verses form a perfect triple chiasm:

A	A *brother* having an unbelieving wife;	AB
B	A wife having an unbelieving husband.	CD
B'	The unbelieving husband sanctified by the wife;	DC
A'	The unbelieving wife sanctified by the *brother*.	BA

[15]The γάρ ("for") is explanatory, modifying the twin imperatives "he/she must not divorce her/him."

[16]So much so that it has elicited considerable scholarly discussion, with nothing close to a consensus, although Conzelmann's despair is probably extreme ("The explanations that have so far been suggested are almost without exception unsatisfactory" [p. 122]; this also seems true of his, that "through the believing partner, the marriage between a pagan and a Christian is withdrawn from the control of the powers of the world"). For an overview of solutions, see Murphy-O'Connor, "Works."

[17]Gk. ἡγίασται, perfect passive indicative (= "is sanctified").

[18]Gk. ἅγιος (cf. 1:2; 3:17).

[19]See the discussion on 1:2, 30 and 6:11. It should be noted that the word-group coheres in this case, that is, it means "holy" whether it be verb, noun, or adjective. For a good overview of Pauline usage, see Murphy-O'Connor, "Works," 352-56.

[20]Two of these require special notice because they have some especially attractive features but finally do not seem to fit the context as well. (1) D. Daube ("Pauline Contributions," pp. 232-41; see n. 28 on 5:2) has argued that the entire passage reflects the rabbinic doctrine that in conversion a proselyte is as a newborn child; hence all former relations have been dissolved. Thus the Corinthian concern had to do with continuing that relationship, which now amounted to living in sexual immorality. Since in the rabbinic materials the verb *qiddēš* ("to consecrate") sometimes meant to consecrate a wife (i.e., a marriage), and since one of the means of such a "consecration" was through sexual

this explanation directly to the Corinthian stance,[21] and (2) finds the clue to Paul's usage here in a similar usage in Rom. 11:16.[22] If we are correct in seeing v. 1b ("It is good for a man not to have relations with a woman") as the grounds for some in Corinth to argue for sexual abstinence within marriage, then in the case of a pagan partner they have even stronger grounds, since Paul himself, in his letter to which they are now responding, had told them not to have close associations with immoral people (see 5:9-11). According to 5:10 they had interpreted that to mean "no intermingling with outsiders," of which the closest kind would be a believer's sharing the marriage bed with a pagan. Thus they would have argued that such an association "defiled" the believing spouse.[23]

To the contrary, Paul now argues, it is not the believer who is *defiled,* but the unbeliever who is *sanctified* in[24] her or his relationship with the believer.[25] This does not mean that they have acquired salvation or holiness. But from Paul's perspective, as long as the marriage is maintained the potential for their realizing salvation remains. To that degree they are "sanctified" in the believing spouse. Such a usage of "holiness" is similar to

---

intercourse (*m.Qidd.* 1.1; *m.Ketub.* 4.4), Daube suggests that the sense of Paul's argument goes: Even though the marriage was dissolved through conversion, one should live on with the spouse in the hope of his/her conversion; by intercourse one "consecrates" the new marriage, otherwise one's children (meaning any born to this relationship) would be "unclean" (illegitimate). Many things are attractive about this option; however, it assumes a Jewish stance on the part of both the Corinthians and Paul that is difficult to sustain.

(2) Murphy-O'Connor ("Works") has argued that "sanctified" is to be understood in light of Paul's usual usage, which he contends means basically to be separated from the world by divine call, but that this must consequently be exhibited in one's behavior. Thus by choosing to stay with the believer the pagan has begun a behavioral pattern that is "holy" and that hopefully will result in actual salvation. Although correctly stressing the behavioral aspect of holiness in Paul, it is less than clear in the context that Paul's use of the perfect tense, modified by the preposition ἐν, will sustain that suggestion.

[21]Cf. esp. Barrett, 164-65.

[22]For this argument see Beasley-Murray, *Baptism,* pp. 195-97.

[23]Murphy-O'Connor, "Works," 350, rightly cautions about making such a reconstruction the basis for one's understanding the text as a whole since a degree of speculation is involved in trying to determine the specific "why" of their conduct. He allows minimally that the best one can say is "that some members of the community were in favour of the dissolution of mixed marriage." This is true; but vv. 14 and 16 seem to be more argumentative (cf. v. 5) than much of the chapter and therefore lend credence to such a reconstruction. The present exegesis is not dependent on this reconstruction; it is only trying to give a viable reason for Paul's unusual use of this language.

[24]Gk. ἐν; probably designating a relationship with the believer rather than a relationship to God "through" the believer.

[25]The idea of some that the physical relationship "sanctifies" is completely foreign to Paul's point of view. See, e.g., Lietzmann, 31.

Paul's analogy in Rom. 11:16: "If the part of the dough offered as firstfruits is holy, then the whole batch is holy; if the root is holy, so are the branches." Although Paul's point in that passage is not completely lucid, the analogy itself seems clear enough. The "consecration" of the part, in the sense of "setting it apart" for God, "sanctifies" the whole. Israel is not yet converted, but because the "firstfruits" and "root" were "holy," that is, because Israel was originally thus "sanctified" unto God, the Israel of Paul's day, though still in unbelief, was nonetheless "holy" in this special sense. Precisely because they belonged to God in this special sense, Paul hoped for their eventually coming to faith. That seems to be the same analogy put forth here. In this case, if the husband/wife is "holy,"[26] then the unbelieving spouse is also "holy," that is, set apart in a special way that hopefully will lead to their salvation (v. 16).

The second part of the verse fits into this same framework.[27] Here in particular Paul seems to be carrying on an argument with the Corinthians. "Otherwise" (meaning "if we allow your position"), he argues, "your children[28] would be unclean. But as it is" (i.e., "allowing my position") "they are holy." The difficult term is "unclean," which also echoes Jewish ritual language. If you are correct, he argues, then your children lie outside the covenant; but as it is, through their relationship with the believer, who maintains the marriage and thus keeps intact the relationship with the children, they too can be understood to be "holy" in the same way as the

[26]Murphy-O'Connor ("Works," 359) objects that the believer is not here called holy; but the implication is in the text itself, not to mention that in this letter in particular believers are referred to as "sanctified in Christ Jesus." The children are "holy," not because of their own behavior but because somehow they are affected by their relationship with the one parent who "has been sanctified in Christ Jesus."

[27]One of the curiosities of the use of Scripture in the church has been the use of this text to support infant baptism. It is argued that children are "holy" either because they have received the Holy Spirit at baptism or because they already participate in the parents' baptismal incorporation into God's holy people. See, e.g., Church of Scotland, *Biblical Doctrine of Baptism* (Edinburgh, 1958), pp. 45ff.; cf. Jeremias, *Infant Baptism,* pp. 38-43, who argues from the language of "unclean" and "holy" that Paul is alluding to the Jewish practice of baptizing the children of proselytes born before their conversion. For a refutation see Beasley-Murray, *Baptism,* pp. 197-99. In a later edition Jeremias himself recognizes the improbability of using this text in this way. See Aland, *Early Church,* pp. 33-35.

[28]Gk. τὰ τέκνα; it is impossible to tell what this means in terms of age or when they were born (before or after the parent's conversion). It probably includes children who have not yet reached maturity, or who are still dependent on their parents. In any case, the matter for Paul is so self-evident that this discussion would probably escape him. See G. Delling, "Lexikalisches zu τέκνον, Ein Nachtrag zur Exegese von I. Kor. 7,14," in *Studien zum Neuen Testament und zum hellenistischen Judentum* (Göttingen, 1970), pp. 270-80; and Murphy-O'Connor, "Works," p. 360.

unbelieving spouse.[29] Thus in both cases Paul is setting forth a high view of the grace of God at work through the believer toward members of his/her own household (cf. 1 Pet. 3:1), and for him that constitutes grounds enough for maintaining the marriage.

15 In keeping with the pattern of the entire argument (vv. 5, 9, 11a, 21, 28, 36, 39), Paul once more qualifies the ideal, "stay as you are," with an exception. The believer may not pursue divorce, "but if"[30] the unbeliever separates, let him or her do so. That is, if the pagan spouse seeks the dissolution of the marriage, then allow the divorce.[31] Except for some differences regarding the nuance of the verb, all are agreed on that much.

The differences begin with the next sentence, in which Paul offers a further explanation of the first one: "The brother or the sister[32] is not bound[33] in such circumstances." That is, they are not bound to the ruling given above about maintaining the marriage. They have wanted to dissolve such marriages. Paul has said No. But now he allows that if the pagan wants out, then one is not enslaved.

This statement is the source of the notorious "Pauline privilege," in which the text is understood to mean that the believer is free to remarry.[34] But despite a long tradition that has so interpreted it, several converging data indicate that Paul is essentially repeating his first sentence: that the believer is not bound to maintain the marriage if the pagan partner opts out. (1)

[29]Cf. the Jewish understanding that the children of proselytes are themselves members of Israel in full standing (*m.Ketub.* 4.3; *m.Yeb.* 11.2).

[30]Except for v. 5, this is the language of each of the exception clauses. Some are present general (vv. 11, 28, 39); the rest are present particular (vv. 9, 15, 21, 36).

[31]In both cases the verb is χωρίζεται ("If he/she separates, let him/her separate"); cf. vv. 10 and 12-13. In this case, see especially the papyrus examples in MM (n. 18 on v. 10), which use this verb for mutual agreement to dissolve a marriage.

[32]This is the actual language of Paul. Since the NIV translates it "brother" in v. 12, one wonders why the change to "believing husband" in v. 14, or to "a believing man or woman" here. This anaphoric usage of brother and sister, which specifically refers back to vv. 12-14, presents insurmountable obstacles to Elliott's and Kubo's view (see n. 8) that Paul is speaking to two different groups in vv. 12-14 and 15-16. This is especially true of Kubo, who continually refers to "the second group" (pp. 543-44). Paul's grammar simply will not allow that.

[33]Gk. δεδούλωται, from δοῦλος, literally meaning "to enslave"; in every case in Paul it is used figuratively (9:19; Rom. 6:18, 22; Gal. 4:3; Tit. 2:3). His ordinary word for being bound to a marriage per se is δέω (7:39; Rom. 7:2), which implies bound by law and duty.

[34]This is canon law in Roman Catholicism. The debate, therefore, has largely been within that communion. The literature is large, and not all of it defends this ancient position. Among others see P. Dulau, "The Pauline Privilige, Is it Promulgated in the First Epistle to the Corinthians?" *CBQ* 13 (1951), 146-52; T. P. Considine, "The Pauline Privilege. (Further Examination of 1 Cor. vii,12-17)," *AusBR* 40 (1963), 107-19; B. Byron, "The Brother or Sister is Not Bound. Another Look at the New Testament Teaching on the Indissolubility of Marriage," *New Blackfriars* 52 (1971), 514-21.

Remarriage is not an issue at all; indeed, it seems to be quite the opposite. In a context in which people are arguing for the right to dissolve marriage, Paul would scarcely be addressing the issue of remarriage, and certainly not in such circuitous fashion. (2) The verb "to be under bondage" is not his ordinary one for the "binding" character of marriage (cf. 7:39; Rom. 7:2); that means that Paul does *not* intend to say one is not "bound to the marriage." One is simply not under bondage to maintain the marriage, which the other person wishes to dissolve. From Paul's point of view, one is bound to a marriage until death breaks the bond (7:39). (3) In v. 11, even though there is a similar exception regarding divorce, he explicitly disallows remarriage. (4) Such a concern misses the theme of the chapter, which has to do with *not* seeking a change in status. The exceptions in each case do not allow a change in partners but in status, either from single to married or vice versa, but not both! All of this is not to say that Paul *disallows* remarriage in such cases; he simply does not speak to it at all. Thus this text offers little help for this very real contemporary concern.

The third sentence in this verse (lit. "But[35] in peace[36] God has called us") is also perplexing. The question is whether the "call to peace" refers to the dissolution of the marriage (v. 15ab) or to its preservation (vv. 12-14). To put that in another way, does all of vv. 15-16 deal with the exception (the dissolution of the mixed marriage), or does only v. 15ab do so, while vv. 15c and 16 return to the question of maintaining the marriage?

It is common to take the clause as a further explanation of the two preceding sentences, the implication being that one should not "contest the divorce"[37] *because* God has called us "to live"[38] in peace. That means either that living in peace "would not be possible if the unbelieving partner were forced to live with the believer,"[39] or that one should let the separation occur in as peaceful a way as possible, not creating unnecessary disturbances.[40] It should be noted that for those who take the "pessimistic" stance

---

[35]Gk. δέ; either adversative ("but, rather"), or consecutive ("and, now," or simply left untranslated).

[36]Part of the difficulty with this sentence is in finding an adequate understanding of ἐν εἰρήνῃ (lit. "in peace"). Most likely this means something close to εἰς (= "unto peace"), or to the admonition "Go in peace"; i.e., depart "in the ways of peace." If the latter, then it would mean something like: "Rather, God has called us into the ways of peace." Cf. Moule, 79: "The preposition may be used 'pregnantly': perhaps *God has called you* into *a peace* in *which he wishes you to live.*"

[37]It should be noted that "divorce" was not a court proceeding with lawyers, etc., but essentially an agreement between two people, frequently legalized by a document of divorce.

[38]These words are added in the NIV to give this sense.

[39]Mare, 231; cf. Goudge, 57; Héring, 53; Holladay, 96.

[40]See, e.g., O-W, 212 ("the separation is to take place without recrimination or anger").

toward v. 16, this is the necessary meaning of the sentence,[41] although not everyone who takes this view subscribes to the pessimistic view of v. 16.

The difficulty with this interpretation is twofold: (1) It tends to run roughshod over the normal sense of Paul's conjunctions; and (2) it misses the Jewish background to Paul's use of the "call to peace." The first problem has to do with the *de* of this sentence, which ordinarily has either adversative or consecutive force.[42] But neither of these makes any sense for this point of view. Thus many leave it untranslated; but that will not do since this view in fact requires a *causal* nuance to this sentence. That is, without the "call to live in peace" being the *cause* of the admonition not to contest the separation, one can make no sense of it at all. The problem, of course, is that *de* simply will not sustain that nuance.[43] More likely, then, the structure of the paragraph is thus:

The ideal:	Do not divorce a pagan spouse (vv. 12-13)
The reason:	*gar* ("for")
	They are sanctified in you (14)
The exception:	*de* ("but")
	If they choose to leave, let it be so (15ab)
The reason (again):	*de* ("rather" than the exception)
	God has called us to peace (15c)
	gar ("for")
	Perhaps you will yet save your spouse (16)

Not only does this give due force to all of the conjunctive words but it also fits the context better, which has to do with urging them *not* to dissolve mixed marriages, not with making peace if they are dissolved.

But what then does it mean for Paul to protest, "Rather (than dissolving the marriage) God has called us[44] to peace"? Very likely this reflects Paul's Jewish heritage, which "for the sake of peace" did certain deeds toward the less favored, or even toward the Gentiles, with a view toward

---

[41]See esp. Kubo, "I Corinthians VII.16," pp. 542-43, who does an end run around this sentence. He maintains that "v. 15c is not crucial since its interpretation is dependent on our understanding of v. 16." It would seem that quite the opposite should prevail. How one understands this sentence, and its relationship to the rest, determines how the explanatory γάρ functions in v. 16.

[42]See n. 35 above.

[43]All the more so when one considers that a piling up of γάρ's is a stylistic feature of this letter (see on 2:10-11; 3:3-4).

[44]For the textual variant see n. 6. It should be added to that discussion that the preferable ἡμᾶς also supports this interpretation. Rather than speaking to them to live in peace by acquiescing to a separation, Paul is calling them to a broader Christian view of their present existence, which in v. 17 he will widen to include all believers, under the rubric of their "call."

winning the favor of Judaism with them.[45] This accords with his concern for Christians' living peaceably with all people (Rom. 12:18).[46] Thus, despite the exception Paul prefers that they follow "God's call into the ways of peace." That means that they should "stay as they are" (in this case, maintain the marriage), and view that on the one hand as God's *calling* (v. 17),[47] and on the other hand as an opportunity for the salvation of the spouse (v. 16).

16 The two questions that conclude the argument are tied to v. 15c with a "for," thus offering a final reason—albeit hypothetical—for maintaining a mixed marriage. Much discussion has centered on whether by these questions Paul expected a positive or negative answer. That is, is he offering them the hope that if they maintain the marriage their partners might be saved, or is he telling them not to fight the separation because they have no assurance that they will ever be saved? In fact the questions are ambiguous and do not lend themselves to either a positive or a negative answer.[48] Probably they are purposely left indefinite, for Paul makes no promises that maintaining the marriage will turn out in their favor. Nonetheless, since the questions give reasons for maintaining the marriage as their response to God's call into the ways of peace, almost certainly they go with vv. 12-14, not with v. 15ab. To that degree they offer yet a further explanation of the pagan mate's "sanctification," and a further reason for maintaining the marriage. They cannot be sure, but perhaps they will be responsible for saving their spouses.

[45]See, e.g., *m.Git.* 5.8-9 ("They do not try to prevent the poor among the gentiles from gathering Gleanings . . . in the interests of peace"; "moreover greetings [meaning 'Shalom'] may be offered to gentiles in the interests of peace"). Cf. the discussion in Daube, "Contributions," pp. 234-35.

[46]Cf. Rom. 14:19, where the strong are encouraged to defer to the weak "for the sake of peace."

[47]This apparent anticipation of v. 17 with this verb also speaks against the common interpretation of v. 15c. The whole point of vv. 17-24 is to justify "staying as one is at the time of one's call" and understanding that *as* one's call. To read v. 15c as referring to peacefully accepting the dissolution of the marriage would make God's call refer to the *exception* to staying as one was at the time of one's call, which hardly makes sense of the argument as a whole.

[48]Cf. Moule, 154, "It is uncertain whether the direct question implied is intended to expect the answer *yes* or *no*." J. Jeremias, "Die missionarische Aufgabe in der Mischehe (I Cor 7 16)," in *Neutestamentliche Studien für Rudolf Bultmann* (ed. W. Eltester; Berlin, 1954), pp. 255-60; and C. Burchard, "*Ei* nach einem Ausdrücke des Wissens oder Nichtwissens Joh 9:25, Act 19:2, I Kor 1:16, 7:16," *ZNW* 52 (1961), 73-82, have mustered considerable evidence in favor of a positive answer. But as Kubo has rightly countered ("1 Corinthians VII.16"), at best they have shown that in some cases it *may* have that sense, but in fact it is generally ambiguous. Kubo goes astray when he argues that if it is ambiguous then it probably expects a negative. To the contrary, as he points out, the context must finally decide, and in this case the context, esp. v. 15c (which Kubo neglects), points toward a sense of "perhaps you will save."

In speaking of "saving one's spouse," Paul is referring to their "evangelizing" or "winning" them, whether by word or deed (cf. 1 Pet. 3:1). This use of "save" is not unique; in 9:22 (cf. Rom. 11:14) Paul speaks of becoming all things to all people so that by every possible means he might "save" some, where "save" is used as a synonym for "winning" people for the gospel. Yet in a similar context in 10:33 he puts the same verb in the passive, "in order that they might be saved." This, of course, is what it means to "save" them in the other sense.

This passage has regularly been consulted in the church for an ongoing concern—divorce and remarriage. But this issue is so complex, and the individual cases so diverse, that this text with its singular focus on maintaining mixed marriages (but allowing them to dissolve if the pagan initiates the action) does not offer much help. It certainly would be an injustice to make it apodictic law ("Thou shalt or shalt not"); on the other hand, one should exercise due caution in using it casuistically (case by case).

Our situation is usually made more complex because our concerns are often the precise opposite of theirs, which caused this to be written in the first place. They wanted to dissolve marriages; we want to know whether remarriage is permitted. Two things, therefore, need to be pointed out. First, Paul does not speak to the question of remarriage. If that is one's concern, then it must be wrestled with in the much larger context of Scripture; and the answer is not clear-cut. In many cases such marriages are clearly redemptive. Even if it is not the ideal situation, God still redeems our fallenness, whether it be individuals or broken marriages. On the other hand, there is nothing redemptive in remarriage that is simply an excuse for legalized lust.

Second, the real point of the passage needs to be given a fair hearing. When a married man or woman hears and responds to the call of the gospel but the married partner does not—at least at the same time—let the new believer consider the spouse sanctified, that is, also set apart for the gospel. And then let him or her so live that in due time they might "save" their spouses. That's the Good News that this passage sets before us.

2. The Guiding Principle—Stay as One Was When Called (7:17-24)

17 *Nevertheless, each one should retain the place in life that the Lord[1] assigned[2] to him and to which God has called him. That is the*

---

[1]The subjects of the two clauses are reversed in the MajT and sy^h; some MSS (א 629 1881 pc) have "God" as the subject in both. Almost certainly this is a conformation to the similar passages in Rom. 12:3 and 2 Cor. 10:13. Unfortunately it misses the subtleties of Paul's sentence. See the commentary.

[2]Both Tischendorf and WH prefer the perfect found in א* B 81 630 1739 pc over the aorist found in the rest (and preferred by UBS³/NA²⁶). If original, then the aorist was

rule I lay down[3] in all the churches. 18 *Was a man already circumcised when he was called? He should not become uncircumcised. Was a man uncircumcised when he was called? He should not become circumcised.* 19 *Circumcision is nothing and uncircumcision is nothing. Keeping God's commands is what counts.* 20 *Each one should remain in the situation which he was in when God called him.* 21 *Were you a slave when you were called? Don't let it trouble you— although if you can gain your freedom, do so.* 22 *For he who was a slave when he was called by the Lord is the Lord's freedman; similarly,[4] he who was a free man when he was called is Christ's slave.* 23 *You were bought at a price; do not become slaves of men.* 24 *Brothers, each man, as responsible to God, should remain in the situation God called him to.*

With this paragraph Paul appears to move afield a bit, but that is true only in content, not overall concern. In v. 15, in the context of staying with a mixed marriage rather than dissolving it, he set forth the general maxim: "God has called us to peace." Now he picks up that theme in order to press home the theological point that controls his response throughout chap. 7. Under the rubric "It is good not to have relations with a woman," they were seeking to change their present status, apparently because as believers they saw this as conforming to the more spiritual existence that they had already attained. Thus they saw one's status with regard to marriage/celibacy as having *religious* significance and sought change because of it. Under the theme of "call" Paul seeks to put their "spirituality" into a radically different perspective. They should remain in whatever social setting they were at the time of their call since God's call to be in Christ (cf. 1:9) transcends such settings so as to make them essentially irrelevant. That is, the call *to* Christ has created such a change in one's essential relationship (with God) that one does not need to seek change in other relationships (with people). These latter are transformed and given new meaning by the former. Thus one is no better off in one condition than in the other.

To make this point Paul illustrates from two other kinds of social settings—circumcision[5] and slavery.[6] The very lack of urgency in these

---

an assimilation to Rom. 12:3 and 2 Cor. 10:13. More likely the early Egyptian MSS were assimilated to the perfect in the next clause.

[3]In place of διατάσσομαι the Western tradition reads διδάσκω (an assimilation to 4:17).

[4]Most of the Western and MajT witnesses add a καί ("also"). This is secondary since there is no good explanation for its omission.

[5]The concern over circumcision in this case, in contrast to that in Galatians, is first of all sociological, then religious; hence the unimpassioned way it finds expression.

[6]Bartchy, 162-65, makes the intriguing suggestion that these two sets of social relationships were regularly linked with male/female relationships in Paul's own thinking, as evidenced in Gal. 3:28, and that is why he chose them.

matters indicates that they are not at issue.[7] What is at issue is the Corinthians' concern over change of status. The argument is structured around the single imperative "remain (walk) as one was when called,"[8] which both opens the paragraph (v. 17) and concludes the two illustrations (vv. 20, 24).[9] The language of "calling"[10] dominates the whole. It forms the heart of each of the imperatives and is repeated for all four of the social conditions addressed (circumcision, uncircumcision, slave, free).

The argument is easily traced. V. 17 sets forth the basic principle: They are to live out their Christian lives in the situation where God called them. Vv. 18-19 apply this to ethno-religious life (being Jew or Gentile), which now counts for nothing. There are no exceptions here: let each one *remain* in his/her calling (v. 20). The principle is next applied to the slave and the free person (vv. 21-24). However, this case is unlike the others in that the slave may not freely choose change of status. So the structure of the argument alters slightly, even though the point remains the same. Paul begins by addressing the slave (v. 21a), but as in each of the preceding marital situations, there is an exception (v. 21b). He never does address the free person directly; rather, in vv. 22-23 he returns to the illustration by showing how one's calling in Christ makes irrelevant being either slave or free, and concludes once again with the statement of the principle (v. 24).[11]

Since the theme of "calling" is central to the argument, it may be helpful to outline it in advance:

---

[7]Cf. Bartchy, 140 n. 491: "He expected the examples in 7:17-24 to support his argument precisely because no tension in the areas of Jew/Greek or slave/free relationships was known to him."

[8]Otherwise Bartchy, 127-59 (following Grosheide, 166-72, who previously followed Bavinck), who argues that the basic imperative means "Live according to your calling from God in Christ," and has nothing to do with where one was at the time of one's call. Therefore, the concern in the imperative is that they continue in their faith given to them at the time of their call and not fall prey to their new theology, which is leading them away from faith in Christ. This view rests finally on (1) the understanding of κλῆσις in v. 20 as referring to "remaining in your Christian calling," with no reference to the circumstances in which that call came, and on (2) the similarities of vv. 17 and 24 to v. 20 that allow Bartchy to neglect their more significant *dis*similarities.

[9]Since the threefold imperative is clearly the framework for the entire paragraph, one could equally see vv. 17 and 24 as giving it opening and closure, with v. 20 functioning simultaneously as the conclusion to vv. 18-19 and the introduction to vv. 21-23.

[10]The verb καλέω appears eight times; the noun κλῆσις once.

[11]Both Paul's present argument and the historical context as a whole seem to be missed rather widely when the lesson Mare, 232, would draw from all this is: "Paul is more afraid of the spirit of anarchy and rebellion, personal and national . . . , than of social inequality." Paul is concerned here with neither of these issues. That is surely to read the text through the eyes of middle-class America in the early 1970s!

1. The concept of call is first of all a way of describing Christian conversion. God calls people to be "in Christ" (1:9).

2. That *call* came to a person in a given social setting. This is the clear emphasis in all the verbs in this passage, especially as it is associated with various social options (vv. 18 [twice], 21, 22 [twice]).

3. These two realities are pressed theologically in various ways:

a. God's call to Christ that comes in these various settings renders the settings themselves irrelevant (vv. 18-19, 22).

b. Because of this, change is not necessary; indeed, one may live out the Christian life in whatever setting that call took place.

c. On the other hand, precisely because the settings are irrelevant, if change does take place, that too is irrelevant. What one is not to do is to seek change as though it had religious significance, which it does not.

d. Although he comes very close to seeing the setting in which one is called as "calling" itself, he never quite makes that jump. At most "calling" refers to the circumstances in which the calling took place.

17 This sentence is tied to what precedes by the excepting conjunction "nevertheless," which itself refers back to the exception in v. 15ab.[12] The brother or sister is not bound in such cases; nevertheless, change is not to be the rule; rather, one is urged to stay in one's social condition at the time of one's conversion. But Paul says this theologically by relating it to God's "call." The imperative in this case (lit. "let each person walk"[13]) has to do with how one lives out the whole of life, especially the Christian life, in the present age (cf. 1 Thess. 4:1; Gal. 5:16). Paul's concern, therefore, is not that they *retain* their present social setting,[14] but that they *recognize* it as the proper one in which to live out God's call.

The two clauses that express this new attitude toward their present situation form a balanced pair in Paul's sentence:[15]

---

[12]Gk. εἰ μή; the closest example to this usage in Paul is Gal. 1:7, where the preceding clause negates the possibility that there really is another gospel; "nevertheless, some are troubling you," he goes on. Since this usage "excepts" a preceding negative, it almost certainly goes back to v. 15b: "The brother or sister is not bound in such cases. . . . Nevertheless. . . ." See Zerwick, BG 470, who would make it the equivalent of ἀλλά; and BDF 376, who see it as the equivalent of πλήν (cf. Lightfoot, 226, who rejects ἀλλά as an equivalent).

[13]Gk. περιπατέω; see on 3:3.

[14]The NIV lacks precision here, both by translating Paul's pregnant verb for Christian life as "retain" and by changing the two ὡς's to *that* and *to which*. Paul's concern is not that they do stay put, but that they see their present married situation as in keeping with God's call and the Lord's assignment.

[15]This structural reality, plus the use of εἰ μή noted above (n. 12), tends to discount the suggestion of Rex, "Attempt," pp. 46-47, that the first of these clauses concludes vv. 12-16 while the second begins the new section.

to each as the Lord[16] assigned,
  each[17] as God has called,
    thus (meaning in accordance with the assignment and calling) let each person conduct his/her life.

Some have argued that the two clauses are synonymous;[18] but the change in subject and verb (including tense[19]) suggests otherwise. The thought is similar to Paul's description of his call to vocation in 1:1, in which he was called to be Christ's apostle (the historical expression of the call) through the prior will of God (the theological ground for it). Here the various social situations are to be understood as something Christ "assigned"[20] to them at the time God called them to salvation. The two clauses together, therefore, help define what is meant by "calling" throughout the passage. The concept of "call" in the clause "as God has called"[21] refers to conversion, that is, to their calling by God to be in fellowship with his Son (1:9; cf. 1:24). But the concern throughout is with their social situation *at the time* of that call, which is now to be seen as that which "the Lord assigned to each."[22] That does *not* mean that one is forever locked into that setting. Rather, Paul means that by calling a person within a given situation, that situation itself is taken up in the call and thus sanctified to him or her. Similarly, by saving a person *in* that setting, Christ thereby "assigned" it to him/her as his/her place of living out life in Christ. In the present context that means being married, whether to a believer or an unbeliever.

---

[16]As usual in Paul this refers to Christ, not God (*contra* Bartchy, 137 n. 484, who actually paraphrases it: "and with the faith that God has distributed to him"). It is difficult to escape the christological implications of this text, where the work of Christ is seen to be in union with the work of God. In Trinitarian terms, God the Father called; God the Son assigned. But both actions are the activity of the one God.

[17]This doubling of ἕκαστος ("each one"), which recurs as the subject in each of the framework sentences (vv. 17, 20, 24), emphasizes both the individual character and the diverse nature of their social settings. "Each" is called in his/her place, which is now "assigned" by the Lord, so they may not insist that the truly spiritual all have one situation.

[18]E.g., Conzelmann, 126; Bartchy, 137 n. 484.

[19]See n. 2 above.

[20]Gk. μερίζω; cf. the similar usage in 2 Cor. 10:13 and Rom. 12:3.

[21]Greek perfect, implying a continuing state from the time of conversion till now. Grammatically there is no way that this clause can be stretched to mean "live according to the fact that God has called you," as Bartchy, 151-55, repeatedly translates. Bartchy's case finally stands or falls on his ability to make vv. 17 and 24 reflect his interpretation of v. 20. At best this attempt in both cases stretches normal usages to the breaking point. Cf. the critique in G. Corcoran, "Slavery in the New Testament II," *Milltown Studies* 6 (1980), 69-72.

[22]Bartchy, 137 n. 484, suggests, on the basis of Rom. 12:3, that what is apportioned to each is "faith," but that puts Paul in a straightjacket; and how could the Corinthians have so understood it?

But this is not to be understood as law, as the various exceptions, and especially the distinction between circumcision and God's commandments in v. 19, indicate. Paul's intent is not to lay down a rule that one may *not* change;[23] rather, by thus hallowing one's situation in life, he is trying to help the Corinthians see that their social status is ultimately irrelevant as such (i.e., they can live out their Christian life in any of the various options) and therefore their desire to change is equally irrelevant—because it has nothing to do with genuine spirituality as their slogan would infer (v. 1b).

That this is a theological statement over against their desire to change status is made clear by the additional clause: (literally) "Even so (i.e., in this same way) in all the churches I give directions." This is the second of four instances in this letter where Paul appeals to what goes on in other churches.[24] The lack of this kind of appeal in his other letters suggests that this is his way of reminding them that theirs is the theology that is off track, not his (cf. 4:17).

Thus he tells them that being in Christ does not negate their present situation; but neither is he arguing that it absolutizes it. Rather, the call to Christ sets them free to live out their new life within it. It is not change per se that he is against, but change *as a Christian*. That is to give significance to one's social setting. Paul's point is that God's call, which comes to them where they are as his gracious gift, totally eliminates social setting as having any kind of religious significance. And how better can he illustrate that than by the one mark of sociological distinction that formerly did have religious significance but does so no more—circumcision.

18 Having theologized their present situation (namely, that those married when converted, whether to believer or pagan, should view that as the place to live out God's calling, assigned to them by Christ), Paul proceeds to illustrate his point by way of another social setting; but in this case the setting also carries religious overtones, which marriage does not. Therefore, it serves as a perfect illustration of the irrelevancy of such things for people who are trying to give religious significance to celibacy. The very lack of passion over this matter indicates that it is not an issue in the church in Corinth,[25] as it was later to become in Galatia and Philippi (Phil. 3:2-11). The gospel absolutely transcends, and thereby eliminates altogether, all

---

[23]Weiss, 183-92, interprets the whole to mean that Paul is laying down the rule that Christians *cannot* change status. But to do so he must make κλῆσις in v. 20 mean "vocation" and must emend the text in v. 24. That is to turn Paul's point on its head.

[24]The others are 4:17; 11:16; 14:33; see also on 1:2 and 16:1.

[25]A Jew-Gentile struggle does not appear in this letter, not even in chaps. 8–10, where one might most expect it. What emerges there is a struggle over *Paul's* way of relating to Jews and Gentiles, probably over the matter of eating idol food in their homes (see 9:19-23).

merely social distinctions. In Christ Jew and Greek together, whether slave or free, make up one body (12:13; cf. Gal. 3:28, which also includes male and female). Since this is so, by analogy it frees one from the urgency to change one's situation, as the Corinthians are trying to do (or to change someone else's, as the Judaizers would do to the Galatian churches!).

Thus he argues, "Was anyone[26] already circumcised when he was called?" That is, were you a Jew when you came to faith in Christ? If so, then "he should not become uncircumcised."[27] One can scarcely imagine a situation in Corinth where Jewish believers might actually have been doing so; rather, this is simply an illustration of the principle that is to be applied to their own concern. So also: "Was anyone uncircumcised when he was called?" That is, were you a Gentile when you came to faith? If so, then "he should not be circumcised." This operation, of course, was being urged by certain sectors of the church on Gentile Christians. But here it is not first of all a religious issue, but a sociological one. Being Jew or Gentile simply means nothing to God; whatever one was when called is what one still is, with no need to change. Christ has made such distinctions obsolete.

What is perhaps more significant is that this is the single social condition in the entire section for which there is no kind of exception. The reason is obvious. This one is not simply sociological; it is inherently theological as well. Paul's own experience of grace (as "calling") on the Damascus road, which came to him quite apart from his circumcision as a Jew, forever stamped his own understanding of the gospel as transcending either circumcision or uncircumcision. Thus, even though it was a matter to which he could acquiesce for pragmatic reasons (Acts 16:3), he was absolutely unyielding when anyone tried to give it religious significance. To do so was to make it count, and that meant to blunt salvation as God's gracious gift. That is the theological point he will make in the next sentence, which gives the reason for no change in this matter.

19 This is the first occurrence of what has to be one of the more remarkable statements that Paul ever made. It will be picked up again in the Galatian controversy as the absolute that disallows the circumcision of

---

[26]Gk. τις; this use of the indefinite pronoun in a terse question, followed by an imperative, further indicates the general nature of the illustration. Cf. E. J. Goodspeed, "The Syntax of I Cor. 7:18, 27," *AJT* 12 (1908), 249-50; *idem,* "A Patristic Parallel to 1 Cor. 7:18, 21," *JBL* 36 (1917), 150.

[27]As difficult as it might be for moderns to imagine, during the period of Hellenization many Jewish men had an operation of a kind that concealed their circumcision. See 1 Macc. 1:14-15: "So they built a gymnasium in Jerusalem, according to Gentile custom, and removed the marks of circumcision, and abandoned the holy covenant" (RSV; cf. Jos., *Ant.* 12.241, who is reflecting on this passage); cf. *As.Mos.* 8:3, where such an operation by Gentiles on Jewish sons is seen as part of God's judgment: "and their young sons will be cut by physicians to bring forward their foreskins" (OTP, II, 931).

Gentile believers (Gal. 5:6; 6:15): "Circumcision is nothing and uncircumcision is nothing." In this basically Gentile church that will be readily understood, precisely because this was never an issue for them. But it is hard for us to imagine the horror with which a fellow Jew would have responded. For not only did circumcision count, it counted for everything. Above all else this was the sign of the covenant, and therefore of their special standing with God. But Paul has seen clearly the implications of this issue for the gospel. Allow change here, and the cross is effectually negated, because such a change for religious reasons attaches significance to status as such. This in effect destroys grace as God's way of salvation. Paul's point, of course, is that they should themselves transfer the principle to their desire to be "demarried": "Marriage is nothing; and celibacy is nothing."[28] These things belong to the category of the irrelevant.

But Paul is quick to add that such a principle does not relativize obedience itself. "What counts"[29] is *not* sociological conditions, but "keeping God's commands"[30] (cf. 9:21). If Paul's fellow Jew would have been scandalized by his former statement, he would have been quite mystified by this one. From his perspective these sentences would be totally non sequitur, indeed contradictory. To be circumcised *is* to keep the commandment of God. But Paul obviously thinks otherwise. It should be noted that more than one theology in the Protestant tradition has equally had difficulty with this statement. How can Paul eliminate "works" (= circumcision) and then turn about and insist on "works" after all? The answer of course is that Paul did not consider obedience to the "commands of God" as "works of the law." That is an unfortunate confounding of terms within Protestant theology that Paul himself would scarcely have understood. Almost certainly this refers to the ethical imperatives of the Christian faith. One's proper response to grace

---

[28]Dungan, 134 n. 1, following Menoud ("Mariage et célibat selon Saint Paul," *RTP* 1 [1951], 33), seems to miss the point of this argument when he says, "In view of his belief that celibacy was a gift of the Spirit, such a formulation [as this present one] would have been impossible." Dungan has gone astray both in believing that Paul was an ascetic—and that therefore celibacy *was* important to him—and in suggesting that only celibacy was a *charisma*. It is clear from v. 7 that *both* marriage and celibacy were *charismata;* it is equally clear from the tenor of the whole argument, and from this analogy in particular, that neither of them amounted to a thing in Christ, any more than circumcision did. And it will not do to appeal to Paul's eschatology here, although that will come in due time. For now it is God's call in itself that transcends—and therefore transforms—one's present station.

[29]The final clause is actually elliptical; but the context indicates that the ἀλλά contrasts the twofold οὐδέν, hence the NIV is quite correct in this translation.

[30]Gk. ἐντολή; Paul tends to use this word ordinarily to refer to the individual commandments (e.g., Rom. 7:8-13, where the individual commandment is distinguished from the whole law; cf. Rom. 13:9). In 1 Cor. 14:37 he uses it to refer to his own instructions.

is obedience to the will of God (see the hermeneutical notes at the end of 3:1-4 and 6:7-11).[31] In a church where spirituality had degenerated into something very close to antinomian behavior, Paul simply cannot allow a religious statement like "circumcision counts for nothing" to be turned into "obedience to the will of God counts for nothing" (cf. 9:21).[32]

20 The first analogy having been given (v. 18), and its theological reason having been stated (v. 19), Paul now repeats the principle with which he began: (literally) "Each one, in the calling[33] in (by)[34] which he/she was called, in this let him/her remain." It has been argued that by this statement Paul intended to emphasize that each one should remain in his/her *Christian* calling, that is, that each one should remain a Christian.[35] Much more likely the word "calling" here carries the same kind of double nuance that it did in 1:26 and that seems to be in view in v. 17.[36] Paul wants them to live out their Christian life (i.e., their "calling" to Christ) in the situation ("calling") where they were when God called them to Christ.[37] The emphasis is on both, that they can be Christians in whatever situation God called them, and therefore that they do not need to change situations—precisely because they are in Christ. Let their "calling" (becoming believers) sanctify the setting of their calling.

---

[31]On the other hand, of course, one must not turn the ethical imperative of the gospel, which is our grateful response to God's mercy, into a new form of law (= obedience in order to gain his favor). This becomes Christian legalism, at which Paul would be equally horrified.

[32]Cf. Barrett, 169: "*That we keep God's commandments* means an obedience to the will of God as disclosed in his Son far more radical than the observance of any code, whether ceremonial or moral, could be."

[33]Gk. κλῆσις, the only occurrence of the noun in the paragraph. See the discussion on 1:26.

[34]The relative here modifies κλήσει; it is not possible to tell whether the sense is locative or instrumental. The locative nature of the similar expression in v. 24 would suggest that it is so here as well, as almost all translations and commentators. But see Parry, 116, "in the calling wherewith he was called."

[35]Grosheide, 169; Bartchy, 132-55 (see above, n. 8). But in order to come to this, one must press the language and sense of vv. 17 and 24 beyond recognizable limits.

[36]Even though the verb is ambiguous in each of the three "framework" imperatives (vv. 17, 20, 24), its usage with each of the four social conditions in vv. 18 and 21-22 makes it certain that the emphasis is not on conversion *per se,* but on a person's social status *at the time* of conversion. And the whole argument is intended to validate that status by the very fact that they were called to Christ in that situation.

[37]Cf. Lightfoot, 229: "[The word] is applied both to the act and (as here) to the circumstances of calling." But it does not mean "vocation." As Lightfoot further comments (228): "The sentiment which underlies this thought is essentially right, but as an interpretation of the apostle's words here it is quite wrong." Unfortunately, it is this latter position against which almost all of Bartchy's argument is raised; but it seems to be a minority view against which he is reacting, and he reacts so strongly that he pushes too hard in another unlikely direction (see n. 8 above).

21 Paul now moves to a second supporting illustration, which in general is structured like the former. It begins with a word to the slave in the form of a question, followed by a command; and this is followed by a theological reason in support of the command. In this case, however, there are also some significant differences. First, he begins with the situation of the slave, but there is no corresponding word to the free person. That is picked up by implication when he comes to the theological reason in vv. 22-23. There are some obvious reasons for this. To correspond with the former, he would need to have said: "Were you a slave when called, do not become a freedman; were you a free person when called, do not become a slave." But for slaves this was not an option; and for free people, although they could—and many did—sell themselves into slavery,[38] that would not be the kind of "change" that one would normally seek. Thus the differences in the two illustrations may be seen by a display of the structure of each argument:

A. First illustration: circumcision (18-20)
1. To the circumcised: do not change (18a)
2. To the uncircumcised: do not change (18b)
   Reason: Neither counts (19)
   Conclusion: Stay in your "calling" (20)
B. Second illustration: slavery (21-24)
1. To the slave: do not be concerned (21a)
   Exception: If granted, make use of freedom (21b)
   Reason: (1) to slave: one is Christ's freedman (22a)
   (2) to free person: one is Christ's slave (22b)
   —Additional theological reason (23)
   Conclusion: Stay in your "calling" *with God* (24)

Second, in contrast to vv. 18-19, but as in vv. 27-28, the question and command are not expressed with the indefinite "anyone," but in the second person singular (cf. 4:7). It is difficult to know what to make of this. On the one hand, it is a standard way in Judaism to express general commands[39] and very well may do so here. On the other hand, the situation in vv. 27-28 seems to be reflecting a real concern in the community that is finally particularized in vv. 36-38. It may be, therefore, that this does indeed strike a note of concern within the community, to which Paul here speaks an *ad hoc* word. Nonetheless, the principle is Paul's greater urgency, so that the

---

[38]Bartchy, 181-82, suggests that v. 23b, "Do not become slaves of men," might carry this nuance in part, but that seems doubtful. See on v. 23.

[39]Besides the OT apodictic laws ("Thou shalt not"), cf. the teaching of Jesus, especially, e.g., the collection of sayings in Luke 6:20-38, which are generally in the second plural but in vv. 29-30 appear in the second singular.

social questions about slavery are eclipsed by the theological reasons of vv. 22-23.

Third, the command is not "Stay as you are," but rather "Don't let it trouble[40] you." Although this gets at the same point that has been raised throughout, it is a significantly different way of saying it. The reason seems clear: Paul realizes that in this case, in contrast to both marriage/divorce and circumcision/uncircumcision, the slave could not choose his/her status. That is, one could sell oneself into slavery, but slaves could not choose freedom. But in some ways this becomes an even more powerful illustration for him because his real concern throughout has not been with change per se, but with those who were desiring change as Christians. His point right along, therefore, has not been simply, "Stay where you are," but precisely as in this case, "Do not let your social condition be a concern to you." Your calling in Christ eclipses such conditions, but thereby also transforms them into situations where you may live out your Christian "calling."

Fourth, in contrast to the two conditions in v. 18, but quite like all the situations in vv. 1-16, an exception is made: (literally) "If indeed (or, even though) you are able to become free, rather (or, by all means) make use of [it]." On its own the sentence is ambiguous, and scholarship has been rather evenly divided[41] as to whether Paul intended, "Even supposing you could go free, you would be better off making the most of your slavery" (NAB), or "Although if you can gain your freedom, do so" (NIV).[42] The problem lies with the verb "make use of," whose object must be understood from the context. The difficulties are best illustrated by the fact that grammar and context are argued as in support of both options.

Those who favor the first, the so-called "negative," option argue (1) that the combination *ei kai* often means "even though"[43] (e.g., 2 Cor. 7:8; 12:11); (2) that the *mallon* ("rather") often carries the adversative sense of

---

[40]Gk. μέλει, "be a concern to someone" (cf. 9:9).

[41]See Bartchy, 6-7, who has a convenient chart, in chronological order, of most significant scholars from Origen in 200 to Hunzinger in 1970. The list of those with whom one would disagree, on either side, is impressive!

[42]Grosheide, 170, and Bartchy, 155-59, offer a third alternative. The verb does not here mean "make use of," but, in keeping with a usage found often in Josephus, "live according to"; and the object to be supplied is "calling." Hence Bartchy: "But if indeed you become manumitted, by all means [as a freedman] live according to [God's calling]." But even though that may well capture some of Paul's sentiment in this section, it seems too obtuse for the Corinthians to have grasped it.

[43]Sevenster, *Paul*, p. 189, argues that "the καί is placed before the δύνασαι and not before ἐλεύθερος γενέσθαι," which in his opinion "excludes the translation: furthermore, if you can gain your freedom." But this quite misses Paul's grammar; the καί goes with the εἰ and forms a strong exception: "if indeed" (cf. vv. 9 and 28). See esp. Thrall, *Particles*, pp. 78-82.

"instead";[44] (3) that the *gar* ("for") that introduces the next clause follows naturally as the reason for staying in slavery;[45] and (4) that the context seems to require it since the whole point is to remain as one is, and to read this text positively is to bring about a change of status.

Despite these arguments and the significant number of scholars who go this way, the so-called "positive" option, which supplies "freedom" as the object of the verb, seems by far the better one. First, for several lexical and grammatical reasons: (1) the normal sense of the combination *ei kai* is not "even though," but "if indeed" (cf. 4:7; 7:11, 28); (2) in an elliptical sentence one would ordinarily supply a word from that sentence—in this case "freedom"—not a word from an earlier sentence;[46] (3) the verb "to make use of" is an aorist infinitive, suggesting a single action, not the present, which would carry the sense needed for "keep on in slavery"; (4) the clause begins with the strong adversative "but," which lends itself to an excepting clause (cf. vv. 9, 11, 15)[47] but makes little sense as the conjunction joining an intensification of the negative imperative, which would expect, "*and* even though . . ."; (5) the word "rather" regularly has an elative sense, that is, "*by all means* make use of it"; and (6) the verb "make use of" does not work well with the negative view, which requires the verb to have a unique meaning ("make the most of," "put up with"); whereas in this view it has Paul's ordinary sense of "make use of" or "take advantage of" (cf. v. 31; and esp. 9:12, 15).[48]

But even more important than these lexical-grammatical considerations are the two that have to do with historical and literary context. First, as Bartchy has shown decisively,[49] the view that a slave could *reject* manumission (being set free) has no historical basis of any kind.[50] That is, a freed

---

[44]Cf. Sevenster, *Paul,* p. 189: "μᾶλλον would be virtually meaningless if Paul were advising: then make use of that opportunity to become free; but it fits in very well if he is advising those who are slaves to do instead the unexpected."

[45]Cf. Barrett, 171: "Particularly important is the *for* (γάρ) with which the next verse begins: You need not hesitate to put up with your servile condition, for. . . ."

[46]Even more difficult is Bartchy's proposal that it picks up κλήσει from yet another sentence earlier.

[47]The word here is ἀλλά; it is δέ in the other examples. But the pattern is constant. "Remain as you are, but. . . ."

[48]Given the proximity of the usage in 1 Corinthians, as well as similar usage in 2 Cor. 1:17; 3:12; and 13:10, Bartchy's disregard of these data in favor of a usage in Josephus does not lend confidence to his interpretation (see n. 42 above).

[49]Pp. 62-120.

[50]Bartchy gives considerable energy to the inclusion of the "positive" view here, too. That is, a slave did not have a choice for freedom either. But his own view, that the protasis means something like "but if indeed you are able to become manumitted," works equally well for this view. It is not that the slave had the *option* of freedom; that was given to him. Paul's word is, "If that be the case, then by all means make the best of it."

slave may continue to serve a master as a freedman, but by the very fact of manumission he or she is no longer a slave.[51] Paul did not intend to suggest that they had the choice between freedom and slavery, but that when, from the slave's perspective, they were able to become free, they should make the best of it because that had been given them by the master. Thus, it is extremely unlikely historically that Paul would have suggested, "Make use of your slavery, even if you are able to become free," since that choice did not exist at all.

Second, the structure of the argument of the entire chapter, and of vv. 17-24 in particular, suggests that the clause is intended to be a genuine exception to the prior imperative. This is the pattern throughout the chapter; it would be highly unusual for this one "exception" to be no exception at all, but rather an intensification of the imperative.[52]

Finally, as the structural display indicates, on the basis of the previous pattern of vv. 18-19, the theological statement of vv. 22-23 does not give a reason for staying in slavery, but for the original imperative. That is, Paul is saying, "Were you a slave when called? Don't let that trouble you, *for* he who was a slave when called by the Lord is the Lord's freedman," to which the exception clause, just as in v. 11, is a parenthesis.

Paul's point, then, is not that one *must* stay where one was when called. Rather, it is precisely as the imperative in this verse implies: *Whatever* your situation was at the time of your call, don't let that become a concern to you. One's calling in Christ raises one above that urgency. In the context, after all, Paul is still addressing those who feel compelled to dissolve their marriages. Change may occur, but one's calling in Christ means that change is unnecessary, and certainly not to be a compulsion.

22 Just as v. 19 gave the theological reason for v. 18 (why Jews should not try to become as Gentiles, and vice versa), so this sentence gives the theological reason for v. 21a, why the Christian slave should not let his/her social situation be the occasion for distress. To which now he adds the situation of the free person. Neither slavery nor freedom counts for anything to the one who is called into fellowship with Christ. Paul makes that point with a wordplay on slave and free in terms of one's relationship to Christ. Thus (literally), "The called-in-the-Lord[53] slave is the Lord's freed-

[51]Corcoran, "Slavery," pp. 73-74, following Weiss, argues "that Paul has directed his admonition against the striving after manumission itself." But that is *not* what the text says; it is doubtful whether one can come to this even by implication.

[52]Corcoran, "Slavery," pp. 66-67, tries to minimize this by arguing that in every other case a *reason* for the exception is given. But that is not so (v. 15c is *not* the reason for 15ab; none is given in v. 11).

[53]Both the NIV and RSV take ἐν κυρίῳ to be instrumental, "called by the Lord"; but that seems to miss the sense of the whole passage. The calling is to be "in Christ," which has to do with one's relationship with him, not that he is the one who

man." That is, the person whose social condition was that of slavery when he/she responded to God's call to be "in the Lord," has by that call been given status with the Lord himself that removes him or her from being someone else's slave—even though that old relationship still obtains. The word "freedman" is the technical term for those who were formerly slaves, but had been manumitted. Under Roman law manumitted slaves ("freedmen") often lived with their former owners, to whom they agreed to continue to render service.[54] But when called to be in Christ, even though one's social status is still that of slave, the relationship of "freedman" has now been established with the Lord. Moreover, the "purchase with a price" metaphor in v. 23 suggests that it is not simply the relationship with the Lord that is in view, but the "freedom" from the bondage of one's former sins.

Likewise, "the person who was free when called is Christ's slave." This person has not heretofore been addressed, although because of the contrasting pairs in the former illustration, one may be sure that he has not been very far away. The implied imperative for which this is now the theological reason would go something like: "Were you a free person when called? Don't let that be a matter of importance to you." And why not? "Because the free person who has been called to be in fellowship with Christ is in fact Christ's slave." That is, even though such people too have been "set free" in Christ, they have come into a relationship with Christ that can best be described by the metaphor of "slavery." Our calling has eliminated the option of belonging to ourselves. We belong to another, Christ.

This imagery, of course, must be understood in light of Greco-Roman slavery, not that of recent American history. Slavery was in fact the bottom rung on the social order, but for the most part it provided generally well for up to one-third of the population in a city like Corinth or Rome. The slave had considerable freedom and very often experienced mutual benefit along with the master. The owner received the benefit of the slave's services; and the slave had steady "employment," including having all his or her basic needs met—indeed, for many to be a slave was preferable to being a freedman, whose securities were often tenuous at best. But the one thing that marked the slave was that in the final analysis, he did not belong to himself but to another. That is Paul's point with this imagery.

By saying that in Christ the slave is freed, and the free person is a slave, Paul is once again minimizing present social status. Since these reversals have already taken place in their call to Christ, neither is of consequence to the one who is in Christ.

---

called. Furthermore, God, not Christ, is the expressed subject of the verb in v. 17 and the implied subject of all the passive expressions of this verb in the letter.

[54]See F. Lyall, "Roman Law in the Writings of Paul—The Slave and the Freedman," *NTS* 17 (1970/71), 78-79; and Bartchy, 70.

23 To reinforce the theological point of v. 22, Paul pushes the metaphors of that verse one step further. He begins by repeating the imagery from 6:20, "You were bought with a price." Only in this case the imagery carries its full double nuance, precisely because it speaks to both people in v. 22.[55] On the one hand, as in 6:20, the basic metaphor is that of becoming the slave of someone through purchase. That speaks directly to the "free person" who through his/her calling to Christ has become "a slave of Christ." On the other hand, for the one who was a slave when called, it is the metaphor of purchase for freedom, as in Gal. 3:3; 4:5; Rev. 5:9. The slave is free and the free person a slave because both have been purchased by Christ through the blood of the cross.[56] Thus the metaphor comes full circle. The slave is still socially a slave, but in Christ he/she is both free and slave: purchased by Christ so as to be set free by him, one has at the same time come under Christ's rightful ownership. The free person is still socially free, but in Christ he/she is both slave and free: purchased by Christ so as to belong to him, one has at the same time experienced the freedom that only he can give.

The final result, therefore, is: "Do not become[57] slaves of men." Again this is not literal, as in "Do not sell yourselves into slavery," but metaphorical.[58] Precisely because the slave is both free and slave in Christ, and the free person is both slave and free in Christ, they must not let themselves come under the bondage of mere humans. They are the slaves of another who has at the same time set them free.[59] With these final words Paul is probably reflecting once again on their penchant to let merely human wisdom, disguised in the form of "spirituality," dictate their present anxieties about the need to be free from certain social settings, especially marriage. Don't come under such bondage, he tells them.

24 With the addition of the vocative, "Brothers [and sisters]" (see on 1:10), Paul concludes by repeating the controlling imperative one more time (see on vv. 17 and 20). In this case the sentence is very close to v. 20, with two modifications:[60] (1) the phrase "in the calling" is replaced by the

---

[55]This is not a universal view, but it seems to make the best sense of its inclusion here.

[56]For the improbable suggestion that sacral manumission is in view, see nn. 73 and 74 on 6:20.

[57]Gk. μὴ γίνεσθαι. Mare, 234, would press this to have its full present tense force, "Stop becoming . . ." (cf. on 4:5; 7:5). But this is such a fixed idiom in Paul's parenesis here that one can scarcely make a point of tense.

[58]Bartchy, *Slavery*, pp. 181-82, suggests that it might also carry a literal nuance; cf. Corcoran, "Slavery," p. 75.

[59]There are *formal* parallels with Stoicism (given in Conzelmann, 128 n. 34), but as Conzelmann comments: "The dialectic of freedom in servitude is alien to them." Cf. Sevenster, *Paul*, pp. 185-92.

[60]By reworking these, Bartchy, 135, makes this say the same thing as v. 20. But that is done by fiat, not by showing how it is grammatically possible.

relative pronoun "in whatever"; (2) the imperative is modified by the prepositional phrase "with God"[61] (NIV, "as responsible to God"). Both of these changes seem to verify our interpretation of vv. 17 and 20, that simultaneously Paul is referring to one's situation when called and to God's call thereby making that situation irrelevant to one's relationship to God (or to put that positively, it sanctifies that situation as a place where one can truly live out God's call in the present age).

First, in the context of the argument the relative clause must have something like the word "situation" supplied (lit. "in whatever [situation] he was called"), and can only mean something like the NEB has translated: "In the condition in which he received his call."[62] The emphasis here is on one's *situation,* not on one's *calling* per se, and the point is that it is all right to stay wherever one was when called. Second, the prepositional phrase "with God" puts the whole issue into perspective. One is not simply to *remain* in one's situation (married, single, circumcised, uncircumcised, slave, free), because in many cases change may come about without one's seeking it. Paul's point right along has been that one should remain *with God;* that is, whether one is slave or free, one's status is finally determined by one's being "before" or "in the sight of" God in that situation. That sets one free both to remain in it and especially to live out the Christian calling therein.

With these words the argument with those who would dissolve their marriages in favor of the higher spiritual status of celibacy is brought to an end. The analogy is that of the slave and the free, and the point is that neither marriage nor celibacy is significant; they should serve God where they are. But the concern raised by the celibates is not over. So in the next section Paul will again apply the principle here argued; but because he disagrees with their reasons, even if he agrees that singleness is best, he turns out to affirm change (i.e., marriage) in rather strong terms.

In an exceedingly mobile culture, in which upward mobility is almost a sacred duty, a passage like this does not get an easy hearing. On the one hand, there are those who think so poorly of their status that they find difficulty seeing it as a place in which to live out their calling as believers. The standard formula begins, "Oh, I'm just a . . . ." On the other hand, the

---

[61]Gk. παρὰ θεῷ, which probably here means something very much as in 3:19, "in the presence of" or "before" God. See BAGD II.2b.

[62]Bartchy, 135, suggests "that here it is equal to the use of ὡς in 7:17," and translates "in accord with." But there is no grammatical evidence for such an understanding (the appeal to Moule, 131, is not accurate). Even more strained is the suggestion that ἐν τούτῳ is masculine because of attraction to this ἐν ᾧ, even though it no longer has masculine force, and that ἐν ᾧ therefore really equals τούτῳ, which refers to the "calling" in v. 20.

tendency of most is to see status as significant, and change as necessary. The two points Paul makes need to be heard anew. (1) Status of any kind is ultimately irrelevant with God. One is simply no better off one way or another. That does not mean that in a culture that provides opportunity one should not seek "to better oneself." But it does mean that one whose life has been determined by God's call should not put any stock in it. (2) Precisely because our lives are determined by God's call, not by our situation, we need to learn to continue there as those who are "before God." Paul's concern is not with change, one way or the other, but with "living out one's calling" in whatever situation one is found. There let one serve the Lord, and let the call of God sanctify to oneself the situation, whether it be mixed marriage, singleness, blue- or white-collar work, or socioeconomic condition.

3. About the "Virgins" (7:25-40)

After telling the married not to seek change, but to remain as they are, Paul now moves to a second, closely related item from their letter: whether some who are called "virgins" *should* get married. But much of Paul's answer is less than certain.[1] Besides a large number of details throughout, the difficulties are basically four: (1) the meaning of the term "virgins"; (2) the structure of the argument, which is especially related to the meaning of vv. 36-38—whether it is the conclusion of the argument begun in v. 25, or whether it is "a special case";[2] (3) the intent and meaning of the central section (vv. 29-35) for the argument as a whole; and (4) the nature of the problem in Corinth as to (a) what was going on, (b) what they said in their letter, and (c) how it relates to the preceding issue (vv. 1-24). The first two matters are interrelated, in that if one thinks vv. 36-38 are a special case, then the word "virgin" may or may not mean the same thing throughout the section. All of this is made more difficult by our uncertainty as to whether Greek or Roman customs prevailed in the Corinth of Paul's day,[3] and the exact nature of these customs in any case.

With the proper degree of hesitation due such difficult texts, this commentary proceeds on the basis of the following reconstruction:

(1) Since the subject matter, "virgins," is specifically mentioned in

---

[1]Evidenced both by the alternative translations in the NIV[mg] and NEB for vv. 36-38, as well as the general hesitance that scholars bring to the text. Cf., e.g., Murphy-O'Connor, 171: "This is probably the most difficult and controverted section of the letter"; and Orr, "Treatment," p. 17, who begins, "I suggest with trembling hesitation. . . ."

[2]The language is Conzelmann's, 134, who believes so.

[3]As throughout, it is unlikely in the highest degree that Paul is addressing a Jewish Christian community, as J. M. Ford, *Trilogy*, and Hurley, 181-82, maintain. See the Introduction, p. 4 n. 12.

the three parts of the argument (vv. 28, 34, 36-38), common sense dictates that unless there are overwhelming reasons to think otherwise, the entire passage is a singular response to one issue. That means that what is begun in v. 26 is brought to its reasonable (for Paul) conclusion with the strong inferential conjunction "so then" in v. 38.[4]

(2) Of the various options for the meaning of "virgins" (see on v. 25), that seems most probable which sees Paul as speaking to some who are betrothed and are now questioning whether to go through with their marriages.

(3) It is also highly likely, given the obvious similarities between this section and the preceding, that the same ascetic stance (namely v. 1b: "It is good for a man not to have relations with a woman") dictates their attitude here. However, in this case, quite in contrast to the former where they were urging a *change* of status, they argued, "It is good for [such a] man to remain as he is" (v. 26), meaning "to keep his 'virgin' a virgin" (v. 37). Indeed, it seems altogether likely that they have either said or implied that going through with the marriage would constitute "sin" (vv. 28, 36); such an idea is totally foreign to Paul's own Jewish heritage.

(4) Thus they have Paul on the horns of a dilemma. On the one hand, he is known to favor celibacy—or perhaps they have appealed to his own example (see v. 7). On the other hand, he totally disagrees with their *ascetic reasons* for such a stance. His problem therefore is how to affirm celibacy without at the same time affirming their asceticism.[5]

(5) This difficulty is increased in light of Paul's immediately preceding argument that people should stay as they are at the time of their call. For the merely single, that would be easy enough. But how do the betrothed stay as they are? Do they bring the betrothal to its normal conclusion (= marriage), or dissolve the relationship altogether? And all of this would become the more difficult if the young woman had been attracted to the ascetic life while the man had not[6] (although this latter is not contended for here).

(6) Probably because of his simultaneous agreement with their stance but disagreement with their theology, Paul's argument takes on a character of its own, quite unlike anything else in his extant letters. He begins with a

---

[4]Thus the section also follows the "a-b-a" pattern of argument noted by Weiss, 192; Allo, 319; and Hurd, 178, in which, just as in 8:1–10:22 and 12–14, Paul begins with a more general statement, follows it with an explanatory digression, and concludes with a very specific response to the problem. See the Introduction, pp. 15-16.

[5]This seems to make better sense of all the data than the suggestion of H. Chadwick ("'All Things to All Men' (I Cor. IX.22)," *NTS* 1 [1954/55], 267-68), that it reflects Paul's approach in Corinth of being "all things to all men"—although on my overall approach to the section I am in general agreement with Chadwick.

[6]See Rex, "Attempt," pp. 48-51, for this suggestion.

caution, that what is about to be said, even though he thinks it trustworthy, is less than a command of the Lord; it is his "opinion" (v. 25). The argument is then laced with "I think" (36), "I am sparing you" (28), "I wish" (32), "I say this for your good" (35), "let him do as he wishes" (36), "he shall do well" (37). What imperatives do appear (v. 27) merely reiterate the stance of vv. 17-24, and as elsewhere are immediately qualified. Whatever else, this is not your standard Paul.

The net result is an argument that does indeed express his own (trustworthy) opinion that in their present situation celibacy is the better option; but it is not the only option. Marriage is a perfectly valid alternative; and whatever else, it is no sin. Despite the confusion of celibacy with asceticism on the part of so many scholars, Paul is no ascetic. Celibate, yes; ascetic, no. His new reasons are basically eschatological (i.e., the truly eschatological person has a radically altered perspective from which he or she views such relationships; vv. 29-31), although they also involve the prospect of "undivided" concern for the things of the Lord (vv. 32b-34). But whether they are married or unmarried he wants them to be "free of anxiety" (v. 32a).

The argument, then, is in three parts: (1) Vv. 25-28 offer the opening statement, in which he picks up their slogan, agrees with it, and then qualifies it. (2) Vv. 29-35 offer two interrelated reasons for his preference for celibacy, neither of which is to be understood as an attempt—as the pneumatics are doing—to put a noose around their necks (v. 35). (3) Rather (vv. 36-38), the two options, to marry or to refrain, are both open to them. If one feels a compulsion to be married, so be it (v. 36); but if one is under no such compulsion, so much the better (v. 37). So then (v. 38), the one does well, and the other, especially in the light of present conditions (v. 26), does even better. He concludes the whole discussion with a final word to the women (vv. 39-40), reminding them that they are bound to their one husband as long as he lives, but that on his decease they, too, have the same two options: to remarry (within the context of the faith) or to stay as widows, of which the latter is preferable. But again, this is his opinion, wherein he also thinks he has the mind of the Lord.

a. Singleness is preferable but not required (7:25-28)

25 *Now about virgins: I have no command from the Lord, but I give a judgment as one who by the Lord's mercy is trustworthy.* 26 *Because of the present crisis, I think that it is good for you to remain as you are.* 27 *Are you* bound to a woman?[7] *Do not seek to be*

---

[7]NIV, "married." See the commentary.

released.[8] *Are you* free from a woman?[9] *Do not look for a wife.* 28 **But if you do marry,**[10] **you have not sinned; and if a**[11] **virgin marries, she has not sinned.** **But those who marry will face many troubles in this life, and I want to spare you this.**

This paragraph both announces the topic to be taken up next and gives Paul's basic response to it. But it also has its share of difficulties. As they have argued, and he agrees, "It is good for the virgins to remain as they are" (v. 26). But his own reason for it, "because of the present crisis," is less than clear. In v. 27 he seems to apply the slogan—by means of terse questions followed by imperatives, similar to those in v. 18. But the precise nature of these questions, both as to who is being addressed and their place in the immediate context, is also not clear. In any case, the final question at least (if not both) is qualified by the reality that marriage is no sin. Paul's own reasons for his opinion are then added to the qualification: The married will have distress in the present life, and Paul wishes to spare them.

25 The new topic is signaled by the second "now about" in the letter (see on v. 1). But who are the "virgins"?[12] There are three basic views,[13] each of which is determined in part by how one understands vv.

---

[8]NIV, "a divorce."

[9]NIV, "unmarried."

[10]The Western uncials D F G, probably influenced by the Latin versions, have λαβῇς γυναῖκα ("take a wife"). See comment on 7:2.

[11]Four MSS (B F G 429) lack the article ἡ with παρθένος, against all the rest. One cannot tell whether the NIV is following B F G here or whether they are generalizing. In either case the translation is ill-chosen. M. Black (*The Scrolls and Christian Origins* [New York, 1961], p. 85) and J. F. Bound ("Who Are the 'Virgins' Discussed in 1 Corinthians 7:25-38?" *Evangelical Journal* 2 [1984], 6-7) consider the anarthrous reading to be original. But that is because they need this reading to support their view that the "virgins" are male celibates, an extremely unlikely option (the noun is feminine throughout; v. 28 is thereby rendered "grossly tautologous" [Barrett, 176]). Bound tries to escape the latter charge by suggesting that vv. 27-28a do not refer to this question, and that only with v. 28b does Paul return to the matter begun in vv. 25-26. But that puts a terrible strain on both the balanced structure of v. 28 (one of 12 such balanced male/female sentences in the chapter) and the sense of the text. The argument that the η was added by dittography (repeating the final η from γήμῃ) carries little force since the omission could equally—far more likely in fact, given scribal habits—have been haplography (accidental omission of a second η).

[12]It will hardly do to answer, as Conzelmann, 131, does: "What is meant by the term παρθένοι is—superfluously enough—hotly disputed: it means virgins." That would be fine if vv. 34 and 36-38 did not exist; but even he must make the latter a "special case" because in these verses it obviously means more than just "virgin."

[13]For the view held by Black and Bound that Paul is addressing male celibates, at least in vv. 25-27 (Black) and throughout (Bound), see n. 11 above. J. M. Ford, "Levirate Marriage in St Paul (I Cor vii)," *NTS* 10 (1963/64), 361-65, followed by Hurley,

36-38, and none of which is completely free of difficulties. (1) The nearly universal tradition of the church up to the twentieth century (cf. the NIV margin for vv. 36-38) has been "that the Corinthians consulted him about the special case of giving virgin daughters in marriage; whereupon St Paul generalised, first stating the guiding principle (ver. 27), then applying it to both sexes (*vv.* 28-35), and finally dealing with the special point which the Corinthians had put to him (*vv.* 36-38)."[14] This position rests on some linguistic features of vv. 36-38 which suggest that the man being addressed has a jurisdictional relationship to the one who is called "his (own) virgin." The crucial item for this point of view is the change of verbs in v. 38 from *gameō* ("to marry") to *gamizō* (which in the Gospels means "to give in marriage"). But despite both this long history and some items in vv. 36-38 that can be seen to favor it, this view has far more difficulties than advantages: (a) Nothing in vv. 25-35 even remotely suggests that Paul is addressing such an issue; indeed, it is fair to say that without v. 38, with its change of verbs, this view would never have arisen, or at least would never have gained popularity. (b) The terms father, guardian, daughter, etc. never appear in the text; furthermore, there is no known evidence for one's speaking of a father-daughter relationship in terms of her being "his virgin." (c) Any number of other items in vv. 36-38 make this view extremely difficult to maintain (see on these verses).

(2) A second view, introduced in modern times by H. Achelis,[15] and adopted by a large number of scholars,[16] including the NEB (see n. 8 on 7:36), understands "virgins" in this verse to refer to both men and women, who are committed to one another in a "spiritual marriage." That is, they are living together but without sexual relations. This has become difficult for some of the men, so they are wondering about the advisability of consum-

---

189-96, proposed that the virgins are young widows who have been married only once, and that the question has to do with the levirate marriage of a sister-in-law. Paul's answer basically releases him from this obligation. Not only does this proposal stretch the meaning of several words (esp. "virgin"!), but it assumes that the Corinthian church was essentially Jewish, concerned with essentially Jewish issues. All of this is highly improbable.

Other proposals are basically modifications of the major three, especially of the "father-daughter" one, such as guardian-benefactor, master-female slave, and adopter-adopted. See J. O'Rourke, "Hypotheses Regarding 1 Corinthians 7, 36-38," *CBQ* 20 (1958), 292-98, who prefers master-female slave.

[14]Lightfoot, 231.

[15]*Virgines Subintroductae: ein Beitrag zum VII. Kapitel des I. Korintherbriefs* (Leipzig, 1902).

[16]Along with Hurd himself, 169-82, see the list in n. 2, p. 170. To that list may now be added, among others, the commentaries by Thrall, Ruef, and Murphy-O'Connor, and esp. R. H. A. Sebolt, "Spiritual Marriage in the Early Church: A Suggested Interpretation of 1 Cor. 7:36-38," *CTM* 30 (1959), 103-19, 176-89.

mating the relationship physically. Although unknown this early elsewhere, this practice prevailed in several quarters of the church from the second century to the fifth,[17] and it is certainly arguable that such an attitude *could* have prevailed in the Corinth of Paul's day. But besides the lack of firm evidence for such a practice as early as this, this view has against it (a) the fact that Paul opposes such a view in vv. 2-6, (b) the lack of any "hard evidence" within the text itself for such a position on the part of the Corinthians, plus (c) even more difficulties than the first view with various parts of vv. 36-38.

(3) The view adopted here[18] (see above, p. 323) is that it was a term that the Corinthians used in referring to some young betrothed women[19] who along with their fiancés[20] were being pressured by the pneumatics and were now themselves wondering whether to go through with the marriage. Paul's response is basically from the man's point of view because it was the cultural norm for men to take the initiative in all such matters. This assumes the influence of Roman culture since by the time of the early Empire it was common for men to act on their own behalf, without the father acting as *patria potestas* as in earlier days.[21] This view has the distinct advantage of seeing both vv. 27-28 and 36-38 as being addressed to the same man, without the need of changing either topics or persons addressed. This view, however, is not without its share of difficulties in vv. 36-38, although they seem to be more easily answered than in the other cases.

Paul's first word is an attempt to put this whole matter into a proper perspective: "I have no command[22] from the Lord."[23] The last items taken

---

[17]See, e.g., *Acts of Paul and Thecla* 5, from the middle of the second century: "Blessed are they who have wives as if they had them not, for they shall inherit God." This is one of six beatitudes that bless continence and virginity.

[18]The most thorough presentation is by W. G. Kümmel, "Verlobung und Heirat bei Paulus (I. Cor 7 $_{36-38}$)," in *Neutestamentliche Studien für Rudolf Bultmann* (ed. W. Eltester; Berlin, 1954), pp. 275-95. It has been adopted by most recent commentaries (Conzelmann, Barrett, Holladay, Senft).

[19]This view does have the advantage that the word is used in the NT to refer to one who is betrothed (Luke 1:27; Matt. 1:18, 23), although in each case she is further described as such. Elliott, "Teaching," p. 221, would also add the "virgins" in the parable of Matt. 25:1-13, but the meaning "betrothed girls" there is questionable.

[20]The plural in v. 25 could possibly refer to both the man and the woman; however, all subsequent uses are singular and feminine.

[21]See J. V. P. D. Balsdon, *Roman Women: Their History and Habits* (London, 1962), pp. 177-79.

[22]Gk. ἐπιταγή (cf. 7:6).

[23]Since this is such unusual talk for Paul, some have argued that the Corinthians themselves have been using some of the sayings of Jesus circulating in their Q form (esp. Luke 20:34-36) and have turned them into support for their asceticism. Paul would then be opposing their use of Jesus in this way by saying that there is *not* a commandment of the Lord on this matter. See J. M. Robinson, "Kerygma and History in the New Testament,"

up in the prior section were prefaced with words similar to these. In v. 10 he did have a command of the Lord, but in the matter addressed in vv. 12-16 he did not. Now he repeats that the Lord did not address this concern of theirs either. But more than that seems to be intended here; the issue itself lies in the category of concerns for which there are no commands of any kind, just advice or judgments[24] (cf. v. 40). The Corinthian pneumatics apparently had turned their slogan into something close to law, the net result of which is that the betrothed would sin against the Spirit if they consummated their marriages. But the Lord did not give commands on this kind of issue; therefore Paul can only give advice.

Paul's judgment is not thereby to be understood as unimportant. Indeed, it is given by "one who by the Lord's mercy is trustworthy[25]." The emphasis is not so much on his being a faithful apostle as on the trustworthiness of his judgment; what makes that so is that he has received mercy from the Lord. In many ways this is a remarkable qualifier. He appeals neither to his apostleship nor to his authority in Christ. Rather, his apostleship, and therefore his judgments on such nonessentials, are viewed in terms of the Lord's mercy to him (cf. 15:9-10), which probably means that they are to understand his advice as an expression of that same mercy. Thus the ultimate appeal is to Christ's mercies, not to his commands. Within this framework Paul will give his own judgment, which has as its aim not their obedience, but their own good (v. 35). In contrast to the Corinthian position that has led them to anxiety, he wishes just the opposite by what he has to say (v. 32).

26 This sentence begins (literally): "I think therefore[26] this to be good[27] because of the present crisis." That is, since I have no command but since my judgment is nonetheless to be considered trustworthy because of the Lord's mercies, "therefore" this is what I think is to your advantage in this matter. But before he gives the content of what is "good" for them, he adds "because of the present crisis." This is the first expression of the reason for his advice. Along with its companion word "troubles"[28] in v. 28, this

---

in *The Bible in Modern Scholarship* (ed. H. P. Hyatt; Nashville, 1965), pp. 127-31; D. L. Balch, "Backgrounds," pp. 351-64.

[24]Gk. γνώμη (see on 1:10; cf. 2 Cor. 8:10; Phlm. 14).

[25]Gk. πιστός; see on 4:2.

[26]Gk. οὖν, infrequent in this letter (see on 4:16).

[27]Gk. καλόν. This usage, which is picked up in its adverb form in v. 37, is sure evidence that it does not have moral connotations for Paul (*contra* Hurd; see n. 33 on 7:1).

[28]The words for "crisis" (ἀνάγκη) and "trouble" (θλῖψις) occur together in Paul's catalogues of suffering in 1 Thess. 3:7 and 2 Cor. 6:4; ἀνάγκη appears without θλῖψις in 2 Cor. 12:10, and θλῖψις without ἀνάγκη in several texts (1 Thess. 1:6; 3:3; 2 Cor. 4:17; 8:2; etc.). Θλῖψις is Paul's ordinary word to express his hardships, although v. 28 is its only appearance in this letter.

phrase probably expresses in its most succinct form what is being elaborated in vv. 29-35. But what exactly it intends is far from certain. Although Paul himself does not use either term in this way, both words are employed elsewhere in the NT to speak of the great eschatological woes that precede the Parousia.[29] In light of v. 29 it is common to suggest that meaning here. Thus the RSV translates, "in view of the impending distress,"[30] suggesting that "present"[31] really means "that which is about to come present." But that seems to fly full in the face of Paul's usage elsewhere, where the term "present" invariably means what is already present in contrast to what is yet to come (see esp. 3:22 and Rom. 8:38). Therefore, whatever the "crisis" is, for Paul it is something they (or the church at large) are already experiencing. But what?

The word literally means "necessity"; it comes to refer especially to that in life which puts one under "compulsion" of any kind, whether from within or without (cf. v. 37; 9:7, 16).[32] But it also is used to express any kind of "distress" or "calamity" that befalls one. Most likely this latter nuance is intended here. Thus there are basically two options, which finally may merge into one: (1) In light of 11:30, where Paul says that *many* of them "are weak and sick, and a number have fallen asleep," it is possible—indeed probable—that they are experiencing considerable "distress" within their community. There is no way to know exactly what it might be, but the death of some is no small matter. (2) In light of v. 28 it is possible that Paul has in view the larger "distress" that is the common lot of those who believe. In this case their own "present distress" is but a part of the larger experience of suffering that the church is undergoing until its final redemption at the coming of Christ. Most likely it is this latter that Paul has in view. His point would be: In light of the troubles we are already experiencing, who needs the additional burden of marriage as well?

But the question remains, How is this related to Paul's eschatology, especially to vv. 29-31? It is commonly argued, or assumed, that Paul is urging them to stay single in light of the imminent coming of Christ, which

---

[29]For ἀνάγκη, see Luke 21:23 (the only known usage of the word in this way in all of Jewish and Christian literature); for θλῖψις, see esp. Rev. 7:14 (cf. 1:9; 2:9-10, 22). For the motif, but not the language, in Jewish apocalyptic see 4 Ezra 5:1-13; 6:18-24; 9:1-12; *Jub.* 23:11-31.

[30]Cf. Montgomery, "in view of the time of suffering now imminent."

[31]Gk. ἐνεστῶσαν (perf. ptc. of ἐνίστημι, "to be present"); cf. 3:22; 2 Thess. 2:2; Gal. 1:4; Rom. 8:38.

[32]This is the meaning preferred by Grosheide, 175-76, but his understanding of the sentence is especially convoluted. He takes the ἀνάγκη to refer to the virgin state of young unmarried women (v. 25). This now is Paul's word of "comfort" to them, that if not asked by a man, they remain single (as though such were a choice under this view) because of the present need to do so.

will be accompanied by a time of great woe. But that seems to miss Paul's own eschatological perspective both in vv. 29-31 and elsewhere. In 2 Thess. 3:6-15 he specifically urged exactly the opposite with regard to work, in a context where the alleged coming of the Day of the Lord (2:2) had caused some to cease working. But more importantly, in Paul's view the End has already begun; the form of this world is already passing away (v. 31). Christians do not thereby abandon the world; they are simply not to let this age dictate their present existence. They are already marked for eternity—in the world but not of it. On the other hand, until the final consummation they also may expect "distress" and "trouble" to be their common lot (1 Thess. 3:3-4). Thus their present eschatological existence should indeed have bearing on the question at hand. But it is not because they are already spiritual, so that as the angels they neither marry nor give in marriage. Rather, it is because they must yet live out their lives "in the present distress." In light of our present existence, with its suffering and trouble, and in light of the increased troubles that will tend to befall the married (v. 28), the single person will do well to remain that way.

Paul's judgment in light of the present distress is that "It is good for a man to remain as he is."[33] Although one cannot be sure, it is probable that this also represents the Corinthian position on this matter,[34] which Paul is citing. This seems to be the best explanation of the awkwardness of the sentence, with its repeated "it is good." (Paul's sentence literally reads: "I think this to be good because of the present distress, namely that it is good for a man to remain thus."[35]) In this case, however, Paul is in full agreement; indeed, that was exactly his point in vv. 17-24. But by adding "because of the present crisis," he posits a different *reason* for it. Furthermore, quite in contrast to them, this new reason does not carry moral weight; therefore, he will also affirm those who do not follow this advice. Thus his answer throughout is both Yes and No.

27 What follows has formal similarities to vv. 18 and 21, including the way those two verses respond to vv. 17 and 20. There is the repeated

---

[33]It is difficult to know what moved the NIV translators to render it, "It is good *for you* to remain as *you are*," especially since they did not do so in v. 1b. Probably it anticipates the questions in v. 27; but any ordinary English reader will read this "you" as plural, whereas what follows is singular, and seems to be addressing the man directly.

[34]Cf. Jeremias, "Gedankenführung," p. 151; cf. Barrett, 174.

[35]Thus the awkward ὅτι here is epexegetic to the τοῦτο ("I think this, namely that . . .") and at the same time serves to introduce the quotation, just as in 8:1 and 4 (twice). Conzelmann's suggestion, 132, that "the expression is not clear" simply is not true. The τοῦτο can only point forward to the ὅτι; and together they point to the slogan itself, whether it be from the Corinthians or from Paul. Cf. Hurd, 178. Grosheide's attempt (see n. 32) to make τοῦτο refer to the virgins of v. 25 and the ὅτι clause become a second object of νομίζω misses the sense of the grammar.

"stay as you are" formula, whose point is immediately pressed with two short questions,[36] marked by asyndeton (no joining particle), followed by their opposite imperatives. Thus he says: "It is good for a man to remain thus: Are you bound to a woman? Stay that way (in this case, lit., 'do not seek to be loosed'). Are you free (i.e., 'loosed') from a woman? Stay that way (in this case, lit., 'do not seek a wife')." All of that seems easy enough. The problem is that the language, being "loosed from a woman," is so highly unusual that it leads one to ask: (1) Who is being addressed? and (2) How do the questions relate to the immediate context?

The nearly universal view is that Paul is speaking in general terms to the married and the unmarried. Thus the NIV: "Are you married? Do not seek a divorce. Are you unmarried? Do not look for a wife." In this view what Paul does at the outset, in light of the formula "stay as you are," is to speak once again on both sides of the issue. First, he repeats what he has already said to the married: "No divorce." But that is not now his concern; rather, he uses that question to set up the second, which speaks to their present circumstances: "Do not seek marriage." What favors this view is the language "bound to a woman (= wife)," which is Paul's ordinary usage for the indissolubility of marriage as long as a mate is living (v. 39; Rom. 7:2). The difficulty lies with the word "loosed,"[37] which is otherwise unknown to denote divorce. If Paul had intended divorce, therefore, why did he use this strange noun? To which the answer is that Paul had both situations in mind, so he chose a word that could express "being loosed" (= divorced) for the married, whose corresponding verb could mean to "be free from"[38] (= never married) for the case in hand—although the second question would then be a word to singles in general, rather than a specific word to the betrothed.

On the other hand, it is possible that both questions speak directly to the present situation.[39] The clue lies with the word "loosed," which is found throughout the papyri as a technical term for discharging someone from the

[36]There is only one question in v. 21; here and in v. 21 the questions are in the second person singular.

[37]Gk. λῦσις, which has a variety of meanings ("unravel" [esp. secrets], "discharge" [as from a contract], or "release").

[38]It should also be noted that the verb λύω is not otherwise used to refer to divorce. For "divorce" verbs, see on vv. 10 and 12. It lies totally outside the present context to suggest that the two questions address the married and the divorced. The qualification of v. 28 makes that nearly impossible: (1) The first sentence would then contradict what is said in vv. 10-11; (2) the second sentence to the "virgins" would be totally irrelevant to such an issue; and (3) it would otherwise require one to separate these two sentences, which in fact form another of the perfectly balanced male-female pairs of this chapter.

[39]This view was argued for, but without noting the linguistic data on λῦσις and λύω, by Elliott, "Teaching," p. 222.

obligations of a contract.[40] If it means that here, then he is speaking first to the betrothed (the "virgins"): "Are you bound (= under obligation to) a woman? Then do not seek to break off the obligation." The second question would then expand the point to include all singles: "Are you free from such obligations? Do not seek a wife." To those who would argue that if Paul intended that, why did he not use "virgin" in the first question (i.e., "Are you bound to a virgin? Do not seek release"), the answer is the same as above. The one term that could cover all possibilities is "woman," which may refer both to a "woman" to whom one is engaged and a "wife" that one is encouraged not to seek.

Either of these is possible, but on balance the second one seems to fit the immediate context better. Otherwise the questions really are generalities and only indirectly address the matter at hand.[41] But if the second view is correct, then the balanced sentences in v. 28, which qualify what is said here, speak to *both* questions; and the subjects, "you" and "the virgin," refer in particular to those who are already under obligation to one another.

28 As with almost all the situations in the preceding section, Paul immediately qualifies v. 27 by allowing its opposite. In this case, however, what is said is so clearly a full qualification that it renders the imperatives of v. 27 to be strictly advice. Furthermore, what is said is so nearly identical to vv. 36-38 that it is difficult to believe that the two are not the same piece of advice to the same people. As throughout the preceding section, even though the final form of the advice in vv. 36-38 speaks directly to the man, the word of exception here is to both parties: "If *you* (i.e., the man spoken to in vv. 26-27) do marry, you have not sinned; and if the (not "a"; see n. 10) virgin marries,[42] she has not sinned."

This is such a remarkable word from a Jewish man, in whose culture marriage was not only normal but in some cases viewed as next to obligatory,[43] that one must ask how it is possible for him even to have thought of using such language in the first place. The best answer, of course, is that it

---

[40]See esp. the data collected in MM, 382.

[41]The traditional view also presents a problem that Grosheide, 176, feels constrained to address. He argues that the first question can scarcely belong to what is merely "good"; in light of vv. 10-11 it must be a true imperative. Yet the second is not an imperative; it is merely advice. But that destroys Paul's balanced clauses.

[42]There is no apparent explanation for the change to the first aorist in this sentence. Elsewhere Paul uses only the second aorist. It may have to do with the change in gender, but that is not likely in view of v. 34. For a full discussion see Lightfoot, 232.

[43]Cf., e.g., *b.Yeb.* 63b: "R. Hama b. Hanina stated: As soon as a man takes a wife his sins are buried; for it is said: *Whoso findeth a wife findeth a great good and obtaineth favour of the Lord"* (Soncino, p. 423); *b.Yeb.* 63a: "R. Eleazar said: Any man who has no wife is no proper man; for it is said, *Male and female created he them and called their name Adam"* (p. 419).

reflects the Corinthian view, which was either specifically suggesting that marriage might be sin or else implying it by the obligatory way they were pressing their ascetic slogans. Thus, this is no grudging condescension to marriage on Paul's part, which by saying it is "no sin" is equal to "damning it with faint praise." To the contrary, Paul recognizes that the question of marriage lies totally outside the category of sin, which is also why there is no "command" of the Lord on this matter (cf. v. 25). Hence he urges that, despite his agreement with their slogan in this case, those who do not accept this advice do not in fact commit sin.

But because he really does believe that his advice is sound, he proceeds to qualify the qualifier, and thereby to repeat in a slightly different way his earlier reason, "because of the present distress" (v. 26). In this case he says: "But those who marry will face many troubles in this life, and I want to spare you this." Thus the argument has gone: (a) I agree, it is good for the "virgins" to remain single, but that is because of the present distress; but (b) it is certainly no sin to marry; nonetheless (a) those who do marry will experience many difficulties (because of the present distress), and I would spare them that. This kind of argument is advice only, and it reflects pastoral concern for them, not principles that would make singleness a better option. That the married will have "troubles in this life"[44] is for Paul a matter of sober reality, almost certainly as the result of "the present distress." What there is about marriage that would cause such tribulation as is not true for the single, Paul does not tell them; and it would be idle speculation to try to read his mind at such a point—especially when we are less than sure about the nature of the present distress. What does seem certain is that this is not a reference to eschatological woes as such, but to real affliction in the present life, probably enhanced by the ordeal that they are currently experiencing.

What follows (vv. 29-30) presents the perspective from which all such matters should be viewed. But in neither part of this explanation is there anything that seems to speak directly to the afflictions of the married as such. What is clear in this opening paragraph is that Paul prefers that the single remain single, but that his reasons for it are strictly pastoral and have nothing to do with the married or single state as such. Hence when he qualifies his preference with an exception here, it is a genuine qualification that affirms marriage as well. This would seem to be a considerable distance from the Corinthian position.

---

[44]Gk. θλῖψιν τῇ σαρκί (lit. "tribulation in the flesh"; cf. 2 Cor. 12:7, σκόλοψ τῇ σαρκί, which must mean literally in the body). It seems unlikely that he means that they will have more physical trials than others; rather, it seems to imply that as long as they are in the present life they will have more trials than others. Grosheide, 177, suggests that it refers to "the bodily difficulties of married women (cf. Mt. 24:19)." But that seems to abuse the plural οἱ τοιοῦτοι, which refers to the subjects of both preceding clauses.

One of the unfortunate things that has happened to this text in the church is that the very pastoral concern of Paul that caused him to express himself in this way has been a source of anxiety rather than comfort. Part of the reason for this is that in Western cultures we do not generally live in a time of "present distress." Thus we fail to sense the kind of care that this text represents. Beyond that, what is often heard is that Paul prefers singleness to marriage, which he does. But quite in contrast to Paul's own position over against the Corinthians, we often read into that preference that singleness is somehow a superior status. That causes some who do not wish to remain single to become anxious about God's will in their lives. Such people need to hear it again: Marriage or singleness per se lies totally outside the category of "commandments" to be obeyed or "sin" if one indulges; and Paul's preference here is not predicated on "spiritual" grounds but on pastoral concern. It is perfectly all right to marry.

Unfortunately, our reading of the text in this way cuts in two ways. Our culture, especially Christian subculture, tends to think of marriage as the norm in such a way that singles are second-class citizens. For such people this text is merely "Paul's opinion," and is seldom listened to at all. That, too, misses Paul's point. Some are called to singleness still; they need to be able to live in the Christian community both without suspicions and with full acceptance and affirmation.

b. Paul's reasons for singleness (7:29-35)

29 *What I mean, brothers, is that[1] the time is short. From now on those who have wives should live as if they had none;* 30 *those who mourn, as if they did not; those who are happy, as if they were not; those who buy something, as if it were not theirs to keep;* 31 *those who use the things of the world,[2] as if not engrossed in them. For this world in its present form is passing away.*

32 *I would like you to be free from concern. An unmarried man is concerned about the Lord's affairs—how he can please the Lord.[3]* 33 *But a married man is concerned about the affairs of this world— how he can please his wife—*34 *and his interests are divided. An unmarried woman or virgin[4] is concerned about the Lord's affairs:*

---

[1]Several Western MSS (and a few others) have an added ὅτι, which could either be epexegetic (as in v. 26: "This I say, namely *that*") or causal ("I say this *because*"). Probably the latter was intended, but in either case it is secondary.

[2]The majority of witnesses have added a τοῦτον (the MajT has the object in the dative case), probably as an assimilation to the sentence that follows.

[3]The Latin tradition reads "God" for "Lord," which may be more pleasing to the ear than the repeated "Lord," but misses Paul's point.

[4]The text here has suffered considerable corruption. The major possibilities are:
1. As the NIV, that the καὶ μεμέρισται goes with v. 33 and the next sentence distinguishes between "the unmarried woman" and "the virgin," who together are the

Her aim is to be devoted to the Lord in both[5] body and spirit. But a married woman is concerned about the affairs of this world—how she can please her husband. 35 *I am saying this for your own good, not to restrict you, but that you may live in a right way in undivided devotion to the Lord.*

The opening words of this section indicate that the apostle herewith intends to explain what has just been said. The section as a whole seems to function, therefore, as a kind of explanatory digression between Paul's opening response (vv. 25-28) and the more specific conclusion of vv. 36-38, both of which say the same thing: It would be good for the "virgins" to remain as they are; but it is no sin for them to marry. Unfortunately, it is an explanation that is no longer clear as to *what* is being explained, what precisely it means, and for whom it is intended.

The argument itself is in two parts (vv. 29-31, 32-35), whose relationship to each other is also something of a mystery. The basic content of the two parts can be fairly easily discerned. Vv. 29-31 present an eschatological framework (the "shortened time") from which they are to view their present existence, especially their relationship to the world, whose present form, including all social, personal, and commercial expressions, is passing away. The question is, For what in vv. 25-28 does this serve as an explana-

---

subject of the verb μεριμνᾷ. This is the reading of P[15] B P 104 181 1962 2495 t x z vg bo Eusebius.

2. A variation of this is read by P[46] ℵ A 33 81 1739 1877 1881 eth, in which the adj. ὁ ἄγαμος ("unmarried") is read twice, modifying both "woman" and "virgin."

3. The Western MSS and the MajT differ from the above in two significant ways. First, they do not have a καί before μεμέρισται; second, ὁ ἄγαμος follows "virgin" and is probably to be understood as the subject of μεριμνᾷ, rather than as an adjective modifying "woman." The net result is a new clause that introduces the pairs about women: "There is also a distinction (μεμέρισται) between the wife and the virgin. The unmarried woman, etc."

This third alternative is vigorously defended by Godet, 381-84 (although he would translate: "The wife is also divided; and the virgin who remains unmarried cares for, etc."), Lightfoot, 233-34, and R-P, 157, on the grounds that it keeps the parallelism of the two sets. That is an attractive argument, but this alternative finally falls short on two grounds: (1) It requires a most unnatural sense to the verb μεμέρισται (Godet tries to circumvent this, but the clause then becomes an intolerable intrusion and the parallelism is broken in any case by the cumbersome "unmarried virgin"). (2) It simply cannot account for the reading of B et al. Given the nice balance provided by the Western text, who would have created from that the text of B? Furthermore, the καί before the μεμέρισται is too well attested across the board to be a later addition; and its presence makes the verb go with v. 33. Its omission came about when Paul's distinction between the "unmarried woman" and the "virgin" was no longer understood and the compound subject with a singular verb was troublesome. Cf. Metzger, 555-56.

[5]A number of early and diverse MSS do not have this first καί (P[46] A D P 33 1175 2495 a t). Zuntz, 199, prefers this reading on stylistic grounds. See also Conzelmann, 131 n. 5.

tion? How does this help them better to appreciate his advice that the "virgins" remain single?

Vv. 32-34 take up the theme of "anxiety." Paul begins (v. 32a) with the general statement that he wants them to be in a state that is free from anxiety *(amerimnous)*. This is followed by two sets of nearly balanced pairs (32b-34), in each of which the cognate verb *merimnaō* (which may be either pejorative, "be anxious about," or positive, "care for") describes the condition of the unmarried and married, both men and women (including the virgin). The questions here are: (1) How does this relate both to vv. 29-31 and to vv. 25-28? (2) To what does *amerimnous* refer? (3) How do the *merimnaō* sentences relate to the opening general statement about being *amerimnous*?

The section concludes with v. 35, in which Paul explains that he has said *this* (apparently all of vv. 29-34) for their advantage, and not to put a noose around their necks. Rather, he wants them to be able to do what is "seemly" and "constant" for the Lord without distraction. This in turn, especially the word "seemly," leads directly into vv. 36-38, where he first affirms those who will go through with their marriage and then those who will not, concluding that both do well, although the latter do "better."

The traditional interpretation of the two parts sees Paul as giving two reasons for remaining single: (1) In light of the imminent Parousia, to marry is to add additional troubles in the present age that is soon to pass away, so why marry? (2) The married man or woman is "distracted" by worldly affairs away from the constant devotion to Christ available to the unmarried, so celibacy is the better option. These may well be correct. But they also leave a number of unanswered questions, particularly as to how this responds to the ascetics who consider getting married as tantamount to sinning, and how this relieves the "anxiety" of the man in v. 36, who *wants* to get married, not to mention the general difficulty with the *amerimnous/merimnaō* interplay in vv. 32-34.

The proper understanding probably lies elsewhere, although precision is difficult to come by. But a few observations can be made: First, there must surely be some interrelationship between (a) remaining single, (b) the present distress, and (c) the eschatological viewpoint of vv. 29-31. What exactly that might be is not clear. In vv. 29-31 Paul does not mention the Parousia, nor suffering, nor living as though the End were tomorrow. Nor does he emphasize the *futurity* of the End vis-à-vis their overrealized eschatology. Rather, in view of the "time" and the fact that the "form" of this present world is passing away, he calls for a radically new understanding of their *relationship to the world*.[6] This seems to fit exactly with the eschato-

---

[6]On this question see esp. D. J. Doughty, "The Presence and Future of Salvation in Corinth," *ZNW* 66 (1975), 61-90, who argues that "Paul's primary concern here has to

logical outlook of 4:1-5 and 6:1-6, where the reality that the future has already begun with Christ and the Spirit determines one's entire existence in the present. If this be so, then it is a general word that requires them to think of *both* marriage and celibacy in light of their new existence. The married will have troubles in this life because of the present hardships, and Paul would spare them that. But such things do not determine one's existence; Christ does. And in him one lives out the present life totally determined by the future that has already come.

Secondly, this leads him to say that he does not want *any* of them to live in anxiety, especially not about the present distress nor about the future, which would mean also no anxiety about whether to marry or not. There are two kinds of existence, he points out. The unmarried either "care for" the things of the Lord (which is good) or are "anxious about" such things (which is bad); so also the married, who either "care for" or are "anxious about" their spouses. The specific difference between them is that the married are also divided, that is, they have the *additional* concern of the spouse. He concludes that all of this has been said for their advantage, so that whichever they are, they may not live in anxiety but in a way that is "seemly" and "constant" before the Lord. Out of such concern, then, he can move on to encourage both marriage and celibacy, even though he concludes finally with his obvious preference for the latter—probably still "because of the present distress."

29a   The presence of the vocative, "brothers [and sisters]" (see on 1:10), indicates that with these words there is a slight turn in the argument. It seems also to broaden the perspective so as to be a word for the whole community on this matter. The sentence begins, literally, "this[7] I say,[8]" pointing forward to what is to be said.[9] The problem lies with trying to determine *what* the following words are intended to explain. On the one hand, it probably gives the eschatological explication of the two phrases "because of the present distress" and "will face many troubles in this life." That is, the "present distress" belongs to the eschatological framework of their present existence, from which they are to understand the advice to stay as one is (unmarried). But at the same time what is said moves considerably beyond a mere concern over celibacy as such. It finally becomes an appeal to

---

do not with speculation about the future of salvation, but rather with the existence of those who, as a consequence of God's salvation deed in Christ, already stand at the end of history. The eschatological language functions to raise up a particular understanding of Christian existence" (pp. 68-69).

[7]The "this" in this case clearly points forward; the next sentence is epexegetic and gives it content. Thus, "*This* is what I mean: The time is short."

[8]Gk. φημι (cf. 10:15, 19; 15:50). This is not Paul's ordinary verb for this expression (as, e.g., in vv. 6, 8, 12, 35). The NIV captures its sense: "What I mean is this."

[9]Otherwise Parry, 120, and R-P, 154, who see it as a kind of solemn declaration.

the entire community to rethink its present existence, and especially seems to insist on their living within an *eschatological* framework as over against, presumably, their current ascetic-spiritual one.

Despite several grammatical difficulties, what follows is probably best understood as a single, complex sentence in Greek, whose structure is:

> The basic premise: The time is compressed, or limited,
> The purpose (or result): so that henceforth[10]
> > [even][11] (1) those who have wives might be
> > as if they did not,
> > and (2) those who mourn (might be)
> > as if they did not,
> > and (3) those who rejoice (might be)
> > as if they did not,
> > and (4) those who buy (might be)
> > as if they possessed not,
> > and (5) those who use the world (might be)
> > as if they did not have full use.
> The reason: For *(gar)*
> > This world in its present form is passing away.

The crucial sentence is the basic premise, "the time is short"; but its intent is not at all easy to determine. Ordinarily, "time"[12] is considered in a quantitative way to refer to "the amount of time left for Christians to do what they have to do."[13] While there is perhaps a dimension of that involved, more likely the noun "time" refers to the eschatological event of salvation, which

---

[10]It is commonplace to see the ἵνα as an example of an "imperatival ἵνα ." See, e.g., Moule, 145; BDF 387 [3]; Turner, *Syntax,* 95; A. P. Salom, "The Imperatival Use of *hina* in the New Testament," *AusBR* 6 (1958), 135. That is probably the result of seeing τὸ λοιπόν as the start of a new clause. But that is not a necessary expedient. Τὸ λοιπόν may be a connecting particle; more likely it carries adverbial force and precedes ἵνα for emphasis (cf. Gal. 2:10). Thus the ἵνα clause expresses the purpose God has for his people in "compressing the time": so that "for the rest" or "from now on" (meaning from the time of their conversion until the End) they might live in the following way. That comes close to an imperative, but is a more standard usage of ἵνα and τὸ λοιπόν. Some of the older commentators took τὸ λοιπόν with the preceding sentence (= "the time is limited as to what remains"), a view reflected by the word order in the Westerns and MajT, τὸ λοιπόν ἐστιν. But that not only weakens the expression but runs counter to Paul's usage elsewhere. For the meaning of τὸ λοιπόν see Thrall, *Particles,* pp. 25-30.

[11]This καί may mean "even the married are to think like celibates" (Godet, 377). But that is an unnecessary inference since the καί forms the first in a series. If there were two members, one would translate "both . . . and." With more than two it simply begins the series. Cf. R-P, 155.

[12]Gk. καιρός, referring to a specific (right, favorable, appointed) time, to be distinguished from χρόνος, which has to do with a period, or duration of time.

[13]Cf. Parry, 120 (this is a paraphrase).

has been set in motion by Christ's death and resurrection and the gift of the Spirit. Their "present distress" is evidence that this time "has been compressed" or "is foreshortened,"[14] that God's people stand at the end of history, as it were. This does not so much mean that the final consummation is imminent (although in a sense that is always true for God's people) as that the future, which was set in motion by the event of Christ and the Spirit, has been "shortened" so that it is now in plain view. And that will absolutely condition how one lives in the present. Paul's concern, therefore, is not with the *amount* of time they have left, but with the radical new perspective the "foreshortened future" gives one with regard to the *present* age. Those who have a definite future and see it with clarity live in the present with radically altered values as to what counts and what does not.[15] In that sense it calls for those who want to get married to rethink what that may mean, especially in light of the present distress.

It may well be that this is a strong word against the Corinthians' general tendency to live and think on the basis of their former pagan past, which generally lacked such an eschatological perspective. Their outlook was that of having arrived (see 4:8)—not in an eschatological sense, but in a "spiritual" sense that made them ascetic with regard to the present age. Paul thus wants them to rethink their existence in terms of "the shortened time," with its certain future that they yet await (cf. 1:7).[16]

---

[14]Gk. συνεσταλμένος ἐστίν, which most likely is to be understood as a periphrastic perfect passive, not "to be" with an adjective. The verb συστέλλω, depending on context, means to constrict, reduce, restrain, or limit in some way. With time it means to "compress" it. The picture is that of one for whom the future was either nonexistent, as for most Greeks, or off in the vague distance; but the event of Christ has now compressed the time in such a way that the future has been brought forward so as to be clearly visible.

In this regard the "shortened time" is often seen to reflect the words of Jesus in Mark 13:20, which indicate that a coming time of suffering will be so great that for the sake of the elect the Lord has "shortened the days." Paul is thus viewed as saying that because the married will have more of these sufferings, the betrothed would do best not to marry. The problem with this view is that Paul himself does *not* make that point in what follows.

[15]The analogy of the terminally ill comes to mind. For those who have made peace with it, the amount of time left is less in the forefront than is the change of perspective. They see, hear, and value in a new way. My former student Dr. J. Camery-Hoggatt suggested the analogy of the one who tells a joke. He alone knows the punch line, and because he knows it, it shapes the telling of the joke in its entirety. Through the resurrection of Christ, Christians know the divine "punch line" (which in this case is no joke but a vivid reality!); they see clearly how the story comes out, and they shape their lives and values accordingly.

[16]It is in this sense that Paul counters their "overrealized eschatology." Thus Käsemann is probably not quite right in saying that "for the Corinthians the end of history has already arrived" (*NT Questions,* p. 106). They had "arrived," to be sure, but more in the sense of what Käsemann says later, "Christian existence here on earth meant for them solely the temporal representation of heavenly being" (p. 124). That is, they were not so

29b-31a   This understanding of the basic premise seems to be borne out by the rhetoric of the purpose clause that follows. God has "compressed the time of salvation" so that "from now on" believers might have a totally new perspective as to their relationship with the world. This perspective is given in the form of five illustrations, expressed in the strongest kind of dialectical rhetoric. Taken literally, the five "as if not" clauses become absurdities, not to mention contradictory to what Paul clearly said earlier about marriage (vv. 2-6) and what he will elsewhere say about sorrowing and rejoicing (Rom. 12:15). But they are not to be taken literally; they are rhetoric, pure and simple. The question is, What is the point of such rhetoric?

These clauses display clear affinities both with Stoicism[17] and Jewish apocalyptic.[18] But Paul is advocating neither the Stoic's "aloofness" from the world[19] nor the apocalyptist's "escape" from the world. What he is calling for is a radical new stance toward the world, predicated on the saving event of Christ that has marked off our existence in a totally new way.[20] Just as in Christ the slave is a freedman and the free man is a slave (vv. 22-23) because one's existence is determined by God, so now one does not so much live "detached" from the world (after all, Paul expects the Corinthians to continue doing all five of these things) as totally free from its control. Therefore, one lives in the world just as the rest—married, sorrowing, rejoicing, buying, making use of it—but none of these determines one's life.

---

concerned about the *future* having come present as with a new spiritual mode of existence that had now become available to them and was already being realized. Thus Paul's concern here is less with the futurity of the Eschaton as with the fact that they must learn to think eschatologically in the first place. Cf. the introduction to 4:1-5.

[17]See, e.g., Epict. 3.22.67-76; 3.24.60; and esp. 4.7.5. Cf. Seneca, *Ep.* 1.2. But it has been regularly pointed out that the eschatological basis of Paul's attitude is radically different from Stoic-Cynic aloofness. See Sevenster, *Paul*, pp. 231-32; Conzelmann, 133; and now especially the brief but helpful overview in D. L. Balch, "1 Cor 7:32-35 and Stoic Debates about Marriage," *JBL* 102 (1983), 429-30.

[18]This has been argued especially by W. Schrage, "Die Stellung zur Welt bei Paulus, Epiktet und in der Apokalyptik," *ZTK* 61 (1964), 125-54. The parallel with *6 Esdras* 16:40-45 (see HSW II, 701) is striking, but the text is so much later than Paul as to give reason for pause as to the direction of influence on Paul's own thinking.

[19]This would also include the concept of "detachment" found in Bultmann (*Theology*, I, 351) and C. Hierzenberger, *Weltwertung bei Paulus nach 1 Kor 7,29-31. Eine exegetisch-kerygmatische Studie* (Düsseldorf, 1967). Paul expects the Corinthians to continue to make use of the world in all of its present expressions. It is not that they are to be "detached" or "aloof." Rather, they are not to be conditioned or controlled by the world or its values. They are as those "having all things, yet possessing nothing" and at the same time "having nothing, yet possessing all things" (2 Cor. 6:10). The world simply does not dictate their existence.

[20]Cf. Doughty, "Presence" (n. 6 above).

The Christian is marked by eternity; therefore, he or she is not under the dominating power of those things that dictate the existence of others.

But what is the point of saying this in the present context? It has been suggested that because "the married" tops the list, this is really a plea for celibacy. That is, since the married should think like celibates, the single should stay celibate. But that is to take the passage too literally. Most likely it is a word to all of them about their entire existence. In this kind of rhetoric it makes no difference whether one is married or celibate. That is, the celibate, too, must live "as if not" in the same sense as all the others, because celibacy too belongs to what is passing away. Granted, Paul does not have a clause to form a pair with "the married"; that would not be possible in the case of "the not married."[21] Paul's concern here seems to go beyond "staying celibate" to the very understanding of Christian existence that caused them to urge celibacy in the first place. The Corinthians think that the unmarried should stay as they are—for ascetic reasons related to their new spirituality. Paul is urging on them a wholly different worldview. Because of the "present distress" and "shortened time," the betrothed may wish to remain single; but being single or married in itself is not the crucial question. Either is all right, he has said and will say again; what is important is that in either situation one live "as if not," that is, without one's relationship to the world as the determining factor.

The final two items need comment since they set up the concluding causal clause. Paul does not discourage buying and selling. As with the other items, the Corinthians are expected to continue doing such things. But Christians do not buy to possess; that is to let the world govern the reason for buying. Those who buy are to do so "as if not" in terms of possessing anything. The eschatological person "has nothing, yet possesses all things" (2 Cor. 6:10; cf. 1 Cor. 3:22). Thus the Christian can at the same time "use the present world." This is the clearest indication that Paul does not have a separatist's bent. The world as such is neither good nor evil; it simply is. But in its present form it is passing away. Thus while one uses the world, one must be "as if not," which in this case does not mean "not abuse" (KJV), but not to make full use of it,[22] that is, be "not engrossed" or "absorbed" in it.

31b   This final clause gives the reason for one's new stance toward

---

[21]Given the *form* this rhetoric takes, with the second part responding "as if not" to the first, he simply could not have used an illustration that already had a negative in its first part. To say "those who are not married, as if they were not" makes no sense at all—not even in rhetoric.

[22]Gk. καταχράομαι (cf. 9:18), the only two occurrences in the NT; see the discussion in Doughty, "Presence," p. 71 n. 47.

the world: "This world in its present form²³ is passing away."²⁴ This is the determinative sentence; it is also eschatological. As elsewhere²⁵ the use of the "progressive present" ("is in the process of passing away") reflects Paul's already/not yet eschatological perspective. The decisive event is the one that has already happened. In Christ's death and resurrection God has already determined the course of things; he has already brought the world in its present form under judgment. And so decisive is that event that it has "foreshortened the time." The result is that even now what others are absorbed in, the Christian is free from. All of these things—marriage/celibacy, sorrowing/rejoicing, buying/using—belong to the world in its present form. Marriage thus belongs to the present scheme of things that is already on its way out. But so does their asceticism. These things may or may not be done, but in either case they belong to what is passing away.

32a With these words Paul now turns to another theme: "Now²⁶ I would like²⁷ you to be free from concern," meaning, apparently, "as long as you are in this present world." The question is, How does this relate to what has preceded (both vv. 29-31 and 25-28) and to whom is it addressed? Traditionally it has been viewed (correctly) as the lead-in to the four sentences that follow, expressing the two kinds of "concern" experienced by the married and unmarried. This view usually treats the adjective "free from concern" as though it were a noun, referring to the "extra cares"²⁸ of married life. Thus it becomes a further exhortation—indeed warning—against marriage. But even though in the sentences that follow Paul may indeed be giving a further reason for encouraging the unmarried to stay that way, "extra cares" is not that reason. And in any case that is not what this opening sentence is about.

²³Gk. σχῆμα, which often means the outward form or appearance that something takes (Phil. 2:7). But here it means more than that; it is not simply the "outward form" that is on its way out, but the total "scheme" of things as they currently exist. Mare, 235, makes the improbable suggestion that it means "material things" here. That is quite to miss its relationship to the rhetoric that has preceded.

²⁴Gk. παράγει; this is its only occurrence in Paul, but cf. 1 John 2:8 and 17. Elsewhere Paul uses καταργέω to express this idea (see 1:26; 2:6; 6:13; 13:8-11; 15:24-26).

²⁵Cf. the discussion on 1:26.

²⁶An untranslated δέ joins this clause to what precedes. It may have adversative force (so Conzelmann, 130), but it is difficult to see how, if our understanding of vv. 29-31 is correct. More likely it is consecutive and flows out of the immediately preceding exhortation to eschatological living.

²⁷Gk. θέλω; if Paul intended that they live free from worldly cares, as the common interpretation has it, then this is a most unusual "wish." In Jesus (Matt. 6:25-34) and elsewhere in Paul (Phil. 4:6) such a concern is addressed as parenesis and is expressly forbidden.

²⁸See, e.g., Mare, 235, whose language this is.

The words "to be free from concern" translate the infinitive "to be" and the adjective "without anxiety" *(amerimnous)*.[29] They have to do with a state of being, not with "cares" as such.[30] The question is, Why this concern here? There seem to be two possibilities. (1) As the common view has it, the "you" may refer now to the "unmarried" of vv. 25-28. But in contrast to that view, the anxiety does not have to do with the worldly cares of marriage, but with the concern over whether or not to get married, especially since some are suggesting that it comes close to sin to do so. That seems altogether likely, but would best be understood as it is subsumed under the next view. (2) Since the sentence flows naturally out of vv. 29-31, Paul's concern most likely still has to do with living in the present age as an eschatological person. That is, because life is determined by one's new existence in Christ (already but not yet, with the "not yet" clearly in view), the believer should be free from the anxiety-ridden existence of those who are determined by the world in its present form. The Christian still buys and marries, but he or she does so "as if not." These things do not determine one's existence; the clear vision of the future does. Thus one is free from anxiety. In this sense the passage does indeed speak to the unmarried who are anxious about marriage. But Paul wants *both* married and unmarried to be this way. Their existences in the present scheme of things differ, as the next sentences point out, but both are to be without anxiety.

32b-33   With the use of the cognate verb *merimnaō,* Paul proceeds to describe the two kinds of existence, married and unmarried, in terms of the object of their "anxiety" or "concern." He begins with the men, and the two sentences he devotes to them are almost perfectly balanced, except for the crucial addition at the end of the second, "and is divided."[31] Thus:

> The unmarried man *merimna* the things of the Lord,
> > how he might[32] please the Lord.
> *de* ("but" or "and")
> The   married man *merimna* the things of the world,
> > how he might please his wife.
> > and he is divided.

---

[29]This word occurs elsewhere in the NT only in Matt. 28:14, where it is probably wrong to translate as "keeping out of trouble." Rather, the lie of the chief priests will save the soldiers from the kind of anxiety properly due to those who have been remiss in their duties. Cf. *T.Jud.* 3:9; Wis. 6:15; 7:23 (the person who obtains wisdom is ἀμέριμνος); and Appian, *Maced.* 19.3. See also the examples in MM, 26. For its usage in Stoic debates about marriage, see Balch, "1 Cor 7:32-35," pp. 434-35.

[30]I owe this important insight, as well as some others in this paragraph, to my son Mark, who during his seminary days wrote his exegesis paper on this passage.

[31]See n. 4 above for the textual discussion.

[32]Gk. πῶς with a deliberative subjunctive. As an independent sentence it would say: "How might I please the Lord?"

What is not clear is how these sentences relate to the opening "wish" that they be "without anxiety," and to the rest of what has preceded as well. There are three options: (1) Traditionally, v. 32a is interpreted as having to do with the worldly cares of married life. Thus the *merimna* of the two clauses, though translated the same, is understood as positive in the first instance and negative in the second.[33] The *de* therefore is adversative ("but"); the married man is not merely concerned for his wife, this concern makes his a clearly inferior existence.[34] The difficulty with this view, however, is that, besides making *merimna* mean two different things in succeeding, nearly identical sentences, it really does seem to undercut what Paul says on either side of it. It is one thing to say that it is no sin to marry; but how is the married man helped to be "free from anxiety" if his existence is subordinated to the celibate's in this way, so that he is indeed "anxious" about the things of the world while the celibate gets to "serve" the Lord in a pleasing way?

(2) Barrett takes the view that in both cases the verb is pejorative.[35] Both the married and unmarried "are anxious about," but neither of them should be. The anxiety to please the Lord is seen as stemming from the Corinthian asceticism. The asceticism itself is an attempt to win favor with God on the basis of a false standard. Thus "the ascetics who decry marriage . . . are not rising above but falling below the Christian standard" (p. 179). This view has the distinct advantage of keeping the same meaning for all the *merimna* cognates. The difficulty with it, as Barrett himself points out, is with the clause "to please the Lord," which Paul elsewhere uses in a good sense (Rom. 8:8; 1 Thess. 2:15; 4:1).

(3) It is possible to read both verbs positively, meaning to "care for" (12:25; Phil. 2:20), and to view them both as legitimate activities.[36] The married man "cares for the things of the world, how to please his wife" in the sense of vv. 30-31. That is a simple statement of reality. But he must do so without anxiety because of the eschatological determination of life in the present. In this case the usage of the verb is something of a play on the adjective in v. 32a: "I want you to be without 'concern' even as you must 'concern yourselves' with life in the present age." The *de* functions as a contrast, but not as an adversative: one is one way, the other is another. The real difference between the two men is that the married man "is divided." That does not mean that he is full of anxieties, but that he "cares for" *both* the Lord and his wife. The "division" may mean that he has less opportunity

---

[33]Repeated most recently by Holladay, 104.

[34]Cf. the translation by Beck: "But once he's married, he worries about earthly things, how he can please his wife."

[35]Favored also by Balch, "1 Cor 7:32-35," pp. 434-35.

[36]This insight also comes from my son Mark. See n. 30 above.

for service than is available to the unmarried; but it does not mean that the one is a superior existence, or that it is more full of anxiety. Had Paul intended that, then the married man would have a right to become anxious despite exhortations to the contrary.

Although either alternative (2) or alternative (3) makes good sense of the text, on balance the latter seems preferable. In light of the "foreshortened time" and the radical new understanding of our relationship to the present world, Paul reminds the Corinthians of the nature of the two kinds of existence. For him this means that celibacy is preferable; but at the same time he is trying to remove any anxiety that marriage might be wrong or "unseemly" in itself. Different, yes; more involved in the present world, yes; but inferior or sinful, no. What is crucial is that either live without anxiety, even though they must continue to "use the world."

34 As throughout the chapter, Paul now repeats for the women what he has just said about the men. But there are three differences, two of them significant: (1) To the "unmarried woman" he adds "the virgin" as the compound subject of the first sentence; (2) in place of "how she might please the Lord," he writes "in order that she might be holy both in body and in spirit";[37] and (3) the verb "is divided" does not appear at the end of the second sentence. The first and third of these differences are related directly to a difficult textual choice (see n. 4). On the one hand, if one were to go with the Majority Text, then the four sentences are all in perfect balance—except for item (2), which is a considerable difference indeed! But the presence of "and" before "is divided" and the nearly impossible meaning required for the verb "divide" rule in favor of the text as the NIV has translated it.

One of the reasons for the textual corruption is almost certainly related to the first of the differences noted above. Why would Paul begin the women's side by distinguishing two kinds of unmarried women? The answer to that must lie with the issue that was raised in vv. 25-28. This is sure evidence that "virgin" does not mean any unmarried woman, but must have a special sense in this section. It also adds support to our interpretation of vv. 32b-33. Paul is making some general statements about the nature of married and unmarried existence in the present age. But as he starts the section on the "unmarried woman," he is brought back specifically to the issue at hand, so he adds "and the virgin," meaning the "virgins" who are the subject under consideration.

The surprising—and more difficult—difference is the second one.

---

[37]On the textual variation see n. 5. Conzelmann suggests that the text of P[46] et al. means "in (the) body and (the) Spirit," but that is both unnecessary and nearly impossible in this case.

There are basically two options as to what it means, depending on how one understands the sentences as a whole (see on vv. 32b-33 above). If the verb means "be anxious about," then this is probably a reflection of the Corinthians' point of view. They are striving to be holy in body as well as in spirit, by avoiding sexual relations.[38] Such an understanding adds weight to the possibility of the "negative" view. If, on the other hand, the verb means "care for" in a positive sense, then Paul probably intends by the phrase "body and spirit" something like "holy in every way" or "completely," with "body and spirit" not to be thought of separately but together, as designating the whole person (see on 5:5; cf. 1 Thess. 5:23; 2 Cor. 7:1).[39] It is also possible, of course, that in the case of the woman this language reflects the cultural ideal of the "chaste woman," so that her chastity is part of her "setting herself apart"[40] for the Lord. In any case, given vv. 2-6 it is not possible that Paul is moving in the direction of the Corinthian asceticism, which viewed sexual relations per se as unholy or not "good." Neither celibacy nor chastity as part of one's "holiness" is the same thing as negating sexual relations as such in the name of holiness,[41] even though these ideas were confused early on in some sectors of the church, partly as the result of this text.

35 This verse functions in two ways. First, it brings closure to the argument of vv. 29-35 by stating the purpose of what has been said; second, by referring to what is "seemly" before the Lord, it serves as a transition to the conclusion in vv. 36-38, which begins by speaking to the one who thinks he might be behaving in an "unseemly" way.

The fact that it brings closure to the explanatory digression is signaled by "this . . . I say," which can only refer to what has preceded. The *touto* ("this") most likely includes all of vv. 29-35, so that the whole is enclosed by the "this I mean" of v. 29, which points *forward* to what is about to be said, and the present "this I say," which points *back* to what has now been said. If so, then it refers to their eschatological existence as determining their life in the present world, including being without anxiety over the matter of whether to marry or not. Although Paul obviously leans toward being celibate, either existence is all right in the present as long as one is neither determined by it nor anxious over it.

[38]See esp. Barrett, 181; cf. Ruef, 65.
[39]Cf. Conzelmann, 134 n. 32.
[40]On the word "holy" see on 1:2 and 7:14.
[41]This confusion of ideas is perpetuated in much of the current literature as well. But celibacy is not the same thing as asceticism. The latter has to do with a worldview that negates the material order; the former may be a stance that emerges from an ascetic point of view, but it can also be the result of other things, including giftedness (7:7). The "gifted" celibate, as Paul was, may have a radically different view of the world from the ascetic, as Paul does.

The *purpose*[42] of what has been said is stated in three parts, first positively, "for your own good" (lit. "for your own advantage"[43]), which is then defined by a negative contrast, followed by a repetition of the purpose phrase with some specific content. The negative contrast, translated "not to restrict you" in the NIV, is a metaphor that literally means, "not to throw a noose[44] around your necks." That seems to mean that Paul's foregoing explanation is intended to benefit them, probably in the direction of having new grounds for celibacy without anxiety. But at the same time what "benefits" is not a commandment; they are not to take his preferences, for any reason, as a burden around their necks. This makes best sense as a word to the betrothed, that they are not "bound" by Paul's word. After all, even if preferable from his point of view, celibacy is first of all a gift (v. 7). Therefore, he wants what has been said to be a liberating word, whichever direction they go. There are two kinds of existence in this present age, but those who have truly entered the new age live now "as if not," and are thereby free from the anxiety that enshrouds all others, including the Corinthian ascetics.

The final phrase, in which the "advantage" is spelled out more specifically, is less than clear. The Greek text literally reads: "but for what is seemly[45] and constant[46] to/for/before the Lord in an undistracted way."[47] The concern appears to flow out of the preceding negative. By these words Paul does not want to restrict them, as the ascetics would do, but to free them for whatever is appropriate in their case (apparently either marriage or celibacy) so that they may have constant and unhindered devotion to the Lord. For the gifted celibate that would mean celibacy; but for the betrothed, whose gift is not celibacy but whose devotion to the Lord has been hindered by the ascetics' demanding that he be so, what is appropriate is marriage. This is not the standard view, which sees this as a final word of commendation for the celibate life, on the basis of vv. 32b-34, that this is the only way

---

[42]The repeated preposition πρός followed by the substantival use of the adjectives marks the two prepositional phrases as the reason or purpose of what has been said.

[43]Not the καλόν of v. 26, but σύμφορον (cf. 6:12; 10:23; 12:7).

[44]Gk. βρόχον, a metaphor from war or hunting. See, e.g., Jos., *War* 7.250: "for a noose was thrown around him by a distant enemy who would have dragged him off, had he not instantly cut the rope with his sword and succeeded in escaping" (Loeb, III, 577). In POxy I.51.16 it is used by a physician to describe a hanging (see MM, 118).

[45]Gk. εὔσχημον ("appropriate, proper, seemly"; cf. εὐσχημόνα, "presentable parts," in 12:24).

[46]Gk. εὐπάρεδρον; a rare adjective, combining εὖ ("well") and παρεδρία ("sitting beside" or "near"). The noun παρεδρία can mean "service" or "constant presence."

[47]Gk. ἀπερισπάστως; cf. Epict. 1.29.59: "nay, sit rather free from distractions and listen" (Loeb, I, 203). This word also played a role in Stoic debates about marriage. See Balch, "1 Cor 7:32-35," pp. 430-34.

one can have unhindered devotion. But the word "seemly" or "appropriate" does not seem to fit well with such a view. Paul has not argued that celibacy is the way of life that is most appropriate or seemly. Rather, he has given eschatological reasons for preferring it. A betrothed person, who is anxious about whether or not to marry, is hardly living appropriately or with unhindered devotion. Thus, at the end, despite his setting forth to give new grounds for preferring celibacy, he again sets that preference in a context that equally affirms the "rightness" of marriage, which is what he will once more spell out in detail in the conclusion that follows.

Paul's point in all of this seems to have been twofold, and everything must be seen in light of his eschatological perspective. First, he really does prefer celibacy, and both the nature of eschatological existence itself—in light of the present distress—and the divided nature of one's caring when married speak in favor of it. But second, celibacy is not the only existence, nor is it to be preferred on moral grounds, only eschatological. All must live as eschatological people, free from anxiety. This is especially true for the betrothed, whose anxiety would have stemmed not from worldly cares but from the Corinthian ascetics. If the present distress and shortened time make celibacy preferable, they do not make marriage wrong. Rather, the married in particular must learn to live as truly eschatological people in a world whose present expression is passing away.

This passage in particular, instead of being viewed as to our advantage, has often been burdensome for the young. But that is probably less Paul's fault than our own. It is hard to perceive that his preference for celibacy does not also make it a superior existence, so that the married feel like second-class citizens in the church. Yet our real failure is to take the main point seriously enough, namely that we are to live out our lives in the present age, whether married or not, as those who have been determined by the "foreshortened time." Being eschatological people is to free us from the grip of the world and its values. We are to live "as if not," that is, as fully in the world but not controlled by its systems or values. Such freedom, which comes only from Christ, removes from one the anxiety about which existence is better. Whichever one is called to is better, as long as it is appropriate and allows one unhindered devotion to the Lord.

The irony of our present situation is that Paul insisted that his own preference, including his reasons for it, were not to be taken as a noose around anyone's neck. Yet we have often allowed that very thing to happen. Roman Catholicism has insisted on celibacy for its clergy even though not all are gifted to be so; on the other hand, many Protestant groups will not ordain the single because marriage is the norm, and the single are not quite trusted. The answer again lies in our becoming eschatological people who live in the present with such a clear vision of our certain future that we are free from such anxiety, and therefore also free from placing such strictures on others as well as on ourselves.

c. But marriage is no sin (7:36-40)

36 *If anyone thinks he is acting improperly toward the virgin he is engaged to, and if she is getting along in years and he feels he ought to marry, he should do as he wants. He is not sinning. They[1] should get married.* 37 *But the man who has settled the matter[2] in his own mind, who is under no compulsion but has control over his own will, and who has made up his mind not to marry the virgin—this man also does the right thing.* 38 *So then, he who marries the virgin[3] does[4] right, but he who does not marry her does even better.[a]*

39 *A woman is bound[5] to her husband as long as he lives. But if[6] her husband dies, she is free to marry anyone she wishes, but he must belong to the Lord.* 40 *In my judgment, she is happier if she stays as she is—and[7] I think that I too have the Spirit of God.*

[a] *Or 36 If anyone thinks he is not treating his daughter properly, and if she is getting along in years, and he feels she ought to marry, he should do as he wants. He is not sinning. They should get married. 37 But the man who has settled the matter in his own mind, who is under no compulsion but has control over his own will, and who has made up his mind to keep the virgin unmarried—this man also does the right thing. 38 So then, he who gives his virgin in marriage does right, but he who does not give her away in marriage does even better.[8]*

[1]A few MSS (D* F G 2495 pc) change the plural to a singular, obviously in the interest of making better sense of the text and probably reflecting the father-daughter interpretation (= "let her marry"; cf. NASB).

[2]The text reads ἕστηκεν ἐν τῇ καρδίᾳ αὐτοῦ ἑδραῖος ("stands firm in his heart"); several MSS (incl. P[46] F G) omit the ἑδραῖος, while the MajT has put it in its more logical position after ἕστηκεν. See the discussion in Zuntz, 96-97.

[3]The text reads τὴν ἑαυτοῦ παρθένον ("his [own] virgin"), which is difficult for any interpretation. The words were eventually omitted, so that the MajT reads, "He who marries does well; he who does not marry does better" (cf. KJV).

[4]For the ποιεῖ of the majority, P[15] P[46] B 6 1739 1881 pc read the future ποιήσει, an assimilation to the future of the next clause—which the NIV translates as a present.

[5]Some Western MSS, followed by the MajT, add νόμῳ ("by law"; K and bo add γάμῳ, "by marriage"), on the basis of Rom. 7:2. It is missing from all the early and best evidence (P[15] P[46] ℵ* A B D* 6 33 81 1175 1739 1881 pc lat Tert Clem Cyp).

[6]A number of MSS (D[2] L Ψ 614 629 1241 2495 pm) add καί, conforming to the earlier pattern ἐὰν δὲ καί ("if indeed"; cf. vv. 11, 21, 28).

[7]For this δέ B 6 33 104 365 630 1739 1881 2495 pc t substitute γάρ. See the discussion in Zuntz, 204.

[8]Cf. NEB: "If a man has a partner in celibacy and feels that he is not behaving properly towards her, if, that is, his instincts are too strong for him, and something must be done, he may do as he pleases; there is nothing wrong in it; let them marry. But if a man is steadfast in his purpose, being under no compulsion, and has complete control of his own choice; and if he has decided in his own mind to preserve his partner in her virginity, he will do well. Thus, he who marries his partner does well, and he who does not will do better."

These two paragraphs together bring the entire argument, including vv. 1-24, to a conclusion. Vv. 36-38 represent a notorious crux, evidenced by the three distinctly different options available in the NIV, NASB (cf. NIV[mg]), and NEB.[9] The best solution is to see this section as flowing directly out of v. 35 and thus bringing to a specific conclusion the argument that began in v. 25, rather than a special case brought in at the end.[10] Thus in v. 36 Paul repeats what was said in v. 28 to the man who *wants* to get married, that marriage is no sin. But for the man who has settled the matter in his *own* mind, staying single is the thing to do (v. 37). Both do well, he concludes (v. 38), although his final preference is for celibacy—for the reasons given in the preceding argument, that is, "because of the present distress."

The final paragraph (vv. 39-40) is something of a puzzle. The question it raises is, What is it doing here as the final word? Two observations need to be made: (1) In keeping with the pattern throughout, this word functions in relation to vv. 36-38, which was addressed to the men, and serve as his balancing word to the women. However, (2) in this case it is not a word just to the virgins themselves—although it will include them—but a final word to the women that reaches all the way back to v. 1. In this way the concerns of both sections are repeated by way of conclusion. First, a woman is not to separate from her husband (vv. 1-24); but second, if he dies, then the same two options noted in vv. 36-38 are available to her. Staying single (in this case as widows) is to be preferred; but marriage is a viable option—as long as it is to a believer.

36 Paul's first directive is for the man who wants to go through with his marriage: "He should do as he wants. He is not sinning. They should get married." That much seems clear enough; but the clause "he should do as he wants" is the apodosis (conclusion) of an extremely complex conditional sentence, whose double protases (one "if" clause imbedded in another) describe the conditions of the man—and perhaps his "virgin"—that lead to this conclusion. The sentence looks like this:

1) Protasis 1:[11]   If anyone thinks he is behaving improperly
                              toward his virgin,
2) Protasis 2:[12]   (if he [or she] be *hyperakmos*
                              and thus it ought to be),

---

[9]See the discussion on v. 25. W. Barclay adopts the expedient of including all three options, one following the other, in his translation (*The New Testament, A New Translation* [London, 1969], II, 46-47).

[10]This is the basic position of the traditional "father-daughter" view; it is still held by Conzelmann, 134, although he takes the view about the "virgins" adopted here.

[11]This first protasis is a present particular (εἰ . . . νομίζει), which implies that Paul knew that an actual situation like this existed in the community.

[12]This protasis, ἐὰν ᾖ, is a supposition, reflecting something that might be so.

3) Apodosis: let him do as he wishes.
4) Explanatory addition: He is not sinning; let them marry.

Since the clause begins with a contrastive "but," and "acting improperly"[13] is the antonym to "what is seemly" in v. 35, it seems probable
that concern for this man was already in view in the argument of vv. 32-35.
From the point of view of the ascetics his desire to consummate the marriage
is "inappropriate"; indeed, they have apparently filled him with anxiety
(v. 32) by their ascetic "noose" (v. 35). Thus Paul addresses this man's
situation specifically, so that his own words in vv. 29-34 will not serve in the
same negative way. What is not clear is what would make this man think his
current behavior toward his betrothed was "unseemly" or "shameful."[14]
Since such an idea probably stems from the ascetics, it could refer either to
his wanting to get married, which they would consider "unseemly," or to
his keeping her betrothed[15] without going ahead with the marriage, which
could make her situation very difficult.

The second protasis interrupts the flow of thought, perhaps as Paul's
own hypothetical contribution as to why the man may think his current
actions are shameful. Under any view it is a particularly difficult clause.
Unfortunately, one cannot be certain as to either the subject of the verb or the
meaning of the adjective *hyperakmos*. The subject may be either the virgin,
who is the one most recently mentioned in the preceding clause, or the man,
since an unexpressed subject in a dependent clause usually picks up the
subject of the preceding clause. Grammatically, the latter seems preferable,[16] but one cannot be sure. Likewise with the adjective. The compound

---

[13]Gk. ἀσχημονεῖν, a particularly pejorative word describing disgraceful, dis-
honorable behavior.

[14]This expression is one of the real difficulties for the "spiritual marriage" view.
If they are already married spiritually, how might he now think he were behaving shamefully toward her? The "father/daughter" view answers this more easily, but not without
difficulty. The father apparently had been considering keeping her a virgin (devoting her
to the Lord on his own volition?), but now he is having some second thoughts. It should be
noted that most commentaries that take this view do not really wrestle with the fact that the
young lady's wishes are not mentioned at all. The father is the prime actor throughout (see
esp. on v. 37), which means that her virginity is not so much *her* "devotion" to the Lord
as *his*.

[15]The language "his virgin" here is one point in favor of the "spiritual marriage"
view since that would be her proper designation. It is sometimes objected that "his virgin"
is a strange way of speaking about one's betrothed, but that would be less so if the term
comes from their letter and Paul is simply using it consistently throughout the argument.
Here it would mean something close to "his girl" (Holladay, 105). It is even more difficult
for the father-daughter view since this is the place in particular where one would expect the
word "daughter" to appear.

[16]Unfortunately, there are no parallels in Paul to help us here. The closest is to be
found in 7:39 and Rom. 7:2, 4, where the second person in the first clause is repeated as
the subject in the ἐάν clause, so that there is no mistaking who died. In 2 Cor. 3:16 and

hyper-akmos is otherwise unknown in the Greek language, but its sense can be discerned from the simple words. *Akmē* refers to the "highest" or "culminating point" of anything. With men it means to be in the "prime of life"; with women it frequently is used to refer to "coming of age," especially puberty. The preposition *hyper* as a compound can either be temporal, "beyond," or intensive, "fully developed" or "exceedingly." For the woman, therefore, it would mean either that she was getting "past her prime" ("bloom of youth," BAGD) or "was fully developed sexually"[17] and therefore ready for marriage. For the man it would most likely be intensive and mean something like "strong passions" (BAGD).[18] On balance, the clause most likely refers to the man;[19] but it may very well refer to the woman. In either case, the second part of the clause, "and thus it ought to be," would mean that his or her being *hyperakmos* leads to a sense that he or she "ought to marry."

The apodosis and its further explanation indicate that the engaged man *wants* to get married: "let him do *as he wishes*." The Corinthian ascetics apparently have led him to believe that it may even be sin if he were to go through with it, which in turn has led to his "anxiety" and "unseemly behavior" toward his fiancée. Paul says, "Not so. If because he or she is *hyperakmos* and marriage ought to occur, then let him do as he wishes. He does not sin."

The final imperative, "let them marry," is particularly difficult for both the other views. For the father-daughter view this is an inexplicable reference to a third party (the groom), who is not otherwise mentioned throughout the passage. If this view were correct, one would expect exactly what the NASB does, "let her marry." If the father is acting as *patria potestas,* it is especially strange that he should be told to "let *them* marry," as if the young man and woman were urging it on him. The verb itself also diminishes the probability of the "spiritual marriage" view, since there is no other evidence that it might mean to consummate sexually a marriage that had taken place much earlier.

Rom. 14:23 the subject of the ἐάν clause is the subject of the main verb in the preceding clause, but there is no ambiguity in those cases. While these data are in no way decisive, they do tend to favor the repetition of the subject of the main clause as the intention here.

[17]This is the suggested translation of LSJ; cf. J. M. Ford, "The Rabbinic Background of St. Paul's Use of ὑπέρακμος (1 Cor. vii:36)," *JJS* 17 (1966), 89-91, who argues on the basis of rabbinic sources that it has to do with fully developed breasts. As with her other suggestions in this chapter, to assume a full rabbinic background for either Paul or the Corinthians is to ask too much of this letter.

[18]Cf. RSV, "if his passions are strong"; NEB, "if, that is, his instincts are too strong"; Barrett, "if he is over-sexed."

[19]Cf. Barrett: "To renounce marriage may be a fine and spiritual act, but in some cases it may be unfair to the girl and impossible to the man" (p. 184).

37 From the one who wishes to marry, which probably reflected a real situation in the church, Paul turns to the one who might opt for the Corinthian and his point of view, that it is better to remain as he is. What is significant here is his description of this man. In no less than four different ways he repeats that such a man must be fully convinced *in his own mind*. First, he "has settled the matter in his own mind";[20] second, he "is under no compulsion";[21] third, "he has authority[22] concerning his own will," meaning no one else is forcing this action on him; and fourth, he "has made up his own mind."[23] This verbal tour de force strongly suggests that outside influences might lead him to take such an action, but *against* his own will.[24] That seems precisely to be the case in Corinth. There were those who were urging such an action on the grounds that "It is morally good for a man not to have sexual relations with a woman, and thus for the betrothed man to remain as he is." Paul agrees with the last part, that he would do well to remain as he is, but not on *moral* grounds. So Paul's word to the man who takes his (Paul's) own position is that he must take control of his own actions and not be "under compulsion," either from the ascetics or from what Paul himself has written in this letter. Hopefully, such a person recognized that he had the *gift* of celibacy in so making up his own mind.

What this man makes up his mind to do is "not to marry the virgin" (lit. "to keep his own virgin"). This tends to be a difficult clause for any view.[25] Most likely he means something like "to keep her a virgin,"[26] hence

---

[20]Gk. καρδία; literally, "who stands firm in his heart." "Heart" here means "mind" (cf. 2:9).

[21]Gk. ἀνάγκη (see on v. 26); here it refers to necessity or compulsion, most likely from outside sources, although it could reflect the opposite of being *hyperakmos*, and "thus it ought to be," in v. 36.

[22]Gk. ἐξουσία (NIV, "control"); cf. 11:10.

[23]Gk. κέκρικεν ἐν τῇ ἰδίᾳ καρδίᾳ; literally, "he has decided in *his own* heart."

[24]This strong emphasis on his making up his *own* mind is especially difficult for both of the other views. Since the Corinthians themselves would *favor* such an action on his part, it is difficult to understand why Paul would so urge the partner in a celibate marriage. And why would Paul so strongly emphasize that a father must make up his own mind in this matter? In any case, it tends to leave the girl out completely, so that her remaining a virgin is scarcely related to her own volition. How can she be "concerned for" holiness in body and spirit (v. 34) when it is forced upon her by her father's will, and not her own choice?

[25]Despite many commentaries to the contrary, this is also a very unusual way for Paul to speak of a father not letting his daughter marry!

[26]Cf. Achilles Tatius 8.17.3 and 8.18.2, where Callisthenes, desiring the hand of Calligone, promises not to touch her sexually until she herself would allow. In the first instance, speaking to Calligone, he says: τηρήσω δέ σε παρθένον ("I will respect your virginity . . ."). In recounting this to Sostratus, he says: παρθένον γὰρ τὴν κόρην μέχρι τούτου τετήρηκα ("I have kept the maiden a virgin to this very hour").

"not to marry" her.[27] It is not clear why he calls her "his own" virgin, but if indeed they are already engaged, then she is his own in that sense, and he would now with his own convictions keep his "virgin" a virgin. If he does come to that conclusion, Paul says, "he will do well."[28]

38 With yet another strong inferential conjunction, "so then,"[29] Paul brings both the argument as a whole and the preceding two verses to a conclusion. The first sentence corresponds to v. 36 but uses language from the end of v. 37: "He who marries his virgin does well." That summarizes vv. 28 and 36: He has not sinned if he marries; indeed, he "does well." The second sentence corresponds to v. 37 and summarizes what he has argued right along: From his point of view, given their present situation, "he who does not marry her will do[30] even better." But *not* because one situation is *inherently* "better" than the other. That is precisely what he has argued against throughout. Therefore, one must go back to v. 26 for what makes it better; it is "because of the present distress."

But in so concluding Paul changes verbs, from *gameō* ("to marry") to *gamizō* (in Mark 12:25 and parallels, "to give in marriage"). Since "giving in marriage" is assumed to refer to a father's giving his daughter, this change of verbs is what brought about the "father-daughter" interpretation of the passage. The verb *gamizō*, however, is not found outside the NT;[31] in classical Greek *gameō* served both purposes. To the question whether the verb *must* carry the nuance "to give in marriage," the answer is No. There is sufficient evidence that the classical distinctions between *-eō* and *-izō* verbs had broken down in the *koinē* period.[32] But that still does not answer the question as to *why* Paul changed verbs in this set of sentences. The usual answer is "for the sake of variety," which may still be the best one. It is at least noteworthy that this is the only case in the chapter where the verb "to

---

[27]This is the clause that offers strongest support for the "spiritual marriage" view. Hence the NEB: "to preserve his partner in her virginity." But there are too many other strikes against this view, and this clause finally will mean nearly the same thing for all views.

[28]This use of the adv. "well" (καλῶς) seems to confirm that the usage "it is good" does not carry moral overtones for Paul (see n. 27 on 7:1), even though it probably did for the Corinthians in their slogans. That makes the NIV's "does the right thing" an unfortunate choice, since "right" in such a sentence can carry strong moral overtones. It is even more unfortunate in the next sentence.

[29]Gk. ὥστε; see on 3:7.

[30]Cf. n. 4. In both instances Paul uses the future for this person.

[31]The 2nd-c. A.D. grammarian Apollonius in fact distinguishes between the two verbs in this way (quoted in MM, 121). But since it is found in no Greek literature or papyri, one cannot tell what his "rule" means; especially so since the Atticists were trying to overcome *koinē* usage. He may very well be trying to "correct" a usage such as Paul's in this passage.

[32]See esp. MM, 121.

marry" has an object. All uses of *gameō* are intransitive; it may be that for Paul *gamizō* carried a transitive nuance, hence its usage here.

So at the end Paul has agreed, and disagreed, with the Corinthians in their letter. They prefer celibacy for "spiritual" reasons; he prefers it for pastoral and eschatological ones. But quite in contrast to them, he also affirms marriage; indeed, he does so strongly: Such a man "does well." But there is one final word. These verses are addressed to the man; but in keeping with his response throughout, there is a final word for married women as well.

39 This final word to the women comes as something of a surprise. It assumes that the woman is married, which is not the perspective of vv. 25-38, but of vv. 1-24, where they were trying to dissolve their marriages. The passage appears, therefore, to function as a concluding word for both sections, by repeating in a different way the word of vv. 1-24, that they should not separate from their husbands, and by urging the same reality on the "virgins" from this section, who are to go through with their marriages.[33]

The first statement, "A woman is bound to her husband as long as he lives," runs so counter to Jewish understanding and practice at this point in history[34] that it almost certainly reflects Paul's understanding of Jesus' own instructions (see on v. 10).[35] As such it is a final word against divorce and remarriage. But there is no argument here, simply a matter-of-fact reiteration of a point made previously (vv. 10, 13). The concern in this case lies ultimately with the second issue, a woman's remarriage, and he repeats the advice just given in vv. 36-38.

The marriage bond is in effect until[36] "her husband dies."[37] After

---

[33]It is often suggested that this final concern is whether widows should remarry. While the advice finally deals with that question, it does not begin that way. Had that been the question, it would have been more appropriate for Paul simply to talk about widows, as in v. 8. Conzelmann, however, sees this opening sentence as "paving the way" for his announcement about widows (p. 136 n. 50).

[34]See n. 12 on v. 10.

[35]In Rom. 7:2-3 the idea is repeated, but in terms of being bound by "the law." That almost certainly means the OT law, but the use of "law" in that case is determined by the context, where death to the "law" is the concern of the analogy (or at least is the point finally derived from it). It is unlikely that Paul is here thinking in terms of the Jewish law. Jesus has the final word on this one.

[36]The Greek clause, ἐάν with the aorist subjunctive, is a future supposition (cf. vv. 10, 28, 36). This seems to run counter to the suggestion of Barrett, 185-86, that it might be speaking of a Christian husband who has already died. Granted that 11:30 implies that many in the community have already died, which may have widowed more than one woman, Paul is nonetheless speaking more generally.

[37]Gk. κοιμηθῇ, lit. "fallen asleep"; a euphemism for death, used by Paul only to refer to believers who have died (1 Thess. 4:13-15; 1 Cor. 11:30; 15:6, 18, 20, 51).

that, she has the same option as the man who wants to get married: "She is free to marry anyone she wishes." This sentence seems to eliminate the possibility that levirate marriage is in view;[38] it also indicates that in this matter at least the woman had full freedom to make her own choice.[39] As before, this is a perfectly valid option. In this case, however, Paul adds a proviso not needed in the previous case. If she chooses to remarry, it should be "only in the Lord."[40] This is not so much a *command* that she may not marry outside the Lord as it is good sense. To be "in the Lord" is to have one's life come under the eschatological view of existence outlined in vv. 29-31. Such a woman lives from such a radically different perspective and value system from that of a pagan husband that a "mixed" marriage, where the "two become one," is simply unthinkable. If she becomes a believer after marriage, then she should maintain the marriage with the hope of winning him to the Lord (vv. 12-16); but it makes no sense from Paul's perspective for one to engage such a marriage once one is a Christian.

40 This final sentence essentially repeats the stance of the foregoing argument, that remaining single is the better option; only in this case the appeal is to her own happiness, with no ground suggested as to why that might be so, except that this is "my own opinion" (see on v. 25). Very much as in v. 25, however, Paul is quick to point out that his opinion is not without good backing. In this matter, "I think that I too have the Spirit of God."

This last sentence may be taken in one of two ways. (1) It is possible that this is one more jab at the Corinthian pneumatics, implying "If you think you have the Spirit, remember that I, too,[41] have the Spirit." (2) Or it may simply be a strengthening of his "opinion," as in v. 25, that he is not simply on his own in this matter. He *also* has the help of the Spirit in making such judgments. Since this is an issue on which they and he would tend to

---

[38]*Pace* Ford, *Trilogy*, p. 98. The clause speaks of her own will in such a way that it is hardly conceivable that she is a young widow obliged by Jewish law to marry her brother-in-law. Dr. Ford seems to disregard the Greek here, which hardly allows that it is the same case as in vv. 36-37 but now from the woman's point of view. Here the question is suppositional, not something that has already happened.

[39]This does not eliminate the father-daughter interpretation for the former paragraph, but it does suggest that since the widow had such freedom of choice, one would need overwhelming evidence to show that a young woman did not have some voice in the matter as well.

[40]Almost certainly this means what the NIV translates, "but he must belong to the Lord." That is, since she is a Christian, her new husband should be from within the community as well. Lightfoot, 235, followed by Barrett, 186, thinks this too limiting for the phrase μόνον ἐν κυρίῳ; but even he (Lightfoot) must allow that his view (simply a word that she remember her own Christian duty in this matter) comes out at nearly the same point.

[41]Gk. κἀγώ (cf. 2:1, 3).

agree, it is more likely that the latter is intended, although it may also be a subtle word against those who were not so sure that he did possess the Spirit.

With these words the two matters relating to marriage are brought to a close. The argument as a whole has generally been against the Corinthian ideal of asceticism. Nonetheless, he agrees with the Corinthians that those who are now single, whether betrothed or widowed, are better off as they are. But since he disagrees with the theology that brought the Corinthians to their stance, he also affirms marriage over against their point of view. In the matter that follows (chaps. 8–10) all of that changes. Not only does he disagree with their stance but also with their reasons for it, as well as the way they have used his own behavior against him. It thus stands in sharp contrast to the relatively mild expression of these two sections.

Paul's judgments in these two paragraphs have often been a source of concern. Does not Scripture say in fact that singleness is *better* than marriage? To which the answer is No. First of all, this reflects Paul's own opinion (vv. 25 and 40), and he is concerned throughout that it not be taken as "Scripture," that is, as some form of commandment or principle. It is an *ad hoc* answer in light of some "present distress." But more importantly, vv. 36-38 are *not* a judgment on marriage or singleness per se at all, but on whether or not engaged couples in that setting should get married. Paul thinks it better for them if they do not; but he also makes it clear that marriage is a perfectly valid option. It has nothing to do with good and evil, or even with better or worse, but with good and better in the light of that situation. It is perhaps noteworthy that the entire discussion is carried on quite apart from one of the major considerations in our culture—love for one another. One can only guess what Paul might have said in a different setting.

B. FOOD SACRIFICED TO IDOLS (8:1–11:1)

The issue that begins with 8:1 continues through 11:1. The topic, "idol food,"[1] is probably related to the warning in 5:10-11 against associating

---

[1]Gk. εἰδωλόθυτα (lit. "things sacrificed to idols"), a word that comes from Hellenistic Judaism; in 10:28 Paul uses the Greek term ἱερόθυτα ("sacred food"). What was sacrificed became part of the meal in the pagan temples and shrines; what was left over from the "god's table" was often sold in the marketplace. Jews were absolutely forbidden to eat such food. See *m.Abod.Zar.* 2.3: "Flesh that is entering in unto an idol is permitted, but what comes forth is forbidden" (Danby, p. 438; cf. *b.Hul.* 13b; 4 Macc. 5.2). It is not certain what the term means in the other instances in the NT. In the Apostolic Decree (Acts 15:29; 21:25) it probably refers to marketplace food, but most likely the issue there is not so much that of eating such food privately, but of eating it at the common meals where Jewish believers would be present. The two passages in Revelation (2:14,

357

with "idolaters."[2] If so, then eating "food sacrificed to idols" refers to a specific form of idolatry against which Paul apparently had already spoken in his previous letter.[3] Most likely in their letter to him they had taken exception to his earlier prohibition.

But not everyone is agreed on the exact nature of the problem and of Paul's response. In the response itself Paul addresses three issues: (1) In 10:1-22 he expressly prohibits the eating of sacrificial food at the pagan temples in the presence of the idol-demons. (2) In 10:23–11:1 he deals with the same food, but now as it is sold in the marketplace, and says that such food may be freely eaten without any question of conscience. (3) In 9:1-27 he offers a strong defense of his apostolic authority, with special emphasis on his apostolic freedom. The questions are, How do these three relate, or do they?[4] and especially, How does 8:1-13 fit into all this?[5] These questions in turn are related to the historical question, What were the Corinthians doing and what have they argued in their letter?

The traditional answer is that Paul is responding to an internal problem in Corinth between the "weak" and the "strong" over the question of marketplace food.[6] In the name of "knowledge" and "freedom" the

---

20) are ambiguous; it could refer to the same thing as in Acts, to private meals, or to temple attendance. The second-century Christian writers who do refer to it forbid it to Christians, and in those cases it almost certainly refers to marketplace food (Justin, *Dial.* 34; Irenaeus, *Haer.* 1.6.3).

[2]The term used in 5:10-11 is εἰδωλολάτραι (cf. 10:7); note the concluding prohibition in 10:14: φεύγετε ἀπὸ τῆς εἰδωλολατρίας.

[3]On this probability see Hurd, 115-49.

[4]These difficulties have been the chief cause of the partition theories for this letter. See the Introduction, pp. 15-16. Cf. Hurd, 42-47.

[5]There are also considerable difficulties with 8:1-13 itself: e.g., the non sequitur nature of the first two paragraphs; how vv. 1-3 respond to the question of idol food; how vv. 7-13 relate to the matters addressed in 10:14-22 and 10:23–11:1.

[6]For a typical, brief expression of this point of view, see Kugelman, 266. This is the position assumed or advocated in the commentaries (Parry excepted), as well as in most of the other literature. Among the more significant items, see H. F. von Soden, "Sacrament and Ethics in Paul," in *The Writings of St. Paul* (ed. W. Meeks; New York, 1972), pp. 257-68 (ET of the article that first appeared in *Marburger Theologische Studien* [Gotha, 1931], I, 1-40); A. Ehrhardt, "Social Problems in the Early Church," in *The Framework of the New Testament Stories* (Manchester, 1964), pp. 275-312; C. K. Barrett, "Things Sacrificed to Idols," *NTS* 11 (1964/65), 138-53; Theissen, 121-43; Horsley, "Consciousness"; Murphy-O'Connor, "Freedom"; and J. Brunt, "Rejected, Ignored, or Misunderstood? The Fate of Paul's Approach to the Problem of Idol Food in Early Christianity," *NTS* 31 (1985), 113-24.

A considerably different point of view has been argued by C. A. Kennedy, "The Cult of the Dead in Corinth" (to appear in the Marvin Pope *Festschrift*), a copy of which the author kindly made available to me. He argues that εἰδωλόθυτα does *not* mean idol food but refers to "memorial meals for the dead." The amassed data are of great interest, but Kennedy's argument as a whole is finally unconvincing since nothing in the text itself hints at funerary rites and his linguistic analysis lacks the one essential ingredient—

"strong" are advocating eating such food (8:7-13), some perhaps even going so far as to attend the cultic meals at the temples (8:10; 10:14-22). Perhaps they are also urging that such eating will "build up" the "weak" on the matter of "freedom" (cf. 8:9-10). The "weak," on the other hand, are arguing against eating idol food as a matter of "conscience." The basic problem, then, is marketplace food, to which Paul responds by first addressing the "strong" and invoking the stumbling-block principle (8:1-13; cf. 10:30–11:1). In 10:23-29, on the other hand, he encourages the "weak" to take a broader view. Chap. 9 functions as an illustration, by way of digression, of his own giving up his freedom for the rights of others. As an aside he also prohibits temple attendance in 10:14-22.

This answer, however, is filled with nearly insuperable difficulties,[7] the most serious of which is the vigorous, combative nature of Paul's answer. This is scarcely the kind of response one would expect if they had simply presented an internal question on which they had asked him to render a decision. As throughout most of the letter, this then is yet another issue on which Paul and they are at odds.[8]

The best solution to all these data is to view 8:10 and 10:1-22 as the basic problem to which Paul is responding throughout. This means that *eidōlothyta* does not refer primarily to marketplace food, but to the eating of sacrificial food at the cultic meals in the pagan temples.[9] In this view all of

---

demonstrable evidence that the word was ever used for funerary rites in Jewish or Christian antiquity.

[7]Among others, (1) it fails to take 8:10 seriously (the only specific mention of their behavior in 8:1-13 deals only with going to the temples, not with marketplace food); (2) it has difficulty with the essentially contradictory nature of 8:1-13 and 10:23-29, if they are both addressed to the same issue (see the next paragraph); (3) it fails to see that 8:4-6 is related to 10:14-22, *not* to 10:23-29; (4) it neglects the combative, apologetic force of chap. 9, not to mention 8:1-13 and 10:1-22; the *effect* (Paul's vigorous argument and defense) is simply not adequate to the *cause* (a letter asking his opinion on issues on which they are internally divided).

Item (2) has always been a source of genuine difficulty for the traditional view, for which a variety of ploys are brought in to salvage the theory (usually that he is addressing two different groups—although nothing in the text suggests as much). Hurd, 148, frankly admits that "therefore, we reach the somewhat strange conclusion that Paul appears to have permitted the Corinthians to continue their current practices concerning idol meat virtually unchanged" and that "Paul devoted the major part of his reply to vigorous disagreement with them, and only at the close did he give them permission to behave as in fact they had been behaving." This is hardly satisfactory. For the fully contradictory nature of 8:7-13 and 10:23–11:1 if they are addressing the same issue, see Fee, "Εἰδωλόθυτα," pp. 176-78.

[8]As elsewhere this does not mean that everyone in the community is so disposed, but that those who are leading the attack against Paul have considerably influenced the whole community. On this issue see the Introduction, pp. 6-10, and the commentary on 1:12 and 4:18-21.

[9]For the advocacy of this position, see Fee, "Εἰδωλόθυτα." In an earlier form it

8:1–10:22 takes up this issue against the Corinthian position that they have the "right" to continue this practice. As with going to the prostitutes (6:12-20), it is forbidden both on theological (10:14-22) and ethical (8:1-13) grounds. Then, in 10:23–11:1 he concludes with the matter of idol food sold in the market and eaten in private homes. On this issue the answer is considerably different; they may do as they wish unless someone else *present at the meal* calls attention to its idolatrous origins.[10]

That going to the temples is the real issue is supported by the fact that the eating of cultic meals was a regular part of worship in antiquity.[11] This is true not only of the nations that surrounded Israel,[12] but of Israel itself.[13] In

---

was adopted by Parry, 125-27; it is assumed in the recent dissertation by Willis (see bibliography).

That this is the real issue is supported by several other data as well: (1) In 8:7 and 10, where Paul focuses on those who are being hurt by the action of the many, he singles out Gentile converts who had formerly been idolaters. It is extremely doubtful whether buying and eating marketplace food would have been a problem for such converts (cf. Acts 15:20, 29, where the presupposition of the Decree is that Gentile converts are not bothered by such things). Such scruples could only have stemmed from Jewish abhorrence of idolatry. There is no reason to believe that Gentiles would have adopted Jewish thinking on this matter when Paul himself had no such scruples (as 10:23-29 makes clear). And in any case, the problem for Jews would not have been with what the Gentile believers were doing on their own, but with community meals where such food might be part of the common meal. But none of this is so much as hinted at here.

(2) In 8:10 Paul specifically says that the problem has to do with temple attendance. In 10:7-8 the specific illustrations of idolatry and sexual immorality from Jewish history both come from settings where the idolatry and sexual immorality were carried on in the context of cultic meals in the presence of the idols. Why these specifics, one wonders, if the issue were simply the contamination of food because it had formerly been on the table of the god at a pagan shrine?

(3) Rhetorically, one might ask, what other kind of setting can be suggested for 8:1-13? In 8:10 he specifically singles out temple attendance as the problem. In 10:25-26 he is absolutely liberal—and just as with circumcision (7:18) quite over against his own Jewish tradition—on the matter of marketplace food eaten in one's own home. In 10:27-29 he takes an equally liberal stance with regard to eating in the home of another, with the proviso of abstention if someone else makes an issue of it. The question is, What other setting is left except the one specifically noted in 8:10?

[10]It has been common to see the introduction of the Apostolic Decree in Corinth (either by Peter, or by Jewish Christians [e.g., Barrett, "Things Sacrificed," 142-43], or by Paul himself in his previous letter [Hurd, 240-70]) as lying behind the whole issue. But this assumes that marketplace food is the issue, which 10:23–11:1 makes clear is no issue for Paul at all. Indeed, Paul's response on this question makes his own relationship to the Decree a matter of some historical difficulty.

[11]For a helpful overview of this phenomenon and the evidence for it, see Willis, 8-64.

[12]For the Canaanites, see Judg. 9:27; for Egyptian practices, which included sexual sins as well, see Exod. 32:6; for Moab (also with sex), see Num. 25:1-2; and for Babylon, Dan. 5:1-4.

[13]The *locus classicus* is Deut. 14:22-26; cf. Exod. 24:11; 1 Sam. 9:13; 1 Kgs.

the Corinth of Paul's time, such meals were still the regular practice both at state festivals and private celebrations of various kinds.[14] There were three parts to these meals: the preparation, the sacrifice proper, and the feast.[15] The meat of the sacrifices apparently was divided into three portions: that burned before the god, that apportioned to the worshipers, and that placed on the "table of the god," which was tended by cultic ministrants but also eaten by the worshipers.[16] The significance of these meals has been much debated,[17] but most likely they involved a combination of religious and social factors. The gods were thought to be present since the meals were held in their honor and sacrifices were made; nonetheless, they were also intensely social occasions for the participants.[18] For the most part the Gentiles who had become believers in Corinth had probably attended such meals all their lives; this was the basic "restaurant" in antiquity,[19] and every kind of occasion was celebrated in this fashion.

The problem, then, is best reconstructed along the following lines. After their conversion—and most likely after the departure of Paul—some of them returned to the practice of attending the cultic meals. In his earlier

---

1:25; Hos. 8:13 (and perhaps Jer. 35:2; Ps. 23:5-6). The fact that this practice stopped in the postexilic period, despite the clear commandment in Deuteronomy, is probably attributable to the two factors of its close association with sexual immorality in Canaanite cults and the destruction of the temple in Jerusalem where such meals had been held.

[14]The description of such a meal in the cult of Asclepius can be found in Aristides, *or.sac.* 2.27 (the cult of Asclepius had a prominent temple in Corinth). Thirteen papyrus invitations to such meals are now extant (11 for the cult of Sarapis; one each for Demeter and Isis; according to Pausanias, *Descriptions of Greece* 4.6, there were two "sacred precincts" in Corinth for both Isis and Sarapis). See the formal analysis of these invitations by C.-H. Kim, "The Papyrus Invitation," *JBL* 94 (1975), 391-402; cf. the discussion in G. H. R. Horsley, *New Documents Illustrating Early Christianity*, I (North Ryde, NSW, Australia, 1981), 5-9. The typical invitation reads: "Chaeremon requests your company at the table of the lord Sarapis at the Sarapeum tomorrow, the 15th at 9 o'clock" (POxy 1.110²); cf. POxy 2791, where the first birthday of a daughter is to be celebrated at a meal in the Sarapeum.

[15]Cf. the description in R. K. Yerkes, *Sacrifice in Greek and Roman Religions and Early Judaism* (New York, 1952), pp. 99-100.

[16]See the description in D. H. Gill, "*TRAPEZOMETA:* A Neglected Aspect of Greek Sacrifice," *HTR* 67 (1974), 117-37.

[17]See the discussion in Willis, 17-61.

[18]On the fundamentally religious character of the meals, see Horsley, *New Documents*, p. 8; Willis, 17-64, on the other hand, argues for their social character, but his argument is directed especially against a sacramental interpretation. His latter point (the lack of a sacramental aspect, which included "partaking of the deity himself") is almost certainly correct; but he has probably pushed the evidence too far in one direction, nullifying the religious aspect altogether. On this point Horsley's brief analysis is an important corrective. See on 10:16-21.

[19]Cf. Ehrhardt, "Social Problems," p. 279.

letter Paul forbade such "idolatry"; but they have taken exception to that prohibition and in their letter have made four points:[20]

(1) They argue that "all have knowledge" about idols.[21] Monotheism by its very nature rules out any genuine reality to idols (8:1, 4)—a point, of course, on which Paul will agree. Apparently this meant for them that attendance at the temples had no significance one way or the other since they were only eating with their friends, not worshiping what did not exist.

(2) They also have knowledge about food, that it is a matter of indifference to God (8:8)—another point on which Paul will agree. But their point seems to be: "Since idols are nonentities, and since food is a matter of indifference to God, it matters not not only *what* we eat but *where* we eat it as well." So how can Paul forbid their going to the temples?

(3) They seem to have a somewhat "magical" view of the sacraments; those who have had Christian baptism and who partake of the Lord's Table are not in any danger of falling (10:1-4).

(4) Besides, there is considerable question in the minds of many whether Paul has the proper apostolic authority to forbid them on this matter. In their minds this has been substantiated by two factors: first, his failure to accept support while with them; and second, his own apparently compromising stance on idol food sold in the marketplace (he abstained when eating with Jews, but ate when eating with Gentiles; cf. 9:19-23).

It seems probable that the advocates of this position are also arguing that others will be "built up" by taking "authority" in this matter (8:9-10).[22] In any case, by pressing for this right in the name of *gnōsis* ("knowledge"), they are abusing some others among them who could not make these fine distinctions. Being invited to join them at the same banquets, these believers with "weak consciences" are being destroyed because for them it is a return to idolatry and an abandoning of Christ.

Thus for Paul four issues need to be squared away. (1) His first

---

[20]As with 6:12 (cf. 10:23); 7:1, 25, one can make the best sense of the argument by assuming that Paul cites their letter at several points. This is especially true of 8:1 and 4, where he actually uses a formula that implies quotation ("we know that . . ."); it is also likely at 8:8. In still other places (e.g., 8:10; 9:1; 10:1-4) he is probably alluding to their argument.

[21]Hurley, 34, makes the thoroughly improbable assertion that "the knowledgeable party is Jewish." This simply fails to take seriously the nature of the present problem. Furthermore, this failure, which Hurley nearly brushes past, is what also calls into question his major thesis, that the Corinthian community was primarily Jewish. See n. 12 in the Introduction (p. 4).

[22]This view has had a long history. It is adopted, *inter alia*, by Weiss, 230; Moffatt, 110-11 (see esp. his translation); Jewett, *Terms*, pp. 422-23; Murphy-O'Connor, "Freedom," 548-49. For an opposing view, see M. E. Thrall, "The Meaning of οἰκοδομέω in Relation to the Concept of συνείδησις (I Cor. 8,10)," in *Studia Evangelica* 4 (TU 102; ed. F. L. Cross; Berlin, 1968), pp. 468-72.

concern is with the attitude that lay behind their behavior and argument. The abuse of others in the name of "knowledge" indicates a total misunderstanding of the nature of Christian ethics, which springs not from knowledge but from love. He begins his response by speaking to this question (8:1-13).[23] (2) Also at issue, as elsewhere in the letter, is a crisis of authority (see on 1:12; 4:18-21; 5:1-5). Paul's own conduct had been called into question and thus his authority and freedom as an apostle (9:1-3). Therefore, in 9:1-27 he launches into a vigorous defense of his apostleship (in this case in terms of his "right" to their support, even if he has given it up; vv. 3-18) and of his freedom (to act as he does about idol food; vv. 19-23). (3) But also at issue is their misunderstanding of the true nature of idolatry and their false security in the Christian sacraments. Hence in 10:1-13 he warns them, on the basis of analogies from Israel, that the Christian sacraments are no sure protection against such disobedience, and in vv. 14-22 he prohibits attendance at cultic meals. Here he expands on 8:4-6 to remind them that idolatry involves the worship of demons. (4) Finally, in 10:23–11:1 he adds a final word about the eating of marketplace food. They may buy and eat at will (v. 25), with the one proviso that they should abstain if in a pagan home someone points out its temple origins (vv. 27-28).

1. The Basis of Christian Conduct—Love, Not Knowledge (8:1-13)

Although Paul will finally forbid their going to the temples, his first concern is with the incorrect ethical basis of their argument. The problem is primarily attitudinal. They think Christian conduct is predicated on *gnōsis* (knowledge) and that knowledge gives them *exousia* (rights/freedom) to act as they will in this matter. Paul has another view: The content of their knowledge is only partially correct; but more importantly, *gnōsis* is not the ground of Christian behavior, love is.

Thus Paul begins by refuting the opening words of their argument, "we all possess knowledge." In vv. 1-3 he insists that that is the wrong basis for Christian behavior. In vv. 4-6 he takes up the partial nature of their "knowledge." These two preliminary words serve as the basis for the argument that follows in vv. 7-13. Since not all do have this knowledge, at least not in the internalized sense of "knowing," their conduct must be based on love. In this case love takes the form of "the stumbling-block principle,"

[23]The chief objection to this reconstruction lies in the tension some see between this section, where he appeals to love, and 10:14-22, where he forbids such behavior outright. How can he begin in this way if in fact he intends finally to forbid it altogether? It should be noted, however, that because of 8:10 this is a problem for all interpreters. The answer lies with Paul's understanding of the relationship between the indicative and the imperative (see on 5:6-8). Paul seldom begins with an imperative. As in 6:12-20; 1:10–4:21; 12:1–14:40, he begins by correcting serious theological misunderstandings and then gives the imperative. See Fee, "Εἰδωλόθυτα," pp. 195-97; and v. 13 below.

which does not have to do with "offending" someone but with causing people to fall by urging on them an action they cannot do freely.

a. The way of love and the way of knowledge (8:1-3)

1 *Now about food sacrificed to idols: We know that we all possess knowledge.ᵃ Knowledge puffs up, but love builds up.* 2 *The²⁴ man who thinks he knows²⁵ something²⁶ does not yet know as he ought to know.* 3 *But the man who loves God²⁷ is known by God.²⁸*

ᵃOr *"We all possess knowledge," as you say*

The most striking thing about this opening paragraph is how non sequitur it seems to be. Paul begins with the regular rubric "now about" (cf. 7:1), having as its present content "food sacrificed to idols." But what immediately follows (vv. 1b-3) says nothing about eating or food or idols; rather, he sets forth knowledge and love in bold relief—words that do not immediately come to mind as natural opposites. Only after this opening salvo does he resume in v. 4 what he began in v. 1a. Since vv. 7-13 conclude this section with a considerable assault on their acting on the basis of knowledge alone, one can be sure that this forms the basis of the Corinthian response to Paul, and that he considers it to lie at the root of the problem.

Paul's response goes right to the heart of things. Their emphasis is totally wrong; the aim of our faith is not knowledge but love. Knowledge and love are thus contrasted in two ways. First, the net effect of each (knowledge puffs up; love builds up); second, the difference it makes for the one doing the knowing or loving. Both sets of sentences are neatly balanced; the sharpness of the contrast is heightened by the asyndeton in each of the first sentences, plus the contrasting "but" *(de)* found between the two members in each set. Thus:

Knowledge puffs up
  but
Love builds up

If any thinks he has come to know [anything],
  he does not yet know as he ought to know;

²⁴The Western MSS, followed by the MajT, add δέ, thus breaking Paul's asyndeton. As Zuntz, 188, argues, this addition "obscures the argument." See the commentary.

²⁵The MajT substitutes the more common εἰδέναι for ἐγνωκέναι, which quite misses Paul's play on the word γινώσκω.

²⁶P⁴⁶ lacks the τι in this clause and (joined by Clement) the τὸν θεόν and ὑπ' αὐτοῦ in the next one. The resultant text reads: "If anyone thinks he has arrived at knowledge, he does not yet know as he ought to; but if anyone loves, this one truly knows (or, is known)." This has all the marks of being the original text, as Zuntz, 31-32, argues. See the commentary.

²⁷P⁴⁶ and Clement lack τὸν θεόν; see the preceding note.

²⁸P⁴⁶ ℵ* 33 and Clement lack the ὑπ' αὐτοῦ. See n. 26 above.

but
If anyone loves [God],
    this one is known [by God].

1 The "now about" that begins the sentence, as well as the completely new content, signals that Paul is picking up yet another item from their letter, "food sacrificed to idols."[29] As in 7:1 (cf. 6:12-13) he begins by citing their letter,[30] apparently intending, as v. 4 indicates, to set forth and qualify the *content* of their knowledge. He begins, "We are aware, along with yourselves,[31] that 'we all possess knowledge.' " But he gets only that far and immediately breaks off to qualify that reality first. There is a sense in which that is true (as vv. 4-6 affirm); but there is another sense in which it is not true at all (v. 7, "but not all have this knowledge"!). This latter reality is what makes their behavior unloving.

One should note that they did not say "we all know," but that "we all possess *gnōsis*."[32] This is one of three places where this word appears in our letter (cf. 1:5; 12:8); here it predominates.[33] Along with *logos* ("speech, rhetoric"; cf. 1:5, 17; 2:1-5) and *sophia* ("wisdom"; cf. 1:17-

[29]For the meaning of this term see above, p. 357 n. 1.

[30]This is confirmed by the structure of the Greek. The repeated οἴδαμεν ὅτι in vv. 1 and 4, and especially the repeated ὅτι (οἴδαμεν ὅτι . . . καὶ ὅτι . . .) in v. 4, makes this certain. When Paul is expressing his own ideas he never repeats with a ὅτι; the simple καί joins such correlative sentences (cf. 15:3-5, ὅτι . . . καὶ ὅτι . . . καὶ ὅτι). Cf. C. H. Giblin, "Three Monotheistic Texts in Paul," *CBQ* 38 (1975), 530. Furthermore, the semiredundancy in v. 4 of the two sentences following ὅτι almost demands that the ὅτι in these cases introduce direct discourse. Finally, this seems to make the best sense of the awkward second "we" in the sentence (see the following note).

[31]This seems to be the best explanation of the awkward double "we." A few of the earlier interpreters suggested that οἴδαμεν should read οἶδα μέν (so also Jeremias, "Briefzitate," p. 151). But this is an unnecessary expedient. See Hurd, 120. More recently Willis, 68-70 (following an earlier suggestion by W. Lock, "I Corinthians viii.1-9, A Suggestion," *Exp* 5th ser. 6 [1897], 65-74), has argued that the citation itself begins with οἴδαμεν. This is possible, but seems to dismiss too easily the formulaic character of οἴδαμεν ὅτι. See BAGD, ὅτι 1e, "The formula οἴδαμεν ὅτι is freq. used to introduce a well-known fact that is generally accepted."

[32]This phrase, along with their apparent insistence that this knowledge gives them ἐξουσία, has led more than anything else to the belief by many that we are here dealing with some form of Gnostic influence in Corinth. See esp. Schmithals, 141-55, 218-29. As useful as this book is for a possible understanding of Corinthian attitudes, its major thesis is flawed by Schmithals's circular reasoning that divides the two Corinthian letters into several letters on the basis of a prior commitment to a Gnostic scheme and then argues for the scheme on the basis of the partitioned letters. The same major flaw also considerably weakens the presentation by Jewett, *Terms,* pp. 23-40. Moreover, to call Paul's Corinthian opponents "Gnostic" is anachronistic since those systems do not emerge until the second century. Much more likely what appears here is part of a stream that became the Gnostic systems of a later period. Others see Jewish backgrounds to the theme. See esp. J. Dupont, *Gnosis,* and Horsley, "Gnosis" and "Consciousness"; cf. Ellis, 45-62.

[33]Five of its ten occurrences are in this chapter (vv. 1 [twice], 7, 10, 11). The cognate verb γινώσκω also occurs four times in vv. 2 and 3.

31), this is almost certainly an "in" word in Corinth. This is made all the more certain by the evidence from 1:5, 12:8, and 13:1-3. *Logos* and *gnōsis* are the two gifts singled out for special mention in the thanksgiving; the *logos* of "wisdom" and the *logos* of "knowledge" appear as the first two items in the list of spiritual gifts (12:8); and "speech" and "knowledge" receive special billing in the contrast with love in 13:1-3 and 8-13. In their minds being spiritual meant to have received *gnōsis,* meaning probably that the Spirit had endued them with special knowledge, which *all* believers should have, and which should serve as the basis of Christian behavior.[34]

Not so, says Paul, and his qualification is a particularly powerful statement about the basic nature of Christian ethics. All the more so if the Corinthians themselves had used the word "build up"[35] in their own slogans, a suggestion made the more plausible by the use of that term in 8:10 and 10:23. They would have urged that by following conduct based on knowledge believers would be "built up" in their *exousia* (rights, freedom; 8:10).[36] Thus for them "knowledge builds up." If so, then Paul is turning all this in on them. Not only does knowledge not "build up," it "puffs up" the individual (v. 1b) and "destroys" others (v. 11); and *exousia* is not the final goal of Christian ethics, but what is "beneficial" and "constructive" is (10:23). The problem with conduct predicated on knowledge is that it results in even greater sinfulness. Knowledge leads to pride; it "puffs up" (cf. 4:6, 18; 5:2).[37] But that is not true of "love."[38] Not only is love "not puffed up"

[34]Some have suggested that the fundamental difference has to do with how each understands the gospel, and that for the Corinthians γνῶσις was the way of salvation. This, of course, is fundamental to Schmithals's view (see n. 32 above); cf. Willis, 71. But the argument that unfolds does not seem to be first of all a question of salvation or existence predicated on knowledge, but of behavior—or the grounds for behavior. The question of existence does surface as fundamental to the argument in 1:10–2:16, where wisdom and the cross are in contrast; but here Paul is dealing with the outworking of their stance in the ethical realm. Their γνῶσις is a gift of the Spirit, which enlightens them to act in a certain way; it is not a way to salvation as such.

[35]Gk. οἰκοδομέω. Although this is clearly a Pauline word, both for his own apostolic ministry (cf. 2 Cor. 10:8; 13:10; Gal. 2:18) and for how believers are to relate to one another (1 Thess. 5:11) and to the community as a whole (1 Cor. 14:6-17), it seems likely to be a term with which the Corinthians are also already familiar. Cf. O. Michel, *TDNT* V, 410-12, and BAGD.

[36]Paul's reworking in 10:23 of the ἔξεστιν slogan that appears in 6:12 further strengthens this suggestion: "All things are permitted (ἔξεστιν = "I have ἐξουσία in all things"), but not all things *build up.*"

[37]One should note how many items in this section are similar to what was said about "wisdom" in chaps. 1–4. They both lead to pride (3:18-21); they both are deceptive and destructive (3:16-18); and he attacks them both with similar irony ("if anyone thinks he is wise" [3:18], "has knowledge" [8:2]).

[38]Gk. ἀγάπη, the basic Christian understanding of ethical behavior. This understanding goes back to Jesus, but becomes thoroughgoing in John and Paul (e.g., 1 Thess. 3:12; 1 Cor. 13; 2 Cor. 2:8; Gal. 5:6, 13, 22; Rom. 13:8; 14:15). Cf. V. P. Furnish, *The Love Command in the New Testament* (Nashville, 1972), pp. 91-117.

(13:4, the final occurrence of this word in the letter), but quite the opposite, it "builds up." The aim of Christian ethics is not Stoic self-sufficiency, which requires proper knowledge; rather, its aim is the benefit and advantage of a brother or sister. Thus it is the opposite of their behavior in vv. 7-12, which sets a stumbling block before others.[39]

2-3 This second set of contrasts between knowledge and love adds yet a further dimension to Paul's qualification of "we all possess knowledge." Unfortunately, these two clauses have caused considerable textual difficulty, leaving us with less than final certainty.[40] The standard text (translated by the NIV) reads:

If anyone thinks he knows (something),
  he does not yet know as he ought to know;
    but
If anyone loves (God),
  this one is known (by God).

The earliest witnesses in Egypt (Clement and P[46]) lack the words in parentheses, resulting in a text that reads:

If anyone thinks he has arrived at knowledge,[41]
  he does not yet know as he ought to know;
    but
If anyone loves,
  this one truly knows (or, is known).[42]

This latter reading fits the context so perfectly that it is either the Pauline original or else the work of an editorial genius.

With either reading the meaning of the first clause (v. 2) is basically the same. The addition of "something," however, tends to put the emphasis on the content of what is known. The "omission," which is more likely original, places the emphasis on the fact of having knowledge as such. The perfect tense of the infinitive implies that they consider themselves to have arrived as far as knowledge is concerned. Paul's point, therefore, is not that "a little knowledge is a dangerous thing" (which is usually true, and does fit their situation); rather, it is biting irony. The one who thinks he is "in the

---

[39]Cf. Rom. 14:13-15 for the same kind of argument; there walking according to love (v. 15) means not to put a stumbling block in the way of a brother (v. 13).

[40]See nn. 26-28 above.

[41]Gk. perfect ἐγνωκέναι, implying having come to the full state of knowledge. This unusual usage may have led to the dropping of τι; more likely τι is not original, and once it was added ἐγνωκέναι was eventually changed to the more common εἰδέναι, which had lost its perfect force.

[42]Gk. ἔγνωσται, either perfect passive or middle. On this reading it is probably middle (has come to know for oneself); if passive, it means "is known" or "recognized," "by God" being the implied subject. Very likely the reading of this verb as a passive led to the double addition of "God" and "by him" in the two parts of this clause.

know" by that very fact has given evidence that he does not yet have the real thing. Like the person who "thinks he is wise" (3:18), the one who thinks he has knowledge is self-deceived; true knowledge has eluded him. Thus the clause "he does not yet know as he ought to know" does not refer to some lack of content, but to the lack of real *gnōsis* itself, which, as the next clause (v. 3) points out, has to do with love.

That leads to the real problem with the standard text of v. 3, which seems to deflect Paul's point. He is not here dealing with loving (or knowing) *God*.[43] Rather, his concern is with their failure to act in love toward some in their midst who do not share their "knowledge." The standard text, it should be pointed out, does indeed reflect Paul's theology of God's prior action in our behalf. That is, our love of God is predicated on God's prior knowledge of us. The problem is in finding a satisfactory reason for him to have said that here.[44] On the other hand, the text of Clement and P[46] reflects exactly the point of the contrast. True *gnōsis* consists not in the accumulation of so much data, nor even in the correctness of one's theology, but in the fact that one has learned to live in love toward all. The final verb may be either middle or passive. If middle it suggests that the person who loves "has reached the fullness of gnosis";[45] if passive it suggests that the person who loves is the one who is truly "known," that is, "recognized" by God as having knowledge. In either case, this shorter text brings Paul's point home so powerfully that it is most likely what he originally wrote.

But why does Paul begin his response to the matter of idol meat in this way? Probably because he does basically agree with the theological premises that he will next take up—although he will have his own unique way of qualifying these as well. But he knows that what they are doing with their knowledge is dead wrong; and this is the more serious problem. So he begins by qualifying their understanding of *gnōsis* itself. Christian behavior is not predicated on the way of knowledge, which leads to pride and destroys others, but on the way of love, which is in fact the true way of knowledge.

---

[43]Otherwise Willis, 82, who concludes that they are seeking "to establish a relationship with God on the basis of knowledge" and that is what Paul is here counteracting. But even if one accepts the standard text, this does not seem to be the issue. See n. 34 above.

[44]The ordinary solution (e.g., Barrett, 190-91; Conzelmann, 141-42; Willis, 78-81), which may well be correct, is that the real question shifts from the Corinthians' acting out of knowledge or love to the ground of their being, in which Paul thus plays on the two words. Thus the one who loves God does so because God has already "known" him or her. Cf. Rom. 8:28, where "loving God" is equated with being called by him. All of this is true, of course, with regard to Pauline theology. But the problem still remains that "knowing God" is *not* the issue raised by the Corinthians in saying "we all possess knowledge."

[45]So Zuntz, 32.

All of this will be spelled out in greater detail in vv. 7-13, and especially in chap. 13.[46]

The tyranny of "knowledge" as the basis of Christian ethics has a long and unfortunate history in the church, from which most likely few who read—as well as the one who writes—this commentary are exempt. Once one's theology is properly in hand, it is especially tempting to use it as a club on others. And in this case, it happens from the theological right as well as from the left. This does not mean that knowledge is either irrelevant or unimportant, but it does mean that it cannot serve as the primary basis of Christian behavior. In Christian ethics "knowledge" must always lead to love. One should always beware of those teachers or systems that entice one by special "revelation" or "deeper insights." Such appeals are invariably to one's pride, not to one's becoming a more truly loving Christian. While it is true that "insight" often leads to "freedom," it is also true that it often results finally in the demand for "freedom" in the form of "rights." This is what had happened at Corinth. In the Christian faith "knowledge" or "insight" is never an end in itself; it is only a means to a greater end, the building up of others.

b. The content of the way of knowledge (8:4-6)

4 *So then, about eating food sacrificed to idols: We know that an idol is nothing at all in the world and that there is no God[1] but one.* 5 *For even if there are so-called gods, whether in heaven or on earth (as indeed there are many "gods" and many "lords"),* 6 *yet[2] for us there is but one God, the Father, from whom all things came and for whom we live; and there is but one Lord, Jesus Christ, through whom all things came and through whom we live.[3]*

With this paragraph Paul resumes what he began in v. 1, after the short qualifying word about the way of love superseding the way of knowledge.

---

[46]One should not miss what seems to be a clear relationship between what is said here and in chap. 13. There again the issue is love toward one's neighbor, not one's relationship with God. In 13:2 γνῶσις without ἀγάπη is nothing; and in v. 8 γνῶσις as a spiritual gift will come to an end, but ἀγάπη is forever. Hence the latter is "greater," without negating the former. Contrary to Willis, 81-82, Paul's struggle in the present passage is not with γνῶσις as such, but with their making it the predicate of Christian ethics, without ἀγάπη.

[1]The MajT follows the Syriac versions in adding ἕτερος ("no other God"). This is a clear gloss based on the OT theme of "other gods" (e.g., Exod. 20:3).

[2]P46 B 33 b sa Irenaeus "clean up" this awkward sentence by omitting the ἀλλ'.

[3]A few later MSS (0142 234 460 618 630) fill out the sentence with a Trinitarian formula ("And one Holy Spirit, in whom are all things, and we in him"). Such a form was known as early as Gregory Nazianzus (early fourth c.), although one cannot be sure it was actually in his bible. See Metzger, 557.

Again he quotes from their letter, in this case two propositions affirming monotheism (v. 4); and again he qualifies what they have said, but in a most unusual way. There is no way, of course, that he could disagree with their propositions. What he does instead is to set off the Christian faith from the pagan religions that are involved in the present conflict. Thus vv. 5-6 form a concessive sentence in which the protasis (v. 5) sets off pagan religions from the Christian affirmations found in the apodosis (v. 6). But v. 5 is stated in such a way that it not only sets up the contrasts in v. 6 but also anticipates the problem of the person with a "weak conscience" in v. 7. At the same time it leaves the door open for the qualification found in 10:19-20.

In both cases Paul does not allow reality to the "gods" of idolatry. What he does rather is to anticipate the argument of v. 7, that such "gods" have subjective reality for their worshipers; that is, they do not objectively exist, but they do "exist" for those who have given them reality by believing in them. Hence there are indeed "gods many" and "lords many." In chap. 10 he will again deny that a "god" is involved; what the Corinthians have not taken seriously is that pagan religion is the locus of demonic activity, and that to worship such "gods" is in fact to fellowship with demons. But that is later; for now the emphasis lies on his agreement with them that in contrast to the "gods many" and "lords many" there is *for us* only one *God,* namely the Father, and only one *Lord,* namely Jesus Christ. The net result is one of the powerful theological statements in our letter.

4 The clearly resumptive force of the "so then"[4] and the repeating of "about eating[5] food sacrificed to idols" indicate that Paul is returning to the topic at hand. With this sentence he picks up the two basic propositions of their argument. He begins as in v. 1, "we know that," meaning that he is affirming as true what they have said.[6]

The two propositions together form a strong affirmation of monotheism over against every form of polytheism or henotheism. Not only is there only one God, but there is a correlative denial that idols have any reality at all. This proclamation would not have been some new thing for them;[7] what is new is how they will use it in their own argument. The order in which the two sentences appear suggests that the Corinthians' main point is that an idol

---

[4]Gk. οὖν.

[5]Gk. βρῶσις; not found in the original rubric in v. 1. It is a verbal noun, emphasizing the actual eating of food. Hence the problem, as Paul sets it forth, is not with the food per se, but with the eating of it. This also points to the temple meals, since that is the place of eating such food.

[6]As noted above (see n. 30 on v. 1), the repeated "that" ("we know that . . . and that . . .") makes it almost certain that he is here quoting them.

[7]This surely reflects what must have been a basic part of the teaching that accompanied the preaching of the gospel in the Greco-Roman world. In this case, of course, the early Christians had been preceded by an aggressive Judaism, which by the time of Paul was generally well known for its monotheism, a faith that repulsed many because of its exclusiveness and insistence on circumcision but at the same time was very

lacks any reality. Although there is some ambiguity as to its precise nuance,[8] what they almost certainly mean is that there is no reality to Isis or Sarapis or Asclepius. Idols, yes; but genuine reality in the world, no. This is so because of the basic theological statement of the Christian faith, "There is no God but one." The Corinthians' point will be that since there is no reality to an idol because there is no God but one, how can we be faulted for eating meals at the temples, since the gods represented by these idols do not in fact exist?

That this is their point seems to be confirmed by the unusual qualification that follows. As a matter of fact, their premise is only partly true, as Paul will explain later in 10:19-20. But for now his concern is completely practical, namely the effect that believing in such "gods" has had on their devotees. Hence in what follows he will both qualify and affirm even more strongly the theological predicate for their behavior. The problem does not lie with its content, but with the unqualified use of it as giving them freedom to do as they will.

5 Vv. 5-6 together form a single sentence,[9] an *anacolouthon* in Greek (it does not follow grammatically), but one whose sense is clear.[10] In fact, even the reason for the *anacolouthon* can be fairly easily traced. The

---

attractive to others because of its higher morality. All of this makes much of the discussion by Horsley ("Gnosis") nearly irrelevant. His concern is to establish that the Corinthian "gnostics" were Hellenistic Jews of the Philonic type, who had converted to Christianity. But even though he has mustered considerable evidence in parallel, nothing in these parallels nor in the present passage demands an "enlightened Judaism" as the background. The early converts had become *Christians,* after all, and that is adequate to inform their present stance.

[8]Gk. οὐδὲν εἴδωλον ἐν κόσμῳ. The οὐδέν can be understood either attributively ("no idol exists in the world") or as a predicate ("an idol is a nothing [i.e., a nonentity] in the world"). The formal correspondence between the two clauses (οὐδὲν εἴδωλον/οὐδεὶς θεός) suggests the former. Otherwise Murphy-O'Connor ("Freedom," 546), who comes out at the same place, but believes one does so best by taking οὐδέν as a predicate.

[9]M. Trèves ("I Corinthiens VIII 5-6," *Cahiers Cercle Ernst Renan* 25 [1977], 22-23) has suggested that the sentence is a post-Pauline interpolation. But the passage sets up the argument of v. 7 so perfectly that one must offer extraordinarily convincing reasons to see it as non-Pauline, which Trèves fails to do.

[10]Some (e.g., Findlay, 841; Parry, 87; Grosheide, 192; cf. the discussion in Hurd, 121-22) have suggested, and Willis, 83-88, has argued at some length, that vv. 5 and 6, excepting the parenthetical ὥσπερ clause, are also part of the Corinthian argument. Willis's argument is based primarily on what he considers the appropriateness of the argument to the Corinthian position, on the one hand, plus the strong qualifying ἀλλ' that begins v. 7, on the other. But that is an unnecessary expedient and rather overlooks the Pauline nature of the grammar and structure: (1) the explanatory γάρ is a strictly Pauline feature, especially in this letter; (2) the *anacolouthon* makes little sense as a Corinthian statement to Paul, but good sense as an *ad hoc* creation by Paul; and (3) most importantly, as the structure of the argument indicates (see the display), the terms "god" and "lord" in the "creedal" statement of v. 6 are dependent on the Pauline interruption with its "gods many" and "lords many," and do not easily follow the original protasis. This latter item seems to make the hypothesis largely untenable.

"for"[11] is explanatory, picking up the theme of the two propositions in v. 4. Thus: "It is true that there is no reality to an idol and that there is only one God; *for* even if[12] there are so-called gods (whether in heaven or on earth) . . ."; but right at that point he breaks off with a parenthetical aside, "just as there are indeed gods many and lords many."[13] Precisely how Paul intended to conclude the sentence when it began cannot be known—perhaps with something like "they do not really have existence." In any case, the interruption calls forth an apodosis that does indeed respond to the opening concession, but does so by sharply qualifying the interrupting clause. Thus:

> *For*
> Even if there are so-called gods,
>   whether heavenly
>   or earthly
> (just as there are indeed gods many   (A)
>   and lords many)   (B)
> *But* for us ["Christians" is implied]
> There is one God [in contrast to the many gods]   (A')
>   namely the Father
>   from whom are all things,
>   and   we for him;
>   and   one Lord [in contrast to the many lords]   (B')
>   through whom are all things;
>   and   we through him.

Thus Paul allows in the first instance that the "gods" are only "so-called."[14] This is true no matter what their abode, whether their natural one, "in heaven," or, as so often happened in the Greek pantheon, where the deities also had a very earthly existence as well, "on earth."[15] Although this could represent the Corinthian position, it makes much more sense as Paul's own construct in which he is basically setting up the argument of v. 7 and anticipating the qualification of 10:19-20. They are "so-called" because they do not have existence in the form their worshipers believe them to have.

But Paul also recognizes the existential reality of pagan worship, and he knows that some within the Corinthian community are going to be af-

---

[11]Gk. γάρ.

[12]Gk. καὶ εἴπερ; see BDF 454 for this concessive usage.

[13]There is a formal correspondence between the original protasis and this insertion that is difficult to translate. Thus:

καὶ γὰρ εἴπερ εἰσὶν λεγόνεμοι θεοὶ . . .
        ὥσπερ εἰσὶν   θεοὶ πολλοί . . .

[14]Gk. λεγόμενοι; cf. the usage in Eph. 2:11.

[15]Even though this anticipates the full qualification in 10:19-20, Conzelmann,

fected by that reality. Thus he interrupts the concession with the affirmation "as indeed there are many 'gods' and many 'lords.'" He does not intend by this that the "gods" exist objectively. Rather, as v. 7 indicates, they "exist" subjectively in the sense that they are believed in. The two terms "gods" and "lords," which set up the Christian confession in v. 6, reflect the two basic forms of Greco-Roman religion as it has been modified by the coming of the Oriental cults. The "gods" designate the traditional deities, who are regularly given this appellation in the literature but are seldom referred to as *kyrioi* ("lords"). The term *kyrios*, on the other hand, is the normal title for the deities of the mystery cults.[16]

6 This clause forms the apodosis of the concession that began v. 5, but it now exists as a sharp contrast to the interruption in v. 5b that allowed that there are many so-called "gods" and "lords." The strong adversative, "but," sets what is true about "us,"[17] that is, us who believe in Christ, over against what has preceded. Although there is no formal equivalent to the words "for us," such as "for them" (meaning the pagans), in the preceding clause, this pronoun makes it clear that all of v. 5 refers not to what really exists, but to what is true "for them." This will be made even more clear in v. 7.

What follows is one of four expressly monotheistic texts in Paul where he uses the traditional formula "one God" (cf. Gal. 3:20; Rom. 3:29-30; 1 Tim. 2:5).[18] Because of its rhythmic character and because there are some parallels both in Hellenism[19] and in Hellenistic Judaism,[20] this sentence is often considered to be a pre-Pauline creedal formulation that had

---

143, probably brings that argument in too soon in his comment on this passage. By "heaven" and "earth" Paul is probably not asserting their "creatureliness," but the whole range of their types and abodes.

[16]See, e.g., the papyrus invitation quoted in the introduction to chaps. 8–10, n. 14, where Sarapis is called κύριος Σάραπις.

A. Feuillet ("La profession de foi monotheiste de 1 Cor. viii,4-6," *Studii Biblici Franciscani Liber Annus* 13 [1962-63], 7-32) thinks v. 5 too contradictory to v. 4 and suggests that Paul here refers not to pagan deities as such, but to the divinization of Hellenistic and Roman emperors who appropriated these titles for themselves. But that tries to "save" Paul by an unnecessary expedient that, in light of vv. 6, 7, and 10:19-20, seems to miss Paul's point.

[17]On the basis of this "for us" H. Lietzmann ("Symbolstudien XI," *ZNW* 22 [1923], 268-71), followed by Conzelmann, 145 n. 51, argued that the creed is basically a "confession." But as Murphy-O'Connor ("Cosmology," 255-57) points out, these words belong to Paul's own sentence, not to the more formal material that looks creedal.

[18]See the thorough discussion of these texts (excepting 1 Tim. 2:5) in Giblin, "Texts."

[19]Cf. Marc.Aur.Ant. 4.23, speaking of Nature, "of you are all things, in you are all things, unto you are all things."

[20]Cf., e.g., Philo, who thinks of God as the origin of all things, which he brought into being through the Logos (*cher.* 127: "we shall see that its [the universe's] cause is God, by whom it has come into being, . . . its instrument the word of God, through which

its origins in Hellenistic Jewish Christianity.[21] That can neither be proved nor disproved.[22] It does indeed have a creedal ring to it, and reflects language found elsewhere in religious texts. But none of this means that it did not originate here with Paul. Most likely it is a Pauline construct, created *ad hoc* in the present argument, but making use of language that he has in common with his Hellenistic Jewish origins. In any case, it so thoroughly fits the present argument that the question of background or origin is ultimately irrelevant.

The text has several remarkable features. First, the formulae "one God" and "one Lord" stand in specific contrast to the "many gods" and "many lords" of the pagans. This means that the emphasis is not on the unity of the godhead, although that may be assumed, but on the uniqueness of the only God. The God whom Christians worship as Father and Son stands in singular contrast to all others who might be thought to be gods but are not. Furthermore, the two parts are in perfect parallel. The formulae "one God" and "one Lord" are followed by the personal designations "the Father" and "Jesus Christ" (the appellation "Son" being implied by the use of "Father" as the personal designation of God). These in turn are followed in each case by a set of prepositional phrases that express both the divine activity characteristic of each and indirectly the functional subordination of the Son to the Father. God the Father is both the ultimate source and the ultimate destiny of all things, including ourselves; the Lord Christ is the divine mediator, through whom God created all things and redeemed us.[23]

The first clause expresses three realities about God that are fundamental to Christian faith. First, Paul picks up the language of Jesus himself, the personal image of "Father," to set forth the Christian understanding of God. Such a designation existed in Judaism before him, but it was Jesus who expressly taught his followers to understand God in this way. For him it was

it was framed"; cf. *leg.all.* 3.96; *op.mund.* 24-25). Cf. the discussion in Horsley, "Background," 130-35, who dismisses the possible Stoic influences altogether (as does Murphy-O'Connor ["Cosmology," 259-62], but for different reasons).

[21]See, e.g., Conzelmann, 144 n. 38: "The phrasing has not been chosen by Paul *ad hoc*. The content is not 'Pauline'; and it reaches far beyond the context." For an overview of opinions on this question see Murphy-O'Connor, "Cosmology," 254-55.

[22]The stylistic considerations that cause Murphy-O'Connor, "Cosmology," 254-55, to view it as pre-Pauline are significant, but not decisive, as he himself admits.

[23]Murphy-O'Connor ("Cosmology") argues that the formula is not cosmological at all, but strictly soteriological. But his argument rests too heavily on a suggestion by M. M. Sagnard ("A propos de 1 Cor. VIII,6," *ETL* 26 [1950], 54-58) that the δι' indicates movement, or direction, on the basis of which he asserts that "the unity of the text derives from the unity of a single movement." He is right in seeing the main concern as soteriology, but that does not preclude that the first member in each clause refers to creation. That the early church easily brought these two ideas together can also be seen in Heb. 1:1-3 and John 1:1-13.

not only a term expressing his own unique self-understanding, but also his gift to his followers. Thus they, too, may have this kind of personal relationship with God. Second, he is the source, the Creator, of all things.[24] After the fact of God's unity, this is the next fundamental theological statement of the Judeo-Christian understanding of God. In contrast to the many gods, themselves often subject to the whims of the cosmos, the Christian God stands apart from all things as their source. Nothing lies outside the jurisdiction of the God with whom we have to do and who invites us to be related to him as child to father. Third, instead of the expected "all things are unto him" (i.e., God is both the source and goal of all created things), Paul says, "and *we* are for/unto him." The emphasis is on the "we," which is the unique feature of this present expression of the creed. The preposition here has a kind of built-in ambiguity to it. Ordinarily in such a creedal formula it is an eschatological term, expressing the fact that God stands at the beginning and end of all things. But precisely because the creed has been personalized, that goal has a very strongly telic (purpose) force to it. God is not only the one to whom we are ultimately heading, along with the whole created order, but our very existence is for his purposes. Thus Paul's concern is not with philosophical theology, but with its practical implications for the matter at hand. Although he does not directly refer to it again, this is the ground of the entire argument that follows. By this phrase he places all of them—the Corinthians, both "gnostic" and "weak," as well as himself—under God's ultimate purposes, which will be spelled out more precisely in the next clause and especially in v. 11.

The second clause places the work of Christ, and our relationship to him, in the closest kind of relationship to God. Although Paul does not here call Christ God, the formula is so constructed that only the most obdurate would deny its Trinitarian implications. In the same breath that he can assert that there is only one God, he equally asserts that the designation "Lord," which in the OT belongs to the one God, is the proper designation of the divine Son. One should note especially that Paul feels no tension between the affirmation of monotheism and the clear distinction between the two persons of Father and Jesus Christ. As with other such statements in the NT,[25] Jesus is the one through whom God both created and redeemed. Thus together the two sentences embrace the whole of human existence. God the Father is the source of all things, which were mediated through the creative

---

[24]Gk. τὰ πάντα (cf. 15:27-28; Rom. 11:36). Murphy-O'Connor ("Cosmology") argues that this term here refers to the new order of salvation, not to the creation of the universe as such.

[25]In the Pauline corpus see Col. 1:15-20; 1 Tim. 2:4-5; elsewhere see John 1:1-3 and Heb. 1:1-3.

activity of the Son; the Son is the one through whom God also redeemed us, so that our existence is now "for" and "unto" God. As with the former clause the emphasis is on Christ's activity in our behalf, and is therefore especially relevant to the Corinthian situation. They are arguing in the abstract, that idols do not exist because there is only one God. Paul agrees; but the redemptive activity of the Father and Son is the basis of Christian behavior—not abstract theology, even if it is true.

In sum: The Corinthians have argued that there is no reality to the "gods" represented by idols since there is only one God. Paul agrees, but he qualifies his agreement in two directions. First, the nonexistent "gods" have a reality of a kind that must finally inform both their relationship with other believers and their own relationship to God himself. That will be spelled out in vv. 7-13. Second, the fuller explication of Christian monotheism argues that "our" God not only exists in uniqueness but that the Corinthians have a relationship to him that must finally determine both their own lives and how they relate to other believers.

Here is a clear example of Christian ethics being grounded in proper Christian theology. It is common today to give a variety of other bases for ethical behavior. For Paul, and therefore for all who would be truly biblical Christians, there is only one ground for such behavior: The unity of God, and the fact that our existence both by creation and redemption is grounded in the one God, whom we serve and with whom we have to do. It is out of this kind of reality that Paul will eventually appeal to the death of Christ as being for others as well as for ourselves (v. 11), and therefore that love, not knowledge, must serve as the motive for Christian ethics.

c. The criterion—care for a brother (8:7-13)

7 *But not everyone knows this. Some people are still so accustomed[1] to idols[2] that when they eat such food they think of it as sacrificed[3] to an idol, and since their conscience is weak, it is*

---

[1]In place of συνηθείᾳ (ℵ* A B P Ψ 33 81 630 1739 1881 pc cop sy^hmg) the Western and Byzantine traditions read συνείδησις, probably an assimilation to the following συνείδησις (so Metzger, 557). Otherwise M. Coune, "Le problème des Idolothytes et l'éducation de la Syneidesis," *RSR* 51 (1963), 515-17 (see the refutation in Murphy-O'Connor, "Freedom," 551-52).

[2]Gk. τοῦ εἰδώλου ("*the* idol"), implying the "god" whom any one of them worshiped and whose temple they frequented.

[3]NIV, "as having been sacrificed." This is quite gratuitous—and probably misleading; no tense is implied in εἰδωλόθυτον.

defiled. 8 But food does[4] not bring us[5] near to God; we are no worse if we do not eat, and no better if we do.[6]

9 Be careful, however, that the exercise of your freedom does not become a stumbling block to the weak. 10 For if anyone with a weak conscience sees you[7] who have this knowledge eating in an idol's temple, won't he be emboldened to eat what is[8] sacrificed to idols? 11 So[9] this weak brother, for whom Christ died, is destroyed by your knowledge. 12 When you sin against your brothers in this way and wound their weak[10] conscience, you sin against Christ. 13 Therefore, if what I eat causes my[11] brother to fall into sin, I will never eat meat again, so that I will not cause him to fall.

With this paragraph Paul returns to the qualification of the *way* of knowledge begun in vv. 1-3, but now by way of the practical qualification of the *content* of knowledge given in vv. 4-6. Even though "all have knowledge," not all

---

[4]The NIV here reflects the Western and Byzantine traditions that read the present tense instead of the future of the Egyptian tradition. This shift (from παραστήσει to παρίστησι) is probably a generalizing tendency in the tradition.

[5]A few MSS (ℵ* Ψ 33 365 1241 1881) read ὑμᾶς.

[6]This reflects the word order of P46 B 81 630 1739 *pc* vg^st cop. Although this reading is confined to Egypt, it seems to be the *lectio difficilior*. The vast majority of witnesses, both East and West, read "*For* we are no better off if we eat, and no worse off if we do not." Zuntz (161-62, 194) argues for both this word order and the γάρ as original—on the grounds that "Paul could not but begin with the claim under discussion." But that is precisely why the original (Egyptian) reading was changed—early and often. Zuntz explains the Egyptian reading as a scribal blunder (haplography due to the double οὔτε, with a later incorrect reinsertion). This seems highly improbable. More recently Murphy-O'Connor ("Food") has argued for the singular reading of A^c (his inclusion of Tischendorf's codex 17 [Gregory 33] is incorrect): "We are no better off if we do not eat, and no worse off if we do." He dismisses the use of external evidence here as "mechanical" and argues that this reading alone accounts for the other two. But that will not do. The external evidence is part of "rational criticism"; readings either have pedigree—which this one does not (the "correction" is by the original hand at the time of copying)—or they arise spontaneously, as this one did. Far from being the original reading to which the scribe had access as he was copying, it represents his confusion between the other two readings, one of which he was copying and the other of which apparently he also knew. In changing from the one to the other he switched verbs but left the negative in its original position.

[7]The σέ is omitted in P46 B F G latt. Zuntz, 92, leans toward the omission, on the grounds that it could have been added on the basis of the σέ in v. 11; but Metzger, 557, has correctly argued that "copyists are more likely to have omitted the pronoun, thus generalizing the apostle's statement, than to have inserted it."

[8]NIV, "has been"; see n. 3 above.

[9]The MajT replaces the γάρ (the more difficult reading under any view) with a καί.

[10]P46 and Clement omit ἀσθενοῦσαν. See Metzger, 557.

[11]Several Western witnesses omit μου in both instances.

believers share that "knowledge" in an experiential way. Their former lives as pagans, in which they believed in the gods, continue to inform their experience in the present (v. 7). Thus they have "weak consciences," and their attendance at the cultic meals would—or does—have the effect of "destroying" them. The first reason Paul gives, therefore, as to why the Corinthians may not go to the temples is that such activity may lead to the destruction of a brother for whom Christ died (vv. 10-12).

To get from v. 7 to vv. 10-12 Paul takes up the next point of the Corinthian argument, with which he fully agrees, that food is a matter of indifference to God (v. 8). But precisely because this is so, they must *not* use it as they are doing, to insist on "rights" and "freedom." Rather, they must move in the opposite direction, not letting "rights" cause the fall of a brother or sister (v. 9). With the concrete example of temple attendance he makes an impassioned plea for the cause of the weak (vv. 10-12). The argument concludes (v. 13) by asserting the stumbling-block principle, in its broadest form, as the criterion of his own action, which serves at once both as paradigm and as the springboard for a vigorous defense of his own actions in such matters (9:1-23).

It should be noted that despite the way the argument proceeds—food as a matter of indifference, the consideration of the weak conscience of another, the implication that they do have "rights" in this matter—the section as a whole has the net effect of prohibition. Some have asserted[12] that if there were no "weak" brother to see the action of those "with knowledge," then the latter might participate in the cultic meals as they wished. But the ensuing argument (10:1-22) quite disallows such an interpretation. Thus the two sections (8:7-13; 10:1-22) indicate that going to the temples is wrong in two ways: it is not acting in love (8:7-13), and it involves fellowship with demons (10:19-22).

7 The strong adversative "but"[13] indicates that Paul is about to qualify what has been said to this point. The present section (vv. 7-13) spells out in detail the principle enunciated in vv. 1b-3, that love, not knowledge, builds up, and therefore that love is what true knowledge is all about.[14] But he makes that point by way of vv. 4-6, where he has already qualified the

---

[12]See n. 74 below.

[13]Gk. ἀλλά. Because of his unique understanding of vv. 4-6 as a quotation from their letter in its entirety, Willis, 87-96, understands v. 7 to belong to vv. 4-6, as Paul's rejoinder. The *content* of v. 7, however, indicates that it introduces what follows.

[14]This is true even though the word "love" does not occur in the section. That is because for Paul love is not some subjective feeling toward others. It is expressed first of all in the death of Christ for us (v. 11), which in turn finds concrete expression in actions toward others. Cf. Conzelmann, 149.

content of their knowledge by insisting that, despite the fact that idols do not really exist as gods, yet for *them* (i.e., the pagans) there are many "gods" and many "lords." Thus, against the Corinthian insistence that "we all possess knowledge" (v. 1), Paul now asserts that "this knowledge is *not* shared by all."[15] As the rest of the verse makes plain, by this he means that even though all may believe at the theoretical level that an idol is no god, not all share this "knowledge" at the experiential, emotional level.[16]

Some of the Corinthian believers are among those for whom the "gods" and "lords" were a genuine reality while they were pagans. Such people are thus "still accustomed to[17] the idol"[18]; that is, even though they now know that the god does not exist, their former association with him or her as a god is still a part of their experience of reality. They may tell their heads all they want that the god is only an idol and that an idol has no genuine reality. The fact is that their former way of life is woven into their consciousness and emotions in such a way that the old associations cannot be thus lightly disregarded. For them to return to the place of their former worship would mean once more to eat "as though it were truly being sacrificed to the god." This seems to make the best sense of the phrase, (lit.) "they eat as though it were idol food." The NIV implies[19] that they are eating food that had *formerly* been sacrificed (thus marketplace food), and that their former idolatrous associations would carry over to this food. But that is to assume that Jewish scruples were promulgated among these Gentile Christians.[20] Paul's language makes far more sense if they are eating the food in the

---

[15]The NIV translates γνῶσις here as a verb, "not everyone knows this." This captures the relationship to vv. 4-6 but misses the formal tie to v. 1 and the play on the word γνῶσις.

[16]This seems to be the most natural explanation of the alleged contradiction between vv. 1 and 7. Paul allows their slogan only theoretically. The knowledge that there is only one God does not immediately eradicate the idolatrous beliefs and practices of a lifetime. Cf. Murphy-O'Connor, "Freedom," 553-56. The difficulty which Willis, 87-88, sees, e.g., which leads him to view all of vv. 4-6 as a quotation, is more apparent than real.

[17]On the textual variant, see n. 1 above. The desire of Coune to read "conscience" here is related to a concern to see the "weak" as Jewish Christians who are being tempted to eat marketplace food. Others who see the problem here as referring to Jewish Christians are Schlatter, 101; T. W. Manson, "Corinthians," pp. 200-203; Dupont, *Gnosis*, pp. 265-377. But Paul's attitude toward that food in 10:25-30 stands in such sharp contradiction to what is said here that such a view seems impossible.

[18]Gk. τῇ συνηθείᾳ ἕως ἄρτι τοῦ εἰδώλου; the dative is causal (= "by reason of"), and the genitive is objective: thus, lit., "by their being accustomed up to this very time to *the idol*." The singular "the idol" suggests that the problem is not with idolatry in general, but with their devotion and allegiance to a given god.

[19]See n. 3 above.

[20]On this issue see the introduction to chaps. 8-10, p. 360 n. 9.

temples, in which case the phrase means not "that they think of it as having been sacrificed to an idol," but that "they eat it as though it were being sacrificed to a god,"[21] just as it had been all their former years.

The final result of such people's return to the temples is that "since their conscience is weak, it is defiled."[22] This clause introduces the two key words ("conscience" and "weak") for the argument that follows. Unfortunately, the precise nuance of the word "conscience"[23] is not easy to capture,[24] nor is it clear from whom the term derives—from the Corinthian letter or from Paul himself. This is its first occurrence in the NT; it is one of the few items in Paul's theological vocabulary that seems to have come from his Greek rather than Jewish background.[25] Because of its frequency in this passage and in 10:25-29 whereas it does not appear elsewhere in 1 Corinthians, and because it is *not* used in the somewhat comparable discussion in Rom. 14, many have argued that the term comes from the Corinthian letter.[26] This may very well be; however, Paul uses the term elsewhere in a variety of ways that should make one properly cautious here.

In any case, the greater issue is what it means. In popular parlance it refers to a kind of inner moral referee that pronounces on the rightness or wrongness of one's actions (as in, "Let your conscience be your guide").

[21]Paul is thus using his Jewish vocabulary to describe what they do: eat *idol* food. But for the participants themselves the "idol" represents a "god."

[22]The weak conscience, it should be noted, has to do with idols, not with food as such. The most likely place for such failure of conscience and "defilement" to take place is at the temple where the idol actually stood.

[23]Gk. συνείδησις. The verb appeared in 4:4. The word occurs eight times in 1 Corinthians, all in 8:7-12 and 10:25-29. In the Pauline corpus it appears three times in Romans, three in 2 Corinthians, and six in the Pastoral Epistles. It also occurs in Acts, Hebrews, and 1 Peter.

[24]The literature here is considerable. Among other items, see H. Osborne, "Συνείδησις," *JTS* 32 (1931), 167-79; C. Spicq, "La conscience dans le NT," *RB* 47 (1938), 50-80; C. A. Pierce, *Conscience in the New Testament* (SBT 15; London, 1955); C. Maurer, *TDNT* VII, 898-919; B. F. Harris, "Συνείδησις (Conscience) in the Pauline Writings," *WTJ* 24 (1962), 173-86; M. Thrall, "The Pauline Use of συνείδησις," *NTS* 14 (1967/68), 118-25; Jewett, *Terms,* pp. 402-46; H. C. Hahn and C. Brown, *NIDNTT* I, 348-53; T. McCaughey, "Conscience and Decision-Making in some Early Christian Communities," *IBS* 5 (1983), 115-31.

[25]Although it is equally clear that (1) the word "heart" in the OT (cf., e.g., Job 27:6) sometimes carries the weight that "conscience" does in Paul, and that (2) the conviction of a former time, that Paul borrowed the term from Stoicism, is no longer tenable. See esp. Pierce, *Conscience,* pp. 13-28.

[26]Besides Pierce, Maurer, and Jewett (see n. 24), this is the position taken by Horsley, "Consciousness," 581-82; Murphy-O'Connor, "Freedom," 548-55; and Willis, 89-90. Pierce argues that it came into Paul's theological vocabulary by way of Corinth and that his later uses stem from this encounter. But that puts too much weight on silence in 1 and 2 Thessalonians. The diversity of later usage suggests that it was a term otherwise available to him.

Although this comes close to Paul's own usage in such passages as Rom. 2:15[27] and 13:5, in the present case the word seems to be closer to its root meaning of "consciousness" as to one's own actions (cf. the verb in 4:4), with a decided moral overtone to that consciousness. Thus "moral consciousness" seems best to capture its sense here. The weakness involved is that their "intellectual conviction that there was only one God had not been fully assimilated emotionally."[28] Thus when encouraged to attend the cultic meals as a form of "edification," they could not cope with the dissonance between their heads and their hearts, as it were, which would ultimately lead them back into idolatry and thus destroy them (see on v. 11). In this way their moral consciousness is being "defiled,"[29] that is, their past associations with idols mean that a return to the worship of the god by eating in his/her honor causes them to defile their new relationship with Christ.[30]

8 With a couple of sentences that are as puzzling as they are abrupt,[31] Paul takes up the cause of those just mentioned as having "weak

[27]Part of the debate has been whether or not συνείδησις pronounces only on past actions (as Pierce argues) or whether it also gives guidance beforehand. The evidence as evaluated in the articles by Osborne, Harris, and Thrall (see n. 24) suggests that it probably does at times function to guide the future, even though most often it pronounces on past actions. Thrall in particular argues that for Paul in Romans it functioned among the Gentiles very much the way the law did for Jews.

[28]Murphy-O'Connor, "Freedom," 554. The context suggests that this is far more likely than the suggestion of BAGD (under συνείδησις) that "weak conscience" means "one that cannot come to a decision." Cf. Horsley, "Consciousness," 581-83, followed by Willis, 90-92, who argues unconvincingly that it means consciousness only, without any moral overtones. Thus, "those who were 'weak' in συνείδησις were simply those who were 'not knowing' (8:7) the truth about idols and idol meat" (Willis, 92). Such a view does not take seriously enough the deep anguish involved for these people, who are "destroyed" by such actions. Their problem is not in coming to a decision, nor in not knowing about idols, but in carrying through with a decision that creates too great a moral dissonance for them, and thus leads them back into idolatry.

[29]Gk. μολύνεται; the only appearance in Paul (cf. the cognate noun in 2 Cor. 7:1). Some (e.g., Dupont, *Gnosis,* p. 284) have seen this usage to indicate that the "weak" are Jewish Christians; but such an argument must be made of stronger stuff.

[30]It is often noted that Paul says nothing about "how the weak consciences could be strengthened" (Conzelmann, 147; cf. Barrett, 194-95: "they are scrupulous where scrupulosity rests on pure error; . . . All this is foolish, and Paul does not defend it"). But that assumes that the problem is basically an internal struggle over marketplace food, not one between them and him over temple attendance. This is precisely what makes this issue differ from that in Rom. 14, where the issue is food per se and he addresses both sides to live together in the community of faith.

[31]The sentence begins with a δέ, which the NIV translates "but" (cf. Hurd, 123). Most likely it is mildly consecutive ("now" or untranslated, as most commentaries). It is in fact very difficult to make sense of it as *Pauline* instruction in *contrast* to what has been said in v. 7, especially if one assumes, as the context demands, that Paul is addressing the "gnostics." In v. 7 he has set up the "weak" as not being able to handle the knowledge of the "gnostics." If this is in contrast to that, then he is here trying to get the latter to "back off" with regard to "idol food" (marketplace food being the assumption), since eating

consciences."[32] The difficulties lie in determining both what the sentences mean and how they function in the argument. Part of the latter problem is related to whether they reflect *ad hoc* instruction from Paul about idol food, or whether they reflect a Corinthian position in some way.

The two sentences have the appearance of aphorisms, the second apparently intended to modify or elaborate the first. Thus: (1) "Food[33] will not present[34] us to God"; and (2) "We are no worse[35] if we do not eat, and no better if we do." The meaning of the first sentence seems easy enough. Even though the verb can be either positive ("present us to God for approval") or negative ("bring us before God for judgment"), the sense in either case is that food as such has nothing to do with our relationship to God.[36] This, of course, would be the perspective of both Paul *and* the Corinthians. What they may well have been urging in their letter is something they could easily have picked up from him.

The puzzle comes in the second sentence. The natural elaboration of sentence 1 would be, "therefore, abstaining is of no advantage to anyone; nor is eating of any disadvantage." Food does not affect our lives one way or

---

such food will not present people before God. But how is such a sentence in contrast unless it reflects a perspective that eating such food *might* so present one? And where would such an idea have come from if not from them, and how does it help Paul's argument over against them at this point?

[32] It is of some importance to note that the word "strong" does not appear anywhere in the argument. The contrast is between those with "weak consciences," as just defined in v. 7, and those "having knowledge." It should not be surprising that Paul takes the side of the "weak" since from his view that is the only proper stance for Christians in the present age (cf. the previous note). This reflects his understanding both of Christ and of his own apostleship (see on 4:8-13). In 2 Corinthians this becomes a key issue in his struggle with this church, who tend to put down weakness as less than Christian.

[33] Gk. βρῶμα (also in v. 13; cf. 6:13). Since Paul does not refer to εἰδωλόθυτα ("idol food"), this word seems to put the argument for a moment into a broader framework (see on v. 13).

[34] Gk. παραστήσει, which as a transitive means "to present" or "offer" something/someone to someone else, and is used as a technical term for bringing someone before a judge. The KJV's "commendeth" (cf. RSV) belongs more properly to the verb παρατίθημι (so also the NIV's "bring near to").

[35] Gk. ὑστερούμεθα; it ordinarily means to lack in some way. Murphy-O'Connor, "Food," 297-98, suggests on the basis of the future tense in the first sentence (which he understands to refer to being brought before the judgment seat of God: eating idol food, the Corinthians have argued, will not do so), and the present in the second, that this refers to "spiritual gifts" (cf. 1:7). Thus the "strong," as he views them, are arguing, "Eating idol food will not bring us under God's judgment; furthermore, if we do not eat (as the weak), we are not abounding in spiritual gifts (as the weak give evidence), and if we do (as ourselves), we are not lacking the same (as is also evident)." But this not only rests on a most improbable textual choice (see n. 6 above) but also is weakened by the complete lack of mention of spiritual gifts in the context.

[36] Cf. Barrett, 195: "to observe food laws does not constitute a claim on God."

the other. So the abstainers, who would usually do so in order to gain God's approval, will not be so advantaged; and those who indulge, who might fear God's disapproval, will not be judged. But that is *not* what Paul says. His elaboration is precisely the opposite: "The one who abstains is not *dis*advantaged; and the one who eats is not advantaged." The problem is, How does this relate to sentence 1 as part of Paul's response to the Corinthians who are challenging him, and especially as part of his taking up the cause of the "weak"?

The contextual problems are equally difficult. (a) Since the context (both vv. 7 and 9-12) does not have to do with "food" as such, but with food eaten in the presence of an idol, hence with idolatry, why is this said at all, and especially why right here? (b) Most striking of all is v. 9, where Paul refers to these aphorisms as "this authority/freedom of *yours,*" as though what was said in v. 8 is not instruction being given for the first time, but a position either for which they have argued or with which Paul knows they will be in agreement. (c) All of this is further complicated by the fact noted above that sentence 1 represents a point of view that can be easily shown to be either Paul's or the Corinthians'.

A variety of solutions has been offered, none of which is totally satisfactory. If this is an *ad hoc* word from Paul,[37] then the strange formulation of sentence 2 remains a problem, as does the apparent rebuttal of v. 9. If this is a Corinthian statement,[38] then the abruptness with which it is brought in, especially in light of how he quotes them in vv. 1 and 4, is equally puzzling, as is the formulation of sentence 2, which seems to be the exact opposite of what one might have expected them to have said.[39]

The solution offered here[40] is that despite the lack of signals, both sentences reflect what the Corinthians were arguing in their letter, whether they are direct quotations or not. The reason for the lack of quotation marks is that they also fully accord with Paul's own point of view. The key lies with

[37]This is the traditional view, but in most cases the contextual question is simply not spoken to and the difficulty with the formulation of sentence 2 is overlooked. One looks in vain for an answer to the question "why," especially in relationship to v. 7.

[38]For a list of some who take this position, see Hurd, 68, to which may be added Holladay (tentatively), and Barrett, Murphy-O'Connor, and Willis (see the next note). Otherwise, Hurd, 123, and Conzelmann, 148, who says that it is "a positive declaration on Paul's part." But neither he nor Hurd wrestles adequately with the contextual question.

[39]This was pointed out long ago by Lietzmann, 38, and has been frequently noted since. Among those who take this position, but recognize the problems, three different solutions have been offered. Barrett, 195, takes sentence 1 as from the Corinthians, with sentence 2 as the beginning of Paul's response. Murphy-O'Connor ("Food") sees the whole as a quotation but opts for an improbable textual solution (see nn. 6 and 35). Willis, 97-98, opts only for sentence 2 but without the οὔτε's, thus making them say, "If we do not eat, we are the worse for it; if we eat, we are the better."

[40]Cf. Fee, "Εἰδωλόθυτα," pp. 190-91, where this was first proposed.

the word "food," which appears again in the conclusion in v. 13 and elsewhere in Paul only in Rom. 14:15-20 (where food laws seem to be in view) and in 1 Cor. 6:13, where it also appears as part of a Corinthian slogan (with which Paul was also in essential agreement).[41] What needs to be noted is that what is here said about food is almost exactly what Paul says elsewhere about circumcision (7:19; Gal. 5:6; 6:15). Very likely this reflects Paul's own position on being "kosher," that food, like circumcision, does not "present us" to God. We are none the worse if we do not eat such food (as with not being circumcised) and we are no better if we do (as with being circumcised). Such are strictly matters of indifference to God. For Paul this would still be true, hence the positive way the aphorisms are presented. This is the "authority/freedom" of the person in Christ. In this view, the Corinthians have picked up one of Paul's own words from a different area and are pressing it to their own purposes; such "freedom," they have argued, can also be applied to the eating of any food, in any circumstance, including the idol temples. For Paul this is the wrong use of "freedom" in regard to food (v. 9)[42]—first of all because of what it can do to a brother or sister (vv. 10-12).

9 This sentence makes it most probable that v. 8 represents part of their argument with Paul. He begins with an adversative conjunction ("but"),[43] followed by the imperative of warning, "be careful."[44] The warning itself sets two words in contrast in such a way that one ("freedom") seems to be the Corinthian view of their present activity, while the other ("stumbling block"[45]) is Paul's. On the crucial term *exousia* ("authority/freedom") see on 6:12.[46] Again, it is almost certainly a Corinthian catchword (cf. also 10:23),[47] and as in 6:12 it means something close to "freedom

---

[41]This usage in 1 Cor. 6:12-13 adds to the probability that Paul is here dealing with a Corinthian position, as does the fact that both sentences, as in vv. 1 and 4, are in the first person plural, in contrast to v. 7 which speaks of the "weak" in the third plural and v. 9 which addresses the "gnostics" in the second plural.

[42]As Conzelmann, 148, nicely put it: "The neutrality of food does *not* mean neutrality of *conduct*" (italics his).

[43]Gk. δέ.

[44]Gk. βλέπετε; cf. 3:10; 10:12; Gal. 5:15.

[45]Gk. πρόσκομμα; found only here in 1 Corinthians (but cf. Rom. 14:13, 20). In v. 13 Paul uses the synonym σκανδαλίζω. Both of these words, as their usage in the Synoptic tradition makes plain, refer not to "offending" someone but to becoming the cause for someone to fall. The context here demands such a meaning as well.

[46]The word ordinarily means "authority," but the substitution of ἐλεύθερος/ἐλευθερία in 9:1, 19 and 10:29 suggests that the ideas are at one point nearly synonymous in this argument.

[47]For an overview of the debate as to its origins in Corinth see Willis, 98-104. He is probably correct in seeing it as an adoption of "popular philosophy" since this is quite in keeping with their attitude as it emerges in 1:10–4:21 (see esp. on 1:12 and 17). As in 6:12 they have possibly taken a Pauline idea and remolded it within the framework of their own

to act as they please without restraint."[48] That this is their own word seems certain from the way Paul speaks of it as "this your authority."[49] The NIV here ("the exercise of your freedom") is too tame and perhaps slightly misleading. Paul is warning them to take heed "lest this authority of yours (promoted in the previous verse)," which Paul would quite agree with in the matter of food laws, be carried over to the eating of the cultic meals and thereby become not "freedom" for others but "a stumbling block" to them. For the Corinthians "knowledge" (= insight) means "rights" to act in "freedom." Thus for them freedom became the highest good, since it led to the exaltation of the individual. For Paul the opposite prevails: "Love" means the "free giving up" of one's "rights" for the sake of others (cf. 9:19-23), and "life together" in community is the aim of salvation.

As noted earlier, latent within the nature of their "authority" is probably a desire to "build up" the "weak." If so, then for them *exousia* is the crucial term. Not only do they want to "free" some of their brothers and sisters from what to them is their current bondage to false notions about the "gods" (which is the point of the specifics in the next verse), but also their view of *exousia* has led them to question Paul's own apostleship and freedom since he does not act with the boldness of such "authority" (which becomes the point of the defense in 9:1-23).

10 Having warned the Corinthians not to use their "rights" as the means for "the weak" to fall, Paul proceeds in the next three sentences (vv. 10-12) to make an impassioned plea for the "rights" of the "weak." He begins in this verse by specifying in detail what they are doing that is bringing about such a fall. Even though the explanation takes the form of a present general supposition, the urgency of the argument suggests that we are dealing with a real, not a merely hypothetical situation.[50] "For," he explains with reference to v. 9, "if anyone (meaning the person with the weak conscience referred to in the apodosis) sees you,[51] the one having

---

views on "wisdom" and "knowledge" so that in its present form it is their own, not Paul's.

[48]The concept of "freedom" in popular philosophy was highly individualized, moving toward self-determination. Thus it meant to be free from restraints imposed by external forces, including other people. Obviously for Paul (9:19) it means exactly the opposite. See H. Schlier, *TDNT* II, 487-502.

[49]Gk. ἡ ἐξουσία ὑμῶν αὕτη.

[50]Otherwise Hurd, 125, who thinks the syntax points to what is hypothetical. But he is arguing that even the so-called "weak" are hypothetical, which does not seem to take seriously enough either the urgency of this response or the still greater urgency of 10:1-22.

[51]Gk. σέ (second person singular). For this usage cf. 4:7; 7:21, 28; 14:17; 15:36. The usage here is very much like that in 4:6-7, where the first sentence has a general introduction in the second plural, followed by a specifying as to how they are being "puffed up" (introduced with an explanatory γάρ) in the second singular.

knowledge, sitting at table in an idol's temple, will not his conscience, being weak (exactly as in v. 7), be 'built up,' leading him to eat[52] sacrificial foods ('himself' being implied)?"

From this question we learn at least three things about the situation in Corinth. First, those with the "knowledge" expressed in vv. 1, 4, and 8 are going to the cultic meals in the temple dining halls.[53] Since this is the only specific expression of the problem in chap. 8, and since this is still the major concern when "idol food" is picked up again in 10:1-22, it seems certain that this is the real issue for which they are arguing against Paul's (apparently) former prohibition.[54]

Second, at the same time they are probably encouraging all others in the community to take their same "knowledgeable" stance on this matter. Hence they seem to be urging others, whom Paul describes as people whose consciences are weak (see on v. 7), to join them at these meals.[55] This seems to be the best way to make sense of two other items in the text: (a) the fact that they "see" the "knowing ones" sitting at table (how could they "see" it if they were not present?)[56]; and (b) the ironic use of the verb "build up"[57]

[52]Gk. οἰκοδομηθήσεται. The translation is from Turner, *Syntax*, 143, who sees this usage as "expressing a measure of effect" (language apparently borrowed from Burton, *Moods*, 411).

[53]Gk. ἐν εἰδωλείῳ κατακείμενον ("reclining at table in the idol's temple"). For the archaeological evidence of these dining rooms in Corinth, see C. L. Thompson, "Corinth," *IBDSup*, p. 180.

[54]The commitment of interpreters to the "marketplace food" view can best be seen from the way this verse is treated. Some simply ignore it altogether (most commentaries); others circumvent it as "an extreme case" (e.g., R-P) to which Paul will return by way of "digression" in 10:14-22. Schmithals, 227, is more candid, dismissing it with a footnote: "Even in 8:10, where of course Paul chooses an extreme example, he is concerned only with the eating of εἰδωλόθυτα, not with participation in the cult as such." To this effect is Paul's one explicit statement in chap. 8, which leads directly to the argument of 10:1-22, ruled to mean something other than what it says in order to fit a prior scheme.

[55]"Freedom" that feels compelled to set others "free" is often an expression of bondage. See on 6:12.

[56]This in itself seems to deal the deathblow to the idea that the "weak" are only concerned with eating marketplace food. Paul does not suggest that they "discover" that others are being so bold as to eat even at the temples, which in turn gives them boldness to eat marketplace food. This frequently repeated idea (e.g., Grosheide, 196; Lenski, 345) needs to be laid to rest. They might be "offended" by what the "gnostics" are doing and most likely would "judge" them for it, but it is difficult to imagine how their discovery of the "gnostics'" action would lead them to take this lesser action of a totally different kind. Such a suggestion takes all the force out of the example by making it a non sequitur. If for the "gnostics" attendance at the temple meals is the issue, then they would scarcely be gratified in encouraging others to buy and eat marketplace food; and if the "weak" were not being pressured into it in some way, what would cause them to do it on their own?

[57]Gk. οἰκοδομέω (NIV, "emboldened," for which there is no known parallel). On this matter see n. 21 in the introduction to chaps. 8-10. Cf. Godet's comment: "He enlightens and strengthens him to his loss! Fine edification!" (p. 426).

with regard to the moral consciousness of the weak. Both of these are understandable if what is "destroying" them (v. 11) is the fact that they are under considerable pressure to accept—or have actually done so—the invitations of the "knowing ones."

Third, the problem with the persons with weak consciences is not that they are "offended" by what the "gnostics" are doing. Their "conscience" is being "built up" in such a way that they are being led also "to eat what is sacrificed to idols." Their problem lies in their inability to handle the "gnostics'" argument (cf. v. 7). They may indeed acknowledge that there is no reality to the idol, but what for the others is "food" only, is for them "food sacrificed to the idol." It is not the food that destroys them, but the idolatry that is inherent in eating in the temples. This is the item that will be picked up and spelled out in greater detail in v. 11.

11 This sentence, which also begins with an explanatory "for" (NIV, "so"), elaborates the *concern* of v. 10 by indicating exactly what happens to the person with a "weak conscience" who would—or has— emulate(ed) the one trying so to "build him up." Such a person "is destroyed by your knowledge."[58] But the person is no longer merely "someone with a weak conscience"; he is "the brother for whom Christ died." Both the emphasis of the word order[59] and the language suggest that for Paul the problem is not merely hypothetical. A Christian life is at stake—all for the sake of their freedom informed by their knowledge. This anticipated—or actual—tragic result of the loss of a brother puts into clearer focus several items from the preceding argument.

In saying that the brother "is destroyed"[60] Paul most likely is referring to eternal loss, not simply some internal "falling apart" because one is behaving contrary to the "dictates of conscience." The latter idea is altogether too modern; and elsewhere in Paul this word invariably refers to eternal ruin.[61] That seems to clinch the argument that real idolatry (i.e., eating cultic meals) is the issue at hand, not simply eating food that formerly had idolatrous associations. What is in view is a former idolater falling back into the grips of idolatry. Only one who takes seriously, as Paul did, the

---

[58]Cf. Rom. 14:15: "Do not by your *eating* destroy (RSV, 'cause the ruin of') your brother for whom Christ died."

[59]The Greek reads literally: "For being destroyed is the weak one by your knowledge, the brother for whom Christ died."

[60]Gk. ἀπόλλυται (cf. 1:18; 10:9-10; 15:18). Note the present tense; already he is experiencing ruin.

[61]Since Paul does not have a prior system to salvage, he sees the danger as real. Cf. Conzelmann, 149 n. 38: "He of course presupposes the idea that the Christian, too, can lose his salvation." This is not a happy thought, but it reflects Paul's own theology with sober realism. Otherwise Bruce, 82, who sees καὶ τύπτοντες (v. 12) as epexegetic, therefore explaining what "destroying" means.

demonic character of idolatry (see 10:19-22) can appreciate the grip it has on the lives of those who are bound by its powers.[62] For such people to return to idolatry means to come back under its power and thus suffer eternal loss. This is why they are destroyed "by your knowledge"—not only because knowledge is the improper basis of Christian ethics but also because the "gnostics'" knowledge about idolatry itself is so defective. For such reasons one can now understand more clearly the nature of Paul's argument to this point, especially vv. 1-3, 4-6, and 7-8 where he has felt impelled at every point to qualify their "knowledge." Knowledge leads to all the wrong actions. It not only fails to "build up" former idolaters; it destroys them—not to mention "puffs up" the one insisting on "rights" and "freedom."

Thus Paul appeals to love in two ways—even though he does not here use the word. First, the person being destroyed is a "brother." Here the interplay on love, knowledge, and building up comes into clear focus. They would "build up" the weak by their "knowledge"; what they do instead is "tear down." Because the people involved are brothers and sisters, they must be built up in the proper way. This means no more insistence on "freedom" since "freedom" moves in the direction of individualized existence, while love moves in the direction of community and care for others. Second, the common basis of their life in Christ is not "knowledge" and "freedom," but the death of Christ. Their arrogance and insensitivity, which would destroy a brother in the name of knowledge and freedom, are thus contrasted with Christ's love "unto death." As in chaps. 1-4, where Paul tries to combat their fascination with wisdom, he brings them back to the cross. Both their lives as individuals and together as a community are predicated on the fact that each of them is someone "for whom Christ died."

12 This sentence brings closure to the present argument by giving a theological expansion of the point of v. 11. "In this way,"[63] that is, in the way described in v. 10, they destroy a brother for whom Christ died (v. 11). That is now expressed in terms of "sin." On the one hand, their activity turns out to be "sin against your brothers and sisters," expressed again in terms of "wounding[64] their weak conscience." On the other hand, so to sin

---

[62]Those who have been involved in the rescue of drug addicts and prostitutes, e.g., or of people involved in various expressions of voodoo and spirit worship, have an existential understanding of this text that others can scarcely appreciate. Many such people must be forever removed from their former associations, including returning to their former haunts for evangelism, because the grip of their former life is so tenacious. Paul took the power of the demonic seriously; hence his concern that a former idolater, by returning to his or her idolatries, will be destroyed—that is, he or she will return to former ways and be captured by them all the more, and thus eventually suffer eternal loss.

[63]Gk. οὕτως, in the first position, correctly translated "in this way," i.e., in the way just described.

[64]Gk. τύπτω, lit. to beat or strike; figuratively, as here, it means to be responsible for the wounds that such a person has received.

against a brother for whom Christ died is to "sin against Christ" himself. This calls to mind the language of Jesus, that to do something against one of the least is to do it against him (Matt. 25:45), or the language of Heb. 6:6, where to return to former sins is to crucify the Son of God all over again and hold him up to public disgrace. To wound a member of Christ is to wound Christ; to sin against one of his own is to sin against the one to whom he belongs.

Because of the switch to the plural ("your brothers") from the singular of vv. 11 and 13, some have suggested that the sin is against the church. That is, this may very well reflect Paul's understanding of the solidarity of Christ with his body. To sin against Christ thus means to destroy his body the church.[65] In either case, the ultimate wrong of the "gnostic" is not simply that he lacks true knowledge, nor even that he is responsible for the loss of a brother, bad as that is, but that in so doing he is directly sinning against Christ himself in some way. The net result of such an argument, of course, is prohibition.

13 With the strong inferential conjunction "therefore,"[66] Paul brings this opening argument to its conclusion, and thereby effects two concerns. First, he brings closure to the immediate argument by generalizing the reference to the stumbling block in v. 9, but does so in terms of his own personal conduct—or at least his willingness to conduct himself henceforth in a certain way for the sake of "my brother." He does this by picking up the language of v. 8 ("food"[67]), which he further narrows specifically to the flesh of animals.[68] Thus, "if food is the cause of my brother's downfall,[69] then I will never eat the flesh of animals again as long as I live,[70] in order that I might not be the cause of my brother's downfall." But why does he generalize in this way? And why does he suddenly use his own conduct as an example of the principle?

[65]This is the position argued by Murphy-O'Connor, "Freedom," 563-64, followed by Willis, 107.

[66]Gk. διόπερ, only here and in 10:14 in Paul (there is a variant in 14:13).

[67]Gk. βρῶμα. Conzelmann, 148 n. 26, makes the unsupported assertion that βρῶμα here means "eating." But βρῶσις (cf. v. 4) is a verbal noun; there is no evidence that βρῶμα can be so used. For the distinction between the two words, see *T.Reub.* 2:7: γίνεται βρῶσις βρωτῶν . . . ὅτι ἐν βρώμασιν.

[68]Gk. κρέα (NIV, "meat"), a word that specifically refers to animal flesh and therefore stands in contrast to the food eaten by a vegetarian (cf. Rom. 14:21). Theissen, 121-45, may be pointing in the right direction when he suggests that part of the problem is sociological. Since the poor would ordinarily eat meat only at such meals, meat itself took on a nearly religious quality for such people.

[69]In this case the language changes from the πρόσκομμα of v. 9 to the synonymous verb σκανδαλίζω, probably because it more truly reflects what has been said in vv. 10-12 about his "being destroyed," and especially "sinning against" him (cf. the usage of this verb in the Synoptic tradition: e.g., Matt. 5:29-30; 18:6-8).

[70]This is an attempt to capture the full force of the future emphatic negative οὐ μὴ φάγω, reinforced in this instance by εἰς τὸν αἰῶνα ("forever").

The answer to the first question seems easy enough. He has been dealing right along with a form of "eating"; but since he generalizes in the first person singular (i.e., with reference to his own conduct), and since he would never have participated in the cultic meals as such, he must broaden the principle to refer to scruples about food in general, and animal flesh in particular. This suggests not only that he is truly generalizing and thus moving quite beyond the specific issue at hand (cultic meals), but also that in some ways the specific issue is only symptomatic of the much greater problem of their insisting on "rights" and "freedom" in the name of knowledge. Thus this conclusion summarizes with a kind of negative general principle the more positive principle with which the argument began ("Knowledge puffs up, but love builds up"). Love, that is, care for a brother, determines Christian ethical life, not "freedom." As 9:19-23 and 10:23-30 make clear, this does not mean that one's *personal* life with regard to food per se is absolutized, but that the first consideration in ethical conduct is not my own "rights" but the good of the other.

Second, at the same time this generalizing conclusion as to his own conduct regarding food leads directly to the argument that follows. In what looks like a digression but is in fact a crucial part of the argument as a whole, Paul makes an impassioned defense of his apostleship, in which his freedom as an apostle to live as he does is the primary issue.[71] The fact that this defense is set up by this concluding word suggests that his conduct with regard to food had become part of the issue as they raised it in their letter.

But that is what chap. 9 is all about. For now a final word needs to be said as to why Paul begins his response to their attendance at cultic meals in this fashion, rather than with the outright prohibition that eventually follows (10:14-22). The answer to that seems to be twofold.[72] (1) This response has been determined first of all by the nature of the argumentation in their own letter. That is, Paul is not simply giving his opinion as to whether one may attend the cultic meals. He will finally say they may not—not under any circumstances. But he begins this way because this is how *they* began.[73] Thus, as has been pointed out, he works his way through their argument point by point, and shows that Christian theology and ethics move in an entirely different direction from theirs. This is argument and appeal *over against them,* not instruction in response to a friendly inquiry.

---

[71]Most often this verse and chap. 9 are regarded as instances of Paul's setting himself up as a model for the conduct argued for in vv. 7-13 (most recently Willis, 108-10, and "An Apostolic Apologia? The Form and Function of 1 Corinthians 9," *JSNT* 24 [1985], 33-48). There is a sense in which that is true; Paul always sets up his own conduct as something to be "imitated" (cf. 11:1). But that is not his *point* in chap. 9. See the introduction and commentary on chap. 9.

[72]Cf. Fee, "Εἰδωλόθυτα," pp. 195-97.

[73]Cf. Willis, 112-22.

(2) Responding in this way also perfectly fits the pattern throughout the letter (see, e.g., 1:10–4:21; 6:12-20; 12–14), where in each case he finally prohibits their present activity, but does so only after he has sought first to correct the problem at a deeper level, namely at the level of their misunderstanding of the gospel. This is also in keeping with his larger understanding of the gospel, that the imperative follows the indicative, that obedience there must be—which sometimes is finally expressed in absolutes as in 6:18 and 10:14-22—but always in terms of response to the gospel.

For this reason Paul invariably treats the imperative in a new way. The divine order still has moral and ethical absolutes; there is conduct that is totally incompatible with life in Christ. Sexual immorality is wrong—absolutely; idolatry is wrong—absolutely.[74] But Paul never begins there. For the person in Christ such behavior is wrong first of all precisely because the person is "in Christ." With Christ one has died; in Christ one has been raised to live a new existence. Such a participant in the new order must realize the fruit of the Spirit. Thus Paul begins with the gospel and its fruit of love and care for brothers and sisters. But he concludes finally (in 10:19-22) with personal conduct, and cultic meals are absolutely forbidden as totally incompatible with life in Christ.

Despite the fact that Western Christianity for over a millennium has had nothing in its culture comparable to this issue, this text has had a long history of use in the church in the form of the "stumbling-block principle." But much that has been said in this regard would derive better from 10:31–11:1 or Rom. 14. A few items need to be noted.

(1) The issue is not that of "offending" someone in the church. It has to do with conduct that another would "emulate"—indeed, in this case apparently is being urged to emulate—to his or her own hurt.

(2) Usually this principle is invoked in more peripheral matters of behavior. But that, too, is not the case here. While it is true that in v. 13 Paul broadens the scope considerably, the specific issue is something that he will eventually forbid altogether. Nonetheless, the greater issues for him in this

---

[74]This is where both von Soden ("Sacrament," p. 264) and Conzelmann, 148-49, seem to miss Paul's argument rather widely. Conzelmann, e.g., says of 8:10: "Paul declares: your conduct does not affect *you;* your inner freedom to go to these places is no problem. The problem is the demonstration you give to your brother, not purposely, but in an objective sense—in other words, the way in which he understands your conduct." Paul declares no such thing, as 10:14-22 makes clear (a passage that Conzelmann seems to find embarrassing to Paul). The problem lies in our inability to think that there might be absolutes without at the same time feeling that Paul is betraying himself by bringing back the law. But no such tension existed in Paul. Imperative there is aplenty in him, but he never lets it be turned into law (meaning as a means of securing oneself before God). Obedience does not secure one before God; nonetheless obedience is expected of one whom God has secured.

section—the attitudinal ones—do need careful hearing: people arguing for behavior on the basis of knowledge and asserting their "authority/freedom" to the detriment of others.

(3) What would seem to be an illegitimate use of the principle, even in the broader terms of v. 13, is for those who feel "offended" to try to force all others to conform to their own idiosyncrasies of behavior. Paul makes it quite clear in Rom. 14 that on matters of indifference people within any given community should learn to live together in harmony, with no group demanding their own behavior of the others.

(4) The real concern of the passage needs a regular hearing in the church. Personal behavior is dictated not by knowledge, freedom, or law, but by love for those within the community of faith. Everything one does that affects relationships within the body of Christ should have care for brothers and sisters as its primary motivation.

2. Paul's Apostolic Defense (9:1-27)

Even though the argument of 8:1-13 is carried on with some vigor, one is scarcely prepared for the rhetoric with which this section begins and which is sustained for the first 14 verses. One rhetorical question follows another with hardly a letup.[1] Equally striking is the argument itself.[2] After an opening salvo in which Paul reasserts his apostleship (vv. 1-2), he sets out to defend himself against those who are calling him into question (v. 3). The "defense" turns out to be a vehement insistence on his "rights" to their material support (vv. 4-14). With every kind of available argument he contends that "If others have the right of support from you, shouldn't we have it all the more?" (v. 12a).[3] Yet after all that, the conclusion in vv. 15-18 is not that they should therefore support him; it is the precise opposite—an explanation, indeed defense, of his policy of not accepting that for which he has just argued so strenuously. That is unusual argumentation under any circumstances.[4]

What follows (vv. 19-23) is an explanation (defense?) of his social behavior, which differed according to setting (Jew or Gentile): he became all

[1]There are 16 in all. Paul begins with four straight (v. 1), followed by eight more beginning with v. 4.

[2]This is another of the sections that has led to theories of partitioning. See the Introduction, pp. 15-16; cf. Hurd, 43-47.

[3]So much is this so that when he begins to explain in v. 12b why he had given up those rights, he breaks off in order to add two more kinds of supporting evidence (vv. 13-14).

[4]Willis, "Apologia," argues that "the claims or illustrations in 9.4-14 can hardly be a defense of Paul's right to support, as if he were called into question by some in Corinth" (p. 35). But his argument is based on unfounded assertions and reverse logic. He fails to take seriously the decidedly defensive nature of most of 1 Corinthians, es-

things to all people so as to win the more. Finally, in vv. 24-27 he turns again to exhortation, now urging self-discipline, for which he serves as an example.

What is one to make of all this, especially in the context of forbidding the Corinthians to attend cultic meals? The traditional answer is that it follows 8:13 as a further example of his willingness to give up his rights for the sake of others. Although Paul's answer may partly function in that way, there are two difficulties with that view as the basic reason for this section: (1) Apart from vv. 26-27, which seem to be moving on to another issue, the text gives no indication that Paul is appealing to them to follow his example.[5] (2) At least one half of the response (vv. 1-14) does not fit this scheme in any way. To suggest that vv. 1-14 merely set up vv. 15-18, where he explains why he gave up these rights, scarcely accounts for the vigor of the rhetoric.[6] Furthermore, vv. 15-18 are so highly personal—and emotionally charged—that they do not seem to function as exemplary.

More likely, as was suggested earlier,[7] this is an integral part of his response to their letter. He had earlier forbidden attendance at the temples. They are challenging that prohibition, both by a set of theological arguments (8:1, 4, 8) and by calling into question his apostolic authority. From this response it would appear that the challenge came from two sources. First, his failure to accept material support is being played off against him, calling into question his apostleship itself (cf. 2 Cor. 12:13!). Second, on the matter of marketplace food he had been known to be of two minds. He ate such food in Gentile settings, but declined when among Jews (vv. 19-22).[8] Such vacillation does not seem worthy of an apostle.

Since a crisis of authority lies behind much of this letter (cf. 4:1-5; 5–6; 14:36-37), Paul takes this occasion, which arose directly from their letter, to hit it head-on. The defense is structured around the opening two questions, which he answers in reverse order: "Yes, I am an apostle" (vv.

---

pecially of chaps. 1–4. On the matter at hand he argues that no one in Corinth would have made an issue of Paul's rejecting their support, but misses the sociological dimension of the problem and fails altogether to note 2 Cor. 11:7-12 and 12:13. The sarcasm of the latter passage is hardly addressed to a nonissue! On the affront his rejecting their support would have been to the Corinthians, see E. A. Judge, "Cultural Conformity and Innovation in Paul: Some Clues from Contemporary Documents," *TynB* 35 (1984), 3-24, esp. 15-23.

[5] In this regard cf. esp. 2 Thess. 3:6-10, where Paul uses some of the same language as here (e.g., v. 9, "not that we do not have the right to such help") and explicitly says that the reason for giving up such rights was to give them an example.

[6] Cf., e.g., Holladay, 113-14, who would attribute it to the style of the diatribe. But that will scarcely do since the defense is so personal and so clearly directed at his relationship with them.

[7] See the introduction to chaps. 8–10, pp. 361-63 above.

[8] Cf. Ruef, 78, and Hurd, 127-28, who have also suggested this possibility.

1b-14); and "My apostleship makes me free to give up my rights to your support" (vv. 15-18) "and to eat or reject food of any kind" (vv. 19-23). Most likely the crucial matter is his freedom to act as in vv. 19-23. But to get there he must first defend his apostleship itself.

a. In defense of his apostleship (9:1-2)

1 *Am I not free? Am I not an apostle?*[9] *Have I not seen Jesus our Lord? Are you not the result of my work in the Lord?* 2 *Even though I may not be an apostle to others, surely I am to you! For you are the seal of my apostleship in the Lord.*

This rhetoric has been set up by the final sentence of the preceding argument (8:13). It is easy to overlook the shift to the first person in that sentence; but once Paul generalizes the principle in this way, it sets off an impassioned defense of his actions. Although the opening question is the crucial one for the context, and follows most naturally from 8:13, the matter of his apostleship itself gets first attention since everything else hinges on that.

1 With unexpected vigor Paul suddenly unleashes a torrent of rhetorical questions, each beginning with the Greek particle *ou*, thus expecting a positive answer: "Of course I am; of course I have; of course you are."[10] The questions fall into their natural order in terms of the argument. The problem has to do with *exousia* ("authority/freedom"; see on 8:9) and *eleutheros* (being "free"; the word used here)—not only theirs, but his, which is what vv. 19-23 and 10:29b-30 are all about. Thus the first question is "Am I not free?"[11] As what follows makes clear, this is not first of all an attempt to set himself up as an example of the proper use of "freedom" (which his response ends up doing in its own circuitous way), but to defend

---

[9]The first two questions are reversed in D F G Ψ Maj a b sy[h], apparently in the interest of putting the more "important" one (that of apostleship) first. But that misses the structure of Paul's argument. The text is read by P[46] ℵ A B P 33 104 365 629 630 1175 1739 1881 pc vg cop Tert.

[10]Willis, "Apologia," p. 34, asserts that because the questions expect an affirmative answer this is therefore not a "real defense." That is reverse logic that quite misunderstands the nature of the rhetoric. The ἀλλά γε ὑμῖν ("but surely *to you* I am!") makes it plain that the opposite prevails. Even more insensitive to the argument here, not to mention the historical situation, is Willis's further assertion that "Paul's apostleship cannot be contested by the Corinthians who are the seal of his authenticity as an apostle" (*ibid.*). If that were the case, one wonders why the problem in 1:12 at all, or why 4:1-21 or 2 Corinthians as a whole!

[11]Gk. οὐκ εἰμὶ ἐλεύθερος. The remarkable similarity with Epict. 3.22.48 has often been noted ("And what do I lack? Am I not without pain? Am I not without fear? Am I not free? [οὐκ εἰμὶ ἐλεύθερος]"). But the parallel is purely coincidental. Epictetus is trying to show the Cynic as the one who knows how to live without things. Paul's is defense pure and simple—of actions that include *eating* marketplace food in given contexts!

his own actions. The second question, "Am I not an apostle[12]?" is the one that gets immediate attention. This is the first direct statement in the letter that his apostleship itself is at stake in Corinth; but such has been hinted at several times before this (1:1, 12; 4:1-5, 8-13, 14-21; 5:1-2).

Paul's own view of apostleship is presented by the second set of questions, which serve to establish that he is indeed an apostle. First, "Have I not seen[13] Jesus our Lord[14]?" Along with 15:8 this question establishes two things: (a) Paul believed that his experience on the Damascus road[15] was more than a mere vision. For him it was a resurrection appearance of a kind with all the others—to be sure, after the ascension and therefore out of due season (15:3-8). (b) But since others who saw the Risen Lord did not become apostles, what most likely legitimized his apostleship was the accompanying commissioning.[16] Although he does not say so here, in Gal. 1:16 the revelation of the Son of God is accompanied by its purpose, "that I might preach him among the Gentiles" (cf. 15:8-11, where the resurrection appearance is followed by discussion of his apostleship).[17]

Second, "Are you not the result of my work[18] in the Lord[19]?" (cf. 3:6, 10; 4:15). This is Paul's second criterion for his apostleship, the establishing of churches in new areas (cf. Rom. 15:17-22). He will pick this up again in 2 Cor. 10:13-16 over against the outsiders who had come in to trouble them. Such people were false apostles in Paul's view, partly because

[12]On the word "apostle" see on 1:1.

[13]Gk. ἑώρακα; cf. ὤφθη in 15:8. There has been considerable debate as to whether this language describes a merely revelatory vision (e.g., W. Michaelis, *TDNT* V, 355-60, and W. Marxsen, *The Resurrection of Jesus of Nazareth* [ET, Philadelphia, 1970], pp. 98-111) or an actual objective seeing (G. O'Collins, *The Resurrection of Jesus Christ* [Valley Forge, 1973], pp. 7-9). Paul surely believed the latter. See the discussion in Kim, *Origin*, pp. 55-66; cf. F. Kerr, "Paul's Experience: Sighting or Theophany?" *New Blackfriars* 58 (1977), 304-13.

[14]This is unusual language in Paul. Cf. Rom. 4:24, which also refers to the Risen Lord. Probably this is semitechnical language for speaking of Christ in his resurrection. He is "Jesus," the name of the Son of God in his incarnation, "our Lord," having become so through his resurrection from the dead.

[15]Although Paul does not mention this experience by name, only the most biased exegete would deny that this is what Paul is referring to here and in 15:8, and probably in Gal. 1:12-16 as well.

[16]So Barrett, 200; Conzelmann, 152; Kim, *Origin*, pp. 56-66.

[17]Luke picks up this aspect of Pauline theology in Acts 1:21-22; cf. the reports of the Damascus road experience in 9:15; 22:10; and esp. 26:15-18.

[18]Gk. τὸ ἔργον μου; lit. "my work," meaning, as the NIV has it, the result of his apostolic labors.

[19]For this ἐν κυρίῳ see on 4:17 and 7:22. The precise nuance is uncertain here. As in the earlier two passages it is probably primarily locative; i.e., their existence is not "in Paul" but "in the Lord." On the other hand, it may have a slightly instrumental ring to it. Even though they are Paul's workmanship, the ultimate responsibility lies with the Lord.

they were laboring in "another man's territory." Paul's point here is that the Corinthians' own existence authenticates his apostleship (cf. 4:15: many guardians but only one father). This point will now be further elaborated in v. 2.

2 This very *ad hominem* elaboration of the final question, and thereby the final three questions, of v. 1 makes it plain that the matter at hand is not simply his "freedom" (i.e., this is not an attempt to explain how an apostle can limit his freedom in the way described in 8:13); rather, his apostleship itself has been called into question. But what we are not quite prepared for is the reference to "others." There are two possibilities: (1) It may refer to other Christians or other communities. That is, he may simply be allowing the hypothetical possibility that others outside their immediate circle may have some reason for not thinking of him as an apostle. This seems to be the implication of the NIV. (2) It may refer to some outsiders, such as those taken on in vigorous confrontation in 2 Cor. 10-12, who have already entered the community and begun to sow seeds of discord.

This is not easy to decide, which is unfortunate since the reconstruction of Paul's relationship to this church rests in part on when the outsiders of 2 Cor. 10-12 made their appearance. Two things may be said: First, from Paul's perspective his present "critics" are from within the Corinthian community itself. Nowhere does 1 Corinthians suggest that the trouble is due to outside agitation. This does not mean that such was not the case, but that Paul sees the problem strictly as an inside affair—as probably their letter gives him full warrant for believing. Yet, secondly, there are indications that others have visited the church. This emerges especially in the slogans of 1:12, and perhaps in such passages as 4:15 ("you have many guardians"[20]) and 9:12 ("if *others* share your *exousia*"). This latter passage seems to suggest outsiders of some kind. If so, then these may include some whom Paul suspects of doubting his apostleship. Thus, "If not to them, surely I am to you![21]"

Even so, as v. 3 and 4:1-5 imply, the problem at this point is from within the community; and the argument here is directed at the church. "If others have doubts," Paul says to them, "you dare not share them because your own existence is the living evidence of my apostleship." That is the point of the final sentence: "For[22] you are the seal of my apostleship[23] in the Lord." Paul thus takes a common metaphor, the "seal" that indicates own-

[20]Although, as was noted there, this may simply refer to those who are currently giving leadership to the community and are leading the charge against him.
[21]Gk. ἀλλά γε ὑμῖν. For this use of ἀλλά in the apodosis see 4:15 and 8:6. With the γε it means, "yet at least to you."
[22]The γάρ here is causal, "for the very reason that."
[23]Gk. τῆς ἀποστολῆς (= the "office" of apostle), found here for the first time in Paul; elsewhere only in Gal. 2:8 and Rom. 1:5.

ership or authentication,[24] and applies it to their relationship to him. Their very existence authenticates his apostleship. As with the final question in v. 1, he adds "in the Lord." Their existence "in the Lord" stamps Paul's ministry with the divine seal of authenticity: it, too, is "in the Lord." Although Paul does not make the point here as he will in chap. 15 (see esp. vv. 12-19), their calling his apostleship into question therefore calls them into question as well. If he is not a true apostle, then they are not truly "in the Lord."

Can anything be said in our day about "apostles"? Given the two criteria expressed here, one would have to allow that apostles do not exist in the sense that Paul defines his own ministry. But it should also be noted that this might be too narrow a view, based strictly on Paul's own personal experience. His more functional understanding of apostleship (see on 1:1) would certainly have its modern counterparts in those who found and lead churches in unevangelized areas. Only when "apostle" is used in a non-Pauline sense of "guarantors of the traditions" would the usage be narrowed to the first century.

b. Paul's apostolic rights (9:3-14)

3 *This is my defense to those who sit in judgment on me.* 4 *Don't we have the right to food and drink?* 5 *Don't we have the right to take a believing wife[1] along with us, as do the other apostles and the Lord's brothers and Cephas[a]?* 6 *Or is it only I and Barnabas who must work for a living?*

7 *Who serves as a soldier at his own expense? Who plants a vineyard and does not eat of[2] its grapes? Who[3] tends a flock and does not drink of the milk?* 8 *Do I say[4] this merely from a human point of*

---

[24]Paul uses the imagery elsewhere to refer to the Spirit as the "seal" of God's ownership (2 Cor. 1:22; Eph. 1:13; 4:30; cf. Abraham's circumcision, Rom. 4:11). Here the emphasis is less on "ownership" than on "legally valid attestation" (Conzelmann, 152 n. 11).

[1]Gk. ἀδελφὴν γυναῖκα (= "a sister for a wife"). Several Western witnesses (F G a b Tert Ambst Pel) apparently take the "we" as a genuine plural and read γυναῖκας ("wives"; without a form of ἀδελφή). Zuntz, 138, contends for the Western reading on the grounds that it fits Paul's "fervour" (cf. J. B. Bauer, "Uxores circumducere [1 Kor 9,5]," *BZ* n.s. 3 [1979], 94-102). But he must also argue that ἀδελφήν is an interpolation—a most improbable option.

[2]This translates the text of P[46] Maj it bo Ambst (ἐκ τοῦ καρποῦ), which is an assimilation to the sentence that follows. Paul's text reads τὸν καρπόν (= "eat its fruit"), supported by ℵ* A B C* D* F G P Ψ 0222 33 1175 1739 pc sa. Cf. Zuntz, 50.

[3]NA[26], following P[46] ℵ A C* Maj sy[p] bo, begins this question with ἤ ("or"). It was removed by an early scribe to conform the clause to the preceding one (B D F G Ψ 81 104 630 1175 1739 pc latt sy[h] sa).

[4]For a discussion of the λαλῶ/λέγω variation see Zuntz, 97.

view? Doesn't the Law say the same thing? 9 *For it is written in the Law of Moses⁵: "Do not muzzle⁶ an ox while it is treading out the grain."ᵇ Is it about oxen that God is concerned?* 10 *Surely he says this for us, doesn't he? Yes, this was written for us, because when the plowman plows and the thresher threshes, they ought to do so in the hope of sharing in the harvest.⁷* 11 *If we have sown spiritual seed among you, is it too much if we reap a material harvest from you?* 12 *If others have this right of support from you, shouldn't we have it all the more?*

But we did not use this right. On the contrary, we put up with anything rather than hinder the gospel of Christ. 13 *Don't you know that those who work in the temple get their food from the temple,⁸ and those who serve at the altar share in what is offered on the altar?* 14 *In the same way, the Lord has commanded that those who preach the gospel should receive their living from the gospel.*

ᵃThat is, Peter
ᵇDeut. 25:4

Although Paul calls this his "defense," the issue is hardly what we might expect in such.⁹ In a series of cascading questions Paul plays variations on a single theme: his right to their material support. Since he goes on in vv. 12b and 15-18 to explain why he has *renounced* this "right," and since this touchy issue is addressed again—in a similarly defensive way—in 2 Corin-

⁵P⁴⁶ f Ambst omit Μωϋσέως; D* F G read simply, "for it is written." Zuntz, 138-39, argues that the Western reading is original but fails to recognize the overwhelming tendency in this tradition toward assimilation. All of the arguments he raises against the longer reading at the same time make it the *lectio difficilior*.

⁶Paul's κωμήσεις has been conformed to the LXX (φιμώσεις; cf. 1 Tim. 5:18) in the entire tradition (incl. P⁴⁶) except for B* D* F G 1739. See Metzger, 558, and Zuntz, 37.

⁷The final words of this "citation" exhibit considerable confusion. The translated text (supported by P⁴⁶ ℵ* A B C P 33 69 81 365 1175 1739 pc sy cop) reads ἐπ' ἐλπίδι τοῦ μετέχειν ("in hope of sharing"). The Western tradition (D* F G a b syʰᵐᵍ) reads τῆς ἐλπίδος αὐτοῦ μετέχειν ("[the thresher ought] to share his hope [i.e., of the plowman]"). This apparently arose because of the ellipsis of ἀλοᾶν after ἀλοῶν. The MajT conflated the two readings ("[the thresher] in the hope of sharing his hope").

⁸This reflects the text of NA²⁶, τὰ ἐκ τοῦ ἱεροῦ (lit. "the things of the temple"), supported by ℵ B D* F G 6 81 1739 pc lat cop. P⁴⁶ A C Ψ Maj b d syʰ do not have the τά, thus reading a text in parallel with v. 14, ἐκ τοῦ ἱεροῦ ἐσθίουσιν (suggesting that they live by means of their priestly office). The question is whether the parallel is Paul's own, which in the former instance was not recognized by scribes, thus causing them to add a τά to make it refer to the food itself (so Zuntz, 51), or whether it is the result of editorializing on the part of scribes (so Conzelmann, 156 n. 2). On the whole the former is to be preferred.

⁹Indeed, it fits the category "defense" so poorly that many believe v. 3 goes with vv. 1-2 and refers only to what has preceded. See the discussion on v. 3.

thians (11:7-12; 12:13), it seems certain that they raised it.[10] And since this occurs in the context of defending his apostleship (vv. 1b-3), most likely his failure to take support has been used against him to call his apostolic authenticity into question.

But how could such a problem have arisen? Most likely it is related to some sociological factors[11]—of a kind also lying behind the problem of division and quarreling suggested for 1:10–4:21.[12] Part of that problem was that they were viewing their various teachers in terms of contemporary popular philosophy. Apparently this involved not only the form and content of their teaching (see on 1:17 and 2:1-5), but also their means of support. Philosophers and wandering missionaries in the Greco-Roman world were "supported" by four means: fees, patronage, begging, and working. Each of these had both proponents and detractors, who viewed rival forms as not worthy of philosophy.[13]

Various bits of evidence from the Pauline letters and Acts suggest that this is an issue with which Paul himself had to struggle, especially in the Greco-Roman cities where he would spend considerable time. The evidence suggests that by the time of his ministry in Thessalonica Paul had generally abandoned patronage (as, e.g., in Philippi in Lydia's household, Acts 16:15) for working (in his case in the trade of tentmaking) as his basic means of support (1 Thess. 2:9; 2 Thess. 3:7-9; 1 Cor. 4:12; cf. Acts 18:3).[14] Why he did this cannot be fully known,[15] although his defense in 1 Thess. 2:1-12 has so many correspondences to the philosophical debates[16] (especially against those receiving fees, and perhaps patronage as well) that one wonders whether something happened in Thessalonica that made him realize his

[10]So also Weiss, 232, and Conzelmann, 154. This is contrary to the suggestion by Daube, *Rabbinic Judaism*, p. 395, that Paul here introduces the theme for the first time and that in v. 8 he somewhat apologizes for it since it ran counter to Jewish practices. But the milieu of this church is Hellenistic, not Jewish.

[11]For this information we are indebted to various studies on the sociology of the early Christians, especially those by Theissen, 50-65; Hock, *Social Context*, pp. 50-65; and Judge, "Conformity," pp. 15-23.

[12]See the introduction to 1:10–4:21, pp. 49-50.

[13]See the discussion in Hock, *Social Context*, pp. 52-59; cf. A. E. Harvey, " 'The Workman is Worthy of His Hire': Fortunes of a Proverb in the Early Church," *NovT* 24 (1982), 214-16.

[14]This is not to say that he did not work earlier, nor that he did not accept provision later, as Hock, e.g., argues (see "The Workshop as a Social Setting for Paul's Missionary Preaching," *CBQ* 41 [1979], 440). Rather, it is to acknowledge that the hard evidence of Acts 18:3; 20:34; 1 Thess. 2:9; and 1 Cor. 4:12 places it for certain from this time on.

[15]One reason may have been that it provided an opportunity for evangelizing, as Hock suggests (see the previous note).

[16]See A. J. Malherbe, " 'Gentle as a Nurse': The Stoic Background to 1 Thess. II," *NovT* 12 (1970), 203-17; and Hock, *Social Context*, pp. 52-59.

need to be more careful about his means of livelihood, lest the gospel itself come into disrepute.[17] In any case, both Luke (Acts 18:3) and Paul (1 Cor. 4:12) bear witness to the fact that in Corinth, apparently by design as much as by need, he obtained his livelihood in Aquila's workshop. His difficulty appears to have arisen when later teachers (Apollos and Cephas[?]) and perhaps some outside agitators, by their own acceptance of patronage, placed Paul's renunciation of it into bold relief. Not only was his working demeaning to himself[18] but to the Corinthians as well (2 Cor. 11:7).[19] From their point of view his apostleship is thereby questionable.[20]

Paul's response to this is not first of all to defend his renunciation of his rights, but to establish that he has such rights. This must be done because they have questioned his authority altogether. From their point of view his activity would not have been the *renunciation* of assumed rights; rather, he must have worked with his hands because he *lacked* such rights. Since, therefore, he did not do as the others—accept patronage—he must not be a genuine apostle. Thus Paul begins with a series of three rhetorical questions whose aim is the point of v. 6, that he has the right *not* to work for a living, and therefore to be supported by them. He then illustrates this with examples from everyday life (v. 7) and from the OT (vv. 8-10). After applying this to his own situation in Corinth (vv. 11-12a), he starts to explain why he has given up this right (v. 12b). But then he remembers two more pieces of supporting evidence for the previous argument, religious practice in general (v. 13) and the teaching of Jesus in particular (v. 14). The net result is a long, impassioned "defense" of his apostleship in which he contends that he had the rights of such even if he had given them up.

3 Having set up the matter with the rhetorical questions of vv. 1-2,

---

[17]Otherwise Dungan, 15, who argues that "in short, it seems that everything depended upon the financial strength of each particular congregation." But two pieces of evidence from Paul quite contradict this. He accepted support from Macedonia (2 Cor. 11:9; Phil. 4:14-20), even though by his own testimony they knew "extreme poverty" (2 Cor. 8:2); yet he rejected support from Corinth, a church that knew abundance (2 Cor. 8:13-14). Not the relative financial strength of the congregations but something more closely akin to the gospel itself is the reason (see on v. 12b).

[18]On Paul's accepting the demeaning character of working with his own hands, see 4:12; cf. Hock, "Paul's Tentmaking and the Problem of His Social Class," *JBL* 97 (1978), 555-64.

[19]This would be even more so for the wealthy among them, who might feel slighted by this refusal on his part. In three of the articles collected in *Social Setting* (chaps. 2–4), Theissen has argued that the basic divisions in the church were between some of the wealthy patrons, who then also demeaned some of the poor both in the matter of idol food and of the Lord's Supper that was celebrated in their homes.

[20]An alternative to this, suggested by C. Forbes ("Comparison, Self-Praise and Irony: Paul's Boasting and the Conventions of Hellenistic Rhetoric," *NTS* 32 [1986], 14-15), is that Paul was offered patronage while he was there, and that his rejection of it led to the anti-Paul sentiment on the part of some.

Paul now states that what follows[21] is "my defense[22] to those[23] who sit in judgment on me" (cf. 4:3-4). For the verb "sit in judgment" see on 2:14-15 and 4:3. The implication in both 4:3-4 and here is that the Corinthians are in process of "examining" or "investigating" him;[24] the evidence of this context makes it certain that the "examination" is related to his apostolic authority. Most likely much of our letter and Paul's relationship to the church is here brought into focus. Any number of items—the "divisions" in chaps. 1–4, the combative nature of so much of the letter, their rejection of his former letter, the continuing ill will that prompted later visits and letters—all make sense when seen in light of this verse.

4-6 Paul begins his defense with a series of rhetorical questions whose *function* in the argument is singular: to force them to recognize, as they should already know, that he has all the rights of an apostle.[25] Less certain is what each of them, especially vv. 4 and 5, specifically refers to. Since the rest of the argument takes up the point of v. 6, that he has the right *not* to work at a trade, most interpreters understand the earlier two questions as variations on the same theme. Indeed, if there were only the first and third questions, probably no one would ever have thought otherwise. The problem lies with v. 5, which does not seem to fit this scheme as well, hence suggesting to some that v. 4 may not either. The alternative is to see the first two as reflecting two other concerns over rights where perhaps he has also been known to deviate from the standard pattern of other apostles, so that together the questions defend his rights on matters of food, marriage, and support. Although this latter suggestion is attractive in a number of ways,[26] a

---

[21]Some have argued that v. 3 goes with vv. 1-2 (e.g., Godet, 5; Ellis, 47 n. 8; Willis, "Apologia," p. 34; and esp. K. Nickel, "A Parenthetical Apologia: 1 Corinthians 9:1-3," *CurTM* 1 [1974], 68-70; cf. Helen Montgomery's translation). But this is ruled out by the word order, which demands that what follows is what αὕτη ("this") refers to. Cf. C. K. Williams: "My vindication of myself to those who are investigating me is *this: . . .*" This captures both the order of the Greek and the present aspect of τοῖς ἀνακρίνουσιν ("those who are investigating"; see n. 24).

[22]Gk. ἀπολογία, a speech or writing in reply to accusations; cf. Acts 22:1; Jos., *c.Ap.* 2.147; Xenophon, *mem.* 4.8.

[23]Conzelmann, 153, suggests that the "critics are (as yet) outside the Corinthian community." He misses the force of 4:3-4 as well. See on 4:18-21; most likely this refers to the leaders of the opposition, who have generally taken the whole church down this path. See the Introduction, pp. 6-10.

[24]Without grammatical warrant the RSV translates this more suppositionally, "those who would examine me." Willis asserts, again without grammatical support, that "τοῖς ἀνακρίνουσιν could legitimately be translated as future. . . . Then we could say that Paul is anticipating criticism rather than answering a previous complaint" ("Form," p. 34). But neither the grammar nor the context supports such an interpretation.

[25]At the same time vv. 5-6 give side glimpses into all kinds of interesting historical tidbits that are otherwise unknown to us, and which are not fully lucid here.

[26]So much so that in my *Study Guide* (1979) I leaned this way.

close look at the three questions, plus the context as a whole, seems to favor the former view, or a modified version of it.

Question 1 (v. 4) asks, "Don't[27] we[28] have the right to food and drink[29]?" The key word in each of the questions is *exousia* (see on 8:7). But in distinction to the usage there, where the nuance of "freedom" predominates, here the emphasis is on "authority" or "rights." This is the word that has caused most interpreters to consider the argument to be setting him up as an example for the "gnostics" of chap. 8 to follow. Just as they have the *exousia* to eat but should curtail it for the sake of the weak, so too Paul has the *exousia* to eat and drink, but he has given it up for the sake of others. The problem with that view, of course, is that the text itself does not suggest it, and the forceful nature of the insistence on "rights" seems to move the concern in a different direction.

But to what does "food and drink" refer? Coming hard on the heels, or nearly so, of 8:13 as it does, it may be that *exousia* really does mean "freedom" and that the issue is his own freedom to eat certain food, even though he has given up this right. Thus it would anticipate the matter spoken to in vv. 19-23.[30] Attractive as that is in terms of its preceding context and the usage of *exousia,* it is nonetheless difficult to sustain. The issue in 8:1-13 is not merely eating idol food; it is eating it in the idol temples; and despite 8:13, other parts of this argument (9:19-23; 10:29b-30; and 10:31) indicate that Paul did not always abstain from such food—which he did in fact in the matter of support from the Corinthians. Furthermore, the combination "food *and drink*" seems to move it out of the arena of the former argument over food to that of sustenance. Most likely, therefore, this is the first in a series of three questions that argue for his right to their support.

Question 2 (v. 5) is the one that is full of puzzles: "Don't we have the

---

[27]In contrast to v. 1 (where there was a simple οὐ), each of these has the double negative μὴ οὐ. Ultimately these also expect a positive response, but they get there in a more circuitous way. The μή expects a negative response to a negatively expressed sentence. Thus (lit.), "Can it be that we do not have the right to food and drink?" This is intensely rhetorical.

[28]This is another puzzling use of the first plural (cf. on 2:6). The entire paragraph, except for v. 8, is in the plural, while all of vv. 1-3 and 15-27 is in the singular. Probably it reflects the fact that Paul and his traveling companions all took this stance toward support. Thus he includes them with himself in this defense. Yet the context, and especially the interchange of "we" and "I" for the same content in vv. 12b and 15, indicates that he is primarily concerned with his own ministry.

[29]Although this may be a legitimate translation, the Greek text has the infinitives of the two verbs: "to eat and to drink."

[30]This has been argued by Bauer, "Uxores," although he thinks vv. 4-5 are picked up again in vv. 24-27, not 19-23. Cf. Dungan, 6 n. 1, who cites this view approvingly. Their further suggestion that the first two questions reflect "eat, drink, and make merry" (= "eat, drink, and make love to one's wife") is farfetched at best.

right to take a believing wife[31] along with us, as do the other[32] apostles and the Lord's brothers and Cephas?" On the one hand, its position between vv. 4 and 6 implies that it at least has to do with his "rights" to their support; on the other hand, the very nature of the question, and especially the contrasts with so many others, implies that the issue here is more than just material support. Those who see this as a second issue over his apostolic rights suggest that all of this means "Don't I have the right to be married?" and that it might thus be related to the issue of his singleness in chap. 7. Again, that has some attractiveness to it, but here such a view is even more difficult to sustain. If that were his intent, then it must be admitted that this is a most circuitous and obtuse[33] way of putting what Paul is perfectly capable of saying directly (cf., e.g., 7:2). Very likely both issues merge here. That is, he is in fact dealing with his rights to their support, but that is here joined to another issue where his (and his companions') way of life is strictly a minority option. Even his fellow tentmakers are a married couple (Acts 18:3). How is it, the Corinthians wonder, given what all others do, that he and his companions are not accompanied by wives? Does this also say something about the authenticity of his apostleship?

The comparisons are as intriguing as they are brief.[34] As 15:7 makes clear, for Paul the word "apostle" was not confined to the Twelve. It is therefore quite impossible to know who all would be included in "the rest of the apostles."[35] Equally intriguing is his setting forth "the Lord's brothers"[36] in this way. This refers to Mary's other children,[37] some of whom are mentioned by name in the Synoptic tradition (Mark 6:3; Matt. 13:55). This passage makes clear that even though they had questions during his earthly

---

[31]Gk. ἀδελφὴν γυναῖκα, which means "a sister as a wife." See n. 1 above. On the question of whether Paul had been formerly married, see n. 7 on 7:8.

[32]Gk. λοιποί (lit. "what remains"; = "the rest of").

[33]The problem lies with the verb προάγω, which means to "lead about," or "go about (in the sense of having someone in close companionship)," and its object "a sister as a wife." Bauer, again followed by Dungan (see n. 30 above), has presented evidence that the verb on occasion could be interpreted to mean "be married." But why prefer an obtuse meaning when the ordinary one can be shown to make good sense in the context?

[34]As Jervell ("Traditions") has cogently argued, this text is sure evidence that traditions about the apostles as well as about Jesus would have been known in the early Christian communities.

[35]Since Paul follows this with "the Lord's brothers" and "Cephas," and since Cephas is indeed one of "the rest," there has been some debate as to whether it also includes the Lord's brothers. Probably so, since Paul by implication includes James as an apostle in 15:7 and Gal. 1:19. Otherwise W. Schmithals, *The Office of Apostle in the Early Church* (ET, Nashville, 1969), pp. 80-81, who quite unconvincingly excludes both James *and* Peter from being apostles in Paul's view.

[36]Paul elsewhere speaks of James as "the Lord's brother" (Gal. 1:19). This is undoubtedly the same James as in 1 Cor. 15:7.

[37]Although Roman Catholic scholarship rejects this. See the bibliographical data in BAGD under ἀδελφός.

ministry (Mark 3:31; John 7:3; but cf. 2:12), they eventually came to believe in Jesus and were among his earliest followers after the Resurrection (cf. Acts 1:14). How widely they may have traveled and how well known they were in the churches remain a mystery.

That he should mention Cephas is less surprising[38] since some in the community are using his name as a rallying point. But does this text suggest that Peter and his wife had in fact visited Corinth? The possibility is enhanced by the argument in 1:10–4:21 (see esp. on 1:12 and 3:22) and by the fact that he is singled out from the other apostles. On the other hand, the fact that some are rallying around his name, whether he had ever been there or not, undoubtedly caused Paul to single him out. It is of some interest that he does this with both Peter and James in 15:4-7, and no one argues seriously that either James or the other brothers of Jesus had ever been in Corinth. Whether Peter had been or not simply cannot be known.

The third question (v. 6) puts the present problem in clearer focus: "Or is it only I and Barnabas who (lit.) do not have the right not to work?"[39] Although this finally comes out where the NIV does, "who must work for a living," the issue is his *right not to work,* meaning work with his own hands at a trade (cf. 4:12). The implication is that the problem for the Corinthians is not simply that he took no support from them (i.e., that he refused to take patronage in the home of one of their wealthier members), but that he supported himself in the demeaning fashion of working at a trade.[40] What kind of activity is this for one who would be an "apostle of our Lord Jesus Christ"? Paul's point of course is that he has the right not to, even though he rejected it.

The mention of Barnabas is especially intriguing.[41] Why not Silas, for example, or Timothy? The answer almost surely does not lie with the suggestion that Barnabas had also visited Corinth,[42] but with the probability that traditions about the apostles were well known. And in this case Paul and Barnabas in particular were known to have worked at a trade when they evangelized.

---

[38]On Paul's use of this name for Peter see n. 41 on 1:12. There is something to be said for the possibility, suggested by Barrett, 204, that the opposition to Paul's apostleship might stem from those who claim to be Peter's people.

[39]Cf. esp. 2 Thess. 3:9, "we did this [worked with our own hands] not because we did not have the right [οὐκ ἔχομεν ἐξουσία] to such help."

[40]On this question see esp. Hock, "Tentmaking."

[41]All the more so since this is written sometime after their falling out recorded in Acts 15:36-41.

[42]Which further qualifies the question of whether Peter ever did. That is, the fact that Barnabas can be singled out like this means that one cannot make too much of the singling out of Peter in the previous sentence, at least as to whether he had visited Corinth or not.

Although the three questions all relate to the same issue, then, that of his right to their support, they pick up various aspects of that concern. He has the right (1) to have them supply his daily needs, (2) to have a wife, who would also accompany him in his ministry, and (3) not to have to work at a trade in order to make ends meet. From here he will present several kinds of illustrations that further demonstrate this right.

7 With yet another set of rhetorical questions Paul proceeds to illustrate the point of vv. 4-6. The questions are all drawn from commonplace realities: the soldier, farmer, and shepherd.[43] Each expects a negative answer. No soldier serves "at his own expense"[44]; every vinedresser eats the grapes (cf. Deut. 20:6; Prov. 27:18); every shepherd "drinks[45] of the milk." Even though as an analogy the first differs slightly from the other two, in each case the point is the same. In everyday life one expects to be sustained by one's labors. So with the apostle. He should expect to be sustained from his "produce" or "flock"—the church that owes its existence to him.

8 Paul is seldom content with an argument based solely on the "way things are," so he supports his "rights" with an appeal to Scripture in the form of yet another rhetorical question. The question is in two parts; the first part, which expects a negative answer, at the same time sets up the second, which expects an affirmative.[46] The NIV captures these nuances by making them two separate questions. In asking "Do I say this from a merely human point of view?" Paul is referring first of all to the immediately

---

[43]Cf. 2 Tim. 2:4-7, where the soldier and farmer are joined with the athlete to make the point that the true soldier, etc., must give wholehearted devotion to the task if they hope to obtain the prize.

[44]C. C. Caragounis, "ΟΨΩΝΙΟΝ: A Reconsideration of its Meaning," *NovT* 16 (1974), 51-52, has argued convincingly for this meaning, with the proviso that "'expense' must not be understood in any sense approximating that of 'wages.'" The word has to do with "provisions," not salary, and is almost certainly both how Paul understood it and what he is here arguing for himself. He is not to be "paid" for services rendered, but "provided for" by those who owe their lives to him. Dungan's insistence, 28-29, that Paul is arguing for the right to a *salary* misses the historical situation by a considerable margin. Cf. Hock, *Social Setting,* p. 50 n. 1 (p. 92).

[45]The Greek verb translated "drink" is ἐσθίει (= "eat"). This suggests that milk is thought of as food for nourishment, not a drink; hence it is "eaten." Nothing is to be made, as R-P (182-83) do, of the ἐκ with γάλακτος in comparison with the straight accusative in the preceding illustration.

[46]Even though the Greek sentence is somewhat awkward, its general sense is clear. It begins with the negative particle μή, thus indicating a negative response ("I do not, do I?"). The ἢ καί (= "or also") both joins the two contrasts ("I λαλῶ these things"/"the Law λέγει these things") and recommends the second alternative (cf. Rom. 4:9). The awkwardness results because the recommended alternative, which is still part of the original sentence, expects a *positive* answer. (The MajT, followed by the TR, cleans all this up by removing οὐ from before λέγει and beginning the second clause with οὐχί.)

preceding illustrations, but beyond them also to the point of vv. 4-6, his right to their support. What is not as clear is the precise nuance of "from a merely human point of view" (cf. 3:3; 15:34).[47] This may mean "Is my right to your support based simply on analogies from everyday life?" But the contrast with the Law in the next clause suggests that it means something more like "Are the analogies I have just given based on a merely human perspective?" "Of course not," is the intended response, leading to the second clause, "Does not *the Law* say these things as well?" Paul does not usually appeal to the OT by this designation,[48] and never so after the Judaizing controversy erupts.[49] As the fuller formula in v. 9 indicates, "Law" here refers more precisely to the Pentateuch rather than to the OT in general (as in 14:21).[50] What Christians call the Old Testament was considered the Word of God by the Jews of the NT era, so an appeal to its words is an appeal to the authority of God himself.

9-10 With an explanatory "for" Paul proceeds to cite what "is written in the Law of Moses."[51] The citation is of Deut. 25:4: "Do not muzzle an ox while it is treading out the grain."[52] The citation itself offers no difficulty; it demonstrates by analogy from the words of Scripture what was argued from everyday analogies in v. 7, that the laborer is permitted to enjoy the material benefits of the harvest. That point Paul himself makes by his application in v. 10. The text reflects the ancient agricultural practice of driving an ox drawing a threshing-sledge over the grain to release the kernels from the stalk. Out of mercy for the laboring animal the Israelites were

---

[47]Daube (*Rabbinic Judaism*, pp. 394-400) argues on the basis of similar usage of the full phrase ("I speak after the manner of men") in Rom. 3:5; 6:19; and Gal. 3:15 that this is a technical phrase from Paul's Jewish background that is "an apology for a bold statement which, without such an apology, might be considered near-blasphemous" (p. 394). That may be true of Rom. 3:5, but it is scarcely so here. Daube assumes a Jewish background for the church as well as for Paul and suggests that the content of vv. 4-7, which is contrary to Jewish practice, is being presented to them for the first time, therefore requiring the "apology." But that seems to miss the historical situation by a wide margin. For a critique of Daube and a more useful study of the phrase, see C. J. Bjerkelund, "'Nach menschlicher Weise rede ich.' Funktion und Sinn des paulinischen Ausdrucks," *ST* 26 (1972), 63-100.

[48]Only here and in 14:21 and (perhaps) 34 in the extant letters.

[49]Rom. 7:7 is no real exception since the argument about the Law in that context calls for the introduction "if the law had not said."

[50]Cf. Rom. 3:21, "the Law and the prophets."

[51]Twice in Romans (10:5, 19) Paul speaks about what Moses "writes" or "says," but he does not again use the formula "It is written in *the Law* of Moses."

[52]Gk. ἀλοῶντα (lit. "while threshing," which is important to note since the word is picked up again in v. 10). This passage aroused great interest among the rabbis, as is attested by the significant number of allusions to it in the Talmud. See Str-B, III, 382-99. Of particular interest are the two passages in which they treat it as an example of "from lesser to greater," i.e., if God shows interest in the animals, how much more in us (see *b.B.Mes.* 88b; *b.Git.* 62a).

forbidden to muzzle the ox, so that he might have some "material benefit" from his labor. Paul now sees that as "written for us."[53]

But Paul's explanation of the OT text has created problems for many.[54] He begins with yet another rhetorical question, similar in form to the preceding one,[55] where the first part expects a negative answer, while the second part expects a positive. The difficulties lie with the first part, where Paul seems to deny that the passage from the Law expressed any concern for the ox, and with the word translated "surely"[56] in the second part, which can mean either "entirely" (RSV) or something like "certainly, undoubtedly, by all means." This in turn has led to considerable discussion—or bald assertions—about Paul's use of the OT.

The difficulty is chiefly of our own making. There is little question that Paul expects a negative answer to the first part of his question, "Is it about oxen that God is concerned?"[57] But that does not mean either that Paul is contradicting the meaning of the OT text,[58] or that he is allegorizing,[59] or

---

[53]Although "us" here could arguably be more inclusive, the use of "we" throughout, and especially again in v. 11, indicates that he intends himself, and perhaps his companions, as in vv. 4-6.

[54]Besides the discussions in the commentaries, see W. Arndt, "The Meaning of 1 Cor. 9,9.10," *CTM* 3 (1932), 329-35; G. M. Lee, "Studies in Texts: I Corinthians 9:9-10," *Theology* 71 (1968), 122-23; A. T. Hanson, *Studies in Paul's Technique and Theology* (Grand Rapids, 1974), pp. 161-66; and W. C. Kaiser, "The Current Crisis in Exegesis and the Apostolic Use of Deuteronomy 25:4 in 1 Corinthians 9:8-10," *JETS* 21 (1978), 3-18.

[55]See n. 46 above. The formal parallel is not precise, but the similarities are noteworthy. (1) Both are in two parts, joined by an ἤ, and the second is preferred to the first; (2) both begin with μή, expecting a negative response to the first part and a positive to the second; (3) both are followed by a γάρ clause that further explains or elaborates the second part, the preferred alternative. The solution by Lee (see the preceding note), in which he tries to make μή positive, may do "no violence to the Greek," as he argues, but it is by all counts a most unnatural meaning.

[56]Gk. πάντως (cf. 9:22; 16:12; and the οὐ πάντως of 5:10).

[57]A passage in Philo is often noted: *spec.leg.* 1.260 ("for the law does not prescribe for unreasoning creatures, but for those who have mind and reason" [Loeb, VII, 251]). But this text does not refer to Deut. 25:4; rather, it reflects Philo's overall attitude. On the other hand, in *virt.* 140-47 he includes this passage (145) among several other "animal" laws as evidence of the splendid mercy of Israel's God toward even the irrational creatures.

[58]This is often suggested (e.g., A. Deissmann, *Paul: A Study in Social and Religious History* [ET, New York, 1957], pp. 102-03; Moffatt, 117), though usually expressed in terms of the "literal" meaning of the OT text, which is already a loaded hermeneutical judgment.

[59]This is also a frequent suggestion. See, e.g., R. N. Longenecker, *Biblical Exegesis in the Apostolic Period* (Grand Rapids, 1975), pp. 126-27; Hanson, *Studies,* p. 166; Ruef, 81; Conzelmann, 155. To call this allegory is to push that term beyond its recognizable boundaries. The OT text was chosen because in its original setting it meant precisely what Paul is arguing for here, that the "worker" should reap material benefit from his labor. The meaning of the text is not allegorized; rather, it is given a new application.

that he is arguing from the "lesser to the greater."[60] To understand Paul's use of Scripture here, three things need to be noted: (1) Paul is not trying to make a statement about the OT text per se. The first part of the question exists strictly to set up the second part: "or does it (the Law)[61] undoubtedly (assuredly, by all means)[62] speak for our benefit?" (2) In keeping with the entire ancient Near East Paul well understood the paradigmatic, analogical character of law. By their very nature the laws, which are limited in number, do not intend to touch all circumstances; hence they regularly function as paradigms for application in all sorts of human circumstances. It should be noted at this point that Paul does not speak to what the law *originally meant*, which tends to be our concern. He is concerned with what it *means*, that is, with its *application* to their present situation. There is a sense in which he clearly keeps the original intent; he simply changes the application.[63] (3) In addition Paul's whole view of the OT was conditioned by his new eschatological existence in Christ. In saying that God is not (now) concerned for the oxen but for us, Paul reflects the same eschatological view of the OT expressed in 10:11, that Scripture ultimately exists for those upon whom the end of the ages has come. That is not so much a denial of concern for animals as it is a recognition that even the Law's concern for the oxen was a way of teaching Israel of God's mercy toward all. And because "we" stand at the end of the ages, toward which and for whom all former things were pointing, Paul argues, "Surely it says this for us, doesn't it?"

Paul's own concern is found in the elaboration of the second part of the rhetorical question: "Yes,[64] this was written for us, because when the plowman plows and the thresher threshes, they ought to do so in the hope[65]

---

[60]This is also frequently suggested (e.g., O-W, 241), but Paul himself does not make this kind of application.

[61]Although no subject is expressed in the sentence, Paul is most likely referring to the Law, not to God, since the same subject is assumed for the verb ἐγράφη ("it was written") in the succeeding sentence; and ὁ νόμος is the subject of λέγει in v. 8b (cf. NEB, Montgomery).

[62]That this is the intent of πάντως is supported not only by the context but by Paul's usage elsewhere. See the discussions in Ellis, *Use,* p. 47, and Longenecker, *Exegesis,* p. 126.

[63]Cf. Kaiser, "Crisis," who uses the paradigm from E. D. Hirsch (meaning and significance) to make this same point. But one is less certain about Kaiser's conclusion as to its "meaning" in the OT passage (following Godet, he suggests it already refers to humans, as well as to oxen, in Deuteronomy; cf. Grosheide, 205). That is an unnecessary expedient in an attempt to salvage the apostle.

[64]This translates (properly) Paul's γάρ; see BDF 452. It is used here to affirm what is asked in the final part of the rhetorical question (= "to be sure").

[65]This phrase is in the emphatic position in the first instance; it appears again in the second clause about the one who threshes. Thus it is the emphatic phrase in the sentence. "In hope" the one plows; and "in hope" the other threshes.

of sharing[66] in the harvest"[67]; that is, they should fully expect to share in the material benefits of their labors. Paul thus applies the analogy of the threshing ox to yet another analogy from farming, both of which together make the point that he has the right to their material support.[68]

11-12a In "his best sermonic style"[69] Paul now picks up the themes from the preceding analogy and applies them specifically to the present argument. He has "sown spiritual seed" among them;[70] it should be "no big thing,"[71] therefore, for him "to reap a material harvest" from them. If "others" have so benefited from them, should not he have that right as well? The language "spiritual" and "material"[72] is the same as that in Rom. 15:27, where he speaks in a similarly reciprocal way of the coming of the gospel to the Gentiles as "spiritual blessings" and their collection for the poor in Jerusalem as "material blessings." His work in Corinth had been that of "sowing" the gospel, which meant for them the "reaping" of the things that have to do with the Spirit. Is it too much that this should now work in reverse, that they should benefit him materially? This application, especially with the use of "is it too much" to begin the apodosis, makes it clear that Paul is contending with them, not simply setting himself forth as an example for them to follow. This becomes even more clear in the next sentence.

The final question (v. 12a) in this long rhetorical argument puts everything into focus. "Others" have been receiving the kind of patronage that Paul is arguing for as his own "right." At this distance we cannot be sure who is intended by these "others." Although it may refer to the "numberless guardians" of 4:15 or the "others" of 9:2, most likely it refers to Apollos and

---

[66]This does not mean that they hope to share together in the harvest, but that each labors "in hope" that he will enjoy a share of the produce.

[67]This is a good attempt to translate a clause that is somewhat difficult because Paul's original sentence (see n. 7 above) is elliptical. One must supply a second ὀφείλει and the infinitive of ἀλοάω to complete Paul's sense.

[68]Some have argued that because of its somewhat poetic style, this final clause is actually a citation of some unknown (perhaps apocryphal) source (cf. Weiss, 237; Lietzmann, 41; Conzelmann, 155). Thus the γὰρ ἐγράφη is understood to introduce the quotation "it is written." But that will not work. Nowhere else does Paul use the aorist passive as an introductory formula to a quotation. The verb refers back to the cited passage in v. 9 and the γάρ has a causal or explanatory sense (cf. Dungan, 11: "Clearly this was written for our sakes *to show that* the plowman, etc.").

[69]Dungan, 11.

[70]One should not miss the strongly personal nature of this application. Note the repeated ὑμῖν, ὑμῶν, ὑμῶν.

[71]Gk. μέγα (NIV, "is it too much," i.e., is it something extraordinary that we should expect this?).

[72]Gk. τὰ πνευματικά and τὰ σαρκικά; they are obviously being used in a different way than in 3:1.

Peter. It seems likely that their accepting material benefits from the Corinthians is what has put Paul on the defensive. On this matter his own failure to accept patronage has made it appear as if he did not have the right to such. So now, on the basis of the preceding analogies, and especially the application of the farming analogy in v. 11, he turns this around on them. If others (= "those reaping"?) have such rights, my having sown the gospel among you only means that "I have them all the more."

The language of this sentence is especially telling. Literally Paul says, "If others share your *authority*, should not rather we?" The verb "share" echoes the harvest metaphor at the conclusion of v. 10;[73] what they have a share in is *exousia,* "authority," or in this context, "rights" (as in vv. 4-6). What is not clear is the nuance of the pronoun "your." Although this may well be a subjective genitive (= "share in the rights you bestow"),[74] it is more likely objective[75] (= "share in rights over you," i.e., "reap the benefits of the rights that are theirs by virtue of their ministry among you"). "Rights" is what the argument is all about, namely "rights" to material support, which are his by virtue of his apostleship. Thus, if others have actually had a share in those benefits, how much more do I have such rights, even if I have never made use of them.

12b With a series of "not/but" contrasts,[76] Paul begins to explain why he "did not use[77] this right *(exousia)*" as "others" had. The fuller explanation will be given in vv. 15-18; but before he gets to that, he will offer yet two more illustrations of the fact of his rights (vv. 13-14).

The explanation here is that rather than "use this right, on the contrary, we put up[78] with anything rather than hinder the gospel of Christ." In saying this Paul indicates both that this was a conscious choice on his part and that it was something that brought a certain amount of hardship. As

---

[73]This unfortunately gets lost in the NIV.

[74]This is the position of R-P, 185-86.

[75]This is affirmed by most interpreters with much more confidence than the evidence warrants. What finally seems to tip the scales is the word order. Elsewhere when Paul uses the possessive, or subjective genitive, with ἐξουσία it follows the noun (cf. 8:9); the enclosed genitive (as here) suggests a slightly different relationship to ἐξουσία.

[76]Gk. οὐ . . . ἀλλά. The sentence begins with an ἀλλ', which sets the clause in contrast to the apodosis of the preceding sentence; the second contrast is within the new sentence itself. Thus (formally): "Should we *not* all the more share in the right of support from you? *But* we did *not* make use of this right, *but* we put up with anything, etc."

[77]Gk. ἐχρησάμεθα (cf. 7:21, 31); the aorist here probably refers to his former stay in Corinth. The perfect occurs in v. 15, implying that even now as he writes this is still his stance.

[78]Gk. στέγω (cf. 13:7; 1 Thess. 3:1, 5). This is not Paul's ordinary word for "endure"; here it seems not to mean "endure sufferings," but to put up with the kinds of hardships that working with one's own hands and evangelizing at the same time would bring on (cf. 4:11-13, where the hungering, etc., may have been related to having to work for his own sustenance). Cf. W. Kasch, *TDNT* VII, 585-87.

noted earlier, this began as early as the mission to Thessalonica, where he refers to laboring with his own hands as something he did "night and day" so as not to burden anyone (1 Thess. 2:9-10; 2 Thess. 3:8).

The reason for this choice is expressed in terms of not causing any hindrance[79] to "the gospel of Christ,"[80] which for Paul would mean not to obstruct evangelizing in any way. Paul is a man of a single passion, "the gospel of Christ." As he will explain in vv. 19-23, everything he is and does is "for the sake of the gospel." When it becomes a choice, therefore, between his "rights" and others' hearing of the gospel, there is no choice at all; anything that would get in the way of someone's hearing the gospel for what it is, the good news of God's pardoning grace, can be easily laid aside.

There has been considerable speculation over what Paul might have had in mind as to the "hindrance."[81] Although he does not specify here, the clue lies in the explanation in vv. 15-18, which this sentence anticipates. By preaching the gospel "freely," that is, without accepting "pay," he is able further to illustrate the "free" nature of the gospel. Almost certainly this stands over against the itinerant philosophers and missionaries, who "peddled" their "wisdom" or religious instruction (cf. 2 Cor. 2:17; 1 Thess. 2:5-10). At the same time, since this protest is inserted here (vv. 13-14 make it clear that the argument is not yet finished), right after mentioning "others" who obviously did *not* follow this practice, Paul most likely intended this to be in contrast to them as well—all the more so if some of these "others" are the opponents of 2 Cor. 11:20, although this is less than certain.

13 But the argument is not over. Either the preceding sentence is an intentional interruption, or else having begun to explain why he gave up those rights, Paul suddenly remembers that there are further illustrations that even more strongly support the argument. In either case, he proceeds to adduce two more reasons—the most telling yet—why he has rights to their support. Up to now the argument, even the one from Scripture, has proceeded on the basis of analogies—the soldier, vinedresser, shepherd, thresh-

[79]Gk. ἵνα μή τινα ἐγκοπὴν δῶμεν (lit. "lest we give any kind of hindrance to"). This is the only occurrence of ἐγκοπή in the NT. The cognate verb occurs three times in Paul (1 Thess. 2:18, "Satan hindered us"; Gal. 5:7; Rom. 15:22).

[80]A phrase that appears elsewhere in Paul in 1 Thess. 3:2; 2 Cor. 2:12; 9:13; 10:14; Gal. 1:7; Rom. 15:19; and Phil. 1:27, always in reference to preaching the gospel to non-Christians, especially Gentiles.

[81]In 1 Thess. 2:9 and 2 Thess. 3:8 he speaks of "not burdening" any of them; but the sarcasm of the similar expression in 2 Cor. 12:13 suggests that it was otherwise with regard to his relationship to this church (cf. n. 18 above). Dungan, 14-15, after reviewing some of the alternatives, suggests that it should be understood in light of 8:9-12, where the Corinthians' actions were an offense, and therefore a sin against a brother. Thus Paul has determined "not to injure" the Corinthians (p. 16). Against this is the language of the passage ("hinder the gospel of Christ"), which, as vv. 19-23 make clear, refers to evangelizing, not relationships with fellow Christians.

411

ing ox, plowman/thresher, and sower/reaper. All of these labor in hope of receiving a share in the benefit of their labor. Before referring to a word from the Lord that speaks directly to this situation (v. 14), Paul has one more analogy, but this time from a very comparable situation—the various ministrants in the temples.

The argument begins with another "Do you not know that?" (cf. 3:16). In this case we can be sure that "they knew that." Both in Jewish and pagan temples (so it matters little as to the background here[82]) the priests who served in making the sacrifices shared in the sacrificial food itself.[83] What makes this analogy pertinent, of course, is that the larger context of this argument is precisely this one, where "those who are employed in the sacred rites[84] get their food from the temple,[85] and[86] those who serve[87] at the altar[88] share in what is offered on the altar." Thus with this analogy Paul is pressing the argument close to home.

14 Finally, on the basis of the preceding analogy ("in the same way"[89]), Paul clinches the argument[90] with a word from the Jesus tradition (cf. 7:10, 25): "The Lord has commanded that those who preach the gos-

---

[82]Dungan, 16-17, insists that the background is Jewish and reflects Qumran motifs; but that cannot be proved, and it quite misses the larger context of the present argument. Undoubtedly Paul speaks out of his own background, but the Corinthians will just as surely hear in terms of theirs.

[83]For Jewish practice see Lev. 6:16-18, 26-28; 7:6, 8-10, 28-36; Num. 18:8-19; for Greco-Roman religions see Willis, 15-17, and the references there.

[84]This seems to be a little more precise for οἱ τὰ ἱερὰ ἐργαζόμενοι than the NIV's "those who work in the temple." Most likely the use of ἐργάζομαι here is intended to recall v. 6.

[85]For the textual question see n. 8 above. Most likely the text reads without τά. If so, then the ἐκ τοῦ ἱεροῦ does not so much mean "from the temple" as "by means of the temple." This is more precisely the analogy for which Paul is arguing and is exactly how he says it in v. 14. For this use of ἐκ see BAGD 3g ("source") or Robertson (*Grammar*, p. 598; "cause" or "occasion").

[86]There is no καί in the Greek text. It is possible, indeed the absence of καί suggests probable, that Paul is not thinking of two kinds of ministrants here, as the NIV implies (cf. Findlay, 850), but that the second clause "repeats the first half in a more definite form" (R-P, 187).

[87]Gk. παρεδρεύω, a NT hapax legomenon. Nor is it an LXX word. It is found in several pagan authors in cultic contexts, referring to doing the work of a priest. See BAGD.

[88]As Robertson (*Grammar*, p. 521) suggests, this is an example of a "pure locative."

[89]Gk. οὕτως καί (cf. 2:11; 11:12; 12:12; 14:9, 12; 15:22, 42).

[90]One should probably not make too much of it one way or the other that Paul *concludes* the argument with a word from the Lord (see the discussion in Dungan, 17-21), especially since one cannot be certain whether vv. 13-14 were in mind at the beginning of the argument (less likely, it would seem), or whether they function as something of an afterthought. The one thing that is certain is that all the prior examples are analogies pure and simple, from which Paul extracts a principle. Here the example is precise, and the "command" a word related directly to his and their situation.

pel[91] should receive their living from the gospel." Paul is here referring to the saying of Jesus that appears in Luke 10:7[92] ("the worker deserves his wages"; cf. Matt. 10:10), spoken originally in the context of his sending out the 72 (the 12 in Matthew's Gospel).[93] But as Matthew's context makes clear, it soon became a word in the church for the larger context of those who were to become the missionaries of the kingdom.[94] Jesus' word itself is not a "command" but a proverb,[95] applied by Jesus to his telling the 72 that they are to eat and drink whatever is given to them. But for Paul such a word of Jesus may be described as a "command" because it has that net effect in the tradition.[96] Whether or not it was previously known in Corinth cannot be known,[97] although the casual way in which Paul introduces it may suggest as much. In any case, for Paul this brings the long argument for his "rights" to their support to its direct and convincing conclusion.

One may properly experience a strange ambivalence toward this text. On the one hand, it serves as one of the key passages that make it clear

[91]This is one of the rare instances where instead of the verb εὐαγγελίζομαι, which itself means "preach the gospel," Paul uses another verb (in this case καταγγέλλω), with the noun εὐαγγέλιον as the object (cf. 1 Thess. 2:9). The reason for this usage here arises out of the second clause, where the noun "gospel" appears again, as the intended source of the missionaries' support.

[92]This version is cited in a similar context in 1 Tim. 5:18.

[93]Since Paul does not actually cite a saying of Jesus here, Dungan, 40-75, takes the entire "mission instructions" of Luke 10:1-12 and its parallels as the "command." He may be right, but the concern here is strictly with their "living by the gospel," which can be narrowed to vv. 4 and 7-8.

[94]As Dungan points out, 42-48, this is also true in Luke's version, although his redaction is more subtle and involves changes and additions in the block itself. In Matthew's Gospel the larger context becomes especially clear in the collection and arrangement of sayings that follow in 10:16-42.

[95]See the discussion in Harvey, "Workman," pp. 209-21.

[96]Dungan, 3-40, makes it a considerable part of his thesis that Paul "set aside" (p. 20), or deliberately disobeyed (p. 3), an explicit command of the Lord. But this is to make far too much of Paul's use of the verb "command" (despite Dungan's remonstrance to the contrary, p. 20 n. 3). Paul certainly did not consider himself to be doing so. It is extremely doubtful that the Corinthians saw him doing such, as Dungan himself admits (p. 39). Since that is so, he can hardly be charged with the kind of duplicity of which Dungan everywhere accuses him. The answer, of course, lies with the nature of the argument itself. In vv. 3-14 he is first of all defending his right to such support, for which analogies of various kinds, as well as Scripture and the "command" of the Lord, all play their part. As "command" the word of Jesus referred to here does not have to do with *his* (Paul's) action but *theirs* (cf. Godet, 23). The command is not given *to* the missionaries, but *for* their benefit. His explanation of his own action, therefore, is not a relativizing of Jesus' command—that would be foreign to Paul's own view—but reflects his own attitude toward his rights and has nothing to do with what the Corinthians should have done.

[97]Dungan, 27, makes a considerable point that the saying was well known to the Corinthians; but that simply cannot be known.

that those who give themselves to the "work of the ministry" are deserving of material support. The whole reason for the argument is to assert that his giving up of these rights does not mean that he is not entitled to them. In a day like ours such rights usually mean a salary and "benefits." On the other hand, the reason he feels compelled to make this kind of defense is that he has given up these rights. Contemporary ministers seldom feel compelled so to argue! The key to everything must be for us what it was for Paul—"no hindrance to the gospel." For every valid ministry in the church of Jesus Christ this must be the bottom line. All too often, one fears, the objective of this text is lost in concerns over "rights" that reflect bald professionalism rather than a concern for the gospel itself.

c. Paul's apostolic restraint (9:15-18)

15 *But I have not used any of these rights. And I am not writing this in the hope that you will do such things for me. I would rather die than have anyone deprive[1] me of this boast.* 16 *Yet when I preach the gospel, I cannot boast,[2] for I am compelled to preach. Woe to me if I do not preach[3] the gospel!* 17 *If I preach voluntarily, I have a reward; if not voluntarily, I am simply discharging the trust committed to me.* 18 *What then is my reward? Just this: that in preaching the gospel I may offer it[4] free of charge, and so not make use of any of my rights in preaching it.*

One is somewhat taken aback that Paul, having so vigorously defended his rights to their support, now argues with similar emotion for his "right" to give it up. Yet the full context indicates that this indeed has been the point right along.[5] The argument itself is one of the more complex in Paul's letters. His overall concern seems clear enough: to explain, in terms of his own unique relationship to the gospel, why he has deliberately not accepted their patronage. But the expression of that concern, both as to how this is his "boast" and how vv. 16-18 serve as grounds for that boast, is less clear.

[1]For the variants here—all attempts to clear up the grammar caused by Paul's breaking off his sentence—see Metzger, 558-59.

[2]A few MSS (א* D* F G; Ambst) substitute χάρις for Paul's undoubtedly original καύχημα.

[3]For the variation between the present and aorist, and the subtle difference the latter makes, see Zuntz, 110.

[4]For the sake of good English the NIV has translated the noun εὐαγγέλιον by the pronoun "it." The Western and Byzantine traditions add τοῦ Χριστοῦ (from v. 12?).

[5]See the introduction to chap. 9 above. In an otherwise helpful study of this passage, E. Käsemann suggests that these verses are a digression ("A Pauline Version of the 'Amor Fati,'" in *New Testament Questions of Today* [ET, Philadelphia, 1969], pp. 217-35, esp. 218). But that is because he rejects either a polemical or an apologetic understanding of chap. 9 as a whole (p. 231).

After repeating from v. 12b that he not only has not used the rights argued for in vv. 3-14, but that he is not now writing in order to secure them (v. 15ab), Paul begins the "explanation" with a surprisingly strong, but unfinished, insistence that he would rather die than. . . , which is broken off by the equally strong assertion that "no one shall nullify my boast" (v. 15c). What follows is a series of sentences that begin with "for,"[6] each explaining or elaborating the former, but also seeming to take the argument astray somewhat. First, he explains what his boast does not consist of—preaching the gospel per se (v. 16a). This is followed by two sentences that explain why evangelizing cannot be his boast; he is under divine compulsion to proclaim the good news (v. 16). But with that he adds a new wrinkle: Since he is under "compulsion," he cannot receive "pay," for "pay" implies voluntary labor. His labor has been "involuntary" in the sense of v. 16, that divine destiny has prescribed his task—he is a "slave" entrusted with a charge (v. 17).[7] What "pay," then, can he expect? With what seems to be something of a wordplay he answers that his "pay" is found in presenting the gospel "without pay" (v. 18a). The final reason for all this echoes the beginning of the paragraph, but with a slight change in verbs, implying that the "use" of his right (*exousia;* v. 12b) in this case would be a "misuse" of his authority (*exousia;* v. 18b).

Although one has the feeling that the argument got away from him a bit, nonetheless the explanations of vv. 16-17 probably help as much as anything in his letters to understand what made Paul tick. Indeed, it would be unfortunate if in the convolutions of the argument one were to miss the fact that his renunciation of his "rights" to material support is attributable to his singular passion for the gospel.[8] Everything is done so as not to hinder the gospel (v. 12b), so as not to misuse his authority in the gospel (v. 18). By presenting the gospel "free of charge" he is himself thereby "free *from* all people"; no one except Christ has a claim on him (v. 19). Although he does not expressly say so here, his presenting the gospel "free of charge" also becomes a lived out paradigm of the gospel itself.

In all of this one must not lose sight of the larger argument. The Corinthians are rejecting his prohibition against going to the pagan temples, contesting his right to do so by his failure to accept patronage. He has the right to such patronage, he has argued, as even the Lord had commanded.

---

[6]Beginning with v. 15c there are five consecutive γάρ's, which are unfortunately modified by the NIV.

[7]Cf. J. D. M. Derrett, *Jesus's Audience* (New York, 1973), pp. 167-74 (Appendix One: "Cultural Ignorance: St. Paul's Boast of Disinterestedness").

[8]See C. Maurer, "Grund und Grenze apostolischer Freiheit," in *Antwort: K. Barth zum siebsigsten Geburtstag* (Zürich, 1956), pp. 636-37, who has especially emphasized this point.

His restraint with regard to that right is not to be understood as not having it, but as related to his own calling. That calling is so interwoven with the gospel itself that he can do nothing that might hinder it, including accepting patronage.

15 Paul now returns to what he began to explain in v. 12b. The argument of vv. 3-14, despite its vigorous, confrontational nature, is not to be understood as an attempt to secure material support; rather, it is a "defense" of his rights to that support, a defense forced upon him by their denial of his apostolic "authority." "But,"[9] he now repeats, even though he has the authority, "I[10] have not used[11] any of these rights."[12] To make sure that this is clearly understood, he adds the further demurrer, "Furthermore, I am not writing[13] this in the hope that you will do such things for[14] me." That is, he is not writing this defense so that they will now begin to do for him what they have been doing in the case of "others" (v. 12).

So strongly does Paul feel about his need to exercise restraint in this matter that his initial response to the idea that someone might think he is here

---

[9]Gk. δέ, which is clearly adversative here (cf. ἀλλ᾽ in v. 12b, which in that case was in an οὐ/ἀλλά contrast).

[10]With this ἐγώ, which stands in the emphatic first position, Paul returns to the first person singular, which he had abandoned in favor of the plural beginning at v. 4 (except for v. 8). The change to the singular in this sentence that is otherwise basically resumptive of v. 12b indicates that vv. 4-14 were about himself personally (cf. n. 28 on v. 4); at the same time the change is especially appropriate because from here on he speaks only for himself and not for his associates or others.

[11]The verb is now in the perfect (cf. n. 77 on v. 12b). Dungan, 22-23, 28-29, 36-40, insists that because Paul did accept gifts from the Philippians (Phil. 4:14-20) he is less than honest here. But that quite misses the nature of the Philippian relationship to Paul. They did not put him on salary, as Dungan suggests, but simply sent him gifts from time to time. That is a far cry from patronage. It is clear from 1 Thess. 2:9; 2 Thess. 3:8; 1 Cor. 4:12; and Acts 18:3 that Paul's material support came from his own hands, not from Philippi. Cf. the critique of Dungan in Hock, *Social Context*, p. 50 and n. 1 (p. 92).

[12]Gk. οὐδενὶ τούτων (lit. "one of these"). Dungan, p. 21 n. 2, translates "I have not used any of these *reasons, arguments*, nor did I write them . . . etc." He argues that the plural τούτων cannot refer to "rights" as such, which is a singular concern, and thus that the first two sentences are formally parallel. But that is unlikely. Paul is repeating the idea of v. 12b, which has to do with *making use of* his ἐξουσία (cf. v. 18), not with using the preceding analogies. The following sentence is not the second member of a synonymous parallelism (τούτων and ταῦτα do not refer to the same thing); it is the further explanation that he is not by this letter trying now to secure what formerly he abstained from. The plural is to be explained on the basis of vv. 4-6, which are the "rights" being contended for even if they are variations on the single concern of his right to their material support.

[13]Gk. ἔγραψα; an epistolary aorist (cf. on 5:11), as the NIV translates. It refers to vv. 3-14, which is past tense from the point of view of the recipients, but present from the point of view of the writer.

[14]Gk. ἐν ἐμοί (lit. "in me"), meaning "in order that *thus* (= what has been argued for in vv. 4-14) it might happen *in my case* (or, with me)." For this usage see Robertson, *Grammar*, p. 587.

trying to secure his rights is to remonstrate, (lit.) "For it is good for me rather to die than. . . ."[15] But with that his sentence breaks off;[16] and it is not certain how he might have intended to finish it—or whether he intended to at all, since the broken clause has power in its own right. He probably did not intend, as some have suggested, that it would be better to die from the kinds of hardships working for his own living imposed on him (cf. 4:11-13) than to accept material support from the Corinthians. Most likely the interrupting sentence is the direction he really wants the explanation to go.

As an apostle he has the "authority" to apostolic "rights." But to have assumed those rights would have meant to put a hindrance in the way of his proclaiming the gospel (v. 12b). Thus he asserts, "no one shall nullify[17] my boast!" But what can that mean, especially in a context in which he is explaining why he has given up his apostolic rights to support? The answer to this is not easy since what follows is an explanation of what his boast is *not*, which is followed by a further explanation that no longer pursues the theme of "boasting" as such. Probably he is indeed referring to his not accepting patronage;[18] but that is to be understood in light of v. 12b (not hindering the gospel in any way) and v. 18 ("that in preaching the gospel I may offer it free of charge"),[19] not in contrast to "others" who accept patronage.[20] That is, Paul is not "boasting" in what he does in contrast to what others have done, but in an indirect way in the gospel itself.[21]

"Boasting" is a particularly Pauline word in the NT.[22] Most often it is a pejorative term (cf. 1:29; 5:6). When Paul uses it positively, his "boast" is ordinarily in things that stand in contradiction to human "boasting" (Christ crucified, weaknesses, sufferings; cf. 1:30-31; 2 Cor. 10–12; Gal. 6:14). The paradox of his boasting in his apostleship is related to this reality:

---

[15]This does not seem to be quite the same thing as the NIV's "I would rather die than. . . ." This is not so much a matter of personal feelings as such as it is a concern for the gospel. It would be better if he were dead than that the gospel were hindered in some way by what he had done.

[16]This is called aposiopesis, a sudden interruption of thought in the middle of a sentence (cf. Gal. 2:6). For its significance in expressing Paul's deep emotion here, see Omanson, "Comments," pp. 136-38.

[17]Gk. κενώσει (= "to make empty").

[18]This is implied in the NIV's "deprive me of *this* boast," which seems to narrow Paul's concern too much.

[19]Cf. Dungan, 23 n. 1.

[20]This is commonly suggested, but the point is moot. If Paul had intended a contrast with the "others" of v. 12, he has not hinted at such in *this* paragraph.

[21]Derrett (*Jesus's Audience*) argues that "boast" here has to do with the Eastern notion of "prestige," which is "upheld by giving much and taking little, and he who takes least is the most prestige-worthy" (p. 167). Such an understanding may have operated in Paul's case, but that is not what *boast* refers to here since that term is conditioned by its meaning elsewhere in 1 and 2 Corinthians.

[22]See n. 28 on 1:29.

God has called him and his churches into being; therefore, he may "boast" in what God does, even through Paul's own weaknesses. Almost certainly this present "boast" is to be understood in these terms. Thus his preaching the gospel without pay is both a calculated decision so as not to hinder the gospel and an expression of his apostolic "weakness."

16 Both the "for"[23] with which this sentence begins and its content suggest that Paul now intends to explain the final clause in v. 15, "no one shall nullify my boast." The explanation itself is given in negative terms— what his boast does not consist of. The content of the explanation, "preaching the gospel," supports the interpretation that Paul's "boast" has to do with the gospel, most likely in activity that does not hinder it. "No one shall nullify my boast," he has asserted, that is, "preaching the gospel without taking 'pay,' without putting a hindrance in its way." Now he must explain: "For if I preach the gospel, which I do all the time,[24] that in itself is no grounds for boasting—at least not for me." In the next two sentences Paul proceeds to explain how this is so.[25]

First, he says, "I am under compulsion"[26] (not "I am compelled to preach," which sounds altogether too much like a Protestant minister with "preacher's itch"). As Käsemann has pointed out, this is not to be understood psychologically, as some "inner compulsion" resulting from his call or from his sense of being "driven" because he was formerly a persecutor.[27] The word "compulsion" here most likely refers to his divine destiny.[28] To preach the gospel of Christ is *not something he chose to do,* which is quite the point of v. 17; it is *something he must do.* God had ordained such a destiny for him from birth and had revealed it to him in the event of the Damascus road (Gal. 1:15-16).[29] From that time on, proclaiming Christ to the Gentiles was both his calling and his compulsion. He "had to" do it because God had so taken hold of him (cf. Phil. 3:12). So much is this so that "Woe to me if I

---

[23]Gk. γάρ; the NIV's "yet" is grammatically unjustifiable.

[24]This paraphrase is an attempt to capture the nature of the present general condition. Preaching the gospel is Paul's regular activity. But doing so in itself offers him no grounds for the "boast" that no one can nullify.

[25]Although both sentences begin with γάρ, the second γάρ elaborates the first, so that both together offer the explanation.

[26]Gk. ἀνάγκη μοι ἐπίκειται ("necessity constrains me"). For ἀνάγκη see on 7:26 and 37.

[27]See "Pauline Version," pp. 228-29, and especially the several variations on the psychological theme noted there.

[28]Although Käsemann ("Pauline Version," p. 229) has shown that the language of this text has close affinities with some pagan parallels, he has also pointed out that in Paul its meaning differs radically. For Paul "necessity" or "destiny" is not some kind of fate to which he must yield; it is divine gift as well as obligation, and leads to freedom and joy, not heaviness.

[29]Cf. in this regard the "call" and divine "necessity" that some of the prophets experienced, especially Amos (3:8; 7:14-15) and Jeremiah (1:4-10; 20:7-9).

do not preach the gospel!" Again, "woe is me" is not to be understood in terms of common parlance, as if he would experience some kind of inner distress if he were to fail to preach.[30] Since this is his divinely appointed destiny, he thereby would stand under divine judgment if he were to fail to fulfill that destiny. His point is a simple one, and it has nothing to do with "inner compulsion." He cannot boast in the task of proclaiming the good news of Christ to the Gentiles because that is what he must do by divine design.

17 What one expects next in this argument is an explanation of what Paul's boast *does* consist of, since it does *not* consist of preaching the gospel as such. Instead we are given yet one more explanation,[31] this time of what has been asserted in v. 16 as to the "compulsory" nature of his task. With his own task clearly in view, he offers two alternatives about "working"—free person and slave—that prevail under ordinary circumstances. One might "perform this task[32] voluntarily," that is, as a free person; or "involuntarily," that is, as a slave.[33] If one is free and does it voluntarily, then one is entitled to "pay" or a "reward."[34] Despite some voices to the contrary who suggest that it reflects Paul's real situation,[35] this first sentence

---

[30]The verb is now aorist, in contrast to the present in the opening sentence. As Zuntz, 110, suggests, this implies, "if I were once not to preach."

[31]The sentence is joined to what precedes by the fifth consecutive explanatory γάρ. See n. 6 above.

[32]Gk. τοῦτο πράσσω (lit. "do this"), which clearly refers to the εὐαγγελίζωμαι ("preach the gospel") of v. 16; hence the NIV's "preach." But that also causes one to miss the metaphorical nature of this verse, which moves over to the broader category of "work" of any kind, with his own specific "task" as the primary exhibit.

[33]The contrast is clear in the Greek (ἑκών vs. ἄκων). That "free" and "slave" are most likely intended emerges in the metaphor in the second sentence, "entrusted with an οἰκονομίαν." Cf. Derrett, *Jesus's Audience*, pp. 169-71.

[34]Gk. μισθός (cf. on 3:8 and 14-15).

[35]This was a long-standing view among older exegetes, especially Roman Catholics, for whom it served as the basis for the doctrine of works of supererogation. See the considerable discussion in Käsemann, "Pauline Version," pp. 218-23. For more modern espousals of this position (that this is Paul's real situation), see *inter alia* Weiss, 241; Grosheide, 210; G. Didier, "La Salaire de Désintéressement (I Cor. ix,14-27)," *RSR* 43 (1955), 235; Reumann, "Οἰκονομία-Terms," p. 159; Hock, *Social Context*, p. 100 n. 113. This view sees Paul as saying in effect, "Even if I *must* preach because of divine compulsion, nonetheless if I now do it voluntarily I have a reward." The rest of the argument is then seen as dealing with "reward" as such. This view is based partly on the form of the conditional sentence (εἰ with the present indicative, which usually expresses a real condition). But that is not helpful in this case since the two clauses are in balanced contrast, the one setting up the other, which is the real condition. Two other matters speak against the view. First, the grammatical structure of the two sentences demands that the first (signaled by γάρ) be explanatory to v. 16, and the second (signaled by δέ) be in contrast to the first. That means, second, that the two sentences together further illustrate v. 16, which has to do with his task as one that "presses upon" him, not one that he has voluntarily taken up.

is intended merely to set up the opposite alternative, which in fact rules out any possibility of "reward" or "pay" in his case.[36] The word translated "reward" is intended to be understood metaphorically as "pay." Paul's point is the one with which he began in v. 16. He cannot boast in preaching the gospel because he does not do so of his own choosing. If he had done so by his own volition, then he is entitled to pay. But he has not done so, so what "pay" is there for him?[37]

That much seems certain; but less clear is how one is to punctuate the second clause. Did Paul intend, "If not voluntarily, I am simply discharging the trust committed to me. What then is my reward?" (NIV), or "If without choice of my own I have been entrusted with a charge, what then is my reward?"[38] Although both come out at nearly the same point, grammatical considerations favor the former.[39] His point is that if his labor is not voluntary, as v. 16 has made clear, then he is not entitled to pay. He makes that point with a metaphor previously used in 4:1. His apostleship is similar to that of a "steward" (usually a slave) who has been "entrusted with" managing a household. Such a person is entitled to no pay, which is exactly the point he will make in the next verse, and therefore is the reason for these two sentences.

18 The argument has gone afield a bit, but with this question, which follows directly from the argument of v. 17, Paul begins to pull the loose threads together. "What then is my reward?" he asks of one who is entitled to no reward. Since his apostolic ministry is his by divine appointment, given to him quite apart from his own choosing, his "pay" in such circumstances is to do something that was not imposed on him, namely "that in preaching the gospel I may offer it free of charge."[40] In one sense his "pay" is in fact to receive "no pay"![41] But in the present argument this nonpayment "payment" also gives him his apostolic "freedom" from all, so that he might the more freely make himself a slave to everyone (v. 19). Thus

---

[36]Along with the answer in v. 18 that his pay is to receive no pay, this set of questions makes quite irrelevant a considerable literature on this text as to the nature of Paul's expected "pay," whether it be eschatological or present. It is obviously neither.

[37]As Käsemann nicely puts it, "One can demand no reward from *ananke*, one can only bow to it or rebel against it" ("Pauline Version," p. 231).

[38]The translation is Barrett's; cf. Bachmann, 320; Munck, *Paul*, p. 22; Reumann, "Οἰχονομία-Terms," p. 159.

[39]The problem lies with the combination εἰ . . . οὖν, which is found nowhere else in Paul. He tends to use the combination εἰ . . . ἄρα for this idiom (cf. 15:14; Gal. 2:21; 3:29; 5:11).

[40]This answer is a clear indication that the question in v. 17a does not reflect his actual situation.

[41]Dungan, 23, suggests that this is a joke; at least it is a play on words.

in terms of his own ministry, his "pay" turns out to be his total freedom from all merely human impositions on his ministry.

At the same time, however, the way the argument is structured implies that his "pay" and his "boast" refer to the same reality, preaching the gospel without accepting support so as to put no hindrance before the gospel.[42] Thus his "reward," as his "boast," is to be found in the "weakness" of working with his own hands so as not to hinder the forward progress of the gospel. In offering the "free" gospel "free of charge" his own ministry becomes a living paradigm of the gospel itself. That seems to be the point of the final result clause, translated in the NIV as, "and so not make use of my rights in the gospel[43]." But that translation makes the argument unnecessarily tautologous[44] and borders on meaninglessness. In fact Paul has here used the intensive form of the verb, which may mean "make full use of," but which in this context most likely has the negative connotation of "abuse" or "misuse."[45] His point is that he offers the gospel "free of charge" so that he will not "misuse his authority *(exousia)* in the gospel" by "making use of his right *(exousia)* to live by the gospel" (vv. 12b and 14). Thus this repeats in its own way Paul's reason for not accepting the material support of his Corinthian friends first expressed in v. 12b. He refuses to do anything that may hinder the gospel. He is an apostle, he has argued in vv. 1-2; therefore he has the "authority/right" to their support, he has further argued in vv. 4-14. But for the sake of the gospel he has not "used" that right (vv. 12b and 15). This is his boast and reward, to make the "free" gospel "free of charge"; and he does so, he concludes, so that he will not "misuse" what is rightfully his in the gospel.

The argument has thus come full circle. They have viewed his re-

---

[42]Cf. Moffatt, 121; Käsemann, "Pauline Version," pp. 231-32; Dungan, 24 n. 1 (from p. 23). This interpretation stands over against all those that would see his reward in terms of his own inner satisfaction over his "unselfish renunciation," which is so often suggested of this text (e.g., H. Preisker, *TDNT* IV, 699; Grosheide, 211). Cf. the discussion in Käsemann, pp. 223-25, of the many who take this stance.

[43]The NIV quite gratuitously translates the final ἐν τῷ εὐαγγελίῳ as "in preaching it." That is not quite Paul's point. His authority comes from the gospel itself, not from his preaching it.

[44]That is, "I did not accept support so that my 'reward' will be that I did not accept support and thereby not make use of my authority in the gospel." The problem is not so much tautology itself (v. 17b seems to border on such), but that the change of verbs indicates that Paul himself did not intend such.

[45]Although this view is often rejected in the commentators, as well as by Käsemann ("Pauline Version," p. 218 n. 5), it is difficult to understand why Paul would have used the stronger construction if he intended nothing by it (so Weiss, 200; cf. Dungan, 24 n. 1; Doughty, "Presence," p. 71 n. 47). The difference may be slight, but the usage in 7:31 indicates that it is real.

straint in making use of his apostolic *exousia* to patronage as not having apostolic *exousia* at all. He does indeed have such *exousia*, he has argued, but for him use might be viewed as misuse. Thus he has refrained for the sake of the gospel. But this policy has also set him free from merely human restraints. He will now return to the theme of freedom (from v. 1) and explain how his nonuse of his rights enhances his freedom to be a servant of the gospel all the more.

Those who are quick to see vv. 4-14 as applicable to today's ministry would probably do well to spend some time with this paragraph as well, and ask in terms of their own ministries how their "use" of their rights might at the same time become a "misuse"—of such a kind that the gospel itself is not so clearly heard in our day. It would not seem to require a lot of imagination to think of several such misuses, even in the most innocent of circumstances. Then the question really does become one of "rights" over against the gospel. The question is not whether one *has* the rights, but whether that is important. Those who see their calling as "necessity laid upon them" should also be glad to readjust their lives for the sake of the gospel.

d. Paul's apostolic freedom (9:19-23)

19 *Though I am free and belong to no man, I made[1] myself a slave to everyone, to win as many as possible.* 20 *To the Jews I became like[2] a Jew, to win the Jews. To those under the law I became like one under the law (though I myself am not under the law[3]), so as to win those under the law.* 21 *To those not having the law I became like one not having the law (though I am not free from God's[4] law but am under Christ's law), so as to win those not having the law.* 22 *To the weak I became weak,[5] to win the weak. I have become all things to all people[6] so that by all possible means I might save some.[7]* 23 *I do all things[8] for the sake of the gospel, that I may share in its blessings.*

[1]NIV, "make," with no grammatical or contextual justification.

[2]A few scribes (F G* 6* 326 1739 pc), apparently feeling the dissonance of a Jew saying that he became *like* a Jew, omitted the ὡς.

[3]This clause is missing in the MajT (hence the KJV), most likely due to homoeoteleuton (cf. the ὑπὸ νόμον of the previous clause). See Metzger, 559; Zuntz, 140 n. 5.

[4]For both θεοῦ and the following Χριστοῦ the MajT reads the dative. This is the easier reading, and probably reflects the sense of the genitive (objective). See the commentary.

[5]In this instance Paul did not use ὡς, although it was added by some early scribes and became the MajT reading. The text is read by P46 ℵ* A B 1739 pc lat Cyp.

[6]NIV, "men."

[7]For Paul's πάντως τινάς the Western tradition (D F G latt), joined by 33 and Didymus, reads πάντας (= that I might save all people).

Paul's argument (v. 3) now broadens its scope considerably. After the extended defense of his rights, and his right to lay them aside, he now sets out to explain his apparently chameleonlike stance in matters of social relationships. In so doing he returns to the opening question of the section, "Am I not free?" (v. 1). Just as with his not accepting patronage, so here he has done all things "for the sake of the gospel" (v. 23), meaning for the sake of sharing the good news with others.

The argument is not difficult and can be easily traced.[9] V. 19, which introduces the new themes, flows directly from the immediately preceding argument, as an essential part of it. Since as Christ's slave (household manager) he cannot receive "pay" (vv. 17-18), he is thereby also "free" from all people (i.e., free from the restrictions that patronage might impose), so that he may "freely" become the "slave" of all. The outworking of this free slavery is then delineated under four categories (Jews, those under/ without the law, the weak), for each of whom Paul has been willing to accommodate himself "in order to win" them (vv. 20-22a). Thus he became "all things to all people so that by all possible means he might save some"

---

[8]In place of πάντα (P[46] ℵ A B C D E F G P 33 69 81 104 365 1175 1739 1881 al latt) later scribes substituted τοῦτο, which became the MajT reading. This narrows Paul's perspective considerably.

[9]The *structure* of the paragraph should be noted. Vv. 19-22 form a unit, for which v. 19 serves as the introduction and 22b as the conclusion. (For the possibility that this is an expression of chiasm, see N. W. Lund, *Chiasmus in the New Testament* [Chapel Hill, 1942], p. 147; if so, it is in form only, not in content, as Weiss, 244, observes.) The four groups illustrate v. 19 and the "all things to all people" of v. 22b. The two middle terms (about law) are qualified with a μὴ ὢν αὐτός ("not being myself"). All six sentences conclude with a ἵνα-clause, the first five with the verb κερδαίνω, the final, generalizing one with the more common synonym, σῴζω. V. 23 then serves as the double reason for all this: for the sake of the gospel; so that Paul might share in its blessings. Thus:

Intro.:   Being free from all, I became slave to all,
            in order to win the many.
1)   to the Jews, as a Jew
            in order to win Jews;
2)   to those under the law, as under the law
        (although not really myself under the law)
            in order to win those under law;
3)   to those not under the law, as not under the law
        (although not lawless)
            in order to win those not under law;
4)   to the weak,   weak
        in order to win the weak.
Concl : I have become all things to all people,
            in order by all means *to* save some.
Reason: I do all things   (1) for the sake of the gospel,
                            (2) *in order to* share its blessings.

(v. 22b). A final sentence (v. 23) puts everything into perspective: He does "all this for the sake of the gospel," that he "might share in its blessings."

The difficulty lies with the contextual question: How does this paragraph function in the present argument as well as in the larger issue of "food sacrificed to idols"? Related to this is the difficulty of identifying the four groups in vv. 20-22. Because of the final item, "to the weak I became weak," most scholars have seen the paragraph as returning to the issue of 8:13, where Paul is depicted as offering himself as an example of willing self-restraint for the sake of others.[10] Others, noting the affinities with vv. 15-18,[11] have seen it as a concluding word on the matter of his not taking material support.[12] That is, his real pay is his "freedom" to "gain" as many as possible for the sake of the gospel.

The solution to this question, however, would seem to lie elsewhere. The affinities with vv. 15-18 seem clear and unmistakable; nonetheless, there are very few parallels in the actual *content* of the two paragraphs. Vv. 15-18 deal with Paul's giving up his right to their material support, vv. 19-23 with his stance on questions of social relationships in various kinds of settings. Most likely, therefore, these affinities are related to v. 3: Paul is still defending his apostleship against those who are calling him into question.[13] He has just brought the one issue, his not accepting patronage, to a conclusion—although what is said in this paragraph will help even more to put that into perspective. But now he is concerned with what they view as conduct too "wishy-washy" for an apostle, and especially for an apostle who would deny them the "right" to attend the cultic meals with their pagan friends. Indeed, Paul's own conduct delineated here could well have been used against him.[14] Paul thus takes the occasion of this defense to explain his conduct, an explanation that rests solely on the cause of evangelism, not his right to do as he pleases.

If this is the proper understanding of the literary context, then the

---

[10]Almost all commentaries. See also Dungan, 25-26; Willis, "Apologia," pp. 36-38 (although in his view the paragraph does not deal with evangelism but with Paul's stance when among Christians). The major difficulty with this view of course, besides the fact that Paul does not himself suggest as much, is that the paragraph does *not* offer a model of *self-restraint,* but of something considerably different—abstinence or indulgence (v. 21 can hardly be understood otherwise), depending on the context!

[11]E.g., the free/slave motif in v. 19; everything for the sake of the gospel; the use of the verb κερδαίνω ("gain, profit") as reflecting his "pay"; and the final purpose clause, that he might share in its blessings.

[12]See esp. Hock, "Tentmaking," pp. 558-61; this is noted also by H. L. Ellison, "Paul and the Law—'All Things to All Men,'" in *Apostolic History and the Gospel, Biblical and Historical Essays presented to F. F. Bruce on his 60th Birthday* (ed. W. W. Gasque and R. P. Martin; Grand Rapids, 1970), pp. 195-202.

[13]Cf. Hurd, 127-31.

[14]So Chadwick, "'All Things,'" p. 263.

question still remains, What specific conduct of Paul's is here in view?[15] Although one cannot be certain, the clear affinities in language and concern between this passage and 10:23-33[16] suggest that the issue has to do in part at least with Paul's stance toward marketplace food. Because on this matter he considered himself free, he ate or did not eat, depending on the situation. In either case, he refused to make an issue of it on its own since he considered it a question of food only, not a matter of idolatry or principle. Given that this was such a "hot issue" elsewhere in the early church (Acts 15:29; Rev. 2:14, 20), one can well understand how Paul's own relaxed attitude toward it could have brought him to grief from several quarters.

19 With these words Paul now returns to the opening question, "Am I not free?" But he does so by way of the immediately preceding argument, where he had used the analogy of a household manager (often a trusted slave) as the reason he could not receive "pay" (vv. 17-18).[17] With an explanatory (or inferential) "for,"[18] he now argues that since he is thus "free and belongs to no man," he has paradoxically used that freedom to become "a slave to everyone." Because he is Christ's slave, he must work without pay; but working without pay also makes him free from any merely human restraints on his ministry, so that he might freely become other

---

[15]On the question of whom the four groups represent, see on vv. 20-22.

[16]Cf. Hurd, 128-30.

[17]The close ties between vv. 17-18 and v. 19 are often overlooked (see the following note). The beginning of v. 19 is so closely related to what precedes that Hock has argued that it concludes vv. 15-18 rather than begins vv. 20-23 (see "Tentmaking," pp. 558-61). Hock understands the phrase "I enslaved myself to all" to mean "by entering the workshop and plying a slavish trade he had made himself available to all people, rich and poor, more in any case than had he accepted support and stayed in a household. The personal loss of status in the eyes of others was worth the gain in converts" (p. 560). In this view vv. 20-22 function as additional illustrations of the length to which Paul was willing to go for the sake of the gospel. This is an attractive option; however, it is dependent on understanding the slavery metaphor as referring to his tentmaking, which attitude is completely lacking in the other passages about working with his own hands, especially those in which he is encouraging other believers to follow his example (e.g., 2 Thess. 3:6-10). Nor does Hock deal adequately with the still closer structural and linguistic ties the verse has with vv. 20-22.

[18]This is omitted in the NIV, as in most contemporary English translations (RSV, JB, NASB excepted)—and for good reason. The almost universal understanding of the participle ὤν as having a concessive relationship to the main verb ("*Though* I am free from all, I made myself a slave to all") makes the γάρ awkward. The γάρ (either as explanatory or inferential, the latter preferred by BAGD 3) implies that the participle must be taken more closely with v. 18, in which case it probably sustains a causal or more strictly circumstantial relationship to the main verb. Thus Paul has argued: "What pay can one like myself, who did not choose this position as God's household manager, expect? Only this: that I can make the gospel 'free of charge' to all so that I not misuse my rights in the gospel. *For* being thereby free from all people [in not accepting 'pay'], I can more freely become everyone's 'slave,' so that I might 'gain' the more."

people's slave as well. In saying that he is "free from all,"[19] therefore, Paul is not referring to inner freedom, nor to freedom from sin or the law. Rather, he primarily means "financially independent of all."[20] In this context that especially means that he is also "free" of those, such as the Corinthians, who would use such material support as a means of manipulating him and his ministry. Because he is Christ's slave, he "belongs to no man"; he is owned by no others.

On the other hand, "freedom" is not his goal; the salvation of others is. Thus, since he is financially independent of all people, he is able freely to put himself at the disposal of all for the sake of the gospel. His language for this servanthood, "I made myself a slave[21] to everyone," not only keeps the present metaphor intact but also is what he and his churches have learned to use about the ministry of Jesus, who became "slave" of all in order to save (cf. Phil. 2:5-8; Gal. 4:4-5). This is why Paul regularly uses the word "servant" (or "slave") to speak of his own ministry (cf. 2 Cor. 4:5), and also why this becomes the basic expression of believers' relationships to one another (e.g., Gal. 5:13): Jesus himself is the paradigm for such servant-hood.[22] Free, in order to become slave to all—this is surely the ultimate expression of truly Christian, because it is truly Christlike, behavior.

In this context his becoming slave of all is to be understood in light of the examples that follow,[23] thus referring to his willingness to accommodate himself to whatever social setting he found himself in, so as "to win[24] as

[19]Gk. ἐκ πάντων (one would ordinarily expect ἀπό for this ablative idea; cf. Rom. 7:3). For this reason some (e.g., Godet, 35) argue that πάντων is neuter (= "free from all things"). The context demands otherwise.

[20]Thus, despite some significant linguistic affinities, "freedom" here means something considerably different than in Gal. 5:13, where "freedom from the law" is in view. For similar expressions of "freedom" as financial independence, see Xenophon, *apol.* 16 (of Socrates): "Who of men is more free (ἀπελευθερία) than I, who accepts neither gifts nor payment (μισθός) from anyone?"; cf. *mem.* 1.2.5-7; Musonius Rufus, *fr.* 11. See also Lucian's satire, "On Salaried Posts in Great Houses," which begins by referring to salaried posts (i.e., living by patronage) as "that sort of slavery."

[21]Gk. ἐδούλωσα; the aorist is particularly significant. Paul is not here speaking in generalities about his *modus operandi;* rather, he is defending past actions. He is known to have conducted himself differently in differing social settings; *his* way of speaking about those actions is that he made himself a slave to everyone in order to win them to Christ.

[22]See esp. Luke 22:24-27. Daube (*Rabbinic Judaism,* pp. 336-51) makes a considerable point that there are parallels in attitude among the Hillelites. Although one would not question that Paul's own liberal understanding of Judaism had been deeply influenced by his Hillelite teacher Gamaliel, on this issue Paul has surely been more deeply influenced by the One whom he insists he imitates. As Barrett, 211, rightly points out, "where [the Hillelites] were willing to make the law no more offensive and burdensome than necessary, Paul was prepared to abandon it altogether."

[23]Otherwise Hock (n. 17), who thinks it points backward and refers to Paul's tentmaking as a slavish trade.

[24]Gk. κερδαίνω, a verb that ordinarily means "to gain, make profit, or gain

many as possible[25]." Such language, as the interchange with "save" in v. 22b makes clear, can only refer to evangelizing.[26] Thus Paul's first concern in such matters is not whether he offends or does not offend— although that too is a concern (10:32)—but whether the gospel itself will get its proper hearing (cf. 10:33).

20 Paul now proceeds[27] to delineate what "making himself a slave to all in order to win as many as possible" means by specifying some of the kinds of social settings in which he practiced evangelism. Although the package seems carefully constructed,[28] its special features suggest that it is an *ad hoc* piece of rhetoric designed to defend his own past actions. Although one cannot be certain about the specifics in some cases ("those under the law" and "the weak"), there can be little question that he is reflecting on his differing conduct in Jewish and Gentile settings, the central issue being questions of Jewish law. To put it in more contemporary terms, when he was among Jews he was kosher; when he was among Gentiles he was non-kosher—precisely because, as with circumcision, neither mattered to God (cf. 7:19; 8:8). But such conduct tends to matter a great deal to the religious—on either side![29]—so that inconsistency in such matters ranks among the greatest of evils.

Paul's policy quite transcended petty consistency—and "religion" itself. His concern was to "win the Jews,"[30] as well as all others; thus "to the[31] Jews I became[32] like a Jew." This opening item serves as the clue for

---

advantage." Daube has demonstrated that its Hebraic counterpart had already been taken over into Judaism as missionary language (*Rabbinic Judaism,* pp. 352-61); cf. 1 Pet. 3:1. Nonetheless, since Paul would ordinarily use "save" for this purpose (cf. v. 22b), he has probably chosen it in keeping with the metaphor, as a play on the "pay" motif. By "gaining" people through his servanthood he brings all the more "profit" to the gospel itself.

[25]Gk. τοὺς πλείονας (lit. "the many"), here meaning not the majority (as in 10:5), but "more than I should have gained by another policy,—the greater number that this policy brings in" (Parry, 142).

[26]Cf. G. Bornkamm, "The Missionary Stance of Paul in 1 Corinthians 9 and in Acts," in *Studies in Luke-Acts* (ed. L. E. Keck and J. L. Martyn; Nashville, 1966), pp. 194-207. Otherwise Willis ("Apologia," p. 37), who thinks Paul is referring throughout to his relationships among Christians. But that is because of his strong stance against chap. 9's being a defense.

[27]The sentence begins with a καί that is probably epexegetic (so R-P, 191).

[28]See n. 9 above; cf. Weiss, 243-44, and Bornkamm, "Stance," pp. 194-95.

[29]The problem in Corinth, it must be kept in mind, did not come from some "weak" who felt abused or, as in Rom. 14, were judging others. Rather, it came from those insisting on "freedom," who wanted to "build up" the weak. See on 8:9-10.

[30]This seems to be sure evidence that Paul never considered himself released from a mission to the Jews, as W. Schmithals has argued on the basis of Gal. 2:9 (see *Paul and James* [ET, London, 1965]).

[31]This is the only occurrence of the article with Ἰουδαῖοι in Paul's letters. BDF 262(1) suggest it particularizes: "those with whom I had to deal on each occasion."

[32]Like the verb "made myself a slave" in v. 19, this aorist must not be over-

understanding the others. How can a Jew determine to "become *like* a Jew"?[33] The obvious answer is, In matters that have to do with Jewish religious peculiarities that Paul as a Christian had long ago given up as essential to a right relationship with God. These would include circumcision (7:19; Gal. 6:15), food laws (8:8; Gal. 2:10-13; Rom. 14:17; Col. 2:16), and special observances (Col. 2:16). On these questions not only was Paul himself free; he also took a thoroughly polemical stance toward any who would impose such requirements on Gentile converts. On the other hand, he had no problem with Jews continuing such practices, as long as they were not considered to give people right standing with God.[34] Nor did he exhibit unwillingness to yield to Jewish customs for the sake of the Jews (cf. Acts 16:1-3;[35] 21:23-26). Although one cannot be certain, from the general context as well as the clear parallels with 10:23-33 one may infer that food laws are the specific issue here, especially the prohibition against eating marketplace food because of its associations with idolatry.[36] Paul himself felt free to eat such food, as 10:23-30 makes certain. The present text suggests that he also willingly refrained when he was in more strictly Jewish settings. It is probably this conduct, more than any other, to which his Corinthian opponents took exception.[37]

The second item is more puzzling. Ordinarily this would obviously refer to Jews; but does it also do so when listed as a second item following "the Jews"? Most likely it does, and is so expressed because the specific issue was related not simply to matters of national origin[38] but especially to

looked. The present would be more fitting if Paul were merely using "a well-crafted piece of rhetorical style" in order to set forth his principles of self-denial for the sake of others (Willis, "Apologia," pp. 37-38).

[33]It is surely the wrong solution to suggest that Paul was not a Jew because no Jew could act so! See G. Ory, "Quelle était l'origine de Paul?" *Cahiers du Cercle Ernest-Renan* 18 (1971), 11-19.

[34]Cf. Conzelmann, 160: "He does not have to deliver the Jews from their practice of the Law, but from their 'confidence' in the Law as a way of salvation."

[35]NT scholarship does not seem to be at its best when the historicity of this event is denied (on the basis of Gal. 2:1-2, where an entirely different context is in view), since it fits so perfectly with this explicit statement of his missionary policy. Here Bornkamm's otherwise helpful article ("Stance") is especially weak.

[36]In any case, every attempt to see this passage as related to the *content* of his preaching seems misguided from the outset. We are here dealing with behavior, not with theology as such. Thus it is not a question of his accommodating the message for the sake of the audience. He may well have done that, but this passage is no evidence for it.

[37]This seems more probable than the more strictly sociological tensions between the rich and poor envisioned by Theissen, 121-43.

[38]Note in particular that when in the next item he turns to speak of his conduct among Gentiles, he omits reference to "Gentiles" or "non-Jews" altogether in favor of one that designates them in terms of their (non-)relationship to the law. This is the answer to Conzelmann's unanswered rhetorical question, "Why does Paul not say, 'To the Greeks'?"

matters of Jewish (religious) legal requirements.[39] Particularly significant is the parenthetical addition,[40] "though[41] I myself am not under the law." By these words Paul intends to clarify his own conduct as a matter of freedom—he "freely" made himself a "slave" for the sake of others—not of obligation. The difference, therefore, between his own behavior and that of his social companions is not in the behavior itself, which will be identical to the observer, but in the reasons for it. The latter abstain because they are "under the law"; it is a matter of religious obligation. Paul abstains because he loves those under the law and wants to win them to Christ. Despite appearances, the differences are as night and day.

21 The third item in the series, "those not having the law,"[42] corresponds to the second as its opposite. Paul is here referring to his conduct among Gentiles, including the majority of the Corinthian believers, and especially those who stand against him within the community. This item, plus the conclusion in v. 22b, "all things to all people," seems to rule out the idea that Paul in this paragraph is offering himself as an example of *self-restraint* since among these people he undoubtedly "ate whatever was put before him without raising any questions of conscience" (10:27). Their knowledge of his conduct in their presence, and of his abstinence when among "those under the law," offers the best solution to the historical occasion of this paragraph.

The qualification in this instance is full of interest. As in the previous clause, he begins, "I became as one without the law, though I myself am not without the law." But he can scarcely resist a play on words. Among Gentiles he behaves as one who is *anomos* (not under Jewish law), but he is not thereby to be considered *anomos* ("lawless" = "godless, wicked"; cf. 1 Tim. 1:9), which point is made by adding the qualifier "toward God."[43]

---

[39]Ellison ("Paul," p. 196) rightly cautions that one not too quickly assume that Paul intends only Jews here since it is a second category—even if in parallel to the first—and may intend to include Gentile god-fearers and proselytes as well. This may well be so, but primarily the category stands in parallel to the first, with emphasis now on the law.

[40]On the textual question see n. 3.

[41]Gk. μὴ ὢν αὐτός; in contrast to v. 19 both the position and context demand that this be concessive.

[42]Gk. ἄνομος. Ordinarily this word means "lawless" (cf. 2 Thess. 2:8), but the fact that it stands in perfect balance with the preceding group as its opposite, not to mention that Paul speaks of himself as ὡς ἄνομος, means that he is not reflecting on their behavior but on their status. The Jews are "under the law"; the Gentiles are "without the law," the Jewish law obviously being intended. Cf. his use of the adv. ἀνόμως in Rom. 2:12.

[43]On genitives after a negative adjective, see Moulton, *Grammar*, pp. 235-36. However, Moulton understands ἄνομος also to mean "without the law" here, and therefore θεοῦ as a subjective genitive. As with Moule, 42, this emphasizes the genitive in relation to νόμος. It seems more likely that Paul is playing on words and that the genitive at least in this first instance is objective. Cf. Barrett, 212-13, who translates, "legal

Indeed, he goes on, I am *ennomos* (lit. "in law" = subject to law) toward Christ. His point is plain: He wishes no misunderstanding of the word *anomos,* which would ordinarily mean to behave in a godless way. To be "as one without the law" does not mean to be "lawless." Like 7:19 this is a clear instance in which Paul can distinguish between keeping "the law" and obeying the ethical imperatives of the Christian faith. For Paul the language "being under (or 'keeping') the law" has to do with being Jewish in a national-cultural-religious sense; but as a new man in Christ he also expects the Spirit to empower him (as well as all of God's new people) to live out the ethics of the new age, which are the "commands of God" (7:19) now written on hearts of flesh (cf. Ezek. 36:26-27).

In this instance the Christian ethical imperative is characterized as being "under Christ's law." Paul uses the word "law," of course, because of the wordplay involving "law" compounds. This does not mean that in Christ a new set of laws has taken the place of the old, although in terms of specifics it would certainly refer to those kinds of ethical demands given, for example, in Rom. 12 and Gal. 5–6, so many of which do reflect the teaching of Jesus.[44] Given the frequency of "lawlessness" among the Corinthians who opposed him, it is not difficult to understand the reason for this significant qualification![45]

22 Since the three preceding items have to do with Jewish or Gentile social settings, what then does Paul intend by this final item, "to the weak I became weak"? On the one hand, this is probably Paul's way of beginning to bring the argument back around to where he left it at 8:13–9:1. This seems all the more likely since it follows hard on the heels of the discussion of the previous group, who almost certainly represent those with whom Paul is in conflict in this church and with whom he has been arguing in this letter. At the same time, however, especially since he speaks also of "winning them,"[46] one must be careful of too specific an identification

---

obligation to God." C. H. Dodd, interestingly enough, argues for the wordplay here, but then goes on to nullify that understanding by making θεοῦ refer to God's law in the sense of obedience to requirements (see "Ἔννομος Χριστοῦ," in *Studia Paulina in Honorem Johannis de Zwaan Septuagenarii* (ed. J. N. Sevenster and W. C. van Unnik; Haarlem, 1953), pp. 96-110, cited here from *More New Testament Studies* (Grand Rapids, 1968), pp. 134-48.

[44]Dodd, "Ἔννομος Χριστοῦ," would understand this phrase to refer to "a code of precepts to which a Christian man is obliged to conform," somewhat analogous to the Torah for Jews (pp. 138-46). As Conzelmann (161 n. 27) points out, however, that seems to be at variance with Paul's use of νόμος.

[45]Dodd ("Ἔννομος Χριστοῦ," p. 137) sees it as a word to imaginary Jewish interlocutors, but that seems to remove the paragraph from its historical context.

[46]Since it is usually assumed that the "weak" here are fully identical with the "weak" of 8:7-13, the repetition of the clause "to win the weak" has generated considerable discussion (see esp. Barrett, 215). Willis ("Apologia") began with this item as his

with the "weak" mentioned in 8:7-13. Perhaps the missing comparative ("like")[47] is more significant than is often allowed.[48] This may well reflect a moment of realism and thereby intentionally be a more generalizing category. For any number of reasons, partly related to his working with his own hands, Paul experienced considerable weakness in Corinth (see on 2:1-5; 4:9-13; cf. 2 Cor. 4:7-18; 11:16–12:10). As noted on 4:9-13, he considered this to be a paradigm of the Christian life; thus "to the weak," that is, the majority of the Corinthian believers (cf. 1:26-31), he "became weak, to win the weak." Thus it is probably a more purely sociological category than a socio-religious one.[49]

In any case, the concluding sentence, "I have become[50] all things to all people so that by all possible means[51] I might save some," summarizes and thereby generalizes the argument. Paul's actions, which appear to them to be inconsistent, have integrity at a much higher level. Whereas he is intransigent on matters that affect the gospel itself, whether theological or behavioral (e.g., 1:18-25; 5:1-5, etc.), that same concern for the saving power of the gospel is what causes him to become all things to all people in matters that don't count.[52] The substitution of the verb "save" in this final clause makes it certain that the verb "win" in the five earlier clauses meant precisely that—eschatological salvation for the perishing through Christ's death and resurrection (cf. 1:18, 21). For Paul everything is subordinated to this central concern of his life, this "destiny" that God has laid upon him (v. 16).

23 The argument concludes[53] with a final, clear affirmation of the

---

way of arguing both for the nonapologetic character of the paragraph and that κερδαίνω throughout means "keep" rather than "win" (see n. 10). Even if the "weak" were identical with those of chap. 8, most likely the repetition is stylistic.

[47]On the textual question see n. 5 above.

[48]Cf. Conzelmann, 161 n. 28, who also makes this observation.

[49]Other alternatives have been offered. Dodd, "Ἔννομος Χριστοῦ," suggests "non-Christians, presumably of Jewish origin," who are "morbidly scrupulous" (p. 134); D. A. Black, "A Note on 'the Weak' in 1 Corinthians 9,22," *Bib* 64 (1983), 240-42, moves in the direction suggested here, but spiritualizes the term too much and thereby misses its sociological implications.

[50]Gk. γέγονα, the perfect instead of the previous aorists in vv. 20a and 22a.

[51]Gk. πάντως (see on v. 10). The NIV does well in bringing out the force of the wordplay in πᾶσιν, πάντα, and πάντως.

[52]On the difficulty in squaring this with his dressing down of Peter in Gal. 2:11-14, see P. Richardson, "Pauline Inconsistency: I Corinthians 9:19-23 and Galatians 2:11-14," *NTS* 26 (1979/80), 347-62. Richardson's solution, that Paul saw our passage primarily as an apostolic function, does not seem adequate. The difference in the Antioch situation is that it has to do with dividing a church in the Gentile mission into Jewish and Gentile factions based on food laws. Precisely because the gospel transcends such, Paul will have none of that in the church.

[53]The sentence is joined to what has preceded by a consecutive δέ ("now then").

singular passion of his life: "All things for the sake of the gospel" (cf. vv. 12b, 15-18). The preceding argument makes it clear that by "the gospel" Paul is not referring to its content as such, but to the proclaimed gospel as God's saving power at work in the world (cf. Rom. 1:16). Thus he means "for the sake of *the progress* of the gospel."[54] But the final purpose clause, (lit.) "that I may be a fellow-participant in it," is less than certain. Is he referring to his participation in the *work* of the gospel,[55] as in the preceding argument (esp. vv. 16-18), or to his sharing with them in its *benefits* ("blessings, promises"), in anticipation of the paragraph that follows? Although the former is an attractive option, Paul's usage elsewhere[56] suggests that he means the latter. The problem, of course, is that that sounds self-serving and seems to undercut what has been said in the preceding verses. But not so. Paul is not so much suggesting that he does all things so that in the end he will receive the benefits of the gospel, as that he places himself alongside those to whom he has preached and to whom he now writes. Along with them, he hopes to share in the final blessings of the gospel.

But such is not guaranteed; he and they must persevere in the gospel to share in its promises. Despite his final confidence in the sovereign work of God's prior grace, he has genuine concern for the Corinthians, whose attendance at the cultic meals in the pagan temples is putting them in real jeopardy. And no false security in the sacraments (10:1-4) will help. Hence this concluding note on his own desire to share in the final blessings of the gospel leads him directly to an exhortation that they, too, as he, "run in such a way as to get the prize" (v. 24b), so that they will not be "disqualified" (v. 27).

This passage has often been looked to for the idea of "accommodation"[57] in evangelism, that is, of adapting the *message* to the language and perspective of the recipients. Unfortunately, despite the need for that discussion to be carried on, this passage does not speak directly to it. This has to do with how one *lives* or *behaves* among those whom one wishes to evangelize (not, it needs to be added in passing, with social taboos among Christians). What needs to be emphasized is the point expressed clearly by Bornkamm:

Godet, 41, thinks this sentence begins a new paragraph; but that seems unlikely. The πάντα, the mention of the gospel as his primary concern, and the concluding ἵνα-clause all indicate that it belongs with what has preceded as the final summation.

[54]Otherwise R-P, 193, who regard διά here as meaning "because of" in the sense of its "being so precious to himself." No doubt it was precious to him, but that is more sentimental than contextual.

[55]So Schütz, *Paul*, pp. 51-52; cf. Parry, 143, who suggests, "that I may have others to share the Gospel with me."

[56]Cf. Rom. 11:17; Phil. 1:7.

[57]For a discussion of accommodation in Paul see P. Richardson and P. W. Gooch, "Accommodation Ethics," *TynB* 19 (1978), 89-142.

"Paul could not modify the gospel itself according to the particular characteristics of his hearers. The whole of his concern is to make clear that the changeless gospel, . . . empowers him to be free to change his stance."[58] This especially needs to be heard among those who would equate certain nonethical behavioral items with the gospel itself.

The greater difficulty for all who would so preach Christ is our inherent resistance, due to the Fall, to the imitation of Christ expressed in v. 19, that freedom leads to making oneself the servant of all in order to win them. Unfortunately, freedom too often is abused in the direction of self-interest rather than expressed in terms of concern for others and for the progress of the gospel.

e. Exhortation and example (9:24-27)

24 *Do you not know that in a race all the runners run, but only one gets the prize? Run in such a way as to get the prize.* 25 *Everyone who competes in the games goes into strict training. They do it to get a crown that will not last; but we do it to get a crown that will last forever.* 26 *Therefore I do not run like a man running aimlessly; I do not fight like a man beating the air.* 29 *No, I beat my body and make it my slave so that after I have preached to others, I myself will not be disqualified for the prize.*

This paragraph is transitional; it brings the long excursus of chap. 9 to its conclusion and at the same time prepares for a return to the argument against going to the cultic meals (10:1-22). The entire passage consists of metaphors from the games.[1] The use of athletic metaphors such as these had a long history in the Greek philosophic tradition, to which Paul is undoubtedly

---

[58]"Stance," p. 196.

[1]For the archaeology and significance of the nearby Isthmian Games (about 14 kilometers from Corinth), see O. Broneer, "The Apostle Paul and the Isthmian Games," *BA* 25 (1962), 2-31; cf. Murphy-O'Connor, *Corinth*, 14-17. See also Dio Chrysostom's imaginary accounts in *or.* 8.6-14 and 9.10-22 of Diogenes's visits to the Games, which undoubtedly reflect his own times (second half of 1st c. A.D.). Conzelmann, 162 n. 31, discounts any connection with these games; but that seems unrealistic, given their undoubted significance for Corinth itself.

These Games, held every two years under the patronage of Corinth and second only to the Olympics, were extravagant festivals of religion, athletics, and the arts, attracting thousands of competitors and visitors from all over the empire. Its sponsors and greater athletes were honored in Isthmia itself by monuments, statues, and inscriptions. Paul would have been in Corinth during the Games of A.D. 51 (in the Spring). Since there were no permanent facilities for visitors until the second century A.D., they had to stay in tents. Broneer (pp. 5, 20) conjectures that Paul would have had ample opportunity to ply his trade and share the gospel with the crowds visiting the Games of that year.

Dio (*or.* 8.12) mentions the six basic athletic events that made up the Games:

indebted.[2] Nonetheless, the usage and application are his own (perhaps based on his own personal observations of the athletes).

He begins with a general observation from the games, with running as the specific example: all run, but only one obtains the prize (v. 24a). He immediately applies that to the Corinthians,[3] urging them so to run (v. 24b). Then he generalizes about the competitors and their prize (v. 25). About the competitors: they exercise self-control in all things so that they may obtain the prize; about the prize: the competitors in the games do so for a perishable wreath, believers[4] for the imperishable one. Next he applies the metaphors to himself (vv. 26-27). Using running and boxing, he insists that he does not "compete" aimlessly but with the goal in mind, thus reflecting the emphasis on the prize. Then, picking up on the boxing metaphor, he redirects it to the emphasis on self-control (discipline), that he not come short of the prize (although the metaphor switches to the idea of being disqualified from the contest).

The primary point of the metaphors[5] is the imperative of v. 24b, which controls the entire paragraph. Paul is urging the Corinthians to "run" the Christian life in such a way, in this case *by exercising proper self-control* (the emphasis in vv. 25-27), as to obtain the eschatological reward.[6] In context the area where they lack "self-control" is that of insisting on the

---

racing, wrestling, jumping, boxing, hurling the javelin, and throwing the discus. On this matter see H. A. Harris, *Greek Athletes and Athletics* (3rd ed., Westport, CT, 1979).

[2]On this question, as well as for the paragraph in hand, see Pfitzner, *Agon Motif*, pp. 23-72 and 82-98.

[3]He first applies the metaphors in the second person plural as an imperative; then he shifts to the first plural in v. 25b, and finally to the first singular in vv. 26-27. They are thus first a word *to* the Corinthians; at the same time, however, they serve to conclude the ἀπολογία of chap. 9.

[4]Note the shift to the first plural, which must now include the Corinthians *and* Paul, thus preparing the way for the first person singulars that follow.

[5]The problem with metaphor is that although it is a marvelous tool of communication, inherent within it is also the possibility of independent application. Fairness in exegesis demands that one "hear" the author's own intent, and neither press it in directions he does not take it, nor allegorize it—the worst of all evils in this case. This paragraph in particular has been one in which Paul's own intent has often been circumvented. Cf. Pfitzner, p. 86.

[6]Otherwise Pfitzner, *Agon Motif*, pp. 87-90, who sees the point more strictly in the motif of self-control, the basic reason for it being Paul's "self-apology." He altogether rejects the idea that it is parenesis (reading the imperative in v. 24b as an indicative; see n. 13 below), but does so mostly in reaction to those who see the parenesis in terms of bland generalities about Christian living (see esp. pp. 97-98). Such interpretations are rightly to be rejected. Paul's concern is much more specific and aims directly at the concern of 10:1-22 (Pfitzner does himself a disservice to reject so totally the close ties to what follows).

right to idolatrous eating in the pagan temples. *Exhortation*, therefore, is Paul's primary purpose; but the passage also serves as a clear *warning* if they fail to "run" properly. As warning it anticipates 10:1-22.[7]

At the same time it conveniently serves as a conclusion to chap. 9. Paul's activities in curtailing his rights, yet exercising his freedom for the singular aim of "all things for the sake of the gospel," are his own brand of exercising self-control in all things, which now surely is intended to serve as a paradigm for them, thus bringing him back to the point of 8:13.

24 The final "Do you not know that?" (see on 3:16) in this letter signals a continuation of the preceding argument, in this case by offering an illustration that will bring the present concerns, going back to 8:7-13, into focus. The imagery is taken from the runners in the games, all of whom in any given race[8] compete for the one prize.[9] Although Paul will elaborate on the theme of the "prize" in v. 25, that is a "complementary" image,[10] not the primary concern. But neither is Paul's point to be found in the imagery of this verse on its own, as though putting forth great effort were the concern;[11] and especially his point does not lie with the fact that only one receives the prize,[12] as though the Christian life were a competition of some sort. All such "meanings" are foreign to Paul, whose intent is found in the way he himself elaborates the imagery in vv. 25-27—the necessity of self-control in order to win the prize.

---

[7]Note the explanatory γάρ that joins 10:1-5 to 9:27. This relationship is emphasized in Senft, 125, who makes 9:24–10:22 a distinct section entitled "Warning against Idolatry."

[8]The NIV has translated ἐν σταδίῳ as "in a race"; it could also mean "at the stadium" (the anarthrous σταδίῳ is similar to our "at home"; cf. ἐν μακέλλῳ in 10:25). The στάδιον was first of all a measure of distance (about 185 meters); it was naturally transferred to the arena itself, which measured the length of a στάδιον, the basic distance in the races.

[9]Gk. βραβεῖον; used specifically for the "prize" in a contest. Cf. the metaphorical usage in Phil. 3:14 and *Mart. Pol.* 17:1.

[10]This is Pfitzner's happy choice of terms (p. 87).

[11]This is a common view, found, e.g., in R-P, 193; Lenski, 383; Grosheide, 215; and even Barrett, 217. Lenski, 383, among others, quite misses the preparatory nature of this first image to the whole paragraph by suggesting that in v. 25 "a further and somewhat different point is added." Even further afield is A. Ehrhardt's idealized suggestion, on the basis of an alleged similarity in an Orphic fragment, that "St. Paul was here referring to a popular conception of man's religious task as a struggle before the face of the Godhead, who had Himself arranged the contest before him"! See "An unknown Orphic writing in the Demosthenes scholia and St. Paul," *ZNW* 48 (1957), 101-10 (the quotation is from p. 109).

[12]Conzelmann, 162, who finally allows that this is only an auxiliary notion, is nonetheless much too prosaic even to suggest "that the moral Paul derives from it—namely that only one wins the prize—appears out of place." Of course it does, since that is to miss Paul's imagery altogether.

Paul's concern is singular: "Run[13] in such a way[14] as to get the prize." This exhortation is the point of the entire paragraph. It first of all picks up the theme of the preceding imagery, of the runner who is intent on winning the prize. Thus he means: "Run as that one runs who wins the prize." At the same time it points forward to the succeeding imagery, which explains both what one must do in order to win the prize and what the prize itself is for which they are running.

25 Paul now displays his concern for the Corinthians by a further elaboration[15] of the imagery. He makes two points: (1) the necessity of "self-control" in order to win the prize; and (2) the nature of the prize. The concerns, of course, are interrelated. Paul is genuinely concerned that they achieve the goal (cf. 6:9-11); what might cause their "disqualification" in this case is their insistence on the right to eat the cultic meals in the pagan temples. Therefore, "everyone who competes in the games[16] goes into strict training," that is (lit.), "exercises self-control[17] in all things[18]." Winning requires discipline, even for the best of athletes. Any athlete entered in the games was required to go into ten months of strict training and was subject to disqualification if he failed to do so.[19] Paul now applies that figure to their— and his—situation. In their case it will mean not simply foregoing some

[13]Gk. τρέχετε, an imperative, not an indicative, as Pfitzner (*Agon Motif*, pp. 88-89) argues. That is simply not a natural reading of the text, and Pfitzner's arguments in its favor are less than compelling. His motivation is given away in the sentence, "If τρέχετε is understood as an imperative . . . the connection between the picture of the Agon and the theme of 'enkrateia' . . . would seem to be impaired" (p. 88). But that is not so (as Conzelmann, 162 n. 35, has also pointed out). Unfortunately, rejecting this imperative also causes Pfitzner to miss the central concern of the paragraph, which is to exhort the Corinthians to the kind of self-control that their demand for *exousia* lacks.

[14]This οὕτως points forward to the ἵνα-clause, making that clause epexegetic: "*So* run *that* you may obtain." At the same time, of course, it refers back to the preceding image.

[15]The δέ is consecutive: "*Now* everyone who, etc.," not adversative, as R-P, 194; Pfitzner, *Agon Motif*, p. 89; Conzelmann, 159.

[16]Gk. πᾶς ὁ ἀγωνιζόμενος; the verb is a technical one for "engaging in a contest," especially an athletic contest. It came to be used by the philosophers as a metaphor for "the heroic stuggle which the pious has to go through in this world" (E. Stauffer, *TDNT* I, 135). It is this metaphorical usage that in turn has caused so many to see Paul as here comparing the Christian life to that same "heroic struggle," and thus (wrongly) to interpret the passage as a piece of general parenesis (see n. 6).

[17]Gk. ἐγκρατεύω; see on 7:5 and 9. For Paul's use of the word see Hill, "'Enkrateia.'" Its basic meaning is to "exercise mastery over oneself."

[18]The πάντα here at least echoes the πάντα of v. 23, if it does not refer to it directly (Pfitzner, *Agon Motif*, pp. 87-88, makes this the "catchword" of chap. 9). As the athlete exercises self-control in "all things" for the sake of the victor's wreath, so Paul does "all things" for the sake of the gospel. By implication they must also do "all things" in order to obtain the prize.

[19]See Plato, *leg.* 840a. This was at least true for the Olympiad; there is no reason

rights for the sake of others (as in 8:7-13), but also foregoing some things altogether because they are inherently incompatible with the Christian "contest" (10:14-22).

To press that point Paul contrasts the forms of the prize. The athlete goes through such discipline to receive the victor's "crown," a "perishable wreath."[20] In contrast to that, Paul tells the Corinthians, "we[21] get a crown that will last forever."[22] In this metaphor the Christian's "crown" is not some specific aspect of the goal but the eschatological victory itself. As with other passages in this letter (e.g., 1:8; 4:5, 8; 6:2, 9; 15:12-19), this may incidentally emphasize the futurity of the Eschaton over against their "over-realized eschatology." In any case, the figure is intended to impress upon them that the goal, being eternal in nature, is of such value that it should affect the way they live in the present.

26 With an inferential "therefore"[23] and an emphatic "I," Paul now elaborates on the preceding metaphors by applying them to his own life. "I therefore so run"—as you also are to run being implied. In part at least he probably intends this application to bring to a conclusion the defense that began in v. 3, and especially as expressed in vv. 15-18 and 19-23. He wants the Corinthians to understand his own conduct in light of the foregoing metaphors, as they are now about to be elaborated. At the same time, however, the imperative in v. 24b, for which this is a further illustration, plus the explanatory "for" that follows in 10:1, indicate that Paul also intends this application to be exemplary. Thus he is returning to the argument of 8:7-13, at the end of which he had set himself forth as an example that they should follow (cf. 11:1).

---

to think otherwise at Isthmia. For athletic training in general, see Harris, *Athletes,* pp. 170-78.

[20]Gk. στέφανος; cf. 2 Tim. 4:8. The Isthmian Games awarded a στέφανος of pine (at least in the 2nd c. A.D.) or withered celery, probably in use at the time of Paul (see Broneer, "The Isthmian Victory Crown," *AJA* 66 [1962], 259-63); cf. his "Apostle Paul," pp. 16-17, where he writes: "It is tempting to see in [Paul's] reference to the perishable wreath . . . a reference to the crown of celery which, when bestowed at the Isthmian Games, was already withered."

The runner, of course, had no thought for the *composition* of the "crown." As with modern athletes, victory meant fame, prestige, and sometimes fortune. The "crown" was the symbol of victory; if it faded, the fame that followed was often more enduring. But even that means nothing in light of the believer's crown.

[21]With this "we" Paul begins to bring exhortation (v. 24b) and example (vv. 26-27) together.

[22]The contrast is between φθαρτός and ἄφθαρτος, what is perishable and what is imperishable (cf. 15:53-54).

[23]Gk. τοίνυν; only here in Paul (elsewhere in the NT only in Luke 20:25; Heb. 13:13; Jas. 2:24).

The two metaphors, from running and boxing, are so clearly parallel that both are no doubt intended to make the same point. He runs, he says, as the runner who is set on winning the prize (v. 24). Only now he puts it negatively, "not like a man running aimlessly."[24] This can only mean "as one who has no fixed goal."[25] People who enter races, of course, do not do such things. Hence the absurdity of the metaphor makes its own point. Paul's actions, which are defended in the preceding paragraphs, are not those of an aimless runner. Everything is for the sake of the gospel, that he too might share in its blessings.

Likewise with the boxer; if he is to win the prize he does not "fight like a man beating the air." But is this a picture of a boxer who fails to land telling blows while in the ring, or of the exercise of shadow-boxing prior to the fight?[26] The one speaks to the effectiveness of his effort, the other its purposefulness. Purposefulness seems to be more in keeping with the parallel in the first sentence. But the former picture could also be interpreted in that sense; that is, to get in the ring with an opponent and only beat air is as useless—and absurd—as the runner who has no eye for the finish line. This seems to make more sense, since shadow-boxing could be seen as a purposeful activity (i.e., part of the training for the fight). In either case, Paul's point is that of v. 25.[27] They are to understand his actions as those of one who has a clear vision of his goal; implied is his exercising self-control as part of that purposefulness. That is the point he will press in the final application of the metaphor in v. 27.

27 In contrast[28] to the absurd boxer, who would merely flag the air and not hit his opponent, Paul "boxes" with real purpose. He aims to win the prize of an imperishable crown. To do so, he argued in v. 25, the athlete exercises self-control. Now he applies that point in a more telling way by elaborating on the boxing imagery just mentioned. As the final clause makes clear, his concern about obtaining the prize is still in view—for himself obviously, but especially for them, as 10:1-22 makes certain.

The metaphor itself gets considerably mixed because Paul is doing two things simultaneously: (1) picking up the theme of boxing from the

---

[24]Gk. ἀδήλως; only here in the NT (cf. the adjective in 14:8).

[25]The translation is from BAGD; cf. NAB, "like a man who loses sight of the finish line." He does not mean "not sure of the goal."

[26]Both ideas can be found in the early Fathers (see W. Foerster, *TDNT* I, 166 n. 8). Philo combines them in *cher.* 81. This may be Paul's point as well; in the ring he doesn't shadow-box. Cf. the discussion in K. L. Schmidt, *TDNT* VI, 915-17, and Pfitzner, *Agon Motif*, pp. 90-91.

[27]It thus serves also to illustrate v. 23: He does all things for the sake of the gospel so that he, with them, might share in its blessings.

[28]Gk. ἀλλά, in an οὐ/ἀλλά contrast.

immediately preceding clause, and (2) going back to the concern about self-control in v. 25. Thus like those of a purposeful boxer, his blows give "bruises."[29] But as is often the case in Paul, his metaphors are fluid (see, e.g., on 5:6-8). Since his concern is self-control, the object of the blows becomes "my body," and since one metaphor calls for another, he leaves athletics altogether and adds, "and make it my slave," i.e., make it serve my purposes in the gospel. But he hardly intends his physical body as such to be the "opponent" he must subdue in order to gain the prize.[30] He uses "body" because of the metaphor; what he almost certainly intends by it is "myself," as in v. 19, which would include the body, but only as it is the vehicle of his present earthly life.[31] His point, after all, is the need for self-restraint, not asceticism (which he thoroughly rejects) or self-flagellation. In his own case, such "bruising of the body" probably refers to hardships to which he voluntarily subjected himself in preaching to the Corinthians, which included working with his own hands, and which in turn meant suffering the privations expressed in 4:11-13.[32] In this way he "disciplined" himself "for the sake of the gospel," so that he, along with them, might share in the promises of the gospel.

That this is Paul's intent is to be found in the final purpose clause, "so that after I have preached to others, I myself will not be disqualified for the prize." Some have seen the reference to "preaching" as continuing the

---

[29]Gk. ὑπωπιάζω, lit. "to strike under the eye," hence "to give a black eye to." The Rheims-Douay translation "I chastise my body," favored by D. R. Fotheringham ("'I Buffet my Body,'" *ExpT* 34 [1922/23], 140), completely circumvents the metaphor in favor of a prior theological position (see the next note).

[30]Any number of quite un-Pauline ascetic practices have been defended on the basis of a crassly literal understanding of this text, for a defense of which see Fotheringham (preceding note). But such an interpretation fails on two counts: it is totally noncontextual (nowhere in the entire passage is there any concern over the treatment of one's body); it is out of character with Paul's theology, who saw the body as mortal yet as destined for resurrection. Sin does not lie in the body; hence it is not to be beaten into submission.

[31]Gundry, 36-37, thinks otherwise. The problem lies with the use of metaphor, both here and in Rom. 12:1. The reason for σώματα in that passage is the metaphor of sacrifice pure and simple. One does not put his or her "soul" or "oneself" on the sacrificial altar, but the carcass (σῶμα) of the animal. Hence σῶμα is the only natural word, but it is a *metaphor* for oneself—not an anthropologically inclusive word, as Bultmann and Robinson have argued (see n. 32 on 6:13-14). The same is true here; Paul is simply keeping the metaphor going. That is not to deny that the body per se is also in view; it is to deny that he is isolating his physical body as the problem area of his life, or the instrument of sin, which needs to be subdued or else he will fail to obtain the prize.

[32]Cf. B. B. Warfield, "Paul's Buffeting of his Body," *ExpT* 31 (1919/20), 520-21; Pfitzner, *Agon Motif*, pp. 92-93. Conzelmann's objection to this view (163 n. 41) misses the point. Paul is indeed still laying emphasis on his own actions, which is exactly how he views his apostolic hardships. They "come with the territory," as it were, but he gives himself totally to such a ministry.

metaphor;[33] but that seems unlikely since this is Paul's regular word for preaching, and the context (vv. 14, 16, 18, 23) indicates that it is to be understood literally, not metaphorically.[34] With this language Paul is bringing the concerns of the foregoing defense back into focus. He exercises self-control in all things, he is telling them with the preceding metaphor, so that after he has fulfilled his task, laid on him by divine necessity (v. 16), he himself will not come short of the prize. To make that point he picks up the athletic metaphor one final time,[35] "lest I be disqualified,"[36] to which the NIV has (correctly) added "for the prize." This has been the point of the metaphors from the beginning, that the Corinthians exercise self-control lest they fail to obtain the eschatological prize. As he often does, and especially so in the context, he uses himself as the example of his concern. That he intends it as a word for them is made clear by the argument that follows.

But does Paul actually mean that one can fail to obtain the prize? Some would say no, but usually because of a prior theological commitment, not because of what the text itself says.[37] While it is true that in 10:13, after the severe warnings spelled out in vv. 1-12, he once again puts his confidence in God to "keep them," it would be sheer folly to suggest thereby that the warnings are not real. Paul keeps warning and assurance in tension. Simultaneously he *exhorts* and, by this and the following examples, *warns* the Corinthians of their imminent danger if they do not exercise "self-control" in the matter of idolatry; yet, as always (cf. on 5:8 and 6:11), he reminds them of their security in the prior activity of God, who has committed himself to them in Christ Jesus.

It is unfortunate when such a powerful text, with its exhortation to discipline as a necessary part of the Christian life—and consequent warning if one take such exhortation lightly—gets sidetracked either in the allegorizing of details or in the kind of bodily discipline exercised in self-imposed asceticism. That is not to say that in an overindulgent culture some of us do

---

[33]A κήρυξ ("herald") summoned the contestants and announced the rules of the contest. See, e.g., Godet, 48; Findlay, 857; R-P, 197.

[34]So Field, *Notes*, pp. 174-75; cf. Barrett, 218; Conzelmann, 163; and the discussion in Pfitzner, *Agon Motif*, pp. 94-96.

[35]Otherwise Pfitzner, *Agon Motif*, p. 96, who rejects any allusion to the contests, on two grounds: that the foregoing use of "preaching" is not metaphorical, and that Paul often uses δόκιμος/ἀδόκιμος ("approved/disapproved") in a theological way. But neither of these is compelling. It is hard to imagine the Corinthians, in light of the entire paragraph, not hearing this as metaphor; on the other hand, even as metaphor it carries the full weight of Paul's theological concerns expressed elsewhere.

[36]Gk. ἀδόκιμος, lit. "unqualified" because one has not passed the test (cf. 2 Cor. 13:5-7; 2 Tim. 3:8; Tit. 1:16).

[37]Cf., e.g., the Geneva Bible, the translation of the Scottish Calvinists in Switzerland: "lest I my self shulde be reproved"!

not need to discipline our bodily appetites. But it is to say that we have been called to a higher life of service that includes self-control and the willingness to endure hardship as concomitants. Perhaps too many contemporary Christians have lost sight of their eschatological goal and are running aimlessly, if they are in the "contest" at all.

3. Conclusion—No Going to the Temples (10:1-22)

With the help of the preceding exhortation—and implicit warning—Paul concludes his apostolic defense and returns to the matter at hand, the insistence of some of their number on attending the cultic meals in the pagan temples. Earlier (8:7-13) he had argued from the perspective of the weak, who were being abused by this falsely "constructive" action (8:10). Now he speaks directly to those who are opposing him on this matter, first by severely warning them on the basis of OT examples of the grave danger they are in (vv. 1-13), and second by expressly prohibiting temple attendance as totally incompatible with the Christian life (vv. 14-22). As the first example (v. 7) explicitly indicates, and the second one (v. 8) implicitly, the content of the biblical exposition of vv. 1-13 is directed specifically at the problem of idolatry, especially in the form of eating in an idol's presence.[1] Since that is also the content of the prohibition in vv. 14-22, there can be little question that the two sections are integral to one another; together they warn against and prohibit attendance at cultic meals because they are expressions of idolatry.

a. The example of Israel (10:1-5)

1 *For I do not want you to be ignorant of the fact, brothers, that our forefathers were all under the cloud and that they all passed through the sea.* 2 *They were all baptized[2] into Moses in the cloud*

---

[1]Failure to recognize this reality has led the majority of interpreters to have considerable difficulty with this section (either vv. 1-13 or 14-22, or both) in its present context. Some have opted for theories of partition; others have seen it as directed to a different group (the weak) from 8:1-13, a most improbable suggestion (on both of these see Hurd, 118-19). The majority see vv. 1-13 as still addressing the question of marketplace food, being a kind of general warning against "complacency." This in turn makes vv. 14-22 a digression—despite the strong διόπερ that joins the two sections (e.g., Conzelmann, 165, 170, who in particular has difficulty with the contextual questions in the entire section that comprises chaps. 8-10).

[2]The MS evidence is divided between the aorist passive ἐβαπτίσθησαν (‭א‬ A C D G Ψ 33 81 104 365 630 2464 2495 al latt Basil Didymus Cyril) and the aorist middle ἐβαπτίσαντο (P46c B K P 614 1739 1881 Maj Origen). Despite the majority of the UBS committee (see Metzger, 559), the middle is more likely the original, since it is nearly impossible to explain how a scribe would have gone from the passive to a middle while the opposite change would have been most natural (cf. Zuntz, 234).

and in the sea. 3 They all ate the same[3] spiritual food 4 and drank the same spiritual drink; for they drank from the spiritual rock that accompanied them, and that rock was Christ. 5 Nevertheless, God[4] was not pleased with most of them; their bodies were scattered over the desert.

In the immediately preceding argument Paul has urged the Corinthians to run (the Christian life is implied) as those intent on obtaining the eschatological prize; the application of the imagery to himself in vv. 26-27 serves as a warning that those who fail to exercise "self-control" may also fail of the prize itself. In the present section (10:1-13) that warning is now vigorously pursued. In a way very similar to such psalms as Ps. 78 and Deut. 32:1-43 or the speech in Neh. 9:5-37 (cf. Acts 7:1-53), in all of which God's rejected mercies in Israel's history serve as warning (or reason for confession of sin) to a present generation, Paul here warns the Corinthians of the dire consequences of persisting in their present idolatry.[5]

The argument is divided into two parts. In the first paragraph (vv. 1-5) Paul sets forth Israel (*"our* fathers") as Exhibit A of those who failed to obtain the prize. The power of the type lies in the fact that they also had their own form of "baptism" and "Lord's Supper," the prefigurement of ours. *All* of them had these privileges; nonetheless, God was displeased with *most* of them and their bodies were scattered over the desert. In the second paragraph (vv. 6-13) he applies this directly to the Corinthians: first by offering four illustrations from the Exodus as to *why* at various times *some* of them were overthrown (vv. 7-10), headed by two examples of idolatry that included table fellowship with the idols; second by using these examples expressly to warn those Corinthians who thought that somehow they were above "falling." Finally, in v. 13 he encourages those who experience true "testing" (as over against those who dare to test God).[6]

---

[3]P[46] and A, plus a few others in each case, omit αὐτό here and in v. 4. Most likely the omission is the result of homoeoteleuton (*TO*AYTO).

[4]A few isolated cursives (81 257 1610) omit ὁ θεός; Zuntz, 232, argues for this as the original on the grounds that it is also the reading of Marcion and Clement. But this patristic evidence is tenuous at best. Textual variation needs a pedigree to be accepted as original, and this one has none.

[5]Some have argued that the material in vv. 1-11 had prior existence as a Jewish or Christian midrash (see, e.g., Conzelmann, 165; W. A. Meeks, "'And Rose Up to Play': Midrash and Paraenesis in 1 Corinthians 10:1-22," *JSNT* 16 [1982], 64-78). But the material has been so thoroughly adapted by Paul, as Meeks admits, that the question of its origin is nearly irrelevant (cf. on chap. 13). One is nonetheless wont to ask rhetorically, Why, given its perfect fit in this context with no clear "seams" and given Paul's own rabbinic background and acknowledged genius, could he not have composed such a Christian "midrash" *ad hoc*? Cf. n. 9.

[6]Roetzel, "Judgment Form," considers 10:1-14 to be another example (along with 3:16-17; 5:1-13) of the OT prophetic judgment form, which Paul has adapted.

The nature of this argument strongly suggests that those who "think they stand" (v. 12) do so on the basis of a somewhat magical view of the sacraments. Otherwise one can scarcely make sense of the present paragraph. Therefore, their argument with Paul most likely included some reference to their own security through the sacraments, which so identified them as Christians that attendance at the idol temples was immaterial since those "gods" did not exist (8:4-6).

1-2   An explanatory "for"[7] and the vocative "brothers [and sisters]" (see on 1:10) indicate that the present argument has close ties with the exhortation and warning that has just preceded. They are to run as those intent on winning; that is, they must exercise self-control in all things lest they end up being disqualified. "For," he now goes on to explain, Scripture itself gives some primary examples of people who did not exercise "self-control" in the matter of idolatry and thereby failed to gain the prize.

The argument begins, "I do not want you to be ignorant of the fact that . . ." (cf. 12:1).[8] One cannot tell what Paul intends by this formula, whether it is to give new information or a new slant on something previously known. The nature of the following argument suggests that they were well aware of the *data* of the OT text; Paul wants to make sure they do not miss its *significance* for their lives.

What follows is one of the apostle's more intriguing uses of the OT.[9] In what appears to be a mixture of type and analogy (see on v. 6),[10] he relates Israel's crossing of the Red Sea and their being sustained by manna

[7]Most commentators either ignore this γάρ (e.g., Conzelmann) or minimize it as having a "loose" connection with what precedes (e.g., Barrett, 220). But that fails to take seriously either the argument itself or Paul's usage throughout this letter.

[8]See also 1 Thess. 4:13; 2 Cor. 1:8; Rom. 1:13; 11:25. This is one of three such formulas. Earlier Paul had repeatedly used the diatribe formula "Do you not know that?" (see on 3:16); later he will say "I make known to you" (15:1), which in that case also means "I remind you."

[9]Cf. Ellis, 156 n. 36, who sees the entire passage (vv. 1-13) as a modified form of midrash ("commentary on the biblical text"); cf., *inter alia*, Weiss, 250; Davies, *Paul*, p. 105; Meeks, "'Rose Up,'" pp. 64-66; C. Perrot, "Les examples du désert (1 Co. 10.6-11)," *NTS* 29 (1983), 437-52. Cf. n. 5.

[10]On this question see Ellis, *Use*, pp. 126-35. Cf. esp. L. Goppelt, *Typos, The Typological Interpretation of the Old Testament in the New* (ET, Grand Rapids, 1982), whose original German edition (1939) set off the modern scholarly debate. For this debate and a defense of the typological use of the OT in the New, see R. M. Davidson, *Typology in Scripture, A Study of hermeneutical τύπος structures* (AUSSDS 2; Berrien Springs, MI, 1981).

In contrast to Davidson, who understands "type" in a more cause-and-effect way, by "type" I mean that *after* the fact one sees a correspondence between earlier biblical events and the present situation. Sometimes these are viewed as nearly "prophetic"; i.e., the earlier event makes the second one inevitable. It is doubtful whether Paul so understood them. He sees the one as divinely given "instruction." They "prefigure" in this sense, but they scarcely happened so as to *demand* further "fulfillment."

and water from the rock in terms of Christian baptism and the eucharistic meal,[11] but concludes that the majority fell under God's judgment in the desert. His point seems to be: They genuinely prefigure us when it comes to our experience of "baptism" and "Lord's Supper"; be sure, therefore, that they do not prefigure us also in their idolatry (which they unfortunately seem to be doing in the case of the Corinthians) and subsequent judgment.

By calling Israel "*our* fathers,"[12] he emphasizes at the outset the Corinthians' continuity with what God had done in the past. Since this is being written to a Gentile congregation, this language is sure evidence of the church's familiarity with the OT as their book in a very special sense,[13] and of Paul's understanding of their eschatological existence in Christ (cf. v. 11) as being in true continuity with the past. God's new people are the true Israel of God, who fulfill his promises made to the fathers.[14] This identification is precisely what gives the warning that follows such potency.

Thus he begins: "*All*[15] were under the cloud and *all* passed through the sea" (see Exod. 14:19-22), which he then interprets as their "undergoing baptism[16] into Moses in the cloud and in the sea." The point seems to be: Just as the Corinthians' Christian life began with baptism, so "our fathers' " deliverance from Egypt began with a kind of "baptism";[17] but that, he will

---

[11]It should be noted that Paul was not the first in Israel's history so to understand the past in light of the present. Isa. 43:19-21 offers a prophetic example of eschatological deliverance from present bondage in terms of Exodus imagery. The allegorical "exegesis" of Qumran and of Philo offer contemporary examples of a different type.

[12]NIV, "forefathers"; cf. Rom. 4:1, where Paul does use the Greek word for forefathers.

[13]In the sense that Christ, in whom they believe and to whom everything points, was already present in those OT events (v. 4).

[14]Such an understanding is thoroughgoing in Paul. See esp. Rom. 2:26-29; 11:17-24; Gal. 3:6-9, 29; 6:16; Phil. 3:3; etc.

[15]The πάντες is repeated five times in vv. 1-4—"*All* were under the cloud; *all* passed through the sea; *all* were baptized; *all* ate; *all* drank"—most likely to emphasize the enormity of their corporate sin and consequent failure to gain the prize. One should note, however, that the four examples in vv. 7-10 all say "*some* of them." Does this reflect the Corinthian situation, where *some* of them (see on 4:18) are leading, or trying to lead, the whole church into these paths?

Those who would use this "all" as an analogy for including infants in Christian baptism (e.g., Jeremias, *Origins,* p. 32) are especially misguided in this instance, since they would have to argue from vv. 3 and 4 that infants also ate the Eucharist (cf. Beasley-Murray, *Baptism,* pp. 183-84).

[16]See n. 2 above. Although Zuntz *(loc. cit.)* probably makes a little too much of it, the force of the middle might imply their willing cooperation in the divine event. For the translation "underwent baptism," see Turner, *Syntax,* p. 57, who calls it an "intransitive active."

[17]Some have argued that the rabbis had already made this equation of Israel's crossing the Red Sea with proselyte baptism. See Longenecker, *Biblical Exegesis,* p. 118; for further bibliography, see A. J. Bandstra, "Interpretation in 1 Corinthians 10:1-11," *CTJ* 6 (1971), p. 6 n. 3. The point is moot.

go on to say, did not keep them from falling into idolatry and thus falling short of the prize.[18] The language "baptized into Moses" is drawn not from the OT but from Christian baptism, where believers were baptized "into Christ" (Gal. 3:27; Rom. 6:3). Therefore, it should not be pressed, as though Paul were trying to say something either about Israel's relationship to Moses[19] or about Moses as a prefigurement of Christ—although the latter is a distinct possibility. As Moses was Israel's deliverer, so Christ is theirs. No further analogy is intended; at least none is drawn. Nor does Paul press any further aspects of the two "baptisms"; it is inherent to the typology that both stand at the beginning of the two existences and that both are with water.

More difficult, therefore, is the reference to the cloud. In the narrative Paul describes them as being "*under* the cloud"[20] and passing "*through* the sea*." In the interpretation (v. 2) the two are joined: They were all baptized "in[21] the cloud and in the sea," the cloud above and the wall of sea on either side together constituting their "baptism." In the Red Sea account the cloud was the means by which the Lord himself "went before them" to lead them (Exod. 13:21) and then moved behind them to separate them from the Egyptians (14:19-20). Is this then a veiled reference to the presence of God in Israel's midst, comparable to the Spirit for Christians?[22] Perhaps; but

[18] All attempts to suggest that Paul saw Israel's experience of the Red Sea, or their eating manna and drinking water from the rock, as something sacramental are misguided and futile. Paul is not concerned with Israel's *experience*, but with the *analogies* they provide. See the refutation of this view by Beasley-Murray, *Baptism*, pp. 181-83.

[19] The various suggestions that by this "baptism" Israel came into some kind of relation with Moses, or devoted themselves in loyalty to him, quite miss the point. See, e.g., Bandstra, "Interpretation," p. 7, and Davidson, *Typology*, p. 215, who (typically) intimates that all available scholarly suggestions were implicit in Paul. But Paul is not concerned about Israel's relationship to Moses, but about the Corinthians' to Christ. Cf. Beasley-Murray, *Baptism*, p. 185; Dunn, *Baptism*, pp. 125-26.

[20] Although in the actual Red Sea narrative the cloud is either before or behind them. But see Ps. 105:39, where the cloud is already seen as a "covering" (cf. Wis. 19:7; in Wis. 10:17 personified Wisdom is the cloud that gave them "shelter").

[21] Although these ἐν's could be interpreted as instrumental, the use of ἐν with βαπτίζω throughout the NT is locative, expressing the element into which one is baptized (see on 13:12). Otherwise, Bandstra ("Interpretation," p. 9), who, incorrectly, it would seem, uses Acts 11:16 as an analogy.

[22] This suggestion goes as far back as Origen; it has been variously adopted by exegetes (e.g., Conzelmann, 166; Dunn, *Baptism*, p. 127). Beasley-Murray (*Baptism*, p. 183) considers such a comparison "gratuitous." Less likely still are the suggestions by A. T. Hanson, *Jesus Christ in the Old Testament* (London, 1965), pp. 11-16, that the cloud is a reference to the preexistent Christ, and by M. G. Kline, *By Oath Consigned, A Reinterpretation of the Covenant Signs of Circumcision and Baptism* (Grand Rapids, 1968), pp. 67-70 (followed by Bandstra, "Interpretation," pp. 8-9), that the cloud and sea refer to "the two elemental ordeal powers," fire and water. Both views demand severe jumps in the symbolism (e.g., in Hanson, "cloud" = angel of the Lord = Christ; in Kline "baptism" = judgment ordeal; "cloud" = fire). Kline and Bandstra argue that their view is supported by the use of the verb βαπτίζω here "in its secondary, technical sense,"

more likely the two images had become so interwoven as a way of speaking of the deliverance event[23] that Paul himself did not "mean" anything by it at all.[24]

3-4a In the same way Paul describes Israel's experience of the miraculous bread (Exod. 16:4-30) and miraculous drinking of water from the rock (Exod. 17:1-7; Num. 20:2-13)[25] as a form of "spiritual eating,"[26] unquestionably viewing it as a type/analogy of the Lord's Supper:[27] "They all ate the same[28] spiritual food and drank the same spiritual drink." But what does he mean by calling their food and drink "spiritual"?[29] That

---

since "none of the non-technical meanings, such as 'to immerse' or 'to dip,' really fit" (Bandstra, p. 8). To the contrary, βαπτίζω has its *primary* technical sense of Christian initiation here, which has simply been used by transfer to refer to Israel's crossing of the sea.

[23]Cf. Neh. 9:11-12; Ps. 78:13-14; 105:38-39.

[24]At the other end of the spectrum is Davidson, *Typology,* pp. 218-21, who argues that "it does not seem possible to limit Paul's intention to a single nuance of meaning," and therefore would view it as such rich symbolism as to encompass several possibilities, including Origen's and Kline's (n. 22). This seems to be a case of "having one's cake and eating it too." In parenesis such as this, Paul is simply trying to establish his point, that Israel had its own form of baptism. To overload the symbols with a vast array of meanings, some of which are in actual conflict, seems to go far beyond the author's intent. Cf. n. 19.

[25]It should be noted that these are not the only references to these events in the OT, but they are the primary historical ones; and in Exod. 16-17 the miraculous feeding and drinking immediately follow one another. Although the two events are mentioned separately in subsequent traditions (e.g., Deut. 8:3, where the bread is already being interpreted "spiritually"), more often they appear together (e.g., Deut. 8:15-16; Neh. 9:15, 20; Ps. 78:15-31; 105:40). Cf. John's Gospel, where the eschatological "bread from heaven" is the theme of chap. 6, followed by the eschatological water in 7:37-39.

[26]Goppelt (*TDNT* VI, 146), following Dibelius, Weiss, and Käsemann, argues on the basis of the Corinthian fondness for this word and the usage in *Did.* 10:3 that this was already a term current in Corinth for the eucharistic elements. If so, it lies beyond certain demonstration. For example, the usage in the *Didache* could be dependent on this passage rather than reflecting widespread common usage in the early church. One simply cannot know.

[27]*Contra* Dunn, *Baptism,* p. 125, whose antisacramental stance causes him to reject any analogical/typological reference to the Eucharist here. Not only does the language nearly demand a eucharistic typology, but in the prohibition of the next paragraph (vv. 14-22) Paul begins with his understanding of the Eucharist as the reason why they *cannot* go to the pagan meals.

[28]Calvin, 204, followed by Edwards, 245, and Hanson, *Jesus Christ,* p. 19, argues that "same" here means "the same which we Christians eat." But that is quite beyond Paul's own concern, which is to emphasize that *all* enjoyed the same privileges, including those whose bodies were scattered about the desert; cf. Héring, 86; Barrett, 221-22. Cf. v. 17; *all* eat the *one* bread.

[29]For a full discussion and critique of the various options, see Willis, 130-42, and Davidson, *Typology,* pp. 225-31, 245-47.

question is perhaps best answered by asking what other word he might have used to accomplish two ends simultaneously: (1) to refer to that food and drink which for Israel were supernaturally given and thus divinely sustained them in the desert; and (2) at the same time to suggest the analogy or type of the Lord's Supper, the special food and drink of Christians. In any case, that is his concern and the reason for this choice of words;[30] whether he intends something more than that is moot. The usage in the next sentence suggests that it points to a "spiritual reality" beyond that which meets the eye. But it is doubtful whether he was trying to say something about the sacramental character of the food, or that in some way it conveyed the Spirit.[31]

4b Paul reinforces[32] the fact of their having received "spiritual food and drink" by interpreting the Israelite experience of water from the rock christologically. In so doing he most likely intends both to indicate how culpable Israel really was (they rejected Christ himself in their headlong plunge after idols) and to tie these prefiguring events even more closely to the Corinthians' own situation (they, too, are testing Christ; vv. 9, 22). That much at least seems to be a reasonable understanding of Paul's intent on the basis of the context. But understanding how he got there is another matter. There are two problems: the statement about the rock accompanying them and the identification of this rock with Christ.

First, he says that "they used to drink[33] from the spiritual rock that followed them." Referring to the "rock" as also "spiritual" and then identifying it with Christ seems further to support what was suggested above as to the meaning of this word. But to what is Paul referring? It is common to see this as a reference to a popular rabbinic interpretation of Num. 21:16-18, to

---

[30]Cf. 15:44-46 for a related adjectival use; there the resurrected body is "spiritual" in nature, being both "heavenly" in origin and nonmaterial in substance. In the present case, "spiritual" does not mean "nonmaterial," but it does seem to point to reality beyond the merely material or historical.

[31]As, e.g., E. Käsemann, "The Pauline Doctrine of the Lord's Supper," in *Essays on New Testament Themes* (ET; SBT 41; London, 1960), pp. 108-35, who is characteristically bold: "βρῶμα and πόμα πνευματικόν undoubtedly mean 'food and drink which convey πνεῦμα.'" In this view he is followed by Jewett, *Terms*, pp. 38-39. But this is to place the emphasis on the sacraments in a way that Paul does not; his concern is with their idolatry, not their false sacramentalism.

At the same time it also seems to go beyond the evidence, and probably beyond Paul's intent, to suggest, as Davidson (*Typology*, p. 246) does, that "the apostle seems to intimate that ancient Israel also partook of sacramental gifts which conveyed the Spirit" (cf. p. 247: "Both are sacraments, charged with πνεῦμα, and salvific"). In this case Davidson's prior interest in typology, not simply as prefiguring but in some way as being *devoir-être* ("must needs be"), goes beyond Paul's concerns in the text itself.

[32]Gk. γάρ, giving the grounds for the previous statement.

[33]Gk. ἔπινον; the imperfect here, in contrast to the preceding aorist, suggesting that they customarily drank from the rock.

the effect that the well (known as Miriam's well and shaped like a rock) accompanied Israel in the desert, serving as a continuous, miraculous source of water.[34] Although several legendary features attached themselves to this tradition as time went on, there can be little question that in its basic form it goes back at least to the time of Paul.[35] From this point in time it is difficult to assess the relationship of Paul's statement with this tradition, especially since he refers only to the "rock" and the rabbinic traditions gathered around the "well" in Num. 21. What they have in common is an understanding of the wilderness experience of Israel in which God continually supplied miraculous water as he did bread. Beyond that we are left to our best guesses, although it is not difficult to understand how such a tradition arose, especially in light of the texts noted above (vv. 3-4a) that joined the miraculous bread and water as they referred back to these events.

Thus, Paul seems to be referring to a common tradition of the continual supply of water; but his interest is not in the water but in its source, the rock, which he goes on to identify with Christ.[36] Some see in this identification the influence of Philo, or more correctly the Hellenistic Judaism of which Philo is the leading figure, who equated the rock with personified

---

[34]The most complete expression of the legend is found in *t.Suk.* 3.11: "And so the well which was with the Israelites in the wilderness was a rock, the size of a large round vessel, surging and gurgling upward, as from the mouth of this little flask, rising with them up onto the mountains, and going down with them into the valleys. Wherever the Israelites would encamp, it made camp with them, on a high place, opposite the Tent of Meeting. The princes of Israel come and surround it with their staffs, and they sing a song concerning it: *Spring up, O Well! Sing to it* (Num. 21:17-18)" (Neusner, p. 220). Although this tosephta is not earlier than the fourth c. A.D., it reflects a tradition that goes much further back, being attested by Rabbi Jose ben Judah (end of 2nd c. A.D.) in *b.Taan.* 9a and by Ps.-Philo, *Biblical Antiquities* 11.14 (end of 1st c. A.D.). It is also mentioned or alluded to in other places: *m.Abot* 5.6 (cf. *b.Pes.* 54a), where the well, along with the manna, is said to have been one of the ten things God created on the eve of the sixth day; *Midr.Num.* 1:2 (which reflects the tosephta, with some additional details); *Midr.Num.* 19:26; *Tg.Ps.-J.* Num. 20:2; 22:15; *b.Sabb.* 35a.

[35]For a discussion of the "legend," its probable sources, and its possible influence on Paul, see esp. Ellis, *Use,* pp. 66-70 (cf. "A Note on First Corinthians 10:4," *JBL* 76 [1957], 53-56). Ellis is disinclined to see a direct relationship between the "legend" as it appears in the later rabbinic materials and Paul; rather, he postulates Paul's having a closer relation to the tradition in the Targum, both of which he sees as borrowing from some prophetic uses of the idea of water from the rock.

[36]The formula used to introduce this identification is similar to that used elsewhere by Paul when he is identifying or interpreting an element from a prior quotation or biblical allusion (see 2 Cor. 3:17; Gal. 4:25; Eph. 4:9). In each of these cases, however, the word being interpreted is given a contemporary application, signaled by the present tense of "to be" (e.g., 2 Cor. 3:17, where "the Lord" mentioned in the preceding OT text refers to "the Spirit"). But that is not the case here, where Paul says in the past tense, "now that rock *was* Christ." Dunn, *Baptism,* p. 125, seems quite mistaken to suggest that the verb "is not significant" and that Paul "is not talking about Christ's pre-existence here."

Wisdom.[37] This is based in part on the misguided perception that Paul has himself already identified Christ with Wisdom in 1:24, 30 (q.v.). But such a point of contact with Philo is remote at best. Far more likely is the suggestion that Paul has made a simple transfer of images from the rock at Horeb to such passages as the Song of Moses in Deut. 32 (vv. 4, 15, 18, 30, 31), where the God of Israel is identified as *the* Rock, whose ways are just and perfect, yet who was rejected by them in the wilderness (see esp. vv. 15, 18).[38] In any case, by this identification Paul is about to make a point similar to that in the Song of Moses, that even though God gave them "spiritual food," they rejected him for their idols.

That Paul now identifies the rock with Christ thus serves his double aim: (1) to emphasize the typological character of Israel's experience, that it was by Christ himself that they were being nourished in the wilderness; and (2) thereby also to stress the continuity between Israel and the Corinthians, who by their idolatry are in the process of repeating Israel's madness and thus are in danger of experiencing their judgment. How much by this identification Paul intended to stress Christ's preexistence is moot, but it seems far more likely that he uses the verb "was" to indicate the reality of Christ's presence in the OT events than that he sees him there simply in a figurative way. To be rejected as missing the context altogether is the suggestion that the identification does not have to do with Israel at all, but with the Corinthians: "He is simply saying that Christ is the source of *our* spiritual sustenance."[39] No doubt that, too, is finally involved, but the typology carries its clout only if Paul understood it to be true first of all for Israel itself. All the more so since v. 5 goes on to "ring the changes" on Israel, and thus bring into focus the *reason* for vv. 1-4 in the first place.

5 Vv. 1-4 form a single long sentence in Paul's Greek, to which v. 5 stands in sharp contrast. "Nevertheless,"[40] he now concludes, "despite these sacred privileges similar in kind to yours, including the presence of Christ himself to 'nourish' them with 'spiritual drink,' they failed to obtain the prize." Thus he sets in motion the following section in which he will

---

[37]See *leg.all.* 2.86: "For the flinty rock is the Wisdom of God, which He marked off highest and chiefest from His powers, and from which He satisfies the thirsty souls that love God" (Loeb, I, 279); cf. *det.pot.ins.* 115. Among those who make this bridge see Barrett, 222-23; Conzelmann, 167; Bandstra, "Interpretation," pp. 12-13. It needs to be noted that only the *fact* that both interpret the rock is in common; but Philo's is pure allegory. Paul is not saying that Christ is now the rock, but that in the rock he was somehow himself actually present in Israel.

[38]This suggestion is made the more plausible by the fact that the language "provoking the Lord to jealousy" and their "sacrificing to demons" in vv. 16-17 of the Song are reflected by Paul in vv. 21-22.

[39]So Dunn, *Baptism*, p. 125; see n. 36 above. Conzelmann, 167 n. 26, rejects the similar notion presented by P. Neuenzeit, *Das Herrenmahl* (Münich, 1960), p. 52.

[40]Gk. ἀλλά, the strong adversative.

specify the reasons for Israel's failure and thereby warn his Corinthian friends that their present idolatry can only have similar consequences.

He expresses Israel's failure in the starkest of forms. "God was not pleased with most of them," as is evidenced[41] by the fact that "their bodies were scattered[42] over the desert." The language of this last clause is taken directly from the LXX of Num. 14:16; the picture intended is probably the vivid one of their corpses being "strewn all over the desert," as the vast majority (all but two in fact!) failed one by one to reach the promised land. Saying that "God was not pleased with the majority of them" is Paul's way of expressing God's judgment upon them and of their resultant forfeiture of election—despite their privileges. Thus, *all* of them had experienced a kind of "baptism" and "Lord's supper," yet the vast majority of them experienced God's judgment and failed of the prize. Therefore, take heed (which is the point of vv. 6-12).

It is easy to get lost in the fascination of texts like these (over the typological understanding of the OT, or the "accompanying rock," or the preexistent Christ in Israel's history) and thereby miss the point of the text itself. Each of those other things is there, and they merit our attention and careful study because they put us in touch with Paul's understanding of the OT as Christian Scripture and of the church as the people of God in the new age. But his point in all this must not be missed: just as God did not tolerate Israel's idolatry, so he will not tolerate the Corinthians'. We deceive ourselves if we think he will tolerate ours.

b. Application of the example—warning against idolatry (10:6-13)

6 *Now these things occurred as examples,[a] to keep us from setting our hearts on evil things as they did.* 7 *Do not be idolaters, as some of them were; as it is written: "The people sat down to eat and drink and got up to indulge in pagan revelry."[b]* 8 *We should not commit sexual immorality, as some of them did—and in one day twenty-three[1] thousand of them died.* 9 *We should not test Christ,[2] as some of*

---

[41] An explanatory γάρ is left untranslated in the NIV.

[42] Καταστρώννυμι, both in classical and *koinē* Greek, means "to spread out," "scatter about." Surely this is the picture intended here, rather than the much more tame "laid low" preferred by BAGD; Barrett, 223; and Conzelmann, 164.

[1] A few witnesses conform the number to Num. 25:9 (24,000).

[2] NIV, "Lord," which is secondary here (supported though it is by ℵ B C P 0150 33 104, plus 34 others and some Fathers), as is the θεόν of A 81 pc. For the full argument in favor of Χριστόν see C. D. Osburn, "The Text of I Corinthians 10:9," in *New Testament Textual Criticism, Its Significance for Exegesis. Essays in Honour of Bruce M. Metzger* (ed. E. J. Epp and G. D. Fee; Oxford, 1981), pp. 201-12; cf. Metzger, 560; Zuntz, 126-27. Cf. n. 34 below.

them did—and were killed by snakes. 10 *And do not grumble,*[3] *as some of them did—and were killed by the destroying angel.*

11 *These things*[4] *happened to them as examples and were written down as warnings for us, on whom the fulfillment of the ages has come.* 12 *So, if you think you are standing firm, be careful that you don't fall!* 13 *No temptation has seized you except what is common to man. And God is faithful; he will not let you be tempted beyond what you can bear. But when you are tempted, he will also provide a way out so that you*[5] *can stand up under it.*

[a]Or *types;* also in verse 11
[b]Exodus 32:6

This paragraph continues the narration of the events of the Exodus in two ways: (1) by explaining that the *reason* for this review is to warn the Corinthians (vv. 6, 11-12), who enjoy blessings similar to those of Israel and who through their idolatry are in danger of incurring similar judgment; and (2) by offering specific reasons for the judgment narrated in v. 5 (vv. 7-10). The concluding sentence (v. 13), which stands out like a rock between the warning of v. 12 and the strong prohibition of vv. 14-22, seems to function both to continue the warning and to offer a word of assurance in the midst of warning and exhortation. The more difficult question is what to make of the four examples. Are they four different reasons for *Israel's* failure to reach the promised land, and thus general examples of sin, or do they each reflect in various ways the present problem in Corinth—the Corinthians' arguing ("grumbling") against Paul over the right to attend the pagan feasts? As the commentary hopes to show, one can make excellent sense of the argument by assuming the latter.

6 This sentence serves to tie the examples that follow to the OT analogy that has just preceded. It begins, "Now these things occurred[6] as examples,"[7] referring to vv. 1-5; it concludes with the purpose of the prior

[3]As Metzger, 560, notes, "Influenced by ἐκπειράζωμεν in ver. 9, the reading γογγύζετε (A B C K P Ψ 81 104 614 1739 *Byz Lect* it[61] vg syr[p,h] cop[sa] eth) was replaced in some witnesses (א D G[gr] 33 it[d] cop[bo] arm) by γογγύζωμεν."

[4]The majority of witnesses add πάντα; but the very fact that they do not do so in the same order (πάντα δὲ ταῦτα/ταῦτα δὲ πάντα) is evidence that it is a later insertion (see Metzger, 560; Zuntz, 166 n. 5). The πάντα is tentatively (but weakly) defended by Davidson, *Typology,* pp. 266-67, but basically for prior exegetical reasons (he wants the ταῦτα to include all of vv. 1-10, not just 7-10).

[5]The original text does not have this "you." It was added later and became the MajT reading for the same reason the NIV has included it—to make a more readable sentence.

[6]Gk. ἐγενήθησαν (lit. "became" or "came to be"); the RSV seems quite wrong in translating "are" (cf. GNB).

[7]Gk. τύποι ἡμῶν (lit. "our examples," or "examples/types for/of us"). The exact nature of this genitive is not easy to determine, but it should not be left out (as the NIV).

examples: "to keep us[8] from setting our hearts on evil things[9] *even as* they did," which anticipates the four following examples, each of which comes in the form "Do not (or 'let us not'), *even as* they did."

The first clause is particularly important in determining how Paul understands the function of these OT examples. Everyone agrees that they function at least as analogies; the question is whether Paul intends something more, something closer to typology, with a kind of latent prophetic sense to the OT counterparts. To put that in another way, did he intend the clause to read "These things have been made our examples," or "These things have happened as types of us"?[10] Most likely the answer lies somewhere in between.[11] That is, Israel, as "our fathers," who had their own form of baptism and Lord's Table, genuinely prefigures "us." It was Christ who gave them their "spiritual drink," just as he does ours. But Paul's concern is that they will *not* prefigure "us" in the tragic circumstances narrated in v. 5. Hence there seems to be a typological sense to *Israel* and its "sacraments," but an analogical sense to the *events* used as warning examples. As typology the passage breaks down precisely at the point of warning. Paul does not want what happened to Israel to be repeated in their case;[12] the danger lies in their repetition of Israel's sins (vv. 7-10), which if persisted in will then lead to similar judgment.

In that case, the emphasis in this verse is based on the analogical character of vv. 1-5. The grammar and language of the clause seem to bear this out. "These things" refer to the two concerns of vv. 1-5: on the one hand, Israel had spiritual privileges comparable to those of the Corinthians;

---

[8]Probably on the basis of 9:24-27, where he has already referred to himself in an exemplary way so as to include himself along with them in the common "race" of the Christian life, Paul continues to use "we/us" in this way throughout the following argument, with the notable exceptions of vv. 7, 10, 12-14, 18-22. On this usage see n. 13 on 2:6.

[9]Gk. ἐπιθυμητὰς κακῶν (lit. "lusters after evil"). The personal noun ἐπιθυμητής occurs only here in the NT. Outside the biblical materials the word can have a positive sense (= a deep desire for something). But here and in its two occurrences in the LXX (Num. 11:34; Prov. 1:22) it is clearly pejorative, as the abstract noun ἐπιθυμία usually is in Paul as well (see Gal. 5:16, 24; Rom. 7:7-8; 13:14).

[10]These questions are borrowed from Findlay, 859. They serve to highlight the difficulty in understanding the force of the verb and the kind of genitive involved in ἡμῶν.

[11]Cf. Bandstra, "Interpretation," pp. 15-17, whose language "hypothetical types" to describe this phenomenon, however, does not seem to be the happiest choice. Davidson, *Typology*, pp. 250-86, in effect comes out at this same place, but his desire to see a "must-needs-be" relationship between the type and antitype has led him to some overstatements, as well as to an overemphasis on type over against parenesis that seems to move far beyond Paul's own concern.

[12]Nonetheless, as noted on v. 1, it is the genuinely typological character of Israel and its "sacraments," which serve existentially to get the Corinthians into the "story," as it were, that gives the warning its potency.

on the other hand, most of them fell under God's judgment in the desert and thus failed to obtain their form of the eschatological prize. The verb "became" probably refers not to those events "becoming" examples in the present, but to their "having happened" in the first place so that by divine providence they may warn the Corinthians. Hence, "these things occurred" precisely so that they may serve as "warning examples for us"; that is, they serve as "our examples" in a negative way, so that we will not be like them.

The verses that follow (7-10), then, give four "examples" of how "privileged" Israel "lusted after evil things,"[13] causing the demise of most of them. Indeed, the common denominator to each example is that they illustrate instances in which "their bodies were scattered over the desert." The exegetical question is whether they were chosen because of Israel or because of Corinth; in other words, were they simply chosen at random to illustrate Israel's fall, and as such become for the Corinthians simply another Pauline sin list,[14] or were they chosen because in a very precise way they reflect the situation in Corinth?[15] Most likely it is the latter; vv. 7-8 are the keys.[16]

7 This first example is clear evidence (1) that the argument that began in 8:1 has not gone astray; (2) that the problem is idolatry per se, not simply the eating of marketplace food; and (3) that the form of idolatry for which the Corinthians were arguing in their letter was attendance at the pagan meals in the idol temples (see the introduction to chaps. 8–10). This first example also differs from the three that follow in one significant way. This one illustrates the actual sin by citing the biblical example, thereby

---

[13]Since there are so many allusions to Numbers in what follows, it is possible that this language, "do not be lusters, as they lusted," is a reflection of Num. 11:34 (LXX); but in fact Paul makes no point here of anything from the Numbers passage. Otherwise Perrot, "Les examples," who thinks that this, rather than idolatry, is the basic sin being addressed.

[14]See Conzelmann, 168; cf. Willis, 144-53, who vigorously contends for this. On the other side, see Perrot, "Les examples," pp. 444-49.

[15]Many commentators take the position that these items reflect the Corinthian situation, but in a more general way. That is, rather than seeing them all as related to the matter at hand, they are viewed as reflecting 1 Corinthians as a whole. See, e.g., R-P, 203-07; Grosheide, 223-25. Willis has rightly pointed out that this is fanciful at times.

[16]A word about structure: Although probably intended as four examples of the "evil things" in v. 6, each clause is joined to v. 6 by a μηδέ ("neither"), as though they were the second through the fifth in a series of five. R-P are probably correct in seeing this usage as reflecting genus/species or class/instance ("another point in which the Greek idiom is rather illogical," p. 203). The four sentences are generally parallel, following the structural form of v. 5. Each begins with an imperative, followed by "even as some of them." The first and fourth are second plural imperatives; the second and third, hortatory subjunctives (first person plural imperatives), thus creating an AB-BA pattern. But that may be incidental to the fact that Paul, by the very nature of the argument, would exclude himself from the first and fourth items.

giving the *content* of the "evil thing" but not the form of the judgment; the others merely allude to the Exodus event, and do so by way of a concluding "and" clause that spells out their demise. It seems possible, therefore, that Paul intended all four to be understood in the same way, that is, that judgment also accompanied the first example, and that the other examples are to be understood in light of the biblical text alluded to. If that may seem too subtle for some, it may on the other hand indicate that these early Christians knew their Bibles better than most moderns do, so that the allusion itself was enough to give them recall of the biblical context.

Thus he begins, "Neither be[17] idolaters, as some of them were." It might be arguable that this is general parenesis against idolatry, were it not for the text that Paul chooses to cite, Exod. 32:6b:[18] "The people sat down to eat and drink and got up to indulge in revelry[19]." More specifically related to "idolatry" per se would be v. 6a, "The people rose up early and sacrificed burnt offerings and fellowship offerings," or v. 31c, "They made themselves gods of gold." Instead he chooses that portion of the narrative which specifically indicates that the people *ate* in the presence of the golden calf, thus, along with 8:10 and 10:14-22, specifically identifying the idolatry as a matter of cultic meals in the idol's presence. The judgment in the case of Israel was the slaying of three thousand by the Levites (v. 28) and a subsequent plague (v. 35), Paul's first example (implicit in this case) of "their bodies being strewn over the desert" (v. 5).

The final verb, "and they rose up to play," is probably also to be understood as part of this concern.[20] Although the verb in the LXX often refers to cultic dancing,[21] and in the Exodus narrative the revelry is further expressed in terms of "shouting" (v. 17), "singing" (v. 18), and "dancing" (v. 19), nonetheless in this case (both in the LXX and in Paul) it almost certainly carries overtones of sexual play.[22] This is suggested by the further description in v. 25 of the people's "breaking loose," or "running wildly

---

[17]One is tempted to see significance to the present imperatives in these four verses (cf. Davidson, *Typology,* p. 256), as though Paul were intending to say, "Stop being idolaters" (cf. 4:5; 7:5). In light of the situation in Corinth that is indeed possible; on the other hand, Paul almost always uses the present with this idiom in parenetic series (see, e.g., Rom. 12:16).

[18]In this instance an exact citation of the LXX.

[19]Gk. παίζειν (lit. "to play"). For reasons that are not clear the NIV adds the adj. "pagan" before "revelry" here but not in the Exodus passage. For the meaning of the word in biblical texts, see G. Bertram, *TDNT* V, 625-30.

[20]Meeks, "'Rose up,'" pp. 69-71, makes the dubious suggestion that "play" here is intended to cover all five forms of sin listed in vv. 6-10.

[21]Cf. 1 Sam. 18:7; 2 Sam. 6:5, 21; 1 Chr. 13:8; 15:29.

[22]The same Hebrew verb and its Greek translation have a clearly erotic sense in Gen. 26:8.

out of control." It was so understood by the rabbis[23] and the early church.[24] Furthermore, in the example that follows eating in the presence of the idol and sexual play are specifically joined in the Numbers narrative (25:1-3). Thus for Paul this verb leads directly to the example of sexual immorality that follows, which is also expressed in the context of cultic eating.

8 This second example, "neither let us commit sexual immorality, as some of them did," is also specifically related to the Corinthian situation (see on 5:1-5, 10-11; 6:9-10, 12-20). In this case the question is whether it is a general word against sexual immorality, with the former cases in mind, or whether it suggests that their feasting in the idol temples also at times involved sexual play. Although proper caution is in order, there are several hints that the latter might be involved.

First, the OT event that is referred to (Num. 25:1-9) specifically joins that particular event of sexual immorality with eating in the presence of the Baal of Peor. Second, the preceding text also alludes to idolatrous eating joined with sexual play. Third, in the prohibition against prostitution in 6:12-20, Paul deliberately reapplies the "temple" imagery of 3:16-17 to the Christian's body that was being "joined" to a prostitute. Does this allude to sexual immorality in connection with the pagan temples? Fourth, every other mention of "idol food" in the NT is accompanied by a reference to sexual immorality (Acts 15:29; Rev. 2:14, 20). Moreover, Rev. 2:14 has the same allusion to Num. 25:1-2. It is highly probable, therefore, that in each case these two sins really belong *together*, as they did in the OT and pagan precedents; and they go together at the meals in the pagan temples.

On the other hand, one cannot be completely certain here. Conzelmann has shown decisively that the temple prostitution in connection with the temple of Aphrodite mentioned in Strabo[25] belongs to a former time.[26] On the other hand, the story narrated in Josephus about the lady Paulina, who "after supper" at the temple had nightlong sex with Mundus, thinking he was the god Anubis,[27] suggests that such possibilities still existed in the shrines of the Hellenistic period.

As with the following two examples, Paul does not here narrate the Exodus event itself, nor does he cite a biblical passage in support. Rather, he

---

[23]Cf. *t.Sot*. 6.6: "R. Eliezer b. R. Yosé the Galilean [mid-2nd c. A.D.] says, '*Playing* stated here refers only to fornication, as it is said, *The Hebrew servant whom you have brought among us came in to me to play with me*' (Gen. 39:17)" (Neusner, p. 172)—although in the same passage Akiba is of the opinion that only idolatry is in view.

[24]Tertullian, *De Jejunio* 6.

[25]*Geography* 8.6.20. But he is probably mistaken. See the Introduction, pp. 2-3.

[26]"Mädchen"; for a summary see his *Commentary*, 12 n. 97.

[27]*Ant.* 18.65-80.

alludes to the OT narrative by mentioning the specific judgment that occurred. The judgment in this instance involves the infamous case of "the missing thousand," for which there is not an entirely satisfactory solution.[28] It is possible that Paul had one event in mind (Num. 25:9) but his memory picked up the number from a different event (the number of Levites in Num. 26:62); or perhaps he had access to an otherwise unknown tradition of this event, which seems unlikely since all other known Jewish sources have 24,000.[29] In any case, this is the second (first explicit) example of "their bodies being scattered over the desert" (v. 5).

9 The third example, "Neither let us put Christ to the test, as some of them did—and were killed[30] by snakes," refers to the Israelites' complaint in Num. 21:4-7,[31] where they "spoke against God and against Moses" because they had to eat manna rather than more ordinary food. This example in particular is often seen as the one that begins the move toward a more general parenesis, prompted more by what actually happened in the Exodus than by the situation in Corinth. To the contrary, Paul seems especially to have adapted it to their present conflict with him over the "right" to attend the cultic meals in the pagan temples. Two things suggest that this is so.

First, the verb "test"[32] does not appear in the OT narrative at this point, although it does in Ps. 78:18, apparently referring to this event.[33] Whether or not Paul was influenced by the Psalm, the clue to his usage is to be found not in the OT narrative, but in vv. 21-22, at the end of the following

[28]Particularly so since a multiple of 23 is so unusual in comparison with a multiple of 24. What is difficult to account for is how such a number might have occurred—or come—to him.

[29]See the evidence in Str-B, III, 410. Most of the "harmonistic" solutions are less than satisfactory at best, e.g., that 23,000 fell on "one day" while the others died later (Mare, 249; this lies beyond the possibility of demonstration, nor does it fit with the plain sense of the text; besides, where did Paul have access to such a tradition?); or that the actual number was 23,500, which the Pentateuch and Paul "rounded off" in different directions (see H. Lindsell, *The Battle for the Bible* [Grand Rapids, 1976], pp. 167-69, which he takes quite seriously; but since Paul had access only to the text that already had it rounded off at 24,000, where did he learn of the "correct" number, and why did he round it off downward?).

[30]The impf. ἀπώλλυντο is difficult to account for. Findlay, 860-61, translates "lay a-perishing," a kind of graphic expression of their scene of misery; R-P, 205, offer the more likely alternative, "perished day by day," implying that in this case the judgment took place over a several-day period.

[31]In light of the specific mention of the snakes, it seems difficult to maintain (as Willis, 151) that "it is probable that Paul does not have a specific text in mind."

[32]Gk. ἐκπειράζω, an intensified form of πειράζω, which appears in the second clause.

[33]The best known occurrence of this idea is Deut. 6:16, cited by Jesus in the temptation narrative in Matthew and Luke. In that case it refers to the waters of Massah/Meribah.

prohibition against temple attendance, where he asks rhetorically in the language of Deut. 32:17, "Are we trying to arouse the Lord's jealousy? Are we stronger than he?" Paul's point is that their challenge of his former prohibition against such cultic meals amounts to "putting Christ to the test."

Second, he refers to it as putting *Christ* to the test. That "Christ," not "Lord," is the word used in the original text is almost certain.[34] That means that Paul once again, as in v. 4, is purposely tying the situations of Israel and Corinth together christologically. It was Christ whom Israel was testing in the desert.[35] At the same time it is Christ whom the Corinthians are putting to the test by trying to eat both at his table and at the table of demons.

10 This final example was probably prompted by the previous one, in which the people complained against both God *and* Moses. In v. 9 the problem with the Corinthians is their "putting Christ to the test"; the problem here is probably their concomitant "grumbling" against Paul in their letter, who, according to 5:9-11, has already forbidden them to engage in idolatry and sexual immorality.[36] This seems to be supported by the OT text alluded to in the judgment clause, either Num. 14:1-38, where the narrative begins with the people "grumbling" against Moses as their leader,[37] or Num. 16:41, where the people grumbled against Moses over God's judgment against Korah and his followers.

It is difficult to decide between these two because in neither case does the narrative refer to the people as being "killed by the destroying angel."[38] In favor of the Korah narrative is the large number of people (over 14,700) killed by *the plague* (hence the association with the destroying angel); against it is the fact that the grumbling motif plays such an insignificant part in the narrative. In favor of the Num. 14 narrative is the prominent

---

[34]It easily has the best external support (the combination of P[46], 1739, Clement, the Egyptian versions in Egypt; all the early Western evidence; the earliest evidence from Palestine [Origen]; and Marcion); one can easily account for the change from Χριστόν to κύριον on two counts: (1) the difficulty with the Israelites' having tested Christ; (2) the ease of conformation to the well-known text of Deut. 6:16, cited in the temptation narratives in the Gospels. For the full argument, see Osburn (n. 2).

[35]It is true, as Parry, 147, notes, that since the καθώς clause has no expressed object, one might supply "God," even if "Christ" is read in the first part. But that seems less likely in light of v. 4.

[36]This may also be reflected in the change back to the second person plural imperative here where, as in v. 7, Paul excludes himself.

[37]Although the verb in v. 2 is ἐγγογγύζω, the verb γογγύζω (as here) is used for the same event in v. 27 and is seen as against both the Lord and Moses (in the LXX).

[38]Gk. ὀλοθρευτής, a noun that occurs only here in biblical Greek and only in Christian writings, apparently dependent on this text, in Greek literature. The LXX speaks of ὁ ὀλοθρεύων, "the destroying one," in Exod. 12:23 (cf. Heb. 11:28) and Wis. 18:25. Although the word "angel" is not in the text, Paul is almost certainly thinking of the destroying angel as responsible for whichever judgment he has in mind (cf. 1 Chr. 21:12, 15, where this actual language does occur). See J. Schneider, *TDNT* V, 160-70.

place of the "grumbling" motif; against it is the fact that in this case only a handful die of a plague (v. 37). Perhaps more significantly, and this is what finally is in its favor, this is the passage where the judgment is pronounced that only Joshua, Caleb, and those under 20 would enter the promised land, and from which the language of v. 5 ("being strewn across the desert") is taken. Using the language of the Destroyer from Exod. 12:23, Paul apparently is alluding to that greater judgment wherein all who had not previously died were condemned to die in the desert. In any case, the grumbling in the OT text is against Moses; and very likely it is the Corinthians' grumbling against Paul, which, as with Moses, involves grumbling against God, that prompted him to include this final example of judgment.

11 Just as Paul concluded vv. 1-5 with an express statement that "these things" occurred so that they might function as examples for "us" (especially the Corinthians), so now he concludes the four examples of judgment in the desert with a similar explicit application: "These things happened to them as examples and were written down as warnings for us." Although the wording has changed from v. 6, the point is the same in both instances, the wording here helping further to clarify that of v. 6. As before Israel does not serve as a "type" of the Corinthians;[39] rather, "these events" that have just been narrated "happened to them[40] by way of example[41]." But[42] they "were written down as warnings for us[43]," thus indicating their divinely ordained reason for being in Scripture. In this sentence one captures a sense of Paul's view that both the historical events and the inscripturated narrative are not simply history or isolated texts in Scripture; rather, behind all these things lies the eternal purposes of the living God, who knows the end from the beginning, and who therefore has himself woven the prefigure-

---

[39]Davidson, *Typology,* pp. 268-69, insists that these examples also serve as "advance-presentation"; but that seems to be asking too much of the text and its wording. That Paul sees a clear corollary seems unquestionable, but one does not need such "typological" language for such an understanding. What Davidson fails to demonstrate is that the more technical usage for this word from a later time is already inherent in Paul's usage here, when there seems to be no contemporary evidence for it.

[40]Gk. συνέβαινεν ἐκείνοις, with emphasis on the fact that something has occurred *to* them. The imperfect is probably used because the string of events is viewed as having occurred separately over a period of time.

[41]Gk. τυπικῶς; the adverb of τύπικος. It does not mean "typologically" here, as the following phrase (lit. "for our warning") indicates. The translation is Barrett's (p. 226). For another view, see Davidson, *Typology,* pp. 267-69.

[42]It seems likely that δέ here is slightly adversative, contrasting what happened to them and what was written for our warning.

[43]Gk. πρὸς νουθεσίαν ἡμῶν; the πρός expresses goal or purpose (= "for the purpose of" or "with a view toward"). The ἡμῶν is an objective genitive (cf. the subj. gen. in Eph. 6:4). Thus the phrase could correctly be translated, "But they were written down to warn us."

ment into these earlier texts for the sake of his final eschatological people.

With the final clause, "on whom the fulfillment of the ages has come[44]," Paul sets everything into his thoroughly eschatological perspective (see especially on 4:1-5 and 6:1-5). If the precise nuance of the wording itself is not certain,[45] there is little question about Paul's point. Through his death and resurrection Jesus Christ marks the turning of the ages; the old is on its way out, the new has begun (2 Cor. 5:17). He has set the future irresistibly in motion; and the new people of God, whether Jew or Gentile, bond or free, male or female, who are his by grace alone, are the people of the End, "upon whom the ends of the ages have come" and "toward whom all history has had its goal." That is what constitutes the typological element in these OT stories; ultimately the whole OT has been pointing toward its eschatological fulfillment in God's new people. And that is why the OT is their book in particular—because it has Christ as its prime actor and final goal. This does not mean that Israel, or its history, was not important in its own right, but that they stand at the beginning of the promises of God that are now finding fulfillment at the end of the ages. Thus all of these now exist in written form for "our" sakes, to warn "us" not to be like them; for Christians stand at the end of history, at the time when God is bringing all of the divine purposes into focus and fulfillment in Christ.

12 With another strongly inferential "so then,"[46] Paul brings this review of Israel's history to its conclusion by directly applying these warnings to the Corinthian situation. The one "who thinks he is standing firm" refers back to vv. 1-4, to those who think their participation in the Christian sacraments has placed them above danger in regard to attending the cultic temple meals—especially since they also have argued that such "gods" do not exist (8:4-6). The warning, which began with the analogies in 9:24-27, is that they, too, might "fall," just as the Israelites who had their own form of "sacraments." This can only mean that the Corinthians, too, as Israel, may fail of the eschatological prize, in this case eternal salvation (see on 6:9-11). Their way of placing themselves in this jeopardy is through their idolatry, which will finally be spelled out in the strongest form of prohibition in the

---

[44]Gk. κατήντηκεν, meaning to have "arrived at" or "come to."

[45]The problem is with the two plurals, τὰ τέλη ("end" or "goal") and τῶν αἰώνων ("age"). For a discussion of the various options, see Davidson, *Typology*, pp. 271-74. Whichever option one takes, almost all agree that Paul's point is that he and the Corinthians belong to the period that marks the end of the ages (translated "fulfillment" in the NIV [cf. NEB] as a way of expressing the nuance "goal"). The suggestion by A. Souter, *Pocket Lexicon of the New Testament* (Oxford, 1916), p. 259, followed by P. Macpherson, "τὰ τέλη τῶν αἰώνων: 1 Corinthians x.11," *ExpT* 55 (1943/44), 222, that it means "the (spiritual) revenues of the ages," has almost nothing to commend it.

[46]Gk. ὥστε (see n. 14 on 3:7).

next paragraph (vv. 14-22). But before that, in typical fashion Paul cannot bring himself to end all of this on such a strong word of threat. Hence he breaks the argument at this point with a corresponding word of encouragement (v. 13).

13 This final sentence of the paragraph is one of the better known in 1 Corinthians, having served generations of Christians as a word of hope in times of difficulty. But it is almost always cited in isolation from its present context, and for good reason—it is difficult to see how it fits into the scheme of the present argument, especially since v. 14 follows vv. 1-12 so nicely. The best solution seems to be to regard it as functioning in two directions at once, both as a continuation of the warning in vv. 1-12 and as a word of assurance leading to the prohibition to "flee idolatry" in v. 14.[47] There is no risk of their falling, he seems to be telling them in response to v. 12, as long as one is dealing with ordinary trials. God will help them through such. But they must "therefore, flee from idolatry" (v. 14) because by implication there is no divine aid when one is "testing" Christ in the way they currently are doing (v. 9).

Thus, following hard on the heels of the warning to "beware lest they fall" in v. 12,[48] Paul reassures his Corinthian friends that they need not fall, at least not in the vicissitudes of Christian life common to all. God has already committed himself to them when it comes to ordinary human trials: "No trial[49] has overtaken[50] you except what is common to our human condition[51]." The "trial" or "temptation" probably harks back to the sins enumerated in vv. 7-10, but now against the backdrop of the larger "trial" that such Gentile converts in Corinth must have undergone through their conversion to this new religion out of the East (cf. esp. 1 Thess. 2:1–3:10).

---

[47]For a discussion of these as alternative views see Willis, 157-59.

[48]The asyndeton of this sentence should be noted. It is possible that the sentence thus begins a new sub-paragraph; more likely it is intended to have the closest possible ties to what is said in v. 12, assuring them that they need not fall.

[49]Gk. πειρασμός, which, depending on context, can have the nuance either of temptation (= "seduction to sin") or trial/test (which can lead to the former if one does not bear up under it).

[50]Gk. εἴληφεν, the perfect of λαμβάνω, with emphasis here on its lying outside their willing or doing; ordinary trials or temptations overtake them, or befall them. This obviously cannot refer to attendance at idol feasts, which they were haughtily doing as their "right"—unless, of course, it is a sudden word to the weak of 8:7-13, which is attractive but unlikely in context since there is no hint that the audience changes for this verse.

[51]Gk. ἀνθρώπινος (= "what is distinctively human"). In this context it could refer to the *origin* of the trial, i.e., attendance at idol feasts is not a God-ordained or God-allowed test; it comes from their own human condition of fallenness. But what follows suggests that it refers to the *nature* of the trial. It does not require superhuman effort for them to abstain since it is a merely human trial.

By persisting in attendance at the cultic meals with pagan friends they have put themselves in grave danger of "falling"; but the "temptation" (cf. n. 49) to do so as part of the "trial" of their new life in Christ is not of such a nature that they must succumb to it.[52]

The divine alternative to succumbing that Paul offers is to remind them of God's prior faithfulness on their behalf. When it comes to the trials common to this human life, "God is faithful" (see on 1:9); he can be counted on to help them, and this in two ways. First, God has pledged himself "not to let you be tested beyond what you can bear."[53] This, of course, speaks not only to the fact of God's prior activity in behalf of his people, Paul's emphasis, but also to the fact that they will be called upon to endure. They must be prepared for "a long obedience in the same direction." In his faithfulness God is pledged not to allow what is beyond that endurance.[54]

Second, and as the other side of the same coin,[55] "when you are tempted,[56] he will also provide the[57] way out (or make an end) so that you can stand up under it." This sounds like a contradiction in terms: finding "the way out" so that you can "continue to bear it."[58] But the problem lies only in the less-than-precise wording. There is a "way out of," or "end to," whatever testing one may undergo; but that is to be seen from the divine perspective. One may yet have to endure before the "end" is realized. In any case, one may trust the faithful God to provide the "end" to a test that he has not necessarily originated, but that he has allowed.

Paul's point, then, is that in ordinary human trials one can expect divine aid. There is no danger of "falling" here. But it is otherwise with

---

[52]Cf. Godet, 69-70: "The Corinthians must be made to understand that they run no risk of sinning and falling away from the faith, if they have only to encounter the temptations God allots to them, but that they have no pledge of victory whatever in the case of temptations into which they throw themselves with light-heartedness."

[53]On the question of God's role in "testing" see H. Seesemann, *TDNT* VI, 24-36.

[54]As Conzelmann, 169, rightly notes, "The measure of the bearable cannot be theoretically determined. It shows itself on each occasion in the measure God appoints."

[55]The two expressions of God's faithfulness are set forth in an οὐ/ἀλλά ("not/but") contrast.

[56]Gk. σὺν τῷ πειρασμῷ (lit. "with the temptation"), which can either be taken with the verb (= "he will provide along with the temptation"—not meaning that he is the author of it, but that he is there with a way out along with the test itself), or temporally, as the NIV (= at the time of the temptation). They both come out at the same point.

[57]It is common for translators and commentaries to skip the article with ἔκβασιν; but as Findlay notes, 862, the article with this word corresponds with ὁ πειρασμός to individualize each: "the temptation" and "the way out."

[58]Cf. Weiss, 255, who argues for "end" as the meaning of ἔκβασις since the clause "so that you may endure" is superfluous if he is providing a "way out."

idolatry. The "way out" in that case is simply put: "Therefore, flee idolatry."[59] That is the concern of the next paragraph.

The final verse of this paragraph helps to put things into perspective. The warning, based on the tragic examples of Israel, is straightforward and powerful. Some sins are so incompatible with life in Christ that sure judgment, meaning loss of salvation, is the inevitable result of persistence in them. These are not matters of being "taken in," as it were, by temptation, thus falling into sin. These are deliberate acts, predicated on a *false* security, that put God to the test, as though daring him to judge one of his "baptized ones." Such heady disobedience, Paul assures us, is headed for destruction. But on the other side is the faithful God, ready to aid those enduring trial, assuring them that there is a way out, an end to it. And in the meantime he is there to apportion the necessary ability to endure, appropriate to the trial.

c. The prohibition and its basis (10:14-22)

14 *Therefore, my dear friends, flee from idolatry.* 15 *I speak to sensible people; judge for yourselves what I say.* 16 *Is not the cup of thanksgiving[1] for which we give thanks a participation in the blood of Christ? And is not the bread that we break a participation in the body of Christ?* 17 *Because there is one loaf, we, who are many, are one body, for we all partake of the one loaf[2].*

18 *Consider the people of Israel: Do not those who eat the sacrifices participate in the altar?* 19 *Do I mean then that a sacrifice offered to an idol is anything, or that an idol is anything?[3]* 20 *No, but the sacrifices of pagans[4] are offered to demons, not to God, and I do not want you to be participants with demons.* 21 *You cannot drink the cup of the Lord and the cup of demons too; you cannot have a part in both the Lord's table and the table of demons.* 22 *Are we trying to arouse the Lord's jealousy? Are we stronger than he?*

---

[59]In Barrett's happy phrase, "The *way out* is for those who seek it, not for those who (like the Corinthians) are . . . looking for a way in" (p. 229).

[1]A few MSS (F G 365 pc) have substituted εὐχαριστίας ("thanksgiving") for the original εὐλογίας ("blessing"). For the translation of the NIV see the commentary.

[2]Due to growing liturgical consciousness, the Western witnesses (D F G 629 it vg^mss Ambrosiaster) add καὶ τοῦ ἑνὸς ποτηρίου.

[3]Several MSS (P⁴⁶ ℵ* A C* Ψ 6 33 945 1881 pc) omit this second question due to homoeoteleuton. The omission is argued for as original by Clark, "Textual Criticism," pp. 52-65.

[4]There are several variants in this clause, all due to the addition of τὰ ἔθνη (properly so in terms of meaning, just as the NIV) as the subject of the sentence, lest a careless reader consider the subject still to be "the people of Israel." See the discussion in Metzger, 560-61, and Zuntz, 102.

With this paragraph Paul finally brings to a conclusion the long argument with the Corinthians that began in 8:1 and that concerned their going to the temple feasts.[5] As was argued above (p. 390), the apparently circuitous route Paul has taken in order finally to reach this prohibition is probably due to the nature of the argument in their letter, which itself set the agenda for Paul's response. In any case, the argument of 8:4-6 (including the citations from their letter), the specific expression of the problem in 8:10, and the immediately preceding argument (vv. 1-13) all lead directly to this paragraph.

In a way similar to the argument in 6:12-20 (see esp. 6:18), Paul finally asserts an absolute prohibition against idolatry (v. 14). Then in an appeal to their good sense (v. 15) he explains from their own experience of the Lord's Table (vv. 16-17) and from the OT sacred meals (v. 18) that the same realities carry over to the pagan meals (vv. 19-20), which therefore makes participation in one meal absolutely incompatible with participation in the other (v. 21). All of which ends on the rhetorical note that, just as with Israel's idolatry (v. 9), they are "testing" Christ, provoking him to jealousy (v. 22).

The basis of Paul's prohibition is twofold: (1) His understanding of the sacred meal as "fellowship," as the unique sharing of believers in the worship of the deity, who was also considered to be present.[6] (2) His understanding, based on the OT, of idolatry as a locus of the demonic.

It should be noted that these two bases for the prohibition bring closure to the two basic arguments from their letter, (1) that since an idol is not real, it matters not not only *what* we eat but *where,* and (2) that as long as we participate in our own sacred meal we remain secure in Christ. In the preliminary qualification of the content of their knowledge in 8:4-6 Paul had allowed that for the pagans there were "gods many and lords many," and that for some these "gods" still had subjective reality. Now he asserts that they do have reality indeed, but not as "gods"; rather, they are the habitation of demons. Likewise, in the immediately preceding argument (vv. 1-13), on the basis of the divinely established example of Israel he argued that there is no inherent safety in the sacraments. Now he moves beyond that to demonstrate the absolute incompatibility of eating both sacred meals. The kind of "fellowship" involved eliminates the possibility.

---

[5]For the difficulties this paragraph poses for other approaches to the historical setting of chaps. 8–10 see, *inter alia,* Grosheide, 229-30; Mare, 251; and Conzelmann (cf. n. 8).

[6]The κοινωνία/κοινωνός word group is obviously the key both to the presuppositional examples in vv. 16-18 (the Lord's Table; the Jewish sacrificial meals) and to the description of the pagan meals in vv. 20-21.

14 With a very strong inferential "therefore,"[7] Paul brings the preceding argument to its logical conclusion.[8] In vv. 1-13 he showed by way of example that Israel's "idolatry" had caused their overthrow in the desert, despite their "sacraments." Having warned Corinth of the same possibility (vv. 11-12), he now concludes the argument with both a tender appeal, "my dear friends,"[9] and a straightforward prohibition, "flee[10] from[11] idolatry." The appeal is an appropriate one to follow the word of warning and assurance in v. 13. "God will provide a way out of genuine trials," he assures them, but, "my dearly loved brothers and sisters, that does not include headlong pursuit of idolatry." This usage is reminiscent of 4:14, where after a long and frequently combative argument with them, he uses similar language to remind them that they are his dear children—despite the vigor with which he has had to argue with them. The word for "idolatry" is the equivalent of the personal noun used in 5:10-11 and 10:7 (cf. 6:9), suggesting both that eating at the temples is involved (10:7)[12] and probably that Paul had previously forbidden the practice in his earlier letter (5:9). On the use of such a prohibition following a primarily theological argument, see on 6:18 and 8:13.

15 The prohibition of v. 14 is both abrupt and absolute. Now Paul seeks to show them how sensible it is, based on their own experience of the Lord's Table. Since the Corinthians had prided themselves in their understanding of things, and surely had intimated as much in their letter to him, Paul allows: "I speak as[13] to sensible[14] people." Although he had used this same language in biting irony in 4:10, it seems less likely that he intends it so here. As in 5:3 the "as" refers to an actual reality, not a merely hypothetical

---

[7]Gk. διόπερ (only here and in 8:13 in the NT).

[8]Conzelmann, 170, asserts that "the train of thought in this section is self-contained" and that "it is hardly possible to discern a strict connection of thought with the preceding section, in spite of διόπερ." To the contrary, not only does it clearly conclude vv. 1-13, but it appropriately concludes the entire argument beginning with 8:1. The relationship of v. 14 to vv. 1-13 is so close that some commentators posit divisions of the section to make that more visible (Findlay and Parry divide it into vv. 1-14 and 15-22; Godet, vv. 1-11 and 12-22).

[9]Gk. ἀγαπητοί μου (lit. "my beloved ones"); cf. 4:14, 17; 15:58; 2 Cor. 7:1; Phil. 2:12; 4:1.

[10]Gk. φεύγετε (cf. 6:18).

[11]Since Paul uses the accusative in 6:18 (cf. 1 Tim. 6:11; 2 Tim. 2:22), it may be that Héring, 93, is correct in seeing in the ἀπό used here "almost a locative sense: '*flee* pagan temples,'" although most commentators think otherwise (e.g., Conzelmann, 171 n. 9).

[12]Godet, 74, is surely wrong in suggesting: "The sacrificial feasts were not idolatry, but they bordered on it and might lead to a fall into it." Paul's whole argument is predicated on the essentially idolatrous nature of these feasts.

[13]Gk. ὡς, unfortunately omitted by the NIV.

[14]Gk. φρόνιμος (cf. 4:10).

one. Since they are sensible people by their own admission, he will, as in 11:13 and 14:20, appeal to them as such: "judge for yourselves what I say," meaning in this case, "what I am about to say."[15] But he does not mean "judge for yourselves" as to its rightness or wrongness.[16] They are to judge for themselves that Paul is right!

16 This is one of two passages (along with 11:17-34) where the apostle refers to the Lord's Supper. For that reason it has received an understandably large amount of attention.[17] In this case it is especially important to observe that this meal is not the focus of Paul's concern; the sacred pagan meals addressed in vv. 19-21 are. This passage serves as the *presupposition* for what he will say in vv. 19-21. On the basis of their (probably) common, and for Paul *proper,* understanding of the nature of their own sacred meal, as well as a biblical understanding of that of Israel (v. 18), he appeals to their common sense that they may not attend the pagan meals. That means, therefore, that one can here learn a great deal about Paul's understanding of the Lord's Table, but since his focus is *only* on what is genuinely similar between the two meals, one cannot learn everything here.

What he argues is that there is something inherent in the nature of the Christian meal that makes participation in the other absolutely incompatible.

---

[15]For a similar use of the more rare φήμι see on 7:29.

[16]As Grosheide, 230, seems to imply.

[17]The literature on this passage (and 11:17-34) is immense. As one might well expect, one's own liturgical or nonliturgical tradition often colors this investigation—on either side (the present commentary is not exempt). Among works (by NT scholars) devoted to the Eucharist in the NT in general, see A. J. B. Higgins, *The Lord's Supper in the New Testament* (SBT 6; London, 1952); O. Cullmann, *Early Christian Worship* (ET, SBT 10; London, 1953); C. F. D. Moule, *Worship in the New Testament* (Richmond, 1961); R. P. Martin, *Worship in the Early Church* (Grand Rapids, 1964; rev. 1974); J. Jeremias, *The Eucharistic Words of Jesus* (ET, Philadelphia, 1966); E. Schweizer, *The Lord's Supper According to the New Testament* (ET, Philadelphia, 1967); W. Marxsen, *The Lord's Supper as a Christological Problem* (ET, Philadelphia, 1970); I. H. Marshall, *Last Supper and Lord's Supper* (Grand Rapids, 1980); G. D. Kilpatrick, *The Eucharist in Bible and Liturgy* (Cambridge, 1982).

Among studies of the Supper in Paul see E. B. Allo, "La synthese du dogme eucharistique chez saint Paul," *RB* 18 (1921), 321-43; J. Jeremias, "Das paulinische Abendmahl—eine Opferdarbringung?" *TSK* 108 (1937/38), 124-41; E. H. Peters, "Saint Paul and the Eucharist," *CBQ* 10 (1948), 247-53; M. E. Boismard, "L'Eucharistie selon Saint Paul," *LumV* 31 (1957), 93-106; P. Neuenzeit, *Das Herrenmahl: Studien zur paulinischen Eucharistieauffassung* (München, 1960); S. Aalen, "Das Abendmahl als Opfermahl im Neuen Testament," *NovT* 6 (1963), 128-52; E. Käsemann, "Pauline Doctrine," pp. 108-35; G. Bornkamm, "Lord's Supper and Church in Paul," in *Early Christian Experience* (ET, New York, 1969), pp. 123-60; A. Doudelet, "L'Eucharistie chez Saint Paul," *Collectanea Mechliniensia* 54 (1969), 33-50; Murphy-O'Connor, "Eucharist"; H.-J. Klauck, *Herrenmahl und hellenistischer Kult. Eine religionsgeschichtliche Untersuchung zum ersten Korintherbrief* (Münster, 1982).

That something he describes as *koinōnia* ("fellowship, participation").[18] Precisely what he intended by that term is problematic; at the same time it is the focal point of one of the deep rifts within the Christian church—namely, over the proper understanding of the *nature* of the Christian sacred meal and of the relationship with Christ that inheres in it. The problem has to do with whether Paul's point—or emphasis—is that in sacred meals one has *koinōnia* with the deity (in the Christian's case, with Christ himself), or with fellow participants in the meal as they worship the deity by sacrifice and by eating in his/her honor. Most likely the solution lies somewhere in between. The linguistic and literary evidence indicates that *koinōnia* has to do with the worshipers themselves; but the basis and focus of their worship were the deity, who in most cases was considered to be present among them.

First, then, there can be little doubt that Paul intends to emphasize the kind of bonding relationship of the worshipers with one another that this meal expresses. V. 17 seems to make this certain. It should be noted that the present sequence, cup–bread, is unique to the NT.[19] The evidence from 11:23-25, however, makes it clear that the standard sequence, bread–cup, prevailed in the Pauline churches. The reason for this order, therefore, seems to be that Paul has chosen to interpret the bread in light of the present argument,[20] an interpretation that emphasizes the solidarity of the fellowship of believers created by their all sharing "the one loaf."[21]

At the same time, however, the distinctively religious nature of these feasts indicates that *worship of the deity* was involved, and therefore that they most likely considered him/her also to be present in some way at the meal. This is especially so in Judaism, in which the Israelites are expressly commanded to eat "in the presence of Yahweh." This at least means in his sanctuary; since sacrifice preceded the meal, Yahweh himself was probably understood to be "present" at that meal in a unique way. So also in the pagan meals, since at least one of the papyrus invitations suggests that the god

---

[18]The basic meaning of the word is "to share with someone in something" (Hauck, *TDNT* III, 804). On its usage in the NT and Paul see Campbell, "Κοινωνία"; H. Seesemann, *Der Begriff Κοινωνία im Neuen Testament* (Giessen, 1933); G. V. Jourdan, "ΚΟΙΝΩΝΙΑ in 1 Corinthians 10:16," *JBL* 67 (1947), 11-24; S. D. Currie, "Koinonia in Christian Literature to 200 A. D." (unpub. Ph.D. dissertation, Emory University, 1962); M. McDermott, "The Biblical Doctrine of ΚΟΙΝΩΝΙΑ," *BZ* 19 (1975), 64-77, 219-33; J. Schattenmann, *NIDNTT* I, 639-44; Panikulam, *Koinōnia*, pp. 17-30; Willis, 167-212.

[19]It is found elsewhere only in *Did.* 9:2-3. On the question whether such an order is known in the "shorter text" in Luke 22:17-20 see Metzger, 173-77.

[20]So also Käsemann, "Pauline Doctrine," p. 110; Barrett, 233; Conzelmann, 172. Some have argued for the opposite, namely that the reversed order is to emphasize the cup (see, e.g., Findlay, 863; R-P, 212).

[21]For this emphasis in the pagan meals, see the discussion in Willis, 188-92.

himself will act as host.[22] But this is especially true of the Christian meal. Not only did Jesus himself host the first of such meals, but the early church understood him to be present by the Spirit in their gatherings (cf. 5:3-5). This is most likely how we are also to understand their use of the prayer *Marana tha* (see on 16:22).

But what the evidence does not seem to allow is a sacramental understanding of the meal itself, as if they were "participating in the Lord" by the actual eating of the food, as though the food were the Lord himself. Neither the language and grammar[23] nor the example of Israel nor the examples from the pagan meals allow such a meaning.[24] The "fellowship," therefore, was most likely a celebration of their common life in Christ, based on the new covenant in his blood that had previously bound them together in union with Christ by his Spirit. But while their "fellowship" was with one another, its basis and focus were in Christ, his death and resurrection; they were thus together in his presence, where as host at his table he shared anew with them the benefits of the atonement. It is this unique relationship *between believers* and *with their Lord,* celebrated at this meal, that makes impossible similar associations with other "believers" at the tables of demons. In this passage the cup seems to focus on the vertical dimension, the bread on the horizontal (cf. v. 21).[25]

Thus Paul begins with the cup: "The cup of blessing which we bless, is it not a sharing in the blood of Christ?" The NIV has translated "the cup of blessing" as "the cup of thanksgiving," apparently because that became the more common word for the Christian understanding of this meal (cf. 11:24). Unfortunately that translation causes one to miss the rich Jewish background of this language. "Blessings" offered to the Creator for his bounty were a common part of Jewish meals.[26] The "cup of blessing" was the technical

---

[22]PKöln 57, pp. 175-77 ("the god invites you to a banquet being held in the Thoereion tomorrow from the 9th hour"); for text and discussion see G. H. R. Horsley, *New Documents 1976,* pp. 5-8. Horsley also notes evidence from coins indicating the presence of the god at such a meal.

[23]See esp. Campbell, "Κοινωνία," pp. 22-25.

[24]See especially the discussion in Willis, 17-64, 168-81.

[25]Cf. Jeremias, *Eucharistic Words,* p. 237: "To share in the atoning death of Jesus and to become part of the redeemed community—that is, according to Paul, the gift of the Eucharist" (the whole sentence is italicized in Jeremias).

[26]Indeed, such blessings were mandatory. Cf. *b.Ber.* 35a: "It is forbidden to man to enjoy anything belonging to this world without a blessing; he who enjoys anything of this world without a blessing commits a violation." H. W. Beyer (*TDNT* II, 760) thus describes the Jewish common meal: "The main part is opened with a blessing usually pronounced by the head of the house with a piece of bread in his hand. The others confirm it with an Amen. After this the head of the house breaks the bread and distributes to those who sit at table with him. . . . There is no question of blessing the food and transforming

term for the final blessing offered at the end of the meal. This was the cup that our Lord blessed at the Last Supper (cf. 11:25, "after supper") and interpreted as "the new covenant in my blood."[27] Hence the early church took over the language of this blessing to refer to the cup of the Lord's Table,[28] adding only that it is "the cup of blessing *which we bless,*" to distinguish it from all others, especially the "cup of demons" (v. 21).

Paul's concern, of course, is that the drinking of this cup is for believers "a sharing in the blood of Christ." As noted above, there is little evidence that the food of sacred meals was understood to be an eating of the deity. Since, therefore, the cup is specifically interpreted by the Lord (cf. Mark 14:24), and continued to be so understood in the early church (1 Cor. 11:25), as "my blood of the new covenant,"[29] this language almost certainly refers to their sharing in the provisions and benefits of that covenant. This also means that they did not consider their table to be an altar where sacrifice was taking place, but a fellowship meal where in the presence of the Spirit they were by faith looking back to the singular sacrifice that had been made and were thus realizing again its benefits in their lives. In this way they shared "in the blood of Christ." Being thus joined together in Christ through his blood makes it impossible to join pagan meals where the focus is equally on the "deity" involved—although Paul must go on to explain that the nonexistent deity is in fact a demon.

Similarly, he speaks of "the bread *that we break.*" This also picks up the language of the Jewish meal, and was used by the earliest Christians to designate their fellowship meal (cf. Acts 2:46; 20:7, 11). What is unique here is that Paul will go on to interpret the bread in terms of the church as his

---

it into something different. He rather praises the Creator who controls the fruits of the earth. At the conclusion of the meal there is a common thanksgiving or praise for the food. Usually the head of the house asks the chief guest to pronounce this. After saying, 'Let us pronounce the blessing,' this guest takes the cup of blessing (τὸ ποτήριον τῆς εὐλογίας) and with his eyes on it pronounces a blessing which consists of four benedictions." Cf. the evidence in the excursus in Str-B, IV, 627-36.

[27]See esp. Jeremias, *Eucharistic Words,* pp. 87, 109-10; and L. Goppelt, *TDNT* VI, 153-58.

[28]There has been considerable discussion as to whether Paul in this passage is using the language of a pre-Pauline tradition. Since Paul himself admits to having received the tradition of the Table from those before him (11:23), it is possible that this language also belongs to the earlier traditions. But there is no good reason why this is not an *ad hoc* construction, even if some of the language is earlier. The greater question, which cannot be answered, is whether the κοινωνία language is also earlier, and whether Paul is herewith appealing to language with which the Corinthians would have been familiar. See the discussion in Willis, 193-96. The point is moot since the Corinthians would certainly have understood such terminology already from their pagan background.

[29]Meaning of course that the new covenant was to be ratified by his death. See on 11:25.

"body." Nowhere else in the NT is the bread interpreted at all.[30] Paul does so here probably because in this context the emphasis lies here. Thus he does not mean that by eating the bread believers have some kind of mystical "participation in" the "broken body" of Christ, but, as he clearly interprets in v. 17, they are herewith affirming that through Christ's death they are "partners" in the redeemed community, the new eschatological people of God.

17 In some ways this sentence looks as if Paul were taking a momentary digression,[31] perhaps anticipating the problem in 11:17-34 and thus taking a sideswipe at their divisiveness. But since the sequence cup–bread most likely came about precisely for the sake of this explanatory word, it probably is crucial to our understanding of the present argument. This explanation is what indicates most strongly that *koinōnia* refers to the common sharing in the Lord's Supper that binds them together as a unique, eschatological community. Their singular existence as the people of God, bound together to their Lord through the benefits of the cross and experienced regularly at his Table, makes all other such meals idolatry.[32] Paul's point, therefore, is not the *unity* of the body that this meal represents (although it probably anticipates that concern as well), but the *solidarity* of the redeemed community as one body in Christ that forbids all other such unions.

He makes that point using the analogy of the bread. In a chiastic pattern, whose logic is not as clear as the actual point being made, he says:

Because there is	one loaf,	A
we who are many are one body;		B
for we all partake		B'
of the one loaf.		A'

The first clause is a direct reflection on the final words of v. 16. At the table they all share a common loaf, which the Lord had identified as his "body" (cf. 11:24). Paul now asserts that the "body" in that identification is to be understood analogically as the church, who even though they "are many" are "one body" because there is one loaf at the table. Even though the

---

[30]Although there is no evidence for it in the NT itself, the close association between the "broken bread" and Jesus' "broken" body on the cross caused the bread eventually to be interpreted in this way (see the textual gloss in 11:25: "my body, which is *broken* for you").

[31]This is suggested by some (e.g., Findlay, 864; Weiss, 258; Moffatt, 135; Grosheide, 234).

[32]Cf. Jewett, *Terms,* pp. 257-59, although his positing of a Gnostic background on the basis of a partitioning of the letter seems quite mistaken.

analogy is clear, the logic of that sentence is not immediate, so he adds the explanation, "for[33] we all partake[34] of[35] the one loaf." By common "participation" in the single loaf, the "body of Christ," they affirm that they together make up the "body of Christ,"[36] which in turn implies that they may not likewise become partners in similar associations that honor demons. He is not thereby suggesting that they *become* that body through this meal;[37] in 12:13 he says that happened through their common "immersion" in the Spirit. Rather, by this meal they affirm what the Spirit has already brought about through the death and resurrection of Christ. On the use of the "body" metaphor see on 11:29 and 12:12-13.

18   As in 9:13-14, but now in reverse order, he adds the further analogy of the sacred meals in Israel. "Consider the people of Israel,"[38] he says, intending to argue his case one step further. "Are not those who eat the sacrifices *koinōnoi* (partners, sharers) in the altar?"[39] The context indicates that Paul is referring to the meals prescribed in Deut. 14:22-27, not to the priests' share of the sacrifice alluded to in 9:13.[40] The language "eat the sacrifices" refers to the meal that followed the actual sacrifice, in which they together ate portions of the sacrificed food. Since there is not the remotest hint in Judaism that the sacrificial food represented God in some way,[41] Paul can only mean by "sharers in the altar" that the participants shared together

---

[33]Another explanatory γάρ.

[34]Gk. μετέχω (cf. v. 21), used here specifically for sharing together in the food of the meal; cf. 9:10 and 12.

[35]Nothing is to be made of the unusual use of ἐκ with ἄρτος; it is a Hebraism: all eat *from* the one loaf.

[36]Perhaps implying further that they are one body because they derive nourishment from the same source (Findlay, 864); but Paul himself does not press this.

[37]*Contra* Conzelmann, 172.

[38]Gk. τὸν Ἰσραὴλ κατὰ σάρκα. This language has elicited some discussion, especially among dispensationalists and their opponents, as to how Paul understands the term "Israel." One thing is certain: he intends to refer to the sacrificial meals in ancient Israel. As BAGD 4 indicate, the usage of κατὰ σάρκα here probably refers to their earthly descent, similar to the usage in Rom. 4:1 and 9:3. Nonetheless, the very usage, which is otherwise unnecessary, seems to imply that there is another Israel κατὰ πνεῦμα.

[39]Some have seen a parallel in Philo, *spec.leg.* 1.221, in a passage explaining why the food of these meals must be eaten in three days. One reason, he says, is that it no longer belongs to the one who made the sacrifice, but to God to whom it was made, who as "the benefactor, the bountiful, . . . has made the convivial company of those who carry out the sacrifices partners (κοινωνόν) of the altar (τοῦ βωμοῦ) whose board they share" (Loeb, VII, 229). Obviously this means to share in the food of the altar.

[40]Otherwise Héring, 95, who says that it refers primarily to the priests, then to the people.

[41]On this matter H. Gressmann, "Η ΚΟΙΝΩΝΙΑ ΤΩΝ ΔΑΙΜΟΝΙΩΝ," *ZNW* 20 (1921), 224-30, led a number of scholars astray by suggesting that "altar" is a circumlocution for "God." For a rebuttal see Campbell, "Κοινωνία," p. 24; and Willis, 184-88.

in the food on the altar. Paul's emphasis seems to be that by this meal they were thus bound together in their common worship of Yahweh. By analogy such people could not also have joined the sacrificial meals of their neighbors, and when they did so, it was clearly considered idolatry (cf. vv. 7-8).

The probable reason for this second example is that it is more closely analogous to the pagan meals, which also involved sacrifice, followed by a meal in which the sacrificial food was eaten. The Christian meal was only an analogy of a sacred *meal;* their sacrifice had been offered once-for-all, and though now celebrated at the meal, was not a part of the meal, as in the Jewish and pagan meals.

19 Paul now proceeds to apply the analogies of vv. 16-18, but does so (rhetorically) by going back to the argument of their letter. They have argued that eating idol food, meaning eating meals at the temples,[42] cannot have any bearing on one's Christian life since there is only one God, which in turn means that an idol cannot have genuine reality (8:4). Since Paul has been arguing that there *is* religious significance to the Lord's Table and to the sacrificial meals of Israel, he must now qualify their argument in light of that reality. "Do I mean[43] then" by the preceding argument "that sacrificial food is anything"?[44] Of course not, is the intended response. That we "share in the blood and body of Christ" does not thereby mean that there is genuine significance to the food eaten at pagan meals, as if it were actually sacrificed to a "god." Nor does he mean to imply that "an idol is anything."[45] No, on this point they are agreed; an idol has no reality, in the sense that an idol does not in fact represent what might truly be called a "god." But what the Corinthians have failed to discern right along is that to say an idol is not a god does not mean that it does not represent supernatural powers. Indeed, it is quite the opposite, as he will now go on to explain in v. 20.

20 To the contrary,[46] Paul says, the preceding argument does not imply reality to idols. Rather, they are to understand idolatry in terms of OT revelation: "The sacrifices of pagans are offered to demons, not to a being

---

[42]The tie in this verse between "idol food" and "idol" at the meal in the pagan temples, which at the same time returns to the argument of 8:4, is sure evidence that εἰδωλόθυτα throughout chap. 8 refers to the temple meals, not to marketplace food. Otherwise Conzelmann, 173 n. 34, who notes that the language recalls chap. 8, but insists that the problem is a different one.

[43]Gk. φήμι; see above on v. 14 and 7:29.

[44]The NIV's "a sacrifice offered to an idol" is misleading here; this is the same word, εἰδωλόθυτον, with which the whole argument began back in 8:1 (cf. 8:4, 7).

[45]On the textual question see n. 3 above.

[46]Gk. ἀλλά, the strong adversative being used "before independent clauses, to indicate that the preceding is to be regarded as a settled matter, thus forming a transition to someth[ing] new" (BAGD 3).

who might rightly be termed God⁴⁷." By changing the tense of the verb,⁴⁸ Paul contemporizes the language of the Song of Moses (Deut. 32:17). Israel in the desert had rejected God their Rock for beings who were no gods, indeed who were demons. Although the OT itself contains no theological reflection on this understanding of idolatry, almost certainly it was the natural development of Israel's realization that the "mute" gods of the pagans did in fact have supernatural powers. Since there was only one God, such power could not be attributed to a god; hence the belief arose that idols represented demonic spirits.⁴⁹

From that piece of revelation Paul proceeds to apply the stinger: "And I do not want you to be⁵⁰ *koinōnous* (sharers, partners) in demons." Now the argument from the table of the Lord, as well as the additional argument from Israel's history, comes into perspective. The food eaten at the pagan meals has been sacrificed to demons; that means that those at the table are sharers in what has been sacrificed to demons in the same way that Israel shared in what had been sacrificed to God. Since at the Lord's Table no sacrifice is now involved, it took the additional illustration from Israel to give clarity to this present assertion. Paul's point is simple: These pagan meals are in fact sacrifices to demons; the worship of demons is involved. One who is already bound to one's Lord and to one's fellow believers through participation at the Lord's Table cannot under any circumstances also participate in the worship of demons. That point will be made explicit in the parallel sentences that follow.

21 But Paul does not merely "not want" them to be participants in the demonic. Using the starkest kind of language he asserts: "You cannot drink the cup of the Lord and the cup of demons; you cannot share at the table of the Lord and the table of demons." These words function as both warning and prohibition. They warn in terms of the following rhetorical questions

---

⁴⁷Although Paul is citing or alluding to the LXX of Deut. 32:17 here, he does not intend to say that "the pagans are not sacrificing to God," meaning the God whom we Christians know and worship. That would be irrelevant at best. Paul means either "not to a god," or "to demons, even to one who is no-god." See esp. Deut. 32:21 (alluded to in v. 22 below), where Israel made God "jealous" by sacrificing to "what is no god." Cf. R-P, 216.

⁴⁸From the aorist ἔθυσαν to the present θύουσιν.

⁴⁹Cf. Ps. 96:5, "all the gods of the nations are idols," which the LXX renders "are demons." See also Ps. 106:37; Isa. 65:3 (LXX); 65:11 (LXX); Bar. 4:7.

It is fashionable among modern scholars to "exonerate" Paul at this point as being a man of his times. He believed in demons as did all his contemporaries; but we do not because we have "come of age." But that takes neither biblical revelation nor spiritual reality seriously. Bultmann's "modern man," who cannot believe in such reality, is the true "myth," not the gospel he set out to "demythologize." The cloistered existence of the Western university tends to isolate Western academics from the realities that many Third World people experience on a regular basis.

⁵⁰Gk. γίνεσθαι, lit. "become."

(v. 22); they prohibit in the sense of pointing out the absolute incompatibility of the two actions. One is not merely eating with friends at the pagan temples; one is engaged in idolatry, idolatry that involves the worship of demons.

One should not make more of rhetoric than an author intends. But it is noteworthy that Paul pronounces this prohibition in terms of the two elements of the Lord's Table, in the sequence given in v. 16. First, one "drinks the cup of the Lord"; therefore, one may not likewise "drink the cup of demons." The parallel in this case does not rest with a cup at pagan meals known as the "cup of Sarapis" or the like. The language is taken from the Christian meal, and drinking the cup of the Lord in particular points to the vertical dimension of that meal, that is, to the binding covenantal relationship one has with Christ through the benefits of his "blood." By analogy one cannot likewise have such a relationship with the "demon" Sarapis. The two are mutually exclusive.

Second, one "shares[51] in the table[52] of the Lord."[53] This echoes the language of vv. 16b-17, where the focus is on the horizontal dimension of the table. Those who eat at the Lord's Table, proclaiming his death until he comes (11:26), are thereby also bound to one another through the death of the Lord that is thus celebrated. So also with pagans. Theirs is a sacred "fellowship" in honor of demons. Those who are bound to one another through Christ cannot also become "fellows" with those whose meals are consecrated to demons.[54]

22 This final set of questions brings the argument as it was resumed at 10:1 to its conclusion as a strong word of warning. The questions are joined to the preceding sentence by an untranslated "or," which implies that it offers some kind of alternative to v. 21. Most likely Paul intends: "*Or* will you continue eating at both meals, and thus arouse the Lord's jealousy, as Israel did in the desert?" That is put in the form of a rhetorical question, "Are we[55] trying to arouse the Lord's jealousy[56]?" With these words Paul

---

[51]Gk. μετέχω again, for the actual act of eating; cf. v. 17.

[52]For the significance of a table for the "god," see n. 16 in the introduction to chaps. 8–10.

[53]The term "the Lord's Table" is dependent on this passage, as "the Lord's Supper" is on 11:20.

[54]The combination of μετέχω and κοινωνία with pagans, in a context forbidding idolatry, suggests that 2 Cor. 6:14–7:1 may be a further reflection on this problem. See G. D. Fee, "II Cor. vi.14–vii.1 and Food Offered to Idols," *NTS* 23 (1976/77), 140-61.

[55]Even at the end, although Paul himself would never have been party to this particular sin, he appeals to them by the inclusive "we." His point seems to be, "Are *we* in our situation to be thought of as any better off than Israel in theirs?"

[56]Gk. παραζηλόω, the same word used in the LXX of Deut. 32:21; cf. Rom. 10:19, but see also 11:11 and 14.

continues the allusion to the Song of Moses (in this case to Deut. 32:21) begun in v. 4 and carried further in v. 20, where precisely for its idolatry Israel was rejected by the Lord.[57] The term "jealousy" is a reflection of the OT motif of God's self-revelation (Exod. 20:5), related to his holiness and power, in which he is to be understood as so absolutely without equal that he will brook no rivals to his devotion.

The precise intent of the final question, "Are we stronger than he?" is more puzzling.[58] Most likely this is the final warning that God's "jealousy" cannot be challenged with impunity. Those who would put God to the test by insisting on their right to what Paul insists is idolatry are in effect taking God on, challenging him by their actions, daring him to act. Secure in their own foolhardiness, they think of themselves as so "strong" that they can challenge Christ himself (cf. Isa. 45:9-10).[59] But their folly, implied in the exhortation of 9:25 and given in the warning of 10:12, is that they will thereby fail to gain the final eschatological prize.

The argument has now come full circle. For modern readers it may seem terribly convoluted; but it probably was not at all so for its first readers, for whom this was a response to their letter. The issue has been singular. They were arguing for the right to attend pagan feasts and were trying to "build up" others by having them attend as well. Paul says No. Not only is the latter action totally unloving—and Christian behavior is based on love, not knowledge—but the action itself is totally incompatible with life in Christ as it is celebrated at the Lord's Table. Thus he appeals, exhorts, and finally warns that such attendance is absolutely forbidden. But the matter is not completely finished. Not everything is absolute; there are still matters of indifference—even about things that are tangentially idolatrous. So Paul must yet speak to the issue of "rights" and "freedom" on those matters, which is the concern of the final section (10:23–11:1).

In a variety of ways this paragraph has continued to be a Word for the church. Converts in Third World settings, of course, often have an immediacy with it that many others do not, as they struggle over the religious intent of meals of various kinds, sometimes even in their ancestral homes, where the meal is eaten in honor of the "god." In Western churches interest

---

[57]Because the OT text refers to Yahweh, some think that God the Father is also in view here; but the immediately preceding references to Christ as Lord (v. 21) suggest otherwise, that Paul has in mind his usual reference to Christ. Cf. on v. 9.

[58]Since Paul probably had Christ in mind in the former question, it is just possible, but highly improbable, that he is reflecting on some aspect of Christ's earthly life, who in his incarnation was totally dependent on the Father, and in the desert refused to put God to the test.

[59]Some see here an indirect ironical mention of the "strong" (cf. Héring, 97; Barrett, 238), but that is unlikely.

in the text has usually been over vv. 16-17, with some passing historical interest in the rest. What Paul is finally forbidding is any kind of relationship with the demonic. How that translates into modern Western cultures may be moot; probably what most Western Christians need to learn is that the demonic is not as remote as some of them would wish to believe.

But at a much deeper level is the hermeneutical issue raised by H. F. von Soden,[60] who suggests that Paul does not really forbid temple attendance per se, but only that which has as its clear intent the worship of idol-demons. He argues that Paul throughout is trying to move both the weak and strong beyond their present positions, by reforming the "magical" view of the sacrament held by the strong (= improper sacramentalism) but at the same time rejecting any legal regulation imposed by the weak (= legalism). While these are proper concerns, it is doubtful that this is Paul's real intent here. Rather, the concern is between what is in fact absolute and what are merely *adiaphora* (matters of indifference) for those who have been radicalized by their new existence in Christ.

Without returning to law, meaning law as a means to right standing with God, the Christian faith has inherent within it something so radical that it absolutizes certain behavior. Being members of one body in Christ makes it quite impossible to be involved in idolatrous practices. Fundamental allegiance is at stake. One cannot serve God *and* mammon—or demons, whatever form they may take in our modern world. Sitting at *the* Table and experiencing its benefits of grace and freedom does not give one license for religious or moral licentiousness. Rather, it binds us to one another in common fellowship around Christ and the new covenant in such a way that our behavior in the new age is radicalized toward "the law of Christ" (9:21).

4. On the Eating of Marketplace Food (10:23–11:1)

23 *"Everything is permissible[1]"—but not everything is beneficial. "Everything is permissible"—but not everything is constructive.* 24 *Nobody should seek his own good, but[2] the good of others.*

25 *Eat anything sold in the meat market without raising questions of conscience,* 26 *for, "The earth is the Lord's, and everything in it."[a]*

27 *If some unbeliever invites you to a meal[3] and you want to go,*

[60]"Sacrament," pp. 261-68.
[1]The MajT has conformed this set of slogans to that in 6:12 by adding μοι in each case. The text without μοι is read by P[46] ℵ* A B C* D F G 81 1739 1881 2464 pc lat co. Cf. Metzger, 561.
[2]Against all the early evidence the MajT has added a subject (ἕκαστος) to this second clause.
[3]The words "to a meal" are not in the Greek text, but are necessary to the sense; cf. the Western addition εἰς δεῖπνον.

eat whatever is put before you without raising questions of conscience. 28 But if anyone says to you, "This has been offered in sacrifice[4]," then do not eat it, both for the sake of the man who told you and for conscience' sake[b]—29 the other man's conscience, I mean, not yours. For why should my freedom be judged by another's[5] conscience? 30 If I take part in the meal with thankfulness, why am I denounced because of something I thank God for?

31 So whether you eat or drink or whatever you do, do it all for the glory of God. 32 Do not cause anyone to stumble, whether Jews, Greeks or the church of God—33 even as I try to please everybody in every way. For I am not seeking my own good but the good of the many, so that they may be saved. 1 Follow my example, as I follow the example of Christ.

[a] Psalm 24:1

[b] Some manuscripts *conscience' sake, for "the earth is the Lord's and everything in it"*[6]

Paul has now basically finished his argument with the Corinthians over the assertions in their letter related to attendance at temple meals. But some loose threads must still be tied together. Eating sacrificial food at the temple meals is absolutely forbidden because it involves the worship of idol-demons. But marketplace idol food, which apparently Paul himself had been known to eat (cf. 9:19-23) and for which he had been judged (9:3; 10:29), is another matter altogether.[7]

It has been common, of course, to see Paul as here returning to the issue raised in chap. 8, as though that, too, were dealing with marketplace

---

[4] The ἱερόθυτον of P[46] ℵ A B H 1175* 1739* b sa Ambrosiaster has been conformed to the εἰδωλόθυτον of 8:1, 4, 7; 10:21 by the rest of the tradition. The latter cannot be original since there is no way to account for ἱερόθυτον if it were. Cf. Zuntz, 134.

[5] A few Western MSS (F G a b d vg[mss] Cyprian) try to make some sense of this interruption by changing ἄλλης to ἀπίστου.

[6] This addition is attested only by the MajT and the Harclean Syriac. It cannot be original because of its weak MS support and because one cannot explain how it would have been deleted in so many early witnesses. Cf. Metzger, 561. It appears to be a clumsy attempt to justify abstinence as well as indulgence on the basis of the same OT text.

[7] Although this, too, may have been raised in their letter, it seems more likely that what is at issue is Paul's own conduct, which they have used against him and his apostleship (see on 9:1-3, 19-23). The affinities of this passage with 9:19-23 are so many and striking (cf. Hurd, 130) that it seems likely that Paul is here returning to an issue to which he has alluded before, but now is putting in the form of a general parenesis for them to follow as well. In any case, he takes a completely different stance toward this question than he did toward the previous one, including the form of argumentation, which is nearly devoid of anything combative (except for vv. 29b-30, where in the first person singular he defends his own conduct).

food. But the difficulties with that view seem insurmountable.[8] What needs to be noted here is how little that is essential to the argument of chap. 8 carries over to this passage.[9] Only the words "edify," "conscience," and "offense" are repeated; but in this case the concern over conscience is so different that one has to posit a different audience (the "weak") in order to make sense of it.[10] On the other hand, the truly important items are all missing: idols, idol food, knowledge, the "weak," temple attendance. Rather, here he deals only with food, food sold in the meat market, although what lies behind this concern is obviously the possibility that some of this food had previously been consecrated to idols—or perhaps butchered by pagan priests.[11]

But the real issues seem to lie deeper than the mere question of eating food. Both the nature of their argument for eating at the temples (8:1, 4, 8) and their criticism of Paul (9:1-3, 19-23) have revealed a basic confusion between absolutes and *adiaphora* (nonessentials). They had tried to make temple attendance an *adiaphoron;* for Paul it was an absolute because it was idolatry. At the same time they had confused the true basis for Christian behavior. For them it was a question of knowledge and rights (*gnōsis* and *exousia*). For Paul it is a question of love and freedom (*agapē* and *eleutheria*). Knowledge and rights lead to pride; they are ultimately non-Christian because the bottom line is selfishness—freedom to do as I please when I please. Love and freedom lead to edification; they are ultimately

---

[8]See above, p. 359, esp. n. 7.

[9]The "parallels" that Hurd, 129, alleges between this passage and 8:1-13 are as strikingly *not* parallel as those between 10:30–11:1 and 9:20-23 are.

[10]This is the most common way of trying to reconcile the obvious differences between this passage and chap. 8. The difficulties with this solution are not adequately addressed by its proponents. (1) Vv. 23-24 must be spoken to the "strong"; so also must be the proviso of vv. 28-29a, since as instruction to the "weak" it makes no sense at all (how can one of the "weak" be told not to eat what would have "destroyed" him had he eaten it in the first place, and that because of the *other* person's conscience?). That also means, therefore, that v. 27 must also be addressed to the "strong." Is one to argue that without a hint Paul shifts his audience in vv. 25-26 to the "weak," especially when v. 27 seems to address the same people? Indeed, any suggestion that Paul changes audiences without the slightest hint of such in the text itself needs to rest on otherwise impregnable exegesis, which is lacking here. All the more so when the audience must change three times in five verses in order to satisfy this point of view. (2) It seems nearly impossible that Paul would now command the "weak" of 8:7-13 to do the very thing that he acknowledges would destroy them, and that without addressing the real issue for them—its idolatrous associations. This solution, as popular as it is, simply does not wash.

[11]The proviso of v. 28, plus the general context of chaps. 8–10, suggests this. Thus Conzelmann, 176, is not quite precise to assert that what kind of meat it is "is a matter of indifference since the principle of freedom is upheld." If it were not for the possibly questionable nature of this meat, the issue would not even have been raised!

Christian because the bottom line is the benefit of someone else—that they may be saved (v. 33).

Paul now addresses these issues by using concrete examples from food purchased in the meat market. Two settings are envisioned: food purchased for eating in one's own home (vv. 25-26), and invitations to meals in a neighbor's home (vv. 27-29a). In the argument as a whole, however, these seem to serve basically to illustrate the greater issue: *exousia* and freedom with regard to nonessentials. Thus Paul has two concerns: (1) to establish that one is truly free in matters that are *adiaphora,* in which as a Christian he would now include circumcision (7:19) and the observance of special days (Rom. 14:5; Col. 2:16), as well as the matter of food addressed here. (2) Yet personal freedom, as important as that is for Paul, is not the summum bonum of the Christian life. Seeking the good of others is. Hence the concrete examples of freedom are sandwiched between parenesis on benefiting others (vv. 23-24, 31–11:1), and even one of the concrete examples is qualified by a hypothetical situation in which one should forbear for the sake of another (vv. 28-29a). What ultimately regulates Christian conduct is not the law, but neither is it the *exousia* for which the Corinthians have been contending (v. 23). What rules is "freedom" set in the context of "benefit" and "edification" on the one hand (vv. 23-24, 32-33), and the glory of God on the other (v. 31).

Because Paul is working his way through these two issues simultaneously, and also because he has some personal investment in these things, there are some difficult jumps in the logic of the argument. This is especially true at v. 25, which does not naturally follow the parenesis of v. 24—indeed, it seems to abandon it altogether—and at vv. 29b-30, which seem to respond in some way to v. 29a yet in content are a defense of the concrete example set forth in vv. 25-26. The best solution to this matter seems to be to view the whole as a kind of chiasmus, alternating between the two concerns (personal freedom and the benefit of others). Thus:

A   (23-24)   The criterion: the good of others;
  B   (25-27)   Personal freedom with regard to food;
    C   (28-29a)   The criterion illustrated: freedom curtailed for the sake of another;
  B′   (29b-30)   Personal freedom defended;
A′   (31-33f)   The criterion generalized: that all may be saved.

23 These opening words, which nearly repeat 6:12, appear as abruptly in the present argument as that verse did after 6:1-11, and as there, they signal a new topic. But it is not totally new. One of the loose ends from the preceding argument is their insistence on *exousia* ("rights"),[12] es-

---

[12]The noun of the verb in the slogan "all things are permissible." See on 6:12.

pecially as that is related to Paul's own freedom to eat idol food sold in the meat market (see on 9:19-23). But what follows is not simply a defense of his actions on this matter; rather, he is about to set up his own attitudes toward this food as a model for Christian behavior, which he insists goes back to Christ himself (11:1).

Thus he begins by taking up the matter of *exousia* once again, and the slogan under which they have been operating: "Everything is permissible."[13] As in 6:12, the slogan receives a double qualification, the first of which is an exact duplication of 6:12: "but not everything is beneficial." In this case, however, in contrast to 6:12, there is no ambiguity as to what this means. It refers to what is beneficial for someone else.[14] This is made clear by the second qualification, which does not make a new point but reinforces the first: "but not everything is constructive[15]." Together the two qualifications in effect bring *exousia* to its knees. For the Corinthians *exousia* meant the "right" to act in freedom as they saw fit. For Paul, as with his own *exousia* in 9:12 and 18, it meant the "right" to become slave of all; or as here, the "right" to "benefit" and "build up" others in the body. For him nothing else is genuine *exousia*.

24 The qualifications of *exousia* in v. 23 are now reiterated in the form of general parenesis: "Nobody should seek his own good, but the good of others." This is the first appearance of this formula in Paul's letters, but it is so basic to his understanding of Christian ethics that it probably had long been part of the instructions he gave to his churches. Both in Rom. 15:1-3 and Phil. 2:4 he bases such a stance on the example of Christ, which is precisely how he approaches it at the end of the present argument (10:33–11:1); later in the letter he will use the formula as part of his description of love (13:5). For Paul the death of Christ, in which he gave himself "for us," is not only God's offer of pardon for sinners, but also the only proper model of discipleship. Hence "freedom" does not mean "to seek my own good"; it means to be free in Christ in such a way that one can truly *seek* to benefit and build up another person.[16]

25 In light of the emphasis in the preceding criterion, we are not

---

[13]For the probability that this is a Corinthian slogan, as well as for further details on its meaning, see the discussion on 6:12.

[14]Otherwise Godet, 93, who thinks it refers to "spiritual good in general, including our own"; cf. Parry, 153, "to the persons themselves, who possess the freedom." But that seems to miss the larger context. As Findlay, 866, notes: "In ch. vi he bade his readers guard the application of the principle for their own sake, now for the sake of others."

[15]Gk. οἰκοδομεῖ, usually translated "build up." See on 8:1 and 10; cf. 14:3-5. In 1 Corinthians, apart from the specific exception in 14:4, it means to help someone else or the community as a whole advance spiritually. That it means that here is made certain by v. 24.

[16]While it is true that this parenesis in effect summarizes 8:1-3 and 7-13 (so

quite prepared for the "applications" that now follow. One would expect illustrations of forbearance for the sake of others;[17] what one gets instead are two concrete examples of personal freedom with regard to the meat market, which are finally defended rhetorically in vv. 29b-30 in a very personal way. Only in vv. 28-29a is there an expression of concern for others. How does one account for this kind of argumentation?[18]

Most often it is either stated or assumed that Paul's real point is the example of forbearance in vv. 28-29a. More likely the real concern of vv. 25-30 is personal freedom with regard to *adiaphora*. On these matters one is truly free, especially in matters of food, since in the prayer of benediction alluded to in v. 30 one acknowledges that the ultimate origin of all food, no matter who butchered it or where it appeared in process, is God himself (which is the point of the supporting text in v. 26). On the other hand, such freedom is not the ultimate good in a believer's life. Therefore, one may also freely abstain in contexts where someone else is concerned. That seems to be why he begins with the parenesis of v. 24, because even in matters of personal freedom this must always be in view. But what this parenesis does *not* do is to lead to rules or obligations of abstinence as a general matter of course. Hence he begins with the criterion of the good of others; but he now proceeds to establish that freedom really is that—freedom—and one's own personal life is not to be judged by others.

Paul's "rule" for everyday life in Corinth is a simple one: "Eat anything[19] sold in the meat market *(macellum)*[20] without raising questions of

---

Weiss, 263), the application Paul will make in the following verses differs radically from the earlier passage. In 8:7-13 it led effectively to prohibition with regard to temple meals; here it qualifies personal freedom but does not have the effect of fencing it in. It thus establishes the greater motivation of behavior without eliminating personal freedom.

[17]Such as one finds, e.g., in Rom. 14:13-23, a passage that seems to be a later reworking of some of the ideas found here; but the parallels presented by R. J. Karris ("Rom 14:1–15:13 and the Occasion of Romans," *CBQ* 35 [1973], 163-69) are overdrawn, especially in terms of what is going on in 1 Corinthians.

[18]One of the more common ways is to assert that Paul is now addressing the "weak," telling them not to be so scrupulous. But that will scarcely work; see n. 10 above.

[19]Paul's word order is emphatic. *Anything* sold in the meat market, eat, etc.

[20]Gk. ἐν μακέλλῳ, thought by most to be a Roman word taken over into the Greek cities; see H. J. Cadbury, "The Macellum of Corinth," *JBL* 53 (1934), 134-41 (although BAGD expresses doubts about this). The lack of the article, as Cadbury points out, probably reflects a common idiom, similar to our "at home" or "in church."

The *macellum* itself was one of the more prominent shops in the Roman and Greek marketplaces, as is evidenced especially by the ruins at Pompeii, and supported by other excavations. It was "a rectangular court of pillars with a fountain in the middle and over it, supported by the pillars, a dome-shaped roof . . . ; the booths on the sides; before them porticos" (J. Schneider, *TDNT* IV, 371). A Latin inscription of the *macellum* in Corinth has been discovered, undoubtedly the very one Paul is referring to here; see the account in Cadbury.

conscience." The reason for addressing this issue is that what was sold in the *macellum* often contained meat butchered by the priests,[21] much of it having been part of the pagan sacrifices. Since such meat was expressly forbidden to Jews, and since in their earliest days followers of "the Way" were considered to be a sect of the Jews, the whole issue of the Christians' relationship to the meat market was a thorny one.[22] As with circumcision, Paul takes a decidedly "liberal" stance on this issue. If the Jewish law allowed one to eat meat *before* it was offered to the idols but not afterward, Paul contended that its ultimate source was God himself (v. 26) and that it was therefore irrelevant whether it had been sacrificed or not.

Thus he tells the Corinthians, all of them, to "buy and eat" and to do so "without raising questions[23] of conscience." Apparently it was possible in some cases,[24] indeed it was required of the Jews, to investigate whether the meat in the *macellum* had been previously sacrificed;[25] so Paul is telling the Corinthians not to conduct such inquiries. Meat is meat; buy and eat. On the other hand, since exactly the same phrase occurs in the second example (v. 27), where such an "inquiry" would be less appropriate, it may be that he intends something more like the NIV: Not only do not conduct an investigation, but simply buy and eat without letting it be an issue. The implication is that since God does not care, neither should you.

But what does Paul mean by (lit.) "for conscience' sake"[26]? On this question there has been a division of the house. Some have argued that the whole participial phrase means that one should not conduct such an investigation, for the sake of one's own conscience. That is, the best way not to create trouble for oneself is not to investigate.[27] But that usually assumes either that Paul is addressing the "weak" or that the real issue is "con-

---

[21]The full story on this matter is not yet fully known. Apparently priests by and large served as the town butchers; whether all meat therefore was "sacrificial" is moot. See the discussion by Ehrhardt, "Social Problems," pp. 276-90, who has argued that the butchering and selling of meat was regulated in the Roman Empire for combined political-religious reasons.

[22]As is evidenced by the Apostolic Decree and Rev. 2:14 and 20. See the discussion in n. 1 on p. 357 above.

[23]Gk. ἀνακρίνω; see on 2:15; 4:3; 9:3.

[24]Cf. M. Isenberg, "The Sale of Sacrificial Meat," *Classical Philology* 70 (1975), 271-73.

[25]On this question see *m.Abod.Zar.* 2.3 (cited in n. 1, p. 357). That food needed to be "investigated" among the Jews is most vividly demonstrated by the fact that an entire Mishnaic tractate (*Hullin*) is devoted to regulations for "animals killed for food."

[26]For the discussion of this word in Paul, see on 8:7; this same phrase occurs three times in this argument (vv. 25, 27, 28).

[27]Cf. R-P, 120, "asking no questions which might trouble conscience. It is wise not to seek difficulties"; and Grosheide, 241, "should it appear later that they had eaten sacrificial meat, they still would not have committed any sin." See also C. Maurer, *TDNT* VII, 915, whose discussion is especially impaired by his dividing this passage into "weak" and "strong."

science," which seems to miss Paul's concern altogether. Rather, he is contending that "conscience" is not involved at all, so an investigation is irrelevant. Thus, do not raise any questions "for conscience' sake" because this matter lies outside the concerns of conscience altogether.

26 Paul now gives the basis[28] for his liberal stance of freedom on this issue by citing Ps. 24:1: "The earth is the Lord's, and everything in it."[29] This is the passage used by the rabbis to support the contention that a blessing must be said over every meal. Since "the earth is the Lord's, and everything in it," one must bless God for one's food; otherwise it is as though one were defrauding the Almighty.[30] By this citation, therefore, Paul is almost certainly reflecting the Jewish use of this text for the blessings over meals, especially since he refers again to the "thanksgiving" in v. 30.

But what Paul here does is full of irony toward his Jewish heritage, whether intended or not. The rabbis saw the text as the reason for thanking God for their food; but the food they thus blessed had been thoroughly "investigated" before the prayer. Paul now uses the text to justify eating *all* foods, even those forbidden by Jews, since God is the ultimate source of the food—even that sold in the *macellum*. For that reason it can be taken with thanksgiving. The clear implication is that nothing contaminates food as such along the way. Apart from his radical statements on circumcision, it is hard to imagine anything more un-Jewish in the apostle than this.

27 In a similar way Paul addresses the other kind of eating available to someone in the Greco-Roman world (apart from the temple meals, which functioned for them as "restaurants")—invitations to someone else's home.[31] In this case there is no question as to the source of the invitation. It comes from one of the "unbelievers."[32] As he has already implied in 9:20-22, the acceptance of such invitations is perfectly legitimate (another place where he would be treading on sacred Jewish traditions[33]); it depends on whether "you want to go."

---

[28]The γάρ is causal, expressing the reason or basis for an action. E. Lohse ("Zu I Cor 10.26, 31," *ZNW* 47 [1956], 277-80) suggests that the γάρ represents "for it is written." That may be so, but it is unnecessary.

[29]LXX 23:1, which is cited here verbatim.

[30]See *b.Ber.* 35a, cited in n. 26 on 10:16; cf. *t.Ber.* 4.1: "[following a cit. of Ps. 24:1] He that getteth enjoyment out of this world without a Benediction, behold, he has defrauded (the Lord), to such a degree that at last all the commands are loosed for him" (Oesterley, p. 45).

[31]As Findlay, 867, observes: "When one buys for himself, the question arises at the *shop;* when he is a guest of another, it arises at the *table.*" Paul's point is that neither location is a legitimate place to inquire about the origin of the food.

[32]Gk. ἄπιστος; see the discussion on 7:12.

[33]See, e.g., the story of Peter in Acts 10:9-23, and esp. 11:2-3; cf. the haggadah in *t.Abod.Zar.* 4.6: "R. Simeon b. Eleazar [late 2nd c. A.D.] says, 'Israelites who live abroad are idolaters.' 'How so?' 'A gentile who made a banquet for his son and went and

Because the verb "invites"[34] is used in a semitechnical way in the papyrus invitations, some have suggested that this meal might be either in a private house or in a temple.[35] But the latter is scarcely possible—for two reasons: (1) In v. 28 the believer has to be informed as to the sacrificial nature of the meat he/she is eating; if they were at the temples, that would be known without the need to be told. (2) Despite von Soden's suggestions to the contrary, Paul has absolutely forbidden attendance at temple meals; it is scarcely possible that he is here taking a more relaxed attitude toward something about which he felt so strongly in 10:1-22. Thus it must be an invitation such as Paul himself would regularly have accepted (cf. 9:21), to dine in a pagan home. There is no reason to assume, nor even to imagine, that Paul was thinking of festivals, and therefore that they were semi-religious.[36]

As with what one buys to eat in one's own home, Paul tells them (in almost identical language): "Eat whatever is put before you without raising questions of conscience."

28-29a   The two concrete examples are assumed to be real conditions for believers in Corinth,[37] and express Paul's understanding of personal freedom in regard to *adiaphora*.[38] But for Paul personal freedom is not absolute; it is always conditioned by the "rule" of v. 24—seeking the good of another. Thus he uses this second instance to offer a hypothetical example[39] of a situation where the criterion of v. 24 would limit one's freedom.[40]

More difficult to determine is what kind of person Paul envisages with this "anyone." The options are:[41] (1) the host; (2) a pagan fellow guest;

---

invited all the Jews who live in his town—even though they eat and drink their own [food and wine], and their own waiter stands over them and serves them, they nonetheless serve idolatry, as it is said, and one invites you, and you eat of his sacrifices (Ex. 34:15).'"

[34]Gk. καλεῖ; the other verb so used is ἐρωτάω.

[35]See, e.g., Conzelmann, 177, following von Soden, "Sacrament," p. 264.

[36]As, e.g., Conzelmann, 177, does. This is purely gratuitous, especially since Paul is creating the situation himself!

[37]The two sentences are asyndetic. The first is a simple imperative since everyone would frequent the marketplace; the second is a real condition (εἰ with the indicative, followed by the imperative).

[38]Although obviously not all would agree with him as to what constitutes *adiaphora*!

[39]Gk. ἐάν τις εἴπῃ, a suppositional condition.

[40]Because of the difficulties in identifying the interlocutor, Willis, 242-45, has offered the unlikely suggestion that vv. 28-29a do not qualify v. 27, but rather *begin* a new section of parenesis that carries through to 11:1. It functions as a "general restriction," predicated on v. 24, to *both* vv. 25 and 27, while vv. 29b-30 function to further the point of vv. 28-29a. But to do this Willis must overlook the clear grammatical tie to v. 27: "*But* (a clearly adversative δέ) if anyone says . . ." (cf. the similar qualifying use of ἐὰν δέ in 7:11, 28, 39; 14:24, 28, 30).

[41]For a fuller discussion of these options, see Willis, 240-43, although he is too

(3) a fellow believer.[42] Each of these has its strengths and weaknesses. Least likely is the possibility of a fellow believer. Although the concern for this person's "conscience" has some affinities with 8:7, where a fellow Christian is in view, nothing inherent in this context suggests such here. Indeed, in v. 32 the possibility of offending non-Christians is explicitly mentioned, and in v. 33 Paul's own actions, which are to serve as a paradigm, reflect 9:20-23 and the clear concern that non-Christians might be saved. But what is most difficult for this option, and accordingly favors one of the others, is that Paul's hypothetical interlocutor speaks from a pagan point of view by referring to "sacrificial meat" (*hierothyton*[43]) rather than the standard Jewish-Christian designation "idol meat" *(eidōlothyton),* which Paul had used earlier in these chapters. It is possible, of course, that a person could be reverting to his/her prior pagan vocabulary; but that misses the fact that this is a Pauline creation, not a report of an actual event. Since Paul himself composed it so that the person speaking uses pagan terminology, it seems unlikely that he would thereby have understood the interlocutor to be a believer. Of the other options, it is less likely that he intended the host since he repeats the indefinite pronoun "anyone." Had he intended the *same* subject as in the preceding sentence, either the demonstrative ("this one") or no expressed subject would be more appropriate (cf. 7:36).

We may assume, then, that Paul intended a fellow guest who was himself a pagan. But that leaves us with two further questions: (1) What does Paul envision to be the motivation behind such an informant? (2) What is the relationship between the believer's forbearance and the pagan's "conscience"?[44] Or to put that in another way, How would a pagan's "conscience" be affected by what a Christian did or did not do? Although the answer to the first question may ultimately be irrelevant to Paul's own concern, it seems likely that he envisions the pagan as trying to "help the Christian out" rather than as putting him/her to the test, as it were. It is not difficult to imagine how such a thing could have happened since all Gentiles

---

prone to minimize serious weaknesses in some and maximize strengths in others. This issue is more resoluble than he allows, apparently because he is pressing for another option altogether. See the preceding note.

[42]Those who take this position usually assume that the fellow Christian is present at the meal and has made earnest inquiry about the meat. One of the acknowledged difficulties with this view is that such a person is unlikely to have accepted the invitation in the first place.

[43]A late word, which does not appear often in the literature; but see Plutarch, *mor.* 729c.

[44]The same question, of course, must be answered if the informant is a believer. How will a *believer's* "conscience" be affected one way or the other by the action of another believer in this matter? Will he/she be offended? Tempted to follow suit against conscience?

would know about Jewish scruples over such food,[45] and since they would also think of Christianity at this stage as a basically Jewish sect.[46]

But the second question is more difficult. Paul's point is that one should forbear "both for the sake of the one who told you[47] and for conscience' sake,"[48] which is immediately clarified in v. 29a: "by conscience I mean the other person's, not yours."[49] The clarification itself seems necessary; otherwise the proviso in v. 28 not only limits freedom but allows what he has already twice disallowed—namely that food can have anything to do with Christian conscience.[50] But how can it have anything to do with a *pagan's* conscience? Probably very little at all. The clue lies in the meaning of "conscience," which is not to be understood as "a moral arbiter" but as "moral consciousness." The one who has pointed out the sacrificial origins of this meat to a Christian has done so out of a sense of moral obligation to the Christian, believing that Christians, like Jews, would not eat such food. So as not to offend that person, nor his/her moral expectations of Christians, and precisely because it is *not* a matter of Christian moral consciousness, one should forbear under these circumstances.

If this is the correct understanding of the text, then what Paul is not referring to is a fellow believer's conscience as restricting the actions of another, as is so often assumed. The significance of this observation is that Paul does not allow *any* Christian to make food a matter of *Christian* concern; he does not even do that in Rom. 14, where he does allow people their differences in such matters.

29b-30   But Paul's present concern is not yet with the limitations of freedom imposed by the criterion of v. 24; he will return to that in vv. 31–11:1. For now the concern is freedom itself. So after the qualification of eating when at table in another's home—the only probable place where someone else could be concerned over one's eating habits—he returns by

---

[45]See the discussion in Ehrhardt (n. 21 above) as to the religious and political importance of butchering and selling meat in the Greco-Roman world.

[46]Note the contemporary example offered by Bruce, 100, over alcoholic content in food or drink in a context where some Christians are total abstainers.

[47]Gk. μηνύω; this word implies private communication.

[48]These two nouns form one idea in Greek, being controlled by the same preposition. However, Paul seems intentionally to have separated "conscience" since he could easily have said "the conscience of the informant." In *this* case, Paul is saying, in contrast to the earlier examples, "conscience" is involved.

[49]Note the very close linguistic ties between these final words and the criterion in v. 24.

[50]This, by the way, seems to be the best answer as to why Paul does *not* appeal to the *conscience* of the weak in Rom. 14: *adiaphora* are not matters of Christian conscience. Thus one cares for the people involved and recognizes the genuine differences in these matters, but there is no appeal to the conscience of the weak in this case.

way of that qualification to speak a final word in behalf of freedom.[51] But the rhetoric with which he does so is so sudden and apparently non sequitur that it has created a notorious crux for interpreters. A variety of solutions has been offered, none of which is fully satisfactory.[52] The best answer seems to be found in the language *"my* freedom," "being judged," and "being denounced,"[53] which recalls Paul's defense of his own conduct in chap. 9. Since so much of the language in the immediately following verses echoes 9:19-23, it seems probable that in dealing with the issue of Christian freedom in regard to *adiaphora* like eating marketplace food, he has felt compelled to offer a final word of defense, precisely because this was the issue on which they were judging him.

The first question is thus linked to what has just been said by a "for," as though he were about to go on to explain further how another's con-

---

[51]Cf. the RSV, which understands the text in a similar way by putting parentheses around vv. 28-29b, suggesting, as here, that that is the material which really intrudes into the present argument. In this view the γάρ of v. 29b refers back to v. 27. Cf. Bruce, 100.

[52]Among the more noteworthy: (1) Some find it so difficult as to deny its authenticity, seeing it as an interpolation by a later hand (e.g., Weiss, 265-66; Zuntz, 17). But that raises more questions than it solves since it does not resolve the contextual issue; it only removes it one step from Paul. (2) Lietzmann, 51 (followed *inter alia* by Pierce, *Conscience,* p. 78; Wendland, 83-84; cf. the NEB, GNB, Montgomery, NAB), sees Paul, in the style of the diatribe, as suddenly introducing the objections of one of the "strong." But that assumes that Paul is dealing with the "weak" and the "strong" here, which is unlikely, and opts for a solution for which there is no internal hint in the text itself. Furthermore, and of even greater difficulty, why should Paul do so and then not provide an answer? (3) Others see it as a response to the aggressive activity of the "weak," who are assumed to be in view in v. 29b; Paul is thus telling them not to take undue advantage of the forbearance of the "strong" (e.g., Grosheide, 244; Héring, 99; Murphy-O'Connor, "Freedom," 570). Besides having against it all the difficulties noted above in n. 10 with regard to sudden changes of audience with no internal clues to such, this makes little sense of the strongly defensive and personal tone of the rhetoric. (4) Others see it as a further elaboration of vv. 28b-29, in which Paul is explaining by way of rhetoric that the person who has thus limited his freedom for the sake of another has not really lost his own freedom on these matters (see Bultmann, *Theology,* pp. 217-19; Barrett, 243). (5) Still others see it as an elaboration of vv. 28-29b, but in the sense that Paul is asking rhetorically how one can consider going ahead with eating if one knows beforehand that it will lead to one's being judged and blasphemed for it; thus it becomes a further reason for foregoing one's privileges to eating (see Findlay, 869; Conzelmann, 178; Willis, 247-50). Although either of the latter two is more satisfactory than the first three, it must be admitted that such an explanation does not immediately come to mind as the purpose of such rhetoric, especially the decidedly defensive tone of the second question. One can generally make good sense of the first question from this perspective (by making it subjunctive, "Why should I let this happen?"); but the second question does not seem to answer the first when it is put in this way. It does not in fact say, as Findlay translates, "What good end will be served. . . ?" (p. 869).

[53]Gk. βλασφημοῦμαι; lit. "being blasphemed, or reviled." This is particularly strong language for this argument.

science, not one's own, modifies behavior in this case. Instead, the idea of another person's conscience[54] as limiting freedom on matters such as these, where God cares not in the least whether one eats or doesn't eat, suddenly causes Paul to burst out in rhetoric against his own accusers: "For why[55] is my freedom being judged[56] by another's conscience?" It is possible, of course, that the subjunctive of the NIV is what Paul intended. That is, "Why should one allow a thing like vv. 28-29a to happen to one's freedom?" The problem with that view is that it receives no answer, certainly not to the second question, which seems difficult to understand in any other way than as rhetorical and apologetic.[57]

Thus he adds, to elaborate the first question, "If I take part in the meal with thankfulness, why am I denounced because of something I thank God for?" This is the question that links this sudden outburst of rhetoric with vv. 25-26, rather than vv. 28-29a. More literally he says, "If I partake[58] with gratitude[59] [referring back to v. 26 and anticipating the "thanksgiving prayer" about to be mentioned], why am I being reviled for that for which I give thanks [meaning, 'offer the thanksgiving prayer']?" What Paul seems to be doing is referring back to v. 26, where in the Jewish home the benediction over the food was given precisely because "the earth is the Lord's, and everything in it." If he has offered that benediction over his food (it seems less likely that it would have been offered in the pagan home of v. 27), then how can the Corinthians, or some of them, be judging him on this matter. He is as a Gentile to Gentiles, and as a Jew to Jews. He can either eat or not eat. But if he eats, he does so in light of the benediction alluded to in v. 26, and he is not to be condemned by anyone.

31-32   With this set of imperatives, which are joined to what precedes by an inferential "therefore,"[60] Paul begins to bring closure to the long argument of chaps. 8–10, and especially of 10:23–11:1. He is currently

---

[54]The Greek literally says, "another conscience," but as Barrett, 242, points out, that is hardly English. The Greek intends the conscience of another person.

[55]Gk. ἱνατί (= "for what reason"); this question is the one that makes possible solutions (4) or (5) (see n. 52 above).

[56]There seems to be no justification for the subjunctive translation of the NIV and RSV ("Why should my freedom be judged?"). Where ἱνατί occurs with the present tense elsewhere in the NT it means, "Why is this going on?" See Matt. 9:4; Luke 13:7; Acts 7:26.

[57]The attempt by Findlay, 869, exhibits the difficulties. He argues that the τί in the apodosis is to be viewed as *prospective* and should be read as εἰς τί or ἱνατί. The suggestion is that one who thanks God as a Christian over idol food is committing blasphemy. Willis, 249-50, tends to skirt the grammatical and lexical difficulties altogether.

[58]Gk. μετέχω; see on v. 17 above.

[59]Gk. χάριτι (dative of manner).

[60]Gk. οὖν; infrequent in this letter. See 4:16; 5:7, etc.

addressing the question of conduct in nonessential matters, which began with the overarching principle that the Christian does not seek her/his own good but that of one's neighbor (vv. 23-24). But that must not be construed as eliminating personal freedom. Using the concrete example of marketplace food, he insists on freedom in these matters, which have nothing to do with Christian conscience. The blessing offered at one's meal, predicated on God's prior ownership of all things, means that no fellow Christian may condemn another on this question. "Therefore," he now concludes in light of both vv. 23-24 and 25-30, two imperatives must control Christian behavior on such questions. First, everything must be to the glory of God (v. 31), and second, one must give no offense to anyone—Jew, pagan, or fellow believer (v. 32). V. 31 thus picks up the theme of freedom and gives it focus; v. 32 picks up the theme of the legitimate limitation of freedom in terms of the effect of one's behavior on others.

The protasis of the first imperative begins by picking up the concrete example of eating, to which is added its companion, drinking, and which is finally expanded to include all such activities, "whatever you do." This could possibly refer to the forbearance of v. 28;[61] more likely it broadens the perspective to include all imaginable *adiaphora*. All such things must finally be "for the glory of God."[62] This seems in particular to pick up on the theme of "thanksgiving" in v. 30, that God is to be blessed because everything is his and thus to his glory; but it also broadens the perspective. One's whole life must be to God's glory, not merely that part which is involved in the acknowledgment of his prior ownership of all things through the thanksgiving. Certainly Paul intends that this "rule" dictate the appropriateness of behavior as well. What is not, or cannot be, for God's glory probably should be excluded from "whatever you do."

As v. 33 makes clear, the second imperative brings the instruction back to the concerns of vv. 23-24, although that concern is now expressed more negatively: "Do not give offense[63] either to Jews, or Greeks, or the church of God." At first blush this would seem to render ineffective the preceding instruction on personal freedom. How can one live so as not to offend someone from one of these categories? Paul's point of course is related to behavior that is intentional. That is, with regard to "eating, drinking, etc." one is not purposely to pursue a path that is to the detriment of

---

[61]R-P, 224, suggest that such is included in this clause.

[62]For this theme in Paul, see S. Aalen, *NIDNTT* II, 44-48; here it means to his praise, i.e., so that the believer's actions will bring him glory, honor, and praise. Otherwise, Murphy-O'Connor, "Freedom," 571-73, who would define it as God's "righteousness." Believers give him "glory" as they become like him in righteousness.

[63]Gk. ἀπρόσκοποι γίνεσθε; the adjective is the negative form of the noun that appears in 8:9.

another.[64] To "give offense," therefore, does not so much mean to "hurt someone's feelings" as to behave in such a way as to prevent someone else from hearing the gospel, or to alienate someone who is already a brother or sister.[65] The categories are intentionally inclusive,[66] and echo the language of 9:20-22. As the next two verses imply, he is here calling on them to follow his example, the example already spelled out in his earlier "defense." Thus he is urging on them the very conduct for which they were judging him: to the Jew as a Jew, to the Greek[67] as a Greek, and to the church of God[68] as loving a brother or sister.

Hence "freedom" does not mean that one does whatever one wishes with no regard for others; nor do the limits on freedom suggested here mean that another's conscience dictates conduct. To the contrary, everything is for God's glory and for the sake of the gospel, that is, for the good of all, which from Paul's point of view means that they might be saved (v. 33). That raises both concerns above mere "rules of conduct." Eating and drinking are irrelevant; the one who insists on the right to eat and drink is thereby making it significant. On the other hand, because it is irrelevant, one can use such freedom to forbear when necessary for the sake of the gospel.

33 As so often happens in Pauline parenesis, he offers himself as a paradigm for the kind of conduct he is urging on others (see esp. 4:15-17). The "even as" that begins this clause very likely is intended to cover both of the preceding imperatives, but in terms of specific content it elaborates especially v. 32. In so doing the negative expression of that imperative is now reexpressed in the language with which this parenesis began in vv. 23-24. Thus, "I try to please everybody in every way." The three categories just mentioned and the final purpose clause, "in order that they may be saved," indicate that he means something very similar to what is found in 9:20-22—or perhaps that passage needs to be rethought in light of this one.

[64]As is often pointed out, ἀπρόσκοπος here, in contrast to Acts 24:16, is transitive. The usage in Phil. 1:10 is ambiguous.

[65]Willis, 255-56, says that Paul's emphasis is "clearly on 'the church of God.'" But in light of the purpose clause that concludes the argument (v. 33), "that they may be saved," that is not at all clear!

[66]Cf. on 1:18 and 22. The old categories Jew and Gentile have given way to the new, "being saved" and "perishing." Both of the former categories now belong to the perishing. In the case of the Jew, partaking would tend to offend; in the case of the Greek, except for a rare few (see Conzelmann, 179 n. 36), abstention might be the cause of the gospel's not getting its proper hearing. On the basis of this passage, some of the early Church Fathers referred to the church as a "third race" (cf. Parry, 155).

[67]As often in Paul, "Greek" represents all non-Jewish pagans within the so-called civilized world. See on 1:22-24.

[68]For this language in reference to the early Christian communities, see on 1:2. It is not clear, as Findlay, 869, suggests, that this usage "transcends a local reference." It may become the source of such usage (e.g., in Colossians and Ephesians), but here it probably refers first of all to the church of God in Corinth.

It is of some importance to note that "pleasing people" in the context of evangelism is otherwise anathema to Paul (1 Thess. 2:4; Gal. 1:10). In those passages he refers to the kind of conduct that often characterized the itinerant philosopher or religious charlatan, those who curried the favor of others in order to gain their approval. Paul's concern is not that he himself be pleasing to them, but that his conduct be such that he may not stand in the way of their being saved. In terms of the category "church of God," Paul's own commentary on this text can be found in Rom. 15:1-3, where "pleasing others" is defined as "for his/her good, to build him/her up," which in turn appeals to the example of Christ in his suffering.

Thus Paul repeats the language of vv. 23-24: "not seeking my own good but the good of many." At the same time this echoes the language of 9:22, with which the sentence now concludes: "so that they may be saved." This is "becoming all things to all people so that by all possible means I might save some."

11:1 This final imperative has suffered from one of the more unfortunate chapter divisions in the NT. The language and argument are such that it seems clearly to conclude the parenesis of 10:23-33. It is not enough for Paul that he appeal to his own example. They are to follow ("imitate") that example,[69] in the same way that he has "imitated" Christ. On this idea in Paul see on 4:16. The emphasis here is certainly on the example of Christ, which for Paul finds its primary focus in his sacrifice on the cross. Thus, as in chaps. 1-4, the antidote to their behavior predicated on wisdom and knowledge is Christ crucified.[70] It is hard to imagine a more telling way to end this long argument.

On this powerful note the long section on "idolatry" and "idol meat" comes to a conclusion. Behavior is not unimportant; but it is not regulated by law, at least not in Christ. Some things are altogether incompatible with life in Christ and must be shunned (10:1-22); but other things are of no consequence whatsoever. One is free with regard to these things; but the example of Christ must be predominant, and he "pleased not himself" but willingly endured the insults of others that they might be saved (cf. Rom. 15:3).

---

[69]Gk. μίμηταί μου γίνεσθε. Godet, 102, rightly notes that the verb here means "become," not "be."

[70]To say that does not mean, however, as Conzelmann asserts, 180, that the imitation of Christ does not take its bearings either on the historical Jesus or his teachings. Lying behind Christ's "saving work" is not only the event of his death but also a life lived for others, as well as his teaching. Even though Paul has not here specifically referred to any single teaching of Jesus, the parenesis itself is permeated by the spirit of that teaching, even if not by the language. On "food," e.g., cf. Mark 7:1-19, which in v. 19b Mark himself interprets for his church as Jesus' "declaring all foods clean." On this matter see on 4:16.

Despite this passage, the issue of personal freedom in matters that are *adiaphora*, and the limitation of freedom for the sake of others, continue to haunt the church. Usually the battle rages over what constitutes *adiaphora*. Conservatives on these issues simply fail to reckon with how "liberal" Paul's own view really is. Hence Paul is seldom heard for the sake of traditional regulations. On the other hand, the assertion of freedom to the hurt of others is not the biblical view either. However, in most contemporary settings the "offended" are not unbelievers or new Christians, but those who tend to confuse their own regulations with the eternal will of God.

C. WOMEN (AND MEN) IN WORSHIP (11:2-16)

After prohibiting the Corinthians from becoming involved in pagan worship, Paul now turns to address three items of abuse in their own assemblies: a concern related to women's head covering or hairstyle when praying and prophesying (11:2-16); the abuse of the poor at the Lord's Table (11:17-34); and the abuse of speaking in tongues in the assembly (chaps. 12-14). Since only the third item begins with the rubric "now about" (12:1), indicating a response to their letter, and since the second item is not from their letter,[1] there is some question both as to the place of the present section in the argument as a whole and how it came to Paul's attention.

On the one hand, the language of v. 2, where he "praises them for keeping the traditions," seems purposely to anticipate v. 17 (and vv. 22-23), where "he has no praise for them." Since vv. 17-34 do not come from their letter, it is at least arguable that both of these items appear here because they fit topically—following the prohibitions of pagan worship and preceding their insistence on tongues as the proper mode of spirituality in Christian worship. On the other hand, how does he know that they have "kept the traditions" (v. 2) unless they have so expressed themselves, most likely in their letter? Furthermore, the style of argumentation (cf. 7:1-40) is much less impassioned than that in vv. 17-34 (indeed, the differences are as night and day).[2] This suggests that Paul may in fact be responding to their letter. But if so, what did they say? If not, how did he learn of this matter and who cared enough to bring it to his attention? All told, it seems most likely

---

[1]See below on 11:17-34.

[2]Murphy-O'Connor, "Sex," seems less than precise to speak repeatedly of "the emotional tone of this passage." To the contrary, it lacks almost all of the evidences of rhetoric and emotion that pervade the rest of the letter (chaps. 7 and 12-13 being excepted). E.g., instead of starting with "Do you not know that?" v. 3 begins "I want you to understand that"; the two rhetorical questions (vv. 13-15) lack "rhetoric"; the appeal is to custom, personal shame, "nature"—hardly the apostle's ordinary kind of argument when he strongly disagrees with them.

that he is here reflecting on something that is being asserted by some of the women in the community, probably in their letter. But one finally cannot be certain.

Along with these larger contextual questions, this passage is full of notorious exegetical difficulties,[3] including (1) the "logic" of the argument as a whole, which in turn is related to (2) our uncertainty about the meaning of some absolutely crucial terms[4] and (3) our uncertainty about prevailing customs, both in the culture(s) in general and in the church(es) in particular (including the whole complex question of early Christian worship[5]). Paul's response *assumes* understanding between them and him at several key points, and these matters are therefore not addressed.[6] Thus the two crucial contextual questions, what was going on and why, are especially difficult to reconstruct. All of which has been further complicated by the resurgence in the 1960s (after being latent for nearly forty years) of the feminist movement, both within and outside the church, so that many of the more recent studies[7] on this text are specifically the result of that movement.[8]

The nature of these difficulties, as well as the "logic" of Paul's

---

[3]This has led some to excise the passage altogether as a non-Pauline interpolation. See W. O. Walker, "1 Corinthians 11:2-16 and Paul's View Regarding Women," *JBL* 94 (1975), 94-110; L. Cope, "1 Cor. 11:2-16: One Step Further," *JBL* 97 (1978), 435-36; G. W. Trompf, "On Attitudes Toward Women in Paul and Paulinist Literature: 1 Corinthians 11:3-16 and Its Context," *CBQ* 42 (1980), 196-215; and the response to Walker by J. Murphy-O'Connor, "The Non-Pauline Character of 1 Corinthians 11:2-16?" *JBL* 95 (1976), 615-21; and to Trompf in "Interpolations," 87-90. This is a counsel of despair and is predicated not on grammatical and linguistic difficulties (*pace* Walker), but on the alleged non-Pauline character of the passage. But there is a certain danger in assuming that one knows so well what Paul could or could not have written that one can perform such radical surgery on a text, especially when nothing in the language or style is non-Pauline!

[4]These include "head" (vv. 3-5); "having down the head" (v. 4); "uncovered" (vv. 5, 13); "glory" (v. 7); "authority over her head" (v. 10); "because of the angels" (v. 10); "in the place of a shawl" (v. 15); "such a custom" (v. 16).

[5]The books written on this subject express far more certainty than the data allow. Chaps. 10–14 serve to remind us how little we really know about early Christian worship, mostly because it was παράδοσις—handed down orally, or simply experienced. There are plenty of hints of various kinds, but hardly a full explanation of anything. We know next to nothing, e.g., about (1) the time/frequency of gatherings, (2) the place(s) of gatherings, (3) the kind(s) of gatherings, or (4) the role of leadership. Thus, e.g., the picture that emerges in 11:17-34 is that the Lord's Supper was eaten in conjunction with a meal; yet in 14:26 the picture of worship is of a considerably different kind. Did these happen at the same gathering? Was the meal one kind of worship, and the teaching, singing, prophesying, and praying of 14:26 another kind altogether? We simply do not have enough information to know. Cf. the Introduction, pp. 18-19.

[6]See further on v. 10.

[7]Besides those mentioned in n. 3, see (Eng. titles only in chronological order): A. Isaksson, *Marriage and Ministry in the New Temple. A Study with Special Reference to Mt. 19:3-12 and 1 Cor. 11:3-16* (ASNU 24; Lund, 1965); W. J. Martin, "I Corinthians 11:2-16: An Interpretation," in *Apostolic History and the Gospel: Biblical and Histor-*

argument, is best seen in this instance by a structural display of the entire argument (in purposefully literal English; **HEAD** = metaphorical usage; **head** = literal):

> 2 *Now* I praise you
>> *because* you remember me in all things,
>>> *and*   *even as* I handed them on to you,
>>> you keep the traditions.

I.   3 *But* I want you to understand *that*—
>>>> the **HEAD** of EVERY MAN is Christ,
>>> (and) THE MAN the **HEAD** of WOMAN,
>>> (and) God   the **HEAD** of Christ.

> 4 Every MAN   shames his **HEAD/head**;
>> praying or prophesying having down/against the **head**
> 5 Every WOMAN   shames her **HEAD/head**;
>> praying or prophesying *uncovered* as to the **head**

---

ical Essays presented to F. F. Bruce on his 60th Birthday (ed. W. W. Gasque and R. P. Martin; Grand Rapids, 1970), 231-41; R. Scroggs, "Paul and the Eschatological Women," *JAAR* 40 (1972), 283-303; N. Weeks, "Of Silence and Head Covering," *WTJ* 35 (1972), 21-27; J. B. Hurley, "Did Paul Require Veils or the Silence of Women? A Consideration of I Cor. 11:2-16 and I Cor. 14:33b-36," *WTJ* 35 (1973), 190-220 (see also his unpublished Cambridge dissertation of the same year, *Man and Woman in I Corinthians,* some of which now appears in revised form in *Man and Woman in Biblical Perspective* [Grand Rapids, 1981], pp. 162-84); W. A. Meeks, "The Image of the Androgyne: Some Uses of a Symbol in Earliest Christianity," *HistR* 13 (1974), 165-208; B. K. Waltke, "1 Corinthians 11:2-16: An Interpretation," *BibSac* 135 (1978), 46-57; Murphy-O'Connor, "Sex"; A. Padgett, "Paul on Women in the Church, The Contradictions of Coiffure in 1 Corinthians 11.2-16," *JSNT* 20 (1984), 69-86; and W. L. Liefeld, "Women, Submission and Ministry in 1 Corinthians," in *Women, Authority and the Bible* (ed. A. Mickelsen; Downers Grove, IL, 1986), pp. 134-54.

I have purposely left out of consideration a large number of books on "women's issues" that have a section on this text, since for the most part they do not break new ground, but rest on the work of others. There are three exceptions. The first is Katherine C. Bushnell, *God's Word to Women* (n.d. [1923?]; repr. R. B. Munson; North Collins, NY), who acknowledges indebtedness to John Lightfoot but whose presentation is frequently bold and unique. The second is Elizabeth Schüssler Fiorenza, *In Memory of Her, A Feminist Theological Reconstruction of Christian Origins* (New York, 1983), pp. 226-30. The third is P. B. Payne, *Man and Woman: One in Christ* (Grand Rapids, 1987? [forthcoming at the time of this writing]), which the author was kind enough to let me see in typescript. I learned much from this helpful study even though I am not fully persuaded of the author's full thesis (see the discussion below).

[8]This is both good and bad for exegesis. It is good because it has caused scholars to look at the text with unusual care, thus supplying us with a wealth of helpful information and possibilities for understanding; it is harmful, however, when the prior conclusions both for and against women's equality determine how one is going to understand the text. On this issue the present writer is also a person of his times, for good or ill. For a helpful overview both of the history of exegesis and how it has been influenced by culture, see Linda Mercadante, *From Hierarchy to Equality, A Comparison of Past and Present Interpretations of 1 Cor 11:2-16 in Relation to the Changing Status of Women in Society* (Vancouver, 1978).

For it is one and the same thing
for her to be one who is shaved.

6   *For* if a WOMAN will not *be covered,*
let her also   be shorn.

But if it is disgraceful for her to be shorn or shaved,
let her   *be covered.*

II. 7   *For*

On the one hand, MAN ought not to have the **head** *covered,*
being the image and glory of God;

On the other hand, THE WOMAN
is the glory of MAN;

8   [A]   *For* MAN is not from WOMAN,
but WOMAN from MAN;

9   [B]   *For* also MAN was not created for WOMAN's sake,
but WOMAN for MAN's

10   For this reason

THE WOMAN ought to have authority over her (own) **head**
because of the angels.

11   *in any case* (nonetheless)
[B']   Neither WOMAN apart from MAN,
nor   MAN   apart from WOMAN,
in the Lord.

12   [A']   For just as the WOMAN (is) from   the MAN,
so also the MAN   (is) through the WOMAN,
but all things   (are) from   God.

III. 13 Judge among yourselves:
Is it fitting for a WOMAN to pray to God *uncovered?*
Does not nature itself teach you *that—*

14   On the one hand,
if a MAN grow long hair,
it is a dishonor to him.

15   on the other hand,
if a WOMAN grow long hair,
it is a glory to her?

Because the hair is given to her
in the place of a covering.

16 *Now* if anyone seems to be contentious,
we have no such custom,
nor do the churches of God.

Several things should be said about this argument. (1) The grammatical/structural signals seem to demand this three-part division.[9] In each instance the situations of the man and woman are distinguished from each other by sets of contrasts, in the final two by the specific grammatical signal

---

[9]This subparagraphing is also found in NA[26], but is followed by no known English translations, nor by commentators.

"on the one hand/on the other hand."[10] (2) Also in each instance the argument seems aimed specifically at the woman—and rests squarely on her "head[11]." (3) The problem has to do with her head being "uncovered" while praying and prophesying, as the two expressions of the problem in vv. 5-6 and 13 make clear. All of this is borne out by the argument itself.

Part I (vv. 3-6) argues from the metaphorical use of "head" that the man would shame his "head" if he were to have (something) "hanging down the head"; whereas the opposite would prevail for the woman: she would shame her "head" if she were to prophesy "uncovered as to the head." The explanatory elaboration in vv. 5b-6, which by way of analogy pursues the question of the woman's shame and concludes with the imperative that she is to be covered, makes it clear that this is where the problem lies.

Although the argument in Part II (vv. 7-12) is more complex—and full of surprises[12]—it again seems to aim at the woman. That the man *ought not* to have his *head* covered since he is God's image and *glory* (v. 7ab) sets up both vv. 7c-9 and 10: first, by the assertion that the woman is *man's glory,* which is then explained in vv. 8-9; second, by the assertion in v. 10 that she *ought* to have authority over her own *head* because of the angels. Vv. 11-12, which correspond in reverse order to the assertions of vv. 8-9, seem to be intended to qualify the latter lest they be misunderstood.

The latter part of this argument seems to go astray a bit, so in Part III Paul takes up the issue one more time, now appealing to their own sense of propriety. Picking up the language of v. 5, he begins with a rhetorical question,[13] which functions as the presupposition for what follows. Again, since the woman alone is singled out, it seems clear that the problem lies here. This is further supported by the question that follows (vv. 14-15), where Paul again uses the man to set up the discussion of the woman, whose

---

[10]Gk. μέν . . . δέ, structural signals that are run over rather roughshod by those who attempt other arrangements. See esp. Murphy-O'Connor, "Sex," who breaks the first paragraph at v. 7b, so that the word to men in v. 7ab is seen as the final response in a paragraph divided as vv. 4-7b. He thus not only disregards the μέν . . . δέ, but also makes an explanatory γάρ read as an adversative: "A man, on the contrary." The grammar will not sustain any of this. Cf. Padgett, "Paul," who likewise breaks the paragraph between v. 7b and 7c, with the μέν clause functioning as the conclusion of the Corinthians' argument (vv. 3-7b) and v. 7c beginning Paul's response. There seems to be no precedent for such usage in Greek literature (Padgett appeals to alleged examples in Rom. 7:25; Gal. 4:8-9; and Heb. 9:23; but these are not parallel to what he advocates, including a break in paragraphs and point of view).

[11]The word κεφαλή appears nine times in vv. 3-10, the metaphorical usage in v. 3 (and probably vv. 4-5) being called forth because that is where the literal problem lay (see on v. 3).

[12]See below on the introduction to this paragraph.

[13]Some (e.g., Bushnell, *God's Word,* par. 249; Padgett, "Paul," p. 82) argue that this is an indicative. See the commentary.

situation alone receives further comment. He then concludes with a word to anyone who would be "contentious" over this matter, that the churches have no "such custom."

But what specifically does it mean for the woman to pray and prophesy "uncovered as to the head"? There are three basic options: (1) The traditional view considered her to be discarding some kind of external covering.[14] This seems to be implied both by the verb "to cover" and by the words about the man in v. 7, which imply an external covering ("he should not have his head covered"). The difficulty with this view comes mostly from understanding v. 15 to say that a woman's long hair is given to her *instead of* a *peribolaion* (lit. "a wraparound," hence something like a shawl).

(2) Because of v. 15, it has been argued that the "covering" contended for in vv. 4-7 and 13 is actually the long hair of vv. 14-15, because some of the women were having their hair cut short.[15] But this has against it the language and grammar of vv. 5-6,[16] where Paul argues by analogy that they should be shaved or shorn if they will not be "covered."

(3) More recently several scholars[17] have suggested on the basis of the usage in the LXX that the adjective "uncovered" refers to "loosed hair," that is, to letting her hair down in public and thus experiencing shame. While this is attractive in many ways, it has its own set of difficulties: how the man's not covering his head in v. 7 is the opposite of this; what to do with v. 15, which implies that long hair, not piled-up hair, serves in the place of a shawl;[18] the fact that there is no sure first-century evidence that long hair in public would have been a disgrace of some kind.[19]

---

[14]The use of the word "veil," most often associated with this view, is an unfortunate one since it tends to call to mind the full veil of contemporary Moslem cultures, which covers everything but the eyes. This is unknown in antiquity, at least from the evidence of paintings and sculpture. Most often the "covering" was either the loose end of an outer garment known at the ἱμάτιον *(himation),* or a loosely fitting light linen cloth. See nn. 60 and 71.

[15]Cf. Martin, "Interpretation"; cf. NIV^mg.

[16]Cf. nn. 26-28 below, plus the commentary on these verses. It is completely forced to make the passive "let her be shaved" read "let her be *for now* with short hair" (as Martin, NIV^mg). Paul could easily have said that, and this imperative does not.

[17]This was first argued by Isaksson, *Marriage,* p. 166, and followed without acknowledgment by Hurley, "Veils," pp. 197-200; cf. Payne, *Man,* pp. 44-47. It was refined by Murphy-O'Connor, "Sex," pp. 488-89, followed by Padgett, "Paul," p. 70. Cf. Fiorenza, *Memory,* p. 227, who offers evidence from the mystery cults that disheveled hair often accompanied the women prophets and liturgists.

[18]The answers to this are varied. See on v. 15.

[19]Since none of these is free from problems, other alternatives have been suggested: (1) Isaksson argues that the problem has to do with hairstyles, but that it was strictly limited to the coiffure of "prophets" and "prophetesses" in the "new temple," the church. But despite his arguments for it, this assumes a distinguishable order of prophets in the early church that is less than convincing. (2) Padgett argues that vv. 3-7b are a Pauline quotation or restating of the Corinthian position, and that vv. 7c-15 are his

Either the first or third of these is the more likely option. In both cases the greater difficulty lies with v. 15. If the traditional view is correct, then vv. 13-15 must serve as an argument by way of analogy. That is, on the analogy of "nature" with regard to hair itself, it seems fitting that a woman should maintain the custom of a covering while praying and prophesying. If "loosed hair" is the problem, then vv. 13-15 are seen to address different problems (Hurley), or the word *peribolaion* is reinterpreted to refer to "put up hair" (Murphy-O'Connor). On the whole, a modified form of the traditional view[20] seems to have fewer difficulties, but "loosed hair" remains a viable option. In either case, the woman's action is considered shameful, and for that reason Paul is willing to offer theological justification for maintaining a custom.

But *why* were some women (apparently) thus disregarding the customary mode of appearance? Traditionally, whenever the question was raised at all, it was suggested that the problem had to do with some women who were being insubordinate to their husbands because of their new-found freedom in Christ. Thus interpreters saw the passage, which rested on a particular understanding of vv. 3 and 7-10, as an attempt to "put women in their proper place" by insisting that they keep the traditional symbol of their subordination, the veil.

More likely the problem is related to the overall historical situation in Corinth, and reflects the theological outlook noted elsewhere in this letter (see the Introduction), especially that of the "eschatological" women noted in chap. 7.[21] There can be little question that in the new age inaugurated by Christ women participated in worship along with men.[22] For the most part,

---

response. Vv. 13-15, therefore, are to be read as indicatives ("It is fitting for a woman to pray to God uncovered; not even nature itself teaches you that if men have long hair it is a disgrace for them, etc."). But there are no hints of any kind that Paul is citing the Corinthians, and to make a paragraph break between v. 7ab and 7c is an unnatural reading of the Greek text (see n. 10 above). (3) Payne suggests that Paul is simply responding to Corinthian questions on the whole matter of dress and hairstyle in the assembly. Thus Paul rules that neither men nor women should wear the traditional *tallith* (prayer shawl; vv. 4, 7 for the men; v. 15 for the women) because through the Spirit one comes to Christ without such a "veil" (cf. 2 Cor. 3:12-18). As for the women, he instructs that although they have authority over their own heads (v. 10), they should not let their hair down in public because of the shame it brings upon both themselves and their husbands. As attractive in some ways as this solution is, it does not seem adequately to deal either with Paul's relationship with the church as a whole (see the Introduction) or with the *structure* of the argument in particular (concern over men's dress does not seem to be in purview).

[20]That is, that the "covering" is a loose shawl, not a veil.

[21]See the introduction to chap. 7.

[22]It was traditional for exegetes, especially in some Protestant traditions, to argue that women did not really pray and prophesy, but that Paul's language had to do only with their being present in divine service when prayer and prophecy were going on, or to their

in these matters Corinth followed the traditions they had received when Paul was among them. But some women either were actually praying/prophesying (most likely), or were arguing for the right to do so, without the customary "head covering" or "hairstyle."[23] Probably this is related to their being *pneumatikos* ("spiritual") and to their somewhat overrealized eschatology. It seems difficult to understand Paul's answer unless their spiritualized eschatology also involved some kind of breakdown in the distinction between the sexes. Already they had arrived in the Spirit; they were already acting as those who would be "like the angels," among whom sexual distinctions no longer existed. As a part of their new "spirituality" they were disregarding some very customary distinctions between the sexes that would otherwise have been regarded as disgraceful. Paul feels strongly enough about the issue to speak to it, even if his argument lacks its customary vigor. Since it is difficult to imagine Paul caring for "custom" per se, especially following 10:23–11:1, it is probably the larger theological issue that leads him to this answer at all.

1. An Argument from Culture and Shame (11:2-6)

2 *I praise you[24] for remembering me in everything and for holding to the teachings[a], just as I passed them on to you.*

3 *Now I want you to realize that the head of every man is Christ, and the head of the woman is man, and the head of Christ is God.* 4 *Every man who prays or prophesies with his head covered dishonors his head.* 5 *And every woman who prays or prophesies with her head uncovered dishonors her[25] head—it is just as though her head were shaved.* 6 *For[26] if a woman does not cover her head, let her also*

---

private praying. This view has been revived in recent times by F. C. Synge, "Studies in Texts—I Cor. 11:2-16," *Theology* 56 (1953), 143; and Weeks, "Silence." But v. 13 completely disallows such a view; the woman "prays to God," and the context makes no sense at all if it is not in the gathered assembly. Cf. the discussion in Isaksson, *Marriage*, pp. 153-57.

[23]That is, the problem is probably not simply with their appearing in the assembly in this way, but with their prophesying improperly "attired." One is tempted to see in this some kind of linkage to what went on in the contexts of pagan "ecstasy" (cf. Bruce, 105; R. and C. Kroeger, "An Inquiry into the Evidence of Maenadism in the Corinthian Congregation," *SBL Seminar Papers*, 4 [1978], 2.331-36; Fiorenza, *Memory*, p. 227).

[24]The Western and MajT traditions have added the vocative ἀδελφοί. As Zuntz, 176, notes: "The pronoun [ὑμᾶς] all but called for the addition. Had the vocative been there originally, its omission by so many outstanding witnesses would be inexplicable." Cf. Metzger, 561-62.

[25]A few MSS (B D² 6 629 945 pm) resolve the issue as to what "head" is being shamed by changing αὐτῆς to ἑαυτῆς.

[26]The NIV omits this very important explanatory "for," and thus alters the sense of the whole verse (see the next note).

be shorn; but[27] *if it is a disgrace for a woman to have her hair cut or shaved off, she should cover her head.*[b]

[a]Or *traditions*

[b]Or *4 Every man who prays or prophesies with long hair dishonors his head. 5 And every woman who prays or prophesies with no covering of hair on her head dishonors her head—she is just like one of the "shorn women." 6 If a woman has no covering, let her be for now with short hair, but since it is a disgrace for a woman to have her hair shorn or shaved, she should grow it again. 7 A man ought not to have long hair.*[28]

After an opening word of praise for their keeping the traditions, Paul begins the argument proper with a theological construct in which he uses the word "head" metaphorically to designate three kinds of relationships—man/Christ; woman/man; Christ/God. This metaphor is the lead-in to the two kinds of covering or hairstyle described in vv. 4-5a, where the "head" specified in v. 3 will be shamed by the man's and woman's actions. The idea of "shame" then leads Paul to elaborate in terms of the woman (where the shame seems to become her own as well as the man's), in an attempt to make her see the validity of being "covered."

The metaphor in v. 3, which has traditionally been interpreted as defending the need for the woman to maintain her place of subordination to her "head," namely her husband, is often seen as the point of the whole passage. More likely, however, this is simply an attempt on Paul's part to remove the problem from the "head" literally by putting it into a broader context of relationships. In any case the literal problem came first, and Paul has used the word metaphorically at the beginning to set the literal problem into a larger theological framework.

2 These opening words seem to flow easily from what has immediately preceded (10:33–11:1). Having exhorted the Corinthians to imitate his imitation of Christ, he now commends them for doing so with regard to the "traditions,"[29] "just as I passed them on to you." Nonetheless these

---

[27]NIV, "she should have her hair cut off; and. . . ." This leaves out the καί ("also"), changes the sense of the verb to a true imperative, and fails to see the δέ as adversative, which is necessary in order to make sense of the corresponding conditional sentence that follows. See the commentary.

[28]How this option made the NIV margin is a great puzzle. It does disservice to the Greek at too many places to be viable. One might allow any one of these, but their cumulative effect requires the acceptance of too many contingent improbabilities.

[29]Gk. παραδόσεις (NIV, "teachings"), which with its cognate verb παραδίδωμι ("I handed down" [NIV, "passed on"]; cf. 11:23; 15:3) is a technical term in Judaism for the oral transmission of religious instruction. In this case it almost certainly does not refer to "teachings" (as it does in 15:3), but to the "traditions" that have to do with worship (as in 11:23). For the term in Judaism, see B. Gerhardsson, *Memory and Manuscript* (ET, ASNU 22; Lund, 1961); for Paul, K. Wegenast, *Das Verständnis der Tradition bei Paulus und in den Deuteropaulinen* (Neukirchen-Vluyn, 1962); *idem*, *NIDNTT* III, 772-74.

words are surprising—in two ways. First, one is scarcely prepared for words of "praise"[30] in this letter, especially "praise for remembering me in everything"; indeed, apart from the opening thanksgiving, little else in this letter remotely resembles praise or commendation. Up to this point it has all been rhetorical argument or exhortation, most of which has been intent on changing either their behavior or their attitudes toward him.[31] Second, although he commends them for "keeping the traditions," nonetheless in what follows in chaps. 11–14 there does not seem to be a single instance of their doing so; indeed, in 11:17-34 they are doing anything but. Moreover, according to 11:34 there are still further concerns in these matters that this letter does not address. How, then, is one to understand these words?

Some have suggested that they are intentionally ironical, or even sarcastic.[32] More likely, (1) they serve in a more general way, as a kind of *captatio benevolentiae* to introduce chaps. 11–14, in which the apostle sets them up with praise with reference to *unmentioned* "traditions" that they are keeping so as to come down on them with greater force in the areas where they are *not*.[33] Or (2) they aim specifically at vv. 3-16, setting up the matter of women's head "coverings" as a contrast to vv. 17-34, a matter in which he cannot praise them.[34] The problems with this latter solution are several: (a) the adversative "but" in v. 3 (see below) implies that the following instruction is not commendation but "correction" of some kind; (b) in vv. 3-16 he is in fact correcting them, not commending them, even if not as strongly as in vv. 17-34; and (c) the word "traditions" is plural; were it referring only to vv. 3-16 one would expect the singular as in v. 17.

Thus, even though he may very well be picking up language from their letter, and perhaps in the first instance (vv. 3-16) speaking to something they are advocating, this opening sentence most likely serves to introduce the whole of chaps. 11–14. Even though they remember him in everything,[35] there are some areas with regard to the "traditions" where praise is not in order. They may be following the "traditions" all right, but not in proper ways.

---

[30]Gk. ἐπαινῶ, a verb that occurs in Paul (apart from an LXX citation in Rom. 15:11) only here and in vv. 17 and 22 (twice).

[31]The obvious solution to this, of course, is that he is here taking up a new topic, as the next words, "holding fast the traditions," imply.

[32]See, among others, Hurd, 182-84; Moffatt, 149.

[33]Cf. Conzelmann, 182 n. 13, who sees the *captatio* as a mere literary device, with no "specific grounds for it." More likely, as with the thanksgiving (1:4-9), this speaks to actual areas where they are continuing the traditions. Thus he can freely correct them where they are not.

[34]Cf. Hurley, "Veils," pp. 191-93.

[35]The word πάντα ("in everything") makes one think he is quoting them. They would tend to have a higher view of their obedience than is realistic.

3 The "but"[36] with which this argument begins suggests that some things are not quite as the Corinthians had portrayed them. Nonetheless, this answer lacks the rhetoric of much that has preceded. Thus Paul begins with the milder "I want you to know that. . . ."[37] What he wants them to know takes the form of a *theologoumenon* (theological statement) that will serve as the point of reference for the response that immediately follows (vv. 4-5). The statement itself is in three parts, each using the word "head" metaphorically to express a different relationship: man/Christ, woman/man,[38] Christ/God. What is not immediately clear, especially to the English reader, is the sense of the metaphor "head," and thus the nature of the relationships that each of the clauses intends.

It should be noted that this theological statement is not something Paul sets out to prove; nor is it the main point of the section. Indeed, after the references to "every man" and "every woman" shaming their "heads" in vv. 4-5, there is no further direct reference to it.[39] Moreover, the first two items (man/Christ, woman/man) appear in that same sequence in vv. 4-5, where Paul takes up the problem itself. This suggests that even though this *theologoumenon* appears as the first item in the argument, the behavioral problem itself really came first, and that that problem, having to do with women's *heads,* dictated both the *fact* and the *form* of the appearance of this construct. Paul seems concerned to shift the problem from one of individual freedom to one of relational responsibility. The problem lay squarely on the

---

[36]Gk. δέ, almost certainly adversative to v. 2 (cf. RSV, JB, NASB, NEB, GNB, Moffatt, Montgomery) rather than consecutive as the NIV's "now" suggests.

[37]Elsewhere only in Col. 2:1. Cf. the rhetorical "Do you not know that?" (see on 3:16), and the more common negative "I do not want you to be ignorant" (see on 10:1). Padgett, "Paul," pp. 78-79, makes the improbable suggestion (1) that "the three-part formula of headship" is a Corinthian rephrasing of a Pauline position on which they are ultimately at odds (they think head = authority; Paul, that it = source of being), and (2) that this introductory formula therefore is Paul's partial affirmation of their formula, which functions similarly to the "we know" formula in 8:1 and 4. Therefore, the phrase "does not indicate that Paul is teaching something new, but that he wishes to bring out a new aspect of what is already known." This puts considerable stress on the plain sense of "I want you to know"; furthermore, this introductory phrase differs altogether from the formula "we know that," which is followed by grammatical clues that he is citing them (see on 8:1 and 4).

[38]It is common to understand this as referring to husbands and wives (cf. RSV: "the head of a woman is her husband"—although they translate the rest of the section as "man" and "woman"!). This is possible, but in light of the argument as a whole it seems less likely (see on v. 5).

[39]The statement in v. 8, repeated in v. 12, that "woman is from man," is very likely an oblique reference to v. 3. V. 7 is often viewed in this way, but with a strange turn of logic that says: (1) Christ is the head of (= authority over) man because (2) man was created in God's image and for God's glory. That seems obtuse at best since man is said to be *God's* image and glory, not Christ's, and the concept of "authority" does not appear in v. 7.

501

women's heads, but it was affecting male/female relationships in the present age. By making their appearance such that it tended to eliminate distinctions between the sexes, they were bringing shame on that relationship, which had not yet been abrogated even though the new age had been inaugurated.[40]

The metaphor itself is often understood to be hierarchical, setting up structures of authority.[41] But nothing in the passage suggests as much; in fact, the only appearance of the word *exousia* ("authority") refers to the woman's own authority (v. 10). Moreover, vv. 11-12 explicitly qualify vv. 8-9 so that they will *not* be understood in this way. Indeed, the metaphorical use of *kephalē* ("head") to mean "chief" or "the person of the highest rank" is rare in Greek literature[42]—so much so that even though the Hebrew word

[40]That is, they are not yet as the angels, without gender, and therefore neither marrying nor given in marriage (cf. 7:1; 13:1; Luke 20:35).

[41]All commentaries up to Barrett and Conzelmann—although even they opt for some form of "subordination" as inherent in the metaphor—as well as some of the studies in n. 6 (Weeks, Hurley). For an early objection to this view, see S. T. Lowrie, "I Corinthians XI and the Ordination of Women as Ruling Elders," *PTR* 19 (1921), 113-30.

[42]Cf., e.g., LSJ, MM; this was first brought to the attention of the scholarly world by S. Bedale, "The Meaning of κεφαλή in the Pauline Epistles," *JTS* 5 (1954), 211-15, who states the problem concisely: "In normal Greek usage, classical or contemporary, κεφαλή does not signify 'head' in the sense of ruler, or chieftain, of a community. If κεφαλή has this sense in the writings of St. Paul (it certainly has it nowhere else in the New Testament) we must suppose it to have been acquired as the result of LXX use of the word to translate [rō'š]" (p. 211). He then goes on to demonstrate that the latter is unlikely. More recent studies have confirmed his initial probings. See R. Scroggs, "Paul and the Eschatological Women: Revisited," *JAAR* 42 (1974), p. 534 n. 8; Murphy-O'Connor, "Sex," 490; B. and A. Mickelsen, "The 'Head' of the Epistles," *CT* 25 (1981), 264-67; *idem*, "What Does *Kephalē* Mean in the New Testament?" in *Women, Authority and the Bible* (ed. A. Mickelsen; Downers Grove, IL, 1986), pp. 97-110; P. B. Payne, "Response," in *ibid.*, pp. 118-32; and K. Kroeger, "The Classical Concept of 'Head' as 'Source,'" in *Serving Together: A Biblical Study of Human Relationships* (ed. G. Gaebelein Hull; New York, 1987), a paper that appears to be decisive. For many of the statistics used here, I am indebted to Payne's "Response."

The two references in BAGD are both quite worthless: The reference from Zosimus dates from the 6th c. A.D. and most likely refers to "dignity," not authority; the word κεφαλή does not even appear in the second instance (Ps.-Aristotle)! Cf. Payne, p. 120.

A contrary view is taken by W. Grudem, "Does κεφαλή ("Head") Mean 'Source' or 'Authority over' in Greek Literature? A Survey of 2,336 Examples," *TrinJ* n.s. 6 (1985), 38-59. For all its attempt at objectivity by means of computer research, this article is quite misleading both in its presentation and conclusions. The number 2,336 in the title is especially so since only a small percentage of these are metaphorical, and these are the only ones that count. Furthermore, Grudem's conclusion that 49 of these mean "authority over" is especially misleading—for several reasons: (1) these 49 include 12 NT examples, which the author prejudges exegetically to mean "authority over" when these are the very passages in question; (2) of the remaining 37, 18 are from Greek translations of the OT, which for reasons outlined below are the exceptions that prove the rule that this is *not* an ordinary meaning for this Greek word (see esp. n. 44); (3) for most of the remaining 19 there is serious exegetical question as to whether the authors intended

rō'š often carried this sense, the Greek translators of the LXX, who ordinarily used *kephalē* to translate *rō'š* when the physical "head" was intended,[43] almost never did so when "ruler" was intended,[44] thus indicating that this metaphorical sense is an exceptional usage and not part of the ordinary range of meanings for the Greek word.

Paul's understanding of the metaphor, therefore, and almost certainly the only one the Corinthians would have grasped, is "head" as "source," especially "source of life."[45] This seems to be corroborated by vv. 8-9, the only place where one of these relationships is picked up further in Paul's argument. There he explicitly states that man was the original source of the woman (cf. v. 12). Thus Paul's concern is not hierarchical (who has authority over whom), but relational (the unique relationships that are predicated on one's being the source of the other's existence). Indeed, he says nothing about man's authority;[46] his concern is with the woman's being

---

a metaphorical sense of "authority over"; and (4) since he used Philo in his calculations, he seems quite mistaken, in light of the passages from Philo cited in n. 45, to conclude that "no instances were discovered in which κεφαλή had the meaning 'source, origin.'" What Grudem has demonstrated is that the metaphorical usage of "leader" can be found (it is not at all clear that it ever means "authority over"); but he is quite wrong to assert that the idea of "source" or "origin" is not to be found. Cf. n. 45.

[43]In 226 of 239 instances. The other 13 are translated differently for a variety of reasons. See Payne, "Response," p. 121 n. 33.

[44]In about 12 of 180 instances, and half of these are variants in a single MS or were required to preserve a head/tail contrast. The only clear instances of *rō'š* = κεφαλή = leader/chief are Judg. 11:11; 2 Sam. 22:44; Ps. 18:43; Isa. 7:8, 9; Lam. 1:5. Cf. Payne, "Response," p. 123 n. 35. As Murphy-O'Connor notes, these "exception[s] (even Homer nods!) do not change the picture." Indeed, these statistics seem to make this a clear case where the exception proves the rule. Grudem's unfortunate failure to note these translational phenomena considerably mars his study (see n. 42).

[45]For this usage see Orphic frag. 168, cited by LSJ: "Zeus is the κεφαλή, Zeus the middle, and from Zeus all things are completed." As Barrett, 248, points out, the fact that some MSS of this fragment have ἀρχή for κεφαλή is especially significant in terms of its meaning. Otherwise Grudem, "κεφαλή," pp. 45-46; but the discussion by Payne, "Response," p. 125, has the better of it here. See also Philo, *congr. qu. er.* 61: "And of all the members of the clan here described Esau is the progenitor, the κεφαλή as it were of the whole creature [meaning the source of the whole clan]" (Loeb, IV, 489); and *praem.* 125: "The virtuous one, whether single man or people, will be the κεφαλή of the human race and all others like the limbs of a body which draw their life from the forces in the κεφαλή at the top" (Loeb, VIII, 389); cf. Artemidorus, *oneir.* 1.2: "Another man dreamt he was beheaded. In real life, the father of this man, too, died; for just as the κεφαλή is the source of life and light for the whole body, he was responsible for the dreamer's life and light" (Teub., p. 16); and 1.35: "For the κεφαλή resembles parents in that it is the cause of one's living" (Teub., p. 34). I am indebted to Payne, "Response," pp. 124-25, for calling these Philo and Artemidorus references to my attention. See esp. Eph. 4:15-16.

[46]Grudem, "κεφαλή," p. 56, makes the unsupported assertion that "head coverings in the first century were a sign of relation to authority." Since the evidence is so ambiguous, both for the wearing of head coverings and the reasons for it, one would need to demonstrate such a universal statement with hard evidence.

man's *glory*, the one without whom he is not complete (vv. 7c-9). To blur that relationship is to bring shame on her "head." This means that the middle clause, "the man is the head of woman,"[47] refers to the creation account also alluded to in vv. 8 and 12. "*The* man" would refer to Adam, and "the woman" to Eve; thus, "the man is the source of the woman's life." But as v. 12 makes plain, that is only part of the story; in a much more significant way, "all things," both man and woman, "come from God."

If this is the meaning of the middle line, and the rest of the context seems to demand such a conclusion, then what about the first and third lines? The first is the more difficult. There are two viable options: (1) In terms of creation, Christ is the source of every man's life;[48] (2) in terms of the new creation, Christ is the source of every Christian man. In favor of the first option are: (a) the possibility that the three clauses are thus chronological— Christ created man; through man came woman; God is the source of Christ in his incarnation;[49] (b) the fact that elsewhere in Paul Christ is viewed as the one through whom all things came to be; (c) this makes good sense of the adjective "every"—through creation he is thus the ultimate source of *every* man; (d) the reference in v. 7 to man's being God's image and glory also refers to the creation narrative (cf. v. 12).

In favor of the second option are: (a) Paul's explicit statement in 2 Cor. 5:17 that the "new creation" is the result of one's being "in Christ" (cf. 1 Cor. 1:30); (b) in Col. 1:18 Paul refers to Christ as the "head" of his body, the church, in a context that implies he is the source of its being; (c) when he picks up this clause in v. 4 he repeats "every man" in a context that refers not to "man" in general, but to believing men in the Christian assembly. On the whole, this seems to be the more likely option.[50] The major objection to this view, besides the language "every man," is that Christ in this sense is also the "head" of every Christian woman. But that is to make too much of the statement as an isolated *theologoumenon*, which it is not. Paul, after all, is not trying to give a theological compendium; this is an *ad hoc* construct, aimed specifically at what he will say in v. 4. Thus the unique

---

[47]Gk. κεφαλὴ δὲ γυναικὸς ὁ ἀνήρ; probably ὁ ἀνήρ is the subject, κεφαλή a definite predicate noun (according to "Colwell's rule"; cf. n. 11 on 3:16).

[48]In the sense of 8:6 or Col. 1:15, that he is the one through whom God created all things. But see the objection by Murphy-O'Connor, "Sex," 494 n. 49. This view can be traced back at least as early as Cyril of Alexandria (*Arcad.* 5.6): "Thus we say that 'the head of every man is Christ.' For he was made by (διά) him . . . as God; 'but the head of the woman is the man,' because she was taken out of his flesh. . . . Likewise 'the head of Christ is God,' because he is of him by nature (ἐξ αὐτοῦ κατὰ φύσιν)."

[49]Argued by Payne, *Man*, p. 41. On the other hand, this order may be only accidentally chronological since it has been set up by vv. 4 and 5.

[50]Cf. Murphy-O'Connor, "Sex," 493-95.

relationship that the Christian man has to Christ as the source of his being disallows him to "have hanging down the head" while praying and prophesying; otherwise he brings shame upon Christ, who gave him life.

This suggests, then, that the final clause, "God is the *kephalē* of Christ," is not a christological statement in the ontological sense; that is, Paul is hardly thinking of the "eternal generation" of the Son from the Father.[51] Rather, it refers to the incarnational work of Christ. God is the source of Christ, who through his redemption became the source of "every man." For the argument that follows, the first two items are all that are necessary; however, in a way reminiscent of 3:22-23, Paul is not content merely to assert the first two relationships, but presses back to the ultimate source of all things, God himself (cf. also 15:22-28). Christ is the "head" of every believing man because lying behind all things is the eternal God, "from whom are all things" (cf. v. 12). With that proper theological point of reference, Paul will now proceed to explain why the women must not be "uncovered" when they pray and prophesy.

4 Paul begins his argument with the men. Although they may also have been involved in "dress" that was breaking down the distinctions between the sexes,[52] that seems unlikely since the argument in each case, and especially in this one, is directed toward the women (vv. 5-6). Rather, Paul seems to be setting up his argument with the women by means of a hypothetical situation for the man that would be equally shameful to his relationship to his "head" as what the women are doing is to theirs.

Thus he asserts, "Every man," meaning every *Christian* man, "who prays or prophesies[53] having down the head dishonors his 'head.' " The two verbs "pray and prophesy" make it certain that the problem has to do with the assembly at worship.[54] One may pray privately; but not so with prophecy. This was the primary form of inspired speech, directed toward the

---

[51]As Cyril, e.g., assumes (n. 48); cf. the discussion in Murphy-O'Connor, "Sex," 493. This is the difficult clause for those who take "head" to mean "authority." The usual solution is to make a distinction between ontological equality and functional subordination. Only in the latter sense is God (= the Father) the one with superior rank within the godhead. Cf. Grudem, "κεφαλή," p. 57.

[52]Perhaps some kind of tonsorial tomfoolery, as argued by Murphy-O'Connor, "Sex," 483-87; see the discussion below.

[53]This is the first occurrence in the letter of this word, which will figure prominently in the argument of chaps. 12–14 (cf. 1 Thess. 5:20). For a discussion of its meaning see on 12:10.

[54]The leading advocate of the contrary view was Bachmann, 350-51. See the refutation in Grosheide, 252-53. What appears to be a new version of Bachmann's view is presented by Ellis, 27, who argues: "The instructions in 1 Cor 11,5 on praying and prophesying probably reflect the procedures used within the prayer sessions of the pneumatics" (cf. p. 36).

community for its edification and encouragement (cf. 14:1-5). The two verbs are neither exhaustive nor exclusive but representative: they point to the two foci of Christian worship—God and the gathered believers.

The "head" that would be shamed is man's metaphorical "head," Christ.[55] Several things make that clear: (1) the asyndeton (no joining particle or conjunction) gives the sentence the closest possible tie to v. 3; (2) Paul uses the personal pronoun "his" rather than the reflexive "his own"; (3) to refer to himself in this way compounds metaphorical usages without warning; (4) otherwise the preceding theological statement has no place in the argument whatever.[56] Therefore, Paul is asserting that if the man were to "have down the head" when praying/prophesying, he would bring shame to Christ in some way, or at least to the relationship established by Christ's being his "head."

The question, of course, is what "having down the head"[57] means, or to put that in another way, "having *what* down the head"? Some have argued that this refers to having long hair "down the head,"[58] a position that has been refined by Murphy-O'Connor, who has shown that disdain for long hair on men was usually in conjunction with homosexuality, where longer hair was artistically decorated to resemble a woman's.[59] The problem with this, however, is that these passages always refer to hair, and never remotely resemble the language Paul uses here. If Paul had intended long hair, this idiom is a most unusual way of referring to it. On the other hand, although Paul's idiom is somewhat unusual, it is not without precedent. In Esther 6:12 Haman is said to have "hurried to his house, mourning and with his head covered" (RSV). The LXX translates this last phrase *kata kephalēs* (= "down the head"). So also Plutarch speaks of Scipio the Younger as begin-

---

[55]Otherwise, Murphy-O'Connor, "Sex," 485. Hurley, "Veils," p. 202, argues for "deliberate double meaning."

[56]Murphy-O'Connor (previous note) too easily dismisses reasons 2 and 3. He argues on the basis of evidence from H. Schlier, *TDNT* III, 674, that since it is possible for "head" to be used as a metaphor for one's person, there should "no longer be any objection" to taking "shames his head" as a synonym for "a dishonor to him" in v. 14. But the *possibility* of "head" as a metaphor for oneself is not the problem. Rather, it is to have this sentence follow v. 3 so closely, with all of the signals that tie it to the metaphorical use in that verse, and then argue that it has a completely different metaphorical meaning here, based on an allegedly parallel sense with v. 14.

[57]Gk. κατὰ κεφαλῆς ἔχων.

[58]E.g., Isaksson, *Marriage*, pp. 166-67; Hurley, *Man*, p. 169; Martin, "Interpretation," p. 233. Hurley's earlier view ("Veils," p. 202) was that the man was prophesying "with his hair up as a woman's." This is similar to Murphy-O'Connor's position (next note), except that he missed the homosexual overtones of having longer hair so that it might be artistically decorated like a woman's.

[59]"Sex," 483-87.

ning to walk through Alexandria "having the *himation* down the head,"[60] meaning that he covered his head with part of his toga so as to be unrecognized by the people. Almost certainly, therefore, by this idiom Paul is ✓ referring to an external cloth covering.

Beyond that everything is more speculative. There is almost no evidence (paintings, reliefs, statuary, etc.) that men in any of the cultures (Greek, Roman, Jew) covered their heads.[61] Since at some point in time the cloak of Deut. 22:12 (LXX, *peribolaion*), mentioned by Jesus in Matt. 23:5, came to be used by Jewish men as the *tallith* ("prayer shawl"), it is tempting to see in this another disavowal by Paul of Jewish customs that divide Jew and Gentile (cf. 7:19; 10:26, 27).[62] This is especially attractive in light of the reference in 2 Cor. 3:12-18 to Moses's "veil" still remaining over the hearts of Jews when the Old Covenant is read;[63] however, in that passage the "veil" is used figuratively of Jewish blindness, and the issue has to do with the face being uncovered, not the head. But the greater problem is that the evidence for the use of the *tallith* in prayer is much too late to be helpful for Jewish customs in the time of Paul.[64] There are other options: since men, as well as women, covered their heads for mourning, one could shame Christ by praying or prophesying in the sign of mourning; since the prophet in the

---

[60]*Mor.* 200F (κατὰ τῆς κεφαλῆς ἔχων τὸ ἱμάτιον). This is identical to Paul's idiom except for the expressed object of the verb. The ἱμάτιον was usually part of a robing garment, either the toga or tunic, although it also could be separate. This was especially so among the Jews, for whom it eventually came to be their *tallith*, or prayer shawl. For a discussion of this phenomenon in these cultures, see E. R. Goodenough, *Jewish Symbols in the Greco-Roman Period*, Vol. IX, *Symbolism in the Dura Synagogue* (New York, 1964), pp. 124-74.

[61]See, e.g., the collection of illustrations in Vol. XI of Goodenough's *Jewish Symbols*. Two notable exceptions, interestingly enough, are in the painting from the Isis temple in Pompeii (fig. 98), where the priest reading the scroll has on a winged hat/helmet, and the relief of the Isis procession (fig. 99), where the "prophet," who is carrying the holy pitcher, has a *himation* (part of his tunic) covering his head (while the priestess herself is uncovered!).

[62]See John Lightfoot, *A Commentary on the New Testament from the Talmud and Hebraica* (Oxford, 1859; repr. Grand Rapids, 1979), pp. 229-31, followed by Bushnell, *God's Word*, par. 241, and Payne, *Man*, pp. 42-44. Payne has easily refuted Hurley's objections to this view, but has also assumed too easily that this was a first-century practice.

[63]That is, it might be an allusion to an actual *tallith* worn at the reading of the law.

[64]The evidence can be found in Str-B, III, 424-26, and John Lightfoot (n. 62). See, e.g., *b.Sabb.* 10a, 12b; *Abot R.Nat.* 6. Unfortunately, some of this evidence is ambiguous as to whether the head itself was actually covered, and in any case none of it is certain for customs of the first century. The possibility that it goes back to the time of Paul is to be found in the basic conservatism of such practices; i.e., that even though these references are late, they may well reflect a tradition that goes way back.

Isis cult wore a head covering,[65] this may be some kind of prohibition against appearing before God in a manner resembling the mysteries. In the final analysis, however, we simply have to admit that we do not know. In any case, it is hypothetical, whatever it was; and whatever it meant, Paul would expect the Corinthians to agree that such a covering for men would bring shame to Christ.

5a By way of contrast[66] Paul now addresses the women with a sentence that is in perfect balance with v. 4, except for the differences in appearance. In place of "having down the head," she brings shame on her "head" if she prays or prophesies[67] "uncovered as to the head." As with v. 4, "her head" must refer to "the man" in v. 3.[68] Although this could mean that she thereby disgraces her husband, more likely, in light of v. 3 and the ensuing analogy in vv. 5-6, as well as the argument of vv. 7-9, this probably refers to bringing shame on "the man" in terms of male/female relationships. That is, their action disregards this relationship by breaking down the distinctions.

But as with v. 4, it is extremely difficult to determine what she was doing in being "uncovered" that would at the same time shame her "head" in this way. The situation here is complicated in several directions: (1) The true opposite of the man's example would seem to be an external covering; but since removal of this in the assembly brings about shame either to the male/female relationship in general or to her husband in particular, the problem lies in determining what is customary that would have caused such shame.[69] In this case, even if we were sure of prevailing customs, we would need to be able to distinguish between Greek, Roman, and Jew customs as well as differences in geography, how one dressed at home, outside the home, and in worship, and differences between the rich and poor.[70] This

[65]See n. 61.

[66]This sentence is joined to its companion (v. 4) by a δέ, which the NIV translates as a consecutive ("and"). That may well be, but more likely it is intended as a contrast, hence "but" (RSV, NASB) or "on the contrary" (NEB); but note the NAB's "similarly."

[67]As in v. 4, this is clear evidence that women participated in the worship and ministering gifts in the Christian communities. Those who argue otherwise (see n. 22) are guilty of special pleading. As A. J. Gordon has correctly argued, "it is quite incredible that the Apostle should . . . spend his breath condemning a forbidden method of doing a forbidden thing" (cited by Bushnell, *God's Word,* par. 242).

[68]In light of vv. 5b-6 it is possible that "her head" is more ambiguous and refers also to her own shame. Nonetheless, as with v. 4, the primary reference must be metaphorical and go back to "the man is the head of the woman" in v. 3. Otherwise there is little reason for Paul's having begun with that statement.

[69]It is always possible that in both cases (i.e., the man's and the woman's) the Corinthians themselves would not have considered the matter shameful, and that that is why Paul felt the need to give his argument the theological starting point of v. 3.

[70]These kinds of problems render generally useless a large amount of the literary

diversity is well illustrated in the various samplings in Goodenough.[71] But it is also this very diversity that makes one wonder how Paul would consider the discarding of the (presumably) customary covering to be the same thing as being shorn (v. 5b).

(2) This has caused some, on the basis of combined evidence both from the LXX and from prevailing hairstyles, to argue that the adjective *akatakalyptos* ("uncovered") refers to "loosed hair," that is, long hair flowing loose down over the shoulders and back. The word *akatakalyptos* occurs only once in the LXX, in Lev. 13:45, where it translates a Hebrew idiom that says the leper's "head shall be unbound."[72] More significantly, a cognate verb[73] is used in Num. 5:18 to translate "he shall loosen the hair of the woman," indicating that the suspected adulteress must wear loosed hair as part of her shame.[74] Since the evidence from Paul's era shows that women did not appear in public with long, flowing hair, it seems altogether possible that "loosed hair" is the "uncovering" that caused shame.[75] The difficulties

---

evidence that is often cited in reference to this text. This is especially true of the large collection of otherwise helpful texts, both Greek and Jewish, in Conzelmann, 185 nn. 39-40, since they deal for the most part with "going out in public." The question is whether women in Christian worship in Corinth would be thought of as "going out in public," or whether, in light of their gathering in homes and calling themselves "brothers and sisters," the wearing of ordinary home "attire" would be proper—not to mention all the difficulties that may obtain from the fact that the gathering is also "religious" and that the women are prophesying.

71See n. 61. Cf. fig. 99 (where a priestess of Isis is uncovered) and 101 (another Isis example, where one woman is covered while the other is not). With this compare the literary evidence from Apuleius, *Met.* 11.10, regarding the Isis festival in Corinth: "The women had their hair anointed, and their heads covered with light linen [cf. fig. 101 in Goodenough]; but the men had their crowns shaven and shining bright" (Loeb, 555). See also the two frescoes from Pompeii (nos. 117 and 118), where in scenes that "unquestionably represent religious ceremonies" (Goodenough, IX, 137) the central figures (women) are covered with the *himation,* while in fig. 117 the flute girl is not. The same ambiguity prevails in fig. 218, where the woman "crowning the dead" is covered while the (apparently slave) woman holding the umbrella is not.

72Cf. Lev. 10:6, where the Hebrew says that Aaron and his sons are not to "unbind their heads." Murphy-O'Connor ("Sex," 488) is probably correct in identifying this, by means of the LXX, with the turban that bound the hair to the top of the head.

73Gk. ἀποκαλύψει τὴν κεφαλὴν τῆς γυναικός ("he shall uncover the head of the woman").

74Philo (*spec.leg.* 3.60), in commenting on this passage from Numbers, uses Paul's exact language (ἀκατακαλύπτῳ τῇ κεφαλῇ). Almost certainly, however (despite Padgett, "Paul," p. 70), he is referring to an external covering, not loosed hair as such, since he says the ritual begins with the priest "removing her kerchief" (τοὐπίκρανον ἀφελών) so that she may be "bareheaded" (ἐπικρίνηται γεγυμνωμένη) during the rite.

75This is made more plausible by the evidence from the rites of Dionysus, Cybele, and Isis that "dishevelled hair and head thrown back were almost trademarks" of the frenzied worship of women in these cults (see Kroeger-Kroeger, "Inquiry," pp.

with this view lie primarily with v. 15, which implies that long hair is a woman's glory and therefore a good thing, and with the imperative "let her be covered" in v. 6 (cf. v. 7; the men should "not be covered"), which does not easily lend itself to the connotation of putting her hair up.[76] It is also true that this does not appear to be the precise opposite of the man's activity in v. 4; but the contrast possibly lies in similarly "shameful" actions, not in precise opposites, since that is not demanded by the context.[77]

As with the man's situation, we must finally admit that we cannot be certain as to particulars.[78] On the basis of what is said of the man in vv. 4 and 7, it seems more likely that some kind of external covering is involved; nonetheless, the linguistic ties with the LXX and the parallels from pagan ecstasy offer a truly viable alternative in favor of hairstyle. But in either case, her action (1) must have been deliberate, (2) must be understood to bring shame on her "head," and (3) probably had inherent in it a breakdown in the distinction between the sexes. Thus Paul wants her to return to what is customary, and will so argue in what follows.

5b-6 Picking up on the theme of shame, Paul offers a nice piece of logic to support his contention, finally spelled out without ambiguity in the final imperative, that the woman "be covered." The common denominator of shame to which he appeals is that of a woman's having her hair cut short or her head shaved.[79] Either of these apparently would constitute such shame

---

331-33; cf. Fiorenza, *Memory*, p. 237). There is also evidence that "sex reversal" (usually by means of dress) played a role in some of these cults. This would also help to explain why "shame" was involved, since part of the "shame" for the men would lie in the widespread appeal of these cults to women, who by their frenzy also received bad press from the predominantly male literary establishment. Hurley ("Veils," p. 202) suggests that the shame was related to their looking like adulteresses. But the problem with that is both the lack of first-century evidence that long, loose hair would have been associated with adultery in any way and the inability to find an adequate reason why the women would have acted so. The connection with the pagan cults would answer the latter question; they had simply carried over to Christian prophecy what they knew about cultic prophecy. See further on 12:1-3 and 14:26-40.

[76]Especially since the evidence shows that "put-up hair" did not always rest in tier fashion on the top of the head, but at times took the form of braids down the back of the neck. Among several examples in Goodenough, *Jewish Symbols*, Vol. XI, see especially the two women in the Isis procession (including the priestess) in fig. 99.

[77]Perhaps the women were doing both, especially if there is a relationship to cultic prophecy. They would be "uncovering" by removing the customary *himation* so that they might "let their hair loose" in the more frenzied fashion of the cultic women.

[78]Nonetheless, the suggestion by Martin ("Interpretation," p. 233) that ἀκατακάλυπτος refers to cut hair has neither linguistic nor contextual evidence in its favor.

[79]The *fact* that a shaved head for a woman constituted shame is found in such diverse texts as Deut. 21:12 (although in this case it is probably also a sign of mourning); Aristot., *Thes.* 837 (the mother of unworthy children should have her hair shorn); and Tacitus, *Germ.* 19, where the husband of an adulterous wife drives her from the house

that they would be unthinkable actions.[80] The shame in this case would seem to be her own; however, since the argument is by way of analogy, Paul probably intends it to carry over from v. 5a. In any case, the shame seems clearly to be related to her becoming like a man with regard to her hair,[81] thus by analogy suggesting that the women were blurring male/female relationships in general and sexual distinctions in particular.

On this common predicate of shame in a woman's having mannish hair, Paul builds a simple, clear argument. First, he asserts that to pray or prophesy "uncovered" makes her (lit.) "one and the same thing with her that is shaven[82]" (v. 5b). He then drives that point home[83] with a pair of conditional sentences,[84] the first of which repeats the point of v. 5a in light of the assertion in v. 5b: "If a woman does not cover herself" (5a), which means that she is bringing shame on her "head," "then let her also be shorn"[85] (5b), that is, let her go the whole way to shame by having her hair

---

shaved and naked. This latter text has been used by some to argue that the shaved head was the sign of an adulteress. But that will not work since Tacitus is referring to customs of Germanic tribes that he thought significantly different enough from Roman customs to relate.

[80]It was commonly suggested that short hair or a shaved head was the mark of the Corinthian prostitutes (cf., e.g., Grosheide, 254). But there is no contemporary evidence to support this view (it seems to be a case of one scholar's guess becoming a second scholar's footnote and a third scholar's assumption). Even Martin, for whose interpretation this possibility would be especially helpful, admits the lack of evidence ("Interpretation," p. 233 n. 4). Nonetheless, on the basis of the article with ἐξυρημένη in v. 5b he postulates "the existence of a specific class to whom this designation could be applied" (p. 234), which in turn apparently "created" such a class for the NIV marginal reading. That is probably more historical weight than one definite article in an *ad hoc* letter can bear. If a "class" is involved, it would certainly be the "masculine" partner in a lesbian relationship. See the next note.

[81]Two texts in Lucian illustrate that short hair on a woman was considered "mannish": of a fugitive wife in the company of three runaway slaves, "a woman with her hair closely clipped (κεκαρμένην) in the Spartan style, boyish-looking and quite masculine" (*fug.* 27; Loeb, V, 85); and of a Lesbian woman Megilla, who after pulling off her wig revealed "the skin of her head which was shaved close (ἀποκεκαρμένη), just as on the most energetic of athletes" (*dial.het.* 5.3; Loeb, VII, 383). The homosexuality involved in this dialogue demonstrates where the "shame" lay.

[82]Gk. τῇ ἐξυρημήνη. Of the two verbs used in this argument (ξυρόω and κείρω), this one would refer to the head being shaved, the other to the hair being cut short. For the differences see an aphorism from Tiberius, quoted in Dio Cassius's *History of Rome:* "I want my sheep shorn (κείρεσθαι), not shaven (ἀποξύρεσθαι)" (15.10.5; Loeb, VII, 137). For ξυρόω in the NT see Acts 21:24; for κείρω, Acts 18:18.

[83]The first clause (v. 5b) is joined to v. 5a with an explanatory γάρ. This first conditional clause is joined to v. 5b by yet another explanatory γάρ; while the second one is contrasted to the first by means of a δέ. See the structural display on p. 494.

[84]These are simple present particulars; see Burton, *Moods,* pp. 102-03.

[85]This is the verb that causes the great difficulty for Martin's interpretation, followed by NIV[mg] (see nn. 26-28 above). His attempt to make the verb "jussive" (pp. 234-39) must be judged as less than successful since it tries to make a remotely possible,

like a man's. Finally, with a second conditional sentence he brings all this together specifically in terms of shame: But if it is a disgrace for a woman either to have her hair cut short (v. 6a) or be shaved (v. 5b)—and it obviously was—then let her be covered (v. 5a). This final imperative, which ordinarily implies an external covering,[86] creates special difficulties for the "put-up hair" view.

This is the closest thing to rhetoric that one finds in the present argument. The point is made by way of analogy. One kind of action (being uncovered) is just like another (having mannish hair). If the latter is shameful, so too is the former. This kind of argument makes one wonder whether the Corinthians sensed the shame of their own actions. In any case, the analogy seems to suggest that the problem lay ultimately with a breakdown in sexual distinctions, which fits the Corinthian theology well.

Although various Christian groups have fostered the practice of some sort of head covering for women in the assembled church, the difficulties with the practice are obvious. For Paul the issue was directly tied to a cultural shame that scarcely prevails in most cultures today. Furthermore, we simply do not know what the practice was that they were abusing. Thus literal "obedience" to the text is often merely symbolic. Unfortunately, the symbol that tends to be reinforced is the subordination of women, which is hardly Paul's point. Furthermore, it would seem that in cultures where women's heads are seldom covered, the enforcement of such in the church turns Paul's point on its head. In any case, the fact that Paul's own argument is so tied to cultural norms suggests that literal obedience is not mandatory for obedience to God's Word.

2. An Argument from Creation (11:7-12)

> 7 For[1] *a man ought not to cover his head, since he is the image and glory of God; but the woman is the glory of man.* 8 *For man did not come from woman, but woman from man;* 9 *neither was man created for woman, but woman for man.* 10 *For this reason, and because of the angels, the woman ought to have* authority over[2] *her head.* 11 *In*[3]

---

but highly improbable, meaning of a verb say something that could have been said easily with a different verb altogether.

[86]Gk. κατακαλύπτω; cf. n. 8 on v. 7.

[1]The NIV omits this explanatory γάρ, which is needed to help the reader see the connection between this and the preceding paragraph. The paragraphing in the NIV (2, 3-10, 11-16) also seems to miss the structures of Paul's argument.

[2]NIV, "sign of authority on"; but with no textual warrant. The difficulty that some have with the plain meaning of Paul's Greek is evidenced in some early versions and Fathers, who variously substitute the word "veil" for ἐξουσία—again with no textual warrant. See Metzger, 562.

[3]The NIV begins a new paragraph here (see n. 1).

the Lord, however, woman[4] is not independent of man, nor is man independent of woman. 12 *For as woman came from man, so also man is born of woman. But everything comes from God.*

The structure and content of this paragraph suggest that Paul is now offering a supporting argument as to why the woman should be "covered" when praying and prophesying, since being "uncovered" in some way brings shame on her "head." But it is supporting evidence that is both complex and full of surprises.[5] The "for" with which the argument begins indicates that Paul intends to reinforce the point of vv. 4-6, that men ought *not* to be covered, while women should be. That in fact is said of the man; but the apparent reason, "being the image and glory of God," is especially surprising in light of v. 3, where Christ, not God, is designated as man's "head." More difficult yet is what is said of the woman, who by way of contrast is called "man's glory," but with no mention of her being covered. What follows rather is an explanation, based on Gen. 2, as to why she is man's glory (vv. 8-9). Then comes the truly surprising text (v. 10), which, because of the verb "ought," seems to correspond to v. 7a (over against "ought not"). But again, instead of mentioning a covering, Paul argues that she should have authority over her ("own" is implied) head because of the angels. This is followed in turn by two sets of male/female clauses (vv. 11-12), which in reverse order correspond precisely, but by way of qualification, to what was said in vv. 8-9. Thus the whole argument points to v. 10 as the crucial text, a text so difficult that it has defied our best scholarly guesses over centuries; at the same time Paul demonstrates considerable eagerness that part of the explanation as to how he got there not be misunderstood.

7 That Paul intends what follows to elaborate on vv. 4-6 (as to why men should not, while women should be covered while praying and prophesying) is made certain both by the explanatory "for" and by the contrasting particles "man on the one hand/woman on the other hand."[6] The elaboration seems designed to explain how the woman's praying or prophesying "uncovered" brings shame on her "head." The argument that follows, however, is so involved that for most readers the explanation tends to muddy the waters rather than to enlighten. Part of the difficulty lies with Paul's syntax: What exactly did he intend to be in contrast in v. 7, and how in turn does that relate to the "conclusion" in v. 10? There are two options. (1) It is

---

[4]The MajT, with no early support, has reversed the order to man/woman, woman/man. See the commentary.

[5]See the structural display on p. 494.

[6]Gk. μέν . . . δέ, omitted in most English translations—for good reason; it is cumbersome English. But something should be done to catch the intended contrast, which the NIV fails to do.

possible that the second part of v. 7 (the woman's part) is elliptical, and that he intended the reader to fill in the missing words from the man's side; in this case v. 10 serves as a conclusion on its own, flowing more directly out of vv. 7c-9.[7] Thus:

A   Man   ought not to have his head covered,
   B   since he is the image and glory of God;
      on the other hand,
A'   The woman [ought   to have her head covered,
   B'   since she] is   the glory of man.

It is likewise possible that vv. 7 and 10 are intended to serve together as the intended contrast, but that the content of v. 10 was modified by the intervening explanation as to how the woman is man's glory. Thus they form an AB-BA chiasm:

A   Man   ought not to have his head covered,
   B   since he is the image and glory of God;
      on the other hand,
   B'   Woman   is   man's glory,
      for this reason
A'   She   ought to have authority on her head because of the angels.

Most likely Paul's syntax is moving in this latter direction, but probably not by intent when the sentence began. What is missing is any reference to the woman's being covered, which is almost certainly to be understood, given the nature of the argument both in what precedes (vv. 4-6) and what follows (v. 13), plus the way the man's argument begins in this verse. This, of course, is what has given rise (probably incorrectly) to understanding her "authority" in v. 10 to be the covering itself.

The first clause is simple and direct: "A man ought not[8] to cover[9] his head." In a very direct way this repeats the point of v. 4. But the reason he now advances, "since he is the image and glory of God," is less than clear

---

[7]Cf. Findlay, 873.

[8]The verb ὀφείλει, which appears again in v. 10, usually carries moral overtones; this is something that should, or should not, be done. The negative in this instance negates the thought of the entire clause.

[9]Gk. κατακαλύπτεσθαι; the same verb as in the preceding imperative about the woman. This verb in particular creates difficulties for the view that the "covering" is "put-up hair," both because the compound verb itself implies an external covering (see LSJ; A. Oepke, *TDNT* III, 561-63) and because it implies that the man's action is to be the opposite of the woman's in v. 6, which can scarcely refer to his not having his hair "put up." Those who advocate this position either ignore the problem or posit a meaning for the verb here for which there is no linguistic evidence.

since he offers no further explanation, and we are left to derive its sense from what he says next by way of contrast about the woman. But a few observations are in order: (1) It is often assumed that this passage is a further reflection on v. 3, that Paul is herewith explaining by means of the creation accounts in Gen. 1:26-28 and 2:18-24 how "headship" (= "authority over") came about.[10] But except for the allusion found in the further explanation in vv. 8-9 as to how woman is man's glory, nothing either in the language of this text or in its explicit statements directly refers back to v. 3. Thus the essential relationship for man posited in v. 3 (Christ being his head) is not so much as alluded to; rather, Paul is here concerned with man's relationship to God.

(2) In saying that man is God's "image" Paul is certainly alluding to Gen. 1:26-28; but he is not trying to interpret that text.[11] Nor does he here offer any further explanation as to the significance of this word. It is often pointed out that in Gen. 1 man and woman together are in God's image and likeness, a point with which Paul certainly would not disagree—after all, he carefully avoids saying that the woman is man's *image*. But in this present argument he appears to be thinking of the two accounts together in a somewhat harmonized way. Hence, the *order* of creation narrated in Gen. 2, where God made the man directly from the dust of the ground, but the woman through the man, has precedence in his thinking (as vv. 8-9 make clear). Thus he can assert that man, because in the order of things he was created directly, is God's image and glory.

(3) Paul's own interest, however, is finally not in man as being God's image, but in his being God's glory,[12] a word that does *not* appear in the creation accounts. This is Paul's own reflection on the creation of man, and it is the word that finally serves as the means of contrast between man and woman. But to define this term is like trying to pick up mercury between

---

[10]See esp. Hurley, *Man*, pp. 171-74, whose arguments from Gen. 1 are without exegetical warrant, yet control his entire discussion. Cf. the circuitous argument in Conzelmann, 183-84, 186-88, where he tries by means of Hellenistic Jewish wisdom texts to tie the κεφαλή of v. 3 to the εἰκών and δόξα of v. 7 as the source of Paul's reasoning. But the ties Conzelmann seeks are not in the text, as he himself admits. There is simply no linguistic tie to v. 3 (except for κεφαλή, which does not count since here it is literal, not metaphorical); it is doubtful whether there is a conceptual tie since there is no logical connection between man's being God's δόξα and Christ's being man's κεφαλή. The fact is that Paul makes nothing at all of the language, which derives directly from Gen. 1 and does not need the mediation of Hellenistic Judaism.

[11]It is on this point especially that Hurley's argument (see the previous note) seems to hang on air. Some have argued that "glory" is an interpretation of the word "likeness" of Gen. 1:26; but that seems unlikely. At best it is a substitution, and even that is doubtful.

[12]Cf. Barrett, 252: "In this context Paul values the term image only as leading to the term glory."

one's fingers. The most frequent suggestion is that man *reflects* God's glory; that is, being in God's image, man is somehow a reflection of God himself. This is perhaps possible, although there is very little linguistic evidence for such a meaning.[13] Moreover, by way of parallel, that would mean that woman is man's glory because she is a reflection of him in some way, which is not how Paul himself explains this second relationship. More likely, therefore, in light of his further reflection in vv. 8-9, and in light of the usage in 10:32, Paul probably means that the existence of the one brings honor and praise to the other.[14] By creating man in his own image God set his own glory in man. Man, therefore, exists to God's praise and honor, and is to live in relationship to God so as to be his "glory." What we are not told here is *why* being God's glory means no covering; v. 4 indicates that it had to do with his not shaming Christ. But that, too, was left unexplained.

As in v. 4, however, this word about man is not the point of the argument; it exists to set up Paul's real concern—to explain why women should be covered when prophesying. But in coming to that concern, he picks up on the word "glory," saying only that "the woman, on the other hand, is man's glory." The implication is that by praying and prophesying in a way that (apparently) disregarded distinctions between the sexes (being already as the angels), she brings shame on the man whose glory she is intended to be. Paul does not hereby deny that woman was created in God's image, or that she, too, is God's glory. His point is singular. She is related to man as his glory, a relationship that somehow appears to be jeopardized by her present actions.

The real difficulty with the argument for us at this distance emerges right here. What one expects next is for Paul to say that the woman therefore should be covered. This is precisely why v. 10 historically has been so interpreted—because the sense of the argument seems to call for it. But even though it seems implied that the woman should be covered because she is man's glory, that is not stated; neither therefore is any explanation offered as to *how* her being his glory calls for a covered head when prophesying. To be sure, interpreters regularly offer reasons,[15] as though to help Paul out with

---

[13]The only evidence is a text first cited by Lietzmann from a Jewish inscription, "blessed Lucilla, the δόξα of Sophronius." See BAGD 1c.

[14]P. B. Payne, in a private conversation, suggested the analogy of a work of art's being an artist's glory, since it both gives expression to a part of herself/himself and at the same time brings praise and honor to her/his skills.

[15]Usually in terms of her subordinate position; but that makes little sense of the argument itself. Appearance does not mark roles of authority or subservience, at least not in this text. Furthermore, at the crucial point, their praying and prophesying, they are clearly not in hierarchical roles. The point is that women must continue to appear as women because they are men's glory and have not arrived at the final spirituality where they are sexless. The most significant alternative to this view has been offered by Morna Hooker, "Authority on Her Head: An Examination of I Cor. xi,10," *NTS* 10 (1963/64),

his argument, but he himself is silent. Rather than move in that direction, Paul feels compelled to offer further explanation of what he has just said, how it is that the woman is man's glory.

8-9   Although both of these sentences begin with an explanatory "for," the second one does not explain the first, but the two together are intended further to explain the sense of v. 7c,[16] that woman is man's glory. The two sentences together are reflections of Gen. 2:23 and 18-20.[17] In the present context they seem to correspond to both vv. 3 and 7. This is how man is the woman's "head"; he is the source of her life: "the woman is from the man." Beyond that, she is also his "glory": "the woman was created for the man's sake."

Although at first blush these sentences sound as if they indicate her subordination to him, vv. 11-12 make clear both that Paul did not intend them to be so, and that he also realized that they could (incorrectly) be taken so. Thus vv. 11-12 are not intended to "correct" these two sentences; they are intended to qualify them so as to limit their application to the immediate argument. Since Paul himself will not allow that "for man's sake" means "for his dominion" or "for him to exercise authority over," what in context is his point? How does the woman's coming from the man and being created for his sake make her his glory?

Most likely the answer lies in what has already been suggested; and in this instance Paul really is reflecting the sense of the OT text to which he is alluding. Man by himself is not complete; he is alone, without a companion or helper suitable to him. The animals will not do; he needs one who is bone of his bone, one who is like him but different from him, one who is uniquely his own "glory." In fact, when the man in the OT narrative sees the woman he "glories" in her by bursting into song. She is thus man's glory because she "came from man" and was created "for him." She is not thereby subordinate to him, but necessary for him. She exists to his honor as the one who having come from man is the one companion suitable to him, so that he might be complete and that together they might form humanity.[18]

Paul's point, of course, is that in the creation narrative this did not happen the other way around—man from woman and for her sake. Hence he

---

410-16, who suggests that the difference in δόξα has to do with being in God's presence. Here man, who reflects God's glory, must not be covered, while woman, who reflects man's glory, must be. This is possible, but see the response in Payne, *Man*, p. 50.

[16]This is made certain by the καὶ γάρ ("for also") that begins the second sentence (v. 9). Cf. BDF 452(3).

[17]The language ἐξ ἀνδρός, repeated in v. 12 as ἐκ τοῦ ἀνδρός, is a direct reflection of LXX Gen. 2:23; in the second instance there are no verbal ties, but the conceptual ties are unmistakable.

[18]For a similar view see A. Feuillet, "L'homme 'gloire de Dieu' et la femme 'gloire de l'homme' (*I Cor.*, XI,7b)," *RB* 81 (1974), 161-82.

is her "head" (her source of origin) and she is his "glory." She must not be uncovered when praying and prophesying, and thereby disregard one of the (apparently) visible expressions of differentiation, because in so doing she brings shame on him by trying to dissolve the rightful male/female relationship that still obtains in the present age.

10 After the brief explanation in vv. 8-9, Paul now brings to a conclusion the argument that began in v. 7. By all counts this is one of the truly difficult texts in this letter. It needs to be noted at the outset that our difficulties are directly related to the *ad hoc* character of the passage.[19] The solution probably lies with what the Corinthians themselves have communicated to Paul; indeed, the key words "authority" and "angels" are very likely from them in some way. Our problem is that at this point we are left on the outside looking in, with these difficult words as our only clues. Hence we must forever be content to "look through a glass darkly" and learn what we can in the midst of admitting how little we know.

Although the difficulty lies primarily in the language, it begins with the syntax. The inferential conjunction "for this reason"[20] with which the sentence begins can point either backward or forward, that is, it can draw an inferred conclusion on the basis of what has been said, or it can anticipate a reason that will be given in what follows. Its role in this sentence is made the more complex as the result of the final prepositional phrase, "because of the angels." Most likely "for this reason" functions here, as it often does in Paul,[21] in both directions at once. It first of all indicates that what is about to be said is the proper inference from what has immediately preceded: the woman ought to have authority over her head because she is man's glory. At the same time it anticipates yet another closely allied reason to be given in the conclusion that is being advanced. The NIV has caught the sense—and the difficulties—by translating, "for this reason, and because of the angels."

But the greater difficulties lie (1) with the content of the conclusion

---

[19]Matters in a letter like this are *ad hoc* to a greater or lesser degree. To the lesser degree that something is *ad hoc*, the more an author will explain to his readers as he writes; to the greater degree, the less he will explain and the more he will assume between himself and them.

[20]Gk. διὰ τοῦτο (cf. 4:17; 11:30).

[21]There are four instances where it clearly points forward only, and each of these cases is followed by an epexegetical ὅτι or ἵνα (1 Thess. 2:13; 2 Cor. 13:10; Phlm. 15; 1 Tim. 1:16). In some cases it points only backward (1 Cor. 11:30); but most often it seems to function in both directions at once; i.e., on the basis of what has just been said, a conclusion is about to be advanced which will also give a further reason or restate the previous ones. Thus in 1 Thess. 3:7 the *reason* for Paul's encouragement is Timothy's report (v. 6), which is restated at the end of v. 7 as διὰ τῆς ὑμῶν πίστεως, which was the *content* of Timothy's report. Cf. 1 Cor. 4:17.

itself, "the woman ought to have authority over her head," and (2) with the second advanced reason, "because of the angels." The first matter, though complicated by several factors, can basically be narrowed down to a single reality, namely, that one is led to expect one thing and gets another. On the one hand, because of the context, and especially because of the repetition of the verb "ought" in contrast to the "ought not" in v. 7, one expects this inferential conclusion to express the opposite of what is said about the man. What one gets, however, is a Greek sentence that by all normal rules of language and grammar says something quite different from that. This sentence, therefore, has been handled in two ways: either to rework what it says so that it means what one expects,[22] or to let it mean what it says and try to understand that in the context.

The problem is twofold: finding a proper sense for *exousia* ("authority"), and determining the nuance of the preposition *epi* ("over" or "on"). The traditional view, which sees the context as referring to the subordination of women, tends to go one of two directions: (1) Some take *exousia* in a passive sense. To "have authority *over* her head" means that she "has" someone else (in this case, her husband) function as authority "over" her. The "covering," though not mentioned, is assumed to be the "sign" that this is so. Thus the NIV translates, "the woman ought to have a sign of authority on her head," while the Living Bible more boldly asserts: "So a woman should wear a covering on her head as a sign that she is under man's authority." The difficulty with this view is that there is no known evidence either that *exousia* is ever taken in this passive sense[23] or that the idiom "to have authority over" ever refers to an external authority different from the subject of the sentence.[24]

(2) Others take *exousia* as a metonym for "veil,"[25] and *epi* as "on." Thus the RSV: "That is why a woman ought to have a veil on her head." The difficulty with this, as Robertson-Plummer candidly admit, is to find an

---

[22]R-P, 232, are candid: "The passage is unique, no satisfactory parallel having been found. There is no real doubt as to the meaning, which is *clear from the context*. The difficulty is to see why Paul has expressed himself in this extraordinary manner. That 'authority' (ἐξουσία) has been put for 'sign of authority' is not difficult; but why does St Paul say 'authority' *when he means 'subjection'*?" (italics mine). What is "extraordinary" is how easily this is said when nothing in the preceding context says a word about women's "subjection." That is based altogether on a faulty reading of "head" in v. 3.

[23]It is not so once in its 103 occurrences in the NT, nor in the LXX, Philo, or Josephus.

[24]Cf. W. M. Ramsay, *The Cities of St Paul* (New York, 1908), p. 203: "[That her authority] is the authority to which she is subject [is] a preposterous idea which a Greek scholar would laugh at anywhere except in the New Testament, where (as they seem to think) Greek words may mean anything that commentators choose."

[25]Cf. R-P (n. 22).

adequate explanation as to why Paul should have chosen *this* word as his metonym.[26] Had Paul intended an external covering, he would surely have said that, since several such words are available to him.[27]

(3) A third alternative has been to understand "to have authority" as "a sign of authority," but in the sense of "as a means of exercising authority." Thus some have argued that the "authority" is to be understood as the woman's new freedom to do what was formerly forbidden, namely to pray and prophesy along with the men.[28] She should therefore continue to be covered, but to do so now as a sign of her new liberty in Christ. Attractive as this solution is, one must finally admit that it is not adequately supported in the text itself. *Why?*

(4) That leads finally to those who understand "to have authority" in its ordinary sense of "freedom or right to choose." In this view *epi* carries its ordinary sense of "over."[29] Thus: "For this reason the woman ought to have the freedom over her head to do as she wishes."[30] The problem with that, of course, is that it sounds so contradictory to the point of the argument to this point.

So where does that leave us? Given the fact that there is no evidence for a passive sense to this idiom, and that such a view basically came into existence for contextual reasons that do not seem to be in the text itself, solution (4) seems to be the best of the possibilities. The problem is to find an adequate sense for it in the context. Perhaps here is where the *ad hoc* nature

[26]The oft-cited passage in Ramsay (n. 24) to the effect that the woman's veil served as her "authority/freedom" to go about freely without fear of molestation fails on two counts: it assumes the veiling of the head from a later period, for which there is no evidence in the NT period; it assumes a custom having to do with a woman's appearance in public, whereas this text deals with a woman's praying and prophesying in the Christian assembly.

[27]It is curious indeed that scholars assume that κάλυμμα ("veil") would be the proper term (this is found only as early as Epiphanius), when Paul himself uses the term περιβόλαιον ("shawl") in v. 15; ἱμάτιον would be the more common term. The attempt by G. Kittel ("Die 'Macht' auf dem Haupt [I Cor. xi.10]," *Rabbinica* [Arbeiten zur Vorgeschichte des Christentums 1/3; Leipzig, 1920], pp. 17-30) to trace both words to a common Aramaic root is hardly tenable. See the refutation in J. A. Fitzmyer, "A Feature of Qumran Angelology and the Angels of I Cor. xi.10," *NTS* 4 (1957/58), 52-53.

[28]E.g., Hooker, "Authority," pp. 415-16, followed by Barrett, 255; cf. A. Feuillet, "Le signe de puissance sur la tete de la femme, 1 Co 11,10," *NouvRT* 95 (1973), 945-54; Fiorenza, *Memory*, p. 228. See Bushnell, *God's Word*, par. 236, who indicates that this interpretation already was well known in her day: "As to the veil, some declare that it is to be worn as an 'authorization' to pray and prophesy."

[29]See, e.g., the five occurrences in the NT of ἔχειν ἐξουσίαν ἐπί (Luke 19:11; Rev. 11:6; 14:18; 16:9; 20:6); cf. ἐξουσίαν ἐπί ("authority over"): Luke 9:1; 10:19; Rev. 2:26; 6:8; 13:7.

[30]Among those who take this position, see John Lightfoot, *Commentary*, pp. 236-39; Lowrie, "Ordination," p. 124; Bushnell, *God's Word*, par. 247; Padgett, "Paul," p. 78; Payne, *Man*, pp. 50-51.

of the answer should come more clearly into focus. There can be little question that *exousia* was one of the Corinthians' own words (see on 6:12 and 8:9). Very likely that is the reason for this choice of words, which otherwise appears to be so unusual. Exactly what they would have asserted, and how Paul now intends this response to be heard in light of that, remains moot. Perhaps he is here affirming their own position, that in these matters they do indeed have *exousia;* nonetheless, in light of the preceding argument, and because of (or for the sake of) the angels, they should exercise that authority in the proper way—by maintaining the custom of being "covered."[31] But finally we must beg ignorance. Paul seems to be affirming the "freedom" of women over their own heads; but what that means in this context remains a mystery.

So too does the perplexing phrase "because of the angels." A common interpretation, that they were "male" angels who on seeing the women unveiled lusted after them after the manner of the "sons of God" in Gen. 6:2,[32] may be ruled out at once, since that assumes a kind of "veiling" on the part of the women for which there is no first-century evidence.[33] But beyond that we are pretty much in the dark.[34] Angels appear in three other texts in 1 Corinthians, which may offer clues of some kind.

(1) In 4:9 angels are understood as part of the "whole universe" before whom Paul's Christian life is on display. Some have therefore argued that the angels were present at the Christian assembly as "watchers of the created order,"[35] or, on the basis of Qumran evidence, as giving assistance in public worship.[36] This would especially be fitting for those who see

---

[31]This is very close to the affirmation of 8:9: "Do not let this ἐξουσίαν of yours (NIV, the exercise of your freedom) become a stumbling block to the weak." He affirms their "authority" about food, but denies their exercising it in the way they were demanding.

[32]This seems to be the way the LXX understood the term. Only Codex Alexandrinus is available here, and the text is that of a corrector. However, it is clearly the text of both Philo (*gig.* 6) and Josephus (*Ant.* 1.73).

[33]On the whole, this interpretation seems foreign to Paul and to the context. How are they envisioned as present so that they should become lustful? And what difference would it make in any case? Would they follow through on their lust? That is, are the women somehow to be understood as being in jeopardy? One is hard pressed to find such ideas in Paul or the rest of the NT.

[34]Padgett, "Paul," pp. 31-32, argues that the term means "human messengers"; but one is hard pressed to find linguistic support in Paul for such a view. Moreover, it overlooks the significance of angels in the Corinthians' own theology. See Fitzmyer, "Feature," p. 53, for a selection of other, mostly farfetched, explanations.

[35]See Hooker, "Authority," pp. 412-13.

[36]See esp. Fitzmyer, "Feature," pp. 55-58, who argues that the unveiled woman is like one who in Qumran has a bodily defect and should therefore be excluded from the assembly "out of reverence for the angels." A similar view was suggested independently by H. J. Cadbury, "A Qumran Parallel to Paul," *HTR* 51 (1958), 1-2.

exousia as a "sign of her authority," although it is difficult to imagine how the angels themselves are affected.

(2) Philip Payne,[37] who sees *exousia* as the woman's own choice as to whether or not to be covered, has suggested that the clue lies in 6:3, where Paul says that the saints will judge angels. Paul's point would then be that in light of the fact that these same women will someday judge angels, they should already exercise authority over their heads in these insignificant matters.

(3) Perhaps, as with *exousia,* the clue lies with their own position. Given their arguments with Paul throughout, and especially the nature of the present problem, this whole sentence may reflect an argument from some of the Corinthian women: that they have *exousia* to be "uncovered" because they were already as the angels (see on 7:1) or perhaps because they were speaking the language of the angels (cf. 13:1).[38] If so, then the following qualification in v. 11 would be directed both to this position of theirs and to v. 9. The order of argument in v. 11, that the *woman* is not independent of the man, would certainly allow such a possibility.

In this case, Paul's argument will have taken a slight turn. Having affirmed that a man should not be covered, and by implication that a woman should because she is man's glory, he turns for a moment to affirm the woman's freedom. But that is not the whole story; since the woman is not independent of the man, he is also arguing that she properly exercise that freedom by continuing the custom of being "covered." But finally, again, we must admit that we cannot be sure.

11-12   With these two sets of sentences, in each of which woman and man are in balanced pairs, Paul qualifies the preceding argument. Both the fact that they immediately follow v. 10 with the adversative "nonetheless"[39] and that he has changed the order from "man/woman" to "woman/man" suggest that they partly function to qualify v. 10 itself in some way. In fact, the sequence "woman/man" makes almost impossible the view that v. 10 has to do with the man's having authority over the woman. In that case the proper qualifier would have been: "Nonetheless, in the Lord man is not independent of woman."[40] But the fact that he says, "woman is

---

[37]*Man*, pp. 51-53.

[38]Fiorenza, *Memory,* p. 228, suggests that "women have such power through the angels, who according to Jewish and Christian apocalyptic theology mediate the 'words of prophecy.'"

[39]Gk. πλήν; common in Luke, but only here and in Eph. 5:33; Phil. 1:18; 3:16; 4:14 in Paul. According to BAGD, Paul tends to use it for "breaking off a discussion and emphasizing what is important" (= "in any case," "nonetheless").

[40]Cf. the MajT reading (see n. 4)! I am indebted to Payne, *Man,* p. 54, for this insight. He also notes that two translations (Phillips, NEB) change the order to fit their understanding of the context (KJV also, but it reflects the TR).

not independent of man," indicates that he is qualifying *her* use of *exousia* in some way. This tends, therefore, to support the suggestion made above that v. 10 represents in part at least the viewpoint of the Corinthians, with which Paul agrees, but which also needs to be qualified toward propriety (vv. 13-15) and not creating shame (vv. 4-6).

Since the two pairs are a perfect double chiasm and correspond precisely to vv. 8-9, however, they seem clearly designed also to set limits on how those verses are to be understood. Thus (literally):

A	Not is man from woman,		a
	but woman from man;		b
B	Not was created man for the sake of the woman,		a
	but woman for the sake of the man.		b
	Nonetheless		
B'	Neither woman without man,		b
	nor man without woman,		a
	in the Lord;		
A'	*For* just as the woman	from the man,	b
	so also the man	through the woman,	a
	and all things	from God.	

This correspondence is so close that it can hardly have been accidental. The qualifiers in the second sets ("in the Lord," "all things from God") are what make the difference. While it is true that woman is man's glory, having been created for his sake (v. 9), Paul now affirms that that does not mean that woman exists for man's purposes, as though in some kind of subordinate position to his aims and will. To the contrary, God has so arranged things that "in the Lord"[41] the one cannot exist without the other, not meaning of course that every Christian man and woman must be married, but that as believers man and woman are mutually dependent on each other.[42]

Some have argued that "in the Lord" does not fully qualify v. 9, but rather sets up the equality of man and woman in Christ in terms of their

[41]For this formula see on 7:22, 39; 9:1, 2. In this case it refers most likely to the "sphere" of their existence in the new age. God has called them to be "in the Lord," and in that new relationship they live out the life of the future, awaiting its consummation. In this new existence man and woman are totally interdependent.

[42]This understanding is a step beyond the actual wording of the text. The problem lies with the lack of a verb. One must supply either "is" or "exists," the latter being the more likely. The preposition "without" ("apart from"; cf. 4:8) then means not simply that they cannot exist without each other, but that they are not intended to exist independent of one another. Cf. the discussion in Payne, *Man*, pp. 53-54. Otherwise, J. Kürzinger, "Frau und Mann nach 1 Kor 11.11f.," *BZ* 22 (1978), 270-75, followed by Fiorenza, *Memory*, pp. 229-30, and Padgett, "Paul," p. 71, who argues that χωρίς here has the sense of "different from," hence a declaration of equality in the Lord.

salvation. But that hardly seems to be Paul's point, especially since in v. 12 he equally qualifies v. 8, but now in more general terms, referring to the fact that man is now born of the woman who at creation came from his side. Furthermore, the final qualifier, "and[43] all things are from God," which includes at least woman and man, puts the whole of vv. 7-9 into proper Pauline perspective. Both man and woman, not just man, are from God. God made the one from dust, the other through man, and now finally both through woman. This seems clearly designed to keep the earlier argument from being read in a subordinationist way.

As pointed out throughout the exegesis, this is a passage in which the apostle has been rather badly handled in the church. Although the paragraph begins with further arguments as to why women should be "covered," Paul seems to leave that concern momentarily to affirm both (1) that women do have authority over their own heads (although that must be exercised in the context of not shaming their "head" and propriety) and (2) that even though in the new age the distinctions between male and female must be maintained, that does not mean that one is subordinate to the other. To read the text as though it said the opposite of what vv. 10-12 seem clearly to say is to do Paul an injustice and possibly to put one in the position of disobeying the intent of God's Word.

3. An Argument from Propriety (11:13-16)

13 *Judge for yourselves: Is it proper for a woman to pray to God with her head uncovered?* 14 *Does[1] not the very nature of things teach you that if a man has long hair, it is a disgrace to him,* 15 *but that if a woman has long hair, it is her glory? For long hair is given[2] as a covering.* 16 *If anyone wants to be contentious about this, we have no such[3] practice—nor do the churches of God.*

In the preceding paragraph Paul's argument moved slightly afield—from a concern over a woman's being "covered" to a concern for her having

[43]Gk. δέ; this could be slightly adversative, but in a continuative, not a contrastive, sense.

[1]Apparently in an attempt to tie the two questions more closely together the MajT added an ἤ ("or").

[2]The NIV adds "to her." It is doubtful whether the αὐτῇ is original (it is not found in P46 D F G Ψ Maj b; Ambst). Two things speak against it: (1) Omission is difficult to account for, especially twice (the only way to account for its absence in both P46 and D F G); whereas (2) an addition is easy to account for, especially since the word occurs in two different positions (after δίδοται: ℵ A B 33 81 365 2464 g syp; before δίδοται: C H P 630 1175 1739 1881 2495). Cf. Zuntz, 127.

[3]NIV, "other"; the Greek is τοιαύτην, which means "such a kind"; there is no evidence that it ever means "other."

"authority" over her head without being either independent of or subordinate to man. With this final paragraph he now returns to the original argument of vv. 4-6, including the motif of "shame." But the appeal in this case is slightly different—to their own judgment and sense of propriety (v. 13), based on "the nature of things" (vv. 14-15). This appeal takes the form of two rhetorical questions: the first one (v. 13b), obviously expecting a negative answer, picks up the language of v. 5 and asks, in terms of propriety, whether a woman should "pray to God with her head uncovered *(akatakalyptos)*"; the second one (vv. 14-15), which expects a positive answer, functions to reinforce or to clinch the first one. Thus he points to the "nature of things," in which man has short hair and woman long. Apparently he intends this appeal to make two points: (1) that "nature" itself has thus distinguished between the sexes, and (2) that a woman's long hair should teach them the propriety of being "covered" when they pray. The question that must be answered has to do with how this question *functions* in the argument, whether this is the actual problem or whether it serves as an analogy to clinch the earlier argument. In any case, Paul can scarcely leave an argument there, so he concludes that the person who is being contentious over this matter needs to reckon with what goes on elsewhere in the churches. They have no "such custom" (apparently of the kind these women are contending for).

13 In a way similar to the argument against attendance at temple meals (10:15), Paul turns at the end to appeal to their own judgments. Although he is certainly trying to get them to agree with him (the nature of rhetorical questions has that built in), the appeal is to their own sense of propriety, as that is further illustrated by nature itself. Once they have thus "judged for themselves," of course, Paul expects them to see things his way.

Also as in 10:15-16, the appeal to their good sense is followed by a rhetorical question.[4] But the rhetoric is not sharp. The issue is one of propriety: "Is it proper[5] for a woman[6] to pray to God[7] with her head un-

---

[4]Both Bushnell (*God's Word*, par. 247) and Padgett ("Paul," p. 82) argue that this is not a question but a declaration, a position taken by Padgett because he has posited that vv. 3-7b are a Corinthian argument that Paul is here combating. See n. 19 on vv. 2-6. But this does not seem to do full justice to πρέπον. If the Corinthians are arguing *for* a certain hairdo (as Padgett maintains), then Paul here is clearly arguing *against* it. Women's authority, therefore, is *not* freedom, as Padgett insists. She *should* do what is πρέπον, which from the present point of view should mean no put-up hair!

[5]Gk. πρέπον (cf. 1 Tim. 2:10; Tit. 2:1).

[6]Gk. γυναῖκα; ordinarily πρέπον takes the dative. But it is probably a step beyond Paul's intent to suggest, as Parry, 162, that the accusative implies that it is fitting "not merely for the woman, but as a Church rule."

[7]This addition of "to God" makes it certain that it is not simply a matter of her being "in church," but that she is an active participant in the worship. Cf. n. 22 on vv. 2-6.

covered?" The question itself clearly picks up the language of v. 5, thus indicating a return to the problem as it was addressed there.[8] The nature of the argument does not differ greatly from the appeal to "shame" in vv. 4-6, although in that case the shame was given a theological basis (v. 3) and accrued to one's "head." Here the propriety (v. 13), disgrace (v. 14), and glory (v. 15) are assumed to have a more universal basis. Whether the Corinthians themselves would have thought it not "fitting" is a moot point, especially since some apparently were doing otherwise.

14 Paul now proceeds, by means of a second rhetorical question,[9] to reinforce the point of the preceding question, and thus to clinch the argument. The appeal in this case is unique in the Pauline corpus: "Does not[10] nature itself[11] teach you?" It is hardly possible for Paul as a Hellenistic Jew not to have known the far-reaching significance that "nature" had in Greek thinking, especially in contemporary popular philosophy, Stoicism in particular.[12] Nonetheless, even though this question has a very Stoic ring to it,[13] Paul makes no theological significance of the idea as one finds it in

---

[8]Hurley, "Veils," pp. 214-15, argues that Paul is either quoting or paraphrasing a question in their letter to him. But that has very little to commend it. He also calls it a rhetorical question, which it is; but if so, how then can he be quoting them? A rhetorical question by definition has its answer implied in the question itself. Hurley also completely disregards vv. 14-15 as a follow-up rhetorical question, making them rather Paul's answer to "each of the three groups involved in the controversy over hair." Positing three groups, when nothing in the text hints at internal conflict in Corinth over this matter, is probably too much weight to place on the preposition ἀντί (v. 15) when there is another viable answer to that problem.

[9]Bushnell (*God's Word*, par. 247) and Padgett ("Paul," pp. 82-83), with even less success, also read these questions as indicatives (cf. n. 4 above). In each case they have considerable difficulty with the final causal clause in v. 15 introduced by ὅτι (Padgett's translation is especially puzzling: "Nature does not teach you that . . . if a woman has long hair it is her glory. For long, loose hair is given to her instead of wrapped-up hair").

[10]Gk. οὐδέ; there is no other example in Paul of this negative conjunction starting a rhetorical question (but see Mark 12:10; Luke 23:40). Most likely, as O-W, 261, suggest, Paul was thinking οὐ δέ.

[11]Gk. ἡ φύσις αὐτή; cf. Rom. 1:26; 2:14, 27; 11:21, 24 (three times); Gal. 2:15; 4:8; Eph. 2:3. Elsewhere in the NT only Jas. 3:7 (twice); 2 Pet. 1:4 (cf. φυσικός in Rom. 1:26, 27; 2 Pet. 2:12). For a discussion of the term see esp. H. Köster, *TDNT* IX, 251-77; cf., on a smaller scale, G. Harder, *NIDNTT* II, 656-61. Köster (p. 271) notes that its rare occurrence in the NT in comparison with its widespread use throughout the entire Hellenistic world must be "a deliberate theological decision which rests on the fact that there is no place for 'natural theology' in the thinking of the NT."

[12]Cf. Marc.Aur.Ant., "Ο φύσις (Nature), from you comes everything, in you is everything, to you goes everything" (4.23; Loeb). Hence for the Stoic the greatest good is to live according to Nature, i.e., according to the given, regular order of things.

[13]Cf. esp. Epict. 1.16.9-14: "Come, let us leave the chief works of nature, and consider merely what she does in passing. Can anything be more useless than the hairs on a chin? Well, what then? Has not nature used even these in the most suitable way possible?

Stoicism.[14] For him this is not an appeal to Nature, or to "natural law," or to "natural endowment"[15]; nor is Nature to be understood as pedagogic (actually "teaching" these "laws"). Rather, for Paul it is a question of propriety and of "custom" (vv. 13, 16), which carries with it "disgrace" or "glory" (vv. 14-15). Hence, this is an appeal to the "way things are" (NIV, "the nature of things"), to the "natural feeling" that they shared together as part of their contemporary culture. Thus Paul is not arguing that men *must* wear their hair short, or that women *must* have long hair, as though "nature" meant some kind of "created order."[16] Indeed, the very appeal to "nature" in this way suggests most strongly that the argument is by way of analogy, not of necessity.

As in the two preceding arguments (vv. 4-6, 7-12), Paul begins with the man in order to set up what he wants to say about the woman. What "nature" thus teaches is that "man, on the one hand,[17] if he has long hair, it is a disgrace[18] to him." This seems to be clear evidence that by "nature" Paul meant the natural feelings of their contemporary culture. After all, according to Acts 18:18 Paul had apparently worn long hair for a time in Corinth as part of a vow. But the very nature of the vow—both letting the hair grow long and cutting it again—demonstrates the "normalcy" of shorter hair on men, as is also evidenced by thousands of contemporary paintings, reliefs, and pieces of sculpture. The "disgrace" lay in the very "unnaturalness" of long hair.

15 For the woman, on the other hand, the opposite prevails. What is dishonor for the one is glory for the other.[19] "Glory" in this instance, since it is the opposite of "dishonor," must mean something like "distinction" or "honor." Long hair does not give her glory; it functions as some-

---

Has she not by these means distinguished between the male and female? . . . Again, in the case of women, just as nature has mingled in their voice a certain softer note, so likewise she has taken the hair from their chins. . . . Wherefore, we ought to preserve the signs which God has given; we ought not to throw them away; we ought not, so far as in us lies, to confuse the sexes which have been distinguished in this fashion" (Loeb, I, 111).

[14]Cf. Köster, p. 273: "The argument is a typical one in popular philosophy and is not specifically Stoic."

[15]After all, what "nature teaches" comes about by an "unnatural" means—a haircut.

[16]As Hurley, "Veils," p. 215, asserts, but without supporting evidence.

[17]This literal rendering tries to catch the emphasis in Paul's Greek: ἀνὴρ μέν . . . γυνὴ δέ, with the conditional clause following.

[18]Gk. ἀτιμία, probably to be distinguished from the αἶσχρον of v. 6. The latter seems to carry the stronger connotation of something base or disgusting, while ἀτιμία comes closer to personal dishonor, here contrasted with δόξα (cf. 2 Cor. 6:8); 15:43 has a similar contrast between exaltation and humiliation.

[19]For the idea that hair is a woman's glory, cf. Achilles Tatius 8.6 (of Leucippe): "She has been robbed of the crowning glory of her hair (τῆς κεφαλῆς τὸ κάλλος; lit. 'the beauty of her head'); you can still see where her head was shaved" (Loeb, p. 399).

thing that distinguishes the splendor of the woman.[20] Although he may be thinking of the hair as it is done up in public, more likely he is not thinking of the public appearance of women but of the more "natural" phenomenon of the hair itself, which at home would more often be on display and without shame. That is, Paul's concern by this analogy is not how people appear, but how they are by the nature of things.

This seems to be the point of the final clause, which is tied to the rhetorical question with a causal conjunction.[21] Long hair is the woman's glory *because* it has been given in the place of a covering. The natural meaning of these words is that her long hair, let down, functions for her as a natural covering. The question is whether the preceding rhetorical question (vv. 14-15) was intended to deal with hair specifically, thus implying that this had been the issue right along, or whether that question functioned as an analogy to reinforce the preceding arguments that the woman should not be "uncovered" when praying or prophesying.

Much has been made of the preposition *anti,* which ordinarily serves for the concept of replacement—one thing *instead of* another.[22] To make *anti* mean that here would tend to force one to take long hair, either loosed or put up, as the "covering" for which Paul has been arguing throughout. We have already noted the difficulties with the "long hair" view.[23] If put-up hair is the concern, then the rhetorical question of vv. 14-15 is not so much trying to reinforce that of v. 13, as it is itself the point of the whole argument, beginning with v. 3. The problem with this view is threefold: (1) If put-up hair has been the issue throughout, why does Paul not say so clearly in vv. 4-6? Why use such ambiguities in the earlier part of the argument when it is clear from this passage that he does not need to? (2) It is difficult to find an adequate reason for this last sentence since, according to this view, nothing in the preceding argument has so much as hinted at the possibility that a woman should have an external covering. Why now should he cap the whole argument with this irrelevancy, that long hair has been given to her *instead of*

[20]Cf. Exod. 28:2, where the splendid garments of the priests are to give them "glory [NIV, dignity] and honor" (LXX, τιμία and δόξα). Thus garments distinguished them, or set them apart from others; but at the same time they gave them dignity and honor for their sacred task.

[21]Gk. ὅτι; it may function here like an explanatory γάρ. But since Paul's argumentation in this letter is full of the latter, he probably intended something more causal in this case.

[22]This serves as part of the argument, e.g., in Isaksson, *Marriage,* p. 185; Martin, "Interpretation," p. 233; Hurley, "Veils," p. 215; Fiorenza, *Memory,* p. 227; and Padgett, "Paul," pp. 82-83. The boldness with which some assert that this is the only meaning of ἀντί outstrips the evidence. See n. 26 below.

[23]See above, n. 85 on v. 6; cf. nn. 26-28 on vv. 2-6.

another covering of some kind?[24] (3) How does one reconcile the clear force of the contrasts in vv. 14-15, that the woman has "long hair" by nature, with the idea that the whole point of the argument is for her to put it up—all the more so since the word "covering" *(peribolaion)* ordinarily refers to a garment that functions as a shawl or "wraparound"?[25] On the whole, this sentence, which proponents of this view see as in its favor, is in fact its Achilles' heel.

Since there is sufficient evidence that *anti* can also mean "that one thing is equivalent to another,"[26] there is no need to force the rigid concept of replacement onto this sentence. Most likely, therefore, just as in vv. 5b-6, Paul is arguing by analogy that since women have by "nature" been given long hair as a covering, that in itself points to their need to be "covered" when praying and prophesying. If the argument is not tight for some modern tastes, it is in fact perfectly understandable.

16 By appealing finally to their own sense of propriety, as "nature" by way of analogy helps them to see that, Paul brings to a close his argument over the "rightness" of the women maintaining the "custom" of being covered. But Paul is never quite comfortable concluding an argument in this fashion. Hence he draws the whole together with a final appeal to what goes on in the "churches of God." That he is dealing strictly with "custom" (church "custom," to be sure) is now made plain, as is the fact that this argument, for all its various facets, falls short of a command as such.

The opening sentence, "If anyone wants to be contentious about this," is one of four such sentences in this letter,[27] each indicating that this is what some are doing. Most likely this refers to some women who are discarding a traditional "covering" of some kind. Paul's final appeal to

[24]Hurley's answer is to posit three groups, a "loose-hair" party, a "hair-up" party, and a "pro-veil" party, who are responsible for this part of the letter by asking Paul's own judgment on these matters. Paul responds by putting it back in their laps (v. 13a). Vv. 14-15 respond to all three. The rhetorical question confirms the rightness of the "hair-up" party; the final sentence is a tack-on response to the "pro-veil" party. Such divisions of a unitary text into parts in itself defeats the proposal.

[25]Hurley does not speak to the problem at all. Murphy-O'Connor, "Sex," 489, has clearly recognized the difficulty and therefore rejects the meaning "instead of" for ἀντί (see his n. 32). But his own solution, that περιβόλαιον does not in fact refer to a garment, but to the put-up hair "wrapped around" her head in plaits, asks for an otherwise unknown meaning for this word (adopted without discussion by Padgett, "Paul," p. 82). Furthermore, his final translation (p. 499, "so that she may wind it around her head") seems to wrench the Greek text beyond recognition.

[26]BAGD 2; cf. LSJ A.III.2. Cf. Murphy-O'Connor, "Sex," 489 n. 32.

[27]Cf. 3:18; 8:2; 14:37, in each case of which the clause picks up one of the Corinthian bywords: σοφία, γνῶσις, πνευματικός.

these women is that "we have no such[28] practice[29]—nor do the churches of God." The words "such practice," therefore, must refer to that which the "contentious" are advocating, and which this argument has been combating.

This is now the third time that Paul has tried to correct Corinthian behavior by appealing to what is taught or practiced in the other churches.[30] As noted on 1:2, this probably reflects something of the independent spirit that is at work in this community. The distinction between "we" and "the churches of God" is most likely between the Pauline (and therefore the "we" includes the Corinthians) and other churches. If so, then Paul is also reminding the Corinthians of how much greater a body it is to which he and they belong.

Even though Paul has now spent considerable effort on this issue, the very nature of his argumentation reveals that it is not something over which he has great passion. Indeed, there is nothing quite like this in his extant letters, where he argues for maintaining a custom, let alone predicating a large part of the argument on shame, propriety, and custom. Two final observations, therefore, need to be made.

First, the very fact that Paul argues in this way, and that even at the end he does not give a commandment, suggests that such a "church custom," although not thereby unimportant for the Corinthians, is not to be raised to Canon Law. The very "customary" nature of the problem, which could be argued in this way in a basically monolithic cultural environment, makes it nearly impossible to transfer "across the board" to the multifaceted cultures in which the church finds itself today—even if we knew exactly what it was we were to transfer, which we do not. But in each culture there are surely those modes of dress that are appropriate and those that are not.

Second, the more casual way Paul argues against this present "deviation" in comparison with what follows, seems to indicate the greater significance—for him at least—of the next one. Here he can appeal to shame, propriety, and custom (as well as theological presuppositions and church practice); in the abuse that follows there is only attack and imperative. What they were doing with the Supper cut at the heart of both the gospel and the church; therefore, much is at stake. But here it is not quite so. The distinction between the sexes is to be maintained; the covering is to go back on; but for Paul it does not seem to be a life-and-death matter.

[28]Gk. τοιαύτην, "such a kind" (cf. 5:1); there is no evidence of any kind that it means "other."

[29]Gk. συνήθεια; cf. 8:7, where it was used in its subjective sense; here it is objective, referring to a specific custom.

[30]See 4:17 and 7:17; cf. on 1:2 and see further 14:33.

D. ABUSE OF THE LORD'S SUPPER (11:17-34)

Paul now takes up a second abuse of Christian worship (cf. 11:2-16), "divisions" at the Lord Supper (v. 18) predicated along sociological lines (v. 22). Apparently Paul had already anticipated this concern in his previous reference to the Table in 10:17,[1] where he reminded them that because they *all* eat of the *one* loaf, they together constitute the *one body* of Christ. Their "divisions" at the Table are giving the lie to the unity that their common partaking of the bread is intended to proclaim.

This problem is the one certain instance in chaps. 7–16 that is not in response to their letter.[2] This means (1) that as in chaps. 1–6 we receive more information from Paul himself as to the nature of the abuse because he tells the Corinthians what he knows about it, and (2) that the level of rhetoric is also more like that of chaps. 1–6 (cf. 8–10), where he took strong exception to what he had heard. Thus in striking contrast to what has immediately preceded (vv. 3-16), here he returns to biting rhetoric (v. 22) and threat and appeal (vv. 28-34), all the while trying to move them from totally unacceptable behavior to that which is more in keeping with the gospel and the fellowship that are proclaimed at this meal.

Although not all are agreed on the precise details of the abuse in this case,[3] its broad parameters are generally clear—and it is not a matter of getting drunk at the Table.[4] In fact the greatest difficulty in reconstructing the problem is to overcome our own familiarity with part of the text (at least vv. 23-26, often vv. 23-32), which usually has been informed within a given liturgical setting.[5] The abuse itself can scarcely be understood apart from

---

[1]These are the only two references to the Lord's Table in the extant Pauline literature. For a select bibliography on the Lord's Table in Paul, see n. 17 on 10:16.

[2]See v. 18. The reason for its place here in the letter is almost certainly topical, having been set up by vv. 2 and 3-16, and thereby also anticipating the final matter on worship in chaps. 12–14.

[3]Some have overlooked the sociological factors altogether, but they have great difficulty with vv. 17-22 and 33-34. It was common at one point, e.g., to suggest that the sacred meal was being profaned by being allowed to become a common, everyday meal, and that Paul's concern is to reinstitute the sacred meal (e.g., Weiss, 283; Lietzmann, 256 [= bad manners]). Similarly, Schmithals, 250-56, sees the problem as coming from spiritualizing Gnostics, who rejected participating in the external elements as though they represented Christ and deliberately substituted a profane meal. Conzelmann, 194, following von Soden ("Sacrament"), takes the opposite view, that the Corinthian *pneumatics* have an "over-heated sacramentalism," an almost magical view that has moved them toward intense individualism at the Table ("each" eating "his own" meal). But none of these can be sustained in light of Paul's own clear expression of the abuse in vv. 22 and 33-34 as a despising of the church by shaming those who have nothing.

[4]This is the most common popular way of reading vv. 17-22; but any careful reading of the text reveals that at best this is incidental to the real problem; indeed, it is not so much as mentioned again after v. 21.

[5]This is true even of—perhaps one should say, especially of—nonliturgical

awareness of two realities: (1) the nearly universal phenomenon of cultic meals as part of worship in antiquity, and (2) the fact that in the early church the Lord's Supper was most likely eaten as, or in conjunction with, such a meal. On the first matter, see the introduction to chaps. 8–10 and the commentary on 10:16-22. The second matter is supported not only by this passage but also by the evidence of Acts (2:42, 46; 20:7, 11), and probably the "love feast" in Jude 12. In contrast to most subsequent Christians, who have kept the "food" but have rather completely lost the symbol of the meal, the Corinthians had kept the meal but were in grave danger of losing altogether the meaning of the food, and thus of the meal as well.

The abuse seems to move in two directions, horizontal and vertical. The primary problem was an abuse of the church itself. This is specifically stated in the rhetorical questions of v. 22: Some are despising the church of God by humiliating those who have nothing. Both the structure of the argument and its details confirm this. The argument is in four parts, which together form a chiasm:

A   Vv. 17-22—The statement of the problem: the rich[6] are abusing the poor ("going ahead with their own [private] meal") at the Lord's Table.
  B   Vv. 23-26—The repetition of the "tradition," the words of institution, with their emphasis on "remembrance of me" and "proclaiming his death until he comes."
  B' Vv. 27-32—"So then"—in response to vv. 23-26, one must "discern the body" as one eats; otherwise one is in grave danger of judgment.
A' Vv. 33-34—"So then"—in response to vv. 17-22, they are to "welcome/receive one another" at the meal, so as not to incur the judgment of vv. 30-32.[7]

Since the matter of vv. 17-22 and 33-34 "sandwiches" vv. 23-32, one must ask how the latter functions in the total argument. The clue lies in

---

Protestant churches, where vv. 27-32 usually serve as a warning against improper participation—meaning "if one has sin in one's life"—and encourage personal introspection.

[6]B. W. Winter, "The Lord's Supper at Corinth: An Alternative Reconstruction," *RefThRev* 37 (1978), 73-82, cautions against dividing the participants too easily into "rich" and "poor" as permanent classes of society; rather, the differences often involved "the secure i.e. those who are guaranteed security by reason of membership of a household, and the insecure i.e. those who had no protection from a patron" (p. 81).

[7]The NIV unfortunately translates the two ὥστε's of vv. 27 and 32 with different English words ("therefore," "so then"), thus causing the reader to miss the double response to the preceding paragraphs. *So then*, because when we eat and drink at this meal we proclaim the Lord's death, we must eat the bread so as properly to "discern the body." *So then*, because otherwise one is subject to judgment, we must "welcome/receive one another at this meal."

v. 29, which in a way similar to the argument of 10:16-17 focuses on the bread (= the body = the church) and thus ties this part of the argument to that of vv. 17-22 and 33-34. Whatever else, they are abusing "the body" at their "fellowship meal," which is a meal eaten at the Lord's Table (10:21) in "honor of the Lord" (v. 20).

At the same time, however, such an abuse of the "body" is an abuse of Christ himself. The bread represents his crucified body, which, along with his poured out blood, effected the death that ratified the New Covenant. By their abuse of one another, they were also abusing the One through whose death and resurrection they had been brought to life and formed into this new eschatological fellowship, his body the church. Thus Paul's need to take them all the way back—to the actual words of institution—so that they will restore the meaning of the food to its rightful place in their meal. "Do this," those words remind them, "in remembrance of *me.*" To which Paul adds, "for as often as we celebrate this meal we proclaim the Lord's death until he comes." Believers eat in the present in fellowship with one another, focusing on Christ's death which brought them life; and they do so as eschatological people, awaiting his return (see on 4:1-5). In that context they must "discern the body"; otherwise they put themselves under the same condemnation as those who crucified him in the first place (v. 27). At his return he will execute judgment on those who do not believe; by their actions the Corinthians are already incurring that judgment (v. 30). They must change so as not to come under the final judgment as well (vv. 31-32, 34).

What is less certain is the specific nature of the abuse, which is made ambiguous for us both by Paul's language[8] and our lack of full understanding of the sociological factors involved in meals in the Hellenistic world.[9] The problem has several dimensions. First, since the church gathered for such meals in the homes of the rich, most likely the host was also the patron of the meal.[10] Second, archeology has shown rather conclusively that the dining room (the triclinium) in such homes would scarcely accommodate many guests;[11] the majority therefore would eat in the atrium (the somewhat

---

[8]The difficult terms are τὸ ἴδιον δεῖπνον προλαμβάνει ("go ahead with his own supper"), ἀλλήλους ἐκδέχεσθαι ("wait for/receive one another"), "having houses to eat and drink in" (v. 22), and "eat at home" (v. 34).

[9]This is further complicated by the fact that Corinth was a Roman colony, and that among the wealthy, Roman customs may have prevailed alongside Greek. Most of the more important literary evidence is from the Roman side. Two of the wealthier converts in fact bore Roman names (Gaius and Titius Justus; unless this is the same person [see on 1:15]).

[10]Cf. Rom. 16:23 (written from Corinth at a later date), "Gaius, who is host to me and *to the whole church.*"

[11]The triclinia average about 36 square meters (about 18 x 18 ft.). If they actually reclined (triclinium = a table with three sides on which to recline) at such meals, there would be room for about 9 to 12 guests at table. Cf. Murphy-O'Connor, *Corinth*, 153-61.

larger entry "courtyard"), which would still seat only about 30 to 50 guests on the average.

These material realities are complicated by a variety of sociological factors. In a class-conscious society such as Roman Corinth would have been, it would be sociologically natural for the host to invite those of his/her own class to eat in the triclinium, while the others would eat in the atrium. Furthermore, it is probable that the language "one's own supper" (v. 21)[12] refers to the eating of "private meals" by the wealthy,[13] in which at the common meal of the Lord's Supper they ate either their own portions or perhaps privileged portions that were not made available to the "have-nots." This is further complicated by the question of the relationship of this "private supper" to the Lord's Supper, especially in light of the language "after supper" for the blessing of the cup (v. 25). Did the wealthy eat their "private meal" *before* or *in conjunction with* the eating of the bread that constituted the Lord's Supper? And how did it affect "those who have nothing"? See further on v. 22.

In any case, the apostle does not eliminate the social distinctions as such: The wealthy still have their own houses in which to eat their private meals (vv. 22, 34). What he will not let them do is to bring such distinctions to the common meal of believers, where Christ had made them all one, signified by their all eating of the one loaf (10:17).[14] By carrying over into these meals a number of "privileged status" aspects of both private and religious meals, the rich were in effect destroying the church as one body in Christ. The net result was to destroy the gospel itself. Hence these especially strong words in behalf of the poor, which at the same time are in behalf of a proper understanding of the Lord's Supper.

1. The Problem—Abuse of the Poor (11:17-22)

17 *In the following directives I have no praise*[15] *for you, for your meetings do more harm than good.* 18 *In the first place, I hear that*

---

[12]Unfortunately missing in the NIV. It is doubtful whether "without waiting for anybody else" is a "dynamic equivalent" of "going ahead with/devouring one's own meal."

[13]See especially the reconstruction by Theissen, 145-74; but note also the caution in Malherbe, *Social Aspects,* p. 84, and some correctives in Winter, "Lord's Supper."

[14]S. C. Barton, "Paul's Sense of Place: an Anthropological Approach to Community Formation in Corinth," *NTS* 32 (1986), 238-39, has argued that the divisions are between households or groups of households, thus positing the same divisions as in 1:10-12. This study contains some helpful insights, but on this crucial point it lacks adequate evidence from the text itself. See below on v. 18.

[15]The text shows considerable confusion here as to which is the main verb and which the participle. The options:

(1) παραγγέλλων οὐκ ἐπαινῶ ("in commanding this, I do not praise"—NIV NA[26] ℵ F G Ψ Maj a d)

*when you come together as a church, there are divisions among you,
and to some extent I believe it.* 19 *No doubt there have to be differences among you[16] to show which of you[17] have God's approval.*
20 *When[18] you come together, it is not the Lord's Supper you eat,*
21 *for as you eat, each of you goes ahead with his own supper.[19] One
remains hungry, another gets drunk.* 22 *Don't you have homes to eat
and drink in? Or do you despise the church of God and humiliate
those who have nothing? What shall I say to you? Shall I praise[20] you
for this? Certainly not!*

This opening paragraph, which is (understandably) seldom read at the Protestant communion service, bursts forth with a rhetorical force altogether
missing from the immediately preceding argument. Paul's point is singular:
to accost the Corinthians with what he knows about the abuse of their
common meal, at which the Lord's Supper is also eaten, and with this very
rhetoric to begin his response to it. The content of the paragraph clusters
around three key ideas or word-groups: (1) "to assemble together" (vv. 17,
18, 22); (2) "to eat" (vv. 20-22); and (3) "divisions among you" (vv. 18-19,
21, 22). As they assemble together to eat the Lord's Supper, instead of being
"together" they are being sundered apart by the activities of some who are
going ahead with their own private meals, thus despising the church by

---

(2) παραγγέλλω οὐκ ἐπαινῶν ("this I command, not praising"—A C 6 33 104
326 365 1175 1739 f vg)

(3) παραγγέλλων οὐκ ἐπαινῶν ("in commanding this, not praising"—B)

(4) παραγγέλλων οὐκ ἐπαινῶ ("I command this; I do not praise"—D* 81 b)
Although eventually these all come out at the same place, the one that best explains the
others is 2, since in light of vv. 3 and 22 that is the more awkward combination. All the
others result from its awkwardness. Here is a place where WH seem to show better textual
judgment than subsequent editors. Cf. A. Fridrichsen, "Non laudo: Note sur I Cor.
11,17.22," in *Mélanges d'histoire des religions et de recherches offerts à Johannes
Pedersen* (Stockholm, 1944-47), pp. 28-32, who, however, makes the ὅτι epexegetic,
thus translating, "disapproving of the fact that. . . ." Otherwise Conzelmann, 192 n. 1;
Barrett, 258 n. 1.

16The ἐν ὑμῖν is omitted in the Western tradition (D* F G lat Cyprian Ambrosiaster). See the discussion in Zuntz, 141.

17A few MSS (P46 C 2464) also omit this second ἐν ὑμῖν, probably because it
comes at the end of Paul's sentence, which would have been complete in the scribe's mind
without it.

18The NIV omits an οὖν ("therefore"), with P46 C* F G b Clement. Most likely
the οὖν is original; the resumptive sense of the sentence (cf. v. 18) seems to require it. Cf.
Zuntz, 192.

19NIV, "without waiting for anybody else." See n. 12 above. This translation is
based on v. 33; but it rather misses the crucial idiom of this passage and the sharp contrast
between the Lord's "supper" and their own private "supper."

20Some important early MSS (P46 B F G lat) read ἐπαινῶ in place of ἐπαινήσω,
probably by assimilation to the following ἐπαινῶ.

535

shaming those who have nothing. The perspective is clearly "from below," taking the side of the "have-nots."

17 Although there is some difficulty in determining Paul's precise wording at the beginning of this sentence,[21] there can be little question as to how it functions: to set the stage for what follows by announcing at the outset that their "gatherings" do "more harm than good." At the same time both the adversative "but"[22] and the participle "not praising" (cf. vv. 2, 22) tie what follows to what has preceded by way of contrast. Thus he begins, "But this[23] I command, not praising [you]." What one expects next is some expression of the content of the "command." What one gets, however, is the reason why he cannot praise them. It has to do with their "coming together"[24] in such a way that it does more harm than good (lit. "not for the better, but for the worse").

The verb "gather together," repeated five times in vv. 17-22 and 33-34, is one of the key words that holds the argument together. Given its similar usage in 14:23 and 26, it had probably become a semitechnical term for the "gathering together" of the people of God for worship. Thus the concern is with what goes on when they "come together *as* the church" (v. 18). The Corinthian problem was not their failure to gather, but their failure truly to be God's new people when they gathered; here there was to be neither Jew nor Greek, slave nor free (cf. 12:13).

18 Paul now proceeds to explain *how* their gatherings are for the worse rather than for the better. He begins as though he were going to list several lapses, "for[25] first of all, on the one hand"; but just as in the preceding sentence, the argument unfolds without following through with either a "second" or "on the other hand."[26] Nonetheless, Paul's concern is

---

[21]See n. 15.

[22]Gk. δέ, not translated in the NIV (cf. NAB, NEB); but see GNB, RSV, NASB (JB makes it consecutive, "now").

[23]This τοῦτο helps to create some of the awkwardness of this sentence. Ordinarily it would, as in 7:6 (q.v.), refer to what precedes, which it can hardly do here (but see Barrett, 260). On the other hand, when it refers to something that follows, Paul tends either to add an epexegetic ὅτι clause (15:50; cf. 2 Thess. 3:10) or to express the content of the "this" (7:29; cf. Gal. 3:2, 17). As in 7:29-35, this τοῦτο and the one in v. 22 enclose the paragraph, although he never does specify the "command" to which τοῦτο refers.

[24]Gk. συνέρχεσθε; cf. vv. 18, 20, 33, 34; 14:23, 26). Except for 7:5, where it has a different meaning altogether, these constitute the total number of usages in Paul's extant letters.

[25]Gk. γάρ; again explanatory. What follows explains how they come together for the worse.

[26]Some have suggested that the expected complement lies with the "further directions" in v. 34 (e.g., Grosheide, 265), or with chaps. 12–14 (cf. Findlay, 877; Parry, 163), or is picked up in v. 20 with the "therefore" (Godet, 137). But all of that

clear, and it is singular: "I hear that when you come together as a church, there are divisions among you," to which he adds the interesting but perplexing words, "and to some extent I believe it."

That he "hears" that there are "divisions"[27] among them is reminiscent of 1:10-12; however, it is doubtful whether this reflects the same reality[28]—for several reasons: (1) The former divisions were further defined as "quarrels" and "jealousy" (1:11; 3:4), which are quite missing from this section, where they are spelled out totally along sociological lines (vv. 21-22; 33-34). (2) In 1:12 Paul mentions at least four names around which the quarrels are taking place; moreover, there is a decidedly anti-Paul sentiment in that quarreling. Here there are only two groups, the "have-nots" and the "haves," with no hint of a quarrel with Paul on this matter. (3) In the present passage Paul says, "When you come together *as a church*,[29] there are divisions among you." This language implies that the "divisions" are especially related to their gatherings, not simply to false allegiances to their leaders or to "wisdom." Finally, (4) the puzzling addition, "I partly believe it," hardly fits the situation described in 1:10–4:21.[30] But it does fit well the present situation. Most likely it was added because Paul is here reflecting the view "from below," whereas the response will be directed toward those "from above." This is Paul's way of crediting his informants[31] with veracity, but also of bridging the sociological gap between them and the wealthy who are guilty of the misdeeds. "To some extent I believe it" means that he really does believe it but also acknowledges that his informants are scarcely disinterested observers.

19 Having mentioned the "divisions" of which he has been informed, and that he is well disposed to believe his informants, Paul adds a theological aside, apparently as a further justification for his believing

---

assumes the letter to be more literary than it is in fact. The best explanation is the simplest one: the πρῶτον μέν is simply not picked up, thus creating something of an *anacolouthon;* cf. BDF 447[4]). Cf. the discussion in Hurd, 79-80.

[27]Gk. σχίσματα; cf. 1:10 and 12:25 (the latter is in the singular).

[28]Cf. n. 14 above.

[29]Gk. ἐν ἐκκλησίᾳ; for the word itself see on 1:1. This usage reflects the original sense of the term, to be "in assembly." Thus even though Paul applies the term to individual local expressions of the people of God, he still uses the term in its primary sense. The people of God may be called the "church/assembly" first of all because they regularly assemble as a "church/assembly." This is further confirmed by the ἐπὶ τὸ αὐτό (in the same place) in v. 20, which is nearly synonymous with this present usage.

[30]Winter, "Lord's Supper," p. 80 n. 16, offers the unlikely suggestion that the informants in this case were one of the "parties" mentioned in 1:10. On the whole matter of "parties," see the introduction to 1:10-17.

[31]It would make a lot of sense in this view for this information also to have come from "those of Chloe's household," especially if they were trusted Christian slaves. The issue then becomes far more a ticklish sociological one than a theological one.

them.[32] One of the reasons he does so is that (literally) "there must also[33] be factions[34] among you so that the approved[35] also might become manifest[36] among you"—a sentence that is one of the true puzzles in the letter. How can he who earlier argued so strongly against "divisions among you" (1:10-17; 3:1-23) now affirm a kind of divine necessity to "divisions"?

The answer lies in two directions. First, although this could possibly be irony ("Given the nature of things in Corinth, it is inevitable that such things happen among you"), more likely it is a reflection of Paul's "already/not yet" eschatological perspective (see on 4:1-5);[37] second, it is probably inserted here in anticipation of vv. 28-32.

In keeping with the teaching of Jesus,[38] Paul expected "divisions" to accompany the End, divisions that would separate true believers from those who were false. Moreover, in v. 30 Paul asserts that some present illnesses and deaths among them are expressions of divine judgment on their "divisions," that is, on their "not discerning the body" at this Supper. In that passage he also urges them to "test" *(dokimazō)* themselves (v. 28) so that they will not incur such judgments. Paul, therefore, probably sees their

---

[32]The sentence is joined to v. 18 with another explanatory γάρ, which seems to function especially to explain the final clause, "and I partly believe it."

[33]The combination γὰρ καί is rare in Paul (cf. 2 Cor. 2:9; Rom. 13:6); it does not seem to mean the same as καὶ γάρ ("for indeed"), despite Findlay, 877. Most likely it is intended to signal an additional reason to the one stated or presupposed in what has already been said. Thus it does not mean "no doubt" (as NIV, GNB, JB), but "There is also this further reason for believing what I heard."

[34]Gk. αἱρέσεις, found elsewhere in Paul only in the vice list in Gal. 5:20; so its precise meaning for him eludes us. It is used elsewhere to distinguish sectarian groups (e.g., Sadducees in Acts 5:17), and later comes to be used of heretical groups. Here it is roughly synonymous with σχίσματα, and must mean something similar: divisions, dissensions, factions. Otherwise, as Barrett, 261, notes, "the connection of thought would break down."

[35]Gk. δόκιμοι (cf. ἀδόκιμος in 9:27), the cognate adjective to the verb δοκιμάζω in v. 28. The implication is that such people have been tested and found to be genuine.

[36]Gk. φανεροί, the adjective of the verb φανερόω, "to reveal, make visible."

[37]Munck, *Paul*, pp. 136-38, sees this sentence as pointing to eschatological "divisions" that are yet future; but the repetition of the idea of "division" and the prepositional phrase "among you" seems to indicate that he is reflecting on what is already present among them.

[38]Cf. (1) his announcement that his coming had the effect of dividing households (Matt. 10:34-37), and (2) his prediction that internecine strife would accompany future tribulation, resulting in the "falling away" of some (Matt. 24:9-13). Indeed, there is a noncanonical saying of Jesus which may well be authentic (it is found in such diverse sources as Justin, *Dial.* 35; the Syriac *Didascalia* 6.5; and the Pseudo-Clementine *Homily* 16.21.4), which uses both words found in vv. 18-19: "There shall be divisions (σχίσματα) and dissensions (αἱρέσεις)." See the discussion in J. Jeremias, *Unknown Sayings of Jesus* (ET, London, 1957), pp. 59-61, and Munck, *Paul*, p. 137.

present divisions as part of the divine "testing/sifting" process already at work in their midst. Such "divisions" are not a good thing, but they are an inevitable part of the Eschaton, which has already been set in motion by Christ. Thus by this evil thing, their "divisions," God is working out his own purposes; those who are truly his, the "tested/approved" (*dokimoi* = those who have passed the "examination"), are already being manifest in their midst, and presumably they will escape the final judgment that is coming upon the world (v. 32).

Thus even though this sentence is something of an aside, it also places their divisions into a framework that is more than simply sociological. They may be acting merely as the rich would always act with poorer guests in their homes; but at the Lord's Table such activities must be seen against the larger divine drama. Such "divisions" have the net effect of revealing those who are genuinely Christ's. And the "proof" lies not in a correct belief system, but in behavior that reflects the gospel.

20 After the brief digression in v. 19, Paul returns to the argument of v. 18 by means of a resumptive "therefore"[39] and the repetition of "when you come together."[40] The new qualifier, "in the same place,"[41] seems to be nearly synonymous with "as a church" in v. 18, both meaning "when you gather together *in assembly*." But now he moves on to give content to the "divisions" about which he had been informed. They well may be "together in the same place," but "it is not the Lord's Supper you eat."

The language "the Lord's Supper" is the only designation given this meal in the NT.[42] One cannot be sure, therefore, whether the present language is traditional or Pauline. At least the noun "supper"[43] is traditional, reflecting both the "Last Supper" of Jesus and the "suppers" in honor of the pagan deities.[44] The question lies with the possessive adjective *kyriakon*,[45]

---

[39]Gk. οὖν (omitted in the NIV); cf. 8:4 and especially the relationship of that verse to 8:1, where an almost identical resumption of the argument occurs.

[40]The repetition is more striking in this case because both clauses are genitive absolutes.

[41]Gk. ἐπὶ τὸ αὐτό (again omitted in the NIV). For this usage see E. Ferguson, "'When You Come Together': *Epi to Auto* in Early Christian Literature," *RestQ* 16 (1973), 202-08, who shows that it means "together" not in the sense of Christian unity, but in the sense of being "in the assembly."

[42]Cf. "the Lord's Table" in 10:21, but that language refers more specifically to the "table of the God" that was part of the cultic meals. Paul there seems to be transferring that language to the Christian's sitting at table in contrast to the pagan table.

[43]Gk. δεῖπνον; the word for the main meal in the Hellenistic world, usually eaten toward or in the evening.

[44]See J. Behm, *TDNT* II, 34-35. Cf. the papyrus invitations to "dine" at the shrines of Sarapis and Isis (n. 14 on 8:1-3).

[45]Cf. Rev. 1:10, where Sunday has been designated ἡ κυριακὴ ἡμέρα.

which ordinarily means "belonging to the Lord," but here probably comes closer to "consecrated to the Lord," or "in honor of the Lord." This meal is uniquely "his own," eaten by the gathered people of God in his presence (by the Spirit) and in his honor. In this passage the adjective stands in sharp contrast to the *idion* ("one's own/private") supper in v. 21. Thus, even though it is *intended* to be the Lord's Supper that they are eating "in assembly," their carrying over to this meal the distinctions that divided them sociologically also meant that it turned out to be "*not* the Lord's Supper you eat."

21 With this sentence Paul ties the statements in vv. 18 and 20 together by explaining both the nature of the "divisions" (v. 18) and why their meal ceases to be "the Lord's Supper" (v. 20): "For as you eat, each of you goes ahead with his own supper. One remains hungry, another gets drunk." At the same time this is the sentence where most of our ambiguities lie. We are told enough to give us some good educated guesses, but not quite enough to give us certainty. The problems are many, and interlocking, having to do with the meaning of every major term in the sentence.

They boil down to three basic options: (1) Some place the emphasis on "each one" and suggest that the picture is that of intense individualism, in which " 'each' enjoys his 'own supper' instead of the Lord's Supper, obviously not only to his bodily enjoyment, but to his spiritual edification."[46] (2) Others emphasize the verb "goes ahead with,"[47] understanding it to mean "to take beforehand." In conjunction with the verb *ekdechomai* (translated "wait for") in v. 33, this is understood to mean that some, apparently the rich, ate their own sumptuous meals before others (slaves and poor freedmen) were able to arrive.[48] (3) Theissen has emphasized the word *idion* ("one's own"), for which he shows evidence that it can mean "private." He posits that the rich were eating their private meals at the Lord's Supper, which included both an earlier starting time and privileged portions not available to the others. A modified version of this position has been offered by Winter, who sees the problem as the rich "devouring" their private meals in the presence of the "have-nots," but more in terms of their simply not sharing with them. Of these options, the first is the least likely since it does not speak to the sociological issue that emerges in "some being hungry" and in "despising those who have nothing."[49] Some form of the

---

[46]Conzelmann, 194.

[47]Gk. προλαμβάνει; only here, Gal. 6:1, and Mark 14:8 in the NT, and in each case with a different nuance.

[48]This is commonly suggested in the literature; see, e.g., Schweizer, *Lord's Supper*, p. 5; Murphy-O'Connor, *Corinth*, pp. 160-61; Holladay, 144-46 (the latter two combine this with option 3). Cf. also my *Study Guide*, p. 199.

[49]It is of some interest that Conzelmann does not speak to these questions at all.

third seems most likely, although one cannot rule out altogether the possibility that something like option 2 is also involved. The details of the sentence seem to support this view.

Given the fact that "some are hungry" (= "those who have nothing"; v. 22), the pronoun "each of you"[50] can hardly refer to every member of the community; rather, its emphatic position highlights the individualistic (i.e., noncommunal) character of the behavior of the rich as they consumed their own meals, in contrast to Paul's emphasis that they are eating *together as the church*. The phrase "as you eat,"[51] which consciously repeats the verb from the preceding sentence, refers to what takes place in the process of the meal. The implication is that the Lord's Supper is eaten in conjunction with a communal meal.[52] Although some have suggested otherwise, Paul does not seem overly concerned by this reality,[53] nor are vv. 33-34 to be understood as prohibiting it. His point is that in eating what is supposed to be a meal consecrated to the Lord, some by their actions are actually eating their own private meals.[54]

The precise nature of these "private meals" is not certain; most likely they were both quantitatively and qualitatively superior to those of the "have-nots." The picture that emerges from such Roman authors as Pliny,

[50]Gk. ἕκαστος; cf. 1:12; 12:7; 14:26, in each case of which it does not necessarily mean "every single person," but is both emphatic and distributive, i.e., it emphasizes the individual as well as the broad character of the activity. When Paul wishes to emphasize "every single person" he uses εἷς ἕκαστος (1 Thess. 2:11; 2 Thess. 1:3; 1 Cor. 12:18; Eph. 4:7).

[51]Gk. ἐν τῷ φαγεῖν, which actually appears at the end of Paul's clause (lit., "for each his own meal goes ahead with in the eating"). Because of the aorist infinitive, this could refer simply to the time of eating the meal, i.e., "whenever you have the Lord's Table." But that could have been said more naturally with a conditional clause (ἐάν or ὅταν).

[52]It is common to assert that "in Corinth this meal is no longer inserted into the Eucharist but precedes it" (Conzelmann, 195 n. 23; cf. Schweizer, *Lord's Supper*, p. 5; Neuenzeit, *Herrenmahl*, pp. 71-72, and the rebuttal in Theissen, 152-53). But nothing in the text itself supports this. On the basis of what Paul says, one cannot determine whether that portion of the meal specifically designated as the "Lord's Supper" was eaten in conjunction with, or after, the communal meal. Both opinions are held. The language "after supper" in the "tradition" (v. 25) does not really help, only suggesting that at the Last Supper, quite in keeping with Jewish meals, Jesus as the "head of the family" started the meal by breaking the bread and blessing it, and concluded the meal with a final blessing over the cup, which in both cases he interpreted in terms of his impending death. It is highly likely that this tradition continued in the early church, under the rubric of "the breaking of bread." This may very well also be the case in Corinth; but one simply cannot be certain. In any case, neither is there evidence that it was otherwise.

[53]Indeed, in light of the tradition, it is unlikely that such should have occurred to him.

[54]For a discussion of ἴδιον as indicating a "private" meal, eaten in conjunction with the "common" meal, see Theissen, 147-50.

Martial, and Juvenal is one in which even at the same table privileged guests received both better portions and far more than others.[55] Thus, the language some "are hungry" and "have nothing" implies that the "meal" of the latter consisted basically of the bread and wine designated as belonging to the Lord.

If this is what was going on in Corinth, the question still remains as to what the verb "goes ahead with" means. Ordinarily the compound *pro* has the temporal sense of "before"; the possibility that it might mean "eat beforehand" would then be supported by one of the common meanings ("wait for") of the verb *ekdechomai* in v. 33. However, there is no clear evidence of the verb *prolambanō*'s being used in this way in the context of eating.[56] In this case the lack of further description by Paul makes a clear-cut decision impossible. Very likely the verb is an intensified form of "take," meaning something close to "consume" or "devour." But one cannot totally rule out a temporal sense. In either case, it is a clear abuse of some who are unable likewise to eat "their own private meal."

The net result is that "one remains hungry, another gets drunk." To many modern minds this is both unthinkable and intolerable. But it tends to be only getting drunk that is so, since in itself this is quite unacceptable behavior (based on a good many biblical texts, one might add), not to mention doing so at the Lord's Supper. More likely, however, Paul is not so

---

[55]Juvenal devotes an entire satire (#5) to excoriating the wealthy for such folly. His is obviously a view "from below," as is the complaint in Martial, *Epigram* 3.60: "Since I am asked to dinner, . . . why is not the same dinner served to me as to you? You take oysters fattened in the Lucrine lake, I suck a mussel through a hole in the shell; you get mushrooms, I take hog funguses; you tackle turbot, but I brill. Golden with fat, a turtledove gorges you with its bloated rump; there is set before me a magpie that has died in its cage. Why do I dine without you although, Ponticus, I am dining with you? The dole has gone; let us have the benefit of that; let us eat the same fare" (Loeb, I, 201; cf. *Epig.* 1.20; 4.85; 6.11; 10.49). The view "from above" may be found in Pliny, *Ep.* 2.6, where he takes exception to being one of the "privileged" at such a meal: "It would take too long to go into the details . . . of how I happened to be dining with a man—though no particular friend of his—whose elegant economy, as he called it, seemed to me a sort of stingy extravagance. The best dishes were set in front of himself and a select few, and cheap scraps of food before the rest of the company. He had even put the wine into tiny little flasks, divided into three categories, not with the idea of giving his guests opportunity of choosing, but to make it impossible for them to refuse what they were given. One lot was intended for himself and for us, another for his lesser friends (all his friends are graded) and his and our freedmen." In response to how he himself could possibly afford to do otherwise, Pliny replies, "My freedmen do not drink the sort of wine I do, but I drink theirs" (Loeb, I, 95-97).

[56]In an inscription from Epidaurus it is used in a context that seems to mean simply "to take." See BAGD, who place this verse under the heading: "in uses where the temporal sense of προ- is felt very little, if at all." Cf. the discussion in Winter, "Lord's Supper," pp. 74-77.

concerned about "drunkenness" per se. What he has done is to take words from both parts of a meal, eating and drinking, and express them in their extremes. The one extreme is to receive nothing to eat, thus to "be hungry"; the other extreme is to be gorged on both food and wine, thus to "be drunk." As the following sentence makes clear, Paul's concern is not with the drunkenness of the one (in other contexts he will condemn that as well), but with the hunger of the other—especially in a context where fellow believers have more than enough to eat and drink.

22 The situation Paul has just described fills him with such indignation that it calls forth a series of rhetorical questions intended to reduce the "sated" to a level of shame similar to that to which they have reduced the poor. The first question responds directly to v. 21, and is full of irony: "For surely it cannot be, can it,[57] that you do not have houses to eat and drink in?" That is, if you really do *not* have houses in which to eat such "private" meals, then you are excused for doing so in the assembly of God's people. But of course if you are eating such meals deliberately in the presence (or absence) of others at the Lord's Table, then a second question must obtain: "Or do you despise the church of God by humiliating those who have nothing?" By this question Paul is getting at what for him is the real nature of their behavior, and so with a third (and fourth) question he brings the argument full circle (cf. v. 17): "What shall I say[58] to you? Shall I praise you for this?" To which, of course, the answer is: "Certainly not!" Or more literally, and in the same language as v. 17: "In this matter I have no praise [for you]."[59]

On its own the first question could simply be a word to the whole church to eat at home those meals necessary for satisfying the appetite. But the second question will not allow such a view. Moreover, the first two questions together indicate that the whole is being addressed to the wealthy. They "*have houses*[60] to eat and drink in." This implies ownership, not simply a place where meals may be eaten, as in v. 34. As such it stands in stark contrast to "those who *have nothing*" in the next question.

The structure of both this argument as a whole and of this series of

[57]This is an attempt to catch the force of the combination μή . . . οὐκ. The γάρ ties it directly to the preceding clause, and forces the irony, since what follows is not true. For the combination μὴ οὐκ see Rom. 10:18.

[58]This may be a future indicative; more likely it is a deliberative subjunctive: "What am I to say to you?"

[59]The NIV (cf. TR, KJV, RV, RSV) punctuates by taking ἐν τούτῳ with the question "Shall I praise you?" NA[26] and UBS[3] (cf. WH, ASV, NEB, Barrett, Conzelmann) take it as part of the concluding statement. What favors the latter is the similarity to v. 17.

[60]Gk. οἰκίας ἔχετε; not "homes," as in the NIV; that word does appear in v. 34.

questions in particular indicates that the second question is where the real problem lies. For those who think of themselves as "keeping the traditions" the actions noted here probably did not register as of particular consequence. They had always acted thus. Birth and circumstances had cast their lots; society had dictated their mores. But for Paul those mores at the Lord's Supper were a destruction of the meaning of the Supper itself because it destroyed the very unity which that meal proclaimed. Thus in the strongest kind of language he asserts that by their actions "they are despising[61] the church of God" (see on 1:2). "The church" is not to be equated with the "have-nots" here, but refers to the community itself as the people of God. Their behavior indicates that the church counts for nothing in their eyes. The way they show such contempt is "by[62] humiliating those who have nothing." The verb "humiliate" is the same as in vv. 4-5, for those who bring shame on their "heads"; but in this case it is far more than dishonor or disrespect; they are degrading, humiliating the "have-nots." No "church" can long endure as the people of God for the new age in which the old distinctions between bond and free (or Jew and Greek, or male and female) are allowed to persist. Especially so at the Table, where Christ, who has made us one, has ordained that we should visibly proclaim that unity.

The Martial and Pliny passages noted above[63] presented opposite solutions to the problem of "privileged portions" at a common meal. The view "from below" (Martial's) is that the poor should eat the same food as the rich; the view "from above" (Pliny's) is that the rich should eat the same fare as the others. Apparently by these questions Paul is adopting the second perspective. Those who want to glut at the common meal are being told to do so at home; the purpose of the Lord's Supper is not to eat to one's fill, but to remember/proclaim the Lord's death until he comes. To the contemporary social ethicist this may be less than a satisfactory response, but Paul's present concern is *not* with penury or gluttony but with their being truly together at the common table, with no class distinctions being allowed on the basis of the kind and amount of food eaten. As with the issue of slavery in Philemon, Paul attacks the system indirectly but at its very core. Be a true Christian at the Table, and the care for the needy, which is also close to Paul's heart (see on 16:1-4), will also become part and parcel of one's life. But that is not his primary concern here; rather, it is the meaning of the Table itself for their unity in Christ. So to that issue Paul now turns,

---

[61]Gk. καταφρονέω, a particularly strong word for expressing contempt for someone.

[62]Gk. καί, which is epexegetical here, so that the second clause gives content to the first.

[63]See n. 55.

and he does so by first reminding them of what the Lord himself said about
this meal.

2. The Problem—Abuse of the Lord (11:23-26)

> 23 *For I received from the Lord what I also passed on to you: The
> Lord Jesus, on the night he was betrayed, took bread,* 24 *and when he
> had given thanks, he broke it and said, "This[1] is my body, which is[2]
> for you; do this in remembrance of me."* 25 *In the same way, after
> supper he took the cup, saying, "This cup is the new covenant in my
> blood; do this, whenever you drink it, in remembrance of me."*
> 26 *For whenever you eat this bread and drink this[3] cup, you proclaim
> the Lord's death until he comes.*

Since this is a "tradition" the Corinthians are *not* keeping (vv. 2, 17, 22),
Paul feels compelled to remind them of its significance by repeating the
actual words of institution. The result is a highly unusual moment in the
extant letters of Paul since it is the only instance where he cites at some
length from the Jesus traditions that would eventually appear in our Gospels.[4] Along with allusions to his teachings in 7:10 and 9:14, this serves as
sure evidence that the Jesus traditions were known in the Pauline churches,
even if the apostle did not often appeal to them in his letters.

Such a citation, however, raises a new set of questions for the interpreter. Since this material had a history of its own before Paul cited it, in the
life-setting of both Jesus and the early church, one of the exegetical tasks has
to do with that history. What did Jesus himself intend by these words? And
how does Paul understand them? At the same time, as always, one must ask
the crucial contextual question, How does this material function as a response to the Corinthian abuse?

---

[1]The MajT, with no early support, begins the institutional words with "Take,
eat," borrowed from Matt. 26:26. This is a "liturgical" assimilation; cf. the next note.
See Metzger, 562.

[2]The Old Latin and Syriac traditions, followed by the MajT, add κλώμενον
("broken"); the Vulgate, Coptic, and Ethiopic versions add "given" from Luke 22:19. It
is missing in P[46] ℵ* A B C* 6 33 1739* Origen Cyprian. The diversity of traditions in itself
indicates that the words are not original. See Metzger, 562.

[3]The τοῦτον (missing in ℵ* A B C* D* F G 33 630 1739* 1881 2464 lat sa
Cyprian) is not original here. It was added, very early and often (P[46] a t sy bo Maj), for the
same reason the NIV has translated it this way—it balances "this bread" so nicely.

[4]This is not to say that he does not elsewhere refer or allude to the teaching of
Jesus. Besides 1 Cor. 7:10 and 9:14, see 1 Tim. 5:18, and the discussion of the concept of
imitating Jesus in 4:16. But this is the single instance where there is a considerable
citation.

The "tradition" of the institution of the Lord's Supper was preserved in the church in two distinct forms, one represented by Mark and Matthew, the other by Paul and Luke. The two forms, and their differences,[5] are best seen in parallel columns (material common to all four accounts is in italics):

Mark [Matthew][6]

While they were eating,
   [Jesus] *took bread,* and after
he had blessed it, *broke it and*
gave it to [his disciples]
and *said:* Take [eat], *This is my
body.*

And he took *the cup*
and after he had given thanks,
he gave it to them /and they all
drank from it. And he said to them/
[Mt.: saying, Drink of it all of
you; for] *This* is *my blood* of the
covenant, which is poured out for
many [for the forgiveness of sins].

{Paul} [Luke][7]

{On the night he was betrayed the
Lord Jesus} *took bread,* and after
he had given thanks, *broke it and*
[gave it to them, saying]
   said: *This is my
body,* which is [given] for you.
This do in my remembrance.
               Likewise
         also *the cup* after supper,

         saying,

This cup, the new
covenant {is} in *my blood* /This do
as often as you drink in my
remembrance/ [Lk: which is poured
out for you]

The basic differences between Mark and Matthew are three: (1) Matthew adds the imperative "eat"; (2) he transforms into an imperative the narrative of their all drinking from the cup; and (3) he adds "for the forgiveness of sins."[8] The differences between this tradition and Paul/Luke are considerable. The more significant are: Paul/Luke (1) have the verb "give thanks" instead of "bless"; (2) lack an imperative with the giving of the bread; (3) with the bread saying have the additional words "which is for you; this do in my remembrance"; (4) have the additional words "after supper"; (5) lack a

---

[5]For a helpful discussion both of the data and of the scholarly debate, see Marshall, *Last Supper,* pp. 30-56.

[6]The text cited is that of Mark, with the Matthean additions/differences in square brackets [].

[7]The text cited is that of Paul; Pauline peculiarities are in brackets {}, Lukan peculiarities in square brackets [].

[8]These differences are expressed in terms of the author's conviction of the priority of Mark (see my *NT Exegesis,* pp. 101-16). These changes in themselves, plus a few incidental stylistic ones, offer further evidence for this view.

blessing over the cup; (6) do not mention their all drinking from the cup; and (7) have a different cup saying: "This cup is the new covenant in my blood"/ "This is my blood of the covenant."[9]

Two judgments may be made in light of these data: First, both traditions are rooted in the same history since their common features, which are the essential items, are very similar. Second, the most significant differences are in the cup saying and the appearance of the "remembrance" motif in Paul/Luke. The more difficult question has to do with the difference between Luke and Paul as to the conclusion of the cup saying, where Luke's version has similarities to that of Mark/Matthew, while Paul's repeats the remembrance motif without mention of the blood being poured out for many.[10] Without making judgments as to which is more likely the actual form used in the Pauline churches, it is at least arguable that the combination of the repeated remembrance motif with the addition of v. 26, which is Paul's own interpretation of the institutional words, gives us our best clues as to where Paul's present concerns lie. By their going ahead with their own private meal, and thereby humiliating the "have-nots," the wealthy have also apparently lost touch with the meaning of the Supper itself. The words of institution are repeated to remind them of why they celebrate such a meal in the first place, a reason that goes back to Jesus himself. They do this to "remember him" in a special way, namely to "proclaim the Lord's death until he comes." Their actions are obviously not in keeping with the essence of that proclamation.

23a   In the immediately preceding sentence (v. 22), echoing v. 17, Paul asserts that he has no praise for them in this present matter. Now he

---

[9]The question as to which at any point represents the more primitive form of the tradition is beyond the proper concerns of this commentary. On this question see esp. Jeremias, *Eucharistic Words*, pp. 138-203; and the discussion in Marshall, *Last Supper*, pp. 30-56. Cf. Conzelmann, 197: "Both in Mark and in Paul we find older and younger elements."

[10]Usually it has been argued that Luke is dependent on the tradition found in Paul, which he conformed at this one place to that found in Mark. H. Schürmann, *Der Einsetzungsbericht Lk 22,19-20* (Münster, 1955), followed tentatively by Marshall, *Last Supper*, pp. 39-40, argues that Luke represents an independent tradition, which seems most unlikely, given that he and Paul have a form that is verbally closer even than that of Mark and Matthew. Most likely they represent adaptations of a common tradition.

This whole problem is further complicated by the liturgical nature of the material; what one does in one's own church will take precedence over whatever one reads in a source. The solution offered here, but in full recognition of the tentative nature of all such solutions, is that Luke represents the actual liturgical tradition of the Pauline churches, or perhaps of the home church at Antioch, while Paul, for the *ad hoc* emphases of this passage, has conformed the cup saying to that of the bread to highlight the "remembrance" motif. See on v. 25.

proceeds to explain *why*. [11] It all has to do with their own self-understanding, expressed in v. 2, that they have been keeping the traditions that had been handed down to them. Insofar as that is true, Paul praises them (v. 2). But not here, for this is one tradition they clearly are not keeping. To demonstrate that, Paul appeals to the tradition itself, as he had "received" it "from the Lord" and had "passed it on" to them.

The verbs "received" [12] and "passed on," [13] which occur again in combination in 15:3, [14] are technical terms from Paul's Jewish heritage [15] for the transmission of religious instruction. [16] His present concern is to establish that the tradition about the Supper they had received from him came from Jesus himself: "I received [it] from [17] the Lord." But it is not certain exactly how we are to understand these words, especially in light of the strong affirmations and denials in Gal. 1:11-12 and 15-17 that he received his gospel directly from the Lord—by revelation and without human mediation. Some have suggested that the same is true here; however, two things suggest otherwise: (1) In Galatians Paul is not referring to the teachings and narratives about Jesus, but to the message of redemption through Christ's death and resurrection, offered freely by God to those who believe. (2) Paul uses the language for transmitting "tradition" to refer to these words of institution, and does not suggest that it came to him "by revelation." Moreover, the Last Supper material is not the kind of thing that belongs to "revelation," but to the church's ongoing tradition from the time of its inception.

Therefore, when Paul says "I received it from the Lord," he probably does not mean that Jesus gave these words to him personally and directly; rather, what he himself "received" had indeed come "from the Lord," but in the sense that Jesus himself is the ultimate source of the tradition. [18] It may also be that latent in such language is his understanding that the Lord, now

---

[11] The sentence begins with another explanatory γάρ.

[12] Gk. παρέλαβον; in Paul see 1 Thess. 2:13; 4:1; 2 Thess. 3:6 (with παράδοσις); 1 Cor. 15:1; 15:3 (with παραδίδωμι); Gal. 1:9, 12; Col. 2:6; Phil. 4:9. Cf. G. Delling, *TDNT* IV, 11-14.

[13] Gk. παρέδωκα; see the discussion on v. 2.

[14] Cf. 2 Thess. 3:6.

[15] While it also occurs in the mysteries and in Gnosticism (see Conzelmann, 195-96), that is irrelevant for Paul's usage, given his rabbinical training.

[16] Heb. *qibbēl/māsar*. See esp. *m.Abot* 1.1: "Moses *received* the Law from Sinai and *committed* it to Joshua, and Joshua to the elders, and the elders to the Prophets; and the Prophets *committed* it to the men of the Great Synagogue" (Danby, p. 446); cf. *m.Peah* 2.6. For other examples see Str-B, III, 444.

[17] Gk. ἀπό. Some (e.g., Grosheide, 269 n. 16) suggest that this preposition (vis-à-vis παρά) reflects a less direct revelation; but it is the context and language, not the preposition, that makes this seem certain.

[18] The question as to *where* Paul received it cannot be answered, but most likely it would have been either Damascus or Antioch. In either case, these churches were founded

risen and exalted, is still responsible by his Spirit for the transmission of such tradition within the church.[19] Thus, the Corinthian meals are not truly the Lord's Supper because they do not reflect or proclaim the meaning of that meal as it came from the Lord himself.

23b-24   The Lord's Supper that Christians celebrate is in fact a continuation of the Last Supper that Jesus ate with his own disciples, probably a Passover meal[20] at which he reinterpreted the bread and wine in terms of his body and blood soon to be given over in death on the cross. At that same meal he announced both their denial of him and his betrayal by Judas. One of the more remarkable features of the words of institution as they were used in the church liturgically[21] and therefore independently of the story of Jesus itself is the singular historical context that was transmitted along with them:[22] "on the night he was betrayed."[23] The verb "betrayed"[24] is just ambiguous enough so that it could mean "handed over" (as in "handed over to death").[25] But most likely its first reference is to the treachery of Judas,[26] which of course led to Jesus' subsequent trials and death. The early Christians thus constantly reminded themselves that even though Jesus was crucified by the Empire, he was nonetheless handed over to them by one of their own—a poignant reminder indeed at the Table where they experienced anew forgiveness and life.

The ordinary Jewish meal began with the head of the house giving

---

by disciples from Jerusalem, so that the tradition must come ultimately from there. Cf. Marshall, *Last Supper*, pp. 32-33.

[19]See, e.g., Bornkamm, "Lord's Supper," p. 131.

[20]For the evidence in its favor, see Jeremias, *Eucharistic Words*, pp. 15-88; cf. the discussion in Marshall, *Last Supper*, pp. 57-75. But see the discussion in Schweizer, *Lord's Supper*, pp. 29-32, for the cautions that cause uncertainty.

[21]Barrett, 264, properly warns that one should not simply assume that such was the case, since nothing Paul says would indicate that the words were used in this way at the meal; but the very fact of their being quoted in this fashion and their being remembered in the church in two clear traditions suggests that they had probably already come to have liturgical usage.

[22]One cannot be certain of course whether this note belongs to the tradition or to Paul himself. Its unusual nature is what suggests that it belongs to the tradition. Since the whole history was not repeated at any given eating of the Supper, this was a way to give the words a context when they were used independently. Cf. Marshall, *Last Supper*, p. 41.

[23]Whatever may have been the meaning of the cultic meals in the mysteries, this little note drives a deep wedge between those meals and the Lord's Supper. This is not the celebration of timeless myths or spiritual truths; it is rooted deeply in the history of Jesus. Cf. Bornkamm, "Lord's Supper," p. 132.

[24]Gk. παρεδίδετο; its proximity to the preceding παρέδωκα is probably completely fortuitous.

[25]So Barrett, 266.

[26]Mostly because Paul is here referring to the "tradition," and the Gospel traditions place the announcement of the betrayal at the time of the Supper. The verb also appears in the LXX of Isa. 53:6 and 12.

the traditional blessing over the bread, breaking it, and giving it to those at table with him. Jesus, as the "Teacher," undoubtedly played that role in meals with the disciples. At the Passover meal the blessing and distribution of the bread came during the meal (cf. Mark 14:18; Luke 22:17-19), immediately following the "Passover liturgy," in which the reasons for this meal were expressed.[27] Hence Jesus' action in blessing[28] and breaking[29] the bread at the Last Supper would have been in the natural course of things. If in fact this was a Passover meal, then the remarkable thing that he did was to reinterpret the meaning of the bread, as he was distributing it, in terms of his own death:[30] "This is my body, which is for you." Several things about this bread saying need to be noted.

(1) The identification of the bread with the body is semitic imagery in its heightened form.[31] As in all such identifications, he means "this signifies/represents my body."[32] It lies quite beyond both Jesus' intent and the framework within which he and the disciples lived to imagine that some actual change took place, or was intended to take place, in the bread itself. Such a view could only have arisen in the church at a much later stage when Greek modes of thinking had rather thoroughly replaced semitic ones.

(2) The use of the term "body" has elicited considerable discussion: does it mean "himself" or his "flesh"?[33] Most likely it means neither, but refers to his actual body, which was about to be given over in death. If there

---

[27]For a brief description of this meal, see Marshall, *Last Supper,* pp. 21-23.

[28]Paul and Luke use the word εὐχαριστέω, rather than εὐλογέω, for the "blessing" (however, see 1 Cor. 10:16). The latter more closely reflects the semitic idiom; but both imply that thanksgiving is being offered to God for the food, and in the case of the Passover God is blessed for Israel's deliverance from Egypt. See esp. *m.Pes.* 10.5, where R. Gamaliel uses a whole series of such words: "Therefore are we bound to give thanks, to praise, to glorify, to honour, to exalt, to extol, and to bless him who wrought all these wonders for our fathers and for us" (Danby, p. 151).

[29]It is common to link the "breaking" of the bread with Jesus' "broken" body; cf. the MajT reading (n. 2). For a brief overview of some who think that this is inherent in the act, see A. R. Winnett, "The Breaking of the Break: Does it Symbolize the Passion?" *ExpT* 88 (1977), 181-82. In fact, of course, Jesus' body was not broken; nor is any point made in the tradition itself linking the *breaking* of the bread with Jesus' death, although one can well understand how the symbolism eventually arose. Cf. Marshall, *Last Supper,* p. 86.

[30]See especially the argument for this in Jeremias, *Eucharistic Words,* pp. 55-61. Bornkamm, "Lord's Supper," pp. 138-39, argues that the words of Jesus do not represent an actual "interpretation" of the event of Jesus' death, and therefore that this does not necessarily support its being a Passover meal. But that seems to have the character of a quibble. What Jesus said about the bread is far more understandable if it was spoken in a context where words were ordinarily spoken over the bread; such a context also best accounts for the words' being remembered by the disciples as they continued such meals.

[31]Cf. 10:4, "the rock *was* Christ," and Gal. 4:25, "Hagar *is* Mount Sinai."

[32]The presence of Jesus with them as he spoke these words would have made any other meaning impossible. Cf. Moffatt, 168.

[33]See the discussion in Marshall, *Last Supper,* p. 86.

is an analogy, it is with the sacrificial victim, whose "body" (carcass) was placed on the altar after the blood had been poured out.[34]

(3) The phrase "which is for you" is unique to the Pauline-Lukan version at this point. Whether it belonged originally to this saying is much debated.[35] In either case,[36] it links the bread and the cup together, both referring to Jesus' death. The words "for you"[37] are an adaptation of the language of Isa. 53:12, where the Suffering Servant "bore sin for many." Thus for Jesus himself this is almost certainly a prophetic symbolic action, by which he anticipated his death and interpreted it in light of Isa. 53 as in behalf of others. By giving them a share in "his body" in this way, he invited his disciples to participate in the meaning and benefits of that death.

(4) Almost certainly Paul also understood the phrase "which is *for* you" in this way. Whenever he uses this preposition in reference to Christ, it expresses either atonement, his death in "our behalf" (e.g., 15:3; Rom. 5:6, 8), or substitution, his death in "our place" (e.g., Gal. 3:13; 2 Cor. 5:21). Thus Paul surely understands this bread saying to refer to Jesus' body as given over in death "in behalf of/in place of" those who are now eating at his Table. What is significant, however, is that in his own interpretation of the bread, Paul does not pick up the theme of "for you," but the imagery of "body" itself. Furthermore, even though there is no further interpretation at this point—since Paul is being faithful to repeat the institutional words themselves—this bread saying is the one that will eventually receive his attention (v. 29), even as it did in 10:16-17.

Also unique to the Paul/Luke version of the bread saying is the command to repeat the action: "Do this[38] in remembrance of me." Because

---

[34]Cf. the use of σῶμα in Rom. 12:1; see also the discussion of this term in 6:13, esp. n. 30.

[35]For the arguments against, see Jeremias, *Eucharistic Words*, pp. 166-68; in favor, see the discussion in Marshall, *Last Supper*, pp. 46-51, although Marshall himself finally takes a position of uncertainty. The focus of the debate is over whether it is more likely that the parallelism of the two sayings was made by Jesus and dropped by the tradition Mark represents (because they would be redundant in light of the cup saying), or whether they were added in the tradition known by Paul and Luke, under the influence of the cup saying, as a way of bringing the two into parallel. On the whole the latter seems more likely, but one cannot be sure.

[36]That is, if original here, they tie the bread and cup together by means of the prepositional phrase "for you," and would have been so understood by those who dropped them from the bread saying, allowing the one prepositional phrase to cover both. On the other hand, if they belong originally only with the cup saying, the proximity of the two sayings in the tradition links the one with the other, i.e., the body and blood together point to his death as "for many/you."

[37]Gk. ὑπὲρ ὑμῶν; cf. 15:3, "for our sins."

[38]There is some discussion as to what "this" means, whether to keep the rite, or to do these acts at a meal. Probably it is the latter. It is of some interest that he did not say "eat this bread," but "*do* this," which must include the blessing, breaking, distributing, and eating, all in light of the interpretative words "This is my body."

these words are missing in Mark/Matthew, there has been some question as to their authenticity.[39] But in this case that is to place a considerable burden on the silence of Mark. What speaks most strongly in its favor is precisely the fact that the early church so soon after Jesus' resurrection and the advent of the Spirit did just this—remember his death in this way, as "for us." The words may have been omitted in the tradition available to Mark for the very reason that such a command is implicit in the continuation of the Supper itself.

The phrase "in remembrance of me" is difficult and has elicited a considerable body of literature.[40] On the basis of Hellenistic parallels, some have argued that the "remembrance" reflects ancient commemorative meals for the dead.[41] The obvious difficulties with this are (a) that this meal, even in its Gentile setting, must be understood in light of Jewish meals, especially the Passover, not pagan meals, and (b) that the meal in honor of Jesus is not for a "dead hero" but for the Risen Lord, through whose death salvation has been wrought for his people. But the greater issue, especially in light of Jewish usage, is the nature of the "remembrance" itself. Does it have a primarily "Godward" reference, in the sense that God is herewith being petitioned to "remember" Jesus' atoning death and thus show mercy to his people,[42] or does it have a primarily "humanward" point of reference, in which his people are to "remember" him and thus reflect again on the mercies of his atoning death? Or is it, as Chenderlin has advanced, inherently ambiguous, so that it can mean either or both?

Although one commonly reads that our remembrance of Christ is the plain sense of the words, the issue is not that easy, having to do with (a) a complex range of usage in the OT and other Jewish literature, (b) Jesus' own intent in light of this usage, and (c) Paul's understanding.[43] The Greek word

[39]E.g., Jeremias, *Eucharistic Words*, p. 168; Barrett, 267.

[40]The modern debate was begun by Jeremias, *Eucharistic Words*, pp. 237-55. Among those works devoted to the question in particular, see D. Jones, "'Ἀνάμνησις in the LXX and the Interpretation of I Cor. XI.25," *JTS* 6 (1955), 183-91; H. Kosmala, "'Das tut zu Gedächtnis,'" *NovT* 4 (1960), 81-94; M. H. Sykes, "The Eucharist as 'Anamnesis,'" *ExpT* 71 (1960/61); and F. Chenderlin, *"Do This as My Memorial." The Semantic and Conceptual Background and Value of* 'Ἀνάμνησις *in 1 Corinthians 11:24-25* (AB 99; Rome, 1982).

[41]This view was advocated most notably by H. Lietzmann, both in his commentary and his monumental *Mass and Lord's Supper* ([1926]; ET, Leiden, 1979). Cf. Barrett, 267.

[42]This is the position of Jeremias (n. 40), to which most of the other studies are in reaction.

[43]One of the great weaknesses in Chenderlin's presentation lies right here. He works through the semantic field with thoroughness and some degree of carefulness—although he does not deal nearly adequately with absolute vis-à-vis qualified uses of the idea—but he fails almost altogether to note that there might be a difference in the life-setting of Jesus and the present understanding of these words in Paul. Indeed, he criticizes

anamnēsis occurs only five times in the LXX,[44] although its cognate *mnēmosynon* occurs numerous times, as does the cognate verb "to remember." Firm examples of both "Godward" and "manward" references abound; however, very few uses are unmistakably "Godward."[45]

In the OT "remembrance" rarely carries the common English nuance of simply a mental activity. Very often "memory" and "activity" go together. God "remembers" and "visits" or "forgives" or "blots out." So also Israel is to "remember" by erecting a "memorial" or by reenacting a rite (cf. Exod. 13:9). Of the various possibilities from the OT the most obvious as to what Jesus intended lies within the Passover and Feast of Unleavened Bread, where the rite of the bread is specifically enjoined as a perpetual "remembrance" before their eyes.[46] Thus just as the Passover meal itself was such a "remembrance" to be kept forever in Israel, so Jesus is now reconstituting the "memorial" for the true Israel that will gather around the table in his name to "remember" its own deliverance through him.[47] That is why he describes it as "*my* remembrance." It is not simply "in memory of *him*," but it is eaten as a "memorial" of the salvation that he has effected through his death and resurrection.

In the same way, it is very difficult to escape the conclusion, based on Paul's own interpretation in v. 26, that for him the "remembrance" was primarily "manward." After all, that is quite the point in the larger context, where the Corinthians' meal had turned into such a fiasco that the "remembrance" of Christ is precisely what is missing. Thus Paul's great concern in repeating these words is to remind them of the "manward" implications of this "remembrance."[48] By this meal they "proclaim" Christ's death

---

Barrett for making this distinction (Barrett allows the "Godward" sense to Jesus but eliminates it from Paul). But in turn Chenderlin fails to address this issue in any significant way, dealing only with the usage in Paul, and even here tends finally to eliminate the context itself in favor of the semantic field on its own. The point, of course, is that whatever semantic range a word may have, it rarely has that whole range in any given context.

[44]Lev. 24:7; Num. 10:10; Ps. 37 (title); 69 (title); Wis. 16:6.

[45]That is, when the "remembering" is "Godward," it is usually clearly so because the text explicitly says so.

[46]Although the rabbis differ over whether the bread represents the distress of "our fathers" in Egypt (*m.Pes.* 10.5) or the haste of their departure (*Mek.Ex.* 12.39; cf. Philo, *spec.leg.* 2.158).

[47]This does not exclude the possibility that Jesus "reminded" God of their need of his forgiveness based on his sacrifice. But it would seem that the primary referent is the "manward" one.

[48]Even though both Jeremias and Chenderlin pay lip-service to the larger context, they seem to abandon it almost totally when they examine the word ἀνάμνησις itself. Paul's concern throughout the passage, and the reason for reminding them of the words of institution, seems altogether to lack a "Godward" dimension. This dimension is precisely what needs to be demonstrated, not the wide semantic range available to Paul.

until he comes, that is, they declare the good news of their salvation that makes them all one. To participate unworthily means to come under judgment for the very reason that it fails to acknowledge the meal as a "memorial" of God's saving event.

25 In the tradition of the Supper available to Paul and Luke the transition to the cup saying is made by the elliptical phrase "likewise the cup after supper,[49] saying," for which the NIV has correctly supplied "he took" from v. 24.[50] The words "after supper"[51] indicate that at the Last Supper the bread and cup sayings were separated by the meal itself (or at least part of it); given their continuing but otherwise unnecessary role in the tradition, it seems probable that this pattern persisted in the early church.[52] As noted earlier,[53] this does not necessarily mean that this was also the Corinthian practice, but neither is there anything in Paul's argument to indicate that the Lord's Supper took place at the *end* of their "love feast," as is so commonly asserted.

The cup saying is the place where not only Paul/Luke differ from Mark/Matthew, but also where, in the second part, Paul and Luke differ from each other. As with the bread saying, both traditions begin with "this," and in both Jesus identifies the cup with his blood in covenantal terms; but there is no scholarly consensus as to which tradition represents the more primitive form. Arguments and counterarguments can be raised on both sides.[54] Rather than trace that discussion, our concern is to note the significance of the differences.

(1) The Markan version, "This is my blood of the covenant, which is poured out for many," is more directly parallel to the bread saying in which the bread signified the Lord's "body." Here the cup signifies "my blood of the covenant." The language "blood of the covenant" is an allusion to Exod. 24:8, where blood, designated by this exact term, was sprinkled over

---

This meal and these words do not urge on them that God remembers Jesus in their behalf, but rather that this meal is a celebration of their common salvation, which their own private meals almost totally ignore.

[49]On the place of this cup in the Passover, see on 10:16.

[50]This is the plain implication of such an ellipsis; it may also, of course, include the blessing, but scarcely the "breaking"—and the distributing is not part of the tradition of Paul and Luke.

[51]Gk. μετὰ τὸ δειπνῆσαι ("after they had eaten"). It is generally agreed that this is a primitive element that reflects a tradition earlier than Mark's. Grosheide, 270, without evidence, argues that the context implies "not after the whole supper was over, . . . but after the eating of the bread." But the language implies otherwise.

[52]J. Moffatt, "Discerning the Body," *ExpT* 30 (1918/19), 19, notes that since they ate a real meal, the Supper for them "was not a 'sacrament' in the modern sense of the term, *i.e.* a gathering at which the eating is only a form."

[53]See n. 52 on v. 21.

[54]Cf. the discussion in Marshall, *Last Supper*, pp. 44-51.

the people to ratify the covenant. To this phrase Jesus added a direct allusion to Isa. 53:12, where the Lord's Servant "poured out his soul to death" and thereby "bore sin for many."

In Paul's version the identification is made directly with the covenant, in this case the "new covenant" of Jer. 31:31: "This cup is[55] the new covenant in my blood." However, that passage also mentions the covenant of Exod. 24 as that which is being replaced. Therefore, in the one version (Mark's), the Old Covenant is referred to explicitly and the New implicitly, while in Paul's it is the reverse, the New being explicit and the Old implicit. In both versions the point is the same, that the wine of the cup signifies Jesus' blood poured out in death, which ratified the new covenant.

(2) In contrast to both Mark and Luke, Paul's version of the cup saying has no allusion to Isa. 53 ("which is poured out for many"), which has already appeared in the bread saying. In the Gospels the tie to Isaiah suggests the additional theological motif of the forgiveness of sins, made explicit in Matthew's version. But in Paul that motif is not tied to the blood as such, but to Christ's death, which point is made in v. 26.

(3) In place of the phrase "which is poured out for many/ you," Paul repeats "Do this in remembrance of me" (see on v. 24), with the addition "as often as you drink." This addition in particular implies a frequently repeated action, suggesting that from the beginning the *Last* Supper was for Christians not an annual Christian Passover, but a regularly repeated meal in "honor of the Lord," hence the *Lord's* Supper.[56]

Although one cannot be certain whether Paul or Luke represents the more primitive form of their common tradition, a good case can be made that Paul is now beginning to move from citation back to his own argument, and has adjusted the institutional words accordingly. Three things suggest this possibility: (a) Since Luke's version is otherwise independent of Mark's, there is no good reason to suppose that he has now abandoned his and Paul's common version for that of Mark. Most likely Luke at this point reflects the unmodified and more primitive expression of their version. After all, his context is that of historical narrative, while Paul's is a vigorous argument with some who are abusing the Table. (b) If that be the case, then Paul repeats the command "do this in my remembrance" precisely because this is where his concern lay—not in the repetition of the words per se, but in their

---

[55]Luke's version has no verb; in Paul it follows the predicate noun. But no point is to be made of its position, as does W. Ellis, "On the Text of the Account of the Lord's Supper in I Corinthians xi.23-32 with Some Further Comments," *AusBR* 12 (1964), 43-51.

[56]But see Barrett, 269, who notes that the phrase has a "limiting effect. Christians must *do this* not every time they have a meal, but whenever they drink wine. Bread was always available; in ordinary households . . . wine was not."

eating the Lord's Supper truly in "Christ's honor," that is, in "remembrance" of the salvation that his death had procured for them. (c) This suggests further that the additional words "as often as you drink," which are not found with the bread saying, are in fact a Pauline insertion into the words of command to bring out his own special emphasis.[57] This seems all the more likely in light of v. 26, where he uses this same language along with an explanatory "for" in order to reínforce his reason for citing the whole tradition in the first place.

If this argument for Pauline "redaction" cannot finally be proved, it does highlight the emphases in Paul's argument. Some of the Corinthians are abusing what is supposed to be the *Lord's* Supper by going ahead with their own private meals in such a way as to humiliate others in the congregation. Paul recalls the words of institution precisely to emphasize that *as often as* they eat this meal it is to be *in the Lord's remembrance*. In the next sentence he will go on to explain what that means for him.

26 With this concluding sentence Paul brings things into perspective. The explanatory "for" suggests that he is now giving his reason for repeating the tradition at this point in the argument.[58] It is not because they have forgotten the words, nor because they have abandoned the Supper. Rather, it is because their version of the Supper gives the lie to its original intent. "Shall I praise you for how you are carrying on?" he had asked. "No," he replied, "for the tradition is this," at which point he repeated the words of institution. The *reason* for repeating those words is now being given. The bread and the cup of this meal together *signify the death* of the Lord; "For," he now explains, "as often as we do this, in *his* remembrance, we are to be reminded through proclamation of the salvation that was effected for us through that death."

That this is Paul's intent is evident from several converging data: (1) the explanatory "for," (2) the word order, which puts the emphasis on his death,[59] (3) the fact that he picks up the precise language of the final repetition command ("as often as you . . ."), (4) which in turn picks up the "eating of this bread" so as to include both parts of the meal in the explana-

---

[57]Against this is the fact that ὁσάκις does not appear elsewhere in Paul, suggesting that it is not part of his regular vocabulary. But one must be cautious in this case, given the limited number of letters one has to draw conclusions from and that no synonymous expression is found.

[58]Holladay, 150, suggests that one cannot be certain whether this sentence also belongs to the tradition or to Paul. The change of person, from first to third, makes it certain that it does not go back to Jesus; the question is whether it belonged to a tradition of the institutional words earlier than Paul. Most likely it is Paul's own elaboration.

[59]Lit. "the *death* of the Lord you proclaim until he comes." Cf. Beverly R. Gaventa, "'You Proclaim the Lord's Death': 1 Corinthians 11:26 and Paul's Understanding of Worship," *RevExp* 80 (1983), 380.

tion, and (5) the emphasis that *both* the bread and the cup proclaim Christ's death.

Thus the focus of Paul's concern is on this meal as a means of proclaiming Christ's death, a point the Corinthians' action is obviously bypassing.[60] Despite the arguments of some to the contrary,[61] the verb "to proclaim"[62] probably does not mean that the meal in itself is the proclamation,[63] but that during the meal there is a verbal proclamation of Christ's death. That seems to be exactly how Paul now understands the two sayings over the bread and cup, and thus why he has repeated the words of institution. With the word over the bread, they "proclaim" that this bread is "Christ's body for you (us)." It points to his death, whereby he gave himself freely for the sake of others. Likewise the cup; it signifies Christ's blood poured out in death, whereby he ratified the New Covenant between God and his people. It seems certain that their version of the meal is less than satisfactory right at this point, probably not so much because they were not "thinking on Christ" properly, or failing to be in right communion with him, but because by their abuse of one another they were negating the very point of that death—to create a new people for his name, in which the old distinctions based on human fallenness no longer obtain.

At the same time, however, Paul is fully aware of the eschatological setting in which this meal was first instituted.[64] Christ's death is not itself the End, but the beginning of the End. Thus at this meal the proclamation is of "the Lord's death until[65] he comes." By these final words Paul is reminding the Corinthians of their essentially eschatological existence (see on 4:1-5 and 6:1-6). They have not yet arrived (4:8); at this meal they are to be reminded that there is yet a future for themselves, as well as for all the people of God.

Because the words of institution are so well known to most of us, and because in reading those words we also include Paul's final comment in

---

[60]Their new spirituality seems to have caused them to miss *both* points Paul makes here—Christ's death (cf. 1:18–2:5), until he comes (cf. 1:7; 15:12).

[61]See esp. Gaventa, "'You Proclaim,'" pp. 381-83.

[62]Gk. καταγγέλλετε (cf. 2:1; 9:14; Rom. 1:8; Phil. 1:17, 18; Col. 1:28), plus 11 more in Acts. In every case it means to preach Christ or the gospel. Cf. J. Schniewind, *TDNT* I, 70-72. The form here could be an imperative, but that is unlikely.

[63]This view is held *inter alia* by Weiss, 288; Lietzmann, 58; Lenski, 474; Héring, 118-19; Thrall, 84; Barclay, 48.

[64]See on 16:22 and the possible use of μαράνα θα in conjunction with this meal.

[65]Jeremias, *Eucharistic Words*, pp. 252-54, argues that this ἄχρι οὗ is not simply a temporal reference, but functions as a kind of final clause. In keeping with his "Godward" view of the "remembrance" motif, and along with the *maranatha* prayer, Jeremias sees this as part of the meal's function as a constant reminder to God to bring about the Parousia.

v. 26, it is easy for us to miss Paul's concern in the argument for our own concern in "actualizing" the Lord's Supper for ourselves. The latter is certainly legitimate, if for no other reason than that the whole paragraph serves as a kind of paradigm of such actualizing for the Corinthian community. The Lord's Supper is not simply a memorial of the Last Supper, nor of Christ's death per se. It is a constant, repeated reminder—and experience—of the efficacy of that death for us. But for Paul, as he will now go on to point out, the concern is not simply personal or introspective. Salvation through Christ's death has created a new community of people who bear his name. We ourselves rather miss the point of this paragraph if we think of the Table only in terms of our needs and not also in terms of those of others.

3. The Answer—Discern the Body (11:27-32)

> 27 Therefore, whoever eats the[1] bread or drinks the cup of the Lord in an unworthy manner[2] will be guilty of sinning against the body and blood of the Lord. 28 A man ought to examine himself before he eats of the bread and drinks of the cup. 29 For anyone who eats and drinks[3] without recognizing the body[4] eats and drinks judgment on himself. 30 That is why many among you are weak and sick, and a number of you have fallen asleep. 31 But[5] if we judged ourselves, we would not come under judgment. 32 When we are judged by the Lord, we are being disciplined so that we will not be condemned with the world.

With this paragraph, and the next, Paul now applies the point of vv. 23-26 to their meals. Their Supper in the Lord's honor is in fact dishonoring to him—in two ways: First, the "haves" have been abusing the "have-nots" by "going ahead with their own private meals." Second, they have thereby

[1]The MajT, anticipated by itᵃ and bo, against all other early evidence (P46 ℵ A B C D F G Ψ 33 1739 pc lat syʰ sa) adds a τοῦτον, giving it a more liturgical (and therefore present) sense.

[2]Some MSS (ℵ D² L 326 al syʰ Ambst) resolve the ambiguity of this adverb by adding τοῦ κυρίου (= "in a manner unworthy of the Lord").

[3]The MajT, following the lead of the Latin and Syriac versions, adds ἀναξίως from v. 27 (cf. the next note). The original text is found in P46 ℵ* A B C* 6 33 1739 pc co. This addition and the next one are understandable attempts to conform this sentence to v. 27, but in so doing they considerably alter the sense. See the commentary.

[4]The NIV adds "of the Lord" (with ℵᶜ C³ D F G K P Maj it sy ["of the Lord Jesus"]; against P46 ℵ* A B C* 6 33 1739 1881* pc co Pel). This is secondary on every count. It was added on the analogy of v. 27. Had it been original it is nearly impossible to account for its omission, especially in a liturgical text, where addition not omission is nearly always the rule. It also destroys the sense; see the commentary. Cf. Metzger, 562-63.

[5]The MajT (against P46 ℵ* A B D F G 33 1739 pc) has changed this δέ to an explanatory γάρ.

been abusing the Lord himself by not properly "remembering" him, especially in terms of the salvation he has wrought through his death, which was intended to make them one, not "divided" as their Supper does. The purpose of the present paragraph, therefore, is to correct the first abuse by warning them of the dire consequences if they persist in behavior at the Supper that reflects failure to understand its true nature.

Because the paragraph has had a long history of being read at the Lord's Supper independent of its original context, its interpretation has also been independent of that context, a problem that is increased by some inherent difficulties with the language. The entire paragraph is dominated by "judgment" motifs, some of which are wordplays not especially easy to put into comparable English. Furthermore, the crucial term ("body") in the crucial sentence (v. 29) is ambiguous enough so that the point of the whole argument is frequently missed altogether, or at least in its main emphasis. The argument in context seems to go as follows:

Paul begins (v. 27) by picking up the language of vv. 23-26, but now in the form of a severe warning that those who eat as they are doing, "in an unworthy manner," will be *liable* for the very death that they are rather to proclaim as *salvation* at this table. That leads to the proposed remedy: self-testing before eating (v. 28), lest they come under divine judgment (v. 29). The "unworthy" eating of v. 27 that brings judgment is now described as eating "without discerning the body," meaning the church (as in 10:16-17; this, after all, is the point of the whole section). This is followed by a prophetic pronouncement (v. 30) that some current illnesses and deaths are present expressions of such judgment, brought about by their failure to discern the body. The argument then concludes (vv. 31-32) with a considerable wordplay on "judgment" themes, in which Paul basically repeats the point of vv. 28-30. On the one hand (v. 31), if they were to "discern themselves" (cf. v. 28), they would not be experiencing the present "judgments" of v. 30; on the other hand (v. 32), the present "judgments" mean that they are being "disciplined" so that they will not come under the final "judgment"—condemnation with the world.

27 With the strong inferential conjunction "so then,"[6] characteristic of the argumentation of this letter (see on 3:7), Paul proceeds to apply what he has just said about the meaning of the words of institution in v. 26 to their abuse of the Table: "Whoever eats the bread and drinks the cup of the Lord[7] in an unworthy manner will be guilty of the body and blood of the

---

[6]Gk. ὥστε. The "therefore" of the NIV is not incorrect, but it misses the close relationship with v. 33.

[7]Even though the two acts of eating and drinking are separated by the disjunctive ἤ, the genitive "of the Lord" refers to both the bread and the cup, just as in the following clause it refers to both the body and the blood.

Lord." Partaking of this meal[8] "in an unworthy manner"[9] is what the entire section is about. Unfortunately, this adverb was translated "unworthily" in the KJV. Since that particular English adverb seems more applicable to the person doing the eating than to the manner in which it is being done, this word became a dire threat for generations of English-speaking Christians.[10]

Paul's concern is related directly to vv. 20-22, where some are abusing others at the Lord's Table by going ahead with their own private meals.[11] Such conduct is unworthy of the Table where Jesus' death is being proclaimed until he comes. So much so, Paul goes on to say, that such a person "shall be guilty of the body and blood of the Lord."[12] What Paul has done here seems clear: Taking the two elements of the Supper, the bread and cup, he has expressed the Corinthians' "guilt" in terms of what the bread and cup signify, the Lord's body and blood. But what he intends by this is less obvious. The adjective "guilty"[13] is a technical legal term to express liability.[14] In genitive constructions such as this one, it can denote either the person sinned against or the crime itself. In this case, therefore, it can mean either "guilty of sinning against the Lord" in some way, or "to be held liable for his death," which the body and blood represent.

Most often this is understood as being a sin against the Lord in terms

---

[8]The context makes it clear that to "eat the bread and drink the cup of the Lord" means simply to participate in the meal known as the Lord's Supper. Paul is not trying to give special significance to the bread and wine per se. Indeed, in Paul's version the cup is *not* identified with the blood in any case, but with the new covenant brought about through the poured-out blood, thus through Christ's death. The reason for spelling it out in this way is related to the reason for reiterating the words of institution in itself: to remind the Corinthians of what this meal is all about, namely a time for experiencing and proclaiming their common salvation in Christ through his "body and blood," i.e., his death "for us."

[9]Gk. ἀναξίως, a NT hapax legomenon (although it is added by later scribes to v. 29).

[10]This is especially true in the more pietistic sectors of the Protestant tradition. People are "unworthy" if they have any sin in their lives, or have committed sins during the past week. This in turn resulted in reading v. 28 personally and introspectively, so that the purpose of one's self-examination was to become worthy of the Table, lest one come under judgment. The tragedy of such an interpretation for countless thousands, both in terms of a foreboding of the Table and guilt for perhaps having partaken unworthily, is incalculable.

[11]Chrysostom clearly recognized this. Unfortunately, a higher interest in the Table per se and in sacramentalism has often caused the text to be read independently of its present context, so that a variety of other options has been suggested for "unworthily": without self-examination, not realizing the real presence, without contemplation of the crucified body of Christ, with any form of sin in one's life, etc. See the list in W. Ellis, "Text," p. 45.

[12]This literal translation follows the KJV, which in this case is to be preferred to the NIV's "guilty of sinning against the body and blood of the Lord."

[13]Gk. ἔνοχος (in the NT: Matt. 5:21, 22 [three times]; 26:66; Mark 3:29; 14:26; Heb. 2:15; Jas. 2:10).

[14]Cf. Parry, 171, "will have to answer for."

of his Table, as though they were "desecrating" (NEB) or "profaning" (Goodspeed) it by their actions. In a sense that may be true, but in light of the whole context and of v. 26 in particular—to which this verse responds—it is doubtful whether this is Paul's intent. That seems to place far more emphasis on the sacred nature of the elements than Paul himself does. His concern is not with the bread and cup in themselves, but with how through these the participants "remember" Christ.

More likely, therefore, the "guilt" Paul has in mind is that of the crime itself. His point is that those who carry on at the Lord's Table as the Corinthians are doing have missed the point of the meal, which is to proclaim salvation through Christ's death, signified in the bread and cup and "proclaimed" in the bread saying and cup saying. To "profane" the meal as they are doing is to place themselves under the same liability as those responsible for that death in the first place.[15] Thus, to be "guilty of his body and blood" means to be "liable for his death." With this word Paul sets in motion the whole chain of forensic language that is to follow.

28 This sentence is joined to v. 27 by an adversative "but,"[16] which intends this imperative to be in contrast to their eating "in an unworthy manner" and thus becoming liable for the very death they should instead be proclaiming: "A man ought to examine himself before he eats of the bread and drinks of the cup." As with v. 27, to "eat of the bread and drink of the cup" means to participate in this meal. The problem lies with the imperative "let a person examine himself/herself," which along with v. 27 has been the cause of untold anxieties within the church. This is not a call for deep personal introspection to determine whether one is worthy of the Table. Rather, it stands in contrast to the "divine examination" to which unworthy participation will lead.

Although not strictly a forensic term, in this context the verb seems to pick up some forensic imagery. Ordinarily it means "to put to the test"[17] (cf. 3:13). Usually such "testing" is done by someone else;[18] but in Paul it also takes on the special sense of believers' "testing" themselves in relation both to their "works" (Gal. 4:6) and to the faith (2 Cor. 13:5). This is the first of such uses, the precise nuance of which is not easy to determine. Probably the verb was chosen in light of the "judgment" theme that runs

---

[15]Cf. Barrett, 273; Conzelmann, 202; see also 8:12, where to sin against a brother is to sin against Christ.

[16]Gk. δέ, omitted in the NIV.

[17]Gk. δοκιμάζω, the cognate of the adjective used in v. 19 to refer to those who "are approved" (= "those who have already been tested and found genuine"). Cf. the discussion by W. Grundmann, *TDNT* II, 255-60.

[18]Cf., e.g., 1 Thess. 2:4, where the God "who tests hearts" has "tested" Paul and entrusted him with this ministry, and 1 Tim. 3:10, where deacons are to be "examined, tested" before being allowed to serve.

through the paragraph. Since they will be "examined" by God at the End—indeed, their present illnesses are part of that "examination" in the present—they should test themselves *now* as to their attitude toward the Table, especially their behavior toward others *at* the Table.[19] This is probably not so much a threat as a call to truly Christian behavior at the Table. It is in this sense that the Corinthians are urged to examine themselves. Their behavior has belied the gospel they claim to embrace. Before they participate in the meal, they should examine themselves in terms of their attitudes toward the body, how they are treating others, since the meal itself is a place of proclaiming the gospel. Although this does not lay a heavy dose of self-introspection on believers, as v. 29 will make plain, it does raise proper cautions about casual participation at this Table by those who are not themselves ready to come under obedience to the gospel that is here proclaimed.

29 With an explanatory "for," Paul now gives the reason for putting oneself to the test before eating: "For anyone who eats and drinks not recognizing[20] the body eats and drinks judgment[21] [i.e., passes sentence] on himself." These are the words that tie the present argument to the problem as it was articulated in vv. 17-22; however, as the textual variations bear witness, they have also been regularly understood in such a way that vv. 23-32 are seen to function as a digression and thus not to speak directly to the problem as it is spelled out in vv. 17-22 and 33-34.

In the Received Text the words "unworthily" and "of the Lord"[22] (cf. NIV) were added respectively to "anyone who eats and drinks" and "the body." This produced a text that reads, "For anyone who eats and drinks unworthily, eats and drinks judgment on himself, not discerning the body of the Lord." This is an unfortunate, if understandable, assimilation to v. 27, to make it say much the same thing.[23] It was thus understood to mean: Whoever eats of the Lord's Table in unworthiness[24] eats one's way right into the very judgment warned against in v. 27, which is now further defined as not properly appreciating the fact that one is eating the body of Christ in this meal (although that is interpreted in different ways). But that is to make the words of institution themselves (vv. 23-25) the point of the section, rather than seeing them as part of the *corrective* to the situation described in vv. 17-22.

---

[19]As Barrett, 273, puts it: "The decision is God's but man may ask himself what decision he is likely to earn."

[20]Gk. μὴ διακρίνων (cf. 4:7; 6:5; 14:29); the participle may sustain either a conditional or a causal relationship to the main verb.

[21]Gk. κρίμα, the noun for the verdict, usually unfavorable as here, handed down by the judge.

[22]See nn. 3-4 above.

[23]But cf. Conzelmann, 202: "This is a variation of v. 27."

[24]See n. 11 for the variety of ways in which that was then understood.

Paul's concern lies elsewhere. Their improper eating brings them under judgment, to be sure; but it is not that of v. 27, where they put themselves under the same kind of liability as those responsible for the death of Christ. That warning had to do with the vertical abuse of the Supper. Here the judgment anticipates v. 30, where Paul asserts that some present illnesses and deaths are the direct result of their violations of the "body" at this Supper.

The phrase "not recognizing the body" in this passage has often been interpreted to mean either[25] (1) failure to distinguish the eucharistic food from the common food of their private meals,[26] or (2) failure to recognize the Lord's body, that is, reflect on his death, as they eat. The first of these must be ruled out as totally foreign to the context.[27] The second has more going for it. Those who adopt it view it as supported by "the parallelism between verses 27 and 29," in which this phrase is to be understood as a shorthand form of "the body and blood of the Lord."[28] But this too seems to miss the argument here, which points in another direction. Most likely the term "body," even though it comes by way of the words of institution in v. 24, deliberately recalls Paul's interpretation of the bread in 10:17, thus indicating that the concern is with the problem in Corinth itself, of the rich abusing the poor. All the evidence seems to point in this direction.

(1) As already pointed out, it is an illusion to see vv. 27 and 29 as parallels. Despite some similarities, the differences are more striking, especially (a) the absolute use of "the body," without a genitive qualifier, and (b) the absence of the heretofore parallel mention of the cup. In v. 26, Paul wrote, "as often as you *eat this bread* and *drink the cup*"; in v. 27, "*eat the bread* and *drink the cup* of the Lord," followed by "*the body* and *blood* of the Lord"; and in v. 28, "so let him *eat the bread* and *drink the cup.*" That combination, it was argued, refers to Christ's death, which this meal is to proclaim. But here Paul says only "the body." One is hard pressed to argue that this is "shorthand" for "the body and blood of the Lord," since Paul otherwise mentions both when he intends both.[29] Furthermore, the absence of the qualifier "of the Lord" seems purposeful since that was the pattern in vv. 26-27 when referring to the elements of the meal itself.

---

[25]A. Ehrhardt, "Holy Sacrament and Suffering," in *The Framework of the New Testament Stories* (Manchester, 1964), pp. 256-74, has offered a unique interpretation, in which "body" is understood to refer to one's own self that should be "separated from" the process of judgment that takes place at the Table. See the critique in Barrett, 275.

[26]Cf., e.g., Weiss, 291; Parry, 171; Héring, 120.

[27]It also runs aground on the probability that 10:1-13 reflects a somewhat magical view of the Table on the part of the Corinthians that would tend to take precisely the opposite stance toward the food.

[28]Barrett, 275; cf. Marshall, *Last Supper,* p. 114.

[29]This point was made many years ago by Moffatt, "Discerning," pp. 21-22.

(2) This sentence now makes sense of what was otherwise an unusual short digression in 10:17, where Paul singled out the bread alone for interpretation and emphatically declared that their all partaking of the "one loaf" was evidence that they themselves were therefore "one body." Since that interpretation played no significant role in the argument of 10:14-22, it is certainly arguable that it was intended to anticipate both this argument and that of chap. 12. It should be noted further that 10:17 offers the only interpretation of the bread as such in the NT. In the words of institution, as we have seen, and when used in conjunction with the cup, the bread does refer to Christ's physical body that was given in death on the cross. But the "meaning" of that "body" at this Table is that those who eat of the one loaf are themselves that one body. Why the absolute use of "body" in this sentence should mean something different from what Paul himself says it means is what needs to be explained if he intended something different here.

(3) If this usage were the only hint in this passage that the church were in view, one might see it as a veiled hint anticipating 12:12-26, but would have to understand it otherwise here. But precisely the opposite prevails. The whole point of the section, beginning with v. 17 and continuing through vv. 33-34, is to correct a considerable abuse of the church as it is visibly portrayed at the Lord's Supper. In light of this context the question ought to be, Why would one think that this absolute use, set up by 10:17, would mean anything else? The usage comes by way of vv. 23-25, to be sure. The Corinthians are missing the meaning of the "body" given in death; but Paul's present concern is with the further sense, the church as that body.

If then Paul is announcing judgment on them for their abuse of the body, why did he use the verb "recognizing/discerning" and what does it mean? The answer to this seems to lie in the wordplays on the theme of "judgment" that dominate the paragraph. No other forms of this verb would be appropriate for expressing the need properly to take cognizance of the whole church that is seated as one body at this meal. The meaning here probably comes close to the English word "discern," meaning to distinguish as distinct and different. The Lord's Supper is not just any meal; it is *the* meal, in which at a common table with one loaf and a common cup they proclaimed that through the death of Christ they were one body, the body of Christ; and therefore they are not just any group of sociologically diverse people who could keep those differences intact at this table. Here they must "discern/recognize as distinct" the one body of Christ, of which they all are parts and in which they all are gifts to one another. To fail to discern the body in this way, by abusing those of lesser sociological status, is to incur God's judgment.[30]

---

[30]Cf. God's judgment of Judah in Isa. 1:14-17: "Your New Moon festivals and your appointed feasts my soul hates. They have become a burden to me. . . . Stop doing

30 With an inferential "therefore"[31] Paul indicates that the verdict pronounced against those who eat the Lord's Supper as they are doing, "not discerning the body," has already begun in their midst, in that "many among you are weak and sick, and a number have fallen asleep[32]." This, too, has often been a troubling passage, especially for those who approach the Table with fear lest they partake "unworthily." But this is neither parenesis nor warning; it is an *ad hoc* reflection on their own situation. Most likely Paul is here stepping into the prophetic role; by the Spirit he has seen a divine cause and effect between two otherwise independent realities: the present illnesses of many, which in some cases have led to death, and the actions of some at the Table of the Lord who are despising the church and humiliating the "have-nots" by "going ahead with their own private meals."[33]

What is intriguing in the passage is what is left unsaid, or what is implied. Most likely Paul does not see the judgment as a kind of "one for one," that is, the person who has abused another is the one who gets sick. Rather, the whole community is affected by the actions of some, who are creating "divisions" within the one body of Christ. Probably the rash of illnesses[34] and deaths that have recently overtaken them[35] is here being viewed as an expression of divine judgment on the whole community. The "judgment" of course, as v. 32 makes clear, does not have to do with their eternal salvation, but with the temporal judgment of sickness and death. Beyond that one may only speculate. Is this related in some way to the "present distress" of 7:26? How many people were in the Corinthian community at this time, and how many of them had fallen ill to this "plague" to cause Paul to say "many of you"? In any case, Paul is not saying that sickness among Christians is to be viewed as present judgment, nor that such sickness is necessarily related to an abuse of the Supper. But these have been prophetically judged to be so.

---

wrong, learn to do right! Seek justice, encourage the oppressed. Defend the cause of the fatherless, plead the cause of the widow."

[31]Gk. διὰ τοῦτο; see the discussion on 11:10.

[32]Gk. κοιμάω; see on 7:39.

[33]On the unlikelihood that this passage is related to 5:5 see the commentary on that verse.

[34]Paul has used two words for illness, ἀσθενεῖς and ἄρρωστοι; the former is the common word for physical weakness of any kind, including sickness. The latter is less common in the NT; it literally means "powerless," but had taken on the more specific meaning of "being sick or ill."

[35]Barrett, 275, suggests a connection to 10:20-21, and says that those "who abused the Lord's table were exposing themselves to the power of demons, who were taken to be the cause of physical disease." But there is no hint of this in the text, and the association with chap. 10 seems quite unwarranted since that involved the "worship of demons" in the idol temples. That is a long way from the abuse recorded in this section.

31-32 As usual, Paul can scarcely bring himself to end an argument on a "down" note, so he concludes by repeating the concerns of vv. 28-30 with a considerable play on the language of "judgment."[36] The two sentences correspond to each other. The first (v. 31) is a contrary to fact supposition. Picking up the theme of self-examination from v. 28 (but now with the verb "discern" from v. 29), Paul says that if they had been examining/discerning themselves, they would not have been experiencing the "judgments" of v. 30. Thus this sentence helps to fill out the sense of the two verbs in vv. 28 and 29. Their "examination" of themselves is to take the form of "discerning" the body.[37] If they had been doing that, they "would not be coming under judgment."[38]

The second sentence (v. 32) responds to the real situation. They are in fact presently being "judged by the Lord" (in the way mentioned in v. 30); but this sentence makes it clear that by "judgment" Paul does not mean that the sick or dead are threatened with eternal loss. Rather, such "judgment" is to be understood as divine "discipline"[39] in which a loving God is correcting his children. The purpose of such discipline is "so that we will not be condemned[40] with the world," when brought to final judgment being implied.

As noted throughout, this paragraph has had an unfortunate history of understanding in the church. The very Table that is God's reminder, and therefore his repeated gift, of grace, the Table where we affirm again who and whose we are, has been allowed to become a table of condemnation for the very people who most truly need the assurance of acceptance that this table affords—the sinful, the weak, the weary. One does not have to "get rid

[36]He also reverts once more to the first person plural—in this case, as often elsewhere, as a means of identifying with them in these theological statements, even if he has had nothing to do with their behavioral aberration. Cf., e.g., 2:7; 5:7-8; 6:3; 8:8; 10:16.

[37]This seems to make more sense in the context than the suggestion that Paul intended that they should "discern" themselves in the "examination," meaning something like "distinguishing between what we are and what we ought to be before coming to the Lord's Supper" (Parry, 171).

[38]The imperfect in both the protasis and apodosis implies action that is in fact going on, and makes it certain that he is referring to the "judgments" and "discerning" that have just preceded.

[39]Gk. παιδευόμεθα (cf. 2 Cor. 6:9 and 1 Tim. 1:20). Inherent in this usage is the idea of "correcting by discipline." On the use of the word in the Greco-Roman world and the NT, see G. Bertram, *TDNT* V, 596-625; cf. D. Fürst, *NIDNTT* III, 775-80.

[40]Gk. κατακρίνω; this is the final wordplay on κριν- words. If we were "discerning" (διακρίνω) ourselves, we would not be coming under judgment (κρίνω); but when we are being judged (κρίνω) it is to correct us by discipline so that we will not be condemned (κατακρίνω) with the world.

of the sin in one's life" in order to partake. Here by faith one may once again receive the assurance that "Christ receiveth sinners."

On the other hand, any magical view of the sacrament that allows the unrepentant to partake without "discerning the body" makes the offer of grace a place of judgment. Grace "received" that is not recognized as such is not grace at all; and grace "received" that does not recognize the need to be gracious to others is to miss the point of the Table altogether.

4. The Answer—Wait for One Another (11:33-34)

> 33 So then, my brothers, when you come together to eat, wait for each other. 34 If[1] anyone is hungry, he should eat at home, so that when you meet together it may not result in judgment.
> And when I come I will give further directions.

Having argued theologically, on the basis of a proper understanding of the Lord's Supper, that the Corinthians should "discern the body" as they eat, Paul now concludes by applying the results of this argument in a very specific way to their situation. The solution is simple and direct: On the one hand, when they come together to eat they should "receive" ("accept," "welcome," "wait for") each other; on the other hand, if they want to eat sumptuously, they should do that at home apart from this meal. As before, this reflects the attitude "from above."[2] Paul does not suggest that all should eat the privileged portions of the well-to-do; rather, he implies that in community the well-to-do should eat what the others do.

As noted in the introductory section, this final conclusion responds to vv. 17-22 in the same way that the first "conclusion" (vv. 27-32) responded to vv. 23-26. The language is thoroughly that of vv. 17-22 ("come together to eat" [vv. 18, 20]; "hungry" [v. 21]; "eat at home" [v. 22]); yet the final warning comes by way of vv. 27-32 ("so that it will not result in judgment"). Thus at the end the pragmatic solution is tied directly to the preceding theological warning.

33 The repeated "so then" (see v. 27), plus the vocative "my[3] brothers [and sisters]" (see on 1:10), leads directly to the final inference to be drawn from this argument. This first pragmatic solution is, "When you come together to eat, receive (or wait for) one another." The difficulty lies with the verb *ekdechomai* ("receive," "wait for"), which has a particularly

---

[1]The MajT adds a δέ, reflecting typical scribal uneasiness with asyndeton. It is missing in P[46] ℵ* A B C D* F G 33 81 pc lat.

[2]See above on v. 22.

[3]This is one of only three occurrences of this more personal note with the vocative in this letter (see 1:11; 14:39; cf. "my beloved brothers [and sisters]" in 15:58).

broad range of meanings, depending strictly on context for its precise nuance.[4] Since it can mean "wait for," it is often taken to mean that here (as in the NIV) on the basis of the verb *prolambanei* in v. 21, which is understood to mean "eat beforehand." But as was noted in the discussion there, it is doubtful whether *prolambanei* carries that nuance in the context of eating, and it probably means something more like "consume" or "devour." If that be the case, then v. 21 refers to their gorging on privileged portions in the presence of the poor, and the verb *ekdechomai* here carries its primary meaning of "receive," which it often does in the context of hospitality (hence, "welcome" or "entertain").[5] Since Paul uses the stronger compound *apekdechomai* for the concept of "await" or "wait for," and since there is no sure evidence that *prolambanei* in v. 21 means to "eat beforehand," it seems most likely that Paul here is urging the wealthy to demonstrate normal Christian hospitality (cf. Rom. 12:13). They are to "welcome" or "receive" one another when they come together to eat.

34a This second piece of practical advice corresponds to the first. As with the rest of the section, it is addressed primarily to the well-to-do in whose homes the church is meeting. To them, not to the "have-nots" who are left hungry at the "private meals" of the rich, Paul says, "If anyone is hungry, he should eat at home." In this context "If anyone is hungry . . ." almost certainly means "If anyone wants to gorge. . . ." That is, if you want to satisfy your desire for the kinds of meals that the wealthy are accustomed to eat together, do that at home, but not in the context of the gathered assembly, where some "have nothing" and are thereby humiliated (vv. 21-22).

That this is Paul's intent is supported by the final purpose clause, which goes back to the "judgment" motif of vv. 28-32: "so that when you meet together it may not result in judgment[6]." With this clause the two sections of the argument are brought together. They are meeting together to eat the Lord's Supper, but in so doing they are "devouring" their own private meals with their privileged portions and thereby humiliating those who have nothing. Because they have treated the Table of the Lord so badly, neither proclaiming the salvation for which this meal is intended nor "discerning the body of Christ, the church," they are presently experiencing

---

[4]The verb occurs elsewhere in Paul only in 16:11, where it has the meaning "expect." Its primary meaning is "receive," like that of the simple form δέχομαι. From there it can take on the meanings "welcome," "receive," "await," "undertake," "take to mean," "encounter," "succeed (in a kingdom) [= receive it from the former king]," "take up (as in an argument)," etc.

[5]For this meaning see such diverse texts as 3 Macc. 5:26; Jos., *Ant.* 7.351; and the Tebtunis Papyrus I.33 (cited by MM and LSJ).

[6]Gk. κρίμα (as in v. 29).

divine judgment. The remedy is simple: "In the gathered assembly, receive one another with full welcome at the Lord's Table." Moreover, as Paul says in v. 22, "Since you have your own houses to eat and drink in, eat your 'private' meals at home." And the reason is to keep from experiencing any further judgment.

34b   Paul signs off this section with one of the more intriguing texts in the letter: "And when I come[7] I will give further directions." How much we are left in the dark because Paul was not writing first of all for us! Indeed, it is not possible even to know to what "the other things" refer: The rest of the matters that have to do with the Lord's Table? Other matters relating to traditions that are being kept but requiring further instruction? Other matters that have to do with relationships between the "haves" and "have-nots"? We simply do not know. What a sentence like this does is to remind us of how little we really do know and to teach us to be grateful for what we have received—even if it had to be at the expense of some unfortunate abuses in this assembly.

If from this section we do not discover the answer to everything that piques our curiosity, we are indeed given more than enough to "examine" us as to our obedience at the Lord's Table. One wonders whether our making the text deal with self-examination has not served to deflect the greater concern of the text, that we give more attention at the *Lord's* Supper to our relationships with one another in the body of Christ. The final imperative is perhaps the most significant one: "Receive/welcome one another." It is the Lord's Supper, after all, not ours. Our task—and joy—is to receive anew the benefits of his grace in the context of truly welcoming others, who are recipients of that same grace. It is not simply by coincidence that Paul begins his corrective on spiritual gifts in the next section by placing that once again in the context of the unity of the body, all members being equally concerned for each other.

E. SPIRITUAL GIFTS AND SPIRITUAL PEOPLE (12:1–14:40)

Since chap. 8 Paul has been dealing with matters related to worship. In 8:1–10:22, despite their protests to the contrary, he absolutely forbids the Corinthians to participate in temple meals—partly on the basis of their own sacred meal. That is followed by three issues involving their own gatherings for

---

[7]Gk. ὡς ἂν ἔλθω ("when I have come, whenever that may be"). Cf. 4:19 and 16:5.

worship. This section is the third of these. It is also probably the most important from Paul's point of view because here in particular the differences between him and them come to a head, especially over what it means to be "spiritual." That seems also to be the reason for the close relationship between these chapters and the final issue—the future bodily resurrection of believers (chap. 15). Together these four chapters bring the letter, with all of its preceding arguments, to a fitting climax. Being "spiritual" in the present means to edify the community in worship (chaps. 12–14), for the perfect has not yet come (13:8-13); and when it does come, it will include the resurrection of the body, albeit as a "spiritual body" (chap. 15).

Most likely the present issue was raised in the Corinthians' letter;[1] nonetheless,[2] both the length[3] and the nature of Paul's response allow for a fairly straightforward reconstruction of the problem.[4] What is more difficult is to determine what they might have said in their letter that called for this response. On the basis of chap. 12 alone,[5] one might think that they were asking questions about spiritual gifts;[6] but chap. 14 indicates that, as throughout the letter, Paul's answer is intended to be *corrective,* not instructional or informational. Thus, even if they presented themselves to Paul with a question (or questions), his response seems to take *exception* to their

---

[1]This is a nearly universal conviction, based on the recurrence of the περὶ δέ ("now about") formula in 12:1. See the discussion in Hurd, 186-95.

[2]When a problem is *reported* to him, Paul feels compelled to tell what he knows (cf. 1:11-12; 5:1; 6:1; 11:17-22); thus we, too, have a better idea of what was going on. When responding to their letter, unless he quotes from it (7:1; 8:1, 4), he picks up right at that point, so we are not always informed as to the precise nature of the problem.

[3]In NA[26] it covers 159 lines of Greek text; chaps. 1:10–4:21 cover 161 lines; chaps. 8–10 cover 143. Hurd, 186, is in error, therefore, when he designates this as the longest item in the letter; cf. J. W. MacGorman, "Glossolalic Error and Its Correction: 1 Corinthians 12-14," *RevExp* 80 (1983), 389, who is probably indebted to Hurd.

[4]Although a glance at the various reconstructions discussed by Hurd, 186-87, 190-91, should make one duly cautious as to what seems "straightforward." R-P's view (257) that the phenomena here dealt with "were to a large extent abnormal and transitory," not being "part of the regular development of the Christian church," probably says more about R-P and their notion of what should be "regular" than it does about either Paul or the primitive church.

[5]Cf. W. J. Bartling, "The Congregation of Christ—A Charismatic Body. An Exegetical Study of 1 Corinthians 12," *CTM* 40 (1969), 67: "If we had only chapter 12, we would probably never have surmised that the focus of Paul's practical concern throughout chapters 12, 13, and 14 of First Corinthians is the tongues phenomenon."

[6]This is the most common view, repeated in a modified form most recently by Martin, 7-8. It is frequently assumed in this view that the Corinthians were divided among themselves on this matter. See, e.g., J. M. P. Sweet, "A Sign for Unbelievers: Paul's Attitude to Glossolalia," *NTS* 13 (1966/67), 240-57, among many others. But this is read into the text from chap. 13; nothing in the argument itself hints of such. There is a tendency among other scholars to see 12:1-3, and the problem of "testing the spirits," as the basic thrust of their letter. See the discussion in Hurd, 186-87.

viewpoint,[7] not simply to inform them in areas where they lack understanding.

The problem is almost certainly an *abuse* of the gift of tongues.[8] This is made clear first of all by the structure of the argument itself, which is basically in three parts, following the A-B-A pattern noted in previous sections[9] (and roughly corresponding to our current chapter divisions). This section begins with a more general word (chap. 12), which is followed by a theological interlude (chap. 13) and a very specific response to the matter in hand (chap. 14).

Since on the basis of this structural pattern the whole argument aims at the specific correctives in chap. 14, it is appropriate to begin our analysis there. This argument is in two parts: (1) In vv. 1-25, using a running contrast between tongues (unintelligible inspired speech) and prophecy (intelligible inspired speech), Paul argues for *the absolute need for intelligibility* in the assembly. This is so both for the sake of fellow believers (vv. 1-19), since only what is intelligible can build them up, and for the sake of unbelievers (vv. 20-25), since only what is intelligible can lead to their conversion. (2) In vv. 26-40, offering some specific guidelines, beginning with tongues, he argues for *the absolute need for order* in the assembly.

Two related concerns emerge from this argument. First, as in 11:2-16 and 17-34, the problem is one of corporate worship. This is specifically indicated by the language "in church" and "when you assemble together" (vv. 18-19, 23, 26); it is also implied throughout.[10] Second, the correctives are all aimed at the abuse of tongues in the assembly, which seems to be both singular in its emphasis and disorderly in its expression (cf. 14:12, 23, 33, 40).

Since this is unquestionably the focus of chap. 14,[11] it is reasonable to assume that the argument in chaps. 12 and 13 leads to these correctives. Thus, after setting forth the basic criterion for distinguishing between what

---

[7]See on vv. 6, 18-19, 23, 33, and esp. 36-38.

[8]Variously called "kinds of tongues" (12:10, 28), "to speak in/with tongues" (14:2, 4, 5, 6, 13, 18, 23, 27, 39), or simply "tongues" or a "tongue" (13:8; 14:22, 26).

[9]See the Introduction, pp. 15-16; and n. 15 on 1:10-17.

[10]In vv. 1-5 by the intelligibility/edification motif; in vv. 6-12 by analogies that require hearers; in vv. 13-17 by the inability of others to respond by saying the Amen to what is said in tongues; in vv. 26-31 by the orderly sequencing of utterances.

[11]Although see D. L. Baker, "The Interpretation of 1 Corinthians 12-14," *EvQ* 46 (1974), 224-34, who thinks the key lies with the Corinthians' use of τὰ πνευματικά, by which they meant "spiritual gifts," and of which only two were of interest to them (prophecy and tongues). Paul's purpose in chap. 14 in this view is simply to answer *their* inquiries about these gifts and to give some guidelines for the use of each. But that does not seem to be an adequate analysis of the argument, especially the insistence on intelligibility over against tongues in the assembly.

belongs to the Spirit and what does not (vv. 1-3), in 12:4-30 Paul emphasizes the need for *diversity* of gifts and manifestations in the unity of the one Spirit.[12] That is the clear concern of vv. 4-11, as well as the major note struck in the analogy of the body in vv. 12-26 and in the concluding reiteration in vv. 27-30. This emphasis is best understood vis-à-vis their singular enthusiasm for tongues.

It should be noted at this point that only tongues is included in every list of "gifts" in these three chapters.[13] Its place at the *conclusion* of each list in chap. 12, but at the beginning in 13:1 and 14:6, suggests that the problem lies here. It is listed last not because it is "least," but because it is the problem. He always includes it, but at the end, after the greater concern for diversity has been heard.[14]

This view of the problem also makes sense of the argument of chap. 13. Their passion for tongues in the assembly was further indication of their failure to love one another (cf. 8:2-3). Love, however, is not set forth in *contrast* to tongues, but as the necessary ingredient for the expression of all spiritual gifts. The reason for the gifts is the edification of the church, which is precisely what love aims at, but uninterpreted tongues does not.[15] Thus he concludes this argument, and therewith begins the final one, by saying (14:1): "Aim at love, which will have as its concomitant that you be zealous for spiritual gifts, especially the intelligible ones, so that the church may be edified."

All of this seems clear enough. Less clear are the *reasons* for this attitude on the part of the Corinthians and *what* they communicated to Paul. Although this point is more speculative, very likely what is going on here between Paul and the Corinthians is the key to much of the rest of the letter. First, there is not a single suggestion in Paul's response that they were themselves divided on this issue[16] or that they were politely asking his

---

[12]It is common to read this section as emphasizing once again the Corinthian need for unity, and for good reason: One has been set up for reading it this way both by the problem of quarreling in chaps. 1–4 and 11:17-34 and by Paul's previous use of body imagery in 10:17 to make that very point, not to mention the fact that vv. 20 and 25 do suggest as much. But a careful reading of the whole indicates that *diversity*, not unity, is Paul's concern; the fact of the body's unity is the *presupposition* of the argument. See on 12:12-14.

[13]See 12:8-10, 28, 29-30; 13:1-3, 8; 14:6, 26.

[14]See G. D. Fee, "Tongues—Least of the Gifts? Some Exegetical Observations on 1 Corinthians 12-14," *Pneuma* 2 (1980), 3-14. It is of some interest that a community that lacked genuine unity should evidence concern for *uniformity* in the manifestation of spiritual gifts. Unity and uniformity are not the same thing, not even close.

[15]It should be noted, however, that this "discussion" on love, which puts gifts into their proper framework, also reflects the larger concerns of the letter, in which their form of spirituality is not marked by proper Christian ethical behavior.

[16]This is the standard view; see n. 6 above. Implied, or indeed more often stated, is the idea that the glossolalists (enthusiasts) were after the more "showy gifts" over

advice. More likely, the crucial issue is their decided position over against him as to what it means to be *pneumatikos* ("spiritual").[17] Their view apparently not only denied the material/physical side of Christian existence (hence the reason why chap. 15 follows hard on the heels of this section),[18] but had an element of "spiritualized (or overrealized) eschatology" as well.

The key probably lies with 13:1, where tongues is associated with angels. As noted elsewhere (7:1-7; 11:2-16), the Corinthians seem to have considered themselves to be already like the angels, thus truly "spiritual," needing neither sex in the present (7:1-7) nor a body in the future (15:1-58). Speaking angelic dialects by the Spirit was evidence enough for them of their participation in the new spirituality, hence their singular enthusiasm for this gift.[19]

But Paul had a different view of life in the Spirit. For him it did not so much remove one from present existence as enable one to live in the present simultaneously in weakness and power (see, e.g., 2:1-5; 4:9-13). Life in the present is conditioned by the life of the future that has already begun with Christ's death and resurrection (cf. 4:1-5; 7:29-31); but that life has only begun, it is not yet consummated. Thus in the present they must cultivate loving, responsible relationships in the body of Christ; and their times of public worship must be for mutual edification, not for heightened individualistic spirituality, which in their case had become a false spirituality.

In so doing Paul does not "damn tongues with faint praise."[20]

---

against others (sometimes viewed as those who preferred prophecy). This is so commonly held that a full bibliography would be tedious. See, e.g., Sweet, "Sign," p. 241; Martin, 20 and *passim*. But not a single sentence in these chapters suggests such an attitude on the part of the Corinthians.

[17]This may be further reflected in his sudden shift to the first person singular at key points in the argument (13:1; 14:6, 14-15, 18, 37), intimating that they may have disapproved of him precisely because of his failure to "come to them speaking in tongues" (14:6). Otherwise, Grudem, 157-62, but his arguments seem to miss the overall nature of the conflict between this church and its apostle; moreover, his contention that πνευματικός basically means "spiritually mature" in the key passages in 1 Corinthians is less than convincing.

[18]See further on 2:6-16; 6:12-20; 7:1-7; 7:25-40.

[19]Although it is not possible from this response to reconstruct what they might have said in their letter, there is much to be said for Hurd's view, 226-28, that this is not the first interchange between them and Paul on this matter—although Hurd's own solution is not fully satisfactory. He follows the many who have argued that the major point of contention is over the "testing" of "spirits." Since Paul's answer reflects little concern over this matter as such, it seems far more likely that it had to do with the value and significance of tongues for spiritual life in the assembly.

[20]This is frequently suggested, because Paul so clearly tries to put tongues in its proper place. But nothing in the argument suggests that he is really trying to eliminate it. If so, then one must allow that he argues out of both sides of his mouth. Among those who take this position see esp. D. Walker, *The Gift of Tongues* (Edinburgh, 1908), p. 72; Chadwick, "All Things," pp. 268-69; Hurd, 188-90; D. W. B. Robinson, "Charismata

Rather, he is concerned to put that gift into a broader context, where it can be used privately as much as one pleases, but in the community only in the context of edification, which requires intelligibility. Hence it must always be accompanied by interpretation; those who speak in tongues must do so in orderly sequence; and in any case, in the assembly prophecy is preferable.

1. The Criterion—Jesus Is Lord (12:1-3)

> 1 *Now about spiritual gifts, brothers, I do not want you to be ignorant.* 2 *You know that when[21] you were pagans, somehow or other you were influenced and led astray to mute[22] idols.* 3 *Therefore I make known to[23] you that no one who is speaking[24] by the Spirit of God says, "Jesus is cursed," and no one can say, "Jesus is Lord," except by the Holy Spirit.*

At first reading this opening paragraph seems quite unrelated to the topic at hand; nonetheless, Paul probably here intends to set the stage for much that follows. Despite some notorious exegetical difficulties in vv. 2 and 3, one thing seems certain: His initial concern is to set their former experience as idolaters in contrast with their present experience as Christians, who speak "by the Spirit of God." The structure of the argument verifies this. He begins by telling them "I do not want you to be ignorant" (v. 1), which is followed by a reminder of something about which they are *not* ignorant, namely what it was like to be pagans (v. 2; led about to mute idols). In light of that experience, therefore, he now makes known to them (v. 3) the proper criterion for what is genuinely the work of the Spirit of God.

---

versus Pneumatika: Paul's Method of Discussion," *RefThRev* 31 (1972), 49-55; and A. C. Thiselton, "The Interpretation of Tongues: A New Suggestion in Light of Greek Usage in Philo and Josephus," *JTS* 30 (1979), 15-36. But see R. Banks and G. Moon, "Speaking in Tongues, A Survey of the New Testament Evidence," *Churchman* 80 (1966), 285, who correctly observe: "He makes it clear, however, that the correct treatment for abuse is not disuse, but proper use," an attitude, they go on to point out, that is "grounded in the belief that the Spirit is the source of the gift"! So also T. W. Harpur, "The Gift of Tongues and Interpretation," *CJT* 12 (1966), 164-71, esp. 165. Cf. W. Richardson, "Liturgical Order and Glossolalia in 1 Corinthians 14:26c-33a," *NTS* 32 (1986), 144-53, esp. 145-46.

[21]The combination ὅτι ὅτε has resulted in the omission of one or the other in a variety of witnesses.

[22]NIV[3]; NIV[2] has "dumb."

[23]NIV, "I tell you." In some cases that may be allowable for γνωρίζω, but not here, where it stands as the complement to ἀγνοέω (to be ignorant) in v. 1.

[24]The Western tradition omits λαλῶν, probably seeing it as redundant, which in this case it is not; rather, it anticipates the discussion of "speaking" in tongues by the Spirit.

What is not certain is (1) the meaning of the term that introduces the matter at hand (whether "spiritual gifts" or "spiritual people"); (2) the significance of the reference to their former idolatry (whether it refers simply to idolatry as such or to "ecstatic"[25] experiences, which Paul thought to be inspired by demonic spirits; cf. 10:20-21); and (3) the meaning of the words of contrast in v. 3, "Jesus is cursed."

When all of that has been sorted out, and especially in light of their special zeal for tongues, it seems most likely that Paul's concern at the outset is singular: To insist that "inspired utterance" in itself does not mark what is truly "spiritual," but the intelligible content of that utterance, content that is ultimately tested by the basic Christian confession of the lordship of Jesus Christ.

1 The new topic is marked both by the repeated "now about" (see on 7:1) and the vocative "brothers [and sisters]."[26] The difficulty lies with the content of the topic, which may be either masculine (= "those who are spiritual") or neuter (= "spiritual gifts"). What favors the former[27] is the usage in 2:15, 3:1, and especially 14:37, where Paul says rhetorically, "If anyone thinks he/she is 'spiritual.' "[28] It would also fit well with the problem in Corinth as we have reconstructed it above, where the conflict with Paul is not simply over spiritual gifts as such but over the significance of the gift of tongues for "spiritual" life. On the other hand, the certain use of the neuter plural in 14:1 in the imperative "Be zealous for *ta pneumatika,*" where it refers at least to prophecy and tongues, plus the overall argument that deals primarily with the manifestation of gifts in the church, not with individual spirituality, has caused most commentators to opt for "spiritual gifts."[29]

---

[25]One of the real difficulties in discussing these matters is the looseness with which many of us use terminology, the term "ecstasy" being a primary case in point. Technically, this should refer to experiential activity in which the person is "beside himself/herself," i.e., either out of control or out of touch with the present surroundings (e.g., a trance of some kind). Cf. T. Callan, "Prophecy and Ecstasy in Greco-Roman Religion and 1 Corinthians," *NovT* 27 (1985), 125-40. But very often it is used as a synonym of "enthusiasm" to denote any number of kinds of spiritually inspired activity or speech. In this commentary I shall use "inspired utterance" or "inspiration" for the latter kinds of spiritual activity and "ecstasy" in its more technical sense.

[26]See n. 22 on 1:10; this is now the twelfth occurrence in the letter, with nine to follow.

[27]See, *inter alia,* Weiss, 294; Hurd, 194; Bruce, 116; Pearson, 47.

[28]For the significance of this formula see on 3:18 (cf. 8:2).

[29]Robinson, "Charismata," has argued that τὰ πνευματικά is a Corinthian word by which they have narrowed the gifts basically to "tongues and other ecstatic utterances"; cf. Baker, "Interpretation." But that probably narrows their usage too much. For more complete arguments in favor of its meaning "spiritual gifts" see Grudem, 157-62, and Martin, 8.

One wonders, however, whether in this instance the options have not been narrowed too rigidly. Most likely the word here is neuter, as in 9:11 and 14:1; but the evidence from 2:13–3:1, Gal. 6:1, Rom. 1:11, and elsewhere suggests that for Paul the primary focus of this adjective is on the Spirit. Paul's immediate—and overall—concern has to do with what comes from "the Spirit of God" (v. 3). Moreover, elsewhere in chap. 12 he uses *charismata* for the specific manifestations of the Spirit's activity. It seems likely therefore that even though at points the two words are nearly interchangeable (as 12:31a and 14:1 would imply), the emphasis in each case reflects the root word (*pneuma,* Spirit; *charis,* grace). When the emphasis is on the manifestation, the "gift" as such, Paul speaks of *charismata;* when the emphasis is on the Spirit, he speaks of *pneumatika.*[30] If so, then both here and in 14:1 the better translation might be "the things of the Spirit," which would refer primarily to spiritual manifestations, from the perspective of the *Spirit's* endowment; at the same time it would point toward those who are so endowed.

On the formula "I do not want you to be ignorant," see on 10:1. As there Paul almost certainly does not intend to give new information, but an additional slant, or a corrective, to their understanding of "the things of the Spirit."

2 Paul begins his correction of their "ignorance" by reminding them of something from their pagan past[31] of which they were well aware. The sentence itself is an *anacolouthon* (it doesn't follow grammatically) since the "when" clause has no main verb. Either something dropped out in the transmission of the text,[32] or else Paul himself intended his readers to supply a second "you were" at some point in the sentence. Literally it reads, "You know that when you were pagans, to mute idols whenever (or however) you would be led, being carried away." The best solution is to repeat the verb "you were" with the final participle "carried away," so that the

---

[30]For another view see Martin, 8, who follows J. Goldingay (*The Church and the Gifts of the Spirit* [Bamcote, 1972]) and J. Koenig (*Charismata: God's Gifts for God's People* [Philadelphia, 1978]) in seeing πνευματικά as the broader term while χαρίσματα refer more specifically to πνευματικά to be practiced in the context of the assembly at worship.

[31]This sentence offers the clearest evidence in the letter of the predominantly Gentile character of the church in Corinth (cf. 6:9-11 and 8:1–10:22). The attempt by J. D. M. Derrett, "Cursing Jesus (I Cor. XII.3): The Jews as Religious 'Persecutors,'" *NTS* 21 (1974/75), 553, to circumvent this so as to give the problem a basically Jewish life-setting is less than convincing. Cf. the earlier, even less convincing, suggestion by J. M. Ford, "The First Epistle to the Corinthians or the First Epistle to the Hebrews," *CBQ* 38 (1966), 410.

[32]One of the more attractive options is that suggested by WH, that ὅτε was probably originally ποτε (= "that at one time you were pagans, carried away to dumb idols, however you were being led").

sentence reads, "When you were pagans, you were carried away, as you were continually[33] being led about to mute idols."[34]

The greater difficulty is to determine the *reason* for this sentence in the argument. There are basically two options: (1) Some have argued for a minimal view, that Paul intends only to contrast their former life as idolaters with their new life as Christians (i.e., pagans are led to idols; Christians are led by the Spirit).[35] A modification of this position sees Paul as contrasting their former experience with idols either (a) as a way to remind them of their "sheer lack of experience with true 'inspired' speech" (thus implying that they have no basis from which to make judgments about speech inspired of the Spirit),[36] or (b) to contrast Christian prophets and their Spirit-inspired utterances with their former experience with totally mute idols.[37] While this view in one of its several forms is certainly possible,[38] the difficulty of finding an adequate reason for making this point in this introductory paragraph has caused most scholars to look elsewhere for an answer.

(2) Others see Paul's larger concern to be setting forth a pagan example against which they are to understand both "inspired utterances" and the significance of "tongues." If so, then it seems probable that what is in view is their former experience of "ecstasy" or "inspired utterances" as pagans. Although neither verb on its own necessarily implies this, the unusual compounding of the verbs,[39] with emphasis on the Corinthians' being

---

[33]This is an attempt to give an iterative force to ὡς ἄν.

[34]The alternative is to read ὡς as a resumption of ὅτι, so that the sentence reads, "You know that, when you were pagans—how you were led to dumb idols, being carried away" (cf. Barrett, 278; Conzelmann, 204). But see the objections in Findlay, 885, and Grudem, 156 n. 69. On the whole question see the discussion in Parry, 175.

[35]As in 1 Thess. 1:9; Gal. 4:8-9. See, e.g., M. Barth, "A Chapter on the Church—The Body of Christ. Interpretation of I Corinthians 12," *Int* 12 (1958), 131, who says, "A short introduction (vss. 2 and 3) reminds the readers that a miraculous operation of the Holy Spirit has freed them from service to dumb idols and makes them confess distinctly that 'Jesus is Lord'"; cf. K. Maly, "1 Kor 12,1-3, eine Regel zur Unterscheidung der Geister?" *BZ* 10 (1966), 82-95.

[36]Grudem, 162-65; his argument is formulated so as to demonstrate the non-ecstatic character of prophecy. He (rightly) makes a considerable point that the sentence must stand in contrast with v. 3, but he fails to show how this minimal view sustains Paul's concern either in these three verses or in the larger argument of chaps. 12–14, which after all is trying to place "tongues" into proper perspective, not give teaching on the nature of prophecy.

[37]See Maly, "Regel"; and Derrett, "Cursing," pp. 552-53.

[38]As such it would be, as Conzelmann points out (205 n. 11), a variation on the theme of "once, but now" (see on 6:11).

[39]The combination ἤγεσθε ἀπαγόμενοι, which is strange at best, seems emphatic, a point generally overlooked by those who take the minimalistic position. Grudem, 162-64, tries to minimize this by looking at each verb separately; but that will not do since it is the combination that is so striking. On this question see Parry, 175; Maly, "Regel"; and J. M. Bassler, "1 Cor 12:3—Curse and Confession in Context," *JBL* 101 (1982), 416-17.

acted upon by others (implied in the two passive verbs), seems to lead in this direction.

In keeping with his Jewish heritage,[40] Paul scorns the idols as mute because they cannot hear and answer prayer; nor can they speak—in contrast to the Spirit of God who can. But he has also argued earlier that the mute idols represent demons (10:20-21)—who can and do speak through their devotees. Most likely, therefore, he is reminding them of what they well know, that in some of the cults "inspired utterances" were part of the worship, despite the "mute idols."[41] If so, then his concern is to establish early on, as v. 3 seems to corroborate, that it is not "inspired speech" as such that is evidence of the Spirit. They had already known that phenomenon as pagans. Rather, what counts is the *intelligible and Christian content* of such utterances.

3 With an emphatic "therefore,"[42] Paul brings this opening argument to a conclusion. The verb "I make known to you" recalls the opening words "I do not want you to be ignorant," but now by way of what was said in v. 2. "Therefore," he says, "since I do not want you to be ignorant about the things of the Spirit, and since you have already known about inspired utterances as pagans, I make known to you what follows." But what follows turns out to be one of the more difficult passages in the letter. In two nearly balanced clauses Paul indicates what one who is speaking by the Spirit *cannot* say, and contrariwise that only by the Spirit can one utter the primary Christian confession. The difficulty lies primarily with the first clause, "No one who is speaking by the Spirit of God[43] says, 'Jesus is cursed.'" But it also has to do with the point of all this for the argument that follows. However one finally responds to the first matter, which is probably "past

---

[40]Cf., e.g., Hab. 2:18-19; Ps. 115:5; 3 Macc. 4:16.

[41]For a thorough discussion of this phenomenon in pagan antiquity, see Aune, *Prophecy*, pp. 23-79. It is unlikely that Paul is also thinking of the frenzied ecstasy and mania of some of the cults (Bacchus, Dionysus, Cybele, etc.; see n. 73 on 11:5) since nothing in the text seems to move in that direction. Paul's concern is not with mania as such, but with pressing the point that "inspired utterances" in themselves are no sure guarantee that one is speaking by the Spirit.

[42]Gk. διό (cf. 14:13); the conjunction emerges as a predominant one in 2 Corinthians.

[43]Parry, 176, 177, following Hort, makes a point of the anarthrous use of πνεῦμα as though it implied an "intermediate sense" in which each manifestation is the work of "a holy spirit." But that is to miss Pauline usage altogether. V. 9 alone indicates that such is not true ("by the same Spirit"; "by the one Spirit"). It is a Pauline idiosyncrasy that πνεῦμα in the dative is almost always anarthrous when referring to the Holy Spirit (see, e.g., Rom. 8:9, 13, 14, surrounded by arthrous uses in other cases), and is usually arthrous when it refers primarily to one's own spirit (see, e.g., 1 Cor. 5:3; 7:34; 14:15; this stylistic feature is probably also the way forward for resolving the ambiguity in Rom. 12:11). See further on 14:2 and the unfortunate translation in the NIV.

finding out," that answer must make sense of two things: (a) how it functions in relationship to v. 2, and (b) how it relates to the larger issue of their apparently inordinate enthusiasm for the gift of tongues.

The problem itself is especially perplexing—in two ways: First, it is difficult for us to imagine either that anyone actually cursed Jesus in the gathered Christian assembly, or that, if he/she did, Paul would take it so casually as to speak to it only here and in this totally noncombative way. Second, how is it possible that Paul would have to "make known to them" that no one speaking in the Spirit would say such a thing as "Jesus is/be[44] cursed"? The solutions are many and varied; none is without difficulties.

(1) An increasingly popular option is that no one in the Christian assembly actually said such a thing; rather, this is a hypothetical alternative, framed in light of v. 2, to the real issue, that "inspired utterances" or true Spirit-possession will be recognized by the criterion of the primitive confession "Jesus is Lord" (cf. Rom. 10:9).[45] The problem with this is the equal difficulty of imagining that the Jewish-Christian Paul created such a blasphemous alternative had it never actually been said.[46] Moreover, the clause "Jesus is/be cursed" has all the earmarks of an actual curse formula.

(2) A second alternative is that this is exactly the kind of thing that those who are "inspired" by demonic spirits may have said in the pagan settings that Paul is alluding to in v. 2. This is an attractive option since it would help us better to understand the reason for v. 2. Furthermore, it would be precisely the kind of contrast between their pagan past and Christian present that would help them to see the difference between "spirits" and *the* Spirit, between "inspired utterance" as such and that which is truly of the Spirit of God. Hence it is not tongues per se that is evidence of the Spirit's

---

[44]It is not easy to determine whether an imperative ("Jesus be cursed") or an indicative ("Jesus is cursed") is intended. Most often an imprecation (imperative) is assumed; but it is likewise generally assumed (for good reason) that the following confession is indicative. Cf. W. C. van Unnik, "Jesus: Anathema or Kyrios (I Cor. 12:3)," in *Christ and Spirit in the New Testament* (ed. B. Lindars and S. S. Smalley; Cambridge, 1973), pp. 115-16, who objects to making this an imperative.

[45]Among others, see Hurd, 193; Conzelmann, 204; Bruce, 118; Pearson, 47-50; Bassler, "1 Cor 12:3"; MacGorman, "Error," p. 392; Aune, *Prophecy*, p. 257.

[46]But see Pearson, 48-50, who insists (correctly, one would think) that "it is impossible for *any* kind of Christian to cu. se Jesus, no matter how erroneous his views or how loose his behavior" (p. 48) and concludes that "Paul's argument is a shocking one, and was undoubtedly intended to be such" (p. 50). Bassler, "1 Cor 12:3," p. 147, has argued that it serves as an *analogy* by way of v. 2 to their "experience in pagan cults when the δαίμων exercised total control over their actions. Thus they should recognize that the Christian likewise does not make the confession of faith by his own will, but shows thereby the controlling presence of the Holy Spirit." In this she is following Weiss, 296, and Conzelmann, 206.

activity, but the intelligible, Jesus-exalting content of such activity. The difficulty with this option lies in the language *anathema*,[47] which seems to reflect a Jewish usage not frequently found among Greeks.[48]

(3) Given the way Paul has set up these contrasts, one must also be open to the possibility that someone had actually uttered such words in the Christian assembly. If so, the problem is to determine how it could have happened, and how it is that Paul is so little taken aback by it. Of the several options that have been suggested,[49] the least likely are those that place the utterance in a context other than pagan temples or Christian worship, which the context seems absolutely to demand.[50] Still other options seem more ingenious than realistic.[51] Of the suggestions that seem even remotely via-

[47]Cf. 16:22. This word in Greek ordinarily refers to a votive offering set up in a temple (cf. Luke 21:5); but it was picked up by the LXX translators to translate *ḥērem*, which more often refers to what is devoted not for consecration but for cursing. Thus it often means "that which is under the *ban*," or "the accursed thing" (cf. Deut. 7:26; 13:17; Josh. 6:18; etc.), referring to "something delivered up to divine wrath, dedicated to destruction and brought under a curse" (J. Behm, *TDNT* I, 354). This usage is known in the Greek world only from a single inscription from the first or second century A.D., in a table of curses (see Deissmann, LAE, pp. 95-96). For Paul's use of the term see esp. van Unnik, "Jesus," pp. 116-21.

[48]However, it is possible that the language is Paul's, while the curse itself could have been part of a pagan setting. Although there is no evidence for such *oracular* imprecations from pagan antiquity (at least none is noted in Aune, *Prophecy*), nonetheless since curses of all kinds abound, there is no good reason to doubt that they could have occurred in the "inspired utterances" of pagan religion. Cf., e.g., Lucian, *Alex.* 38, where Alexander begins with a "cursing" of Christians. For Christian examples, see Gal. 1:8-9; Rev. 22:18-19. Those who think that the curse is hypothetical also generally assume that it would have been spoken in some setting outside the Christian community, not within (cf. Aune, *Prophecy*, p. 257).

[49]For overviews see Derrett, "Cursing Jesus," p. 544; R. P. Martin, *The Worship of God: Some Theological, Pastoral, and Practical Reflections* (Grand Rapids, 1982), pp. 175-78; and Bassler, "1 Cor 12:3," pp. 415-16.

[50]Among these are (a) the suggestions by Schlatter, 333; Moffatt, 178; and Derrett, "Cursing Jesus," who in various ways place it in the context of the Jewish synagogue; and (b) those who see it as taking place in the context of persecutions or trials (e.g., O. Cullmann, *Les premières confessions de foi chrétiennes* [Paris, 1948], pp. 22-23, who suggests that those who so recanted claimed the Spirit taught them to say this; cf. V. Neufeld, *The Earliest Christian Confessions* [Grand Rapids, 1963], p. 6). All such settings are noncontextual.

[51](a) This is especially true of those who see it as a Gnostic formula, in which an exaltation Christology allowed them to curse the earthly Jesus, but confess (the heavenly) Christ as Lord. See W. Schmithals, 124-30; Wilckens, 121 n. 1; N. Brox, "*ANATHEMA IĒSOUS* (1 Cor. 12:3)," *BZ* 12 (1968), 103-11. See the refutation in Pearson, 47-50; cf. Conzelmann, 205 n. 10, who calls this view "fantastic."

(b) Van Unnik, "Jesus," offers the intriguing, but finally less than convincing, suggestion that the term *anathema* is intended to be more positive, in the sense of Gal. 3:13, where Jesus is seen as becoming a "curse" for us in his death. For Paul, however,

ble, the two most common are: (a) That the real issue is a matter of "testing the spirits" because some Christians have actually been uttering this curse;[52] for Paul such an utterance means that these people "have become the mouth and instrument of demonic powers"[53] and he is here giving them the criterion by which to judge the authentic from the inauthentic. (b) That some who think of themselves as inspired of the Spirit are making such an utterance, either being carried away by the freedom of the Spirit[54] or else attempting to resist the onset of an ecstatic experience.[55] But the difficulties with these still remain: How could a *believer* under any circumstances say such a thing in the Christian assembly, and how is it that he or she would need such instruction? Morever, if this were actually happening in the Corinthian assembly, one is hard pressed to explain both how this introduces the rest of the argument and why Paul does not pursue such blasphemy with his usual vigor.

In the final analysis, therefore, it seems more likely that it is either hypothetical, perhaps serving as an analogy to their pagan past, whose point is its shock value, or else it is something that some of them had actually experienced in their pagan past. In either case, Paul's point in context is not to establish a means of "testing the spirits," but to remind them that "inspired utterance" as such is not evidence of being "led of the Spirit."

Paul's insistence that "no one can say, 'Jesus is Lord,' except by the Holy Spirit" has also troubled later readers, since it would seem possible for anyone to say these words at will. But that misses the radical nature of this confession for the earliest Christians. The use of "Lord" in such a context meant absolute allegiance to Jesus as one's deity and set believers apart from

---

this is inadequate because it emphasizes his death in such a way as to miss the significance of his resurrection.

(c) W. F. Albright and C. S. Mann, "Two Texts in I Corinthians," *NTS* 16 (1969/70), 271-76, suggest a textual emendation, in which the original text read *"Ana athe, emar maran Iēsous"* ("I am coming, said our Lord Jesus"), which was mistaken for *anathema Iēsous*.

(d) T. Holtz, "Das Kennzeichen des Geistes (1 Kor. xii. 1-3)," *NTS* 18 (1971/72), 365-76, suggests that the confession is less a matter of utterance than it is a matter of behavior. The one who "curses Jesus" does so by living a life that rejects Jesus as Lord.

(e) Here, too, I must place Bassler's suggestion ("1 Cor 12:3," pp. 417-18) that even though it is probably hypothetical, Paul "is drawing on his own personal biography to support his argument."

[52]For a typical presentation see Parry, 176.

[53]H. Aust and D. Müller, *NIDNTT* I, 414; cf. Martin, 9-10.

[54]Cf. Grosheide, 280-81; R. Scroggs, "The Exaltation of the Spirit by Some Early Christians," *JBL* 84 (1965), 359-73.

[55]Allo, 321-22; Barrett, 280.

both Jews, for whom such a confession was blasphemy,[56] and pagans, especially those in the cults, whose deities were called "lords."[57] Thus this became the earliest Christian confession,[58] tied in particular to Jesus' having been raised from the dead and therefore having become the exalted One.[59] Paul's point, of course, is that just as formerly they had been "led about and carried away" to mute idols, so now one who is possessed by the Spirit of the living God is led to the ultimate Christian confession: "Jesus (the crucified one) is (by his resurrection) Lord (of all the universe)." As in 2:10-13, only one who has the Spirit can truly make such a confession because only the Spirit can reveal its reality.

Because of its less than clear relationship to the rest of chaps. 12–14, especially for those whose chief interest in this section is in learning about spiritual gifts, this paragraph is generally passed over quickly. But if our interpretation is correct, then it continues to stand as a particularly important word for the church, in which many of these spiritual phenomena are recurring. The presence of the Spirit in power and gifts makes it easy for God's people to think of the power and gifts as the real evidence of the Spirit's presence. Not so for Paul. The ultimate criterion of the Spirit's activity is the exaltation of Jesus as Lord. Whatever takes away from that, even if they be legitimate expressions of the Spirit, begins to move away from Christ to a more pagan fascination with spiritual activity as an end in itself.

2. The Need for Diversity (12:4-31)

Paul began his argument with the Corinthians by placing the phenomenon of "inspired utterances" in the broader context of the Spirit's role in their confession of Jesus as Lord.[1] Now he proceeds to zero in on the specific problem in Corinth by emphasizing the need for a wide variety of manifestations of the one Spirit within the church. The argument is in three parts, each emphasizing the need and value of diversity within unity.

[56]Cf. Acts 7:54-60.

[57]See on 8:5-6. Eventually, of course, it would set them in opposition to the cult of the emperor as well, but that comes at a later time. But it came precisely because of the absolute nature of this confession for Christians.

[58]Cf. Rom. 10:9-10; Phil. 2:6-11; and Acts 2:36. See the discussions in Neufeld, *Confessions*, pp. 42-68, and W. Kramer, *Christ, Lord, Son of God* (ET, SBT 50; London, 1966), pp. 65-107.

[59]See especially the motif of humiliation-exaltation and the tie to the resurrection in the passages mentioned in the preceding note.

[1]Martin, 10-11, observes that v. 3 puts them in the orbit of the *gift* of the Spirit, whereby they confess Jesus as Lord and become one of his; now he will move on to talk about the *gifts* of the Spirit for the building up of the life of the community. The gift is one; the gifts are many.

Paul begins his discussion by putting the whole question in its ultimate theological context—diversity within unity belongs to the character of God himself (vv. 4-11). Although there is but one Spirit, one Lord, and one God, a great variety of gifts and ministries characterizes each of the divine Persons (vv. 4-6). Such diversity in God manifests itself, Paul argues further, by his distributing to the many of them different manifestations of the Spirit for the common good (v. 7). Several of these are then put forth as illustrations (vv. 8-11).

In vv. 12-26 Paul reinforces all this by means of a common political-philosophical analogy—the "body" politic now viewed as the "body" of Christ. He begins the analogy by highlighting the two essentials, unity and diversity (one body, with many parts; vv. 12, 14), and by focusing on their *common* experience of the Spirit in conversion as the key to unity (v. 13). But the essence of elaborations of the analogy (esp. vv. 15-20) is the need for diversity if there is to be a true body and not simply a monstrosity. By its very nature the analogy shifts focus momentarily from the gifts per se to the diversity of people who make up the community in vv. 21-26.

Finally, all of this is replayed once more by means of yet another list (given twice, though not precisely) that combines both gifts and persons (vv. 27-31a). The point of emphasis once again is that "not all" are the same, nor are all "gifted" in the same way.

Paul's point seems clear: Diversity, not uniformity, is essential for a healthy church. At the same time he urges that all of this is God's doing and part of his divine purposes, a point he repeats throughout (vv. 6, 7, 11, 18, 24, 28). The one God who is himself characterized by diversity within unity has decreed the same for his church. Very likely this emphatic theological framework is part of the corrective. Had their emphasis on spirituality, manifested by tongues, become an end in itself, so that they were focusing more on these things than on God himself? In any case, the opening paragraph (vv. 1-3) put the work of the Spirit into a proper christological perspective; this section puts it into a proper theological one. Everything, absolutely everything—gifts, persons, church—owes its origin to the one God who works all things in all of his people (v. 6).

a. Diversity in the Godhead and the gifts (12:4-11)

4 *There are different kinds of gifts, but the same Spirit.* 5 *There are different kinds of service, but the same Lord.* 6 *There are different kinds of working, but the same God*[2] *who works all of them in all* people.[3]

---

[2]B 1739 and the MajT add ἐστιν (at different places), a clearly secondary addition (cf. Zuntz, 187).

[3]NIV, "men," which is needlessly sexist—and not carried through in vv. 7-10, but repeated again in v. 11.

> 7 *Now to each one the manifestation of the Spirit is given for the common good.* 8 *To one there is given through the Spirit the message of wisdom, to another the message of knowledge by means of the same Spirit,* 9 *to another faith by the same Spirit, to another gifts of healing by that one⁴ Spirit,* 10 *to another miraculous powers,⁵ to another prophecy, to another distinguishing between⁶ spirits, to another speaking in different tongues,ᵃ and to still another the interpretation of tongues.ᵃ* 11 *All these are the work of one and the same Spirit, and he gives them to each person,⁷ just as he determines.*

ᵃOr *languages;* also in verse 28

Everything in this opening paragraph[8] revolves around the two ideas expressed in the opening sentence: "There are different kinds of gifts, but the same Spirit." This can best be seen by means of a structural display of the whole, given in a very literal translation (the emphasis on "diversity" is CAPITALIZED; the emphasis on "the same Spirit" *italicized*):

⁴ DIVERSITIES of gifts   there are, but *the same Spirit;*
⁵ DIVERSITIES of service there are, but *the same Lord;*
⁶ DIVERSITIES of workings there are, but *the same God,*
                    who works ALL THINGS IN ALL PEOPLE.

⁷ TO EACH is given the manifestation *of the Spirit*
                                 for the common good.

   for
⁸ TO ONE is given a message of wisdom,   *through the Spirit;*
  TO ANOTHER   a message of knowledge, *by the same Spirit;*
⁹ TO ANOTHER⁹   faith,   *by the same Spirit;*
  TO ANOTHER   gifts of healings,   *by the one Spirit;*

⁴The majority of witnesses (ℵ D F G 0201 Maj) conform this ἑνί to the preceding twice-repeated αὐτῷ (A B 33 81 104 630 1175 1739 1881 2464 pc lat); P⁴⁶ omits altogether. See Metzger, 563.

⁵One cannot tell what text the NIV here translates, since this would be the appropriate translation of the text of P⁴⁶ (ἐνεργήματα δυνάμεως, with the genitive being understood as descriptive; cf. the Western tradition, ἐνεργεία δυνάμεως = "miraculous power"). Zuntz, 100, also prefers the reading of P⁴⁶, arguing that the plural δυνάμεων has been conformed to the preceding ἰαμάτων. More likely P⁴⁶ and the Westerns reflect an attempt to "improve" a difficult plural that seemed tautologous.

⁶The original here (supported by P⁴⁶ A B Ψ Maj syʰ bo) is plural (διακρίσεις), not found in any known English translation. The English tradition reflects the move toward the singular found in ℵ C D F G P 0201 33 1175 pc latt syᵖ sa.

⁷NIV, "man."

⁸The NIV breaks the paragraph into subparagraphs—as part of its (commendable) attempt to be "international" (a readable translation for those for whom English is a second language). But in this case the two parts need to be seen together or too much is lost.

⁹This enumeration follows standard Hellenistic patterns (ᾧ μέν, followed by ἄλλῳ δέ, ἄλλῳ δέ), except for two idiosyncrasies: (1) The third and eighth items (faith and kinds of tongues) are enumerated by the synonym ἑτέρῳ. This stylistic variation is not

¹⁰ TO ANOTHER   workings of miracles;
   TO ANOTHER   prophecy;
   TO ANOTHER   discernments of spirits;
   TO ANOTHER¹⁰ kinds of tongues;
   TO ANOTHER   interpretation of tongues;

¹¹ ALL THESE THINGS works *the one and the same Spirit,*
         DISTRIBUTING to EACH ONE,
         even as he wills.

The emphasis and flow of the argument are easy to see. Diversity has its roots in God himself (vv. 4-6); he in turn by his Spirit has given diverse manifestations (gifts) to different people for the common good of the community (v. 7), which point is illustrated in vv. 8-10. V. 11 concludes by repeating, and thereby reinforcing, all the prior themes.

Since contemporary interest in these texts is often related to the list of "gifts" in vv. 8-10, some preliminary observations need to be made: First, Paul's argument is entirely *ad hoc,* reflecting the Corinthian situation itself;[11] therefore his own concern is not with instruction about "spiritual gifts" as such, their number and kinds. Indeed, the list of nine items in vv. 8-10 is neither carefully worked out nor exhaustive; it is merely *representative* of the diversity of the Spirit's manifestations.[12] Paul's concern here is to offer a *considerable* list so that they will stop being singular in their own emphasis.

---

unknown (cf. Matt. 16:14; Heb. 11:35-36), but in these cases it is a simple twofold enumeration, ἄλλος δέ . . . ἕτερος δέ. (2) Although there is some textual variation in each case, what is most likely Paul's original text also lacks the ordinary δέ in the two instances where he has ἕτερος. This may be simply variety for variety's sake; but it is also arguable that this most unusual expression of variety has some purpose to it. Very likely this is Paul's own clue—subtle though it might be and therefore not terribly significant— as to how the list is to be "grouped." See the commentary; cf. Findlay, 888-89; Conzelmann, 209. (For a different, but overly simplified, view of the textual question, see Zuntz, 106.)

[10]See the preceding note.

[11]Note especially that the list begins with language (λόγος, σοφία, γνῶσις) that reflects the opening thanksgiving (1:5-7), where he thanked God that they had been enriched in all λόγος and γνῶσις, lacking no χάρισμα. Speech, wisdom, and knowledge, of course, are part of the *problem* in this church (see on 1:17 and 8:1); it is hardly accidental that they now head Paul's list—in the same way that it is hardly accidental that tongues comes at the end!

[12]This is demonstrated in two ways: (1) The fact that Paul has six other lists in this argument (12:28, 29-30; 13:1-3, 8; 14:6, 26), each of which is also *ad hoc* (simply spun off at the moment for the purpose of the argument) and no two of which (even 12:28 and 29-30!) are exactly alike either in language, number, or character. (2) There is considerable flexibility in Paul's use of language on these matters, both here and in the rest of the NT. For example, (a) in v. 4 he speaks of the Spirit's χαρίσματα, which in v. 7 are called "manifestations," while χαρίσματα appears again in v. 9 (and vv. 28, 29) narrowly confined to "healings," only to reappear in v. 31 in reference to the broader categories;

All of this suggests not only that we do not have here a systematic discussion of "spiritual gifts," but also that there is some doubt as to whether the apostle himself had precise and identifiably different "gifts" in mind when he wrote these words. In any case, he would almost certainly not recognize some of the schematizing that later interpreters have brought to these texts.

4-6 These opening sentences seem intended to give the theological context within which all that follows is to be understood. Each begins with "different kinds of,"[13] making clear where Paul's emphasis lies; and each is followed by a noun that characterizes the activity of one Person of the Trinity.[14] The repetition of "same" with each divine Person seems to emphasize that the *one* Spirit/Lord/God manifests himself in a great variety of gifts and ministries. Thus the unity of God does not imply uniformity in gifts; rather, the one and the same God is responsible for the variety itself.

Given the flexibility of language noted above (see n. 12), one should probably not make too much of the different words used to describe the individual activities of the divine Persons:[15] "gifts,"[16] "ministries" or "ser-

---

(b) in v. 6 the activities of God are called ἐνεργήματα ("workings") which he ἐνεργεῖ ("works"), yet ἐνεργήματα occurs again in v. 10 as one of the Spirit's "manifestations," and in v. 11 the Spirit is said to ἐνεργεῖ all these things; (c) the "workings of miracles" is simply "miracles" in vv. 28-29; (d) one finds the λόγος of "knowledge" in v. 8, "knowing all mysteries and all knowledge" in 13:2, and simply "knowledge" in 13:8 and 14:6; (e) "prophecy" is a "manifestation" in v. 10; the prophets themselves are mentioned in vv. 28-29 (cf. 14:29 and 37); but it is not at all clear that "prophecy" is the private province only of some who are called "prophets" (cf. "teachers" and "teaching" in 12:28 and 14:6, 26); (f) in v. 5 the activities associated with the Lord are called διακονίαι, a word that appears again as a χάρισμα in Rom. 12:6-7, but in a context where the Spirit (though perhaps assumed on the basis of chap. 8) is not mentioned. It is fair to say at this point that far greater confidence is often expressed on some of these matters in both the scholarly and popular literature than the evidence itself warrants.

[13]Gk. διαιρέσεις. Because of the appearance of the cognate verb διαιρέω in v. 11, where it means "apportion" or "distribute," BAGD suggest the meaning "allotments" for these three occurrences of the noun; cf. Barrett, 283, and most commentators. But the meaning "difference" or "variety" is also well established; the context rules in favor of the latter here. Cf. Parry, 177, who would combine the ideas: "there are varieties of gifts assigned." Martin, 12-13, makes the intriguing suggestion that διαιρέσεις might be a wordplay on the αἱρέσεις of 11:19.

[14]I recognize that this language may be anachronistic for Paul, but as will be noted below, this kind of construction is part of the "stuff" out of which the later articulations and language arise. As Barth has rightly said, "Trinity is the Christian name for God."

[15]But see A. Bittlinger, 20-21, who sees χάρισμα as reflecting the source of the gifts (the divine χάρις), the διακονίαι as reflecting the way in which they become real in practice, and the ἐνεργήματα as indicating their results (definite effects); cf. Findlay, 887; and Dunn, *Jesus,* p. 411 n. 51.

[16]Gk. χαρίσματα (see on 1:7; cf. 7:7). This is a distinctly Pauline word (16 of 17 NT occurrences). See Dunn, *Jesus,* pp. 205-06. It does not mean "spiritual gift" as such;

vices,"[17] "workings."[18] Most likely they are simply three different ways of looking at what in v. 7 Paul calls "manifestations" of the Spirit.[19] This is supported by the fact that (1) both "gifts" and "workings" occur again in the list itself (associated with "healings" and "miracles" respectively) and that (2) both "God" and "the one and the same Spirit" are respectively the subjects of the same verb ("works") in vv. 6 and 11. In any case, the word *charisma* is probably too narrow to embrace the great variety of things mentioned in this argument. Apostles and prophets, for example, would better be described as "ministries," whereas "prophecy" itself is a *charisma*. But all such distinctions belong to our interests, not Paul's, for whom the emphasis is simply on their great variety and divine origin.

At the same time, however, the three nouns probably do reflect what for Paul would be a primary aspect of the three divine Persons. Thus, even though elsewhere the word *charisma* is not ordinarily associated with the Spirit,[20] the central concern of the present argument (chaps. 12–14) is with the Spirit and his "gifts." Hence it is appropriate that the argument begin with this association.[21] Likewise, the correlation of "kinds of service" (or "ministries") with "the same Lord"[22] is especially appropriate since this word group is used everywhere in the NT to describe the "servant" ministry of both Christ and his "ministers." The triad climaxes with the sentence about God the Father.[23] The noun used in his case is somewhat rare; but its cognate verb, which appears in the qualifying clause, usually carries the

---

indeed, it picks up that connotation in Rom. 1:11 by the addition of the adj. πνευματικόν. The emphasis in this word lies with the idea of something's being freely, graciously bestowed; such "gifts" are simply expressions of the divine favor. Thus in its broadest usage (as in Rom. 6:23) it refers to the "gift" of salvation; more narrowly (as in 1 Cor. 7:7) it refers to a "given" capacity or ability. In these chapters (at least in vv. 4 and 31), *contra* Grosheide, 283, it probably refers to the more concretely visible manifestations of the Spirit's activity, such as those listed in vv. 8-10.

[17]Gk. διακονία, the emphasis being on "service." Paul regularly calls his own ministry in the gospel a διακονία (e.g., 2 Cor. 3:7-9; 4:1) and himself and his coworkers διάκονοι of the gospel (see on 3:5). But so, too, is the collection for the poor saints in Jerusalem a διακονία to them (2 Cor. 8:4; 9:1, 12-13). See further 16:15 and 2 Tim. 4:11.

[18]Gk. ἐνεργήματα, found only here and in v. 10 in the NT. The emphasis seems to be on the "effects" produced by work, not simply on activity in and of itself (*contra* BAGD); cf. Findlay, 887.

[19]Cf. Bruce, 118: "*Gifts, service* and *working* are not distinct categories."

[20]Most often it is associated with God; see, e.g., 1 Cor. 1:5-7; 7:7; Rom. 6:23; 11:29; 2 Tim. 1:6. But see Rom. 1:11, where the adj. πνευματικόν modifies the noun χάρισμα.

[21]Thus it is quite irrelevant to suggest, as some do (e.g., Lietzmann, 61), that the sentences represent an ascending order of rank.

[22]As usual in Paul, the term κύριος refers to Christ.

[23]Although God is not called "Father" here, Paul regularly does so; see esp. 8:6 and the salutations ("God our Father and our Lord Jesus Christ"). Yet see 2 Cor. 13:13.

connotation of "effective" or "effectual" working. Something is accomplished by the effort put forth. Thus it is probably not so much individual "gifts" or "manifestations" that Paul has in mind with this noun, but the fact that *all things* done in the church are ultimately effected by the powerful working of God. This is further suggested by the final qualifying clause, "who works (or effects) all of them[24] (meaning the 'gifts' and 'ministries' as well) in all people[25]." With this final clause Paul redirects the focus from the statements about God to the diverse ways ("all of them") and the many different people ("in all people") God uses to minister in his church, which he will now spell out in detail in vv. 7-11.

In passing one must note the clear Trinitarian implications in this set of sentences, the earliest of such texts in the NT.[26] As Barrett notes, "The Trinitarian formula is the more impressive because it seems to be artless and unconscious" (p. 284). It is not in fact a Trinitarian construct as such; that is, Paul's interest is not in the unity of the *Persons* of the Godhead: the relationships are not spoken to at all, nor does he say that the Father, Son, and Spirit are one. Nonetheless, such passages as this are the "stuff" from which the later theological constructs are correctly derived. Paul's use of language is somewhat fluid. On the one hand, in these sentences, as elsewhere in this letter (e.g., 3:22-23; 11:3; 15:23-28), the unity of God dominates his thinking in such a way that the Son and Spirit are subsumed under that unity, and their own activities are seen as functionally subordinate (e.g., God gives gifts "through the Spirit," vv. 8-9). On the other hand, there can be little question that he thinks of Christ and the Spirit in terms of their full deity. For Christ see, for example, on 1:3 and 8:6, plus the title "Lord" in the immediately preceding verse. For the Spirit the interchange of subjects in vv. 7 and 11 is the strongest kind of evidence. The combination of texts like this one plus the full attributions of divine activities and attributes to the Son and Spirit become Paul's contribution to the later formulations.

7 Having grounded his appeal for diversity in the Triune God himself, Paul proceeds to articulate how that diversity is worked out in the life of the church. This sentence states his thesis, which is then illustrated by the representative examples in vv. 8-10 and concluded in v. 11 by a restatement of the concern of this sentence, but with a slightly different emphasis.

---

[24]Gk. τὰ πάντα; this combination in Paul generally means "the whole of everything," depending on the context. Sometimes it refers to the whole created order (as in 8:6; 15:27-28), but other times, as here, it refers in a more limited way to the subject at hand (cf., e.g., 2:15; 11:12; 12:19). Martin, 5, prefers to take it adverbially, "in every way."

[25]Gk. ἐν πᾶσιν, which could mean "in every case" (TCNT), but the context seems to require "in all people" in this instance.

[26]In Paul cf. 2 Cor. 13:13 and Eph. 4:4-6.

This thesis sentence is simply stated; Paul's emphasis is to be found in holding together its three leading ideas. First, "each one," standing in the emphatic first position as it does, is his way of stressing diversity; indeed, this is how that diversity will be emphasized throughout the rest of the paragraph.[27] He does not intend by this to stress that every last person in the community has his or her own gift.[28] That may or may not be true, depending on how broadly or narrowly one defines the word *charisma*. But that is simply not Paul's concern. This pronoun is the distributive (stressing the individualized instances) of the immediately preceding collective ("in all people"), which emphasizes the many who make up the community as a whole.

Second, what "each one" is given in this case is not a "gift," but a "manifestation of the Spirit." One should not make too much of this change of words, as if the following items would be wrongly called "gifts" because they are now called "manifestations."[29] Most likely the change reflects Paul's own emphasis throughout these chapters, which is on the Spirit himself, not on the "gifts" as such. Thus each "gift" is a "manifestation," a disclosure of the *Spirit's* activity in their midst.[30] These first two items together, therefore, are Paul's way of repeating the theme of diversity from vv. 4-6. His urgency, as vv. 8-10 make clear, is not that each person is "gifted," but that the Spirit is manifested in a great variety of ways. His way of saying that is, "to each one is given the manifestation of the Spirit."

Third, probably to give a proper balance to "each one," he concludes with the reason for this great diversity: "for the common good."[31] By so doing he anticipates the concern of chaps. 13 and 14, that the gifts are for the building up of the community as a whole, not primarily for the benefit of the individual believer.[32]

---

[27]It is spelled out in particular in the unusual ninefold repetition in vv. 8-10 of "to one, to another," etc.

[28]When Paul wants to make that point he usually says εἷς ἕκαστος ("every single one"). Cf. n. 50 on 11:21. Grosheide, 284, makes the opposite error: "Paul's words *'to each one is given'* must mean: to everyone who has special gifts of the Spirit is given." Hardly.

[29]Especially so since in 1:5 he has already designated as *charismata* two words found on the following list, "speech" *(logos)* and "knowledge" *(gnōsis)*.

[30]This is so whether the genitive is subjective or objective. In favor of an objective genitive is the verb δίδοται, which has "God" as its implied subject. Thus God gives to each, i.e., to the community at large, different gifts by which the Spirit is visibly evident in their midst. In favor of a subjective genitive is v. 11, where the Spirit himself is the one who distributes to each as he wills. The former seems the more likely since the concern is not with the gifts, but with the manifestation of the Spirit through the gifts. Cf. Dunn, *Jesus*, p. 212: "It is difficult to exclude either sense."

[31]Gk. πρὸς τὸ συμφέρον; cf. 6:12; 7:35; 10:23, 33.

[32]This is not to say that the building up of the individual believer is no concern of

8-10 To illustrate[33] the thesis of v. 7 Paul proceeds to offer a sizable list of ways in which the Spirit is manifested in the Christian assembly. Because this is the first of several such listings of "gifts" in the Pauline corpus,[34] considerable interest has been generated over this passage in terms of the nature and meaning of the various gifts themselves.[35] But as noted above,[36] that lies outside Paul's own interest, which is simply to illustrate the *diversity* of the Spirit's activities/manifestations in the church.[37]

Attempts to classify the several items are numerous and varied.[38] Some have suggested that they reflect a descending order of value,[39] while others have rearranged the items conceptually.[40] A popular grouping is (1) gifts of instruction (wisdom and knowledge); (2) gifts of supernatural power (faith, healings, miracles); and (3) gifts of inspired utterance (prophecy,

---

his. To the contrary (see on 14:4). But the concern throughout this entire argument is on the effect of gifts in building up the community.

[33]Note especially the γάρ; cf. BAGD 1d, "the general is confirmed by the specific."

[34]Besides the others in these chapters (cf. n. 12 above), see Rom. 12:4-8 (apparently a later reflection on some items from this chapter) and Eph. 4:11.

[35]As one might expect, the popular literature on this passage is immense, especially among Pentecostal and charismatic groups. Two items from this material are worth noting. The first is by the prominent British Pentecostal, Donald Gee, *Concerning Spiritual Gifts* (Springfield, MO, n.d. [in an appendix dated Nov. 4, 1947, the author indicates that the present printed edition had appeared ten years earlier]). Although untrained in the "school" sense, Gee showed remarkable exegetical skills; this book is worthwhile both for its own insights and for understanding traditional Pentecostalism. The second is by George Mallone *et al.*, *Those Controversial Gifts* (Downers Grove, 1983), a collection of seven essays by four pastors within the more traditional evangelical framework who have experienced in their churches the renewal of some of the more visible gifts in this list.

[36]See the introduction to this paragraph, pp. 585-86.

[37]Paul is capable of simply listing gifts; but he does not do so here. In each case there is the prior "to one," "to another," etc. That is part of his emphasis.

[38]One wonders, e.g., what motivated our present verse divisions, which were created in the sixteenth century in the Greek text. Although there are a large number of unfortunate choices, by and large they make enough sense of things that one cannot believe they were done willy-nilly. In this case the clue lies in the first instance in the similarity in content of the first two (hence v. 8); the second break was probably motivated by the presence of the phrase "by the same Spirit," which the second two share with the first two (hence v. 9). What remained was a list of five gifts with no qualifier (thus v. 10).

[39]E.g., Bruce, 119.

[40]E.g., J. W. MacGorman, *The Gifts of the Spirit: An Exposition of I Corinthians 12-14* (Nashville, 1974), p. 35, who arranges them in categories of (1) intelligible utterance (wisdom, knowledge, prophecy); (2) power (faith, healings, miracles); (3) spiritual discernment; and (4) ecstatic utterance (tongues, interpretation). Cf. the "traditional Pentecostal" view expressed by W. R. Jones, "The Nine Gifts of the Holy Spirit," in *Pentecostal Doctrine* (ed. P. S. Brewster, 1976), pp. 47-61, who has the divisions: (1) illumination (wisdom, knowledge, discernment); (2) action (faith, miracles, healings); (3) communication (prophecy, tongues, interpretation).

discerning prophecies, tongues, interpretation of tongues).[41] The seventh item (discernment of spirits) is the one that tends to give trouble to most of these arrangements. If grouping is legitimate at all, it is most likely to be found in some clues Paul himself has given, by starting the third and eighth items (faith and tongues) with a different word for "another."[42] If so, then the first two are chosen for very specific *ad hoc* purposes; "wisdom" and "knowledge" held high court in Corinth. He then adds a random list of five items that have as their common denominator a supernatural endowment of some kind, and concludes with the "problem child" and its companion, tongues and interpretation.

What distinguishes this listing is the concretely visible nature of these items, especially of the last seven. These, after all, are not only "gifts"; they are above all *manifestations* of the Spirit's presence in their midst,[43] most likely chosen because they are, like tongues itself, extraordinary phenomena. It would scarcely do for Paul at this point to attempt to broaden their perspective by listing less visible items. That will come in time (especially through the analogy of the body and in the lists in vv. 28-30); but for now the emphasis is on the supernatural. Indeed, the truly remarkable feature of this list is the attribution to "each one" of a whole gamut of supernatural activities—in the same matter-of-fact way that contemporary churchmen would list positions on an organizational chart![44] How, then, are the individual items to be understood?

(1) *The message (logos) of wisdom (sophia).* This language clearly harks back to the problem addressed in 1:17–2:16, where in the name of wisdom the Corinthians were rejecting both Paul and his gospel. Indeed, in contrast to their own criterion for "spiritual" excellence, Paul says he deliberately rejected coming to them either in "wisdom characterized by word (rhetoric)" (1:17) or "with excellence of word or wisdom" (2:1, 5). With a considerable stroke of inspiration Paul now does two things: (a) He uses one of their own terms[45] to begin his list of "manifestations" in the assembly that demonstrate the great diversity inherent in the one Spirit's activities; and (b)

---

[41]E.g., Baird, *Church,* p. 149; Martin, 12.

[42]See n. 9 above.

[43]Note that the emphasis on "the same/one Spirit" carries through the first four items; Paul surely intends that it should carry through to the end.

[44]One is reminded of the words of J. B. Phillips, penned in the introduction to his translation of the Book of Acts (*The Young Church in Action* [New York, 1949], p. vii): "Yet we cannot help feeling disturbed as well as moved, for this surely is the Church as it was meant to be. . . . If they were uncomplicated and naive by modern standards, we have ruefully to admit that they were open on the God-ward side in a way that is almost unknown today."

[45]The probability that both σοφία and γνῶσις were Corinthian terms taken over by Paul only increases our difficulty in determining the specific nature of these two gifts in Paul's own thinking. Cf. the discussion in Dunn, *Jesus,* pp. 217-21.

he reshapes that term in light of the work of the Spirit so as to give it a significantly different content from their own.[46]

The phrase means either "a message/utterance full of wisdom" or "an utterance characterized by wisdom."[47] In either case its content is probably to be understood in light of Paul's own argument in 2:6-16. There the "message of wisdom," revealed by the Spirit, is not some special understanding of the "deeper things" or "mysteries" of God.[48] Rather, it is the recognition that the message of Christ crucified is God's true wisdom,[49] a recognition that comes only to those who *have* received the Spirit. For only the Spirit, Paul says, whom we have received, understands the mind of God and reveals what he accomplished in Christ (2:10-13). Thus in the present case the "utterance of wisdom" comes "through the Spirit," and in Corinth it is almost certainly to be found among those who give spiritual utterances that proclaim Christ crucified in this highly "wisdom"-conscious community. It is of some interest, therefore, that this particular "gift" does not appear again in any further list or discussion.

(2) *The message (logos) of knowledge (gnōsis).*[50] As with the first item, this is first of all Paul's way of rescuing this gift of the Spirit[51] from their own fascination with "knowledge" and its concomitant pride (see on 8:1-3, 7). In this case, however, Paul's own understanding of the gift as a "manifestation" of the Spirit is more difficult to determine, since "knowledge" as gift recurs in the ensuing discussion in three significant texts (13:2, 8-12 and 14:6), which also display some ambiguities. Some have suggested that Paul here has in mind a supernatural endowment of knowledge, factual

[46]As Martin, 13, says of these first two items: "He now rescues both terms from the Corinthian pneumatics and gives them a fresh stamp."

[47]The interpretation in LB, "the ability to give wise advice," has nothing to do either with the context in Corinth or with the Greek word σοφία.

[48]In Pentecostal and charismatic circles this "gift" is often understood to be that special word of insight given by the Spirit when the community is going through a time of difficulty or decision. See, e.g., Bittlinger, 28, who thus defines this gift: "In a difficult or dangerous situation a word of wisdom may be given which resolves the difficulty or silences the opponent." One need not doubt that the Holy Spirit speaks so to today's church, but it is unlikely that Paul had this in mind by this "gift." If he were to "label" such a phenomenon, it would probably be ἀποκάλυψις ("revelation"); cf. 14:6. The same is true of the so-called word of knowledge that has become such a frequent occurrence in these communities.

[49]Cf. Gee, *Gifts*, pp. 20-26, who affirms that this is the primary meaning for Paul, although he goes on to add the possibility mentioned in the preceding note on the basis of Jesus' word to his disciples in Luke 21:15.

[50]See on 1:5, where these two words individually are singled out as illustrations of the Corinthians' giftedness.

[51]Conzelmann, 209, distinguishes between διὰ τοῦ πνεύματος and κατὰ τὸ αὐτὸ πνεῦμα as the Spirit's being both the source and the norm; but he also allows that the distinction cannot be taken strictly. BAGD give evidence that κατά means "by way of."

information that could not otherwise have been known without the Spirit's aid,[52] such as frequently occurs in the prophetic tradition and is assumed to be true in the pagan prophetic oracles. But since here it is a descriptive genitive with the word *logos,* others see it as referring to something more akin to inspired teaching,[53] perhaps related to receiving Christian insight into the meaning of Scripture.[54]

Since this word has also been taken over from the Corinthians and is so closely tied to the preceding "utterance of wisdom," the two should probably be understood as parallel in some way. Most likely, therefore, it is a "spiritual utterance" of some revelatory kind.[55] This is suggested by its place between "revelation" and "prophecy" in 14:6 and by the fact that, along with prophecy and tongues, it will cease at the Eschaton (13:8). How the content of such an utterance makes it *gnōsis* as distinguished from "wisdom" or "revelation" is perhaps forever lost to us.[56]

(3) *Faith.*[57] With this word Paul moves on to include several more clearly supernatural manifestations of the Spirit.[58] While it is true that Paul considers the "faith" that leads to salvation to be the work of the Spirit in the believer's life,[59] what he has in mind here is the special gift of supernatural faith that can "move mountains," mentioned again in 13:2. It probably refers to a supernatural conviction that God will reveal his power or mercy in a special way in a specific instance.[60] Although it is listed separately, as given "to another," there is a sense in which this and the following two items belong together—and indeed would at times seem not quite possible to

[52]Peter's "knowledge" of Ananias and Sapphira's misdeed in Acts 5:1-11 is often looked upon as this gift in action. That may well be (although "revelation" would be as fitting a label); but Luke himself does not so indicate. In fact, the word "know" or "knowledge" does not occur in the narrative.

[53]Somewhat surprisingly, this is the position argued for at some length by Gee, *Gifts,* pp. 27-34 and 110-19, who insists that the list does not require this gift to be a supernatural manifestation.

[54]Cf. Bittlinger, 30, who says it "consists of the old message spoken in the new situation in such a way that it still remains the old message." This may be so, but it lacks an exegetical basis.

[55]Cf. Dunn, *Jesus,* p. 218, who suggests that the "utterance" in 8:4, "an idol is nothing in the world," may be a Corinthian "*logos* of knowledge."

[56]In any case, as Dunn (*Jesus,* p. 221) has rightly argued, "for Paul wisdom and knowledge as such are not thought of as charismata; only the actual utterance that reveals wisdom or knowledge to others is a charisma."

[57]On the question of the relationship of this gift to "the measure of faith" in Rom. 12:3, see Dunn, *Jesus,* pp. 211-12.

[58]The difference between αὐτῷ and ἑνί in the two prepositional phrases in this verse is purely rhetorical; cf. v. 11, where the two are joined.

[59]Cf. also Gal. 5:22, where "faith" (= faithfulness) is listed as a "fruit" of the Spirit; cf. 1 Tim. 4:12 and 6:11.

[60]Both Gee, *Gifts,* p. 36, and Bittlinger, pp. 32-33, suggest the story of Elijah at Carmel (1 Kings 18) as an OT example of such a gift in operation.

differentiate. Faith that "moved a mountain" could also rightly be called the working of a miracle.

(4) *Gifts of healings*.[61] What this refers to needs little comment. Jesus, Paul, and the rest of the early church lived in regular expectation that God would heal people's physical bodies. This expectation was based in part on the OT promises that in the messianic age God would "heal" his people.[62] According to Acts, such healings accompanied Paul's own ministry; and Paul himself probably referred to them in "the signs of an apostle" in 2 Cor. 12:12.[63] Only among the intellectuals and in a "scientific age" is it thought to be too hard for God to heal the sick.[64]

What is of interest here is the language "gifts of healings," which recurs in the two lists in vv. 28 and 30. Probably this language reflects two things: (a) The use of *charisma* itself suggests that the "manifestation" is given not to the person who is healed, but to the person God uses for the healing of another;[65] (b) the plural *charismata* probably suggests not a permanent "gift," as it were, but that each occurrence is a "gift" in its own right.[66] So also with the plurals in the next item.

(5) *Miraculous powers* (lit. "workings[67] of miracles"[68]). Although Paul would probably include gifts of healings under "workings of miracles," this manifestation most likely covers all other kinds of supernatural activities beyond the healing of the sick. The word translated "miracles" is the ordinary one for "power," and as was pointed out in 2:4-5 it is especially associated in Jewish antiquity with the Spirit of God. The present context suggests that it covers a broad range of supernatural events that ordinary

[61]Gk. χαρίσματα ἰαμάτων; both are plural, as are "workings of miracles," "discernments of spirits," and "kinds of tongues."

[62]Cf., e.g., Matthew's use in 8:17 of Isa. 53:4 to refer to Jesus' ministry of healing the sick. The Isaiah passage itself is ambiguous; it is clearly a metaphor for salvation, but in the prophetic tradition such salvation also included the healing of the people's wounds incurred in their judgment. Thus in the NT this passage is understood both as a metaphor for salvation (1 Pet. 2:24) and as a promise of physical healing (Matt. 8:17).

[63]Cf. 1 Thess. 1:5; Rom. 15:19.

[64]Although this is also unfortunately true of many contemporary Christians, whose theology has made a severe disjunction between the "then" and "now" of God's working. This seems to be a seriously flawed understanding of the kingdom, which according to the NT was inaugurated by Christ in the power of the Spirit, who continues the work of the kingdom until the consummation.

[65]Otherwise Dunn, *Jesus*, p. 211.

[66]Cf. the similar suggestion by Bittlinger, 37: "Every healing is a special gift. In this way the spiritually gifted individual stands always in new dependence upon the divine Giver."

[67]Gk. ἐνεργήματα; see on v. 6.

[68]Gk. δύναμις; see on 2:4-5. Cf. 2 Cor. 12:12, where Paul claims the "signs of an apostle" were "effected" (κατειργάσθη) among them in the form of "signs (σημεῖα), wonders (τέρατα), and miracles (δυνάμεις)."

parlance would call miraculous.[69] In the duplicated list of vv. 28-30, the word appears by itself in the plural.

(6) *Prophecy*.[70] With this word Paul returns to verbal manifestations. In light of the running contrast in chap. 14 between this gift and tongues, he is probably also consciously moving toward the conclusion of this list with its mention of tongues. Also because of that running contrast, we have a fairly good idea as to how Paul himself understood this phenomenon. Several things need to be noted: First, although prophecy was an especially widespread phenomenon in the religions of antiquity,[71] Paul's understanding—as well as that of the other NT writers—was thoroughly conditioned by his own history in Judaism. The prophet was a person who spoke to God's people under the inspiration of the Spirit. The "inspired utterance" came by revelation and announced judgment (usually) or salvation. Although the prophets often performed symbolic acts, which they then interpreted, the mainstream of prophetic activity, at least as it came to be canonized, had very little to do with "ecstasy," especially "frenzy" or "mania."[72] For the most part the prophets were understood only too well! Often the word spoken had a futuristic element, so in that sense they also came to be seen as "predicters"; but that was only one element, and not necessarily the crucial one.

Second, with the outpouring of the Spirit at the end of the age, the early Christians understood the prophecy of Joel 2:28-30 to have been fulfilled, so that "prophecy" not only became a renewed phenomenon but was also potentially available to all, since all now possessed the Spirit in fullness (cf. Acts 2:17-18). This seems especially to fit what we learn in the Pauline letters. It seems to have been a widespread phenomenon (cf. 1 Thess. 5:19-22; Rom. 12:6); the evidence in chap. 14 indicates that it consisted of spontaneous, Spirit-inspired, intelligible messages, orally delivered in the gathered assembly, intended for the edification or encouragement of the people.[73] And those who prophesied were clearly understood to be "in control" (see 14:29-33). Although some people are called "proph-

---

[69]Weiss, 301, and Héring, 126, see it as referring especially to exorcisms. It would certainly include but not be limited to these. See Dunn, *Jesus*, p. 210.

[70]Because of the more universal nature of this gift in antiquity, it has received considerable attention among scholars. The more significant studies for understanding this phenomenon in Paul are H. Krämer, R. Rendtorff, R. Meyer, and G. Friedrich, *TDNT* VI, 781-861; D. Hill, *New Testament Prophecy* (Atlanta, 1979); Grudem, *Gift;* and Aune, *Prophecy*. Aune includes a considerable review of both the *TDNT* article and Hill.

[71]See Aune, *Prophecy*, pp. 23-88.

[72]However one is to understand the "ecstasy" of Saul and the others in 1 Sam. 19:19-24, e.g., it scarcely belongs to the canonical understanding, and the latter is what influenced Christ and the early Christians.

[73]Thus it is *not* the delivery of a previously prepared sermon.

ets," probably because they were frequent speakers of "prophecies,"[74] the implication of chap. 14 is that it is a gift available—at least potentially—to all.[75]

(7) *Distinguishing between spirits* (lit. "discernments of spirits"). This is language over which scholars have engaged in considerable debate, but with little agreement. The question is, To what does it refer? To the phenomenon associated with "testing the spirits, to see whether they be of God" (1 John 4:1), meaning the ability to discern what is truly of the Spirit of God and what comes from other spirits?[76] Or to the phenomenon noted in 14:29, "and let the others weigh carefully (i.e., discern or judge rightly) what is said," in which the cognate verb of this noun appears?[77]

Most likely, given Paul's own use of language in chap. 14, it refers to both, but particularly to the phenomenon of "discerning, differentiating, or properly judging" prophecies in 14:29.[78] There are several reasons for taking this position: (a) Both 1 Thess. 5:20-21 and 1 Cor. 14:29, the two places where Paul mentions the functioning of prophecy in the church, call for a "testing" or "discerning" of prophetic utterances; it therefore seems likely, given that the noun used in this passage is the cognate of the verb in 14:29, that the same is true here, since it immediately follows "prophecy." (b) That seems all the more likely in this case since these two are followed immediately by "tongues" and "interpretation." This same pattern of tongues plus interpretation and prophecy plus discernment is found again in the instructions on order in 14:26-29. (c) The real difficulty lies with the word "spirits." The probable key to understanding lies not in 1 John 4:1,[79] but with Paul's own usage in 14:12, 14, and especially 32, where he tends to use the term in a much more flexible way than most of us are comfortable

---

[74]Although this may also have become a term for some who emerged as "charismatic leaders" within the communities; cf., e.g., Acts 13:1 and Eph. 2:20.

[75]See on 14:1-5, 23-24, 29-31. This does not mean that all do (cf. 12:29), but that it is not limited strictly to "prophets," as is so often suggested in the literature.

[76]E.g., as Paul does in Acts 16:16-18. This position is taken, *inter alia,* by Bittlinger, 45; Grudem, 58-60 and 263-88; and most Pentecostal interpreters.

[77]See, e.g., Findlay, 888-89; Moffatt, 182; Holladay, 161; Hill, *Prophecy,* p. 133; and Martin, 14. A unique view is offered by G. Dautzenberg, "Zum religionsgeschichtlichen Hintergrund der διακρίσεις πνευμάτων (I Kor. 12.10)," *BZ* 15 (1971), 93-104 (cf. his *Urchristliche Prophetie* [Stuttgart, 1975], pp. 122-48), who argues that it means "interpreting the utterances of the prophets." Grudem, 263-88, has thoroughly refuted Dautzenberg, but he is less than convincing in arguing as well that the term does not have to do with "discerning" prophecies.

[78]Similarly Barrett, 286; Dunn, *Jesus,* p. 233.

[79]Where among those who have "charisms" (2:27) they are told to "test the spirits to see whether they are of God." But one must not make the prior assumption that what is going on in 1 John is a well-known phenomenon by which this present passage is to be understood. Very likely that passage is to be understood in light of these chapters in Paul.

with. The Spirit who speaks through the prophets is understood to be speaking through "the spirit" of the prophet; when Paul is praying in the Spirit, he speaks of "my spirit" praying (cf. on 5:3-4). The Corinthian zeal for "spirits" in 14:12, therefore, is zeal for manifestations of the Spirit (especially tongues) as he quickens their spirits to pray.

Thus in this present listing, it seems most likely that Paul is referring to the same phenomenon as in 14:29, but is using the language of "spirits" to refer to the prophetic utterances that need to be "differentiated" by the others in the community who also have the Spirit and can so discern what is truly of the Spirit.

(8) *Different kinds of tongues*. This is obviously the "controversial gift," both then and now.[80] If our interpretation of chap. 14 is correct,[81] then the Corinthians' singular preference for this manifestation is what lies behind this entire argument. Thus, after listing several equally visible and extraordinary manifestations of the Spirit, Paul includes their favorite as well,[82] along with its companion, "interpretation." As with prophecy,

---

[80]The literature here is immense, especially since the outbreak of this phenomenon in the traditional churches in the late 1950s. Before 1960 there were basically two studies in the scholarly journals devoted solely to tongues: C. Clemens, "The 'Speaking with Tongues' of the Early Christians," *ExpT* 10 (1898/99), 344-52; and I. J. Martin, "Glossolalia in the Apostolic Church," *JBL* 63 (1944), 123-30. See also the monograph by G. B. Cutten, *Speaking with Tongues* (New Haven, 1927).

Since 1960 nearly every major journal has had at least one article. The following is a highly selective representation of these (Eng. titles only, in chronological order): R. H. Fuller, "Tongues in the New Testament," *ACQ* 3 (1963), 162-68; F. W. Beare, "Speaking with Tongues," *JBL* 83 (1964), 229-46; W. G. MacDonald, "Glossolalia in the New Testament," *BETS* 7 (1964), 59-68; S. D. Currie, "'Speaking in Tongues.' Early Evidence Outside the New Testament Bearing on 'Glossais Lalein,'" *Int* 19 (1965), 174-94; Banks-Moon, "Tongues"; R. H. Gundry, "'Ecstatic Utterance' (N.E.B.)?" *JTS* 17 (1966), 299-307; Harpur, "Tongues"; E. L. Kendall, "Speaking with Tongues," *CQR* 168 (1967), 11-19; Sweet, "Sign"; J. M. Ford, "Toward a Theology of 'Speaking in Tongues,'" *TS* 32 (1971), 3-29; B. L. Smith, "Tongues in the New Testament," *Churchman* 87 (1973), 183-88; S. Tugwell, "The Gift of Tongues in the New Testament," *ExpT* 84 (1973), 137-40; R. A. Harrisville, "Speaking in Tongues— Proof of Transcendence?" *Dialog* 13 (1974), 11-18; D. M. Smith, "Glossolalia and Other Spiritual Gifts in a New Testament Perspective," *Int* 28 (1974), 307-20; E. Best, "The Interpretation of Tongues," *SJT* 28 (1975), 45-62; R. A. Harrisville, "Speaking in Tongues: A Lexicographical Study," *CBQ* 38 (1976), 35-48; V. S. Poythress, "The Nature of Corinthian Glossolalia: Possible Options," *WTJ* 40 (1977), 130-35; T. L. Wilkinson, "Tongues and Prophecy in Acts and 1st Corinthians," *VoxR* 31 (1978), 1-20. See also the unpublished dissertation by N. I. J. Engelsen, "Glossolalia and Other Forms of Inspired Speech According to 1 Corinthians 12-14" (Yale, 1970).

For further bibliography, including a helpful bibliographical essay, see W. E. Mills, *Glossolalia: A Bibliography* (New York, 1985).

[81]See the introduction to chaps. 12–14 (pp. 571-74).

[82]But it is purely prejudicial to say, as Conzelmann, e.g., "Paul indicates his criticism by the very order of the enumeration" (209).

enough is said in chaps. 13–14 to give us a fairly good idea as to how Paul understood it. The following seem certain: (a) It is Spirit-inspired utterance; that is made explicit both in vv. 7 and 11 and in 14:2. (b) The regulations for its use in 14:27-28 make it clear that the speaker is not in "ecstasy" or "out of control."[83] Quite the opposite; the speakers must speak in turn, and they must remain silent if there is no one to interpret. (c) It is speech essentially unintelligible both to the speaker (14:14) and to other hearers (14:16).[84] (d) It is speech directed basically toward God (14:2, 14-15, 28);[85] one may assume, therefore, that what is "interpreted" is not speech directed toward others, but the "mysteries" spoken to God.

What is less certain is whether Paul also understood the phenomenon to be an actual language. In favor of such a view are (a) the term itself, (b) the need for "interpretation," and (c) the evidence from Acts 2:5-11.[86] In the final analysis, however, this question seems irrelevant. Paul's whole argument is predicated on its unintelligibility to both speaker and hearer; he certainly does not envisage someone's being present who would be able to understand it because it was also an earthly language. Moreover, his use of earthly languages as an *analogy* in 14:10-12 implies that it is not a known earthly language, since a thing is not usually identical with that to which it is analogous. Most likely, therefore, the key to Paul's—and their—understanding lies in the term "the language of angels" in 13:1 (q.v.).[87] On its usefulness or lack thereof to the community and the individual, see on 14:1-5 and 13-19.

(9) *The interpretation of tongues.* This is the obvious companion to "tongues," precisely because of the unintelligibility of the latter. Although this term could mean something close to "translation," it can also mean "to put into words";[88] in this context it probably means to articulate for the benefit of the community what the tongues-speaker has said. The evidence

---

[83]*Contra* Callan, "Prophecy," and many others. Callan tries to distinguish between prophecy and tongues in terms of prophecy's being nonecstatic and tongues's being "accompanied by trance" (p. 137). But he is guilty of a loose use of the idea of trance and seems to miss the point of the evidence in 14:27-28.

[84]Bruce, 119, taking his clue from Acts 2, suggests that this includes languages "intelligible to some hearers." But nothing in 1 Cor. 12–14 suggests that Paul thought of it in these terms.

[85]Cf. Bittlinger, 48-51, who discusses this gift under the heading "praying in the Spirit."

[86]See esp. Gundry, "Utterance," who is followed by Ford, "Theology"; cf. also Wilkinson, "Tongues." Dunn, *Jesus,* p. 244, concludes: "It is evident then that Paul thinks of glossolalia as language. But can we go on from that to conclude that he equates glossolalia with 'human language foreign to the speaker' (Gundry)? I think not"; cf. Richardson, "Order," p. 148.

[87]Cf. Barrett, 299-300; Conzelmann, 209; Dunn, *Jesus,* p. 244.

[88]See especially the discussion by Thiselton, "Interpretation," pp. 15-36.

from 14:5, 13, and 27-28 indicates (a) that this, too, is a "Spirit-inspired" gift of utterance, and (b) that it may be given either to the tongues-speaker or to another.

11 After the considerable list of manifestations illustrating the thesis of v. 7, Paul closes this section of the argument by summing up what has been said thus far. The language "one and the same Spirit" echoes both vv. 4-6 and 8-9, again emphasizing that the diversity is the product of the one God, who by his Spirit "works" (the same verb that was used with "God" in v. 6) "all these," referring to the preceding list of manifestations.[89] The participial phrase "distributing[90] to each person"[91] picks up the noun translated "different kinds of" in vv. 4-6, emphasizing here both the variety and the active work of the Spirit in apportioning out to the many these manifestations. Only the final clause is new: "just as he determines[92]," which in this context might best be translated, "just as he sees fit (or pleases)." The emphasis is less on the Spirit's deliberation in action as on his sovereignty in distributing the gifts, or perhaps in manifesting himself. Thus the gifts, even though they are "given" to "each person," are ultimately expressions of the Spirit's own sovereign action in the life of the believer and the community as a whole.[93] This is the Pauline version of "the wind/Spirit blows where it/he wills" (John 3:8).

Thus, from beginning to end the single emphasis of the paragraph is the great diversity of gifts that the one God distributes/manifests through his one Spirit for the sake of the community. The reason for such emphasis is not immediately clear from what is said here, but before Paul finishes, the Corinthians should have no doubt about Paul's concern, and the *corrective* nature of this present argument.

Apart from the traditional Pentecostal movement, the church at large showed very little interest in this paragraph until the outbreak of some of these phenomena both in Roman Catholic and in traditional Protestant circles in the late 1950s. The result has been a considerable body of literature, both scholarly and popular, on the gifts enumerated in vv. 8-10. Most of this literature assumes that such gifts are available to Christians in all ages of the church. Although some have taken a dim view of the phenomena, most have been moderately cautious, suggesting openness to what the Spirit might do,

---

[89]R-P, 268, note that the πάντα is very emphatic.

[90]The NIV's "gives them" lacks the precision that the English verbs "distributes" and "apportions" carry with them.

[91]Gk. ἰδίᾳ ἑκάστῳ; the addition of ἰδίᾳ emphasizes the individual nature of the Spirit's dealings with each; cf. Barrett, "individually to each one"; Conzelmann, "to each in particular."

[92]Gk. βούλεται; by the *koinē* period it was roughly synonymous with θέλω.

[93]Cf. Conzelmann, 209, "This denies the pneumatic any power of his own."

but usually offering correctives or guidelines as well. However, there has also been a spate of literature whose singular urgency has been to justify the limiting of these gifts to the first-century church. It is fair to say of this literature that its authors have found what they were looking for and have thereby continued to reject such manifestations in the church. It can also be fairly said that such rejection is not exegetically based, but results in every case from a prior hermeneutical and theological commitment.[94]

Perhaps the greater tragedy for the church is that it should have lost such touch with the Spirit of God in its ongoing life that it should settle for what is only ordinary and thus feel the urgency to justify itself in this way. The hope, of course, lies with v. 11, that the one and the same Spirit will do as he pleases, despite the boxes provided for him by those on both sides of this issue.

b. The body—diversity in unity (12:12-14)

12 *The body is a unit, yet[1] it is made up of many parts; and though all its[2] parts are many, they form one body. So it is with Christ.* 13 *For indeed[3] we were all baptized by[a] one Spirit into one body— whether Jews or Greeks, slave or free—and we were all given one Spirit[4] to drink.* 14 For indeed[5] *the body is not made up of one part but of many.*

[a]Or *with;* or *in*

In order to press the point made in the previous paragraph, the need for diversity within unity, Paul adopts a common analogy from antiquity and

---

[94]This is true even of a book like R. Gaffin's *Perspectives on Pentecost* (Phillipsburg, NJ, 1979). Gaffin's exegetical skills are obvious, but he has nonetheless set up the questions and gone after the results in terms of his prior questions quite apart from Paul's own interests.

[1]NIV, "though"; the Gk. καί has some degree of flexibility, but it can scarcely mean "though," which in this case yields a nonsensical tautology ("even though composed of many parts, the body is one; even though composed of many parts, the body is one").

[2]The Greek text reads τοῦ σώματος, to which the MajT (also D b Ambrosiaster) adds τοῦ ἑνός (= all the parts of the *one* body).

[3]The NIV omits the intensive καί that goes with the γάρ. This would be acceptable here were it not for the parallel in v. 14. The NIV totally disregards the latter by translating "now," which it cannot possibly mean.

[4]A few late MSS (630 1881 2495 pc sy[h]) read πῶμα for πνεῦμα, thus making this a reference to the Lord's Supper: "We were all given one drink to drink."

[5]See n. 3. In failing to see this καὶ γάρ as parallel to v. 13 and the two verses as alternately elaborating on the two points of v. 12, the NIV has made v. 14 the beginning of the next subparagraph. In some ways that would be acceptable, since the first application of the analogy does indeed reinforce the point of v. 14. However, that isolates vv. 12-13 to make a different point, which is to miss the argument by too much.

applies it to the Corinthian situation. In so doing, as often happens with such rich metaphors, he also makes further points about attitudes that need correcting in Corinth. Since good analogies by their very nature are open to independent application, and since this one is so well known in the church, one must be especially careful to read the text with Paul's concerns in view.

The argument is in three parts (vv. 12-14, 15-20, 21-26).[6] This first paragraph sets forth the basic presupposition of the imagery (the body is one) and its urgency (but has many members). This is followed by a twofold elaboration of the metaphor, the first part emphasizing diversity, the second unity. Paul's primary concern with this imagery is not that the body is one *even though* it has many members,[7] thus arguing for their need for unity despite their diversity. Rather, his concern is expressed in v. 14, that *even though the body is one*, it does not consist of one member but of many, thus arguing for their need for diversity, since they are in fact one body.[8] The structure of the argument in vv. 12-14 bears this out. The opening sentence somewhat redundantly strikes both notes with equal force:

For just as	the body is one,	A
yet[9]	has many members,	B
and	all the members, though many,	B'
	are one body,	A'
So also is	Christ.	

Thus the first clause (AB) strikes the note of diversity; the second (B'A') the note of unity.

The two following sentences (vv. 13 and 14) both begin with the identical, but unusual, "for indeed,"[10] suggesting that in turn they will elaborate (or explain) what has just been said. Thus v. 13 takes up the presuppositional statement (the body is one) and explains *how* the many of them became one body: They were all immersed in and made to drink the same reality—the Spirit. V. 14 then picks up the second theme, but rephrases it so as to emphasize the real urgency of the analogy: The one body is not one member but many.

12 The "for" with which this sentence begins indicates that what

---

[6]Not vv. 12-13, 14-20, 21-26 as in the NIV and NA[26].

[7]See n. 1 above.

[8]Cf. Conzelmann, 212, commenting on v. 14: "Now the accent again lies (as in vv. 4-11) upon the notion of differentiation." This stands over against both the NIV and a large number of interpreters, who, despite the structure and all the signals to the contrary, see the passage as emphasizing unity. See most recently, C. H. Talbert, "Paul's Understanding of the Holy Spirit: The Evidence of 1 Corinthians 12-14," *PRS* 11 (1984), 98-99.

[9]Gk. καί; see n. 1 above.

[10]Gk. καὶ γάρ; see on 5:7.

follows is intended to offer further explanation of the point made in vv. 4-11. The explanation returns to the imagery of the church as the "body of Christ," first used in 10:17 and picked up again in 11:29.[11] The imagery itself was common in the ancient world,[12] and was therefore probably well known to the Corinthians. It suits Paul's present concern perfectly.[13]

In its first instance (10:17) Paul's point was that the many are one body, a point made on the basis of the many of them eating of the one loaf at the Lord's Table. That note is struck again here, but now as the presupposition; this is not what Paul will argue *for,* but argue *from.*[14] As noted above, in this passage the emphasis shifts to the many who make up the one body. Nonetheless, in this opening sentence both points are made: The body is one, yet the body has many members.[15] In saying that it is one, his concern is for its essential unity. But that does not mean uniformity. That was the Corinthian error, to think that uniformity was a value, or that it represented true spirituality. Paul's concern is for their unity; but there is no such thing as true unity without diversity. Hence the need to strike that note so strongly.

[11]On the possible "sources" or "origin" of this term in Paul, see Best, *Body*, pp. 83-95. The very commonness of the imagery makes much of that discussion irrelevant. Less likely still is the suggestion that the "source" was the temple of Asclepius with its many clay replicas of "dismembered" parts of the body. See A. E. Hill, "The Temple of Asclepius: An Alternative Source for Paul's Body Theology?" *JBL* 99 (1980), 437-39; and G. G. Garnier, "The Temple of Asklepius at Corinth and Paul's Theology," *Buried History* 18 (1982), 52-58.

[12]It should be noted that in none of the other known usages is the same point made as in Paul. Thus the fable of Menenius Agrippa (*ca.* 494 B.C.), recorded in Livy, *Hist.* 2.32 (the parts are upset with the stomach and choose not to feed it, resulting in their common emaciation), stresses the *interdependence* of the many on one another (in his case the need for the plebs not to be seditious). Jos., *War* 4.406, uses the analogy in a negative way to describe the spread of sedition; his usage is comparable to 12:26 ("if one part suffers, all parts suffer together"), but his concern is radically different from Paul's. So also with the Stoic philosophers, whose concern is that any one part is ultimately subservient to the whole, which is the greater. Cf. Marc.Aur.Ant. 2.1; 7.13; Epict. 2.10.3-4; Seneca, *Ep.* 95.52, whose language comes the closest to Paul's: "All that you behold, that which comprises both god and man, is one—we are the parts of one great body." He is also concerned that the parts are mutually interdependent.

[13]Much of the theological discussion of the metaphor, as to whether Paul is concerned with some "mystical" truth of the church as a living organism, is quite irrelevant. For Paul it is metaphor pure and simple, whose point is not the nature of the church per se but the need for it to experience its proper diversity in unity. This, of course, stands over against the vast majority of Roman Catholic interpreters. For an assessment and challenge of that view, see Best, *Body,* pp. 98-101, and B. Daines, "Paul's Use of the Analogy of the Body of Christ—With Special Reference to 1 Corinthians 12," *EvQ* 50 (1978), 71-78.

[14]Best, *Body,* p. 96 n. 1, faults Robinson, *Body,* pp. 59-60, for making this same point; but in this instance Best's reading of the full context of chaps. 12–14 seems especially unsatisfactory. His interest in the topic "body of Christ" seems to have gotten in the way of reading the text in light of chap. 14.

[15]Gk. μέλος; see on 6:15.

In saying "So it is with Christ," Paul is probably using metonymy. Thus "Christ" means the church as a shortened form for the "body of Christ." Clear evidence for this is found in v. 27: "Now you are the body of Christ, and each one of you is a part of it," followed by v. 28, "And in the church God has appointed. . . ."[16]

13 This verse and the next pick up the two parts of v. 12 by way of explanation/elaboration. The present sentence further explains the presupposition "the body is one." In keeping with the preceding argument, as well as with the section as a whole, the explanation is given in terms of the Spirit. But one suspects that this is not simply an *ad hoc* theological construct, but rather is inserted precisely because it reflects the heart of Pauline theology.[17] What makes the Corinthians one is their common experience of the Spirit, the very Spirit responsible for and manifested in the great diversity just argued for in vv. 4-11. For Paul the reception of the Spirit is the *sine qua non* of Christian life. The Spirit is what essentially distinguishes the believer from the nonbeliever (2:10-14); the Spirit is what especially marks the beginning of Christian life (Gal. 3:2-3); the Spirit above all is what makes a person a child of God (Rom. 8:14-17). Thus it is natural for him to refer to their unity in the body in terms of the Spirit. Indeed, despite the considerable literature on this text suggesting otherwise, Paul's present concern is not to delineate how an individual becomes a believer, but to explain how they, though many, are one body.[18] The answer: The Spirit, whom all alike have received.

To make that point Paul refers to their common reception of the Spirit at the beginning of their Christian experience by means of parallel sentences:

"We[19] all were baptized in the one Spirit,"
  and
"We   all were caused to drink one Spirit."

The first clause is further qualified by the prepositional phrase "unto/into[20]

---

[16]For a discussion of the church as the body of Christ, see Best, *Body*, pp. 83-159; and E. Schweizer, *TDNT* VII, 1067-80.

[17]Cf. Dunn, *Jesus*, pp. 199-202. So also E. Käsemann, "The Theological Problem Presented by the Motif of the Body of Christ," in *Perspectives on Paul* (ET, London, 1971), p. 104, who, however, sees the "heart" to be the sacramental aspect rather than the Spirit.

[18]Missing this point is what mars Beasley-Murray's—and others'—discussion of this text (*Baptism*, pp. 167-71).

[19]For this use of "we" in the middle of an argument where Paul begins to identify with the Corinthians, especially in their common experience of life in Christ, see on 2:7; 5:7-8; 6:3; 8:8; 10:16; 11:31.

[20]Gk. εἰς, which can either be local, indicating that into which all were baptized, or denote the goal of the action, indicating the purpose or goal of the baptismal action (= "so as to become one body").

one body," which in turn is modified by the parenthetical addition "whether Jews or Greeks, slave or free."

But there is considerable difference of opinion as to what experience(s) this language refers to. Because of the verb "baptize," it is often assumed[21] that Paul is referring to the sacrament of water baptism,[22] and it is then often argued further that this text supports the close tie of the reception of the Spirit with baptism itself.[23] But that assumes more than is actually said. While it is true that early on this verb became the technical term for the Christian initiatory rite, one may not thereby assume that *Paul* intended its technical sense here. In fact he does not use "baptized" absolutely, which by itself would imply "with water," but specifically says, "baptized in the Spirit."[24] Moreover, it is *not* baptism but the *one* Spirit, repeated in both clauses, that in Paul's present argument is the basis for unity (cf. vv. 4-11). In any case, one is hard pressed to find an equation between baptism and the reception of the Spirit in Paul's letters.[25] Both are assumed to be at the beginning of Christian experience, to be sure, but the two are not specifically tied together in such a way that the Spirit is received at baptism. This text supports such a view *only* on the unsupported grounds that Paul himself makes that assumption.

But the greater difficulty for this view lies with the second clause, "and we were all given one Spirit to drink." Some have argued that this clause points to a *second* experience of some kind,[26] but the lack of such usage elsewhere in Christian literature militates against it. Rather, as indicated above, this is most likely a piece of semitic parallelism, where both

---

[21]This is the stance of most commentaries, which for the most part do not even raise the question.

[22]See the argument for this position in Beasley-Murray, *Baptism*, pp. 167-71, whose "considerations" that seem to "demand" this view are less than convincing. In Paul's argument it is not *baptism* that makes them one, but the *one Spirit*.

[23]Even Beasley-Murray backs off here: "There is nothing automatic about this association of baptism and the Spirit" (*Baptism*, p. 170).

[24]For the Corinthians, of course, the point of reference for the metaphor would be their own baptism (immersion) in water. But that is not the same thing as suggesting either that Paul intended the rite here or that they would have thought him to be referring to it.

[25]See the assertion by R. Schnackenburg, *Baptism in the Thought of St. Paul* (ET, New York, 1964), p. 83: "That baptism and the reception of the Spirit are associated is not to be doubted, according to I Cor. vi.11; xii.13." But that is precisely what is to be doubted in both cases (see the commentary on 6:11). The argument thus becomes circular.

[26]Some (including Calvin, Luther, Käsemann, Conzelmann; for a more complete list see Schnackenburg, *Baptism*, p. 84) have suggested the Lord's Supper, which has nothing in its favor except the verb "to drink." Nowhere is such a metaphor used for the Table; there is not a hint that anyone in the early church ever thought of drinking the cup as imbibing the Spirit; the tense of the verb is aorist, indicating that a single action is in view. A traditional Pentecostal view sees the two clauses as referring to conversion and Spirit-baptism (see, e.g., R. E. Cottle, "All Were Baptized," *JETS* 17 [1974], 75-80, defending a view put forth by R. Riggs, *The Spirit Himself* [Springfield, MO, 1949]). The

clauses make essentially the same point.[27] It is the clearly *metaphorical* sense[28] of this parallel clause[29] that argues most strongly for a metaphorical, rather than literal, meaning for "baptism" in the first clause.[30]

If so, then to what do the two clauses refer? For what Christian experience do they serve as metaphors? Some have argued for "Spirit-baptism," by which they mean a separate and distinguishable experience from conversion.[31] But this has against it both Pauline usage (he does not elsewhere use this term, nor clearly point to such a second experience[32]) and the emphasis in this context, which is not on a special experience in the Spirit beyond conversion, but on their *common* reception of the Spirit.

Most likely, therefore, Paul is referring to their common experience of conversion, and he does so in terms of its most crucial ingredient, the receiving of the Spirit. Such expressive metaphors (immersion in the Spirit and drinking to the fill of the Spirit), it needs to be added, do imply a much greater experiential and visibly manifest reception of the Spirit than many have tended to experience in subsequent church history (see on 2:4-5).

If this is the correct understanding of these two clauses, and the full context seems to demand such, then the prepositional phrase "in the Spirit" is most likely locative,[33] expressing the "element" in which they have all

---

traditional Roman Catholic view is that it refers to confirmation (see Schnackenburg, p. 84; cf. J. Hanimann, " 'Nous avons été abreuvés d'un seul Esprit.' Note sur 1 Co 12, 13b," *NouvRT* 94 [1972], 400-05). These views reflect vested interests that lie beyond the concern of Paul's argument.

[27]This is a common device in Paul; cf., e.g., vv. 15-16, 17, 21, 22-23 below.

[28]Cf. the usage in the Gospel of John, where "water" is used as a symbol for the Spirit (4:10, 14; 7:37-39). An attractive option that has been gaining adherents suggests that the metaphor reflects the idea of "watering" (cf. 3:6-7), referring especially to OT motifs of the "pouring out" of the eschatological Spirit on the land, as in Isa. 29:10. Thus, "we were all saturated with the one Spirit." See the considerable argument in its favor by Schnackenburg, *Baptism,* pp. 84-86, and Dunn, *Baptism,* pp. 130-31; cf. Wendland, 97; Beasley-Murray, *Baptism,* p. 170; Cottle, "All," p. 79; G. J. Cuming, "ἐποτίσθησαν (I Corinthians 12.13)," *NTS* 27 (1981), 283-85; Martin, 24. The most crippling blow to this position is the accusative ἓν πνεῦμα; the LXX of Isa. 29:10 has the dative, which one would certainly expect here had Paul intended πνεῦμα to be instrumental. See further E. R. Rogers, "ἐποτίσθησαν Again," *NTS* 29 (1983), 139-42.

[29]There is, after all, no experience called "drinking the Spirit"!

[30]Among others who adopt this view, see Wendland, 97; Dunn, *Baptism,* pp. 127-31; Talbert, "Understanding," pp. 98-99.

[31]Most recently H. Hunter, *Spirit-Baptism, A Pentecostal Alternative* (Lanham, MD, 1983), pp. 39-42.

[32]Which does not mean that he did not know of such. *Pace* Hunter (*Spirit-Baptism,* pp. 30-63) whose texts are all exegeted on the prior assumption that such *may* be the case, there is no clear statement in Paul that speaks to such a question.

[33]It is possible, as the NIV, to see it as instrumental, especially in light of v. 9; cf., e.g., Moffatt, 186; O. Cullmann, *Baptism in the New Testament* (ET, London, 1950), p. 30. But usage elsewhere in the NT suggests otherwise.

been immersed, just as the Spirit is that which they have all been given to drink. Such usage is also in keeping with the rest of the NT. Nowhere else does this dative with "baptize" imply agency (i.e., that the Spirit does the baptizing),[34] but it always refers to the element "in which" one is baptized.[35]

In this sentence the *goal* of their common "immersion" in the one Spirit is "into/unto one body." The precise nuance of this preposition is not certain. It is often given a *local* sense, suggesting that all are baptized "into" the same reality, namely the body of Christ, the implication being that there is a prior entity called the body of Christ, of which one becomes part by being immersed in the Spirit.[36] But with verbs of motion like "baptize" this preposition most often has the sense of "movement toward so as to be in."[37] In the present case the idea of "goal" seems more prominent. That is, the purpose of our common experience of the Spirit is that we be formed into one body. Hence, "we all were immersed in the one[38] Spirit, so as to become one body." This phrase, of course, expresses the reason for this sentence in the first place. How did the many of them all become one body? By their common, lavish experience of the Spirit.

To emphasize that the many ("we all") have become one through the Spirit, Paul adds parenthetically, "whether Jews or Greeks, slave or free." As in 7:17-24, these terms express the two basic distinctions that separated people in that culture—race/religion and social status.[39] In Christ these old distinctions have been obliterated, not in the sense that one is no longer Jew or Greek, etc., but in the sense of their having *significance*. And, of course, having significance is what gives them value as distinctives. So in effect their common life in the Spirit had eliminated the significance of the old distinctions, hence they had become one body.

[34]The usage in 6:11 that is often suggested is not parallel. See the commentary.

[35]This is always true of "water" (Matt. 3:11; Mark 1:8; Luke 3:16; John 1:26, 31, 33; Acts 1:5; 11:16; cf. Matt. 3:6; John 3:23;); it is likewise true in the other instances of "Spirit-baptism," which are always set in contrast to water baptism (Matt. 3:11; Mark 1:8; Luke 3:16; John 1:33; Acts 1:5; 11:16); cf. Paul's usage in 10:2. See Dunn, *Baptism*, pp. 127-28.

[36]See, e.g., Schnackenburg, *Baptism*, p. 26. One need not doubt the general truth of such a statement. The question is whether Paul intended it here since his question is not "How do people become believers?" but "How do the many believers become one body?"

[37]Dunn, *Baptism*, p. 128.

[38]Note the repetition of this qualifier from vv. 4-11 (esp. vv. 9 and 11). The basis of their unity is still the unity of God himself, expressed here in terms of the "one Spirit."

[39]In 7:17-24 the same four groups are mentioned in the same order. Cf. Gal. 3:28, where Paul adds the final separation between people, "male and female." For a different expression of this kind of list, see Col. 3:11.

14 With another "for indeed"[40] Paul proceeds to elaborate the second motif of v. 12, that even though they are one body, made so by their common experience of the Spirit (v. 13), the body itself, though one, is not one "part" but "many." Though picking up that theme from v. 12, this is not simply reiteration. In v. 12 it is stated matter-of-factly: "The *body* is *one;* the *one body* has *many* members." Here Paul mixes the two themes with a negative contrast: "The *one body* is *not* one member; *rather,* it is composed of *many* constituent parts." This negative way of reiterating v. 12 is surely the point of the whole; otherwise why say it at all, especially in this sentence which intends to elaborate v. 12?

From here Paul proceeds to develop the imagery of the "body" (referring always to the church) in two slightly different directions (vv. 15-20, 21-26), which will apply both parts of the figure (one body, many members) to their situation; but the primary concern, as this verse indicates, is with the "many parts."

It is easy to understand how in the later church the emphasis of this text shifted from Paul's concern over diversity to the concern over unity. It should be noted, of course, that our later concern really is there, especially in v. 13. What is disconcerting, however, is that what for Paul is the basis of unity, namely their common life in the Spirit, has in later times become the point of so much tension. Two things perhaps need to be emphasized: (1) If the work of the Spirit appears to be the cause of disunity among some, it is certainly not the Spirit's fault. Our common fallenness unfortunately often causes both pride and suspicion or distrust to prevail when it comes to the work of the Spirit. (2) Nonetheless, unity is the result of our common life in the Spirit, not of our human machinations. Is it our lack of the Spirit that has forced us to attempt unity on other grounds? Paul saw the Spirit as the key to everything in the Christian life. It seems mandatory that such prevail again if there is to be effective Christianity in our day. But let the one who says that not force his/her own brand of "spiritual unity" on the church as simply another human machination. Our desperate need is for a sovereign work of the Spirit to do among us what all our "programmed unity" cannot.

c. A twofold application of the metaphor (12:15-26)

15 *If the foot should say, "Because I am not a hand, I do not belong to the body," it would not for that reason cease to be part of the body.* 16 *And if the ear should say, "Because I am not an eye, I do not belong to the body," it would not for that reason cease to be part*

---

[40]See n. 5 above.

of the body. 17 *If the whole body were an eye, where would the sense of hearing be? If the whole body were an ear, where would the sense of smell be?* 18 *But in fact[1] God has arranged the parts in the body, every one of them, just as he wanted them to be.* 19 *If they were all one part, where would the body be?* 20 *As it is, there are many parts, but one body.*

21 *The eye cannot say to the hand, "I don't need you!" And the head cannot say to the feet, "I don't need you!"* 22 *On the contrary, those parts of the body that seem to be weaker are indispensable,* 23 *and the parts that we think are less honorable we treat with special honor. And the parts that are unpresentable are treated with special modesty,* 24 *while our presentable parts need no special treatment. But God has combined the members of the body and has given greater honor to the parts that lacked[2] it,* 25 *so that there should be no division[3] in the body, but that its parts should have equal concern for each other.* 26 *If one part suffers, every part suffers with it; if one part is honored, every part rejoices with it.*

By further extending the imagery of the body, these two paragraphs illustrate the two concerns of vv. 12-14, diversity in unity. The first takes up the point of v. 14, but concludes by once more stressing unity (v. 20), which point is then taken up in the second illustration. These elaborations, it should be noted, become analogies in their own right, and are capable of independent application (as often happens to them). However, even though in Paul's hands analogies are often less than precise—the analogy seems to make one point while Paul's own application makes another[4]—nonetheless we must go with Paul, not with the imagery as such.

Part of the key to understanding these analogies lies in their structure. In each case Paul begins with a personification of some of the parts of the body, in which they are disallowed to say things either about themselves (vv. 15-16) or about others (v. 21) because what is said is absurd in terms of the body. The absurdity is pressed in the first instance with rhetorical questions (v. 17) and in the second with observations about how certain parts of the body are treated (vv. 22-24a). Paul then "applies" these pictures to the

---

[1]Gk. νυνί (logical "now"), read by P46 ℵ C Ψ Maj; A B D* F G 2496 read the temporal νῦν, probably an assimilation to v. 20.

[2]Both the passive (ὑστερουμένῳ; ℵ* A B C 048 6 33 630 1739 1881 pc) and active (ὑστεροῦντι; P46 D F G Ψ Maj) can mean "to be in need"; but only the active can have the further meaning "to be inferior." Zuntz, 128, favors the latter; but he seems to miss Paul's concern here.

[3]Some MSS (ℵ D* F G L 323 2464 pm a) anticipate the application to the church and make this singular plural.

[4]Cf. the imagery of the "great house" in 2 Tim. 2:20-21, where the same kind of problem exists. Cf. Fee, *1 Timothy*, pp. 210-12.

body itself (vv. 18-20, 24b-26), thus keeping the imagery alive. But in each case one recognizes that they are also intended now to be applied to the situation in Corinth, that *they* are the "body" being spoken about. The ultimate exegetical concern is to determine how the Corinthians were expected to hear and apply these pictures, and thus to see the place of this imagery in the total argument.

Thus in the first picture Paul makes his point not in the imagery itself, that is, in what the foot and ear say to the hand and eye, but in the set of rhetorical questions that follow in vv. 17 and 19: that all members are necessary if there is to be a body and not a monstrosity. Vv. 18 and 20 respond to the rhetoric by indicating the true nature of the body as it was divinely ordained: one body with many parts. Thus Paul intends this first elaboration of the analogy to illustrate the point of v. 14, "the body is not *one* member [= the whole body is not to assemble and only speak in tongues], but *many* [= the other gifts mentioned in vv. 8-10]." The language of v. 18 in particular indicates that the "application" to their situation harks back to vv. 7-11 and the insistence on diversity with regard to *gifts and manifestations of the Spirit,* not to kinds of *persons* within the Corinthian community.

In the second instance, however, the apostle picks up and drives home a point *not* made previously in *this* argument, but somewhat intrinsic to the metaphor. Probably this slight digression, which many interpreters see as the point of everything,[5] is a direct reflection of the divided situation in Corinth—especially so if Theissen is correct that much of the tension in the community is the result of social status.[6] Paul begins this argument (v. 21) with three of the members from vv. 15-16, but now with clear implications of alleged superiority. His point here is found in the imagery itself: the apparently superior cannot say to the apparently inferior, "We can get along without you." This is demonstrated by the further elaborations in vv. 22-24a, which emphasize the strictly *apparent* nature of such "hierarchy." He argues that the apparently weaker, the internal organs, are the more necessary, and that the apparently less seemly, the sexual organs, are accorded the higher honor (of clothing being implied). In vv. 24b-26, still keeping the metaphor intact, he seems clearly to be pursuing the problem of their internal divisions. In this case, therefore, the conclusion drawn is less the need for diversity than the need for unity and mutual concern, with a decided emphasis on God's own care for the one who lacks. This in effect moves the analogy from gifts to people, a concern that will spill over into the next listings in vv. 27-31.

---

[5]Most recently, Martin, 19-21.
[6]See *Social Setting,* pp. 69-119.

15-16 Paul begins his elaboration of the analogy by personifying some parts of the body, in this case the extremities of the two limbs (foot/ hand) and two of the sensory organs (ear/eye). In both cases these parts carry on comparable functions in the body; there is no hint that one is superior to the other. In two virtually identical sentences he disallows that some parts can deny their own place in the body.[7] Thus: "If the foot/ear should say, 'Because I am not a hand/eye, I do not belong to the body,' it would not for that reason[8] cease[9] to be part of the body." That is obviously absurd.

The question, of course, is the intent of this picture. As noted above, this becomes an analogy in its own right and thereby can have independent force. For example, there can be little question that the disquieting desire on the part of many to be something in the body other than what they are is a plague on our house. But what the analogy does not suggest is that some envy what they are not because they feel *inferior*.[10] It is precisely this kind of application, based on the metaphor alone, that seems to do injustice to Paul's own concern, which will be made by the following rhetorical questions (vv. 17 and 19) and the affirmation in v. 18.

17 With a set of parallel rhetorical questions, Paul begins to apply the analogy, but does so by keeping the analogy itself alive. Taking up the two members of v. 16 (eye/ear), he asks: "If the whole body were an eye, where would the sense of hearing be?" Then, keeping to the sensory organs, he adds: "If the whole body were an ear,[11] where would the sense of smell be?" This interchange of the sense organs makes it clear that Paul's point is

---

[7]The sentences are almost certainly statements (as NIV; cf. UBS[3], RSV, NASB, NEB), not interrogatives (as KJV; cf. NA[26]). What makes this certain is the fact that they are present general conditions, which do not lend themselves to being interrogatives without some internal clues.

[8]Gk. παρὰ τοῦτο, expressing cause. The τοῦτο points to the fact of their saying it, not to their position in the body. Cf., e.g., Godet, 213, who suggests that the reason is its "inferior" status in the body. There is no hint here of inferiority/superiority.

[9]This is an excellent translation. In the Greek there are two negatives, one before παρὰ τοῦτο and one before the verb ἐστιν. But this is not a case of double negative; the former negates παρὰ τοῦτο only (= "not by asserting this"), the latter negates the rest of the sentence.

[10]E.g., Grosheide, 294, "They failed to appreciate the unity of the body. . . . In both cases the inferior member seems to suppose that the superior member certainly must belong to the body"; cf. Godet, 215, and many others. Neither in the analogy itself nor in Paul's own application (vv. 17-20) is there a hint that one of these is superior to the other. That comes in the second application (and then he allows that it is only *apparent*), but it is totally lacking here, where the parts are of the same kind in each case (limbs, sensory organs).

[11]The Greek repeats the ἀκοή (sense of hearing) from the preceding sentence. But the words for the sense perceptions in Greek are often used for the organ itself. See BAGD.

not the "inferiority" of one to the other. The point is the *need* for all members; otherwise some function of the body would be missing.

18   In this and the following verses Paul makes his own application of vv. 15-16, but he does so still in terms of the imagery of the body. This first sentence brings the analogy itself to a conclusion with its opening words "but in fact,"[12] implying that Paul is responding to his own rhetorical questions put forward in v. 17. The sentence also reminds the reader that Paul is still carrying on the argument that began in v. 4, since it repeats so much of the language and ideas from v. 11.

The diversity in the body, Paul says, is by God's own design. "God has arranged[13] the parts in the body, every one of them, just as he wanted them to be." That could sound like an argument for the orderly arrangement of the body; but not so. The emphasis is on the fact that each member is there by divine placement. In the Corinthian context, this probably refers back to vv. 7-11, where the Spirit gives these various manifestations to "each person, just as he pleases." As in that opening paragraph, and as he will do again in vv. 24 and 27, Paul emphasizes that the diversity, the "many parts of the one body," is God's design.

19   This rhetorical question functions in relationship to v. 18 in the same way as those of v. 17 do to vv. 15-16. The form is identical to v. 17, except that his point is spelled out in plain Greek, so that there can be no missing it. There he asked, still within the boundaries of the analogy of vv. 15-16, "If the whole body were an eye, where would the hearing be?" That suggests that if all were one part, other functions would be lacking. Now Paul presses his concern even further, especially in light of their singular enthusiasm over tongues: "If all the parts were of one kind, there would be no body at all, only a monstrosity!" The concern for diversity can scarcely be missed.

20   With another logical "but now,"[14] Paul brings this first application of the analogy to its conclusion by repeating the themes of vv. 12 and 14. Since he has been stressing the "many parts," he begins with that motif; but since diversity is not an end in itself, but is to function within their essential unity, he concludes with that reminder. Thus, "there are many parts, but one body."

---

[12]Gk. νυνὶ δέ. The δέ is adversative, indicating a response to the rhetorical questions of v. 17; the νυνί is "logical," not temporal, "but now as the situation is" (BAGD). Ct. n. 1 above.

[13]Gk. ἔθετο (cf. v. 27). In Hellenistic Greek this verb does not differ basically in meaning from the active (BAGD); thus it lacks the classical force of "appoint" and here (as in v. 27) means something close to "set" or "arranged."

[14]Only in this case it is the simple νῦν δέ; see n. 1 above.

21 With this verse Paul returns to the personification of the parts of the body, but now to make a considerably different point. The thought probably flows out of the final statement in v. 20, the repetition of the theme of "one body," although the emphasis on the need for diversity is certainly not lost. The parts of the body personified include three from vv. 15-16 (eye/hand, feet), but in a new mix that has one of the sensory organs (the eye) speaking to one of the external limbs (the hand), while the ear has been replaced by the "head," which speaks to the feet. Both the direction and content of what is said imply a view "from above," where those who consider themselves at the top of the "hierarchy" of persons in the community suggest that they can get along without some others, who do not have their allegedly superior rank. That this is the thrust of the present analogy is made certain by the rest of the paragraph. At the same time, of course, in its own way this new analogy continues the theme of the need for variety. Indeed, in v. 22 the absolute necessity of parts that others would scorn is specifically asserted.

It is common to see in this analogy a reference to those who speak in tongues as considering themselves superior to those in the community who do not. If so, then this is the only hint of such in the entire argument. Nothing in chap. 14 itself suggests as much. That guess, therefore, as common as it is, is probably considerably off the mark in terms of Paul's own concerns. Since the implication of the analogy as Paul proceeds with it is that some *people* consider themselves superior to others, not that some *gifts* are superior,[15] it seems more likely that one is to find the historical situation here addressed in a broader context within the church. But that context is not the problem of chaps. 1–4 since no hierarchy of persons is implied in those divisions and disputations. The most obvious setting, therefore, is that which immediately preceded this one, 11:17-34, where exactly this kind of problem is in view. In that passage the "haves" are abusing the "have-nots" at the Lord's Table and thereby despising the church itself. This suggestion seems all the more probable in light of (1) Paul's own use of "body" imagery in 11:29 to call into question their abuse of others in the church, and (2) the inclusion of "whether slave or free" in the affirmation in v. 13 about their common experience of Spirit as what makes them one body. The stench, it should be noted, is not simply in their pride. One can sometimes tolerate that in the "aristocracy." Rather, it is both in their self-sufficiency

---

[15]Moreover, nothing inherent in a person's having one gift of the Spirit would necessarily lead to his/her thinking that he/she could get along without other members of the community. They might have pride, but that does not mean eliminating the others, as the analogy in this verse specifically indicates. Indeed, the "superior proud" need the inferior around in order that their pride may have meaning for them. But not so with regard to social status. The "haves" can get along very nicely without the "have-nots" as their equals in the same community.

and in their demeaning of others to the point of saying, "I have no need of you."

22 With a considerable change of metaphors, but still using "bodily parts," Paul proceeds to pursue the point of v. 21, that some people of allegedly superior rank think they can get along without some others in the community. "On the contrary,"[16] says Paul, "those parts of the body that seem to be weaker are the more indispensable[17]." In terms of the analogy Paul almost certainly has in mind the internal organs, which are full of "weakness," but are indispensable to there being any bodily functions at all. Crucial to this argument is the fact that they only "seem" to be weaker. There is a sense, of course, in which that is true; they are weak and thus protected internally. Paul's point seems to be that such apparent weakness has no relationship to their real value and necessity to the body. One must be careful at this point not to allegorize and try to find people who are like this.[18] This is not allegory but analogy. Appearances deceive, Paul is saying. If one removed an organ because it appeared weak, the body would cease to be whole. So with the church. All the parts are necessary, no matter what one may think.

23-24a In typical fashion, while on this theme Paul adds a parallel metaphor, with which he appears to be making a point similar to that of v. 22. Both of these points together are then intended to respond to the absurdity expressed in v. 21. He mentions some parts of the body as appearing "less honorable" and "shameful,"[19] saying of the former that we bestow on them the "greater honor," and of the latter that they have "greater decorum." It is nearly impossible to transfer Paul's play on words into good English. Literally he says:

And what parts of the body we esteem less honorable (*atimotera*),
  on these greater honor (*timēn*) we bestow;
And our shameful parts (*aschēmona*)
  greater decorum (*euschēmosynē*) have;
But our decorous parts (*ta euschēmona*) do not have need.

Paul is undoubtedly referring to the sexual organs, on which we bestow greater honor, and which therefore have greater decorum, because we cover

---

[16]Gk. ἀλλά, the strong adversative.

[17]Gk. πολλῷ μᾶλλον . . . ἀναγκαῖα (lit. "by how much more . . . are necessary").

[18]Cf. Best, *Body*, p. 103, who, after suggesting "those that do the work in the background and attract no attention," admits that "perhaps this is too fanciful; it is only a metaphor and we must not try to fit every detail into the life of the Church in Corinth."

[19]Gk. ἀσχήμονα (NIV, "unpresentable," which is not bad since discretion on the part of Paul calls for discretion in our own language). For this usage of the word to refer to sexual shame, see Deut. 24:1 (LXX).

them, while the more decorous parts (e.g., the face) do not have such need. Although the analogy with the preceding sentence is not precise, Paul's point seems to be similar. Bodily appearances are deceiving; all the parts are necessary, which is reflected in this case by the very way we treat some parts of our bodies that seem "lesser" to us.

24b As in vv. 18-20,[20] Paul now proceeds to apply the preceding observations to the physical body, keeping the imagery intact to the end, but at the same time intending the Corinthians to apply it to their own situation (as v. 27 makes clear). In this case the concluding application is in three parts: a sentence (v. 24b) that affirms God's role in so ordaining the body; a purpose clause in two parts (v. 25) that tells them why the body is so composed; and a concluding illustration (v. 26) of the positive half of the purpose clause, that all the parts may have mutual concern for one another.

This opening sentence, which has obvious similarities to v. 18, attributes the observations of vv. 22-24a to the way God himself has "composed"[21] the body. He "has given greater honor to the parts that lacked[22] it." This latter verb, which in the active means not to be "inferior" but "in need," seems to pick up both kinds of bodily parts from the preceding sentences. Both the "weak" and the "less honorable" are in their own way "in need." It is less clear, however, precisely what Paul had in mind by "greater honor." Most likely he means that the parts that appear to be weak and less worthy are in fact accorded the greater honor of having important functions or receiving special attention. In any case, this point is not pressed. It is sufficient for Paul that the body is so composed by God himself. His intended application of it to the situation in Corinth is found in the purpose clause that follows (v. 25).

25 This sentence expresses the reason for God's having composed the body as illustrated in vv. 22-24. The clause is in two parts, in the form of a "not . . . but" contrast. In a sense both parts come as something of a surprise, partly because the preceding metaphor did not seem to be heading in this direction, and partly because the contrast between "division" and "equal concern for each other" does not seem immediately appropriate to the present context. The logic itself, however, is not too difficult to follow, especially if one thinks of the body as such, and does not allegorize it in terms of the church. Not only can some parts not say that they can get along without others (v. 21), but even parts that appear to be "lesser" get special treatment, since all are so vital to one another (vv. 22-24a). God has arranged things (v. 24b) in such a way that there should be no strife among the

---

[20]But in this case with the more emphatic ἀλλά ("but as it is").

[21]Gk. συγκεράννυμι, which means to mix (together), blend, or unite. The NIV's "combined" tends to lean toward "mix together"; Paul's emphasis is on God's "uniting" the parts with one another so as to form a body.

[22]On this verb see n. 2.

members of the body, who mutually need each other in order to function as a body (v. 25).

The contrast between "division"[23] and "equal concern[24] for one another"[25] is especially appropriate to the situation of the Lord's Table described in 11:17-34, where the "division" is precisely in terms of some abusing others by not caring for their needs. On the other hand, it has almost no significance for the matter of their high estimate of the gift of tongues. Not only does this context suggest that persons, not gifts, are in view, but chap. 14, where Paul corrects their position with regard to tongues, says nothing to indicate that this gift was causing internal strife of any kind. Nor is there any suggestion that the Corinthians who spoke in tongues had an elitist view or considered themselves superior to others. That is read into the text on the basis of this analogy, and then this analogy is read on the basis of that reading of chap. 14—a purely circular argument.

26 Paul rounds off the application by elaborating the positive side of v. 25, namely "that its parts should have equal concern for each other." The analogy is easily understood, especially the first part. It is difficult to study when one has a toothache; the whole body suffers with the part that is aching. More difficult is the second part,[26] "if one part is honored,[27] every part rejoices with it."[28] Does it suggest that the adulation of some part of one's body (eyes, face, physique, etc.) causes momentary forgetfulness of other difficulties, even bodily ones? Or does it refer to a part receiving special care?[29] In any case, one can see the net drawing closer around the Corinthians. This is how they are to be toward one another, precisely because, as Paul will spell out clearly in v. 27, they are the one body of Christ and individually members of it, and therefore members of one another.

Paul has come a long way from where all this began as illustrations of v. 14. But his point is not irrelevant. Their lack of unity, demonstrated most clearly at their Supper, is scarcely commendable, all the less so in light of their arrogance over wisdom and knowledge. Yet in their eagerness for

---

[23]Gk. σχίσμα, as in 1:10 (but not 3:3) and 11:18.

[24]Gk. μεριμνάω; see on 7:32-34. The verb is positive in this instance.

[25]Gk. ἀλλήλων. It is remarkable that in a church where there is alleged to be so much internal strife this word appears so seldom (only here and in 11:33 in this way). Yet it is one of Paul's favorites in the parenetic sections of his other letters, both before (1 Thessalonians) and after (Galatians, Romans) this one.

[26]Barrett, 291-92, doubts that this part applies to the body at all. But given v. 27, which finally applies the whole of what has preceded to themselves, it seems better to hear it still as part of the metaphor—although it obviously points rather directly at them.

[27]Gk. δοξάζεται, which, since it can mean "clothed in splendor" with regard to our heavenly existence, most likely carries that connotation here. Some part is "honored" or "praised" in some way.

[28]In terms of application to the church, it should probably be noted that the former is usually much easier than this one.

[29]E.g., in North American culture something akin to a back rub or full stomach.

spiritual things (14:12) they have focused singularly on tongues. They need both unity and diversity. But they cannot have the one without the other. Thus this concern for unity; the rest of the chapter is devoted to diversity, to which he will now return in the next paragraph.

This is one of the sections of the letter that is ready-made for present-day application. The caution that must be raised, however, is that one not neglect altogether Paul's own concerns in favor of those kinds of easy, independent ones that are so quickly available from such rich metaphors. Paul's concern is for diversity, on the one hand, and for mutual concern in the body, on the other. According to the analogies themselves, that means (1) that there must be a greater acceptance of a variety of gifts in the church. The singular focus on one gift, be it tongues, prophecy, or healing in charismatic churches or strictly cerebral gifts in others, destroys the diversity God intended for the body. But it also means (2) that, in terms of people, we must stop negating others as less important than ourselves. That is to destroy unity.

d. Once more—the fact of diversity (12:27-31)

27 *Now you are the body of Christ, and each one of you is a part of it.* 28 *And in the church God has appointed first of all apostles, second prophets, third teachers, then workers of miracles, also those having gifts of healing, those able to help others, those with gifts of administration, and[1] those speaking different kinds of tongues.* 29 *Are all apostles? Are all prophets? Are all teachers? Do all work miracles?* 30 *Do all have gifts of healing? Do all speak in tongues[a]? Do all interpret?* 31 *But eagerly desire[b] the greater[2] gifts. And now[3] I will show you the most excellent way.*

[a]Or *other languages*
[b]Or *But you are eagerly desiring*

[1]The first edition of the NIV added "finally," which was both pejorative and misleading.

[2]The Westerns and MajT substituted the misleading κρεί(ττ)ονα ("better") for Paul's clearly original μείζονα ("greater"), read by P46 ℵ A B C 6 33 81 104 326 630 1175 1739 1881 pc co. See Zuntz, 135, who is worth quoting in full: "The 'non-Alexandrian' reading makes Paul end on a truism: if there are any charismata 'better' than others, of course they ought to be sought; it moreover credits him with a use of the word κρεῖσσον for which there is no parallel in his writings. . . . The essence of Paul's exhortation is that some spiritual gifts are 'greater' than others (cf. xiv.5) because they benefit the wider community. Even so, he opposes outright the notion that any one is superior or inferior to another." On the other side see A. Harnack, "The Apostle Paul's Hymn of Love (1 Cor. XIII.) and its Religious-Historical Significance," *Exp* 8:3 (1912), 385-408, 481-503 (esp. pp. 387-88), which appeared originally in *Sitzungsberichte der Preussischen Akademie der Wissenschaften* (Berlin, 1911), pp. 132-63.

[3]Gk. ἔτι (= "still" or "yet"); it is difficult to justify the NIV here. The difficulty with this adverb is demonstrated by the reading of P46 (and perhaps D* F G), εἴ τι (= "If

This paragraph brings to a conclusion the argument that began in v. 4 by tying together its two parts (vv. 4-11 and 12-26) and thus returning to the emphasis with which it began. In v. 27 the preceding imagery of the body (vv. 12-26) is applied specifically to the church in Corinth, again with emphasis on the many who make it up. In vv. 28-30, now by way of v. 27, Paul returns one more time to the concern of vv. 4-11, the need for diversity, not uniformity, in gifts and ministries.

He makes this point by means of another *ad hoc* list, which this time includes persons and their ministries as well as some of the *charismata* from vv. 8-10. As before, his concern is neither with *instruction* about gifts and ministries nor with *ranking* them. Rather, the preceding illustrations implied that the body has both different kinds of parts and differences within the same kind. The former dealt with gifts (vv. 15-20), the latter with persons (vv. 21-26). Now he simply combines them all, beginning with "persons" and ending again with "tongues." But he has not lost sight of his goal, which comes out forcefully in the rhetoric of vv. 29-30: "Are all one thing?" "Do all have the same gifts?" "Of course not," is the intended reply. This is simply v. 19 being applied directly to the situation of the church. Diversity within unity is Paul's concern; and diversity *includes* tongues, though it will not allow tongues to be *exclusive*.

27 This sentence, which ties all the preceding pieces together, spells out what the Corinthians must have known right along, that the foregoing analogies were all about them. In v. 12 Paul asserted that the body, with its diversity in unity, is like Christ. Now he says plainly, "*you*[4] are the[5] body of Christ," meaning that collectively in their common relationship to Christ through the Spirit they are his one body[6] (vv. 12-13). At the

there is anything beyond, I point out the way to you"). But this reading is almost certainly a corruption. Cf. the discussion in Zuntz, 90-91, who is tantalized by it but admits the difficulties.

[4]The pronoun takes the emphatic first position.

[5]There is no definite article in the Greek text. Paul is not trying to say something about their relationship to other churches, but about their relationship to Christ and to one another. Thus he does not mean *the* body, as if they were the whole, nor does he mean *a* body, as if they were one among many (true as that might otherwise be). Rather, he means something like "Your relationship to Christ (vv. 12-13) is that of being his body." The genitive "of Christ" is possessive. Cf. Parry, 185. So intent is Mare, 266, on making this passage refer to the church universal that he limits his discussion to this anarthrous usage and quite disregards the emphatic ὑμεῖς δέ!

[6]Although the concern is a good one, it is doubtful whether E. Schweizer has captured Paul's concern here in emphasizing the "missionary" character of the church as his "body," meaning that it is to function "as the instrument by which Christ did his continuing service to the world" (see "The Church as the Missionary Body of Christ," *NTS* 8 [1961/62], 1-11). All of this is true, of course, but in this text even the enumeration of ministries points to functions within the church for building it up, not to ministry without.

same time "each one of you[7] is a part of it," meaning that individually they make up the many parts (v. 14). As the next verses make plain, this means that individually they are members with a variety of "assigned" parts. As before, the emphasis lies on the many who give the one body its necessary diversity.

28 With this sentence Paul proceeds to give substance to the preceding application, that individually they are parts of the one body of Christ. In so doing he reiterates two points from the preceding argument: First, he reasserts that God is responsible for the diversity that makes up the one body (cf. vv. 4-6, 11, 18, 24b).[8] The sentence begins on this emphatic note (literally)[9]: "And[10] those whom[11] God has placed[12] in the church[13] [are]."

Second, he illustrates that diversity by means of another considerable list (cf. vv. 8-10), which has several remarkable features: (1) He begins with a list of *persons* (apostles, prophets, teachers), whom he ranks in the order of first, second, third. (2) With the fourth and fifth items (lit. "miracles" and "gifts of healings") he reverts to *charismata,* taking two from the list in vv. 8-10. These are both prefaced by the word "then," as though he intended the ranking scheme to continue. (3) The sixth and seventh items (lit. "helps" and "guidances"), which are deeds of service, are noteworthy in three ways: (a) they are the only two not mentioned again in the rhetoric of vv. 29-30; (b) they are not mentioned again in the NT; (c) they do not appear

---

[7]Gk. ἐκ μέρους, meaning here "each for his/her part" a member. Cf. BDF 212.

[8]The correspondence with v. 18 is especially noteworthy. As in that verse, the emphasis here is on God's responsibility for the diversity, for "arranging" the many parts in the body as he wished.

[9]Although Paul's intent seems clear enough, the grammar breaks down some, making a literal translation difficult at best.

[10]Gk. καί, probably coordinate here, developing not "the thought of the church as an organic structure" (Barrett, 293), but that of the many kinds of parts that make up the one body.

[11]Gk. οὓς μέν, which expects a coordinate οὓς δέ ("some of one kind, . . . others of another"; see on 7:7). Instead Paul abandons this construction for an ordinal enumeration, which creates something of an anacoluthon.

[12]Gk. ἔθετο; see n. 13 on v. 18. Since this verb is identical to that in v. 18, and since the two sentences correspond so closely, it is difficult to justify the NIV's use of a different word here.

[13]Since this sentence is coordinate with v. 27, with its emphatic "you are," meaning the church in Corinth, there can be little question that by this phrase Paul also primarily intends the local assembly in Corinth. Cf. Dunn, *Jesus,* pp. 262-63. But its use in this kind of context seems also to prepare the way for its broader use in the Prison Epistles to refer to the church universal—especially so since the first item "God has placed in the church" are "apostles" (plural). Cf. Martin, 31, who says this in reverse, that "what Paul had in view was the universal church of which the Corinthian Christians formed a local outgrowth." His entire exegesis, as with most interpreters, is then predicated on the more universal nature of the ministries at the head of this list. On the other side see R. Banks, *Paul's Idea of Community* (Grand Rapids, 1980), pp. 35-37, who would limit the term strictly to the local community.

to be of the same kind, that is, supernatural endowments, as those on either side (miracles, healings, tongues).

Thus, whether intended or not, this list has been presented so as to include personal ministries, *charismata,* and deeds of service, concluding with tongues. These represent a whole range of "ministries" in the church and were probably chosen for that reason. What one is to make of this mix is not certain. At best we can say that the first three emphasize the persons who exercise these ministries, while the final five emphasize the ministry itself.[14] The NIV has tried to overcome this by making the entire list personal: "miracles" becomes "workers of miracles," and "helps," "those who help others." This may be justifiable in light of vv. 29-30, where the nature of those questions demands a more personal expression.[15] But in fact he lists gifts and deeds, not persons. That probably suggests that the first three items are not to be thought of as "offices" held by certain "persons" in the local church, but rather as "ministries" that find expression in various persons; likewise the following "gifts" are not expressed in the church apart from persons, but are first of all gracious endowments of the Spirit, given to various persons in the church for its mutual upbuilding.

That leads to the further question, Does Paul intend that *all* of these be "ranked" as to their role or significance in the church? To which the answer seems to be No. He certainly intends the first three to be ranked. One might argue also for the rest on the basis of the "then . . . then" that prefaces the next two. But that seems unlikely since (1) he drops the enumeration with the sixth item, (2) the fourth and fifth items are in reverse order from their earlier listing, and (3) there seems to be no special significance as to whether miracles precedes healings or vice versa, or whether these precede or follow helpful deeds and acts of guidance. The gift of tongues, as noted earlier, is not listed last because it is least but because it is the problem. As before, Paul includes it because it is a part of the necessary diversity; but he includes it at the end so that the emphasis on diversity will be heard first.

Why, then, does Paul rank the first three? That is more difficult to answer; but it is almost certainly related to his own conviction as to the role these three ministries play in the church. It is not so much that one is more important than the other, nor that this is necessarily their order of au-

---

[14]It is common to assert, as, e.g., Parry, 187, that "a marked line is drawn . . . between the permanent functions already enumerated and the occasional manifestations of spiritual power." Whether some functions were permanent or occasional may or may not be true, but the text itself does *not* make that claim. It is an assertion only, no matter how often it is repeated.

[15]See on vv. 29-30, where Paul seems to sense the difficulty himself. He tries to keep to the "gifts" as such, but the question "Are all miracles?" makes so little sense (in Greek or in any other language) that he makes the final three personal by adding a verb. The fact that he begins by simply listing a gift suggests that the emphasis is still on the gift, rather than on the persons who express that gift.

thority,[16] but that one has precedence over the other in the founding and building up of the local assembly.[17] In light of 14:17 and the probability that those who have taken the lead against Paul are considered "prophets," one is tempted to see here a subordinating of such people to the apostle, who is giving them "the Lord's command" (14:37) over against their "prophets." It is perhaps noteworthy that none of these "ranked persons" is *addressed* in this letter, nor are they assumed to be "in charge" of the worship, which according to these texts is still under the sovereign authority of the Spirit.

As to the individual items:

(1) *First, apostles.* On this term see on 1:1 and 9:1-2. It is no surprise that Paul should list "apostles" first. The surprise is that they should be on this list at all, and that he should list them in the plural. As noted on 1:1, for Paul this is both a "functional" and "positional/official" term. In keeping with the other members on this list, it is primarily "functional" here, probably anticipating the concern for the "building up" of the body that he has already hinted at in v. 7 and will stress in chap. 14.[18] Most likely with this word he is reflecting on his own ministry in this church;[19] the plural is in deference to others who have had the same ministry in other churches.[20] In any case, there is no other evidence that Paul thought of a local church as having some among it called "apostles," who were responsible for its affairs.

(2) *Second, prophets.* On this term see on vv. 8-10. The question is whether Paul is here thinking of a specific group of people known as "prophets" vis-à-vis "apostles" and other members of the community, or whether this is a purely functional term for him, referring to any and all who would

---

[16]Although that would certainly be true of "apostles." But the question of "authority structures" is not asked here, and in terms of the argument it is altogether irrelevant. It is of some interest that those most interested in this question have relegated the first two ministries to the first century only (although some, without textual warrant, would make "prophet" equal "preacher"), so that the third, teacher, now assumes the first position (see, e.g., MacArthur, 322-24). One wonders whether a teacher first designed this hermeneutics!

[17]Cf. Grudem, 56-57, although his term is not "precedence" but "usefulness in building up the church." Nothing in the text supports the oft-repeated suggestion that these three are itinerant ministries, while the rest would be local. See, e.g., Martin, 32-33. On this debate in German scholarship see Conzelmann, 215.

[18]Cf. the list in Eph. 4:11, which also begins with apostles and includes prophets and teachers, whose reason for being "given" to the church is "the equipping of the saints for the work of the ministry" and the "building up of the body of Christ."

[19]Note especially that in 9:1-2 the "authority" of "apostles" from Paul's perspective was *not* over the church universal, but over the churches he founded. On this point see Dunn, *Jesus,* p. 274.

[20]On the basis of 9:6, Dunn, *Jesus,* p. 275, would limit the term here to Paul and Barnabas.

exercise the gift of prophecy. The answer is probably Yes and No. As noted on v. 10, the evidence of chap. 14 suggests that all "Spirit people" were potentially "prophets," in the sense that they could prophesy. But this list, as well as the similar kind of language in Eph. 2:20 and 4:11, suggests that for Paul, as for Luke, there were some who, because they regularly functioned in this way, were known as "prophets." The term here is probably a designation for the latter, although the emphasis would still be on their *function*, namely to build up the community.

(3) *Third, teachers.* This is the first mention of this ministry in the extant Pauline letters. All attempts to define this ministry from the Pauline perspective are less than convincing since the evidence is so meager.[21] As with prophecy, the noun "teaching" will appear again as a gift (14:6, 26; q.v.) without concern for the person of the teacher. Probably the same relationship obtains between teaching (as an inspired utterance) and the teacher as between prophecy and the prophet. There were some who regularly gave a "teaching" in the communities, and thus came to be known as teachers. But again, as chap. 14 indicates, the concern here is with their *function*, not their office.[22]

(4, 5) *Then, miracles; then, gifts of healings.* On these gifts see on vv. 8-10. It is of interest that these two appear in reverse order from vv. 9-10, thus suggesting the irrelevancy of rank from here on. As noted above, the emphasis is not on the people who have these gifts, but simply on the presence of the gifts themselves in the community.

(6) *Helpful deeds.*[23] This word occurs only here in the NT, although it is known in the LXX, where it functions as a verbal noun meaning to help, assist, or aid someone.[24] Perhaps it is similar to the final three items in the list in Rom. 12:8 (service, giving to the needs of others, doing acts of mercy).[25] In any case, it implies that some minister to the physical and spiritual needs of others in the community.

---

[21]See, e.g., Dunn, *Jesus,* pp. 282-84, who sees their primary functions as "passing on and interpreting the traditions." This is attractive, and may be correct, but it lies beyond our ability to demonstrate from the evidence alone.

[22]Since the emphasis in each case is on the function of these first three terms, it is very likely that in terms of persons there was some overlap. That is, the apostle Paul, e.g., is among those in Antioch known as "prophets and teachers" (Acts 13:1). Probably the terms finally came to be attached to certain people on the basis of their own most common function in the church.

[23]NIV, "those able to help others."

[24]Usually of divine aid, or in the papyri of help sought from a king. But it is purely gratuitous to argue on the basis of this usage, as Parry, 187, does, that "it has therefore the definite suggestion of assistance given by governing authorities."

[25]An observation made also by Dunn, *Jesus,* p. 252; the oft-repeated suggestion that these would be the duties of the "deacons" speaks to the concerns of a later time. Cf. the list of "good deeds" attributed to the "genuine widow" in 1 Tim. 5:10.

(7) *Gifts of administration.*[26] Although the cognate personal noun of this word occurs in Acts 27:11 and Rev. 18:17, meaning "steersman" or "pilot," this noun occurs three times in the LXX,[27] where it carries the verbal idea of giving "guidance" to someone. Since the word "administration" in contemporary English conjures up the idea of "administrative skills," which is a far cry from what Paul had in mind, the better translation here might be "acts of guidance," although it is likely that it refers to giving wise counsel to the community as a whole, not simply to other individuals.[28]

(8) *Different kinds of tongues.* On this gift see on v. 10. As noted above, it is no surprise that it is listed last; what is unusual is that it stands rather by itself at the end of this list as a gift of utterance. It surely seems out of place after the preceding four items. This increases the probability that our interpretation is correct, that it is not at the bottom of a descending list but is finally included in a truly heterogeneous listing of gifts and ministries in the church.

29-30 Paul now concludes the argument of this chapter with a crescendo of rhetorical questions. His concern throughout has been the need for diversity, which of course must function in unity. With these questions that is made plain. "Are all one thing? Do all function with the same ministry?" The intended answer is, "Of course not." Paul's point, then, is: "Correct; so why don't you apply this to yourselves and your singular zeal for the gift of tongues?" Tongues are fine, he will go on to affirm, provided they are interpreted. But not everyone should speak in tongues when the church assembles for worship. That makes everyone the same, which is like a body with only one part.

The list itself repeats the items from v. 28,[29] with the omission of "helpful deeds" and "acts of guidance," and the addition of the "interpretation of tongues" at the end. Nothing should be made of these differences since the rhetoric itself indicates the point Paul is trying to make. The addition of the verbs "have" and "speak" with "gifts of healing" and "tongues"[30] is simply a way of avoiding the awkwardness that began with the fourth question, "Are all miracles?"[31] The next three questions make it certain that he intended, "Do all work miracles?"

---

[26]Gk. κυβερνήσεις; also a NT hapax legomenon. Equally gratuitous to the linking of "helps" with "deacons" (see the preceding note) is that of linking this word with "bishops."

[27]Prov. 1:5; 11:14; 24:6.

[28]Cf. Dunn, *Jesus*, p. 252, who translates, "giving counsel."

[29]Making it clear that this is the point of that list, not the number or rank of ministries.

[30]Cf. also the use of the verb instead of the noun for "interpretation."

[31]Cf. Barrett, 296, "Paul's sentence breaks down." Yes and no. As noted above, it is atrocious Greek, as it is English. But it keeps the emphasis on the gifts, not on persons as such.

The tension that some feel between this rhetoric and the question as to whether anyone is therefore excluded from any of these gifts is again related to our own concerns for precision. The "wish" in 14:5 that all speak in tongues (apparently "privately" is intended) and the imperative of 14:1, "eagerly desire spiritual gifts, especially that you may prophesy," plus the statement in 14:31 that "all may prophesy," suggest that such gifts are potentially available to all. But that is *not* Paul's point or concern here. His rhetoric does not mean, "*May* all do this?" to which the answer would probably be, "Of course." Rather, it means, "*Are* all, *Do* all?" to which the answer is, "Of course not." The singular concern of this argument has led to this rhetoric, which concludes in a resounding fashion as a plea for diversity.

31 After the argument of vv. 4-30 and especially after the rhetoric of vv. 29-30, the imperative with which this verse begins, "But eagerly desire[32] the greater gifts," is a puzzle. It is not so for many, of course, since it is common to read v. 28 as *ranking* the various ministries and gifts, so that Paul might place tongues as the last and least of the gifts.[33] This imperative is then read as urging them to seek the gifts at the top of the list as opposed to those at the bottom, which the argument in chap. 14 is seen to support (prophecy as the "greater" and tongues as the "least"). The difficulties with this view, however, are simply too many to make it viable;[34] indeed, it must finally be rejected as contradictory both to the spirit and the intent of the preceding argument. But if so, then what does one do with this imperative, which likewise seems contradictory to what has preceded? Three alternatives[35] have been offered.

---

[32]Gk. ζηλοῦτε (cf. 14:1, 39 and ζητεῖτε in 14:12), which may very well have the full force of the present tense, "keep on eagerly desiring." With its adj. ζῆλος (see on 3:3) it can be used either in a positive sense (as here; cf. 2 Cor. 11:2) or in a negative one ("have rivalry, be jealous," as in 13:4).

[33]On this as a misunderstanding of Paul's use of μείζονα, see the quotation from Zuntz in n. 2 above.

[34](1) Paul's own emphasis throughout the preceding argument is consistently on the need for diversity, not on ranking some gifts as "greater" than others. (2) This is confirmed by the rhetoric of vv. 29-30, which quite disregards any concern for rank, and has only to do with variety. (3) By the same reasoning that puts tongues as the least, "apostles" should be the "greater" gift, yet all are agreed that this is the one gift that none of them may properly "eagerly desire." (4) Although prophecy is used as the primary example of intelligibility in chap. 14, its place in the two lists in chap. 12 is ambiguous—sixth on the first one, second on the other. (5) The lack of concern for ranking is manifest by Paul's failure to include five of the nine items from the first list in the second one; and of the four he does include, the first three are in reverse order. (6) Such a view seems to run full in the face of the concern in the second application of the body imagery (vv. 21-26), where Paul stressed their mutual interdependence, no one being "superior" to others.

[35]Harnack, "Hymn," p. 388, boldly argues that by "gifts" here Paul meant the fruit of the Spirit listed in Gal. 5:22-23. The weakness of this argument, which even he sensed, lies in its total lack of support in the present passage. Harnack thus appeals: "yet every heart must feel and know what he had in mind."

(1) Some have suggested that this is a citation from the Corinthian letter, as though Paul were saying, "But 'earnestly desire the greater gifts,' you say; well, I will show you a way far superior to that."[36] This is supported not only by the fact that in previous places Paul seems to cite their letter,[37] but by the language of 14:12 as well: "Since you *are* zealots for 'spirits.' " The difficulty with this option is the lack of signals at this point in the argument that would suggest either that Paul is quoting them or that what follows is a qualification of the kind found, for example, in 6:13-14; 7:2; or 8:2-3.

(2) It is possible to read the verb as an indicative (cf. NIV margin).[38] Thus Paul, after arguing for diversity against their own singular enthusiasm for tongues as the premier evidence of being "spiritual," has remonstrated, "But you are seeking the so-called greater gifts. Rather I will show you a 'more excellent way.' " He then proceeds to urge the pursuit of love, and that in that context they eagerly desire not "greater gifts," but simply "spiritual gifts."[39] And when one does both—pursues love and desires spiritual gifts—he or she will seek an intelligible gift such as prophecy (or others listed in 14:6), for only what is intelligible will edify the community. This is supported further, as with the prior option, by Paul's statement to this effect in 14:12. What basically stands against this option[40] is the appearance of the same verb form in 14:1 and 39, where it can only be an imperative and not an indicative.[41]

(3) Despite some attractive features to this second option, the more likely alternative is that the verb is an imperative, as in 14:1, but that it is not intended to be in contrast to 12:4-30, nor to the preceding listings of gifts.

---

[36]See, e.g., Baker, "Interpretation," pp. 226-27; following M.-A. Chevallier, *Esprit de Dieu, Paroles d'Hommes* (Neuchâtel, 1963), pp. 158-63.

[37]See, e.g., 6:12, 13; 7:1, 25; 8:1, 4.

[38]For this argument see G. Iber, "Zum Verständnis von I Cor. 12:31," *ZNW* 54 (1963), 43-52. Cf. Bittlinger, 73-75, who also adopts this alternative. Martin, 34-35, combines these first two options, following Chevallier in making a considerable distinction between τὰ χαρίσματα in this verse and τὰ πνευματικά in 14:1. See the next note.

[39]However, Chevallier, Baker, and Martin (see nn. 36 and 38) make a considerable point that πνευματικά in 14:1 is a deliberate change of words on Paul's part, reflecting the heart of the controversy between him and them. The difficulty with this view is that it makes χαρίσματα the Corinthian word, which Paul then tries to put into a new context with the use of πνευματικά. But that seems to run counter to the rest of the evidence of this letter, namely that πνευματικός was the *Corinthian* word, which they used vis-à-vis Paul.

[40]Although one would also expect the emphatic pronoun ὑμεῖς δέ ("but as for you") if this were Paul's intent.

[41]But as Iber points out, when it does reappear as an imperative in 14:1, it lacks what he views as the pejorative qualifier "greater." Thus Paul is saying, "You are seeking the *greater* gifts; you should be simply seeking spiritual gifts in the context of love."

Rather, the preceding argument has concluded with the rhetoric of vv. 29-30. With these words Paul is about to launch on his next argument, namely 14:1-25 and the need for intelligibility in the community; and in the community *all* the intelligible gifts are "greater" than tongues because they can edify while tongues without interpretation cannot.[42] But before he gets to that point, Paul interrupts himself to give the proper framework in which the "greater gifts" are to function—love. In this view 14:1 is resumptive. "Pursue love," he commands, "and in that context eagerly desire the things of the Spirit, especially those gifts that are intelligible and will thus edify the community."

If this is the correct view of things, then the words "and now I will show you the most excellent way" serve to interrupt the argument in order to put the entire discussion into a different framework altogether. It is often suggested that Paul is setting forth love as the greatest of all the gifts, and therefore the "greater gift" that all should pursue. But this is not quite precise. Not only does Paul not call love a gift, either here or elsewhere, but this clause stands in *contrast* to the immediately preceding imperative, not as its proper complement. What Paul is about to embark on is a description of what he calls "a *way*[43] that is beyond comparison."[44] The way they are going is basically destructive to the church as a community; the way they are being called to is one that seeks the good of others before oneself. It is the way of edifying the church (14:1-5), of seeking the common good (12:7). In that context one will still earnestly desire the things of the Spirit (14:1), but precisely so that others will be edified. Thus it is not "love versus gifts" that Paul has in mind, but "love as the only context for gifts"; for without the former, the latter have no usefulness at all—but then neither does much of anything else in the Christian life.

3. The More Excellent Way (13:1-13)

This is one of the greatly loved passages in the NT, and for good reason.[1] It is one of Paul's finest moments; indeed, let the interpreter beware lest too

---

[42]See especially on 14:5, where prophecy is specifically called μεῖζον for this very reason.

[43]Cf. the brief excursus on the concept of ὁδός in Conzelmann, 216; see also C. Spicq, *Agape dans le Nouveau Testament* (EBib; Paris, 1959), II, 64-66 (ET [but without the copious notes], *Agape in the New Testament* [St. Louis, 1965], II, 143). (In further notes page numbers refer to the French original; the English translation is in parentheses.)

[44]See BAGD under κατά, II.5bβ.

[1]For a discussion of the significant literature from 1910 to 1950, howbeit with the considerable omission of Spicq's *Agape*, see J. T. Sanders, "First Corinthians 13, Its Interpretation Since the First World War," *Int* 20 (1966), 159-87.

much analysis detract from its sheer beauty and power. Unfortunately, however, the love affair with this love chapter has also allowed it to be read regularly apart from its context, which does not make it less true but causes one to miss too much. Even worse is that reading of it in context which sees it as set over against "spiritual gifts." Paul would wince.

Both the imperative in 12:31a and the resumptive nature of the imperatives in 14:1 indicate that this is something of a digression in Paul's argument. But as with all such "digressions,"[2] it is fully relevant to the context, and without it the succeeding argument would lose much of its force. Because of the exalted nature of its prose,[3] however, along with some obvious changes in style,[4] many have questioned whether it was composed for the first time for this argument.[5] Some have argued that it had independent existence before having been adapted and inserted here.[6] Although that is certainly possible,[7] one must note finally that in its present form it is not only fully Pauline,[8] but also has been so thoroughly adapted to the context that such questions seem ultimately irrelevant.[9]

[2]Cf. the "B" section in the various A-B-A arguments in this letter (see n. 9 on 12:1-3): 2:6-16; 7:29-35; 9:1-27.

[3]With unguarded enthusiasm it is often called poetry, or even a "hymn to love" (cf., e.g., Héring, 135, and many others). But only vv. 1-3 fit a poetic mold. There is no question that it "soars"; but prose can do that as well as poetry. Cf., e.g., 3:21-23; 15:51-56; Rom. 8:28-39. See also the judgment of Spicq, *Agape,* "The passage is not a psalm or hymn, properly speaking, but rather a parenetic exhortation" (p. 59 [141]).

[4]Particularly in vv. 1-3 and 4-7.

[5]This discussion has a long history, especially in German scholarship. See most recently Oda Wischmeyer, *Der höchste Weg. Das 13. Kapitel des 1. Korintherbriefes* (Gütersloh, 1981). Cf. the presentation in Conzelmann, 217-20, who is especially enamored by some "parallels" that seem to him to suggest a "topos," i.e., a common scheme used by many authors to present what they believe is the "highest good." But the alleged parallels are of dubious value; praise of "virtue" or "eros" is not quite the same thing as an exhortation to ἀγάπη. At best they serve as "counterparallels." Equally difficult to sustain is the notion of Sanders that the passage in its present context is displaced, having been put here by a redactor ("First Corinthians 13," pp. 181-87).

[6]That also raises the question as to whether it was originally by Paul or not. Most believe so; but some have questioned whether even in its present place it is by Paul (see, e.g., E. L. Titus, "Did Paul Write I Corinthians 13?" *JBR* 27 [1959], 299-302, who argues that it is an elaborate editorial addition); but that seems to be criticism run amok.

[7]The one thing such a view may help explain is the inclusion of a few items in vv. 3-7 that do not otherwise seem immediately to the point of the letter. On the other hand, Spicq, *Agape,* pp. 55-56 (140-41), rejects it altogether.

[8]It is often suggested that its lack of christological emphasis is unusual for Paul; cf. Conzelmann, 220. But one must be wary of circular reasoning here—that lack of Christology suggests it is not by Paul; therefore, Paul is not its original author because it lacks Christology. In its present form it is in fact by Paul; therefore, one may rightly presuppose the thoroughly theological, christological understanding of ἀγάπη that he demonstrates everywhere.

[9]In any case, Conzelmann, 218, seems quite wrong, both in terms of assump-

What is relevant is its structure and place in the present argument. In a series of three paragraphs, Paul sets out to put their zeal for tongues within a broader *ethical*[10] context that will ultimately disallow uninterpreted tongues in the assembly. That context is love for others[11] over against self-interest; in chap. 14 such love will be specified in terms of "building up" the church.

At the same time, however, much of the language suggests that Paul is picking up on some of the differences between himself and them that have emerged throughout the letter.[12] Thus the structure of the argument, lyrical as it is, also reflects his continuing argument with them. At issue have been opposing views of "spirituality." They speak in tongues, to be sure, which Paul will not question as a legitimate activity of the Spirit. But at the same time they tolerate, or endorse, illicit sexuality, greed, and idolatry (5:9-10; illustrated in 5:1-5; 6:1-11; 6:12-20; 8:1–10:22). They spout "wisdom" and "knowledge"; but in the former they stand boldly against Paul and his gospel of a crucified Messiah, and in the latter they are willing to "build up" a brother by destroying him (8:10-11). In short, they have a spirituality that has religious trappings (asceticism, knowledge, tongues) but has abandoned rather totally genuinely Christian ethics, with its supremacy of love.

Thus he begins by setting forth several "religious" activities, many of them from the list in 12:8-10, as not benefiting the person doing them if that person's life is not also characterized by love (vv. 1-3). He follows that with a description of love that seems to have been especially adapted to the

---

tions and exegetical method, to argue, "at all events the passage must be expounded in the first instance on its own." To the contrary, whatever one may learn from "formal" considerations, its meaning "in the first instance" is predicated strictly on its present context. Vv. 1-3 make sense *only* in this context, as do vv. 8-13, which under any view do not fit well as part of a self-contained unit; furthermore, the language "self-contained unit" (which even Martin, 42, is willing to use) would appropriately fit only vv. 4-7, which, however, also reflect a choice of words especially tailored to the Corinthian situation.

[10]Whatever else, it must be remembered that this is not a "hymn to love," as though "love" were an abstraction, or worse, simply a beautiful sentiment. For Paul, just as in 8:2-3, this is ethical instruction, as the imperative in 14:1 makes plain. To miss the parenetic thrust of this chapter is to miss the point altogether. See n. 3 above.

[11]There has been some discussion as to whether "love" in this chapter has to do with love for God or for people. Because he has abstracted the passage from its context, Conzelmann, 221, considers the question irrelevant. To the contrary, the context and parenetic nature of the whole demand that the concern be love for others. On the whole question, see Spicq, *Agape*, pp. 108-11 (172-74).

[12]Cf. M. Miguens, "1 Cor. 3:8-13 Reconsidered," *CBQ* 37 (1975), 80, who also makes the point that it has ties to the letter as a whole as well as to the immediate context of chaps. 12–14.

627

Corinthian situation[13] and their differences with Paul (vv. 4-7).[14] This in turn leads him to contrast love with selected *charismata,* including tongues, in terms of the absolute, eternal nature of the one and the relative, temporal nature of the other, placed within the context of their "already/not yet" eschatological existence (vv. 8-13). This does not make *charismata* less valuable for life in the present as one awaits the consummation, but it posits against their "overrealized" spirituality that these things have a relative life span (for the "already" only), while love is both for now and forever. Thus vv. 1-3 urge the absolute *necessity* of love; vv. 4-6 describe the *character* of love; and vv. 8-13 illustrate the *permanence* of love[15]—all to the one end that they eagerly desire "the things of the Spirit" (14:1) for the sake of the common good (12:7).

Two further points must be made: First, because of the lyrical nature of this section, it is easy to think of love as an abstract quality. That is precisely to miss Paul's concern. Love is primary for him because it has already been given concrete expression in the coming of Jesus Christ to die for the sins of the world.[16] Love is not an idea for Paul, not even a "motivating factor" for behavior.[17] It *is* behavior. To love is to act; anything short of action is not love at all. Second, love is not set over against the gifts, precisely because it belongs in a different category altogether. For Paul it is not "gifts to be sure, but better yet love"; rather, love is the *way* in which the gifts are to function. To desire earnestly expressions of the Spirit that will build up the community is *how* love acts in this context.

a. The necessity of love (13:1-3)

1 *If I speak in the tongues[a] of men and of angels, but have not love, I am only a resounding gong or a clanging cymbal.* 2 *If I have the gift of prophecy and can fathom all mysteries and all knowledge, and if I have a faith that can move mountains, but have not love, I am*

[13]See, e.g., R-P, 285-86: "Most of the features selected as characteristic of [love] are just those in which the Corinthians had proved defective"; and Spicq, *Agape,* p. 77 n. 3 (150 n. 123): "[These characteristics] are neither exhaustive nor arbitrary, but were chosen with reference to the virtues most neglected by the Corinthians." Cf. the less than adequate reconstruction by I. J. Martin, "I Corinthians 13 Interpreted by its Context," *JBR* 18 (1950), 101-05, who perceives Paul as opposing glossolalists—at best a fanciful caricature—without a single *linguistic* tie to the context.

[14]See the commentary on vv. 4-7 for this point of view.

[15]Cf. the oft-quoted words of K. Barth, *Church Dogmatics* IV/2, pp. 824-40: "It is love alone that counts; it is love alone that triumphs; it is love alone that endures."

[16]Cf. Rom. 5:6-8; 8:30-31; Eph. 5:1-2.

[17]As will be pointed out, this is not quite the point of vv. 1-3, although such is often suggested. The "religious" activities in themselves have value and for the most part can benefit others; but for the "religious" who do these and do not *also* have the kind of love for others described in vv. 4-7, all is religious show, with no genuinely Christian substance.

nothing. 3 *If I give all I possess to the poor and surrender my body to the flames,*[b18] *but have not love, I gain nothing.*

[a]Or *languages*
[b]Some early manuscripts *body that I may boast*[18]

Paul begins his description of "the way that is beyond comparison" with a series of three conditional sentences[19] whose powerful cadences—and order of appearance—should have had a sobering effect on the Corinthians. He begins with tongues because that is where the problem lay; and for that reason it also gets individual treatment. He then expands his list to include a variety of the *charismata* from chap. 12, which he himself had argued for so vigorously as part of the need for diversity. Finally, he includes examples of self-sacrificial deeds. In each case the conditional clause presupposes that both he and they are agreed that the activity has value. Thus what is at stake is not the activity without love, but the person himself/herself. These are good things; what is not good is religious performance, gifts on display by one who is not otherwise acting as described in vv. 4-7. It is not a matter of these things *or* love, or even these things motivated *by* love, but these things by a person whose whole life is otherwise also given to love. If not, that person's life before God adds up to zero.

[18]The textual choice in this instance is one of the truly difficult ones in the NT. There are three readings:

1) καυχήσωμαι P[46] ℵ A B 6 33 69 1739 cop Origen Jerome
2) καυθήσωμαι K Ψ 614 1881 Maj Chrysostom Cyril Theodoret
3) καυθήσομαι C D F G L 81 104 630 1985 latt arm

Although Zuntz, 35-37, favors 2, few others do since it is a grammatical monstrosity (future subjunctive; otherwise unknown in the *koinē* period, but occurring in the Byzantine). The choice then is between a basically Western (3) or Egyptian (1) reading, with the Western reading finally having prevailed. Given the generally excellent quality of the Egyptian tradition, the external evidence favors 1. So, too, does transcriptional probability: It is difficult to imagine that in a time when martyrdom by burning was common someone with καυθήσομαι before him would change it to καυχήσωμαι, either accidentally or deliberately, especially since the basic difficulty that anyone has ever had with reading 1 is to find an adequate sense for it. But these matters are finally indecisive in themselves; the question must finally be determined on the basis of intrinsic probability. On this see the commentary. For arguments in favor of 1 see Clark, "Textual Criticism," pp. 61-62, and Metzger, 563-64. For arguments favoring 3 see J. K. Elliott, "In Favour of καυθήσομαι at I Corinthians 13:3," *ZNW* 62 (1971), 297-98 and R. Kieffer "'Afin que je sois brule' ou bien 'Afin que j'en orgueil'? (1 Cor. xiii.3)," *NTS* 22 (1975/76), 95-97 (cf. Barrett, 302-03, and Conzelmann, 217 n. 1).

[19]Each is a present general (if ever the one condition prevails, so does the other). Each is carefully structured in three parts: (a) a protasis (in the second and third instances a double protasis), (b) an adversative clause, "but have not love," and (c) an apodosis. The balance is maintained by having a longer apodosis in v. 1, where the protasis is shorter, and the briefest possible apodosis in vv. 2 and 3, where the protasis is elaborated. The whole is a work of art, with marvelous cadences and dramatic effect.

It is hard to escape the implication that what is involved here are two opposing views as to what it means to be "spiritual." For the Corinthians it meant "tongues, wisdom, knowledge" (and pride), but without a commensurate concern for truly Christian behavior. For Paul it meant first of all to be full of the Spirit, the *Holy* Spirit, which therefore meant to behave as those "sanctified in Christ Jesus, called to be his holy people" (1:2), of which the ultimate expression always is to "walk in love." Thus, even though these sentences reflect the immediate context, Paul's concern is not simply with their over-enthusiasm about tongues but with the larger issue of the letter as a whole, where their view of spirituality has caused them to miss rather widely both the gospel and its ethics.

1 This opening sentence is the reason for the entire argument: "If I speak in the tongues of men and of angels." One may be quite sure that the Corinthians believed they did; indeed, this best accounts for the sudden shift to the first person singular (cf. 14:14-15).[20] On its own this could mean nothing more than "speak eloquently," as some have argued and as it is popularly understood. But since it is not on its own, but follows directly from 12:28-30 and anticipates 14:1-25, most likely this is either Paul's or their understanding (or both) of "speaking in tongues." "Tongues of men" would then refer to human speech,[21] inspired by the Spirit but unknown to the speaker; "tongues of angels" would reflect an understanding that the tongues-speaker was communicating in the dialect(s) of heaven.

That the Corinthians at least, and probably Paul, thought of tongues as the language(s) of angels seems highly likely—for two reasons: (1) There is some evidence from Jewish sources that the angels were believed to have their own heavenly language (or dialects) and that by means of the "Spirit" one could speak these dialects. Thus in the *Testament of Job* 48–50 Job's three daughters are given "charismatic sashes";[22] when these were put on they allowed Hemera, for example, to speak "ecstatically in the angelic dialect, sending up a hymn to God with the hymnic style of the angels. And as she spoke ecstatically, she allowed 'The Spirit' to be inscribed on her garment."[23] Such an understanding of heavenly speech may also lie behind

[20]That is, Paul uses himself as the hypothetical person precisely because many of the Corinthians were like this in reality. Bringing them into the argument in this more indirect way is its own form of powerful argumentation. At the same time, as in 14:6, this use of the first person could reflect an undercurrent of their disapproval of him for *not* being known to speak in tongues, hence of his not being truly πνευματικός; cf. on 2:15.

[21]See on 12:10. Martin, 43, along with many others, sees the two genitives as suggesting "eloquence and ecstatic speech," with eloquence reflecting the Corinthian interest that one finds in chaps. 1–2. That is certainly possible, but it seems more likely in this context that Paul is simply describing "tongues" in two different forms.

[22]The language is that of R. P. Spittler, "The Testament of Job," in OTP, I, 865. For a discussion of the other possible reflections of this phenomenon see p. 866 n. "f."

[23]*T. Job* 48:3 (Spittler's transl.).

the language of 1 Cor. 14:2 ("speak mysteries by the Spirit"). (2) As has been argued elsewhere,[24] one can make a good deal of sense of the Corinthian view of "spirituality" if they believed that they had already entered into some expression of angelic existence. This would explain their rejection of sexual life and sexual roles (cf. 7:1-7; 11:2-16) and would also partly explain their denial of a future bodily existence (15:12, 35). It might also lie behind their special interest in "wisdom" and "knowledge." For them the evidence of having "arrived" at such a "spiritual" state would be their speaking the "tongues of angels." Hence the high value placed on this gift. ⏋

⌐ But Paul's concern lay elsewhere. Their "spirituality" showed evidence of all kinds of behavioral flaws. Their "knowledge" led to pride and the "destruction of a brother for whom Christ died" (8:2, 11). Their "wisdom" led to quarrels and rivalry (1:10; 3:4). Their "tongues" were neither edifying the community nor allowing pagans to respond to the prophetic word (14:1-25). In short, theirs was a spirituality that lacked the primary evidence of the Spirit: behavior that could be described as "having love." ⏌

⌐ In saying "but have not love[25]," Paul does not mean to suggest that love is a possession of some kind. The language has been formed by the elevated style of the prose. To "have love" means to "act lovingly," just as to "have prophecy" in v. 2 means "to speak with the prophetic gift."[26] And to act lovingly means, as in the case of Christ, actively to seek the benefit of someone else. For Paul it is a word whose primary definition is found in God's activity in behalf of his enemies (Rom. 5:6-8), which was visibly manifested in the life and death of Christ himself. To "have love," therefore, means to be toward others the way God in Christ has been toward us. Thus, in the Pauline parenesis, for those who "walk in the Spirit" the primary ethical imperative is "love one another." This is found at the heart of every section of ethical instruction,[27] and the other exhortations are but the explication of it. ⏌

The final coup in this sentence is the language "resounding gong" and "clanging cymbal." Although what the former designates is uncer-

---

[24]See especially on 7:1-7 and 11:2-16; cf. the rejection of future somatic existence in 15:12.

[25]Gk. ἀγάπη, rare but not unknown in Greek literature. The LXX often uses this word to speak of God's love, which probably became the source of its use among the early Christians. For them it designated a love differing especially from ἔρος ("desiring love") and also from φιλία ("natural sympathy" or "mutual affection"). See the discussion by W. Günther and H.-G. Link, *NIDNTT* II, 538-47; and by G. Quell and E. Stauffer, *TDNT* I, 221-54. See also the important monographs by J. Moffatt, *Love in the New Testament* (New York, 1930); A. Nygren, *Agape and Eros* (ET, London, 1932, 1939); and esp. Spicq, *Agape* (1959).

[26]Otherwise Ellis, 52 n. 29, who argues that it "here includes the perception of mysteries."

[27]See 1 Thess. 4:9; Gal. 5:13, 22; 12:9; 13:8; Col. 3:14; Eph. 5:2.

tain,[28] at least it is a metaphor for an empty, hollow sound.[29] The latter in fact was an "instrument" expressly associated with the pagan cults.[30] Perhaps, then, this is an allusion to 12:2 and their former associations with such cults.[31] To speak in tongues as they were doing, thinking that they were "spiritual" but with no concern for building up the community, is not merely to speak unintelligible words; it makes one sound like the empty, hollow noises of pagan worship.

2 In this second sentence Paul widens the perspective to include three of the *charismata* from 12:8-10, a list which in that argument came from Paul himself as his way of expanding their own horizons as to the work of the Spirit. Thus he includes *prophecy,* the gift he regularly considers to be of primary significance for the community (cf. 1 Thess. 5:19-20; 1 Cor. 14:1-25); *knowledge,* which was another of the Corinthian favorites (cf. 1:5; 8:1); and *faith,* which, together with its qualifier, "that can move mountains," means the gift of special faith for mighty works (see on 12:9).[32] In order to make this point as emphatic as possible, Paul thrice emphasizes "all": *all* mysteries, *all* knowledge, *all* faith. If one person could embrace the whole range of *charismata* and the full measure of any one of them, but at the same time would fail to be full of love, such a person would be *nothing* in the sight of God.[33]

But what did Paul intend by the second item, "fathom[34] all mysteries and all knowledge"? These terms appear together as a regular feature of

---

[28]Gk. χαλκὸς ἠχῶν (= lit. "echoing bronze"). Of the two items, this is the more puzzling since there is no known evidence for its use as an "instrument." Recently it has been suggested that it reflects the bronze "amplification" systems of the stone amphitheatres. See W. Harris, "Echoing Bronze," *Journal of the Acoustical Society of America* 70 (1981), 1184-85; *idem,* "'Sounding Brass' and Hellenistic Technology," *BARev* 8 (1982), 38-41; cf. Murphy-O'Connor, *Corinth,* pp. 76-77; and W. W. Klein, "Noisy Gong or Acoustic Vase? A Note on I Corinthians 13.1," *NTS* 32 (1986), 286-89.

[29]Cf. K. L. Schmidt, *TDNT* III, 1037-39, and Spicq, *Agape,* pp. 69-70 (146), who suggest that it may reflect a commonplace scoffing at the empty sophist or rhetorician (cf. 1:10–4:21).

[30]In particular with the cult of Cybele, where some of the more bizarre forms of "ecstasy" also occurred. See the evidence in E. Peterson, *TDNT* I, 227-28; and K. L. Schmidt, *TDNT* III, 1037-39; cf. J. Quasten, *Musik und Gesang in den Kulten der heidnischen Antike und christlichen Frühzeit* (Münster, 1930).

[31]Cf. H. Riesenfeld, "Note supplémetaire sur I Cor. XIII," *Coniectanea Neotestamentica* 10 (1946), 50-53.

[32]This qualifier is another sure evidence of Paul's acquaintance with the teaching of Jesus, reflecting a saying found variously in Mark 11:25 and Matt. 17:30 (cf. Luke 17:6). On this question see on 4:16; 7:10, 25; and 9:14.

[33]This latter idea is not in the text per se, but is surely what Paul means by "nothing" in this sentence and "profit nothing" in the next. Cf. Spicq, *Agape,* p. 71 (147).

[34]The verb εἰδῶ controls both nouns, "all mysteries" and "all knowledge." Here it must mean "understand"; hence the NIV's "fathom."

Jewish apocalyptic,[35] especially with regard to the unfolding of God's final eschatological drama. Paul now uses this language to refer to God's present revelation of his ways,[36] especially in the form of special revelations by means of the eschatological Spirit whom Christians have received (cf. 14:6).[37] This is most likely how we are also to understand both the "utterance of knowledge" in 12:8 and the "knowledge" that accompanies tongues and prophecy in vv. 8-13 that follow.

Given the longer protasis, Paul concludes with a shorter apodosis, "I am nothing." That speaks eloquently for itself. As before, possession of *charismata* is not the sign of the Spirit; Christian love is.

3 Enlarging his perspective yet further, this time quite beyond *charismata,* Paul next offers examples of great personal sacrifice.[38] The first item literally says, "If I parcel out[39] all my property[40] for food," to feed "the poor" being implied. In light of the word about "faith" in v. 2, Paul is probably once again reflecting on the teaching of Jesus.[41] How, then, can he say that such a "loving deed" gains nothing? Here in particular Paul's own point comes to the fore. As with the *charismata,* the deed in itself is a good thing, commanded by Jesus of his would-be followers, and surely of benefit for the recipients. Paul's point is that such an action by one who is not otherwise characterized by the love described in the next four verses is of no benefit[42] whatever to the giver.

The final item, which is undoubtedly intended to climax the series, also presents us with the greatest difficulties in understanding. Some form of self-sacrifice seems to be in view, but because of the difficult textual variation (see n. 13 above), one cannot be sure which. The majority of interpret-

[35]See, e.g., Dan. 2:19-23, 28 where in the LXX the repeated language includes σοφία, γνῶσις, μυστήρια, and ἀνακαλύπτω; cf. also the recurring "he showed me all the mysteries of . . ." in 1 Enoch (41:1; 52:2; 61:5; 63:3; 68:5; 71:4).

[36]See above on 4:1.

[37]Friedrich, *TDNT* VI, 853-54, asserts, but without textual support: "*Gnosis* is one of the 'rational gifts of the Spirit.' It is attained speculatively, by thinking about the mysteries of the faith. . . . In contrast, prophecy rests on inspiration. Knowledge is given to it by sudden revelation. The prophetic thought or image strikes the prophet from without." This is hard to square with Paul's own language in 12:7-11 and 14:1-6.

[38]Spicq, *Agape,* p. 71 (147), suggests a connection with ἀντίλημψις in 12:28; this is doubtful since the emphasis here is not on helping others as such.

[39]Gk. ψωμίσω (cf. the reference in Rom. 12:20 to "feeding one's enemy"). The verb literally means "to feed by putting little bits into the mouth" (LSJ); cf. Num. 11:4; *T.Lev.* 8:5.

[40]Gk. τὰ ὑπάρχοντα; see the next note.

[41]Especially so since the language τὰ ὑπάρχοντα does not appear elsewhere in Paul, but is used by Jesus in a saying very similar to this one (Matt. 19:21//Luke 12:33; cf. Luke 12:15).

[42]Harnack, "Hymn," p. 394, suggests that Paul is here reflecting on his Jewish background, in which good deeds "profit" one before God.

ers prefer the reading "to burn," and view it either as martyrdom or an extreme example of giving oneself up to the most painful of deaths for some great cause. But there are several difficulties with this option: (1) Even though martyrdom by fire was not unknown among the Jews,[43] this had not yet become a Christian phenomenon; the fiery persecutions of Nero are still at least a decade away. It seems unlikely, therefore, that Paul had martyrdom in mind. (2) This is made even less likely by the language itself. One does not "give over one's body" to martyrdom; rather, such is taken from one. Moreover, the language "if I give over my *body*, so that I might be burned" is highly unusual under any circumstances.[44] One would expect rather "that *it* might be burned." (3) The basic reason for adopting this reading is *not its own intrinsic merit;* rather, it tends to win by default, in light of what is perceived to be the still greater difficulty of making good sense of "that I might boast." It is regularly assumed[45] that this latter is pejorative language and, therefore, that such an action is already so unloving that Paul's apodosis becomes redundant. (4) Given the difficulty with this alternative and the frequency of Christian martyrdom in the early church after Paul, one can well understand why a scribe would have changed "boast" to "burn"[46]; whereas under the same circumstances it is nearly impossible to account for the opposite change.[47]

What that means, therefore, is that Paul most likely wrote, "if I hand over my body that I might boast." The question is, What could that mean? If we were limited only to a pejorative sense for "boast," then despite all the above arguments we would probably have to assume that Paul wrote "burned" and try to find an adequate meaning for it. But in fact we are not so limited in Paul. As noted in the discussion of this word in 1:29-31 and 9:15, for Paul this can be a positive idea, as long as it is brought under the gift of

[43]See esp. Dan. 3 and 4 Macc. 9:17-25.

[44]Elliott, "In Favour," pp. 297-98, sees this difficulty as the *reason* for the change to καυχήσωμαι.

[45]Cf., e.g., Elliott, "In Favour," where this assumption itself underlies the rejection. The view of Harnack (n. 48 below) is simply not noted.

[46]A passage in Clement of Rome's letter to the church in Corinth (*ca.* A.D. 96) is of considerable interest: "We know of many among us who have delivered (παραδε-δωκότας) themselves to bondage in order to ransom others; many have sold themselves into slavery and used the price paid for themselves to feed (ἐψώμισαν) others" (55:2 [Grant-Graham transl.; New York, 1965]). This usage of the two verbs from 13:3 in a passage shortly after his referring to 1 Corinthians and the command to love (chaps. 47–50) seems too remarkable to be accidental. If so, then the absence of καυθήσομαι ("burning"), but the giving up of oneself in other ways for the sake of others, implies that Clement knew nothing of a text that had "burn" in it.

[47]The most frequent suggestion is the *frequency* of the verb καυχάομαι in Paul and the relative infrequency of καίω (e.g., Spicq, *Agape,* pp. 57-58; Elliott, "In Favour," p. 298). But this will not do since scribes who would be trying to make sense of the text would be little influenced by word frequency.

grace. That is, Paul will boast in the very things that are his weaknesses so that the gospel might be the more glorified.[48] For him this usage had eschatological overtones; he expected to have a legitimate "boast on the day of the Lord" (2 Cor. 1:14; cf. Rom. 5:2-3). If that is the meaning here, then this final item is most likely a genuine reflection on his own ministry, in which he is referring to the kinds of bodily sufferings of which he "boasts" in 2 Cor. 11:23-29 and 12:10, which also help to bring about his greater "boast," their salvation. But if he does not also have love, even these reasons for boasting, he says, "profit me nothing."[49]

The inclusion of the examples in v. 3 makes it clear that love is not being set in contrast to gifts; rather, Paul is arguing for the absolute supremacy and necessity of love if one is to be a Christian at all. Paul will continue to "give his body so that he might boast"; he will especially urge the Corinthians to desire prophetic utterances; and he will encourage tongues in their life of personal prayer. But these things must be brought forth in lives that above all "have put on love"; for without love one quite misses the point of being Christian in the first place. The easiest way to move this paragraph from their situation to ours is simply to give it a new *ad hoc* expression, in terms of how one thinks of his/her own life to be spiritually significant. For example, "If I preach with the brilliance of Paul or Chrysostom, but have not love . . ."; or perhaps, "If I write a commentary on 1 Corinthians 13, but have not love . . . ," etc.

b. The character of love (13:4-7)

4 *Love is patient, love[1] is kind. It does not envy, it does not boast, it is not proud.* 5 *It is not rude, it is not self-seeking,[2] it is not easily*

---

[48]For a considerable presentation of this argument, see Harnack, "Hymn," pp. 401-04.

[49]Cf. Harnack, "Hymn," p. 404: "Thus without love all reason for glorying, even the greatest, is profitless."

[1]One cannot be certain how Paul structured the beginning of this enumeration. This second ἀγάπη, which follows χρηστεύεται, could go either with that verb or with οὐ ζηλοῖ that follows. This is further complicated by the presence or absence of a third ἀγάπη between οὐ ζηλοῖ and οὐ περπερεύεται (missing in P46 B 33 104 629 1175 2464 pc [also lat sa bo, but one cannot tell whether this represents a translational "improvement"]). Thus one has four options (besides P46, which adds an ἀγάπη after οὐ περπερεύεται):

    1) "Love is patient; love is kind; does not envy, etc."
    2) "Love is patient, is kind; love does not envy, does not boast; etc."
    3) "Love is patient; love is kind; love does not envy; etc."
    4) "Love is patient; is kind; love does not envy; love does not boast; is not proud; etc."

Zuntz, 68, argues vigorously for 2 on the grounds of rhythmical style (one who thinks otherwise is "blind to its obvious, well-balanced structure"). Obvious or otherwise, it is

angered, it keeps no record of wrongs. 6 Love does not delight in evil
but rejoices with the truth. 7 It always protects, always trusts, always
hopes, always perseveres.

With a series of fifteen verbs (some with objects) Paul proceeds to describe
the love that he has just insisted is the *sine qua non* of Christian behavior.
Although some think this listing is the giveaway that the whole chapter had
prior existence as a self-contained unit, in its present form (especially the list
of negatives in vv. 4b-5) it is so tailored to the Corinthian situation[3] that it
would be quite impossible to reconstruct an earlier expression of it.[4] Nonetheless, as is often true of such lyrical moments (as, e.g., 3:21-23; Rom.
8:31-39), this passage easily transcends that immediate situation as well,
which is what gives it such universal appeal (if not universal obedience!).

⌐ The enumeration is basically in three parts: It begins with two positive expressions of love (patience and kindness); these are followed by eight
verbs expressing what love is not like or does not do, the last of which is
balanced by its positive counterpart (v. 6); finally, there is a staccato of four
verbs, each with the object "all things," two of which pick up the other two
cardinal Christian virtues, "faith and hope," and the last of which recalls the
first item (patience) by means of its synonym, endurance. ⌐

⌐ **4a** These first two clauses, "Love is patient,[5] love is kind[6]," represent respectively love's necessary passive and active responses toward others. The one pictures long forbearance toward them—indeed, it is difficult to
improve on the KJV's "suffereth long"; the second pictures active goodness
in their behalf. In Pauline theology they represent the two sides of the divine
attitude toward humankind (cf. Rom. 2:4).[7] On the one hand, God's loving
forbearance is demonstrated by his holding back his wrath toward human
rebellion; on the other hand, his kindness is found in the thousandfold

---

also possible that Paul was not thinking rhythm, but used the noun for the first three items,
then dropped it thereafter.

[2]For the τά of the rest, P[46c] and B read τὸ μή, resulting in "does not seek that
which is not her own."

[3]See n. 12 on vv. 1-3. Holladay, 171-72, sees this in a slightly different way, as a
continuation of the "I" formula of vv. 1-3. That is, Paul is here setting forth his own
apostolic ministry, many items of which are expressed in light of the Corinthians' attitudes
toward him. Although a few items seem forced, there is much to be said for some of this.

[4]Cf. in this regard the clear echo of this passage in 1 Clem. 49, where in v. 5
Clement thoroughly adapts the language to fit the new situation.

[5]Gk. μακροθυμεῖ; cf. 1 Thess. 5:14.

[6]Gk. χρηστεύεται (a NT hapax legomenon); the verb is found only in Christian
writings. Since it occurs twice in Clement of Rome (once in a saying of Jesus), Harnack
conjectured that Paul derived it from a "Q" saying of Jesus. The noun and adjective occur
regularly in the LXX to describe the character of God.

[7]The two cognate nouns appear together also as fruit of the Spirit in Gal. 5:22 (cf.
Col. 3:12), as well as in the description of Paul's apostolic ministry in 2 Cor. 6:6.

expressions of his mercy.[8] Thus Paul's description of love begins with this twofold description of God, who through Christ has shown himself forbearing and kind toward those who deserve divine judgment. The obvious implication, of course, is that this is how his people are to be toward others.

4b-5   The two positive expressions are followed by seven verbs that indicate how love does *not* behave, the first five of which are taken right out of the Corinthian file. It is as though Paul were saying, "You must have love; without it you are simply not behaving as Christians. And what is love? It is to behave in ways opposite to yourselves!"

(a) *Love does not envy.*[9] This verb is ordinarily used by Paul in a positive sense;[10] but its cognate adjective[11] appears in 3:4, in conjunction with "strife,"[12] to denote the "rivalry" expressed in the Corinthians' divisions over their teachers that is being carried on in the name of wisdom. More pointedly it probably reflects those who stand against Paul as his "rivals" for the affection of the community (see on 4:18). Love does not allow fellow believers to be in rivalry or competition, either for "vaunted positions" or to curry people's favor in order to gain adherents. Indeed, it seeks quite the opposite: How best do I serve these for whom Christ died, whatever my own desires?

(b) *Does not boast.*[13] This rare word means literally to "behave as a braggart," or "be a windbag." It suggests self-centered actions in which there is an inordinate desire to call attention to oneself. Although Paul's use of this word is often viewed as his being critical of the desire on the part of some Corinthians to have the more "showy gifts," more likely it again reflects those in the community who are especially Paul's "rivals" or "op-

---

[8]Cf. especially the Pauline testimony in 1 Tim. 1:12-17 that is intended to illustrate the "sound teaching of our Lord Jesus Christ." After the litany of his own former attitudes toward God (v. 13), what receives emphasis is that to the chiefest of sinners God has shown mercy, so that in saving him the full extent of God's forbearance might be manifest to all who would later believe in Christ (v. 16).

[9]Gk. ζηλόω; to be distinguished from its synonym φθονέω, which is always pejorative and is the baser evil, implying not covetousness (the evil desire for what another possesses), but displeasure at another's good fortune—indeed, begrudging such a person to the point of wishing her/him deprived of it. The verb ζηλόω is a "middle term," referring to a human attitude that can either be base or noble. When noble, it "earnestly desires" something nobler for oneself; when base, it "jealously longs" for the betterment of oneself to the detriment of another.

[10]See 12:31; 14:1, 39; cf. 2 Cor. 11:2. For the distinctions see esp. Gal. 4:17-18, where Paul's opponents are accused of "courting the favor" of the Galatians for their own ends, so that the Galatians in turn will "court them." Nonetheless, he goes on to say in v. 18, it is always right to be "courted" with honorable intentions.

[11]Gk. ζῆλος; it may also be used positively, as in 2 Cor. 7:7, 11; 9:2; Col. 4:13; cf. Phil. 3:6.

[12]Cf. 2 Cor. 12:20; Gal. 5:20; and Rom. 13:13.

[13]Gk. περπερεύεται; a NT hapax legomenon, this is its first occurrence in Greek literature (cf. Marc.Aur.Ant. 5.5.4).

ponents," who in effect are leading the whole church down the wrong paths. Over against Paul, they think of themselves as having "wisdom" (3:18) and "knowledge" (8:2), and especially as being "spiritual" (14:37).[14] It is not possible to "boast" and love at the same time. The one action wants others to think highly of oneself, whether deserving or not; the other cares for none of that, but only for the good of the community as a whole.

(c) *Is not proud*. This verb literally means to be "puffed up," carrying with it overtones of arrogance. It is used exclusively in this letter to describe the Corinthians themselves, especially in contexts where they stand over against the apostle.[15] For Paul this is their greater sin, to be arrogant in the face of so much that is unholy and unloving, and therefore unchristian.

(d) *Is not rude*.[16] If the KJV is a bit stilted here ("doth not behave itself unseemly"), it does seem to capture Paul's sense better than does the English word "rude." The verb means to "behave shamefully or disgracefully." In this letter it recalls (i) the activities of the women in 11:2-16, who are bringing shame on their "heads" by attiring themselves so as to disregard the distinctions between the sexes, or (ii) the actions of the "haves" at the Lord's Table, who are humiliating (shaming) "those who have nothing." Christian love cares too much for the rest of the community to behave in such "unseemly" ways.

(e) *Is not self-seeking*. This is the fifth consecutive item that specifically echoes earlier parts of the letter, this time 10:24 and 33. In a context where he will urge freedom to eat whatever one wants, because the earth and everything in it is the Lord's, Paul prefaces that discussion as he concludes it, that the *prior* consideration is not what's right, or even all right, but rather that they should not seek their own good but that of others. In some ways this is the fullest expression of what Christian love is all about.[17] It does not seek its own; it does not believe that "finding oneself" is the highest good; it is not enamored with self-gain, self-justification, self-worth. To the contrary, it seeks the good of one's neighbor—or enemy (cf. Phil. 2:4).

(f) *Is not easily angered*.[18] With this verb Paul begins to move beyond the immediate situation in Corinth,[19] at least as it is reflected in the present letter.[20] In the active the verb means to arouse someone to anger, to

[14]Cf. H. Braun, *TDNT* VI, 94: "The immediate context puts περπερεύεσθαι in the setting of defiant conduct through the proximity of ζηλοῦν."

[15]Gk. φυσιόω; see on 4:6, 18-19; 5:2; 8:1. Its only other occurrence in the NT is Col. 2:18.

[16]Gk. ἀσχημονέω; cf. 7:36.

[17]Thus Paul describes our Lord as "not pleasing himself" but taking on the "insults" of others for their sakes (Rom. 15:1-3).

[18]Gk. παροξύνομαι; cf. Acts 15:39; 17:16.

[19]Although "anger" and "quarreling" are often closely related vices.

[20]Bittlinger, 86, observes that with this verb the list begins to speak to how one responds to the evil in others, since the first five deal basically with the evil in oneself.

provoke. In the passive, as here, it suggests that the one who loves is not easily provoked to anger by those around him or her. This is a further expression of the forbearance with which the list began.

(g) *Keeps no record of wrongs.* Literally this says that love "does not reckon the evil." Since the language is very close to the LXX of Zech. 8:17, it is possible, as the KJV does ("thinketh no evil"), to understand this to mean "love does not devise evil against someone else." More likely, however, the object, "the evil," refers to that done to one by another person. The verb then could mean, "does not think on it (i.e., take notice of it)." Since in Paul this verb very often means to "put to one's account," it seems probable that the nuance suggested by the NIV moves in the right direction. Just as God in Christ does not "reckon our sins against us" (2 Cor. 5:19), so the one who loves does not take notice of the evil done against him/her in the sense that no records are kept, waiting for God or man to settle the score. Here Paul reflects the tradition of Jesus' word on the cross as found in Luke's Gospel (23:34), where the Savior extends forgiveness to those crucifying him.

6 The first clause in this verse is actually the final item in the preceding list, "does not delight in evil"; however, since it is balanced by its opposite, "but rejoices with[21] the truth," it is probable that they are to be understood together, as two sides of the same reality. Evil and truth, therefore, are probably thought of here in their larger sense of the gospel and all that is opposed to it. Here again by his use of *agapē* Paul is especially reflecting the character of God, which is now to be displayed by his people. The person full of Christian love joins in rejoicing on the side of behavior that reflects the gospel—for every victory gained, every forgiveness offered, every act of kindness. Such a person refuses to take delight in evil, either in its more global forms—war, the suppression of the poor—or in those close to home—the fall of a brother or sister, a child's misdeed. Love absolutely rejects that most pernicious form of rejoicing over evil, gossiping about the misdeeds of others; it is not gladdened when someone else falls. Love stands on the side of the gospel and looks for mercy and justice for all, including those with whom one disagrees.

7 This final staccato of verbs brings the present description to a summary and conclusion. In each case the verb is accompanied by the object "all things," a rhetorical repetition which here comes very close to an adverbial use ("in everything," or "always").[22] Most likely they form a chiasm, the first and fourth dealing with present circumstances, the second

---

[21]The simple verb χαίρει with the preposition ἐπί ("on the basis of" or "over") appears in the first clause; the compound συγχαίρει in this one. It is doubtful that σύν is intended to go with "truth," as though the latter were personified. More likely it means something like Barrett's translation, "joins in rejoicing at (or in) the truth."

[22]So also Martin, 51.

and third looking to the future.[23] Thus it is the character of love to "put up with everything,"[24] the sense perhaps best captured by the NEB: "there is nothing love cannot face." So too the final verb, "love always perseveres." Love has a tenacity in the present, buoyed by its absolute confidence in the future, that enables it to live in every kind of circumstance and continually to pour itself out in behalf of others.[25] Paul's own ministry was a perfect example of such love.

The middle verbs reflect the other two members of the triad found in v. 13. In saying "love always believes" and "hopes," Paul does not mean that love always believes the best about everything and everyone, but that love never ceases to have faith; it never loses hope. This is why it can endure. The life that is so touched by the never-ceasing love of God in Christ (cf. Rom. 8:39) is in turn enabled by the Spirit to love others in the same way. It trusts God in behalf of the one loved, hopes to the end that God will show mercy in that person's behalf.

With these final rhetorical phrases Paul has rhapsodized somewhat beyond his immediate concern, both in this section on spiritual gifts and in the letter at large. But not totally so. The passage has some affinities with 3:21-23, where the earlier items are especially to the point, but the later ones lift their horizons to take in a much larger picture. Paul has not lost sight of his argument, however, so with the next paragraph he brings this description of love into focus in terms of its permanence, over against the gifts of the Spirit that belong only to the present age. And in so doing he leads the Corinthians back to the concern at hand, that they should above all "make love their aim" and at the same time "eagerly desire the gifts of the Spirit."

It is often pointed out that in this paragraph Paul seems best to capture the life and ministry of Jesus. So much so that one could substitute his name for the noun "love" and thereby describe love in a more personal way. After doing so, however, one does not want to miss Paul's point, which ultimately is description for the purpose of exhortation. Perhaps that point could best be captured by putting one's own name in place of the noun "love," and not neglecting thereafter to find a proper place for repentance and forgiveness.

[23]This suggestion comes from Findlay, 899; it seems to make the best sense of the rhetoric.

[24]Gk. πάντα στέγει; cf. 9:12, where Paul uses this same verb and object to mean "put up with" the kinds of hardships that have befallen him as a minister of the gospel. See n. 78 on 9:12. There seems to be no good reason to make it go in another direction here, although its range of meanings would allow "protect [NIV], cover [Conzelmann, in his translation, but not in the commentary], supports [Barrett]."

[25]One is reminded of Shakespeare's famous line, "Love is not love that alters when it alteration finds."

c. The permanence of love (13:8-13)

8 *Love never fails.*[1] *But where there are prophecies, they will cease; where there are tongues, they will be stilled; where there is knowledge,*[2] *it will pass away.* 9 *For we know in part and we prophesy in part,* 10 *but when* what is complete[3] *comes, what*[4] *is in part disappears.* 11 *When I was a child, I talked like a child,*[5] *I thought like a child, I reasoned like a child. When*[6] *I became a man, I put childish ways behind me.* 12 *Now we see but a poor reflection as in a mirror; then we shall see face to face. Now I know in part; then I shall know fully, even as I am fully known.*

13 *And now these three remain: faith, hope and love. But the greatest of these is love.*

Paul's concern in this interlude on Christian love is twofold: (1) to redirect their thinking on the true nature of spirituality, on which he and they are at such odds (see pp. 572-73 above); and (2) to place even their emphasis on tongues within the framework of the primacy of love in Christian ethics, so that their eagerness for "spirits" (14:12) will be redirected toward edifying the community rather than directed toward "spirituality" as such.

Thus the argument began with a set of contrasts in which Paul insisted that *charismata* and good works do not benefit the speaker or doer if he or she does not also have Christian love. Now, following the lyrical description of *agapē* in vv. 4-7, he brings this argument to its conclusion with another set of contrasts: Love is the "way that is beyond comparison" because, in contrast to the *charismata,* which function within the framework of our present eschatological existence only, *agapē* characterizes our existence both now and forever. Thus its primacy, not because what is only for

---

[1]The Westerns and MajT read the compound ἐκπίπτει; P⁴⁶ ℵ* A B C 048 243 33 1739 pc read πίπτει. The latter is almost certainly original, despite Harnack, "Hymn," p. 481 n. 2. The former presupposes the meaning "come to an end" for πίπτω; see the commentary.

[2]A few MSS (ℵ A F G 33 365 pc a) make this plural, conforming it to the preceding plurals and thus making it clear that it refers to the "utterances of knowledge" in 12:8.

[3]NIV, "perfection"; plus "imperfect" for the next clause. But these tend to mislead since the latter is the same phrase translated "in part" in v. 9, with the article making it a substantive. See the commentary.

[4]The MajT, with no early support, adds τότε, probably under the influence of v. 12. But it misses the point of the later τότε altogether, which is not a logical "then" but a contrast between the present "now" and the eschatological "then."

[5]For the argument for the word order of P⁴⁶ and the MajT, "as a child I talked, etc.," as the original, see Zuntz, 128-29, who is almost certainly correct. As he notes, Paul's emphasis lies not on the verbs, but on the repeated ὡς νήπιος.

[6]The MajT, with some Western support, adds a δέ, which is spurious by all counts. See Zuntz, 189 n. 8.

now *(charismata)* is lesser, but because what is both for now and forever *(agapē)* must dictate *how* the gifts function in the present life of the church.

The greater urgency of this present argument, however, is with the "*only*-for-the-present" nature of the gifts, not with the permanence of love—although that is always lingering near the surface. Love is scarcely mentioned (vv. 8a, 13 only); the fact that the gifts will pass away forms the heart of the entire argument (vv. 8b-12). The clue to this emphasis lies with the Corinthians' understanding of tongues as evidence of their spirituality. The problem is with an "overspiritualized" eschatology, as if tongues, the language of the angels, meant that they were already partakers of the ultimate state of spiritual existence.[7] Hence the underlying polemical tone of this passage.[8] This is not a condemnation of the gifts; it is a relativizing of them. In 1:7 Paul had already stated his own perspective: "You do not lack any spiritual gift as you eagerly wait for our Lord Jesus Christ to be revealed." Now he urges over and again that gifts do *not* belong to the future, but only to the present. On this they are deluded. The irony is that the gifts, their evidence of their future existence, will pass away (v. 8a); they are "partial" (v. 9); they are as childhood in comparison with adulthood (v. 11); they are like looking into a mirror in comparison with seeing someone in person (v. 12).[9]

One must not mistake this emphasis with a devaluation of the gifts themselves.[10] The fact is that we are still in the present; and therefore in chap. 14 Paul will go on not only to correct an imbalance with regard to the gifts, but to urge their proper use. Pursue love (14:1), he says, because that alone is forever (13:8, 13); but that also means that in the present you should eagerly desire manifestations of the Spirit that build up the community (14:1-5).

8 This paragraph begins with the famous line, "Love never fails[11]," but it is not immediately clear what Paul intends. On the one hand, the combination of the adverb "never" and the present tense of the verb suggests that it stands in continuity with the preceding list, bringing the

---

[7]The close proximity of the argument in chap. 15 is especially relevant here.

[8]This paragraph in particular, with its concern for the "present only" nature of the gifts, hardly fits the view that the whole chapter is a self-contained unit extolling the greatness of love.

[9]For those who take a noneschatological view of this passage, seeing it rather as dealing with immaturity and maturity, see below, n. 23.

[10]Something like this is suggested all too frequently by scholars whose skills should serve them better. That for Paul the Spirit is the source of the gifts and that he himself holds prophecy in such high regard make this an impossible position. See also n. 20 on 12:1-3.

[11]Gk. πίπτει, which literally means "to fall," is used figuratively to refer to "falling" into guilt, sin, or apostasy (cf. 10:8, 12) or to "become invalid, deprived of its force" (Luke 16:17). See the discussion by W. Michaelis, *TDNT* VI, 164-66.

whole to its conclusion. In this case it would mean something like "Love is never defeated, is never brought to the ground; it persists even when rebuffed."[12] On the other hand, several items indicate that it serves as the beginning of the present paragraph[13] and is intended to be set in contrast both to the verb "remain" in v. 13 and the verbs "pass away" and "cease" in v. 8. If so, then it would mean something like "never comes to an end, becomes invalid," and thus extends the sense of the final verb in v. 7, "always endures."[14] Perhaps Paul's intent is to be found in the very ambiguity of such figurative language, so that both are in view. There is a sense in which love is never brought down; it reflects God's character, after all, and cannot fluctuate from what it is. Yet that very reality is what also gives it eternal character, so that it "remains" even after all other things have come to their proper end.

Despite the majestic description of love that has just preceded, Paul has not lost sight of his overall argument. Thus he sets forth three *charismata*[15] which, by way of contrast to the nonfailing character of love, are destined "to come to an end." If there is any significance to this choice of gifts, it lies with the fact that the first, "prophecies," is his own preference for the edification of the community,[16] while the other two are Corinthian favorites. In both cases, and therefore in all cases, these are manifestations of the Spirit for the church's present eschatological existence, in which God's new people live "between the times"—between the inauguration of the End through the death and resurrection of Jesus with the subsequent outpouring of the Spirit and the final consummation when God will be "all in all" (see 15:20-28). Thus the basic verb chosen to describe the temporal, transitory nature of the *charismata* is an eschatological one, used elsewhere in the letter to refer to the "passing away" of what belongs merely to the present age.[17] This choice of verbs, which recurs in v. 10, is already the

---

[12]Cf. Michaelis, *TDNT* VI, 166, who suggests the former alternatives, and Barrett, 305, who prefers the latter but in contrast to Michaelis sees the sentence as the beginning of the present paragraph.

[13]Especially (1) the repetition of the subject ἡ ἀγάπη, suggesting in the strongest way that it is no longer part of the preceding series; (2) the δέ and repeated εἴτε before the three gifts, indicating that these are intended to be in contrast to this sentence; and (3) the verb πίπτει, standing in contrast to the μένει with which the paragraph concludes.

[14]See esp. Spicq, *Agape*, pp. 93-95 (160-61).

[15]All three appear in the original list in 12:8-10; they also reappear in the present argument in 13:1-2.

[16]Not because it is superior to any of the others, but because it is representative of intelligible utterances, which can edify, in contrast to uninterpreted tongues, which cannot.

[17]Gk. καταργέω (cf. 1:28; 2:6; 6:13; 15:24-26; 2 Thess. 2:8), used here with both "prophecy" and "knowledge." Some (e.g., MacArthur, 359; cf. S. D. Toussaint, "First Corinthians Thirteen and the Tongues Question," *BibSac* 120 [1963], 311-16) have argued that the change of verbs (including the change of voice) with tongues (παυ-

indicator that the contrasts in the passage have to do with eschatology, not with maturity of some kind.

It needs only be noted further that "knowledge" in this passage does not mean ordinary human knowing or learning, but refers rather to that special manifestation of the Spirit, the "utterance of knowledge" (12:8), which understands revealed "mysteries" (13:2).[18] It has to do especially with "knowing" the ways of God in the present age. This is made certain by vv. 9 and 12b, where this form of "knowledge" is referred to as "partial," in contrast to a "face-to-face" knowing at the Eschaton that is "complete," that is, of the same character as God's knowledge of us.

9-10 Paul now sets out to explain[19] what he has asserted in v. 8. He does so by using the language "in part"[20] to describe the "for now only" nature of the gifts[21] (repeating the verb "pass away" from v. 8 to indicate what happens to them) and "the perfect/complete"[22] to describe the time when what is "in part" will come to an end. The use of the substantive "the perfect/complete," which sometimes can mean "mature," plus the ambiguity of the first analogy (childhood and adulthood), has led some to think that the contrast is between "immaturity" and "maturity."[23] But that will hardly

---

σονται) has independent significance, as though this meant that tongues might cease before prophecy and knowledge. But that misses Paul's concern rather widely. The change of verbs is purely rhetorical; to make it otherwise is to elevate to significance something in which Paul shows no interest at all. Just as one can scarcely distinguish between "cease" and "pass away" when used in the same context, neither can one distinguish between καταργέω and παύω in this context (although the NIV's choice of "be stilled" for tongues is felicitous). The middle voice came along with the change of verbs.

[18]Cf. Johansson, "I Cor. xiii," p. 389, and Miguens, "Reconsidered," p. 82, although they differ considerably as to the *content* of such *gnōsis*.

[19]Note the return of the explanatory γάρ, last seen in 12:12-14 (cf. its frequency in chaps. 1–11), evidence that Paul is returning to his argumentative style, which will predominate throughout chap. 14.

[20]Gk. ἐκ μέρους; cf. 12:27.

[21]The choice of prophecy and knowledge from the preceding verse does not "mean" anything. Partly this is due to style, partly to the fact that "tongues" does not lend itself easily to the way these sentences are expressed. "We speak in tongues in part" is not particularly meaningful; but tongues, as well as all the other *charismata* in 12:8-10, are to be understood as included in the argument. Otherwise Miguens, "Reconsidered," p. 90, and Martin, 53-54, who suggest that "knowledge," the Corinthians' prized gift, is basically being taken to task here. The argument of chap. 14 (esp. v. 6) refutes this.

[22]Gk. τὸ τέλειον; cf. 2:7. This is the adjective of the verb τελειόω. Both mean to "bring to an end, to complete" something, although they also carry the further sense of "making" or "being perfect." That is, the completing of something is the perfecting of it. God may thus be described as τέλειος (Matt. 5:48), which can only mean "perfect." The meaning in the present instance is determined by its being the final goal of what is ἐκ μέρους, "partial." Thus its root sense of "having attained the end or purpose" (BAGD), hence "complete," seems to be the nuance here.

[23]This has taken several forms, depending on how one understands τὸ τέλειον. (1) Some see it as referring to love itself. In this view the Corinthian desire for gifts reflects

do since the contrast has to do with the *gifts'* being "partial," not the believers themselves.[24] Furthermore, that is to give the analogy, which is ambiguous at best, precedence over the argument as a whole and the plain statement of v. 12b,[25] where Paul repeats verbatim[26] the first clause of v. 9, "we know[27] in part," in a context that can only be eschatological. Convoluted as the argument may appear, Paul's distinctions are between "now" and "then," between what is incomplete (though perfectly appropriate to the church's present existence) and what is complete (when its final destiny in Christ has been reached and "we see face to face" and "know as we are known").[28]

That means that the phrase "in part" refers to what is not complete, or at least not complete in itself.[29] The phrase by itself does not carry the connotation of "temporary" or "relative"; that comes from the context and the language "now . . . then" in v. 12. But the implication is there. It is "partial" because it belongs only to this age, which is but the beginning, not

---

their immaturity; when they have come to the fullness of love they will put away such childish desires (e.g., Findlay, 900; Bruce, 128; Johansson, "I Cor. xiii," pp. 389-90; Miguens, "Reconsidered," pp. 87-97; Holladay, 174). (2) Others see "the perfect" as referring to the full revelation given in the NT itself, which when it would come to completion would do away with the "partial" forms of charismatic revelation. Given its classical exposition by B. B. Warfield, this view has been taken over in a variety of ways by contemporary Reformed and Dispensationalist theologies. It is an impossible view, of course, since Paul himself could not have articulated it. What neither Paul himself nor the Corinthians could have understood can possibly be the meaning of the text. (3) Still others see it as referring to the maturing of the body, the church, which is sometimes also seen to have happened with the rise of the more regular clergy (Eph. 4:11-13 is appealed to) or the coming of Jews and Gentiles into the one body (see, e.g., J. R. McRay, "*To Teleion* in I Corinthians 13:10," *RestQ* 14 [1971], 168-83; and R. L. Thomas, "'Tongues . . . Will Cease,'" *JETS* 17 [1974], 81-89). This view has nothing to commend it except the analogy of v. 11, which is a misguided emphasis at best.

It is perhaps an indictment of Western Christianity that we should consider "mature" our rather totally cerebral and domesticated—but bland—brand of faith, with the concomitant absence of the Spirit in terms of his supernatural gifts! The Spirit, not Western rationalism, marks the turning of the ages, after all; and to deny the Spirit's manifestations is to deny our present existence to be eschatological, as belonging to the beginning of the time of the End.

[24]Even though Paul says "*we* know in part," the emphasis is not on the immaturity of the Corinthians, but on the relative nature of the gifts. This is demonstrated (1) by the γάϱ that ties it to v. 8, where it is said of these gifts that *they* will pass away, not that the Corinthians need to grow up, and (2) by the clause "we prophesy in part," which makes sense only as having to do with the prophecies, not with the prophets.

[25]Such a procedure is to make "the tail wag the dog."

[26]With the exception of the change from the plural to the singular.

[27]No significance can be attached to the use of the verb instead of the noun. The usage in 8:1-2 indicates that the verb here means "to have knowledge," which in this context means to have the gift of knowledge.

[28]Cf. Grudem, 148-49, especially the discussion of ἐϰ μέϱους in n. 59.

[29]On the translation in the NIV see n. 4 above. "In part" and "imperfect" do not carry the same connotations to most English readers.

the completion, of the End. These gifts have to do with the edification of the church as it "eagerly awaits our Lord Jesus Christ to be revealed" (1:7). The nature of the eschatological language in v. 12 further implies that the term "the perfect" has to do with the Eschaton itself, not some form of "perfection" in the present age.[30] It is not so much that the End itself is "the perfect," language that does not make tolerably good sense; rather, it is what happens at the End, when the goal has been reached (see n. 22). At the coming of Christ the final purpose of God's saving work in Christ will have been reached; at that point those gifts now necessary for the building up of the church in the present age will disappear, because "the complete" will have come. To cite Barth's marvelous imagery: "*Because* the *sun* rises all lights are extinguished."[31]

11 Picking up the themes of "in part" and "the complete," plus the verb "pass away"[32] from v. 10, Paul proceeds to express the point of vv. 9-10 by way of analogy. The analogy itself is commonplace.[33] The adult does not continue to "talk" or "think" or "reason" like a child.[34] Because of the use of the verb "talk," which elsewhere in this section is used with tongues, and the contrast in 14:20 between thinking like children and adults, it is common to see this analogy as referring to speaking in tongues,[35] which is then also considered "childish" behavior that the Corinthians are now being urged to set aside in favor of love. Such a view flies full in the face of the argument itself, both here and in 12:4-11 and 14:1-40.[36]

Paul's point in context does not have to do with "childishness" and "growing up," but with the difference between the present and the future. He is illustrating that there will come a time when the gifts will pass away.[37] The analogy, therefore, says that behavior from one period in one's life is not appropriate to the other; the one is "done away with" when the other comes. So shall it be at the Eschaton. The behavior of the child is in fact

[30]Cf. the discussion in Grudem, 210-19, which also includes a refutation of the views in n. 23.

[31]*The Resurrection of the Dead* (ET, London, 1933), p. 86.

[32]But now in the active. This is the only instance in the letter where it is not necessarily eschatological. It was chosen in this instance because of its use in the preceding sentences. Here it means "do away with," or in keeping with the imagery "set aside."

[33]See Conzelmann, 226 n. 84.

[34]Gk. νήπιος, which ordinarily, as here, refers to a very young child.

[35]But as Conzelmann, 226 n. 85, notes, that breaks down with the use of the past tense and the first person singular. After all, Paul speaks in tongues more than all of them (14:18).

[36]Although the "childishness" is seen in their eagerness for tongues, the net result is that spiritual gifts, which for Paul are "manifestations of the Spirit," are disparaged.

[37]Cf. Parry, 195: "It is an illustration merely: no ref. to the metaphorical use of νήπιος and τέλειος."

appropriate to childhood. The gifts,[38] by analogy, are appropriate to the present life of the church, especially so since from Paul's point of view they are the active work of the Spirit in the church's corporate life. On the other hand, the gifts are equally inappropriate to the church's final existence because then, as he will go on to argue in v. 12, "I shall know fully, even as I am fully known." Hence the implicit contrast with love, which will never come to an end. Love does not eliminate the gifts in the present; rather, it is absolutely essential to Christian life both now and forever. The gifts, on the other hand, are not forever; they are to help build up the body—but *only* in the present, when such edification is needed.

12 Paul now proceeds to another analogy, to which he appends an immediate application. With their repeated "now, but then" language, these sentences bring out more sharply the contrast between the Corinthians' present existence and that of the future. The fact that they are tied to v. 11 by an explanatory "for"[39] further indicates, as we have argued, that the preceding analogy has basically to do with two modes of existence, not with "growing up" and putting away childish behavior.

The first sentence, which literally reads "For at the present time[40] we look through[41] a looking-glass *en ainigmati*[42], but then[43] face to face[44]," is particularly relevant to their setting, since Corinth was famous as the pro-

---

[38]Not simply tongues, which is not taken up as such in the argument after v. 8. Tongues at this point is but one among all the Spirit-inspired gifts (note the special emphasis on the Spirit's role in 12:7-11) that are part of the present life of the church.

[39]Unfortunately untranslated in the NIV.

[40]Gk. ἄρτι, an adverb that in classical Greek meant "just now" (cf. Matt. 9:18), but in Hellenistic Greek took on the further connotation of "now in general," referring especially to "the present time." This is the predominant usage in the NT, and can mean nothing else when set in contrast with τότε, as here.

[41]This is a bit stilted; because of the peculiar nature of the reflection in a mirror, the Greeks thought of one as looking "through" the glass, in contrast to our looking "in" or "into" it.

[42]This Greek word, which appears only here in the NT, literally means "in a riddle, or figurative way." Very likely this is an echo of Num. 12:8 (LXX), where God spoke with Moses directly ("mouth to mouth"), not as to the prophets, to whom he spoke through visions or dreams (v. 6), "in figures," implying that they received "pictures" of the truth that were not as clear as the direct words to Moses. The problem here is whether it means "indistinctly" (thus, "obscurely," "dimly," etc.) or "indirectly" (thus "in riddle" as over against "direct speech"), referring to the form rather than the content. The majority of interpreters have taken the former position, but cf. the critique by S. E. Bassett, "I Cor. 13:12, βλέπομεν γὰρ ἄρτι δι᾽ ἐσόπτρου ἐν αἰνίγματι," *JBL* 47 (1928), 232-36; and esp. N. Hugedé, *La métaphore du miroir dans les Epitres de Saint Paul aux Corinthiens* (Neuchâtel, 1957); there is an English synopsis by F. W. Danker, "The Mirror Metaphor in 1 Cor. 13:12 and 2 Cor. 3:18," *CTM* 31 (1960), 428-29.

[43]The coming of Christ is implied.

[44]A biblical idiom for direct personal communication. See Gen. 32:30; cf. Num. 12:8, "speak 'mouth to mouth.'"

ducer of some of the finest bronze mirrors in antiquity.[45] That suggests that the puzzling phrase *en ainigmati* is probably not as pejorative as most translations imply.[46] More likely the emphasis is not on the *quality* of seeing that one experiences in looking into a mirror—that would surely have been an affront to them—but to the *indirect nature* of looking into a mirror[47] as opposed to seeing someone face to face.[48] The analogy, of course, breaks down a bit since one sees one's own face in a mirror, and Paul's point is that in our present existence one "sees" God (presumably),[49] or understands the "mysteries," only indirectly. It is not a *distorted* image that we have in Christ through the Spirit; but it is as yet *indirect,* not complete. To put all this in another way, but keeping the imagery, "Our present 'vision' of God, as great as it is, is as nothing when compared to the real thing that is yet to be; it is like the difference between seeing a reflected image in a mirror and seeing a person face to face." In our own culture the comparable metaphor would be the difference between seeing a photograph and seeing someone in person. As good as a picture is, it is simply not the real thing.

With the second set of sentences in this verse, Paul brings into focus all that has been argued since v. 8. Picking up the words of contrast from v. 12a ("at the present time," "then") but the *content* of v. 9, he concludes, "Now I[50] know in part, but then I shall know fully,[51] even as I am fully known." By this Paul intends to delineate the difference between the "knowing" that is available through the gift of the Spirit and the final eschatological knowing that is complete. What is not quite clear is the exact nuance of the final clause that expresses the nature of that final knowing,

---

[45]See, e.g., *Corinth, A Brief History of the City and a Guide to the Excavations,* published by the American School of Classical Studies in Athens, 1972, p. 5. It is thus surely not by accident that this analogy occurs only in the Corinthian correspondence among the Pauline letters (cf. 2 Cor. 3:18); cf. in a similar way the relevance of the analogy in 9:24-27.

[46]As, e.g., by "darkly" (KJV), "we are baffled" (Montgomery); "only blurred" (Norlie); "dimly" (TCNT). In fact the idea that their mirrors were of poor quality and therefore one did not get a true image is a purely modern idea. See Hugedé, *Métaphore,* pp. 97-100.

[47]Cf., among others, Bassett, "I Cor. 13.12"; Barth, *Resurrection,* p. 85; Hugedé, *Métaphore,* pp. 145-50; Danker, "Mirror," p. 429; Conzelmann, 228.

[48]This imagery has elicited considerable discussion, with a whole range of suggestions, most of which seem quite unrelated to the context, and especially to the *point* of the analogy, which is made plain in the second half of the verse. The most likely of these options is that of G. Kittel, *TDNT* I, 178-80, who argues that both terms, "through a mirror in riddles," refer to "seeing in the Spirit," meaning to "see prophetically." See the critique of the other suggestions in Hugedé, *Métaphore,* pp. 37-95.

[49]Otherwise Miguens, "Reconsidered," p. 87.

[50]For this sudden switch to the singular see on v. 1.

[51]The verb in this final clause is the compound ἐπιγινώσκω, which probably is intended to carry its precise nuance, "to know exactly, completely, or through and through" (BAGD).

"even as[52] I am fully known." It is often suggested that the passive, "as I am fully known," "contains the idea of electing grace."[53] Attractive as that is theologically, most likely it simply refers to God's way of knowing. God's knowledge of us is immediate—full and direct, "face to face,"[54] as it were; at the Eschaton, Paul seems to be saying, we too shall know in this way, with no more need for the kinds of mediation that the mirror illustrates or that "prophecy" and the "utterance of knowledge" exemplify in reality.

Thus Paul's point with all of this is now made. In v. 8 he argued that love, in contrast to *charismata,* never comes to an end. Precisely because the gifts have an end point, which love does not, they are of a different order altogether. This does not make them imperfect, although in a sense that too is true; it makes them relative. Paul's concern in vv. 9-12 has been to demonstrate the strictly "present age" nature of these gifts. They shall pass away (v. 8); they are "in part" (v. 9); they belong to this present existence only (vv. 10-12). Most likely the purpose of all this is simply to reinforce what was said in vv. 1-3, that the Corinthians' emphasis on tongues as evidence for spirituality is wrong because it is wrongheaded, especially from people who do not otherwise exhibit the one truly essential expression of the Spirit's presence, Christian love. Good as spiritual gifts are, they are only for the present; Christian love, which the Corinthians currently lack, is the "more excellent way" in part because it belongs to eternity as well as to the present.

13 This sentence, which is related to v. 8 through its use of the verb "remain," is at once both the best known and most difficult text in the paragraph. There can be little question that it is intended to bring the argument of the present paragraph to a conclusion, and probably the entire chapter as well. But how? There are five interrelated problems: (1) Whether the words "and now" carry a temporal or logical force; (2) in conjunction with that, whether "remain" has to do with the present or the future; (3) the sudden appearance of "faith and hope" in an argument that heretofore has had to nothing to do with these virtues, but with love and spiritual gifts; (4) how love is "greater than" these other two; and (5) how, then, this sentence concludes the paragraph.

Despite the long debate over the temporal or logical force of the combination "and now,"[55] it is difficult under any circumstances to divest

---

[52]Gk. καθώς; Spicq, *Agape,* p. 102 (166), notes that Paul uses this word 25 times, always with the connotation "exactly as," i.e., "it makes an exact comparison."

[53]The language is Conzelmann's (p. 228), but the suggestion is found throughout the literature (cf., e.g., Martin, 54).

[54]Cf. Gen. 32:31.

[55]Gk. νυνὶ δέ; see 12:18 and 15:20; cf. 2 Cor. 8:11, 22; Rom. 3:21; 6:22; 7:6, 17; 15:23, 25; Phlm. 9, 11; Col. 1:22; 3:8.

the adverb "now" of some temporal sense. That is, even if its basic thrust is logical (= "but as it is"),[56] it carries the force "as it is in the present state of things." This seems to be all the more so here, given the present tense of the verb "remain" and the fact that these three opening words stand in immediate conjunction to the eschatological words that have just preceded. Thus, however we finally translate them, these opening words seem to imply some kind of *present* situation over against what is yet to be, when "I shall know fully, even as I am fully known."

The real issue, then, has to do with the sudden appearance of "faith and hope" with love, and in what sense these three "abide." First, there is good evidence to suggest that this was a familiar triad in early Christian preaching, and therefore that it would have been well known to the Corinthians.[57] Together these words embrace the whole of Christian existence, as believers live out the life of the Spirit in the present age, awaiting the consummation. They have "faith" toward God, that is, they trust him to forgive and accept them through Christ. Even though now they do not see him (or see, as it were, "a reflection in a mirror"), they trust in his goodness and mercies. They also have "hope" for the future, which has been guaranteed for them through Christ. Through his resurrection and the gift of the Spirit, they have become a thoroughly future-oriented people; the present age is on its way out, therefore they live in the present "as if not" (cf. 7:29-31), not conditioned by the present with its hardships or suffering. They are on their way "home," destined for an existence in the presence of God that is "face to face." And they have "love" for one another as they live this life of faith and hope in the context of a community of brothers and sisters of similar faith and hope. In the present life of the church "these three remain (or continue): faith, hope, and love."[58]

---

[56]The debate is carried on, of course, by those who want to interpret the sentence eschatologically, i.e., that faith, hope, and love all remain forever, even into eternity. This view demands a logical force to νυνὶ δέ, since a strictly temporal sense eliminates it as a possibility. But it must be noted that adopting a "logical" sense to νυνὶ δέ does not demand an eschatological view, it merely makes it possible.

[57]In Paul see 1 Thess. 1:3; 5:8; Gal. 5:5-6; Rom. 5:1-5; Col. 1:4-5; Eph. 4:2-5 (cf. Tit. 2:2). Beyond Paul see Heb. 6:10-12; 10:22-24; 1 Pet. 1:3-8. Beyond the NT see Barn. 1:4; 11:8; Polycarp, *Phil.* 3:2-3. Cf. the discussion in A. M. Hunter, *Paul and his Predecessors* (London, 1961²), pp. 33-35, who has argued convincingly that the formula antedates Paul, and suggests that the words τὰ τρία ταῦτα might be translated "the well-known three."

[58]Those who interpret the passage as eschatological would not disagree with most of this; the question is whether for Paul "remain" meant "forever." The obvious difficulty with the eschatological view—with which all who adopt it struggle in some way—is how Paul could envision "faith" and "hope" as continuing into eternity, especially since in 2 Cor. 5:7 he contrasts faith with the final glory in the words "for we walk by faith and not by sight," and in Rom. 8:24 he says that "hope that is seen is not hope." Despite a variety of suggestions as to how these two virtues could still be a part of

But why this triad in the present context where the contrast has been between gifts and love? The answer probably lies with Paul's concern to emphasize that love is *not* like the gifts, in that it is both for now and forever. The preceding argument might leave the impression that since the gifts are only for the present, love is basically for the future. But not so. Love never comes to an end; it always remains. So now he concludes the argument by emphasizing the presentness of love as well. In so doing, since he is trying to emphasize the nature of *their present life* in Christ, he adds faith and hope to love somewhat automatically, since for him these are what accompany love, not spiritual gifts. They simply belong to different categories.

That also, then, explains why he adds at the end, "But the greatest[59] of these is love." Even though love "continues" in the present, along with its companions faith and hope, love is the greatest of these three because it "continues" on into the final glory, which the other two by their very nature do not.

Thus with this sentence Paul is basically bringing the present argument to its conclusion. The concern has been over the "only for now" aspect of the gifts, which stands in contrast to love. The gifts are "in part"; they belong to the "now," which will be brought to an end with the "then" that is to be. Love, on the other hand, is not so. It never fails; it will never come to an end. Along with its companions, faith and hope, it abides in the present. But it is greater, at least as the point of this present argument, because it abides on into eternity.

It is not difficult to bring the final verse of this paragraph into the contemporary church; these are still the "three imperishables" for those who would live a truly Christian life in the present age. Nor is it difficult to emphasize the eschatological dimension of the paragraph, that our present existence, for all its blessings, is but a foretaste of the future. This present partial existence shall someday give way to that which is final and complete. What is more difficult is the way the emphasis on the "present only" aspect of the gifts has been treated. Most have simply yielded to historical reality

---

our eternal existence, I find the idea especially incompatible with Rom. 8:24. "Hope" does not seem to be a meaningful concept once it has been realized. Among those who argue for an eschatological sense for μένει, see Parry, 196-98; R-P, 300; Barrett, 308-10; M.-F. Lacan, "Les Trois qui demeurent (*I Cor.* xiii,13)," *RSR* 46 (1958), 321-43; F. Neirynck, "De Grote Drie. Bij een nieuwe vertaling van I Cor. XIII 13," *ETL* 39 (1963), 595-615.

[59]Gk. μείζων, as in 12:31b and 14:5; here it probably takes the place of the superlative, as it often does in Hellenistic Greek. Otherwise, R. P. Martin, "A Suggested Exegesis of 1 Corinthians 13:13," *ExpT* 82 (1971), 119-20, who gives it its true comparative force, suggesting it should be translated "but greater than these [three] is [the] love [of God]."

and have tried to make a virtue out of that reality, that for the most part these extraordinary gifts have already ceased for so many. The irony, of course, is that our present view is almost the precise opposite of that of the Corinthians, who thought of these things as eternal and therefore needed to have that view corrected. One wonders how Paul would have responded to present-day cerebral Christianity, which has generally implied that we can get along quite well without the Spirit in the present age, now that the church has achieved its maturity in orthodoxy. It seems likely that he would not be pleased to see this text used to support such a view of things.

4. The Need for Intelligibility in the Assembly (14:1-25)

With this section (vv. 1-25) and the next (vv. 26-40) Paul proceeds at last to offer specific correctives to the Corinthians' apparently unbridled use of tongues in the assembly. He began his argument with them by setting forth the broader theological framework in which these specifics are to be understood.[1] In chap. 12 he argued for diversity, tongues being only one among many manifestations of the Spirit, who gives gifts to each as he wills for "the common good" (vv. 7-11). In chap. 13, reflecting on the theme of "the common good," he insisted that none of them, himself included, counts for anything, no matter how "spiritual" they are, if they do not likewise manifest love. Now he puts these together by insisting that in the gathered assembly the single goal of their spiritual zeal should be love (v. 1), which, as in 8:1, is expressed in the language of "building up" the church (vv. 3-5, 12, 17, 26).[2] This latter theme is developed in two ways: by insisting on *intelligibility* in the gathered assembly and by giving guidelines for *order*.

This first section (vv. 1-25) takes up the issue of intelligibility. The argument is in two parts: Vv. 1-19 argue for intelligibility for the sake of fellow believers—that they might be edified; vv. 20-25 make the same point for the sake of unbelievers—that they might hear the word of the Lord and be converted. To make this point Paul argues in two ways: (1) In vv. 1-5 and 20-25 he urges that they seek prophecy vis-à-vis tongues because, being understandable, it can both edify and lead to conversion. However, both the list of gifts in v. 6 and the argument of vv. 6-19 indicate that the real issue is not tongues and prophecy per se, but the building up of the community, which can only be effected by understandable utterances, prophecy being the primary representative.

(2) In vv. 6-19 Paul directly addresses the issue of tongues, as to its unintelligibility and therefore inability to edify the community. After a

---

[1]See n. 9 on 12:1-3 for this stylistic feature.

[2]*Contra* Conzelmann, 233, whose view that chap. 13 is an editorial intrusion allows him to say of this opening: "A unified line of thought can be discovered only with difficulty."

series of analogies illustrating the basic lack of benefit from what is unintelligible (vv. 7-12), he applies this point to their situation, arguing that prayer and praise must be intelligible if the community is to be edified (vv. 13-17). This section begins (v. 6) and ends (vv. 18-19) on personal notes that suggest that Paul is perhaps also offering an apologetic for his not comporting with their standard for spirituality. For him to come to them speaking in tongues would not benefit them; thus, even though he speaks in tongues more than all of them, *in church* he will do only what edifies, that is, only what is intelligible.

a. The "greater gift"—prophecy (14:1-5)

1 *Follow the way of love and eagerly desire spiritual gifts, especially the gift of prophecy.* 2 *For anyone who speaks in a tongue[a] does not speak to* people[3] *but to God. Indeed, no one understands him; he utters mysteries by the Spirit.[4]* 3 *But everyone who prophesies speaks to* people *for their strengthening, encouragement and comfort.* 4 *He who speaks in a tongue edifies himself, but he who prophesies edifies the church.* 5 *I would like every one of you to speak in tongues,[a] but I would rather have you prophesy. He who prophesies is greater than one who speaks in tongues,[a] unless he interprets, so that the church may be edified.*

[a]Or *another language;* also in verses 4, 13, 14, 19, 26 and 27

This opening paragraph sets forth the basic contrasts and the central themes of what follows. The concern is edification (vv. 3-5), the issue intelligibility. Tongues is not understandable (v. 2), hence it cannot edify the church (v. 4). Prophecy is addressed to people precisely for their edification (v. 3), and in that sense is the greater gift.

Although there can be little question that Paul prefers prophecy to tongues in the gathered assembly, v. 5 indicates that the real issue is not tongues per se, but *uninterpreted tongues* (cf. v. 13), since an interpreted tongue can also edify. That means, therefore, as vv. 2-3 imply, that the real issue is intelligibility in the assembly. Furthermore, it is clear from vv. 2-5 that Paul is not "damning tongues with faint praise."[5] In both cases the contrasts between tongues and prophecy do not have to do with their inherent value, but with the direction of their edification. The edifying of oneself is not a bad thing; it simply is not the point of gathered worship.

1 These opening imperatives have a single purpose: to serve as a transition from the preceding argument(s) to the issue at hand, namely their

[3]NIV, "men." Also in v. 3.
[4]This is the reading of the NIV[mg]; the text reads "with his spirit," apparently under the influence of v. 14. Cf. n. 43 on 12:3. See the commentary.
[5]See n. 20 on 12:1-3.

abuse of tongues in the gathered assembly. Thus in chiastic order[6] Paul says "Follow the way of love," namely chap. 13, and in that context "eagerly desire spiritual gifts," resuming the argument from 12:31a that was interrupted by the exhortation to love. In the earlier exhortation (12:31a) he had said "eagerly desire the *greater* gifts"; now he indicates (v. 5) that by the greater gifts he means those that edify the community. Thus his choice to represent those greater gifts is "especially that you may prophesy."[7] A further word about each of these.

The command to "Follow[8] the way of love" puts into imperative form what was implied throughout the preceding argument. The "love" that they are to pursue, of course, is that described in 13:4-7, since without it the "spiritual" person amounts to zero (vv. 1-3); furthermore (vv. 8-13), it is the great imperishable: it alone—not the gifts—will abide into eternity.

The imperative "eagerly desire spiritual gifts,"[9] although it resumes the argument from 12:31, is nonetheless not a precise repetition. The verb remains the same, but the object is no longer "the greater *charismata*," but *ta pneumatika*, which probably means something like "utterances inspired by the Spirit" (see on 12:1). Some have argued for more significant differ-

---

[6] Thus: (12:31) Be zealous for τὰ χαρίσματα   A

             Yet I point out the superior way   B

     (13)   Description/exhortation on love   C

     (14:1)   Pursue love   B′

             Be zealous for τὰ πνευματικά   A′

[7] It should be noted that the imperatives are here spoken to all, not to a select group of "prophets." One may assume, therefore, that even though not all will be "prophets" (12:29), nonetheless the gift of prophesying is as available to all as is the command to pursue love, and the wish that *all* may speak in tongues (v. 5); cf. Barrett, 315. Otherwise Ellis, 24-27, who argues that only "pneumatics" are in view in chap. 14.

[8] Gk. διώκετε, lit. "pursue, strive for, seek after, aspire to" (BAGD). The word most often means to pursue in a negative sense, thus "persecute." But in Paul it is a favorite metaphor for spiritual effort (cf. 1 Thess. 5:15; Rom. 9:30-31; 12:13; 14:19; Phil. 3:12; 1 Tim. 6:11; 2 Tim. 2:22). The present imperative implies continuous action, "keep on pursuing love."

[9] Martin, 65-66, following Chevallier and Baker (see on 12:31), argues that these words are best understood as a quotation from the Corinthian letter. Although this option has some attractive features, it has several strikes against it: (1) The form of the verb is imperative; it is not easy to imagine why the Corinthians would have spoken to Paul in this manner, especially in a setting where they are basically in opposition to him. (2) To make this work Martin suggests that the following ἵνα is imperatival; but that will not do since it is grammatically dependent on ζηλοῦτε, which means further that both verbs must be part of *Paul's* exhortation. That is, one could well understand how he could quote them and then qualify their position with an imperative—but not with a ἵνα-clause that is grammatically dependent on the quotation itself. (3) That the ἵνα-clause is *not* imperatival is further demonstrated by the exact repetition of the μᾶλλον δὲ ἵνα προφητεύητε in v. 5, where it cannot be so.

ences between these two words;[10] more likely it is a matter of emphasis. At the end of chap. 12, where he had been speaking specifically of the *gifts* themselves as gracious endowments, he told them, "eagerly desire the greater *charismata.*" Now in a context where the emphasis will be on the activity of the Spirit in the community at worship, he says, "eagerly desire the things of the Spirit."

What must be emphasized is that this imperative is now to be understood singularly in light of the exhortation to love that has preceded it. If the two imperatives are not kept together, the point of the entire succeeding argument is missed. Thus he immediately qualifies the imperative with a clause that literally says, "but rather[11] that[12] you prophesy."[13] In the following sentences Paul gives the reasons for this qualification.

2-4   This argument may best be analyzed in light of its structure. With two balanced pairs (vv. 2-3) Paul first contrasts tongues and prophecy as to who is addressed (in bold) and therefore as to their basic purpose (in italics); the second pair (v. 4) then interprets the first pair in terms of who is being edified. Thus:

> *For*[14]
> a) The one who speaks in tongues speaks *not* to people,
> > *but* **to God.**
> > Indeed,[15] no one understands[16] him;
> > > he speaks *mysteries* by the Spirit.
> *On the other hand,*[17]
> b) The one who prophesies   speaks   **to people,**
> > *edification,*
> > *encouragement,*
> > *comfort.*
>
> a) The one who speaks in tongues edifies himself;
> > *on the other hand,*
> b) The one who prophesies   edifies the church.

[10]See the discussion on 12:1; cf. n. 39 on 12:31.

[11]Gk. μᾶλλον δέ, which could be intensive. as implied by the NIV, "especially." More likely, in light of the exact repetition in v. 5, Paul intends it to be slightly adversative, introducing "an expr. or thought that supplements and thereby corrects what has preceded" (BAGD). The "correction" in the present case is toward specifying with greater exactness the point of the preceding imperative.

[12]Gk. ἵνα, which in this case is probably epexegetic, functioning like a ὅτι. Thus, "Be eagerly desiring the things of the Spirit, but rather *namely that* you prophesy." That is awkward Greek as well as English, but the point seems clear enough.

[13]On the gift of prophecy, see on 12:10. It should be noted that throughout the present argument, both for prophecy and tongues, the verbs "prophesy" and "speak in tongues" predominate over the mention of the gifts themselves. The verb "prophesy" appears in vv. 1, 3, 4, 5 (twice), 24, 31, and 39; the noun "prophecy" in vv. 6 and 22, and

Paul's emphasis—and concern—is unmistakable, the edification of the church. The one activity, tongues, edifies the speaker but not the church because it is addressed to God and "no one understands him." The other activity, prophecy, edifies the church because it is addressed to people and speaks "edification, encouragement and comfort" to them.

Although trying to cool their ardor for congregational tongues-speaking, Paul does not disparage the gift itself; rather, he seeks to put it in its rightful place.[18] Positively, he says three things about speaking in tongues,[19] which are best understood in light of the further discussion on prayer and praise in vv. 13-17: (1) Such a person is "speaking to[20] God," that is, he or she is communing with God by the Spirit. Although it is quite common in Pentecostal groups to refer to a "message in tongues," there seems to be no evidence in Paul for such terminology. The tongues-speaker is not addressing fellow believers but God (cf. vv. 13-14, 28), meaning therefore that Paul understands the phenomenon basically to be prayer and praise.[21]

(2) The content of such utterances is "mysteries" spoken "by the Spirit."[22] It is possible that "mysteries" means something similar to its usage in 13:2; more likely it carries here the sense of that which lies outside the understanding, both for the speaker and the hearer. After all, "mysteries" in 13:2 refers to the ways of God that are being revealed by the Spirit to his people; such "mysteries" would scarcely need to be spoken back to God.[23]

"prophet" in vv. 29, 32 (twice), and 37. The combination "speak in tongues" occurs in vv. 2, 4, 5 (twice), 6, 13, 18, 23, 27, and 39; the noun "tongue(s)" in vv. 14, 19, 22, and 26.

[14]A causal γάρ, giving the reason for the final clause in v. 1.

[15]Gk. γάρ, almost certainly inferential in this case.

[16]Gk. ἀκούει; although this usage does not occur often in the NT, it is otherwise well attested. It combines the two ideas of "hearing with the understanding."

[17]Gk. δέ; even though there is no μέν in the previous clause, the two sets are so clearly set up in contrast that such a translation makes that point the clearer.

[18]Cf. n. 20 on 12:1-3.

[19]On the nature of the gift itself, see on 12:10.

[20]Grosheide, 317, understands this to be a dative of advantage, but the standard usage with the verb "to speak" makes this especially difficult to sustain.

[21]Cf. Dunn, *Jesus,* p. 245.

[22]Not "with his spirit," as the NIV (cf. Godet, 266; Héring, 146; Parry, 200; Morris, 191). That is not precise even for vv. 14-15. On the absence of the article with Spirit in the dative see n. 43 on 12:3. It is clear from 12:7-11 that tongues is the manifestation of the Spirit of God through the human speaker. It does not seem remotely possible that in this context Paul would suddenly refer to speaking "with one's own spirit," rather than by the Holy Spirit. Cf. Holladay, 175.

[23]Although it is a moot point as to whether Rom. 8:26 reflects glossolalia, the main thrust of that passage echoes what is said here.

(3) Such speech by the Spirit is further described in v. 4 as edifying to the speaker. This has sometimes been called "self-edification" and therefore viewed as pejorative.[24] But Paul intended no such thing. The edifying of oneself is not self-centeredness, but the personal edifying of the believer that comes through private prayer and praise. Although one may wonder how "mysteries" that are not understood even by the speaker can edify, the answer lies in vv. 14-15. Contrary to the opinion of many, spiritual edification can take place in ways other than through the cortex of the brain.[25] Paul believed in an immediate communing with God by means of the S/spirit[26] that sometimes bypassed the mind; and in vv. 14-15 he argues that for his own edification he will have both. But *in church* he will have only what can also communicate to other believers through their minds.

But despite these favorable words about tongues, Paul's present concern is not with private devotion but with public worship. Therefore, he urges by implication that they *not* speak in tongues in worship (unless it be interpreted, vv. 5, 13, 27), but rather that they seek to prophesy (or in light of v. 6 bring forth any form of intelligible utterance). The reason for prophecy is that it speaks "edification, exhortation and comfort" to the rest of the people.[27] These three words[28] set forth the parameters of the divine intent of prophecy, and probably indicate that in Paul's view the primary focus of a prophetic utterance is not the future, but the present situations of the people of God.

The first word, "edification,"[29] controls the thought of the entire chapter. In 8:1 Paul had said, "love builds up"; now the sequence runs, "Pursue love, and in that framework seek the things of the Spirit, especially

[24]See, e.g., O. Michel, *TDNT* V, 141: "It is thus wrong for the man who speaks in tongues to edify himself"; cf. Gromacki, 168. MacArthur, 372, whose biases intrude on his interpretation, considers it sarcastic here.

[25]See Bittlinger, 100-06, for a discussion of the gift of tongues in terms of its psychological benefits; but such discussions lie quite beyond what one can say exegetically.

[26]On this way of translating the concept of the Divine Spirit speaking through the human spirit, see on 5:3-4 (pp. 204-05).

[27]There is some ambiguity as to whether the edifying of others is to be viewed in terms of edifying the other individuals who are present, or whether it refers to the community corporately. V. 3 implies the former; v. 4 the latter. Probably they run together in the apostle's mind. The edification of the whole at the same time includes the edification of the various parts.

[28]They function grammatically as the compound direct object of the verb λαλεῖ, hence the given translation. Some see the second two as defining the first (e.g., Wendland, 109; Conzelmann, 233-34; Ellis, 132 n. 13). Otherwise, Findlay, 902 (explicitly) and most commentators implicitly.

[29]Gk. οἰκοδομή; see on 3:10; 8:10; and 10:23. One can appreciate the interest in stylistic diversity in the NIV; nonetheless the translation "strengthening" causes the English reader to miss the tie with the verb "edify" in v. 4.

prophecy, because prophecy builds up." Thus the reason for the preceding chapter:[30] Since love builds up, in their zeal for gifts they are to seek prophecy because it is intelligible and thus builds up the body. The second word[31] is more ambiguous, meaning alternatively "encouragement,"[32] "comfort,"[33] or "exhortation (appeal)."[34] It is joined in this instance by its companion "comfort."[35] The question is whether these two words are, as in other instances, near synonyms meaning to encourage or comfort, or whether they embrace the broader categories of exhorting and comforting.[36] In either case, the aim of prophecy is the growth of the church corporately, which also involves the growth of its individual members.

5 This verse summarizes vv. 1-4 by making explicit Paul's preference for prophecy over tongues in the assembly. As in vv. 2-4, he begins with tongues: "I would like every one of you to speak in tongues." This sentence is often viewed as "merely conciliatory," especially in light of 12:28-30 where he argues that all will not speak in tongues.[37] But that is not quite precise. Paul has already indicated that tongues have value for the individual, meaning in private, personal prayer (cf. vv. 14-15 and 18-19). Now he says of that dimension of spiritual life that he could wish all experienced the edification that came from such a gift of the Spirit. But that of course is not his present point; thus he quickly qualifies that "wish" by repeating the language of v. 1: "but rather that you prophesy."

After such a summary one would expect that it might be followed by an explanatory "for" and a reason given. In this case, however, he concludes with the proposition, "Greater is the one who prophesies than the one

---

[30]Conzelmann, 233, in his desire to isolate chap. 13 from the present context, makes the curious comment: "The criterion is no longer ἀγάπη, 'love,' but οἰκοδομή, 'edification, upbuilding.'"

[31]Gk. παράκλησις; cf. especially the combination of verbs in v. 31: "you can all *prophesy* in turn so that all may learn and all παρακαλῶνται." Note also the collocation of the two nouns, παράκλησις and παραμυθία, probably as near synonyms, in Phil. 2:1.

[32]So translated here by NIV, RSV, GNB, NAB, JB, Moffatt, Montgomery, and Beck. For this usage in Paul see, e.g., Rom. 15:4-5.

[33]See the many examples in 2 Cor. 1:3-7.

[34]So translated here by KJV and NASB. For this usage in Paul see 1 Thess. 2:3; 2 Cor. 8:17, and the cognate verb frequently.

[35]Gk. παραμυθία; cf. the combination of the cognate verbs in 1 Thess. 2:12 and cognate adjectives in Phil. 2:1.

[36]Cf., e.g., Findlay, 902, who sees παράκλησις as addressing duty, παραμυθία sorrow or fear; Dunn, *Jesus*, pp. 229-30, implies that the two words *together* suggest both exhortation and encouragement/comfort. See also Hill, *Prophecy*, pp. 122-32, who tries, not totally successfully, to build a case from these words that the basic function of prophecy in Paul was "pastoral teaching."

[37]See, e.g., H. W. House, "Tongues and the Mystery Religions of Corinth," *BibSac* 140 (1983), 135-50.

who speaks in tongues." With these words two items from the preceding argument are brought into focus. First, this defines the meaning of "greater gift" in the exhortation in 12:31; second, the *reason* why prophecy is greater is related to the edification of the community, as the preceding argument makes clear. Thus it is not inherently greater, since all gifts come from the Spirit and are beneficial. It is greater precisely because it is intelligible and therefore can edify.

This last point is made certain by the final qualifying clause added to speaking in tongues: "unless[38] he interprets,[39] so that the church may be edified." The problem is not speaking in tongues per se but speaking in tongues without interpretation—which from the context seems very likely what the Corinthians were doing. The interpretation of the tongue brings it within the framework of intelligibility, which in turn means that it too can edify the community. This does not imply that such a tongue is to be understood as directed toward the community, but that what the person has been speaking to God has now been made intelligible, so that others may benefit from the Spirit's utterance.[40]

Thus, even though from Paul's perspective prophecy is clearly preferable, it seems equally clear that the real urgency is not with tongues and prophecy, but with intelligible utterances in the gathered assembly, so that all may be edified.

At a time in history when there is a broad range of opinion about speaking in tongues in the church, both its validity and its usefulness, the point of this text needs to be heard again—on both sides of that question. It is sheer prejudice to view Paul here as "demoting" tongues as such. Uninterpreted tongues in the assembly, yes; but for the edification of the believer in private, no. Anyone who would argue that what is spoken to God by the Spirit for the edification of a believer is of little value is hardly reading the apostle from Paul's own point of view. On the other hand, there is a tendency on the part of some Pentecostals to fall full into the Corinthian error, where a "message in tongues," interpreted of course, is often seen as the surest

---

[38]Gk. ἐκτὸς εἰ μή (cf. 15:2; 1 Tim. 5:19), a redundancy that belongs to the Hellenistic period (found, e.g., in Plutarch, Dio Chrysostom, Lucian).

[39]This is not in conflict with 12:30 or 14:28, as some imply, since the former verse says that not *all* are or do the same thing, not that anyone may do *only* one thing; and the latter text allows for interpretation from others than the tongues-speaker. According to 12:10, this too is a gift of the Spirit; therefore, it is potentially available to anyone, including the tongues-speaker (cf. v. 13, where the tongues-speaker is encouraged to pray for this gift, so that his tongue might edify).

[40]Dunn, *Jesus*, pp. 247-48, wants to raise the question, If this is the case, why then tongues at all? implying that "Paul is trying to rationalize a form of charismatic worship in Corinth with which he is not altogether happy." Paul himself certainly does not suggest as much.

evidence of the continuing work of the Spirit in a given community. Paul would scarcely agree with such an assessment. He allows tongues and interpretation; he prefers prophecy.

At the same time Paul's clear preference for prophetic utterances is often neglected throughout the church. By prophecy of course, as the full evidence of this chapter makes clear, he does not mean a prepared sermon, but the spontaneous word given to God's people for the edification of the whole. Most contemporary churches would have to be radically reconstructed in terms of their self-understanding for such to take place. Again, Pentecostal and charismatic groups, where such utterances are more often in evidence, continually need to "test" the spirits in terms of v. 3, that the utterance be for the edification, exhortation/encouragement, and comfort of the community.

b. Analogies that argue for intelligibility (14:6-12)

6 *Now, brothers, if I come to you and speak in tongues, what good will I be to you, unless I bring you some revelation or knowledge or prophecy or[1] word of instruction?* 7 *Even in the case of lifeless things that make sounds, such as the flute or harp, how will anyone know what tune is being played unless there is a distinction in the notes?* 8 *Again, if the trumpet does not sound a clear call, who will get ready for battle?* 9 *So it is with you. Unless you speak intelligible words with your tongue, how will anyone know what you are saying? You will just be speaking into the air.* 10 *Undoubtedly there are all sorts of languages in the world, yet none of them[2] is without meaning.* 11 *If then I do not grasp the meaning of what someone is saying, I am a foreigner to the speaker, and he is a foreigner to me.[3]* 12 *So it is with you. Since you are eager to have spiritual gifts,[4] try to excel in gifts that build up the church.*

[1]Each of these nouns appears with an ἐν (= in the form of a revelation, etc.). The ἐν is missing with διδαχῇ in P⁴⁶ ℵ* D* F G 0243 630 1739 1881 pc, which then would tie it more closely with prophecy (= with a prophecy or teaching). This is not an easy textual choice. On the one hand, it is difficult to account for its omission by scribes, either accidentally or intentionally; on the other hand, it is equally difficult to account for Paul's having omitted it in this instance when the rest of the list is so carefully balanced. On the whole it seems more likely that Paul himself omitted it, but it is unlikely that he "meant" anything by it. See the discussion in Barrett, 312 and 317.

[2]The NIV here reflects the addition of αὐτῶν in the MajT, an addition that came about for the same reason that the NIV so translated it, smoothness.

[3]This translation reflects the ἐμοί of P⁴⁶ D F G 0243 6 81 365 1175 1739 1881 al b vg bo. As Zuntz, 104, notes, this is almost certainly a harmonization to the preceding τῷ λαλοῦντι. The original (ℵ B A Ψ Maj lat sy bo) has the preposition ἐν (ἐν ἐμοί = "in my view"); cf. Barrett, 312.

[4]Paul wrote πνευμάτων ("spirits"); the change to πνευματικῶν was actually made by P 1175 pc a r syᵖ co. See the commentary.

The argument of this present paragraph extends through v. 19. It is an elaboration of the concern over the unintelligible, and therefore nonedifying, character of uninterpreted tongues in the assembly. This first paragraph makes that point with the use of analogies. The opening rhetorical question (v. 6) sets the agenda: Hearers do not benefit at all from what is not understandable. This is followed by a series of examples from musical instruments (vv. 7-9) and foreign languages (vv. 10-12), each of which is applied to the Corinthians with a similar, "So it is with you" (vv. 9 and 12). The final application concludes on the same note with which the paragraph began— the edification of the church, which should rule their zeal for spiritual utterances.

At the same time one perceives an undercurrent of apologetic between Paul and the Corinthians. If our reconstruction is correct, that not only are they high on tongues as evidencing true spirituality but at the same time negative toward Paul for his shortcomings at this point, then the form of v. 6 is especially relevant: "If *I come to you* speaking in tongues, how shall I benefit you?" This motif seems to carry through v. 19. Paul has not lost his primary focus of putting their gift into proper perspective, especially as the community gathers for worship. At the same time he takes the opportunity to put his own practice into perspective for them. Even though he speaks in tongues more than all of them (v. 18), and determines to pray and sing both in the Spirit and with his mind (v. 15), he likewise refuses to "come to them" as they might prefer, speaking in tongues, because that will not benefit *them*.

6 A turn in the argument is indicated both by the vocative "brothers [and sisters]" (see on 1:10) and by the conjunctive combination "but as it is."[5] This opening sentence functions as a transition: It carries forward the argument of vv. 1-5; at the same time it sets the stylistic pattern for the first set of analogies ("If . . . , how shall . . . ?"[6]), which argue vigorously against unintelligibility (= tongues) since it has no usefulness for its hearers.

Even though the sentence is probably intended to present a hypothetical setting for the argument,[7] both the combination "but as it is" and the

---

[5]Gk. νῦν δέ, which in this case, in contrast to the clearly temporal usage in 5:11 and 7:14, seems to function in a logical sense, as in 12:20 (cf. the νυνὶ δέ in 12:18; 13:13; and 15:20). See the discussion on 13:13; the present sense is never quite missing from this use of the adverb. Thus, "But (δέ) as it is (νῦν), brothers and sisters, . . ."

[6]Cf. vv. 6, 7, 8, and 9, each of which basically follows the same form: an ἐάν clause, followed by an interrogative particle (τί, πῶς, τίς), followed by a future indicative.

[7]Cf. Conzelmann, 235, who sees it as rhetorical, in diatribe style.

language "if I come to you"[8] support[9] the suggestion made above that this is more than merely hypothetical; probably it also indicates the way things presently are between them and him, implying his rejection of their criterion for being *pneumatikos* ("spiritual"). Paul in effect refuses to "come to [them] speaking in tongues." The reason for this echoes the motif of edification from vv. 3-5. By following their criterion he would not "profit them."[10]

The alternative[11] is for him to come speaking some form of intelligible utterance, which he illustrates with yet another list of *charismata*. This list is both illuminating and intriguing.[12] On the one hand, the appearance of prophecy in the third position intimates, as has been argued in vv. 1-5, that the real issue is not tongues and prophecy as such, but tongues and intelligibility, for which prophecy serves as the representative gift. On the other hand, as with the other lists in this argument,[13] this one is also especially *ad hoc*. His concern is to specify various kinds of Spirit-inspired utterances that have intelligibility as their common denominator. Thus he includes two items from previous lists, "knowledge" and "prophecy" (see 12:8-10; 13:2, 8). The other two call for additional comment.

Paul uses the word "revelation" in a variety of ways,[14] but only in the present argument to suggest some kind of utterance given by the Spirit for the benefit of the gathered community.[15] Precisely what its content might be and how it would differ from "knowledge" or "prophecy" is not at all

---

[8]Cf. 2:1; 4:18-19, 21; 16:2, 5. Apart from 2:1 each of these refers to his anticipated next visit. The choice of this language for the hypothetical setting is striking.

[9]Perhaps this is true of the vocative as well, since this sudden very personal address does not otherwise seem to fit with an appeal whose main content will be a series of analogies.

[10]Gk. ὠφελέω (cf. 13:3); cf. the concern in 12:7 for "the common good."

[11]Gk. ἐὰν μή. Although there can be little doubt as to Paul's point, the Greek syntax is a little awkward. This ἐὰν μή clause is probably intended as a second protasis, for both of which the τί ὑμᾶς ὠφελήσω serves as the apodosis (as the NIV).

[12]Some (e.g., Calvin, 438; R-P, 308; Ruef, 148; Grudem, 138-39, with qualification) see an "artful" arrangement in which there are two pairs, the latter two expressing the "administration" of the former two. But given Paul's usage throughout this argument, this is a discovery that would most likely come as a surprise to him. On the basis of 13:2 ἀποκάλυψις would correspond more with γνῶσις than with prophecy. In any case the list is too *ad hoc* for such schemes.

[13]Cf. 12:8-10, 28, 29-30; 13:1-2, 8; 14:26.

[14]Gk. ἀποκάλυψις (cf. v. 26). It sometimes refers to visible disclosures associated with the return of Christ (1:7; 2 Thess. 1:7; Rom. 2:5; 8:19). In other places it refers to the "revelation" of the gospel given to Paul by Christ (Gal. 1:12), or of God's will in his life (Gal. 2:2). The latter may well be associated with the kind of charismatic utterance referred to in this passage. On the other hand, there are the "revelations" of the Lord given to Paul in the visionary experiences of 2 Cor. 12:1, 7, which he was not allowed to share with others.

[15]Those who equate Gal. 2:1-10 with the famine visit recorded in Acts 11:27-29 see the reference in Gal. 2:2 to his going up to Jerusalem "by revelation" as related to the

clear. For example, along with "teaching" it appears in the final list in v. 26, a list that includes neither "prophecy" nor "knowledge." Yet in the subsequent discussion of the ordering of utterances (vv. 27-33), Paul takes up tongues and prophecy, not "revelation," although its cognate verb does appear in the discussion of prophecy in v. 30. This latter passage in particular suggests that there is a general lack of precision in Paul with regard to these various items.[16] Perhaps in the final list (v. 26) this word covers both prophecy and knowledge as the more inclusive term. In any case, it implies the disclosure of divine "mysteries," either about the nature of the gospel itself (cf. 2:10) or perhaps about things otherwise hidden to the "natural man."[17]

Equally intriguing is the appearance of "teaching,"[18] which corresponds to "the teacher" in 12:28 as prophecy does to the prophet. Probably this has to do with a Spirit-inspired utterance that took the form of instruction,[19] rather than with the more common usage that implies formal teaching of some kind. Again, how this differs in terms of content from the other items on this list is a matter of speculation since the data are so meager. See the discussion on 12:28.

Despite our lack of certainty about the precise nature and content of these various forms of utterance, however, their common denominator is their intelligibility, and to that question Paul now turns in the form of analogies.

7-8 The analogies seem self-evident.[20] The first (v. 7) is taken from "lifeless things that give sounds,"[21] that is, from musical instruments.

---

prophecy of Agabus in the Acts account. But that will hardly do since the "prophecy" was about the famine, not about those who would go up to Jerusalem. Moreover, Paul's usage implies a personal "revelation" to himself, not a prophecy about a famine.

[16]Cf. Barrett, 317: "All these activities . . . shade too finely into one another for rigid distinctions."

[17]Cf. the discussion in Dunn, *Jesus,* p. 230.

[18]Gk. διδαχή; referring to the utterance itself, not to "doctrine" (KJV).

[19]This is supported by three pieces of evidence: (1) Its appearance here in a list of items that are otherwise unquestionably to be understood as Spirit-inspired *charismata;* (2) the fact that the whole section has to do with πνευματικά (v. 1) and the Corinthians' zeal for "spirits" (v. 12); and (3) its appearance in v. 26 in a similar context of inspired utterances. Cf. Dunn, *Jesus,* pp. 236-37.

[20]The only real difficulty is with the introductory ὅμως (cf. Gal. 3:15), which ordinarily means "nevertheless." If it means that here, the explanation is to be found in some form of displacement, where it qualifies the following clause. More likely it carries the sense of "likewise." See BAGD; cf. J. Jeremias, "ὅμως (1 Cor 14,7; Gal 3,15)," *ZNW* 52 (1961), 127-28; R. Keydall, "ὅμως," *ZNW* 54 (1963), 145-46.

[21]Gk. τὰ ἄψυχα φωνὴν διδόντα. For musical instruments as "inanimate" see Euripides, *Ion* 881 and Plutarch, *lib.educ.* 9c. The use of φωνή with musical instruments reflects common usage (cf. Plut., *mor.* 713c), including the LXX (cf. Exod. 19:16; Isa. 18:3; Ps. Sol. 8:1).

The two instruments, flute and harp, are commonplace in the Hellenistic world.[22] Paul's point is to be found in the "how" clause: "How will anyone know what tune is being played[23] unless there is a distinction in the notes[24]?" This example calls to mind another use[25] of a musical instrument: "If the trumpet does not sound a clear call,[26] who will get ready for battle[27]?"

The analogy is clear. Tongues, Paul is arguing, is like the harpist running fingers over all the strings, making musical sounds but not playing a pleasing melody,[28] or like a bugler who blows the bugle without sounding the battle cry. In both cases sounds come from the instrument, but they make no sense; hence they do not benefit the listener. So it is with tongues.

9 This application to their situation follows the form of the two preceding examples.[29] Referring specifically to speaking in tongues, he asks, "Unless you speak intelligible words[30] with your tongue,[31] how will anyone know what you are saying?"[32] To which he adds the biting words, echoing the irresponsible bugler, "You will just be speaking into the air."[33] All of this, of course, assumes the perspective of the hearer in the community at worship.

10-11 This third analogy, the phenomenon of different languages, would also have been commonplace in a cosmopolitan center such as Corinth. It is also the one most closely related to the immediate problem. The analogy is not that the tongues-speaker is also speaking a foreign language, as some have suggested,[34] but that the hearer cannot understand the one

[22]These instruments were played individually, not in "orchestras," and used in various settings: dance, drama, pagan worship, etc. See C. Sachs, *The History of Musical Instruments* (ET, New York, 1940).

[23]Lit., "how will what is being fluted or harped be known?" The point is that of the NIV.

[24]Gk. διαστολὴν τοῖς φθόγγοις, which may refer either to pitch or the interval between notes; probably in Paul it is a nontechnical usage for hearing a melody.

[25]Joined to the preceding by καὶ γάρ; cf. 11:9; 12:13-14.

[26]This time ἄδηλον φωνήν (an indistinct sound, so that the battle call is not recognizable).

[27]Gk. εἰς πόλεμον; for this use see Field, *Notes,* p. 178.

[28]In modern culture the appropriate analogy would be the cacophony of the symphony orchestra tuning instruments and warming up just before the conductor raises the baton.

[29]The protasis is very close to the form of v. 8; the apodosis to that in v. 7.

[30]Gk. εὔσημον λόγον (= a clear, distinct, recognizable word).

[31]Here referring to the organ of speech, hence διὰ τῆς γλώσσης, not the γλώσσαις of v. 6. Nonetheless, the close relationship of the two is pointed.

[32]Lit., as in v. 7, "how will what is said be known?"

[33]Cf. our idiom, "talking to the wind"; note also the non-purposeful boxer in 9:26.

[34]E.g., Gundry, "Utterance?" p. 306. The point of the analogy is that "tongues" functions *like* this. Cf. Dunn, *Jesus,* p. 244: "That which is not self-evident

speaking in tongues any more than he can the one who speaks a foreign language.

The form of the analogy differs from the preceding ones. In v. 10 there is the simple statement of fact, that there are who-knows-how-many[35] different languages[36] in the world, none of which is without meaning to those who speak them.[37] This analogy also emphasizes the perspective of the hearer. It is not that the different languages do not have meaning to their speakers; rather, they do not have meaning to the hearers.

This latter point is pressed in v. 11 by means of the inferential conjunction "therefore."[38] That is, the inference to be drawn from the reality stated in v. 10 is that "If I do not grasp the meaning[39] of what someone is saying,"[40] then we are as foreigners to one another.[41] Again, the application to their setting and "speaking in tongues" is obvious. Just as the hearer of one speaking in a foreign language cannot understand what is said, so the other worshipers in the community cannot understand what is spoken "in tongues." Thus it is of no value to them.

12 This final application begins exactly as in v. 9: "So it is with you." But in this instance instead of applying the obvious point of the preceding analogy, Paul ties all this together by picking up two motifs from vv. 1-5. First, (lit.) "since you are zealots[42] for spirits[43]." As many have

---

(the uselessness of unintelligible glossolalia in the assembly) is illuminated by that which is self-evident (the uselessness of unintelligible foreign language in the assembly)." See also the discussion on 12:10.

[35]This is an attempt, following Conzelmann, 232, to render Paul's εἰ τύχοι (cf. 15:37) a little more closely to his sense than the NIV's "undoubtedly"; cf. Barrett, 319, "I don't know how many." Literally the idiom means, "if it should turn out that way" (BAGD); hence "perhaps" or "probably."

[36]Gk. τοσαῦτα γένη φωνῶν; the use of φωνή in this context is classical. It is probably chosen in place of γλῶσση because the latter is used throughout this passage to refer to "speaking in tongues," that special "utterance" inspired by the Holy Spirit. This usage, rather than supporting the idea that γλῶσση also means "a foreign language" in this section, suggests the opposite. See n. 34 and the discussion on 12:10.

[37]Gk. οὐδὲν ἄφωνον (lit. "nothing is without speech"). This can mean either (1) "nothing is without its own language" (Barrett; cf. Conzelmann), or (2) "nothing is without meaning." In context the latter seems more likely.

[38]Gk. οὖν; NIV, "then."

[39]Gk. δύναμιν; as our "the *force* of the word." Used only here in the NT in this sense, but a good classical usage. Cf. BAGD.

[40]Lit., "know the meaning of the language."

[41]Lit., "I shall be a βάρβαρος to the one speaking, and the one speaking a βάρβαρος in my view (see n. 3)." The word βάρβαρος originally was onomatopoeic, meaning something like speaking gibberish. It came to refer to anyone who was non-Greek, hence a foreigner; it was sometimes used derogatorily (= "barbarian"), but not always (as here). Cf. Rom. 1:14.

[42]Gk. ζηλωταί, the cognate noun of the verb ζηλόω ("eagerly desire") in v. 1.

[43]Gk. πνευμάτων; see the discussion on 5:3-4.

seen, this clause probably holds the key to much. Whatever else it means, it explicitly indicates that zeal for the things being talked about in these chapters is a Corinthian trademark. This has caused some, therefore, to read the two imperatives in 12:31 and 14:1 as quotations from the Corinthian letter. But that is an unnecessary expedient. Paul was not commanding them in those cases to do what they were already doing. Rather, just as in this verse, he was urging them to direct that zeal toward gifts that edify (14:5).

The more difficult concept is their zeal for "spirits." On the basis of 14:1, this is almost universally understood, as in the NIV, to refer to their alleged zeal for "spiritual gifts" in general. But that seems unlikely, both in terms of this choice of words and of the historical context as a whole. More likely this refers especially to their desire for one particular manifestation of the Spirit, the gift of tongues, which was for them the sure evidence of their being *pneumatikos* (a person of the Spirit, hence "spiritual").[44] This plural does not mean that the "one and the same Spirit" of 12:7-11 is now to be understood as a multiplicity of spirits.[45] Rather, this is Paul's way of speaking about the Spirit manifesting himself through their individual "spirits." The clue lies in the usage in v. 32, where the "spirits of the prophets" refers to the Holy Spirit's speaking prophetic utterances through the one who is prophesying. Likewise in vv. 14-15, Paul will pray with "my spirit," meaning "by means of the Holy Spirit through my spirit." Hence they have great zeal for their own spirits, through speaking in tongues, to be the mouthpiece of the Spirit.

Paul's present concern is to capitalize on their zeal, or more accurately, as before, to redirect their zeal. Thus the second motif from vv. 1-5, and the point of everything: "Try[46] to excel[47] in building up the church." This was the explicit concern of vv. 1-5; it has been the implicit concern in the several analogies of this paragraph. Utterances that are not understood, even if they come from the Spirit, are of no benefit, that is, edification, to the hearer. Thus, since they have such zeal for the manifestation of the Spirit, they should direct that zeal in corporate worship away from being "foreigners" to one another toward the edification of one another in Christ.

[44] Cf. Dunn, *Jesus*, p. 234, who interprets it to mean "eager to experience inspiration, . . . particularly the inspired utterance of glossolalia." Ellis, 31, suggests that it implies "an interest in the powers that lie behind and attend those manifestations."

[45] As suggested by Weiss, 326-27, who quite misses Paul's point and the larger context.

[46] Gk. ζητεῖτε (cf. 10:24, 33; 13:5), the more common verb for the notion of "striving for."

[47] Gk. ἵνα περισσεύητε, where a ἵνα clause functions as an infinitive of purpose.

In a time when charismatic utterances are experiencing something of a revival in the church, this paragraph is especially important to those in that renewal. The point of everything in corporate worship is not personal experience in the Spirit, but building up the church itself. Much that comes under the banner of charismatic or pentecostal worship seems very often to fail right at this point. However, it is not so much that what goes on is not understood by the others, but that it fails to have this final verse as its basic urgency. The building up of the community is the basic reason for corporate settings of worship; they should probably not be turned into a corporate gathering for a thousand individual experiences of worship.

c. Application to the believing community (14:13-19)

13 *For this reason anyone who speaks in a tongue should pray that he may interpret what he says.* 14 *For[1] if I pray in a tongue, my spirit prays, but my mind is unfruitful.* 15 *So what shall I do? I will pray with my spirit, but I will also pray with my mind; I will sing with my spirit, but I will also sing with my mind.* 16 *If you are praising[2] God by the Spirit,[3] how can one who finds himself among those who do not understand[a] say "Amen" to your thanksgiving, since he does not know what you are saying?* 17 *You may be giving thanks well enough, but the other* person[4] *is not edified.*

18 *I thank God that[5] I speak in tongues more than all of you.* 19 *But in the church I would rather speak five intelligible words to instruct others than ten thousand words in a tongue.*

[a]Or *among the inquirers*

[1]This γάρ (not found in P[46] B F G 0243 1739 1881 pc b sa) is by all counts not original. Its omission would be almost impossible to account for, either accidentally or deliberately—even more so independently across two early traditions (Egyptian and Western). One can easily account for the addition, given both the frequency of this conjunction in this letter and the apparent awkwardness of the asyndeton. Cf. Zuntz, 194, who adds the note that both here and in v. 18, where Paul suddenly brings in his own person, the text is asyndetic. See the commentary.

[2]P[46] F G 048 and the MajT read the aorist εὐλογήσῃς here, almost certainly in error. The aorist, which is the more common nonindicative "tense" in Greek (cf. vv. 6, 7, 8, and 9), is the one toward which change most often occurs. As in v. 14, this sentence is most likely a present general condition.

[3]NIV, "with your spirit." Even though the original text is either πνεύματι (P[46] ℵ* A F G 0243 33 629 1739 1881) or ἐν πνεύματι (ℵ[2] B D P 81 365 1175 pc)—probably the former—against the τῷ πνεύματι of the MajT, Paul intends the Holy Spirit, just as in 14:2 (q.v.). This usage is determined by 12:3 and the context. See the commentary.

[4]NIV, "man."

[5]There is no conjunction in the Greek; a ὅτι is supplied in the Latin tradition (F G lat) for the same reason the NIV has in English. The lack of a conjunction tends to heighten the significance of the second sentence. See R-P, 413.

This paragraph continues the argument of vv. 6-12. Paul now applies the point of the analogies to their corporate worship by indicating the specific effect unintelligibility has on gathered worshipers.[6] After urging the one who speaks in tongues to pray for the gift of interpretation (v. 13), he argues in vv. 14-15, on the basis of his own experience, that since praying in the Spirit means that the understanding is unfruitful, he will do both—pray in the Spirit and with the mind—adding that he will do the same in praise (in this case, singing). As vv. 16-17 demonstrate, this latter item is his basic concern, praising God with the mind (= intelligibly) for the sake of others, who cannot otherwise say the corporate "Amen" to what is said. Vv. 18-19 conclude on another personal, and probably apologetic, note (cf. v. 6), putting the whole into perspective: For the sake of others, only what is intelligible in church; thus no uninterpreted tongues.

The entire section deals with tongues; prophecy is not mentioned, although perhaps it is alluded to at the end (v. 19).[7] Tongues becomes intelligible through interpretation, as already suggested in v. 5. Here in particular it is evident that for Paul "tongues" is an expression of prayer and praise, not a word directed primarily toward the community. As far as the one speaking is concerned, everything said here about tongues is quite positive; nonetheless, as before, the purpose of the whole is to check the unbridled use of uninterpreted tongues in the assembly.

13 The strong inferential conjunction "for this reason"[8] indicates a close relationship between this sentence and v. 12. It functions both to conclude vv. 6-12 and to apply the principle "building up the church."[9] Its content, therefore, comes as something of a surprise. In light of the total argument to this point, one might have expected, "For this reason let the one who speaks in tongues seek rather to prophesy." But prophecy is not Paul's concern, intelligibility is; thus he moves toward that concern by urging that "the person who speaks in a tongue should pray that he may interpret[10] what he says."[11] The point is that of v. 5:[12] The interpretation of the tongue

---

[6]Cf. Holladay, 180: "The movement of thought advances from the general need for clarity to the specific need for clarity in the assembly."

[7]Dunn, *Jesus,* p. 228, suggests that "praying with the mind" in v. 15 is to be equated with prophecy. This is doubtful. It may have the same effect—intelligibility—but all of vv. 14-17 deals with God-directed utterances.

[8]Gk. διό (cf. 12:3).

[9]This observation, plus the asyndeton in v. 14 (see n. 2 above), suggests that the subparagraphs should perhaps be vv. 6-13, 14-17, and 18-19.

[10]On the matter of the tongues-speaker also interpreting, see n. 38 on v. 5.

[11]Some of the older interpreters suggest a different meaning for this sentence, viewing "prayer" as "praying in a tongue" in v. 14 and the ἵνα clause as telic (purpose). Thus, "Let him that has the gift of tongues pray with tongues, but let him do so with the purpose of interpreting his utterance afterwards" (Edwards, 365; cf. Godet, 277-78). But this breaks down both grammatically and contextually.

[12]This verse seems to function in relationship to vv. 6-12 as v. 5b did to vv. 1-5.

makes it an intelligible utterance;[13] therefore it can satisfy the concern of v. 12, the edification of the church. As before, the Corinthians' practice of uninterpreted tongues is what is being challenged, not tongues as such. This is further confirmed by vv. 27-28, which again disallow uninterpreted tongues, but otherwise *regulate* the expression of the gift *when there is interpretation.*

14 With this sentence Paul begins the specific application of the argument against unintelligibility in vv. 7-13. He does so, as he will again in v. 18, by referring to his own experience of speaking in tongues.[14] But the *point* of this sentence is less than certain. Probably he is using his own experience to point up a basic principle, which will be elaborated in v. 15 and then applied to their assembly in vv. 16-17.

This seems to make the best sense of what is otherwise a very difficult sentence in the middle of this argument,[15] made the more so by the addition of the explanatory "for" found in the majority of witnesses (and the NIV).[16] Paul is not arguing that the tongues-speaker should also interpret for the benefit of his or her own understanding. That would be a considerable "rock" in the middle of this argument for the edification of others through intelligibility. It would also tend to contradict what is said in vv. 2 and 4 and intimated in v. 15, that the one who speaks in tongues is edified by his or her communion with God through the Spirit, without the need of perceptual understanding. Paul's point is a simple one, and one that they themselves should fully recognize: When I pray in tongues[17] I pray in the Spirit, but it does not benefit my mind—the implication being, as he will go on to argue in vv. 16-17, that neither does it benefit the minds of others.

---

[13]But not necessarily having "the effect of converting it into prophecy, or teaching," as Barrett, 319, suggests.

[14]As suggested on v. 6, this probably also carries an undercurrent of apologetic. He does indeed speak in tongues—more than all of them (v. 18)—despite what they may think.

[15]This is seldom noted by interpreters; nevertheless the contextual difficulties are considerable if the γάρ is original and the intent is that the tongues-speaker should pray for the gift of interpretation for the benefit of his/her own understanding, a view espoused by, *inter alia,* Calvin, 292; Grosheide, 325-26; Morris, 194; Ruef, 150; Mare, 273. Not only does this contradict vv. 2, 4, and 15, but it places a premium on the mind as the only means whereby one may be edified personally. Furthermore, it seems out of keeping with the whole context, which has the edification of the church in view.

One way out of this difficulty has been to make ἄκαρπος "active" in meaning; thus "my mind produces no results for anyone" (Williams; cf. Goodspeed, Moffatt, Conzelmann). Although that moves the concern in the right direction, it seems unlikely that the intended contrast (Gk. δέ) between "my spirit" and "my mind" is that between "what benefits me and what benefits others."

[16]See n. 2 above.

[17]The conditional sentence is a present general; hence, whenever I am praying in a tongue, this is the consequence.

As suggested before,[18] in the present context the difficult wording "my spirit prays" seems to mean something like "my S/spirit prays." On the one hand, both the possessive "my" and the contrast with "my mind" indicate that he is here referring to his own "spirit" at prayer. On the other hand, there can be little question, on the basis of the combined evidence of 12:7-11 and 14:2 and 16, that Paul understood speaking in tongues to be an activity of the Spirit in one's life; it is prayer and praise directed toward God in the language of Spirit-inspiration. The most viable solution to this ambiguity is that by the language "my spirit prays" Paul means his own spirit is praying as the Holy Spirit gives the utterance.[19] Hence, "my S/spirit prays."

As v. 15 makes certain, Paul does not mean that praying in the Spirit is a bad thing because it does not benefit his understanding; rather, this states the way things are. What he does go on to say is that he will do *two* things— one apparently for his own sake, the other for the sake of others.

15 Paul now elaborates the principle set forth in v. 14, with an eye toward turning it into application in vv. 16-17. In light of the simple reality stated in v. 14, he asks rhetorically, "So what shall I do?"[20] His answer is that he will do both. On the one hand, "I will pray with my S/spirit[21]," meaning, as vv. 14 and 19 make certain, "I will pray[22] in tongues." Although this is obviously not Paul's present concern, it joins with v. 18 in suggesting that such was his regular practice and that he was edified thereby even if his mind did not enter into such praying.[23] On the other hand, the combination "but also"[24] indicates that the emphasis lies here, "I will *also* pray with my understanding,"[25] meaning "I will also pray and praise in Greek for the sake of others."

---

[18]See on 5:3-4; 12:10; and 14:12.

[19]Cf. the language of Acts 2:4: "They began to speak in other tongues, as the Spirit gave them utterance" (RSV). This is not far removed from, but seems to be a preferable way of stating, the alternative favored by Barrett, 320, and others, that "my *spirit* is the spiritual gift entrusted to me."

[20]Gk. τί οὖν ἐστιν (cf. 14:26); cf. also the simple τί οὖν of Rom. 3:9; 6:15; 11:7, which is the more classical form. The idiom means, "What then is the upshot of what has just been said?"

[21]Gk. τῷ πνεύματι. If the analysis offered above (n. 43 on 12:3) is correct, then this arthrous usage does not refer directly to the Holy Spirit, but to "my spirit" in v. 14. To the degree that it recognizes this relationship with v. 14, the NIV is correct here. But the usage in v. 16 is anarthrous and probably refers more directly to the Spirit himself.

[22]This future must be understood as volitive, not temporal, expressing determination.

[23]This in itself speaks against an understanding of v. 14 that sees Paul as encouraging the tongues-speaker to pray for the gift of interpretation so that his or her mind might also benefit from what is said. Obviously for Paul the latter is not always necessary.

[24]Gk. δὲ καί; cf. 15:15.

[25]Gk. νοῦς, as in v. 14; the NIV has "mind," but Paul's concern is with the "understanding" involved, not the "location," as it were.

Although it is not explicitly stated here, this contrast between praying and singing with my S/spirit and my mind ultimately aims at relegating the former to the setting of private praying, while only the latter is to be exercised in the assembly. This is implied both in vv. 16-17, where he allows that the tongues-speaker is praising God all right, but to no one else's benefit, and especially in v. 19, where this distinction is made explicitly.

To "praying" Paul adds "singing[26] with the S/pirit" and "with the understanding." Singing was a common part of worship in Judaism and was carried over as an integral part of early Christian worship as well, as v. 26 and Col. 3:16//Eph. 5:19 illustrate.[27] The evidence from Colossians and Ephesians suggests that some of the singing was corporate; the language of these passages[28] further indicates that besides being addressed as praise to God, such hymns served as vehicles of instruction in the gathered community. Furthermore, both passages, as well as this one, indicate that some of the singing might best be called "a kind of charismatic hymnody,"[29] in which spontaneous hymns of praise were offered to God in the congregation, although some may have been known beforehand. The present passage, as well as v. 26, indicates that some of this kind of singing was "solo." This text also adds a dimension to our understanding of "speaking in tongues." Not only did one *pray* in this way, but one also *praised* God in song in this way. Hence the verbs in vv. 16-17 that pick up this theme are "bless" and "give thanks."

16 With an untranslated "otherwise"[30] Paul makes the transition from his own determination to praise in both ways—in tongues to be sure, but *also* with his understanding—to their need to do especially the latter in the assembly: "Otherwise, if you[31] are praising[32] God[33] by the Spirit[34]

---

[26]Gk. ψαλῶ; cf. 14:26, ἕκαστος ψαλμὸν ἔχει.

[27]See, e.g., G. Delling, *TDNT* IX, 489-503; K. H. Bartels, *NIDNTT* III, 668-75 (who, however, quite misses the point of this text); R. P. Martin, *Worship,* pp. 39-52; Dunn, *Jesus,* pp. 238-39.

[28]"Speaking to one another" (Eph. 5:19) and "teaching and admonishing one another" (Col. 3:16).

[29]The language is Dunn's; see his *Jesus,* p. 238.

[30]Gk. ἐπεί, which ordinarily is causal ("since"; cf. v. 12). For the usage here cf. 5:10 and 7:14, where it functions in a similar way.

[31]This "you" is singular; for this sudden shift to the second singular in applicational or parenetic sections see on 4:1; 7:21 and 27. Probably Paul is here supposing an interlocutor, who is understood to be taking the opposite position of his own.

[32]The sentence, like v. 14, is a present general condition: "Whenever you praise God in this way, you may expect these results." The verb εὐλογέω is most frequently used in the LXX to translate the Heb. *bārak,* "bless." Thus it is often thought to refer here to specific kinds of prayers, such as the blessings in the Jewish synagogue. But that will not work here, of course, since it is the verb for "praising" in tongues. Most likely it covers in a more general way both activities mentioned in v. 15.

[33]This word is not in the Greek text, but is obviously implied.

[34]On this usage see on vv. 14-15, and n. 43 on 12:3.

[meaning here, praising God in tongues in the assembly], how can [another] say 'Amen' to your thanksgiving,[35] since he will not know what you are saying?" Saying the (customary)[36] "Amen"[37] assumes the setting of corporate worship, where this word, also taken over from the Jewish synagogue, indicated wholehearted response to and endorsement of the words of another.[38] Paul's point, the same one he has been making throughout, is clear enough: Praising God (or praying) in tongues, even though it is by the Spirit, does not build up anyone else in the assembly (v. 17) since what is said is unintelligible.

Paul's description of the person who cannot say the "Amen," however, is puzzling: (literally) "the one who fills the place of the *idiōtēs*." The problem is twofold: (1) whether the expression "fills the place of"[39] is to be taken literally or figuratively; and (2) what *idiōtēs* itself means here. The problem is complicated by two factors: (a) Although the word ordinarily means "nonexpert," hence "an ordinary person" in contrast to one who is skilled, there is also evidence that it was a technical term in religious life for nonmembers who still participated in the pagan sacrifices.[40] (b) In the present context this same person in v. 17 is referred to as being "built up," which in Paul has to do with believers, yet the word *idiōtēs* reappears in v. 23 in close connection with unbelievers.

Those who presuppose that the word refers to the same person both here and in v. 23 most often[41] consider the *idiōtēs* to be a person who stands somewhere between nonbelievers and "full-fledged Christians."[42] Hence

---

[35]Gk. εὐχαριστία; the cognate verb appears in v. 17. Thus the two verbs, εὐλογέω and εὐχαριστέω, are nearly interchangeable here, as in 10:16 and 11:24.

[36]This is implied by the use of the article τό before ἀμήν. The continuation of the practice in the early church is noted by Justin, *Apol.* 65: "When he has finished the prayers and the thanksgiving, the whole congregation present assents, saying, 'Amen.'"

[37]A word borrowed from the Hebrew, meaning "that which is sure and valid." In the NT it most often appears at the conclusion of doxologies to God or Christ. See Gal. 1:5; Rom. 1:25; 9:5; 11:36; 16:27; Phil. 4:20; Eph. 3:21; 1 Tim. 1:17; 6:16; 2 Tim. 4:18; Heb. 13:21; 1 Pet. 4:11; 5:11; Jude 25. Cf. the magnificent scene in Rev. 5, where at the conclusion of the hymns of praise to God and to the Lamb, the four living creatures say, "Amen" (v. 14). On the use of this word in early Christian worship, see H. Schlier, *TDNT* I, 336-38; and R. P. Martin, *Worship*, pp. 36-37.

[38]See Dunn, *Jesus*, p. 282, who emphasizes the importance of the corporate sense of the worship, in which all joined together, both in the "ministry" of the gifts and in the response to what God was saying. The "Amen" would function as the affirmation following the "testing" of the utterances.

[39]Gk. ὁ ἀναπληρῶν τὸν τόπον. The verb ordinarily means to "fill up," or "fill a gap, replace."

[40]See the evidence in BAGD; cf. H. Schlier, *TDNT* III, 215-17.

[41]A few consider the person to be an "outsider" (RSV) in both cases.

[42]"As a kind of proselytes or catechumens" (BAGD). This has been the traditional stance of German scholarship in general. Cf. Schlier (n. 40); see also Morris, 195-96; Martin, 71.

the translation "inquirer" in the NIV margin. Very often he/she is also viewed as having a special place reserved for him/her in the Christian assembly. But there are considerable difficulties with these positions. First, even though such language was used at a later time for catechumens, it is almost certainly an anachronism to assume that there were already "nonbaptized converts" who had special "places" reserved for them in the early house churches. Second, the context as a whole seems to be against it. The concern to this point has been the edification of *the church*. In v. 17 this *idiōtēs* is referred to as "the other person" who "is not edified" by hearing praise in tongues. Elsewhere in this argument such language refers to a believer. Moreover, Paul says this person is unable to say the customary "Amen" *to your thanksgiving,* which implies wholehearted endorsement by one who regularly affirms the praise of the living God.

The alternative is to take the verb in the figurative sense of "one who finds himself in the place or role of an *idiōtēs,*" with the latter word being used in its nontechnical sense to refer to such a person's inability to comprehend the tongues-speaker. This does not mean, as is often suggested, that such people do not have spiritual gifts, so that they are also being "put down" by the one speaking in tongues.[43] Rather, it refers to any and all in the community who become *idiōtai* to the tongues-speaker—perhaps in the further sense of being "untrained" (cf. Acts 4:13) in the "language" being spoken—precisely because they do not understand what is being said.[44] The reason for the singular is that it corresponds to the second person singular of the person being addressed. Thus, rather than speak to all in the second plural, Paul's point is better made in the singular, with the person addressed representing those speaking in tongues in the community, and the "person taking the place of the unlearned" representing all the rest in the community who at any time must listen to the uninterpreted tongues without understanding. This, after all, is Paul's concern throughout the argument, and is further supported by his own follow-up explanation in v. 17.

17 This sentence, which is joined to v. 16 by an explanatory "for,"[45] spells out why that situation is unacceptable. The contrasts are emphatic. Still keeping to the singulars, he says (literally): *"You, to be*

---

[43]Despite the frequency of this suggestion (among others, Goudge, 127; R-P, 313; Lenski, 594; Grosheide, 327; Héring, 151), it has almost nothing to commend it. The issue is not between those who do and don't have this gift, but between intelligibility and this gift in the assembly. Even other tongues-speakers will be *idiōtēs* in the sense that Paul is using the word, since they, too, will be unable to understand what is being said by the others.

[44]Cf. Godet, 282: "Paul thus designates all the members of the Church, because in this situation they play the part of unintelligent hearers in relation to the glossolalete." See also Barrett, 321.

[45]Gk. γάρ; again untranslated in the NIV.

sure,[46] are giving thanks[47] well enough, but *the other person* is not being edified." The "you" and the "other person" are the two mentioned in v. 16, the one praising God in tongues and the one who takes the place of the "unlearned" because he/she does not understand. Thus, as in vv. 1-5 and 6-12 intelligibility and edification are tied together. In the assembly the latter cannot happen without the former.

There is no good reason to translate the first clause with an English subjunctive, "You may be giving thanks well enough[48]." Paul is simply affirming what he has already said in vv. 15 and 16: "To be sure, you are giving thanks." But that is not adequate in the assembly, he is telling them. What is needed is to give thanks *intelligibly,* so that others may benefit as well.

18 Paul concludes the argument on yet another personal note, which in itself is not surprising since both the larger section (beginning with v. 6) and the more immediate subparagraph (beginning with v. 14) begin on such a note.[49] What is surprising is its *content:* "I thank God[50] I speak in tongues more than[51] all of you." Indeed, one wonders who is more greatly surprised, the Corinthians themselves or the contemporary reader.

It has been common to treat the earlier personal references as rhetorical and therefore hypothetical; this one, however, indicates that those references do indeed reflect Paul's own spirituality. Along with vv. 14-15 and 2 Cor. 12:1-10, this assertion lets us in on aspects of Paul's personal piety for which we otherwise would have been quite unprepared.[52] Apparently his life of personal devotion was regularly given to praying, singing, and praising in tongues. Granted that this is probably somewhat hyperbolic;[53] it thereby only makes the reality more emphatic. The fact that he can say it at

---

[46]Gk. μέν, followed in this case by the stronger ἀλλά (= "to be sure . . . but").

[47]Gk. εὐχαριστεῖς. On the basis of vv. 15 and 16 this is a straightforward statement of fact: "You are giving thanks well enough." Cf. Barrett, 321, who is one of the few English translators to catch this: "You indeed are giving thanks well enough."

[48]Nor is there cause to make the καλῶς ironical here, as R-P, 314, suggest. That fails to take v. 15 seriously, as well as the language of "praise" and "thanksgiving" to God associated with this gift.

[49]As with v. 14, this one is asyndetic; the argument concludes on the same abrupt note with which it began.

[50]For the lack of a conjunction here, and its significance, see n. 5 above.

[51]Gk. μαλλόν, used with the genitive of comparison, rather than the customary ἤ. One cannot tell whether the intent is primarily qualitative (Bruce, 132, "a richer endowment") or quantitative (with greater frequency). Although it is not necessary to decide, it is probably the latter.

[52]These passing references in the Corinthian correspondence should give us reason to pause whenever we think we know about as much about the apostle as can be known. More likely the extant correspondence is but the tip of the iceberg.

[53]After all, one may legitimately ask how he knew, to which the answer would be that he probably didn't.

all, and say it as a matter for which he can thank God, and say it without fear of contradiction to some who are quite taken by this gift, must be taken seriously.

If our suggestion has been correct, that there is an undercurrent of apologetic in these references, where Paul is both defending his own status with regard to their criterion—the gift of tongues—and rejecting their use of it, then these sentences are intended to fall like something of a bombshell in Corinth. Despite what they may think, he can assert—with thanksgiving to God![54]—"I speak in tongues more than all of you." His concern throughout has been with uninterpreted tongues in the assembly, because they cannot edify the church. With this sentence he outmaneuvers the Corinthians altogether. He herewith affirms their gift in the strongest of terms; but he does so in order to reorder their own thinking about what was going on in the assembly.

Thus this sentence corresponds to the first clause in v. 17. "When praising in tongues, you are thanking God well enough. Indeed, I do this more than all of you. But what goes on in church is another story altogether." Hence v. 19 will be his own personal response to v. 18, which in turn corresponds to the second clause of v. 17—the edification of others in the assembly.

19 Having set them up with the surprising words of v. 18, he now drops the other shoe. When it comes to tongues as such, he has just asserted, I surpass all of you. But so what? The crucial question is not whether one speaks in tongues or not, but *what is appropriate in the assembly.* Heretofore one may only have suspected that Paul was making distinctions between private devotion and public worship; this sentence makes it explicit.

The contrasts, which return in part to the language of v. 15, are stark. In church[55] "five intelligible words"[56] are to be preferred to "ten thousand[57] words in a tongue."[58] Only the language for edification has

---

[54]This asseveration is probably to be understood in part as something of a mild oath, a way of calling on God to be witness to the absolute truthfulness of what follows (cf. his use of "I tell the truth, I am not lying" in Rom. 9:1; Gal. 1:20; 1 Tim. 2:7; cf. also 2 Cor. 1:23; 11:10). At the same time it says something about his own attitude toward this gift.

[55]There is no article in the Greek. "In church" is to be preferred to the "in the church" of the NIV as the more appropriate English idiom for the actual gathering together of God's people; in contemporary English the addition of the article tends to move the idiom toward the concept of the *place* of gathering, which is totally foreign to its sense here.

[56]Gk. τῷ νοΐ μου ("with my understanding"), exactly as in vv. 14-15.

[57]Gk. μυρίους (cf. 4:15), the adjective for "ten thousand," the largest word for numbers available in Greek. As an adjective it means "countless, innumerable, tens of thousands."

[58]This use of the singular γλώσσῃ, following immediately on the plural

changed: "to instruct[59] others."[60] This language suggests that "the intelligible words" in this sentence are moving away from the prayer and singing (praising) of vv. 15-16, including the interpretation of such praise, back toward the other intelligible gifts mentioned in v. 6.

Thus the section has come full circle. If Paul came to them as they wished, speaking in tongues, it would not benefit them. He must speak in intelligible ways. Now he affirms that he does speak in tongues—more than all of them; but in church, so that others might be instructed, he would[61] rather speak just five words that could be understood than countless words in a tongue. The obvious implication is that they should wish to do the same.

As with the preceding paragraph, this one needs to be heard well by those on both sides of the "tongues issue." Those who tend to discount it as meaningful because of Paul's strong words against it in the assembly need to pay closer attention to his own determination to pray and praise in this way—and his thanksgiving for it. On the other side, those who have rediscovered this gift as a meaningful expression in their personal lives of devotion need to be especially conscious of the greater concern of this paragraph that the gathered assembly be a time for the building up of others individually and the body as a whole.

d. Application for the sake of unbelievers (14:20-25)

20 *Brothers, stop thinking like children. In regard to evil be infants, but in your thinking be adults.* 21 *In the Law it is written:*

> "With other[1] *tongues*
> *and through the lips of foreigners[2]*
> *I will speak to this people,*
> *but even then they will not listen to me,"[a]*

says the Lord.

γλώσσαις in v. 18, is a sure indication that there is no real significance to the singular or plural. It scarcely now means "a foreign language"; probably it implies "in any given instance of speaking in tongues."

[59]Gk. κατηχέω (cf. Gal. 6:6; Rom. 2:18); it is not the ordinary word for "teach"; rather, it has to do with "informing" or "instructing" another in religious matters.

[60]Paul now shifts back to the plural from the singulars of vv. 16-17.

[61]Gk. θέλω (cf. v. 5); here it means something close to "prefer."

[1]NIV, "through men of strange tongues." Apparently this is in the interest of OT parallelism; but it is not what Paul said—nor intended. His emphasis is not on "*men of* strange tongues," but on the phenomenon of "other tongues" itself.

[2]In place of ἑτέρων (א A B Ψ 0201 0243 6 33 81 104 326 1739 2464 pc), P[46] D[s] F G Maj lat co have ἑτέροις, making it modify "lips" and thus equivalent to ἑτερογλώσ- σοις ("other tongues and other lips"). As Zuntz, 174 n. 4, points out, this is less suited to Paul's argument, which implies by ἑτέρων "that 'others' (i.e., believers) will vainly speak in tongues to nonbelievers."

22 *Tongues, then, are a sign, not for believers but for unbelievers; prophecy, however, is for believers, not for unbelievers.* 23 *So if the whole church comes together and everyone speaks in tongues, and some who do not understand[b] or some unbelievers come in, will they not say that you are out of your mind?* 24 *But if an unbeliever or someone who does not understand[c] comes in while everybody is prophesying, he will be convinced by all that he is a sinner and will be judged by all,* 25 *and[3] the secrets of his heart will be laid bare. So he will fall down and worship God, exclaiming, "God is really among you!"*

[a]Isaiah 28:11, 12; Deut. 28:49
[b]Or *some inquirers*
[c]Or *or some inquirer*

Having challenged the Corinthians' apparently exclusive use of tongues as incapable of edifying the church, Paul now concludes by noting the effect of this gift on unbelievers as well. The structure of the present argument is plain, despite some notorious difficulties involving v. 22:[4]

20 Exhortation: Redirect your thinking (about the function of tongues)
21 OT text: Tongues do not lead people to obedience
22 Application: So then—
  Assertion 1—Tongues a sign not for   believers   A
                                  but for unbelievers   B
  Assertion 2—Prophecy [a sign] not for unbelievers   B
                                  but for   believers   A
23 Illustration 1—Effect of tongues (1) on unbelievers   (B)
24-25 Illustration 2—Effect of prophecy (2) on unbelievers   (B)

Although one is led to expect something else from the assertions, Paul's basic concern is easily discernible, both from the flow of thought and from the fact that both illustrations deal with unbelievers only. As in the preceding section, it has to do with the effect of unintelligibility in the corporate setting. Uninterpreted tongues do not edify believers; nor do they benefit unbelievers who may visit their assembly. Indeed, the effect would be quite the opposite. As the illustration in v. 23 points out, instead of leading to conviction of sin and thus to repentance, the use of tongues in the assembly turns out to fulfill the word of Isa. 28:11-12 (cited in v. 21), that "even then [by speaking in tongues] they will not obey me." But that is not

---

[3]The MajT, against all the early evidence, adds a premature καὶ οὕτως to the argument (see the next clause).

[4]Cf. the structural analysis in B. C. Johanson, "Tongues, a Sign for Unbelievers?: A Structural and Exegetical Study of I Corinthians xiv.20-25," *NTS* 25 (1979), 180-203, esp. 186-90.

the final word. As with believers, prophecy on the other hand will have the opposite effect; it will lead to their conversion.

Thus even though in v. 22 Paul speaks of the effect of both tongues and prophecy on *believers,* he has already dealt with that, so in this paragraph he addresses only how each affects *unbelievers.*[5] Although this analysis does not resolve all the difficulties with the language of v. 22, it does point out the direction in which the resolution must lie.

20 Another turn in the argument is marked by the vocative (cf. v. 6)[6] and the rather abrupt appearance of this exhortation to stop being[7] children[8] in their thinking.[9] Although some have seen this as related to 13:10-11 and have thus argued that Paul considered speaking in tongues itself as childish behavior to be outgrown,[10] both the preceding argument— especially vv. 15 and 18—and the structure of this sentence suggest otherwise.[11] With the familiar A-B-A pattern of argument,[12] Paul uses this imagery to appeal in two directions: that they cease being like children *in their thinking;* and that they be as innocent as babies *in their behavior.* In Paul's sentence this is the basic contrast, brought out in the first two clauses, while the third balances the first as its opposite. Thus (literally):

Do not be children	in your thinking;[13]	A
but[14] be infants[15]	in evil.[16]	B
rather *(de)*	in your thinking be adults.	A

[5]Cf. Johanson, "Tongues," p. 187: "The main concern of *vv.* 21-5 has to do with the relation of tongues to unbelievers in contrast to the relation of prophecy also to unbelievers." In an otherwise helpful study, P. Roberts, "A Sign—Christian or Pagan?" *ExpT* 90 (1978/79), 199-203, makes a crucial leap of logic so that the concern turns out to be with the Corinthians themselves rather than with the ineffectiveness of unintelligibility in the community.

[6]For this usage in 1 Corinthians, see on 1:10.

[7]The NIV has probably caught the correct nuance of the present imperative here.

[8]Gk. παιδία, the only occurrence of this word in Paul; in 3:1-2 he uses νήπιος (cf. 13:11).

[9]Gk. φρεσίν (only here in the NT), referring to understanding or discernment. Cf. the similar appeal to their thinking sensibly that begins the final prohibition against idolatry in 10:15. Although this exhortation begins the present paragraph, it undoubtedly is intended also to apply to all that has been said since v. 1. In fact, some (e.g., Findlay, 908; Martin, 72) break the paragraph after v. 20.

[10]Perpetuated as recently as Martin, 71.

[11]Cf. R. Schnackenburg, "Christian Adulthood According to the Apostle Paul," *CBQ* 25 (1963), 365: "Not that glossolaly itself is childish behavior, but rather it is childish to have an unreasonable preference for this gift of the Spirit."

[12]For this pattern in the larger structure of the argument, see n. 9 on 12:1-3; for an example of this structure within a single sentence, see on 1:10.

[13]In each case this is a dative of reference.

[14]Gk. ἀλλά, which with the preceding μή is the indication that *Paul's* contrasts

As in the usage of this same imagery in 3:1-2, a degree of irony is probably intended.[17] Their childishness consists of *thinking* improperly that tongues serves as evidence of their new transcendent spirituality and thus marks off the spiritual quality of their gathering,[18] while in fact they evidence all kinds of ethical/behavioral aberrations.

In the context of the OT passage Paul is about to cite, the prophet Isaiah prefaces the cited words with this rhetorical question: "To whom is he explaining this message? To children weaned from their milk?" In Isaiah this was probably spoken to the prophet by his mockers. It seems possible that Paul has this context in mind; for him the Corinthians are in danger of playing the role of those "children," who rejected the word of the Lord. Thus this exhortation serves both to get them to reconsider their own evaluation of tongues and at the same time to prepare the way for the final argument against unintelligibility in the community.

21 Paul begins redirecting their thinking by adapting a passage from Isa. 28:11-12, which he introduces as a citation from "the Law."[19] The citation itself is not precise;[20] it seems to have been chosen for two interre-

---

lie here. Otherwise Johanson, "Tongues," p. 186, who sees the second clause as parenthetical.

[15]Gk. νηπιάζετε; probably no significance is to be attached to the differences between παιδία and νήπιος, especially since in 13:11 Paul refers to thinking like a νήπιος (infant). The fluidity of Paul's images is reflected in his positive use of the "infant" metaphor here, which was negative in 3:1-2 and neutral in 13:11. Here it implies the need for innocence with regard to evil.

[16]Gk. τῇ κακίᾳ; cf. 10:6.

[17]Because of the abrupt nature of the transition from v. 19 to v. 20, R. M. Grant suggests that Paul is here taking up another topic from Corinth, i.e., their justification for their "childish behavior" as having "the sanction of the Lord's command," as found in Mark 10:15 and parallels ("Like Children," *HTR* 39 [1946], 71-73). The possibility that Paul is here taking on their own point of view seems viable, but more likely it is in irony than in direct refutation of an alleged use of a Jesus word.

[18]See the introductions to chaps. 12–14 and to 14:1-25, as well as the commentary on 13:1. Thus it fits again with the overall argument of the letter. Both Johanson, "Tongues," and Sweet, "Sign," see this paragraph, as well as the whole of chaps. 12–14, to be dealing with internecine strife between glossolalists and prophets. This view fails at a number of significant points (see n. 16 on 12:1-3, as well as the commentary on 1:10-17); this presupposition, which in both cases is integral to their analysis of the paragraph, mitigates what are otherwise helpful insights.

[19]On the use of this formula in Paul, see on 9:9; cf. the discussion on 14:34. Citing the prophets as "in the Law" is a carry-over from his Jewish heritage (cf. Rom. 3:19; John 10:34). Cf. W. Gutbrod, *TDNT* IV, 1036-78.

[20]Paul follows neither the LXX nor the MT, although he is closer to the latter. Since there are some correspondences between this citation and the later (*ca.* 100 years) translation of Aquila (in the combined form ἑτερόγλωσσος, and in the inversion of "tongues" and "lips," including the form ἐν χείλεσιν ἑτέρων), it is possible that Paul and he were both dependent on an earlier form of Greek text no longer available. See the argument in Harrisville, "Study," pp. 42-45.

lated reasons: the occurrence of the language "other tongues"[21] and the fact that in the OT context this "speaking in tongues" by foreigners did not effect belief in Israel[22]—indeed, it both led to and was part of their judgment.[23] To bring out his own concerns Paul does four things with the Isaiah passage. (1) He inverts the order of "stammering lips" and "other tongues" to put his interest, "other tongues," in first position. (2) He changes "stammering lips" to "the lips of others"; the "others" now being the Corinthian believers, whose speaking in tongues would have a deleterious effect on unbelievers.[24] (3) In keeping with the MT, but against the LXX, Paul changes "the Lord will speak" to "I will speak" and concludes with the formula "says the Lord," probably to increase its impact on the Corinthians.[25] (4) Most significantly, he skips a considerable section in the Isaiah passage, picking up at the end of v. 12, where he changes "and they would not hear *(akouō),*" referring to the intelligible words of the Lord, to "and even so [referring now to the 'other tongues'] they *will not obey (eisakouō)* me." In Paul's context this refers to the outsiders of v. 23, who on hearing the Corinthians speaking in tongues would declare them mad. Paul's point seems to be that such a reaction would be a "fulfillment" of this "word of the Lord" to the effect that tongues do not lead sinners to obedience.

22 With the strong inferential conjunction "so then,"[26] Paul

---

[21]Gk. ἐν ἑτερογλώσσοις; only here in the NT. The LXX has διὰ γλώσσας ἑτέρας (cf. Acts 2:4: ἑτέραις γλώσσαις).

[22]Cf. Roberts, "Sign," p. 201: "There seems to be little similarity between the situation which evoked Isaiah's words, and the circumstances which caused Paul to quote them here, except for the strange tongues and their ineffectiveness"; and Johanson, "Tongues," p. 182.

[23]How much of the OT context Paul was consciously bringing to this citation is a matter of debate, which is not otherwise significant unless one thinks that the "sign" in v. 22 is related to the "judgment" of Israel in the Isaiah passage (e.g., R-P, 317). See also O. P. Robertson, "Tongues: Sign of Covenantal Curse and Blessing," *WTJ* 38 (1975), 45-53, who makes a number of unsupported assertions and theological judgments based on the OT texts and some parallels in Acts 2, but not on what Paul himself actually says. At best one can say that despite his several adaptations, Paul does not radically alter the sense of this text in Isaiah; but it goes quite beyond the evidence to argue that Paul also brings with the citation Isaiah's use of this phenomenon—as evidence of Israel's receiving the covenantal curse of Deut. 28:49 (cf. Jer. 5:15). For a full discussion of the OT passage and its possible relevance to Paul's citation see Grudem, 185-201, which appeared earlier as "1 Corinthians 14.20-25: Prophecy and Tongues as Signs of God's Attitudes," *WTJ* 41 (1979), 381-96.

[24]But see n. 20 above; this may simply reflect the tradition he had available. So Conzelmann, 242. Even so, his *choice* of this tradition over against the MT would be significant.

[25]On this usage, see Ellis, 182-87, and *Use,* pp. 107-12. He advances the (highly speculative) hypothesis that this formula may indicate the utterances of Christian prophets.

[26]See on 3:7 (incl. n. 14). Johanson, "Tongues," p. 189, considers it consecutive, but his own discussion implies otherwise.

deduces two antithetical assertions from the Isaiah passage just quoted.[27] But what he says has become a notorious crux. The problem is twofold: (1) the meaning of "sign," including whether he intended it to be repeated for the second assertion, and if so, what it also meant there; and (2) how to square what is said here with the illustrations that follow,[28] especially the second assertion with the second illustration.[29] As noted above, the solution to this lies primarily in the recognition that Paul's point in the paragraph is made in vv. 23-25 and especially in the way v. 23 "fulfills" the Isaiah passage. This means that, contrary to many interpretations, this text (v. 22) needs to be understood in light of what follows, not the other way around.

The first assertion flows directly from the quotation itself: "Tongues are a sign,[30] not for[31] believers[32] but for unbelievers[33]." Although it cannot be finally proven, the flow of the argument from v. 20, including the strong "so then" of this sentence, suggests that Paul is setting up this antithesis with the Corinthians' own point of view in mind.[34] That is, "In contrast to

[27]Martin, 72, would resolve the difficulties by viewing v. 22 as a midrash on v. 21, without its pointing forward to vv. 23-25. But this seems to break down on the structural analysis presented above.

[28]Johanson, "Tongues," pp. 190-91, has made the helpful distinction that the assertions express the relation of tongues and prophecy to the two groups in terms of *function*, whereas the OT citation and the illustrations do so in terms of *effect*.

[29]This is so severe that J. B. Phillips, without textual warrant, opted for radical surgery and transposed "believer" and "unbeliever" in his translation. He noted: "This is the sole instance of the translator's departating from the accepted text. He felt bound to conclude, from the sense of the next three verses, that we have here either a slip of the pen on the part of Paul, or, more probably, a copyist's error" (p. 346). Cf. Parry, 205, who would prefer to see v. 22 as a gloss.

[30]Gk. εἰς σημεῖον; this is a possible rendering and is favored by Grudem, 192-93, esp. n. 23. The evidence in its favor, however, is basically semitic—even the passages in Paul that are brought forward as evidence are all citations of the LXX (e.g., 1 Cor. 6:16; 15:45). On the other hand, it is possible to give the preposition its more ordinary telic force (= "tongues are meant as a sign"), as Moule, 70; Johanson, "Tongues," p. 190 n. 5; cf. 1 Cor. 4:3. On the whole, the latter seems preferable, although the meaning is not greatly affected.

[31]Dative of advantage/disadvantage.

[32]Gk. τοῖς πιστεύουσιν, a common designation for Christians in Paul's letters (he never uses πιστός in this way); cf. 1:18; 1 Thess. 1:7; 2:10, 13; 2 Thess. 1:10; Gal. 3:22; Rom. 4:24.

[33]Gk. τοῖς ἀπίστοις (see on 6:6; 7:12; 10:27); as in those texts it can refer only to those who are outside the Christian faith. Perhaps the ἄπιστοι referred to in 7:12 are the kind Paul could envision being present at a Christian gathering, especially if the Christian meal was being eaten at the same time. On this probability see Barrett, 325.

[34]This has also been suggested, but with differing agenda in mind, by Sweet, "Sign," p. 241; Johanson, "Tongues," pp. 193-94; and Roberts, "Sign," p. 201. Johanson sees the *whole* of v. 22, including the internal antitheses in each assertion, as the point of view of the Corinthian glossolalists, which Paul is reproducing here in the form of rhetorical questions. Thus σημεῖον is positive (because it expresses their outlook); Paul's response is found in the illustrations of vv. 23-25, which stand in opposition to the

what you think, this word of the Lord from Isaiah indicates that tongues are *not* meant as a sign for believers. They are not, as you make them, the divine evidence of being *pneumatikos,* nor of the presence of God in your assembly. To the contrary, in the public gathering uninterpreted tongues function as a sign for unbelievers." The question is, What kind of sign? In light of v. 21, for which this is the inferential deduction, "sign" in this first sentence can only function in a negative way. That is, it is a "sign" that functions to the disadvantage of unbelievers, not to their advantage.

Most likely Paul is using the word in a way that is quite in keeping with his Judaic background, where "sign" functions as an expression of God's attitude;[35] something "signifies" to Israel either his disapproval[36] or pleasure.[37] In this case, it is his disapproval that is in view; but not in the sense that God *intends* unbelievers during this time of grace to receive his judgment. To the contrary, tongues *function* that way as the result of their *effect* on the unbeliever, as the illustration in v. 23 will clarify. Because tongues are unintelligible, unbelievers receive no revelation from God; they cannot thereby be brought to faith. Thus by their response of seeing the work of the Spirit as madness, they are destined for divine judgment—just as in the OT passage Paul has quoted. This, of course, is not the divine intent for such people; hence Paul's urgency is that the Corinthians cease thinking like children and stop the public use of tongues, since it serves to drive the unbeliever away rather than to lead him or her to faith.

With a balancing antithetical clause Paul adds that "prophecy, however," also functions as a sign,[38] but "not for unbelievers, but for believers."[39] With this sentence he once again picks up the contrast between tongues and prophecy that was last expressed in vv. 1-6 (although it is alluded to in v. 19 in anticipation of this argument). This is also the clause in which all the difficulties have arisen, since in the illustration that corresponds to this assertion (vv. 24-25) he does not so much as mention believers

---

glossolalists, and in favor of those who prefer prophecy. Although this has some attractive features, it finally breaks down both grammatically (Paul's use of ὥστε in 1 Corinthians—the alleged analogous usage in Gal. 4:16 is not similar) and contextually (there is otherwise not a hint in this chapter, nor throughout 12–14, that Paul is responding to an in-house division over this matter—not to mention that in chaps. 1–4, where there is internal division, Paul refuses to take sides).

[35]For the argument in favor of this point of view see Dunn, *Jesus,* pp. 230-32, and Grudem, 194-202 (apparently independently of Dunn, given the nature of the addendum to n. 25, p. 196).

[36]See, e.g., Num. 26:10 (those who died in Korah's rebellion became a sign); cf. Deut. 28:46. See further, Grudem, 195.

[37]E.g., Gen. 9:12 (the rainbow); Exod. 12:13 (the blood on the doorpost).

[38]The Greek text does not specifically say this; but the sentence is most likely an ellipsis since the verb εἰσιν is omitted as well. This means that the two sets of antitheses are to be understood as in perfect balance. Cf. Grudem, 193-94.

[39]The NIV reverses the order of the antithesis, for no apparently good reason.

but indicates only how prophecy affects unbelievers, and in a way that would make one think that it is really a sign for *them,* that is, to *their* advantage.

The solution again lies first of all in the nature of the conflict between Paul and the Corinthians. Over against their preference for tongues, he asserts that it is prophecy, with its intelligibility and revelatory character, that functions as the sign of God's approval, of God's presence, in their midst.[40] The evidence of this is to be found in the very way that it affects unbelievers. By the revelatory word of prophecy they are convicted of their sins, and falling on their faces before God they will exclaim, "God is really among you!" That exclamation as a response to prophecy is a "sign" for believers, the indication of God's favor resting upon them.[41]

Thus, tongues and prophecy function as "signs" in two different ways, precisely in accord with the *effect* each will have on unbelievers who happen into the Christian assembly.

23 With this sentence and the next Paul proceeds[42] to illustrate the two assertions of v. 22 in terms of the effect of each on unbelievers. Both sentences take the same form: a present general condition in which the protasis expresses the hypothetical situation of the gathered church into which unbelievers enter and the apodosis expresses their response—first to tongues, then to prophecy. Although hypothetical, and probably overstated, the protases must nonetheless be taken seriously as real possibilities; otherwise the argument is to no avail. Thus these illustrations give us several insights into an early Christian gathering for worship.

(1) The language for their assembling together is nearly identical to that found in 11:20: "the whole church comes together at the same place."[43] Along with the salutation[44] and the evidence from Rom. 16:23,[45] this implies that all the believers from all the house churches met together in some way.[46] Given the limitations of size in even the most commodious of well-

---

[40]Barrett, 324, sees prophecy as a sign of "judgment" on the Corinthian believers since they prefer tongues to the very kind of intelligibility that can lead to salvation.

[41]Cf. such OT passages as Isa. 29:10; Mic. 3:6; Lam. 2:9 for indications that the absence of prophecy is a sign of judgment, or the loss of God's favor.

[42]The illustrations are joined to v. 22 by means of an inferential οὖν, translated "so" in the NIV. As with the two assertions, the two illustrations are connected by an adversative δέ ("on the other hand").

[43]As in 11:20 the NIV omits the additional qualifier ἐπὶ τὸ αὐτό, probably as a redundancy. As noted there, this probably means "together," although here it may mean in a single gathering over against multiple gatherings in various house churches.

[44]See 1:2; the letter is written to *the* church in Corinth.

[45]Writing from Corinth, Paul sends greetings from "Gaius, host to me and to *the whole church.*"

[46]Cf. Banks, *Paul's Idea,* p. 38, who argues that the use of ὅλη ("whole") here implies a more regular meeting of smaller groups. Parry, 207, allows that it could refer to "the whole of any particular congregation"; but that seems doubtful in light of all the evidence.

to-do homes,[47] does this imply that the church was somewhat smaller than we might tend to think? Or is it possible that one of the houses was considerably larger than archeology has uncovered in Corinth to this point? We simply do not know.

(2) Both this text and v. 26, as well as 11:2-16, where women are praying and prophesying in the assembly, indicate that at least one expression of their worship was "charismatic," in the twofold sense that there was general participation by all the members, including the women, and that there was considerable expression of the more spontaneous gifts of utterance.

Two things should be noted in regard to the language "and all speak in tongues." (a) Even though this is probably overstated, one can hardly escape the implication that all of the believers could potentially do so. This means that Paul's point in 12:29-30, as we noted there, was to discourage "all" from doing so; he did not mean that only a few could be so gifted (cf. v. 5). The same is true of prophecy.[48] (b) Again, even though it is overstatement, this is probably a generally realistic description of the current scene in Corinth. Not that all were necessarily speaking in tongues at the same time; nonetheless the guidelines in vv. 27-33 seem to imply that many were doing so on a regular basis.[49] If so, then not only did the unintelligibility lead to the exclamation of "madness," but so also would the general chaos of so much individualized worship with no concern for the general edification of the body as a whole.

(3) These gatherings of the "whole church" were also accessible to unbelievers. The term "unbeliever" is the same as in v. 22, making it certain that these verses serve as illustrations for those assertions. Added to "unbeliever" in both instances is the word *idiōtēs* from v. 16.[50] The close ties of this word with "unbeliever" and the nature of their response to tongues and prophecy indicate that such people are not believers. It is also doubtful for the same reasons that it is a technical term for an "inquirer," someone who stands in some kind of halfway position. Most likely, as before, it carries the nontechnical sense of anyone who is "unlearned," in

---

[47]See the introduction to 11:17-22 (pp. 533-34).

[48]See on vv. 24 and 29.

[49]So also Barrett, 324. R-P, 317, object that since πάντες cannot mean all simultaneously in v. 24, it also cannot here. But that has Paul's argument in reverse. V. 24 receives its *form* from v. 23; it is not necessary to think that Paul would have envisioned "all prophesying" as being in disarray, which apparently he did of their speaking in tongues.

[50]In this first instance he has ἰδιῶται ἢ ἄπιστοι; in v. 24 they are in reverse order and singular. Nothing significant is to be made of these differences (as, e.g., Findlay, 911; R-P, 318; Barrett, 325; Conzelmann, 243 n. 28). Both changes are stylistic (the transposition creates a chiasm).

this case "untutored" with regard to the Christian faith.[51] Indeed, it is possible that Paul did not intend to designate a second kind of person at all;[52] rather, he simply begins his description of unbelievers in general with this word. Thus, the visiting "unbeliever" is also "untutored" in the faith.[53] As noted earlier, Paul may very well have in mind an unbelieving spouse accompanying the believer to his or her place of worship. Such a person is both outside of Christ and as yet uninstructed in Christ.

(4) The response of the unbeliever to the community's collective speaking in tongues is to equate the Christian gathering with the mania that attended some of the mystery cults.[54] "Madness,"[55] they will say. For Paul such a response is totally unworthy of the gospel of Christ. Hence tongues fulfills the prophetic word of Isaiah, that with "other tongues" God will speak to "this people," yet even so they will not obey. This is Paul's final word about uninterpreted tongues in the assembly; with it he is once more urging them to stop such activity. Not only do tongues not edify; they are also not the "evidence" the Corinthians think they are. To the contrary, this response would be sure evidence that they have quite missed what it means to be God's "Spirit people" in the new age that has dawned with Christ.

24-25   Once more prophecy is set forth as the alternative to the unintelligibility of uninterpreted tongues. In this case it is viewed as leading directly to the conversion of the visiting unbeliever. This passage in particular implies that prophesying is *potentially available* to all believers since all are Spirit people.[56] That is, Paul does not say, "If the prophets all prophesy . . . ," but, "If *all* prophesy . . . the unbeliever will be convicted by *all* [not all the prophets] . . . and he will be judged by *all*." The nature of this argumentation seems to exclude the option that this gift was limited to a group of authoritative people who were known in the community as "the prophets." Again, as with tongues, it does not mean that Paul expects

---

[51]Cf. Findlay, 910: "unacquainted with Christianity." Since the term in both cases is nontechnical, there can be no objection to its referring to believers in v. 16, who are "unacquainted" with the meaning of the "tongue" and therefore cannot say the "Amen," and to unbelievers here, who are quite "untutored" with regard to the Christian faith and would see their corporate tongues-speaking as "madness."

[52]So Barrett, 324, who joins the two words into one by translating "unbelieving outsiders." Cf. Conzelmann, 243.

[53]This makes far more sense than the NIV's "someone who does not understand," which seems to break down on the matter of prophecy.

[54]See nn. 23 and 75 on 11:2-6.

[55]Gk. μαίνεσθε; cf. John 10:20; Acts 26:24, 25. The cognate noun is μανία, which occurs in various texts reflecting the ecstasies of the mysteries. E.g., Pausanias 2.7.5: "These women they say are sacred to Dionysus and maddened by his inspiration" (Loeb, I, 285); cf. Herodotus 4.79.

[56]This kind of language expresses the prophetic ideal that in the coming age of the Spirit all of God's people will be "prophets" (cf. Joel 2:28-30 and especially the citation on the Day of Pentecost in Acts 2:17-18).

everyone to prophesy; it does imply the extensive involvement of the whole community in worship, especially in the manifestation of the gifts of inspired utterance.

In contrast to the negative response in v. 23, here Paul offers a considerable description of the unbeliever's response to such prophesying. One cannot tell from what is said whether these prophecies would be similar to those in v. 3 that edified believers, or whether some of the prophecies would be more specifically directed toward the unbeliever as such. In either case, quite in keeping with the OT view of prophecy, Paul views the inspired word as penetrating deeply into the moral consciousness of the hearers. There are several dimensions to this.

First, the unbeliever is "convicted[57] by all, is called to account[58] by all." These two verbs together imply the deep probing work of the Holy Spirit in people's lives, exposing their sins and thus calling them to account before the living God. Lying behind the word "convicted" is the OT view that one is exposed before the living God through the prophetic word; inherent in such "exposure" is the call to repentance,[59] the summons to have one's exposed sins forgiven by a merciful God.

The second word appeared previously in this letter to describe the Corinthians' "examination" of Paul and his apostleship (4:3-4; 9:3); it is also used in 2:14-15 to describe the proper sphere of activity of the "spiritual person," meaning something like "discern." Perhaps there is an intended deflection by the use of this word here. Instead of "examining" Paul on their grounds of spirituality, they should seek to prophesy in the assembly so that the proper "examining" might take place, that of the Spirit in the heart of the unbeliever, bringing him or her to a place of repentance.

The result of this convicting process begins as an internal work in the sinner: "the secrets of his heart will be laid bare."[60] The emphasis here is on the revelatory aspect of the prophetic utterance.[61] The story of the Fall suggests that one of its first effects on humanity is their great sense of need to

---

[57]Gk. ἐλέγχεται; in Paul cf. Eph. 5:11, 13; 1 Tim. 5:20; Tit. 1:9, 13; 2:15; 2 Tim. 4:2. Cf. also John 16:8-11. For a discussion of biblical usage see F. Büchsel, *TDNT* II, 473-76.

[58]Gk. ἀνακρίνω; only in 1 Corinthians (ten times) in Paul. See the discussion on 2:15.

[59]Büchsel, p. 474: It means "to show someone his sin and to summon him to repentance." Hence the basic correctness of the NIV's "he will be convinced by all that he is a sinner."

[60]Cf. 4:5, where nearly identical language describes the eschatological judgment of God. Now he uses it to refer to the judgment that takes place in the present through the Spirit.

[61]The Greek for "laid bare" is φανερός; it is the adjective of the verb "to reveal." See n. 33 on 4:5 for references in Paul and Judaism that the living God knows and searches the human heart.

hide from the living God; it is the folly of our sinfulness that allows us to think we can. Thus, one of the sure signs of the presence of God in the believing community is this deep plowing work of the Spirit, whereby through prophetic revelation the secrets of the heart are laid bare.[62] No wonder the Corinthians preferred tongues; it not only gave them a sense of being more truly "spiritual" but it was safer!

The final result of such exposure before God is conversion, which is what Paul's language unmistakably intends. The language is thoroughly steeped in the OT. First, "he will thus fall on his face[63] and worship God." This is biblical language for obeisance and worship. That Paul intends this to mean conversion is indicated by the final exclamation, which is a conscious reflection of Isa. 45:14 (cf. Zech. 8:23): God, speaking through the prophet, says that the Egyptians will come over to you, and "will worship" before you, and say, "Surely God is with you." Paul simply changes the singular "with you," referring to Israel, into a plural, "among you,"[64] referring to the gathered community.[65] This final confession of the unbeliever is thus the "sign" that prophecy is for "believers"; it is sure evidence of God's favor resting on his people.

With these powerful words Paul brings to a conclusion his argument against both the use of uninterpreted tongues in the assembly and the thinking that lay behind it. He insists that in the gathered community only what is intelligible is permissible—because what is intelligible, especially prophecy, both edifies God's people and leads to the conversion of others. But this is only part of the problem. Their use of tongues was apparently also disorderly, so to that question he now turns before concluding the argument with a direct confrontation with the Corinthians over his right so to order them and over who in fact is truly *pneumatikos*.

Along with the great need for local communities to be edified, the reason set forth in this paragraph ought to be sufficient to lead the church to pray for the renewal of the prophetic gift in its ongoing life. It is not simply the presence of prophecy itself that signifies God's presence among his gathered people, but the powerful revealing work of the Spirit that convicts

---

[62]It is characteristic of the biblical view that sin is first of all a matter of the heart. Therefore, conversion includes not only the forgiveness of one's sins but the regenerating work of the Spirit in the heart, from whence are the issues of life.

[63]Gk. πεσὼν ἐπὶ πρόσωπον; in the LXX see, e.g., Gen. 17:3, 17; Lev. 9:24; Num. 16:22; Ezek. 11:13; and many others. In the NT see Matt. 17:6; 26:39 (of Jesus in Gethsemane); Luke 5:12; 17:16; Rev. 7:11; 11:16.

[64]Gk. ἐν ὑμῖν; cf. on 3:16.

[65]The thoroughly biblical language used throughout vv. 24-25 to describe the effect of prophecy on the unbeliever is further evidence that this phenomenon in Paul is to be understood in light of his Jewish heritage and not similar phenomena in Hellenism.

of sin and leads to repentance. Perhaps in our domestication of the Spirit we have also settled for a "safer" expression of worship, one in which very few are ever led to exclaim that "Surely God is among you." Seeing that actually take place leads to prayer that v. 1 might be the church's ongoing portion: love, spiritual gifts, especially prophecy.

5. *The Ordering of Gifts (14:26-40)*

The basic problem Paul has with the Corinthians' singular zeal for the gift of tongues has now been addressed (vv. 1-25); because the gift is unintelligible, it neither edifies saints nor converts sinners. But that is not the only concern. What was hinted at in v. 23 is implied more strongly in vv. 27-28. Apparently there was a degree of disorderliness to their speaking in tongues as well. Although the evidence is not conclusive, the argument of this section suggests that more than one of them was accustomed to speaking forth at the same time. Thus there appears also to have been a high degree of individualized worship in their corporate gatherings. Paul, however, does not press this latter theme here, so one must be duly cautious. His antidote is to offer guidelines for regulation that, taken together, suggest orderliness, self-control, and concern for others.[1]

Thus, the opening paragraph of this section brings the argument of the chapter to its conclusion. Paul begins with a descriptive exhortation (v. 26): Each one has something to contribute, and everything must be done to edify. This is followed by guidelines, first for tongues and interpretation (vv. 27-28) and then for prophecy and discernment (vv. 29-31). The concluding word on prophecies (vv. 32-33) probably functions as a concluding word for the whole section. Christian inspiration is not out of control, for God himself is not like that; and this holds for all the congregations of the saints.[2]

As noted throughout, the issue right along has been not only their incorrect assessment of tongues and spirituality, but also their rejection of his authority because (probably) he failed to pass their test on this point (see on vv. 6, 14-15, 18). Thus before bringing the whole of chaps. 12–14 to a summary conclusion (vv. 39-40), Paul turns *ad hominem* one more time.

---

[1]Ellis, 38, makes the improbable suggestion that Paul's coworkers were the original subjects of these regulations and that in their present form they are applied only to a certain class of pneumatics who have spiritual gifts (p. 26).

[2]In most Greek MSS, but not in the Western church where they appear after v. 40, there follows a word about the silence and submission of women (vv. 34-35), which intrudes in the present argument like a "rock." The questions of both transcriptional and intrinsic probability raise considerable doubt as to its authenticity. See the commentary.

With a series of rhetorical questions that flow directly from the mention of all the churches, he asks how it is that they consider themselves alone to have the word of God on these matters, and concludes with a direct confrontation with them over his own status as apostle and *pneumatikos* (vv. 36-38).

a. The ordering of tongues and prophecy (14:26-33)

26 *What then shall we say, brothers? When you come together, everyone[3] has a hymn, or a word of instruction, a revelation, a tongue or an interpretation. All of these must be done for the strengthening of the church.* 27 *If anyone speaks in a tongue, two—or at the most three—should speak, one at a time, and someone must interpret.* 28 *If there is no interpreter, the speaker should keep quiet in the church and speak to himself and God.*

29 *Two or three prophets should speak, and the others weigh carefully what is said.* 30 *And if a revelation comes to someone who is sitting down, the first speaker should stop.* 31 *For you can all prophesy in turn so that everyone may be instructed and encouraged.* 32 *The spirits[4] of prophets are subject to the control of prophets.* 33 *For God is not a God of disorder but of peace, as in all the congregations of the saints.*

If this material were in a nonpolemical letter, it would look very much like instruction on the regulation of spiritual gifts. Its appearance here, however, indicates that, even though instructional, it is primarily correctional, especially in light of the argument that has preceded and the rhetoric that follows (vv. 36-38). The section is in four parts: an opening exhortation (v. 26) and final admonition (vv. 32-33) surround the regulation of tongues (vv. 27-28) and prophecy (vv. 29-31). The two regulatory sections are quite similar, both in structure and in content: Paul begins with a word about the number of speakers (two or three at the most); they must speak "one at a time"; tongues must be interpreted and prophecy "discerned"; under certain conditions silence is enjoined; and each section concludes with words similar to the instruction in vv. 2-4 (without interpretation the tongues-speaker must speak privately to God; if properly regulated, prophecies will bring instruction and encouragement).

What is said here about tongues is precisely in keeping with what Paul has argued throughout; it serves as further evidence that he has not been

---

[3]The Westerns and MajT have the understandable, but secondary, addition of ὑμῶν. It is missing in P⁴⁶ ℵ* A B 0201 33 81 630 1175 1739 1881 pc, an "omission" that can scarcely be accounted for.

[4]A few MSS (D F G Ψ* 1241ˢ pc a b syᵖ) try to alleviate the difficulty of this plural by making it singular—although in some cases this could be the result of an accidental dropping of a τά.

after tongues as such, but after uninterpreted tongues in the assembly. Here he regulates the use of tongues *with* interpretation.

26 The combination of the formula "What then is the upshot of all this?"[5] and the vocative "brothers [and sisters]"[6] signals a shift in the argument, but in this case one that seems intended to tie together several loose ends. The verb "you come together," spoken now in the second person plural (as in 11:18, 20, 33-34), picks up the argument from vv. 23-25.[7] The first sentence, which offers a description of what should be happening[8] at their gatherings, echoes the concerns of chap. 12, that *each one*[9] has opportunity to participate in the corporate ministry of the body. The second sentence, the exhortation that all of the various expressions of ministry described in the first sentence be for edification,[10] echoes the basic concern of chap. 14—as well as of chap. 13. Thus these concluding guidelines bring both sections of the preceding argument into focus.

Like all the former lists in these chapters, this final one is *ad hoc;* it is intended neither to give the "order" of service[11] nor to be exhaustive of what "each one has" to offer by way of ministry. Given the fact that neither prayer nor prophecy and "discernment" is listed (cf. 11:4-5) yet in the following sentences the latter two are "regulated," this list in particular seems capable of yielding to an *et cetera* at the end. Each of these items has appeared in the previous discussion; most likely they represent various *types* of verbal manifestations of the Spirit that should occur in their assembly. Since the latter three are Spirit-inspired utterances, and are therefore spontaneous, it is likely that the first two are to be understood in that way as well,[12] although that is not certain.

For a discussion of the "hymn" see on v. 15; very likely this word stands for "prayer" as well, although the interpreted tongue could also fit

[5]See n. 20 on v. 15.

[6]See on 1:10; cf. vv. 6 and 20.

[7]See on v. 23. This repetition of the verb in terms of what should be happening further supports the suggestion made there that v. 23 gives a generally realistic picture of what they were doing in fact.

[8]It is possible that some of this was already going on; but the rest of the context, including chap. 12, suggests that this is a corrective word rather than a merely descriptive one. Martin, 78, offers the possibility that the repeated "has" may be a form of reproof; however, nothing in the text itself mildly hints at disapproval here.

[9]Reinforced in this case not by the repetition of ἕκαστος but of the verb ἔχει. Cf. 12:8-10.

[10]The preposition πρός with οἰκοδομήν in particular indicates the purpose of all these things. The NIV's "for the strengthening of the church" is permissible, but one wonders why so here, when this exact phrase, plus the qualifier "of the church," appears in v. 12 and is translated "build up the church." That will hardly help the average reader trace ideas through the chapter.

[11]So also Conzelmann, 244; cf. R-P, 320; otherwise, Findlay, 912.

[12]See the discussion on vv. 6 and 15.

that category. For "word of instruction" and "revelation" see on v. 6. As suggested there, the latter could very easily be a cover word for all other forms of intelligible inspired speech, including the "prophecies" of vv. 29-32, especially since the verb "revealed" occurs in the context of prophecy and discernment in v. 30. For "tongue" and "interpretation" see on 12:10. On the "charismatic" nature of this worship, see on v. 23. What is striking in this entire discussion is the absence of any mention of leadership or of anyone who would be responsible for seeing that these guidelines were generally adhered to. The community appears to be left to itself and the Holy Spirit.[13] What is mandatory is that everything aim at edification.

27 Having commanded that "all things (i.e., the various ministries in the preceding list) be done for the edification of the church," Paul proceeds to show how this may be accomplished for tongues and prophecy, the two gifts that have been at the forefront of the preceding discussion. He begins with the problem child, tongues.[14] Three guidelines are given.

First, "two—or at the most three—should speak." One cannot be sure whether this means "at any one service" or "before there is an interpretation." In favor of the former is the phrase "at the most," plus the overall concern of the chapter that tongues not dominate the assembly; therefore in this guideline Paul is suggesting that such manifestations be limited in any given meeting. In favor of the latter is the similar recommendation for prophecies in vv. 29-31, which on the basis of vv. 24 and 31 is intended to limit the number of speakers in sequence, not the number of prophecies at any given service. On the whole, this is not easy to decide, but probably the word "at the most," which is missing in the guidelines for prophecies, tips the balance in favor of the former.[15]

Second, "and[16] one at a time[17]." Two observations are in order. (a) There seems to be no good reason for such a word unless it is intended to be

---

[13]But see Parry, 209, who says of vv. 27-28 that "these are rules for the chairman"!

[14]The sentence begins with an εἴτε, implying that he intended to "regulate" several items: "whether it be a tongue, do it thus; whether it be prophecy, etc." However, the first one apparently ended up longer than the εἴτε anticipated, especially with the qualifying sentence about interpretation in v. 28. Hence the discussion of prophecy skips εἴτε and picks up with the guideline about two or three in succession.

It should also be noted that the sentence is a simple condition; as Richardson, "Order," p. 148, notes, "It is not a question of contingency, but an introduction to directives; not a matter of whether, but when."

[15]The factor of "amount of available time" that is often brought into this discussion is probably altogether too modern—and Western—to be relevant. Anyone who has sat through several hours of worship in Romania, West Africa, or Latin America will recognize such language as a Western phenomenon.

[16]This καί, omitted in the NIV, indicates a second directive.

[17]Gk. ἀνὰ μέρος; for this idiom see BAGD, under ἀνά 2. Parry, 209, suggests "share and share alike," which sounds too modern and has no support.

corrective. Along with v. 23, the implication is that the Corinthians were doing otherwise. Not only did they have a singular passion for this gift, but apparently they had allowed it to dominate their gatherings in a way that reflected pagan ecstasy far more than the gospel of Christ. (b) This guideline clearly removes tongues from all forms of pagan ecstasy, as far as Paul's understanding is concerned. The admonition in v. 32 is probably intended as much for this gift as for prophecy. Whatever else, Christian inspiration, including both tongues and prophecy, is not "out of control." The Spirit does not "possess" or "overpower" the speaker; he is subject to the prophet or tongues-speaker, in the sense that what the Spirit has to say will be said in an orderly and intelligible way. It is indeed the Spirit who speaks, but he speaks through the controlled instrumentality of the believer's own mind and tongue. In this regard it is no different from the inspired utterances of the OT prophets, which were spoken at the appropriate times and settings.

Third, "and someone must interpret." This simply repeats what has already been said in vv. 6 and 13, except that in those two passages it is assumed that the tongues-speaker will also receive the interpretation; whereas here and in 12:10 and 28-30 it is assumed that the interpretation will be given to someone else.[18] What cannot be decided is whether "one" is to interpret after each utterance in tongues[19] or whether both of the first guidelines are also intended to limit the number of expressions in tongues before there is an interpretation. Probably the latter, but there is no way to determine. This guideline receives further qualification in the next verse.

28 This qualification serves to underscore what has been said throughout vv. 1-25. First, "If there is no interpreter,[20] the speaker should keep quiet in the assembly." This puts into the form of a regulation what was said in different ways in vv. 5, 6-13, and 14-19. It also accounts for the conclusion in v. 13 of the discussion in vv. 6-12 that urges the tongues-speaker to pray that he or she might also interpret. If they have not themselves experienced the gift of interpretation, and if no one is present who is known to have this gift, then they are to remain silent.

But as before, Paul does not forbid the gift itself. Repeating the ideas

---

[18]Although the εἷς in this case could refer to one of the two or three tongues-speakers.

[19]So Bittlinger, 119; Martin, 78.

[20]Gk. διερμηνευτής, the *nominal subject* for the verb διερμηνεύω that appears in v. 27 (cf. 12:30), which in turn refers to the activity described by the noun ἑρμενεία γλωσσῶν ("the interpretation of tongues") in 12:10. As with "tongues," all of this is functional language. There was no group in Corinth known as "the interpreters of tongues"; the language of 14:5, plus the exhortation of v. 13, tells against such a possibility. See the discussion in v. 29 for how this affects our understanding of the word "prophet" in that passage.

of vv. 2 and 4, he admonishes that the tongues-speaker "speak to himself and God." Speaking "to himself"[21] stands in contrast to "in the assembly" in v. 27, meaning that he or she should pray "to God" in this way in private.

Apart from the final admonition in v. 39, this is the final word about tongues in this argument. Paul has been consistent throughout. It is the language of prayer and praise, directed toward God, but because it is unintelligible and therefore cannot edify, it should remain in the setting of personal prayer and devotion. Only when someone known to be gifted with interpretation is present may it be exercised in the assembly.

29 Paul now turns to give similar guidelines for the exercise of the gift of prophecy.[22] Because of the similarities with what was said about tongues, some have suggested that there were difficulties with this gift in Corinth as well. More likely, however, he advances these guidelines because this is the gift he has been arguing for throughout vis-à-vis tongues; since he has just "regulated" their gift, he goes on to do the same for the one he has been plumping for in its place. Hence the similarities.

He begins with the same ordering as in v. 27: "Two or three prophets should speak."[23] This does not mean that in any given gathering there must be a limit of two or three prophecies. Even though that is commonly suggested, it lies quite beyond Paul's concern[24] and makes little sense at all of v. 24 ("when you come together and *all* prophesy"), nor of the concern in v. 31 that *all* have opportunity to participate. Rather, it means that there should be no more than three at a time before "the others weigh carefully what is said." This latter item is the verb for "distinguishing between spirits" in 12:10 (q.v.). As noted there, this is probably to be understood as a form of "testing the spirits," but not so much in the sense of whether "the prophet" is speaking by a foreign spirit but whether the prophecy itself truly conforms to the Spirit of God,[25] who is also indwelling the other believers. Other than in 12:3, no criterion is here given as to what goes into the "discerning"[26] process,[27] although in Rom. 12:6 we are told that prophecies are to be "according to the analogy of faith," which probably means "that

---

[21]Gk. ἑαυτῷ; cf. BDF 188 (2): dative of advantage.

[22]Grosheide, 337, in a discussion lacking exegetical basis, argues that the "regulating" of prophecy in itself has the effect of putting it below preaching.

[23]The verb is λαλέω, the same used throughout in conjunction with tongues. This usage tells heavily against those who have regarded this verb as a somewhat technical term for tongues, indicating its less-than-articulate nature.

[24]See above on v. 27.

[25]Cf. Bittlinger's happy phrase: "The Spirit recognizes the Spirit" (121).

[26]Cf. Grudem, 58-60, who translates "evaluating." He also separates this activity from that of 12:10 more than seems warranted—or necessary.

[27]But see the useful discussion in Dunn, *Spirit,* pp. 293-97.

which is compatible with their believing in Christ."[28] Nor is there any suggestion as to how it proceeds. At best one can argue that prophecies did not have independent authority in the church, but must always be the province of the corporate body, who in the Spirit were to determine the sense or perhaps viability of what had been said.

Some have argued, on the basis of 12:28, that "prophets" refers to the special group of authoritative persons in the community who have been given this gift.[29] "The others"[30] in this case means "the other prophets,"[31] so that the whole text is intended to regulate the activities of the prophets, vis-à-vis regulating "prophecies" per se. But nearly everything else in the argument stands over against such a view. (a) The argument from v. 1 has been in the second plural, addressing the entire community. He urges all of them "eagerly [to] desire spiritual gifts, especially that *you* prophesy," without a hint that this gift is limited to the "prophets." (b) So with the rest of the argument; for example, in v. 12 he exhorts, "Since you are zealous for spiritual manifestations (referring to their collective enthusiasm for tongues), seek to excel in the building up of the church (meaning especially the gift of prophecy)." (c) The evidence in v. 24, even though hypothetical, is especially telling. As in v. 23, Paul implies a situation that could conceivably occur, namely that "all prophesy," so that the unbeliever is convicted by *all* and judged by *all*. (d) So also in v. 31 he urges orderliness, "for you may *all* prophecy in turn so that *all* may learn and *all be* encouraged/exhorted." It is gratuitous to suggest that the first "all" means "all the prophets" while the next two refer to the whole community.[32]

This does not mean, of course, that all *will* or *do* prophesy. It is simply to note that Paul's concern here is not with a group of prophets, but with the functioning of prophecy in the assembly. The noun "prophets," therefore, is to be understood as functional language, similar to the use of

---

[28]So also Cranfield, *Romans,* II, 621.

[29]This has become an increasingly popular view. See, *inter alia,* Ellis, 139 n. 48; Hill, *Prophecy,* pp. 120-21.

[30]Gk. οἱ ἄλλοι; cf. on 12:8 and 10. This word basically means "others different from the subject." Whereas it could mean "the rest," had Paul intended that idea the more correct term would have been οἱ λοίποι (cf. 9:5, οἱ λοίποι ἀπόστολοι). To put that in another way, the use of οἱ λοίποι would almost certainly have meant "the rest of the same class," i.e., prophets. Paul's word could mean that but ordinarily does not, referring simply to "someone else" or, in the plural, "the others that make up the larger group." Cf. Barrett, 328; Grudem, 60-62.

[31]Cf. Grosheide, 338; Lenski, 611; Friedrich, *TDNT* VI, 855-56; H. Greeven, "Propheten, Lehrer, Vorsteher bei Paulus. Zur Frage der 'Ämter' im Urchristentum," *ZNW* 44 (1952-53), 6; Hill, *Prophecy,* p. 133. See the refutation in Grudem, 60-62.

[32]The lack of the definite article with προφῆται seems to clinch this argument. The sentence begins with this word—"prophets," not *the* "prophets"—implying, on the basis of the structure of v. 27: "If some speak as prophets. . . ."

"interpreter" in v. 28, and means, as in v. 3, "the one who is prophesying." Although he uses a noun in this case, which he does not do with "the one who speaks in a tongue,"[33] the structure of the two sentences (vv. 27 and 29) calls for a similar understanding in both cases and does not imply that he is now speaking about a special group of persons.

30-31 These two sentences offer a further guideline for this gift, so that everything will be "done in a fitting and orderly way" (v. 40). The requirement seems to be aimed at those who might tend to dominate the meeting, although that is not certain. In any case, Paul presupposes that while one is speaking, "a revelation[34] [may come] to someone who is sitting down."[35] The use of the verb "reveal" in this context suggests that for Paul this was the essential character of what was spoken in a prophecy. See on vv. 6, 24-25, and 26. When this happens then "the first speaker," meaning the one already speaking, "should stop."[36] The grounds for such a regulation will be given in v. 32; neither the tongues-speaker *nor* the prophet is out of control.

The "for" that begins v. 31 may be either explanatory, offering an elucidation of what has just been said, or causal, giving its reason. In either case, Paul now offers a justification for the preceding regulation: "you can all prophesy in turn[37]." As noted above, (1) "all" does not mean that everyone has this gift; the implication is that it is potentially available to everyone; and (2) this language makes almost no sense at all if he is referring to what should take place over several different meetings; the concern throughout, beginning with the verb "you assemble" in v. 26, is with what takes place in a given gathering.

The appeal is both to self-control and to deference. It is difficult to imagine two people prophesying simultaneously. But since they apparently were doing so with tongues, this at least anticipates their also doing so with prophecy—as well perhaps as keeping it in the category of "controlled" speech in contrast to pagan varieties.

The reason for such orderliness is given in a final purpose clause. Paul is emphatic: "*All* may prophesy, so that *all* may be instructed and *all*[38]

---

[33]In English we are thus forced to use such infelicities as "glossolalist" or "tongues-speaker."

[34]Gk. ἀποκαλυφθῇ; lit. "it is revealed (to another)." This is the verb for the noun ἀποκάλυψις in vv. 6 and 26.

[35]The clear implication is that the one prophesying stands while doing so; probably this would be true of the other manifestations as well. Cf. the Jewish rabbi who taught sitting down.

[36]Gk. σιγάτω; lit. "let (the first) be silent" (cf. v. 28). See also vv. 34-35.

[37]Gk. καθ' ἕνα; distributive usage = one by one.

[38]By omitting this πάντες, as well as by changing the translation from "all" to "everyone," the NIV obscures Paul's emphasis on "all."

may be encouraged." As in chap. 12, and again in v. 26 with which this paragraph began, this reflects a concern for edification in which everyone contributes. Since the whole of the divine revelation is not given to just one or a few—or in simply one kind of manifestation—the concern is that all, including those who speak prophetically, should learn from[39] and be encouraged or exhorted by[40] what the Spirit has given to others. The result of such orderliness, therefore, is that the opening exhortation is fulfilled, that "everything be done for the edification of the church" (v. 26).

32 With this crucial sentence Paul offers his justification for the preceding regulations of the activities of both speaking in tongues and prophesying. Along with its theological basis given in the next verse, these two sentences bring this section to a fitting conclusion. With these words Paul lifts Christian "inspired speech" out of the category of "ecstasy" as such and offers it as a radically different thing from the mania of the pagan cults. There is no seizure here, no loss of control; the speaker is neither frenzied nor a babbler.[41] If tongues is not intelligible, it is nonetheless inspired utterance and completely under the control of the speaker. So too with prophecy.

As noted earlier,[42] the phrase "spirits of prophets" means "the prophetic Spirit" by which each of them speaks through his or her own spirit.[43] Paul's point is that the utterances are subject to the speakers in terms of timing; the content is understood to be the product of the Divine Spirit who inspires such utterances. Thus he justifies their speaking one at a time, being silent with regard to tongues when no interpreter is present, and ceasing for the sake of another when a prophetic revelation is given to someone else. All of this is possible because "the spirits of prophets are subject to prophets."

33 To conclude Paul adds a significant theological justification for the foregoing guidelines. Everything has to do with the character of God and what God has already established to be true of his divine activity in the rest of the churches. First, "for[44] God is not a God of disorder[45] but of peace." This

---

[39]Gk. μανθάνω (see on v. 35; cf. 1 Tim. 2:11); it means to *receive* instruction (= to learn) as over against giving it (= to teach).

[40]Gk. παρακαλέω; see on v. 3.

[41]For descriptions of the Hellenistic view of prophecy involving "ecstasy," see Plato, *Phaed.* 243e-245c; Philo, *spec.leg.* 4.49; *quis rer.div.* 4.265. See especially the discussion in Aune, *Prophecy*, pp. 19-22, 33-34.

[42]See on vv. 12; 14-15; cf. 5:3-4 and 12:10 on "the discerning of spirits."

[43]Ellis, 36-42, makes the unlikely suggestion that "spirits" here refers to "angelic spirits." See the refutation in Grudem, 120-22 (see pp. 120-36 for a discussion of other views as well).

[44]The γάρ in this case is clearly explanatory.

[45]Gk. ἀκαστασίας; cf. esp. 2 Cor. 12:20, where it occurs in the list of sins Paul fears may yet be going on in Corinth. There it may mean something closer to "distur-

sentence, along with the final appeal in v. 40, seems to corroborate the
suggestion made on v. 23 that the Corinthian assembly had become unruly
in its expression of tongues. Now Paul is arguing that the basis of all these
instructions is ultimately theological. It has to do with the character of God,
probably vis-à-vis the deities of the cults, whose worship was characterized
by frenzy and disorder. The theological point is crucial: the character of
one's deity is reflected in the character of one's worship.[46] The Corinthians
must therefore cease worship that reflects the pagan deities more than the
God whom they have come to know through the Lord Jesus Christ (cf.
12:2-3). God is neither characterized by disorder nor the cause of it in the
assembly.

The interesting opposite of "disorder," however, is not quietness or
propriety, or even "order," but "peace."[47] Minimally this refers to the
sense of harmony that will obtain in a Christian assembly when everyone is
truly in the Spirit and the aim of everything is the edification of the whole
(v. 26). It is tempting once again, as in 7:15 (q.v.), to see here a reflection of
Paul's Jewish background, in which God's people are called to live, in this
case worship, "for the sake of peace," that is, in such a way as to win the
favor of others.

Second, what is true of God in terms of Christian worship is so "in all
the congregations of the saints."[48] Because of some apparent awkwardness
in speaking of God in this way, the NIV follows a number of scholars who
prefer to take this final phrase with vv. 34-35. But there are a number of
reasons for taking it as the concluding word to these instructions on "order."
(a) As will be noted in the next section, there is substantial evidence that vv.
34-35 are not authentic, and therefore that Paul could not have intended it to
go with what he did not write. In any case, the very early textual evidence in
the Western church indicates that this phrase was not considered to be part of
vv. 34-35.[49] (b) The two rhetorical questions in v. 36, both of which begin
with "or," make best sense when understood as referring directly to this
statement. That is, "All the churches of the saints are intended to be orderly
as we have just described, *or* did the word of God originate with you?" This

---

bances," as it seems to in the list of his apostolic hardships in 6:5 of that same letter. See
also Jas. 3:16 where it stands in contrast to peace among other virtues.

[46]Which probably says something about somber Christian worship as well, since
joy is the order of the early church, indicating that God is a God of joy, who delights in the
worship of his people as they delight in him.

[47]See on 1:3 and 7:15.

[48]This is the only occurrence of this combination in the NT, but that is not
surprising in light of 1:2 (q.v.).

[49]Cf. Chrysostom, *hom. 36 and 37 in 1 Cor.*, who breaks these two homilies
between vv. 33 and 34 and joins v. 33b to v. 33a. The idea that v. 33b goes with v. 34
seems to be a modern phenomenon altogether.

seems to be the proper understanding of the rhetoric of v. 36, even if vv. 34-35 are authentic. (c) To take this phrase with v. 34 creates an even clumsier sentence: "As in all the churches of the saints women should remain silent in the churches." That is a redundancy that is nearly intolerable[50]—even the NIV tries to alleviate it with a different translation for the two clauses.[51] (d) This is now the fourth appeal of this kind in the letter (see 4:17; 7:17; 11:16); in each of the other instances this appeal *concludes* its sentence, and in two cases (4:17; 11:16) it functions as an addendum just as it does here. (e) Finally, and most importantly, this concern that they be like the other churches is more fitting at the conclusion of the major concern of this argument, as in chaps. 1–4 and 11:2-16, than with something that if authentic is an aside at best.

Thus, this final appeal continues the theological word with which the sentence began.[52] God is not only like this, but he has so ordered that his character be appropriately displayed in worship in all the churches. This particular appeal, which in this letter began with the opening words of salutation (see 1:2), is an indication to the Corinthians that their view of tongues and spirituality that has allowed this kind of disorderly conduct is out of keeping with what God is doing elsewhere through the gospel. They are marching to their own drum; Paul is urging them not only to conform to the character of God, but also to get in step with the rest of his church.

By and large the history of the church points to the fact that in worship we do not greatly trust the diversity of the body. Edification must always be the rule, and that carries with it orderliness so that all may learn and all be encouraged. But it is no great credit to the historical church that in opting for "order" it also opted for a silencing of the ministry of the many. That, it would seem, is at least the minimal point of the paragraph.

The most important word in this paragraph is the final one. Some Pentecostal and charismatic assemblies would do well to heed these directives; confusion and disorder is simply not in keeping with the character of God. On the other hand, v. 26 makes it clear that the "peace" and "order" of v. 33 do not necessarily mean somber ritual, as though God were really something of a "stuffed shirt." If our understanding of God's character is revealed in our worship, then it must be admitted that God is not often thought of in terms of allowing spontaneity or of joy.

[50]Although see Martin, 76 n. "f," who allows that "maybe this is Paul's emphasis as it was needed." But one must admit that it lacks precedent.

[51]Some suggest that the second phrase means, "in every congregational meeting in Corinth"; but that runs counter to Pauline usage. See the commentary on v. 34.

[52]Grosheide, 341, objects that the words of the first clause in v. 33 "refuse to take any further qualification." But that assertion is unsupported either theologically or grammatically in Paul. See further on vv. 34-35, p. 701 n. 14.

[[b. The ordering of women (14:34-35)[1]]]

34 *Women[2] should remain silent in the churches. They are not allowed to speak, but must be in submission,[3] as the Law says.* 35 *If they want to inquire about something, they should ask their own husbands at home; for it is disgraceful for a woman to speak in the church.*

Although these two verses are found in all known manuscripts, either here or at the end of the chapter, the two text-critical criteria of transcriptional and intrinsic probability combine to cast considerable doubt on their authenticity.[4]

First, on the matter of transcriptional probability,[5] Bengel's first principle must rule: That form of the text is more likely the original which best explains the emergence of all the others. In this case there are three options: Either (1) Paul wrote these words at this place and they were deliberately transposed to a position after v. 40; or (2) the reverse of this, they were written originally after v. 40 and someone moved them forward to a position after v. 33; or (3) they were not part of the original text, but were a very early marginal gloss that was subsequently placed in the text at two different places. Of these options, the third is easily the one that best fits Bengel's first principle. One can give good historical reasons both for the gloss itself and for its dual position in the text;[6] but one is especially hard pressed to account for either options 1 or 2 had the other been original.

[1]Most MSS (including P[46] A B K Ψ 0243 33 81 1739 Maj) include these verses here; they are found after v. 40 in D F G 88* a b d f g Ambrosiaster Sedulius-Scotus, thus the entire Western tradition.

[2]The MajT, along with D F G a b, adds ὑμῶν ("your women").

[3]Codex A adds "to their husbands"; it is not at all clear that this is what the author intended.

[4]For a thorough presentation of this position see G. Fitzer, *Das Weib Schweige in der Gemeinde* (Munich, 1963). Among others see also Weiss, 342; Zuntz, 17; Bittlinger, 110-11; Barrett, 332-33; Conzelmann, 246 (who without textual warrant also includes vv. 33b and 36); Scroggs, "Eschatological Women," pp. 294-96; Ruef, 154-55; Murphy-O'Connor, 133 (and "Interpolations," 90-92); E. E. Ellis, "The Silenced Wives of Corinth (I Cor. 14:34-5)," in *New Testament Textual Criticism, Its Significance for Exegesis: Essays in Honour of Bruce M. Metzger* (ed. E. J. Epp and G. D. Fee; Oxford, 1981), pp. 213-20, who, however, thinks that the marginal gloss came from Paul himself, a view also adopted by Barton, "Sense," 229-30.

[5]This has to do with what a copyist is most likely to have done.

[6]Various reasons have been given for the gloss, all relating to the known situation of the church at the end of the first century or the beginning of the second (e.g., the attempt to check a rising feminist movement [cf. 1 Tim. 2:9-15; 5:11-15]; to reconcile 1 Cor. 14 with 1 Tim. 2). The insertions are both explicable; one comes at the end of the guidelines on "order" and before the *ad hominem* argument of vv. 36-38; the other simply occurs at the end.

Although the majority of interpreters assume that option 1 is original, they generally do so without asking the historical question as to how then the Western text came into existence. The solution that is sometimes offered, that someone in the early second century[7] "edited" the text in this fashion "to find a more appropriate location,"[8] seems to be unhistorical— on two grounds: (a) displacements of this kind do not occur elsewhere in the NT;[9] and (b) no *adequate* reason can be found for such a displacement were these words originally in the text after v. 33. It is simply a modern invention that someone in the early church would have been troubled by the *placement* of these words in the text, since all who comment on it find the arrangement very logical.[10] It is therefore most highly improbable that with this text before him it would ever have occurred to a copyist to take such an unprecedented step as to rearrange Paul's argument—especially so since in this case one can scarcely demonstrate that the "displacement" makes better sense![11] The Western text may not be shunted aside. All the surviving evidence indicates that this was the only way 1 Corinthians appeared in the Latin church for at least three hundred years. Those who wish to maintain the authenticity of these verses must at least offer an *adequate* answer as to how this arrangement came into existence if Paul wrote them originally as our vv. 34-35.

[7]Since this is the universal reading of the Western church until the influence of the Vulgate, which in this case reflects the text of the Eastern church, the position of these verses in this tradition must go back to a very early source. Godet, e.g., cannot be right in suggesting that "several Latin copyists" made this transposition. One may with difficulty possibly account for it *once,* but not twice under any circumstances. This also discounts his suggestion that the scribes of F and G therefore added διατάσσομαι at the end of v. 33 after they made the transposition. That simply is not so. These MSS bear single witness to an earlier addition of this word, based on 1 Cor. 7:17, in a MS that never had vv. 34-35 here but only at the end of the chapter.

[8]Cf. Metzger, 565.

[9]Except, of course, in the case of the inauthentic adulterous woman pericope, which found its way into the NT text at five different locations. The transpositions in the Gospels (Matt. 5:4-5; Luke 4:5-10), where immediately joining verses are transposed for obvious harmonistic reasons, are of a completely different kind. This is not to say that it *could not* happen in the Epistles, but that it *did not;* and one would therefore need particularly strong reasons for arguing that in fact it did in this one instance.

[10]See, e.g., Chrysostom, *hom. 36 and 37 in 1 Corinthians;* cf. Theodoret, Ps.-Oecumenius, John of Damascus.

[11]The point is that *if it were already in the text after v. 33,* there is no *reason* for a copyist to make such a radical transposition. He would simply have copied the text before him with no questions asked. This is not to say that copyists did not think; it is to argue that the history of Christian interpretation of the text in its Eastern position makes it clear that it would never have occurred to anyone to "help" Paul out in this way. Hurley's comment (*Man,* p. 185 n. 12) that "the transposition of 14:33b[sic]-35 is obviously for the purpose of easier reading" fails to take the historical question seriously. In fact, his entire note is both prejudicial and an inadequate exercise in textual criticism.

700

Second, once one recognizes the improbability of authenticity on transcriptional grounds, then several questions of intrinsic probability[12] are more easily answered: (1) One can make much better sense of the structure of Paul's argument without these intruding sentences. As noted above,[13] the balanced guidelines for tongues with interpretation and prophecy with discernment are fittingly brought to a conclusion on the twin notes of vv. 32-33, that the "spirits of prophets are subject to prophets" and that orderly worship fits the character of God, being what is found (or laid down)[14] in "all the churches of the saints." Then, in typical fashion, the mention of "all the churches" sends Paul off on an *ad hominem* argument against those in the community who in the name of being *pneumatikos* ("spiritual") are leading this church in another direction. Thus, in light of the "other churches," he asks rhetorically, "*Or* did the word of God originate with you? Or are you the only people it has reached?" This rhetorical aside (vv. 36-38), which at the same time is a direct confrontation between him and them over the crucial matters that divide them, is then followed (vv. 39-40) by a concluding wrap-up of the whole matter of chaps. 12-14. This reading of the text makes so much sense of all the data that even if one were to conclude that vv. 34-35 are authentic, they would appear to be best understood as something of an afterthought to the present argument.

Furthermore, very little in the two verses fits into the present argument, which to this point has only to do with manifestations of the Spirit in the community. Any mention of people as such (e.g., "the one speaking in tongues") is quite subordinate to the larger concern of intelligibility and edification in the community through prophecy and related gifts, which by the same token disallows uninterpreted tongues. These verses, on the other hand, have to do with people only—women in this case, with no correspond-

[12]That is, what an author is most likely to have written. Since this can be a more subjective criterion, it can seldom stand on its own. But in this case, contrary to the suggestion of some (e.g., Grudem, 241, "[this view] depends on the conviction that they seriously conflict with 11.5 and other passages in Paul"]), it does not stand on its own. The transcriptional question comes first, and has always been the primary reason for thinking it an interpolation. To put that another way: As with many other difficult passages in this letter, undoubtedly someone would eventually have suspected the authenticity of these verses (see those discussed in Murphy-O'Connor, "Interpolations"), but not on *textual* grounds. Suspicions as to authenticity on textual grounds arose precisely because of the external evidence.

[13]See on v. 33.

[14]The alleged grammatical problem with this clause being attached to v. 33a was never a problem in the early Greek-speaking church. For example, even though Chrysostom did not have a verb in his text (as the citation in *hom.* 37.2 makes certain), in commenting on this verse he simply added a διδάσκω (see *hom.* 36.7 [twice]), indicating that this is what he understood the apostle to have meant even though the verb must be supplied by the reader.

ing word to men as in 7:1-35 and 11:4-15. Moreover, there is not a single internal hint that they deal with gifts or manifestations of the Spirit in any way. The linguistic ties that do exist ("speaking, silence, submission") are used in such completely different ways as to make them suspect in any case. For example, there is not a single absolute use of the verb "to speak" in its other 21 occurrences in this chapter, yet it is twice so used here; and the enjoined "silence" in vv. 28 and 30 is of an otherwise legitimate activity that in some circumstances is being curtailed, whereas here the injunction to silence is absolute. Thus, these two verses simply lack any genuine correspondence with either the overall argument of chaps. 12–14 or the immediate argument of vv. 26-40.

(2) Of even greater difficulty is the fact that these verses stand in obvious contradiction to 11:2-16, where it is assumed without reproof that women pray and prophesy in the assembly, not to mention that such is also assumed in the repeated "all" of vv. 23-24 and 31 and the "each one" of v. 26.[15] This problem is so manifest that most interpretations that consider these words authentic[16] engage much of their energy in "getting around" their plain meaning so as to allow the two passages to exist side by side in the same letter.

(3) Finally, as will be noted in the commentary on the individual verses that follow, some usages in these two verses seem quite foreign to Paul.

Taken together these data are more than sufficient reasons for considering these verses inauthentic. Nonetheless, since they are missing from no known manuscripts and are found in the majority of witnesses at this point,[17] there have been several attempts to make sense of them in this context, none of which, however, is free of difficulties.

Historically the passage was taken as part of a long series of instructions on "order" in the churches. After some "rules" for tongues and prophecy, Paul laid down a further rule about women because they, too,

[15]The problem is even more severe if our reading of many of the earlier passages is correct, that some "eschatological women" (the designation is from R. Scroggs) were the source of many of the difficulties Paul was facing in this community (see on 7:1-7; 11:2-16). If so, then one could well understand his eliminating the problem by this blanket rejection of their speaking out in the assembly; but that leaves one with the considerable difficulty of making sense of 11:2-16, where he not only does not forbid it but seems positively to affirm it.

[16]Some, of course, have tried to rework 11:2-16 so that that passage disallows women's praying and prophesying; but these meet with even less success (see n. 22 on 11:2-16).

[17]The words of Martin, 84, are typical: "We should strive to excel in the gift of interpreting the text as it stands before we embrace [interpolation]." But to interpret "the text as it stands" is to resolve the textual question without engaging in textual criticism. One could as easily say this of the interpolation in John 5:4. Their appearance in the majority of witnesses at this point does not guarantee their authenticity.

were apparently out of order. The argument in 11:2-16 was usually dismissed as not really permitting women to prophesy, but as insisting on submission to their husbands by wearing the traditional head covering, or as referring to "private" meetings over against "official services" of the church.[18] As already noted, the extreme difficulty of reconciling these two passages has led to other options, of which there are three major types.

(1) The most commonly held view is that which sees the problem as *some form of disruptive speech.*[19] Support is found in v. 35, that if the women wish to learn anything, they should ask their own husbands at home. Various scenarios are proposed: that the setting was something like the Jewish synagogue, with women on one side and men on the other and the women shouting out disruptive questions about what was being said in a prophecy or tongue; or that they were asking questions of men other than their own husbands; or that they were simply "chattering"[20] so loudly that it had a disruptive effect.

The biggest difficulty with this view is that it assumes a "church service" of a more "orderly" sort than the rest of this argument presupposes. If the basic problem is with their "all speaking in tongues" in some way, one may assume on the basis of 11:5 that this also included the women; furthermore, in such disarray how can mere "chatter" have a disruptive effect? The suggestion that the early house churches assumed a synagogue pattern is pure speculation; it seems remote at best.[21]

(2) Others consider the passage to be a prohibition of *some form of inspired speech other than prophecy.* This has taken one of two forms: (a) Some have suggested that the ban is on the "discerning" of prophecies mentioned in v. 29.[22] It is assumed in this model that women did prophesy, but they are now being excluded from the weighing of prophecies because

---

[18]This is the view of most, but not all, Protestant interpreters before the twentieth century. For more recent expressions of it, cf. Grosheide, 342; and Ridderbos, *Paul,* p. 462. It may be fairly said of this view that it reflects the situation of the church in which the interpreter finds himself more than that of Paul and the Corinthians. That is, they reflect church settings where charismata are unknown and where women are not allowed public expression.

[19]Among others see Sevenster, *Paul,* p. 198; Bruce, 135; and Barrett, 332 (if it is in fact authentic).

[20]The verb λαλεῖ, which probably was originally an onomatopoeic word, meant "to chatter" in classical usage.

[21]The appeal to similar problems in contemporary Middle Eastern churches says nothing about first-century Greco-Roman culture, but only that such churches are heavily influenced by the mores of the semitic, usually Muslim, cultures in which they are found.

[22]This appears to have been suggested first by Thrall, 102; it has been contended for rather vigorously by Hurley, "Veils," pp. 217-18; and Grudem, 239-55. Cf. Hill, *Prophecy,* pp. 134-35, who leans this way. It has also been adopted by D. Carson, *Exegetical Fallacies* (Grand Rapids, 1984), p. 40; it does not strengthen this otherwise helpful book that the author points out the fallacy in another's argument by adopting a position that is itself most highly questionable.

that could possibly put them in the "unbiblical" position of sitting in authority over their own husbands. This has against it (i) the extreme difficulty of being so far removed from v. 29 that one wonders how the Corinthians themselves could have so understood it;[23] (ii) the fact that nothing in the passage itself even remotely hints of such a thing; and (iii) the form of v. 35, "if they wish to learn anything," which implies not "judging" their husbands' prophecies but failing to understand what is going on at all. Furthermore, despite arguments to the contrary, it is less than convincing that "discerning" the prophetic utterance of a husband is to sit in authority over him in a greater way than by a prophetic utterance. That seems to make the dependent, and therefore lesser, item (discerning prophecies) more significant than prophecy itself.

(b) Others have argued that the "speaking" here being banned is "tongues" itself, the implication being that it is the eschatological women who are primarily responsible for the disorder brought about by this gift in the church.[24] In this view the verb "to speak" assumes its regular role in this chapter;[25] and "to be in submission" means, as in v. 32, that their "spirits" are to be kept in submission. This view has the attraction of trying to place the passage within the larger historical problem and to see the answer as within the context of the present argument. But it also seems to face insuperable difficulties: the verb "speak" is invariably accompanied by "tongues" in this argument when that is meant; the prohibition takes a more absolute form here than this view allows; v. 35 implies the asking of questions for the sake of learning, not the alleged thrusting on the congregation of their own revelations.

(3) Because of the very Jewish nature of this passage, others have argued that it does not represent Paul's point of view at all, but rather is a quotation or restatement of the view of some Corinthians who were imposing it on the community.[26] Usually this is associated with the "Cephas party" of 1:12. Vv. 36-38 are then viewed as Paul's own response to this

[23]Grudem, 250-51, tries to resolve this by a structural analysis that must finally be judged as not altogether successful since it misses the balanced nature of the two items on tongues and prophecy, it fails to see the "closure" aspect of vv. 32-33 to the preceding argument, and it does not take seriously enough the abrupt nature of this interruption, with no prior hint in the text itself.

[24]For the most recent advocacy of this position, see Martin, 85-88, which has what appears to be a valid understanding of the historical problem itself, but a view of this text that leaves too many unresolved exegetical questions.

[25]Although it is not quite precise to argue as Martin does that this is what the verb basically means in this chapter. In fact it is used of prophecies in vv. 3 and 29, of foreigners speaking to one another in vv. 10-11, and of speaking "intelligible words" with one's tongue in v. 9.

[26]See especially the translation by Helen Barrett Montgomery; cf. Bushnell, God's Word, par. 189-215. More recently it has been advocated, inter alia, by W. C.

imposition of "the Law" on the church. This is attractive in that it removes the difficulties of the previous views, which must find ways to "get around" what is said if Paul is the author. On the other hand, it also has considerable difficulties: There is no hint in v. 34 that Paul has suddenly taken to quoting them; there is no precedent for such a long quotation that is also full of argumentation (two explanatory "for's"); it presupposes the unlikely scenario that some in the church were forbidding women to speak—and especially that the quotation would come from the same Corinthian letter that is otherwise quite pro-women (see on 7:1-7; 11:2-16).

On the whole, therefore, the case against these verses is so strong, and finding a viable solution to their meaning so difficult, that it seems best to view them as an interpolation. If so, then one must assume that the words were first written as a gloss in the margin by someone who, probably in light of 1 Tim. 2:9-15, felt the need to qualify Paul's instructions even further. Since the phenomenon of glosses making their way into the biblical text is so well documented elsewhere in the NT (e.g., John 5:3b-4; 1 John 5:7), there is no good historical reason to reject the possibility here. The fact that it occurs in all extant witnesses only means that the double interpolation had taken place before the time of our present textual tradition, and could easily have happened before the turn of the first century. In the commentary that follows, this is the assumed point of view; but other options are noted as well.

34 These two verses together have a singular concern, that women "remain silent" in the congregational meetings, which is further defined as "not being permitted to speak" (v. 34) because it is "shameful" for them to do so (v. 35). The structure of the argument bears this out. It begins with "a sentence of holy law," the absolute nature of which is very difficult to get around.[27] Two reasons are then given for such a proscription, which are intended to be two sides of the same reality. On the one hand, "it is not permitted for them to speak"; on the other hand, "let them be in submission." To this final reason there is added the further justification, "even as the Law says." This is followed by the allowance that they should learn at home by asking questions of their own husbands, for which the concluding reason is that "it is shameful for them to speak in the church." Thus:

Kaiser, "Paul, Women, and the Church," *Worldwide Challenge* 3 (1976), 9-12; N. M. Flanagan and E. H. Snyder, "Did Paul Put Down Women in 1 Cor 14:34-36?" *BTB* 11 (1981), 10-12; D. W. Odell-Scott, "Let the Women Speak in Church, An Egalitarian Interpretation of 1 Cor 14:33b-36," *BTB* 13 (1983), 90-93; and Talbert, "Understanding," pp. 105-07.

[27]On this score, the older interpreters seem to have the better of it. Their problem lay with the way they tried to get around 11:2-16.

The rule	The women must be silent
	in the churches.
The reasons:	For[28]
	1) It is not permitted them to speak;
	2) But let them be in submission,
	even as the Law says.
The provision:	If they wish to learn,
	let them ask their own husbands at home.
The reason:	For
	It is shameful for a woman to speak
	in the assembly.

Despite protests to the contrary, the "rule" itself is expressed absolutely. That is, it is given without any form of qualification. Given the unqualified nature of the further prohibition that "the women"[29] are not permitted to speak, it is very difficult to interpret this as meaning anything else than all forms of speaking out in public. Someone apparently was concerned to note by way of a gloss that all the previous directions given by the apostle, including the inclusive "each one" of v. 26 and the "all" of v. 31, were *not* to be understood as including women.

The problems with seeing this as authentic are obvious. If Paul himself is responsible for such a "corrective," it is surprising that he should add it here, yet allow them to pray and prophesy in 11:5 and 13. What is also surprising is the sudden shift from the problem of disorder in the congregation in Corinth to a rule that is to be understood as universal for all the churches. The problem is not so much with Paul's setting forth such a rule as with his suddenly doing so here in the present argument. Some, who have also taken v. 33b as the beginning of this sentence, have argued that "in the churches" means "in all the congregational meetings of the Corinthian church."[30] But that will not work. Paul invariably says "in assembly" when that is what he means; both the plural and the definite article indicate that the author (whether Paul or an interpolator) intended this to be a rule for all Christian churches. We have already noted above that this rule of unqualified silence stands in a considerably different category from the two expressions of "silence" in vv. 28 and 30.

The first reason for the rule comes in the form of a prohibition: "They are not permitted to speak." What kind of speaking is intended depends on one's view, both of authorship and, if authentic, of its place in

---

[28]The NIV curiously leaves this causal γάρ untranslated, although it does translate the next one.

[29]Gk. αἱ γυναῖκες; probably all women, although the author assumes a culture in which most women are married.

[30]E.g., Barrett, 330; Martin, 84.

the present argument. The only internal suggestion is that of v. 35, that they should ask questions at home if they wish to learn. If authentic, this unqualified use of the verb seems to tell against the probability that only a *single form* of speech is being prohibited. Elsewhere Paul has said "speak *in tongues*" when that is in view, and when he means "discern" he says "discern," not "speak." Again, as with the opening "rule," the plain sense of the sentence is an absolute prohibition of all speaking in the assembly. This again makes sense as the glossator's concern, but very little as Paul's.

More difficult yet is the flip side of the reason,[31] namely that they "must be in submission, as the Law says." Some have argued that "let them be in submission" refers to v. 32, that their "spirit of prophecy" is to be in submission.[32] But that plays havoc with the grammar, which points to the women themselves as being in subjection, not to their having control over their own "prophetic spirit." What is not clear is whether the women are to be subject to their own husbands or to the church as a whole in its worship. More likely it is the latter.

Real problems for Pauline authorship lie with the phrase "even as the Law says." First, when Paul elsewhere appeals to "the Law," he always cites the text (e.g., 9:8; 14:21), usually to support a point he himself is making. Nowhere else does he appeal to the Law in this absolute way as binding on Christian behavior. More difficult yet is the fact that the Law does *not* say any such thing. Gen. 3:16 is often appealed to,[33] but that text does not say what is here argued. If that were the case, then one must admit that Paul is appealing not to the written Torah itself but to an oral understanding of Torah such as is found in rabbinic Judaism.[34] A similar usage is reflected in Josephus, who says, "The woman, says the Law, is in all things inferior to the man. Let her accordingly be submissive."[35] This usage suggests that the provenance of the glossator was Jewish Christianity. Under any view this is difficult to reconcile with Paul.[36]

The author of this piece seems intent on keeping women from joining in the vocal worship of the churches. The rule he wishes to apply he sees as

---

[31]It should be noted that even though Paul regularly uses the οὐ/ἀλλά contrast, this one is not in his style, which is usually to set two balanced propositions over against one another.

[32]E.g., Martin, 87.

[33]Mare, 276, suggests three NT texts as well, all later than this one!

[34]See, e.g., S. Aalen, "A Rabbinic Formula in I Cor. 14,34," in *Studia Evangelica* 2 (TU 87; Berlin, 1964), pp. 513-25.

[35]*C.Ap.* 2.200-201 (Loeb, I, 373).

[36]Some (e.g., Martin, 87) have argued that "law" here does not mean the Torah, but simply "principle" or "rule," thus referring to Paul's earlier instruction. But in an unqualified form that lacks Pauline precedent.

universal and supported by the Law. It is difficult to fit this into any kind of Pauline context.

35 But the author is not against women finding their "proper place," as he understands it, within the Christian community.[37] The implication of this provision is twofold: First, the author assumes that the women would not understand what is being said in the community, probably with regard to the spiritual utterances being addressed in this chapter. Second, he wants them to learn, but they are to do so at home from their own husbands. It is certainly possible that for the glossator some form of asking questions was going on in the church that he wanted to stop. But that is not a necessary implication from what is said. It is also possible that this is simply a proviso: "If their wanting to learn is the reason for them to speak out, then. . . ."

On the other hand, if Paul is the author, this seems yet to be the best of all the options, that some form of disruptive speaking out was going on, which then qualifies the apparent absolutes of v. 34. Nonetheless, as noted above, such a view is loaded with its own set of difficulties.

The final reason given for their being silent in the assembly is that speaking in church, apparently for the reasons given in v. 34, is "shameful," in the sense of being inconsistent with accepted standards of modesty. Again, as with the rule and prohibition in v. 34, the statement is unqualified: It is shameful for a woman to speak in church, not simply to speak in a certain way.

Thus, in keeping with the textual questions, the exegesis of the text itself leads to the conclusion that it is not authentic. If so, then it is certainly not binding for Christians. If not, the considerable doubts as to its authenticity ought to serve as a caution against using it as an eternal prohibition in a culture where such speaking by women in the assembly would not be a shameful thing. What seems hermeneutically questionable is the denial of all the surrounding matter as applicable to the church on prior hermeneutical grounds while selecting this single and probably inauthentic passage as a word for all time in all settings.

c. Conclusion—confrontation and summary (14:36-40)

36 Or[1] did the word of God originate with you? Or are you the only people it has reached? 37 If anyone thinks he is a prophet or a person of the Spirit,[2] let him acknowledge that what I am writing to you is

---

[37]On this matter see esp. Barton, "Sense," pp. 229-34, although he attributes it to Paul as a marginal afterthought.

[1]The NIV omits the conjunction ἤ that ties these questions to what has preceded.

[2]NIV, "spiritually gifted."

the Lord's command.[3] 38 *If he ignores this, he himself will be ignored[4].[a]*

39 *Therefore, my[5] brothers, be eager to prophesy, and do not forbid speaking in tongues.* 40 *But everything should be done in a fitting and orderly way.[6]*

[a]Some manuscripts *If he is ignorant of this, let him be ignorant*

Paul's long response to the Corinthians' enthusiasm for tongues is now finished. The basic issue is over what it means to be *pneumatikos* ("spiritual"); and on this issue Paul and they are deeply divided. They think it has to do with speaking in tongues, the language(s) of the angels, the sure evidence that they are already living the pneumatic existence of the future. For this reason they have great zeal for this gift (cf. v. 12), including an insistence on its practice in the gathered assembly. Apparently in their letter they have not only defended this practice, but by the same criterion have called Paul into question for his lack of "spirituality." Hence the undercurrent of apologetic for his own speaking in tongues in vv. 6, 15, and 18.

Paul's response to all this has been twofold. First, they are to broaden their perspective to recognize that being Spirit people by its very nature means a great variety of gifts and ministries in the church (chap. 12). Second, the whole point of the gathered people of God is edification, the true expression of love for the saints. Whatever they do in the assembly must be both intelligible and orderly so that the whole community may be edified; thus it must reflect the character of God, which is how it is (or is to be) in all the churches of the saints (v. 33).

Paul is now about to wrap all this up, which he does in vv. 39-40 with a final summation of the argument, reaffirming the priority of prophecy

[3]The singular ἐντολή is read by P[46] (ℵ) B 048 0243 33 1241[s] 1739* pc vg[ms]. Various attempts were made to ameliorate this difficult reading (following the plural ἅ). Some witnesses (D* F G b Ambst) omit the word altogether; the majority change it to a plural. Otherwise Zuntz, 139-40 (cf. Barrett, 314; Bruce, 136; Murphy-O'Connor, 133), who thinks the Western text best explains how the others came about; but in this case one has considerable difficulty explaining how a scribe would have created the singular ἐντολή as a "clarifying addition." See Metzger, 566.

[4]The early MSS go back and forth across "party lines," some favoring ἀγνοεῖται (ℵ* A*[vid] D [F G] 048 0243 b 33 1739 pc b bo; favored by NIV[txt] and Metzger, 566) and others ἀγνοείτω (P[46] ℵ[2] A[c] B D[2] Ψ Maj sy; NIV[mg] and Zuntz, 107-08). The former is easily the "more difficult" reading—from any perspective—as even Zuntz, who thinks it is too difficult, acknowledges. See the commentary.

[5]Although the μου is missing in many witnesses (P[46] B[2] D* F G 0243 Maj lat), Zuntz, 179, has noted that in every case in this letter where the pronoun occurs, some MSS omit it; whereas the opposite does not occur.

[6]For a discussion of the various readings that make up this final clause, but with differing results, see Zuntz, 29-31, and Metzger, 566-67. Zuntz makes an unconvincing attempt to derive "meaning" from what he considers to be the original form.

without forbidding tongues (vv. 1-25), yet insisting that all must be done in a fitting and orderly way (vv. 26-33). But before that, the mention of how things are in "all the churches of the saints" spins off into a moment of *ad hominem* rhetoric in which he not only dresses the Corinthians down for "marching to their own drum" (v. 36) but also confronts them directly on the matter of who is truly *pneumatikos*, they or he (v. 37), concluding with a prophetic sentence against any who reject the corrections given in this response (v. 38). All of this is reminiscent of the final parting shot in 4:18-21 and the defense in 9:1-23.

36 These two questions are a direct confrontation with the Corinthians over their attitude toward Paul on some issue,[7] in which he tries to give them perspective by reminding them of their own place in the history of "the word of God" (i.e., the gospel of Christ).[8] "Did the message of Christ originate with you?" he asks with sarcasm. "Are you the fountainhead from which all Christian truth derives that you can act so in this matter?" "Are you the only ones to whom it has come," he asks further, "so that you can carry on in your own individualistic way, as if there were no other believers in the world?" This is biting rhetoric, which flows directly from the (probably immediately) preceding clause, "as in all the churches of the saints." Who do they think they are anyway? is the implication; has God given them a special word that allows them both to reject Paul's instructions, on the one hand, and be so out of touch with the other churches, on the other?

But to what does this rhetoric refer? Probably not to vv. 34-35,[9] which are unlikely to be authentic; in any case, one can make far better sense of the argument by seeing this as referring to the larger matter at hand, namely to their and his disagreements over the nature of being *pneumatikos* and the place of tongues in the assembly. Both questions begin with the conjunction "or," implying that the first question flows directly from the immediately preceding sentence.[10] This conjunction in fact goes very poorly with v. 35,[11] but makes excellent sense following v. 33: "For God is not a God of disorder but of peace, as in all the churches of the saints; or did the

---

[7]Both in style and content these questions are so thoroughly Pauline, and fit the context so well, that one is puzzled by Conzelmann's including them as part of the interpolation of vv. 34-35—all the more so since there is no textual warrant for it.

[8]Cf. the usage in 1 Thess. 2:13; 2 Cor. 2:17; 4:2; Col. 1:25 (in Rom. 9:6 it refers to God's former "word" spoken in Scripture); cf. "the word of the Lord" in 1 Thess. 1:8; 2 Thess. 3:1. In each case this means "God's message" or "the message that comes from God."

[9]This is the traditional view, as though the Corinthians were allowing women to speak in the assembly against Paul's own instructions and the custom of the churches elsewhere.

[10]As elsewhere in this letter; see, e.g., 6:2, 9, 16, 19; 9:6.

[11]So much so that the KJV and others (RSV, Montgomery, TCNT) resorted to translating it "What!"

word of God originate from you? Or are you the only people it reached?" They are dead wrong on this matter; this rhetoric, therefore, is not only an attempt to get them to see that they are out of step with the other churches, but also leads directly to the two conditional sentences that follow.

37 This is now the third instance in this letter where Paul attacks their own position head-on with the formula "If anyone thinks he is . . ." (see on 3:18 and 8:2).[12] Each occurs in one of the three major sections of the letter (chaps. 1–4; 8–10; 12–14); and the argument in each case indicates that by this formula Paul is zeroing in on the Corinthians' perspective as to their own spirituality. They do indeed think of themselves as "the wise" (3:18) and as "having knowledge" (8:2), probably in both cases because they also think of themselves as being *pneumatikoi* (see on 2:15 and 3:1).

In this case, however, it is probably not the Corinthians as a whole whom he is taking on, although they are certainly in view as well; more likely, as in 4:18 and 9:3, he is speaking directly to those who have been leading the church in its anti-Pauline sentiments. These people consider themselves to be "prophets" and "Spirit people." These two words are probably to be understood as closely linked. In contrast to the functional use of "prophet" in the immediately preceding argument, the word "prophet" here reverts back to the usage in 12:28, where it refers to those who had a "ranked" position of ministry in the local assembly. Crucial here is the addition "or *pneumatikos*" (= "spiritual" or "a person of the Spirit"). As argued throughout the commentary,[13] this is the central issue. There seems to be no other good reason for Paul to have spoken to them in this way if they did not consider themselves to be "spiritual," the primary evidence of which was the gift of tongues. They were sure that they themselves were Spirit people; they were less sure of the apostle.

But in 12:28 Paul has already anticipated what he says here. God has placed in the church *first* apostles, *second* prophets. He is not denying that those who oppose him are prophets, nor that the Corinthians as a whole are *pneumatikoi*. He seems to be arguing that he is first of all an apostle, that he is therefore also a prophet, and that thus he is "writing to you the Lord's command[14]." The emphasis in Paul's word order is on "the Lord" (referring of course to Christ) as the source of what he has been writing. The word "command" therefore is most likely a collective singular referring to all that

---

[12]See also on 11:16.

[13]See the Introduction, pp. 10-15; see also the introduction to chaps. 12–14, as well as the commentary throughout this section.

[14]Gk. κυρίου ἐστὶν ἐντολή; BAGD are probably incorrect to list this usage under the category of "the precepts of Jesus." Paul is almost certainly referring to the instructions of the preceding argument. But see the discussion by Dodd, "Έννομος," p. 142 n. 3. On the textual question see n. 3 above.

he has written on this present matter, especially their need for intelligibility and order in the assembly so that all may be edified. Since both he and they have the Spirit, the true "person of the Spirit" will thus "acknowledge"[15] that what Paul writes is from the Lord.

38 With the authority of the same Lord from whom he received the "command," Paul pronounces sentence on those who do not recognize the Spirit in what he writes: "If anyone (i.e., the one who thinks he is a Spirit person) ignores[16] this, he himself will be ignored."

Paul's point is clear; the precise meaning of the repeated verb is slightly less so. He seems to be making a double play on words. The verb "to ignore" is here the antonym of "acknowledge" in v. 37. Thus, a spiritual person should "recognize" what Paul writes as "from the Lord"; if anyone "fails to acknowledge" it as such, that person will in turn not be "recognized/acknowledged." Although it is possible that Paul meant the subject of this last clause to be himself or the church (= "not recognized to be a prophet or spiritual"), more likely "God" is intended.[17] That is, failure to recognize the Spirit in Paul's letter will lead to that person's failure to be "recognized" by God (cf. 8:2-3). Hence it is a prophetic sentence of judgment on those who fail to heed this letter.[18]

39-40 Since the rhetorical confrontation in vv. 36-38 is something of an aside—although in Paul never irrelevant!—he brings the preceding argument to a conclusion by way of a three-part summation. It is signaled by the strong inferential conjunction "so then," common to this letter,[19] and yet another vocative. After the rhetoric of the preceding verses, in this case he adds the personal possessive, "*my* brothers [and sisters]" (see on 1:10).

The first clause repeats the imperative with which Paul began in v. 1: "eagerly desire to prophesy." The second speaks to their favorite: "and do not forbid speaking in tongues." As in the argument itself, he is not to be understood as forbidding tongues, nor will he allow anyone else to take the preceding correction as prohibition. Tongues are permissible in the assembly when accompanied by interpretation, and may be experienced as much as one wishes in private. These two clauses together thus summarize vv. 1-25.

[15]Gk. ἐπιγινωσκέτω (cf. 13:12); here it means "recognize to be so," hence "acknowledge."

[16]Gk. ἀγνοεῖ; cf. 10:1; 12:1.

[17]Cf. Käsemann, "Sentences," pp. 68-69; so also Conzelmann, 246; otherwise Barrett, 334.

[18]This also makes better sense of the sentence than does the variant reading (see n. 4), which makes the play on words in the second clause go in a different direction: If he/she fails to recognize Paul's word as the Lord's command, let him/her continue on in ignorance. In a more circuitous way that, too, is a form of judgment; but the indicative seems to be the more likely option.

[19]See on 3:7 and the note there.

The third clause (v. 40) summarizes the argument of vv. 26-33: "Everything should be done in a fitting and orderly way." The word "fitting"[20] argues again for propriety in the assembly (cf. 11:13); the word "orderly"[21] echoes its opposite, "disorder," from v. 33, and along with that verse strongly implies that the assembly in Corinth was in disarray. The implication of the argument throughout has been that speaking in tongues is the guilty party. With these words, therefore, the argument is brought to a fitting conclusion.

But the letter itself is not finished. Lying behind their view of spirituality is not simply a false view of spiritual gifts, but a false theology of spiritual existence as such. Since their view of "spirituality" had also brought them to deny a future resurrection of the body, it is fitting that this matter be taken up next. The result is the grand climax of the letter as a whole, at least in terms of its argument.

It is of some interest that people who believe so strongly in the Bible as the Word of God should at the same time spend so much energy getting around the plain sense of vv. 39-40. Surely there is irony in that. What Paul writes in these chapters he claims to be the command of the Lord; one wonders how he might have applied v. 38 to those who completely reject this command.

F. THE RESURRECTION OF BELIEVERS (15:1-58)

Although this chapter constitutes an abrupt change of subject matter, it is nonetheless significantly related both to the immediately preceding concern of chaps. 12–14 and to many other matters in the letter as a whole. The issue itself is clear: "How can some of you say that there is no resurrection of the dead?" (v. 12).[1] In other words, "Given that you believed in the resurrection of Christ (vv. 1-2, 11), how is it that some of you are denying the future bodily resurrection of believers?"[2] Furthermore, even though he mentions "some of you" (v. 12), nothing in Paul's response suggests that the Corinthians are divided among themselves on this matter. As before, the issue seems to be between some of them—who have influenced the whole—and

---

[20]Gk. εὐσχημόνως; cf. 1 Thess. 4:12; Rom. 13:13. Cf. the use of εὐσχημοσύνη in 12:23, which moves into the area of propriety.

[21]Gk. κατὰ τάξιν, only here in Paul.

[1]Cf. the repeated "if the dead are not raised" in vv. 16, 29, and 32.

[2]Otherwise Schmithals, 155-59, who argues that they are denying the resurrection of Christ; but his view is predicated on several questionable assumptions, which this argument aims to prove.

the apostle Paul. What is less certain is whether Paul has learned of this problem from their letter, which seems less likely, or from a report.[3]

Paul's response is in three parts. He begins (vv. 1-11) by reestablishing their commonly held ground, that *Christ* was raised from the dead. This is presented in such a way as to emphasize the objective reality of both Christ's death and resurrection.[4] At the same time he repeats two themes from the immediately preceding argument (14:33-38): (a) that this is the common ground of *all* who believe in and preach Christ, and (b) that his own apostolic ministry is the source of their life in Christ.

In Part II (vv. 12-34) Paul takes up what for him are two contradictory positions on their part (belief in Christ's resurrection and denial of their own) and sets out to demonstrate their logical—and therefore absurd—consequences. This section is also in three parts, which revolve around a hypothetical allowance of their position, that the dead are *not* raised. First (vv. 12-19), that would mean that Christ was not raised (vis-à-vis vv. 1-11); and if Christ was not raised, then everything is false. They cease to exist altogether as Christians since both their past and future are predicated on what they now deny. Next (vv. 20-28) he takes up the reverse position. Since Christ *has* been raised from the dead, the inevitable corollary is the resurrection of believers. Christ's resurrection is the firstfruits of the full harvest, having set in motion the defeat of death itself, a defeat that the very nature of God demands be brought to consummation. Finally (vv. 29-34), Paul once more picks up their position and shows the absurdity of their and his present activities if they are right. All of this together argues for the inevitability of a resurrection of believers from the dead.

Part III then takes up a new issue, namely *how* the dead are raised (v. 35), meaning not by what power but in what form. The answer? Bodily, but in a body adapted to the new conditions of the future. There is both continuity and discontinuity. The present body is earthly, "natural," subject to decay; the raised body is heavenly, "spiritual," and incorruptible. The final result, therefore, is a glorious resurrection-transformation of both the dead and the living wherein the final enemy, death, is swallowed up in victory.

---

[3]On this matter see the discussion in Hurd, 91-92. The reason for thinking it comes by way of report is the language "some among you," which is found again in what appears to be the anticipated response in v. 35: "Someone will ask, ..." This does not sound like language responding to their letter.

[4]This seems to be the point of the otherwise unnecessary inclusion of the burial (as a matter of first importance) and the considerable catalogue of appearances. Otherwise, Barth, *Resurrection,* pp. 150-51; and W. Marxsen, *The Resurrection of Jesus of Nazareth* (ET, Philadelphia, 1970), p. 95, who see the section as an attempt to trace back the later faith of all the church(es) to Jesus himself. But that seems to miss Paul's concern.

Both this analysis and the language of the argument indicate that the Corinthians' problem had to do with the resurrection *of the dead,* meaning, in light of vv. 35-58, that they had especially objected to the corporeal features of such an idea.[5] But how did believers in Christ come by such a denial? Although several answers have been given to this question,[6] the most likely is related to what has been argued right along, that it reflects the conflict between them and Paul over what it means to be *pneumatikos* ("spiritual"). In their view, by the reception of the Spirit, and especially the gift of tongues, they had already entered the true "spirituality" that is to be (4:8); already they had begun a form of angelic existence (13:1; cf. 4:9; 7:1-7) in which the body was unnecessary and unwanted, and would finally be destroyed.[7] Thus for them life in the Spirit meant a final ridding oneself of the body, not because it was evil but because it was inferior and beneath them; the idea that the body would be raised would have been anathema.[8] It is also possible that they saw the sacraments as the magical way of securing this new existence, which may further explain why some of them were being baptized for the dead—not because they expected the dead to be raised but because they saw in it a way of offering similar spiritual existence to the

---

[5]All 14 occurrences of νεκρός in this letter are in chap. 15. As Pearson (15; cf. 94 n. 3) points out, to the person whose native tongue was Greek this would mean the resurrection of "corpses," an idea that "would probably be repugnant."

[6]There has been a long debate with a considerable bibliography. Although there are variations on each, and hybrid forms of each, basically the positions are five: (1) that the opponents were some Jews who had a Sadducean theology that rejected resurrection altogether; (2) that the Corinthians had imbibed Greek philosophy so that they believed in the immortality of the soul but rejected the resurrection of the body; (3) that some of them had adopted Gnostic views and actually denied the resurrection of Christ; (4) that they were the forerunners of the "overrealized" eschatology advocated later by Hymenaeus and Philetus in Ephesus (2 Tim. 2:17-18), arguing that the resurrection has already occurred in a spiritual sense; (5) that in their sacramental union with Christ they believed they had received present immortality, and that what they denied therefore was the possibility of death itself, a position sometimes held in conjunction with 4. The most complete critical discussion of these views and others can be found in the unpublished dissertation by D. J. Murphy, "The Dead in Christ: Paul's Understanding of God's Fidelity: a Study of I Corinthians 15" (Union, NY, 1977), pp. 9-161. For briefer overviews see J. H. Wilson, "The Corinthians Who Say There Is No Resurrection of the Dead," *ZNW* 59 (1968), 90-107; B. Spörlein, *Die Leugnung der Auferstehung: eine historisch-kritische Untersuchung zu I Kor 15* (Regensburg, 1971), pp. 1-19; A. J. M. Wedderburn, "The Problem of the Denial of the Resurrection in I Corinthians XV," *NovT* 23 (1981), 229-41; and K. A. Plank, "Resurrection Theology: the Corinthian Controversy Reexamined," *PRS* 8 (1981), 41-54.

[7]For this thoroughly Greek view of the body see further on 6:13-14.

[8]It is altogether likely that they held a similar view of Jesus' resurrection. That is, they believed in his "resurrection" but they had spiritualized it in their own terms. For a presentation of this view, see R. J. Sider, "St. Paul's Understanding of the Nature and Significance of the Resurrection in I Corinthians XV 1-19," *NovT* 19 (1977), 124-41.

departed (15:29).[9] Although one cannot be certain of this reconstruction, it is in keeping with what we have seen throughout to be their position vis-à-vis Paul.[10]

Two historical realities probably merged to bring about their actual denial of a bodily resurrection. First, it seems unlikely that an articulated doctrine of resurrection belonged to the earliest Christian preaching, especially among Gentiles.[11] Christ's resurrection was central, but that said something primarily about *him* (cf. Rom. 1:3-4). For believers it secured salvation and gave hope for the future, but that hope would not necessarily have been thought of in terms of a resurrection.[12] After all, few of them would have died—and in any case their hope was in an imminent Parousia. The evidence from 1 Thess. 4:13-18 suggests that even as late as A.D. 48-49 Paul had not yet addressed this question—at least not in that church. When he does so, apparently because some have died, it is in terms similar to our present chapter.[13] Since 1 Thessalonians was written from Corinth, is it at this time that he began to teach the resurrection of believers here as well?

Second, apparently soon after Paul's departure from Corinth things took a turn for the worse in this church. A false theology began to gain ground, rooted in a radical pneumatism that denied the value/significance of the body and expressed in a somewhat "overrealized," or "spiritualized," eschatology. Along with this there arose a decided movement against Paul. These two matters climax in this letter in their pneumatic behavior (chaps. 12–14) and their denial of a resurrection of the dead (chap. 15), which included their questioning of his status as *pneumatikos* (14:36-38) and perhaps their calling him an "abortion" or a "freak" (15:8). Thus, as elsewhere, Paul sets out not only to correct some bad theology but at the same time to remind them of his right to do so.

Furthermore, all of this is integrally tied to the matters of behavior that have preceded. It is of more than merely passing interest that both major sections of this argument conclude with exhortation to proper behavior. Part II concludes (vv. 33-34) with an especially strong appeal that belief in

---

[9]For similar, but not identical, reconstructions, see Wedderburn, "Problem," and Lincoln, 33-37.

[10]See the Introduction, pp. 10-15.

[11]Since the first believers were Jews, and had experienced the Risen Christ, they would naturally have assumed a Jewish confidence in their own resurrection as well. However, on the matter of lack of a monolithic view in contemporary Judaism, see H. C. C. Cavallin, *Life After Death, Part I* (Lund, 1974).

[12]For example, in the creedal argument in vv. 3-5, the matters of "first importance" center in Christ and have "for our sins" as the human benefit.

[13]Cf. 1 Thess. 4:14: "For if we believe that Jesus died and rose again, thus will God also bring with him those who have fallen asleep through Jesus."

the resurrection should serve to mend their aberrant ways, while Part III concludes (v. 58) on a more positive note, exhorting them to continue the work of the gospel in which they already stand (v. 1).

At all events, the net result of their errors is one of the great theological treasures of the Christian church.[14] If for Paul, and therefore for us, there is an element of mystery to the concept of a "spiritual body" (v. 51), there can be little question that for him Christ's resurrection is central to everything. It is the ultimate eschatological event. By raising him from the dead God set in motion the final overthrow of death itself. Hence the inevitable fact (vv. 12-28) and nature (vv. 35-49) of our own resurrection.

1. The Basis—The Resurrection of Christ (15:1-11)

1 *Now, brothers, I want to remind you of the gospel I preached to you, which you received and on which you have taken your stand.* 2 *By this gospel you are saved, if you hold firmly to the word I preached to you.*[15] *Otherwise, you have believed in vain.*

3 *For what I received*[16] *I passed on to you as of first importance*[a]: *that Christ died for our sins according to the Scriptures,* 4 *that he was buried, that he was raised on the third day according to the Scriptures,* 5 *and that he appeared to Peter,*[b] *and then*[17] *to the Twelve.*[18] 6 *After that, he appeared to more than five hundred of the brothers at the same time, most of whom are still living, though some have fallen asleep.* 7 *Then he appeared to James, then to all the apostles,* 8 *and last of all he appeared to me also, as to one abnormally born.*

9 *For I am the least of the apostles and do not even deserve to be called an apostle, because I persecuted the church of God.* 10 *But by*

[14]As Conzelmann, 250, notes: "Paul's theses are in essence understandable even if we cannot reconstruct with certainty the views prevailing in Corinth on this world and the next, on death and the afterlife."

[15]The Western tradition (D* F G a b t Ambst)—and probably (as Zuntz, 254-55, argues) the *Vorlage* of P46 as well—has the spurious substitution of ὀφείλετε κατέχειν for the εἰ κατέχετε of Paul. Martin, 89, 92, seems to prefer this reading, but it has little to commend it as the original.

[16]Not surprisingly, Marcion omitted this clause; in this he is followed by b and Ambrosiaster.

[17]Apparently as part of a theological tendency to heighten the role of Peter, the Western tradition substituted καὶ μετὰ ταῦτα for Paul's εἶτα, suggesting that the "tradition" ends with the appearance to Peter. Then, "after these things" he appeared to the rest. They also substitute "the Eleven" for "the Twelve." One cannot tell whether this is a "pedantic correction" (so Metzger, 567) because of the demise of Judas, or whether it meant the "eleven," minus Peter, who had already received his own resurrection appearance.

[18]See the preceding note.

the grace of God I am what I am, and his grace to me was not without effect.[19] No, I worked harder than all of them—yet not I, but the grace of God that was with me. 11 *Whether, then, it was I or they, this is what we preach, and this is what you believed.*

[a]Or *you at the first*
[b]Greek *Cephas*

Although the enumeration of appearances might suggest otherwise, Paul is not here setting out to *prove* the resurrection of Jesus. Rather, he is reasserting the commonly held ground *from which* he will argue against their assertion that there is no resurrection of the dead.[20] To do so he appeals to "the tradition" of the whole church, which he preached and they believed, namely that Christ died, was buried, and was raised on the third day. The emphasis is threefold: First, he reiterates both at the beginning (vv. 1-2) and the end (v. 11) that this tradition is something they have indeed believed. Two points are made here: (a) In keeping with the emphasis at the end of the preceding argument (14:33, 36), what Paul preached and they believed is the common ground of the whole church (cf. vv. 3-5, 11). (b) Alongside that emphasis is the reminder that their very existence as believers is at stake on this matter. That is, any deviation from this gospel which "saved them" and "in which they stand" puts them in danger of "believing for naught."

Second, beginning with v. 3, Paul reiterates the tradition itself. For several reasons[21] it is generally agreed that in vv. 3-5 Paul is repeating a very early creedal formulation that was common to the entire church,[22] to which he adds other traditions about several resurrection appearances. Paul's use of this material seems to have a twofold concern: (a) The combination in the creed of "buried" and "raised on the third day" emphasizes the resurrection of a dead corpse, not the "spiritual" renewal of life after death. Whatever

---

[19]The Western tradition (D* F G b Ambst) reads πτωχή for κενή, resulting in "his grace was not beggarly (or impoverished, impotent)." As Zuntz argues, 89-90, on transcriptional grounds this is so difficult that it well may be original. Thus, God's "rich" grace did not prove to be "poor" in his case.

[20]Sider, "Understanding," p. 132, suggests otherwise, that the list of eyewitnesses is included because some in Corinth had come to doubt the teaching of Christ's resurrection. But it is not clear whether Sider means that they have come to doubt his bodily resurrection, or the resurrection altogether. It would seem to be the former.

[21](1) The fact that he says it is something he both "received" and "passed along" to them; (2) the stylized form of four statements in two balanced sets; (3) the repeated ὅτι before each clause, which implies a kind of quotation and (4) the appearance of several non-Pauline words in such a short compass. On this question see esp. Jeremias, *Eucharistic Words*, pp. 101-03.

[22]Not so Lenski, 630, on the grounds that in Gal. 1:11–2:2 Paul rejects having received his gospel from men; cf. Grosheide, 349. But the context of Galatians indicates that "his gospel" in that case has to do with its being law-free and for the Gentiles. The concern is different here. See on v. 11.

the precise nature of the Corinthian view, this citation of the creed is a reminder that the nature of Christ's resurrection is genuine and corporeal. (b) So also with the catalogue of resurrection appearances (vv. 5-7), the like of which there is nothing else in the early literature. Since this catalogue is unlikely to be part of the creed itself, its inclusion seems emphatic. Christ *was seen* by all these people, meaning he was corporeally visible this side of the grave.

Third, the catalogue of appearances concludes with his own experience (v. 8), which leads him to a brief word about his apostleship (vv. 9-10). Since these words are otherwise unnecessary to the argument, one must ask what caused them to appear here. The best answer seems to be that they reflect the conflict between him and them[23] last addressed in 14:36-38. In relating his own experience of the Risen Christ he describes himself as "one who is *ektrōma,*" a word that means "miscarriage" or "abortion" and probably refers to his "lowly" status as "least" among the apostles, which was perhaps hurled at him as an epithet by some of the Corinthians. In any case, as in 4:8-13 where he also sets forth his own view of apostleship over against theirs, he capitalizes on his lowliness in order to exalt the grace of God in his life—not the least of which is evidenced in their coming to faith through such an *ektrōma* as he (v. 11)!

Thus this introductory section functions both to ground the argument that follows in Christ himself and to ground Paul's authority in his having seen the risen Lord and in their being the result of his ministry (cf. 9:1-2). At the same time it serves to illustrate once more his own understanding of apostleship as modeled after the Crucified One (cf. 2:1-5; 4:8-13; 9:15-23).

1-2   This opening sentence serves to introduce most of the concerns that will be spelled out in the argument that follows, at least through v. 28. At the same time it ties what follows to what has immediately preceded. The verb "I make known,"[24] although finally meaning "I remind" (as the NIV), is probably a nice piece of irony that picks up the verb in 14:38, "if anyone *does not know* (lit. 'is ignorant'!)."[25] To those who think of themselves as "spiritual" over against Paul, he pronounces the judgment that their "ignorance" of his word as the commandment of the Lord meant they would be "ignored" by God himself. Now he "makes known" to them what they already know, but seem to have forgotten.

---

[23]Cf. P. von der Osten-Sacken, "Die Apologie des paulinischen Apostolats in 1 Kor 15:1-11," *ZNW* 64 (1973), 245-62; cf. also M. J. Harris, *Raised Immortal: Resurrection and Immortality in the New Testament* (Grand Rapids, 1982), p. 13.

[24]Gk. γνωρίζω; cf. 12:3 and esp. Gal. 1:11, where this sentence is repeated nearly verbatim.

[25]Cf. the same combination in 12:1 and 3, where the lack of a chapter break makes the connection more visible. Conzelmann, 250, prefers to see the usage as "ceremonious."

Even though the sentence itself is somewhat convoluted, so that some have despaired of making grammatical sense of it,[26] the flow of Paul's thought can be easily discerned. The argument has an A-B-A-B structure:[27]

I make known to you the gospel	} A
which I preached to you,	}
which also you received,	}
in which also you stand,	} B
through which also you are being saved,	}
(that is)	
with what word I preached to you	} A'
provided you hold fast	}
unless you received it in vain	} B'

By this analysis A' repeats the basic statement of A, while B expresses their response to the gospel and B' serves as its negative counterpoint, indicating the net result of their present stance with regard to resurrection. Thus Paul begins, "Now[28] I make known to you, brothers [and sisters],[29] the gospel that I preached to you." In terms of the argument proper, these words anticipate vv. 3-5, which give the *content* of the gospel Paul preached, and could easily have followed. Instead, he digresses momentarily (B) to remind them that the gospel he preached is also the one on which their past ("you received"[30]), present ("you stand"[31]), and future ("you are being saved"[32]) are predicated.[33] Having thus stressed that the gospel *he* preached is also the one to which *they* owe their very existence, he resumes the opening clause, but now by means of an indirect question. Leaving out the "digression," the A-A' sentences read: "I make known to

---

[26]F. Blass, e.g., considered the final two clauses a gloss (see BDF 478). The most common solution is to reverse the final two clauses, so that they read, "If you hold fast what I preached to you." But none of these expedients is necessary.

[27]Adopted by RV; cf. Edwards, 391; Findlay, 919; Bachmann, 429. The objection by Héring, 157, that this leaves κατέχετε without an object is irrelevant.

[28]Gk. δέ; probably consecutive, as the NIV translates.

[29]On this vocative in 1 Corinthians, see on 1:10.

[30]Gk. παρελάβετε (see on 11:23). Although this is the language of the "transmission" of tradition, in this case it also refers to their having received it in a saving way, hence to their conversion.

[31]Gk. perfect (ἐστήκατε); the NIV catches the perfect with "you have taken your stand," but seems to miss Paul's nuance by implying that it is the gospel *on* which they stand; more likely Paul means the gospel is that "in which they currently stand as believers." Cf. esp. Rom. 5:2.

[32]Gk. σῴζεσθε; cf. 1:18, where the same futuristic nuance of the present tense may be seen; salvation is now, but it is also in process, to be completed at the Day of the Lord. See esp. Rom. 5:9; 1 Thess. 5:9-10. So also Findlay, 918; Barrett, 336.

[33]Cf. R-P, 331.

you the gospel I preached to you, that is, with what word[34] [namely, the tradition that will follow in vv. 3-5] I preached to you." But this repetition of the opening statement leads to a second "digression" (B'), the counterpoint to B: "Provided[35] you hold fast,[36] unless[37] you have believed in vain[38]." Grammatically this last clause goes with A'; conceptually it modifies B.[39]

Despite their qualification of the clauses in B, the final clauses (B') are not to be understood as doubt on the apostle's part. Rather, the whole sentence nicely introduces the three concerns of vv. 3-28. First, the opening sentence both serves as a transition from 14:36-38, as already noted, and anticipates the apologetic note in vv. 8-11. Second, the repeated phrase "gospel which I preached to you" introduces vv. 3-7, the "tradition" that has the death and resurrection of Christ as its heart and soul and in turn becomes the predicate of the entire argument in vv. 12-28. Third, the two "asides" (B-B') anticipate the logic of vv. 12-19, that their own existence as believers argues for the truth of the resurrection of the dead. On the one hand, the clauses in part B reassert that the Corinthians owe their entire existence as believers to the gospel Paul preaches, with its central affirmation of Christ's resurrection. On the other hand, the final clause in B' is surely irony, and is intended to anticipate the argument in vv. 14-19. If they do not hold fast to the gospel, that is, if their current position as to "no resurrection" is correct, then Christ did not rise, which in turn means that they did indeed believe in vain. If they are right, everything is a lie, and they cease to exist as believers altogether.[40]

3a With an explanatory "for" Paul proceeds to introduce the "word" (v. 2) of the "gospel I preached." The language is nearly identical to that in 11:23. These two texts together make it clear that this is technical vocabulary from Paul's Jewish heritage for the transmission of religious instruction.[41] As with the tradition of the Lord's Supper, this language indicates that the essential matters go back to the very beginnings of things. Of crucial importance here is the clear implication that the two basic tenets of the Christian faith, atonement through the death of Christ and a high Chris-

---

[34]Gk. τίνι λόγῳ; cf. the usage in 1 Thess. 4:2.

[35]Gk. εἰ ("if"); the suggested translation is appropriate when the "if" clause follows the clause it modifies, as here. Cf. 1 Tim. 2:15.

[36]Gk. κατέχετε; cf. the affirmation in 11:2.

[37]Gk. ἐκτὸς εἰ μή; see on 14:5.

[38]Gk. εἰκῇ; used only by Paul in the NT (Rom. 13:4; Gal. 3:4 [twice]; 4:11; Col. 2:18). Some would make it mean here "without consideration" or "idly" (e.g. Findlay, 919; R-P, 332). This is possible, but it misses the irony and the close tie to v. 14.

[39]This is the point missed by those who see this analysis as "untenable" (e.g., R-P, 332).

[40]Thus the Western text (see n. 11) quite misses Paul's point.

[41]See on 11:23, esp. n. 16.

tology based on his resurrection,[42] were well formed before Paul came on the scene. For all the shaping that Christian theology underwent in his hands,[43] the basic elements were there before and after him. This is what he "received" and what he "passed on."

What is less certain is the meaning of the prepositional phrase translated "as of first importance."[44] As the marginal reading indicates, this could also mean priority in time. Although a case can be made for the latter (he would be stressing that this is what he preached and they believed from the very beginning of their coming to Christ), both the form and language suggest that the former is Paul's concern.[45] Among all the things he proclaimed and taught while he was with them, these are the matters of "first importance." Here is the "bare bones" content of the gospel that saves.

3b-5 Even though the material in vv. 6-7 is "traditional" by its very nature, and therefore probably belongs to "what Paul received and passed on" to them, it seems unlikely that it also belonged to the "gospel I preached to you." For this reason, plus the balanced structure of vv. 3b-5, most scholars consider these verses to be an expression of a very early Christian creed,[46] while vv. 6-7 represent further traditions that Paul adds at the end to fill out his personal concerns.

As to the creed itself, there has been considerable discussion over several issues:[47] its unity;[48] the extent of its content;[49] and its original

[42]While it is true that there is no explicit Christology in this creed, the resurrection is the primary experiential catalyst for such theologizing in the early church. See, e.g., Acts 2:36; Rom. 1:3-4; and the implicit Christology in this argument in vv. 22-28 and 45-49. On this matter see G. Delling, "Die bleibende Bedeutsamkeit der Verkündigung des Anfangs im Urchristentum," *ThLZ* 95 (1970), 801-09.

[43]Particularly the clear insight that such an atonement nullifies all other grounds for relationship with God, so that Gentile and Jew together are accepted freely by grace.

[44]Gk. ἐν πρώτοις.

[45]The preposition with the plural πρώτοις seems especially to point in this direction. One would expect ἐν ἀρχῇ if he intended "at the beginning" (cf. Phil. 4:15). Cf. a similar usage in Plato, *Statesman* 522c.

[46]In this regard cf. the instructions of the risen Jesus in Luke 24:45-47, where he "opened their minds so they could understand the Scriptures," which say that "the Christ will suffer and rise from the dead on the third day." These two passages give further credence to the likelihood that the author of the Third Gospel was a companion of the apostle Paul. Cf. also the "model" sermon for the Hellenistic synagogue recorded in Acts 13:16-41, esp. 28-31, where the same four points are made.

[47]For a bibliography up to 1970 see Conzelmann, 254 n. 54. For an overview of the issues and debate see J. Kloppenborg, "An Analysis of the Pre-Pauline Formula in 1 Cor 15:3b-5 in Light of Some Recent Literature," *CBQ* 40 (1978), 351-67; and J. Murphy-O'Connor, "Tradition."

[48]The unity of the "creed" was rejected by U. Wilckens, "Der Ursprung der überlieferung der Erscheinungen des Auferstanden: Zur traditionsgeschichtlichen Analyse von 1 Kor 15, 1-11," in *Dogma und Denkstrukturen* (ed. W. Joest and W. Pannen-

language.[50] On these matters one is referred to the literature. In its present form it has four lines, each introduced with a *hoti* ("that"),[51] thus emphasizing the content of each line. The four lines are in two nearly perfect sets of semitic parallels. Lines 1 and 3, which describe the death and resurrection of Jesus, correspond formally, including the phrase "according to the Scriptures"; lines 2 and 4 respond respectively to lines 1 and 3, warranting their content. Thus:

1)   that Christ died for our sins
                      according to the Scriptures;
2) and that   he was buried;
3) and that   he was raised on the third day,
                      according to the Scriptures;
4) and that   he was seen by Cephas [and][52] the Twelve.

Line 1. That "Christ died for our sins" is the primary tenet of the Christian faith. Several items need to be noted: (a) In 1 Thess. 4:14 Paul simply said, "We believe that Jesus died and rose." But the creed uses[53] the

---

berg; Göttingen, 1963), pp. 81-95; he was followed by R. Fuller, *The Formation of the Resurrection Narratives* (London, 1972), pp. 13-14. For a response see Murphy-O'Connor, "Tradition," 583-84.

[49]Although most consider it to go through v. 5, some have argued that it goes only through v. 4 (Héring, 158; P. Winter, "I Corinthians XV 3b-7," *NovT* 2 [1957], 142-50), while others have argued that it goes only as far as the first εἶτα in v. 5 (E. Bammel, "Herkunft und Funktion der Traditionselemente in I Kor. 15:1-11," *TZ* 11 [1955], 401-19; and H.-W. Bartsch, "Die Argumentation des Paulus in I Cor 15:3-11," *ZNW* 55 [1964], 261-74). Neither of these has gained a wide following.

[50]This also has to do with its original provenance, whether Palestinian (hence originally in Aramaic) or Hellenistic (hence originally in Greek). Jeremias ("Eucharistic Words," pp. 101-03, and "Artikellos *Christos*. Zur Ursprache von I Kor 15:3b-5," *ZNW* 57 [1966], 211-15) and B. Klappert ("Zur Frage des semitischen oder griechischen Urtextes von 1. Kor. xv.3-5," *NTS* 13 [1966/67], 168-73) have been the leading advocates of the former. H. Conzelmann ("On the Analysis of the Confessional Formula in I Corinthians 15:3-5," *Int* 20 [1966], 15-25) and P. Vielhauer ("Ein Weg zur neutestamentlichen Christologie," *EvT* 25 [1965], 56-57) are the leading exponents of the latter. For further bibliography see Kloppenborg, "Analysis," p. 352 n. 5.

[51]Actually καὶ ὅτι in lines 2-4. This is the matter that convinced Wilckens (n. 48 above) that the creed lacked unity; Murphy-O'Connor has argued that the formula reflects Paul's quotational method found in 8:4 and is his way of stressing each line from a common source.

[52]One cannot tell whether this second appearance belonged to the creedal formula or not; if so, then it probably would have been introduced with a καί, which Paul has changed to an εἶτα in order to make it the second in his list of six such appearances.

[53]This is debated in the literature since Paul uses the anarthrous title Χριστός to refer to Jesus at least 126 times. Thus it is argued that the title is a Pauline adaptation. This of course can neither be proved nor disproved. But there is good reason to believe that the

divine title as a name, *"Christ* died." Although by now this had become Jesus' divine name, it undoubtedly still carried messianic overtones. In Christian understanding, the Messiah is characterized first of all by this reality: "He died to take away our sins" (cf. 1:23; 2:2).

(b) The language "for our sins"[54] is a direct reflection of the LXX of Isa. 53.[55] Since Judaism did *not* interpret this passage messianically, at least not in terms of a personal Messiah,[56] and since there is no immediate connection between the death of Jesus and the idea that his death was "for our sins," it is fair to say that whoever made that connection is the "founder of Christianity." All the evidence points to Jesus himself, especially at the Last Supper with his interpretation of his death in the language of Isa. 53 as "for you" (see on 11:23-25).

(c) This is the language of atonement. In saying "Christ died for our sins," the creed presupposes alienation between God and humans because of human rebellion and sinfulness, for which the just penalty is death. Death "for our sins" means that one died on behalf of others to satisfy the penalty and to overcome the alienation. Thus, even though there is no "theory" of atonement here, just the affirmation, the concept of substitution is woven into the very earliest of the Christian creeds.[57] In Pauline theology this

original creed expressed itself in terms of the Messiah rather than simply with the name of Jesus. After all, that is where the theological impact lay. The evidence from Luke 24:46 also suggests that the title belongs to the tradition. If so, it may be that Paul simply used the anarthrous form. Cf. the debate between Jeremias and Conzelmann (n. 49).

[54]Gk. ὑπὲρ τῶν ἁμαρτιῶν ἡμῶν; this combination is unusual in Paul, but not unknown. The identical phrase appears again in Gal. 4:1 (probably, since there is textual variation). The plural appears again in v. 17, as well as in Gal. 1:4; Rom. 4:7; Col. 1:14; Eph. 2:1. Thus it is not quite true to assert, as is frequently done, that this usage is un-Pauline. This assertion is accomplished by the unusual methodology of starting with Romans and Galatians, where the usage is primarily singular, dismissing Colossians and Ephesians as non-Pauline (partly on the grounds of this usage!), and considering the usage in Gal. 1:4 and Rom. 4:7 to be from "traditional material." But that will not quite work since both of these passages are now free Pauline compositions and since he has shown himself well able to adapt traditional material (cf. on 11:23-25).

[55]The plural "our sins" occurs in vv. 4, 5, and 6; "for sins" occurs in v. 10; and "their sins" in vv. 11 and 12. Some have doubted that this reflects the LXX since the LXX does not use the preposition ὑπέρ; but it does use περί, and these two have become nearly interchangeable in *koinē*. Cf. Conzelmann, 253 n. 48.

[56]See A. Neubauer, ed., *The Fifty-Third Chapter of Isaiah According to Jewish Interpreters*, 2 vols. (repr., New York, 1969).

[57]Cf. R-P, 333. Conzelmann, 255, would distinguish between "atonement sacrifice" and "vicarious sacrifice"; but it is doubtful whether this would have had meaning to the early Christians, whose history in Judaism already had inherent in it the idea of vicarious sacrifice in the atonement itself. On this matter see also H. Ridderbos, "The Earliest Confession of the Atonement in Paul," in *Reconciliation and Hope* (ed. R. Banks; Grand Rapids, 1974), pp. 76-89, esp. 79-81.

includes not only forgiveness from past sins, but in a very real sense deliverance from the bondage of one's sinfulness as well.

(d) Finally, the added phrase, "according to the Scriptures," probably is not intended to point to a single passage or set of passages but to the larger reality of the OT, where "Scripture is seen as a whole."[58] According to "the Scriptures" God had provided that the death of a spotless lamb should be part of Israel's rescue from the bondage of Egypt. This in turn became part of the sacrificial system in which animals "bore the sins" of the people on the Day of Atonement. And this language is picked up once more in Isa. 53 to describe the one who "as a lamb led to slaughter" took away the sins of the people.

Although this first line is almost certainly to be understood as part of the creed,[59] hence the reason for its inclusion, at the same time it serves to emphasize the reality of his death and perhaps to press the concern of chaps. 1–4 one more time, that the gospel is not "wisdom" humanly conceived but the story of a crucified Messiah who died on behalf of sinners.

Line 2. This addition to line 1, "and that he was buried," functions to verify the reality of the death.[60] In the present context it emphasizes the fact that a dead corpse was laid in the grave, so that the resurrection that follows will be recognized as an objective reality, not merely a "spiritual" phenomenon. Therefore, even though the point is incidental to Paul's own concern, this very early expression of Christian faith also verifies the reality of the empty tomb stories.[61] It is common in some quarters of NT scholarship to deny this latter;[62] but that seems to be a case of special pleading. The combined emphasis on death, burial, and third-day resurrection would have had an empty tomb as its natural concomitant, even if not expressed in that way. Given this language, embedded in the heart of the earliest tradition, the early Christians and Paul would find it unthinkable that some would deny

[58]So Conzelmann, 255. This does not exclude the idea that there are particular passages in mind as well; but the plural probably does not so much refer to individual passages as to the OT wholistically conceived.

[59]For the combination "died" and "rose" in the NT see esp. 1 Thess. 4:14; 2 Cor. 5:15; Rom. 4:25; 14:9; Acts 3:15; 1 Pet. 1:19-21; Rev. 1:5.

[60]But not necessarily that death is the precondition of resurrection (as, e.g., Martin, 98).

[61]So the majority of commentators; cf. Sider, "Understanding," p. 38; R. Stein, "Was the Tomb Really Empty?" *JETS* 20 (1977), 27-29; and W. L. Craig, "The Historicity of the Empty Tomb of Jesus," *NTS* 31 (1985), 39-67, esp. 39-42. For the debate see J. Mánek, "The Apostle Paul and the Empty Tomb," *NovT* 2 (1957), 276-80.

[62]See, e.g., Conzelmann, 255, and "Analysis," p. 21; cf. E. L. Bode, *The First Easter Morning* (AB 45; Rome, 1970), pp. 98-100. For others, especially in German scholarship, see Craig, "Empty Tomb," p. 69 n. 10.

that they believed that the tomb was also empty, or that those stories were the creation of a later generation that needed "objective verification" of the resurrection. One may not believe that Jesus rose and that the tomb was therefore empty; but one may scarcely on good historical grounds deny that they so believed.[63]

Line 3. With this line Paul comes to his present concern. Nonetheless he keeps to the language of the creed, "that he was raised on the third day according to the Scriptures." In distinction from the two previous lines, the verb in this instance is a perfect passive ("he has been raised"), implying that he was both raised and still lives.[64] The difficulty for us is to determine precisely what was meant by "on the third day according to the Scriptures."

The problem with the first phrase, "on the third day," has to do both with its origin and its significance for the creed. Although several solutions have been offered, the most likely is that "on the third day" came into the creed primarily because this was in fact the day of the discovery of the empty tomb and of the first resurrection appearances.[65] One may surmise that the event had such an impact on those who saw Jesus alive after his crucifixion that it was simply carried over into the creed, in somewhat the same manner that the Lord's Supper tradition carried with it "on the night that he was betrayed" (see on 11:23). Added to that would be the disciples' after-the-fact understanding, as referring to his resurrection, of the otherwise enigmatic saying that Jesus "would destroy the temple and in three days build it again" (John 2:19-22; cf. Mark 14:58//Matt. 26:61; Mark 15:19//Matt. 27:40). That is, their own experience of the risen Lord "on the third day," plus their later remembrance that he himself had so predicted such an occurrence,[66] combined to fix the phrase in the creed.

The phrase "according to the Scriptures" has posed even greater

---

[63]Cf. Harris, *Raised*, pp. 37-40.

[64]The perfect is repeated throughout the chapter when referring to Christ (vv. 12, 13, 14, 16, 17, and 20). The passive is an example of the "divine passive," with God as the implied subject (see v. 15); cf. on 1:5-8; 12:7. It should be noted here that it is absolutely crucial to Paul's view of things that Jesus did not so much rise as that God raised him, thus vindicating him. See esp. vv. 20-28.

[65]For other options, see Craig, "Empty Tomb," p. 42. Harris, *Raised*, pp. 11-12, also argues for a combination of several factors. The basic alternative is that the language "according to the Scriptures" implies that the formula rests primarily on some particular scriptural passages, which became the basis for its origin (cf., e.g., Conzelmann, 256 [whom see also for other alternatives]; H. K. McArthur, " 'On the Third Day,' " *NTS* 18 [1971/72], 81-86). This is based in part on the preceding construct, in which "for our sins" is not based on their experience but on their understanding of Jesus' death as fulfilling Scripture.

[66]As the three passion predictions in Mark (8:31; 9:31; 10:34) explicitly indicate. The predictions are doubted in many quarters because they are so explicit in their lan-

difficulties. Since neither the tradition of the third day nor the Resurrection is well attested in the OT, several theories have been offered: (a) that it modifies "on the third day" and refers to some specific OT texts;[67] (b) that it refers either to early Christian attempts to write passion and resurrection narratives[68] or to Testimony Books containing OT citations that were interpreted prophetically as referring to the third day;[69] (c) that it reflects a popular Jewish belief that corruption set in only after the third day, so that Jesus was raised on the third day to fulfill Ps. 16:9-11 (LXX) that his body would not suffer "corruption";[70] (d) that it modifies only the verb "he was raised" and does not include "on the third day";[71] and (e) that it has the same force here that it did in line 1, asserting that the OT as a whole bears witness to the resurrection on the third day. This latter seems the most likely option. If so, then an early tradition saw the combined evidence of Pss. 16:8-11 and 110:1 as bearing witness to the Messiah's resurrection (cf. Acts 2:25-36); and that it happened "on the third day" was probably seen in terms of the

---

guage. But there is no good reason to doubt that Jesus predicted both his death (after all, he as much as precipitated it by going to Jerusalem and cleansing the Temple at Passover) and his vindication by God through resurrection. How much of the precise language belongs to Jesus' own words and how much to the after-the-event memory of the disciples is moot. "After three days" may very well have been part of his own language, reflecting an OT motif, supported by midrash and targum, that the third day was "the day of divine salvation, deliverance and manifestation" (Bode, *Easter,* p. 125).

[67]Most frequently Hos. 6:2 ("After two days he will revive us; on the third day he will restore us, that we may live in his presence"); and sometimes Jon. 1:17 (on the basis of Matt. 12:40) and 2 Kings 20:5 (the promise of restoration to Hezekiah, "on the third day you shall go up to the house of the Lord"). The Hosea text is the most promising in this regard, especially since it has been demonstrated that from a very early time (at least the 2nd c. A.D., although probably earlier) the rabbis interpreted this text in terms of resurrection. See McArthur, " 'Third Day,' " 81-86. The difficulty with all of these is the silence of the early church. Nowhere in the NT or soon thereafter does anyone appeal to any of these texts as referring to the resurrection on the third day. Cf. Craig, "Empty Tomb," p. 45.

[68]W. Bussmann, *Synoptische Studien, iii, Zu den Sonderquellen* (Halle, 1931), pp. 186-91. Besides the inherent improbability of this proposal, it has against it the parallel in v. 3 that certainly refers to the OT and the fact that the phrase αἱ γραφαί invariably refers to the OT and only much later (2nd-3rd c.) to Christian documents.

[69]Cf. D. Plooij, *Studies in the Testimony Book* (Amsterdam, 1932), pp. 6-7, and V. Taylor, *The Formation of the Gospel Tradition* (New York, 1933), p. 49 n. 2. But even if such books existed, this scarcely removes the difficulty, since one must still find appropriate OT texts that might have been included.

[70]D. Hill, "On the Third Day," *ExpT* 78 (1966/67), 266-67.

[71]B. M. Metzger, "A Suggestion Concerning the Meaning of I Cor. XV.4b," *JTS* 8 (1957), 118-23. On its own this would be a readily acceptable solution to a difficult crux; but it is not on its own here. The phrase "according to the Scriptures" in line 1 only makes sense as modifying the full clause that precedes. By analogy it most likely does so here as well.

variety of OT texts in which salvation or vindication took place on the third day.[72]

Line 4. Not only was Jesus raised, but "he appeared to Cephas, and then to the Twelve." Just as line 2 functions to warrant line 1, so this line warrants line 3 and thereby also emphasizes the objective reality of the Resurrection. He "was raised" and he "was seen."[73] This is so crucial for the present argument that Paul will append four more appearances to these first two (vv. 6-8). Paul's point seems emphatic. The resurrection of Jesus from the dead was not a form of "spiritual" existence. Just as he was truly dead and buried, so he was truly raised from the dead bodily[74] and seen by a large number of witnesses on a variety of occasions.

In the Gospel narratives, the first appearances are to women;[75] in this "tradition" these appearances are passed over for those to Peter and the Twelve, which are also recorded in the Gospel tradition.[76] Since Peter is

---

[72]See Hill, "Third Day"; cf. K. Lehmann, *Auferwecht am dritten Tag nach der Schrift* (Freiburg, 1968), pp. 262-90; and Bode, *Easter,* pp. 119-26, who see this phenomenon as the *origin* of the third-day tradition. Without a historical event, however, this seems extremely unlikely. See the critique in Craig, "Empty Tomb," pp. 45-49, who adopts a position similar to the one taken here; also Harris, *Raised,* pp. 10-11.

It should be noted, however, that at least as early as the Gospel of Matthew the "sign of Jonah" was interpreted as referring to the "three days and three nights" that Jonah was in the belly of the fish, which in turn was seen as a prediction of Jesus' resurrection.

The "sign of Jonah" saying occurs in Matthew both in a parallel with Mark (Matt. 16:4//Mark 8:12) and in a "Q" parallel with Luke (Matt. 12:39-40//Luke 11:29-30). In the Markan parallel, which has no mention of Jonah (no sign at all shall be given), the Matthean redaction adds "except the sign of Jonah," which at that point is left uninterpreted. In the "Q" saying, Luke's version indicates that Jonah himself is a "sign" to the Ninevites, which in Matthew's Gospel receives the additional explanation based on his three days and nights in the fish.

[73]Gk. ὤφθη. There has been considerable discussion as to whether this verb implies a kind of "revelation" or a true "seeing." But most of that discussion is either irrelevant or simply prejudicial (as Kim, *Origin,* p. 55 n. 1, correctly notes of Marxsen's discussion [in *Resurrection,* pp. 98-111]). The form of the creed, which has Christ as the subject throughout, has determined that the verb is passive. While this implies that the initiative was indeed his (therefore, "he appeared"), that does not mean that he was any less visible to those who saw him. See also the discussion in G. O'Collins, *The Resurrection of Jesus Christ* (Valley Forge, 1973), p. 7.

[74]*Contra* E. Güttgemanns, *Der leidende Apostel und sein Herr* (Göttingen, 1966), 53-94, who sees Paul as responding to Gnostics and using *sōma* not so much to emphasize the corporeal nature of the Resurrection as to distinguish between Christ himself and later Christians, since the Gnostics were merging the two into one spiritual reality.

[75]This is true of Mark, Matthew, and John, plus the spurious ending of Mark (cf. 16:9). It is of some interest that this is another point where Luke and Paul correspond.

[76]For Peter see Luke 24:34; for the Twelve see Luke 24:36 (although this could be taken to include more), John 21:19, and Matt. 28:16-17. The spurious ending of Mark (16:9-14) reflects the Mary Magdalene tradition of John's Gospel, the appearance to the two (cf. Luke 24:13-34), and an appearance to "the Eleven."

here called "Cephas," which is *Paul's* usual appellation for him (see on 1:12), one must be cautious as to whether this name was actually in the "tradition" that Paul cites. It may mean, as some have argued,[77] that the tradition ends with the verb "was seen." More likely it means simply that Paul has substituted his own preference for whatever was in the tradition.[78]

One cannot tell whether the addition "then to the Twelve" belonged to the creed itself or whether it is the beginning of Paul's expansion on the final line. In either case, the reference is to an appearance such as that found in John 21:19. The use of the term "the Twelve" is a clear indication that in the early going this was a title given to the special group of twelve whom Jesus called to "be with him" (Mark 3:14). Thus this is their collective designation; it does not imply that all twelve were on hand, since the evidence indicates otherwise. This designation for Jesus' disciples, plus the fact that Paul will later refer to another appearance to "all the apostles" (v. 7), suggests most strongly that the joining of these two terms into the title "the twelve apostles" had not yet taken place in the church. That is, in Paul's view "the Twelve" were a distinct entity, no doubt considered apostles,[79] but the latter designation covered a much larger group of people.[80] The idea that there were only twelve apostles belongs to a later—or different—stratum of Christian tradition.

6 The language of the three additional appearances (vv. 6-7) is so thoroughly Pauline that it seems probable that these items have been added by Paul himself, probably from a different "tradition."[81] By "tradition" one does not here mean another creed, but simply information available to him from whatever source. After all, the clear implication of v. 6 is that the eyewitnesses were around to be consulted, and one would scarcely need some special source for such information. These additional items seem to function in two ways: first, further to emphasize the veracity of the tradition that in Jesus' case a real resurrection was involved; second, to form a bridge

---

[77]See n. 49 above.

[78]In the Lukan account he is called "Simon" (Luke 24:34).

[79]Otherwise Schmithals, *Office,* pp. 73-79, who argues unconvincingly that the language of v. 7, "then to all the apostles," excludes Peter, James, and the Twelve since they would not in Paul's view have been accounted worthy of a second manifestation (p. 79).

[80]Including himself, James (Gal. 1:19), Andronicus and Junia (Rom. 16:7; probably Andronicus and his wife); by implication also Silas and Timothy (1 Thess. 2:7), and Barnabas (Gal. 2:7-9; 1 Cor. 9:5-6).

[81]Not all would agree. Some have suggested the improbable thesis that these reflect two "rival" traditions from Jerusalem (Peter and the Twelve, James and the apostles). See esp. A. Harnack, "Die Verklärungsgeschichte Jesu, der Bericht des Paulus (I. Kor. 15.3ff.) und die beiden Christusvisionen des Petrus," *Sitzungsberichte der Preussischen Akademie der Wissenschaften, philosophisch-historische Klasse* (1922), p. 67; followed by Wilckens, "Ursprung"; Winter, "I Corinthians XV 3b-7," p. 145; Ruef, 160. But see the refutation in Schmithals, *Office,* p. 74.

of tradition between the Twelve and himself, since when he gets to his own experience the concern shifts for a moment from the resurrection of Jesus to Paul's own place in the tradition. The fact that none of these next three enumerations is otherwise known from our available sources is but a reminder that the literature we have from the early church, including the NT documents, is a small collection that at best gives us a slice of the early history, but scarcely anything bordering on the whole picture.

Of the appearance to "more than five hundred of the brothers at the same time"[82] nothing more is known. Probably, as elsewhere in Paul (see on 1:10), the designation "brothers" includes women as well, since it is the unanimous witness of the various traditions that Jesus had women as well as men among his disciples. The adverb "at the same time" can hardly be explained except as an attempt to emphasize the reality and objectivity of this appearance.[83] But beyond that, in terms of time and place, all is speculation.[84]

Everyone agrees that the words "most of whom are still living, although some have fallen asleep," are a Pauline addition. But not all agree as to their significance. The usual understanding is that it functions as a kind of open-ended invitation for the Corinthians to inquire for themselves, as it were, thus putting the emphasis on "most of whom are still living," with a slight note of regret that some have indeed already fallen asleep.[85] Others put the emphasis on "although some have fallen asleep" as a kind of anticipation of the argument that begins in v. 12, implying that the Corinthians who say there is no resurrection of the dead are also asserting that they themselves do not expect to die.[86] But since the latter is not specifically

---

[82]Gk. ἐφάπαξ, which ordinarily, and elsewhere in the NT, means "once for all" (Rom. 6:10; Heb. 7:27; 9:12; 10:10). For this reason P. J. Kearney, "He Appeared to 500 Brothers (I Cor. XV 6)," *NovT* 22 (1980), 264-84, reconstructs vv. 6-7 to read as a doxology: "He appeared above (ἐπάνω) to 500 brothers, once for all to all the apostles." But the suggestion is based on too many congruent improbabilities.

[83]As Murphy-O'Connor ("Tradition," 586) has noted: "A small group of close acquaintances might be accused of self-deception, but this is a much less plausible hypothesis when it is a question of a very large crowd."

[84]Some (e.g., Findlay, 920) have suggested Matt. 28:17, while others have speculated that it is another version of the Pentecost narrative in Acts 2 (E. von Dobschütz, *Ostern und Pfingsten: Eine Studie zu I Korinther 15* [Leipzig, 1903], pp. 33-43; Craig, 218-19; S. M. Gilmour, "The Christophany to More Than Five Hundred Brethren," *JBL* 80 [1961], 248-52). For a feasible reconstruction of such an appearance in Galilee, see E. F. F. Bishop, "The Risen Christ and the Five Hundred Brethren (1 Cor 15,6)," *CBQ* 18 (1956), 341-44.

[85]For this verb as signifying Christian death, see n. 37 on 7:39.

[86]This has become an increasingly popular view. Among others, see Bartsch, "Argumentation," pp. 264-66; Conzelmann, 257-58; Schütz, *Paul*, p. 85; B. Schneider, "The Corporate Meaning and Background of 1 Cor 15,45b—'O ESCHATOS ADAM EIS PNEUMA ZOIOPOIOUN," *CBQ* 29 (1969), 450-67; see also n. 22 on v. 35. See the refutation in Murphy-O'Connor, "Tradition," 586.

brought out in the argument that follows, and since Paul seems to exhibit considerable concern to demonstrate the objective reality of Christ's resurrection, the traditional interpretation is most likely the correct one.

7   Finally, he adds an appearance[87] "to James" and "then to all the apostles," both of which are also unknown elsewhere in the canonical tradition, although an appearance to James is recorded in the apocryphal Gospel of the Hebrews,[88] and Acts 1:6-11 reflects a tradition of several appearances to those who would come to be known as apostles.[89] This James is the Lord's brother, who, along with his other brothers, "did not believe in him" during Jesus' earthly ministry (John 7:2-9) but who appear with the disciples after the Resurrection. At some early stage he became a leader in the church in Jerusalem.[90] Paul's first contact with him occurred on his first brief visit to Jerusalem as a Christian (Gal. 1:19), in which passage he also refers to James as an "apostle."[91]

The final item in the catalogue, "then to all the apostles," is the most puzzling of all, both in terms of who is intended by this designation and of the "event" itself, whether Paul intended a single appearance to all or appearances to each of them.[92] On the second matter, even though there is no "at once" as in v. 6, the enumerating conjunction "then" and the fact that the appearance to the Twelve was collective, not individual, combine to suggest that a collective appearance (probably with a commissioning) is in view here. Moreover, one would expect the apostle to have written "and then to *each* of the apostles," had he intended such.

But whom does Paul understand "all the apostles" to include? There have been three ways of taking this: (a) That it means "then to *all* the apostles," implying that besides the individual appearances to Peter, the Twelve, and James, Jesus appeared again to the entire group who came to be known as apostles, including Peter, etc.;[93] or (b) that it is simply another

---

[87]The verb ὤφθη is repeated in the case of James; some have made a point of this, as though it might indicate the beginning of yet another tradition. But that seems unlikely; the reason for the repetition of the verb is probably related to the length of the aside in v. 6b about the more-than-five hundred. In returning to the enumeration of appearances, the original verb is now at some distance and has been interrupted by v. 6b, so he simply repeats the verb from v. 5, which he will do again in his own case in v. 8 for emphasis.

[88]According to Jerome, *vir.ill.* 2; see HSW, I, 165.

[89]Cf. Findlay, 921.

[90]Cf. Acts 12:17; 15:13; 21:18; see also the corroborating data from Paul (Gal. 1:19; 2:9, 12).

[91]Otherwise Schmithals, *Office,* pp. 73-79, who denies that Paul intended to include either Peter or James as apostles. But it is almost impossible to get around the natural reading of Gal. 1:19, that Paul intended to include James among the apostles, whoever their full number might have been.

[92]See Schmithals, *Office,* pp. 74-79, for a vigorous defense of this point of view.

[93]This is the more common view. See, *inter alia,* Parry, 217; Héring, 162; Grosheide, 352; Barrett, 343; Holladay, 195.

way of speaking of "the Twelve" and refers to a second, commissioning appearance to them;[94] or (c) that it means "then to all the *apostles*," implying that this is yet another group not heretofore mentioned.[95] Although the scheme of enumeration itself tends to favor (c), Paul's usage of the term "apostle" elsewhere, especially in Gal. 1:17-19, implies that both Peter and James were "apostles before him."[96] The further inclusion of John in Gal. 2:1-10 implies that Paul considered him an apostle as well. Therefore, even though there are some difficulties with (a), this probably refers to a tradition similar to that recorded in Acts 1:6-11. Such an appearance would have included Peter, the Twelve, and James, plus a larger group who came to be known as apostles. Most likely this designation, as elsewhere in Paul, is a functional term rather than an official one.[97] Or to put that in another way, "the Twelve" were a definite group who had a special relationship to Jesus and in the early church probably served in some kind of authoritative capacity. But the "apostles," a term that included the Twelve, were a larger group who in Paul's understanding had seen the risen Lord and were commissioned by him to proclaim the gospel and found churches (cf. 9:1-2). They, too, had authority in the churches, especially those they founded, but they scarcely formed a "body" or served as a "council." Their authority was that of ministry rather than jurisdiction.

8 The mention of the appearance to "all the apostles" leads Paul directly to his own experience: "and last of all[98] he appeared to me also, as to one abnormally born."[99] As noted on 9:1, Paul is here referring to his having seen the risen Lord on the Damascus Road, which he did not consider a visionary experience but an actual resurrection appearance of a kind with the others in this series. The sure evidence of that is (a) his actually including his experience in this enumeration, (b) the repetition of the verb "appeared," and (c) the language he uses to describe his inclusion, that it is "last of all" and "as to one abnormally born."

But it is not at all clear what *ektrōma* ("abnormally born") means. Traditionally, it has been understood to mean that Paul recognized his own

---

[94]E.g., R-P, 338; most recently Murphy-O'Connor, "Tradition," 587-89.

[95]See Schmithals, *Office*, pp. 73-79.

[96]See also on 4:9 (n. 47), where by implication Apollos is also included.

[97]See the discussion on 1:1; 9:1; and 12:28 for Paul's usage of this term.

[98]This phrase is somewhat ambiguous. Schütz, *Paul*, pp. 104-06, argues for a nontemporal meaning, comparable to 4:9 (= last of all in the sense of least significant); cf. G. B. Kelley, " 'He Appeared to Me,' " in *Critical History and Biblical Faith* (ed. T. J. Ryan; Villanova, 1979), pp. 108-35, esp. 114. But that will scarcely do here in a context of enumerations. P. R. Jones, "Last Apostle," argues for the meaning "last of all the apostles." This is possible, but it does not seem to be Paul's own emphasis. More likely it is the final link in the chain that began with Peter and means "finally."

[99]The emphasis in Paul's sentence lies on the final phrase, "even to me." Lit. it reads, "And last of all, as to one abnormally born, he appeared even to me."

experience to lie outside the "normal" process. His was a unique and gracious gift that occurred after the time when such appearances were understood to have ceased. This lends credence to the suggestion that the preceding appearance "to all the apostles" refers to the tradition of Christ's appearing to them at the time of the Ascension, which "event" occurred not for his sake, to get him to heaven as it were, but for their sakes, both to enable them to see his ascending to the place of authority at the Father's right hand and to bring to a conclusion the time of resurrection appearances. From that point on, the divine visitation was in their experience of the Spirit. Hence the Risen Lord's appearance to Paul was "as to one abnormally born."

The problem with that view is twofold. First, Paul includes the article with the noun, hence "as to *the ektrōma*"; second, the word literally refers to any kind of premature birth (abortion, stillbirth, or miscarriage).[100] Thus the word comes to be used figuratively to refer to something horrible or "freakish." Since this is such an unusual term of deprecation, and since it occurs with the article, *the* "abortion," it has often been suggested that the Corinthians themselves have used the term to describe Paul, as one who because of his personal weaknesses is something of a "freak" in comparison with other apostles, especially Apollos and Peter.[101] Others have suggested that the term is a play on Paul's name—*Paulus*, "the little one." Hence they dismissed him as a "dwarf."[102] This has the advantage of helping to explain the unusual "digression" in vv. 9-10, where he in fact allows that he is "least" of all the apostles; nonetheless God's grace worked the more abundantly in his behalf.

In any case, whether it originated with them, which seems altogether likely, or with Paul himself in a sudden outburst of self-disparagement, it seems hardly possible to understand this usage except as a term that describes him vis-à-vis the Corinthians' own view of apostleship. That is made more certain by the explanatory digression that follows in vv. 9-10. As we have noted throughout,[103] this tension between him and them over their

---

[100]See, e.g., LXX Job 3:16; Eccl. 6:3; and Num. 12:12, where it reflects the idea of the "ugliness" or "monstrous" nature of such a "birth"; cf. Philo, *leg.all.* 1.76, where the soul of the worthless man is said to bring forth "wretched abortions and miscarriages (ἐκτρώματα)." See the discussion in J. Schneider, *TDNT* II, 465-67.

[101]See, e.g., Weiss, 351-52; Parry, 218; Harnack, "Verklärungsgeschichte," p. 72; Schneider, *TDNT* II, 466; A. Fridrichsen, "Paulus abortivus. Zu 1 Kor. 15,8," in *Symbolae philologicae O. A. Danielsson octogenario dicatae* (Uppsala, 1932), pp. 79-85. Fridrichsen understands it to refer to Paul's pre-Christian life, which seems unlikely.

[102]This is one of the options suggested by J. Munck, "Paulus tamquam abortivus," in *New Testament Essays: Studies in Memory of Thomas Walter Manson* (ed. A. J. B. Higgins; Manchester, 1959), pp. 180-93; and taken up especially by T. Boman, "Paulus abortivus (1. Kor. 15,8)," *ST* 18 (1964), 46-50; and Martin, 92-93

[103]See the Introduction, pp. 6-15. See the commentary on 1:10-17; 2:1-5; 3:5-15; 4:1, 6, 7, 8-13, 14-21; 5:1-13; 8:1; 9:1-17; 10:29-30; 11:17-22; 14:6, 18, 33-38.

activities—and theological justification for them—has also brought about the anti-Pauline sentiment that is in part responsible for their divisions as well as their attitude toward him and his apostleship. As in 4:9-13, he once more goes on the "attack" in this matter by asserting as a value what they would disparage, namely his "untimely birth" or his "dwarf" status as a real "paulus" of an apostle. What they see as weakness and therefore as evidence of a lesser standing, he sees as the true evidence that his apostleship is from the Lord. Thus, in 2 Cor. 10–13 where all this comes to a head, he defends himself once again by glorying in his weaknesses (cf. 1 Cor. 2:1-5 and 9:1-27).

9 With this verse and the next Paul offers an explanation[104] of the self-deprecating words of v. 8, which serve at the same time as an apologetic of his apostleship and especially of his ministry among them. The opening words, "I am the least of the apostles," affirm both that he *is* an apostle and that, as they probably view him, he is the least ranking of them all. As noted above, this is very likely a play on his own name in light of their view of him as something of a "freak." Indeed, he will take them a step further. He does "not even deserve to be called an apostle"—a view many of them probably also held. But his reasons for it would be different from theirs. They have difficulty with his weaknesses and lack of spirituality, as judged by their own criteria.[105] In the earlier passages where he defended his ministry among them he gloried in his weaknesses, through which the power of the Spirit could be manifested (2:1-5; 9:15-18). But his reason here has to do with his former way of life: "because I persecuted the church of God."

Frequently when Paul mentions God's grace in his behalf, he refers to himself in this way (Gal. 1:13-15; Phil. 3:6-8; 1 Tim. 1:13-16).[106] While a persecutor, of course, he thought he was doing God a favor; for him this was "zeal" for the Lord and "advancement" in Judaism. But on this side of his encounter with the risen Lord he saw himself for what he really was, the chief of sinners (1 Tim. 1:15) and persecutor of the church *of God*,[107] thus standing over against God himself and what he was doing in the world through Christ. Out of this encounter comes the basis of his theology of grace. Since God was gracious to him, God's enemy, in this way, he came eventually to realize that this is the way God is toward all, Jew and Gentile

---

[104]Note the explanatory γάρ.

[105]See, e.g., on 1:10-17; 2:1-5; 4:1-5; 13:1; 14:6, 18, 36-38.

[106]Cf. Acts 26:9-11, a paragraph that can scarcely be explained except on the grounds of authentic tradition on the part of Luke.

[107]This is one of the rare instances in Paul's earlier letters where he uses ἡ ἐκκλησία with the qualifier τοῦ θεοῦ to refer to the church in a more universal sense rather than to a local body (cf. Gal. 1:13 and the plural in v. 22). Ordinarily in this kind of context Paul refers to "the churches of God" (cf. 1 Thess. 2:14). Such a usage is at least possible in 10:32 as well. Cf. also the discussion on 12:28.

alike, making no distinctions. Since all alike are sinful, all alike are potential recipients of God's grace. In like manner he views his apostleship. It is a matter of grace, and grace alone. Since they have not given him his authority, they can neither take it from him nor deny it to him. It has been given him by a gracious act of God, which point he will make in the next verse.

10 Paul proceeds to give the reason why he is indeed an apostle: "by the grace of God I am what I am." Although this is true of his being a believer as well, the concern here has to do with his undeserved apostleship. Even though he is admittedly something of an "abortion" and the least of the apostles, Paul is nonetheless an apostle—"by the grace of God." Thus, "grace" in this sentence does not so much refer to God's gracious favor on behalf of sinners, although that is not very far behind, but in a way similar to 1:4 to the concrete expression of that grace in his apostleship. Thus he speaks in the succeeding clauses of God's "grace *to* me"[108] and finally of "the grace of God that was *with* me."[109] In these sentences he makes two points: First, God's grace in his case "was not without effect."[110] That is, it did not become something given "in vain." Most likely this sentence points in two directions. On the one hand, it points back to v. 2 and forward to v. 14, where there is considerable danger that if they persist in their present folly, God's grace to them will have turned out to be "in vain." On the other hand, it points directly to their own existence in Christ; they themselves are the sure evidence that God's grace in terms of Paul's apostleship was not without effect.

Second, although God's gracious gift of apostleship was the result of divine initiative, hence all of grace, nonetheless it required Paul's response. Thus he can also say, "No, I worked harder than all of them,"[111] referring to "the apostles" in v. 9. In Paul's view this is the sentence that balances his being "the least." He is so because he deserved least to be one at all; not only was his birth "untimely" but it turned out that in his former zeal he had been God's avowed enemy. But although least in this sense, he does not consider his work itself to be one whit less than anyone else's. Paul is sometimes given to expansive statements, and "I worked harder than all of them" is one of these. His point, however, is not that of comparison, as if to say "I am better than they because I worked harder." Rather, his concern is to say something about his own ministry as such, including his having come to Corinth with the gospel.[112] To make sure that he is not misunderstood, he

---

[108]Gk. ἡ χάρις αὐτοῦ ἡ εἰς ἐμέ.

[109]Gk. ἡ χάρις τοῦ θεοῦ ἡ σὺν ἐμοί (= "the with-me grace of God").

[110]Gk. κενή (= empty, in vain); cf. the double occurrence in v. 14.

[111]Meaning not all of them together, but any one of them.

[112]That is, it is not referring to his sufferings (e.g., 2 Cor. 11:23-27), but to his continually reaching out to new frontiers with the gospel (cf. 2 Cor. 10:13-17).

quickly qualifies with "yet not I, but the grace of God that was with me."[113] That is, even my intense labors in the gospel are ultimately not the result of a personal need to compensate God for his grace, but are themselves the reflection of that very grace at work in my life. Thus, in Pauline theology, even though his labor is a response to grace, it is more properly seen as the effect of grace. All is of grace; nothing is deserved. Neither therefore can he lay claim to his own ministry nor can they reject it; it is God's activity in him in their behalf.

11 By concluding the considerable enumeration of resurrection appearances with his own, which in turn led to a short digression about his apostleship, Paul's argument has gotten away from him a bit. Not that these things are unimportant—or irrelevant. To the contrary, the enumeration of witnesses is crucial to the argument that will follow and the defense of his apostleship integral to the whole reason for the argument, namely some strong differences between him and them on this matter. But the argument itself has to do with their denial of the resurrection of the dead. To that matter he is about to turn. He does so by coming back to the point of the present paragraph, namely that belief in the resurrection of the dead is predicated first of all on the reality of the resurrection of Christ. His point has been that this is something that they have believed (even if in an unsatisfactory way); it is the foundation of their existence in Christ.

Thus he concludes all these matters (literally): "Therefore, whether I or they, this is what we preach, and this is what you believed." The NIV has missed some subtleties here by putting the opening phrase ("whether I or they") in the past tense. Had this conclusion come directly out of v. 8, as it logically could have, Paul would have said, "Thus we (or I) *preached,* and thus you believed." In the meantime, however, he has made the short excursion through vv. 9-10, so he concludes, "Whether I or they, thus we *preach.*" With these words, therefore, he is not simply identifying the gospel they believed with the creed of vv. 3-5, but he is also tying it both to his own apostleship and to the common preaching of all the apostles—and therefore by implication suggesting that this is the gospel held in common by all who believe in Christ. Once more, therefore, he is pressing on them that their current behavior and theology are out of step with those of the other churches (cf. 1:2; 4:17; 7:17; 11:16; 14:33). Thus, "what they believed" through his preaching when he was among them is the same gospel preached presently by him and by all the apostles. On the matter of their denial of the resurrection, therefore, they are following neither Apollos, nor Cephas, nor Christ; they are simply going off on their own.

---

[113]Cf. Conzelmann, 260: "At once the reference to his own achievement has a brake put on it."

On the basis of this common faith, Paul will next turn to a direct confrontation with the Corinthians over their denial of the resurrection of the dead. The nature of that argument makes it plain that the purpose of this opening paragraph is not to *prove* Christ's resurrection but to reestablish that fundamental premise as the common denominator from which to argue with them, as he will in vv. 12-34. The reason for the catalogue of witnesses is therefore not to prove that Jesus rose but to emphasize that the resurrection of Christ, which they believed, had objective reality.

Unfortunately, in today's church many claim to be believers who deny what for Paul was the same as denying the faith itself. Such a denial meant to believe "for naught." It was the Resurrection after all that made it possible for them to say, "Christ died for our sins." And it was the Resurrection, as he will go on to argue in vv. 20-28, that guarantees our own future as the people of God. To deny the objective reality of Christ's resurrection is to have a faith considerably different from Paul's. One wonders whether such faith is still the *Christian* faith.

On the other hand, there are those who use this passage to try to prove the Resurrection to unbelievers. What they fail to recognize is that such "proofs" are valid only to those who believe. Either one believes the witnesses or one does not. But the resurrection of Christ itself finally lies outside the ordinary categories of historical proof. What one may prove is that *they* believed in the bodily resurrection of Christ, and that such belief took an extraordinary (i.e., miraculous) event in order for it to have come into being. Nonetheless, our calling is to *proclaim* the Resurrection as those who, with Paul, are absolutely convinced of its reality and significance. Such conviction leads also to the proclamation of the gospel itself, the good news that God loves sinners and has made provision through Christ's death and resurrection to overcome their alienation, so that they too may know divine forgiveness and have a sure hope for the future. This, it would seem, is the lasting significance of this argument and its content for today.

2. The Certainty of Resurrection (15:12-34)

Having reasserted the resurrection of Christ as the common ground of all Christian preaching and faith, Paul now moves from that base to refute those who deny the resurrection of the dead. The argument proceeds along two lines, an appeal to logic (vv. 12-28) and an appeal *ad hominem* (vv. 29-34). In each case Paul indicates the logical consequences, and therefore illogical nature, of their position. On the one hand, he argues in vv. 12-19, if they are right that there is no resurrection of the dead, then Christ was not raised, which not only contradicts the common faith of vv. 1-11 but logically means that he and they cease to exist as believers altogether. On the other hand, he continues in vv. 20-28, since Christ is raised from the dead, that means that God has set in motion two irreversibles: the resurrection of all who are "in Christ" (vv. 20-22) and thus the final destruction of death itself (vv. 23-28). Likewise, he goes on in vv. 29-34, if there is no resurrection of the dead, then both they and he are playing the role of fools. Significantly, he concludes this present argument with a strong appeal to them to stop their sinning as well (vv. 33-34).[1]

Thus Paul's concern is to demonstrate from their commonly held position—the resurrection of Christ—both the absurdity of their present position (vv. 12-19) and the splendor of his (vv. 20-28). And in case that is not fully heard, there are always the practical absurdities of both their and his daily lives if there is no resurrection of the dead (vv. 29-34).

a. If Christ is NOT raised (15:12-19)

12 *But if it is preached that Christ has been raised from the dead, how can some of you say that there is no resurrection of the dead?* 13 *If there is no resurrection of the dead, then not even Christ has been raised.* 14 *And if Christ has not been raised, our preaching is useless and so is your[2] faith.* 15 *More than that, we are then found to be false witnesses about God, for we have testified about God that he raised Christ from the dead. But he did not raise him if in fact the dead are not raised.* 16 *For if the dead are not raised, then Christ has not been raised either.* 17 *And if Christ has not been raised, your faith is futile; you are still in your sins.* 18 *Then those who have fallen asleep in Christ are lost.* 19 *If only for this life we have hope in Christ, we are to be pitied more than all* people[3].

With this paragraph the reason for the present argument is stated for the first time: Some of them are saying that there is no resurrection of the dead. With a piece of compelling logic, Paul takes up first the awful consequences of that position by showing how it affects the argument that has just preceded. The logical force of their position is that Christ is not raised from the dead if the dead are not raised (v. 13). The rest of the argument takes up that hypothetical position, that Christ is not raised if the dead are not raised, and

---

[1]J. Lambrecht, "Paul's Christological Use of Scripture in I Cor. 15.20-28," *NTS* 28 (1982), 502-27, sees here another example of the A-B-A' form of argumentation common to this letter (see n. 15 on 1:10-17). This is certainly true of its *form* (e.g., both A-A' are predicated on the hypothetical "if the dead are not raised" [vv. 13, 16, 29, 32]); but the *nature* of the argument itself is considerably different in vv. 29-34 than in the present paragraph.

[2]Several witnesses, including B D* 0243 0270* 6 33 81 1241ˢ 1739 1881 *al* a, read ἡμῶν, an assimilation to the preceding clause, which tends to destroy the structure of the argument. See below.

[3]NIV, "men."

spells out its net results: both his preaching and their believing are to no avail. Paul's point is a simple one: If their present position prevails, they have neither a past nor a future.

The structure of the argument is as follows:[4]

I. Vv. 12-13 represent in chiastic fashion the gospel (A) and their current position (B), followed by the hypothetical allowance of their position (B′) and its logical consequence as to Christ himself (A′):

> A We preach: Christ has been raised from the dead,
>> B Some of you say: there is no resurrection of the dead.
>>> *but*
>> B′   If there is no resurrection of the dead,
> A′   neither has Christ been raised.

II. Vv. 14-16 pick up the hypothetical consequence of A′, indicating its net results (R[1] and R[2]); the point here is that the faith itself is otherwise false:

> A′ *If*   Christ has not been raised,
> R[1] *then* both our preaching
>>   and your believing are to no avail.
> *More than that*[5]
> R[2] we are found to be false witnesses of God,
>> *because*
>> A We bore witness about God, that he raised Christ,
>>> A′ Whom he did not raise,
>>>> B′ If indeed the dead are not raised
>>>> *for*
>>> B′ If   the dead are not raised,
>> A′ not even   Christ has been raised.

III. Vv. 17-19 repeat the hypothetical consequence of A′ and then elaborate R[1], with emphasis on the futility of the effects of their believing:

> A′ *If*   Christ has not been raised,
> R[1] your faith is futile:
>> R[1](a) You (the living) are still in your sins,
>>   *and furthermore*
>> R[1](b) Believers who have died have perished.

---

[4]Schütz, *Paul,* pp. 87-88, suggests a chiastic structure for vv. 13-15; but that tends to treat this much of the argument as a piece while ignoring or minimizing Paul's own structural signals (e.g., the explanatory γάρ in v. 16). Schütz sees the structural key as the phrase "if the dead are not raised." But that clause only leads to the repeated hypothetical "if Christ is not raised" in vv. 14 and 17, which begins both parts of the argument and ties it all together.

[5]Gk. δὲ καί (= but also); see on 14:15.

Conclusion (resulting from R¹[b]):

> If we have hoped in Christ in this life alone, then we are to be pitied above all others. [That is, if we have believed in Christ's resurrection as giving us hope for the future when there is no hope for the future, then we are truly to be pitied.]

By this form of logic, called *modus tollens*,[6] the Corinthians are being forced to agree that there is a future resurrection of believers on the basis of their common faith in the resurrection of Christ. The argument is irrefutable, given their acceptance of Christ's resurrection and its effects in their lives. Hence the significance of vv. 1-11.

12 An adversative "but" contrasts the preceding argument, "It is preached[7] that Christ[8] is raised from the dead" (vv. 1-11), with their present position, "Some of you say there is no resurrection of the dead."[9] The present contrast takes the form of a question: How is it in light of what has just been said that some of you now say . . . ? Although this is the position of only "some among you," most likely the "some" are the same as those in 4:18 and elsewhere (e.g., 9:3) who have had a significant influence within the community and are responsible for its prevailing anti-Pauline sentiment.

Even though in vv. 1-11 Paul did not use the language that Christ was raised "from the dead,"[10] this is in fact what he intended and is his regular way of speaking of Christ's resurrection.[11] Thus, as the creed says, Christ died and was buried, and as Paul regularly says, he was also raised *from the*

---

[6]See the series of articles by T. C. Bucher: "Die logische Argumentation in 1. Korinther 15,12-20," *Bib* 55 (1974), 465-86; "Auferstehung Christi und Auferstehung der Toten," *MTZ* 27 (1976), 1-32; "Nochmals zur Beweisführung in 1. Korinther 15,12-20," *TZ* 36 (1980), 129-52; "Allgemeine überlegungen zur Logik im Zusammenhang mit 1 Kor 15,12-20," *LingBib* 53 (1983), 70-98. Cf. the responses by M. Bachmann, "Zur Gedankenführung in 1. Kor. 15,12ff.," *TZ* 34 (1978), 265-76; and "Rezeption von 1. Kor. 15 (V. 12ff.) unter logischem und unter philologischem Aspekt," *LingBib* 51 (1982), 79-103. Bachmann agrees with Bucher as to the mode of logic; he disagrees, rightly it would seem, that Paul's argument is not for a general resurrection (as Bucher), but for the particular resurrection of the believing dead. The other concern is simply not in Paul's purview.

[7]Greek present, κηρύσσεται (= it is being continually preached by all).

[8]Lit., "if Christ is preached, that he is raised." As Findlay, 922, notes, "The preaching of Christ *is* the preaching *of His resurrection*."

[9]On the possible background and nature of their position see the introduction to the chapter (pp. 715-17). That this represents a thoroughly Greek view of the world, see Aeschylus, *Eumenides* 647-48: (in the mouth of Apollo) "When the dust hath drained the blood of a man, once he is slain, there is no resurrection (ἀνάστασις)" (Loeb, p. 335, adapted); cf. *Agamemnon* 1360; Herodotus 3.62; Sophocles, *Electra* 137.

[10]Gk. ἐκ νεκρῶν.

[11]Cf. 1 Thess. 1:10; Gal. 1:10; Rom. 1:4; 4:24; 6:4, 9; 8:11 (twice), 34; 10:9; Col. 1:18; 2:12; Eph. 1:20; 2 Tim. 2:8.

dead, referring not to his being raised from death itself[12] but from among those who have died. The Corinthians' position, "There is no resurrection of the dead," means that the dead do not rise, implying both that those who are currently dead and those who shall yet die will not have a future existence that involves their present *bodily* form. Thus they are not denying that they shall die, nor is Paul arguing that people *must* die in order to be raised, as some have argued.[13] The problem for the Corinthians is with *the dead* and their *rising,* that the dead have a future existence in some somatic form— probably from their point of view taken literally to mean the reanimation of a corpse to continue bodily existence in its *present* form. Paul himself will go on to reject that view (vv. 42-50); but before he does so he must affirm the reality of resurrection itself, including the implicit fact that it is "bodily."

13 Paul now sets out to show how their premise would affect the preaching of vv. 1-11. "For the sake of argument," he is suggesting, "let's allow that your position is correct, that there is no resurrection of the dead." That logically means, he argues, that no one has or ever will rise from the dead, which means that "not even[14] Christ has been raised."[15] This may possibly mean that a general repudiation of the resurrection would thereby render a single instance to be impossible; more likely Paul already has in mind the causal connection between Christ's resurrection and that of believers. That is, to deny the resurrection of the dead is to deny the resurrection of the one who makes any and all resurrections possible.[16] At this point, however, Paul chooses not to refute their position on the basis of vv. 1-11, that is, since Christ has been raised, as he preached and they believed, there must be a resurrection of the dead. That will come in vv. 20-28. Rather, he chooses first to show the further logical consequences of their position, which he takes up in the rest of the paragraph.

14 The hypothetical allowance of their position in v. 13 concluded

[12]As Parry, 219, e.g., suggests. Cf. the data in Conzelmann, 265 n. 16, including the evidence there that νεκρός without the article means "the dead."

[13]See nn. 6 and 86 on 15:1-11. Cf., e.g., Conzelmann, 258, 262-63; Schütz, *Paul,* pp. 85-93; Martin, 95. The argument for the transformation of the living in vv. 50-53 seems to stand quite against this view, not to mention the fact that the problem the Corinthians would have had with resurrection is the implication of a future bodily existence inherent in the idea of resurrection itself. Furthermore, some of their number have in fact already died (11:30) and they do not seem to be concerned as to what happened to them.

[14]Gk. οὐδέ (= not either) for the NIV's "not even" (see also NASB, Montgomery; cf. NAB, "Christ himself has not been raised" [cf. JB]). R-P, 347, reject this translation as misleading.

[15]Greek perfect, and throughout. See n. 64 on v. 4. The emphasis seems to fluctuate between the past event, "was raised," and its present reality, "is raised."

[16]So R-P, 347, and Conzelmann, 265 n. 18. Otherwise, M. Dahl, 25-26.

that if they are right, then he and all the apostles are wrong: Neither has Christ been raised. That apodosis now becomes the hypothetical premise for the rest of the argument. "But if Christ has not been raised, then,[17]" he argues, what was hinted at in vv. 1-2 has come to pass: literally, "empty (without basis)[18] [is] our preaching; empty (without basis) also is your believing."[19] Both his preaching that led to their faith and their faith itself are to no avail. Paul will elaborate the second item, the futility of their faith in terms of its effects, in vv. 17-19; for now the emphasis lies on the futility or baselessness of his preaching.

It is not certain what Paul intends by "our preaching,"[20] whether he is pointing to the content of the preaching given in vv. 3-7 and suggesting that it has no foundation whatever if Christ is not raised, or whether he is pointing to the futility of their preaching as an activity since it has no basis in truth. Perhaps here it is a case of both-and since both are equally true. In either case it comes out at the same point, having the net effect that "their believing is therefore also to no avail" since it is based on preaching that has been divested of its content—if they are right.

15-16 Paul elaborates. The logical conclusion of their position (v. 12), with its consequence that Christ is not raised (v. 13), is not only that Paul's and the other apostles' preaching (v. 11) is to no avail (v. 14), but that it turns out to be a lie. If the fact itself is untrue, then the testimony to the fact is equally untrue. Even worse, it is a lie carried out in God's name, so that by implication their denial of the resurrection of the dead finally implicates God himself: "More than that (i.e., what is said in v. 14)," Paul says, "we are also found[21] to be false witnesses of God, because we have borne witness against God[22] by saying that he raised Christ[23] from the dead, whom he did not raise, if indeed the dead are not raised." Although it is possible that the genitive "of God" is objective (= we are false witnesses about what God did or did not do), it is also possible that it is possessive (= we are bearing false witness in God's name, as those sent from God). The causal

---

[17]Gk. ἄρα, frequently used in the apodosis of unreal conditional sentences to strengthen the "if . . . then" inference (in Paul see Gal. 2:21; 3:29).

[18]Gk. κενόν; cf. v. 10.

[19]The two nouns κήρυγμα and πίστις refer back to the verbs in v. 11 ("we preach" and "you believed").

[20]Gk. κήρυγμα; see on 1:21 and 2:4.

[21]Gk. εὑρισκόμεθα, the implication being that they are "found out" to be false witness.

[22]Gk. κατὰ τοῦ θεοῦ. Although there is evidence that this preposition can mean "about," that seems unnecessary since the ordinary meaning of "witnessing against" makes sense here.

[23]Here "Christ" has the article; perhaps it is anaphoric (= the Christ of whom we are speaking). More likely the title is always implied in the name. Hence "Christ the Messiah."

clause that follows tends to support the former: "because we have borne witness against God that he raised Christ from the dead" (= we have accused God falsely of doing something he did not in fact do, if the Corinthians are right). Since for Paul Christ's resurrection is not his (Christ's) own doing, but God's vindication of the work of the Son, that means that a denial of the resurrection of the dead leads ultimately to a denial of the gospel altogether and levels an accusation against God himself that he did what in fact he did not do—if they are correct.[24]

But more significantly, the final two clauses in v. 15, "whom he did not raise, if in fact[25] the dead are not raised," repeat the argument, if not the precise language, of v. 13, which is then further reinforced in v. 16 by yet another, this time almost verbatim, repetition of v. 13.[26] By thus bringing the argument back to their position with regard to the resurrection of the dead, Paul seems to be implying that ultimately the false witness against God is to be laid not at the apostles' feet but at the feet of those who deny the resurrection.

17-18 Just as v. 16 repeats v. 13, so the opening clause in this sentence repeats the hypothetical protasis that begins v. 14: "If Christ is not raised." The apodosis in this case picks up the last clause of v. 14 ("empty is your believing") in order to elaborate on it. By the change of adjectives with which the clause now begins,[27] Paul emphasizes the utter futility of their own situation if their basic premise is correct. The futility of their "faith" has to do with both the living and the dead.

First, as to themselves (the living), "you are still in your sins." If Christ is not raised, there is no longer any possibility of saying, "Such *were* some of you, but now you are washed, etc." (6:11). The reason for quoting the creed in full in vv. 3-5 now comes into sharper focus. The denial of their future, that they are destined for resurrection on the basis of Christ's resurrection, has the net effect of a denial of their past, that they have received forgiveness of sins on the basis of Christ's death. As in Rom. 4:25 and 5:10, the death of Jesus as "for us," including both justification and sanctifica-

---

[24]Even more than in vv. 5-8, this clause stands as the strongest kind of evidence that Paul believed in the Resurrection as an objectively verifiable reality. He simply would not have understood the double-talk of Christian existentialism, which affirms "resurrection language" theologically but denies that anything actually happened as an event in history.

[25]Gk. ἄρα; see on v. 14.

[26]The two sentences read:

v. 13 εἰ δὲ ἀνάστασις νεκρῶν οὐκ ἔστιν,
οὐδὲ Χριστὸς ἐγήγερται·

v. 16 εἰ γὰρ νεκροὶ οὐκ ἐγείρονται,
οὐδὲ Χριστὸς ἐγήγερται·

[27]From κενή ("empty") to ματαία ("useless, futile").

tion, is inextricably bound together with his resurrection. To deny the one is to deny the other. Thus, as hinted at in v. 2, Paul is urging that their present position with regard to the resurrection means that they cease to be believers altogether. This, of course, is a *reductio ad absurdum;* since their experience is otherwise, he expects them to read the logic in reverse and admit therefore that there must be a resurrection of the dead.

Second, "Indeed,[28] also those who have fallen asleep[29] in Christ [i.e., those who were believers when they died (cf. 11:30)] are lost."[30] It is crucial to note that this clause is a continuation of v. 17. The net result of the Corinthian position is that the dead in Christ, those who at the time of their death had put their hope in Christ, have in fact "perished" because, as with the living, they were still in their sins when they died. In saying that they "have perished" Paul means that there is for them no future of any kind. Because they would thus have died in their sins, they perish along with the rest of fallen humanity.

Such a conclusion probably stands directly over against that of the Corinthians. Although they have denied that there is a resurrection of the dead, it is unlikely, in light of their baptizing for "the dead" in v. 29, that they also thought there was no future for people who have died. Most likely in their view the believing dead have simply shed their bodies (cf. 6:13) so as to have entered into the final spiritual (heavenly) existence.[31] Not so, says Paul, they have perished; they have no future at all. For if Christ did not rise, which he did not if they are correct, then there is no provision for sins, and believers who have "fallen asleep" have died in their sins. Thus Paul's point is that to deny the resurrection of the dead is not only to deny one's past but finally to deny any real future as well. Thus the whole Corinthian existence, past, present, and future, has come to nothing, if they are correct.

19 This verse adds a final addendum to the point of vv. 17-18 and flows especially from the conclusion reached in v. 18. But the precise nuance of the protasis is not easy to determine. Literally it reads, "If in this life in Christ we are those who hoped[32] only." Does the "only" modify the phrase "in this life" (NIV), or more specifically the verb itself, emphasizing that in this life we have only hoped in Christ but with no real future? More likely it is the former since "hope" is always a positive term in Paul's extant letters and the second option makes it somewhat negative. This way of

---

[28]Yet another inferential γάρ (see vv. 14, 15); this time it "is used to emphasize a further result, and continues the apodosis of vs. 17" (BAGD).

[29]For this verb, see above on v. 6.

[30]Gk. ἀπώλοντο; cf. 1:18.

[31]So also Gundry, 170.

[32]Gk. ἠλπικότες ἐσμέν; there is some debate as to whether this is a periphrastic perfect (= we have hoped) or a copula with a participle functioning as a substantive (= we are people who have hoped; cf. Weiss, "we are hopers"). This tends to have significance only if μόνον is understood to modify the verb.

stating it, however, has given some later generations difficulty since it is often understood to imply that Christian faith is interested only in life in the future, or that somehow the Christian life is a mean existence at best, so there had better be a future reward; otherwise it was terribly unkind of God to exact such payment, promise reward, and then have none to offer.

Paul's point, however, is other than this, and embraces the reality of v. 17 as well as of v. 18. It is still based on the hypothetical protasis that began v. 17. By believing in Christ's death and resurrection, we (meaning both he and they) have placed our trust in Christ to forgive us our sins. But if Christ is not raised from the dead, that means we not only do not have present forgiveness but have lost our hope for the future as well. And if we have believed in the future when there is no future, then of all human beings we are the most to be pitied—not because Christian existence is interested only in the future, but because the loss of the future means the loss of the past and present as well.

Both this final sentence and the whole argument of this paragraph are especially troublesome to those within the Christian faith who have done what is here only hypothetical for the Corinthians—denied Christ's resurrection and thus ours as well. There seems to be little hope of getting around Paul's argument, that to deny Christ's resurrection is tantamount to a denial of Christian existence altogether. Yet many do so—to make the faith more palatable to "modern man," we are told. But that will scarcely do. What modern man accepts in its place is no longer the Christian faith, which predicates divine forgiveness through Christ's death on his resurrection. Nothing else is the Christian faith, and those who reject the actuality of the resurrection of Christ need to face the consequences of such rejection, that they are bearing false witness against God himself. Like the Corinthians they will have believed in vain since the faith is finally predicated on whether or not Paul is right on this issue.

On the other hand, the word for those who accept Christ's resurrection as reality is a blessed one indeed. It includes not only the forgiveness of sins, and therefore fullness of life in the present, but it also means a glorious future, including a resurrection like Christ's. Since Christ is indeed raised from the dead, neither our faith nor our preaching is in vain—which is the point Paul will proceed to make next.

b. But Christ IS raised (15:20-28)

20 *But Christ has indeed been raised from the dead, the firstfruits of those who have fallen asleep.[1] 21 For since death came through a*

---

[1]The MajT (followed by the KJV) added an ἐγένετο, thus making two clauses ("and become the firstfruits").

man, the resurrection of the dead comes also through a man. 22 *For as in Adam all die, so in Christ all will be made alive.* 23 *But each in his own turn: Christ, the firstfruits; then, when he comes, those who belong to him.* 24 *Then the end will come, when he hands over the kingdom to God the Father after he has destroyed all dominion, authority and power.* 25 *For he must reign until he has put all his enemies under his feet.* 26 *The last enemy to be destroyed is death.* 27 *For he "has put everything under his feet."* [a] *Now when it says that "everything" has been put under him, it is clear that this does not include God himself, who put everything under Christ.* 28 *When he has done this, then*[2] *the Son himself will be made subject to him who put everything under him, so that God may be all in all.*

[a]Psalm 8:6

In the preceding paragraph Paul attempted to show the irresponsibility of their arguing that there is no resurrection of the dead by pointing out the consequences, if they are right, in terms of their own existence. But since all of that was hypothetical, Paul now turns to demonstrate that Christ's resurrection, which both he and they believe (vv. 1-11), has made the resurrection of the dead both necessary and inevitable.

In order to understand how this is so, and therefore also the logic of the present argument, one must keep in mind two realities about Paul's theological outlook: (1) Whatever else, Paul's thinking is thoroughly eschatological.[3] He understood both the death and resurrection of Christ and the subsequent gift of the Spirit as eschatological realities. That is, he recognized that in those events God had set in motion the events of the End in such a way that they must of divine necessity be brought to consummation. The absolutely crucial matter in this view is the resurrection of Jesus from the dead. In Paul's Jewish eschatological heritage resurrection belonged to the final events of the End.[4] The fact that *the* Resurrection had already taken place within history meant that the End had been set inexorably in motion; the resurrection of Christ absolutely guaranteed for Paul the resurrection of all who are "in Christ." This is the point he makes in vv. 20-22, using the metaphor of firstfruits and the Adam-Christ analogy.

(2) As noted above (vv. 4, 15), it is basic to Paul's view of things that

---

[2]Most MSS have a καί following τότε (= even the Son himself); it is missing in B D* F G 0243 33 1175 1739 pc b cop. Although this one could go either way, more likely the shorter text is original (the addition is easily explained as intensifying the point of the text; independent and early omission is less easy to account for).

[3]For this matter in 1 Corinthians see especially on 4:1-5; 6:1-11; 7:29-31.

[4]On this see G. E. Ladd, *I Believe in the Resurrection of Jesus* (Grand Rapids, 1975), pp. 51-59.

Christ did not rise from the dead, but that God raised him. Therefore, the inevitable chain of events set in motion by Christ's resurrection has ultimately to do with God's own absolute authority over *all things,* especially death.[5] For Paul, Christ's resurrection and ascension mean that Christ now rules (v. 25); but it is also clear that despite his rule the enemy is still at work since people still die. Thus for Paul there is a divine necessity to the resurrection of the dead since that alone is the evidence of the final overthrow of the last enemy, death itself. Christ's resurrection, therefore, also set in motion the defeat of death, the final form of which is the overpowering of its stranglehold on humanity in the form of resurrection. When that occurs, that is, when the final enemy is thus defeated through resurrection, then God becomes "all in all."

This is the point of vv. 23-28,[6] which are not a digression, as some have suggested, nor an apocalyptic working out of the chronology of resurrection.[7] Rather, they are crucial to the whole argument: Christ's resurrection demands our resurrection; otherwise death is never defeated and God cannot be "all in all." Thus the concern is ultimately theological; not just the death of individuals concerns Paul here, but death itself as the final enemy of God and his sovereign purposes in the universe.[8] The work of Christ is therefore the key to everything, both the resurrection of believers, set in motion by his own resurrection, and at the same time through that resurrection the consummation of the "saving acts of God," including the utter defeat of all of God's enemies.

Thus, in a passage of "epic grandeur,"[9] Paul responds to the Corinthians' denial of the resurrection of the dead. Their form of spirituality, which allows such a denial, stems not only from a false view of the nature of

---

[5]This emphasis on God's sovereignty, including the work and rule of Christ, is found in the repetition of πᾶς/πάντες in vv. 24-28 (ten times); Christ destroys *every* dominion and *every* authority and power (v. 24); he rules until he has placed *all* his enemies under his feet (v. 25); he subjects *all* things to Christ (vv. 27-28), so that God might be *all* in *all.* Cf. G. Barth, "Erwägungen zu 1. Korinther 15,20-28," *EvT* 30 (1970), 515-27, esp. 523.

[6]Some suggest that Paul's purpose in these verses is to assert the reality of the *future* vis-à-vis the Corinthians' overrealized eschatology. See, e.g., Lincoln, 38; Martin, 112-13; Güttgemanns, *Apostel,* pp. 70-77; G. Barth, "Erwägungen," p. 521. This may be so, but as an urgency it does not arise in the actual statements of the text itself. So also Lambrecht, "Christological Use," p. 515.

[7]So K. Barth, *Resurrection,* p. 150; Grosheide, 364; and in effect Barrett (by making vv. 1-22 one paragraph and vv. 23-28 another). On the other side, see W. Dykstra, "I Corinthians 15:20-28, an Essential Part of Paul's Argument Against Those Who Deny the Resurrection," *CTJ* 4 (1969), 195-211; and G. Barth, "Erwägungen."

[8]Cf. J. D. McCaughey, "The Death of Death (I Cor. 15:26)," in *Reconciliation and Hope, New Testament Essays on Atonement and Eschatology* (ed. R. Banks; Grand Rapids, 1974), pp. 246-61.

[9]The words are Parry's (p. 222).

humanity but also from a less than adequate view of God as the sovereign Lord of history.

20 This opening sentence of affirmation picks up the theme of vv. 1-11, in the language of v. 12 ("Christ has been/is raised from the dead"); at the same time both the content ("the firstfruits of those who have fallen asleep") and the introductory "but, as a matter of fact"[10] make it clear that it stands in contrast to the twice repeated hypothetical clauses in vv. 14 and 17, especially the latter, to which this sentence stands as the logical response: "If Christ is not raised, as the logical consequence of your present position requires, then the further consequence is disaster for both the living and the dead. Believers are still in their sins and the dead in Christ have perished." In contrast to that Paul asserts, "But as it is, Christ has indeed been raised from the dead, the firstfruits of those (mentioned in v. 18) who have fallen asleep."[11] The point of course is that those who have fallen asleep *in Christ* (v. 18) will not perish, but are destined for resurrection.

This is the final mention of Christ's resurrection in the argument, but everything that follows is predicated on it. Paul's present concern is to demonstrate not only that the resurrection of Christ stands logically against their view that there is no resurrection of the dead (vv. 12-19), but that his resurrection has inherent in it that which makes the resurrection of the believing dead inevitable.[12] He does this first by calling Christ the "firstfruits[13] of those who have fallen asleep."[14] Although this term has a rich OT

---

[10]Gk. νυνὶ δέ (NIV, "indeed"; the translation is that of BAGD); see the discussion on 12:18 and esp. 13:13. Although this is a logical νυνὶ δέ, it underscores the point made in 13:13 that this combination is never without a temporal sense. Here by way of emphatic contrast it expresses the way things really are at the present moment (cf. BAGD: "introducing the real situation after an unreal conditional clause or sentence"). Hence, "but as it is . . . indeed." That overloads the adverb somewhat, but it helps to keep both the logical and temporal force of the word.

[11]This tie to v. 18 is missed by Conzelmann, 268, who suggests that Paul purposely does not say "the first of those who have been raised, but: of those who have fallen asleep," his point being that Paul is thus emphasizing the necessity of death before resurrection.

[12]Thus it does not seem quite precise to call this a christological apology, as does G. L. Borchert, "The Resurrection: 1 Corinthians 15," *RevExp* 80 (1983), 407-09.

[13]Gk. ἀπαρχή; cf. 16:15; 2 Thess. 2:13 (for several reasons, almost certainly the original text; see Metzger, 636-37); Rom. 8:23; 11:16; 16:5. On the usage see G. Delling, *TDNT* I, 484-86, and esp. R. Murray, "New Wine in Old Wineskins XII. Firstfruits," *ExpT* 86 (1975), 164-68.

[14]On this verb see on v. 6; here in particular Paul's consistent use of this verb to refer to believers who have died comes into focus. Not all who have died (ἀποθνήσκω, v. 22) are raised to life in Christ, but only those who have fallen asleep in him. Cf. J. C. Bowmer, "A Note on ἀποθνήσκω and κοιμάω in I Corinthians 15:20, 22," *ExpT* 53 (1941/42), 355-56. This distinction, of course, is denied by those who see πάντες in v. 22 as referring to a general resurrection, or to a resurrection in two stages. See n. 19 below.

history,[15] Paul's interest is not in its biblical overtones,[16] which have to do with consecrating the firstfruits of the harvest to God (cf. Lev. 23:9-14), but in its function as a metaphor for the first of the harvest serving as a kind of guarantee for the full harvest. In his usage, therefore, the metaphor functions similarly to that of the "down payment" or "earnest money" of the Spirit in 2 Cor. 1:22 and 5:5 (cf. Eph. 1:14); both serve as a present pledge on the part of God for the final eschatological harvest or payment. Thus the Thessalonians (2 Thess. 2:13) and the household of Stephanas (1 Cor. 16:15) are the "firstfruits" in a given geographical area, which means not only that they are the first converts but the first of a much larger harvest that is yet to be realized. So too with Christ. He is God's "firstfruits," God's own pledge that there will be a full harvest of those who will be raised from the dead. By calling Christ the "firstfruits," Paul is asserting by way of metaphor that the resurrection of the believing dead is absolutely inevitable; it has been guaranteed by God himself.[17]

21-22   With these two sentences Paul proceeds to explain further[18] the metaphor of v. 20 and its inherent implication of the inevitability of the resurrection of the believing dead. The two sentences are set forth in perfect double parallelism, the first (v. 21) explaining by way of analogy how God's raising Christ as "firstfruits" makes the resurrection of the believing dead an inevitable concomitant, the second (v. 22) further elaborating v. 21 so that its point cannot be missed. Thus:

> *for* (explaining how Christ's being firstfruits leads inevitably to the
>   resurrection from the dead)
>
> Since through a man,   death,
>   also   through a man, the resurrection of the dead;
>
> *for* (explaining how so)
>
> Just as in Adam   all die,
>   so also in Christ   all will be made alive.

It must be noted at the outset that the general resurrection of the dead is not Paul's concern, neither here nor elsewhere in the argument.[19] Both the

---

[15]On this see Murray (n. 13), pp. 164-66.

[16]So also Conzelmann, 267.

[17]Martin, 110 (cf. Conzelmann, 268), sees the metaphor as partly polemical, that *only* Christ is thus far raised. But that seems doubtful since their proposition (v. 12) does not imply that a form of resurrection has already taken place (one places far too much confidence in one's interpretation of the very obscure v. 29 to suggest that it is found there), but that resurrection (which would always mean, for them, "bodily") does not happen.

[18]Both sentences begin with an explanatory γάρ.

[19]*Contra*, e.g., R. D. Culver, "A Neglected Millennial Passage from St. Paul," *BibSac* 113 (1956), 141-52; W. B. Wallis, "The Problem of an Intermediate Kingdom in

context and Paul's theology as a whole make it clear that in saying "in Christ all will be made alive," he means "in Christ all *who are in Christ* will be made alive."[20] The lack of such a qualifier in the sentence itself is the result of both the balanced style and the fact that he expected it to be read in the context of his argument with them, not as a piece of abstract theology. In the present context these two sentences are still part of his response to vv. 17-19, begun in v. 20. In v. 18 Paul referred to "those who have fallen asleep in Christ," making it certain that even that paragraph was concerned only with the resurrection of believers. In v. 20 he asserts the inevitability of their resurrection by calling Christ the "firstfruits of those who have fallen asleep," meaning those mentioned in v. 18. The present Adam-Christ analogy is thus a further attempt to show how Christ's resurrection makes inevitable the resurrection of those who have fallen asleep *in Christ.*[21]

This is the first use of the Adam-Christ analogy in Paul's extant letters.[22] He will pick it up again, but in a different way, in vv. 45-49, as well as in Rom. 5:12-21. His varied use of this theme suggests that it is a commonplace with Paul, for whom Christ stands at the beginning of the new

---

1 Corinthians 15:20-28," *JETS* 18 (1975), 229-42. The latter in particular (p. 234) argues that if a portion of Adam's race is left permanently in death, then Paul's argument is incomplete. But that is to put one's own logic ahead of Paul's concerns. There can be *no* question that his concern is with the resurrection of believers; this is clearly stated in the words "then those who are his"; had he shown a similar interest in all the dead, one might expect that also to be explicit, not something that one must find by means of several circuitous exercises in what one deems to be "logical" for Paul.

The difficulties with this view are several and insuperable. It requires (a) that Christ be the firstfruits even of the perishing; (b) that "those who have fallen asleep in Christ" (v. 18) include the perishing, since that is the point picked up in v. 20; (c) that the verb "shall be made alive" be a synonym for resurrection rather than having to do with "life" itself; (d) that the Adam-Christ analogy have nothing to do with the creation of a new humanity, but have to do strictly with death and resurrection. Furthermore, it runs aground on the parallel in vv. 50-57, where the swallowing up of death in victory is limited strictly to the resurrection/transformation of believers.

[20]This is the usual view since it alone fits the context. Cf. the discussion in W. V. Crockett, "The Ultimate Restoration of all Mankind: 1 Corinthians 15:22," in *Studia Biblica 1978: III. Papers on Paul and Other New Testament Authors* (ed. E. A. Livingstone; Sheffield, 1980), pp. 83-87, who despite the title also argues for this view.

[21]Cf. the similar expression in 1 Thess. 4:16, "the dead in Christ shall rise first." This does not mean that Christians who have died will be raised before all others, but that *the dead* who are Christians will rise as the first item on the eschatological agenda, after which *the living* who are Christians will be caught up with them. There is simply no interest of any kind in these passages in a general resurrection of the dead, or in a final raising to life in Christ of those who are not his. Prior theological commitments in this case have created some strange bedfellows, e.g., dispensationalists and universalists, who for radically different reasons want Christ's resurrection to be the firstfruits of all human beings.

[22]Conzelmann, 268, is representative of many who see Paul as using a "mythical schema" of a "primal man"; but since the sources for this schema are of doubtful value as

humanity in a way analogous to, but not identical with, the way Adam[23] stood at the beginning of the old order, both temporally and causally. Paul's interest here is twofold: (a) in death and the overthrow of death through resurrection—the motif that will dominate the rest of the argument, and (b) in the *human* mediation of both death and life, and therefore in the genuine humanity of Christ. Whatever the Corinthians may have believed about Christ's resurrection, it cannot be argued to be of a different order because he was divine. Rather, just as death, so resurrection is *through a man*.

Thus the analogy begins by stating that "death came through a man." Paul's point is that death is inevitable because of our sharing in the humanity and sinfulness of the one man, Adam. But believers' sharing in the resurrection from the dead through the second Man, Christ, who in his resurrection effected the reversal of the process begun in Adam, is equally inevitable. That this is Paul's intent is made clear by the second set of clauses, which explain how the first set works out in fact. In saying that "all die in Adam," Paul means that this common lot of our humanity is the result of our being "in Adam," that is, being born of his race and thereby involved in the sin and death that proceeded from him (cf. Rom. 5:12-14, 18-19). In saying that "in Christ all will be made alive," Paul means that those who are "in Christ," those who have entered the new humanity through grace by means of his death and resurrection, will just as certainly "be made alive"[24]; they will be raised from the dead into the *shared life* of the risen One. Thus Christ is the firstfruits; he is God's pledge that all who are his will be raised from the dead. The inevitable process of death begun in Adam will be reversed by the equally inevitable process of "bringing to life" begun in Christ. Therefore, it is not possible for the Corinthians to say there is no resurrection of the dead. Such a resurrection is necessitated by Christ's.

23-24 Although the preceding analogy was expressed in terms of Adam and Christ, Paul is less concerned with the outworking of this analogy per se (which he will pick up again in vv. 45-49) than he is with the *fact* that Christ's resurrection makes absolutely necessary the resurrection of believers from the dead. What lies behind Paul's reasoning here is the ongoing

---

saying anything about Paul's own milieu, and since Conzelmann himself admits that Paul has modified it (radically, one might add), one wonders about the exegetical usefulness of such language. Cf. J. Gillman, "Transformation into the Future Life. A Study of 1 Cor. 15:50-53, its Context and Related Passages" (unpub. Ph.D. diss.; Catholic University, Leuven, 1980), pp. 314-15, cited by Lambrecht, "Christological Use," p. 516.

[23]Although Paul's stress is on the common humanity all share in Adam, there can be little question that he considered Adam to be a real person in the same sense as Christ.

[24]Gk. ζωοποιηθήσονται (cf. vv. 36, 45). This verb is used instead of ἐγείρω because it offers the proper contrast with ἀποθνῄσκω; it is difficult, however, to escape the conclusion that the nuance "to give life to" means more than simply the resuscitation of a corpse. They rise to "life" because they already have been given "life" in Christ.

reality of death. Through the Fall Adam began the process of *death* (note that emphasis in both vv. 21 and 22); that process has now been overturned through the Resurrection, which means that by raising Christ from the dead God has in fact triumphed over death. The problem is that despite Christ's resurrection (= triumph over death), believers still die. Hence they *must* be raised, (a) because they are "in Christ," who is already raised, and (b) only so will death, the last enemy, finally be subdued, so that through the work of Christ God will finally be "all in all." The argument in the rest of this paragraph makes it clear that this is Paul's real concern.

In these two verses (a single sentence in Greek) he begins by setting forth the "order" of events that leads to "the End." At that time[25] Christ will do two things: (1) "he [will] hand over the kingdom (reign)[26] to God the Father"; and (2) "he [will] bring to an end all dominion and all authority and power." As the rest of the argument indicates, these two items logically occur in reverse order (hence the NIV's "after he has destroyed").[27] In Paul's sentence, however, they are coordinate and without a conjunction; most likely he intended them to be in double apposition to "the end." Thus the whole sentence looks like this:

But[28] each in his/its own order:
    (1)   the firstfruits, Christ;
    (2) Then   at the Parousia
             those who belong to him;
    (3) Then the end (= the goal):
        (A) When he hands over the kingdom to God the Father,
        (B) When he brings to an end all other dominions.

Some have seen this as slightly discursive from the argument in the interest of spelling out a Jewish (now Christian) apocalyptic scheme about the end times;[29] but in fact it is both relevant and crucial to the argument, and has little to do with apocalypticism.[30] Paul's concern is singular: to demon-

---

[25]Both clauses begin with the indefinite ὅταν, indicating a future reality whose time is not known. Cf. the similar use in 13:10; 15:27, 28, 54.

[26]Gk. βασιλεία, the noun for "the kingdom of God." Its cognate verb βασιλεύω appears in the next sentence by way of further explanation as to what this means. Hence the need to use a cognate noun and verb in English ("reign") to make this clear.

[27]It is often suggested that this is also inherent in the use of the aorist in the second clause; but that runs aground grammatically, and in any case is unnecessary since the succeeding context makes this perfectly plain.

[28]Gk. δέ, here slightly adversative to "all shall be made alive."

[29]See n. 7 above.

[30]Here is a case of the loose use of language, where "apocalyptic" and "eschato-logical" tend to become synonyms. What little might be considered apocalyptic in this passage is purely conceptual (an alleged schematization of history [!]; the authority of the evil powers; the "intermediary" reign of the Messiah), and even then is neither predomi-

strate on the basis of Christ's resurrection the necessity of the resurrection of the dead by tying that event to the final events of the End, particularly the defeat of death (cf. vv. 54-55).

Having asserted that "in Christ all will be made alive," Paul sets out to explain "but each (event)[31] in his (its) own order[32]." The first "order" is the one already mentioned in v. 20, that on which the entire argument is predicated—Christ's resurrection as "firstfruits." God himself has thereby set in motion a series of events that have to do with resurrection and the defeat of death. Thus the next event in this scheme happens at the *coming*[33] of Christ,[34] when he raises from the dead those who are his.[35]

Although the third item is prefaced with another "then," it is unlikely that Paul intends by this yet another *event* in the sequence begun by Christ's resurrection.[36] The "order" of resurrections is only two: Christ the firstfruits; the full harvest of those who are his at his Parousia.[37] Paul shows no interest here in anything beyond these. The "then" in this third instance is sequential to be sure, but in a more logical sense,[38] meaning that following

nant nor linguistically related to apocalyptic materials. This is Pauline eschatology, undoubtedly influenced by his Jewish heritage, but it lacks the essential "stuff" of apocalyptic.

[31]The ἕκαστος is singular, referring first to Christ and then to the dead in Christ.

[32]Gk. τάγμα, a military technical term for bodies of troops in various numbers, but eventually simply a term for a class or group. In this case it perhaps means something close to "in turn" (cf. Arrian, *Tacitus* 28.2), but more likely it keeps its basic sense of class (= each in his own company).

[33]Gk. παρουσία (cf. 1 Thess. 2:19; 3:13; 4:15; 5:23; 2 Thess. 2:1, 8, 9). In the political sphere it had to do with the arrival of a ruler, in religion the epiphany of a deity (as here). This is its last occurrence in Paul with reference to the "coming" of Christ.

[34]The ἔπειτα is thus defined by the prepositional phrase "at his coming." This is precisely in keeping with 1 Thess. 4:14-18, where the resurrection of the dead in Christ also takes place at his coming.

[35]Gk. οἱ τοῦ Χριστοῦ = "those who are of Christ," i.e., who belong to him.

[36]This has been a matter of long debate. Among commentators who think otherwise see Weiss and Lietzmann; cf. the articles by Culver and Willis (n. 19 above). On the other side, see esp. J. Héring, "Saint Paul a-t-il enseigné deux résurrections?" *RHPR* 12 (1932), 300-320; and H.-A. Wilcke, *Das Problem eines messianischen Zwischenreichs bei Paulus* (ATANT 51; Zurich, 1967).

[37]This is not to say that Paul *denied* a resurrection of the unjust (Acts 24:15 suggests otherwise), but that it simply lies totally outside his concern in *this* passage.

[38]As with the preceding ἔπειτα, this εἶτα is defined by the two ὅταν clauses that follow. Since these say nothing whatsoever of resurrection, but only of what transpires at the end, it is pure presumption to read into this text a third resurrection. So also is the concern to find here an intermediate stage between the resurrection of "those who are Christ's" and the final handing over of the kingdom to God the Father. Paul may have believed in such, but it lies quite outside his present concern. The point is that he neither explicitly nor allusively speaks of such, which he was fully capable of doing, had it been of any interest to him. What he says is, "then the end." Without a verb this can only mean that following the resurrection of believers is the end, which then is described in its two parts.

the resurrection of believers at the Parousia the final two "events" transpire. With the resurrection of the dead, the end, or goal,[39] has been reached; an "end" that has two sides to it. On the one hand, the resurrection of the dead will mean that Christ has subjugated,[40] and thereby destroyed, the final enemy death, expressed in this case in the terminology "every dominion" and "every authority and power."[41] That this destruction of the "powers" refers to the defeat of death is made certain by the supporting argument from Scripture that follows. On the other hand, with the final defeat of the last enemy the subjugation of all things has taken place, so that Christ might turn over the "rule" to God the Father.[42] The rest of the argument spells out how this is so.

25 The argument that begins with this verse and carries through v. 28 is Paul's explanation of the how and why of the two "events" of the End, mentioned at the end of v. 24. The explanation is based on his use (interpretation?) of two passages from the Psalms (110:1 and 8:6 [LXX 8:7]), which have the similar theme of "placing his enemies (subjecting all things) under his feet."[43] Although the argument gets somewhat complex, primarily because one is not always sure of the antecedent of all the pro-

---

[39]Weiss, 358, and Lietzmann, 80, suggest that τέλος means "the rest" here (= the resurrection of the unrighteous dead). But not only is there no evidence for such a meaning for this word (cf. Héring, "Saint Paul," p. 304 n. 3), but Paul is perfectly capable of saying οἱ λοίποι when that is what he intends.

But "the End" is perhaps not fully adequate since there is a purposive ("telic") force to the basic sense of this word. Thus, Paul is not speaking of an "end" to Christ's rule, but that its goal will have been achieved with the resurrection and its concomitant defeat of death and subsequent handing over the kingdom to the Father. Nevertheless, it is also the "end" of history as we now know it.

[40]But see T. Aono, *Die Entwicklung des paulinischen Gerichtsgedankens bei den Apostolischen Vätern* (Bern, 1979), pp. 26-28, who argues, on the basis of his exegesis of v. 25, that God should be understood as the subject of this verb. But that is unlikely since nothing prepares the reader for such a radical shift in subjects.

[41]Gk. ἀρχή, ἐξουσία, and δύναμις. This is the first time Paul uses this terminology to refer to the "spiritual powers." Cf. Eph. 1:21, where the same three terms (plus κυριότης) appear in combination; at least two of them appear together in Rom. 8:38; Col. 1:16; 2:10, 15; Eph. 3:10; 6:12. These other passages make it clear that Paul sees them as malevolent, demonic powers. In the cross Christ has already spelled their doom (Col. 2:15), which will be brought to completion at his coming.

[42]Paul does not use "kingdom" language often (see on 4:20 and 6:9-10); when he does, most often it is the traditional language "kingdom of God" (2 Thess. 1:5; 1 Cor. 4:20; 6:10; 15:50; Gal. 5:21; Rom. 14:17; Col. 4:11; cf. 1 Thess. 2:12). But see Col. 1:13; Eph. 5:8 ("the kingdom of Christ and God"); 2 Tim. 4:18. For Paul the interchange is related to his christological soteriology. God's rule is presently manifest in the lordship of Christ.

[43]It should be noted that Paul does not use "citational" language in either case, although he seems more bound to the OT text in the second instance (the NIV is curious here, using quotation marks in v. 27 but not in v. 25). The allusions are certain; in fact the similar combination of "citations" in Heb. 1:13 and 2:6-9 suggests that these were well-

nouns, whether Christ or God, the point of the whole seems plain enough. God himself stands as both the source and goal of all that is; and since he has set in motion the final destruction of death, when that occurs he will be "all in all." Christ's role is to bring about this destruction through the resurrection, which is inherently tied to his own. When that occurs, all of God's enemies will be subjected to Christ, so that in turn he may be made subject to God, who, it turns out, has been the one who subjected all things to him in any case.[44]

Paul thus begins by picking up the theme of "Christ's rule" from v. 24. This rule is currently in effect, but at "the end," when he has destroyed all the powers, he will "hand [it] over to God the Father." Paul now puts that into biblical perspective. Christ's rule, which by implication began with his resurrection (or subsequent ascension), *must continue*[45] until Ps. 110:1 is fulfilled, "until he has put all[46] his enemies under his feet."

What is not certain is the intended subject of the verb "until he has put."[47] In favor of "Christ" is (a) the grammar itself, since the natural antecedent is the subject of the preceding "he must reign," referring to Christ; and (b) the fact that this serves as an explanation of v. 24, where Christ is the subject of the clause "when he destroys all dominion, etc."[48] In favor of "God" is (a) the fact that in the psalm itself God places all things under the Messiah's feet, and (b) that in v. 28 God is finally designated as the subject of Ps. 8:6, as the one who has subjected all things to Christ.[49]

---

established messianic texts in early Christianity (Ps. 110:1 is the most cited OT passage in the NT; see the discussion in D. M. Hay, *Glory at the Right Hand: Psalm 110 in Early Christianity* [Nashville, 1973]). Nonetheless Paul does not actually cite, but reworks, the language of the OT texts into his own sentences. On this matter see esp. Lambrecht, "Christological Use," pp. 506-11.

[44]The question of whether the passage is basically christo- or theocentric is perhaps a red herring. It is both. That is, God is the ultimate source of all things; but he works out his purposes in history through Christ. Hence both Christ and God can alternatively function as the subject of most of the verbs in this paragraph. Christ is the subject of the verbs at least through v. 26; God is the "subject" of the passives in vv. 27c-28. What is not clear is how one is to understand v. 27ab. See the discussion in Lambrecht, "Christological Use," pp. 506-12.

[45]Gk. δεῖ; cf. v. 53. The "must" has to do with the divine purposes, not with the necessity of "fulfilling" Scripture, since no introductory formula is given. Paul's theological concern has to do with the continuing reality of death. Christ *must rule* until he has brought the rule of death to its end.

[46]This word is a Pauline addition to the psalm, perhaps under the influence of Ps. 8:6, which he will cite next. In any case it reflects a clear emphasis in this passage (see n. 5 above).

[47]See the discussion in Lambrecht, "Christological Use," pp. 509-10.

[48]Indeed, this is so natural a reading of the Greek text that most commentators do not even raise the question.

[49]This position has been argued for or adopted by F. W. Maier, "Ps 110,1 (LXX 109,1) in Zusammenhang von 1 Kor 15,24-26," *BZ* 20 (1932), 139-56; Aono, *Ent-*

Almost certainly we must go with the grammar here and see Christ as the subject.[50] Thus, he must reign (as he is now doing by virtue of his being Lord) until he places all his enemies (especially death, as v. 26 makes clear) under his feet. By subjecting death to himself through the resurrection of the dead, which is causally related to his being the firstfruits, Christ will thus have brought Satan's tyranny to its conclusion.

Paul's concern is therefore not with "two reigns," but with the Messiah's bringing to completion his work of redemption.[51] The further explanation in vv. 27-28 makes it clear that God ultimately lies behind this final action of the Messiah. The reason for this is that the destruction of death takes place in the raising of the dead itself, an event that occurs because those who are in Christ are in solidarity with him, so that his resurrection becomes the foundation of theirs; and God is the ultimate "cause" of the resurrection, which takes place in two "orders."

26 The grammar of this sentence is somewhat puzzling; nonetheless, its point is certain. This is Paul's own interpretation of the "last enemy" that must be put under the reigning Messiah's feet, death itself, and thus is the reason for this entire explanation in the first place. The sentence literally reads, "The last enemy is being destroyed,[52] namely death." The difficulty lies with the present tense and passive voice of the verb, plus the fact that no conjunction or particle joins it to what has preceded. F. C. Burkitt[53] suggested that it serves as the apodosis of the two "when" clauses in v. 24, with "the end" being understood adverbially (= "at the end") and v. 25 as a parenthesis explaining the twin protases of v. 24. Thus: "Then at the end, when he hands over the kingdom to God the Father, when he has destroyed all dominion, authority, and power (for he must reign until he has put all his enemies under his feet), the last enemy is being destroyed, death itself." Attractive as that is as a way out of the grammatical difficulty, the

---

wicklung, pp. 26-28; Grosheide, 367; Barrett, 358 (hesitantly); Holladay, 203; Wallis, "Problem," p. 236.

[50]Especially so since this is *not* a citation but an adaptation of the psalm to Paul's own grammar, and a reader (or hearer) could not possibly have understood "God" to be the subject until he or she came to v. 27c. Had Paul intended "God" at this point, it is almost demanded grammatically that he would have inserted a ὁ θεός.

[51]The later theological concern as to what happens to the "humanity" of Christ is simply not in Paul's purview. For a comparison of three later struggles (Marcellus of Ancyra, Calvin, A. A. van Ruler) with this issue in light of this text, see J. F. Jansen, "1 Corinthians 15:24-28 and the Future of Jesus Christ," in *Texts and Testaments: Critical Essays on the Bible and Early Church Fathers* (ed. W. E. March; San Antonio, 1980), pp. 173-97.

[52]Gk. καταργεῖται (cf. v. 24).

[53]"On I Corinthians xv 26," *JTS* 17 (1916), 384-85. This had previously been suggested in the commentary by von Hofmann (see the discussion in Héring, 166).

reading of v. 25 as a parenthesis when the content of v. 26 is dependent on it seems to nullify it.

Nonetheless, Burkitt is probably on the right track in terms of understanding Paul's intent. The asyndeton (lack of conjunction) gives the sentence a "strong and decisive prominence" between the two scriptural adaptations.[54] The present passive is best understood as referring to what takes place at the time of v. 24; that is, it refers to Christ's destroying "every dominion, authority and power." In a sense death, the final enemy to be subdued, is already being destroyed through the resurrection of Christ; but Paul's concern here is with its final destruction, which takes place when Christ's own resurrection as firstfruits culminates in the full harvest of the resurrection of those who are his. Death is the final enemy. At its destruction true meaningfulness is given to life itself. As long as people die, God's own sovereign purposes are not yet fully realized. Hence the necessity of the resurrection—so as to destroy death by "robbing" it of its store of those who do not belong to it because they belong to Christ! This is precisely the point made again at the end of the argument in vv. 53-57.

27 With this verse and the next Paul proceeds, on the basis of Ps. 8:6, to show how it is that God is ultimately responsible for this whole chain that began with Christ's resurrection and culminates in the destruction of death through the resurrection of believers. The verse begins with an explanatory "for," referring to vv. 25-26, and an adaptation of Ps. 8:6: "He has subjected all things under his feet."[55] But it is not at all certain either who is the intended subject (Christ or God) or how this past tense further explains vv. 25-26. There are two options.

First, it is possible that this is simply a further reiteration of the point of vv. 25-26, with Christ as the subject and the past tense retained from the psalm but explained in the following clause to refer only to the Eschaton.[56] This would ordinarily be the natural reading of the subject of the verb. The case for this view is especially strengthened by the introduction of the next clause with the same conjunction as in vv. 24 and 28.[57] Thus Christ is also the subject of the next verb, which should then be translated, "Whenever he

---

[54]Cf. McCaughey, "Death," p. 251.

[55]In the psalm this refers to humankind. Some have seen this "interpretation" therefore as an abuse of the plain meaning of the OT text. But that fails to reckon with Paul's perspective, where Christ as *man* is thus the representative "Man" to whom all things are subjected.

[56]This is the view of Findlay, 929; it was vigorously defended by Parry, 226-27. For a full presentation, see Lambrecht, "Christological Use," pp. 510-11.

[57]Gk. ὅταν, with the sense of an indefinite time in the future. This usage is easily the most difficult grammatical point for the next option. Even if it only means "whenever," as in 14:23, this is an odd way of referring specifically to a psalm that has just been "cited."

shall have said, 'All things have been subjected.' " The two verses then look like this:

27(a) For "he (Christ) has subjected all things under his feet."
　　　 but
　(b) *Whenever* he (Christ) shall have said:
　　　　　"All things have been subjected" [referring to v. 25]
　(c) (of course excepting Him who subjected to him all things),
28　　 but
　(a) *Whenever* all things shall have been subjected to him,
　(b) 　*then* even the Son himself shall be subjected
　　　　　　　　to Him who subjected to him all things,
　(c) 　　　　so that God might be all in all.

The difficulty for this view lies with the third clause (v. 27c), which must be understood as something of an awkward parenthesis that anticipates v. 28b, while v. 28a functions as the resumption of v. 27b.

　　Second, it is possible that this "citation" of the psalm, including the retaining of its past tense, is now moving on to the point that will be made explicit in v. 28, that ultimately it is God who has subjected all things to Christ. In this case, vv. 25-26 and 27-28 respectively serve as the scriptural explanation for the two "whenever" clauses in v. 24: Vv. 25-26 explain v. 24c ("when he destroys all dominion, authority and power") in terms of Ps. 110:1; and vv. 27-28 explain v. 24b ("when he hands over the kingdom to God the Father") in terms of Ps. 8:6. Thus, when death is finally destroyed (vv. 25-26), the way is paved for the final "handing over of the kingdom to God the Father" (vv. 27-28). In this view God is the subject of the verb in the scriptural citation in v. 27, which is then explained in the succeeding clause (= "when it [Scripture] says"), to which the final clause then serves as the apodosis. Thus:

27(a) For "he (God) has subjected all things under his (Christ's) feet."
　　　 Now
　(b) When it (Scripture) says:
　　　　　"All things have been subjected,"
　(c) 　it is clear that "all things" excludes the One who
　　　　　　did the subjecting to him.
28　　 But
　(a) Whenever it shall be that all things are subjected to him,
　(b) 　then even the Son will be subjected to the One who
　　　　　　　　subjects all things to him,
　(c) 　　　　so that God might be all in all.

758

It is difficult to choose between these two options. The first is especially attractive since (1) it keeps the flow of thought with vv. 25-26, and (2) it gives the conjunction in v. 27b its natural meaning in this context. Nonetheless, the difficulty in finding an adequate reason for v. 27c (one is naturally suspicious of solutions that require parentheses) and the fact that the rest of vv. 27-28 after the quotation seems to be an interpretation of Ps. 8:6 tend to make one lean in the direction of the second option.

If so, then the explanation begins by commenting on the text of the Psalm itself. The key for Paul lies in the fact that an external subject is responsible for the act of subjecting all things to Christ. Thus, "When it says that 'everything has been subjected,' it is clear that 'everything' excludes the one (i.e., God) who did the subjecting to him (i.e., Christ)." As the next verse makes clear, this has to be explained because in Paul's view a twofold act of subjecting is going on in the raising of the dead. On the one hand, death itself will thereby finally have been subjected to Christ (v. 24c); on the other hand, with that final subduing of death the time of Christ's reign comes to its end, so that he may hand over the "rule" to the Father (v. 24b), who thus becomes "all in all" (v. 28).

28 This final sentence in the argument ties together all that has preceded. First, it serves as a further elaboration of Paul's interpretation of Ps. 8:6; second, it further explicates the twin clauses of v. 24, which state that at the end Christ will hand the kingdom over to God the Father, having subdued all the "powers." Although it is not specifically said here, it therefore also serves as the culminating word on the necessity of the resurrection of the dead. Paul's point is that in raising Christ from the dead God has set in motion a chain of events that must culminate in the final destruction of death and thus of God's being once again, as in eternity past, "all in all."

The first clause thus repeats the point of the final clause of v. 24, but now in the language of the Psalm. "When all things have been subjected (by God, is implied) to him" is thus the new way of saying, "when he has destroyed all dominion, authority and power." By means of the Psalm Paul is pointing out that *God* is responsible for that subjection *through Christ*. As vv. 20-22 and 26 make certain, "all things" here refers especially to death.

The second clause likewise repeats the first clause of v. 24, also through the language of the Psalm. "Then the Son himself is subjected to the One (God) who subjected all things (death) to him (the Son)" is the new way of saying, "when he hands over the kingdom to God the Father." This is made clear by the final purpose clause, "so that God may be all in all." The last words "all in all" are a Pauline idiosyncrasy,[58] and must be understood

---

[58]Cf. Col. 3:11 (of Christ) and esp. Eph. 1:22.

in light of vv. 54-57 or Rom. 11:36. In any case, as Barrett notes, they are to be understood soteriologically, not metaphysically. Most likely he here intends that at the time of the resurrection of the dead, when through Christ God has subdued his people's final enemy, God's will will be supreme in every quarter and in every way. In Paul's view the consummation of redemption includes the whole sphere of creation as well (cf. Rom. 8:19-22; Col. 1:15-20). Nothing lies outside God's redemptive purposes in Christ, in whom all things finally will be "united" (Eph. 1:9-10). Therefore, at the death of death the final rupture in the universe will be healed and God alone will rule over all beings, banishing those who have rejected his offer of life and lovingly governing all those who by grace have entered into God's "rest."

As in 3:22-23 and 11:3, the language of the subordination of the Son to the Father is functional, referring to his "work" of redemption, not ontological, referring to his being as such. The unity of God lies behind all such language.

This is one of the great passages in the NT, not only in terms of Paul's own argumentation, but especially in terms of the true significance of Easter. It is therefore unfortunate that at times this powerful demonstration of the certainty of our own resurrection is overlooked in favor of an apologetic of trying to prove the resurrection to unbelievers. First of all, that is not what Paul is trying to do. What he has going for him is the common ground of their common faith in the resurrection of Christ. There is a place for apologetics, that is, the defense of Christianity to the unconverted; but Easter is not that place. Easter, which should be celebrated more frequently in the church, and not just at the Easter season, calls for our reaffirming the faith to the converted. The resurrection of Christ has determined our existence for all time and eternity. We do not merely live out our length of days and then have the hope of resurrection as an addendum; rather, as Paul makes plain in this passage, Christ's resurrection has set in motion a chain of inexorable events that absolutely determines our present and our future. Christ is the firstfruits of those who are his, who will be raised at his coming. That ought both to reform the way we currently live and to reshape our worship into seasons of unbridled rejoicing.

c. Ad hominem *arguments for resurrection (15:29-34)*

29 *Now if there is no resurrection, what will those do who are baptized for the dead? If the dead are not raised at all, why are*

*people baptized for them¹? 30 And as for us, why do we endanger
ourselves every hour? 31 I die every day—I mean that, brothers²—
just as surely as I glory over you³ in Christ Jesus our Lord.⁴ 32 If I
fought wild beasts in Ephesus for merely human reasons, what have I
gained? If the dead are not raised,*

> *"Let us eat and drink,*
> *for tomorrow we die."ᵃ*

*33 Do not be misled: "Bad company corrupts good character."
34 Come back to your senses as you ought, and stop sinning; for there
are some who are ignorant of God—I say⁵ this to your shame.*

ᵃIsaiah 22:13

This paragraph makes it clear that the issue of their denying the resurrection
is no small matter. Paul has just rung the changes on a powerful and, given
their common faith in Christ's resurrection, conclusive theological argument for both the inevitability and necessity of the resurrection of the dead.
Nonetheless, with this paragraph he comes at the issue yet again, this time
with very little in the way of theology. It is pure *ad hominem*. As usual in
such arguments (cf. 14:36-38), Paul proceeds by way of rhetorical questions, to which he appends his own rhetorical responses before turning to

---

¹Against all the early evidence the MajT has changed this pronoun to τῶν
νεκρῶν, apparently in conformity to the preceding clause. J. C. O'Neill's preference for
the singular reading of codex 69, αὐτῶν τῶν νεκρῶν, is without textual warrant (see
"1 Corinthians 15²⁹," *ExpT* 91 [1979/80], 310). Readings must be shown to have pedigree, and this one has none; cf. the textual argument in n. 6 on 8:8.

²Although found in significant early MSS (ℵ A B K P 33 81 104 365 1175 1241ˢ
2464 pc lat sy co), it is especially difficult to account for the omission of this vocative by a
widely scattered group of witnesses (P⁴⁶ D F G Ψ 075 0243 Maj b Ambst Pel) had it been
in the text originally. The addition would be natural in such an appeal. Cf. Zuntz, 176-77;
otherwise Metzger, 568.

³This translates (correctly) Paul's ὑμετέραν as an objective usage (*contra* Zuntz,
176 n. 2; Parry, 230; Ruef, 168). Some scribes (A 6 365 614 629 1241ˢ al) misunderstood
that and, on the basis of the qualifying "which *I have,*" changed it to ἡμετέραν (cf.
Metzger, 568). As Godet, 392, points out, ἡμετέραν fits very poorly indeed between the
two first person *singular* verbs that surround it. The nature of the scribal change is
unwittingly illustrated by the argument in its favor in J. D. Joyce, "Baptism on Behalf of
the Dead, An Interpretation of I Corinthians 15:29-34," *Encounter* 26 (1965), 269 n. 2.
See the commentary.

⁴Chiefly on the basis of what he considers to be a mixture of additions, plus what
he sees as a Pauline formula, Zuntz, 182, argues that the shorter form, ἐν κυρίῳ (D* b
Ambst Pel), is original. In fact, it has almost nothing to commend it.

⁵As further evidence that λαλέω in chap. 14 is not technical language for utterances or "chatter," Paul uses the verb here in this solemn asseveration (it was changed to
λέγω in the later MajT).

exhortation.[6] The actions of some of them (v. 29), not to mention of himself (vv. 30-32), border on absurdity if the dead are not raised. But even more importantly, he concludes (vv. 33-34) with an exhortation to righteous living, which strongly implies that there are some close ties between this particular issue and the aberrant behavior he has been attacking throughout the letter.[7]

Thus the paragraph is in three parts, signaled by three (or four) changes in personal pronouns. The first two parts are rhetoric, and conclude on the identical note from vv. 12-19, "if the dead are not raised," while the third is a series of three imperatives; each part flows out of the former. Thus:

I.   Otherwise (if vv. 20-28 are not true),
        What shall **they** do, **those who** are being baptized for the dead?
            If the dead are not raised at all,
                    why indeed are **they** being baptized for them?

II.   *Why indeed* do **we ourselves** face danger every hour?
            I die every day
                —by my "boasting" in you,
                        which **I** have in Christ Jesus our Lord—
            If **I** fought "wild beasts" in Ephesus,
                    for merely human reasons,
                What have **I** gained?
            If the dead are not raised,
                Let **us** eat and drink,
                    for **we** die tomorrow.

III.   [**You**] Stop being misled:
                "Bad company corrupts good character."
            [**You**] Come back to your senses rightly;
            [**You**] Stop sinning; for some are ignorant of God.
                I say this to **your** shame.

By reason of their personal nature, *ad hominem* arguments are usually *ad hoc* to a very high degree. The result is that Paul mentions activities in both cases (I and II) that are especially difficult to decipher in terms of specifics. So much is this so that at least forty different solutions have been suggested for the first item (baptism for the dead).[8] One may consider it as

[6]On vv. 12-34 as another example of Paul's A-B-A' form of argumentation, see n. 1 on 15:12-19.

[7]A. Malherbe, "The Beasts at Ephesus," *JBL* 87 (1968), 71-80, esp. pp. 72-73, has demonstrated convincingly that the whole paragraph has features of the diatribe, the moralistic "preaching" of the Roman Empire. Probably Paul's Corinthian opponents were also familiar with the style and would have recognized themselves as the antagonists.

[8]For overviews and critiques of the majority of these see B. M. Foschini, " 'Those Who Are Baptized for the Dead,' I Cor. 15:29, An Exegetical Historical Disser-

axiomatic that when there is such a wide divergence of opinion, no one knows what in fact was going on. The best one can do in terms of particulars is point out what appear to be the more viable options, but finally admit to ignorance. What is certain is how the text *functions* in the argument. Whatever it was that some of them were doing, those actions are a contradiction to the position that there is no resurrection of the dead (v. 12).

29 This rhetoric follows naturally, although not necessarily logically, from the preceding argument in which Paul pressed for the necessity of the resurrection, given the fact of Christ's resurrection and its having set in motion the final defeat of death. "Otherwise,"[9] he now urges, implying that if what has been argued is not true, then (literally) "what shall they do,[10] those who are being baptized (or are having themselves baptized) for[11] the dead[12]?" In typical fashion, and to make certain that his point is clear, he repeats the question, once again using the language of their assertion: "If the dead are not actually[13] raised, why at all[14] are they being baptized for them?"

The normal reading of the text is that some Corinthians[15] are being

---

tation," *CBQ* 12 (1950), 260-76, 379-88; 13 (1951), 46-78, 172-98, 276-83 (hereafter cited by article no./page no. [e.g., III/75]); and M. Rissi, *Die Taufe für die Toten* (Zürich, 1962). See also the helpful discussions in Schnackenburg, *Baptism,* pp. 95-102; and Beasley-Murray, *Baptism,* pp. 185-92.

[9]Gk. ἐπεί; for this use of the conjunction to precede questions and in response to what has just been argued, see on 14:15 (cf. Rom. 3:6).

[10]Gk. ποιήσουσιν, the future indicative, not deliberative subjunctive; the future is probably "logical" (= when they realize what they are doing and that there is no real future for the dead, how will it affect them?), although as Barrett, 362, notes, the verb here could also mean "accomplish" (= "what will they accomplish," or "what will they hope to achieve"), a view adopted by Joyce, "Baptism," p. 271; O'Neill, "1 Corinthians 15²⁹"; and Martin, 120.

[11]Gk. ὑπέρ; cf. the discussion on v. 3. Much of the debate hinges on the meaning of this preposition, which ordinarily means "in behalf of, for the sake of"; especially so in Pauline usage with persons as the object (see, e.g., 11:24; Gal. 2:20; Rom. 5:6, 8; 8:32; Eph. 5:25). See the discussion below.

[12]Here the article is used with νεκροί (see also vv. 35, 42, 52). This usage in particular excludes the translation "death." See also n. 12 on v. 12.

[13]Gk. ὅλως. See the discussion on 5:1; with the negative it can mean, as the NIV, "not at all," which makes good sense here. O'Neill, "1 Corinthians 15²⁹"; and Murphy-O'Connor, "Baptized," independently object to this translation on the basis of word order. Since as in 6:7 ὅλως immediately precedes the noun νεκροί, they argue that it should here be translated "the really dead," in contrast to those in the first clause. But that is to place too much confidence in too little evidence when it comes to word order. More likely, in each case this word comes first in the Pauline sentence for emphasis; the verb appears last here because that is the fixed formula throughout. Nor is it clear that ὅλως modifies the noun in 6:7; see the translation suggested there ("it is altogether a defeat").

[14]For this rendering of τί καί see BDF 442(14).

[15]This is one of the rare instances in the letter where Paul addresses a community matter only in the third person plural. In other instances (e.g., 4:18-21; 15:12-19), even

baptized, apparently vicariously, in behalf of some people who have already died. It would be fair to add that this reading is such a plain understanding of the Greek text that no one would ever have imagined the various alternatives were it not for the difficulties involved.[16] The problem is twofold: (1) There is no historical or biblical precedent for such baptism. The NT is otherwise completely silent about it; there is no known practice in any of the other churches nor in any orthodox Christian community in the centuries that immediately follow;[17] nor are there parallels or precedents in pagan religion.[18] This is a genuinely idiosyncratic historical phenomenon. For that reason, if in fact some were actually practicing such a baptism, we are left quite in the dark on all the essential questions: (a) *Who* was being baptized? (b) *For whom?* (c) *Why* were they doing it? (d) *What effects* did they think it had for those for whom it was being done? It is impossible to give a definitive answer to any of these.

(2) The second problem is theological and has to do with how Paul can appeal, without apparent disapproval,[19] to a practice that stands in such contradiction to his own understanding both of justification by grace *through faith,* which always implies response on the part of the believer, and of baptism as personal response to grace received. It smacks of a "magical" view of sacramentalism of the worst kind, where a religious rite, performed

---

when "some" are specified, the rest of the argument is directed at the community as a whole in the second person plural. Since that does not happen here, one may surmise that this is the activity of only a few.

[16]This still seems to be true, despite Murphy-O'Connor's gentle chiding of those who say this (" 'Baptized,' " 532). Whether it is either *probable* or *correct* is another issue, but the plethora of opinions exists precisely because this is what it *appears* to say vis-à-vis some inherent difficulties with it as it appears. Cf. the opinion of A. Oepke, *TDNT* I, 542 n. 63: "All interpretations which seek to evade vicarious baptism for the dead . . . are misleading" (cf. H. Riesenfeld, *TDNT* VIII, 512-13); and Parry, 228: "[This is] the plain and necessary sense of the words."

[17]Chrysostom, *hom. 40 in 1 Cor.* 1, describes such a practice among the Marcionites. This is an especially strong argument against the Mormons, e.g., who would justify their practice on alleged "biblical" grounds (which is of some interest in itself since the exegesis of the biblical text generally holds very little interest for them). How can such a practice be so *completely* unknown if in fact it had had any authorization within the churches of the first century? This complete silence in all other sources is the sure historical evidence that, if such a practice existed in fact, it did so as something purely eccentric among some in the Corinthian community.

[18]Although the History of Religions School noted some examples of vicarious rites in the mysteries. See Foschini, "Baptized," III/51 n. 118.

[19]Foschini, " 'Baptized,' " III/64-65, argues that the structure of vv. 29c and 30, namely the repeated "Why indeed," implies approval of the one because of the certain approval of the other. But that is not a necessary inference, any more than Jesus' parable about the shrewdness to act on the part of the corrupt household manager implies tacit approval of his financial shenanigans (Luke 16:1-8).

for someone else, can have saving efficacy. That lies quite outside the NT view of things.

This combination of difficulties has led to a variety of alternative solutions, which at best are difficult to categorize, but which for the most part have in common the attempt to find an alternative meaning to the plain sense of one or more of the words (either "baptized," "for," or "the dead").

(1) One option is to understand "baptize" metaphorically in light of Mark 10:38 and Luke 12:50. Either (a) some were "being baptized into the ranks of the dead" by martyrdom,[20] or (b) the apostles "were being destroyed by their labors on behalf of the dead (i.e., those who are lost),"[21] a view recently revived by J. Murphy-O'Connor, but who takes v. 29a as a Corinthian gibe at Paul's labors, to which Paul responds in the rest of the paragraph.[22]

(2) Others take "baptized" as referring to Christian baptism but give the preposition "for" different shades of meaning; sometimes these views suggest special meanings for "the dead" as well. These run the gamut: (a) that they are being baptized "over" the graves of the dead;[23] (b) that they are being baptized "with death before their eyes" as it were;[24] (c) that it means "with a view toward," suggesting that the departed are Christians and those being baptized are new converts who are being baptized with a view toward their being reunited with their departed loved ones;[25] (d) that it means "concerning," or "with reference to," having to do with the symbolic meaning of baptism, that it is in reference to death, burial, and resurrection;[26] (e) that the prepositional phrase goes with the verb "do," not "bap-

[20]See, e.g., Godet, 391.

[21]For older commentators who held this view, see Foschini, "'Baptized,'" I/266-67. See pp. 264-76 for other less viable metaphorical options, plus Foschini's critique.

[22]"'Baptized.'" Besides the inherent difficulties of having νεκροί change meaning in the two juxtaposed lines, especially without some kind of adversative, and the improbability of their using such a metaphor to describe apostolic hardships (*pace* Murphy-O'Connor; the influence of Philonic Judaism is questionable at best), there seems to be no contextual preparation for this (again *pace* Murphy-O'Connor; how this flows logically from v. 28 remains a mystery). Nor is there any hint in the text either that (a) Paul is quoting (which of course they would have known if it were so), or more importantly (b) that the rest is a response, when there is no adversative of any kind.

[23]A view held by Luther, and supported by Grosheide, 373, as one of the two best options.

[24]The view of Bengel; on the unlikelihood of "the dead" meaning "death," see n. 12 above.

[25]See M. Raeder, "Vikariatstaufe in I Kor. 15:29?" *ZNW* 46 (1956), 258-60, and supported by her mentor, J. Jeremias, "Flesh and Blood cannot inherit the Kingdom of God," *NTS* 2 (1955/56), 155-56; cf. also J. K. Howard, "Baptism for the Dead, A Study of 1 Corinthians 15:29," *EvQ* 37 (1965), 137-41. For older, and slightly different, expressions of this view see Findlay, 930-31, and R-P, 359-60.

[26]See A. G. Moseley, "'Baptized for the Dead,'" *RevExp* 49 (1952), 57-61.

tized," and should read, "What will the baptized do in behalf of the dead (in the future, given that they do not believe in resurrection)?"[27]

(3) Another set of solutions attempts to find a meaning for "the dead" that will be more compatible with Pauline theology. These include: (a) that "the dead" refers to the "(soon to be) dead bodies" of the Christians themselves, and that they were being baptized for the sake of that part of them that was dying and about to become a corpse;[28] and (b) that "the dead" refers to those among whom Christ was named, hence "What shall they do who have sworn allegiance to one who on their showing must be numbered among the dead?"[29]

(4) Finally, some have offered alternative punctuation: either (a) "In that case, what are the baptized to do? (It is) for the dead (= merely in death), if there is no resurrection of the dead at all. Why then are they baptized for them (= and whatever is the use of that?)";[30] or (b) "Otherwise what shall they do who are baptized? for the dead? (i.e., are they baptized to belong to, to be numbered among the dead, who are never to rise again)? Indeed, if the dead do not rise again, why are people baptized? For them? that is, are they baptized to be numbered among the dead who are never to rise again?"[31]

Partly because of this very plethora of options, none of which is compelling as a natural reading of the text, the majority of scholars think that Paul is referring to some form of vicarious baptism. But again, there is no unanimity as to what "form" this may have taken. Some things, however, seem to be necessary prerequisites. First, as already noted (n. 15), this unusual use of the third person plural, when elsewhere Paul always turns such references into a word to the community as a whole (e.g., vv. 12-13, 35-36), suggests that it is not the action of the whole community. On the

[27]Bachmann, 457.

[28]This was the view of most of the Greek Fathers. See, e.g., Chrysostom, *hom. 40 in 1 Cor.* 2. See further the collection of evidence in K. Staab, "1 Kor 15,29 im Lichte der Exegese der griechischen Kirche," in *Studiorum Paulinorum Congressus Internationalis Catholicus* (Rome, 1963), I, 443-50. This view was advocated by A. B. Oliver, "Why Are They Baptized for the Dead? A Study of I Cor. 15:29," *RevExp* 34 (1937), 48-53; it has been recently revived by O'Neill, "1 Corinthians 15²⁹," and, with slight modifications, Martin, 120-21. This view in particular has great difficulty accounting for the use of the third person, since Paul would in fact be addressing the congregation itself if this view is correct.

[29]P. J. Heawood, "Baptism for the Dead," *ExpT* 55 (1943/44), 278. For earlier expressions of this view see Foschini, "'Baptized,'" IV/181-82.

[30]This was put forth by Sir Robert Anderson, *The Bible or the Church?* (London, 1905), p. 234; this is the translation of F. J. Badcock, "Baptism for the Dead," *ExpT* 54 (1942/43), 330.

[31]This is the view (and transl.) of Foschini, "'Baptized,'" V/276-83; cf. K. C. Thompson, "I Corinthians 15,29 and Baptism for the Dead," in *Studia Evangelica* 2 (1964), 647-59, who offers a slightly different translation and nuance for "the dead," taking it to refer to "dead bodies."

other hand, there is no reason to deny that it was happening with the full
knowledge of the community and probably with their approval. Second,
Paul's apparently noncommittal attitude toward it, while not implying approval, would seem to suggest that he did not consider it to be as serious a
fault as most interpreters do.[32] On the other hand, it is difficult to imagine
any circumstances under which Paul would think it permissible for living
Christians to be baptized for the sake of unbelievers in general. Such a view,
adopted in part by the Mormons, lies totally outside the NT understanding
both of salvation and of baptism. Therefore, the most likely options are (a)
that it reflects some believers' being baptized for others who either were or
were on their way to becoming believers when they died (e.g., as in 11:30),
but had never been baptized;[33] or (b) that it reflects the concern of members
of households for some of their own number who had died before becoming
believers.

What they may have expected to gain from it is not quite clear, but
one may guess that at least they believed baptism to be necessary for entering
the final eschatological kingdom.[34] In any case, and everything must be
understood as tentative, this probably reflects the Corinthian attitude toward
baptism in general, since 1:13-17 and 10:1-22 imply a rather strongly sacramental stance toward baptism on their part, with some apparently magical
implications. Perhaps they believed that along with the gift of the Spirit
baptism was their "magical" point of entrance into the new pneumatism that
seems to have characterized them at every turn. If so, then perhaps some of
them were being baptized for others because they saw it as a way of offering
similar spirituality to the departed. But finally we must admit that we simply
do not know.

In any case, whatever they were doing and for whatever reason, Paul
saw it as a clear contradiction to the present stance of the community at large
that "there is no resurrection of the dead." If so, Paul argues, then this other
action by some of their number is the highest expression of absurdity. From
his point of view, Christ's resurrection makes any other form of spiritual
existence beyond the grave a non sequitur.

30   While on this kind of tack, Paul reverts to another question that

[32]Perhaps this is the significance of the passage in 2 Macc. 12:39-45 in which
Judas Maccabeus offers prayer and takes an offering to provide for the sin offering for
those of his men who had been slain while wearing "sacred tokens of the idols of Jamnia."
This is not so much vicarious sacrifices for the dead as an appeal to God to have mercy on
circumcised Jews who at the time of their death were wearing expressions of idolatry.
Could it be that "baptism for the dead" fell into something of this general category of
"innocence" so that Paul felt no great urgency to "correct" it?

[33]This is the view advocated by Rissi, *Die Taufe*, and adopted by Barrett, 364,
and Bruce, 148-49, among others.

[34]So also H. V. Martin, "Baptism for the Dead," *ExpT* 54 (1942/43), 192-93.

lies behind so much of this letter—their view of his apostleship vis-à-vis his own—which he will now defend in a most circuitous way. As noted throughout,[35] the Corinthians oppose Paul's *point of view* in so many things because they stand in opposition to him. Their opposition is based in part on conflicting views of what it means to be *pneumatikos,* which had inherent in it their taking a less than enthusiastic view of his weaknesses and sufferings as an apostle. What Paul seems to do in the next three verses is to capitalize on his weaknesses once more (cf. 2:1-5; 4:10-13; 15:9-10), this time, however, agreeing that if they are right on the one count (there is no resurrection), then they are surely also right on the other (his apostleship is of no profit whatsoever). But of course they are not right on the former (vv. 20-28), and his apostleship has to do with their being his "boast" in Christ Jesus.

The new train of thought thus proceeds in the style of the final sentence in the preceding verse: "Why indeed do we ourselves[36] face mortal danger every hour[37]?" This question serves as a significant comment on Paul's view of his own life. As he will detail on more than one occasion,[38] his apostolic ministry was a constant round of hardship and danger of all kinds. The emphasis here is on its continual (= "every hour") dangers (cf. 2 Cor. 11:26), for which the next two verses serve as commentary. His point, of course, is that he is indeed crazy to put his life in constant jeopardy for the sake of others, if neither he nor they have hope in the resurrection. But even more, this sentence also indicates the absolutely central and crucial place that Christ's resurrection played in his life. One must remember throughout that to deny the resurrection of the dead meant to deny the resurrection of Christ (vv. 12-19), which meant for Paul the denial of Christian life altogether. Thus everything Christians do as Christians—and especially the labors of an apostle—are an absurdity if there is no resurrection.

31 Paul's point could have been made by his simply adding v. 32b at this point.[39] Instead, for their sake he elaborates on the continual dangers

---

[35]Cf. the discussion on 1:10-17; 2:1-4; 3:18-23; 4:1-21; 5:1-5; 9:1-27; 14:6, 15-19, 36-38; 15:8-10.

[36]This is a rare case of the appearance of the nominative personal pronoun. Thus the use of the intensive pronoun to bring that out; the NIV does this by means of a reflexive, which is not quite precise. This emphatic "we" immediately following v. 29 excludes the Corinthians themselves (*contra* R-P, 361); it may include other apostles (as in v. 11; so Findlay, 931; Lenski, 692), but the following elaboration suggests that it is editorial and means "I myself."

[37]Gk. πᾶσαν ὥραν. This is a literal translation. The accusative implies "extent of time"; the phrase is an idiom that means "all the time."

[38]See on 4:11-13; cf. 2 Cor. 4:8-9; 6:4-5, 8-10; 11:23-29; 12:10.

[39]That is, all he needed to say in order to make his point, comparable to v. 29, was: "Why indeed do we ourselves face dangers every hour? If there is no resurrection of the dead, then let us eat and drink, for tomorrow we die."

mentioned in the opening sentence: "Daily[40] I die." Taken as an elaboration of v. 30, this means something like "On a daily basis I face the reality of death."[41] Although one cannot be sure as to what this refers specifically, there are several hints in this letter and in 2 Corinthians that his stay in Ephesus was anything but an Aegean holiday. In the next sentence he refers to "fighting wild beasts in Ephesus"; in 16:9 he notes that even though a great door was open for ministry, many stood in opposition to him. Then, sometime later when writing our 2 Corinthians, shortly after leaving Ephesus, he thanks God for being delivered from a deadly peril in which he had actually despaired of his life (1:8-11), while the rest of the letter is a litany of hardships and sufferings that seem too fresh in mind to be simply general catalogues. One wonders at moments like these what a different picture of both the apostle and the early church we might have received if Paul had kept a journal of his stay in Ephesus!

What follows comes as something of a surprise. It is a kind of oath, the first word serving as the affirming particle (= "I swear by"),[42] and the next words serving as that by which one swears. Literally it reads "I swear by your boasting," which he quickly qualifies as "(boasting) which I have in Christ Jesus our Lord."[43] The NIV's "I glory over you" translates the possessive adjective "your"[44] plus the noun for the act of "boasting."[45] Although grammatically this could refer to their boasting in him, that fits neither the immediate context (especially the following qualifying phrase) nor the context of the letter as a whole. Rather, the possessive is here objective and refers to Paul's "boast" in the Corinthians as believers,[46] a "boast" that probably does not so much refer to his telling others about the

---

[40]Gk. καθ' ἡμέραν, which stands in the emphatic first position: "Why are we exposed to danger every hour? *Daily* I am subject to death."

[41]Cf. his citation of Ps. 43:23 (LXX) in Rom. 8:36; cf. also 2 Cor. 4:10; 11:23 ("in deaths many"). Thus it has nothing to do with piety and the daily dying to self and sin—although constant exposure to danger may have that effect as well!

[42]Only here in the NT; see the examples in LXX Gen. 52:15 ("I swear by the health of Pharaoh"), and Jos., *c.Ap.* 1.255 ("I swear by Zeus").

[43]Moffatt seems to catch the sense: "Not a day but I am at death's door! I swear it by my pride in you, brothers, through Christ Jesus our Lord."

[44]Gk. ὑμετέραν; in Paul see 16:17; 2 Cor. 8:8; Gal. 6:13; and Rom. 11:31. Although an objective use of this pronoun is rare, it does occur. See esp. Thucydides 1.69.5 ("the hopes they have placed in you"; Loeb); cf. also 1 Cor. 11:24, "in my remembrance" (= in remembrance of me).

[45]Gk. καύχησιν, which occurs throughout 2 Corinthians (1:12; 7:4, 14; 8:24; 9:4; 11:10, 17). On the use of this word group in Paul, and especially in 1 and 2 Corinthians, see on 1:29-31; cf. on 5:6; 9:15-16.

[46]Cf. 1 Thess. 2:19 and Phil. 2:16 (καύχημα) and the eschatological perspective of this kind of "boast."

Corinthians[47] as to their very existence as the result of his apostolic labors (cf. 9:2, 15-16).

What a telling oath this is. To make sure that they understand the truth of his constant facing of death, he swears by that which is dearest to him, their own existence in Christ, which also came about by labors that had exposed him to such dangers.[48] That seems also to be the point of the qualifying addition, "which I have in Christ Jesus our Lord." The boast is his, but it is not self-serving nor self-exalting. It rests completely on what Christ had done among them through his labors (cf. vv. 9-10).[49] Thus they are his boast; but for Paul that ultimately means boasting in Christ.

32 The first sentence in this verse further elaborates vv. 30-31 by way of a specific instance; the second sentence ties it all back into the argument with the same form of conditional clause as in v. 29. The fighting "with wild beasts in Ephesus" must be understood metaphorically,[50] not only because Paul otherwise lived to tell about it if it was literal(!),[51] but because (a) such a metaphor was a common phenomenon in the moralistic literature of Hellenism,[52] and (b) his Roman citizenship should have ex-

---

[47]As suggested, e.g., by Holladay, 205; Bruce, 149.

[48]As Barrett, 365, notes, for Paul "this is worth many deaths."

[49]MacDonald, "Emendation," has offered the imaginative, but unconvincing, proposal that v. 31c is an interpolation by someone who was trying to harmonize 1 Corinthians with the Pastoral Epistles (in this case, 2 Tim. 4:17). In his view, the Pauline original takes up a position of the Corinthians, that they had believed a legendary story about his having fought with a lion in Ephesus. Besides being speculative at every key point, the author in particular neglects Paul's own argument of vv. 30-31a and requires too many contingent grammatical and lexical improbabilities to make it work. See also the critique in Murphy-O'Connor, "Interpolations," 93.

[50]Héring, 171-72, following Weiss, argues for a hypothetical usage: "If I ever were to have to fight, etc." But it is difficult to see how something that never happened would serve as an adequate elaboration of the point in v. 31. For a useful summary of the arguments pro and con for a metaphorical or literal understanding, see R. E. Osborne, "Paul and the Wild Beasts," *JBL* 85 (1966), 225-30.

[51]To be sure, many have taken the verb θηριομαχέω (a NT hapax legomenon) literally, as if Paul had actually fought with wild animals in the arena. The argument usually is predicated on an understanding of a relationship with v. 31 that sees this verse as climactic (e.g., Godet, 394), a view that was vigorously defended by C. R. Bowen, "'I Fought with Beasts at Ephesus,'" *JBL* 42 (1923), 59-68. But that is probably a false hypothesis, as well as a failure to reckon seriously with the nature of the opposition noted in 16:9.

[52]See especially the discussion by Malherbe, "Beasts," whose balanced presentation helps to bring some order out of the chaos of much that has preceded. Cf. also the well-known parallel in Ignatius, *Rom.* 5:1, referring to his captors: "From Syria to Rome I am fighting with wild beasts, by land and sea." Conzelmann, 277 n. 130, suggests that this is not a real parallel since his impending death was close at hand. But Ignatius's usage is in fact metaphorical, no matter how much what lay before him prompted the metaphor.

cluded him[53] from what would have meant certain death if it were a literal "fight" in the arena.[54] But the metaphor is not a word about his struggle with opponents in general; rather, he specifies that it was with "wild beasts" in *Ephesus*. Since he is in Ephesus at the time of writing, and since a few paragraphs later (16:9) he refers to many who oppose him there, this is probably a reference to that struggle. The language of v. 31 would suggest that it was not simply an ideological struggle but, as often in his life, one that had exposed him to severe physical dangers as well. Beyond that, one would only be speculating.

With this understanding of the metaphor, the much debated prepositional phrase "according to man" is also easily decided.[55] Its meaning is not "for merely human reasons" (NIV), but exactly as in 3:3, where Paul, in contrast to their boasting of being truly "in Spirit," accuses the Corinthians of acting "according to man," that is, as "mere human beings" who do not have the Spirit of God.[56] Here he means that if there is no hope in the resurrection, then his life or death struggle against the opponents of his gospel is carried on at the merely human level—he is nothing more than a "mere man" among other "mere humans."[57] His point of course is, What sense does it make to live like *this* if we live only at the merely human level as others who have no hope for the future?

The concluding apodosis, "what have I gained?" is often seen as

---

[53]It is often pointed out that according to Acts 19:31-40 Paul has some well-placed friends in Ephesus, who protected him on one occasion. It is hard to believe that they would have allowed him, as a Roman citizen, to be thrown to wild beasts in the arena.

[54]On the basis of archeological evidence from Corinth J. W. Hunkin ("1 Corinthians xv.32," *ExpT* 39 [1927/28], 281-82) suggested that the metaphor might not be a reference to condemned persons (although see on 4:9), but to that class of gladiators (*venatores* or *bestiarii*) who were trained to give exhibition fights with wild animals. Thus it is a picture not of one condemned to the arena, but of a well-trained fighter, hardened by long training. MacDonald, "Emendation," p. 273, rightly calls the view "as unsatisfactory as it is romantic."

[55]The suggestions are many and varied: "in the nature of man" (= seeking the rewards for which people risk their lives); "humanly speaking" (= to use a figure); "as far as the will of man is concerned" (= those trying to execute Paul acted contrary to God's will); "according to human folly" (proposed by MacDonald, "Emendation," to support his interpretation); "in human form" (= contending with wild beasts in human form), a view proposed by C. P. Coffin, "The Meaning of 1 Cor. 15$_{32}$," *JBL* 43 (1924), 172-76.

[56]MacDonald, "Emendation," pp. 269-70, seems quite wrong in seeing this and 3:3 as comparable to the usage in 9:8 or Rom. 3:5. No speaking is involved here; the verse has to do with how one lives.

[57]Cf. Malherbe, "Beasts," p. 80: "If there were no resurrection of the body, his struggle at Ephesus had been in vain. It would have been κατὰ ἄνθρωπον, a struggle on a merely human level, without a hope of resurrection." This makes so much sense of the phrase in context that one wonders why there has been so much struggle over its nuance.

reflecting on his own personal life. While there is a degree of truth to that, more likely he is once again putting his ministry, and in that sense his personal life, into perspective. No resurrection means he has played the fool with his life; all of his labor has been in vain after all. This comes very close to the point of vv. 9-10 and 14-15, that their existence is predicated on his ministry, which had the resurrection of Christ as its heart and soul. Thus, without the resurrection his earthly struggle is without meaning; he has gained nothing, not only now but in the life to come, and not only for himself but for all those who have come to Christ as a result of that struggle.

To cap the argument Paul once more repeats the protasis against which this entire argument struggles, namely the Corinthian position, "if the dead are not raised." The apodosis in this case offers the logical conclusion as to the direction in which one's life ought to go, in contrast to the daily struggles, even to the point of facing death, that characterize his own life. If there is no resurrection, then instead of "fighting wild beasts in Ephesus," one may as well go the route of despair—and dissolution—and "eat and drink, for tomorrow we die." This word is one of those happy ambivalences in Paul that point simultaneously in two directions.[58] On the one hand, this is a verbatim citation of Isa. 22:13, and is surely intended as the logical alternative to his own kind of "daily dying." If there is no resurrection, he has argued, such a "death-facing" life is without gain. One may as well go the way of despair and eat and drink, for "tomorrow" we die anyway. To be without hope in the resurrection life is a constant round of nothing.

On the other hand, this citation of Isa. 22:13 also reflects contemporary anti-Epicurean sentiments, which (not altogether fairly) believed the Epicureans taught this very philosophy.[59] In Plutarch's anti-Epicurean writings, for example, the language of "eating and drinking" was a formula for the dissolute life.[60] Since Paul immediately follows this quotation with a series of imperatives that call the Corinthians from the errors of their ways to a "sober" life in Christ in which they "stop sinning," these words of despair also serve as transition to what follows. The Corinthians, aware of his own apostolic struggles on the one hand, and their own less-than-disciplined lifestyle on the other, would have to be in a true stupor (cf. v. 34) not to catch his point and see the application.

33 In typical diatribe style, the *argumentum ad absurdum* turns truly *ad hominem,* and becomes a word of exhortation for the Corinthians to mend their ways. When one considers that the point of the whole argument is

---

[58]Many commentators (e.g., Godet, 394; Findlay, 932) see it as introducing what follows, which it does; but one misses too much to fail also to see its formal role as a conclusion to vv. 30-32, just as the similar clause in v. 29.

[59]See especially the discussion in Malherbe, "Beasts," pp. 76-79.

[60]See, e.g., *mor.* 1098C, 1100D, 1125D.

to get them to change their views as to the resurrection of the dead, it is difficult not to see in these words a direct connection between much of the behavior being corrected by this letter and this denial of theirs. Paul's concern is a simple one: They are to adopt the kind of behavior that should be expected of those for whom the future is both "already" and "not yet," who have been "washed from their sins" through Christ Jesus (cf. 6:11; 15:3) and who yet await the final destruction of death (vv. 24-28). They are to live as people who not only have a past in Christ, but a future as well.

This opening exhortation, therefore, repeats the imperative of 6:9 (cf. 3:18): "Stop deceiving yourselves" (or "allowing yourselves to be misled"). Their present path is one of delusion, both in terms of their theology and its consequent behavior. In this case the delusion is spelled out in the language of an epigram from Menander's *Thais*, "Bad company corrupts good character,"[61] which comes into the argument as something of a jolt. On the one hand, as countless generations in every culture and clime have experienced, this epigram is independently true and carries much the same effect as the more Jewish proverb he cites in 5:6. Keeping company with evil companions can have a corrosive influence on one's own attitudes and behavior. But why that word here, in the middle of an argument against their denial of the resurrection of the dead?

It may be that this is simply a matter of style, that in keeping with the diatribe Paul is merely generalizing about their own behavioral patterns. But more likely this is a very direct word to their present situation. Since the word translated "company" can mean either "companionship" or "conversation,"[62] one wonders whether the emphasis here is more on the "company" of "evil conversation" that denies the resurrection, than on simply associating with people who so deny.[63] In that case, it would mean here something like, "Evil conversations such as those that deny the resurrection of the dead can only have a corrupting effect on your good character." Otherwise, he would seem to be pointing to the "some" in v. 12 who are denying the resurrection. By implication, they should thus dissociate from them.

34 The concluding two imperatives suggest that the "evil company" is in fact their denial of the resurrection, which undoubtedly had a role in the corrosion of their Christian behavior. Thus he exhorts them to "Sober

---

[61]As both Conzelmann, 278 n. 139, and Malherbe, "Beasts," p. 73, point out, one cannot make too much of Paul's own acquaintance with such literature from this quotation, since it had become a popular epigram by the time of Paul. See Conzelmann and Malherbe for the evidence.

[62]Gk. ὁμιλία, which is the word for a "speech" as well, hence our "homily."

[63]Some (e.g., Godet, 395) think it refers to being seduced by their pagan friends (as in chaps. 8–10), but the interpretation offered here makes more sense of the present context.

up[64] as you ought[65] and stop sinning." The verb "sober up" may be a metaphor either for to awake from sleep[66] or to be aroused from a drunken stupor[67]. One cannot be sure which is mind here, although both the context ("let us eat and drink") and the compounded form of the verb suggest that it is the latter.[68] In any case, it is a telling metaphor for their present state of delusion, in which they both deny the resurrection and behave as if there were no future to the kingdom of God. Thus, coming to their senses, they must "stop sinning." The present prohibition implies the cessation of action already going on; and apparently it is not the action of one or a few. The letter is replete with examples of sinning to which this could refer.

What is less clear is the final reason of this double-sided exhortation, "for (literally) ignorance of God some have." It is possible that this is a word that points outward, to those outside their community who do not know God and, given the present theological delusion and behavioral aberrations of this Christian community, are not likely to.[69] Nonetheless, in the present context this is almost certainly a word of irony, the ultimate "put-down" of those responsible for taking this church down its present disastrous course. Those who are leading others into a new understanding of Spirit, wisdom, and knowledge are here said to be as the pagans that surround them, being ultimately "ignorant of God." Most likely this is to be understood in light of the preceding paragraph (vv. 20-28), that those who deny the resurrection ultimately live in ignorance of God, who through Christ's resurrection has set in motion that chain of events which leads to his finally being all in all. It is also possible, however, since the clause functions as the explanation of "stop sinning," that Paul intends a much broader perspective (e.g., as in 8:2-3, where their lack of love also exhibits failure to know God). In any case, he says this "to their shame," probably in much the same way as in the first occurrence of this clause in 6:5, where his argument itself is an attempt to "shame" them into a change of thinking and behavior.

---

[64]Gk. ἐκνήφω, a NT hapax legomenon; cf. the noncompounded form used in 1 Thess. 5:6, 8, where the context demands the metaphor of sleep rather than drunkenness.

[65]Gk. δικαίως; cf. 1 Thess. 2:20 and Tit. 2:12, where it means to live in an upright manner. The KJV so translates it here, and probably that moves in the direction Paul is intending. Nonetheless, that use of the adverb does not go well with the imperative "Sober up." Hence BAGD suggest, "as you ought" (perhaps, "as is fitting" or "right").

[66]It is so used literally in Hab. 2:7, 19.

[67]As in Gen. 9:24 and 1 Sam. 25:37 (literally) and Joel 1:5 (metaphorically).

[68]Although Martin, 124, perhaps narrows the metaphor too much to make it refer to their "'intoxication' with their spiritual exuberance."

[69]So, e.g., Gromacki, 192. Although this is not a popular view among commentators, it should not be lightly dismissed, especially in light of the language that concludes the next section (v. 58), where abounding in the work of the Lord most likely refers to evangelism.

Thus the long argument that began in v. 12 comes to a conclusion on this very strong hortatory word. Their position means the end of their existence as believers (vv. 14, 17) and hopelessness for the dead (v. 18); it also means that the activities of some of them and especially of his own apostolic labors are living contradictions. Thus they need to come to their senses, as he will urge again at the conclusion of the letter (16:13). But before that conclusion he must bring the present matter to its full conclusion, by addressing the issue of what the resurrection means in relationship to our present bodily existence.

Probably because most people have had such a difficult time knowing what to do with v. 29, there has been a strange silence in the church with regard to this paragraph. Yet it stands as one of the more significant texts pointing to a genuine relationship between what one believes about the future and how one behaves in the present (cf. 2 Pet. 2–3). This is not to say that the future is the only motivation for correct behavior, but it is to plead that it is a proper one because it ultimately has to do with the nature and character of God. We should be living in this world as those whose confidence in the final vindication of Christ through our own resurrection determines the present. On this matter see also on 7:29-31. It is a matter of sober historical record that slippage at this key point of Christian theology is very often accompanied by a relaxed attitude toward the Christian ethic. It is no wonder that the world fails so often to "hear" our gospel, which must look at times like anything but the good news it really is—that Christ delivers people from the bondage of sin and guarantees their future with him in a life where neither sin nor death shall have a foothold.

3. The Resurrection Body (15:35-58)

Paul's concern to this point has been to refute those who deny the resurrection of the dead by urging its absolute necessity if there is to be any Christian faith at all. Everything is up for grabs—Christ's death as a saving event, forgiveness of sins, hope for the future, Christian ethics, the character of God himself—if there is no resurrection. But almost certainly lurking behind that denial is a view of the material order that found the resurrection of material bodies (or dead corpses) to be a doctrine most foul.[1] To that issue Paul now turns.

The turn in the argument is signaled both by the two questions that

---

[1]Some (e.g., Schmithals, 155-57; Conzelmann, 280) have questioned whether this part of the problem came from the Corinthians themselves. But both the language (ἄφρων) and the energy expended in response to it make little sense if the questions are merely hypothetical.

begin this section (v. 35) and by the decided shift in language. The word *nekros* ("dead") appeared eleven times in vv. 1-34, six in the phrase "if the dead are not raised." That word occurs only three times in the present section (vv. 35, 44, 52)—at key points where the two sections are tied together. The word that now dominates is *sōma* ("body"), which occurs ten times here but not once in vv. 1-34. Nonetheless, these are related ideas. "The dead" refers not simply to people who have died, but also to their dead bodies that have been laid in the grave. This is made clear by three pieces of evidence:[2] (a) In the opening set of questions, the second is best understood as specifying the first; thus: "How are *the dead* raised?" that is, "With what kind of *body* will they come?" (b) The significant verb "is raised" occurs in both sections, in vv. 1-34 to speak of the raising of the dead, in vv. 35-58 to speak of the raising of bodies. (c) The final occurrence of "the dead shall be raised"—in v. 52—is now qualified by the word "imperishable," the key word from the argument in vv. 42-49, which responds to the opening questions of how and with what kind of body.

All of this suggests that the real concern behind their denial of the resurrection of the dead was an implicit understanding that that meant the reanimation of dead bodies, the resuscitation of corpses. Paul's response in turn is driven by two concerns. First, denial of the resurrection for him meant the denial of any genuine continuity between the present and the future. The point of continuity lay with the body;[3] therefore there must be a resurrection of the body.[4] Second, and even more importantly, the reality of the resurrection of Christ absolutely dominated his thinking at every turn.[5] Since Christ was raised bodily—he was *buried,* raised, and *seen*—there must of necessity

---

[2]See n. 38 below on vv. 42-43. Cf. the evidence for this same kind of usage in Philo mustered by Horsley, "Elitism."

[3]*Contra* Conzelmann, 281 n. 15 and passim. But to deny this Conzelmann simply ignores the emphasis on σῶμα in this section.

[4]One of the curiosities of a preceding generation of NT scholarship was its readiness to adopt so wholeheartedly the view of Bultmann (and Robinson; see n. 29 on 6:13-14) that by σῶμα Paul meant the essential person ("Man does not *have* a *sōma;* he *is sōma"; Theology,* I, 194). Yet that proved so difficult for Bultmann to maintain in the light of this passage that he accused Paul of betraying himself—never allowing that it may have been his reconstruction of Paul that was at fault. See the critique in R. J. Sider, "The Pauline Conception of the Resurrection Body in I Corinthians xv.35-54," *NTS* 21 (1974/75), 428-39, esp. 438; and Gundry, 164-69.

[5]Cf. C. F. D. Moule, "St Paul and Dualism: The Pauline Conception of Resurrection," *NTS* 12 (1965/66), 107: "Paul steered a remarkably consistent course between, on the one hand, a materialistic doctrine of physical resurrection and, on the other hand, a dualistic doctrine of the escape of the soul from the body; . . . the secret of his consistency here is his tenacious grasp of the central theme: Jesus, Son of God."

This also explains his essential differences from his contemporaries in rabbinic Judaism. For this discussion among the Hillelites and Shammaites, see Cavallin, *Life,* pp. 171-92; cf. R. Morisette, "La condition de ressuscité. 1 Corinthiens 15,35-49: structure littéraire de la péricope," *Bib* 53 (1972), 208-28.

be a bodily resurrection of believers. Nonetheless, Paul was equally convinced that Christ's resurrection was not the resuscitation of a corpse, but the transformation of his physical body into a "glorified body" (Phil. 3:21) adapted to his present heavenly existence. It is this reality that ultimately controls the present argument. Thus, the long debate over whether the stress lies on continuity or discontinuity is a bit misguided.[6] Paul's concern obviously lies with both; however, it is far better to speak of continuity and transformation. With what kind of body? As with Christ, the same yet not the same; this body, but adapted to the new conditions of heavenly existence; sown one way, it is raised another, but the same body is sown and raised.[7]

The argument, which shows continuous development in its line of thought,[8] is in three parts, enclosed by the questions of v. 35 and the final exhortation of v. 58. In Part I (vv. 36-44) Paul prepares the way for the idea of a "spiritual" (= heavenly, or glorified) body through two sets of analogies: seeds and kinds of bodies. The analogies are intended to take them from the known to the unknown. That of the seeds (vv. 36-38) illustrates both the genuine continuity of the future body with the present one and the reality of its transformation, in which a "body" for each mode of existence is given by God himself; that of the differing kinds of "bodies" (vv. 39-41) further illustrates the latter point, that bodies differ and have a different "glory." In vv. 42-44 the two analogies are applied to the resurrection of the dead, the key word for the new body being "imperishable."

Part II (vv. 45-49) further illustrates the two themes of "bodies sown one way but raised another" and "the transformed body adapted to its new conditions" by picking up the Adam-Christ analogy from vv. 21-22. Just as believers have shared the earthly body of the first man, so also will they bear the heavenly body of the second man. This of course is the key to everything. The ultimate reason for Paul's faith lies with the resurrection of Christ and the fact that he was thus raised in incorruption, glory, and power. The continuity existed because he who had been crucified was also seen, visibly and corporeally, after his resurrection; but his current heavenly existence also meant for Paul that there was obvious transformation. So with ourselves, he argues. We do and shall bear the likeness of both Adam and Christ.

The argument is brought to a resounding climax in Part III (vv.

---

[6]Some tend to stress one to the exclusion of the other; this is especially so with regard to discontinuity. See, e.g., Conzelmann, 281; for correctives to this see M. E. Dahl, *Resurrection*, and Sider, "Conception." For a view similar to the one argued here, see J. Gillman, "Transformation in 1 Cor 15,50-53," *ETL* 58 (1982), 309-33, esp. 322-33.

[7]Cf. M. E. Dahl's term (10, 94-95) "somatically identical," which stresses continuity but is to be differentiated from "materially identical."

[8]So also K. Usami, "'How are the dead raised?' (1 Cor 15,35-58)," *Bib* 57 (1976), 474. Cf. n. 15 below.

50-57), where Paul argues for the absolute necessity of transformation in order for believers to enter their heavenly existence. Quite in contrast to those who think Paul's major point in the argument is that believers must die in order to be raised,[9] his concern in fact is that transformation must take place in order for believers, whether dead or alive, to enter into heavenly existence: "This corruptible *must* be clothed with incorruptibility." Thus, whatever they may think about their present spirituality, it is not the heavenly existence that is to be. Moreover, when the transformation does take place, then the point of the argument in vv. 24-28 is realized—death is not only defeated, it is swallowed up in victory!

This section, therefore, is absolutely crucial to the argument of chap. 15, since it responds to the real issue that led to their denial of the resurrection. At the same time, it is crucial to the entire letter. The key issue has to do with being *pneumatikos*. The Corinthians are convinced that by the gift of the Spirit, and especially the manifestation of tongues, they have already entered into the spiritual, "heavenly" existence that is to be. Only the body, to be sloughed off at death, lies between them and their ultimate spirituality. Thus they have denied the body in the present, and have no use for it in the future.[10] Not so, says Paul. As with Christ, so with us. This corruptible *must* put on incorruption; only then does the End come. At stake is the biblical doctrine of creation. According to Scripture, God created the material order and pronounced it good. But in the Fall it also came under the curse. In Paul's view, therefore, the material order must also experience the effects of redemption in Christ, and that involves the physical body as well. Since in its present expression it is under the curse, it must be transformed; and that happens at the Eschaton, so that beginning and end meet in Christ Jesus.

a. Analogies of seeds and "bodies" (15:35-44)

35 *But someone may ask, "How are the dead raised? With what kind of body will they come?"* 36 *How foolish! What you sow does not come to life unless it dies.* 37 *When you sow, you do not plant the body that will be, but just the seed, perhaps of wheat or something else.* 38 *But God gives it a body as he has determined, and to each kind of seed he gives its own body.* 39 *All flesh is not the same:* People[11] *have one kind of flesh, animals have another, birds another and fish another.* 40 *There are also heavenly bodies and there are earthly bodies; but the splendor of the heavenly bodies is one kind, and the splendor of the earthly bodies is another.* 41 *The sun has one kind of splendor, the moon another and the stars another; and star differs from star in splendor.*

---

[9] See n. 22 on v. 36 below.
[10] On this whole question see especially on 6:12-14.
[11] NIV, "men."

42 *So will it be with the resurrection of the dead. The body that is sown is perishable, it is raised imperishable;* 43 *it is sown in dishonor, it is raised in glory; it is sown in weakness, it is raised in power;* 44 *it is sown a natural body, it is raised a spiritual body. If[12] there is a natural body, there is also a spiritual body.*

This initial response to the opening set of questions (v. 35) is in two parts. In vv. 36-41 Paul offers two sets of related analogies that are applied in vv. 42-44 to the resurrection of the dead. The analogy of the seed (vv. 36-38) illustrates from their everyday experience that one living thing, through death, can have two modes of existence. As the application in vv. 42-44 indicates, the stress lies on its being sown (in death) one way, and being raised another. Inherent in that analogy is the other, that "bodies" exist in a great variety of forms, some adapted for one existence, others for another. As the later Adam-Christ illustration makes plain, this too is of great significance for the argument. It will explain how the *same* body can move from one form of existence to another. God has already so arranged the universe that "bodies" are adapted to a variety of kinds of existence. Thus the first analogy, that of the seeds, stresses both continuity and transformation; the second analogy, that of the kinds of bodies, is intended to illustrate the phenomenon of bodies' being adapted to their existence. Both are applied to the resurrection in vv. 42-44.

35 The strong adversative[13] with which these questions begin indicates that Paul knows his task to here is but partly done; there still remains the philosophical objection that must have lain behind their denial of the resurrection in the first place. Even though these questions continue the form of diatribe from vv. 29-34, in which an author uses an interlocutor ("but someone will ask"[14]) to raise the question that he wishes next to address, in this case it seems most highly probable that Paul knew by firsthand information that this is the real issue. Inherent in their denial of the resurrection was the assumption that it had to do with reanimating corpses. Therefore, because they could not handle the *how,* they had given up the *that*—the resurrection itself. Having spoken at length with all of his rhetorical and theological skills to the latter question, he now turns to the former.

---

[12]The NIV begins the new paragraph with this sentence. This is fine for reading, but it is less useful for a commentary. A few MSS, followed by the TR (and KJV), omit the εἰ (preferred by Godet, 415), thereby missing the punch in Paul's argument.

[13]Gk. ἀλλά.

[14]There seems to be no good reason for the English subjunctive of the NIV. This implies that the question is merely anticipated. In fact it is almost certainly the real issue, even if the question as such has not been communicated to Paul. Given the way he addresses the questioner, "Foolish man," it seems nearly impossible that he did not know that this was what lay behind the denial.

As noted above, the two questions are probably to be understood as corresponding to one another. The first, "How are the dead raised?" is made specific in the second, "With what kind of body do they come?"[15] Inherent in the first is the scepticism of the interlocutor, "How is it possible that the dead are raised at all?"[16] scepticism that is further elaborated by the incredulity of the second question, "With what kind of body?" As noted above, it is this connection of "body" with "the dead" that makes the concept of resurrection so difficult for those Corinthians who are leading the church down these paths.

36-37   Paul now responds to his interlocutor in the strongest of terms, beginning with the vocative, "Foolish man!" an appellation so harsh to Christian ears that it tends to get modified in translation (NIV, "How foolish!").[17] The implication is not simply that such questions suggest one to have taken leave of his senses,[18] but that one stands as the "fool" in the OT sense—as the person who has failed to take God into account.[19] Thus the contrast is being set up with v. 38, where God gives the dead seed a new body as he wills.

This vocative is followed immediately in the Greek text by the personal pronoun, which ordinarily is not expressed, and is usually emphatic when it is, especially in the first position. Thus Paul says, "Foolish man, you, what you sow. . . ." In other words, "*You* hold the answer in your *own* hands. Simply look at the way God has arranged the natural order of plant life. In the everyday occurrence of the seed you have the evidence to answer your question."

The two clauses that follow are especially awkward, but thereby reveal Paul's own emphases: "You, what you sow does not *come to life*[20] unless it *dies;* and what you sow, not *the body that shall be* you sow, but a

---

[15]Jeremias, "Flesh and Blood," p. 157, proposes that the whole section, vv. 35-58, is a chiastic response to the two questions of v. 35. Vv. 36-49 (B') respond to the second question (B), "With what kind of body?"; vv. 50-58 (A') respond to the first question (A), "How are the dead raised?" While there is a degree of truth to this, it seems to miss both the progression of the argument and the climactic nature of vv. 50-58.

[16]Cf. Sider, "Conception," p. 429, who points out that πῶς frequently introduces rhetorical questions that challenge or reject an idea.

[17]Gk. ἄφρων, not the more pejorative μωρός that appears in 3:18 and 4:10 (and Matt. 5:22).

[18]Although in a community where wisdom and knowledge rule (cf. 1:10–4:21; 8:1-13), this may well have been heard differently from the way a modern reader would (ἄφρων implies a person without wisdom).

[19]Cf. Ps. 14:1; 53:1; 92:6; and especially in the Wisdom literature, where ἄφρων appears in the LXX to describe such people. Cf. Luke's usage in the parable of Jesus (12:16-21), where the rich man is called ἄφρων for precisely the same reason. Cf. Martin, 132.

[20]Gk. ζωοποιεῖται; cf. v. 22, where it is used of the activity of Jesus in bringing the dead to life in resurrection (so also in v. 45); cf. Rom. 4:17; 8:11.

naked seed, perhaps[21] of wheat or something else." The two sentences are coordinate, each beginning with the relative clause "what you sow," and joined by an unusual (for Paul) paratactic "and." Together they pick up the twin themes of "the dead" and "body" from the two questions of v. 35.

The first clause is reminiscent of John 12:24, but the point is different here. There the emphasis is on the necessity of death for fruit. Despite several contemporary scholars who would see the necessity of death as the point here too,[22] that concern is not picked up anywhere in the succeeding argument, and vv. 50-53 stand quite against it. Paul's concern is with death as the precondition of life, not in the sense that *all must die* but in the sense that the seed itself demonstrates that *out of death* a new expression of life springs forth. God's purposes are not thwarted by death; as with the seed, what is sown in death is brought forth into life. His point, therefore, in response to their scepticism as to the resurrection is that it is possible for the dead to rise again, as their own experience of sowing grain gives evidence.

But as he says in the next sentence (v. 37), and this is his concern, the life that comes forth does so in a transformed "body."[23] The use of "body" at this point in the analogy,[24] and especially "the body that will be,"[25] indicates that this is where everything is leading. It matters not whether one speaks of "wheat" or any other grain, Paul says, one plants a "naked seed," bare grain. Although Paul will later speak of the body as "weak and subject to decay" (2 Cor. 4:7-12), there is no hint of that in this imagery. The emphasis is not on its weakness but on its being simply a seed, with no vestige of its "afterlife" visible in the seed itself.[26] Thus the emphasis is on the transformed nature of the "body" of the seed after its "resurrec-

---

[21]Gk. εἰ τύχοι; see the discussion on 14:10.

[22]See above, n. 86 on v. 6, a view that has been stressed for this verse especially by H. Riesenfeld, "Paul's 'Grain of Wheat' Analogy and the Argument of 1 Corinthians 15," in *The Gospel Tradition* (ET, Philadelphia, 1970), pp. 171-86, esp. 174-78. Cf. Conzelmann, 281; Martin, 132.

[23]For a different use of this analogy, cf. Rabbi Meir, whose response to whether the dead will be raised clothed is: "The answer is given . . . by taking the case of a grain of wheat. If a grain of wheat was buried naked and comes out of the ground abundantly clothed, how much more will the righteous be dressed in their clothes" (*b.Sanh.* 90b). That assumes not only a materialistic view of resurrection but a Jewish view of nakedness! Paul's experience of the risen Lord moved him to understand resurrection in terms of transformation.

[24]Schneider, "Corporate Meaning," p. 452, makes the improbable suggestion that "body" here means "nature." To the contrary, it means "body"—even if that does not fit seeds so well—because the concern is not with seeds but with the nature of the resurrection *body*.

[25]Gk. τὸ γενησόμενον, the rare future participle.

[26]He will pick up this imagery again, however, in 2 Cor. 5:1-5, where he looks forward with longing to the mortal body's being "overclothed" with a resurrection body, since one is left "naked" at death.

tion." Nonetheless, inherent in the imagery, and crucial to it, is the fact of continuity. The one "life" is in two modes, one before and one after death and resurrection.[27]

38 As is his custom, Paul proceeds to take the "natural" phenomenon he has just described and attributes it to God.[28] In saying that "God gives it [the naked seed] a body as he has determined" (cf. 12:11), he means of course "the body that shall be," hence the "resurrection body." Even though he is still in the middle of the analogy, his point is clear: The answer to the question "With what kind of body will the dead come?" is ultimately to be understood as an activity of God. That is why the interlocutor is called a fool in v. 36; such a question has left God out of account. God does as he pleases;[29] and what pleases him is to "transform our lowly bodies so that they will be like Christ's glorious body" (Phil. 3:21).

But Paul is not yet ready to make that application; that will come in vv. 42-49. For now he keeps to the analogy of the seeds. However, the mention of God's giving to the "naked seed" a "resurrected" body as he pleases reminds him of the great variety of "bodies" there are in the plant world. Thus, "and to each kind of seed God gives its own body," meaning that each of the kinds of grain is different, not only from its naked seed, but from others as well. It is this last point that he feels compelled to elaborate in the next series of analogies.

39-41 With these verses Paul elaborates on the last clause of v. 38, that God has given to each seed its own kind of body. His present concern is to point out the great variety and kinds of "bodies" there are in the world, all of which is God's doing in creation. Although it is not clearly specified, the applications that follow suggest that Paul's concern is to emphasize that each is adapted to its own peculiar existence, that "body" does not necessarily mean one thing (= flesh and blood) since there are many kinds of bodies. At the same time, even though he means something different with the language "heavenly and earthly bodies" here than in vv. 45-49, he seems to be anticipating the language of that argument.[30] In vv. 36-38 the use of the word "body" was limited to that which was "raised," a usage that had been determined by the second question in v. 35. In the present series, even though Paul uses the word "flesh" for the first group, he uses the word "body" to describe both the heavenly and earthly "bodies." The series seem to begin with "earthly bodies" (v. 39), followed by "heavenly bodies"

---

[27]Those who stress discontinuity at the expense of continuity will wince at this; but their emphasis is a false dichotomy that Paul would not understand.

[28]Cf. Gen. 1:11: "Then God said: 'Let the land produce vegetation: seed-bearing plants . . . according to their various kinds.' And it was so."

[29]For this meaning of καθὼς ἠθέλησεν see on 12:11. In Paul's sentence the verb is aorist and refers first of all to the divine decrees of creation. Seeds die and come to life with a given "body" because God decreed that that be so.

[30]So also Lincoln, 39.

(v. 41), with v. 40 standing as the middle term that expressly ties the two together. All together they form a nearly perfect chiasm:

A   Not all "flesh" is the same;   [earthly bodies]

  B   People have one kind;
    Animals another;
    Birds   another;
    Fish   another.

    C   There are heavenly bodies [B']
    There are earthly   bodies [B]

    C'   The splendor of the heavenly bodies is of one kind;
    The splendor of the earthly   bodies is of another.

  B'   The sun   has one kind of splendor;
    The moon   another kind of splendor;
    The stars   another kind of splendor;

A'   And star differs from star in splendor. [heavenly bodies]

Thus the first and final sentences (A-A') emphasize differences within kinds; the two B sentences emphasize the differences within "genus" (the earthly expressed in terms of "flesh"; the heavenly in terms of "splendor"); while the two middle sentences (C-C') simply state the realities of earthly and heavenly "bodies."[31]

The first series (v. 39) calls attention to the phenomenon of animal life. Here Paul uses the term "flesh" because his concern is not with the *form* of their bodies but with the different *substance* of each, thus also anticipating the difference between the earthly and heavenly existence of believers. These are the "earthly bodies" mentioned in v. 40. The four "kinds" are standard expressions of "animal" life (human beings, beasts, birds, fish).[32]

Even though the affirmations of v. 40 seem clearly to refer to the sets spoken of in vv. 39 and 41, by their very expression they also anticipate the argument of vv. 45-49. What is important to note is that each has its own kind of "glory," so that in this argument, even though the earthly body must die, it is not without its own glory. Nonetheless, it is scarcely accidental that the description of the "heavenly bodies" in v. 41 is carried through, not

---

[31]Some have suggested that "heavenly bodies" cannot refer to the sun, etc. in v. 41 on the grounds that such usage is unknown in Greek antiquity, and therefore that Paul is referring to angelic beings (Findlay, 935; Parry, 236) or "the stars being equated with angelic powers" (H. Traub, *TDNT* V, 541; cf. Héring, 174; Conzelmann, 282). But the latter is pure speculation, with no basis in the text. This is to do word study precisely backwards. The context must prevail here. The question of v. 35b has already determined Paul's language; and in v. 37 Paul has already used "body" for a stalk of wheat. To insist, therefore, that "heavenly bodies" does not refer to the sun, etc. in v. 41, which the context clearly demands, is to make a Procrustean bed for Paul's use of language.

[32]These are the four specifically mentioned, in reverse order, as being created on the fifth and sixth days of creation (Gen. 1:20, 24, 26). Cf. Rom. 1:23, where "reptiles" replaces "fish" because that was a common expression of idolatry.

with the word "flesh," which would make no sense at all, nor with the word "body," which might. Rather, the heavenly triad of sun, moon, and stars is described in terms of the "glory" (here = radiance) of each.[33] In the application in v. 43, it is the resurrected (heavenly) body that has "glory." The fact that each star differs from others in radiance illustrates the well-known observations of the heavens that fascinated the ancients.

42-43 Paul now proceeds to apply both analogies to the present concern, which is expressed again in the language of their denial: "So also[34] is[35] the resurrection of the dead." Paul again resorts to rhetoric.[36] With a series of four staccato clauses, each repeating the verbs "it is sown, it is raised," he applies first the analogy of the seed (the first three clauses, vv. 42b-43) and then the analogy of the differing kinds of bodies (v. 44a). In so doing, he keeps alive the metaphor of the seed through the first verb ("it is sown"), but expresses the language of resurrection with the second ("it is raised"). The clauses have no expressed subject; "body" is most likely intended[37] as the subject for *both* verbs in each set,[38] thus implying genuine continuity between the present body and its future expression.

The first three sets of contrasts are intended to describe the essential differences between the "naked seed" and "the body that is to be" (v. 37); that is, despite the verb "sown," they are not intended to describe the "dead body" that is buried, but to contrast the present body with its future expression. The first set is primary, describing the essential difference between the present, earthly body and the future, heavenly one.[39] As the Corinthians well know, the present body is subject to decay; indeed, in death it "is sown in a perishable state,[40]" which is precisely why they are disenchanted with it

---

[33]The Fathers, with their love of allegory, were fond of "identifying" these as various grades of saints and sinners, etc. (cf. Tertullian, *res.* 52).

[34]Gk. οὕτως καί; for similar usage in applying a metaphor or analogy in Paul, see 2:11; 12:12; 14:9, 12; Gal. 4:3; Rom. 6:11.

[35]There is no verb in the Greek text; since the verbs that follow are expressed in the present, that seems preferable here as well. These are gnomic presents, and therefore timeless.

[36]This in itself should make one cautious about pressing the antitheses. Some work better than others; but each describes the humble, earthly nature of the one and the glorious, exalted nature of the other.

[37]Hence the NIV. This is in fact specified in the fourth set, where "body" is the subject or predicate apposition. Otherwise, Findlay, 936; Barrett, 372; and Gillman, "Transformation," p. 327, who would make them impersonal passives ("the sowing takes place in corruption").

[38]This is another clear indication, noted in the introduction to this section (vv. 35-58), of the interchange between "the dead" and "the body." It points to the fact that the problem expressed in the former lies with the latter.

[39]Cf. Lincoln, 39-40, who uses the language "the pre-eschatological state of the body over against the eschatological."

[40]Gk. ἐν φθορᾷ; its opposite is ἐν ἀφθαρσίᾳ ("in an imperishable state"). It is perhaps a reflection on our fallenness that the "positive" word is the negative one (perishable), whose opposite "positive" is formed with an *alpha*-privative (nonperishable).

(cf. 6:13). But what they have failed to reckon with is the transformation that God will effect: "it is raised imperishable." So important is this basic set of contrasts to Paul's argument that this is the only language picked up in the description of the final transformation in vv. 50-54, where it is repeated three times (vv. 50/52, 53, 54).

The second set picks up the theme of "glory" from vv. 40-41 in order to describe the resurrected body. But now it does not mean "radiance." Rather, this reflects Jewish eschatological language for the future state of the righteous.[41] Paul has already used it of Christ's personal reign (1 Thess. 2:12). In Phil. 3:21 it is the word used to describe Christ's resurrection body. This usage is what here controls Paul's thinking. Its opposite is "dishonor" (better, "humiliation"). This, too, the Corinthians would readily agree to. For Paul, it is not so much a pejorative term to describe the body as shameful, as it is a description of its present "lowly" state in comparison with its glorified one.

Likewise with the third set, "weakness and power." In this case the language has been determined by its present state of "weakness," a word that particularly recurs in 2 Cor. 10-13 to describe not only the body, but Paul's whole present existence. Its opposite, "power," in this case less describes its permanent heavenly state than the nature of its being raised.

44 With this fourth set of contrasts Paul now applies the analogy of the differing kinds of "bodies" from vv. 39-41. Thus, instead of describing *how* the body is sown, the two adjectives "natural" *(psychikos)* and "spiritual" *(pneumatikos)* are used with the noun "body" *(sōma)* to describe its present earthly and future heavenly expressions respectively. At the same time, however, this use of language must have had special shock value in Corinth, where the word *pneumatikos* is most likely what set them apart from Paul and was a catchword for their antisomatic understanding of Christian existence. They would probably have had little trouble with the description of the present body as *psychikos*.[42] But the use of *pneumatikos* to describe *sōma* must have been troublesome indeed.[43]

---

[41]E.g., Dan. 12:3; 1 Enoch 62:15; 105:11, 12; 2 Bar. 51:10.

[42]On the basis of word statistics it is difficult to escape the conclusion that *pneumatikos* was a Corinthian term. The same cannot be said of *psychikos*. See the discussion on 2:14. On the whole *psychikos* seems unlikely as their term; it was probably chosen because of the usage in Gen. 2:7 that Paul is about to cite with reference to Adam (so also Martin, 136). If the term was theirs, one cannot be sure of its origins. Despite some conceptual similarities with Philo (cf. Pearson, *Terminology*, and Horsley, "Pneumatikos"), this specific linguistic contrast does not occur. That Paul and the Corinthians were at odds over the interpretation of Gen. 2:7, as Pearson (17-26) suggests, is a thesis that cannot be proved or disproved.

[43]But see E. Schweizer, *TDNT* VI, 420; cf. H. Clavier, "Brèves remarques sur la notion de πνευματικὸν σῶμα," in *The Background of the New Testament and Its Eschatology* (ed. W. D. Davies and D. Daube; Cambridge, 1964), pp. 342-62.

These are the same two adjectives used in 2:14 to describe the basic differences between believer and unbeliever. In this case, therefore, as the next analogy (vv. 45-49) will make clear, they do not describe the "stuff" or composition of the body; nor are they value words as in 2:14, describing the essential difference between those who belong to God and those who do not. Rather, they describe the one body in terms of its essential characteristics as earthly, on the one hand, and therefore belonging to the life of the present age, and as heavenly, on the other, and therefore belonging to the life of the Spirit in the age to come. It is "spiritual," not in the sense of "immaterial" but of "supernatural,"[44] as he will explain with the help of Scripture in v. 45, because it will have been recreated by Christ, who himself through his resurrection came to be "a life-giving Spirit."

The transformed body, therefore, is not composed of "spirit"; it is a *body* adapted to the eschatological existence that is under the ultimate domination of the Spirit. Thus for Paul, to be truly *pneumatikos* is to bear the likeness of Christ (v. 49) in a transformed body, fitted for the new age. The problem that the Corinthians would have had with this idea seems to be the best explanation for the unusual final sentence in this argument: "If there is a *psychikos* body [a matter on which there would be no quibble], there is also a *pneumatikos* body."[45] But that would be precisely the problem for the Corinthians, so Paul turns next to explain how so, and does so on the basis of the Adam-Christ analogy, which has Christ's supernatural, that is, "spiritual," body as its presupposition.

Thus, with this set of analogies and applications Paul has argued first with illustrations from everyday life that God has already so arranged the universe that there are bodies of all kinds adapted to their various existences. And in one case, the analogy of the seed, the same "life" itself finds expression in two different "bodies." But that analogy must not be pressed because the seed and the full stalk with grain have only their life in common. In the case of the resurrection body, there is genuine continuity, a point made by using the same noun "body" to describe its twofold expression. Thus the way is prepared for the next analogy, that of Adam and Christ, since the entire argument is predicated on the resurrection of Christ.

b. Analogy of Adam and Christ (15:45-49)

45 *So it is written: "The first Adam[1] became a living being"*[a]*; the last Adam, a life-giving spirit.* 46 *The spiritual did not come first, but*

---

[44] The language is Héring's, 176; it is preferred also by Martin, 137.

[45] As Lincoln, 43, points out, the argument is neither *a fortiori* (given the one, then all the more the other) nor from inference (the existence of the one is inferred from the existence of the other), but typological, based on the inferences drawn from Gen. 2:7 in v. 45.

[1] The Greek reads ἄνθρωπος Ἀδάμ, a redundancy omitted by the NIV for the same reason as did a few MSS (B K 326 365 pc Iren).

the natural, and after that the spiritual. 47 *The first man was of the dust of the earth, the second man[2] is of[3] heaven.* 48 *As was the earthly man, so are those who are of the earth; and as is the* heavenly man[4], *so also are those who are of heaven.* 49 *And just as we have borne the likeness of the earthly man, so let us[5] bear the likeness of the man from heaven.*

aGen. 2:7

This paragraph break is quite arbitrary. The first sentence continues the argument of vv. 42-44, serving as an elaboration of v. 44b. Nonetheless, since the content of vv. 45-49 is so different from what has preceded,[6] it is fitting to isolate this material as a paragraph and see its place in the overall argument, which unfortunately is not easy to see in English because of the inherent difficulty in translating some of the key words and concepts.

To understand the argument one must keep in mind two crucial contextual matters: First, the concern is *not* christological;[7] rather, its function in the argument is to demonstrate from Scripture the reality of v. 44, that just as there is a *psychikos* body, so there is a *pneumatikos* body. As noted above, this must have come as something of a shock to the Corinthian pneumatics. Second, the Adam-Christ analogy presupposes its prior use in

---

[2]In the interests of piety, several changes were made to this text. Marcion substituted ὁ κύριος for ἄνθρωπος (this is also the reading of 630, but most likely as a deviation, by way of omission, from the MajT). The MajT (thus the KJV) has conflated by adding ὁ κύριος, thus creating a christological text ("the second Man is the Lord from heaven"), instead of Paul's eschatological-soteriological one. P46 has the singular addition of πνευματικός (= "the second man is spiritual from heaven"); F G latt add ὁ οὐράνιος after οὐρανοῦ. Both of these are attempts to balance the first clause.

[3]NIV, "from"; see the commentary.

[4]NIV, "man from heaven."

[5]This is the reading of NIVmg (also Tischendorf, WH, von Soden, Vogels); the text reads "shall we" (supported by B I 6 630 1881 al sa, and the majority of commentators); cf. Metzger, 569, who notes: "Exegetical considerations (i.e., the context is didactic, not hortatory) led the Committee to prefer the future indicative, despite its rather slender external support." But the UBS committee abandoned its better text-critical sense here. If the reading of B *et al.* were original, given that it makes so much sense in context, how is one to account for such a nearly universal (P46 ℵ A C D F G Ψ 075 243 Maj latt bo Clement Origen Epiphanius) change to the hortatory subjunctive? (It can only be accounted for as an extremely early itacism that affected the entire tradition; B *et al.* would thus inadvertently have the original, not as "copies" of it but as independent attempts to correct the "error.") Far better to make sense of what best explains how the other came about than to assume that the context cannot here be hortatory (so also Grosheide, 389; Héring, 179; Sider, "Conception," p. 434; Lincoln, 50). See the commentary.

[6]Widman, "Einspruch," pp. 47-48, considers vv. 44b-48 an interpolation. See the response in Murphy-O'Connor, "Interpolations," 94.

[7]A considerable amount of scholarly energy has been expended on both vv. 45 and 47 in terms of their christological implications. But these are quite beside Paul's point, which, as in vv. 21-22, has to do with Christ's *resurrection* being the ground of ours. The *language* has been dictated by the argument itself, especially the use of Gen. 2:7.

vv. 21-22, and therefore deals with the effects of the resurrection of Christ, now in terms of the resurrection body. All of that is to say, therefore, that Paul's concern throughout has to do with the question, "With what kind of body?" (v. 35). Just as the resurrection of Christ is the ground of our resurrection (vv. 1-11, 20-28), so it is the ground of the resurrection body.

The argument is basically in two parts, both of which are based on a kind of midrashic interpretation of Gen. 2:7 in light of the resurrection of Christ. In vv. 45-46 Paul cites the text, in which the key word, *psychē,* is used of Adam and the implied word *pneuma* ("God breathed"), is applied to Christ, and insists that what is *pneumatikos* comes after what is *psychikos.* In vv. 47-49, again in the language of Gen. 2:7, the contrast between Adam and Christ is made in terms of the nature of their humanity: One by virtue of creation is "of earth," the other by virtue of resurrection is "of heaven" (v. 47), which point is then applied to the Corinthian believers (v. 48). Finally, in v. 49 they are urged to bear the likeness of the one who is now "heavenly." Since believers have all shared the existence of the first Adam, they are being called to bear the image of the last Adam, which in its eschatological expression will be a "heavenly" body such as he now has.

45 In vv. 21-22 Paul had argued that "as in Adam all die, so in Christ all will be made alive." He now returns to that analogy by way of Scripture to support his contention in v. 44, that believers will be raised with a "spiritual body," that is, a "supernatural" body acquired through resurrection and adapted to the life of the Spirit in the coming age. He begins by citing the LXX of Gen. 2:7 in a kind of midrash pesher (= a quotation that is at once citation and interpretation; cf. 14:21).[8] Thus:

| The first man, Adam, became a living | *(zōsan)* | *psychē;* |
| the last | Adam | a life-giving *(zōiopoioun) pneuma.* |

Several observations need to be made about this citation: (1) The modifications in the first line, namely the additions of the adjective "first" and of the name "Adam," are designed to lead to the second line, where Paul's concern lies. (2) The two words that describe Adam and Christ respectively are the cognate nouns for the adjectives *psychikos* and *pneumatikos* in v. 44. This clear linguistic connection implies that the *original bearers* of the two kinds of bodies mentioned in v. 44 are Adam and Christ.[9] (3) Even though the second line is neither present nor inferred in the Genesis text, it nonethe-

[8]See Ellis, *Use,* pp. 141-43; it is doubtful whether Paul is here citing a midrash that had already taken hold in Christian circles (pp. 95-97). He is perfectly capable of such pesher. For a vigorous rejection of all such ideas, see Lenski, 717-21.

[9]Cf. J. D. G. Dunn, "I Corinthians 15:45—last Adam, life-giving Spirit," in *Christ and Spirit in the New Testament, Studies in Honour of Charles Francis Digby Moule* (ed. B. Lindars and S. Smalley; Cambridge, 1973), p. 130.

less reflects the language of the prior clause in the LXX, "and he *breathed* into his face the breath of life *(pnoēn zōēs)*." (4) At the same time the language "life-giving" repeats the verb used of Christ in the Adam-Christ analogy in v. 22, indicating decisively, it would seem, that the interest here is not in his incarnation[10] nor in his creational activity, but as before in his resurrection as the ground of ours ("in Christ all will be made alive").

Although some subtleties are at work here, from these observations one may draw the following conclusions about Paul's intent. First, the *reason* for the citation lies with Paul's desire to demonstrate the reality of the resurrection body on the basis of the prior Adam-Christ analogy. The use of *psychē* to describe Adam gives Paul a biblical base for the distinctions he wants to make between the two kinds of *sōma* and at the same time allows him to connect that with what he had already said in vv. 21-22.

Second, as the further explanation in vv. 47-48 makes clear, the overriding urgency in this passage is to show in an analogical way that the two kinds of bodies "sown" and "raised" in v. 44 are already represented in the two archetyphal "Adams." The first Adam, who became a "living *psychē*," was thereby given a *psychikos* body at creation, a body subject to decay and death. This Adam, who brought death into the world (vv. 21-22), thus became the representative man for all who bear his *psychikos* likeness. The last Adam, on the other hand, whose "spiritual (glorified) body" was given at his resurrection, not only became the representative Man[11] for all who will bear his *pneumatikos* likeness, but he is himself the source of the *pneumatikos* life[12] as well as the *pneumatikos* body.[13]

Therefore, third, the shift from "living" with regard to Adam (he is merely life-receiving) to "life-giving" seems to have a double *entendre* with regard to Christ. In his resurrection whereby he assumed his "supernatural body," he also became the giver of life to all who will ever follow after.[14]

[10]This has been a common interpretation, but seems to miss Paul's point altogether. See, *inter alia,* Edwards, 444; Parry, 239.

[11]Hence the reason he is called the "last Adam," meaning not just the final such representative, but the "eschatological" Adam—and "Adam," not "man," because he is representative, not simply a model or pattern. Schneider, "Corporate Meaning," suggests that "Adam" in this verse should be understood in a corporate sense. That seems unlikely.

[12]Cf. Dunn, "Last Adam," p. 132; however, his emphasis on the verb ζωοποιέω as referring primarily to the present misses its clear tie to v. 22, where it is used of the resurrection.

[13]Lincoln, 43, follows Vos (*Eschatology,* p. 169) in suggesting that by this collocation of Adam and Christ on the basis of Gen. 2:7 Paul implies that at creation a different kind of body was already in view. Thus, "the Corinthians should not view the idea of a bodily form appropriate to spiritual existence as something so novel and unimaginable, for in fact this has always been God's purpose."

[14]Cf. Lincoln, 43-44: "The last Adam however has a new quality of life, for as πνεῦμα ζωοποιοῦν he is no longer merely alive and susceptible to death but rather has now become creatively life-giving."

Paul's point seems to be that one can assume full *pneumatikos* existence only as Christ did, by resurrection, which includes a *pneumatikos* body. The concern of line 2, therefore, is not christological, as though Christ and the Spirit were somehow now interchangeable terms for Paul.[15] The concern is soteriological-eschatological;[16] the language has been dictated both by the Genesis text and the concern to demonstrate that Christ is the foundation of believers' receiving a "spiritual body."

Part of Paul's point in all of this seems to be to deny, on the basis of Christ's resurrection, that they are completed pneumatics now. They, too, must await the resurrection (or transformation, v. 52) before their "spirituality" is complete, since as with Christ it *must* include a somatic expression. This is the point he will pick up with the second use of this text and the Adam-Christ analogy in vv. 47-49; but before that he takes another swipe at their misguided, overspiritualized eschatology.

46 Since v. 47 follows so naturally from v. 45, the present verse is a truly puzzling text in the argument, both as to what "spiritual" and "natural" here refer (Christ and Adam, or the two kinds of bodies) and why it is said at all, especially with the adversative "but"[17] and the "not/but" contrast that emphatically declare that the "spiritual" comes second. Of several suggestions the best solution seems to lie in the preceding citation of Gen. 2:7, and almost certainly is to be understood over against the Corinthians themselves. On the one hand, in asserting that the last Adam became "a life-giving spirit," Paul was alluding to the prior act of God in breathing life into the first Adam. Now Paul corrects any misimpressions that allusion may have created. The "last Adam" refers to the *eschatological* reality of Christ's resurrection and of his subsequently giving life to his own at their resurrection. Thus the *pneumatikon* comes after the *psychikon*, in terms both of Adam and Christ and of the two forms of somatic existence people will bear. The debate over Adam/Christ or the two bodies, therefore, is probably too narrowly conceived. The words most likely refer to the two orders of

---

[15]It is sometimes suggested, on the basis of this text and 2 Cor. 3:17, that Paul "does not draw any hard and fast line between the Spirit and Christ" (Ruef, 173). But that reflects a very poor understanding of Paul's Christology, not to mention of 2 Cor. 3:17, which is not saying something about Christ at all. The Spirit there is being identified in a midrashic way with "the Lord" mentioned in the Exodus passage cited in v. 16. Although he has correctly rejected the improper use of 2 Cor. 3:17, Dunn ("Last Adam") has unfortunately perpetuated this kind of "Spirit Christology" for the present text. Since such an idea is found only in such a pesher as this, far better it would seem to allow fluidity in Paul's use of *language* than to argue that he tends basically to identify the Risen Christ with the Spirit—especially since he does not do so elsewhere, where the language is more straightforward.

[16]Some would say, "anthropological"; e.g., R. Scroggs, *The Last Adam, A Study in Pauline Anthropology* (Philadelphia, 1966), p. 87. The issue, however, is not with the "nature" of humanity, but with eschatological salvation as including a somatic expression.

[17]Gk. ἀλλ', untranslated in the NIV.

existence connoted by this language, of which Adam and Christ are the representatives and the two bodies the concrete expressions.[18]

At the same time, however, the emphatic "not/but" suggests that he is asserting this order of things over against the Corinthians themselves. This does not mean, as some have suggested, that the Corinthians were asserting some kind of Philonic[19] or Gnostic[20] understanding of the priority of the spiritual to the physical. After all, in neither of those systems is there a concern for the chronology of the one in relation to the other. The order here is that set out in v. 23, which insists that each comes in its own order, Christ first, then those who are his. Against the Corinthians, who assumed that they had already entered into the totality of pneumatic existence while they were still in their *psychikos* body, Paul insists that the latter comes "first," that is, that they must reckon with the physical side of their present life in the Spirit. "Then,"[21] meaning at the Eschaton, comes the *pneumatikos;* and they must reckon with the reality that since the *psychikos* comes first and has a body, so too the *pneumatikos* that comes after will have a body, a transformed body appropriate to eschatological spiritual life.[22]

47 But Paul is not done with the Adam-Christ analogy, nor with his use of Gen. 2:7 as the biblical text from which to make his point. In v. 45 he used the Genesis text to demonstrate that just as Adam was the representative man for all who bear a *psychikon* body, so Christ in his resurrection became the representative Man for all who will bear the *pneumatikon* body. In v. 46 he insisted that the one prevails until the eschatological arrival of the other. Now he takes up the language "dust from the earth"[23] from the account of Adam's creation and offers an appropriate opposite for Christ, "of heaven." Thus Paul is once again using the Genesis text to refer to something charac-

---

[18]Cf. Lincoln, 44: "What started out as a comparison between two forms of bodily existence moved to a comparison between the two representatives of those forms and now proceeds to include the two world-orders which the first and last Adam exemplify."

[19]Among those who view this as a response to Philonic views, see Allo, 427-28; Héring, 178; Barrett, 374-75; Davies, *Paul*, pp. 51-52; Pearson, 17-23; Horsley, "Pneumatikos." This view has been (rightly) rejected by Scroggs, *Last Adam*, pp. 115-22; A. J. M. Wedderburn, "Philo's 'Heavenly Man,'" *NovT* 15 (1973), 301-26; and Lincoln, 44.

[20]Cf. Schmithals, 169-70; Jewett, *Terms*, pp. 352-56; E. Brandenburger, *Adam und Christus* (WMANT 7; Neukirchen, 1962). See the critique, especially of Brandenburger, in Kim, *Origin*, pp. 162-93, based in part on the unpublished dissertation of Wedderburn, "Adam and Christ" (Cambridge, 1970).

[21]Gk. ἔπειτα, as in v. 23.

[22]Cf. Wedderburn, "Heavenly Man," 302, and Lincoln, 45. In Wedderburn's words: "Taken in this way the verse becomes a polemic against an unrealistic spiritualizing of this present life, a blending of heaven and earth that does away with the earthiness of the latter; the Corinthians erred in holding to a *one-stage soteriology*, rather than in reversing the order of a two-stage one" (italics mine).

[23]The LXX has χοῦν ἀπὸ τῆς γῆς; Paul says ἐκ γῆς χοϊκός.

teristic of Adam, for which he will say something about Christ that is its
eschatological counterpart. In so doing he reverts to the language "man" for
each, as in v. 21, but picks up, by implication, the language "first" and
"second" from v. 45.

Unfortunately this use of language has led to a considerable amount
of misunderstanding, which the NIV helps to foster. Paul's sentence reads,
literally:

> The first   man of earth   made of dust;[24]
> The second man of heaven.

There is a history of interpretation that sees these clauses as referring
to the *origin* of Adam and Christ.[25] That is, the first man's origin is "from
the earth," therefore he is "earthly," while the second man "*comes*[26] from
heaven" and is therefore "heavenly." More likely, however, these prepositions, which have come about by way of Gen. 2, are intended to be synonyms of *psychikos* and *pneumatikos* and are thus intended to be qualitative,
having to do with *human*[27] life that is characterized by being either "of
earth" or "of heaven." Several considerations support this view of things:[28]

(1) The context nearly demands such an understanding. Paul's concern here, as in v. 45, is not with Christ's origins, but with his present
(heavenly) *somatic* existence as the ground of believers' similar heavenly
existence at their resurrection. Thus his is "of heaven" in the same way that
Adam's—and ours now—is "of earth." (2) The grammar also supports this
contextual understanding. The adjective "made of earth" is nominative and
follows "of the earth" as its duplicate, so that together they modify "man"
as predicate adjectives; the adjective seems to have been added to show that
it is in fact with regard to the body that Paul thus speaks.[29] That means,
therefore, that the verb "to be" must be supplied, and that it must be
supplied after "man." Thus what characterizes the first man is that his life is
of the present earth, earthly, whereas what characterizes the second man is
that his life is "of heaven," that is, heavenly. (3) The following verses,
which elaborate this one, indicate most clearly that Paul did not intend to
identify Christ as having *come* from heaven. The same adjective, "made of

[24]Gk. χοϊκός, the adjective of the noun χοῦς used in the LXX. The use of the
adjective indicates that Paul's interest is not in the "stuff" or dust of the earth per se, but in
describing Adam's body as being "earthy," that is, subject to decay and death.
[25]See, e.g., Parry, 240; Grosheide, 388; Barrett, 375-76; Martin, 137.
[26]This is the verb supplied by Barrett, 375.
[27]Thus the use of "first and second *man*," the emphasis here being on Christ's
humanity now being "of heaven" by virtue of his resurrection.
[28]Cf., *inter alia,* Godet, 427-30; Findlay, 939; Bruce, 153; Lincoln, 45-46.
[29]So also Godet, 427, whose language has been borrowed.

earth," is repeated in Adam's case; the counterpart used of Christ is now "heavenly"—which qualitatively describes his resurrected existence—not "from heaven." The reason for this is simple: Believers are said to share both kinds of existence, that of Adam through their humanity, that of Christ through their resurrection. They do not share Christ's heavenly existence because, *as he*,[30] they are *from* heaven, but because at the resurrection they will receive a heavenly body that is just like his. (4) Finally, for Paul now to refer to Christ's preexistence and incarnation would be to contradict the very point just made in vv. 45-46, that the *pneumatikos* comes second.[31]

Thus in both passages the concern is the same. At the resurrection the "last Adam," whose resurrection marks the beginning of the End and whose somatic existence as the "second man" is now "of heaven," will change our "humble bodies into the likeness of his glorified body" (Phil. 3:21). That point is precisely what is elaborated in the final two sets of clauses in the paragraph.

This also means that an enormous amount of discussion that has surrounded this verse is nearly irrelevant since it has been concerned with the background (or origin) of the idea of "the man from heaven" in Pauline thinking, as though he were influenced by myths of a Primal Man or a "redeemed Redeemer."[32] Since he is not thinking in those terms at all, the true question has to do with the origin of his seeing Christ's present humanity as "of heaven." In this case those are surely right who have seen the background as lying in his own encounter with the "heavenly Christ" on the Damascus Road, coupled with the theme of the restoration of Adam to heavenly existence found in Jewish apocalyptic literature.[33]

48-49   With this set of perfectly balanced sentences Paul now applies the Adam-Christ analogy of v. 47 to their situation. They also make plain that the point of vv. 45-47 is to explicate the assertion of v. 44, that the body "sown" in death is *psychikon*, while the one raised at the resurrection is *pneumatikon*. Using the language of v. 47, slightly modified in the case of

---

[30]The correlatives οἷος . . . τοιοῦτοι are crucial here: "of such nature as the one, of such nature also the other."

[31]Some have suggested that Paul's intent in v. 47 is to qualify v. 46, so that the Corinthians will not be led astray into thinking that Christ is really second to Adam, since he was in fact before him. But that theological nicety is beside Paul's present concern. If so, why then the emphasis in v. 46 at all? And why not a genuine qualifier about Christ instead of this sentence that begins with a word about the genuineness of Adam's humanity? And how will a reference to the Incarnation help Paul's argument at all? After all, the point of everything is v. 44, and Paul's concern to show by way of analogy that at the resurrection believers will assume a "spiritual body" that is like Christ's.

[32]See the helpful discussion of this debate in Lincoln, 46-50.

[33]See, e.g., Wedderburn, "Adam," pp. 66-112; Lincoln, 47-50; Kim, *Origin*, pp. 187-93. For apocalyptic as the background see also J. L. Sharpe, "The Second Adam in the Apocalypse of Moses," *CBQ* 35 (1973), 35-46.

Christ, Paul argues that Adam and Christ are representative of those who belong to them, first to an earthly order of existence and then through Christ to a heavenly one. Thus:

Such as	the man	of earth,
such also	the people	of earth;
Such as	the man	of heaven,
such also	the people	of heaven.

   and

even as we have borne the likeness
         of the man of earth,
let us also   bear   the likeness
         of the man of heaven.

The first pair in particular indicate that the description of Christ in v. 47 did not have to do with his incarnation, but with his resurrection. The first man's progeny are as he is. They "bear his likeness."[34] He is of earth, earthly; so also are they. As Adam died, so like him they sow at death a corruptible body that is "of earth." This is the *psychikon* body, which belongs only to the present existence. As noted above, that would scarcely have disturbed the Corinthians; they would be glad to have it sown in the earth so as to get on with the truly "spiritual," that is, nonsomatic, existence that their present experience of the Spirit has already made available for them. But not so, says Paul. For those who are "in Christ" (v. 22) also share the likeness of the man of heaven, whose resurrection has guaranteed that they shall share a heavenly body as well.

But in this case the question remains as to whether their sharing of the "heavenly" existence has not already begun, that is, whether their corresponding to the man of heaven refers only to the resurrection body that they are to assume at the Eschaton, or whether Paul is here intending also a broader sense, including behavioral implications, involved in their sharing in his likeness now. Under ordinary circumstances, one would see the latter as a secondary idea at best, brought in circuitously by way of vv. 21-22 through the later discussion in Rom. 5.[35] But in this case the question arises on the basis of the final verb in v. 49. If Paul had written the future, "we shall bear," the case would be closed; the whole discussion would then

---

[34] Gk. ἐφορέσαμεν τὴν εἰκόνα; the verb is a metaphor for putting on clothing. Cf. the same metaphor with the verb ἐνδύω in vv. 53-54 and 2 Cor. 5:1-4. The phrase probably means, as BAGD interpret, "represent in one's own appearance." Thus, even though εἰκών here may perhaps reflect Genesis (in this case 1:26-27), it is probably not fraught with theological overtones. In our earthly bodies we are like the one, Paul says; in our heavenly bodies like the other.

[35] In fact it is expressly denied by Barrett, 377.

involve the heavenly body and have to do only with the Eschaton. One can well understand, therefore, why the majority of those who have written on this passage opt for this reading. Nonetheless, the future is found in only a few disparate MSS and is easily accounted for on the very same grounds that it is now adopted by so many, while it is nearly impossible to account for anyone's having changed a clearly understandable future to the hortatory subjunctive so early and so often that it made its way into every textual history as the predominant reading.[36] For that reason it must be the original, and if original it must be intentional on Paul's part as a way of calling them to prepare now for the future that is to be.

If so, then the exhortation is not that the Corinthians try to assume their "heavenly body" now; both the argument of vv. 23-28 and of vv. 50-57 insist that such happens only at the Eschaton. Rather, they are being urged to conform to the life of the "man of heaven" as those who now share his character and behavior. As in vv. 33-34 and v. 58, the concerns over their denial of the resurrection with its heavenly body and over their unchristian behavior merge. The implication is that not only are they not fully *pneumatikos* now, but they will not be fully *pneumatikos* at all if they do not presently also "bear the likeness of the man of heaven." Thus we have another expression of Paul's "already/not yet" eschatological framework. They are being urged to become what they are by grace; but as vv. 50-57 make plain, what they presently are by grace will not be fully realized until this mortal puts on immortality and the final defeat of death is realized.

The problem is that the Corinthians believed that they had already assumed the heavenly existence that was to be, an existence in the Spirit that discounted earthly existence both in its physical and in its behavioral expressions. What Paul appears to be doing once again is refuting both notions. They have indeed borne—and still bear—the likeness of the man of earth. Because of that they are destined to die. But in Christ's resurrection and their being "in him" they have also begun to bear the likeness of the man of heaven. The urgency is that they truly do so now as they await the consummation when they shall do so fully.

4. The Assurance of Triumph (15:50-58)

50 I[1] *declare to you, brothers, that flesh and blood cannot[2] inherit the kingdom of God, nor does the perishable inherit the imperish-*

---

[36]See n. 3 above.

[1]In place of the δέ with which this paragraph begins (not transl. in NIV; cf. KJV, "now"), the Western witnesses (D F G b Ambst) substitute a γάρ, making this verse the conclusion of vv. 45-49.

[2]In conformity (apparently) to 6:9-10, some Western witnesses omit the δύναται (A C D Maj have δύνανται) and change the infinitive to a future indicative.

able. 51 *Listen, I tell you a mystery: We will not all sleep, but we will all be changed—*[3] 52 *in a flash, in the twinkling*[4] *of an eye, at the last trumpet. For the trumpet will sound, the dead will be raised imperishable, and we will be changed.* 53 *For the perishable must clothe itself with the imperishable, and the mortal with immortality.* 54 *When the perishable has been clothed with the imperishable, and the mortal with immortality,*[5] *then the saying that is written will come true: "Death has been swallowed up in victory."*[a]

> 55 *"Where, O death, is your victory?*
> *Where, O death, is your sting?"*[b][6]

56 *The sting of death is sin, and the power of sin is the law.* 57 *But thanks be to God! He gives us the victory through our Lord Jesus Christ.*

58 *Therefore, my dear brothers, stand firm. Let nothing move you. Always give yourselves fully to the work of the Lord, because you know that your labor in the Lord is not in vain.*

[a]Isaiah 25:8
[b]Hosea 13:14

[3]This text has suffered considerable corruption in transmission. There are five basic text forms:

1. We shall not all sleep,
   but we shall all be changed (B Maj)
2. We shall all sleep,
   but we shall not all be changed (ℵ C)
3. We shall not all sleep,
   and we shall not all be changed (P[46] A[c])
4. We shall all sleep,
   and we shall all be changed (A*)
5. We shall all be raised,
   but we shall not all be changed (D* Marcion)

The best solution is to see #1 as responsible for the others, either in view of Paul's own death or as a reflection of later Christian eschatology (e.g., #2, "all men must die, but transformation is for believers only"). P[46] is a conflation of #1 and #2. Cf. Zuntz, 255-56; Metzger, 569; Conzelmann, 288 n. 1. H. Saake, "Die kodikologisch problematische Nachstellung der Negation (Beobachtungen zu 1 Kor 15 $_{51}$)," *ZNW* 63 (1972), 277-79, argues for #2 as original, but would change the punctuation so that it meant the same as #1 (πάντες μὲν κοιμηθησόμεθα οὐ, πάντες δὲ ἀλλαγησόμεθα); but the alleged parallel of a postpositive οὐ in Rom. 7:18 is not quite precise.

[4]For a full discussion of the variant ῥοπῇ found in P[46] D* F G 1739 and the majority of witnesses in his time, according to Jerome, see Zuntz, 37-39.

[5]Several omissions and subsequent transpositions occurred in the MS tradition due to homoeoteleuton/arcton. See the discussion in Metzger, 569.

[6]Later MSS, in partial conformity to the LXX of Hos. 13:14, change the order of the clauses and substitute ᾅδη for θάνατε in the second instance (cf. KJV, "O death, where is thy *sting*? O *grave*, where is thy *victory*?"). The text is read by P[46] ℵ* B C 088 1739* pc lat co.

With this magnificent crescendo Paul brings to a conclusion the argument that began in v. 35. Having argued both for the reasonableness of a resurrection body (through the analogies of vv. 36-44) and for its certainty (on the basis of Christ's heavenly body, vv. 45-49), he now emphasizes: (1) the absolute necessity of transformation in order to enter the heavenly mode of existence (vv. 50, 53); (2) the fact that both the living and the dead must be so transformed (vv. 51-52); and (3) that the resurrection/transformation, which will take place at the Parousia (v. 52), will signal the final defeat of death (vv. 54-55). Never one to let a theological moment pass without an exhortation, Paul concludes on the high note of Christ's present victory over sin and the law as well (vv. 56-57), which leads to a concluding exhortation to work in the context of hope (v. 58).

This is Paul's final, triumphant response to the questions of v. 35, "Is it possible for the dead to raised? With what kind of body will they come?" The answer: a transformed body, in which the perishable and mortal are clothed with imperishability and immortality. At the same time, however, since the emphasis is not now on resurrection per se, but on the necessity of transformation, Paul adds—and emphasizes—the revelation of a mystery: Transformation will happen to *the living* as well as to the dead. It is difficult to assess the impact this revelation may have had on them; but surely it was not without purpose for Paul. In a community where being *pneumatikos* ("spiritual") appears to have been understood as a present full realization of what is to be, for whom the thought of somatic existence, either present or future, was repugnant, the revelation of this "mystery" must have come as no small jolt.

Two further notes: (1) Although he does not say so here, the preceding argument makes it certain that this revelation is predicated on the resurrection of Christ, who in his present heavenly existence has assumed a transformed, glorified body. (2) Since for Paul correct theology always leads to proper behavior, one is not surprised to have this eschatological argument conclude with affirmation and exhortation about the present. The one who will swallow up death at his Parousia (vv. 54-55) has already through his death and resurrection prevailed victoriously in our behalf over sin and the law (vv. 56-57). Hence the exhortation in v. 58. The framework is thus the same throughout: Eschatology that is both already and not yet. Through Christ the End has begun; but they are not there yet, as many of them think. So they must live in hope, not in a false triumphalism that leads to aberrant behavior.

50   Although some have seen this verse to be the conclusion of vv. 45-49,[7] there can be little question that it serves rather to introduce this final

---

[7]Among translations, the RSV; among Greek editors, B. Weiss; among commentators, Calvin, 341; Héring, 180; Lietzmann, 86; Gromacki, 196; Wilson, 235; cf. also E. Schweizer, *TDNT* VII, 128-29.

paragraph.[8] This is confirmed by the conjunction *de* (= "now");[9] the vocative, "brothers [and sisters]" (see on 1:10); the opening assertion, "This I say . . . that," which is identical to 7:29,[10] in which a new thought is also begun; as well as its clear linguistic ties to what follows. On the other hand, of course, it picks up the argument up to v. 49 and begins to carry it to its final conclusion. Paul's point is that which he has been making since v. 37, that "the body that shall be" is a transformed expression of the one that was "sown." He now spells that out in terms of its present incompatibility with the future. What is said negatively here is reasserted positively in v. 53.

The two lines are most likely to be understood as synonymous parallelism,[11] so that the second makes the same point as the first.[12] Together they declare most decisively that the body in its present physical expression cannot inherit the heavenly existence of vv. 47-49. Of the two terms that describe present physical existence, the second, "the perishable," was used in v. 42 and will be repeated in vv. 52-54. Contrary to Jeremias, it does not refer to what is already dead, but to that which in its present form is subject to decay, which in itself rules out its possibility for eternal longevity.

This is probably also how we are to understand the more ambiguous

---

[8]This is even more so if the hortatory subjunctive is the correct reading at the end of v. 49, as we have argued.

[9]Had it summarized what has been said to this point, as some maintain, then one would have expected the explanatory γάρ (as in v. 53), which some MSS substitute for this very reason (see n. 1).

[10]As there, it is not certain whether this is a solemn declaration about what is to be said (so, e.g., Conzelmann, 289) or a kind of summation of what has been said to this point, "what I mean is this" (NEB, Barrett).

[11]Jeremias, "Flesh and Blood" (followed by Barrett, 379-80), has argued that they express synthetic parallelism, and therefore that the first has to do with the living, the second with the dead. He then sees this antithesis repeated throughout vv. 51-54, in a form of chiasm. Although he is probably generally correct that "flesh and blood" refer to the living—although, as will be noted, that, too, needs to be qualified—the real difficulty with this proposition lies with his identifying the abstract noun ἡ φθορά with the already dead. That forces Paul's language into such a narrow sense that it simply cannot be sustained. Furthermore, as J. Gillman ("Transformation," pp. 320-22) has shown convincingly, the chiastic structure that Jeremias sees must yield to a structure that appears to be two sets of A-B-A'; cf. R. Morisette, " 'La chair et le sang ne peuvent hériter du Règne de Dieu' (*I Cor., XV, 50*), *ScEs* 26 (1974), 39-67, esp. 46-48.

[12]So most of the older commentaries. See also Morisette, " 'La chair,' " pp. 46-48; Usami, "How," p. 489; Schweizer, *TDNT* VII, 218-19; Gillman, "Transformation," pp. 316-18; and Conzelmann, 289. But the latter seems quite mistaken in suggesting that the first is a piece of traditional material taken over by Paul somewhat intact, while the second is Paul's exposition of it. In fact, the language "flesh and blood" and "inherit the kingdom of God" are both Pauline. The former is found in Gal. 1:16 and Eph. 6:12, while the latter is found only in Paul in the NT (1 Cor. 6:9, 10; Gal. 5:21; the usage in Matt. 25:34 is not identical and lacks the nuance of the Pauline usage). At best, as Morisette argues, the first is traditional Jewish language that has been transformed into Hellenistic terminology in the second clause.

"flesh and blood." On the one hand, this could refer to the *composition* of the present body; a body so composed cannot enter the Eschaton.[13] Very likely a dimension of this understanding must be included. On the other hand, Jeremias (see n. 11) popularized the view that it means "the living" in contrast to "the dead";[14] the living cannot enter the kingdom as they are. Although this seems to move in the right direction, both of these are probably too narrowly conceived. Most likely it refers simply to the body in its present form, composed of flesh and blood, to be sure, but subject to weakness, decay, and death, and as such ill-suited for the life of the future.[15]

The description of the future in terms of "inheriting the kingdom of God" indicates how varied was the language used to describe the future. Paul had already used this terminology in 6:9-10; its appearance here echoes vv. 24-28, where the future is described in terms of the Son's handing over the kingdom to God the Father (v. 24) so that God may be "all in all" (v. 28). Thus those who are currently in Christ's kingdom (v. 25) are thereby also destined for God's final eschatological kingdom. There can be little question that in Paul's view this refers to our final heavenly existence, in which believers "inherit" the "heavenly" likeness of Christ himself (vv. 48-49).

51 The concern of Paul's argument is with the nature of the body that believers will assume *at the resurrection*. The contrasts that have been set up, however, are not between the corpses of the dead and their reanimated bodies, but between bodies in their present earthly expression vis-à-vis their transformation into the likeness of Christ's glorified body. Thus he asserted (v. 50) that the body *in its present form* cannot "inherit the kingdom." Even though this may still refer to the body "that is sown," the logical consequence is that what is true of the dead is equally true of the living. The perishable body, either dead or alive, cannot inherit the imperishable life of the future. Paul, therefore, now turns to emphasize that point with regard to the living. They, too, must be changed before they are fitted for immortality. The Corinthians, of course, would have been plumping for

[13]So, e.g., Godet, 433.

[14]Jeremias notes that Schlatter had taken this view before him. In fact it has a much longer history. Cf. Godet, 434. See the discussion in Gillman, "Transformation," pp. 310-12.

[15]Cf. Parry, 241: "the embodiment of the human life to fit its earthly sphere"; and R. Meyer, *TDNT* VII, 116: "From the very outset . . . the idea of mortality and creatureliness seems to be especially bound up with the phrase." In this sense it indeed refers to the living, since it cannot possibly refer to dead corpses in the grave.

On the other hand, the ethical view found in Patristic exegesis (e.g., Chrysostom, *hom. 42 in 1 Cor.* 2) and favored by Edwards, 450, and Morisette, "'La chair,'" pp. 46-48, has little to commend it. Both the terminology and the argument as a whole stand quite against it. Cf. the refutation in Gillman, "Transformation," pp. 318-19.

a nonsomatic immortality; but for Paul the resurrection of Christ and his present somatic heavenly existence exclude their option. Hence the solemn asseveration: "Listen,[16] I tell you a mystery."

As elsewhere in the Pauline corpus, "mystery" does not refer to what is currently hidden, but to what was once hidden but has now been revealed through Christ.[17] The heavenly existence of Christ in a *pneumatikon sōma* ("supernatural body") means that yet another "mystery" is now revealed to God's people. The content of that mystery is found in the pair of clauses that follow, the first of which probably sustains a concessive relationship to the second: "Even though we will not all[18] sleep,[19] nevertheless we will all be changed."[20] Two further observations need to be made.

First, Paul has already expressed himself similarly in 1 Thess. 4:13-18. There in particular it is difficult to avoid the plain sense of the language, that he expected to be among the living at the Parousia. That does not mean that he lived in intense, eager anticipation of it, as is sometimes maintained, but that he simply expected it to happen within his lifetime. Similar language prevails here, but on an even lower key in terms of expectation. He uses "we" chiefly because nothing else would make sense, especially in the first clause. In a letter where he easily falls in and out of this usage, especially when he wants to include himself with them in the benefits of salvation,[21] it is hardly possible that this clause could have been expressed in either the second or third person. Thus it says very little about Paul's expectations with regard to the Parousia; what it says is that he is *currently* among the living.

Second, Paul's emphasis is on the necessary "change"[22] that will

---

[16]Gk. ἰδού; excluding quotations, found in Paul only in 2 Cor. 5:17; 6:9; 7:11; 12:14; Gal. 1:20.

[17]See the discussion of this word in the commentary on 2:7. Although one cannot be certain, the usage here probably reflects that of 13:2, where as a prophet Paul has been given special revelation, a kind of charismatic knowledge (cf. 12:8). On the other hand, it could belong to the great "mystery," the plan of salvation as now revealed through Christ, of which this is the final event. Cf. the discussion in Brown, *Semitic Background,* pp. 47-48.

[18]The unusual word order πάντες οὐ can probably best be explained stylistically, as anticipating the next clause, πάντες δέ. It can only mean, "not all." So Robertson, *Grammar,* 423 (*contra* his own note on p. 753!); Moule, 168.

[19]On this word as a metaphor for the death of Christians, see on 7:39; 11:30; 15:6, 18, 20.

[20]On the basis of its similarities to 1 Thess. 4:14-17, G. Löhr has argued for a common oral tradition between them ("1 Thess 4:15-17: Das 'Herrenwort,'" *ZNW* 71 [1980], 269-73), while D. Gewalt sees here the reworking of a Jesus *logion* ("1 Thess 4,15-17; 1 Kor 15,51 und Mk 9,1—Zur Abgrenzung eines 'Herrenwortes,'" *LingBib* 51 [1982], 105-13). The latter is unlikely, the former unnecessary.

[21]See, e.g., v. 49; cf. on 1:18, 30; 2:7, 12-13; 6:14; 9:25; etc.

[22]Gk. ἀλλάσσω, used only here and in v. 52 in the NT to refer to such a transformation. The word used of Jesus' transfiguration in Mark 9:2 (//Matt. 17:2) is

happen to all, both the living and the dead. Not all will die since by the nature of things some will be alive at the return of Christ; but *all,* including those alive at the time of the Parousia, must be transformed so as to bear the likeness of the man of heaven. It is probably this latter reality that is the content of the "mystery." It may be that Paul is pressing this point as a direct word against the Corinthian point of view; however, it is just as possible that it flows naturally as the logical concomitant of the argument to this point. In either case, such a word is unlikely to be received enthusiastically in Corinth.

52 With the three prepositional phrases that begin this verse Paul indicates the nature and time of the transformation. It is clear from similar usage in 1 Thess. 4:16 that he intends the time of the Parousia. However, since the emphasis here is on the transformation that all experience, there is no mention of the coming of the Lord himself or of believers' rising to be with him.[23] Thus, in place of language referring to the shout of victory, the emphasis here is on the instantaneous nature of the transformation: "We will all be changed in a flash,[24] in the twinkling[25] of an eye."

What marks the Parousia is the blowing of "the last trumpet," imagery that had been taken up into Jewish prophetic-apocalyptic in a variety of senses to herald the Eschaton:[26] to sound the last battle cry (e.g., Jer. 51:27), to warn of the approaching day of judgment (Joel 2:1), to announce the coming of the Lord (Zech. 9:14), to summon the people of God from the four corners (Isa. 27:13). Since it is such common imagery for the heralding of

---

μεταμορφόω, a word Paul uses of the present "transforming" of our lives into the likeness of Christ (2 Cor. 3:18: Rom. 12:2). For the idea of "transformation" in Judaism, see 2 Bar. 51:10, in which, however, it happens not at the resurrection but at the final judgment.

[23]G. Luedemann sees considerable differences between this and the 1 Thessalonians passage, thus suggesting changes in Paul's own perspective. See "The Hope of the Early Paul: From the foundation-preaching at Thessalonika to 1 Cor. 15:51-57," *PRS* 7 (1980), 195-201. But that is to make more than seems permissible from two *ad hoc* statements that have quite different concerns.

[24]Gk. ἐν ἀτόμῳ, which literally means "uncut," hence "indivisible" because of smallness (cf. "atom"). The English equivalent would be "in a split second."

[25]Gk. ἐν ῥιπῇ ὀφθαλμοῦ, the equivalent of the Eng. "at the blink of an eye." It is of interest that this physical phenomenon was picked up in more than one culture to express the speed with which something can happen.

[26]See the discussion in G. Friedrich, *TDNT* VII, 71-88. Its origins may have been the original theophany at Sinai (Exod. 19:16), now transformed eschatologically. On the other hand, the blowing of the trumpet accompanied a variety of special occasions (in the cultus; for warfare; for warning; at the "parousia" of a significant person). For its use in eschatological contexts see *inter alia* (in the OT) Isa. 18:3; 27:13; Jer. 4:5; 51:27; Hos. 5:8; Joel 2:1; Zech. 9:14; (in apocalyptic) 4 Ezra 6:23; *Apoc.Mos.* 22, 27; *Or.Sib.* 8.239; *Apoc.Abr.* 31:1-2; (in rabbinics) *b.Rosh.Hash.* 11b; *Midr.Qoh.* 1:7; (in the NT) Matt. 24:31; 1 Thess. 4:16; Rev. 4:1; 8:2–9:14. Conzelmann seems to reflect a theological bias in noting only the apocalyptic tradition.

the End, it may carry no metaphorical freight whatever in this instance. On the basis of the next clause, however, it is arguable that the imagery is that of summoning the dead from their graves. It is the "last" trumpet not because it is the final in a series, but because it signals the End.

With an explanatory "for," the next clause basically repeats the concerns of vv. 51-52a by spelling out what they entail. First, "the trumpet will sound," repeating what has immediately preceded. With that, secondly, "the dead will be raised imperishable." Although this language has not been frequent in this section of the argument (vv. 35-58), its appearance here, as in v. 42, indicates that this has been the concern right along. People die partly because they live in perishable bodies. But with the coming of Christ, all of that changes. They are raised, still with bodies, but bodies that have been made over into their "imperishable" form. Third, along with the resurrected dead, "we [= the living][27] will be changed." These last two clauses, which in their own way repeat v. 51, have no interest in chronology, although they are expressed in the same order as in 1 Thess. 4:16-17. For all practical purposes the events transpire at the same time—at the sound of the eschatological trumpet.

53 These words bring closure to the present argument, that both the living and the dead must[28] have transformed bodies in order to enter their final, heavenly existence. In Christ Jesus, God has already decreed such; and therefore it must be so. Again, as in v. 50, the two clauses are synonymous parallels,[29] in this case made certain by the repeated demonstrative "this"[30] and the neuter adjectives used as substantives (= "this perishable [body]").[31] Both lines emphasize the same reality, the first word in each case referring to our present existence in bodies that are *subject to* decay and death.[32] Their opposites are bodies that are "clothed"[33] in the likeness of

---

[27]For the debate as to whether this means, as in v. 51, both the living and the dead, see Gillman, "Transformation," pp. 319-20. The contrast here with the resurrected dead, plus the use of πάντες in the former passage, argues for "the living" here.

[28]Gk. δεῖ; cf. v. 25. Not a necessity of natural order but of divinely ordained eschatology.

[29]Again, *contra* Jeremias, "Flesh and Blood," p. 153, who in this case simply asserts without evidence.

[30]This demonstrative would make little sense as referring to those already dead. At the same time it implies continuity, even though there is transformation. It is *this* mortal body that is clothed in immortality. Cf. Gillman, "Transformation," p. 331.

[31]See also Gillman, "Transformation," pp. 316-17, who has demonstrated conclusively from usage in Plutarch (*mor.* 960B), Philo (*op.mund.* 119), and Wisd. 9:14-15 that these two terms (τὸ φθαρτόν and τὸ θνητόν) were generally used synonymously in antiquity, and frequently, as here, in parallel sentences. The neuter could be used abstractly (= this perishability of ours); but it seems far more likely that it is referring back to the "body."

[32]It should be noted, of course, that even though Paul speaks in terms of the present conditions of the living, the argument by its very nature also embraces the dead.

[33]For this clothing imagery see on v. 49. The imagery stands in sharp contrast to

Christ, with imperishability and immortality. The long chain of decay and death inaugurated by the first Adam will finally be irrevocably broken by the last Adam.

54 With the rhetorically powerful full repetition of the two clauses from v. 53, Paul advances the argument by indicating the net results of the Parousia-resurrection-transformation process—the abolition of death itself. In vv. 23-28 he had argued that resurrection is a divine necessity, inaugurated through the resurrection of Christ, as God's way of destroying the last enemy, death. Now he returns to that theme, not so much in terms of its necessity as in exultation and triumph. "Take that, death," he exults, "for when mortality is clothed with immortality, you have lost both your victory and your sting." No more can death tyrannize, because it has been "swallowed up" by resurrection.

Paul makes this point in significant fashion by citing two OT texts (Isa. 25:8; Hos. 13:14) that he understands as yet to be fulfilled: "Then the saying[34] that is written will come true." This is the only instance of his citing yet unfulfilled prophecy; but as always he cites the OT in light of the death and resurrection of Jesus. So these two passages are in fact fulfilled in Christ; they simply have yet to be realized.

The citations themselves, both of which vary from the LXX, are brought into collocation by the key words "death" and "victory." It is of interest, therefore, that the word "victory" is not found in either OT passage. At this distance we can only surmise how all of this came about. The citation of Isa. 25:8 is the key and is most likely the "saying" (singular) to which Paul is referring. In this case the citation is precisely in keeping with its OT context, where the prophet proclaims that on the great day of salvation "God will swallow up death forever,"[35] for which Paul reads: "Death has been swallowed up in victory." In so doing he is reflecting a common LXX idiom for the translation of the Hebrew "forever";[36] but as the next citation

---

the Greek view, in which one is naturally endowed with immortality. But not so Paul; immortality is the investiture of resurrection.

[34]Gk. λόγος; note the singular, which at least refers to Isa. 25:8, perhaps to both, understood as belonging together as one whole. But see on v. 55.

[35]Cf. Rev. 21:4, which alludes to both lines (incl. wiping away of tears) of the Isaiah text (in reverse order). See *m.Moed Qat.* 3.9 for the use of this text as part of the "lamentations" at funerals during Dedication and Purim, making it clear that it was already interpreted by the rabbis as referring to the eschatological elimination of death.

[36]For this complex issue see R. Morisette, "Un Midrash sur la Mort (*I Cor.*, xv, 54c à 57)," *RB* 79 (1972), 161-88, esp. 168-70. The Heb. *lāneṣaḥ* derives from the verb *nṣ*, which means "to overcome, prevail over." The adverb is variously translated in the LXX, as well as in Theodotion, Aquila, and Symmachus, either with εἰς τέλος ("to the uttermost"); εἰς τὸν αἰῶνα (χρόνον) ("forever"); or εἰς νῖκος (lit. "in victory," which is probably an idiom for "forever"; see LSJ). The LXX has translated here as though it were the verb form ("having prevailed"), while both Theodotion and Aquila have εἰς

makes clear, he means it finally in terms of "victory," not just "forever." At the resurrection-transformation God will abolish death forever, just as he promised in the words of the prophet.

55 In light of the swallowing up of death in the victory of the resurrection-transformation, Paul proceeds to taunt death in the language of Hos. 13:14 (somewhat modified). Whether Paul intended to "cite" this passage as such, as part of the fulfilled word of v. 54, is moot. By a series of modifications, Paul seems to be taking over the text of Hosea so as to make it his own derision of death in light of the argument of vv. 51-53 and the citation of Isa. 25:8 in v. 54.[37] He does this in three ways: (1) by changing the LXX word *dikē* ("penalty") to *nikos* ("victory"), thus bringing it into verbal agreement with the previous quotation from Isaiah; (2) by substituting in the second line the vocative "O death" for the "O grave" of the LXX, thus making both lines a derision of death itself; and (3) by bringing forward the possessive pronoun "your" to first position (after "where"), followed immediately by the vocative, thus emphasizing the personification (lit., "where your, O death, victory?" which replaces the LXX's "where the penalty of you, O death?").

The net result is a powerful taunt of death that looks in two directions at once. First, it completes the argument of the paragraph as a whole as well as the citation in v. 54. Even though he still lives in the "already," and in his own body experiences both the perishability and mortality of the present age that is passing away,[38] Paul has also seen the risen Lord, and with a clear vision of what is to be he mocks the enemy, whose doom has been sealed through Christ's own death and resurrection. And it is precisely because of Christ's victory that the mockery obtains, even if in the meantime believers "fall asleep." Thus it is Paul's way of looking forward to the triumph of the ages. Death's victory has been overcome by Christ's victory; and death's deadly sting has been detoxicated—indeed, the stinger itself has been plucked—through Christ's resurrection. Death, therefore, is "powerless over the dead";[39] God's people will be raised and changed into the likeness of Christ himself.

Second, even though the taunt has to do with the future resurrection of believers, it is expressed in the present tense, precisely because the beginning of the End has "already" set in motion the final victory that for us

---

νῖκος. But the idiom is obviously common enough that it makes little sense to refer to Paul's text as "pre-Theodotion."

[37]Cf. Barrett, 383: "He is not however here grounding an argument upon Scripture, but writing freely, in scriptural language, of the ultimate victory over death."

[38]See especially the language of 2 Cor. 4:7-18.

[39]Holladay, 211.

is still "not yet." The mention of the word "sting,"[40] therefore, leads Paul from the future to the present; what is to be has in effect already begun. Thus, he concludes this exalted description of the "not yet" with an appropriate reminder of the victory that is "already" theirs in Christ (vv. 56-57). As Holladay (p. 111) further notes: "Death is also powerless over the living."

56 Anyone who has heard this paragraph read at a Christian funeral senses the dissonance these words seem to bring to the argument.[41] For our purposes the taunt of v. 55 is climactic. But Paul is not quite finished. Granted that the argument proper is now over; however, much as in vv. 33-34, the final word is one of application to their present situation. That word will come partly by way of the exhortation in v. 58. Before that, however, the final words of the taunt in v. 55 apparently touch off a theological chord that must be given a moment's hearing. With a piece of step-parallelism, Paul moves from the final line of the Hosea "quotation" to a brief compendium of his own theology as to the relationship of sin and the law to death. Not only has *death* been overcome by resurrection; but *mutatis mutandis* so have the enemies that have brought death to all—sin and the law.[42] Thus:

> "Where, O *death,* is your *sting*?"
> Now
> (1) the *sting*   of *death* is **sin**;
>   and
> (2) the power of **sin**   is the law.

The first line requires little comment. In Pauline theology sin is the deadly poison[43] that has led to death. Although this word group has not occurred frequently in the letter to describe the Corinthian behavioral aberrations,[44] there can be no question that Paul considered their actions sinful and

---

[40]Gk. κέντρον. The word is used of a "goad" (Acts 26:14; Prov. 26:3) and may be so intended by the LXX translator; however, it also is used of the sting of insects (4 Macc. 14:19) and scorpions (Rev. 9:10), and is clearly the sense that Paul is picking up here.

[41]So much so that some (e.g., Weiss, Moffatt) have argued that this verse is a gloss, either by Paul himself at a later time or by a later editor (e.g., Moffatt, 268, "They are a prose comment which could not have occurred to him in the passionate rush of triumphal conviction"). But such a comment says far more about the commentator than about Paul: Paul could not be imagined to write differently from our better selves!

[42]This seems preferable to the suggestion by M. Gertner, "Midrashim in the New Testament," *JSS* 7 (1962), 282-83, that Paul is using "hidden midrashim" to derive two different senses from the words of Hosea.

[43]Cf. Martin, 191. Some see the word "sting" here as referring to human "feelings" in the face of death; but that is to psychologize Paul and miss his theology by too much.

[44]See 6:18; 7:28 (36); 8:12.

in need of divine forgiveness. The word occurs with greater frequency in this chapter. The reason Christ died is "for our sins" (v. 3); and if he did not rise, they are still in their sins (v. 17). In the exhortation that concludes the first section of the argument they are urged to "stop sinning" (v. 34). The full explication of this sentence will emerge in the Epistle to the Romans; its appearance here in this fashion is the sure indication that this essential dictum of Pauline theology had long been in place. Although something of an aside, it is not difficult to see its relevance. This is the deadly sting that has led to death. Thus, Christ's victory over the latter is evidence that he has overcome the former as well.

The second line is the puzzler, especially since in this Gentile community the relationship of sin to the law has not seemed to emerge as a problem. Nowhere do the issues that have arisen, either between him and them or between them internally, reflect concern over the law.[45] That means that the statement belongs to the first one as a theological construct, not as an issue in this church. If so, this also means that the essential matters that surface in a thoroughgoing way in Galatians and are spelled out at length in Romans had been essential to Paul's theology long before the Judaizing controversy erupted—at least in the tangible form in which we know it from Galatians.[46] Its point is simple, and is spelled out in detail in Rom. 7: The relationship of law to sin is that the former is what gives the latter its power. In Rom. 5:13 Paul explains: "Sin is not imputed (NIV, 'taken into account') where there is no law." That is, the law not only makes sin observable as sin, but also, and more significantly, demonstrates that one's actions are finally over against God, and thus leads to condemnation (cf. 2 Cor. 3:6). The law, which is good, functions as the agent of sin because it either leads to pride of achievement, on the one hand, or reveals the depth of one's depravity and rebellion against God, on the other. In either case, it becomes death-dealing instead of life-giving.[47]

Paul's point in this theological aside is that death is not simply the result of decay through normal human processes. Rather, it is the result of the deadly poison, sin itself, which became all the more energized in our

[45]Indeed, this is the only use of this term in a theological sense in the two epistles—although see 2 Cor. 3:4-18, which implies that the Corinthians were not untrained in this kind of understanding of the law.

[46]For the radically different viewpoint held in rabbinic Judaism see the discussion in Morisette, "Midrash," pp. 176-83.

[47]On the much larger issue of "Paul and the law," which is currently front and center in Pauline studies, but which lies beyond the scope of this commentary, see *inter alia* E. P. Sanders, *Paul and Palestinian Judaism* (Philadelphia, 1977); idem, *Paul, the Law, and the Jewish People* (Philadelphia, 1983); H. Hübner, *Law in Paul's Thought* (1978; ET, Edinburgh, 1984); J. D. G. Dunn, "The New Perspective on Paul," *BJRL* 65 (1982), 94-121; H. Räisänen, *Paul and the Law* (ET, Philadelphia, 1983).

lives through acquaintance with the law. Hence, in exulting in Christ's victory over death, Paul is reminded that that victory is the *final* triumph over the sin that brought death into the world, and over the law that has emboldened sin. But since both sin and the law have already been overcome in the cross, this compendium prefaces a final doxology that thanks God for present "victory" as well.

57 As just noted, this final doxology first of all expresses gratitude that God through "our Lord Jesus Christ" presently gives his people victory over sin and the law, which lead to death. At the same time, however, it embraces the entire argument, especially as it climaxes in this paragraph. Thus, Paul exults in God's victory over death through resurrection (v. 55) and now in the conquest of the sin that leads to that death (v. 57). As at the beginning (vv. 3-5), so at the conclusion, Christ is the one through whom God has wrought this triumph.

58 In light of the sure hope of resurrection, and now especially in light of Christ's triumph over sin and the law as well, Paul concludes, as is his wont, on a strong word of exhortation. The opening "so then" (NIV, "therefore") is the last of the long series of these inferential conjunctions in this letter.[48] For its use with this vocative see 11:33 and 14:39.[49] The vocative in this case is accompanied by the term of endearment, "my dear (= beloved) brothers [and sisters]."[50] Despite his misgivings over their theology and behavior, and despite their generally anti-Paul stance on so many issues, from his own point of view they are ever his "dear brothers and sisters," and that because, even though in one sense they are his dear children in the Lord (4:15), in the much greater sense predicated on the theology of the preceding doxology he and they are brothers and sisters, with the same divine parent.

The surprising feature of this exhortation is that, unlike vv. 33-34, it is not directed toward ethical behavior as such, but toward the work of the gospel. Probably, therefore, it is to be understood as a word to the congregation as a whole vis-à-vis those who are leading them astray by denying the "resurrection of the dead" (v. 12). On the contrary, Paul urges, not only must they not go that route because of what Christ has effected (vv. 20-28, 45-49, 54-57), but they must in general remain loyal to the gospel as he preached it among them. He makes this point in two ways.

First, on the negative side, "Let nothing move you." This transla-

---

[48]See on 3:7.

[49]Cf. 7:24, the only other instance of the vocative in a conclusion. Cf. n. 21 on 1:10.

[50]Cf. 10:14, where it appears by itself in the vocative. This full, and most affectionate, form is found only here and in Phil. 4:1.

tion combines two Greek words, "steadfast"[51] and "immovable,"[52] which together urge that they not be "shifting from the hope of the gospel which you heard" (Col. 1:23, RSV). This urgency is almost certainly in direct response to the denial of the resurrection by some. It urges by way of exhortation what was affirmed in vv. 1-2, that the gospel of Christ is that in which they do in fact stand.

Second, on the positive side, "Always[53] give yourselves fully[54] to the work[55] of the Lord." It is not absolutely certain what kind of activity Paul had in mind by the phrase "the work of the Lord." Minimally, it may refer more broadly to whatever one does *as a Christian*, both toward outsiders and fellow believers; but along with the next word, "labor,"[56] Paul frequently uses it to refer to the actual ministry of the gospel. Probably in their case it covers the range but leans more toward the former. That is, there are those kinds of activities in which believers engage that are specifically Christian, or specifically in the interest of the gospel. This seems to be what Paul has in mind here.

With a marvelous stroke of genius, whether intentional or not, Paul concludes on the same note with which he began in vv. 1-2. There he was concerned, because of the denial of the resurrection by some, whether his own "labor"—namely their own existence in Christ—was in vain. Now, after the strong evidence for the resurrection presented throughout, he concludes with such faith as the ground for their continued labor: "because you know that your (own) labor in the Lord is not in vain." Thus the entire chapter is tied together. The implication in all this, of course, is that if they continue their present route, they have good grounds for lacking any confidence that what they do as Christians has any meaning (vv. 14-19). But Christ has been raised from the dead, and they too shall be raised to share his likeness; therefore they may not only abound in his service, but know assuredly that what they do is not in vain.

---

[51]Gk. ἑδραῖοι (cf. 7:37); it is used similarly in Col. 1:23.

[52]Gk. ἀμετακίνητοι, a NT hapax legomenon.

[53]Gk. πάντοτε, usually found in Paul's prayer reports in his thanksgivings (e.g., 1:4; 1 Thess. 1:2; 2 Thess. 1:3, 11; 2:13; Rom. 1:10; Col. 1:3; 4:12; Phlm. 4; Phil. 1:4), but also used in exhortation (e.g., 1 Thess. 5:15, 16; Gal. 4:18; Eph. 5:20; Phil. 4:4).

[54]This translates the Gk. ptc. περισσεύοντες (= "abound" or "overflow"); cf. 14:12; used frequently of the overflow of God's grace toward us in Christ (Rom. 5:15; 2 Cor. 1:5; 4:15; 9:8; Eph. 1:8), and therefore often of the overflow toward God and one another that God's people should/do have (1 Thess. 3:12; 4:1, 10; Rom. 15:13; 2 Cor. 8:2; 9:12; Phil. 1:9; Col. 2:7).

[55]Gk. ἔργον. For this noun as referring to the work of the gospel see on 3:13-15 and 9:1; cf. 1 Thess. 5:13; 2 Tim. 4:5.

[56]Gk. κόπος; for this combination as referring to the ministry of the gospel see especially on 4:12, where the two verbs appear together; and 16:16, where they appear as συνεργέω and κοπιάω. For the noun as referring to the work of the gospel see also 3:8; 1 Thess. 3:5; 2 Thess. 3:8; 2 Cor. 6:5; 10:15; 11:23.

It is of some interest that Paul's own moment of hesitation in vv. 1-2 is answered for him by his own arguments, so that this concluding paragraph exudes with confidence and triumph. There is little doubt as to why it is read regularly at Christian funerals. Read without comment, it has its own power. Here the Word has its own regenerative power because it expresses the truth of Christ himself. But here, too, it is a word for all seasons. Our present existence in Christ, and our present labors, are not in vain. Standing beneath them is the sure word of Christ's own triumph over death, which guarantees that we shall likewise conquer. Victory in the present begins when one can, with Paul, sing the taunt of death even now, in light of Christ's resurrection, knowing that death's doom is "already/not yet." Because "death could not hold its prey, Jesus our Savior," neither will it be able to hold its further prey when the final eschatological trumpet is blown that summons the Christian dead unto the resurrection and immortality. What a hope is this. No wonder Paul concluded on a note of exhortation that we may confidently continue on our way in the Lord.

G. ABOUT THE COLLECTION (16:1-11)

With the triumphant words of 15:50-58, Paul has brought the essential matters between him and them, both by way of report and by letter, to their conclusion. But two items from their letter (presumably) still require a brief word. Apparently they have written for further instructions as to their part in the collection for the poor in Jerusalem, especially how they are to go about it and how it is to get to Jerusalem. So he gives instructions similar to those given in other churches. Since these instructions included a word about his coming to pick up the collection, he digresses to speak about his own travel plans in coming to them (vv. 5-9). This is turn reminds him that Timothy may very well be arriving in the meantime, so he includes a word about their reception of him (vv. 10-11). While on travel plans, he then returns to the final item from their letter: their request that Apollos return soon, which he addresses in v. 12.

Unlike most of the letter, this part has little that is openly confrontational; nonetheless, in light of what has preceded, one may see hints of tension here as well, especially since some of these items are the very ones that explode on him between this letter and the writing of our 2 Corinthians.[1] Thus the way the apostle defuses potential trouble in some workaday, personal matters becomes both a lesson in Christian tact and instructive about how Paul managed his everyday relationships with his churches.

---

[1]Cf. Hurd, 200-206, who, however, seems to read far more between the lines than is found in the text itself. This is particularly true of his treatment of vv. 5-9 and Paul's change of plans. On Hurd's view one seems forced to the conclusion that Paul was less than honest in his present dealings with them.

1. Arrangements for the Collection (16:1-4)

1 *Now about the collection for God's people: Do what I told the Galatian churches to do.* 2 *On the first day of every week, each one of you should set aside a sum of money in keeping with his income, saving it up, so that when I come no collections will have to be made.* 3 *Then, when I arrive, I will give letters of introduction to the men you approve and send them with your gift to Jerusalem.* 4 *If it seems advisable for me to go also, they will accompany me.*

This is the first of three, perhaps four,[2] instances in Paul's letters where he mentions the collection for the "poor" among the "saints" in Jerusalem.[3] According to Gal. 2:9-10, part of the agreement reached with the "pillars" in Jerusalem regarding their mutual spheres of ministry included his willingness to "continue to remember the poor."[4] Apparently this collection was a major part of his concern during his third missionary tour,[5] which functioned

---

[2]See also 2 Cor. 8–9; Rom. 15:25-32. Many scholars consider 2 Cor. 8 and 9 to be two different letters about the collection. For two different views from this perspective see Martin, *2 Corinthians*, pp. 249-52, who thinks that chaps. 1–8 form one letter, and that chap. 9 is another letter on the same issue written to Corinth very shortly thereafter; and H.-D. Betz, *2 Corinthians 8 and 9* (Hermeneia; Philadelphia, 1985), who considers them two separate letters, neither of which belongs with any part of chaps. 1–7, chap. 8 being addressed to Corinth and chap. 9 to the Achaian churches not including Corinth. The most recent presentation that sees them as belonging together as part of chaps. 1–7 is Furnish, *II Corinthians*, pp. 429-33.

[3]That it is intended for Jerusalem is stated in v. 3. The fact that it was intended for the poor is not mentioned in this letter; it is implied in 2 Cor. 8:13; 9:9, 12, and made explicit in Rom. 15:26. It is idle speculation to try to determine how this church became poor. Two things are mentioned in Acts: the fact that the gospel apparently reached a large number of widows in Jerusalem (Acts 6:1-6) and the failure of crops during famine (Acts 11:27-30).

There is little to commend K. Holl's suggestion that "the poor" was another word for "the saints" in Jerusalem and that the collection, therefore, was really a Christian form of the Temple tax being imposed on the Gentile churches by Jerusalem (see "Der Kirchenbegriff des Paulus in seinem Verhältnis zu dem der Urgemeinde," in *Gesammelte Aufsätze zur Kirchengeschichte* [Tübingen, 1928; repr. of 1921 art.], II, 44-67). The basic perspective of this view has been revived by B. Holmberg, *Paul and Power, The Structure of Authority in the Primitive Church as Reflected in the Pauline Epistles* (Philadelphia, 1978), pp. 35-43. Since Paul stresses the *voluntary* nature of this collection and the *willingness* of those who participated, this view seems quite untenable. Cf. the refutation in Furnish, *II Corinthians*, pp. 412-13.

[4]The NIV rightly captures the thrust of the present subjunctive by translating "continue to remember." Probably this reflects the previous relief for the poor mentioned in Acts 11:27-30.

[5]Given its apparent importance to Paul, one is surprised that it gets scant attention in Acts, which at least says something about how material is selected and shaped by an author's own purposes. That Luke knows about the collection is evident from Paul's speech before Felix (24:17) and the representatives from the churches who accompanied him (20:4).

for him not only to bring relief to the poor, but also as his own attempt to bring unity between Gentile and Jewish Christianity.[6] For Paul it was a matter of reciprocity, similar to his argument for support in 9:10-12: "For if the Gentiles have shared in the Jews' spiritual blessings, they owe it to the Jews to share with them their material blessings" (Rom. 15:27)—not to mention the fact that such generosity overflowed in expressions of thanksgiving and mutual prayer (2 Cor. 9:12-14).

None of this, however, is mentioned in our present passage, which makes one wonder as to (1) how and what the Corinthians had previously heard about this collection, and (2) what they may have said in their letter about it. On these questions we are left with our best guesses since Paul hardly alludes to such things here. Since so many other items in their letter appear to be responses to his previous letter (5:9), it seems probable that this, too, had been broached in that letter. Perhaps there he had explained its purpose and that the churches in Galatia had already agreed to participate.[7] In any case, what Paul does here is to give some matter-of-fact directions about how they are to go about it (vv. 1-2) and what will happen to it when he comes (vv. 3-4).[8]

1 This is the fifth "now about"[9] since 7:1 and, as before, suggests that Paul is responding to their letter. This is confirmed by several further items. First, the whole phrase "now about the collection for God's people[10]" implies a new topic. But the fact that the *destination* of the collection is not mentioned in this phrase, and only indirectly in v. 3, implies that they well knew for whom it was intended. The same holds true for the fact that Paul here offers so little information about the collection itself—its purpose, for whom, and its theological significance. Finally, this is probably the best explanation for the use of the word "collection" here and in v. 2,[11] which is

---

[6]For full discussions of the collection, its relationship to Jewish backgrounds (e.g., Temple tax, almsgiving), and its probable theological motivations, see K. Nickle, *The Collection, A Study in Paul's Strategy* (SBT 48; London, 1966), and D. Georgi, *Die Geschichte der Kollekte des Paulus für Jerusalem* (Hamburg-Bergstedt, 1965). For further discussion of the possible theological motivation, see also Munck, *Paul*, pp. 282-308. For helpful overviews of all these matters see the commentaries on 2 Corinthians by Barrett (pp. 25-28), Furnish (pp. 409-13), and Martin (pp. 256-58); cf. also Panikulam, *Koinōnia*, pp. 31-57.

[7]Barrett, 385, takes the alternative view that they had heard of the collection from others, perhaps from some Galatians.

[8]On the complex issue of the relationship of this instruction and Paul's proposed visit to what actually happened, as it can pieced together from our 2 Corinthians, see the commentaries on 2 Corinthians (Barrett, Furnish, Martin) and the proposal by G. D. Fee, "ΧΑΡΙΣ in II Corinthians 1:15: Apostolic Parousia and Paul-Corinth Chronology," *NTS* 24 (1977/78), 533-38. See the commentary on vv. 5-9.

[9]Gk. περὶ δέ; see on 7:1, 25; 8:1 (4); 12:1; cf. 16:12.

[10]Gk. τοὺς ἁγίους ("the saints"); see on 1:2.

[11]Gk. λογεία; the plural in v. 2 puts emphasis on the activity itself, as do most of

the technical term for the actual activity of "taking up" the contributions. Since this word is not used again by Paul in any of the discussions of this "collection," its use here is most likely a reflection of the Corinthian letter, and of their concern for how to go about the actual "collecting" of the money.

Elsewhere Paul speaks of this collection in terms that are full of theological content: "fellowship,"[12] "service,"[13] "grace,"[14] "blessing,"[15] and "divine service."[16] All of this together suggests that the "collection" was not some mere matter of money, but was for Paul an active response to the grace of God that not only ministered to the needs of God's people but also became a kind of ministry to God himself, which resulted in thanksgiving toward God and in a bond of fellowship between "God's people" across the Empire.

It is probably this aspect of "fellowship," as well as perhaps a concern that the Corinthians see the collection within the broader framework of the church,[17] that brings about the initial word of instruction: "Do what I told[18] the Galatian churches to do." Since Paul had just recently come through Galatia on his way to Ephesus (Acts 18:23), most likely at that time he also informed them of the collection and how they could best go about laying it aside. And since he did not plan to return to Jerusalem by way of

---

the examples in MM. Thus its connotations in Greek are very much like those of the word "collection" in English, where it refers not so much to the money itself as to the actual activity of "taking it up," as it were.

[12]2 Cor. 8:4; 9:13; Rom. 15:26. This usage probably indicates Paul's basic hope for this ministry in terms of Jew-Gentile relationships. Cf. Panikulam, *Koinōnia,* pp. 49-57.

[13]Gk. διακονία (2 Cor. 8:4; 9:1, 12, 13; Rom. 15:31; cf. v. 25). See the discussion of this word in 12:5. The implication is that loving service in behalf of others is an essential feature of Christian κοινωνία.

[14]Gk. χάρις; this is the most common term (see on v. 3); cf. 2 Cor. 8:4, 6, 7, 19. The most vivid commentary on its usage in this regard is 2 Cor. 8:9; they are to respond to the benefits of God both exemplified and made available to them in Christ in this tangible way.

[15]Gk. εὐλογία; see 2 Cor. 9:5, where there is something of a play on the word. Their "bounty" becomes a "blessing" to others, who in turn offer the "blessing" of thanksgiving to God.

[16]Gk. λειτουργία; 2 Cor. 9:12 (cf. Rom. 15:27). The monetary gift is seen as an act of service to God. Since this is often a technical term for "divine service" (cf. our derivative, "liturgy"), many think there is a link between this word and an actual collection taken during the service of worship. But this is extremely doubtful, especially in light of the very private nature of the setting aside of the money in v. 2.

[17]On this matter in this letter, see on 1:2 and esp. 14:33.

[18]Gk. διέταξα (cf. 7:17; 9:14; 11:34), a word that can go the range from "command" to "arrange." Here it means "ordered" in the sense of "directed" rather than "commanded."

these churches, the contribution was probably to be brought to him by one of their own.[19]

2 With this sentence Paul proceeds to detail the instructions he had given to the churches of Galatia, which the Corinthians are now to follow as well. For them it is all very matter-of-fact; for us there are some intriguing items for which there is a degree of uncertainty. This is particularly true of the first two phrases, "on the first day of every week"[20] and (literally) "let each one by himself."[21] Some have argued that "by himself" means "let him take to himself what he means to give";[22] in other words, each is to bring to the assembly what he or she has determined "privately" to give. But there is very little linguistic warrant for such a suggestion, not to mention that the participle translated "saving it up"[23] implies that "each person" is to store up what is set aside until the designated time. The phrase "by himself" almost certainly means "at home."[24]

If so, why then does Paul mention "on the first day of every week"? Traditionally this has been one of three NT texts that have been used to support Christians' use of Sunday, rather than the Jewish Sabbath, as their day of worship.[25] Although one should not assert more than such a passing reference allows, some observations need to be made: (1) The fact that Paul makes such a reference at all implies that there is some significance to their setting money aside on *this day* rather than, for example, "once a week." (2) Although that significance may have been only a matter of when people were paid,[26] it seems far more likely that it is a weekly reckoning with religious

[19]Although one cannot be certain, this may be the role of Gaius of Derbe (Acts 20:4).

[20]This is the proper understanding of the Gk. κατά as distributive.

[21]Gk. παρ' ἑαυτῷ. See the discussion in BAGD, παρά II.1bα; and ἑαυτοῦ 1g.

[22]Cf. Hodge, 364, whose words these are; cf. Morris, 238; Mare, 293; Gromacki, 200. But this assumes a contemporary picture of the church, including church officials, regular offerings, and a building.

[23]Gk. θησαυρίζω (= storing something up as a treasure); this word in particular assumes the accumulation of many smaller amounts.

[24]See, e.g., Xenophon, *mem.* 3.13.3 ("who complained that the drinking water at home [παρ' ἑαυτῷ] was warm"); Philo, *cher.* 48 ("rather, as stewards guard the treasure [θησαυρόν] in your own keeping [παρ' ἑαυτοῖς]"); *leg. ad Gai.* 271 ("cheer up, you are staying at home [παρ' ἑαυτῷ]").

[25]The other two are Acts 20:7 and Rev. 1:10. On this whole question, and especially the relationship of this text to the larger question of Sunday worship, see W. Rordorf, *Sunday, The History of the Day of Rest and Worship in the Earliest Centuries of the Christian Church* (ET, London, 1968), pp. 193-96; D. A. Carson, ed., *From Sabbath to Lord's Day, A Biblical, Historical and Theological Investigation* (Grand Rapids, 1982), pp. 184-86 (chap. by D. R. De Lacey); and from a sabbatarian perspective, S. Bacchiocchi, *From Sabbath to Sunday, A Historical Investigation of the Rise of Sunday Observance in Early Christianity* (Rome, 1977), pp. 90-101.

[26]Deissmann, LAE, p. 361, put forth this suggestion but acknowledged that it had no known support. It seems altogether too modern to have merit.

significance, especially since it reflects the Jewish tradition of counting days with reference to the Sabbath. (3) This language is well remembered in the Gospel traditions in relationship to the resurrection of Jesus from the dead. The fixed place of this terminology in those narratives implies that it had more than simply historical interest for the early church. This is verified further by the note in Acts 20:7, which implies most strongly that Paul and the others waited in Troas until the "first day of the week" precisely because that is when the Christians gathered for the breaking of bread, that is, their meal in honor of the Lord.

All of this together, therefore, implies that this is the day when believers from a very early time gathered for their specifically Christian celebration of worship, which included the Lord's Table. Thus, even though they were not necessarily to bring their gift to the assembly on this day, it was the fact that this day marked for them the specifically Christian day in their week that probably made it convenient for Paul to note it as the time for them to remember the poor among the brothers and sisters in Jerusalem.

What is less clear is the clause that apparently is intended to refer to the amount set aside each week. The NIV translates, "in keeping with his income."[27] But that is probably a bit too modern, especially for a culture where a number of the community were slaves and had no "income." More likely it is intentionally ambiguous and does not mean that each should lay aside all his or her "profits," which a literal rendering of the Greek text would allow, but that in accordance with "whatever success or prosperity may have come their way that week," each should set aside something for this collection. There is no hint of a tithe or proportionate giving; the gift is simply to be related to their ability from week to week as they have been prospered by God.

The purpose of this arrangement is simple: "so that when I come no collections will have to be made." Although he does not say as much, such a plan will also ensure a greater gift than a single collection at the time of his arrival.[28] His concern, therefore, seems to be in part that by their weekly setting aside from their "success" of that week, there will be a sum worth the effort of sending people all the way to Jerusalem, which is the matter he speaks to next.

3 That Paul is anticipating a sizable gift is to be seen in this further explanation as to how the gift will get to Jerusalem. When Paul himself

---

[27]Gk. ὅ τι ἐὰν εὐοδῶται. The verb is probably present subjunctive; hence Barrett translates, "whatever profit he makes."

[28]Hurd, 201-02, reads into this urging of a weekly setting apart of money a reluctance on the part of the Corinthians to contribute as much as they were capable of giving. But that goes quite beyond the evidence. This is, after all, the same advice as has been given to the churches of Galatia—for obvious reasons. A one-time gift simply will not meet needs in the same way that a gift prepared over a long span will.

comes, he will write[29] "letters of introduction" for those whom the Corinthians themselves approve[30] to "bear their gift *(charis)* to Jerusalem." This is now the second clear reference to his own proposed visit (cf. 4:18-21), the details of which will be spelled out in the next paragraph (vv. 5-9). Such letters of introduction, or commendation, were a regular part of business dealings in antiquity. Helpful examples may be found in the NT in Acts 15:23-29, Rom. 16:1-2, and especially 2 Cor. 8:16-24, where the final paragraphs function as such a letter.[31]

What is significant is that Paul had determined to send[32] along representatives of the congregations, probably from key churches in larger geographical areas, to accompany the gifts. A number of reasons, partly practical and partly theological, probably lie behind this decision. On the one hand, they would probably be carrying a considerable sum—all in coin!— and there is some safety in numbers. At the same time it would be a practical way of assuring the various churches of the basic integrity of the entire enterprise.[33] On the other hand, surely for Paul the personal representation would be as important as the gifts themselves in his greater concern for the unity of the church. Much more than in modern Western cultures real life in ancient cultures often happened at the anecdotal level; and living persons accompanying such gifts carry the stories of "giver" and "recipient" alike, thus giving a sense of genuine tangibility to such gifts. In any case, whether Paul went along or not, representatives from the church(es) would "bear your gracious gift."[34]

4 At this stage of the planning, Paul is uncertain as to whether he will also go to Jerusalem with the gift. His own present hesitation is found in the words "if it seems advisable for me to go also." The word translated

---

[29]The phrase δι' ἐπιστολῶν could go with the verb δοκιμάσητε, hence the RSV (cf. Montgomery; Findlay, 946): "those whom you accredit by letter." But given the verb "I will send" and the uncertainty expressed in v. 4 as to his accompanying them, more likely he is the source of the letters.

[30]Gk. δοκιμάζω; it means more than simply "select" or "determine" but, as in the NIV, "approve." For this usage in a similar context see 2 Cor. 8:22.

[31]On this matter see esp. Betz, *2 Corinthians 8 and 9,* whose literary analyses are very helpful even if the author is perhaps overly confident that the two chapters therefore represent two separate letters.

[32]Note the πέμψω, "I will send." In the final analysis the project is his, not theirs.

[33]See, e.g., the implications in 2 Cor. 11:14-19 that such accusations lie just below the surface of their relationship with Paul.

[34]It is difficult to know how to interpret the evidence from Acts 20:4, which does not mention any representatives from Achaia. The implication of Rom. 15:26 is that the collection in Corinth had succeeded; but there Paul does not mention Asia or Galatia. Were the gifts of these latter provinces already sent on with representatives? What, then, of the evidence of Acts 20:4 and 21:29? The best guess is that, for reasons that are not quite clear, all of these passages are only partial listings of the people and areas involved.

"advisable" also bears the meaning "worthy."[35] Some, therefore, have felt inclined to see the gift as the subject of the clause, implying that if the gift is worthy of it, that is, an amount substantial enough,[36] then Paul might himself accompany it. But the grammar does not seem to allow such a view;[37] rather, the question is one of appropriateness. What is not clear is, "Appropriate" or "advisable" from what perspective? Some think, From the Corinthians'; hence, "if it is your mind that I should go."[38] More likely the clause is much more ambiguous and reflects Paul's own concerns about his ministry in the West and perhaps his reception in Jerusalem (cf. Rom. 15:23 and 31). In any case, by the time he wrote 2 Corinthians he had decided to accompany the gift (2 Cor. 1:16; cf. Rom. 15:25) and have the brothers accompany him.[39]

What happens next with regard to this collection lies properly beyond the bounds of this commentary since it is a matter for 2 Corinthians and Romans. But two points may be noted. First, the evidence of Rom. 15:26-27 makes it clear that the collection from this church was finally received, and "they were pleased" to do it, according to Paul.[40] Second, according to 2 Cor. 8:10-11 they had made a good beginning, but had failed to follow through with it. Hence Titus was dispatched—twice—to help them bring it to completion. Their reluctance in the meantime is almost certainly the result of the crisis brought about by Paul's sudden, "painful" visit noted in 2 Cor. 2:1, which also caused the (second) change of travel plans explained in 1:15–2:13 and 7:2-16. Most likely the proposed return portion of that visit is when he intended to pick up the collection; but the visit had been so painful that he went on to Ephesus from Macedonia instead, and in his place dispatched Titus with a letter. On their meeting again in Macedonia, Titus reported to him that things were basically better between him and the church in general, but the matter of the collection was strictly on hold. Hence in our 2 Corinthians he sends Titus and three others, part of whose purpose is to get the collection ready for Paul's arrival. The evidence of Rom. 15 is that, despite these momentary setbacks, the Corinthian contribution was finally collected.

---

[35]Gk. ἄξιον; cf. 2 Thess. 1:3.

[36]See, *inter alia,* Godet, 457; Findlay, 946; Parry, 246; Morris, 239.

[37]The adjective is impersonal and followed by an articular infinitive of purpose. It can only mean, "if it be fitting (proper, worthwhile, advisable) that I also go along."

[38]The translation is Conzelmann's, 294; cf. Georgi, *Kollekte,* p. 41.

[39]Obviously now without need of the letters of v. 3.

[40]Indeed, had only 1 Corinthians and Romans been preserved, these two texts would be seen as totally complementary. This is another piece of evidence that should cause scholars to be a bit less dogmatic about conclusions based on documents that are so limited in scope.

Although this is not a primary text in the NT on Christian giving, at least in comparison with 2 Cor. 8:1-15 or 9:6-15, something can still be learned here. The worthiness of the project itself and the proper theological motivation for giving must be found elsewhere. What is significant here is the very matter-of-fact way the issue is taken up. On a weekly basis they should set money aside, as the Lord has prospered them. No pressure, no gimmicks, no emotion. A need had to be met, and the Corinthians were capable of playing a role in it. In a day of highly visible campaigns for money on every side, there is something to be said for the more consistent, purposeful approach outlined here.

2. Travel Plans—Paul's and Timothy's (16:5-11)

> 5 *After I go through Macedonia, I will come to you—for I will be going through Macedonia.* 6 *Perhaps I will stay with you awhile, or even spend the winter, so that you can help me on my journey, wherever I go.* 7 *I do not want to see you now and make only a passing visit; I[1] hope to spend some time with you, if the Lord permits.* 8 *But I will stay on at Ephesus until Pentecost,* 9 *because a great door for effective work has opened to me, and there are many who oppose me.*
>
> 10 *If Timothy comes, see to it that he has nothing to fear while he is with you, for he is carrying on the work of the Lord, just as I am.* 11 *No one, then, should refuse to accept him. Send him on his way in peace so that he may return to me. I am expecting him along with the brothers.*

In 4:17 and 18-21, in the heat of an argument with the Corinthians over his authority, Paul announced that Timothy had been dispatched to Corinth to remind them of his ways in the Lord and that he himself would be coming "very soon." Now the mention of his coming to make the final arrangements for their collection to be sent to Jerusalem (vv. 3-4) leads Paul to explain his travel plans in getting there, and to add a word about the coming of Timothy and of their reception of him. Such travel information regularly appears in his letters either about himself (Rom. 15:22-33; Phil. 2:24; Phlm. 22; Tit. 3:12) or about his companions (Phil. 2:19-30).[2]

The information in this case is straightforward. He is currently in Ephesus (vv. 8-9), where he plans to stay at least until Pentecost. That means he is probably writing in early spring. According to these plans he would not

---

[1]Paul has an explanatory γάρ; the MajT reads δέ.

[2]In some additional cases he also explains why he did not come as expected or hoped (1 Thess. 2:17–3:5; 2 Cor. 1:15–2:13).

take the direct route (by sea; v. 7), but would come by way of Macedonia (v. 5), where he would apparently spend the better part of summer and early fall, since he hopes to winter in Corinth. Although this fits precisely with the picture in Acts 20:1-3, the latter can scarcely be referring to the realization of these present plans.[3] Indeed, according to 2 Cor. 1:15–2:4 Paul did exactly the opposite of this. Apparently he paid them a quick visit by sea, hoping that they would send him on his way to Macedonia; from Macedonia he would return to Corinth so that they would also send him on his way to Jerusalem (1 Cor. 1:15-16).[4] But this brief visit developed into a major crisis in Paul's relationship with this church, which took at least two more letters and two visits from Titus to straighten out.

The straightforward way in which Paul gives his own plans offers no hint that there is some tension between him and them on this matter.[5] To be sure, this letter reflects such tensions in nearly every section; but Paul probably also expects this letter to function in his place and prepare the way for his own coming.[6] Hence his somewhat relaxed attitude as to his own coming. But those very tensions fill him with more than just a little anxiety about Timothy and their reception of him (vv. 10-11). Given the nature of the abuse Paul himself apparently has been taking from some quarters in the church, and given Timothy's own apparently less than forceful personal mien, he urges them to take Timothy in as they would the apostle himself. Of this visit we know nothing more, not even whether it materialized.

5 Paul begins the outline of his itinerary by telling them that he is taking the overland route through Macedonia.[7] Although these churches (at least Philippi, Thessalonica, and Berea) by and large seem to have maintained his ways, it has been several years since he has visited them, so at the moment he apparently plans to spend late spring and summer among them. The language "pass through"[8] implies not that he intends simply to be there overnight, as it were, but that he is on a tour of supervision through these various churches. The added "for I will be going through[9] Macedonia" is

---

[3]Mare, 294, makes this equation, as if the evidence in 2 Corinthians did not exist.

[4]On this whole question see Fee, "ΧΑΡΙΣ."

[5]Otherwise Hurd, 202-03, who considers the "casualness" of these plans to be something of a ploy on Paul's part to dissociate himself from the collection personally lest the Corinthians suspect his motives.

[6]On this question see on 4:17 and especially the article by Funk noted there (n. 38).

[7]Gk. ὅταν . . . διέλθω (= "whenever I shall have passed through Macedonia").

[8]Cf. 2 Cor. 1:16. This verb is used frequently in Acts to describe missionary activity in places where they did not stay an extended time (cf. 8:4, 40; 11:19; 13:6, 14).

[9]Gk. διέρχομαι, an example of the futuristic use of the durative present. Apparently an incorrect understanding of this verb is responsible for the subscript of the KJV:

probably intended to emphasize his desire both to return to these churches and to let the Corinthians know that the "very soon" of 4:19 has this degree of delay to it.

6-7   These two sentences together stress Paul's eagerness to spend considerable time among them. It may be that lying behind this is some concern as to how he will find the church when he comes and whether it may take some time for him to square away the breakdown in relationships between him and them. But if so, we must conjecture it from what else we know from this letter. The sentences themselves reflect a straightforward desire, couched in terms of just enough uncertainty to preclude its being a promise. The hope is first expressed as "Perhaps[10] I will stay with you awhile, or even spend the winter." Given the problems of travel during winter[11] and the open-ended nature of his going to Macedonia, this probably reflects nothing more than a generally realistic hope of how things very well could turn out.

But the purpose of his spending time turns out to be something of a surprise: "so that you can help me on my journey, wherever I go." The "wherever I go" corroborates the doubt expressed in v. 4 as to his destination following Corinth. Most likely lying behind this hesitation is the double yearning to take the collection to Jerusalem and to visit Rome. The verb "help me on my journey"[12] is a technical one for providing a person with food, money, and traveling companions so as to ensure a safe and successful arrival at his or her destination. It seems to be a key means of Christian hospitality in antiquity.[13] In light of the tensions over his refusal to accept monetary support while among them (see on chap. 9), this has all the earmarks of being a peace offering on this matter. Although he has refused to take money while with them so that his gospel might be offered "free of charge," he now offers them the opportunity to assist him on his further journeys, so that in this way they, too, can have a share in his ministry.

"The first epistle to the Corinthians was written from Philippi by Stephanas, and Fortunatus, and Achaicus, and Timotheus." V. 8 absolutely rules this out.

[10]Gk. τυχόν; cf. the εἰ τύχοι of 14:10; 15:37. The absolute use of the neuter participle as here tends to express much more hope regarding the outcome. Thus, "It may actually turn out that I will be able to spend time with you, even the winter."

[11]Cf. 2 Tim. 4:21. The danger is vividly illustrated in Acts 27:9-44. For a full presentation of the difficulties of travel on the Mediterranean in winter, see F. Brandel, *The Mediterranean and the Mediterranean World in the Age of Philip II* (New York, 1966), 248-56.

[12]Gk. προπέμπω; it appears again in v. 11. It is found in the NT with this meaning in 2 Cor. 1:16; Rom. 15:24; Tit. 3:13; Acts 15:3; 3 John 6. Outside the NT cf. 1 Macc. 12:4; 1 Esdr. 4:47; see also the entry in MM.

[13]Cf. Fee, *1 Timothy*, p. 167 (on Tit. 3:13).

The next sentence (v. 7) begins with an explanatory "for,"[14] indicating his sense of need to elaborate on this concern to spend time with them. Hence he simply repeats this dimension of v. 6 in new words. He doesn't want to see them "now"[15] because he intends to go to Macedonia (v. 5), and that would mean to "make only a passing visit."[16] Rather, he repeats, he hopes to spend some time with them, but this time he qualifies, "if the Lord permits" (cf. 4:19). As always, Paul's own plans are ultimately subject to Christ.

8 First he explained his determination to go to Macedonia (v. 5), then his desire to spend considerable time in Corinth (vv. 6-7). Now he offers a final word about the present situation in Ephesus. He plans to "stay on" there "until Pentecost." This latter is an especially intriguing note, given that both the Ephesian and Corinthian churches were predominantly Gentile. Minimally, it is a reflection of Paul's Jewish heritage in which, just as the week is divided by days from the Sabbath (v. 3), so the year is divided by the annual feasts. Therefore, it does not necessarily imply that he and the churches kept this feast, but that it is a convenient time reference to a period in mid-spring. On the other hand, such a casual mention of it in this way (cf. Acts 20:16) may suggest that the church very early saw Christian significance to this feast, probably as a result of the birth of the church on the Day of Pentecost.

Some have suggested on the basis of this reference and the allusion to Christ as the Paschal lamb in 5:7 that the letter must have been written near Passover/Easter.[17] That may well be, but it could just as easily have been before, as after, Easter. Although "Pentecost" technically refers to the "feast of fifty days" that followed Passover, it came to be used as a shortened form for "the day of Pentecost," the celebration of the fiftieth day. Most likely that is what Paul is here referring to.

9 With this verse Paul explains why he intends to stay on for a while longer in Ephesus: On the one hand, "a great door[18] for effective work[19] has opened to me," while on the other hand, "there are many who oppose me." In a sense these two sentences describe Paul's lifelong labors

---

[14]Gk. γάρ, untranslated in the NIV.

[15]Gk. ἄρτι, "at the present moment." For its usage in this letter, see 4:11, 13; 13:12; 15:6. It has been a matter of considerable debate whether this adverb implies an earlier short visit, i.e., "I do not want to pay another 'in passing' visit." But the grammar does not require this, nor does the historical evidence support it.

[16]Not now διέρχομαι but ἐν παρόδῳ, a word he avoids in 2 Cor. 1:15-16 in explaining what motivated him to do this very thing. Rather, he was hoping to offer them the "grace" of helping him on his journey twice.

[17]See the discussion in n. 15 on 5:7. See also Rordorf, *Sunday*, pp. 195-96.

[18]For this metaphor see also 2 Cor. 2:12; Col. 4:3.

[19]Gk. ἐνεργής (cf. Heb. 4:12; Phlm. 6). Lit. the text reads, "for a door has opened to me, great and effective."

as a Christian missionary. Since no specifics are given here and the material in Acts cannot be dated, one properly hesitates to identify any of this with the latter material. Nonetheless, some significant correspondences should be noted. In Acts 19:22, Paul has already sent Timothy on ahead of him— although Luke has probably telescoped a bit the account of Paul's plans in v. 21. Furthermore, Paul's imagery does coincide with the picture Luke portrays of the considerable success of Paul's mission in this city that finally brought about the conflict with the hawkers of souvenirs at the temple of Artemis (Acts 19:23-41). It is certainly possible, therefore, and especially so in light of 1 Cor. 15:32, that at the time this letter was written Paul was fully anticipating a ruckus similar to that which Demetrius would finally instigate. In any case, these passages together give a clear picture of opposition to the gospel from outsiders. That it might have come in this case from pagan religion should offer no surprises.

10-11   From his own travel plans and the momentary reflection on the opposition, Paul is reminded of Timothy and the likelihood that he will be arriving in Corinth at some point along the way. In 4:17 Paul explicitly said that he had sent Timothy to them. The protasis of this conditional clause, therefore, probably does not intend to imply doubt as to whether he would come or not. Rather, it expresses uncertainty as to his actual time of arrival; and in any case, given the nature of travel in antiquity, it also allows for the proper hesitation as to the event itself. Thus, Paul probably means, "whenever Timothy comes."[20] There seems to be little question that he expected him eventually to come.

What is of interest, however, is Paul's concern for Timothy's reception. If there have not been many overt hints of the tensions between Paul and this church in vv. 1-9, these sentences about Timothy bring that issue back into focus, especially so in light of the fact that Timothy worked with Paul in the founding of this church for well over a year. Why, then, should Paul fear that an old friend might not be well received? Most likely (1) because he knew that the sentiment against himself in this church was strong indeed and that it would almost certainly overflow toward Timothy, and (2) because Timothy had been specifically dispatched to "remind them of Paul's ways" (4:17). Thus, he urges that they "see to it that he has nothing to fear while he is with you." The very fact that such a strong warning is issued is evidence enough of Paul's own concern.

The second clause is intended to put the first into perspective: "For he is carrying on the work of the Lord,[21] just as I am." That is, they are to

---

[20]See BAGD, 1d: "At times the mng. . . . approaches close to that of ὅταν whenever."

[21]Gk. τὸ ἔργον κυρίου ἐργάζεται. For this word as referring to the ministry of the gospel see on 3:13-15; 4:12; and 15:58.

treat Timothy as one who is there in Paul's place, ministering in Paul's stead. But a word that would ordinarily be one of commendation and security may not be so in this case, so Paul adds a further warning: "No one, then, should treat him with contempt."[22] Again it is difficult to find a reason for such a word unless Paul was fearful that the contempt some of them have for him will spill over onto his younger colleague.

Since Timothy would be coming as Paul's personal delegate, he asks the community to afford him the same treatment he hoped to receive from them himself (v. 6), namely that they "help him on his journey[23] in peace." The addition "in peace" probably reflects the traditional Jewish *shalom;* thus he wants them to provide for his needs so that he may return to Paul and be sent on his way with the traditional blessing of "peace." All of this "so that he may return to me," although there is no hint here as to whether this means in Ephesus or Macedonia.

Also unclear is what is intended by "along with the brothers." In the Greek text this could mean "I, along with the brothers, am expecting him." Those who take this position usually consider it to refer to the same brothers mentioned in v. 12, therefore to the three Corinthians mentioned in v. 15. But that makes very little sense since if they wait for Timothy to return before this letter is sent, why say it at all—unless one also wants to argue that this letter was sent back to Corinth without these three men, which is most highly unlikely. On the other hand, those who take it to refer to brothers who are expected to come with Timothy are equally at a loss. In Acts 19:22 Erastus is said to accompany him. Does this reference include some others as well whom Luke fails to mention, who accompanied Timothy during the entire trip? If so, which seems likely, then the concern for Timothy's own treatment stands out the more. If not, then we have absolutely no way of knowing to whom he is referring.[24]

One is left to wonder how this visit by Timothy turned out since there is no further mention of it in Paul's letters. In any case, two things are certain. First, shortly after this letter Paul goes absolutely contrary to the plans here laid out and pays a sudden, unexpected visit to Corinth. Why he did so is purely a matter of conjecture, but that he should so radically alter his plans suggests that perhaps the return of Timothy gave him reason for even

---

[22]Gk. ἐξουθενήσῃ; see on 1:28 and 6:4. The word basically means "to despise" or "hold in contempt." The NIV's "refuse to accept" is a euphemism at best, and seems not to take seriously enough the conflict between this church and its apostle.

[23]Gk. προπέμψατε, as in v. 6.

[24]Speculations include some Ephesians who are accompanying the three Corinthian delegates back to Corinth with this letter (see v. 17), and may be expected to return with Timothy.

greater alarm with regard to this church. The fact that the visit turned out to be such a blowup, apparently under the leadership of one person in particular,[25] and that the visit was so painful for Paul that he refused to return for the time being, seems to give this suggestion some merit. Second, what Paul did do was to send Titus back to Corinth instead of either himself or Timothy (2 Cor. 2:13; 7:6-7). For the present, neither of them is a *persona grata* to the community; it also means that Titus must have been a person of extraordinary grace. This, at least, is one viable attempt to make some sense of these very fragmentary pieces of historical data.

H. ABOUT THE COMING OF APOLLOS (16:12)

12 *Now about our brother Apollos:[1] I strongly urged him to go to you with the brothers. He was quite unwilling to go now, but he will go when he has the opportunity.*

Following these personal matters relating to his and Timothy's travel plans, one might well expect Paul now to bring the letter to its conclusion, which in fact he will begin to do in v. 13. But before that, he needs to address one final item from their letter. Apparently they have requested him to ask Apollos to return and minister among them. The fact that he did so probably says as much about his self-understanding as an apostle as anything in this letter. Although it is a brief sentence, and is easily overlooked in light of some of the thundering moments in this Epistle, here indeed is a chunk of Paul's life that puts a considerable number of things in this letter into their proper perspective.

12 The sixth and final "now about"[2] with which this sentence begins implies that this passage is also in response to their letter. Its content further supports such a view. Given the nature of the problem addressed in 1:10–4:21, it is difficult to imagine any circumstances in which Paul himself

---

[25]This is based on an understanding of 2 Cor. 1–7 that sees the material from 1:8 to 2:14 and 7:2 to 16 as basically a chronological recounting of Paul's and their most recent exchanges. If so, then the man in 2:5-11 who needs their restoration is probably the same as the one in 7:12 who injured someone else. If the injured party is Paul, all of this makes a great deal of sense.

[1]The Western witnesses (D* F G a Ambst) and ℵ* add δήλω ὑμῖν ὅτι (= "I make known to you that"). One could make good sense of this as the original text since Paul would thus be protesting his own innocence in the failure of Apollos to come. But if original, it is difficult to account for its deliberate omission in the rest of the textual tradition. Most likely, therefore, it is an attempt to improve on Paul's sentence, which is a bit awkward due to the opening περὶ δέ phrase.

[2]See on 7:1 (cf. v. 1 above).

would have initiated a request for Apollos[3] to return to Corinth! What this means, therefore, is that in their letter to Paul the Corinthians have requested Apollos's return. What is remarkable is that Paul acceded to it: "I strongly urged[4] him to go to you with the brothers." The "brothers" in this case are almost certainly the three mentioned in v. 17, who presumably brought the Corinthian letter to Paul and are now returning with his letter to them. Since they are going, and since Apollos is obviously well-loved by many in the congregation, Paul urges him to go along as well, perhaps as a display on his part of the complete harmony between the two of them.

But for the present Apollos resists the imploring, both of Paul and of the church. But what is not as clear as the NIV suggests is whose "will" is involved in this rejection, Apollos's or God's. The Greek sentence is quite ambiguous, reading literally, "And not at all was[5] the will that now he come." Although a good case can be made for this to refer to God's will,[6] the lack of qualifiers suggests that it should be understood within its immediate context. Since Apollos is the subject of the final clause, "when he has the opportunity," one may rightly assume that he is the one who has also determined not to come now. If so, then this refusal probably says as much about Apollos's own character as it does of Paul's in asking him in the first place. Most likely he would have turned it down precisely because with Paul he resisted any implication that either of them was party to the internal strife being carried on in the church in their names.

Two things about this request are especially significant for this letter. First, this is sure evidence that Paul did not consider Apollos himself responsible for the trouble that is addressed in chaps. 1–4. Furthermore, both the request itself and the designation "our brother" indicate that Paul's view of their unity in ministry expressed in 3:5-9 paints the picture as Paul *really* sees it, not as he would say it in some idealistic fashion. They are coworkers under God; from Paul's point of view there is no rivalry between them.

Second, this is a particularly important text in our piecing together Paul's view both of his own ministry and his true relationship to the church.

---

[3]Lit. "Apollos the brother." On the absolute use of "brother" for Paul's companions see on 1:1.

[4]Gk. παρεκάλεσα (see on v. 15); cf. the usage in 1:10; 4:13, 16.

[5]As several have pointed out (e.g., Conzelmann, 297), both this unusual past tense and the lack of a greeting from Apollos in 1:1 or 16:20 suggest that he may not be present at the time of writing. Was he urged to go to Corinth, but then moved on to another area of ministry in the meantime?

[6]The strongest argument in its favor is also the strongest argument for Apollos, the absolute use of the word without a qualifier. Cf. Rom. 2:18. Those who take this position include Moffatt, 185; Héring, 185; Ruef, 184; Barrett, 391; Bruce, 160; G. Schrenk, *TDNT* III, 59.

There can be little question that for him several of the issues spoken to in this letter in various ways pose threats to his apostolic authority in this community. At times he takes up this challenge in such vigorous ways (e.g., 4:18-21; 9:1-27) that one could get the impression that Paul, as so often happens in the church, had so identified the gospel and the church with his own ministry that a threat to the one (his ministry) is a threat to the other (the gospel). At times this seems to be precisely what he says. But in 3:5-23, and again in 4:1-13, he puts all of this into perspective. The gospel is God's thing, and his alone, and so too, therefore, is the church. The church, he argues strenuously, belongs neither to himself, nor to Apollos, nor to them. The church belongs to God through Christ, and all of its ministers, including the founders (!), are merely servants. This final word about Apollos is living evidence that Paul is as good as his word. If the church in Corinth were Paul's, the last person in the world he would want to return would be Apollos. Indeed, the real pressure would be to keep him away for some time while things cooled off. But not so Paul. Apollos watered what Paul had planted (3:6); and "all things are theirs" in Christ Jesus, including Apollos (3:21-22). So for the sake of the growth of the community he can urge Apollos to return, despite some of the inherent difficulties that would entail. Here is another piece of clear evidence, along with Phil. 1:12-18, of the incredible bigness of the Apostle to the Gentiles—far greater than that of many of his detractors, one is wont to add.

IV. CONCLUDING MATTERS (16:13-24)

In 1:1-9 it was noted that a threefold salutation appears on almost all letters from the Greco-Roman period, often followed by a thanksgiving and/or prayer, and that Paul followed this standard form but thoroughly adapted it to the realities of the gospel. The conclusions of letters, on the other hand, lacked a standard form; various elements are found, but not all of them appear in any one letter.[1] The one rather constant element was a final wish; other elements include greetings, a health wish, the date, a concluding autograph, and postscripts.

As before, Paul uses some of these conventions and freely adapts them to his own concerns. Since the form itself was not constant, it is no surprise that there is no standard form in his own letters; he uses some of the elements already available, but he also adds some of his own. Generally speaking his conclusions contain (1) hortatory remarks, (2) a wish of peace, (3) greetings, including (4) the exhortation to greet one another with a holy

---

[1]For a detailed analysis of this material, see Gamble, *Textual History*, pp. 56-83.

kiss and (5) an autographic greeting, and (6) a grace-benediction. Our letter follows this form with the following exceptions: (a) there is no wish of peace;[2] (b) a brief word of warning is inserted between the autographic greeting (v. 21) and the grace-benediction (v. 23); and (c) the grace-benediction, which is the final item in all his letters, is followed in this instance by the personal wish of Paul's love (v. 24).

Thus beginning with v. 13, Paul is bringing the letter to its conclusion. In this case the elements include:

(1) vv. 13-18 Hortatory remarks
[(2) missing—the wish of peace]
(3) vv. 19-20a Greetings
(4) v. 20b The holy kiss
(5) v. 21 Autographic conclusion
(*) v. 22 Interruptive word of warning
(6) v. 23 Grace-benediction
(*) v. 24 Personal wish of love

As always in Paul, these not only reflect the present circumstances of this letter but also are thoroughly marked by Paul's singular commitment to the gospel.

A. CONCLUDING EXHORTATIONS (16:13-18)

13 *Be on your guard; stand firm in the faith; be* people[3] *of courage; be strong.* 14 *Do everything in love.*

15 *You know that the household of Stephanas[4] were the first converts in Achaia, and they have devoted themselves to the service of the saints. I urge you, brothers,* 16 *to submit to such as these and to everyone who joins in the work and labors at it.* 17 *I was glad when Stephanas, Fortunatus and Achaicus arrived, because they have supplied what was lacking from you.* 18 *For they refreshed my spirit and yours also. Such men deserve recognition.*

This hortatory part of the conclusion is in three parts. The first (vv. 13-14) is a series of five seriatim imperatives that appear to be a kind of generalized parenesis that could fit any of Paul's letters; at the same time, however, some of them in particular seem to reflect the Corinthian situation. These are followed (vv. 15-16) by a *parakalō*-period (= I beseech you)[5] of a kind that

---

[2]This is also missing in Colossians, Philemon, and the Pastoral Epistles.
[3]NIV, "men."
[4]Various assimilations to v. 17 occurred in the Western tradition: D 104 629 1175 2464 pc add "and Fortunatus"; C*vid F G 365 2495 pc a Pelagius add "and Fortunatus and Achaicus."
[5]On this matter see on 1:10 (n. 20 in particular).

appears elsewhere in Pauline conclusions.[6] As in other instances they are concerned with relationships within the community addressed, in this case with the proper recognition of the household of Stephanas. To this is added a word about the presence of Stephanas, Fortunatus, and Achaicus (vv. 17-18), who are almost certainly the bearers of the Corinthian letter to Paul, and probably will return to Corinth with this letter.

The matters in vv. 15-18 are full of interest, both in terms of how these men relate to Paul, on the one hand, and to the quarrels of 1:10-12, on the other. Both the fact that Paul devotes this amount of space to this matter and that Stephanas at least probably represents someone who is loyal to Paul suggest that this is one more reflection of the tension between him and the church. But on these matters no certain word can be given.

13 This first series of imperatives is as surprising as it is abrupt. Their presence is probably best explained formally: As noted above, and especially in the earlier letters,[7] Paul seems to have developed the habit of beginning his conclusions with words of exhortation, as though reluctant to sign off without a final word of urgency. These first four imperatives are related in that they all call to watchfulness and steadfastness as to the faith itself (cf. 15:58).[8] In light of all that has preceded Paul is probably urging loyalty to the gospel as they received it from him.

First, the Corinthians are urged to "be watchful" or "alert." This imperative occurs elsewhere in the NT, including Paul, in eschatological contexts, urging watchfulness in light of the Lord's return.[9] But it can also be a call to watchfulness with regard to the enemy (1 Pet. 5:8) or to corrosive influences (Acts 20:31). Given the full context of 1 Corinthians, the latter is most likely what is intended, hence "be on your guard." This seems the more so in light of the second imperative, "stand firm[10] in the faith," which is a modified version of the concern expressed in 15:1 and 58 (cf. 10:12). In Paul this verb invariably has the sense of "standing" firm in Christ, as opposed to "falling." The use of "in *the* faith"[11] in place of "the gospel" is

---

[6]See 1 Thess. 5:12-14; Rom. 16:17-20; cf. Phil. 4:2-3. Cf. Bjerkelund, *Parakalô*, p. 113.

[7]Cf. 1 Thess. 5:16-22; 2 Cor. 13:11.

[8]Spicq, *Agape*, p. 181 (120-21), suggests that they reflect military commands; cf. Godet, 464.

[9]Gk. γρηγορεῖτε. See 1 Thess. 5:6, 10 and Col. 4:2, its only other occurrences in Paul; cf. Mark 13:34, 35, 37 and parallels, and Rev. 3:3.

[10]Gk. στήκετε, a verb found first in Paul in all of Greek literature; apparently a new form from the perfect of ἵστημι. Cf. 1 Thess. 3:8; 2 Thess. 2:15; Gal. 5:1; Rom. 14:4; Phil. 1:27; 4:1. See the discussion in W. Grundmann, *TDNT* VII, 636-38.

[11]The RSV translates "in your faith," a position taken also by Parry, 249; Grosheide, 402; and Barrett, 393, who allows that the other may be in view, but suggests that it finally makes little difference since it "would then mean the Christian religion, the religion which (on the human side) is marked by trust and obedience." This is true, of

clear evidence that in Paul from the very beginning this noun can refer to the content of what is believed as well as to the activity of trusting itself.[12]

The third and fourth imperatives in this list are calls to courage, in which Paul seems to be recalling the language of Ps. 31:24.[13] Ordinarily, one would expect such imperatives in a context of outside opposition; but in the present context Paul is probably urging them to remain steadfast in the gospel he preached, and to do so courageously in the face of the errors and behavioral aberrations that are rife among them.

14 The preceding imperatives have basically to do with their remaining faithful to the gospel itself, this final one with their relationships to one another. "Do all things in love" echoes chap. 13. Apart from that chapter this word does not occur frequently in this letter, but its appearance there and in the crucial passage in 8:1-3, as well as at the heart of all of Paul's ethical instructions,[14] makes it certain that in Paul's understanding this is the imperative that covers much that has preceded. "All things" would include the quarrels in the name of leaders in chaps. 1-3, their attitude toward him in chaps. 4 and 9, the lawsuits in 6:1-11, husband-wife relationships in chap. 7, the abuse of the weak by those with "knowledge" in 8:1-10:22, the abuse of the "have-nots" at the Lord's Supper, and the failure to edify the church in worship in chaps. 12-14. If they were to "do *all things* in love," then these other things would not be happening. It is therefore no surprise that this is the final expression of parenesis in the letter.

15 The appeal of this brief paragraph (vv. 15-18), that they honor Stephanas's household and others like him who labor among them, has its precedent in 1 Thess. 5:12-14. However, as with vv. 13-14, this material is not to be explained simply on formal grounds. This is made clear in the present case by the very awkwardness of vv. 15-16, through which Paul's emphases emerge. The clause in v. 16 is properly the (objective) complement of the opening verb, "Now I urge you, brothers [and sisters]."[15] But it

course, but the combination of the preposition ἐν (which makes the usage in 2 Cor. 1:24 not comparable) and the article τῇ indicates that it means "in the faith" (= locative of sphere; cf. Ellis, 170 n. 88); the context suggests that it is thus comparable to "the gospel."

[12]This is especially noteworthy in light of the oft-repeated, but inaccurate, assertion with regard to the Pastoral Epistles that the use of "faith" in those letters does not reflect Paul's "distinctive" use of this word. That is to judge everything in light of Galatians and Romans, and even there is to overlook Gal. 1:23. Cf. Fee, *1 Timothy*, p. 8.

[13]LXX Ps. 30:25; cf. 26:14; 2 Sam. 10:12. This seems all the more likely since of the two verbs, ἀνδρίζομαι occurs only here in the NT and κραταιόω elsewhere in Paul only in Eph. 3:16, with a considerably different sense. The verb ἀνδρίζομαι means to "play the role of a man," an idea that is frequent in antiquity as a call to courage in the face of danger.

[14]See n. 38 on 8:1 and n. 27 on 13:1.

[15]See n. 22 on 1:10.

is suspended to make room for the explanatory parenthesis that gives the *reason* they should submit to Stephanas and his household: "You know the household of Stephanas, that they are, etc." The result is a singular emphasis on Stephanas, and the Corinthians' need especially to recognize him, to which then is added that they need to be in submission to all who so labor among them. This strong commendation of Stephanas implies that he had been loyal to Paul in the present tensions within the community. The language of v. 16 further makes certain that he is a leader in the church. Very likely he is also a source of further information about the condition of the church, quite apart from their letter.

In calling attention to the "household of Stephanas,"[16] Paul reminds them of two things about Stephanas that they already well know.[17] First, his "household" were "the first converts[18] in [the province of] Achaia."[19] It is impossible to determine who would have made up the household, which included at least two or more adult members, since the second verb is plural, "*they* have devoted themselves to the service of the saints." It is possible, though not provable, that Fortunatus and Achaicus were themselves members of his household, perhaps as slaves or attached freedmen.[20]

Second, Stephanas and his household are noted among the Corinthian believers for having "devoted themselves[21] unto service for[22] the saints."[23] Here are people who in self-dedication took it upon themselves to

[16]On this "household" see on 1:16.

[17]Gk. οἴδατε; for this verb as a reminder see on 1:16 and 12:2.

[18]Gk. ἀπαρχή, "firstfruits" (see on 15:20), thus not just the "first converts," but as "firstfruits" the promise of more to come. For this usage to refer to first converts in a province or city, see 2 Thess. 2:13 and Rom. 16:15. The fact that they were among his first converts in this city accounts for the fact that he baptized them (1:16). Ellis, 20, suggests that ἀπαρχή here means "the consecrated first-born who, like the Levites, are set apart for the work of God." But that runs aground on the other Pauline uses of the term. However, see C. Spicq, "'ΑΠΑΡΧΗ. Note de lexicographie neo-testamentaire," in *The New Testament Age, Essays in Honor of Bo Reicke* (ed. W. C. Weinrich; Macon, GA, 1984), II, 493-502, who also sees the metaphor in a more active than passive sense (= "the firstfruits who are consecrated to Christ in such and such a region").

[19]This is true for Paul despite the evidence of Acts 17:34. Most likely Paul used the term here in its more limited sense to refer to the Peloponnesus, and especially to Corinth as the capital of the province.

[20]See further on v. 17. For the discussion of slaves and freedmen in these settings see on 7:21 and 22.

[21]Gk. ἔταξαν ἑαυτούς (lit. "they appointed themselves"), a combination commonly used to express this idiom.

[22]Gk. dative, not genitive as in the NIV, indicating the *people for whom* their service was rendered.

[23]The nearly identical phrase "the service of the saints" appears in 2 Cor. 8:4 and 9:1 to refer to the collection for the saints in Jerusalem. Ruef, 186, thinks that this is in view here as well. But the aorist of the verb, the content of v. 16, and the context of the paragraph as a whole are against it; the "saints" here are the Corinthians themselves, as in 1:2, and the "ministry" has been among them.

minister to others in Corinth. One cannot be certain as to the specifics of this "service" since the word is ambiguous enough to cover a number of "ministries," including that of teaching and preaching.[24] It may be that Stephanas's house also served as one of the places of meeting, in which case he would also be one of the "patrons" of the Lord's Supper. But that, too, cannot be known. The content of v. 16, including both the urging of "submission" to "Stephanas's household" and the addition of "everyone who joins in the work and labors at it," implies that their ministry was probably not limited to good deeds of service among the believers, but also included some responsibility for the ministry of the Word.

16 This sentence functions as the object of the verb "I urge," with which v. 15 began.[25] Paul's concern is that the Corinthians give proper recognition to Stephanas and his household. Thus, "I urge . . . that you also[26] submit[27] to such as these and to everyone who joins in the work, and labors at it." The verb "submit" is used only here in the NT to refer to the relationship of a Christian community to those who labor among them.[28] Although this could possibly mean to be in submission to them in some form of obedience,[29] both the context and the similar passage in 1 Thess. 5:12-13 suggest rather that it means "submission in the sense of voluntary yielding in love" (BAGD), much the same as in Eph. 5:21, where all are urged to be "subject to one another out of reverence for Christ."

In the first instance this refers to "the household of Stephanas,"[30] which is what the words "to such as these" must mean. That is, Paul is not

---

[24]Gk. διακονία; see n. 17 on 12:5 and n. 13 on 16:1.

[25]Zerwick, *BG*, 415, suggests that this use of ἵνα is imperatival. That would make v. 15a an independent clause with no object; but since the verb παρακαλῶ demands some kind of object, either expressed or implied, this ἵνα clause functions as that object, even if one goes the route of Zerwick as to grammatical nomenclature.

[26]Gk. καί, omitted by the NIV but without good reason (although cf. Conzelmann, 298, who warns against overloading the word). Paul is urging that they not only "recognize" them for their service for the saints, but that they *also* submit themselves to such people. Or perhaps the καί picks up the service of Stephanas's household (= "you in your turn"). See the next note.

[27]Gk. ὑποτάσσησθε; cf. 15:27-28. There is probably something of a play on words here. They "appointed themselves" (ἔταξαν ἑαυτούς) as your servants; you in your turn "submit yourselves" (ὑποτάσσησθε) to them.

[28]Holladay, 215, incorrectly cites Tit. 3:1, which, like Rom. 13:1-6, refers to the ruling authorities.

[29]The verb does seem to mean that in Rom. 13:1 and 5, although in 1 Pet. 2:13 and 18 it means to submit to undeserved brutality in the sense of not fighting back, as over against submission = obedience.

[30]If this includes Fortunatus and Achaicus in the next verse, and the plural "to such as these" makes that a possibility if not a probability (in v. 18 it clearly refers to the three of them), then in the Christian church a whole new order has been established in which believers lovingly submit themselves to one another out of love and respect for their labors. This could include slaves as well.

simply generalizing with this language; that is what the next phrase will do. Here he is referring particularly to Stephanas and other members of his household, which very well might include his wife and slaves and/or freedmen. In any case, for Paul the key to such respect or "submission" is not sex or socioeconomic status but ministry, as becomes clear in the addition "and to everyone who joins in the work, and labors at it." The collocation of these two words almost certainly refers to the ministry of the gospel.[31] This final addition expands the appeal that began in v. 15 to include all who so labor among them for the sake of the gospel. But the fact that it occurs merely as an addition implies that the real urgency of the passage has to do with their attitudes toward Stephanas. Although as in vv. 10-11 one cannot be certain, this looks like one more attempt on Paul's part to urge the Corinthians not only to accept him and his own ministry, but also to extend that acceptance to those who are his colaborers.

17 This sentence helps to put some things from the two preceding verses into perspective.[32] Paul "rejoices[33] over the coming[34] of Stephanas, Fortunatus, and Achaicus." Of the latter two men nothing more is known.[35] Fortunatus is a common Latin name, meaning "blessed" or "lucky"; it appears to have been common especially among slaves and freedmen. Whoever this Fortunatus was, he was undoubtedly from among the large number of Romans who made up this Roman colony. Achaicus means "one who is from Achaia." This name, too, appears to be the kind that is given to slaves, or taken sometimes by freedmen. Such derivations may mean little or nothing as to their present socioeconomic status. On the other hand, they do add weight to the possibility that these two men are attached to Stephanas in some way.[36] In any case, that is as probable as the oft-repeated assumption that the three men were independent of one another as members of the church

---

[31]See on 15:58. Although this is the only occurrence of the verb συνεργέω in this sense, Paul uses the noun σύνεργος regularly to refer to his fellow workers in the gospel. See on 3:9. That it also includes women is made certain from its usage in Phil. 4:2-3. For the verb κοπιάω see on 4:12 and 15:10; cf. esp. Rom. 16:6 and 12. For the latter word see also A. Harnack, "ΚΟΠΟΣ," *ZNW* 27 (1928), 1-10.

[32]The δέ could be slightly adversative to the preceding sentence. Thus, when these men return to Corinth, they should give respectful deference to them, "but for now I am rejoicing in their coming."

[33]Gk. χαίρω (NIV, "I was glad"); the present tense implies that he is still rejoicing over their coming and therefore over their continuing presence with him. *Contra* Conzelmann, 298 n. 9, who argues that it means "'arrival' (not 'sojourn')."

[34]Gk. παρουσία; see on 15:23 to refer to the Second Coming of Christ.

[35]Clement of Rome mentions a Fortunatus in his letter (65:1), but he can scarcely be the same man. The name was very common in Rome.

[36]Cf. Lenski, 779-80; Moffatt, 278; Grosheide, 403. According to Godet, 467, who thinks it probable, the suggestion goes back at least to Weizsäcker, *Die apostolische Zeitalter* (1886), p. 632.

in Corinth. If they belonged together in some way, as members of Stephanas's household, then they might very well have been traveling together to Ephesus, perhaps on business, in which case the church would have asked them to carry their letter to Paul. In that sense the three together would become a kind of "official delegation" from the church.

That at least is how Paul himself treats them. By their coming to be with Paul, "they have supplied what was lacking from you." The words "to fill up your lack"[37] mean that Paul's absence from Corinth had left a gap in his life; in these three men, therefore, he has in effect welcomed the whole congregation, of whom they are the representatives, even if they do not in themselves truly "represent" the various elements and points of view in the community. That is, as bearers of the Corinthian letter, they are "officially" from the church, even if they do not represent the point of view of the letter itself. If this is the correct view of things, then there is a degree of irony in this accolade.

18 With two sentences Paul concludes these brief words about the brothers from Corinth. First he explains how it is that they have made up for his not being able to see the whole church in person: "For[38] they have refreshed[39] my spirit." This sentence scarcely needs comment for any who have ever been thus visited by longtime friends in the faith, especially those with whom one has worked. Such visits are always "seasons of refreshing" in the Lord, both because of the personal relationships involved and the news of other believers. But what they did for Paul is no surprise; they had already often done so to the Corinthians themselves, as the words "and yours also" attest.

"Therefore,"[40] Paul concludes, "recognize[41] such men." Although the NIV captures the sense of this with its "Such men deserve recognition," it misses too much by omitting the imperative and inferential conjunction. These words at the conclusion of this paragraph further add to the supposition that even though they have come on behalf of the church, they are among Paul's people in the community. Thus, this final sentence has the effect of being a "letter of commendation" (see on v. 3) for the very ones who came to Paul from the church in the first place. In any case, the language implies that they are now the bearers of Paul's letter back to the church.

---

[37]Gk. ὑμέτερον [see on 15:31] ὑστέρημα . . . ἀνεπλήρωσαν. R-P, 396, give equal weight to the possibility that ὑμέτερον could be subjective, but the nearly identical, and unambiguous, passage in Phil. 2:30 rules that out.

[38]The final explanatory γάρ in this letter, which has an especially large number of them.

[39]Gk. ἀναπαύω, used always in this sense by Paul: 2 Cor. 7:13; Phlm. 7 and 20.

[40]Gk. οὖν, omitted by the NIV.

[41]Gk. ἐπιγινώσκετε; cf. the οἴδατε in v. 15 and the ἐρωτῶμεν . . . εἰδέναι of 1 Thess. 5:12.

Although one cannot be certain of the reconstruction here suggested, it has the advantage both of fitting the letter as a whole and of making good sense of the language and apparent concern that Stephanas continue to be well received in his own community. If so, then one should probably also be somewhat cautious as to the usefulness of the paragraph in helping us understand the role of leadership in the local church. It seems unquestionable that Stephanas at least was a leader in the church in Corinth; probably also Fortunatus and Achaicus, even if they were attached to Stephanas's household in some way. That the church should honor and submit itself in love to such is first of all a local concern, probably related to their relationship to Paul and the church's somewhat antagonistic attitude toward the apostle. On the other hand, there is no reason why such should not always be so in the church, provided of course that one is talking of those who lead by serving the saints (v. 16) and refreshing them (v. 18). Such people, whether in leadership or otherwise, are always worthy of proper recognition in the community of believers.

B. FINAL GREETINGS (16:19-24)

19 *The churches in the province of Asia send you greetings. Aquila and Priscilla[a1] greet you warmly in the Lord, and so does the church that meets at their house.[2]* 20 *All the brothers here send you greetings. Greet one another with a holy kiss.*

21 *I, Paul, write this greeting in my own hand.*

22 *If anyone does not love the Lord—a curse be on him. Come, O Lord![b]*

23 *The grace of the Lord Jesus[3] be with you.*

24 *My love to all of you in Christ Jesus.[4]*

[a]Greek *Prisca*, a variant of *Priscilla*
[b]In Aramaic the expression *Come, O Lord* is *Marana tha*

---

[1]The form Πρίσκα (P[46] ℵ B P 0121a 0243 33 1175* 1739 1881* pc r sa bo) is almost certainly original. This is the form used by Paul (Rom. 16:3; 2 Tim. 4:19); Luke prefers the diminutive "Priscilla," by which she is better known. A similar textual variation occurs in Rom. 16:3, but in fewer MSS. Cf. the discussion in Metzger, 570.

[2]The Western witnesses (D* F G it) add the spurious note, "with whom I am lodging."

[3]Most of the witnesses add Χριστοῦ (except ℵ* B Ψ 33 pc sa). On this addition see also on 5:4-5. See the discussion in Metzger, 570.

[4]The vast majority of MSS reflect the use of this letter in the church by adding the liturgical ἀμήν (absent from B F 0121a 0243 33 81 630 1881 pc sa Ambst). Cf. Metzger, 571.

The later MajT also adds a spurious—and obviously incorrect—subscription: "The first letter to the Corinthians was written from Philippi by Stephanas, Fortunatus, Achaicus, and Timothy."

The letter now concludes with a series of standard (for Paul) greetings[5] (vv. 19-21) and the grace-benediction (v. 23). But Paul cannot quite give up the urgency of the letter, so he interrupts these two rather constant elements of his conclusions with one final word of warning to those who have been causing him grief, this time in the form of an extraordinary curse formula (v. 22). The apparent harshness of this warning is matched by the equally unusual addition of a final word of affirmation of his love for them (v. 24), found only here in his extant letters. Thus even to the end the unique concerns that have forged this letter find their expression.

It is frequently suggested, especially because of v. 22, that Paul deliberately shaped this conclusion to function as the transition from the public reading of the letter to the celebration of the Eucharist.[6] But that is unlikely. There can be little question that Paul expected the letter to be read publicly—although whether in this case that would be done in a single setting is another question. The obvious setting for such a public reading is the gathered assembly. But it is tenuous at best to argue backward to this letter from the presence of the kiss in the eucharistic celebration of Justin's *Apology* (chap. 65) and the use of *Maranatha* in a concluding eucharistic prayer in the *Didache* 10:6, and see these various elements as the actual preparation for the Lord's Supper in Corinth. In the *Didache* the *Maranatha*

---

[5]Found in every letter except Galatians, Ephesians, and 1 Timothy, each for reasons peculiar to the individual letters, although this is the first of the extant letters in which greetings from those with Paul are sent to the recipient(s) of the letter. For the full discussion of this feature both in the Hellenistic letters and Paul, see Gamble, *Textual History*, pp. 59-60 and 73-75.

[6]Apparently this was first suggested by R. Seeburg, *Aus Religion und Geschichte* (Leipzig, 1906), pp. 118-20; it was adopted by Lietzmann, *Mass*, p. 186, and by many scholars thereafter, e.g., K. M. Hofmann, *Philēma Hagion* (Gütersloh, 1938), pp. 23-26; G. Bornkamm, "The Anathema in the Early Christian Lord's Supper Tradition," in *Early Christian Experience* (1950; ET, New York, 1966), pp. 169-79; O. Cullmann, *Early Christian Worship* (1950; ET, SBT 10; London, 1953), pp. 13-14; J. A. T. Robinson, "Traces of a Liturgical Sequence in 1 Cor. 16[20-24]," *JTS* 4 (1953), 38-41; Wiles, *Intercessory*, pp. 42, 70, 150-55.

This view has been rejected by Gamble, *Textual History*, pp. 143-44, who rightly notes: "A liturgical *form* may indeed be derivative, but in the letters may perform a strictly epistolary function. . . . To the extent that such formulae can be seen to serve purely epistolary needs and/or to possess contextual relationships, and thus to be integral to the letters *as letters*, there is no reason to seek out a non-epistolary rationale for their use." This is surely the crucial point. One may as well argue that the creedal formula of 15:3-5 at that point served liturgically in the assembly as the place in worship for the citing of the creed. And to go beyond that and argue, as Robinson does, that we have here the very sequence—indeed, the earliest evidence for such—of the liturgy is to outstrip the evidence altogether. Cf. also W. C. van Unnik, "*Dominus Vobiscum:* The Background of a Liturgical Formula," in *New Testament Essays, Studies in Memory of Thomas Walter Manson* (ed. A. J. B. Higgins; Manchester, 1959), p. 272, who correctly warns against such "pan-liturgism," which finds evidence of later liturgies behind every conceivable passage in Paul's letters.

comes at the *end* of the celebration as an eschatological cry for the coming of the Lord, and in this letter, however these elements are worked out in the actual life of the community, they nonetheless conclude the letter *as a letter*—even if some derive from worship and may actually take place in such a setting.

19-20a   Such greetings as these become another way (besides the mutual collection for Jerusalem) that Paul keeps the churches aware of, and thus in relationship to, one another. The greetings in this case are threefold: from (a) all the churches of Asia, (b) Aquila and Prisca and the church that meets in their house, and (c) all the brothers presently with him.

(a) The greeting from all the churches of a province occurs only here in Paul's extant letters.[7] One cannot tell from such language, of course, how much of the province this entails. We know from Rev. 2–3 that by the end of the first century there were churches in many of its cities. The implication of Acts 19:10 and 26 is that this had already begun with Paul's ministry.

(b) The greeting from Aquila and Prisca probably reflects a twofold reality. First, these were former Corinthians (cf. Acts 18:2-3), who now join Paul in "warmly"[8] greeting old friends; second, this is most likely the house church[9] in Ephesus to which Paul himself is attached. Hence the greeting comes not only from their friends, but from the church as well.

Aquila and Prisca[10] are among the companions of Paul about whom there is a bit more information than for some others. Fellow Jews and tentmakers, they first met Paul in Corinth (Acts 18:1-3). They then accompanied him to Ephesus, where they led Apollos to Christ (Acts 18:18-26), and where they still are at the time of this writing. A little later they are apparently again in Rome, where they have another house church (Rom. 16:3-5);[11] but in 2 Tim. 4:19 they are back in Ephesus.[12] Both their mobility

---

[7]Thus in yet another, albeit subtle, way Paul tries to lift their vision to recognize that they belong to a much larger "family" of believers. See on 1:2; 4:17; 11:16; 14:33, 36; 16:1.

[8]Gk. πολλά (= "very much"), an unusual intensification that indicates a strong desire to be remembered by their friends in Corinth.

[9]Gk. τῇ κατ᾽ οἶκον αὐτῶν ἐκκλησίᾳ; this is the first appearance of this expression in Paul's writings. Cf. Rom. 16:5; Col. 4:15; Phlm. 2. This is probably also the meaning of Acts 8:3. On this phenomenon see F. V. Filson, "The Significance of the Early House Churches," *JBL* 56 (1939), 105-12; Malherbe, "House Churches and Their Problems," in *Social Aspects*, pp. 60-91; Banks, *Idea*, pp. 33-42.

[10]Ordinarily the names appear in reverse order (cf. Rom. 16:3; 2 Tim. 4:19; Acts 18:18, 26), indicating the considerable prominence of Priscilla. Only here and in Acts 18:2, where they are first introduced, do they appear in this order.

[11]For a cogent argument that Rom. 16 belongs to that Epistle, see Gamble, *Textual History*.

[12]This "movement" of these two people has led in part to the doubts as to whether Rom. 16 belongs to that letter and to whether 2 Timothy is authentic. But there is no good reason to doubt the *possibility* of such mobility.

and their patronage of house churches (in Corinth, Ephesus, and Rome) indicate that they were well-to-do.

(c) One cannot be sure whether "all the brothers" in v. 20a is a redundant generalizing of those mentioned in v. 19, or whether, more likely, it refers to Paul's various coworkers and traveling companions.[13] If the latter, of course, we cannot name any except Sosthenes (1:1), since Timothy is not with him and one cannot be sure of who else is, although it is possible that Titus would currently be working with him (see 2 Cor. 2:13).

20b From greetings *to* the Corinthians *from* Asia, Paul turns to encourage them to "greet one another," and to do so "with a holy kiss." This is the second of five such appeals in the NT.[14] There can be little doubt that this form of greeting prevailed in the church from the very beginning.[15] Most likely it was a carryover from Judaism and from the culture in general. Its background in Judaism can be found in the greeting of both family (e.g., Gen. 27:26; cf. Luke 15:20) and friend (1 Sam. 20:41); it was also the evidence of reconciliation (Gen. 33:4).

By the time of Justin,[16] the "kiss of peace" had become a part of the liturgy in Rome. Some have suggested, therefore, that it has liturgical significance here as well, where the kiss of peace, indicating an expression of reconciliation or unity, preceded the Lord's Table.[17] More likely, however, it is simply the common form of greeting, reflecting both the culture (thus "the kiss" as such) and the special relationship that believers had to one another as the family of God (thus a "holy" kiss, that is, a kiss that belonged to the saints, God's holy people[18]).[19]

21 With this sentence Paul proceeds to a third kind of greeting, his to them. In so doing he also begins the autographic conclusion. Thus (literally): "This greeting is in my own hand, Paul."[20] This means that the letter

---

[13]So also Ellis, 14.

[14]See 1 Thess. 5:26; 2 Cor. 13:12; Rom. 16:16; and 1 Pet. 5:14, where it is called "the kiss of love." On this matter see, *inter alia*, Hofmann, *Philēma Hagion;* G. Stählin, *TDNT* IX, 138-41; G. Dix, *The Shape of the Liturgy* (London, 1945), pp. 105-07; N. J. Perella, *The Kiss Sacred and Profane* (Berkeley, 1969), pp. 12-18; Gamble, *Textual History,* pp. 75-76.

[15]This is evidenced by the fact that it occurs not only in the letters to Pauline churches (Thessalonica and Corinth), but also in Romans and in 1 Peter.

[16]*Apol.* 65: "On finishing the prayers we greet each other with a kiss." This is followed by the Eucharist itself.

[17]See the studies by Hofmann, Bornkamm, Robinson, and Wiles in n. 6 above.
[18]See on 1:2.

[19]Cf. Gamble, *Textual History,* p. 76: "We should think only of an act of mutual greeting, a visible sign and seal of fellowship within the congregation on any occasion."

[20]On this phenomenon see esp. G. J. Bahr, "The Subscriptions in the Pauline Letters," *JBL* 87 (1968), 27-41 (who, however, is probably more ambitious than the evidence warrants as to how much makes up this signature, taking it in this case back to v. 15); and Gamble, *Textual History,* pp. 76-80.

to this point has been inscribed by someone else, probably Sosthenes (see on 1:1), and that the rest, from here through v. 24, would be in Paul's own "large print"[21] handwriting.[22] This means of authentication was a common feature in letters and reports in antiquity.[23] Although it does not occur in all of Paul's letters, the possibility that someone had forged a letter in his name (2 Thess. 2:1) caused him to adopt such a procedure in 2 Thessalonians, and in other later letters as well.[24] His reason for doing so here can only be surmised, but most likely it is related to the questioning of his authority by some in this church.

22 With pen in hand, immediately following his signature, Paul apparently feels impelled to take one last shot at his Corinthian opponents, in the form of a curse: "If anyone does not love[25] the Lord, let him be *anathema*[26]." Because of the un-Pauline character of the language[27] and of the alleged eucharistic setting for the following *Maranatha,* it has been argued that this is a ban formula, intended to exclude certain people from the Lord's Table.[28] But to arrive at that conclusion requires several leaps with the evidence. It seems quite probable that Paul has here borrowed something traditional; that its setting is a "fencing of the Table" for the Lord's Supper seems highly unlikely, especially in light of 11:17-34, where his judgments on their actions require a change, to be sure, but scarcely result in a ban.

The clue to its meaning lies in two places: (1) Paul's own usage of a similar "curse" in Gal. 1:8-9, where it is pronounced on those who deviate from the gospel that Paul preached. There is no good reason to think it means otherwise here, especially in light of the frequent warnings of this letter, some of which take even stronger expression than this.[29] (2) The similar warning that moves toward exclusion in 2 Thess. 3:14-15, where the warning is precisely for those who "do not obey our instruction in this letter."

Thus, using traditional language whose origin is uncertain, Paul offers one last warning to those who persist in deviating from his gospel, and

---

[21]See Gal. 6:11.

[22]The very fact of this change of hands, as well as the content of this greeting, indicates that this is primarily an epistolary, not a liturgical, phenomenon. See n. 6 above. Robinson, "Traces," p. 39, suggests that this is Paul's way of "being present" at the Table. But that stretches epistolary forms beyond recognition.

[23]See the evidence in Bahr, "Subscriptions."

[24]See Gal. 6:11 and Col. 4:18; cf. Rom. 16:22. See also 1 Pet. 5:12.

[25]Gk. φιλεῖ; this verb is found only here and in Tit. 3:15 in the entire Pauline corpus.

[26]For this word see on 12:3, esp. n. 47.

[27]Paul elsewhere uses the verb ἀγαπάω for "love"; in the similar formula in Gal. 1:8, he has ἀνάθεμα ἔστω rather than the ἤτω ἀνάθεμα that appears here (in fact this is the only occurrence of ἤτω in his letters); *Maranatha* is a NT hapax legomenon.

[28]See n. 6 above, especially the argument in Robinson.

[29]Cf. 3:17; 5:4-5; 6:9-10; 11:29; 14:38.

now especially to those who might refuse to obey the injunctions of this letter. He has just authenticated the letter with his signature. That leads him to assert their need to obey; but instead of putting it in terms of their obeying him, he puts it in the ultimate language of Christian obedience: "If anyone does not love the Lord." That covers the whole letter. To insist on human wisdom over against the gospel of the Crucified One is to "not love the Lord"; so with living in incest, attendance at idol feasts, and so forth. The ultimate issue for Paul, therefore, is not their obedience to his word, but their love, or lack thereof, for the Lord himself. Failure to obey him is lack of love for him; to reject him in this way is to place oneself under the *anathema*.[30]

But what, then, is the meaning of *Maranatha*? This is a particularly complex issue, both because of the ambiguity as to its meaning in Aramaic and because of its place here in the letter.[31] The Aramaic lying behind this Greek (and English) transliteration can be pointed either *Marana tha* (= "Our Lord, come!") or *Maran atha* (= "Our Lord has come"). In either case its use in a context like this can only be explained on the basis of its prior use in the Aramaic-speaking church, almost certainly in the context of worship. Whether or not it belonged to the "liturgy" of the Lord's Table in such an early setting is moot. If so, then it probably meant "Come, O Lord" (as the NIV), and is to be understood as an early eschatological prayer, similar to that in Rev. 22:20, "Come, Lord Jesus."[32] This is precisely its function in the concluding eucharistic prayers in the *Didache* 10:6.[33]

But it is not certain that in this context Paul intended it as a prayer, or if he did, whether he intended it eschatologically. Some have argued that his intent is to reinforce the preceding "ban formula," as an invocation of the

[30]Cf. C. Spicq, "Comment comprendre φιλεῖν dans I Cor. xvi,22?" *NovT* 1 (1956), 200-204, who sees the sentence not as a liturgical formula, but as describing the state of a person who has rejected Christ and is thereby excluded from the church and finally the heavenly kingdom. He is followed by W. Dunphy, "Maranatha: Development in Early Christology," *ITQ* 37 (1970), 294-308, esp. 302.

[31]The bibliography is considerable. Among the more significant items, see K. G. Kuhn, *TDNT* IV, 466-72; C. F. D. Moule, "A Reconsideration of the Context of *Maranatha,*" *NTS* 6 (1959/60), 307-10; S. Schulz, "Maranatha and Kyrios Jesus," *ZNW* 53 (1962), 125-44; P.-É. Langevin, *Jésus Seigneur et l'eschatologie* (Bruges/Paris, 1967), pp. 168-208; Albright and Mann, "Two Texts"; Dunphy, "Maranatha"; M. Black, "The Maranatha Invocation and Jude 14, 15 (I Enoch 1:9)," in *Christ and Spirit in the New Testament* (ed. B. Lindars and S. S. Smalley; Cambridge, 1973), pp. 189-96.

[32]Gk. ἔρχου κύριε Ἰησοῦ, which would be nearly the Greek equivalent of the Aramaic *Marana tha*.

[33]This stands in direct opposition to those, such as Robinson, "Traces," who think it functions as a prayer of invitation for the Lord's presence at the beginning of the Eucharist proper. That is to force the sure evidence of the *Didache* and the Revelation to conform to a dubious historical reconstruction, namely the "sequence" of the conclusion of this letter.

Lord's presence to hear and bear witness, as it were, to the pronounced *anathema*.[34] It is also possible that it functions in this same capacity as an indicative. In light of the inherent warning in the words "If anyone love not the Lord, let him be *anathema*," he concludes by affirming that the Lord whom they reject has indeed come.

At this distance, and especially with a word that would have had special significance for worship, one cannot be certain as to Paul's own intent. In light of its later use in the *Didache*, supported by the prayer at the end of the Revelation, it seems most likely that it is in fact an eschatological prayer. If so, in the present context it would seem to function as a response to the *anathema* on those who do not love the Lord, affirming that the Lord whom they reject is indeed coming, and those who do not love him are under the *anathema* and in danger of being rejected by him. It needs only to be added that this prayer is clear evidence that in the very earliest days the Aramaic-speaking church referred to Jesus by the title that in the OT belongs to God alone.[35]

23-24 All of Paul's letters conclude with the grace-benediction.[36] The standard "good-bye" in ancient letters was *errōso* (lit., "be strong"),[37] found in the NT in the letter of James (Acts 15:29).[38] As with the salutations, this standard conclusion is also Christianized. It is "grace," the favor of God that is theirs through "the Lord Jesus," that he wishes for them.[39] Thus the letter begins with the salutation "Grace to you" and concludes the same way.[40] Grace is the beginning and the end of the Chrstian gospel; it is the single word that most fully expresses what God has done and will do for his people in Christ Jesus.

Given that reality, the concluding expression of Paul's own love for

---

[34]See, e.g., Moule, "Reconsideration"; Bornkamm, "Anathema," pp. 170-71; Wiles, *Intercessory*, p. 152.

[35]*Pace* W. Bousset, *Kyrios Christos* (ET, Nashville, 1970), p. 129, who argues that the title first arose in the Greek-speaking church, and for whose theory this prayer is a "rock" that he rather lightly steps around instead of taking seriously; cf. Bultmann, *Theology*, I, 52.

[36]See the discussion in Gamble, *Textual History*, pp. 65-67.

[37]See the scores of examples in Exler, *Form*, pp. 69-77 and 111-13.

[38]Cf. also the letters of Ignatius of Antioch; 2 Macc. 11:21, 23; Josephus, *Life* 227, 365.

[39]Since no verb is expressed, it could be either an indicative (= "grace is yours") or an optative ("grace be yours"). Both van Unnik, *"Dominus Vobiscum,"* p. 291, and G. Delling, *Worship in the New Testament* (ET, Philadelphia, 1962), p. 75, argue for the indicative. However, since it takes the place of the standard ἔρρωσο, most likely the optative is intended. As Gamble, *Textual History*, pp. 66-67, points out, it functions as a benediction or blessing.

[40]This phenomenon tends to make the question of its prior origin in the liturgy of the church especially tenuous, all the more so since all the other evidence is later than Paul.

them is all the more striking. Most likely it is added to soften the blow of what at times, including v. 22, have been very strong words. To write as he has does not mean he loves them less, but more. Thus, along with the benediction of grace from the Lord, he affirms that his love is also "with them." It is more difficult to determine whether Paul here intends an indicative or an optative, but it matters little. His love is always "with them," hence he offers it to them as the final matter of this otherwise very strong letter, in which he and they have been at odds on almost all issues. What makes all of this possible are the final words of the letter, "in Christ Jesus." Just as he began in 1:1-3, so he concludes, by reminding them that their common life together, and thus his love for them, takes place as they are together "in Christ Jesus."

Thus the letter ends on a note similar to its beginning, full of the same tensions between what they are by grace and what they yet need to become in terms of obedience to Christ. They are greeted with warmth, and assured of Christ's grace and Paul's love. Along with him they await the coming of the Lord. They should continue to greet one another with the kiss of love. However, they are not yet fully there, so even here there is the word of warning (v. 22). Christians must continually live in the tension between the "already" and the "not yet"; what they must not allow themselves to do is to excuse themselves from obedience because they are not yet fully there. The grace of the Lord and the hope of his coming should cause all to heed the words of this letter so as to be watchful and to do all things in love (vv. 13-14).

INDEX OF SUBJECTS

Adam 504, 749ff., 777, 779, 786ff., 803

Adiaphora 477f., 480, 483, 485f., 488, 491

Adultery 239, 243, 250, 292f., 296, 510

Angels 11f., 175, 234, 269, 276, 451, 457, 495, 498, 513, 516, 518f., 521f., 573, 598, 630, 642, 715

Antioch 548

Anxiety 336f., 342ff., 348

Aphrodite 2

Apollos 8ff., 14, 31, 47ff., 55ff., 60f., 127, 129ff., 136ff., 151, 153f., 156, 158f., 166, 169f., 185, 190, 400, 409, 733, 736, 809, 823ff., 835

Apostolic Ministry 9, 28ff., 50ff., 125, 128, 137f., 156, 158, 160, 165, 174ff., 193, 195, 205, 221, 229, 328, 358, 362f., 366, 382, 385, 390, 392ff., 399ff., 416ff., 420ff., 424, 587, 616, 618, 620, 636, 711, 714, 717, 719, 729ff., 733ff., 768, 770, 823

Aquila 56, 400, 833, 835

Arrogance (see Pride)

Asceticism 273ff., 279, 296, 323f., 339, 341f., 344, 346ff., 351ff., 357, 439f., 627

Asia 1f., 815

Athens 1, 92

Atonement 551, 724f.

Authority 6ff., 50ff., 156, 159, 183, 194, 196, 207, 221, 229, 247, 252f., 270, 280, 291f., 328, 358, 362f., 383ff., 393, 396, 400ff., 406, 410, 414ff., 421f., 495, 502f., 513, 515ff., 620, 688, 704, 747, 752, 754, 758f., 837

Baptism 53, 61ff., 246f., 301, 362, 442, 444ff., 450, 452, 462, 604ff., 716, 762ff.; Spirit 604f.

Barnabas 397, 404, 620

Berea 818

Boasting 11, 38, 48, 50, 59, 66, 78f., 84, 87, 128ff., 148, 150, 153, 165f., 169, 171, 173, 186, 192f., 201, 214f., 220, 414f., 417ff., 421, 634f., 637f., 769f.

Body 11f., 16, 110, 211, 249ff., 253ff., 266, 276, 279, 346, 439, 550f., 559, 563f., 573, 608ff., 614ff., 714f., 728, 741, 775ff., 778ff., 788ff., 797ff.

Calling 307ff., 314ff., 318ff., 322, 416, 418f.

Celibacy 269f., 273, 275, 277, 284f., 286f., 290, 307, 313, 321f., 341ff., 349, 323ff., 330ff., 335ff., 341ff., 349, 353, 355, 357, 403

Cephas (see Peter)

Charismatic Movement 46, 590, 592, 660, 667, 698

Church 7, 18ff., 31f., 34, 40, 46, 50, 60, 66, 128, 136ff., 145ff., 151, 164, 194, 214f., 227, 228, 230, 258, 260, 264, 266, 389, 450, 469, 489f., 504, 530, 532f., 536f., 541, 543, 559, 564, 568, 572, 582f., 588, 600ff., 606f., 608ff., 616ff., 625, 642, 646, 650, 652f., 656ff., 660f., 666f., 668f., 673, 675f., 677, 689ff., 694, 698, 707, 712, 734, 815, 825

Circumcision 18, 252, 268, 307f., 311ff., 427f., 481f.

Conscience 158, 162, 358f., 362, 370, 376ff., 380ff., 385ff., 429, 476f., 481ff.

Covenant 301, 313, 468, 554f., 557

Creation 778

Cross, Crucifixion 14, 17, 37, 39, 49ff., 61, 63ff., 66ff., 80, 83f., 89, 91f., 96, 98ff., 102, 104ff., 117, 120, 128, 131, 137, 138, 140, 151, 153f., 156, 158, 165, 172, 175f., 180, 215, 218, 241, 263, 265, 313, 366, 389, 417, 490, 549, 754

Cynicism 252
Cynics 252, 275

Damascus 548
Deacons 130, 621
Death 17, 154, 210ff., 218, 355, 555f.,
  559, 565, 714, 725, 730, 738, 741, 744,
  745ff., 759f., 763, 769f., 773, 781,
  784, 796f., 800ff., 803ff.
Demons 103f., 106, 113, 358, 363, 370,
  378, 388, 457, 462f., 467f., 470ff.,
  565, 575, 579, 581, 754
Denominations 155f.
Discipleship 172, 174, 181, 184, 186, 479
Discipline 20, 118, 183, 192f., 197, 203,
  213f., 226ff., 566
Divisions 5f., 8f., 47ff., 52ff., 63, 66,
  121f., 144, 146, 148, 401, 531, 537ff.,
  565, 609, 614f.
Divorce 287, 290ff., 296ff., 302ff., 306,
  321, 331, 355
Drunkenness 225, 239, 531, 540, 542f.,
  774

Easter 760, 820
Ecumenism 66
Egypt 2
Election 29, 79, 82, 450
Ephesus 6, 15, 31, 54, 190f., 761, 769ff.,
  812, 816ff., 820, 832, 835
Epicureanism 772
Eschatology 12, 16f., 32, 36f., 41ff., 46,
  69ff., 83, 100, 103, 106, 143, 147, 151,
  154, 157, 161, 163, 172f., 175, 178,
  181f., 212f., 228, 230ff., 238ff., 242,
  248, 255, 269, 324, 329f., 335ff., 348,
  355f., 408, 437, 441, 442, 444, 453,
  459, 469, 498, 533, 538f., 557, 633,
  635, 642ff., 648, 650f., 716f., 746ff.,
  752, 757, 785, 790ff., 795, 796f., 839
Ethics 17f., 32, 87, 124, 127, 179, 183,
  187f., 194f., 197, 202f., 215, 217ff.,
  224, 228, 241, 248, 252, 291, 313f.,
  360, 363, 366f., 369, 388, 390f., 430,
  475, 478ff., 544, 572, 627, 630, 641,
  775, 807
Evangelism 306, 411, 422, 423f., 427,
  431f., 489f.
Excommunication 208f., 212ff.
Exodus 443ff., 451, 454ff., 550
Exorcism 595

Faith 96, 120, 131, 584, 590f., 593f.,
  632f., 636, 640, 641, 649ff., 738,
  742f., 764, 827
Fall (of man) 170, 285, 433, 686, 752, 778

Feast of Unleavened Bread 216ff., 224
Fellowship 466f., 469, 473, 531, 812
Feminist Movement 492
Financial Support 393ff., 398ff., 403ff.,
  409ff., 414ff., 426, 819
Flesh 209ff.
Forgiveness 218, 549, 553, 555, 640, 745
Fornication 6f., 278
Freedom 251ff., 358f., 363, 366, 369,
  377f., 383ff., 394, 402, 422ff., 429,
  433, 474, 477ff., 482ff.

Galatia 86, 311, 812, 815
Gentleness 193
Gifts, Spiritual (see Spiritual Gifts)
Glory 515ff., 522, 527f.
Gnosticism 5, 11, 57f., 99f., 103f., 106,
  111, 116, 177, 211, 252, 365, 371, 375,
  402, 469, 548, 580, 728, 791
Gossip.639
Grace 18, 34f., 37f., 44, 52, 82, 113, 137,
  143ff., 171, 217, 248, 312f., 566, 635,
  718f., 734ff., 764, 812, 833f., 839
Greed 224, 239, 241

Head 495, 499, 501ff., 513, 515
Healing 584, 587, 590, 594, 616, 618f.,
  621f.
Heaven 782ff., 787f., 791ff., 798ff.
Hell 144
Holiness 118, 149f., 203, 218, 299ff.,
  345f. (see also Sanctification)
Holy Spirit 10ff., 16ff., 29, 40, 42, 45, 50,
  64, 72, 90, 94ff., 98ff., 105f., 109ff.,
  114ff., 123ff., 127, 141, 147f., 150, 157,
  172, 191ff., 201f., 204ff., 214, 224,
  228, 239, 245, 247f., 249, 260f., 263f.,
  339, 356f., 366, 430, 445, 447, 470,
  572, 574, 576ff., 581ff., 603ff., 609,
  611, 619, 630, 633, 640, 642f., 645,
  650, 652, 655ff., 667, 686f., 690ff.,
  701, 712, 733, 746, 749, 778, 786
Homosexuality 200, 239, 243f., 506, 511
Hope 636, 640f., 649ff., 744
Hospitality 819
Humility 171, 180

Idolatry 4, 7, 9, 14, 17f., 57f., 74f., 147,
  160, 223, 239, 242f., 260, 267, 357ff.,
  364ff., 369ff., 376ff., 402, 424f., 428,
  440ff., 450ff., 453ff., 457ff., 462ff.,
  471ff., 476ff., 565, 838
Illness 93, 538 (see also Sickness)
Incest 194ff., 199ff., 220f., 250, 838
Inheritance (of saints) 192, 229, 239f.,
  242, 245

Israel 33, 301, 360, 363, 442ff., 451ff., 457ff., 462, 465, 470ff., 553
Isthmian Games 433f., 436

James 58, 403f., 717, 729, 731f.
Jealousy 126, 127
Jerusalem 13, 409, 549, 662f., 727, 731, 809f., 812, 814ff., 817ff.
Jews 2ff., 7, 13f., 57f., 65, 68f., 71, 74ff., 92, 111, 147, 216, 218, 231, 308, 311ff., 318, 355, 357, 360, 370, 379, 399, 422, 427f., 481f., 489, 507, 548f., 606, 811
Joy 697f.
Judgment 72, 83, 141ff., 146, 148, 151, 156ff., 161ff., 197, 208, 221, 226f., 228, 230, 232, 234ff., 242, 289, 342, 382, 451, 454, 456, 458, 462, 533, 538f., 558f., 562f., 565f., 567ff., 595, 682
Justice 639
Justification 86, 239, 245ff., 743

Kindness 636f.
Kingdom of God 16, 173, 192, 239, 242, 245, 594, 752ff., 758f., 795, 799
Knowledge 11, 38ff., 358, 362ff., 369ff., 377ff., 385ff., 477, 584, 590ff., 616, 630ff., 639, 644, 648f., 662f.

Law 17f., 43, 71, 187, 252, 311, 355, 391f., 398, 406ff., 422, 427, 429f., 475, 478, 481, 490, 679, 699, 705, 707f., 796f., 805ff.
Lawsuits 228ff., 231ff., 239ff., 248
Leadership 128, 130f., 134ff., 145, 153, 691, 833
Leaven 215ff.
Lord's Supper 11, 15, 17, 19, 82, 209ff., 218, 226, 243, 362, 400, 442, 444, 446ff., 450, 452, 457, 462ff., 465ff., 491f., 530, 531ff., 534ff., 545f., 558f., 567ff., 600, 602, 604, 612, 615, 638, 721, 726, 814, 830, 834, 836ff.
Love 154, 193, 212, 214, 296, 363ff., 369, 378, 385, 388, 390ff., 477, 572, 624f., 626ff., 635ff., 641ff., 652, 654f., 658, 688, 828, 833, 838ff.

Macedonia 188, 400, 816ff.
Marriage 4, 20, 201, 267ff., 273ff., 286ff., 290ff., 297ff., 307, 310f., 313, 318, 321ff., 334, 335ff., 341ff., 349ff., 401, 403; Levirate 326, 356; Spiritual 351f.
Martyrdom 634, 765
Mercy 328, 639f.
Ministry 130ff., 134f., 160, 194, 619

Miracles 14, 584, 587, 590, 594, 616, 618f., 621f.
Mormonism 764, 767
Moses 444ff., 456ff.
Mystery 104f., 158ff., 508, 632, 644, 648, 653, 656f., 663

Parousia 16, 37, 42, 71, 142, 157, 163, 192, 329, 336, 557, 716, 752ff., 797, 800f.
Passover Feast 216ff., 549f., 553, 727, 820
Patience 636
Peace 34f., 297, 303ff., 307, 697, 710, 822
Pentecostal Movement 46, 590, 592, 599, 659f., 667, 698, 820
Peter 47, 49, 55, 57f., 60, 138f., 153, 156, 158, 185, 360, 397, 400, 403f., 410, 593, 717, 728f., 731ff., 736
Philippi 311, 399, 416, 818
Poor 3f., 15, 19, 81f., 182, 491, 532, 534, 536f., 539ff., 547, 558, 563, 565, 568, 612, 639, 810, 814
Power 69, 74ff., 80
Power of God 69, 74ff., 80, 90, 95, 191, 192f., 194, 207, 209, 213f., 734
Prayer 271, 273f., 282, 284, 491, 495ff., 505ff., 513, 516ff., 524f., 597, 653, 656f., 667ff., 690, 693, 811
Preaching 64ff., 73, 89ff., 94ff., 101f., 110f., 114, 126, 158, 191, 415, 418ff., 440, 740, 742, 830
Predestination 105
Pride 49, 165, 169ff., 189, 191ff., 194ff., 199, 201ff., 366, 477, 612, 630f., 635, 638
Priscilla 56, 833, 835
Prophecy 8, 10, 18, 39, 194, 205, 207, 292, 491, 495ff., 505ff., 513, 516ff., 571, 574, 577, 584, 587, 590, 593, 595f., 616, 618ff., 623f., 628, 631f., 635, 641ff., 645, 652ff., 657ff., 660, 662, 666, 668, 677f., 682ff., 685ff., 688ff., 693ff., 701ff., 706ff., 709, 711f.
Prostitution 2, 4, 18, 149, 200, 239, 243f., 249ff., 253ff., 271, 276, 278, 289, 360, 455, 511
Purgatory 137, 144

Redemption 86
Remarriage 290ff., 302f., 306, 324, 355f.
Repentance 194, 202f., 229, 640, 677, 686, 688
Resurrection 4, 12, 16ff., 69, 123, 142, 151, 154, 157, 173, 181, 192, 211, 249, 251, 253, 255ff., 265f., 267, 269, 339,

Resurrection (continued)
342, 395, 459, 570, 713ff., 717ff., 736, 737ff., 746ff., 760ff., 775ff., 778ff., 787ff., 797, 799ff.

Revelation 42f., 72, 102, 106, 109ff., 142, 548, 593f., 662f., 687, 800

Rewards 133, 136, 141ff., 163, 419ff., 424, 434ff., 440, 474

Rome 1f., 319, 819, 835

Rulers 103f., 106ff.

Sabbath 813f.

Sacraments 362f., 432, 443, 447, 459, 475

Saints 231ff., 242

Salvation 17f., 29, 32, 42, 45, 63, 69, 73, 105ff., 110, 113, 128, 132, 160, 191f., 209, 212f., 246f., 251, 257, 299f., 305f., 310, 312f., 338, 340, 366, 431, 459, 462, 478, 524, 554, 556, 558, 559f., 565, 587, 595, 720, 767, 800

Sanctification 29, 32f., 86f., 96, 132, 139, 143f., 203, 218f., 239, 245ff., 264, 266, 296f., 299ff., 305f., 310, 314, 322, 630, 743 (see also Holiness)

Satan 72, 104, 175, 191, 204f., 208ff., 213, 281ff., 411, 756

Security 137, 248; Eternal 462

Self-Control 434ff., 438ff., 441ff., 695

Servanthood 7, 128ff., 133f., 153, 156, 158ff., 186, 426, 433, 587, 833

Sexual Immorality 2f., 6, 12, 18, 20, 195ff., 199ff., 219, 220ff., 239, 242f., 249ff., 261ff., 267, 277, 283f., 289, 299, 360f., 391, 450, 454f., 457

Sickness 210f., 559, 562, 565 (see also Illness)

Signs and Wonders 95f.

Silas 30, 404

Singleness (see Celibacy)

Slander 179f., 225, 239

Slavery 2f., 81f., 86, 159, 263ff., 268, 307, 312, 315ff., 340, 419, 423ff., 545, 606, 612, 830

Spirit (see Holy Spirit)

Spirit Baptism (see Baptism, Spirit)

Spiritual Gifts 10f., 36ff., 46, 95f., 171ff., 277, 284f., 366, 382, 569, 570ff., 575ff., 583ff., 609, 616ff., 626, 628, 632f., 635, 640, 641f., 645ff., 654f., 659f., 662, 666, 667ff., 688f., 694, 702, 709

Spiritual Marriage (see Marriage, Spiritual)

Stoicism 102, 154, 173, 175, 177, 200, 252, 320, 340, 343, 347, 367, 374, 380, 526f., 602

Suffering 93, 177ff., 210, 329f., 336, 417, 490, 635

Support, Financial (see Financial Support)

Teachers/Teaching 50, 128, 145, 164, 184, 616, 618, 621, 663, 830

Temptation 282f., 451, 460ff.

Thanksgiving 476, 482, 487f., 667, 672, 674, 811

Thessalonica 92, 188, 399, 411, 818

Timothy 9, 28, 30, 92, 157, 183, 186, 188f., 191, 404, 809, 817f., 821f., 823, 836

Titus 816, 818, 823, 836

Tongues 10f., 14, 39, 42, 95f., 267, 491, 571ff., 574ff., 577, 579, 612, 615, 616f., 619, 622f., 625, 627ff., 630ff., 635, 641f., 644, 649, 652ff., 656ff., 660ff., 667ff., 674f., 676ff., 688f., 691ff., 698, 701ff., 705ff., 709ff., 712f., 715, 778

Transfiguration 800f.

Trinity 61, 110, 112, 246, 310, 374f., 586, 588

Truth 636, 639

Unity 53, 66, 122, 130, 133, 469, 544f., 572, 582f., 600ff., 606f., 608, 615f., 617, 815, 836

Virginity 268f., 287f., 322ff., 329, 331, 334ff., 345, 349ff.

War 639

Wealthy 2ff., 15, 19, 80f., 182, 400, 404, 534, 537, 539ff., 547, 558, 563, 565, 567f., 612

Widows 269, 287ff., 291, 324, 350, 355, 357

Wisdom 8f., 11, 13ff., 19, 32, 39, 48ff., 56f., 59, 63ff., 66ff., 79f., 82ff., 90f., 94, 96, 98ff., 101ff., 119f., 121f., 124, 126, 128f., 136ff., 145f., 150ff., 158, 169, 171f., 176, 180, 182, 186, 192f., 195, 201, 237, 320, 365ff., 385, 388, 449, 584, 590ff., 616, 630f., 638, 725, 838

Women 81, 270, 290, 294, 345ff., 491ff., 499ff., 508ff., 512ff., 524ff., 698, 699, 702ff., 705ff.

World 71f.

Worship 19f., 267, 466, 471, 491ff., 497, 505f., 531f., 569ff., 573, 620, 622, 654f., 657, 661ff., 666f., 668, 671, 675, 683ff., 688, 691, 697f., 707, 760, 814, 839

Zeal 652, 666, 694, 734

INDEX OF AUTHORS

Aalen, S. 465, 488, 707
Achelis, H. 326
Agnew, F. H. 30
Ahern, B. M. 258
Aland, K. 63, 301
Albright, W. F. and Mann, C. S. 581, 838
Alford, H. 241
Allo, E. B. 36, 58, 180, 217, 261, 294, 323, 465, 581, 791
Anderson, R. 766
Aono, T. 754, 755
Arens, E. 287, 288
Arndt, W. 407
Aune, D. E. 148, 579, 580, 595, 696
Aust, H. and Müller, D. 581
Ayles, H. H. B. 232

Bacchiocchi, S. 813
Bachmann, P. 58, 93, 253, 420, 505, 720, 766
Bahr, G. J. 30, 836, 837
Baird 591
Bailey, K. E. 67, 188, 196, 240, 243, 246, 253, 256, 258, 265
Baker, D. L. 571, 575, 624, 654
Balch, D. L. 273, 276, 292, 328, 340, 343, 344, 347
Baljon, J. M. S. 167, 168
Balsdon, J. V. P. D. 327
Bammel, E. 723
Bandstra, A. J. 444, 445, 446, 449, 452
Banks, R. 618, 683, 724, 747, 835
Banks, R. and Moon, G. 574, 597
Barclay, W. 79, 136, 200, 210, 350, 557
Barker, D. C. 293
Barré, M. L. 178, 288, 289
Barrett, C. K. 13, 29, 34, 39, 41, 43, 44, 45, 54, 55, 56, 57, 71, 74, 79, 82, 85, 88, 89, 91, 93, 95, 102, 103, 106, 111, 113, 132, 138, 139, 143, 147, 148, 154, 160, 164, 166, 168, 173, 178, 180, 182, 201, 202, 204, 209, 210, 215, 217, 233,

247, 253, 263, 284, 286, 288, 300, 314, 317, 325, 327, 330, 344, 346, 352, 355, 356, 358, 360, 368, 381, 382, 383, 395, 404, 420, 426, 429, 430, 435, 440, 443, 446, 449, 450, 458, 462, 466, 474, 486, 487, 502, 503, 515, 520, 535, 536, 538, 543, 549, 552, 553, 555, 561, 562, 563, 565, 577, 581, 586, 588, 596, 598, 599, 615, 618, 622, 629, 638, 640, 654, 660, 663, 665, 666, 669, 670, 673, 674, 681, 683, 684, 685, 694, 699, 703, 706, 709, 712, 720, 731, 747, 756, 760, 763, 767, 770, 784, 791, 792, 794, 798, 804, 811, 814, 827
Bartchy, S. S. 29, 79, 264, 265, 268, 269, 307, 308, 310, 314, 315, 316, 317, 319, 320, 321
Bartels, K. H. 671
Barth, G. 747
Barth, K. 586, 628, 714, 747
Barth, M. 276, 577
Bartling, W. J. 259, 570
Bartmann, B. 144
Barton, S. C. 534, 699, 708
Bassler, J. M. 577, 579, 581
Batey, R. 259
Bauer, J. B. 397, 402, 403
Bauer, W., Arndt, W. F., Gingrich, F. W., and Danker, F. 29, 31, 38, 39, 53, 67, 71, 73, 75, 79, 88, 93, 103, 126, 130, 139, 143, 148, 158, 160, 161, 162, 163, 171, 180, 209, 210, 231, 234, 275, 293, 321, 352, 365, 366, 381, 403, 412, 425, 438, 450, 470, 471, 502, 516, 522, 529, 542, 586, 587, 590, 592, 610, 611, 625, 654, 655, 663, 665, 691, 711, 774, 830
Baur, F. C. 57
Bavinck, H. 308
Beare, F. W. 597
Beasley-Murray, G. R. 63, 64, 245, 247, 300, 301, 444, 445, 603, 604, 605, 763

845

Beck, W. F. 344, 658
Bedale, S. 502
Behm, J. 53, 184, 539, 580
Bengel, J. A. 765
Berger, K. 109
Bernard, J. H. 195, 228
Bertram, G. 71, 454, 566
Best, E. 261, 274, 597, 602, 603, 613
Betz, H. D. 187, 193, 810, 815
Beyer, H. W. 130, 467
Bishop, E. F. F. 730
Bittlinger, A. 586, 592, 593, 594, 596, 598, 638, 657, 692, 693, 699
Bjerkelund, C. J. 52, 406, 827
Black, D. D. 431
Black, M. 325, 838
Blass, F., Debrunner, A., and Funk, R. W. 140, 234, 309, 338, 408, 517, 537, 618, 720
Bode, E. L. 725, 727, 728
Boismard, M. E. 465
Boman, T. 733
Borchert, G. 748
Bornkamm, G. 91, 102, 104, 160, 427, 428, 432, 465, 549, 550, 834, 836, 839
Boswell, J. 243, 244
Bound, J. F. 325
Bousset, W. 168, 839
Bowen, C. R. 770
Bowmer, J. C. 748
Boyd, W. 103
Brandel, F. 819
Brandenburger, E. 791
Brandon, S. G. F. 58
Branick, V. P. 66, 67
Braun, H. 155, 638
Broneer, O. 433, 437
Brooten, B. 294
Brown, C. 380
Brown, R. E. 91, 104, 160, 800
Brox, N. 580
Bruce, F. F. 62, 103, 138, 147, 180, 274, 387, 485, 486, 498, 575, 579, 587, 590, 598, 674, 703, 709, 792
Brun, L. 208
Brunt, J. 358
Büchsel, F. 86, 686
Bultmann, R. 99, 100, 103, 177, 187, 232, 247, 256, 340, 439, 472, 486, 776, 839
Burchard, C. 305
Burkill, T. A. 259
Burkitt, F. C. 756, 757
Burton, E. D. 140, 295, 386
Bushnell, K. C. 493, 495, 507, 508, 520, 525, 526, 704
Bussmann, W. 727

Byrne, B. 262
Byron, B. 302

Cadbury, H. J. 480, 521
Cadoux, C. J. 282
Caird, G. B. 103
Callan, C. T. 575, 598
Calvin, J. 42, 209, 446, 604, 662, 669, 797
Cambier, J. 212
Campbell, J. Y. 45, 466, 467, 470
Campbell, R. C. 293
Caragounis, C. C. 405
Carr, W. 103, 104
Carson, D. 703, 813
Catchpole, D. R. 292
Cavallin, H. C. C. 716, 776
Cerfaux, L. 70, 258
Chadwick, H. 323, 424, 573
Chance, J. B. 49, 50
Chenderlin, F. 552, 553
Chevallier, M. A. 624, 654
Clark 462, 629
Clavier, H. 785
Clemens, C. 597
Coenen, L. 45
Coffin, C. P. 771
Collins, G. O. 728
Collins, J. 16
Colson, F. H. 167
Considine, T. R. 302
Conybeare, W. J. 261
Conzelmann, H. 3, 29, 38, 42, 55, 58, 59, 70, 71, 74, 83, 84, 85, 86, 88, 89, 90, 93, 99, 100, 103, 106, 112, 113, 130, 132, 133, 136, 140, 147, 158, 159, 160, 167, 168, 169, 173, 175, 180, 197, 199, 201, 202, 205, 208, 216, 218, 219, 220, 223, 225, 233, 241, 247, 252, 260, 265, 273, 276, 280, 283, 284, 286, 292, 295, 299, 310, 320, 322, 325, 327, 330, 335, 340, 342, 345, 346, 350, 355, 368, 372, 373, 374, 378, 381, 383, 384, 387, 389, 391, 395, 397, 398, 399, 401, 407, 409, 428, 430, 431, 433, 435, 436, 439, 440, 441, 442, 443, 445, 449, 450, 453, 455, 461, 463, 464, 466, 470, 471, 477, 483, 486, 489, 490, 500, 502, 509, 515, 531, 535, 540, 541, 543, 547, 548, 561, 562, 577, 579, 580, 585, 592, 597, 598, 599, 601, 604, 620, 625, 626, 627, 629, 640, 652, 657, 658, 661, 665, 669, 680, 684, 685, 690, 699, 710, 712, 717, 719, 722, 723, 724, 725, 726, 730, 736, 748, 749, 750, 751, 770, 773, 775, 776, 777, 781, 783, 796, 798, 801, 816, 830, 831

Cope, L. 492
Corcoran, G. 310, 318, 320
Cottle, R. E. 604, 605
Coune, M. 376, 379
Craig, C. T. 36, 38, 138, 192, 231, 275, 725, 726, 727, 728, 730
Cranfield, C. E. B. 53, 111, 694
Crockett, W. 750
Crook, J. 229
Cullmann, O. 57, 61, 103, 465, 580, 605, 834
Culver, R. 749, 753
Cuming, G. J. 605
Currie, S. D. 466, 597
Cutten, G. B. 597

Dahl, M. E. 777
Dahl, N. A. 48, 49, 50, 57, 59, 186, 190, 194
Daines, B. 602
Danby, H. 289, 294
Danker, F. 206
Daube, D. 192, 202, 252, 299, 300, 305, 399, 406, 426, 427, 785
Dautzenberg, G. 596
Davidson, R. M. 443, 445, 446, 447, 451, 452, 454, 458, 459
Davies, W. D. 187, 443, 785, 791
Davis, J. A. 4, 13, 14, 65, 66, 70, 73, 81, 116
de Boer, W. P. 187
Deissmann, A. 40, 206, 208, 225, 243, 265, 293, 407, 580, 813
De Lacey, D. R. 813
Delcor, M. 232
Delling, G. 62, 142, 301, 548, 671, 722, 748, 839
Derrett, J. D. M. 294, 415, 417, 419, 576, 577, 580
Dibelius, M. 446
Didier, G. 419
Dinkler, E. 237
Dix, G. 836
Dodd, C. H. 31, 430, 431, 711
Donfried, K. 137, 143, 144, 211
Doudelet, A. 465
Doughty, D. J. 336, 340, 341, 421
Dulau, P. 302
Dungan, D. L. 187, 276, 290, 292, 293, 294, 295, 298, 313, 400, 402, 403, 405, 409, 411, 412, 413, 416, 417, 420, 421, 424
Dunn, J. D. G. 35, 42, 61, 64, 95, 245, 247, 260, 285, 313, 445, 446, 448, 449, 586, 589, 591, 593, 594, 595, 596, 598, 603, 605, 606, 618, 620, 621, 622, 656,

658, 659, 663, 664, 668, 671, 672, 682, 693, 788, 789, 790, 806
Dunphy, W. 838
du Plessis, P. J. 102, 103, 122
Dupont, J. 252, 365, 379, 381
Dykstra, W. 747

Edwards, T. C. 446, 668, 720, 789, 799
Egan 175
Ehrhardt, A. 358, 361, 435, 481, 485, 563
Elert, W. 264, 265
Elliott, J. K. 268, 293, 297, 302, 327, 331, 629, 634
Ellis, E. E. 8, 31, 48, 65, 66, 69, 75, 89, 95, 100, 101, 109, 113, 130, 134, 152, 160, 169, 172, 259, 365, 401, 408, 443, 448, 505, 631, 654, 657, 666, 680, 688, 694, 696, 699, 788, 827, 829, 836
Ellis, P. F. 51
Ellis, W. 555, 560
Ellison, H. L. 424, 429
Engelsen, N. I. J. 597
Evans, O. E. 33
Exler, F. X. J. 27, 839

Farrar, F. W. 273
Fascher, E. 57, 58
Fee, G. D. 28, 97, 104, 114, 208, 223, 268, 271, 275, 276, 278, 359, 363, 383, 390, 401, 473, 540, 546, 572, 608, 811, 818, 819, 827
Ferguson, E. 539
Feuillet, A. 109, 373, 517, 520
Field, D. H. 265
Field, F. 55, 92, 167, 236, 240, 241, 440, 664
Filson, F. V. 835
Findlay, G. G. 41, 93, 171, 173, 204, 217, 223, 226, 235, 252, 263, 265, 267, 273, 283, 290, 371, 412, 440, 452, 456, 461, 464, 466, 469, 470, 479, 482, 486, 487, 489, 514, 536, 538, 577, 585, 586, 587, 596, 640, 657, 658, 678, 684, 685, 690, 720, 721, 730, 731, 757, 765, 768, 772, 783, 784, 792, 815, 816
Fiore, B. 156, 167, 184, 186
Fiorenza, E. S. 493, 496, 498, 510, 520, 522, 523, 528
Fishburne, C. W. 136, 141
Fitch, W. O. 58
Fitzer, G. 699
Fitzmyer, J. A. 520, 521
Flanagan, N. M. 705
Flint, A. J. 182
Foerster, W. 253, 438
Fohrer, G. 68

Forbes, C. 400
Ford, J. M. 4, 146, 287, 297, 298, 322, 325, 352, 356, 576, 597, 598
Forkman, G. 203, 209
Foschini, B. M. 762, 764, 765, 766
Fotheringham, D. R. 439
Francis, J. 100, 124
Frid, B. 105, 108
Fridrichsen, A. 30, 535, 536, 733
Friedrich, G. 73, 595, 633, 694, 801
Fuller, R. H. 597, 723
Fung, R. Y.-K. 86, 245, 246, 247
Funk, R. W. 60, 91, 100, 101, 102, 115, 122, 189, 818
Furnish, V. P. 59, 93, 134, 175, 185, 212, 289, 366, 810, 811
Fürst, D. 566

Gaffin, R. 600
Gamble, H. 62, 825, 834, 835, 836, 839
Garland, D. E. 268, 283, 287
Garnier, G. G. 602
Garnsey, P. 229
Gärtner, B. E. 100, 102, 110, 146, 147
Gaventa, B. R. 556, 557
Gee, D. 590, 592, 593
Georgi, D. 811, 816
Gerhardsson, B. 499
Gertner, M. 805
Gewalt, D. 800
Giblin, C. H. 253, 273, 287, 365, 373
Gill, D. H. 361
Gillman, J. 751, 777, 784, 798, 799, 802
Gilmour, S. M. 730
Gnilka, J. 144
Godet, F. 28, 40, 44, 71, 72, 82, 85, 91, 93, 111, 134, 148, 209, 273, 275, 335, 338, 386, 401, 408, 413, 426, 432, 440, 461, 464, 479, 490, 536, 610, 656, 668, 673, 700, 761, 765, 770, 772, 773, 779, 792, 799, 816, 827, 831
Goldingay, J. 576
Gooch, P. W. 432
Goodenough, E. R. 507, 509, 510
Goodspeed, E. J. 115, 312, 669
Goppelt, L. 443, 446, 468
Gordon, A. J. 508
Goudge, H. L. 99, 138, 273, 303, 673
Grant, R. M. 679
Grayston, K. 52, 187
Greeven, H. 694
Gressmann, H. 470
Gromacki, R. G. 140, 657, 774, 797, 813
Grosheide, F. W. 34, 39, 93, 138, 142, 210, 223, 231, 250, 267, 273, 275, 278, 279, 280, 283, 308, 314, 316, 329, 330,

332, 333, 371, 386, 408, 419, 421, 435, 453, 463, 465, 469, 481, 486, 505, 511, 536, 548, 554, 581, 587, 589, 610, 656, 669, 673, 693, 694, 698, 703, 718, 731, 747, 756, 765, 787, 792, 827, 831
Grudem, W. A. 118, 502, 503, 505, 573, 575, 577, 595, 596, 620, 662, 680, 681, 682, 693, 694, 696, 701, 703, 704
Grundmann, W. 35, 124, 275, 561, 827
Guelich, R. 193
Guerra, M. 31
Guhrt, J. 72
Gundry, R. H. 255, 256, 260, 261, 262, 263, 439, 597, 598, 664, 776
Günther, W. 631
Gutbrod, W. 679
Güttgemanns, E. 728, 747

Hahn, H. C. 380
Hamerton-Kelly, R. G. 71
Hanimann, J. 605
Hanna, R. 281
Hanson, A. T. 180, 407, 445, 446
Harder, G. 116, 148, 526
Harmon, A. M. 152
Harnack, A. 616, 623, 633, 635, 636, 729, 733, 831
Harpur, T. W. 574, 597
Harris, B. F. 380, 381
Harris, H. A. 434, 437
Harris, M. J. 719, 726, 728
Harris, W. 632
Harrisville, R. A. 597, 679
Hart, J. H. P. 56
Hartman, L. 89, 90, 91, 93, 94, 95
Harvey, A. E. 160, 399, 413
Hauck, F. 45, 180, 200, 466
Havener, I. 206, 212
Hay, D. M. 755
Heawood, P. J. 766
Hengel, M. 45, 75, 76
Héring, J. 29, 38, 54, 73, 91, 103, 114, 168, 180, 199, 218, 241, 249, 254, 267, 303, 446, 464, 470, 474, 486, 557, 563, 595, 626, 656, 673, 720, 723, 731, 753, 754, 756, 770, 783, 786, 787, 791, 797
Hierzenberger, C. 340
Higgins, A. J. B. 465, 733, 834
Hill, A. E. 602
Hill, D. 86, 595, 596, 658, 694, 703, 727, 728
Hill, M. 278, 283, 289, 436
Hirsch, E. D. 408
Hock, R. F. 93, 179, 399, 400, 404, 405, 416, 419, 424, 425, 426
Hodge, C. 279, 283, 813

Hodgson, R. 177
Hofmann, K. M. 834, 836
Holl, K. 810
Holladay, C. 91, 115, 138, 162, 252, 303, 327, 344, 351, 383, 393, 540, 556, 596, 636, 656, 668, 731, 756, 770, 804, 805, 830
Holmberg, B. 810
Holtz, T. 581
Hooker, M. 125, 126, 166, 167, 169, 516, 520, 521
Horsley, R. A. 4, 13, 49, 64, 65, 74, 81, 100, 102, 116, 276, 358, 361, 365, 371, 374, 380, 381, 467, 776, 785, 791
Horst, J. 258
Hort, F. J. A. 578
House, H. W. 658
Howard, J. K. 216, 765
Howard, W. F. 168
Howson, J. S. 261
Hübner, H. 806
Hudson, J. T. 168
Hunkin, J. W. 771
Hunter, H. 605
Hunzinger 316
Hurd, J. C. 7, 13, 15, 16, 47, 49, 56, 58, 194, 197, 201, 217, 222, 223, 228, 231, 233, 250, 254, 267, 275, 287, 288, 323, 326, 328, 330, 358, 359, 360, 365, 371, 381, 383, 385, 392, 393, 424, 425, 441, 476, 477, 500, 537, 538, 570, 573, 575, 579, 714, 809, 814, 818
Hurley, J. B. 4, 252, 253, 254, 255, 257, 259, 261, 270, 297, 322, 325, 362, 493, 496, 497, 500, 502, 506, 507, 510, 514, 526, 527, 528, 529, 700, 703

Iber, G. 624
Isaksson, A. 492, 496, 498, 506, 528
Isenberg, M. 481

Jansen, J. 756
Jensen, J. 278
Jeremias, J. 62, 217, 273, 288, 301, 305, 330, 365, 444, 465, 467, 468, 538, 547, 549, 551, 552, 553, 557, 663, 718, 723, 724, 765, 780, 798, 802
Jervell, J. 57, 403
Jewett, R. 11, 205, 211, 362, 365, 380, 447, 469, 791
Joest, W. 722
Johanson, B. C. 677, 678, 679, 680, 681
Johnson, S. E. 203
Jones, D. 552
Jones, P. R. 30, 732
Jones, W. R. 590

Jourdan, G. V. 466
Joyce, J. D. 761, 763
Judge, E. A. 81, 393, 399

Kaiser, W. C. 113, 115, 407, 408, 704, 705
Karris, R. J. 480
Kasch, W. 410
Käsemann, E. 148, 149, 205, 210, 262, 339, 414, 418, 419, 420, 421, 446, 447, 465, 466, 603, 604, 712
Kearny, P. J. 730
Kee, H. C. 83
Kempthorne, R. 250, 253, 258, 261, 264
Kendall, E. L. 597
Kennedy, C. A. 358
Kerr, F. 395
Keydall, R. 663
Kieffer, R. 629
Kilpatrick, G. D. 168, 465
Kim, C. H. 361
Kim, S. 105, 395, 791, 793
Kirk, J. A. 30
Kittel, G. 175, 520
Klappert, B. 723
Klauck, H. J. 465
Klein, W. W. 632
Kline, M. G. 445, 446
Kloppenborg, J. 722, 723
Knox, W. L. 57, 222
Koenig, J. 576
Kosmala, H. 552
Koster, H. 526, 527
Kramer, H. 595
Kramer, W. 582
Kroeger, K. 502
Kroeger-Kroeger, R. and C. 498, 509
Kubo, S. 297, 302, 304, 305
Kugelman, R. 358
Kuhn, K. G. 838
Kümmel, W. G. 73, 327
Kürzinger, J. 523

Ladd, G. 746
Lake, K. 58
Lambrecht 747, 751, 755, 757
Lampe, G. W. H. 210
Lang, F. 142
Langevin, P. V. 34, 838
Lee, G. M. 230, 407
Legault, A. 168
Lehmann, K. 728
Lenski, R. C. H. 250, 279, 386, 435, 557, 673, 694, 718, 768, 788, 831
Lias, J. J. 218

Liddell, H. C., Scott, R., and Jones, H. S. 502, 514, 529

Liefeld, W. L. 493

Lietzmann, H. 64, 88, 91, 103, 138, 217, 267, 300, 373, 383, 409, 486, 516, 531, 552, 557, 587, 753, 754, 797, 834

Lightfoot, J. B. 36, 40, 41, 71, 82, 85, 91, 93, 111, 115, 138, 143, 180, 185, 188, 192, 199, 210, 216, 217, 223, 233, 252, 258, 273, 277, 278, 281, 298, 309, ·314, 326, 332, 335, 356, 493, 507, 520

Lincoln, A. T. 716, 747, 782, 784, 786, 787, 789, 791, 792, 793

Lindsell, H. 456

Link, H. G. 631

Lock, W. 365

Lohr, G. 800

Lohse, E. 482

Longenecker, R. N. 407, 408, 444

Lowrie, S. T. 502, 520

Luedemann, G. 801

Lund, N. W. 423

Lütgert, W. 58

Luther, M. 604, 765

Lutz, C. 280

Lyall, F. 319

MacArthur, J. 115, 131, 136, 148, 149, 620, 657

MacArthur, S. D. 206, 209, 211

MacDonald, D. R. 168, 770, 771

MacDonald, J. I. H. 66

MacDonald, W. G. 597

MacGorman, J. W. 570, 579, 590

MacGregor, G. H. C. 103

MacPherson, P. 459

MacRae, G. W. 41

Maier, F. 755

Malherbe, A. J. 258, 399, 534, 762, 770, 771, 772, 773, 835

Malina, B. 278

Mallone, G. 590

Maly, K. 577

Mánek, J. 725

Manson, T. W. 166, 379

March, W. 756

Marcion 249, 787

Mare, W. H. 85, 89, 91, 122, 138, 139, 169, 199, 231, 238, 273, 283, 303, 308, 320, 342, 456, 463, 617, 669, 707, 813, 818

Marshall, I. H. 86, 274, 465, 546, 547, 549, 550, 551, 554, 563

Marshall, P. 175

Martin, D. W. 110

Martin, I. J. 597, 628

Martin, R. P. 465, 570, 573, 575, 576, 582, 586, 588, 591, 592, 596, 605, 609, 618, 620, 624, 627, 630, 639, 654, 671, 672, 678, 681, 690, 692, 698, 702, 704, 706, 707, 717, 725, 733, 747, 749, 763, 766, 767, 774, 780, 781, 785, 786, 792, 805, 810, 811

Martin, W. J. 492, 496, 506, 510, 511, 528

Marxsen, W. 395, 465, 714, 278

Maurer, C. 380, 415, 481

McArthur, H. K. 726, 727

McCaughey, T. 380, 747, 757

McDermott, M. 466

Meeks, W. A. 269, 442, 443, 454, 493

Menoud, P.-H. 313

Mercadante, L. 493

Metzger, B. M. 27, 88, 98, 129, 135, 136, 145, 198, 249, 272, 296, 297, 335, 369, 398, 414, 422, 441, 450, 451, 469, 475, 476, 498, 512, 545, 558, 584, 629, 700, 709, 717, 727, 748, 761, 787, 796, 833

Meuter, S. 238

Meyer, R. 595, 799

Michaelis, W. 186, 187, 189, 395

Michel, O. 146, 366, 657

Mickelsen, A. and B. 502

Miguens, M. 250, 253, 259, 627

Miller, G. 104

Miller, J. I. 259

Mills, W. E. 597

Minear, P. S. 194

Mitton, C. L. 216

Moffatt, J. 40, 91, 103, 108, 138, 153, 167, 171, 172, 206, 207, 223, 282, 290, 362, 407, 421, 469, 500, 501, 550, 554, 563, 580, 596, 605, 631, 658, 669, 769, 805, 831

Moiser, J. 268, 269, 285, 287, 291, 297

Montefiore, H. 218

Montgomery, H. 54, 206, 329, 401, 486, 658, 815

Morisette, R. 776, 798, 803, 806

Morris, L. L. 86, 134, 210, 213, 223, 273, 275, 283, 656, 669, 672, 813, 816

Moseley, A. G. 765

Moule, C. F. D. 73, 132, 160, 202, 261, 281, 282, 303, 305, 321, 338, 429, 465, 681, 776, 800, 838, 839

Moulton, J. H. 124, 230, 429

Moulton, J. H. and Milligan, G. 293, 294, 302, 343, 347, 354, 502

Munck, J. 47, 48, 49, 59, 65, 80, 130, 138, 185, 420, 538, 733, 811

Murphy, D. J. 715

Murphy-O'Connor, J. 1, 2, 3, 5, 58, 89,

100, 168, 204, 205, 206, 207, 208, 209, 210, 212, 253, 254, 255, 256, 258, 261, 262, 268, 271, 274, 275, 278, 290, 293, 295, 299, 300, 301, 322, 326, 358, 362, 371, 373, 374, 375, 376, 377, 379, 380, 381, 382, 383, 389, 433, 465, 486, 488, 491, 492, 493, 495, 496, 497, 502, 503, 504, 505, 506, 509, 529, 533, 540, 632, 699, 701, 709, 722, 723, 730, 732, 763, 764, 765, 770, 787
Murray, R. 748, 749

Neubauer, A. 724
Neuenzeit, P. 449, 465, 541
Neufeld, V. 580, 582
Neusner 448, 455
Nickel, K. 401
Nickle, K. 811
Nygren, A. 631

O'Brien, P. 36, 39, 40, 42, 43, 45, 276
O'Collins, G. 395
Odell-Scott, D. W. 705
Oepke, A. 514, 764
Oesterley, W. O. E. 482
Oliver, A. B. 766
Omanson, R. L. 291, 417
O'Neill, J. C. 761, 763, 766
O'Rourke, J. 326
Orr, W. F. 268, 283, 287, 322
Orr, W. F. and Walther, J. A. 38, 91, 114, 138, 205, 218, 303, 408, 526
Ory, G. 428
Osborne, H. 380, 381
Osborne, R. E. 770
Osburn, C. D. 450, 457

Padgett, A. 493, 495, 496, 501, 509, 520, 521, 523, 525, 526, 528, 529
Pagels, E. 206
Panikulam, G. 45, 466, 811, 812
Pannenberg, W. 722
Parry, R. St John 138, 142, 143, 160, 169, 185, 216, 218, 223, 233, 265, 273, 314, 337, 338, 358, 360, 371, 432, 457, 464, 479, 489, 525, 536, 560, 563, 566, 577, 578, 581, 586, 617, 619, 621, 656, 681, 683, 691, 731, 733, 747, 757, 761, 764, 783, 789, 792, 799, 816, 827
Payne, P. B. 493, 496, 497, 502, 503, 504, 507, 516, 517, 520, 522, 523
Pearson, B. A. 4, 11, 13, 65, 81, 100, 102, 103, 116, 295, 575, 579, 580, 715, 785, 791
Perella, N. J. 836

Perrot, C. 443, 453
Peters, E. H. 465
Peterson, E. 70, 632
Pfitzner, V. C. 175, 202, 434, 435, 436, 438, 439, 440
Phillips, J. B. 591, 681
Phipps, W. E. 269, 274
Pierce, C. A. 380, 381, 486
Plank, K. A. 715
Plooij, D. 727
Poythress, V. S. 597
Preisker, H. 143, 421
Prior, D. 136
Prümm, K. 5

Quasten, J. 632
Quell, G. 631

Raeder, M. 765
Räisänen, H. 806
Ramsey, W. M. 54, 519, 520
Reitzenstein, R. 103
Rendtorff, R. 595
Rengstorf, K. H. 30, 159
Reumann, J. 159, 419, 420
Rex, H. H. 290, 291, 309, 323
Richards, J. R. 13
Richardson, P. 196, 228, 241, 270, 292, 431
Richardson, W. 574, 598, 691
Ridderbos, H. 69, 142, 703, 724
Riesenfeld, H. 131, 133, 632, 764, 781
Riggs, R. 604
Rissi, M. 763, 767
Roberts, P. 678, 680, 681
Roberts, R. L. 293
Robertson, A. and Plummer, A. 41, 93, 111, 124, 138, 142, 143, 148, 180, 199, 210, 217, 250, 252, 265, 273, 279, 283, 293, 335, 337, 338, 386, 405, 410, 412, 427, 432, 435, 436, 453, 456, 466, 472, 481, 488, 519, 570, 599, 662, 667, 674, 684, 720, 721, 724, 732, 765, 768
Robertson, O. P. 119, 185, 412, 416, 680, 800
Robinson, D. W. B. 573, 575
Robinson, J. A. T. 256, 439, 776, 834, 836, 837, 838
Robinson, J. M. 292, 327
Robinson, W. C. 75, 95
Roetzel, C. J. 148, 206, 442
Rogers, E. R. 605
Romaniuk, K. 261
Rordorf, W. 813, 820
Ross, J. M. 168

Ruef, J. 34, 44, 73, 326, 346, 393, 407, 662, 669, 699, 729, 761, 790, 829
Russell, K. C. 289
Ryan, T. J. 732

Sachs, C. 664
Sagnard, M. M. 374
Salom, A. P. 338
Sanders, B. 184, 186
Sanders, E. P. 141, 806
Sanders, J. T. 45, 52, 625
Sänger, D. 80
Sasse, H. 72
Schattenmann, J. 466
Schlatter, A. 79, 379, 580, 799
Schlier, H. 40, 385, 506, 672
Schmidt, K. L. 178, 438, 632
Schmiedel, P. W. 168
Schmithals, W. 11, 58, 211, 275, 365, 366, 386, 403, 427, 531, 580, 713, 729, 731, 732, 775, 791
Schmitz, E. D. 72
Schmitz, O. 291
Schnackenburg, R. 30, 604, 605, 606, 678, 763
Schneider, B. 730, 781, 789
Schneider, C. 192, 193
Schneider, J. 210, 457, 480, 733
Schnelle, U. 256
Schniewind, J. 557
Schoeps, H. J. 57
Schrage, W. 177, 340
Schreiner, K. 81
Schrenk, G. 73
Schubert, P. 36
Schulz, S. 200, 838
Schürer, E. 231
Schürmann, H. 547
Schütz, J. H. 50, 69, 91, 432, 730, 732
Schweizer, E. 79, 95, 116, 205, 465, 540, 541, 549, 603, 617, 785, 797, 798
Scott, C. A. A. 246
Scroggs, R. 12, 64, 99, 100, 102, 103, 243, 244, 269, 493, 502, 581, 699, 702, 790, 791
Sebolt, R. H. A. 326
Seeburg, R. 834
Seesemann, H. 127, 282, 461, 466
Senft, C. 91, 138, 147, 167, 327, 435
Sevenster, J. 175, 282, 316, 317, 320, 340, 703
Sharpe, J. L. 793
Sider, R. J. 715, 718, 725, 776, 777, 780, 787
Smalley, S. S. 838
Smith, B. L. 597

Smith, D. M. 597
Snyder, E. H. 705
Snyder, G. 251
Souter, A. 459
Spicq, C. 251, 380, 625, 626, 627, 628, 631, 632, 633, 634, 827, 829, 838
Spittler, R. P. 630
Spörlein, B. 715
Staab, K. 766
Stählin, G. 180, 836
Stanley, D. M. 187
Stauffer, E. 101, 436, 631
Stein, A. 236, 725
Stone, M. and Strugnell, J. 109
Stowers, S. K. 232
Strack, H. and Billerbeck, P. 184, 406, 456, 468, 507, 548
Strobel, A. 62
Strugnell, J. 168
Stumpff, A. 126
Sweet, J. M. P. 570, 573, 597, 679, 681
Sykes, M. H. 552
Synge, F. C. 498

Talbert, C. H. 601, 605, 705
Taylor, V. 727
Thackeray, H. St. John 70
Theissen, G. 3, 15, 54, 59, 62, 80, 81, 176, 177, 358, 389, 399, 400, 428, 534, 541, 609
Thiselton, A. C. 12, 172, 211, 574, 598
Thompson, C. L. 386
Thompson, K. C. 766
Thrall, M. E. 160, 261, 295, 316, 326, 338, 362, 380, 381, 557, 703
Tischendorf, C. von 306, 787
Titus, E. L. 626
Townsend, J. T. 144
Traub, H. 783
Treves, M. 371
Trites, A. A. 91
Trompf, G. W. 492
Tugwell, S. 597
Turner, N. 102, 114, 126, 160, 163, 164, 185, 202, 263, 286, 338, 386, 444

Usami, K. 777, 798

van Unnik, W. C. 34, 36, 579, 580, 834, 839
Versnel, H. S. 174
Vielhauer, P. 57, 723
Vischer, L. 238
Vogels, H. J. 787
Vögtle, A. 225
von Campenhausen, H. 30, 211

von der Osten-Sacken, P. 719
von Dobschütz, E. 730
von Hofmann 756
von Soden, H. F. 31, 358, 391, 475, 483, 531, 787
Vos, G. 142, 789

Wagner, G. 104
Walker, D. 573
Walker, W. O. 492
Wallis, W. 749, 756
Waltke, B. K. 493
Warfield, B. B. 439
Wedderburn, A. J. M. 73, 716, 791, 793
Weeks, N. 493, 498, 502
Wegenast, K. 499
Weiss, J. 33, 103, 138, 144, 146, 147, 155, 168, 173, 180, 189, 199, 204, 211, 217, 256, 294, 311, 318, 323, 362, 399, 409, 419, 421, 423, 427, 443, 446, 461, 469, 480, 486, 531, 557, 563, 575, 579, 595, 666, 699, 733, 753, 754, 770, 797, 805
Weizsäcker, C. von 831
Wendland, H. D. 486, 605, 657
Wenthe, D. O. 217
Westcott, B. F. and Hort, F. J. A. 576
White, J. L. 52
Wickert, U. 33
Widmann, M. 100, 787
Wilcke, H. A. 753
Wilckens, U. 11, 65, 69, 71, 91, 99, 100, 103, 106, 116, 119, 580, 722, 723, 729

Wiles, G. P. 43, 218, 834, 836
Wilkinson, T. L. 597, 598
Williams, C. K. 163, 168, 401, 669
Willis, W. L. 45, 360, 361, 365, 366, 368, 369, 371, 378, 379, 380, 381, 383, 384, 389, 390, 392, 394, 401, 412, 424, 427, 428, 430, 446, 453, 456, 460, 466, 467, 468, 470, 483, 486, 487, 489, 753
Wilson, G. B. 797
Wilson, J. H. 715
Wilson, R. McL. 11
Winnett, A. R. 550
Winter, B. W. 532, 534, 537, 542, 723, 729
Wischmeyer, O. 626
Wiseman, J. 1
Wuellner, W. 66, 69, 81, 89, 101
Würthwein, E. 143

Yarbro Collins, A. 206, 208, 211, 212
Yerkes, R. K. 361

Zerwick, M. 53, 162, 202, 309, 830
Zuntz, G. 27, 28, 35, 39, 88, 97, 98, 121, 129, 135, 136, 183, 198, 230, 249, 272, 335, 349, 364, 368, 377, 397, 398, 414, 419, 422, 441, 442, 444, 450, 451, 462, 476, 486, 498, 524, 535, 583, 584, 585, 608, 616, 617, 623, 629, 635, 660, 667, 676, 699, 709, 717, 718, 761, 796

INDEX OF SCRIPTURE REFERENCES

GENESIS

1:11	782
1:20	783
1:24	783
1:26	515, 783
1:26-27	794
1:26-28	515
2	513, 515, 792
2:7	785ff.
2:18	275
2:18-20	517
2:18-24	515
2:23	517
2:24	257, 259
3:1-15	282
3:16	707
4:26	34
6:2	521
9:12	682
9:24	774
12:8	34
17:13	687
17:17	687
20:6	275
26:8	454
27:26	836
32:30	647
32:31	649
33:4	836
39:12	260
39:17	455
40:8	115
40:16	115
40:22	115
41:12	115
41:13	115
41:15	115
52:15	769

EXODUS

2:1	278
12:6	216
12:13	682
12:14-20	216
12:15	216
12:23	457f.
13:9	553
13:21	445
14:19-20	445
14:19-22	44
15:16	93
16–17	446
16:4-30	446
17:1-7	446
18:22	240
19:5-6	32
19:16	663, 801
20:3	369
20:5	474
20:6	108
21:1	231
21:20	193
24	555
24:8	554
24:11	360
28:2	528
32:6	360, 451, 454
32:17	454
32:18	454
32:19	454
32:25	454
32:28	454
32:31	454
32:35	454
34:15	483

LEVITICUS

6:16-18	412
6:26-28	412
7:6	412
7:8-10	412
7:28-36	412
9:24	687
10:6	509
13:45	509
18:7-8	200
20:11	200
23:9-14	749
24:7	553

NUMBERS

5:18	509
10:10	553
11:4	633
11:34	452f.
12:6	647
12:8	647
12:12	733
14	457
14:1-38	457
14:2	457
14:16	450
14:27	457
14:37	458
15:34	115
16:41	457
18:8-19	412
20:2	448
20:2-13	446
21	448
21:4-7	456
21:16-18	447
21:17-18	448
22:15	448
25:1-2	360, 455
25:1-3	455
25:1-9	455
25:9	450, 456
26:10	682
26:62	456

DEUTERONOMY

4:10	32

5:10	108
6:4	155
6:16	456f.
7:9	44, 108
7:26	580
8:3	446
8:15-16	446
13:17	580
14:22-26	360
14:22-27	470
17:7	220f., 227
19:19	220
20:6	405
21:12	510
21:23	76
22:12	507
22:21	220
22:24	220
24:1	293, 613
24:7	220
25:4	398, 406f.
28:30	278
28:46	682
28:49	677, 680
32:1-43	442
32:4	449
32:15	449
32:16-17	449
32:17	457, 472
32:18	449
32:21	472ff.
32:30	449
32:31	449

JOSHUA

6:18	580

JUDGES

8:16	231
9:27	360
11:11	503

RUTH

2:9	275
4:2	231

1 SAMUEL

2:10	80
9:13	360
16:7	111, 163
18:7	454
19:19-24	595
20:41	836
25:37	774

2 SAMUEL

6:5	454
6:21	454
7:14	193
10:12	828
22:44	503

1 KINGS

1:25	360f.
18	593

2 KINGS

20:5	727
22:11	203
22:19	203
23:4-5	203

1 CHRONICLES

13:8	454
15:29	454
21:12	457
21:15	457
22:14	140
22:16	140
28:9	163
29:2	140f.

2 CHRONICLES

3:6	140f.
11:21	278

EZRA

10:1	203
10:3	203
10:6	202

NEHEMIAH

9:11-12	446
9:15	446
9:20	446
9:35-37	442

ESTHER

6:12	506

JOB

2:4-10	210
2:6	208
3:16	733
5:13	150, 152
27:6	380
29:7-8	231
38	171
38–42	70

PSALMS

6:10	83
8:6	754f., 757ff.
8:7	754
14:1	780
16:8-11	727
16:9-11	727
18:43	503
23:5-6	361
24:1	476, 482
26:14	828
30:25	828
31:17	83
31:24	828
33:10	70
35:4	83
35:26-27	83
37	553
43:23	769
50:15	34
53:1	780
69	553
78	442
78:13-14	446
78:15-31	446
78:18	456
92:6	780
93:12	152
94:11	150, 152
96:5	472
98:2	109
105:38-39	446
105:39	445
105:40	446
106:37	472
110:1	727, 754f., 758
114:2	147
115:5	578
135:6	83
139:1	111, 163
139:2	111
139:11-12	163
139:23	111
144:13	44

PROVERBS

1:5	622
1:8	184
1:10	184
1:22	452
2:1	184
3:1	184
6:29	275
8:1–9:6	65

10:13	193
11:14	622
21:18	180
22:15	193
24:6	622
26:3	805
27:18	405

ECCLESIASTES

6:3	733
12:12	184

ISAIAH

1:14-17	565
1:25	289
3:3	138
6	203
7:8	503
7:9	503
10:24	193
13:16	278
18:3	801
19:11-12	70
19:16	93
19:22	70
22:13	761, 772
25:8	796, 803f.
27:13	801
28:11	677
28:11-12	677, 679
28:12	677
28:16	147
29:10	605, 683
29:14	68f.
31:8	240
33:18	70
40:12-14	70
40:13	98f., 119
40:14	171
40:25	70
43:19-21	444
45:9-10	474
45:14	687
53	551, 555, 724f.
53:2-3	181
53:4	594
53:6	549
53:12	549, 551, 555
54:1	278
64:4	98, 108
65:3	472
65:11	472
65:16	108

JEREMIAH

1:4-10	418
1:10	133
4:5	801
5:15	680
9:7	289
9:23	80
9:23-24	70, 78, 84
9:24	78, 87
17:10	163
20:7-9	418
31:31	555
35:2	361
51:27	801

LAMENTATIONS

1:5	503
2:9	683
3:1	193
3:45	180

EZEKIEL

11:13	687
36:26-27	430
40–48	147
43:9	147
47:1-12	147

DANIEL

2:19	109
2:19-23	633
2:20-23	111
2:22	109, 111
2:28	109, 633
3	634
5:1-4	360
5:7	115
7:18-27	32
7:22	233
7:27	173
11:35	289
12:3	785

HOSEA

5:8	796
6:2	727
7:8	222
8:13	361
13:14	796, 803

JOEL

1:5	774
2:1	801
2:28-30	595, 685

2:31	43
3:5	34

AMOS

2:7	200
3:8	418
4:11	144
5:18-20	43
7:14-15	418

JONAH

1:17	727
4:3	275
4:8	275

MICAH

3:6	683

HABAKKUK

2:7	774
2:18-19	578
2:19	774

HAGGAI

2:8	140

ZECHARIAH

3:2	144
8:17	639
8:23	687
9:14	801
12:1	111
12:10-14	203
13:2	20

MATTHEW

1:18	327
1:23	327
3:6	606
3:11	606
5:4	202
5:4-5	700
5:5	193
5:11-12	187
5:21	560
5:22	560, 780
5:29-30	389
5:32	292
5:48	644
6:4	163
6:6	163
6:18	163
6:24	170

6:25-34	342	3:31	404	12:15	633
7:1-5	227f.	4:11	226	12:16-21	780
8:17	594	6:3	403	12:23	633
8:29	163	6:18	278	12:50	765
9:4	487	7:1-19	490	13:7	487
9:18	647	7:21-22	225	15:20	836
10:10	413	7:22	225	16:1-8	764
10:16-42	413	8:11	74	16:16	292
10:34-37	538	8:12	728	16:17	642
11:29	193	8:15	216	17:6	632
11:38-39	74	8:31	726	17:16	687
12:39-40	728	8:34f.	182	17:34	170
12:40	727	9:2	800	18:10	170
13:55	403	9:31	726	19:11	520
16:4	728	10:11	292	19:17	173
16:14	585	10:15	679	20:25	437
16:18	139	10:19	241	20:26-27	175
17:2	800	10:34	726	20:28	278
17:6	687	10:38	765	20:34-36	327
17:30	632	10:41-45	130	20:35	12, 269, 502
18:6-8	389	10:42	130	21:5	580
18:20	207	10:45	130	21:15	592
19:9	292	11:25	632	21:23	329
19:18	168	12:10	526	22:17-19	550
19:21	633	12:25	354	22:17-20	466
19:28	233	12:33	278	22:19	545
20:33	278	13:20	339	22:19-20	546
21:37	184	13:34	827	22:24-27	426
22:28	278	13:35	827	22:25-27	130
23:5	507	13:37	827	22:27	130
24:9-13	538	14:1	217	22:29-30	173
24:19	333	14:8	540	22:30	233
24:31	801	14:16	217	22:37	168
25:1-13	327	14:18	550	23:34	179, 639
25:21	143	14:18-24	546	23:40	526
25:23	143	14:24	468	24:13-34	728
25:34	798	14:26	560	24:20	103
25:45	389	14:58	147, 726	24:34	728f.
26:26	545	15:19	726	24:36	728
26:26-28	546	16:9-14	728	24:45-47	722
26:39	687			24:46	724
26:61	726	**LUKE**			
26:66	560	1:27	327	**JOHN**	
27:40	726	3:16	606	1:1-3	375
28:14	199, 343	4:5-10	700	1:1-13	374
28:16-17	728	5:12	687	1:26	606
28:17	730	6:20-38	315	1:31	606
28:19	61	6:22-23	187	1:33	606
		6:28	179	2:19-21	147
MARK		9:1	520	2:19-22	726
1:8	606	10:1-12	413	3:8	599
1:19	54	10:7	413	3:23	606
2:1	199	10:19	520	4:10	605
2:21	54	11:2	31	4:14	605
3:14	729	11:16	74	4:18	278
3:29	560	11:29-30	728	5:3-4	705

5:4	702
6	446
6:30	74
6:45	114
7:2-9	731
7:3	404
7:37-39	446, 605
7:40-43	54
8:1-11	201
9:16	54
10:19-21	54
10:20	685
10:34	679
12:3	104
12:24	781
14:30	104
16:8-11	686
16:11	104
17:15-16	223
21:19	728f.

ACTS

1:5	606
1:6-11	731f.
1:14	404
1:21-22	395
2	598, 680, 730
2:4	670, 680
2:5-11	598
2:17-18	595, 685
2:22-25	106
2:25-36	727
2:36	582, 722
2:38	61, 113, 247
2:42	532
2:46	468, 532
3:15	106, 725
3:17	103
4:13	673
4:28	105
5:1-10	210
5:1-11	593
5:2	162
5:17	538
6:1-6	810
6:13	147
7:1-53	442
7:26	487
7:48-50	147
7:54-60	582
8:3	835
8:4	818
8:16	61
8:40	818
9:14	34
9:15	395

10:9-23	482
10:47	113
10:48	61, 247
11:12-13	482
11:16	445, 606
11:19	818
11:27-29	662
11:27-30	810
12:17	731
13:1	596, 621
13:6	818
13:14	818
13:16-41	722
13:26-42	92
13:27	103
13:28-31	722
15	222
15:3	819
15:13	731
15:20	360
15:23	34
15:23-29	27, 815
15:29	13, 357, 360, 425, 455, 839
15:36-41	404
15:39	638
16:1-3	428
16:3	312
16:15	399
16:16-18	596
16:37-39	232
17:16	638
17:16-34	92
17:34	92, 829
18	6
18:1-3	835
18:1-8	3, 92
18:2	835
18:2-3	835
18:3	399f., 403, 416
18:5	188
18:7	62
18:8	62
18:9-11	94
18:12	5
18:12-17	229
18:17	31
18:18	7, 15, 511, 527, 835
18:18-26	835
18:23	812
18:24	56
18:24-28	56
18:26	835
19:2	113
19:5	61
19:8-10	190

19:10	835
19:21	821
19:22	188, 821f.
19:23-41	821
19:26	835
19:31-40	770
19:35	71
19:39	32
20:1-3	818
20:4	810, 813, 815
20:7	468, 532, 813f.
20:11	468, 532
20:16	820
20:31	184, 827
20:34	399
21:18	731
21:23-26	428
21:24	511
21:25	357
21:29	815
22:1	401
22:10	395
22:16	245f.
24:15	753
24:16	489
24:17	810
25:5	80
25:10-12	232
26:9-11	734
26:14	805
26:15-18	395
26:24	685
26:25	685
27:9-44	819
27:11	622

ROMANS

1	225
1–11	53
1:3-4	716, 722
1:4	257, 740
1:5	396
1:8	37, 557
1:9	204
1:10	808
1:11	43, 576, 587
1:13	443
1:14	665
1:16	77, 432
1:18-31	72
1:22-28	722
1:23	783
1:25	672
1:26	243, 526
1:26-27	244
1:27	526

1:29	55	6:9	740	9:3	470
1:29-30	225	6:10	730	9:5	672
1:29-31	225	6:11	784	9:6	710
1:32	198	6:12	173	9:30-31	654
1:45-49	722	6:15	670	10:5	406
2:2-3	198	6:16	146	10:9	579, 740
2:4	636	6:18	302	10:9-10	582
2:5	662	6:19	406	10:18	543
2:12	429	6:22	302, 649	10:19	406, 473
2:14	526	6:23	42, 113, 587	11:7	670
2:15	381	7	806	11:11	473
2:16	163	7:1-3	296	11:12	240
2:18	676, 824	7:2	302f., 331, 349, 351	11:14	306, 473
2:23	84	7:2-3	355	11:16	300f., 748
2:26-29	444	7:3	426	11:17	432
2:27	526	7:4	209, 351	11:17-24	444
3:5	406, 771	7:5-6	212	11:21	526
3:6	763	7:6	649	11:24	526
3:9	670	7:7	406	11:25	176, 443
3:19	679	7:7-8	452	11:29	587
3:21	406, 649	7:8-13	313	11:31	769
3:24	87	7:11	151	11:33	45, 111
3:27	84	7:17	649	11:35	152
3:29-30	373	7:18	796	11:36	375, 672, 760
4:1	444, 470	7:25	495	12	430
4:4-5	143	8	80, 586	12:1	53, 439, 551
4:7	724	8:1	127	12:2	801
4:9	405	8:4	127	12:3	135, 306f., 310, 593
4:11	397	8:8	344	12:4-8	590
4:17	780	8:9	119, 123, 578	12:6	37, 42, 595, 693
4:24	395, 681, 740	8:11	740, 780	12:6-7	586
4:25	725, 743	8:13	578	12:8	621
5	794	8:14	578	12:11	578
5:1	770	8:14-17	603	12:13	32, 568, 654
5:1-5	650	8:15	31, 113	12:14	179
5:2	720	8:17	106, 181	12:15	340
5:2-3	634	8:17-27	93	12:16	176, 454
5:3	84	8:19	42, 662	12:17	179, 241
5:6	551, 763	8:19-22	760	12:18	305
5:6-8	628, 631	8:23	42, 263, 748	12:20	633
5:8	551, 763	8:24	650f.	13:1	830
5:9	231, 720	8:25	42	13:1-6	830
5:10	743	8:26	656	13:3	104
5:12-14	751	8:27	111	13:4	721
5:12-21	750	8:28	108, 368	13:5	381, 830
5:13	806, 808	8:28-39	626	13:6	538
5:14	173	8:29-30	105f.	13:8	366
5:15	808	8:30-31	628	13:9	168, 313
5:15-16	42	8:31-39	636	13:13	55, 126f., 226, 637, 713
5:17	173	8:32	763	13:14	452
5:18-19	751	8:34	740	14	276, 381, 391f., 427,
5:21	173	8:35	178		485
6:2-3	61	8:36	769	14:3	235
6:3	61, 445	8:38	154, 329, 754	14:4	827
6:3-7	63	8:39	640	14:5	478
6:4	127, 209, 740	9:1	675	14:9	725

14:10 235
14:13 367, 384
14:13-15 367
14:13-23 480
14:15 366f., 387
14:15-20 384
14:17 192, 428, 754
14:19 305, 654
14:20 384
14:21 389
14:23 352
15 816
15:1-3 479, 490, 638
15:3 108, 490
15:3-4 97, 109
15:4-5 658
15:11 500
15:13 95
15:14 184
15:16 209
15:17-22 395
15:18 141
15:19 95, 411, 594
15:20 138
15:22 411
15:22-23 817
15:23 649, 816
15:24 819
15:25 649, 812, 816
15:25-32 810
15:26 62, 810, 812, 815
15:26-27 816
15:27 409, 811f.
15:29 90
15:31 812, 816
16 54, 62, 835
16:1 130
16:1-2 815
16:3 833, 835
16:3-5 835
16:5 835
16:6 831
16:7 729
16:12 831
16:15 748, 829
16:16 836
16:17-20 827
16:18 151
16:22 837
16:23 62, 533, 683
16:25 43
16:33 3

1 CORINTHIANS
1 128, 169
1–2 630

1–3 16, 48, 828
1–4 8, 11, 39, 47, 50, 56,
    59, 125, 138, 184, 194,
    229, 366, 388, 393, 401,
    490, 572, 612, 682, 698,
    711, 725, 824
1–6 195, 531
1–7 810
1–11 644
1:1 28ff., 45, 52, 75,
    105, 174, 183, 188, 310,
    395, 397, 537, 620, 732,
    824, 836f.
1:1-2 77, 79
1:1-3 840
1:1-9 825
1:2 29, 31ff., 38, 45,
    85f., 149, 189, 203, 206,
    219, 231, 247, 299, 311,
    346, 489, 530, 544, 630,
    683, 697f., 736, 811f.,
    829, 835f.
1:3 34f., 588, 697
1:4 137, 170, 735, 808
1:4-5 125
1:4-7 96
1:4-8 17
1:4-9 500
1:5 37ff., 41, 42, 90,
    172, 365f., 589, 592,
    632
1:5-7 37, 585, 587
1:5-8 12, 726
1:6 37, 40f., 43f., 88, 91
1:7 36f., 40ff., 284, 339,
    382, 557, 586, 642, 646,
    662
1:8 36, 37, 41, 43f.,
    141f., 437
1:9 29, 37, 44ff., 77, 79,
    307, 309f., 461
1:10 52ff., 79, 90, 123,
    126, 129, 166, 180, 183,
    186, 189, 246f., 320,
    328, 337, 443, 537, 567,
    575, 615, 631, 661, 678,
    690, 712, 720, 730, 790,
    807, 824, 826, 828
1:10-12 5, 47ff., 127, 153,
    534, 537, 827, 829
1:10-13 121
1:10-17 3, 50ff., 537f.,
    571, 679, 733f., 738,
    768
1:10–2:5 16
1:10–2:16 366

1:10–4:13 184, 186
1:10–4:21 5, 8, 9, 47ff.,
    68, 193, 195, 363, 384,
    391, 399, 404, 537, 570,
    632, 780, 823
1:10–6:20 46f., 270
1:11 5, 7, 47, 54f., 126,
    194, 537, 567
1:11-12 127, 570
1:12 5, 8, 55ff., 127, 138,
    153, 166f., 169, 359,
    362, 384, 394ff., 404,
    537, 541, 704, 729
1:13 53, 56, 58ff., 63
1:13-15 247
1:13-17 52, 59, 767
1:14-15 61, 62
1:14-16 60, 61, 63
1:15 533
1:15-16 818
1:15–4:21 60
1:16 3, 62, 63, 829
1:16-17 49
1:17 9, 30, 61ff., 66ff.,
    89, 90, 94, 101, 111, 114,
    117, 158, 186, 191, 237,
    365, 384, 399, 585, 591
1:17-18 39
1:17-25 61, 89
1:17-31 365f.
1:17–2:2 67
1:17–2:16 121, 591
1:18 65, 68f., 72, 74, 76,
    94, 96, 101, 111, 117,
    387, 431, 489, 681, 720,
    744, 800
1:18-25 40, 50, 66f., 79,
    89, 92, 152, 176, 431
1:18-31 89, 186
1:18–2:5 51, 66f., 98,
    100f., 106, 116, 123, 156,
    191, 557
1:18–2:16 60, 64, 139,
    150f., 166
1:18–3:4 150, 152
1:18–3:23 53
1:18–4:21 245
1:19 69f., 111, 152, 169
1:20 65, 70ff., 79, 103f.,
    112, 151f.
1:21 68f., 72ff., 76, 94,
    98, 111, 207, 431, 742
1:22 14, 67, 69, 71, 74f.,
    489
1:22-23 77, 85
1:22-24 489

1:22-25   69f., 73, 82, 90
1:23   30, 67, 75f., 89, 92,
      117, 139, 725
1:23-24   102, 113
1:23-25   89, 95
1:24   29, 45, 65, 67, 69,
      73, 76f., 79f., 85, 98,
      310, 449
1:25   65, 75f., 80, 89, 93,
      95
1:26   3, 5, 79ff., 83, 90,
      104, 176f., 190, 314, 342
1:26-28   17, 106, 176
1:26-29   62, 82, 85
1:26-31   50, 67, 70, 78,
      89, 96, 431
1:27   73, 80, 184
1:27-28   67, 79, 82f.
1:27-29   84, 151
1:28   103, 235f., 255, 643
1:28-29   209
1:29   79, 84f., 153, 169,
      201, 215, 417
1:29-31   48, 171, 201, 215,
      634, 769
1:30   32, 65, 77, 79, 87,
      98, 102f., 203, 246f.,
      299, 449, 504, 800
1:30-31   84ff., 417
1:31   71, 84, 87, 90, 93,
      96, 153, 169, 201, 215
2:1   40, 65f., 90ff., 123,
      356, 557, 591, 662
2:1-2   40, 89, 93
2:1-3   176
2:1-4   39, 768
2:1-5   9f., 50, 56f., 64f.,
      67, 88f., 99, 101, 114,
      191, 365, 399, 431, 573,
      719, 733f., 768
2:1-3:4   49
2:2   27, 67, 75, 89ff.,
      102, 113, 139, 725
2:3   89f., 92ff., 158, 356
2:3-4   90
2:3-5   89, 176
2:4   89, 91, 110, 742
2:4-5   94ff., 98, 101, 114,
      147, 176, 191, 206, 594,
      605
2:5   66, 89f., 96, 591
2:6   9, 75, 83, 101ff.,
      105ff., 113f., 116, 123ff.,
      151, 342, 402, 452, 643
2:6-8   109
2:6-9   112

2:6-10   99
2:6-13   114
2:6-16   5, 16, 30, 48, 65,
      72f., 77, 85, 91, 96ff.,
      102, 122f., 125, 128, 136,
      138, 160, 176, 573, 592,
      626
2:6-3:4   50f., 156
2:6-3:20   14
2:7   83, 88, 91, 101f.,
      107f., 112, 114, 123,
      159f., 177, 217, 566,
      603, 644, 800
2:7-8   104ff.
2:7-10   112
2:7-13   101
2:8   102ff., 107f., 113, 151
2:8-9   116
2:9   101f., 107ff., 112f.,
      353
2:10   98, 101f., 106f.,
      109ff., 112f., 118, 663
2:10-11   110ff., 304
2:10-12   114, 126
2:10-13   99, 110, 115, 147,
      582, 592
2:10-14   603
2:11   97, 113, 117, 412,
      784
2:12   99, 102, 110, 112ff.,
      404
2:12-13   204, 800
2:13   88, 110, 113ff., 123
2:13-14   800
2:13-3:1   576
2:14   99, 110, 115ff., 124,
      785f.
2:14-15   115, 122, 401,
      686
2:14-16   99, 110, 115, 158
2:15   9, 99, 102, 116f.,
      160, 190, 481, 575, 588,
      630, 686, 711
2:15-16   112, 117ff.
2:16   53, 101, 112
3   169
3:1   9, 90, 102, 116, 121f.,
      127, 409, 575, 711
3:1-2   123ff., 172, 678f.
3:1-3   11
3:1-4   50, 99, 101, 115,
      117, 121ff., 128f., 136,
      314
3:1-9   57
3:1-23   16, 538
3:1-4:21   60

3:2   122, 158
3:2-3   126f.
3:3   54f., 111, 121, 124,
      154, 189, 309, 406, 615,
      623, 771
3:3-4   48, 304
3:3-9   63
3:4   111, 127ff., 132, 153,
      537, 631, 637
3:4-5   5
3:4-9   56
3:5   129ff., 145, 148, 587
3:5-9   7, 48, 55f., 128ff.,
      136, 138, 145, 150, 153f.,
      158f., 824
3:5-15   122, 289, 733
3:5-17   50, 122, 128f., 151
3:5-23   48, 51, 825
3:5-4:5   156, 165f.
3:5-4:13   184, 191
3:6   131ff., 135, 183, 395,
      825
3:6-7   130, 605
3:6-8   131
3:7   129, 132, 152, 163,
      218, 354, 459, 559, 680,
      712, 807
3:8   130, 132f., 136, 138,
      143, 419, 808
3:9   31, 130ff., 137, 158,
      831
3:9-15   146
3:10   133, 136ff., 147,
      158, 183, 384, 395, 657
3:10-15   128, 134, 135ff.,
      148, 164
3:11   27, 57, 136, 138ff.,
      153
3:12   136, 139ff.
3:12-13   136, 148
3:12-15   139, 190
3:13   136, 140ff., 161, 561
3:13-15   12, 43, 133,
      139f., 146, 148, 158,
      808, 821
3:14   133, 136, 163
3:14-15   136, 140, 142ff.,
      419
3:15   68, 136, 142, 144,
      148, 158, 164, 213
3:16   137, 146ff., 205f.,
      215, 232, 249, 257,
      263f., 411, 435, 443,
      501, 504, 687
3:16-17   18, 122, 129, 134,
      136, 139, 141, 145f., 197,

219, 237, 442, 455
3:16-18   366
3:17   12, 19, 139, 144,
  148ff., 151, 162, 190,
  299, 837
3:18   10f., 151f., 190,
  237, 242, 366, 368, 529,
  575, 638, 711, 773, 780
3:18-19   176
3:18-20   150f.
3:18-21   48, 366
3:18-23   9, 50, 122, 129,
  150f., 156ff., 768
3:19   321
3:19-20   152, 169
3:21   48, 84, 132, 152ff.,
  163, 201, 215
3:21-22   153f., 825
3:21-23   150, 153, 158,
  626, 636, 640
3:21ff.   252
3:22   17, 56f., 159, 166,
  329, 341, 404
3:22-23   245, 504f., 588,
  760
3:23   153ff., 157
4   50, 150, 167, 828
4:1   91, 158ff., 162, 420,
  671, 733
4:1-2   48, 159
4:1-5   7, 17, 28, 51, 65,
  118, 130, 133, 156ff.,
  230, 337, 340, 393,
  395f., 459, 533, 538,
  557, 573, 734, 746
4:1-13   825
4:1-21   9, 49, 56, 156f.,
  394, 768
4:1-23   51
4:2   105, 158, 160ff., 189,
  328
4:3   8f., 117, 158, 160f.,
  163, 183, 190, 227f.,
  401, 481, 681
4:3-4   117, 119, 401, 686
4:3-5   141, 159, 170, 232
4:4   117, 158, 161ff., 247,
  380f.
4:4-5   143
4:5   12, 132, 143, 158,
  161ff., 213, 245, 281,
  320, 437, 454, 686
4:6   8, 9, 11, 48f., 55ff.,
  159, 164ff., 170f., 184,
  190f., 201, 209, 215,
  366, 638, 733

4:6-7   190, 201, 385
4:6-8   165
4:6-13   51, 156, 164ff.,
  184
4:7   6, 36, 38, 48, 60, 84,
  163, 165, 170ff., 182,
  201, 215, 232, 295, 315,
  317, 385, 562, 733
4:7-13   166
4:8   12, 39, 42, 96, 103,
  110, 125, 157, 165, 171,
  174, 178, 339, 437, 523,
  557, 715
4:8-9   175
4:8-11   82
4:8-13   36, 39, 93, 159,
  182, 382, 395, 719, 733
4:8-17   135
4:9   165, 173f., 176ff.,
  180, 234, 521, 715, 732,
  771
4:9-11   199
4:9-13   10, 13, 20, 93, 96,
  431, 573, 734
4:10   81, 96, 165, 175,
  464, 780
4:10-13   17, 768
4:11   178, 820
4:11-12   178
4:11-13   90, 165, 176f.,
  186, 193, 410, 417, 439,
  768
4:12   178f., 187, 225,
  399f., 404, 416, 808,
  821, 831
4:12-13   178f., 241
4:13   175, 178, 180, 244,
  820, 824
4:14   123, 172, 183f., 189,
  237, 464
4:14-16   125
4:14-17   166, 178, 192,
  245
4:14-21   7, 37, 51, 156,
  182ff., 194, 199, 395,
  733
4:15   28, 59, 183ff., 192,
  395f., 409, 675, 807
4:15-17   138, 489
4:16   30, 52, 180f., 183f.,
  186ff., 291, 328, 487,
  490, 545, 632, 824
4:16-17   18, 175, 183, 185,
  224, 241
4:17   33, 127, 157, 183,
  186ff., 307, 311, 395,

464, 518, 530, 698, 736,
  817f., 821, 835
4:17-7:40   188
4:18   8, 10, 11, 49, 59, 96,
  169, 185, 189f., 193, 201,
  205, 222, 366, 444, 637,
  711, 740
4:18-19   48, 194, 638, 662
4:18-20   8, 192
4:18-21   166, 183, 359,
  362, 401, 710, 763, 815,
  817, 825
4:19   569, 819f.
4:19-20   191f., 194f., 206
4:20   16, 173, 192, 242,
  754
4:21   192ff., 195, 662
5   11, 47, 190, 195, 228
5-6   9, 50, 194, 393
5-16   47
5:1   5, 18, 47, 194, 197,
  199ff., 231, 240, 250,
  278, 530, 570, 763
5:1-2   197, 199, 395
5:1-5   32, 191, 198ff.,
  214, 250, 362, 431, 455,
  627, 768
5:1-8   221, 230
5:1-13   8, 19, 20, 47, 192,
  195ff., 229, 231, 243,
  248, 250, 267, 442, 733
5:1-6:20   194ff.
5:2   11, 194, 197, 199,
  201ff., 215, 221, 299,
  366, 638
5:3   202, 226, 247, 464,
  578
5:3-4   193, 202ff., 226,
  260, 597, 657, 665, 670,
  696
5:3-5   96, 197, 203, 220,
  227, 467
5:4   95, 194, 205f., 208,
  247
5:4-5   147, 197, 239, 833,
  837
5:5   12, 43, 68, 142, 143,
  201, 203, 206, 208ff.,
  216, 221, 346, 565
5:6   11, 146, 194, 201,
  215f., 218, 417, 769,
  773
5:6-7   227
5:6-8   44, 197, 209, 214ff.,
  247, 363, 438
5:7   197, 215ff., 221, 224,

228, 234, 239, 245, 487, 601, 820
5:7-8 17f., 566, 603
5:8 132, 215f., 218ff., 246, 440
5:9 6, 13, 15, 197, 200, 220, 267, 274, 464, 811
5:9-10 221ff., 226, 232, 243, 273
5:9-11 7, 199, 260, 300, 457
5:9-13 197, 220ff.
5:10 6, 224f., 300, 407, 671
5:10-11 227, 241f., 245, 267, 357f., 455, 464
5:11 179, 188, 209, 212, 218, 221ff., 227, 416, 661
5:12 163, 221, 226, 233
5:12-13 17, 221, 226ff.
5:13 197f., 221, 226
6 4, 190, 195f., 479, 730
6:1 196, 229ff., 237, 240ff., 246, 570
6:1-5 60, 459
6:1-6 17, 229ff., 337, 557
6:1-11 4, 8, 47, 192, 195f., 224, 226, 228ff., 478, 627, 746, 828
6:2 146, 175, 227f., 230, 232, 234ff., 242, 249, 263, 437, 710
6:2-4 161, 220, 229, 232
6:2-6 229
6:3 146, 217, 232, 234f., 263, 522, 566, 603
6:3-4 230, 234ff.
6:4 83, 235, 239, 242, 295, 822
6:5 8, 163, 184, 229f., 236f., 240, 562, 697, 774
6:5-6 229ff.
6:6 229, 232, 237f., 240, 298, 681
6:7 18, 199, 229, 238, 239ff., 246, 248, 763
6:7-8 281
6:7-11 239f., 314
6:8 232, 239ff., 246
6:8-10 229, 240, 245, 248
6:8-11 229
6:9 146f., 151, 173, 229,

232, 239f., 242, 246, 249, 263, 437, 464, 710, 773, 798
6:9-10 192, 197, 225, 250, 289, 455, 754, 795, 799, 837
6:9-11 14, 18, 44, 128, 196, 212, 436, 459, 576
6:9-20 196
6:10 239, 241ff., 754, 798
6:10-11 4, 16, 225
6:10-14 260
6:11 32, 61, 86, 110, 144, 162, 203, 207, 229, 239, 242, 244ff., 251, 299, 440, 577, 604, 743, 773
6:12 138, 251ff., 262, 276, 280, 347, 362, 366, 384, 386, 478f., 521, 589, 624
6:12-13 201, 250f., 261, 276, 365, 384
6:12-14 211, 251, 778
6:12-20 4, 12, 18, 20, 195ff., 228, 240, 242f., 249ff., 267, 271, 273ff., 360, 363, 391, 455, 463, 573, 627
6:13 12, 83, 250f., 253ff., 260, 276, 342, 382, 384, 551, 624, 643, 744, 785
6:13-14 12, 251, 253ff., 439, 624, 715, 776
6:14 17, 251, 253ff., 800
6:14-17 18
6:15 146, 257ff., 263, 602
6:15-16 250, 253
6:15-17 250f., 257, 262
6:16 146, 263, 280, 681, 710
6:16-17 257, 259f.
6:17 204, 250f.
6:18 250f., 257f., 260ff., 265, 463f., 805
6:18-20 251, 260, 262
6:19 110, 146f., 204, 249, 260, 710
6:19-20 149, 251, 256, 258, 260, 263ff.
6:20 245, 320
7 4, 10, 12, 47, 201, 267f., 307, 403, 491, 497, 828

7-16 5, 221, 250, 531
7:1 5, 215, 221f., 228, 262, 267, 269, 271, 273ff., 284, 290, 298, 300, 311, 323, 325, 328, 330, 350, 354, 362, 364f., 502, 522, 570, 624, 811, 823
7:1-6 12
7:1-7 195, 250, 268f., 271ff., 287, 289, 290f., 573, 631, 702, 705, 715
7:1-16 47, 269ff., 288, 316
7:1-24 267f., 322, 350, 355
7:1-25 289
7:1-35 702
7:1-40 4, 5, 8, 20, 267ff., 491
7:1–16:12 266f.
7:2 197, 200, 250, 268, 273f., 276ff., 283, 287, 325, 403, 624
7:2-4 274, 277
7:2-5 274, 283, 291
7:2-6 273, 285, 327, 340, 346
7:2-7 271
7:3 274, 279, 283
7:3-4 250, 274, 277ff., 286
7:3-5 276, 279
7:4 253, 262, 280
7:5 47, 209, 241f., 250, 272ff., 278ff., 283, 286, 290, 300, 302, 320, 436, 454, 536
7:6 270, 272ff., 283f., 298, 327, 337, 536
7:7 271ff., 277, 283ff., 287f., 313, 323, 346f., 586f., 618
7:8 215, 268, 270, 273, 275f., 287f., 290, 297f., 337, 403
7:8-9 268, 271, 273, 284f., 286f., 291, 298
7:9 273, 278, 283, 287ff., 302, 316f., 436
7:10 268ff., 286, 289, 291ff., 298, 302, 328, 331, 355, 412, 545, 632
7:10-11 268, 271, 290f., 297f., 331f.
7:10-16 285

7:11   268, 288, 290, 294ff., 298, 302f., 317f., 349, 483
7:12   268, 286, 291ff., 302, 331, 337, 482, 681
7:12-13   293, 297ff., 302, 304
7:12-14   297, 302f., 305
7:12-16   268, 271, 291f., 296ff., 309, 328, 356
7:13   355
7:14   32, 297ff., 304, 346, 661, 671
7:15   290, 294, 297f., 302, 307, 309, 317f., 697
7:15-16   297, 302f.
7:15-24   29
7:15-28   16
7:16   68, 297ff., 303ff.
7:17   127, 189, 304f., 308ff., 314, 319ff., 330, 530, 698, 700, 736, 812
7:17-24   79, 268, 305, 306ff., 318, 324, 330, 606
7:18   309, 311f., 314ff., 318, 325, 330, 360
7:18-19   308f., 315, 318
7:19   17f., 311, 314f., 318, 384, 427f., 430, 478, 507
7:20   308, 310f., 314f., 320f., 330
7:20-24   3, 5
7:21   6, 302, 308f., 315ff., 330f., 349, 385, 410, 671, 829
7:21-22   314
7:21-23   308
7:21-24   308, 315
7:22   264, 309, 315, 318ff., 395, 523, 829
7:22-23   308, 315f., 318, 340
7:23   315, 319f.
7:24   52, 308, 310f., 314f., 320ff., 807
7:25   53, 162, 267f., 270, 274, 287, 291f., 298, 322ff., 327, 329, 330, 333, 350, 356f., 362, 412, 624, 632, 811
7:25-26   325
7:25-27   325

7:25-28   324ff., 335f., 342f., 345
7:25-35   326
7:25-38   268f., 273, 285, 287f., 355
7:25-40   16, 51, 267f., 271, 322ff., 573
7:26   215, 262, 270, 275f., 283, 323ff., 333f., 347, 353f., 418, 565
7:26-27   268, 332
7:26-31   12
7:26-38   284
7:27   6, 324ff., 330, 332, 671
7:27-28   170, 315, 325, 327
7:28   269, 276, 278, 295, 302, 316f., 323ff., 328ff., 332ff., 349f., 354f., 385, 483, 805
7:28-35   326
7:29   278, 329, 337ff., 346, 465, 471, 536, 798
7:29-30   333
7:29-31   17, 72, 275, 324, 329f., 335f., 340ff., 356, 573, 650, 746, 775
7:29-34   336, 351
7:29-35   16, 322, 324, 329, 334, 346, 536, 626
7:30-31   344
7:31   17, 317, 330, 341f., 410, 421
7:32   324, 328, 336, 342ff., 351
7:32-33   343ff.
7:32-34   324, 336, 347, 615
7:32-35   335, 351
7:33   334f.
7:33-34   282
7:34   288, 290, 323, 325, 332, 345f., 353, 578
7:35   275, 298, 324, 328, 336f., 346ff., 350f., 589
7:36   269, 276, 302, 323f., 336, 350ff., 484, 638, 805
7:36-37   356
7:36-38   315, 322f., 325ff., 332, 335f., 346, 350, 355, 357
7:36-40   16, 349ff.

7:37   268, 323f., 328f., 350f., 353f., 418, 808
7:38   132, 323f., 326, 350, 354
7:39   295f., 302f., 331, 351, 355f., 483, 523, 565, 730, 800
7:39-40   268, 288, 290, 324, 350
7:40   53, 268, 270, 291, 298, 328, 356f.
8   237, 386, 402, 431, 471, 476f., 569, 810
8-10   4, 5, 11, 16, 57, 147, 223, 254, 260, 267, 311, 357, 373, 379, 386, 393, 441, 453, 463, 473, 477, 487, 531f., 570, 711, 773
8:1   11, 39, 137, 267, 274, 276, 330, 357, 360, 362, 364ff., 369f., 379, 383f., 386, 393, 453, 463, 471, 476f., 479, 501, 539, 570, 585, 624, 632, 638, 652, 657, 733, 811, 828
8:1-2   645
8:1-3   358, 363ff., 377f., 388, 479, 539, 592, 828
8:1-13   15f., 39, 358ff., 363ff., 392, 402, 441, 477, 780
8:1-10:22   4, 14, 51, 196, 323, 569, 576, 627, 828
8:1-11:1   5, 8f., 47, 243, 357
8:2   10, 151, 365ff., 529, 575, 631, 638, 711
8:2-3   367ff., 572, 624, 627, 712, 774
8:3   108, 365, 368
8:4   267, 274, 276, 330, 362, 364f., 370ff., 383f., 386, 393, 471, 476f., 501, 539, 570, 593, 624, 723, 811
8:4-6   359, 363, 365, 369ff., 377ff., 388, 443, 459, 463
8:5   3, 370ff.
8:5-6   370f., 582
8:6   35, 155, 370f., 373ff., 396, 504, 587f.
8:7   4, 14, 58, 147, 162, 360, 365, 370ff., 378f.,

381ff., 386f., 402, 471, 476, 483f., 530, 592
8:7-8 388
8:7-12 367, 380
8:7-13 358f., 363f., 369, 376ff., 390, 430f., 435, 441, 460, 477, 479f.
8:8 254, 362, 381ff., 386, 389, 393, 427f., 477, 566, 603, 761
8:9 79, 252, 378, 383ff., 389, 394, 410, 488, 521
8:9-10 6, 170, 359, 362, 427
8:9-12 383, 411
8:10 47, 137, 359f., 362f., 365f., 385ff., 391, 441, 454, 463, 479, 657
8:10-11 627
8:10-12 378, 384f., 389
8:11 68, 365f., 375f., 378, 381, 387ff., 631
8:12 158, 387ff., 561, 805
8:13 363, 378, 382, 384, 389ff., 393f., 396, 402, 424, 435, 464
8:13–9:1 430
9 8f., 359, 390, 414, 427, 433ff., 486, 810, 819, 828
9:1 141, 362, 384, 392, 394ff., 402, 422f., 523, 732, 808
9:1-2 28, 138, 392, 394, 398, 400f., 421, 620, 719, 732
9:1-3 183, 363, 399, 402, 476f.
9:1-14 393
9:1-17 733
9:1-19 15, 162
9:1-23 28, 378, 385, 710
9:1-27 16, 358, 363, 392, 626, 734, 768, 825
9:2 396f., 409, 523, 770
9:3 8ff., 117, 161, 163, 392, 396, 398, 400f., 422, 424, 437, 476, 481, 686, 711
9:3-14 3, 9, 397ff., 413, 415f.
9:3-18 252, 363
9:4 392, 401ff., 413, 416
9:4-5 402

9:4-6 401ff., 405, 407, 410, 416
9:4-7 406
9:4-14 392, 416, 421f.
9:4-18 179
9:5 57, 288, 401f., 694
9:5-6 401, 729
9:6 400f., 403f., 412, 620, 710
9:7 329, 400, 405f.
9:7-8 413
9:8 399, 402, 405f., 416, 707, 771
9:8-10 400
9:9 316, 406, 409, 679
9:9-10 406ff.
9:10 406, 410, 431, 470
9:10-12 811
9:11 407, 410, 576
9:11-12 400, 409f.
9:12 8, 317, 392, 396, 398, 400, 402, 409ff., 414ff., 421, 432, 470, 479, 640
9:13 146, 400, 411f., 470, 740
9:13-14 392, 410ff., 470
9:13-19 17
9:14 91, 291, 400, 412ff., 421, 440, 545, 557, 632, 812
9:15 111, 317, 402, 410, 415ff., 420, 634
9:15-16 769f.
9:15-18 392ff., 398, 410f., 414ff., 424f., 432, 437, 734
9:15-23 719
9:15-27 402
9:16 111, 329, 415, 418f., 431, 440
9:16-17 415
9:16-18 414, 432
9:17 111, 159, 415, 418ff.
9:17-18 423, 425
9:18 341, 415ff., 420ff., 425, 440, 479
9:19 302, 384f., 415, 420, 423ff., 429, 433, 439
9:19-22 393, 423
9:19-23 9, 18, 276, 311, 362f., 385, 390, 392, 394, 402, 411, 422ff., 437, 476f., 479, 486

9:19-27 219
9:20 427ff., 431
9:20-22 423ff., 482, 489
9:20-23 425, 477, 484
9:21 17, 313f., 424, 429ff., 475, 483
9:22 68, 306, 407, 423f., 427, 429ff., 490
9:23 423, 431ff., 438, 440
9:24 146, 432, 434ff.
9:24-27 2, 393, 402, 433ff., 452, 459, 648
9:24–10:22 435
9:25 434ff., 474, 800
9:25-27 434f.
9:26 158, 437f.
9:26-27 393, 434, 437, 442
9:27 432, 435, 438ff., 538
10 370
10–14 492
10:1 437, 452, 473, 501, 576, 712
10:1-2 443ff.
10:1-4 362, 432, 444, 449, 459
10:1-5 11, 435, 441ff., 451f., 458
10:1-6 61
10:1-10 451
10:1-11 442, 464
10:1-12 440, 460
10:1-13 128, 363, 441ff., 463f., 563
10:1-14 442, 464
10:1-22 16, 243, 358f., 378, 385f., 433ff., 438, 441ff., 483, 490, 767
10:2 445, 606
10:3 444
10:3-4 446f.
10:4 442, 444, 447ff., 457, 474, 550
10:5 427, 449f., 452f., 458
10:6 443, 451ff., 458, 679
10:6-10 454
10:6-12 450
10:6-13 442, 450ff.
10:7 258, 358, 441, 452ff., 457, 464
10:7-8 360, 453, 471

10:7-10   442, 444, 451ff.,
           460
10:8   197, 258, 441,
           455f., 642
10:9   447, 451, 456f.,
           460, 463, 474
10:9-10   68, 387
10:10   452, 457f.
10:11   17, 175, 184, 408,
           444, 451, 458f.
10:11-12   451, 464
10:12   132, 384, 443, 451,
           459f., 474, 642, 827
10:12-14   452
10:12-22   464
10:13   44, 245, 440, 442,
           451, 460ff., 464
10:14   184, 258, 260, 358,
           389, 460, 463f., 471,
           807
10:14-22   18, 223, 358ff.,
           363, 386, 390f., 437,
           441, 446, 451, 454, 460,
           462ff., 564
10:15   337, 463ff., 525,
           678
10:15-16   525
10:15-22   464
10:16   45, 465ff., 473,
           482, 531, 550, 554, 566,
           603, 672
10:16-17   463, 473, 475,
           533, 551, 559
10:16-18   463, 471
10:16-21   361
10:16-22   532
10:17   19, 446, 466,
           469f., 473, 487, 531,
           534, 563f., 572,
           602
10:18   79, 463, 465, 470f.
10:18-22   452
10:19   337, 471
10:19-20   370ff., 463
10:19-21   465
10:19-22   378, 388, 391
10:20   471f., 474, 533
10:20-21   463, 565, 575,
           578
10:21   463, 467f., 472ff.,
           476, 533, 539
10:21-22   449, 456
10:22   60, 447, 463,
           472ff.
10:23   137, 251f., 347,

362, 366, 384, 478f.,
           589, 657
10:23-24   477f., 488ff.
10:23-29   359f.
10:23-30   18, 390
10:23-33   15, 425, 428,
           490
10:23–11:1 358ff., 363,
           474, 475ff., 487, 498
10:24   478ff., 483, 485,
           638, 666
10:25   117, 363, 435,
           478ff., 483
10:25-26   276, 360,
           477f., 487
10:25-27   478
10:25-29   380
10:25-30   379, 480, 488
10:26   480ff., 487, 507
10:27   117, 298, 429, 477,
           481ff., 486f., 507, 681
10:27-28   363
10:27-29   360, 478
10:28   357, 477, 481,
           483, 485, 488
10:28-29   477f., 480,
           483ff.
10:29   384, 476, 478,
           485f.
10:29-30   8, 276, 394,
           402, 476, 478, 480, 483,
           485ff., 733
10:29-33   9
10:30   9, 51, 480, 482,
           488
10:30–11:1 359, 477
10:31   402, 478, 488
10:31-32   487ff.
10:31-33   18, 478
10:31–11:1 391, 477, 485
10:32   18, 237, 427, 484,
           488f., 516, 734
10:32-33   478
10:33   68, 252, 306, 427,
           478, 484, 488ff., 589,
           638, 666
10:33–11:1 479, 499
11   12
11–14   500
11:1   18, 183, 187, 292,
           357, 390, 437, 479, 484,
           489f.
11:2   7, 491, 499ff., 512,
           531, 536, 545, 548,
           721

11:2-6   498ff., 525, 528,
           685
11:2-16   4f., 8, 10, 12, 47,
           52, 267, 269f., 491ff.,
           531, 571, 573, 631, 638,
           684, 698, 702f., 705
11:3   35, 491, 495, 497,
           499ff., 506, 508, 513,
           515, 517, 519, 526, 528,
           535, 588, 760
11:3-5   492
11:3-6   495
11:3-7   495f., 525
11:3-10   495, 512
11:3-16   500, 531
11:4   492, 497, 505ff.,
           510, 514, 516
11:4-5   495, 499, 501,
           544, 690
11:4-6   513f., 523, 525ff.
11:4-7   495f.
11:4-15   702
11:5   492, 495, 501, 505,
           508ff., 525f., 578, 701,
           703, 706
11:5-6   495f., 505, 508,
           510ff., 529
11:6   510, 512, 514, 527f.
11:7   492, 495ff., 501,
           504, 510, 512, 513ff.,
           517ff.
11:7-9   495, 504, 508,
           514, 524
11:7-10   497
11:7-12   495, 512ff., 527
11:7-15   496
11:8   501, 504, 524
11:8-9   495, 502f., 513,
           515ff., 523
11:9   517, 522f., 664
11:10   353, 492, 495, 497,
           502, 513f., 516, 518ff.,
           522f., 565
11:10-12   524
11:11   522
11:11-12   495, 502, 512,
           517, 522ff.
11:11-16   512
11:12   412, 501, 503ff.,
           517, 524, 588
11:13   19, 465, 492,
           495f., 498, 514, 525ff.,
           706, 713
11:13-15   491, 497, 523
11:13-16   524ff.

11:14   506, 526f.
11:14-15   495f., 525ff.
11:15   492, 496f., 510, 520, 526ff.
11:16   33, 151, 189, 311, 492, 527, 529f., 698, 711, 736, 835
11:17   283, 291, 491, 500, 535f., 543, 545, 547
11:17-22   82, 531ff., 536, 567, 570, 684, 733
11:17-34   3, 5, 19, 226, 267, 465, 469, 491f., 500, 531ff., 571f., 612, 615, 837
11:18   5, 32, 53, 531, 534ff., 539f., 567, 615, 690
11:18-19   5, 535, 538
11:19   141, 537ff., 586
11:20   272, 473, 536f., 539f., 567, 683, 690
11:20-22   47, 535
11:21   531, 534f., 540ff., 567f., 589
11:21-22   537, 568
11:22   19, 500, 531ff., 540, 543ff., 545, 547, 567, 569
11:22-23   491
11:23   291, 468, 499, 547ff., 720f., 726
11:23-24   549ff.
11:23-25   179, 466, 724
11:23-26   531f., 545ff., 567
11:23-32   531
11:24   467, 469, 554f., 672, 763, 769
11:25   468f., 534, 541, 547, 554ff.
11:26   12, 16f., 473, 547, 553, 555ff.
11:27   132, 532f., 567
11:27-32   532, 567
11:27-34   163
11:28   538
11:28-32   538, 568
11:28-34   531
11:29   19, 470, 533, 551, 568, 602, 612, 837
11:30   17, 148, 329, 355, 518, 533, 538, 741, 744, 767, 800
11:30-32   210, 211, 532
11:31   234, 603

11:31-32   533
11:32   12, 245, 532, 539
11:33   52, 132, 535f., 540, 542, 567f., 615, 807
11:33-34   531ff., 536f., 540, 567ff., 690
11:34   500, 533f., 536, 543, 568f., 812
12   16, 53, 564, 570f., 576, 623, 629, 652, 655, 690, 696, 709
12–13   491
12–14   5, 10f., 16, 39, 42, 51, 159, 267, 323, 391, 491, 505, 531, 536, 570, 577, 582, 587, 597f., 602, 627, 679, 682, 688, 701f., 711, 713, 716, 828
12:1   267, 274, 443, 491, 570, 574, 654f., 712, 719, 811
12:1-3   14, 510, 570, 572, 574, 583, 626, 642, 652, 656, 678f.
12:1-5   571
12:1-19   571
12:1-25   571
12:1–14:40   363
12:2   4, 14, 574, 576ff., 632, 829
12:2-3   697
12:3   58, 110, 574ff., 578ff., 582, 653, 656, 667, 670f., 693, 719, 837
12:4   42, 284, 585, 587, 611, 617
12:4-6   35, 110, 583, 585ff., 599, 618
12:4-11   36, 572, 583ff., 601ff., 606, 617, 646
12:4-30   572, 623f.
12:4-31   582ff.
12:5   586, 830
12:6   571, 583, 586f., 594, 599
12:6-12   571
12:7   36, 347, 541, 583, 585, 587ff., 590, 598f., 620, 625, 628, 662, 726
12:7-10   583
12:7-11   588, 609, 611, 633, 647, 652, 656, 666, 670
12:8   39, 48, 102, 237,

365f., 586, 590, 633, 641, 644, 694, 800
12:8-9   588, 599
12:8-10   572, 585, 587ff., 590ff., 599, 609, 617f., 620f., 627, 632, 643f., 662, 690
12:8-11   40, 582
12:9   578, 585, 590, 605f., 632
12:9-10   621
12:10   505, 571, 586f., 590, 621f., 630, 655f., 659, 665, 670, 691ff., 696
12:11   36, 583, 585ff., 593, 598ff., 606, 611, 618, 782
12:12   60, 412, 583, 600ff., 607, 611, 617, 784
12:12-13   470, 600f., 617
12:12-14   572, 608ff., 608, 644
12:12-26   19, 258, 564, 572, 583, 617
12:13   3, 5, 19, 172, 247, 312, 470, 536, 583, 600f., 603ff., 607, 612
12:13-17   571
12:14   583, 600f., 607, 608f., 611, 615, 618
12:14-20   601
12:15-16   605, 608ff.
12:15-20   19, 583, 601, 607, 617
12:15-26   607ff.
12:16   610
12:17   605, 608ff.
12:17-20   610
12:18   541, 583, 609ff., 614, 618, 649, 661, 748
12:18-19   571
12:18-20   609
12:19   588, 609ff., 617
12:20   572, 608ff., 612, 661
12:20-25   571
12:21   605, 608f., 612ff.
12:21-25   236
12:21-26   19, 583, 601, 607, 617, 623
12:22   612f.
12:22-23   605
12:22-24   608f., 614
12:23   571, 713

12:23-24   613f.
12:24   347, 583, 611, 614,
                618
12:24-26   609
12:25   53, 344, 537, 572,
                614f.
12:26   571, 602, 614ff.
12:26-31   571
12:26-40   571
12:27   603, 611, 615,
                617f., 644
12:27-30   572
12:27-31   583, 609, 616ff.
12:28   571f., 583ff., 594,
  603, 618ff., 622f., 633,
  662f., 694, 711, 732, 734
12:28-29   586
12:28-30   591, 595, 617,
                630, 658, 692
12:29   585, 596, 654
12:29-30   572, 585,
  617ff., 622f., 625, 662,
                684
12:30   594, 659
12:31   576, 585, 587,
  623ff., 626, 637, 651,
                654, 659, 666
13   16, 366, 369, 442,
  570ff., 589, 635, 652,
  654, 658, 690, 828
13–14   589, 598
13:1   11, 42, 175, 269,
  502, 522, 572f., 598,
  629ff., 648, 715, 734,
                828
13:1-2   643, 662
13:1-3   366, 572, 585,
  626ff., 636, 649, 654
13:1-13   20, 625ff.
13:2   39, 105, 159, 369,
  586, 592f., 629, 631ff.,
  644, 656, 662, 800
13:3   629, 633ff., 662
13:3-7   626
13:4   126, 367, 623, 636
13:4-5   636ff.
13:4-6   628
13:4-7   626ff., 635ff.,
                641, 654
13:5   479, 666
13:6   636, 639
13:7   410, 639f., 643
13:8   83, 369, 571f.,
  585f., 593, 642ff.,
                648f., 662
13:8-11   342

13:8-12   40, 592, 642
13:8-13   36, 366, 570,
  627f., 633, 641ff., 654
13:9   641f., 644f., 648f.
13:9-10   644ff.
13:9-12   649
13:10   83, 643, 752
13:10-11   678
13:10-12   649
13:11   642, 645ff., 679
13:12   125, 445, 641f.,
  644ff., 647ff., 712, 820
13:13   640, 642f., 649ff.,
                661, 748
14   8, 16, 570f., 589,
  595ff., 602, 612, 615,
  620f., 623, 627, 642,
  644, 654, 690, 699, 761
14:1   572, 574ff., 623ff.,
  626ff., 637, 642, 653ff.,
  656, 658, 665f., 688,
                694, 712
14:1-4   658
14:1-5   506, 596, 598,
  625, 642, 652ff., 661f.,
  665f., 668, 674
14:1-6   40, 633, 682
14:1-19   652
14:1-25   625, 630ff.,
  652ff., 679, 688, 692,
                710, 712
14:1-33   20
14:1-40   646
14:2   105, 159, 571, 578,
  598, 631, 653, 656,
                669f., 693
14:2-3   653f.
14:2-4   655ff., 689
14:2-5   653
14:3   653, 655, 657, 660,
  686, 695f., 704
14:3-5   137, 479, 652f.,
                662
14:4   479, 571, 590, 653,
  655ff., 669, 693
14:5   36, 571, 599, 616,
  623, 625, 651, 653ff.,
  658ff., 666, 668, 676,
  684, 692, 721
14:6   39, 365, 571ff.,
  585f., 592f., 621, 624,
  630, 633, 644, 652f.,
  655ff., 661ff., 667ff.,
  674, 678, 688, 690ff.,
  695, 709, 733f., 768
14:6-12   668, 674, 692

14:6-13   668, 692
14:6-17   366
14:6-19   652
14:7   661, 663f., 667
14:7-8   663f.
14:7-9   661
14:7-12   653
14:7-13   669
14:8   438, 661, 664, 667
14:9   412, 661, 664f.,
                667, 704, 784
14:10   665, 781, 819
14:10-11   664f., 704
14:10-12   598, 661
14:11   665
14:12   137, 412, 571,
  596f., 616, 623f., 641,
  652, 661, 663, 665ff.,
  668ff., 680, 690, 694,
  696, 709, 784, 808
14:13   389, 571, 578, 599,
  653, 656f., 659, 668f.,
                692
14:13-14   656
14:13-17   652, 656
14:13-19   598, 667ff.
14:14   204, 596, 598,
  653, 656, 667ff., 671,
                674
14:14-15   193, 205, 573,
  598, 630, 656ff., 666,
  668, 671, 674f., 688
14:14-17   19, 668
14:14-19   692
14:15   578, 661, 668f.,
  670f., 674f., 678, 690,
                709, 739, 763
14:15-16   676
14:15-19   768
14:16   168, 598, 670ff.,
                674, 684f.
14:16-17   6, 170, 668ff.,
                675
14:17   137, 385, 620, 652,
                672ff.
14:18   61, 571, 573, 646,
  656, 661, 667, 669,
  674ff., 678, 709,
                733f.
14:18-19   653, 658, 668
14:19   185, 653, 656, 661,
  668, 670f., 675f., 679,
                682
14:20   103, 125, 465, 646,
  677ff., 681, 690
14:20-25   652, 676ff.

14:21   406, 677, 679ff.,
         707, 788
14:21-25   678
14:22   132, 571, 655f.,
        677f., 680ff., 684
14:22-24   298
14:23   10, 18, 32, 272,
   536, 571, 656, 672, 677,
   680ff., 683ff., 686, 688,
      690f., 694, 697, 757
14:23-24   596, 702
14:23-25   681, 690
14:24   117, 163, 483, 655,
      677, 684, 691, 693f.
14:24-25   19, 677, 682,
           685ff., 695
14:25   141, 163, 677
14:26   19, 137, 492, 536,
   541, 571f., 585f., 621,
   652f., 656, 662f., 671,
   684, 688ff., 695ff., 702,
                          706
14:26-29   596
14:26-33   689ff., 710, 713
14:26-40   510, 652,
              688ff., 702
14:27   571, 653, 656f.,
               691ff.
14:27-28   598f., 669,
           688f., 691
14:27-33   663, 684
14:28   483, 598, 656,
   659, 691ff., 695, 702,
                          706
14:29   562, 586, 596f.,
     656, 692ff., 703f.
14:29-31   596, 688f., 691
14:29-32   691
14:29-33   595
14:30   483, 663, 691,
               702, 706
14:30-31   695
14:31   623, 655, 658, 691,
      693ff., 702, 706
14:32   596, 656, 666,
     692, 695f., 704, 707
14:32-33   688f., 701, 704
14:33   33, 189, 311, 530,
   571, 696ff., 699ff., 706,
   709f., 713, 718, 736,
               812, 835
14:33-35   700
14:33-38   714, 733
14:34   406, 679, 697f.,
        705ff., 708

14:34-35   688,   695,
       697f., 699ff., 710
14:35   696, 703ff., 707f.,
               708, 710
14:36   33, 60, 189, 697f.,
       710f., 718, 835
14:36-37   393
14:36-38   689, 699, 701,
   704, 712, 716, 719, 721,
               734, 761, 768
14:36-40   708ff.
14:37   8, 10f., 151, 313,
   529, 573, 575, 586, 620,
   638, 656, 710ff.
14:38   710, 712f., 719,
                          837
14:39   52, 132, 567, 571,
   623f., 637, 655f., 693,
                          807
14:39-40   688, 701, 709,
                      712f.
14:40   571, 688, 695,
     697, 699, 713
15   5, 173, 255f., 397,
   570, 573, 642, 715f.,
                          778
15:1   443, 548, 717,
        718ff., 827
15:1-2   713, 718ff., 742,
                          808
15:1-11   40, 160, 714,
   717ff., 737, 740f., 746,
               748, 788
15:1-22   746
15:1-28   17
15:1-34   776
15:1-35   776
15:1-58   4, 573, 713
15:2   68, 659, 718ff., 744
15:3   203, 499, 548, 551,
   718, 721ff., 763, 773,
                          806
15:3-5   365, 716, 718,
   720ff., 736, 743, 807,
                          834
15:3-7   721, 742
15:3-8   395
15:3-28   721
15:4   723, 741, 746
15:4-7   404
15:5   57, 722ff., 731
15:5-7   30, 719
15:5-8   743
15:6   355, 729ff., 744,
   748, 781, 800, 820

15:6-7   722, 729
15:6-8   729
15:7   174, 403, 729, 731
15:8   395, 716, 719,
        732ff., 736
15:8-10   768
15:8-11   10, 395, 721
15:9   29, 734f.
15:9-10   137, 328, 733,
   736, 768, 770, 772
15:10   735f., 742, 831
15:10-11   75
15:11   713, 718f., 736f.,
               742, 768
15:12   8, 10, 12, 42, 123,
   256, 276, 557, 631, 713,
   724, 726, 730, 740ff.,
   748f., 763, 773, 775,
                          807
15:12-13   739, 766
15:12-19   397, 437, 714,
   721, 737ff., 748, 762f.,
                          768
15:12-28   17, 717, 721,
                          737
15:12-34   714, 737f., 762
15:13   726, 738, 741ff.
15:14   73, 420, 721, 726,
   735, 739, 741f., 744,
               748, 775
15:14-15   772
15:14-16   739
15:14-19   721, 808
15:15   670, 726, 743f.,
                          746
15:16   713, 726, 738
15:17   724, 726, 739,
   744f., 748, 775, 806
15:17-18   743f.
15:17-19   739, 750
15:18   68, 355, 387,
   744f., 748f., 775, 800
15:19   744f.
15:20   355, 649, 661,
   726, 748f., 750, 753,
               800, 829
15:20-22   738, 746, 759
15:20-28   16, 643, 714,
   726, 737f., 745ff., 762,
   768, 774, 788, 807
15:21   749, 752, 792
15:21-22   749f., 777,
        787ff., 794ff.
15:22   412, 734, 748ff.,
   752, 780, 789, 794

869

15:22-28   505
15:23   16, 791, 831
15:23-24   751ff.
15:23-28   154f., 588,
        738, 747, 795, 803
15:24   12, 83, 192, 747,
        754ff., 758f., 799
15:24-26   342, 643
15:24-28   17, 747, 773,
        778, 799
15:25   173, 747, 754ff.,
        799, 807
15:25-26   757f.
15:26   83, 755ff., 759
15:26-28   35
15:27   755ff.
15:27-28   155, 375, 588,
        758f., 830
15:28   45, 719, 754, 757,
        759ff., 765, 799
15:29   12, 61, 199, 713,
        716, 738, 744, 749,
        762ff., 768, 770, 775
15:29-31   775
15:29-34   714, 737f.,
        760ff., 779
15:30   767ff.
15:30-31   770
15:30-32   762, 772
15:31   768f., 771
15:31-32   168, 191
15:32   713, 738, 770ff.,
        821
15:33   151, 242, 772ff.
15:33-34   5, 716, 738,
        762, 795, 804, 807
15:34   184, 236, 406,
        773ff., 806
15:35   631, 714, 730, 763,
        776f., 779f., 782, 788,
        797f.
15:35-36   766
15:35-38   17, 715, 775ff.
15:35-44   778f.
15:35-49   717
15:35-58   776f., 780,
        784, 802
15:36   170, 385, 751
15:36-37   6, 780ff.
15:36-38   777, 779, 782
15:36-41   779
15:36-44   797
15:36-49   780
15:37   665, 784, 798, 819
15:38   780, 782

15:39   782f.
15:39-41   782ff., 785
15:40   783
15:40-41   785
15:41   783
15:42   412, 763, 798, 802
15:42-43   784f.
15:42-44   779, 787
15:42-49   255, 776, 782
15:42-50   741
15:43   527
15:44   212, 784ff., 787ff.,
        793
15:44-46   116, 447
15:44-48   787
15:45   681, 730, 751, 780,
        786, 787ff., 791f.
15:45-46   788, 793
15:45-47   793
15:45-49   750f., 777,
        782f., 786ff., 795f., 807
15:46   790f., 793
15:47   787, 790ff., 794
15:47-48   789
15:47-49   798
15:48   788
15:48-49   793ff., 799
15:49   786, 788, 794,
        798, 800, 802
15:49-53   16
15:50   16, 192, 337, 536,
        754, 785, 797ff., 802
15:50-53   741, 781
15:50-54   785
15:50-57   750, 778, 795
15:50-58   780, 795ff.,
        809
15:51   105, 355, 717,
        799ff., 802
15:51-52   797, 802
15:51-53   804
15:51-54   798
15:51-56   12, 626
15:52   763, 776, 785,
        790, 797, 800ff.
15:52-54   798
15:53   755, 785, 797f.,
        802f.
15:53-54   437, 794
15:53-57   757
15:54   752, 785, 803f.
15:54-55   753, 797
15:54-57   17, 760, 807
15:55   804f., 807
15:56   805ff.

15:56-57   797, 805
15:57   807
15:58   5, 52, 132, 141,
        184, 464, 567, 717, 774,
        777, 795, 797, 805,
        807ff., 821, 827, 831
16   267
16:1   32, 267, 274, 311,
        811ff., 823, 830, 835
16:1-2   811
16:1-4   544, 810
16:1-9   821
16:1-11   809ff.
16:2   662, 811ff.
16:3   37, 811f., 814ff.,
        820, 832
16:3-4   811
16:4   815ff., 819
16:5   569, 662, 818ff.
16:5-9   189ff., 809
16:5-11   817
16:6   820, 822
16:6-7   819f.
16:7   191, 820
16:8   15, 217, 819f.
16:9   191, 728, 769ff.,
        820f.
16:10   79, 92f., 141, 188
16:10-11   188, 809, 818,
        821ff., 831
16:11   568, 819
16:12   10, 31, 48, 55, 267,
        274, 407, 809, 811,
        822ff.
16:13   775, 823f., 826ff.
16:13-14   826, 840
16:13-18   826ff.
16:13-24   825ff.
16:14   828
16:15   32, 52, 62f., 298,
        587, 748f., 822, 824,
        828ff., 831, 836
16:15-16   826, 828
16:15-17   3, 7, 54, 62f.
16:15-18   827f.
16:16   63, 808, 828ff.,
        830f., 833
16:17   769, 822, 824,
        826, 829, 831f.
16:17-18   827
16:18   832f.
16:19   836
16:19-20   826, 835f.
16:19-21   834
16:19-24   833ff.

16:20	824, 826, 836	4:3	295	8:10	328
16:20-24	45	4:4	298	8:10-11	816
16:21	31, 826, 836f.	4:5	426	8:11	649
16:22	12, 467, 557, 580,	4:7	93	8:13	810
	826, 834, 837ff., 840	4:7-12	93, 781	8:13-14	400
16:23	826, 834	4:7-18	431, 804	8:14	209
16:23-24	839f.	4:7–5:10	93	8:16-24	815
16:24	826, 834, 837	4:8-9	177, 179, 768	8:17	658
		4:10	93, 769	8:19	812
2 CORINTHIANS		4:15	808	8:22	649, 815
1–7	810, 823	4:16-17	181	8:23	134
1–8	810	4:17	328	8:24	769
1:1	31, 33, 188	5:1-4	794	9	810
1:3-7	658	5:1-5	781	9:1	587, 812, 829
1:5	808	5:5	749	9:4	769
1:8	443	5:7	650	9:5	812
1:8-11	769	5:14-17	224	9:6-15	817
1:8–2:14	823	5:15	725	9:8	808
1:12	121, 219, 769	5:17	459, 504, 800	9:9	810
1:12-24	190	5:19	639	9:12	808, 810, 812
1:14	142, 635	5:21	551	9:12-14	811
1:15	811	6:4	130, 328	9:13	411, 812
1:15-16	818, 820	6:4-5	177, 768	10–12	396, 417
1:15–2:4	817	6:4-10	93	10–13	8, 57, 734, 785
1:15–2:13	816, 818	6:5	808	10:1	193
1:16	816, 818f.	6:6	636	10:1–13:10	175
1:17	317	6:8	527	10:7	59
1:18	44	6:8-10	177, 768	10:8	366
1:21	40	6:9	566, 800	10:10	235, 259
1:22	397, 749	6:9-10	151	10:10-11	205
1:23	34, 675	6:10	39, 340f.	10:12	115, 231
1:24	134, 828	6:13	125, 184	10:12-16	138
2:1	816	6:14-15	298	10:13	306f., 310
2:1-4	8	6:14–7:1	473	10:13-16	395
2:3	823	6:16	146, 264	10:13-17	735
2:5-11	212, 823	7:1	346, 381, 464	10:14	411
2:8	366	7:2-16	816, 823	10:15	808
2:9	538	7:4	769	11:2	623, 637
2:12	411, 820	7:6-7	823	11:2-3	151
2:13	204f., 835	7:7	637	11:3	151
2:14	175	7:8	316	11:4	113
2:14–6:13	90, 175	7:9	143, 295	11:7	400
2:17	219, 411, 710	7:11	637, 800	11:7-12	393, 398f.
2:17–3:4	162	7:12	823	11:8-9	9
3:1-3	138	7:13	832	11:9	179, 400
3:3	121	7:14	769	11:10	675, 769
3:4-18	806	7:15	94	11:13-15	167
3:6	130, 806	8	810	11:14-19	815
3:7-9	587	8–9	37, 62, 811	11:16–12:10	431
3:12	317	8:1-15	817	11:17	769
3:12-18	497, 507	8:2	328, 400, 808	11:17–12:10	93
3:16	351	8:4	587, 812, 829	11:19	176
3:17	448, 790	8:6	812	11:20	411
3:18	648, 801	8:7	38, 812	11:21	231
4:1	587	8:8	769	11:23	59, 130, 769, 808
4:2-4	163	8:9	39, 812	11:23-27	735

11:23-29	177ff., 635, 768	2:1-2	428	5:6	313, 366, 384
11:26	768	2:1-10	53, 662, 732	5:7	411
11:27	178	2:2	662	5:9	214, 216
11:29	178, 289	2:6	417	5:11	420
11:30	93	2:7-8	57	5:13	366, 426, 631
12	810	2:7-9	729	5:14	168
12–13	587	2:8	396	5:15	384
12:1	662	2:9	57, 135, 427, 731	5:16	127, 189, 309, 452
12:1-10	674	2:9-10	810	5:19-21	225
12:7	93, 178, 210, 333,	2:10	338	5:20	55, 121, 126, 538,
	662	2:10-13	428		637
12:7-10	93	2:11	57	5:21	192, 754, 798
12:9	84	2:11-14	431	5:22	366, 593, 636
12:10	177, 328, 635, 768	2:12	731	5:22-23	623
12:11	316	2:14	57	5:24	212, 452
12:12	95, 594	2:15	526	6:1	193, 212, 540, 576
12:13	9, 393, 398f., 411	2:18	366	6:3	151
12:13-17	179	2:20	763	6:6	676
12:14	184, 800	2:21	420, 742	6:11	837
12:17-18	188	3:1	92, 151	6:13	769
12:20	55, 126, 225, 637,	3:2	113, 536	6:14	417
	696	3:2-3	123, 603	6:15	313, 384, 428
12:20-21	225	3:3	320	6:16	444
12:21	197	3:4	721		
13:4	93	3:6-9	444	**EPHESIANS**	
13:5	561	3:13	76, 265, 551, 580	1:1	32
13:5-7	440	3:14	113	1:3-11	29
13:10	317, 366, 518	3:15	406, 663	1:5	105
13:11	827	3:17	536	1:8	808
13:12	836	3:20	373	1:9	105
13:13	45, 587f.	3:22	681	1:9-10	760
		3:24	185	1:10	153
GALATIANS		3:27	445	1:11	105
1:4	29, 329, 724	3:28	31, 247, 270, 307,	1:13	397
1:5	672		312, 606	1:14	749
1:7	309, 411	3:29	420, 444, 742	1:20	740
1:8	837	4:1	724	1:21	754
1:8-9	580, 837	4:3	302, 784	1:22	759
1:9	548	4:4-5	426	2:1	724
1:10	490, 740	4:5	265, 320	2:2	104
1:11	719	4:6	31, 561	2:3	298, 526
1:11-12	548	4:8	526	2:10	127
1:11–2:2	718	4:8-9	495, 577	2:11	372
1:12	548, 662	4:11	721	2:20	596, 621
1:12-16	395	4:13-14	93	2:21	137, 146
1:13	734	4:14	235	2:21-22	264
1:13-14	76	4:16	682	3:3	105
1:13-15	734	4:17-18	637	3:4	105
1:15-16	418	4:18	808	3:7	130
1:15-17	548	4:19	125, 184	3:9	105
1:16	395, 798	4:25	448, 550	3:10	754
1:17-19	732	5	80	3:16	828
1:18	57	5–6	430	3:21	672
1:19	403, 729, 731	5:1	827	4:1	127
1:20	675, 800	5:5	42	4:2-5	650
1:23	828	5:5-6	650	4:4-6	588

4:7	541
4:8	152
4:9	448
4:11	590, 620f.
4:11-13	645
4:29	225
4:30	397
5:1-2	628
5:2	127, 631
5:3-5	225
5:3-13	197
5:4	225
5:5	192
5:8	754
5:11	686
5:13	686
5:18	226
5:19	671
5:20	247, 808
5:21	830
5:22-33	296
5:25	763
5:25-33	259, 276
5:33	522
6:4	184, 458
6:5	94
6:12	104, 754, 798
6:19	105
6:21	130

PHILIPPIANS

1:1	19, 31, 33, 130
1:3	37
1:3-11	29
1:4	808
1:6	142
1:7	432
1:9	808
1:10	142, 219, 489
1:12-18	825
1:15	55
1:17	557
1:18	522, 557
1:27	411, 827
1:29	181
1:29-30	93
2:1	45, 658
2:4	479, 638
2:5-8	426
2:6-11	582
2:7	342
2:12	94, 464
2:16	142, 769
2:19-23	189
2:19-30	817
2:20	344

2:22	125
2:24	817
2:25	134
2:30	141, 832
3:2-11	311
3:3	444
3:4	151
3:6	637
3:6-8	734
3:8	143, 244
3:10	181
3:12	418, 654
3:14	435
3:16	522
3:20	42
3:21	167, 255, 777, 782, 785, 793
4:1	464, 807, 827
4:1-3	52
4:2-3	827, 831
4:3	31, 134
4:4	808
4:6	342
4:9	548
4:12	178
4:14	522
4:14-20	400, 416
4:15	722
4:20	672

COLOSSIANS

1:3	37, 808
1:4-5	650
1:7	130
1:13	192, 754
1:14	87, 724
1:15	504
1:15-20	375, 760
1:16	104, 754
1:18	504, 740
1:22	43, 649
1:23	130, 808
1:24	93, 180
1:24-27	93
1:25	130, 710
1:26-27	105
1:28	184, 557
2:1	501
2:2	105
2:2-3	77, 85
2:5	204
2:6	127, 548
2:7	808
2:10	754
2:12	740
2:12-15	61

2:15	104, 754
2:16	428, 478
2:18	638, 721
2:20-21	276
3:5	224f.
3:5-7	197
3:5-11	224
3:8	225, 649
3:11	606, 759
3:12	636
3:14	631
3:16	184, 671
3:17	207, 247
4:2	827
4:3	105, 820
4:5	226
4:6	225
4:7	130
4:11	134, 192, 754
4:12	808
4:13	637
4:15	835
4:18	837

1 THESSALONIANS

1:1	188
1:2	37, 808
1:2-5	27, 42
1:3	650
1:5	40, 64f., 110, 594
1:6	328
1:7	681
1:8	710
1:9	577
1:10	740
2:1-10	92
2:1-12	162, 399
2:1–3:10	460
2:3	658
2:3-6	64
2:4	163, 490, 561
2:5-10	411
2:7	30, 125, 729
2:9	179, 399, 411, 413, 416
2:9-10	411
2:10	681
2:11	125, 184, 541
2:12	106, 127, 658, 754, 785
2:13	37, 64, 518, 548, 681, 710
2:14	734
2:15	344
2:17–3:5	190, 817
2:18	191, 411

2:19	753, 769
2:20	774
3:1	409f.
3:1-6	188
3:2	43, 134, 411
3:3	181, 328
3:3-4	330
3:5	282, 410, 808
3:6	518
3:7	328, 518
3:8	416, 827
3:11	35
3:12	366, 808
3:13	43, 753
4:1	52, 127, 187, 292, 309, 344, 548, 808
4:1-8	197
4:2	721
4:3	32
4:9	274, 631
4:10	52, 808
4:11	179, 291
4:11-12	222, 292
4:12	127, 226, 713
4:13	274, 298, 443
4:13-15	355
4:13-18	716, 800
4:14	716, 723, 725
4:14-17	800
4:14-18	753
4:15	753
4:16	750, 801
4:16-17	802
5:1	274
5:1-11	233
5:2	43, 142, 198
5:4	142
5:6	298, 774, 827
5:8	650, 774
5:9-10	720
5:10	827
5:11	170, 366
5:12	184, 832
5:12-13	830
5:12-14	827f.
5:13	141, 808
5:14	52, 184, 222, 636
5:15	179, 241, 654, 808
5:16	808
5:16-24	827
5:19-20	632
5:19-22	595
5:20	235, 505
5:20-21	596
5:23	32, 346, 753
5:24	44

5:26	836
2 THESSALONIANS	
1:3	37, 541, 808, 816
1:5	192, 754
1:7	42, 662
1:8	142
1:10	40, 106, 681
1:11	808
1:11-12	209
2:1	753, 837
2:2	142, 198, 329f.
2:3	151
2:8	429, 643, 753
2:8-12	73
2:9	753
2:10	91
2:13	37, 748f., 808, 829
2:14	73
2:15	827
2:17	43
3:1	710
3:3	43, 44
3:4	291
3:6	53, 207, 247, 291, 548
3:6-10	393, 425
3:6-13	179
3:6-15	213, 330
3:7-9	399
3:8	411, 808
3:9	393, 404
3:10	291, 536
3:12	291
3:14	222
3:14-15	212, 837
3:15	184, 226
1 TIMOTHY	
1:3	291
1:9	429
1:9-11	225
1:12-17	637
1:13	637
1:13-16	734
1:15	734
1:16	518
1:17	637, 672
1:20	208, 566
2	699
2:4-5	375
2:7	675
2:9-15	699, 705
2:10	525
2:11	696
2:14	151

2:15	721
3:3	226
3:8	130, 226
3:10	43, 561
4:3	276
4:6	130
4:11	291
4:12	593
5:10	621
5:11-15	699
5:14	286
5:18	179, 291, 398, 413, 545
5:19	659
5:20	686
6:2	237
6:4	55, 225
6:11	464, 593, 654
6:13	291
6:16	672
6:17	291
2 TIMOTHY	
1:6	587
1:8	40
2:4-7	405
2:8	740
2:17-18	715
2:20-21	608
2:22	260, 464, 654
3:2-5	225
3:8	440
4:2	686
4:5	808
4:8	437
4:11	587
4:17	770
4:18	192, 672, 754
4:19	833, 835
4:21	819
TITUS	
1:5	226
1:6	43
1:7	43
1:9	686
1:13	686
1:16	440
2:1	525
2:2	650
2:3	302
2:8	237
2:10	237
2:12	774
2:15	686
3:1	237, 830

3:3	225	**JAMES**		6	819
3:5-7	123	1:1	34		
3:9	55	1:5	85	**JUDE**	
3:10	184	2:10	560	6	234
3:12	817	2:24	437	12	226, 532
3:13	819	3:1-12	225	25	672
3:15	837	3:7	526		
		3:16	697	**REVELATION**	
PHILEMON		4:15	191	1:5	725
1	134	5:4	241, 281	1:9	329
2	835			1:10	539, 813
4	37, 808	**1 PETER**		2–3	835
6	820	1:3-8	650	2:9-10	329
7	832	1:19-21	725	2:14	357, 425, 455, 481
8	52	2:1	225	2:20	358, 425, 455, 481
9	649	2:13	830	2:22	329
10	125, 184	2:18	830	2:26	520
11	649	2:19-21	241	3:3	827
14	328	2:23	225	3:17	172
15	518	2:24	594	4:1	801
20	832	3:1	302, 306, 427	5	672
22	817	3:15-16	225	5:9	265, 320
24	134	4:3	225	5:10	173
		4:11	672	6:8	520
HEBREWS		5:8	827	7:11	687
1:1-3	374f.	5:11	672	7:14	329
1:13	754	5:12	837	8:2–9:14	801
2:6-9	754	5:14	836	9:10	805
2:15	560			11:6	520
4:12	820	**2 PETER**		11:16	687
4:12-13	163	1:4	526	13:7	520
6:6	389	2–3	775	14:3	265
6:10-12	650	2:4	234	14:18	520
7:27	730	2:12	526	16:9	520
9:12	730			18:17	622
9:23	495	**1 JOHN**		20:4	173, 233
10:10	730	2:8	342	20:6	173, 520
10:22-24	650	2:17	342	21:4	803
11:13-16	179	2:27	596	21:8	225
11:28	457	4:1	596	22:5	173
11:33-38	177	5:7	705	22:15	225
11:35-36	585			22:18-19	580
13:13	437	**3 JOHN**		22:20	838
13:21	672	2	27		

INDEX OF EARLY
EXTRABIBLICAL LITERATURE

Note: If necessary, see ABBREVIATIONS (pp. xiii-xx).

JEWISH LITERATURE

APOCRYPHA

1 Esdras
4:47	819
8:69	202
9:12	278
9:18	278

Tobit
4:12	278

Wisdom
3:7-8	233
6:15	343
7:23	343
9:14-15	802
10:17	445
16:6	553
18:25	457
19:7	445

Sirach
1:4	65
1:9	65
1:30	163
19:2	259
23:7-15	225
23:16	289
49:7	133

1 Maccabees
1:14-15	312
12:4	819

2 Maccabees
7:28	83
11:21	839
11:23	839
12:39-45	767

3 Maccabees
4:16	578
5:26	568

4 Maccabees
5:2	357

PSEUDEPIGRAPHA

Apocalypse of Abraham
31:1-2	801

Apocalypse of Moses
22	801
27	801

Assumption of Moses
8:3	312

2 Baruch
51:10	785

3 Baruch
4:17	225
8:5	225
13:4	225

1 Enoch
1:9	233
62:15	785
67-69	234
91:6-7	225
91:13	147
91:15	234
95:3	233
105:11	785
105:12	785

2 Enoch
66:6	177

Epistle of Aristeas
188	186
210	186
281	186

6 Esdras
16:40-45	340

4 Ezra
5:1-13	329
6:18-24	329
6:23	801
9:1-12	329

Joseph and Asenath
8:15	83

Jubilees
1:17	147
23:11-31	329

Psalms of Solomon
8:1	663
17	33

Sibylline Oracles
2.254-83   225
8.239   801

Testament of Abraham
13   141

Testament of Job
48–50   630
48:3   630

Testament of Judah
3:9   343
14–16   225

Testament of Levi
9:9-10   278

Testament of Naphtali
8:8   281f.

Testament of Reuben
1:10   202
2:7   389

DEAD SEA SCROLLS

1QpHab
5:4   233

1QS
6:24–7:25   203

4QFlor   147

RABBINIC
LITERATURE

Abot R.Nat.
6   507

Bar.Rosh.Hash.
16b-17a   144

Bar.Sota
3a   163

b.B.Mes.
88   406

b.Ber.
35   467, 482

b.Git.
62   406
88   231

b.Hul.
13   357

b.Ketub.
75   293

b.Pes.
54   448

b.Rosh.Hash.
11b   801

b.Sabb.
10   507
12   507
35   448

b.Sanh.
19   185
54   200
90b   781

b.Taan
9   448

Mek.Ex.
12.39   553

Midr.Num.
1:2   448
19:26   448

Midr.Ps.
14:1   163

Midr.Qoh.
1:7   801

m.Abod.Zar.
2.3   357, 481

m.Abot.
1.1   548
1.5   289
5.6   448

m.Git.
5.8-9   305
9.10   293

m.Ketub.
4.3   302
4.4   300

m.Moed Qat.
3.9   803

m.Peah
2.6   548

m.Pes.
1.1   216
10.5   550, 553

m.Qidd.
1.1   300

m.Sanh.
6.4   76
7.4   200

m.Yebamoth
11.2   302
14.1   294

t.Ber.
4.1   482

t.Sot.
6.6   455

t.Suk.
3.11   448

Tg. Ps.-J. Num.
20:2   448
22:15   448

PHILO

Abr.
261   173

agric.
9   124

cher.
48   813
92   225
92-93   226
127   373

congr.qu.er.
19   **124**
61   **503**
70   **187**

det.pot.ins.
34   225
115   449

gig.
6   521
30   137

leg.ad Gai.
53   185
271   813

leg. all.
1.76   733
2.86   449
3.96   374
3.111   172

Mos.
1.49 — 80
1.278 — 222

omn.prob.lib.
160 — 124

op.mund.
24-25 — 374
119 — 802

post.Cain.
145 — 172

praem.
125 — 503

sacr.AC
32 — 225

somn.
2.8 — 137f.
2.164-69 — 225

spec.leg.
1.221 — 470
1.260 — 407
2.158 — 553
3.12-21 — 200
3.37-39 — 243
3.60 — 509
4.187 — 83

virt.
66 — 186
140–47 — 407
174 — 180

JOSEPHUS

Ant.
1.73 — 521
1.163 — 275
3.274 — 200
7.351 — 568
12.241 — 312
13.75 — 236
15.259 — 294
18.65-80 — 455

c.Ap.
1.255 — 769
2.147 — 401
2.200-201 — 707

Life
227 — 839
365 — 839

War
1.242 — 80
2.151-53 — 177
4.165 — 177
4.406 — 602
5.413 — 163
7.132-57 — 174
7.250 — 347

EARLY CHRISTIAN

Acts of Paul and Thecla
5 — 327

Aristides
Sacred Discourses
2.27 — 361

Barnabas
1:4 — 650
4:7 — 472
11:8 — 650

Chrysostom
hom. 9 in 1 Cor. — 144
hom. 15 in 1 Cor. — 216, 224
hom. 36 & 37 in 1 Cor. — 697, 700f.
hom. 40 in 1 Cor. — 764
hom. 40 in 1 Cor. 2 — 766
hom. 42 in 1 Cor. 2 — 799

1 Clement
47:1-4 — 47
49:5 — 636

Clement
Letter to Corinth
55:2 — 634

Clement of Rome
65:1 — 831

Pseudo-Clementine *Homily*
16.21.4 — 538

Didache
9:2-3 — 466
10:3 — 446
10:6 — 834, 838

Didascalia (Syriac)
6.5 — 538

Ignatius
Ephesians
18:1 — 71

Romans
5:1 — 770

Irenaeus
Haer.
1.6.3 — 358

Jerome
vir.ill.
2 — 731

Justin
Apol.
65 — 672, 834, 836

Dial.
34 — 358
35 — 538

Martyrdom of Polycarp
17:1 — 435

Origen
Contra Celsum
3.44 — 81

Polycarp
Phil.
3:2-3 — 650

Tertullian
De Jejunio
6 — 455

pudic.
13–15 — 212

res.
52 — 784

GRAECO-ROMAN

Achilles Tatius
8.6 — 527
8.17.3 — 353
8.18.2 — 353

Aeschylus
Agamemnon
1360 — 740

Eumenides
647-48 — 740